Handbook of
Modern
Accounting

ACCOUNTING AND FINANCE PRACTICE SERIES

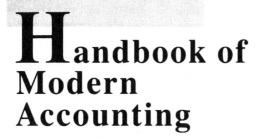

Handbook of Modern Accounting

Third Edition

Edited by

Sidney Davidson, CPA
Arthur Young Professor of Accounting
Graduate School of Business, University of Chicago

and

Roman L. Weil, CPA, CMA
Professor of Accounting
Graduate School of Business, University of Chicago

PRENTICE HALL
Englewood Cliffs, New Jersey 07632

Prentice-Hall International, Inc. *London*
Prentice-Hall of Australia, Pty. Ltd., *Sydney*
Prentice-Hall of Canada, Inc., *Toronto*
Prentice-Hall of India Private Ltd., *New Delhi*
Prentice-Hall of Japan, Inc., *Tokyo*
Prentice-Hall of Southeast Asia Pte., Ltd., *Singapore*
Whitehall Books, Ltd., *Wellington, New Zealand*
Editora Prentice-Hall do Brasil Ltda., *Rio de Janeiro*
Prentice-Hall Hispanoamericana, S.A., *Mexico*

PRENTICE-HALL, INC

Englewood Cliffs, N.J.

10   9   8   7   6   5   4   3   2   1

Library of Congress Cataloging in Publication Data

Main entry under title:

Handbook of modern accounting.

Includes index.
1. Accounting–Handbooks, manuals, etc.
I. Davidson, Sidney, date.   II. Weil, Roman L.
HF5635.H23   1983   657   83-952
ISBN 0-13-380916-1   KGP 89876

ISBN 0-13-380916-1

PRENTICE HALL
BUSINESS & PROFESSIONAL DIVISION
A division of Simon & Schuster
Englewood Cliffs, New Jersey 07632

PRINTED IN THE UNITED STATES OF AMERICA

Contents

Index follows Appendix

Contributors

HECTOR R. ANTON Retired Partner, Deloitte Haskins & Sells, and Director, V. C. Ross Institute of Accounting Research, New York University (CHAPTER 35)

THEODORE M. ASNER Partner, Alexander Grant & Company (COAUTHOR CHAPTER 23)

DENNIS R. BERESFORD Partner, Ernst & Whinney (COAUTHOR CHAPTER 21)

R. GLEN BERRYMAN Professor of Accounting, University of Minnesota (CHAPTER 30)

HORACE R. BROCK Director, Extractive Industries Accounting Research Institute, North Texas State University (CHAPTER 18)

BRYAN CARSBERG Arthur Andersen Professor of Accounting, The London School of Economics and Political Science, and Director of Research, Institute of Chartered Accountants in England and Wales (CHAPTER 6)

JOSEPH D. COUGHLAN Partner, Price Waterhouse & Co. (CHAPTER 16)

SIDNEY DAVIDSON Arthur Young Professor of Accounting, University of Chicago (CHAPTER 20)

GORDON B. DAVIS Professor of Accounting and Honeywell Professor of Management Information Systems, University of Minnesota (CHAPTER 8)

ALLAN R. DREBIN Professor of Accounting and Information Systems, Northwestern University (CHAPTER 41)

THOMAS R. DYCKMAN Professor of Accounting, Cornell University (CHAPTER 22)

ROBERT K. ELLIOTT Partner, Peat, Marwick, Mitchell & Co. (CHAPTER 7)

BARRY JAY EPSTEIN Blackman, Kallick and Company, Ltd. (COAUTHOR CHAPTER 23)

OSCAR S. GELLEIN Retired Partner, Deloitte Haskins & Sells, and Former Member, Financial Accounting Standards Board (COAUTHOR CHAPTER 28)

MICHAEL H. GRANOF Professor of Accounting, The University of Texas at Austin (COAUTHOR CHAPTER 2)

DAVID O. GREEN Professor of Accounting and Vice President for Administration, Baruch College, City University of New York (CHAPTER 5)

ERNEST L. HICKS Retired Partner, Arthur Young & Company, and Adjunct Professor of Accounting, The Ohio State University (COAUTHOR CHAPTER 27)

RICHARD N. HILDAHL Partner, Ernst & Whinney (CHAPTER 40)

RONALD J. HUEFNER Professor of Accounting, State University of New York at Buffalo (CHAPTER 15)

YUJI IJIRI Robert M. Trueblood Professor of Accounting and Economics, Carnegie-Mellon University (CHAPTER 13)

MONROE J. INGBERMAN Assistant Professor of Accounting, New York University (CHAPTER 3)

VIRGINIA ERDWIEN JONES University of Kansas (COAUTHOR CHAPTER 12)

ROBERT S. KAPLAN *Professor of Industrial Administration, Carnegie-Mellon University* (CHAPTER 11)

THOMAS F. KELLER *R. J. Reynolds Industries Professor of Business Administration and Dean of The Fuqua School of Business, Duke University* (CHAPTER 14)

DAVID L. LANDSITTEL *Partner, Arthur Andersen & Co.* (COAUTHOR CHAPTER 26)

JAMES A. LARGAY, III *Arthur Andersen & Co. Alumni Professor of Accounting, Lehigh University* (CHAPTER 34)

BARUCH LEV *Professor, Tel Aviv University and University of California, Berkeley* (CHAPTER 4)

JOHN LESLIE LIVINGSTONE *Vice President, Management Analysis Center, Inc.* (CHAPTER 19)

JAMES K. LOEBBECKE *Professor of Accounting, University of Utah* (CHAPTER 10)

MICHAEL W. MAHER *Associate Professor Accounting, University of Michigan* (CHAPTER 39)

R. K. MAUTZ *Director, Paton Center for Accounting Education and Research, University of Michigan* (CHAPTER 1)

TERENCE E. McCLARY *Vice President, Corporate Financial Administration, General Electric Company* (CHAPTER 32)

DENNIS W. MONSON *Partner, Peat, Marwick, Mitchell & Co.* (CHAPTER 24)

RICHARD H. MOSELEY *Manager, Ernst & Whinney* (COAUTHOR CHAPTER 21)

LOREN A. NIKOLAI *Professor of Accountancy, University of Missouri* (CHAPTER 29)

HUGO NURNBERG *Professor of Accountancy, Baruch College, City University of New York* (CHAPTER 36)

MELVIN PENNER *Partner, Arthur Young & Company* (COAUTHOR CHAPTER 27)

TIMOTHY J. RACEK *Partner, Arthur Andersen & Co.* (CHAPTER 42)

AURORA M. RUBIN *Partner, Deloitte Haskins & Sells* (COAUTHOR CHAPTER 28)

KATHERINE SCHIPPER *Associate Professor of Industrial Administration, Carnegie-Mellon University* (CHAPTER 25)

GORDON SHILLINGLAW *Professor of Accounting, Graduate School of Business, Columbia University* (CHAPTER 38)

DANIEL G. SHORT *Associate Professor of Accounting, The University of Texas at Austin* (COAUTHOR CHAPTER 2)

K. FRED SKOUSEN *Director, School of Accountancy, Brigham Young University* (CHAPTER 37)

MORTON B. SOLOMON *Partner, Main Hurdman* (CHAPTER 17)

JOHN E. STEWART *Partner, Arthur Andersen & Co.* (COAUTHOR CHAPTER 26)

CLYDE P. STICKNEY *Professor of Accounting, The Amos Tuck School of Business Administration, Dartmouth College* (CHAPTER 31)

MICHAEL H. SUTTON *Partner, Deloitte Haskins & Sells* (COAUTHOR CHAPTER 28)

ARTHUR L. THOMAS *Arthur Young Professor of Accounting, University of Kansas* (COAUTHOR CHAPTER 12)

ROMAN L. WEIL *Professor of Accounting, University of Chicago* (CHAPTER 9)

ARTHUR R. WYATT *Partner, Arthur Andersen & Co.* (CHAPTER 33)

Preface

Accounting is an information system—an information system designed to communicate meaningful economic information about an entity to interested parties. The communication process involves preparers and users of the information. This handbook is designed to help both the preparers and the users of accounting information. For preparers—mainly accountants—there is a vast array of accounting topics and suggested treatments. For users—managers, shareholders, and others seeking to understand a firm—there is a simple but comprehensive explanation of the meaning of accounting terms and of financial statements.

The accounting message frequently summarizes substantial compilations of data. The analysis of accounting data and financial statements is increasingly being carried on by means of mathematical and statistical techniques. The title, *Handbook of Modern Accounting*, emphasizes the decision to incorporate descriptions of the newest concepts and techniques that are reshaping accounting as well as to provide the time-tested theories and procedures of accounting. The volume offers a balanced coverage of the new and the old, the emerging and the traditional topics.

This handbook provides comprehensive and authoritative information on accounting in a conveniently organized and succinctly stated form. Those faced with accounting problems can find guidance toward answers. The handbook contains many practical, how-to-do-it forms and information. However, the contributors have avoided a "cookbook" approach and have spiced their sections with observations on the philosophical background and likely development of each accounting topic.

There will be occasions, of course, when the reader will wish to know more about a specific subject than is set forth here. Although it is obvious that a complete book could be written on any of the subjects dealt with in a chapter, the contributors were limited in space. To compensate for this, each author has included a bibliography at the end of the chapter so that the reader who is interested in a subject will be directed to further sources of authoritative information. The bibliography lists a few books or articles that the author believes will be helpful in acquiring a deeper understanding of the subject.

This handbook is the work of many people. The contributors were selected because of the knowledge they possess of the subjects assigned to them. As a group, they form a good cross section of accounting thought, representing accounting professors, public accounting, and industry. To each of them, we express our appreciation.

Much credit for the completion of the handbook must be given to Sandra

Myers. She was indefatigable in her styling and efforts and in dealing with the vast amount of correspondence involved in the preparation of the handbook. She was assisted in these efforts by Raymonde Rousselot and K. Xenophon-Rybowiak. Lynne Lackenbach, a consultant to McGraw-Hill, worked expertly and cooperatively on copy editing and book production.

To all who participated—chapter authors, editorial assistants, copy editors, proofreaders, and publisher—goes our appreciation. Without them, this handbook would not have been possible.

SIDNEY DAVIDSON
ROMAN L. WEIL

Handbook of
Modern
Accounting

CHAPTER 1

Accounting Concepts

and Principles

and Auditing Standards

and Opinions

R. K. Mautz
*Director, Paton Center for Accounting Education
and Research, University of Michigan*

ACCOUNTING CONCEPTS

Accounting's claim to status as an intellectual discipline depends largely on its emergence as the primary analytical discipline concerned with providing information about enterprise status and progress. Accounting is analytical in the sense that it takes a great mass of transaction data and, through classification and summarization, reduces that mass of data to a relatively small number of highly significant and interrelated items, which, if presented properly, tell much about the status and progress of the given enterprise. Any type of analytical classification depends on a few basic concepts supported by a large number of subordinate concepts. Accounting is no exception. Without an understanding of these concepts, one can neither apply accounting effectively nor understand the reports produced by accountants.

To some, accounting appears to be primarily procedural in nature. Emphasis appears to be placed on record keeping and preparation of financial statements, rather than on conceptually based analysis. This appearance is deceiving. Recording is preceded by transaction analysis. From the development of a chart of accounts for a given enterprise to preparation of its financial statements, accounting is concerned primarily with analyzing the nature and effect of its transactions. Thus recognition and development of the conceptual foundation of accounting is of first importance to all those concerned with it.

The Nature of Concepts. Concepts are essential ideas that permit the identification and classification of phenomena or other ideas. Thus we must have a concept of an asset to separate assets from those items that are not assets. In turn, we must have a concept of current assets in order to separate current assets from noncurrent assets. Not until the essential nature of such concepts is known can one recognize the differences and similarities necessary to make the desired separations. Neither can one understand reports that include some classification unless one is informed as to the meaning of or the essential differences between each of the several classes. Accounting is in large measure a classificatory art, depending for its classifications on a variety of distinctions and differences that have been found useful to those evaluating the status and progress of business enterprises.

To be complete, a concept must state all that the given class includes and all that it excludes—all that it is, and all that it is not. This is no small task. For example, one may start with a definition of an asset, which states simply that an asset is "anything of value owned," a satisfactory concept for simple situations. One who is familiar with business activities finds that certain types of leases give to the lessee such rights to use the property that for some purpose the lessee has the equivalent of ownership. We tend to modify our rudimentary concept of an asset to include such lease arrangements. Other arrangements suggest other modifications of the basic concept until it becomes complex rather than simple. Because so many of the concepts with which accounting deals are both abstract and very complex, they are not easily stated in any complete sense. We find it necessary to use broad, general terms to describe most concepts and rarely meet the requirements of a complete statement.

Expressed concisely, concepts are definitions. Rarely are these complete, although definitions are often extremely useful in conveying one's understanding to another.

Kinds of Concepts. A more complete understanding of the nature of concepts may be obtained by examining some of their characteristics, which provide separation of concepts into different classes. Thus, we have "ideal" and "real" concepts. Ideal concepts are established for the purposes of theoretical discussion and do not necessarily bear any direct relationship to the real world. For example, lawyers use the concept of "the prudent man" in discussing the rights and obligations of parties to certain contracts. Economists use the concept of "an economic man" to describe the assumed action of an individual in certain circumstances. One cannot go to the real world and pick out either a prudent man or an economic man who fits completely the characteristics included in the concept. Nevertheless, these are important concepts for discussion purposes, particularly in working out theoretical explanations of behavior.

Real concepts represent phenomena or ideas in the real world, such as one's concept of an automobile or of a building or of the Supreme Court. Real-world concepts can be tested against actual observable things or actions.

Accounting must deal with both abstract and real-world phenomena, but accounting to date has given very little attention to ideal concepts, finding its chief usefulness in the world of reality. Ideal concepts are likely to become more useful as accountants give more attention to the development of theory.

The distinction between "native" and "borrowed" concepts is also useful to our understanding. Native concepts are those that are indigenous to the field itself. Borrowed concepts are used within the field but are taken from other disciplines. Accounting's concept of retained earnings, for example, is a native concept; that is, it has been developed by accountants for accounting purposes and is not particularly relevant to other fields of interest. The concept of opportunity cost, however, used by cost accountants in discussing decision theory, is largely borrowed from economics. Accounting has a great number of borrowed concepts taken from law, from economics, and from finance. It also has a substantial number of native concepts, some of which are well developed and some of which are still rudimentary in nature. In this chapter, our concern is primarily with concepts native to the field of accounting.

Another distinction among concepts may be pointed out in terms of the fields of interest within accounting. There are concepts relevant to financial accounting, to managerial accounting, to tax accounting, and to auditing. Certain concepts are relevant to all these fields. Other concepts have a very specialized usefulness. In this chapter, we are concerned primarily with concepts of general interest throughout accounting.

The Importance of Changes in Accounting Concepts. As a subject of study, accounting would be much easier to master if its concepts were fixed and established for all time. It would also be a much less interesting field and certainly less useful. Accounting concepts are continually evolving and changing. This is particularly true of its native concepts. Two reasons may be cited for this evolutionary situation. First is that, as a relatively new field, accounting continues to understand its concepts better year by year as it works with them more intensively and thoughtfully. Even our most experienced practitioners and our most advanced theorists have not yet had the opportunity to exhaust the possible applications of all accounting concepts, so that our understanding increases from time to time as new applications are made available to us. This becomes particularly evident when innovative businesspeople devise new transactions or new modifications of old transactions. Often these bring to light aspects of a concept that had not previously been sufficiently explored.

A second reason is that some concepts, particularly abstractions that cannot be tested against real-world phenomena, tend to change as the perceptions, needs, and expectations of those affected by the application of the concepts change. For example, a historical study would establish that the quantity and quality of information included in the published financial statements of corporations have increased significantly in this country over the last 30 years and the trend appears to be continuing. An increased interest in financial data by investors, creditors, financial analysts, and others together with recognition of the securities market as a major means of resource allocation affecting all interests in the economy has greatly influenced our views of what should be disclosed and thereby some important concepts.

This change is both quantitative and qualitative. Not only is a broader range and a larger amount of detail called for, some critics insist that the fundamental basis of financial reporting should be modified. Accounting first developed as a simple record of transactions. The monetary amounts of transactions provided a ready means of quantifying, recording, and accumulating completed transactions. To separate "reality" from speculation, wishful thinking, and outright misstatement, rules were established restricting accounting to completed transactions, and the concepts of historical cost (transaction price) and stewardship reporting became important influences in accounting theory and practice.

More recently, in the face of continuing inflation and dramatic changes in specific price levels over long periods of time, historical cost and stewardship reporting have been criticized as irrelevant to investment decisions, and a strong case has been made for some form of current value as a more relevant basis for corporate financial reporting. A number of authoritative bodies have indicated an awareness of this recommended change in emphasis and its effect if implemented. General price-level adjustments, greater disclosure of current values, and changes in the realization concept have been proposed. For the foreseeable future, the most likely prospect appears to be a period of probable experimentation and change. Whatever may be the situation in other disciplines, it appears highly likely that in accounting we shall have a continuing study and reevaluation of our essential concepts.

Interrelatedness of Accounting Concepts. Another characteristic of great importance is the interrelationship among concepts. Very few of our native concepts stand by themselves; most of them depend to a considerable extent on others. The concept of full disclosure is related to the idea of fair presentation. Our idea of fair presentation in turn is based on concepts of financial position and results of operations. These in turn are influenced by our notions of what constitutes a transaction, what is an asset, and what is a liability. A change in our notion of an asset might have considerable influence on either or both of our concepts of revenue and expense, which in turn influence the concept of net income. One could carry on with this sort of explication endlessly, but it may be enough to emphasize that many concepts are tightly interrelated one with another, and that as any one of them grows and evolves or is modified, there is likely to be a series of influences on related concepts.

This suggests that any attempt to discuss concepts in an orderly fashion is necessarily difficult. No single concept can be discussed by itself without some attention to those related to it. One scarcely knows where to begin with such a discussion, because it is hard to demonstrate that any single concept is so basic to all other concepts that it can be discussed separately from them.

Relationship of Postulates to Concepts. An adequate appreciation of the nature and limitation of our concepts requires that we give some attention to the postulates that lie at their roots. Postulates are assumptions—not arbitrary, deliberate assumptions, but necessary and often unrecognized assumptions, which typically reflect our best judgment of the facts of a situation or the trend of events. For example, in recognizing a liability, we assume that the creditor will hold the debtor for payment, and that the debtor will make such payments. These are assumptions. They are assumptions that have been borne out in the past by the facts, and they are supported by legal institutions making them to some extent enforceable. Yet, in a number of cases, creditors have not held debtors to payment and, in even more cases, debtors have been unable to pay. Thus there is an element of assumption in recognizing a liability as a real obligation. Where such an assumption seems invalid, that is, where we have evidence to believe that a liability will not be paid, we would not recognize it as a valid liability. Thus any postulate, any assumption, should be observed only if there is no persuasive evidence to the contrary. Where evidence to the contrary does exist, the most reasonable assumption in the circumstances should be made, and we should account accordingly.

Some people object to the term "postulates" and particularly to interpretation of that term as assumptions, on the grounds that accounting should not be based on assumptions. Although one can be sympathetic with the attitude that we should not make arbitrary or unfounded assumptions, a more realistic approach is to recognize that postulates unavoidably exist in a world of uncertainty.

Accounting statements must be prepared and issued before the ultimate consequences of certain actions can be known. Assumptions about the future course of events cannot be avoided under such circumstances.

A Conceptual Framework. A recent development of great importance is a continuing effort by the Financial Accounting Standards Board (FASB) to construct a "conceptual framework" for financial accounting and reporting. The project is at once an exploration of basic concepts and a discussion of pervasive principles, and extends beyond the scope of this chaper. Four Statements of Financial Accounting Concepts have been published:

No. 1 *Objectives of Financial Reporting by Business Enterprises*
No. 2 *Qualitative Characteristics of Accounting Information*
No. 3 *Elements of Financial Statements of Business Enterprises*
No. 4 *Objectives of Financial Reporting by Nonbusiness Organizations*

Additional topics to be added as the conceptual framework effort continues include:

Accounting Recognition Criteria for Elements of Financial Statements
Measurement of the Elements of Financial Statements
Reporting Earnings and Fund Flows
Financial Reporting by Small and Closely Held Business Enterprises
Reporting the Performance of Nonbusiness Organizations

To illustrate the nature and interrelatedness of accounting concepts, and to provide an understanding of accounting and some of its problems and potential, a brief introduction to a small number of important accounting concepts follows.

BASIC CONCEPTS

Five basic concepts will be discussed; for most of these, the discussion will include some description of related concepts. The five basic concepts follow, with a parenthetical indication of some of the major subsidiary concepts that are necessary to an understanding of the basic concepts.

1. Financial condition (asset, liability, shareholders' equity)
2. Results of operations (revenue, expenses, losses, net income, matching)
3. Enterprise (corporate entity, consolidated financial statements)
4. Continuity
5. Present fairly (generally accepted accounting principles, consistency, materiality, full disclosure)

Financial Condition. It is easy to misinterpret the term *financial condition* because many people use it in ordinary conversation referring to their own financial condition. When used by accountants, however, it is a technical term and typically refers to a profit-directed business enterprise. As used by accountants, financial condition refers to the impression or conclusions one might draw from a balanced array of a company's assets and the claims against those assets. In such an array, the assets and the claims against the assets are described in a semistandardized fashion; that is, certain terms and certain classifications are conventionally used. Conventional methods are also used in measuring or evaluating the assets and the claims against those assets. Unless one has an understanding of the classification and measurement conventions applied in presenting such an array, one could easily come to erroneous conclusions about their meaning and significance. Thus, to explain the concept of financial condition properly, one must move on to some explanation of the concept of assets, liabilities, and shareholders' equity, together with the conventional methods of classifying and measuring these items.

Asset. An *asset* may be defined as anything of use to future operations of the enterprise, the beneficial interest in which runs to the enterprise. FASB Statement of Financial Accounting Concepts No. 3 [1980, par. 19] says that "assets are probable future economic benefits obtained or controlled by a particular entity as a result of past transactions or events." Assets may be monetary or nonmonetary, tangible or intangible, owned or not owned. So long as they can make a contribution to future operations of the company and the company has the right to so use them without additional cost in excess of the anticipated amount of that contribution, they constitute assets and are so treated in accounting.

Accountants tend to dichotomize assets basically between current and noncurrent assets. The technical definition of current assets approved by the Accounting Principles Board of the American Institute of Certified Public Accountants reads as follows [CAP, 1953, chap. 3A]:

> For accounting purposes, the term *current assets* is used to designate cash and other assets or resources commonly identified as those which are reasonably expected to be realized in cash or sold or consumed during the normal operating cycle of the business.

Any asset not meeting the terms of this definition is excluded from the current assets classification. Noncurrent assets are typically reported under a variety of headings, such as long-term investments, fixed assets, tangible assets, and other assets. Current assets are set off from noncurrent assets because of their importance in a company's current position. Current position is another concept, subsidiary to the overall notion of financial condition, which has to do with a company's ability to meet its immediate maturing obligations in the ordinary course of business with the assets at hand.

Within the classification of current assets, one typically finds the following:

1. Cash, that is, coin, currency, and bank deposits that are readily available for any purpose the company management chooses

2. Marketable securities intended for conversion into cash within the operating cycle

3. Accounts and notes receivable that will be collected within the normal operating cycle of the business[1]

---

[1] "The average time intervening between the acquisition of materials or services entering this process and the final cash realization constitutes an *operating cycle*" [CAP, 1953, chap. 3A].

4. Inventories of raw materials, work in process, and finished goods

5. Any prepaid expense that if not prepaid, would be a drain on other resources within the next operating cycle (infrequently, substantial in amount).

Asset measurement. The general rule for asset measurement is that assets be valued at transaction price, reduced proportionately for observed and/or estimated consumption of use value. As used in the expression "transaction price," a transaction refers to an arms'-length exchange transaction between independent parties in which the specific company is one of the parties. Typically, such a transaction has a stated price, which provides the basis for recording the asset acquired. If no stated price exists, a price is inferred from such surrounding circumstances as exist. For example, prices in transactions that are equivalent in terms of quantity and timing may be used. If no transaction price either exists or can be inferred from surrounding circumstances with any degree of validity, accountants sometimes measure the asset received in the same terms as the asset given up. Thus, transaction prices constitute the basic date of accounting.

When used in operations, assets are consumed either physically or in terms of their total available service. To reflect this, the amount recorded for the asset is reduced accordingly so that, over its useful life, an asset's recorded valuation declines from the original transaction price to the price expected to be received upon its retirement or to zero, as the case may be.

There are significant exceptions to this general rule for measuring assets. If the anticipated recovery from use or sale of an asset falls below the transaction price, accountants generally write down the carrying value of the asset to the anticipated recovery amount. Note that these are write-downs only. Accountants are loath to write up an asset to a higher anticipated recovery value. This is the most apparent application of the doctrine of conservatism, which is fairly common in accounting. Conservatism holds that, given a situation in which exact measurement is not possible, accountants should err on the side of understatement of assets and overstatement of expenses, rather than vice versa. Obviously, such a doctrine can be misused; for example, it may be employed to continually understate assets. The extent to which such understatement does exist is not easily determinable, although some suspect that it is not uncommon.

This rule of reducing the carrying value of an asset because of an anticipated reduced recovery is typically applied to marketable securities and to inventories, although it may be extended to other assets as well. If marketable equity securities currently held have market value lower than acquisition cost, they are written down to their present market value for financial statement purposes.[2] The same treatment is applied to inventories, but with an important modification. Inventories are not written down to a lower present realization price but are valued in terms of a rule commonly described as *the lower of cost or market*. In this expression, the term "market" is not the sales market but the replacement market. Thus, inventories are typically valued for financial statement purposes at the lower of cost or replacement market.

The argument offered in support is that unless an inventory will bring to the

---

[2]See FASB Statement No. 12 [1975].

company not only an amount equivalent to its cost, but also the anticipated gross profit, it has lost some of its usefulness, and this usefulness should be recognized through a decrease in its carrying value. Any asset that has lost its utility should be written down, goes the argument, and replacement market is a convenient lay method of determining the utility of inventories.

Challenges to the general rule for asset valuation. Although transaction price accounting for assets is well established and generally accepted for accounting purposes, modified, of course, for the valuation of certain assets as described, there are substantial criticisms directed against it. The critics fall into two quite separate groups. One group of critics directs its objections to the fact that transaction prices, once established, are unaffected by general price-level changes and thus transaction price data tend to become obsolete. The second group would not be satisfied with adjustment of transaction price data for general price-level changes; it charges that accounting should use a valuation method that measures assets in terms as close to current economic value as possible.

Continuing inflation in this and in other countries provides a basis for contending that transaction price data become obsolete over time. This is particularly true of the prices for long-lived assets, such as land, buildings, and equipment, although to some extent it may also be true for inventories. During a period of rising prices, not only is the carrying value of fixed assets stated in terms of higher-value dollars, but the proportional amount written off to reflect the cost of using the asset during the period is also usually well below the cost of using a similar asset purchased more recently. Thus not only the balance sheet but the calculation of income is influenced. The recommended remedy is that a general price-level index of some kind be applied against the historical transaction prices to obtain an updated transaction price stated in terms of current dollars.

The severest critics of accounting, however, would not be content with general price-level adjustments. They feel that accounting has made about as much progress as it can based on historical transaction prices, whether adjusted or not. Their contention is that accounting should now shift its base of measurement for assets to the closest approximation to current value possible. To the extent available, they would use quoted market prices for investments, inventories, and used machinery. Where no quoted price exists, they would use a replacement market or, failing this, an index-number adjustment of historical cost. At the least it appears that increased disclosure of current value information may be required and that modification of the conventional realization test is less likely but possible.

The Financial Accounting Standards Board, acting to meet such criticisms, has issued its Statement of Financial Accounting Standards No. 33, *Financial Reporting and Changing Prices* [1979], which requires no changes in the basic financial statements, but calls for supplementary information about the effects of both general inflation and changes in the prices of certain specific types of assets in the reports of certain large, publicly held enterprises.

Liabilities. The claims against the assets of a company are typically classified under two headings: liabilities and shareholders' equity. The FASB has offered the following definition of liabilities: "Liabilities are probable future sacrifices of economic benefits arising from present obligations of a particular entity to transfer assets or provide services to other entities in the future as a result of past transactions or events."[3] Like assets, liabilities are generally classified as current or noncurrent. Current liabilities are those that will be paid from among the assets listed as current assets. Thus, there is a direct relationship between current liabilities and current assets, generally described as expressing the current position of the company. Noncurrent liabilities do not have the same extent of variety as do noncurrent assets. However, a number of peculiarities might be pointed out.

Included within the general liability section may be found items described as *deferred credits*. The expression "deferred credits" reminds the reader that ultimately some part or all of the item will be credited to income. This is because the deferred credit includes an element of profit. For example, a company may receive an advance payment on a future sale to a customer. The advance payment may be sufficient to cover not only the cost of delivering the product to the customer but a margin of profit also. For this reason the item may be considered a deferred credit to income. Magazine subscriptions collected in advance are often referred to as deferred credits, as are such items as interest income collected in advance, rent collected in advance, and so on.

An unusual item included among liabilities is deferred federal income tax, which in some cases amounts to a very substantial sum. Because of differences in computing taxable income and income for general business reporting purposes, companies may have reported income in a current year not subject to the current rate of federal income tax. However, if the company continues to operate at a profit and if tax rates remain in effect approximately as they currently exist, there is every expectation that sometime in the future the company will have to pay taxes, not only on all future income, but also equal in amount to the taxes not paid on the current year's reported income. Under current standards of accounting, it is required that in such a case the company include, as an expense of the current year, tax expense in an amount proportional to its reported income even if not currently taxed. The difference between what must be paid to the government and the amount considered to be an expense of the current year is carried as a deferred credit until such future date as it must be paid as taxes. Many accountants do not agree that deferred federal income taxes constitute a liability item that ought to be recognized as such, but the consensus within accounting has established this as required practice.

Liability measurement follows the general rule of using transaction price, with the exception, however, that if the amount received at inception of the obligation is substantially below the amount that must be paid at its maturity, the difference may be amortized or allocated over the intervening years. Thus, one may have either a premium or a discount on a long-term debt, which will be reduced gradually until at maturity the amount of the debt is stated at the amount that must then be paid.

Shareholders' equity. The second major class of claims against the assets of an enterprise is commonly described as *shareholders' equity*, a term one must

---

[3]FASB Statement of Financial Accounting Concepts No. 3 [1980, par. 28].

interpret with care, as noted in a subsequent paragraph. The amount reported in a balance sheet as the shareholders' equity is the arithmetic difference between the total of the enterprise assets and the total of its liabilities. Thus, in a sense, shareholders' equity is a balancing figure. The amount can also be determined in another way as the sum of the original investment by the shareholders plus the amount of undistributed earnings accumulated since the inception of the company. In current practice, the shareholders' equity section of a balance sheet reports these two items separately, the amount paid in on capital stock and the amount of retained earnings. Somewhat different terminology is used if the enterprise is unincorporated.

The purpose of reporting these amounts separately is to give some indication of the extent to which the company is being financed through the retention of past earnings in comparison with the issuance of shares. When a company has paid stock dividends, the distinction between these two categories becomes blurred, because amounts of retained earnings equal to the stock dividend are transferred to capital stock. Some accountants argue that the distinction between what was originally invested by shareholders and the accumulated earnings they have left in the business is not a significant one in any case, and that the two amounts might be combined for reporting purposes with no loss of important information.

In practice, the distinction is maintained and often elaborated by showing such items as discounts and premiums on the issuance of shares, amounts of shareholders' equity arising from transactions in the company's own stock, the results of asset revaluations, and the effect of quasi-reorganizations. Most of these are sufficiently unusual to be encountered only on relatively rare occasions.

To understand the significance of the amount of the shareholders' equity, one must remember that the assets have been recorded in the balance sheet at cost, reduced proportionally for estimated use value of each asset consumed to date, either through operations or otherwise. In contrast, the economic value of the shareholders' interest in a company is actually based on anticipated earnings, not on the past cost of its assets. Those who are trading in the company's shares on the market take into account, as best they can, the anticipated future success of the company in providing its product or service to its customers at a profit. Thus stock market values are directly influenced by estimates of future events. Balance sheet amounts are not. One must therefore expect to find the balance sheet amount for shareholders' equity to be different than the amount that would be obtained by multiplying the outstanding shares of stock by the quoted price per share on the market. Only if each asset could be priced for accounting purposes at an amount that accurately reflects its future earning power could the shareholders' equity in the balance sheet be said to reflect the worth of the shareholders' interest in the corporation.

Results of Operations. As generally used, the expression *results of operations* refers primarily to profit-directed enterprises; it will be so used in this chapter. This is a general term suggesting a presentation of those accounting data that together indicate how well an enterprise has succeeded in fulfilling its profit-seeking purpose during a given period of time. The presentation attempts to show what the enterprise has accomplished and what efforts or costs have been expended in obtaining that accomplishment.

Revenue. Revenue is the measure of the product or service transferred to customers during the period at the price paid or promised to be paid by those customers. Thus it represents the accomplishment of the enterprise. The FASB describes revenues as "inflows or other enhancements of assets of an entity or settlements of its liabilities (or combinations of both) during a period from delivering or producing goods, rendering services, or other activities that constitute the entity's ongoing major or central operations."[4] Traditionally, revenue is not measured or reported until accepted by the market. The realization test for revenue is based on the existence of an arms'-length transaction between the selling enterprise and its customers. Until production has passed this test, that is, until it has been sold, traditional accounting refuses to accept it as realized. It is not enough that other transactions by other companies indicate what the product is worth. Until the company itself has been successful in selling the product, no revenue has been realized, in the ordinary accounting sense of the term.

There are those who criticize the present realization test, pointing out that other tests of equal objectivity might be established. They note that the realization test may place undue emphasis on the sale, whereas for some companies some other effort such as production or, in some cases, obtaining orders, or just holding an asset while its market value increases, might be equally or more important. This view is consistent with the arguments for pricing assets at economic value rather than transaction price.

Expenses. The efforts made by a company to obtain revenues are described in accounting terms as *expenses*, or sometimes as *costs and expenses*. The FASB describes expenses as "outflows or other using up of assets or incurrences of liabilities (or a combination of both) during a period from delivering or producing goods, rendering services, or carrying out other activities that constitute the entity's ongoing major or central operations."[5] Expenses tend to fall into three general groups, of which the first is the cost of goods or services sold to produce the revenues. There typically is a direct relationship between cost of goods sold and revenues obtained from their sale. Second are those costs of selling and administration which, although not as related directly to the sales of the period, can often be clearly associated with them. Finally, there are other costs of doing business, which do not necessarily have any direct relationship with specific revenues. These include the payment of federal income and other taxes, charitable contributions, asset expirations due to catastrophes, and the like.

In some cases there is a causal relationship between efforts (expenses) and accomplishments (revenues). Note that this is not a cause-and-effect relationship in the sense that certain causes always bring about certain effects. Rather, expenses are incurred with the intent and often the effect of producing reve-

---

[4]*Ibid.,* par. 63.

[5]*Ibid.,* par. 65.

nue, but there is no absolute assurance that revenue will follow. In the same sense, revenue may be causal of some expenses. If, for example, the company includes a guarantee or service agreement of some kind in its sales agreement, certain *aftercosts* may almost automatically follow the production of revenue. Other items of expense have no such causal relationship; their only connection with revenue is the time relationship, that is, that both occurred within the same accounting period.

Losses. The term *loss* is used to describe a concept in accounting that is not well defined. Indeed, the term is used in two ways. It is used first to describe the results when the expenses for a period exceed the revenues. A company is said to have "incurred a loss" when its expenses are greater than its realized revenues. The term is also used to describe those efforts that are unsuccessful in producing revenue. If, for example, certain items of merchandise that have been purchased with the expectation of sale are later found to be unmarketable, the cost of these items would be treated as a loss and charged against the revenue of the period although they themselves did not represent a successful effort in obtaining such revenue.

Relationship of assets and expenses. Note the close relationship between expenses and assets. Theorists have pointed out that all expenses are at least momentarily assets; that is, they are first acquired with the intent that they will benefit operations of a company either immediately or in the future. The purpose of acquiring almost all assets is so that they may be used to make a contribution to revenue. As this contribution is made, they pass from an asset stage into an expense stage. Thus there is a continual cycling of assets into expense which, in turn, produces revenue represented by new assets which can then be used for further operations.

Net income. Net income is one of the most important concepts in accounting. It is calculated as the difference between realized revenue for a period and those expenses that are related directly to that revenue or that, for some other reason, must be recognized as occurring within the period. The calculation of net income is typically made in a statement of income, which commences with revenues and subtracts the various classifications of expense, generally cost of goods sold, then selling and administrative expenses, and finally those other expenses that must be covered by the revenue of the period. All expenses must be covered if net income is to result. Thus, whether asset decreases are successful in producing revenue and therefore are treated as expenses or are unsuccessful and termed "losses," they must be exceeded in total amount by the revenues of the period. Otherwise, a net loss rather than net income is shown as the result of operations for that accounting period.

Matching. The term *matching* is used to describe the appropriate association of related revenues and expenses. Accounting presentations strive to associate data on an interpretive basis, that is, those items that are related one to another are presented together, those items that are different from one another are separated. The matching of revenue and related expenses is a specific application of this general principle of associating like items. Matching is applied on a total company basis in that all revenues and all expenses for the company are presented together in the income statement for the period, with the final figure showing the net results of operations. Matching may also be applied to specific parts of the company, to divisions, or to groups of transactions, or for whatever other segment it is useful to report the results of operations. In such cases, the reported revenues and expenses may have a more intimate relationship than they do for the company as a whole. Effective matching, whether on a total company basis or on a less than total company basis, is an essential step in presenting the results of operations. Any failure to reveal significant interrelationships between revenues and expenses to that extent does not present the results of operations fairly.

Enterprise. The concept of an *enterprise* or entity is another one of the very few central concepts in accounting. The enterprise is the focus of accounting attention. Accounts are kept, transactions are analyzed, and reports are prepared from the point of view of a specific enterprise. As noted earlier, transactions are usually at least two-party propositions, but the accountant's interest is in only one side of such transactions. The accountant is always concerned with a specific enterprise and its participation in transactions, largely ignoring the effects of the transaction on the other party or parties.

Accounting is flexible enough to adapt itself to almost any kind of unit that has transactions. Occasionally, in the professional literature, much has been made of the idea of an accounting unit. Actually the only requirements for the application of accounting are that the specific unit be identifiable and that it enter into transactions. Given these two conditions, accounting can record the results of those transactions and present useful, interpretive, decision-oriented data.

Accounting may focus on the legal organization or on some part of the legal organization. For example, accounts may be kept for a corporation or, if the corporation engages in a variety of activities, individual profit centers may be established for which accounts can be kept. A simple illustration would be a chain of stores. Accounts could be kept for each of the several stores so that the results of their operations could be determined individually. In addition, the results of all the stores taken as a whole for the total company could also be accounted for and reported.

Corporate entity. Accounting can serve sole proprietorships, partnerships, corporations, trusts, and any other form of legal organization. As a matter of fact, most business activity is carried on under the corporate form, and corporation accounting is a major part of the field of accounting. The corporate entity is used in different ways by different companies. Some large companies manage to operate a substantial number of divisions in widely diversified activities under a single corporate organization. Others use different corporate forms for different purposes within what is essentially a single economic entity. In some cases, differing legal requirements among states, tax provisions, or other reasons encourage a company to form a large number of individual legal entities, all of which effectively are parts of the same total company. In such cases, accounting can provide information about them individually or in total, or preferably both.

The corporate form of organization permits companies to own parts of other companies. Thus, a parent company is one that has a controlling interest in another; that is, it owns a majority of the voting shares of a subsidiary corporation. The terms *parent* and *subsidiary* are typically used when one company has a controlling interest in another. In theory, a controlling interest must be something more than exactly 50 percent of the voting stock of the subsidiary. Practically, this is not always necessary. If a company's outstanding stock is widely disseminated so that no shareholder owns a very large proportion of it, a relatively small holding may have effective control. The point has been made frequently that in such conditions management may perpetuate itself almost indefinitely without holding a majority of the outstanding shares.

Orthodox accounting requires that control be defined in terms of something over 50 percent of the outstanding stock. Critics of orthodox accounting on this particular point contend that the existence of control should be measured on some more realistic basis, whatever the proportionate holding may be. When a company holds an important but less than controlling interest in another company, the second one is referred to as an *affiliate*.

Consolidated financial statements. State corporation laws require that each corporate entity maintain accounting records and prepare financial statements. If a single economic entity includes more than one legal entity, the financial statements of the legal entities must be *consolidated* into one set to represent the total company. In the preparation of consolidated financial statements, those companies that are controlled by the parent will generally have their accounts consolidated with it. (Important exceptions to this rule include subsidiaries in foreign countries, particularly if exchange or currency restrictions influence profit withdrawals.) Those that are not controlled will not be consolidated. In consolidated financial statements, all transactions between controlled members of the family group are eliminated, on the theory that they do not meet the realization test of transactions at arm's length between independent opposing interests. Transactions with uncontrolled companies are considered to be arms'-length transactions outside the family group and, therefore, a proper basis for recognizing revenue and expense. Thus, consolidated financial statements present the combined financial position and results of operations of a group of companies controlled by a single managerial body with all intracompany relationships and transactions eliminated, so that, in effect, we see the family group as if it were a single enterprise dealing only with the outside world.

Business acquisition. In a *business acquisition,* two or more formerly independent business entities are combined into one. If certain technical requirements are met, the combination is treated as a *pooling of interests;* otherwise it is a *purchase.* In accounting for a pooling of interests, the accounts of the two companies are added together, including their retained earnings. When one company purchases another company, however, the retained earnings of the purchased company cannot be carried forward because of the accepted theory that income must be earned, not purchased. In accounting for a business acquisition treated as a purchase, the shareholders' equity of the acquired company disappears; only its assets and liabilities appear in the balance sheet of the purchaser. When the net assets so acquired exactly match the amount paid, the former substitutes for the latter in the purchaser's balance sheet. If the amount paid by the purchaser exceeds the net assets received, the acquiring company is considered to have purchased an intangible asset commonly described as *goodwill.*

Price paid by purchaser		$1,000,000
Company acquired:		
Assets	$1,200,000	
Liabilities	400,000	800,000
Goodwill		$ 200,000

Under the theory that the excess payment would be made only if expected future earnings justified it, goodwill is often described as the price paid for excess future earnings and is required to be amortized as an expense against revenues over a period not to exceed 40 years.

The Continuity Concept. Oversimplification has distorted the nature of the continuity concept in some discussions. Some say that the continuity, or going-concern, concept means that the enterprise is considered to exist indefinitely into the future. There is just enough truth in this view to make it misleading. Actually, the continuity concept sees the enterprise continuing in its present form, and, with its present purpose, sufficiently far enough into the future so that its assets will be used for the purpose for which they were acquired and the obligations against them will be paid in due course.

This conception of the continuity idea is the foundation for one of the basic postulates of accounting. Properly expressed, that postulate would be stated somewhat as follows: "Unless and until there is evidence to the contrary, an enterprise must be considered as continuing largely in its present form and with its present purposes."

The opening qualification is of prime importance. Unless there is evidence to the contrary, accountants have no alternative except to treat an enterprise as continuing. If they operated on a contrary assumption, they would have to treat every enterprise as if it were about to liquidate. This would have a severe influence on the valuation of assets, the treatment of liabilities, and all presentations of financial position and results of operations. Actually, experience tells us otherwise. Experience tells us that most enterprises do continue in business. Obviously, when there is evidence to the contrary—when the specific enterprise in which the accountant is interested appears to be liquidating or to have no continuing life—he or she should value the assets and present the liabilities on an entirely different basis, one that reflects the more likely possibility. Thus, the continuity concept actually requires that in certain fairly rare cases, the accountant adopt a liquidation point of view rather than a going-concern point of view.

There may be a little confusion in terming a given item both a concept and a postulate, as has been done here with enterprise continuity. In expressing any accounting postulate, one must use accounting terms, each of which represents a concept of greater or lesser importance. We must comprehend the concept of continuity before we can use the term in stating the postulate.

Present Fairly. The expression *present fairly* is used in a short-form auditor's opinion to suggest that the financial statements examined are satisfactory. It is a difficult term to define, and one that itself relies on a substantial number of other quite important concepts. *Present fairly* is generally coupled with another expression, *generally accepted accounting principles*; that is, a set of financial statements either does or does not present fairly in accordance with generally accepted accounting principles. Accountants have been known to argue over whether this means that the financial statements present fairly *and* are in accordance with generally accepted accounting principles, or that they present fairly *on the basis of* generally accepted accounting principles. The distinction is a fine one, but an important one.

Generally accepted accounting principles. Generally accepted accounting principles include a number of conventions and practices that are currently subject to criticism. There are those who contend that certain generally accepted accounting principles do not present fairly, that their application in some circumstances is something less than useful. To such critics, the expression "presents fairly in accordance with generally accepted accounting principles" is merely a defensive term used to protect accountants from attacks on their reports. The majority of accountants, however, feel that the expression "generally accepted accounting principles" describes those practices and procedures that over time have been found to be most useful, and although they are not necessarily the preferred treatment in every case, in combination they do present a satisfactory picture of the status and progress of the enterprise reported upon.

Consistency. One of the primary purposes of accounting is to present reports on a comparable basis. By themselves, individual accounting figures are seldom informative. Coupled with other figures, for example, reports for the same company for prior periods, they become much more useful. If comparisons are to be made, however, it becomes imperative that reports be prepared on a consistent basis, one year with another. Accountants thus place great reliance on consistency as a required virtue of accounting data. *Consistency* means that the same transactions have been treated the same way this year and last year so that the financial statements for the current year can be compared with preceding years without erroneous conclusions being drawn from them. If an inconsistency exists between the presentations of successive years, fair presentation demands that this be disclosed.

Materiality. Obviously it is not required that all transactions, however minor, be handled on a consistent basis; only transactions of material significance require such attention. A *material* transaction or event or item is one the knowledge of which might influence the judgment of an informed reader. If an informed reader would not be concerned with the item because it was not of sufficiently consequential nature or amount, the item is regarded as immaterial.

No objective tests of materiality have been established, although there seems to be a general feeling that an item running in excess of 5 to 10 percent of an appropriate base is likely to be considered material in most cases. Thus, if we found consistency in all cases except for treatment of a given item that constituted, say, 15 percent of the net income for the year, most accountants would agree that the assertion "presents fairly in accordance with generally accepted accounting principles applied on a basis consistent with the preceding year" would require mention of the inconsistent treatment.

Full disclosure. The term *full disclosure* is a common one in accounting. Although recommendations have been made for substitution of the term *adequate disclosure,* the older term is still widely used. It means that the presented information includes everything that an informed reader should know to come to appropriate conclusions—that nothing of substance has been concealed or omitted. Accountants face a dilemma in summarizing information for reporting purposes. If they were to report the total amount of detail available to them, most readers would be overwhelmed. On the other hand, in condensing and classifying the total mass of transaction detail, they must be careful not to bury or hide items or events that would influence the reader's judgment.

Full disclosure relates especially to transactions between an enterprise and those who are in positions of authority within the enterprise. Thus, any transactions between an enterprise and its officers should be disclosed, as should all other transactions that have any unusual bearing on the company's financial position or results of operations.

In describing financial statements as presenting fairly, the description typically refers to the financial statements *taken as a whole.* The idea here is that although there may well be minor inaccuracies within the financial statements, overall they present a satisfactorily realistic expression of the company's progress and status. No one can guarantee that every item in the balance sheet and income statement is accurate or correct. One can be reasonably certain, however, that any errors that may be included are not sufficiently important to mislead those who read the statements. Thus, when each item is read in context with the others, an overall impression is gained of the company's activities and current position that is satisfactorily objective and fully and fairly disclosed.

ACCOUNTING PRINCIPLES

Accounting concepts are implemented through accounting principles that may be described as guides to proper action. Other things being equal, sound concepts lead to right actions. But not everyone who keeps accounts necessarily has an adequate understanding of accounting concepts. Deficiencies or limitations in one's concepts will affect the propriety of one's accounting. Accounting is a method of analysis designed to represent certain aspects of reality as truthfully as possible. We apprehend reality in terms of our concepts. To the extent that all accountants understand the same concepts, they should account for the same transactions in the same way. To aid those who do not have an adequate understanding of concepts to account on a basis comparable to those who do, principles have been established to indicate consensus. Accounting Principles Board Statement No. 4 [1970] rightly describes accounting principles in these terms:

> Generally accepted accounting principles incorporate the consensus at a particular time as to which economic resources and obligations should be recorded as assets and liabilities by financial accounting, which changes in assets and liabilities should be recorded, when these changes should be recorded, how the assets and liabilities and changes in them should be

measured, what information should be disclosed and how it should be disclosed and which financial statements should be prepared.

Accounting data have a variety of uses. They are used as a basis for operating and investment decisions within the company, for credit and investment decisions external to the company, for taxation and regulation, and for a variety of other uses. Some users of accounting data are able to control the data they receive; some are not. For example, internal operating and investment decisions are made by members of the company's management who are able to control the accounting department directly and to obtain the information they require prepared on any basis they consider appropriate. Taxation and regulatory bodies have the power to establish rules and regulations to be followed by those subject to their control and to conduct examinations and enforce observance of those rules and regulations. In contrast, decisions to extend credit to the company and to make investments in it are made by people with no direct control over the accounting information they receive. They must use what they get. Creditors of various kinds, shareholders, labor union representatives, economists, financial analysts, planners, and others must rely on the company for accurate and realistic data.

Accounting principles are thus required for two reasons: first, to guide those who prepare financial statements so they know what the consensus is on appropriate accounting for transactions and events; second, to assure some degree of uniformity and comparability in the data received and relied on by those who have no direct influence over the accumulation and presentation of the accounting data on which they rely. The expression "generally accepted accounting principles" applies almost completely to the guides followed in preparing accounting data for those without influence. Management, regulators, and taxing bodies are well advised to follow the same accounting principles, but are quite free to deviate therefrom if they so desire.

Meaning of Generally Accepted Accounting Principles. The term *generally accepted accounting principles*, or GAAP, is one used by accountants since the 1930s and is now deeply embedded in accounting literature. Its meaning is not well defined, but the phrase is generally interpreted to include those accounting practices accepted as satisfactory by a significant number of recognized accountants. There is no single reference to which one can turn for a complete exposition of GAAP, a number of different organizations having been recognized at different times as authoritative sources.

As business becomes more complex and new kinds of transactions and business relationships are invented, the application of general principles to specific sets of actions and circumstances requires difficult judgments. Two important issues relate to these conditions. One is the uniformity-flexibility issue; the other is the standards overload question.

The Uniformity-Flexibility Issue. A continuing question in establishing accounting principles is the extent to which such propositions should be stated as detailed prescriptions or only as general guides. Proponents of flexibility argue that the great variety in business situations and circumstances is such that strict uniform rules would result in only superficial uniformity, that detailed prescriptions applied to substantively different transactions and events supply no true comparability. On the other hand, there are those who can point to serious abuses of the flexibility now permitted in accounting. For example, practices first developed to meet a given set of circumstances have been extended to other circumstances for which they were never originally intended. A study entitled *Effect of Circumstances on the Application of Accounting Principles* [Mautz, 1972], notes that "Flexibility in accounting and reporting has been availed of by some for purposes other than those related to obtaining the fairest possible corporate financial reporting," and "Disciplinary elements in the corporate financial reporting process have not been as effective in curbing the misuse of present provisions for flexibility as some desire." The same report further notes: "Comparability and uniformity are not equivalent terms. Uniformity stresses application of the same or similar methods of accounting or reporting to all apparently similar transactions, conditions, or events. Comparability is dependent upon presentations responsive to the substance of the transactions, conditions, and events to be reported and the circumstances in which these occur."

Thus, those charged with the responsibility of establishing accounting principles that others are expected to follow must continually be alert to the necessity of steering a fine line between excessively detailed and rigid requirements that may fail to reflect reality in unusual situations and guides stated in such general terms that they lend themselves to misinterpretation and abuse.

Standards Overload. The so-called *standards overload* arises from at least two separate tendencies. One is the continuing request from practicing accountants to the authoritative body to explain how and to what extent a general principle applies to a range of transactions that, although somewhat similar, vary from clearly subject to the principle through those that might be subject and finally to those that are probably outside its scope. The second is the apparent concern of the standard setters, often born of sad experience, that a principle will be misapplied. Hence they use illustrations and add specific provisions to cover special transactions and conditions. Together these tendencies over time convert broad guidelines into something akin to detailed rule books.

Establishment of Accounting Principles. A variety of efforts to state the principles underlying corporate financial reporting have been made by individuals and committees with and without special commissions from organized bodies. In *The Search for Accounting Principles* [1964], Reed K. Storey points out that the earliest principles formally established by the American Institute of Certified Public Accountants (at that time the American Institute of Accountants) evolved out of correspondence between committees of the American Institute of Certified Public Accountants and the New York Stock Exchange in 1932. The American Institute of Certified Public Accountants established a committee for the purpose of pronouncing on important accounting problems in 1939. During the 20-year period of its existence, that Committee on Accounting Procedure issued 51 Accounting Research Bulletins on a variety of topics. The Committee on Accounting Procedure was replaced by the Accounting Principles Board and an Accounting Research Division, both as units of the American Institute of Certified Public Accountants, in 1959. The Accounting Research Division was intended to provide special research resources in an attempt to strengthen the procedure for establishing authoritative principles. Membership on the Accounting Principles Board varied from 18 to 21 at different times during its life and included representatives of the major public accounting firms, smaller firms, and geographic areas of the country as well as representatives from industry and academia.

The Financial Accounting Standards Board. Since 1973, the Financial Accounting Standards Board has been the designated organization in the private sector for establishing standards of financial accounting and reporting. FASB standards are officially recognized as authoritative by the Securities and Exchange Commission [Accounting Series Release No. 150, December 1973] and the American Institute of Certified Public Accountants [Rules of Conduct, as amended May 1973 and May 1979].

The seven members of the FASB serve full-time. They have diverse backgrounds, but they must possess "knowledge of accounting, finance, and business, and a concern for the public interest in matters of financial accounting and reporting." They are aided by a staff of technical specialists plus administrative and other support personnel. Board members are appointed for 5-year terms and are eligible for reappointment to one additional 5-year term.

The FASB is the operating part of a tripartite structure that includes the Financial Accounting Foundation and the Financial Accounting Standards Advisory Council. The Foundation's board of trustees raises funds to support the Board, appoints the members, and exercises general oversight. Its members are made up of nominees from the following sponsoring organizations:

American Accounting Association (academe)
American Institute of Certified Public Accountants
Financial Analysts Federation (investors and investment advisors)
Financial Executives Institute (corporate executives)
National Association of Accountants (primarily management accountants)
Securities Industry Association (investment bankers, brokers)

There also is a trustee at large.

The advisory council has responsibility for consulting with the Standards Board as to major policy questions, technical issues on the Board's agenda, the assigning of priorities to projects, matters likely to require the attention of the FASB, selection and organization of task forces, and such other matters as may be requested by the FASB chairman. The council has a membership that varies between 40 and 45, broadly representative of preparers, auditors, and users of financial information. It has its own chairman.

The Financial Accounting Standards Board has the authority not only to issue standards but also to issue interpretations of Opinions of the Accounting Principles Board and Accounting Research Bulletins of the Committee on Accounting Procedure. Members of the American Institute of Certified Public Accountants are required by that organization's rules of conduct to accept statements by the Financial Accounting Standards Board as authoritative.

Public-sector establishment of accounting principles. The Financial Accounting Standards Board organization, like that of the Accounting Principles Board and the Committee on Accounting Procedure before it, is an effort to retain the authority for formulating and establishing accounting principles in the private sector. Some accounting principles, however, are issued within the public sector. The Securities and Exchange Commission (SEC) has authority to establish the accounting principles required in filings to be made with it. In general, the Securities and Exchange Commission has relied on the accounting profession for the development of accounting principles, but on occasion has differed with the promulgations of the accounting profession and has issued requirements of its own. Recently the Securities and Exchange Commission expressed its approval of the procedures and organization of the Financial Accounting Standards Board and indicated its desire to rely on statements from that Board whenever possible.

In 1971, the Congress of the United States established a five-member Cost Accounting Standards Board (CASB) with the Comptroller General of the United States as chairman. The function of the Board was to promulgate cost accounting standards to be followed by contractors and government agencies in the negotiation, administration, and settlement of negotiated defense contracts. Promulgations by the CASB accepted by Congress have the full force and effect of law. Failure to renew funding in 1980 resulted in the demise of the CASB.

Certain regulatory agencies, such as the Interstate Commerce Commission, the Civil Aeronautics Board, the Railroad Accounting Principles Board, and others, also issue accounting rules and regulations applicable to the companies subject to their control.

A number of organizations with different kinds of authority and different functions are thus active in the general field of accounting principles. The extent to which the work of one of these authorities will overlap or conflict with that of another is yet to be determined. Efforts to establish liaison among the several groups have been made in good faith. It is hoped that these will be sufficiently effective that conflicting standards will not appear.

Informal establishment of accounting principles. In addition to these relatively formal methods of establishing accounting principles and standards, informal methods exist. When an industry or even a company faces a new situation, one that no present principle seems to cover, it must develop the best solution it can. The relatively lengthy procedures required by the duly established authorities may take so long that the company or industry facing the problem cannot wait. In such cases, principles are established on an informal, ad hoc basis by the reporting company or an industry group, and if adopted by a number of companies may become "generally accepted" until they are reviewed and either more formally accepted or rejected by the appropriate authoritative body.

Because business is a dynamic rather than a passive type of activity, with new agreements, transactions, and practices developing continually and on a random basis, it seems unlikely that any body or group of bodies can state with final authority all generally accepted accounting principles. On the contrary, we shall continually find situations sufficiently different that they appear to justify special principles, and we shall continually be adding to and refining those principles, practices, and procedures referred to as "generally accepted accounting principles."

AUDITING STANDARDS AND OPINIONS

The Role of Auditing. In a credit economy such as that in the United States and other economically developed nations, accounting data are one of the bases on which a company's creditworthiness is decided. But accounting data are produced by the reporting company, so additional steps are necessary to establish their reliability. Independent auditors are professional experts in the examination of the financial statements and underlying accounting records of corporations and other business organizations. An audit is a professional examination meeting certain standards on the basis of which the auditor expresses an independent professional opinion respecting the fairness of presentation of the financial statements at issue. Because of the flexibility permitted by generally accepted accounting standards and the many judgments and estimates necessary to prepare a set of financial statements, any assertion about financial statements more specific than that they "present fairly" is considered by auditors and their legal advisors to be unwise.

To give what is known as an unqualified opinion, the kind that companies most like to receive, an auditor must make the examination in accordance with generally accepted auditing standards.

Generally Accepted Auditing Standards. Auditing standards differ from auditing procedures in that *procedures* relate to acts to be performed, whereas *standards* deal with measures of the quality of the performance of those acts and the objectives to be attained by the use of the procedures undertaken. *Auditing standards* as distinct from *auditing procedures* thus concern themselves not only with the auditor's professional qualities but also with the judgment exercised by the auditor in the performance of the examination and in the report.

The generally accepted auditing standards as approved and adopted by the membership of the American Institute of Certified Public Accountants are as follows:

General standards

1. The examination is to be performed by a person or persons having adequate technical training and proficiency as an auditor.

2. In all matters relating to the assignment an independence in mental attitude is to be maintained by the auditor or auditors.

3. Due professional care is to be exercised in the performance of the examination and the preparation of the report.

Standards of field work

1. The work is to be adequately planned and assistants, if any, are to be properly supervised.

2. There is to be a proper study and evaluation of the existing internal control

as a basis for reliance thereon and for the determination of the resultant extent of the tests to which auditing procedures are to be restricted.

3. Sufficient competent evidential matter is to be obtained through inspection, observation, inquiries, and confirmations to afford a reasonable basis for an opinion regarding the financial statements under examination.

Standards of reporting

1. The report shall state whether the financial statements are presented in accordance with generally accepted principles of accounting.

2. The report shall state whether such principles have been consistently observed in the current period in relation to the preceding period.

3. Informative disclosures in the financial statements are to be regarded as reasonably adequate unless otherwise stated in the report.

4. The report shall either contain an expression of opinion regarding the financial statements, taken as a whole, or an assertion to the effect that an opinion cannot be expressed. When an overall opinion cannot be expressed, the reasons therefor should be stated. In all cases where an auditor's name is associated with financial statements the report should contain a clear-cut indication of the character of the auditor's examination, if any, and the degree of responsibility he or she is taking.

Kinds of Audit Opinions. Upon completion of an examination, an auditor can give an unqualified opinion, a qualified opinion, an adverse opinion, or disclaim an opinion. The standard short-form unqualified opinion recommended by the American Institute of Certified Public Accountants consists of a statement describing the nature of the examination, usually referred to as the scope of the examination, and an expression of the auditor's opinion.

Unqualified opinion. Wording for the standard short-form report follows:

(Scope)

We have examined the balance sheet of X Company as of (at) December 31, 19XX, and the related statements of income, retained earnings and changes in financial position for the year then ended. Our examination was made in accordance with generally accepted auditing standards and, accordingly, included such tests of the accounting records and such other auditing procedures as we considered necessary in the circumstances.

(Opinion)

In our opinion, the financial statements referred to above present fairly the financial position of X Company as of (at) December 31, 19XX, and the results of its operations and the changes in its financial position for the year then ended, in conformity with generally accepted accounting principles applied on a basis consistent with that of the preceding year.

Typically the report is addressed to the company whose financial statements are being examined or to its shareholders or board of directors.

In some circumstances, a departure from the auditor's standard report is recommended, generally for one or more of the following reasons:

1. The scope of the auditor's examination is affected by conditions that preclude meeting some requirement included in generally accepted auditing standards.

2. The auditor's report is based in part on the report of another auditor.

3. The financial statements are affected by a departure from generally accepted accounting principles.

4. Accounting principles have not been applied consistently.

5. The financial statements are affected by uncertainties concerning future events, the outcome of which is not susceptible to reasonable estimation at the date of the auditor's report.

6. The auditor wishes to emphasize a matter regarding the financial statements.

Qualified opinion. Statement on Auditing Standards No. 2, issued in October 1974 by the American Institute of Certified Public Accountants, describes a qualified opinion in the following words:

> A qualified opinion states that, "except for" or "subject to" the effects of the matter to which the qualification relates, the financial statements present fairly financial position, results of operations and changes in financial position in conformity with generally accepted accounting principles consistently applied. Such an opinion is expressed when a lack of sufficient competent evidential matter or restrictions on the scope of the auditor's examination have led him to conclude that he cannot express an unqualified opinion, or when the auditor believes, on the basis of his examination, that
>
>   *a.* the financial statements contain a departure from generally accepted accounting principles, the effect of which is material,
>
>   *b.* there has been a material change between periods in accounting principles or in the method of their application, or
>
>   *c.* there are significant uncertainties affecting the financial statements,
>
> and he has decided not to express an adverse opinion or to disclaim an opinion.

The statement illustrates a number of qualified opinions, which vary with the reason for the qualification but which in every case try to point out why the opinion must be qualified and the importance of that qualification.

Adverse opinion. An adverse opinion states that the financial statements do not present fairly the financial position, results of operations, or changes in financial position of the reporting company in conformity with generally accepted accounting principles. Statement on Auditing Standards No. 2 requires that an auditor who expresses an adverse opinion should disclose in a separate paragraph of the report all the substantive reasons for that adverse opinion and the principal effects of those reasons on the financial position, results of operations, and changes in financial position to the extent that this can be determined. The opinion paragraph should include a direct reference to the separate paragraph that discloses the reason for the adverse opinion.

Disclaimer of opinion. A disclaimer of opinion states clearly that the auditor does not express an opinion on the financial statements. The auditor who disclaims an opinion is required to state in a separate paragraph of the report all of the substantive reasons for doing so. In most cases the reason for disclaimer of opinion is that the auditor has not made an examination sufficient to provide a basis for expressing an opinion. A disclaimer of an opinion is not appropriate if an auditor has reason to believe that the financial statements do not present fairly what they purport to represent. Thus the auditor who has any reservations regarding fair presentation in conformity with generally accepted accounting principles or in the consistency of their application should so state in the separate paragraph.

Piecemeal opinions, that is, expressions of opinion by the auditor as to certain identified items in financial statements without an overall opinion on the financial statements taken as a whole, were at one time accepted. Statement on Auditing Standards No. 2 makes it clear that piecemeal opinions are no longer appropriate and that they should not be issued in any situation.

Negative Assurance. A negative assurance is a statement to the effect that "nothing came to our attention that would indicate that these amounts or statements are not fairly presented." Reports containing negative assurances as a result of examinations by external auditors are not approved by the American Institute of Certified Public Accountants with one exception. Negative assurances are permissible in letters required by security underwriters in which the independent auditor reports on limited procedures followed with respect to unaudited financial statements or other financial data pertinent to a registration statement filed with the Securities and Exchange Commission. These are viewed as a special kind of report and the one situation in which a negative assurance would not be misleading. The argument against the use of a negative assurance in an audit report is that the less work one does, the stronger the assurance that can be given. But unless the reader has a very sound and specific understanding of the extent of the auditor's work, the negative assurance is not informative.

Professional Ethics Regarding Accountants' Opinions. It is generally recognized that (1) financial statements are representations by management, (2) the CPA has the responsibility for conducting the examination in accordance with generally accepted auditing standards, and (3) the CPA has the sole responsibility for writing the report stating, among other things, whether the financial statements are presented in accordance with generally accepted principles of accounting (reporting standard number 1).

Further light on the responsibilities of the CPA may be gained by reference to the Restatement of the Code of Professional Ethics adopted by the membership of the American Institute of Certified Public Accountants [1973]. The specific rules in that Code are based on the following five broad concepts stated as affirmative Ethical Principles:

> *Independence, integrity, and objectivity.* A certified public accountant should maintain his integrity and objectivity and, when engaged in the practice of public accounting, be independent of those he serves.
> *Competence and technical standards.* A certified public accountant should observe the profession's technical standards and strive continually to improve his competence and the quality of his services.

Responsibilities to clients. A certified public accountant should be fair and candid with his clients and serve them to the best of his ability, with professional concern for their best interests, consistent with his responsibilities to the public.

Responsibilities to colleagues. A certified public accountant should conduct himself in a manner which will promote cooperation and good relations among members of the profession.

Other responsibilities and practices. A certified public accountant should conduct himself in a manner which will enhance the stature of the profession and its ability to serve the public.

BIBLIOGRAPHY

Accounting Principles Board (AICPA), *Basic Concepts and Accounting Principles underlying Financial Statements of Business Enterprises*, Statement No. 4 (APB, 1970).

American Institute of Certified Public Accountants, *Code of Professional Ethics* (AICPA, 1973).

————, Auditing Standards Executive Committee, *Reports on Audited Financial Statements*, Statement on Auditing Standards No. 2 (AICPA, 1974).

————, *Codification of Statements on Auditing Standards*, first issued in 1973; reissued periodically.

Committee on Accounting Procedure (AICPA), *Restatement and Revision of Accounting Research Bulletins*, Accounting Research Bulletin No. 43 (CAP, 1953).

Financial Accounting Standards Board, *Accounting for Certain Marketable Securities*, Statement of Financial Accounting Standards No. 12 (FASB, 1975).

————, *Objectives of Financial Reporting by Business Enterprises*, Statement of Financial Accounting Concepts No. 1 (FASB, November 1978).

————, *Financial Reporting and Changing Prices*, Statement of Financial Accounting Standards No. 33 (FASB, September 1979).

————, *Qualitative Characteristics of Accounting Information*, Statement of Financial Accounting Concepts No. 2 (FASB, May 1980).

————, *Elements of Financial Statements of Business Enterprises*, Statement of Financial Accounting Concepts No. 3 (FASB, December 1980).

————, *Objectives of Financial Reporting by Nonbusiness Organizations*, Statement of Financial Accounting Concepts No. 4 (FASB, December 1980).

Mautz, R. K., *Effect of Circumstances on the Application of Accounting Principles* (Financial Executive Research Foundation, New York, 1972).

Storey, R. K., *The Search for Accounting Principles* (AICPA, New York, 1964).

CHAPTER **2**

Financial Statements:

Income Statements

and Balance Sheets

Michael H. Granof
Professor of Accounting, The University of Texas at Austin

Daniel G. Short
Associate Professor of Accounting, The University of Texas at Austin

This chapter focuses on the income statement, the balance sheet, and the statement of changes in retained earnings. Disclosure of changes in other owners' equity accounts is also discussed. A third primary statement, the statement of changes in financial position, is discussed in Chapter 3.

DEFINITION

Financial statements periodically communicate to interested parties the data that have been recorded, processed, and summarized by a firm's accounting system. Financial statements include not only the main numerical tables themselves but also the information and explanations incorporated into footnotes and other supplementary sections.

According to Accounting Principles Board (APB) Statement No. 4 [1970], if financial statements are to present fairly the financial position and results of operations of an enterprise in conformity with generally accepted accounting principles, they must include the following:

1. Balance sheet
2. Income statement
3. Statement of changes in retained earnings
4. Statement of changes in financial position
5. Disclosure of changes in other categories of shareholders' equity

A *balance sheet* (or *statement of financial position*) presents the financial status of an enterprise at a *particular time*. It sets forth a firm's (1) assets, (2) liabilities, and (3) owners' equity.

An *income statement* indicates the results of an enterprise's profit-directed activities *during the period of time covered*. It reports on the firm's revenues, expenses, gains, losses, and the resultant net income (or loss).

A *statement of changes in retained earnings* summarizes the transactions that occurred during the accounting period that affected retained earnings. Retained earnings represent the cumulative earnings of the enterprise that have not been distributed to owners. Changes in retained earnings are brought about by the recognition of income, the payment of dividends, and the adjustment of income of prior periods. The statement of changes in retained earnings reconciles the retained earnings at the beginning of the period with those at the end.

Changes in other owners' equity accounts may be reported in a variety of ways, including a separate statement. These changes are attributable to the issue and retirement of shares, stock dividends, stock splits, and any other adjustments that affect the interests of the owners.

BALANCE SHEET AND INCOME STATEMENT: IMPORTANCE OF ARTICULATION

The balance sheet provides a detailed description of the fundamental accounting equation,[1]

$$\text{Assets} = \text{Liabilities} + \text{Owners' Equity}$$

Assets are probable future economic benefits obtained or controlled by a particular entity as a result of past transactions or events.

Liabilities are probable future sacrifices of economic benefits arising from present obligations of a particular entity to transfer assets or provide services to other entities in the future as a result of past transactions or events.

Owners' equity is the residual interest in the assets of an entity that remains after deducting liabilities. In a business enterprise, the owners' equity represents the claims of the owners against the firm's assets.

Owners' equity can be decomposed into two classes: investments by owners and retained earnings. Investments by owners are increases in net assets result-

---

[1] For definitions of the major components of financial statements, see FASB *Statement of Financial Accounting Concepts No. 3* [1980b].

ing from contributions of cash, other assets, or services. Retained earnings are the cumulative changes in the net assets of the enterprise resulting from net increases from operations (income) and decreases from disbributions of net assets to owners (dividends).

THE BALANCE SHEET AS A STATEMENT OF RESIDUALS

In the years prior to the 1930s, the balance sheet was considered the financial report of central concern. Indeed, many firms prepared only a balance sheet. Since then emphasis has shifted from the balance sheet toward the income statement. The objectives of financial reporting articulated by the Financial Accounting Standards Board (FASB) in Statement of Financial Accounting Concepts No. 1, *Objectives of Financial Reporting by Business Enterprises* [1978] indicate specifically that "the *primary* focus of financial reporting is information about an enterprise's *performance* provided by *measures of earnings* and its components" (emphasis added). Earnings are of significance because they provide a basis for assessing future cash flows.

Generally accepted accounting principles require that income, assets, and liabilities be determined by way of accrual accounting. *Accrual accounting* records the financial effects of transactions in the periods in which they have their primary economic impact, rather than only when cash is received or paid. Accrual accounting assures that recognition is given to the receipt and consumption of all resources, not just cash. Insofar as flows of noncash resources eventually result in receipt or disbursement of cash, income calculated on an accrual basis is considered to be a more reliable indicator of future cash flows than is income computed on a cash basis.

Central to accrual accounting is the concept that resources received or expended should be recorded as revenues or expenses in periods in which they can be associated with the firm's production or sales activities. Resources may be received or consumed in periods other than those in which related production or sales activities have occurred. These resources require accounting recognition, but they cannot be recorded as revenue or expenses under accrual accounting. As a result, they must be reflected on the balance sheet as either assets or liabilities; that is, as future economic benefits or sacrifices. For example, when a firm acquires production equipment, the equipment is given accounting recognition when acquired by recording its cost as an asset. Only as it is used in the production of goods or services is the cost charged as an expense. The periods in which the expense is recognized are independent of those in which the cash payments are made for the equipment.

Owing to the application of the accrual concept as well as to the primacy accorded measurements of income, the balance sheet may be interpreted as a statement of residuals—that is, as a compendium of benefits and sacrifices that have not yet been recognized on the income statement. The balance sheet does not, and is not purported to, indicate the current values of assets and liabilities. The purpose of the balance sheet is not to indicate the amounts for which assets could be sold or replaced or the amounts for which liabilities could be liquidated. For example, the net amount at which equipment is presented is indicative of its acquisition cost, less the amount that has not yet been charged off as an expense. Seldom would such an amount be representative of the market price of the asset.

OBJECTIVES OF FINANCIAL STATEMENTS

Financial accounting can be understood and evaluated only by considering the needs of those who will rely on financial statements to facilitate the decisions they are required to make. The most useful form or content of financial reports depends on the information required by users.

The FASB, in Statement of Financial Accounting Concepts No. 1 [1978], has expressed three primary objectives of general-purpose financial reporting:

1. To provide information that is useful to present and potential investors and creditors and other users in *making rational investment, credit, and similar decisions.*

2. To provide information to help present and potential investors and creditors and other users in *assessing the amounts, timing, and uncertainty of prospective cash receipts* from dividends or interest and from the sale, redemption, or maturity of securities or loans that they will receive. Because investors' and creditors' cash flows are related to enterprise cash flows, financial reporting should provide information to help investors, creditors, and others assess the amounts, timing, and uncertainty of prospective net cash inflows to the related enterprise.

3. To provide information about the *economic resources of an enterprise; the claims to those resources* (obligations of the enterprise to transfer resources to other entities and owners' equity); and *the effects of transactions, events, and circumstances that change its resources and claims to those resources.*

The objectives were selected from a large set of possible objectives. They are intended to limit the scope of general-purpose financial reports. The objectives, for example, indicate that the financial reports should be directed to "potential investors and creditors and other users in making rational investment, credit, and similar decisions." By implication, general-purpose financial reports are not intended specifically for managers to rely on in making routine operating decisions. The content and form of special-purpose financial statements to be used to make internal management decisions need not be governed by official pronouncements.

The objectives also state that financial reports should provide information to enable investors and creditors to assess the amounts, timing, and uncertainty of prospective cash flows. They are not intended to provide data on the liquidation or current market values of a business enterprise, either taken as a whole or as individual components. For decisions that require such information, supplementary data are needed.

GENERAL STANDARDS FOR FINANCIAL REPORTING

Two primary qualities that make accounting information useful to those who rely on it are relevance and reliability. These and other qualities that accounting information should possess are discussed by the FASB in Statement of Financial Accounting Concepts No. 2, *Qualitative Characteristics of Accounting Information* [1980a].

Relevance is the capacity of information to make a difference in a decision by helping users to make predictions about the outcome of past, present, and future events or to confirm or correct prior expectations.

Reliability is the quality of information that assures that information is reasonably free from error and bias and faithfully represents what it purports to represent.

Information that is the most reliable may not always be the most relevant. As a rule, for example, data on historical costs—those based exclusively on transactions of the past—are more reliable than those on current market values. Yet for many decisions, information with respect to the current value of an asset is more pertinent than that regarding the amount paid to acquire the asset in the past. Generally accepted accounting principles balance the competing standards, sometimes sacrificing attainment of one for the other. As a result, financial reports are neither as relevant nor as reliable for some decisions as both accountants and users would like.

Two additional qualities that enhance the utility of accounting information are comparability and consistency.

Comparability is the quality of information that enables users to identify similarities in, and differences between, two sets of economic phenomena. The need for comparability suggests the importance of conforming the content and arrangement of particular financial statements to statements of other organizations that are likely to be used concurrently.

Consistency is the quality of information that assures conformity from period to period with unchanging policies and procedures. Consistency of practice facilitates comparisons of information from one period to the next and enables users to decipher trends and relationships among measurements over time. The Accounting Principles Board stated, in APB Opinion No. 20, that "in the preparation of financial statements there is a presumption that an accounting principle once adopted should not be changed in accounting for events and transactions of a similar type."

GENERAL RECOMMENDATIONS

The guidelines that follow are applicable to financial reports as a whole. Guidelines pertaining to each of the basic statements, as well as the supplementary sections, are presented later in this chapter.

Accounting period. Financial statements are normally presented for an accounting period of 1 year. (Issues of reporting over shorter periods of time are discussed in Chapter 5.)

Comparative statements. Financial statements for two or more periods are normally presented for comparative purposes. The AICPA Committee on Terminology explained the need for comparative statements in Bulletin No. 1:

> The presentation of comparative financial statements and other reports enhances the usefulness of such reports and brings out more clearly the nature and trends of current changes affecting the enterprise. Such presentation emphasizes the fact that statements for a series of periods are far more significant than those for a single period and that the accounts for one period are but an installment of what is essentially a continuous history.

Business enterprises that are subject to Securities and Exchange Commission (SEC) rules must provide shareholders with balance sheets for the ends of each of the last 2 years and statements of changes in financial position and income statements for each of the last 3 years. In addition, selected financial data must be presented for each of the preceding 5 years.

Consolidated financial statements. If one enterprise in a group owns more than 50 percent of the outstanding voting stock of another enterprise, there is a presumption that the financial statements are more meaningful when they are consolidated. Specific rules as to when consolidated statements should be presented are contained in Accounting Research Bulletins (ARBs) No. 43 and 51.

Foreign operations. A business enterprise with foreign operations should translate amounts stated in a foreign currency into U.S. dollars. Conversion procedures are explained in FASB Statement No. 52.

Form of financial statement presentation. The accounting profession has not identified a particular format for financial statements as being best for all purposes. As a result, a variety of forms are used in practice. Several widely used forms are illustrated in this chapter.

Classification. Information contained in financial statements should be classified based on the presumed needs of users. If an item that would otherwise be required to be shown is immaterial in amount, it need not be reported separately.

Materiality. Of overriding concern to a preparer of financial statements is their relevance to the parties relying on them. Generally accepted accounting principles apply only insofar as their effect will be material. Financial statements need not disclose information that is immaterial. But generalizations as to when information should be considered material have proved illusive.

The materiality of an item must be evaluated within the context of the information requirements of the parties who can be expected to use the financial statements. The FASB has defined materiality in Statement of Accounting Concepts No. 2 as "the magnitude of an omission or misstatement of accounting information that, in light of surrounding circumstances, makes it probable that the judgment of a reasonable person relying on the information would have been changed or influenced by the omission or misstatement." The SEC (Regulation S-X, rule 102) has indicated that a material matter is one "about which an average prudent investor ought reasonably to be informed."

At least three questions relating to materiality face the preparer of financial statements:

1. Is an item of information sufficiently material that it should be disclosed at all? Details of adverse contingencies, for example, must be reported upon either in the income statement or balance sheet or in notes thereto.

2. Is an item sufficiently material that it must be taken into account in required calculations? The computation of earnings per share, for example, must incorporate shares of common stock the firm has commitments to issue in the future. But the additional shares need be taken into account only so far as they will have a material impact on earnings per share.

3. Is an item of information sufficiently material that it should be disaggregated (shown separately) from other data? In order to avoid "information overload," individual revenue and expense accounts may be combined with other accounts of similar nature.

There are presently no rules as to dollar amounts or percentages of totals that can be considered material. Materiality depends on much more than quantitative measures alone. Because they may reflect on the integrity of management, for example, receivables from related parties, such as corporate officers, may be of greater significance than corresponding amounts of receivables from customers.

To date, none of the major rule-making authorities has issued *general* guidelines as to what constitutes materiality. However, in a number of pronouncements materiality guidelines for the application of specific accounting principles are provided. Several of these guidelines are pointed out in this chapter. For a detailed discussion of the meaning of materiality, as well as numerous examples of specific guidelines, the reader is referred to Statement of Financial Accounting Concepts No. 2, *Qualitative Characteristics of Accounting Information* [FASB, 1980a]. A discussion of materiality as it applies to the auditor's reporting obligation is contained in Auditing Research Monograph No. 1, *The Auditors Reporting Obligation, The Meaning and Implementation of the Fourth Standard of Reporting*, Chapter 4, "Central Reporting Concepts." Guidelines as to specific accounts or principles can be found by consulting the indices to compendiums of FASB pronouncements and SEC Accounting Series Releases under both "materiality" and the specific accounting principle in question.

INCOME

From the perspective of an economist, income represents the change in *real* wealth between two periods of time. Because of the difficulties of measuring real wealth, the accountant defines income as the difference between revenues and expenses (plus gains or minus losses). Revenues and expenses are calculated in accordance with established procedures designed to result in a statement that can be used by outsiders to make their own assessments of future cash flows.

Revenues are increases in owners' equity caused by inflows of assets (or reductions in liabilities) from delivering or producing goods, rendering services, or carrying out activities that constitute the entity's primary activities.

Expenses are decreases in owners' equity caused by outflows of assets (or increases in liabilities) from delivering or producing goods, rendering services, or carrying out other activities that constitute the entity's primary activities.

Gains and *losses* are similar to revenues and expenses but result from transactions that are incidental to the entity's primary activities.

Central to accrual accounting is the concept of *matching.* Revenues should be recognized as goods or services are delivered or produced; expenses should be matched with the revenues that they generate and should be included in the determination of income in the same period. Because there may be uncertainty as to which period revenues and expenses should be assigned, rule-making authorities have promulgated general guidelines, as well as specific rules, for revenue and expense recognition. These are described in greater detail in Chapter 12, as well as in the chapters devoted to the various types of revenues and expenses.

CURRENT OPERATING VERSUS ALL-INCLUSIVE CONCEPTS

Among the more fundamental issues of reporting that have caused both controversy and diversity of practice is whether net income should reflect all transactions that have an impact on retained earnings or merely revenues and expenses from normal operations. The dispute centers around whether gains or losses that cannot be expected to recur with regularity should be included in the measurement of net income or charged directly to retained earnings.

The *current operating concept* holds that net income should be the difference between ordinary revenues and expenses. Those who favor this concept believe that by comprising only those flows of resources that are likely to recur in the normal course of business, net income provides the more reliable basis on which to assess cash flows of the future. The *all-inclusive concept* holds that all flows of resources that have an impact on retained earnings (with the exception of dividends and selected adjustments to owners' equity accounts) should be included in the computation of net income. Those who support this concept aver that it is preferable because it eliminates the need to distinguish between usual and unusual transactions. They also maintain that a series of income statements over time should provide a complete history of the transactions and events (excluding selected transactions with owners) that affect the entity's assets and liabilities. All-inclusive, but not current operating, statements provide this comprehensive record.

In APB Opinion No. 9, the Accounting Principles Board supported the all-inclusive concept, with slight modification. It stated that *net income should reflect all items of profit and loss* with the exception of prior period adjustments. As a result of this opinion, as well as FASB Statement No. 16, prior period adjustments, which would be accounted for as direct charges or credits to retained earnings, are permitted only to correct errors in the financial statements of prior periods and to record tax adjustments relating to preacquisition loss carry-forwards of subsidiaries.

EXTRAORDINARY ITEMS

APB Opinion No. 30 sets forth specific criteria as to what constitutes extraordinary items and prescribes how they should be reported. Extraordinary items are transactions and events that are *both* unusual in nature and infrequent in occurrence. *Unusual in nature* means that the underlying event or transaction should possess a high degree of abnormality and be unrelated or only incidentally related to ordinary activities of the entity. *Infrequency of occurrence* suggests that the event or transaction should be of a type that would not reasonably be expected to recur in the foreseeable future. Among gains or losses that would *not* satisfy the criteria are write-downs or write-offs of receivables and inventories, effects of a strike, gains or losses from disposal of a segment of a business, and gains or losses on currency revaluations. By contrast, among those that would meet the criteria are losses resulting from major casualties such as an earthquake or from prohibitions of products under newly enacted laws or regulations.

The nature and the amount of each individual extraordinary item should be presented on the face of the income statement (or in notes if adequate disclosure on the face is impracticable). The extraordinary items should be reported *net* of applicable income taxes, but the applicable income taxes should be indicated. The income from operations line of the income statement is labeled "net income before extraordinary items" (or comparable words), and the presentation of the extraordinary item follows. For example:

Income before extraordinary charge	$4,203,000
Extraordinary charge—flood loss net of	
applicable income taxes of $202,000	(262,000)
Net income	$3,941,000

In accord with APB Opinion No. 15, per-share data on income before and after extraordinary items would also be presented at the bottom of the income statement.

DISCONTINUED OPERATIONS

APB Opinion No. 30 also provides guidance as to how the results of discontinued operations should be reported. The income or loss from operations of a business segment that has been disposed of should be reported as a separate component of income, after income from continuing operations but before extraordinary items.

A business segment is a component of an entity whose activities represent a separate major line of business or class of customer. It may be in the form of a subsidiary, a division, or a department so long as its assets, results of operations, and activities can be clearly distinguished physically and operationally from those of other areas of the business.

Any profit or loss earned during the period from the operation of the activity that is being discontinued is combined with the gain or loss upon discontinuation rather than being included in income from continuing operations. Similarly, the income taxes associated with the profit or loss from the discontinued operations and the gains or losses upon disposal should be reported along with the results of discontinued operations rather than as part of the income tax expense associated with income from continuing operations.

A segment should be considered as being discontinued as soon as a firm has committed itself to a formal plan of disposal, even though the segment might not actually be sold or abandoned until a later date. Gains or losses from disposition should be reported as of that same date, even though they may have to be estimated. Presentation can take a form similar to the following:

Income from continuing operations	$ 161,555
Discontinued operations	
Income from discontinued operations, less applicable income taxes of $8,208 .	$ 9,164
Loss on disposal, less applicable income tax benefit of $29,341	(32,104)
Income (loss) from discontinued operations	$ (22,940)
Net income	$ 138,615

ACCOUNTING CHANGES

APB Opinion No. 20 directs that changes in accounting principles should be recognized by including the cumulative effect of the change in net income. Examples of changes in accounting principles are shifts from the first-in, first-out (FIFO) to the last-in, first-out (LIFO) cost flow assumption for inventory, and from straight-line to an accelerated method of depreciation. In the year of the change the firm must make a "catch-up" adjustment so that balance sheet accounts indicate the amounts that would have been reported had the firm previously employed the new principle. For instance, if the firm shifts to double-declining-balance from straight-line depreciation, the accumulated depreciation account must be adjusted by way of a charge to income so that it reveals the amount of depreciation that would have accumulated had the firm consistently used the double-declining-balance method.

The amount of the change should be shown in the income statement between the captions "extraordinary items" and "net income." This amount, says APB Opinion No. 20, "is not an extraordinary item but should be reported in a manner similar to an extraordinary item." In addition, pro forma effects of retroactive application (total as well as per share) should be shown on the face of the income statement (or in notes, if space does not permit) for income before extraordinary items and net income.

THE INCOME STATEMENT

Title. Official pronouncements do not specify the words to be used in the title of income statements. Of the 600 firms reported on in *Accounting Trends and Techniques* [AICPA, annual], a majority use the term *income*. A substantial minority choose *earnings,* and a small percentage select *operations* or some other key word (e.g., *loss*).

If the statements are those of a consolidated enterprise, it is common to use *consolidated* in the title, as in Statement of Consolidated Income or Consolidated Statement of Earnings.

Format. Income statements are most commonly presented in one of two basic formats: the single-step or the multiple-step. In the pure single-step format, expenses are deducted from revenues in a single step to arrive at income before extraordinary items. There are no intermediate balances. Commonly, however, the single-step format is modified so that income before federal income taxes is indicated and federal income taxes is shown as a separate, last item. Exhibit 1 illustrates the modified single-step format. In the multiple-step format, expenses are deducted from revenues in a series of steps, each one representing a preliminary stage in the determination of income. Among the typical preliminary stages that are reported are gross margin on sales, income from operations, and income before taxes. Exhibit 2 illustrates a multiple-step format.

The primary advantages of the single-step format are as follows: (1) It minimizes classification problems (gross margin, for example, is not indicated, and hence there is less concern with whether a cost is included in cost of goods sold

---

EXHIBIT 1   Modified Single-Step Income Statement

ILLUSTRATIVE CO. A
Income Statement
Years Ended December 31, 19X2 and 19X1
(dollars in thousands)

	19X2	19X1
Revenues:		
Net sales	$84,580	$75,650
Other income	80	100
	$84,660	$75,750
Costs and expenses:		
Cost of goods sold	$60,000	$55,600
Selling expenses	2,000	1,700
General and administrative expenses.	3,000	2,900
Interest expense	180	190
Income tax.	9,350	7,370
	$74,530	$67,760
Income before extraordinary items	$10,130	$ 7,990
Extraordinary gains (losses) net of applicable income tax		
reduction of $1,880,000 in 19X2 and zero in 19X1.	(2,040)	(1,280)
Net income.	$ 8,090	$ 6,710
Per share of common stock:		
Income before extraordinary items	$1.73	$1.37
Extraordinary items, net of tax	(.34)	(.22)
Net income.	$1.39	$1.15

EXHIBIT 2.   **Multiple-Step Income Statement**

ILLUSTRATIVE CO. A
Income Statement
Years Ended December 31, 19X2 and 19X1
(dollars in thousands)

	19X2	19X1
Net sales	$84,580	$75,650
Cost of goods sold	60,000	55,600
Gross margin	$24,580	$20,050
Operating expenses:		
Selling expenses	$ 2,000	$ 1,700
General and administrative expenses	3,000	2,900
Total operating expenses	$ 5,000	$ 4,600
Operating income	$19,580	$15,450
Nonoperating income................................	80	100
Subtotal	$19,660	$15,550
Nonoperating deductions (interest)	180	190
Income before income taxes and extraordinary items.........	$19,480	$15,360
Income taxes	9,350	7,370
Income before extraordinary items	$10,130	$ 7,990
Extraordinary gains (losses) net of applicable income tax reduction of $1,880,000 in 19X2 and zero in 19X1	(2,040)	(1,280)
Net income...	$ 8,090	$ 6,710
Per share of common stock:		
Income before extraordinary items	$1.73	$1.37
Extraordinary items net of tax...........................	(.34)	(.22)
Net income...	$1.39	$1.15

or some other expense category); (2) it discourages inferences that some costs (e.g., cost of goods sold) take precedence over others (e.g., administrative costs) and are somehow related more closely to reported revenues; (3) it is less cluttered with captions and, hence, clearer. The multiple-step format, on the other hand, highlights intermediate differences (such as gross margin and income before taxes) that are conventionally computed by analysts. It thereby spares users the inconvenience of making their own calculations.

Recent surveys reported in *Accounting Trends and Techniques* indicate that approximately 60 percent of firms favor the single-step format and 40 percent the multiple-step one.

Disclosure of Revenues and Expenses. APB Statement No. 4 prescribes that "the income statement of a period should include and properly describe all revenue and expenses as defined by generally accepted accounting principles." It does not, however, dictate how the various items of revenue and expense should be summarized and reported. Decisions as to the extent to which data are aggregated and how they are classified are left to the reporting entity. Official pronouncements, however, require that certain types of information be *dis-*

closed, although the form of disclosure (e.g., body of statement or footnotes) may not be specified. Among the disclosures required by the pronouncements of the APB and FASB are the following:

Pension expense (APB Opinion No. 8)
Depreciation expense (APB Opinion No. 12)
Effects on operations of poolings and purchases (APB Opinion No. 16)
Income taxes (APB Opinion No. 11)
Earnings of subsidiaries when the equity method is used (APB Opinion No. 18)
Gain or loss on the early extinguishment of debt (FASB Statement No. 4)
Gains or losses from nonmonetary transactions (APB Opinion No. 29)
Rental expenses (FASB Statement No. 13)
Research and development expenses (FASB Statement No. 2)
Foreign currency gains and losses (FASB Statement No. 52)
Gains and losses (realized and unrealized) on marketable securities (FASB Statement No. 12)

The specific items of revenue and expense included in the income statement are a function of the magnitude of the amounts as well as their significance to the particular firm. For guidance as to common practice, the reader is referred to *Accounting Trends and Techniques,* which reports the percentages of firms that include specific revenues and expenses and provides numerous illustrations of income statements drawn from a variety of industries.

Operating Revenues. By convention, the first section of the income statement indicates operating revenues. Operating revenues are those from the ordinary activities of the firm and usually exclude interest, dividends, and incidental gains from the sale of noncurrent assets. The majority of firms reported on in *Accounting Trends and Techniques* present *net sales*—that is, sales after provisions for returns, discounts, and uncollectibles. A provision for uncollectibles may also be classified as an expense rather than a direct reduction of sales, but because an uncollectible account represents a sale that is never fully realized, categorization as a reduction of revenues is theoretically preferable.

In a single-step income statement, nonoperating revenues are reported directly beneath the operating revenues. In a multiple-step statement they are reported in a section devoted to nonoperating revenues and expenses, which is inserted below the caption, "income from operations."

Cost of Goods Sold. Cost of goods sold represents costs that are considered to "attach" to the products sold. Consistent with the principle that costs should be associated with the revenues they generate, they are reported as expenses in the period in which the product is sold. The distinction between costs that attach to a product and those that do not is not sharp, and is left largely to the discretion of management. As a rule, cost of goods sold in a manufacturing concern comprises direct labor, direct materials, and overhead. Overhead includes depreciation on factory equipment, supervision costs, repair and maintenance costs, and plant operating costs. By contrast, it does not include interest on funds borrowed to finance the manufacture of the product, selling costs, and administration costs incurred outside of the factory. Conventions pertaining to the measurement of cost of goods sold are discussed in Chapter 16 of this handbook. Although it is permissible to report on the income statement the various specific costs that make up cost of goods sold, an overwhelming percentage of firms reported on in *Accounting Trends and Techniques* combine the costs into a single amount.

Operating Expenses. Operating expenses are the regular, normal expenses associated with operating revenues. The most commonly reported categories of operating expenses are

Selling expenses (which include those costs related directly to the sale and delivery of goods or services)
General and administrative expenses
Research, development, engineering, etc.
Advertising
Rent
Maintenance and repairs
Employee benefit plans
Depreciation, amortization, and depletion

To the extent that any costs can be associated directly with products manufactured, they should be included in cost of goods sold rather than as operating expenses.

Other Revenues and Expenses. Other (nonoperating) revenues and expenses are those that arise from transactions not related directly to the major income-earning operations of the enterprise and are of a recurring nature so that they cannot be characterized as extraordinary.

The distinction between operating and nonoperating accounts is not sharp. Proper classification is dependent on the nature of an enterprise's business and the specific facts and circumstances that gave rise to the revenue or expense. Examples of items frequently reported as nonoperating revenues and expenses are interest, rent, commissions, gains or losses from foreign exchange fluctuations, gains or losses from sale (or recovery of previous declines in market value) of marketable securities, gains or losses upon sales of long-lived assets, share of subsidiary earnings or losses (under the equity method of accounting), and dividends received.

Whereas firms combine and summarize nonoperating revenues and expenses in a variety of categories, interest expense (which may also be classified as an operating expense) is of sufficient importance that it is reported as a separate line item by most companies.

Income Taxes. APB Opinion No. 11 requires that income taxes be allocated among the accounting periods (*interperiod* tax allocation) as well as the various components of income reported on the statement with which they are associated (*intraperiod* tax allocation).

Interperiod tax allocation matches income taxes to the earnings to which they relate. Reported income tax expense is based on *reported* pretax income rather than on taxable income. As a consequence, reported tax expense may not reflect the amount of tax for which the firm is obligated, per its tax return. Instead, it would indicate the amount of tax that will eventually be (or has already been) paid on the reported earnings. The difference between the tax expense to be reported (that based on reported pretax earnings) and the amount to be paid per the current tax return is carried forward on the balance sheet as a deferred credit or charge.

The need for *intraperiod* tax allocation arises because the required tax payment may be based on items of revenue and expense that are classified as extraordinary items, income from discontinued operations, prior period adjustments, other direct charges to shareholders' equity accounts, and ordinary pretax income. In order to make certain that statement users can relate tax expenses with the income on which it is based, the tax expense associated with ordinary income and each other source must be separately computed and identified.

Earnings per Share. Because of the significance that investors attach to them, earnings-per-share data should be shown on the *face* of the income statement. In accord with APB Opinions No. 15 and 30, earnings per share should be computed and reported for income from continuing operations, earnings before extraordinary items, and net income. It is also desirable to present earnings-per-share data for extraordinary items, the results of discontinued operations, and the gain or loss from disposal of business segments.

STATEMENTS OF CHANGES IN RETAINED EARNINGS AND OTHER OWNERS' EQUITY ACCOUNTS

If a firm has engaged in certain transactions with its owners, the statement of income will not fully explain the changes in owners' equity during a period. Two other statements may be used to supplement the statement of income:

EXHIBIT 3   Statement of Changes in Retained Earnings

ILLUSTRATIVE CO. B
Consolidated Statements of Earnings and Retained Earnings

	19X2	19X1
Net earnings	$ 16,742,000	$16,006,000
Retained earnings at beginning of year	89,099,000	78,886,000
Dividends declared:		
5% cumulative preferred stock—$5 per share	(64,000)	(65,000)
$2.75 convertible preference stock—$2.75 per share . .		(6,000)
Common stock—$1.85 per share	(5,744,000)	(5,722,000)
Retained earnings at end of year	$100,033,000	$89,099,000

EXHIBIT 4   Combined Statement of Income and Changes in Retained Earnings

ILLUSTRATIVE CO. C
Consolidated Statements of Earnings and Earnings Retained in the Business

	19X2 (000 omitted)	19X1 (000 omitted)
Earnings:		
Net sales	$1,769,132	$1,634,762
Costs and expenses:		
Cost of products sold	$1,360,790	$1,259,776
Marketing and administrative expenses	201,739	182,247
	$1,562,529	$1,442,023
Earnings before taxes	$ 206,603	$ 192,739
Taxes on earnings	99,500	91,700
Net earnings for the year	$ 107,103	$ 101,039
Net earnings per share (based on average shares outstanding) . .	$3.28	$3.07
Earnings retained in the business:		
Beginning of year	$ 690,980	$ 633,701
Net earnings for the year	107,103	101,039
Cash dividends ($1.45 per share in 19X2 and $1.33 per share in		
19X1	(47,394)	(43,760)
End of year	$ 750,689	$ 690,980

(1) a statement of retained earnings and (2) a statement of other changes in owners' equity. Both statements serve to reconcile beginning and ending balances in the accounts to which they pertain.

The statement of changes in retained earnings reports net income as per the income statement, dividends declared, prior period adjustments, and transfers to or from appropriations of retained earnings. Exhibit 3 illustrates one form of the statement of changes in retained earnings. As an alternative, many firms combine the statement of changes in retained earnings with that of the statement of income. This type of presentation, which is illustrated in Exhibit 4, has particular appeal when the change in retained earnings during the period can be attributed entirely to income and dividends. Still other firms combine the statement of changes in retained earnings with the statement of changes in other owners' equity accounts.

The statement of other changes in owners' equity reports on the issue of additional shares of stock (both common and preferred), the retirement of shares, the purchases and sale of treasury stock, stock dividends, stock splits, and any other adjustments that affect the equity section of the balance sheet. Many firms use a tabular form of presentation, in which a column is provided for each of the shareholder's equity accounts (e.g., preferred stock, common stock, capital in excess of par, and retained earnings). This form typically encompasses the statement of changes in retained earnings. Exhibit 5 illustrates the tabular presentation. If there are only a few changes in shareholders' equity, they can be

EXHIBIT 5. Combined Statement of Changes in Retained Earnings and Other Owners' Equity Accounts

ILLUSTRATIVE CO. D
Statement of Consolidated Shareholders' Equity

	6% cumulative first preferred stock	5% cumulative second preferred stock	Common stock Number of shares	Common stock Amount	Additional paid-in capital	Retained earnings	Treasury stock Number of shares	Treasury stock Amount
Balance at September 28, 19X1	$175,500	$650,000	766,816	$766,816	$1,364,090	$5,445,114	2,000	$5,500
Exercise of stock options under qualified stock option plan			14,700	14,700	10,950			
Net income for the period						1,517,238		
Cash dividends paid:								
$6.00 per share on 6% cumulative preferred stock						(10,530)		
$5.00 per share on 5% cumulative preferred stock						(32,500)		
$.123 per share on common stock						(116,061)		
10% stock dividend ($ 186 paid in cash in lieu of fractional shares)			77,842	77,842	287,042	(365,070)		
Balance at September 26, 19X2	$ 175,500	$650,000	859,358	$859,358	$1,662,082	$6,438,191	2,000	$5,500

presented in notes to the other financial statements rather than in a separate statement.

Restatement of the data of prior years is necessary in some circumstances. Among them are the following:

1. There has been a change in selected accounting principles. Although the Accounting Principles Board, in Opinion No. 20, ruled that most changes in accounting principles do not justify restatement of the reports of prior periods, it set forth three changes for which the advantages of retroactive adjustment outweigh the disadvantages. These changes are

    (a) A change from the LIFO method of inventory pricing to another method

    (b) A change in the method of accounting for long-term construction-type contracts

    (c) A change to or from the "full cost" method of accounting, which is used in the extractive industries

2. There has been a pooling of interests. Financial statements of the separate companies should be restated on a combined basis.

3. There has been a prior period adjustment. The net income, retained earnings, and all other affected balances of the periods reported on should be restated to reflect retroactive application of the prior period adjustment.

4. There have been discontinued operations. The operations of business segments that were discontinued in the current year should be reclassified and reported as income (loss) from discontinued operations in the income statement of not only the current year, but the prior periods as well.

Explanations of the changes should accompany the comparative statements in notes thereto.

CONCEPTS OF ASSETS, LIABILITIES, AND EQUITIES

Characteristics. The FASB (in Statement of Financial Accounting Concepts No. 3) has identified three essential characteristics of an *asset:* (1) It embodies a probable future benefit that involves a capacity to contribute to future cash flows; (2) a particular enterprise can obtain the benefit and control others' access to it; (3) the transaction giving rise to the enterprise's right to the benefit has already occurred.

If an item lacks one of these essential characteristics, it cannot be recorded as an asset. General scientific knowledge, for example, may be an asset to an enterprise, but the firm cannot record it as such because it cannot control others' access to the knowledge.

A *liability* also has three essential characteristics: (1) It embodies a present responsibility to one or more entities that entails settlement by probable future transfer or use of assets at a specified or determinable date; (2) the responsibility obligates a particular enterprise, leaving it little or no discretion to avoid the future sacrifice; (3) the transaction or other event obligating the enterprise has already happened.

In order to remain in business, an enterprise may need to replace inventory that has been sold. This responsibility is not recorded as a liability, because it is not an unavoidable obligation.

Equity is the residual after liabilities are subtracted from assets. Although there are often different forms of equity, each represents a residual interest. No form of equity has the essential characteristics of a liability.

Valuation. Assets, liabilities, and equities are initially recorded at prices that are established in exchange transactions. Changes in the value of assets and liabilities generally are not recognized, except for certain downward adjustments such as the reduction of inventory under the lower-of-cost-or-market rule.

Several alternatives to historical costs have been advocated (see, e.g., *Objectives of Financial Statements* [AICPA, 1973]). Under *exit value* accounting, assets and liabilities are recorded at the amount that would be paid or received in a nondistress liquidation. *Current replacement* cost accounting requires that assets and liabilities be recorded at prices representing replacement values. *Discounted cash flow* accounting necessitates that assets and liabilities be stated at the present value of their expected future cash flows. *Constant dollar* accounting maintains the original historical costs of assets and liabilities but adjusts these costs for changes in the purchasing power of the dollar.

Generally accepted accounting principles require that the principal financial reports be based on historical costs. Statements prepared on other bases may be included in supplementary sections of the financial report. In fact, FASB Statement No. 33 mandates certain current cost and constant dollar disclosures for corporations above a specified size. FASB Statement No. 33 is discussed in detail in Chapter 31.

THE BALANCE SHEET

Title. *Accounting Trends and Techniques* reports that approximately 90 percent of the firms surveyed use the title *Balance Sheet*, whereas the other companies use either *Statement of Financial Position* or *Statement of Financial Condition*. For those enterprises that report on a consolidated basis, the term "consolidated" appears as part of the title of the balance sheet.

Format. The balance sheet may be presented in a variety of formats. The format used most often is the *account form*. This format gives clear expression to the accounting equation, with assets reported on the left-hand side and liabilities and shareholders' equity on the right-hand side. An example of the account form appears in Exhibit 6.

The second most widely used format is the *report form*, of which there are two variations. In the more popular variation, assets are listed and totaled, followed by liabilities and shareholders' equity. An example appears in Exhibit 7. In the alternative variation, total assets minus total liabilities are shown as being equal to shareholders' equity.

A few companies use the *financial position form*. In this form, working capital

EXHIBIT 6   Account Form Balance Sheet

ILLUSTRATIVE CO. E
(A Delaware Corporation)
Consolidated Balance Sheet
December 31, 19X2 and 19X1
(dollars in thousands)

Assets

	December 31	
	19X2	19X1
Current assets:		
Cash	$ 25,000	$ 24,000
Marketable securities—at cost (market value of $40,000 in 19X2, $32,000 in 19X1)	20,000	15,000
Receivables (less allowance for uncollectible $3,000 in 19X2; $2,500 in 19X1)	150,000	145,000
Inventories—at cost under first-in, first-out method	180,000	170,000
Prepayments	15,000	16,000
Total current assets	$390,000	$370,000
Investments—at cost	18,000	20,000
Property, plant, and equipment—at cost less accumulated depreciation of $20,000 in 19X2, $15,000 in 19X1	430,000	435,000
Patents—at cost less $1,000 amortization	12,000	
Total assets	$850,000	$825,000

Liabilities and shareholders' equity

	December 31	
	19X2	19X1
Current liabilities:		
Accounts payable—trade	$160,000	$170,000
Notes payable	80,000	90,000
Accrued liabilities	30,000	30,000
Income taxes payable	40,000	35,000
Total current liabilities	$310,000	$325,000
Long-term liabilities:		
9% bonds payable—at par (due in 19X9)	200,000	200,000
Total liabilities	$510,000	$525,000
Shareholders' equity:		
Common stock (no par value; 100,000 shares authorized and outstanding)	$100,000	$100,000
Retained earnings	240,000	200,000
Total shareholders' equity	$340,000	$300,000
Total liabilities and shareholders' equity	$850,000	$825,000

EXHIBIT 7.   Report Form Balance Sheet

ILLUSTRATIVE CO. E
Balance Sheet
December 31, 19X2 and 19X1
(dollars in thousands)

	December 31, 19X2	December 31, 19X1
Current assets:		
Cash	$ 25,000	$ 24,000
Marketable securities—at cost (market value $40,000 in 19X2, $32,000 in 19X1)	20,000	15,000
Receivables (less allowance for uncollectibles of $3,000 in 19X2; $2,500 in 19X1)	150,000	145,000
Inventories—at cost under first-in, first-out method	180,000	170,000
Prepayments	15,000	16,000
Total current assets	$390,000	$370,000
Investments—at cost	18,000	20,000
Property, plant, and equipment—at cost less accumulated depreciation of $20,000 in 19X2; $15,000 in 19X1	430,000	435,000
Patents—at cost less $1,000 amortization	12,000	
Total assets.	$850,000	$825,000
Less: Liabilities		
Current liabilities:		
Accounts payable—trade	$160,000	$170,000
Notes payable.	80,000	90,000
Accrued liabilities	30,000	30,000
Income taxes payable—estimated	40,000	35,000
Total current liabilities	$310,000	$325,000
9% bonds payable—at par (due in 19X9).	200,000	200,000
Total liabilities	$510,000	$525,000
Shareholders' equity (net assets)	$340,000	$300,000
Sources of shareholders' equity:		
Common stock (no par value: 100,00 shares authorized and outstanding).	$100,000	$100,000
Retained earnings	240,000	200,000
Total shareholders' equity	$340,000	$300,000

is first presented by subtracting current liabilities from current assets. Then noncurrent assets are added and noncurrent liabilities are subtracted to arrive at total shareholders' equity. An example of this form appears in Exhibit 8.

Classification of Accounts. APB Statement No. 4 establishes the general requirement that information contained in financial statements should be classified according to the presumed needs of investors. However, it provides little guidance as to how best to meet these needs.

To facilitate assessment of solvency, the balance sheet indicates assets in order of when they will be transformed into cash and liabilities in order of when they will be liquidated.

EXHIBIT 8 **Financial Position Form of Balance Sheet**

ILLUSTRATIVE CO. F
Statement of Financial Position
For Years Ended December 31, 19X2 and 19X1
(dollars in thousands)

	19X2	19X1
Current assets:		
Cash..	$ 25,000	$ 24,000
Marketable securities—at cost (market value $40,000 in		
19X2, $32,000 in 19X1)	20,000	15,000
Receivables (less allowance for uncollectibles of $3,000 in		
19X2; $2,500 in 19X1)	150,000	145,000
Inventories—at cost under first-in, first-out method	180,000	170,000
Prepayments	15,000	16,000
Total current assets...............................	$390,000	$370,000
Less: Current liabilities		
Accounts payable trade	$160,000	$170,000
Notes payable	80,000	90,000
Accrued liabilities..................................	30,000	30,000
Income taxes	40,000	35,000
Total current liabilities	$310,000	$325,000
Net working capital	$ 80,000	$ 45,000
Investments—at cost.................................	18,000	20,000
Property, plant, and equipment—at cost less accumulated		
depreciation of $20,000 in 19X2; $15,000 in 19X1	430,000	435,000
Patents—at cost less $1,000 amortization..................	12,000	
Total assets less current liabilities....................	$540,000	$500,000
Less: 9% bonds payable—at par (due in 19X9)	200,000	200,000
Net assets	$340,000	$300,000
Source of net assets (shareholders' equity):		
Common stock (no par value; 100,000 shares authorized and		
outstanding)	$100,000	$100,000
Retained earnings	240,000	200,000
Total...	$340,000	$300,000

Assets and liabilities are classified as to whether they are *current* or *noncurrent*. ARB No. 43 states "the term *current assets* is used to designate cash and other assets or resources commonly identified as those which are reasonably expected to be realized in cash or sold or consumed during the normal operating cycle of the business." Examples of current assets are (1) cash, (2) marketable securities, (3) accounts and notes receivable, (4) inventories, and (5) prepayments. Cash that is not available for withdrawal and investments in securities that have been made for the purpose of control are not listed as current assets.

Current liabilities, according to ARB No. 43, "designate obligations whose liquidation is reasonably expected to require the use of existing resources properly classifiable as current assets, or the creation of other current liabilities."

Other liabilities that are expected to be liquidated within 12 months should also be included.

Short-term obligations are excluded from the current liability classification if two conditions are satisfied:

1. The enterprise intends to refinance the obligation on a long-term basis.
2. The enterprise's intent to refinance the obligation is supported by an ability to consummate the refinancing (see FASB Statement No. 6 for specific requirements).

Except for the requirement that accounts be grouped as to their current or noncurrent status, official pronouncements do not mandate any specific scheme of classification. Regulation S-X, however, provides that an account may be combined with others if it is less than 10 percent of total assets and it has not increased or decreased by more than 25 percent from the previous balance sheet presented. Raw materials, work in process, and finished goods, though, should always be reported separately.

The following section provides guidelines pertaining to specific accounts.

Current Assets. *Cash* balances available for withdrawal are normally shown in a single account with the title *Cash* or *Cash Including Time Deposits.* Some enterprises combine cash and marketable securities into a single account. Separate disclosure should be made of cash that is restricted as to withdrawal. Cash may be restricted as a result of contractual arrangement (such as a compensating balance agreement) or by simple management declaration.

Marketable securities represent temporary investments made to secure a return on funds that might otherwise be unproductive. Whether an investment is classified as temporary or not depends largely on management intent. To be considered a temporary investment, a security must not only be marketable, but management must plan to dispose of it if it needs to raise cash.

Marketable securities are normally shown on the balance sheet at their original acquisition cost. If, however, cost is greater than current market value, a valuation allowance must be established to reduce the net carrying value to market (see FASB Statement No. 12). Increases in the value of short-term investments over cost are not given recognition in the accounts, but the current market value of the portfolio should be reported parenthetically as part of the balance sheet caption or in footnotes.

FASB Statement No. 12 does not specifically require that the lower-of-cost-or-market rule be applied to bonds. For marketable securities not covered by FASB Statement No. 12, Regulation S-X requires disclosure of both cost and market value.

Receivables encompass monetary claims against debtors of the firm. They should be separated by source—those arising from (1) customers, (2) parent and subsidiary corporations, (3) other affiliated corporations, (4) certain related parties such as directors, officers, employees, and major shareholders. The term *accounts receivable* is commonly used to refer to receivables from trade customers that are not supported by written notes.

Receivables should be stated at the present value of the net amount to be collected. The face value of receivables should be reduced by an estimate of the amount that will be defaulted upon as well as by unearned interest. Procedures for discounting receivables to reflect unearned interest (whether such amounts are actually stated in the notes or have to be "imputed" by comparing stated interest rates with those on comparable obligations) are discussed in APB Opinion No. 21. Receivables are typically presented at face values, with the required reductions for uncollectible accounts and unearned interest reported in adjacent contra accounts. Current trade receivables due within 1 year need not, however, be discounted to give recognition to imputed interest.

APB Opinion No. 10 precludes offsetting of assets and liabilities in the balance sheet except where a specific right of offset exists. Thus it generally would be improper to net a party's account payable with its account receivable.

Inventories, according to ARB No. 43, include those items of tangible personal property that (1) are held for sale in the ordinary course of business, (2) are in process of production for such sale, or (3) are to be currently consumed in the production of goods or services to be available. Inventory is recorded at cost except "when the utility of the goods is no longer as great as its cost." The cost of inventory includes all expenditures that were incurred directly or indirectly to bring an item to its existing condition and location.

Several cost flow assumptions may be used to allocate costs between cost of goods sold and ending inventory. The most widely used are (1) LIFO, (2) FIFO, and (3) average cost. The assumption that is selected by an enterprise must be fully disclosed in footnotes. Chapter 16, on inventories, discusses the impact of alternative cost flow assumptions on the calculation of net income and asset values.

In unusual cases, inventory may be stated at an amount that is greater than cost. ARB No. 43 provides the example of precious metals with a fixed monetary value and minimal selling costs. Currently some enterprises value agricultural commodities at current (exit) market value.

Prepayments include prepaid rent, insurance, and interest. They are not current assets in the sense that they will be converted into cash; rather they are items that if not prepaid would have required the use of cash. They are sometimes referred to as *deferred charges*, because the charge to income resulting from the prepayment is delayed until it can be properly matched with appropriate revenues.

Other current assets represent those accounts that could not be included in other captions and may include deferred income taxes, unbilled costs, advances or deposits held by a supplier, and property held for resale.

Noncurrent Assets. *Long-term investments* are securities that management plans to hold for a period longer than the firm's current operating cycle. Investments may be carried on either the cost or equity basis, depending on the percentage-of-ownership criteria set forth in APB Opinion No. 18. If the investment is carried on the cost basis, the lower-of-cost-or-market rule (as described in FASB Statment No. 12) must be applied.

If the investment is carried on the equity basis, then complete disclosure must include: (1) the name of each investee and the percentage ownership of common stock; (2) summarized information as to assets, liabilities, and results of operations, if material; (3) the difference, if any, between the amount at which an investment is carried and the amount of underlying equity in net assets, and the accounting treatment of the difference. APB Opinion No. 18 contains complete disclosure requirements.

Property, plant, and equipment are tangible assets used in the production of goods and services. They are stated at cost, less accumulated depreciation. APB Opinion No. 12 requires disclosure of:

1. Depreciation expense for the period
2. Balances of major classes of depreciable assets, by nature or function, at the balance sheet date
3. Accumulated depreciation, either by major classes of depreciable assets or in total, at the balance sheet date
4. The method or methods used in computing depreciation with respect to major classes of depreciable assets

APB Statement No. 4 notes that in unusual circumstances the utility of productive facilities may have been impaired, and as a result the firm will be unable to recover their original cost. In such situations, the amount at which these facilities are carried must be reduced to recoverable cost.

The current market value of property, plant, and equipment is not typically reported on the face of the balance sheet. However, those corporations subject to SFAS No. 33 are required to report the current cost of property, plant, and equipment as part of the supplementary current cost disclosures.

Intangible assets include goodwill, patents, trademarks, copyrights, franchises, and organization costs. According to APB Opinion No. 17, all intangibles eventually lose value and must therefore be amortized.

Before FASB Statement No. 2 became effective, many business enterprises capitalized research and development costs as intangible assets. With the exception of those of contract research, all research and development costs must now be expensed as incurred.

Other noncurrent assets include those assets that are not properly classified under another caption and are not significant in amount. SEC Regulation S-X requires that any individual item that is in excess of 5 percent of total assets should be stated separately on the balance sheet or in a footnote.

Current Liabilities. *Accounts and notes payable* are conventionally subdivided into amounts due to the following: (1) banks; (2) factors or other financial institutions; (3) holders of commercial paper; (4) trade creditors; (5) related parties; and (6) underwriters, promoters, and employees (this classification is required by Regulation S-X, rule 5-02.19, for corporations that must file reports with the SEC).

APB Opinion No. 21 requires that notes and accounts payable be recorded at the present value of expected future cash payments. However, as with receivables, this opinion does not apply to payables arising from transactions with customers or suppliers in the normal course of business that are due in customary trade terms not exceeding approximately 1 year. (See APB Opinion No. 21 for additional exceptions.)

Other current liabilities include accrued payroll, accrued interest, taxes, customer advances, the current portion of long-term debt and warranty obligations. Regulation S-X requires that any item in excess of 5 percent of total current liabilities should be stated separately in the balance sheet or reported in a footnote.

Federal income taxes payable must be apportioned into current and noncurrent amounts. The current liability includes the actual current tax obligation as well as the current portion of deferred tax credits. Deferred tax credits are the cumulative differences between the tax expense based on pretax accounting income and tax liability based on taxable income. Deferred tax credits are reported as a current liability when they relate to assets or liabilities that are classified as current.

Noncurrent Liabilities. *Long-term obligations* are usually subdivided into notes payable, bonds payable, and capitalized leases. Disclosure should be made of (1) the general character of each type of debt, including the rate of interest; (2) the date of maturity; (3) contingencies that may have a bearing on the amount or timing of principal or interest payments; (4) payment priorities; (5) convertible features; and (6) the combined amount of maturities and sinking fund requirements for all issues, each year for 5 years following the date of the balance sheet. These disclosures are required by rule 5-02.22 of Regulation S-X.

A premium or discount is associated with long-term debt whenever the rate of interest specified in a loan agreement (the coupon rate) differs from the "true" interest rate (the yield) prevailing at the time the debt was issued. If the book value is not reported directly, then premiums and discounts should be reported beneath the debts with which they are associated. Discounts, even though they have debit balances, are not assets.

Long-term leases that satisfy specified criteria must be capitalized and reported on the balance sheet. The present value of the required payments is classified as a liability. The criteria as well as disclosure requirements are set forth in FASB Statement No. 13.

Minority interest in consolidated subsidiaries represents the equity of minority shareholders in firms in which the reporting entity owns a controlling interest. It may be reported either among the noncurrent liabilities or as a single item between noncurrent liabilities and owners' equity. Advocates of the entity theory would show minority interest among the owners' equitites.

Equities. The *shareholders' equity* section of the balance sheet includes preferred stock, common stock, paid-in capital, and retained earnings. APB Opinion No. 15 requires that financial statements describe the pertinent rights and privileges of the various securities outstanding. Examples of features that should be disclosed are (1) number of shares authorized, issued, and outstanding; (2) par or stated value; (3) dividend rates; (4) dividend and liquidation preferences; (5) participation rights; (6) call prices and dates; (7) conversion or exercise prices or rates and pertinent dates; (8) sinking fund requirements; and (9) voting rights.

Preferred stock may be recorded at a variety of amounts. Although par value is the most widely used, many corporations show preferred stock at liquidation or redemption value. APB Opinion No. 10 recommends that any excess of involuntary liquidation value over par value be disclosed in the financial statements. The statements should also disclose the amounts at which preferred shares may be called or are subject to redemption through sinking fund operations (APB Opinion No. 10), as well as the amount of arrearages in cumulative preferred dividends (APB Opinion No. 15).

Most companies report *common stock* at par or stated value. The difference between par or stated value and the amount received from the sale of common stock is reported as *additional paid-in capital*. The distinction between par value and additional paid-in capital has little economic significance. It is made because corporation laws of some states require firms to maintain a minimum amount of legal capital based on the par value of common stock.

Retained earnings may be described by a variety of captions, but *Retained Earnings* is by far the most popular. Even though Accounting Terminology Bulletin No. 1 recommends that the term "earned surplus" no longer be used, a few corporations continue to use that caption. A few corporations classify a portion of retained earnings as appropriated for some purpose. This practice is acceptable (see FASB Statement No. 5), as long as appropriated retained earnings is shown within the shareholders' equity section of the balance sheet and no costs are charged to the account. The practice of appropriating retained earnings is not recommended and is gradually dying out.

Treasury stock is typically shown as a contra equity account (an account that reduces total shareholders' equity). A small number of corporations report treasury stock as a noncurrent asset when the shares are held for later use in compensation plans, such as stock options for employees. Accounting Research Bulletin No. 43 requires that when state laws relating to the acquisition of treasury stock restrict the availability of retained earnings for payment of dividends, adequate disclosure be made of the restriction.

The shareholders' equity section may also contain a contra equity account, *net unrealized loss on investments in securities*. This account is created when a business entity has a holding loss on a portfolio of equity securities that are held as noncurrent assets. Under FASB Statement No. 12, this holding loss is recorded as a reduction of shareholders' equity, rather than as a reduction of net income.

SUPPLEMENTAL DISCLOSURE

In addition to the basic fundamental statements, a business enterprise is expected to report certain information in footnotes and schedules. APB Statement No. 4 explains the need for additional disclosure:

> . . . The information given on the face of the statement is largely restricted to that which can be represented by a number described by a very few words. Normally information of that type needs amplification to make it most useful, and the financial statements, descriptions of accounting policies, and notes are necessary for adequate disclosure.

Several types of supplemental disclosures were indicated in the discussion of specific accounts. Others include the following.

Accounting policies. APB Opinion No. 22 requires a description of all significant accounting policies adopted by an enterprise, including consolidation,
depreciation, amortization of intangibles, inventory pricing, recognition of
profit on long-term construction contracts, and recognition of revenue from
franchising and leasing operations.

Accounting changes. APB Opinion No. 20 prescribes that the nature and
impact of an accounting change should be disclosed in the financial statements for the period in which the change is made.

Inflation adjustments. FASB Statement No. 33 requires detailed disclosure of
the impact of inflation. These requirements are discussed in detail in Chapter 31 of this handbook.

Contingencies. FASB Statement No. 5 requires disclosures of contingencies.
A contingency is a condition that exists on the date of the financial statements and involves an uncertainty that will be resolved when a future event
occurs.

Subsequent events. An important event affecting an enterprise may occur
after the end of an accounting period but before financial statements have
been issued. Such an event should be disclosed if knowledge of that event
might affect interpretation of the financial statements. Subsequent events
are described in AICPA Statement on Auditing Standards 1.

Business segments. Many enterprises engage in activities in a variety of types
of business. A single set of financial statements may obscure facts related to
these varied activities. FASB Statement No. 14 requires disclosure of the
revenues, earnings, and assets of significant industry segments (defined as a
component of an enterprise engaged in providing a product or service primarily to unaffiliated customers for a profit).

Oil and gas reserves. FASB Statement No. 19 requires enterprises to disclose
the quantity of their interests in proved reserves and proved, developed
reserves of crude oil and natural gas.

BIBLIOGRAPHY

Accounting Principles Board (AICPA), *Basic Concepts and Accounting Principles underlying Financial Statements of Business Enterprises*, Statement No. 4 (APB, 1970).

American Institute of Certified Public Accountants, *Accounting Trends and Techniques*
(AICPA, annual).

Financial Accounting Standards Board, *Objectives of Financial Reporting by Business
Enterprises*, Statement of Financial Accounting Concepts No. 1 (FASB, 1978).

————, *Qualitative Characteristics of Accounting Information*, Statement of Financial
Accounting Concepts No. 2 (FASB, 1980a).

————, *Elements of Financial Statements of Business Enterprises*, Statement of Financial
Accounting Concepts No. 3 (FASB, 1980b).

Granof, M. H., *Financial Accounting Principles and Issues* (Prentice-Hall, Englewood
Cliffs, N.J., 1980).

CHAPTER 3

Funds Statements

Monroe J. Ingberman
**Assistant Professor of Accounting,
New York University**

INTRODUCTION

There are three basic financial statements: the balance sheet (or statement of financial position), the income statement, and the funds statement (or statement of changes in financial position). The balance sheet has been called a statement of "stocks," whereas the other statements have been called statements of "flows."

Because these terms are seldom explained, and have inappropriate connotations, it is advisable to discard such vague terminology. Instead, we can view the balance sheet as a dated listing of those rights and responsibilities of the reporting enterprise that result from previously recognized accounting events.

A comparative balance sheet presents balance sheets for the beginning and end of the most recent accounting period. The income statement and the funds statement explain some of the differences between the two balance sheets.

The balance sheets reveal the cumulative effects of all accounting events that occurred during the life of the firm, from inception until the balance sheet date, whereas the income statement and the funds statement provide more direct descriptions of selected accounting events that occurred in the current period. Conventionally, all events reported directly in the income statement and funds statement are also reported indirectly in the balance sheet, and the same measurement methods are employed whenever an event affects more than one statement. This relation between the statements is called *articulation*.

Both the income statement and the funds statement are sources of highly regarded performance measures: The income statement provides income numbers and earnings per share, and the funds statement discloses the amount of funds provided by operations.

We begin by describing the development of current practice, and we conclude by analyzing recent proposals for revising the content and format of the funds statement.

EVOLUTION OF THE FUNDS STATEMENT

The first textbook to include a funds statement was *Accounts: Their Construction and Interpretation*, by W. M. Cole, published in 1915. Cole classified all balance sheet changes under two headings, "Where-Got" and "Where-Gone." His emphasis was on qualitative changes:

> Certain kinds of assets are always good, certain kinds are sometimes bad, and a few kinds are usually bad. Certain kinds of liabilities are not suspicious, and certain other kinds are often so. A summary table showing the changes . . . indicates whether good assets are exchanged for less good, and whether troublesome liabilities are exchanged for those that are less exacting.

For Cole, the funds statement was a means of evaluating the changes in successive balance sheets. Much the same approach was taken by Paton and Stevenson in their 1918 book, *Principles of Accounting:*

Some accountants make a statement of this sort an end in itself, but it can readily be seen that such statements would be of very little use to the average investor in the enterprise. The comparisons (between successive balance sheets) which were discussed in the preceding paragraphs could be quite readily obtained from this statement, and it is the comparisons that are ultimately desired.

As the statement evolved, certain events were excluded, and others were grouped together, as shown by Homer Gregory in his 1928 textbook, *Accounting Reports in Business Management:*

There are, however, a large number of changes in balance-sheet items found in practice, which find their way into the reports, that are nonpecuniary in nature. These changes are not "funds" in the strict sense of the word, but are the result of bookkeeping entries made in the ledger. They have no real value, and since their presence tends to give an erroneous reading to the source and utilization of funds, it is necessary to determine what these adjustments are, and also in what manner they cause false conclusions regarding the actual changes in the financial structure.

The notion that the funds statement should describe only those events that affect working capital became popular during the 1920s, largely through the efforts of H. A. Finney, author of leading accounting textbooks and former editor of the Students' Department in the *Journal of Accountancy.*

During the next decade, the funds statement became a standard topic in all accounting textbooks, and by 1941, as seen in Paton's *Advanced Accounting,* the funds statement had virtually attained its final form, as seen in today's annual reports.

The first authoritative pronouncement dealing with the funds statement was Accounting Principles Board (APB) Opinion No. 3, *The Statement of Source and Application of Funds,* issued in 1963. The APB recommended, but did not require, inclusion of a funds statement in the annual report.

By 1970, the Securities and Exchange Commission (SEC) had modified Regulation S-X to require a funds statement in Form 10-K, the annual report presented by registrants to the commission. Following the SEC's lead, the APB issued Opinion No. 19 in 1971, requiring inclusion of a funds statement in the annual report prepared for shareholders. In that year the American Institute of Certified Public Accountants (AICPA) issued Statement on Auditing Procedures No. 50, *Reporting on the Statement of Changes in Financial Position,* mandating coverage of the funds statement in both the scope and opinion paragraphs, and providing specific guidance for auditing and reporting.

In 1972, the AICPA issued three brief interpretations of Opinion No. 19, and in the following year the SEC issued Accounting Series Release No. 142, *Reporting Cash Flows and Other Related Data.*

No further developments in the funds statement have taken place since that time, but it appears that the Financial Accounting Standards Board (FASB) is planning the first major changes since APB Opinion No. 19 was issued in 1971.

In 1980, the FASB issued a Discussion Memorandum, *Reporting Funds Flows, Liquidity, and Financial Flexibility,* considering various proposals for modifying the funds statement, and on November 16, 1981, the FASB issued an

Exposure Draft of a proposed Statement of Financial Accounting Concepts, *Reporting Income, Cash Flows, and Financial Position of Business Enterprises.* We turn next to a detailed description of current practice as required by APB Opinion No. 19, which is still in force.

PREPARATION OF THE FUNDS STATEMENT— WORKING CAPITAL BASIS

A Comprehensive Example. The following comprehensive example will be used to illustrate the preparation of a statement of sources and uses of funds (working capital).

The beginning-of-the-year balance sheet for the Oakdale Company is given in Exhibit 1. The balance sheet, income statement, and retained earnings statement for 19X2 are shown in Exhibits 2, 3, and 4, respectively.

The transactions for the year 19X2 are summarized below.

1. Operations for the year include credit sales of $200,000 and cash sales of $100,000. Collection of receivables amounts to $180,000.

EXHIBIT 1

OAKDALE COMPANY
Balance Sheet
December 31, 19X1
Assets

Cash		$ 30,000	
Marketable securities (at cost; market $50,000)		20,000	
Accounts receivable	$150,000		
Allowance for bad debts	2,500	147,500	
Inventory		35,000	
Prepaid expenses		5,000	
Total current assets			$237,500
Investment in Riverbank, Inc. (at equity)		$ 80,000	
Plant assets	$160,000		
Accumulated depreciation	(55,000)	105,000	185,000
Total assets			$422,500

Equities

Accounts payable		$ 70,000	
Notes payable		30,000	
Dividends payable		4,000	
Total current liabilities			$104,000
Bonds payable			100,000
Deferred income taxes			20,000
Common stock ($5 par value)		$ 30,000	
Retained earnings		168,500	198,500
Total equities			$422,500

EXHIBIT 2

OAKDALE COMPANY
Balance Sheet
December 31, 19X2

Assets

Cash		$ 108,000	
Marketable securities (at cost; market $42,000)		15,000	
Accounts receivable	$168,600		
Allowance for bad debts	4,100	164,500	
Inventory		95,000	
Prepaid expenses		3,500	
Total current assets			$386,000
Investment in Riverbank, Inc.			95,000
Plant assets—owned		$ 200,000	
Plant assets—leased		114,700	
		$ 314,700	
Accumulated depreciation		60,000	254,700
Patents			36,000
Total assets			$771,700

Equities

Accounts payable		$ 80,000	
Interest payable		10,000	
Total current liabilities			$ 90,000
Bonds payable		$ 200,000	
Less: Bond discount		3,600	
		$ 196,400	
Lease obligations		114,700	
Total long-term liabilities			311,100
Deferred income taxes			23,000
Common stock		$ 88,000	
Capital contributed in excess of par		59,000	
Retained earnings		202,600	
		$ 349,600	
Less: Treasury stock at cost		2,000	347,600
Total equities			$771,700

2. The appropriate adjustment to the allowance for bad debts is estimated at 1 percent of total sales for the period. During the year, $1,400 of delinquent accounts were actually written off to the allowance account.

3. Inventory purchases amounted to $180,000 for the year; $150,000 of the purchases were on account and $30,000 for cash. The cost of goods sold was calculated to be $120,000. Payments on accounts payable were $140,000.

4. Operating expenses paid in cash amounted to $55,000; in addition, $1,500 of the prepaid expenses were written off to operating expenses.

5. The note payable of $30,000 was repaid during the year.

6. Ten-year bonds of $200,000 were issued at the beginning of the year for

---

EXHIBIT 3

OAKDALE COMPANY
Income Statement
For the Year Ending December 31, 19X2

Sales		$300,000
Expenses:		
Cost of goods sold	$120,000	
Bad debt expenses	3,000	
Amortization of patent	4,000	
Depreciation expense	12,000	
Other operating expenses	56,500	195,500
Operating profit before taxes		$104,500
Other income:		
Profit of subsidiary	$ 25,000	
Gain on sale of marketable securities	7,000	32,000
		$136,500
Other expenses:		
Interest expense	$ 10,400	
Loss on sale of plant assets	2,000	12,400
Income before taxes		$124,100
Income taxes		68,000
Net income		$ 56,100

$196,000 cash proceeds. The coupon rate of interest is 5 percent, payable annually. Straight-line amortization of discount is used, because the amount is not material.

7. The $100,000 bonds payable at the beginning of the year were retired by paying $60,000 in cash and converting $40,000 of the bonds to common shares on a dollar-for-dollar basis (8,000 shares at $5 par value).

8. A 10 percent stock dividend (on 6,000 shares) was declared and issued to shareholders of record at the beginning of the year. At the time the market value of the stock was $20.

EXHIBIT 4

OAKDALE COMPANY
Retained Earnings Statement
For the Year Ending December 31, 19X2

Beginning balance		$168,500
Deduct:		
Stock dividend	$12,000	
Cash dividend	10,000	22,000
		$146,500
Add: Income for 19X2		56,100
Ending balance		$202,600

9. One thousand common shares were issued during the year. The cash proceeds were $25 per share. Also during the year, the company acquired 100 shares of its own stock from a retired officer at $20 per share.

10. A patent was acquired at the beginning of the year in exchange for 2,000 shares of common stock, which at the time of issue had a market value of $20 per share. The useful life of the patent was estimated to be 10 years, and $4,000 was written off as an expense for the year.

11. Plant assets originally costing $10,000 were sold for $1,000 at the beginning of the year. The accumulated depreciation was $7,000.

12. Plant assets were purchased for $50,000 cash.

13. The investment in Riverbank, Inc., is carried at equity. During the year, Riverbank earned profits of $25,000; $10,000 was remitted to the Oakdale Company in the form of a cash dividend. Oakdale owns 100 percent of Riverbank's stock.

14. During the year marketable securities costing $5,000 were sold for $12,000.

15. The Oakdale Company uses straight-line depreciation for reporting purposes and sum-of-the years'-digits depreciation for tax purposes. The income tax differential is deferred. The estimated straight-line depreciation for the year is $12,000. The sum-of-the-years'-digits depreciation is $18,000. The income taxes paid in cash are $65,000; the income tax reported on the income statement is $68,000.

16. At the end of the year, the Oakdale Company acquired a new plant asset by using a long-term lease (20 years). The annual rentals are $10,000 per year, payable at the end of each year. The company decided to capitalize the lease using a 6 percent discount rate, which gives a capitalized value of $114,700 (= $10,000 × 11.47).

17. At the end of the year, the Oakdale Company paid cash dividends of $10,000. During the year, the company also paid the dividends payable at January 1, 19X2.

These transactions cover most of the situations that prove to be troublesome in funds flow analysis. Also, the example is comprehensive enough to serve as a basis for the discussion in later sections.

We will show how to prepare a funds statement on a working capital basis. We begin by recording all the information given in the income statement and the statement of retained earnings, bearing in mind that events normally calling for a debit or a credit to a current account are now recorded with a debit or credit to "working capital." Working capital is not a ledger account—it appears only on worksheets used to prepare a funds statement.

(1) Dr. Working Capital   297,000
        Cr. Income Summary   297,000
        Adjusted net sales of $297,000 = $300,000
        (sales) minus $3,000 (bad debt adjustment).

(2) Dr. Income Summary   120,000
        Cr. Working Capital   120,000
        Cost of goods sold.

(3) Dr. Income Summary   12,000
      Cr. Accumulated Depreciation   12,000
      Depreciation expense.

(4) Dr. Income Summary   56,500
      Cr. Working Capital   56,500
      Selling and administrative expenses excluding depreciation.

(5) Dr. Income Summary   4,000
      Cr. Patent   4,000
      Amortization of patent.

(6) Dr. Investment in Riverbank   25,000
      Cr. Income Summary   25,000
      Equity method income from investment.

(7) Dr. Working Capital   7,000
      Cr. Income Summary   7,000
      Gain on sale of marketable securities. Gain on sale = cash received (current) less cost of securities sold (current), so the gain equals the net increase in working capital.

(8) Dr. Income Summary   68,000
      Cr. Working Capital   65,000
      Deferred Taxes   3,000
      Income tax expense. Tax expense of $68,000 is obtained from the income statement. Deferred taxes increased by $3,000, as can be seen from the balance sheets: $3,000 = $23,000 (December 31, 19X2) − $20,000 (December 31, 19X1). Taxes payable must equal the difference between tax expense and deferred taxes, so taxes payable must be $65,000, which is recorded as a credit to working capital.

(9) Dr. Income Summary   10,400
      Cr. Working Capital   10,000
      Bond Discount   400
      Interest expense. Interest expense of $10,400 is obtained from the income statement. Comparison of the balance sheets reveals that interest payable increased by $10,000. If no interest was paid during the year, then the increase in interest payable represents the payable portion of this year's interest expense, recorded as a credit to working capital. Because interest expense exceeds interest payable, the plug must be to bond discount.

(10) Dr. Working Capital   1,000
      Income Summary   2,000
      Accumulated Depreciation   7,000
      Cr. Plant Assets   10,000
      Loss on disposal of plant assets. This entry cannot be derived exclusively by analysis of the financial statements, but the cost and accumulated depre-

ciation of the disposed plant assets are disclosed
in Schedules V and VI of the SEC's Form 10-K.

(11)	Dr. Income Summary........................	56,100	
	Cr. Retained Earnings		56,100
	Closing entry.		

(12)	Dr. Retained Earnings	10,000	
	Cr. Working Capital		10,000
	Declaration of a cash dividend.		

(13)	Dr. Retained Earnings	12,000	
	Cr. Common Stock........................		3,000
	Additional Paid-in Capital		9,000

Declaration of a stock dividend. This entry cannot
be derived entirely from the statement of retained
earnings: It is also necessary to know that the market price per share was $20 at the time of the stock
dividend.

The worksheet for preparing the funds statement can take various forms. We illustrate a version of the T-account method developed by Kester [1946] and Vatter [1944]. All current accounts are combined in a single "working capital" T-account, and separate T-accounts are prepared for the remaining balance sheet items and the income summary. For every account except the income summary, the beginning and ending balances are included in the T-accounts, and the effects of current period events are posted between the two balances. After posting the first 13 entries shown above, we obtain the T-accounts shown in Exhibit 5.

The beginning balance of the working capital account is taken from the December 31, 19X1, balance sheet: $133,500 = $237,500 (current assets) minus $104,000 (current liabilities). At December 31, 19X2, working capital equals $296,000 = $386,000 (current assets) minus $90,000 (current liabilities). As can be seen, most of the changes have not been explained by the events taken from the income statement and statement of retained earnings. Additional events can be inferred by analyzing the T-accounts.

(14)	Dr. Working Capital	10,000	
	Cr. Investment in Riverbank		10,000
	Equity method dividends from investment.		

The balance in this account increased by $15,000. If Oakdale did not sell part of its investment in Riverbank, then the $25,000 debit recorded in the investment account under the equity method must be offset by a $10,000 credit, representing equity method dividends from the investment.

(15)	Dr. Plant Assets...........................	50,000	
	Cr. Working Capital		50,000
	Purchase of plant assets.		

The plant assets account increased by $40,000, so the $10,000 credit previously recorded must be offset by a debit of $50,000, representing the purchase of plant assets.

EXHIBIT 5

Working Capital	
Bal. 133,500	
(1) 297,000	120,000 (2)
(7) 7,000	56,500 (4)
(10) 1,000	65,000 (8)
	10,000 (9)
	10,000 (12)
Bal. 296,000	

Investment in Riverbank	
Bal. 80,000	
(6) 25,000	
Bal. 95,000	

Plant Assets	
Bal. 160,000	
	10,000 (10)
Bal. 200,000	

Income Summary	
(2) 120,000	297,000 (1)
(3) 12,000	25,000 (6)
(4) 56,500	7,000 (7)
(5) 4,000	
(8) 68,000	
(9) 10,400	
(10) 2,000	
(11) 56,100	

Capitalized Leases	
Bal. 0	
Bal. 114,700	

Accumulated Depreciation	
	55,000 Bal.
(10) 7,000	12,000 (3)
	60,000 Bal.

Patent	
Bal. 0	4,000 (5)
Bal. 36,000	

Bonds Payable	
100,000 Bal.	
200,000 Bal.	

Bond Discount	
Bal. 0	
	400 (9)
Bal. 3,600	

Lease Obligations	
	0 Bal.
	114,700 Bal.

Deferred Taxes	
	20,000 Bal.
	3,000 (8)
	23,000 Bal.

Common Stock	
	30,000 Bal.
	3,000 (13)
	88,000 Bal.

Retained Earnings	
	168,500 Bal.
(12) 10,000	56,100 (11)
(13) 12,000	
	202,600 Bal.

Treasury Stock	
Bal. 0	
Bal. 2,000	

Additional Paid-in Capital	
	0 Bal.
	9,000 (13)
	59,000 Bal.

(16) Dr. Capitalized Leases	114,700	
Cr. Working Capital		114,700
Acquisition of plant assets under capitalized leases.		

Acquisition of plant assets by signing a capital lease is equivalent to a purchase.

(17) Dr. Patent	40,000	
Cr. Working Capital		40,000
Acquisition of a patent.		

Because a $4,000 amortization of a patent was reported in the income statement and the balance in the patent account was $36,000 after the $4,000 amortization, a patent must have been purchased during the year for $40,000.

```
(18)  Dr. Bonds Payable..........................   100,000
          Cr. Working Capital ......................              100,000
      Retirement of bonds.
```

From analysis of the income statement, it would not be apparent that bonds with a face value of $100,000 were retired during the year.

```
(19)  Dr. Working Capital ..........................   196,000
          Bond Discount .........................     4,000
          Cr. Bonds Payable......................              200,000
      Bond issue.
```

The balance in the bond discount account increased from zero to $3,600 after the $400 amortization recorded in entry (9), so bonds must have been issued during the year at a $4,000 discount. In the absence of additional information, analysis of the T-accounts would have led to the erroneous conclusion that there had been no bond retirements, and additional bonds with a face value of $100,000 had been issued at 96.

```
(20)  Dr. Working Capital ..........................   114,700
          Cr. Lease Obligations ....................              114,700
      Financing from long-term leases.
```

Signing a capital lease is treated as a long-term loan combined with a cash purchase. The obligation will be discharged with interest by future lease payments.

```
(21)  Dr. Working Capital ..........................   105,000
          Cr. Common Stock.......................               55,000
          Additional Paid-in Capital ..............               50,000
      Stock issue.
```

Contributed capital increased by $117,000. The stock dividend accounted for $12,000 of this increase, so the remainder describes the issue of stock for cash. Observe that the increase in working capital recorded in entry (21) depends only on the total amount of the stock dividend, and does not require the additional details obtained from knowledge of the market price per share, as recorded in entry (13).

```
(22)  Dr. Treasury Stock ..........................     2,000
          Cr. Working Capital ......................                2,000
      Acquisition of treasury stock.
```

With this entry, all the changes in the noncurrent accounts have been explained. After these entries have been posted to the T-accounts, this will be the working capital T-account, which is shown in Exhibit 6.

EXHIBIT 6

Working Capital

Bal. 133,500	
(1) 297,000	120,000 (2)
(7) 7,000	56,500 (4)
(10) 1,000	65,000 (8)
(14) 10,000	10,000 (9)
(19) 196,000	10,000 (12)
(20) 114,700	50,000 (15)
(21) 105,000	114,700 (16)
	40,000 (17)
	100,000 (18)
	2,000 (22)
Bal. 296,000	

EXHIBIT 7   Funds Statement—Direct Method

OAKDALE COMPANY
Statement of Changes in Financial Position
For the Year Ended
December 31, 19X2

Sources of funds

From operations:

Adjusted sales...............................		$297,000	
Less: Expenses decreasing working capital:			
Cost of goods sold.....................	$120,000		
Other operating expenses	56,500		
Interest	10,000		
Taxes	65,000	251,500	
Funds provided by operations			$ 45,500
From sale of marketable securities			7,000
From sale of plant assets			1,000
From bond issue			196,000
From assumption of lease obligation			114,700
From stock issue..............................			105,000
From dividends on investment in Riverbank			10,000
Total sources of funds			$479,200

Uses of funds

Retirement of bonds	$100,000	
Purchase of plant assets	50,000	
Acquisition of leased assets.....................	114,000	
Purchase of patent	40,000	
Purchase of treasury stock......................	2,000	
Cash dividends	10,000	
Total uses of funds	$316,700	
Increase in working capital	$162,500	

These entries must also explain the increase in working capital, and it can be seen that this requirement has been satisfied. Only entries (10), (13), (18), and (19) were based on information external to the financial statements.

By analyzing the working capital account, a funds statement can be prepared as shown in Exhibit 7. In this presentation, funds from operations is shown as the difference between revenues increasing working capital [entry (1)], and expenses decreasing working capital [entries (2), (4), (8), (9)]. This is called the *direct method*.

According to *Accounting Trends and Techniques* [1979], only one out of 600 firms surveyed use the direct method. Most firms use the indirect (or *add-back*) method, described as follows in APB Opinion No. 19:

> The Statement for the period should begin with income or loss before extraordinary items, if any, and add back (or deduct) items recognized in determining that income or loss which did not use (or provide) working capital or cash during the period.

Using the indirect method, funds from operations for the Oakdale Company in the year 19X2 would be presented as shown in Exhibit 8. The remainder of the funds statement is identical to that shown in Exhibit 7.

The worksheet entries to derive funds from operations by the indirect method are shown below:

(a)	Dr. Working Capital from Operations	56,100	
	Cr. Retained Earnings		56,100
	Net income.		
(b)	Dr. Working Capital from Operations	4,000	
	Cr. Patent		4,000
	Add back amortization of patent.		

EXHIBIT 8   Funds from Operations—Indirect Method

Sources of funds		
From operations:		
Net income		$ 56,100
Add back expenses not requiring use of working capital:		
Depreciation	$12,000	
Amortization of patent	4,000	
Amortization of bond discount	400	
Deferred taxes	3,000	19,400
Add back losses:		
Loss on sale of plant assets		2,000
		$ 77,500
Deduct other income and gains:		
Equity method income from investment	$(25,000)	
Gain on sale or marketable securities	(7,000)	(32,000)
Funds from operations		$ 45,500

(c) Dr. Working Capital from Operations   12,000
      Cr. Accumulated Depreciation   12,000
      Add back depreciation.

(d) Dr. Investment in Riverbank   25,000
      Cr. Working Capital from Operations   25,000
      Deduct equity method income from investment.

(e) Dr. Working Capital from Operations   3,000
      Cr. Deferred Taxes   3,000
      Add back deferred taxes.

(f) Dr. Working Capital from Operations   400
      Cr. Bond Discount   400
      Add back amortization of bond discount.

(g) Dr. Working Capital from Operations   2,000
       Working Capital   1,000
       Accumulated Depreciation   7,000
      Cr. Plant Assets   10,000
      Add back loss on disposal of plant assets.

(h) Dr. Working Capital   7,000
      Cr. Working Capital from Operations   7,000
      Deduct gain on sale of marketable securities.

A separate "working capital from operations" T-account is established to record these entries, as shown in Exhibit 9. This account is closed to the "working capital" account:

(i) Dr. Working Capital   45,500
      Cr. Working Capital from Operations   45,500

Funds from operations, as shown above, does not include dividends from investments, gains, and losses. APB Opinion No. 19 is unclear about the proper treatment of dividends from investments, so many companies include this item in funds from operations. For the Oakdale Company,

Equity in earnings of Riverbank $25,000
Dividends received from Riverbank   10,000
Equity in undistributed earnings of Riverbank $15,000

If Oakdale chooses to include the dividends from Riverbank in funds from operations and if funds from operations is computed by the indirect method, then the following worksheet entry would replace equity method income by equity method dividends:

Dr. Investment in Riverbank   15,000
    Cr. Working Capital from Operations   15,000
Deduct equity in undistributed earnings of Riverbank.

EXHIBIT 9   Partial Worksheet for Indirect Method

Working Capital from Operations

(a) 56,100	25,000 (d)
(b) 4,000	7,000 (h)
(c) 12,000	
(e) 3,000	
(f) 400	
(g) 2,000	

APB Opinion No. 19 seems quite clear on the proper treatment of gains and losses:

> In addition to working capital or cash provided from operations ... the Statement should clearly disclose ... [p]roceeds from sale of long-term assets not in the normal course of business ... [par. 14].

This appears to indicate that disposal of noncurrent assets should be distinguished from operations as a source of funds. Nevertheless, some companies include gains and losses upon disposal of noncurrent assets in funds from operations; the book value of the disposed assets is then reported as a separate source of funds.

The Oakdale Company sold plant assets for $1,000 that cost $10,000 and had accumulated depreciation of $7,000, so a loss of $2,000 was recognized as a consequence of the sale.

If the loss is included in funds from operations, then the book value of $3,000 must be recorded as a separate source of funds by the following worksheet entry for the indirect method:

Dr. Working Capital	3,000	
Accumulated Depreciation......................	7,000	
Cr. Plant Assets		10,000

To record the book value of disposed plant assets as a source of funds.

Although this treatment is confusing and contrary to APB Opinion No. 19, it is encountered occasionally in published annual reports.

Funds statements nominally record only those events that alter working capital. Events that have two current effects do not change the balance of working capital; for example, collection of accounts receivable is recorded by the entry

Dr. Cash...	
Cr. Account Receivable	

which leaves working capital unchanged.

Equally, events that have two noncurrent effects cannot alter the balance of working capital. Only events having one current effect and one noncurrent

EXHIBIT 10

A. Dr. Noncurrent Asset 　　Cr. Noncurrent Liability	=	Dr. Working Capital 　Cr. Noncurrent Liability Financing event.	+	Dr. Noncurrent Asset 　Cr. Working Capital Investing event.
For example,				
Dr. Land 　Cr. Mortgage Acquisition of land for a mortgage.	=	Dr. Working Capital 　Cr. Mortgage	+	Dr. Land 　Cr. Working Capital
B. Dr. Noncurrent Asset 　　Cr. Contributed Capital	=	Dr. Working Capital 　Cr. Contributed Capital Financing event.	+	Dr. Noncurrent Asset 　Cr. Working Capital Investing event.
For example,				
Dr. Patent 　Cr. Common Stock Acquisition of a patent for common stock.	=	Dr. Working Capital 　Cr. Common Stock	+	Dr. Patent 　Cr. Working Capital
C. Dr. Noncurrent Liability 　　Cr. Contributed Capital	=	Dr. Working Capital 　Cr. Contributed Capital Financing event.	+	Dr. Noncurrent Liability 　Cr. Working Capital Investing event.
For example,				
Dr. Bonds Payable 　Cr. Common Stock Conversion of bonds to common stock.	=	Dr. Working Capital 　Cr. Common Stock	+	Dr. Bonds Payable 　Cr. Working Capital
D. Dr. Contributed Capital 　　Cr. Contributed Capital	=	Dr. Working Capital 　Cr. Contributed Capital Financing event.	+	Dr. Contributed Capital 　Cr. Working Capital Investing event.
For example,				
Dr. Preferred Stock 　Cr. Common Stock Conversion of preferred stock to common stock.	=	Dr. Working Capital 　Cr. Common Stock	+	Dr. Preferred Stock 　Cr. Working Capital

effect can change working capital—for example, financing events such as stock issues, and investing events such as purchases of plant assets.

However, restricting the funds statements to events having one current and one noncurrent effect would be contrary to the purpose of the funds statement as expressed in APB Opinion No. 19:

> The objectives of a funds statement are (1) to summarize the financing and investing activities of the entity. . . . The Statement of each reporting entity should disclose all important aspects of its financing and investing activities regardless of whether cash or other elements of working capital are directly affected. For example, acquisitions of property by issuance of securities or in exchange for other property, and conversions of long-term debt or preferred stock to common stock, should be appropriately reflected in the Statement.

To achieve these objectives, certain events having two noncurrent effects must be reported in the funds statement. Because the funds statement is prepared by analyzing changes in working capital, these events must be viewed as combinations of financing and investing events, as shown in Exhibit 10. These events are reported twice, once under sources, and once under uses of funds. For this reason they are sometimes called "in-and-out" events.

PREPARATION OF THE FUNDS STATEMENT—CASH BASIS

APB Opinion No. 19 allows great latitude in the format and approach adopted in preparing a funds statement:

> The Statement may be in balanced form or in a form expressing the changes in financial position in terms of cash, of cash and temporary investments combined, of all quick assets, or of working capital.

Despite the flexibility offered by the APB, the 1979 survey of 600 firms published in Accounting Trends and Techniques [Shohet and Rikert, 1979] reveals that 558 firms based the funds statement on changes in working capital, and 42 used a cash, or cash and cash-equivalent, basis.

Having examined the working capital basis in the last section, we turn now to the cash basis.

Funds from operations can easily be transformed from a working capital basis to a cash basis. The necessary adjustments can be illustrated by returning to the Oakdale Company example shown previously. The adjustments make use of certain balance sheet changes, as shown in Exhibits 11 and 12.

In general, to transform funds from operations from a working capital basis to a cash basis, begin with funds from operations, working capital basis, then add credit changes and subtract debit changes in current operating accounts except cash: accounts receivable, estimated uncollectibles, inventory, prepayments, accounts payable, and accrued liabilities (wages, interest, taxes, etc.). Analysis of the T-accounts explains the necessity for these adjustments; see Exhibit 13.

From the financial statements it is known that sales were $300,000 with a bad debt adjustment of $3,000. These events increased working capital by a net of $297,000. From the estimated uncollectibles account we see that there were write-offs of $1,400, so collections from customers were only $280,000. The

---

EXHIBIT 11

OAKDALE COMPANY
Partial Comparative Balance Sheet

	12-31-X1	12-31-X2	Debit change	Credit change
Accounts receivable	$150,000	$168,600	$18,600	
Estimated uncollectibles	2,500	4,100		$ 1,600
Inventory	35,000	95,000	60,000	
Prepayments	5,000	3,500		1,500
Accounts payable	70,000	80,000		10,000
Interest payable		10,000		10,000

EXHIBIT 12

OAKDALE COMPANY
Funds from Operations
For the Year Ended December 31, 19X2

Working capital basis		$45,500
Add credit changes:		
Estimated uncollectibles	$ 1,600	
Prepayments	1,500	
Accounts payable	10,000	
Interest payable	10,000	23,100
		$68,600
Deduct debit changes:		
Accounts receivable	$(18,600)	
Inventory	(60,000)	(78,600)
Cash basis		$(10,000)

$17,000 difference between the increase in working capital and the increase in cash equals the difference between the $18,600 debit change in accounts receivable and the $1,600 credit change in estimated uncollectibles.

Because inventory increased $60,000, despite cost of goods sold of $120,000, there must have been inventory purchases of $180,000, but accounts payable increased only $10,000, so suppliers of inventory must have been paid $170,000. Thus cash payments exceed cost of goods sold by $50,000, the difference between the debit change of $60,000 in inventory and the credit change of $10,000 in accounts payable.

The $1,500 decrease in prepayments and the $10,000 increase in interest payable decrease working capital by $11,500 without having any effect on cash. In the list of adjustments shown above, these credits changes are shown as addbacks.

EXHIBIT 13

Accounts Receivable		Estimated Uncollectibles		Inventory	
Bal. 150,000			2,500 Bal.	Bal. 35,000	
300,000	1,400	1,400	3,000	180,000	120,000
	280,000				
Bal. 168,600			4,100 Bal.	Bal. 95,000	

Prepayments		Interest Payable		Accounts Payable	
Bal. 5,000			10,000 Bal.		70,000 Bal.
	1,500			170,000	180,000
Bal. 3,500			10,000 Bal.		80,000 Bal.

EXHIBIT 14

Dividends Payable		Notes Payable	
	4,000 Bal.		30,000 Bal.
	10,000		
	0 Bal.		0 Bal.

The analysis of balance sheet changes cannot distinguish between cash and credit transactions, but this distinction is irrelevant as far as the adjustments are concerned.

There are two more differences between the cash statement and the working capital statement, and these can be derived by analyzing the T-accounts in Exhibit 14. The $10,000 credit to dividends payable records the declaration of a cash dividend. Because the ending balances are zero in both accounts, there must have been dividend payments of $14,000, and $30,000 of notes payable must have been repaid.

The funds statement on a cash basis can be prepared directly. The procedures are similar to those shown previously, and they are summarized in the T-accounts in Exhibit 15. The complete funds statement on a cash basis is shown in Exhibit 16.

COMPARISON BETWEEN WORKING CAPITAL AND CASH

The income statement is based on the accrual principle: Cash-significant events are reported, whether or not they coincide with actual cash flows. The accrual principle necessarily involves the use of estimates and artificial allocations in seeking to predict future cash effects of current events, and attempting to measure the current consequences of the past cash flows.

Working capital provided by operations is derived from the income statement by omitting certain items that do not affect working capital. For this reason, working capital provided by operations depends on many of the same estimates and conventions that enter into the measurement of net income. Over time, cumulative amounts of income, working capital, and cash should coincide—the only difference should be the timing of the reported flows. Because most financial decisions must be based on annual data, and timing differences between the reported annual flows can be substantial, these differences have a significant impact on the actions taken by decision makers.

Because few companies prepare funds statements on a cash basis, little empirical research has been devoted to comparisons between working capital from operations and cash from operations, and not much is known about cash-based funds statements.

One of the few studies comparing income, working capital, and cash, "Cash

EXHIBIT 15

Cash

Bal. 30,000	
(7) 12,000	170,000 (14)
(11) 1,000	40,000 (15)
(17) 280,000	50,000 (18)
(20) 114,700	114,700 (19)
(22) 105,000	65,000 (21)
(25) 196,000	55,000 (23)
(31) 10,000	30,000 (24)
	100,000 (26)
	2,000 (27)
	14,000 (29)
Bal. 108,000	

Inventory

Bal. 35,000	
	120,000 (10)
(13) 180,000	
Bal. 95,000	

Capitalized Leases

Bal. 0	
(19) 114,700	
Bal. 114,700	

Interest Payable

	0 Bal.
	10,000 (9)
	10,000 Bal.

Lease Obligations

	0 Bal.
	114,700 (20)
	114,700 Bal.

Common Stock

	30,000 Bal.
	55,000 (22)
	3,000 (30)
	88,000 Bal.

Notes Payable

	30,000 Bal.
(24) 30,000	
	0 Bal.

Marketable Securities

Bal. 20,000	
	5,000 (7)
Bal. 15,000	

Investment in Riverbank

Bal. 80,000	
(6) 25,000	10,000(31)
Bal. 95,000	

Accounts Payable

	70,000 Bal.
(14) 170,000	180,000 (13)
	80,000 Bal.

Patent

Bal. 0	
(15) 40,000	4,000 (3)
Bal. 36,000	

Bonds Payable

	10,0000 Bal.
(26) 100,000	200,000 (25)
	200,000 Bal.

Taxes Payable

	0 Bal.
(21) 65,000	65,000 (8)
	0 Bal.

Additional Paid-in Capital

	0 Bal.
	50,000 (22)
	9,000 (30)
	59,000 Bal.

Dividends Payable

	4,000 Bal.
(29) 14,000	10,000 (28)
	0 Bal.

Accounts Receivable

Bal. 150,000	
(1) 300,000	1,400 (16)
	280,000 (17)
Bal. 168,000	

Estimated Uncollectibles

	2,500 Bal.
(16) 1,400	3,000 (2)
	4,100 Bal.

Plant Assets

Bal. 160,000	
(18) 50,000	10,000 (11)
Bal. 200,000	

Accumulated Depreciation

	55,000 Bal.
(11) 7,000	12,000 (4)
	60,000 Bal.

Bond Discount

Bal. 0	
(25) 4,000	400 (9)
Bal. 3,600	

Deferred Taxes

	20,000 Bal.
	3,000 (8)
	23,000 Bal.

Treasury Stock

Bal. 0	
(27) 2,000	
Bal. 2,000	

Retained Earnings

	168,500 Bal.
	56,100 (12)
(28) 10,000	
(30) 12,000	
	202,600 Bal.

EXHIBIT 15   (*Continued*)

Income Summary		Payables for Services		Prepayments		
	300,000 (1)		0 Bal.			
(2) 3,000	25,000 (6)	(23) 55,000	55,000 (5)	Bal. 5,000	1,500 (5)	
(3) 4,000	7,000 (7)	-------------	-------------	-------------	-------------	
(4) 12,000			0 Bal.	Bal. 3,500		
(5) 56,500						
(8) 68,000						
(9) 10,400						
(10) 120,000						
(11) 2,000						
(12) 56,100						

EXHIBIT 16

OAKDALE COMPANY
Statement of Changes in Financial Position
For the Year Ended 19X2

Sources of cash

From operations
Collections from customers		$ 280,000	
Less:			
Payments for inventory.	$(170,000)		
Payments for services	(55,000)		
Payments for taxes	(65,000)	(290,000)	
Cash deficit from operations			$(10,000)
From sale of marketable securities			12,000
From sale of plant assets.			1,000
From bond issue.			196,000
From stock issue			105,000
From investment in Riverbank			10,000
From assumption of lease obligation.			114,700
Total sources of cash.			$428,700

Uses of cash
For retirement of bonds	$100,000
For purchase of treasury stock	2,000
For purchase of plant assets	50,000
For purchase of patent	40,000
For payment of dividends	14,000
For repayment of notes payable	30,000
For acquisition of leased asset	114,700
Total uses of cash	$350,700
Increase in cash	$ 78,000

Flows, Ratio Analysis and the W. T. Grant Company Bankruptcy," by Largay and Stickney, was published in 1980. They compared net income, working capital provided by operations, and cash provided by operations for the W. T. Grant Company in the years 1966–1975, the 10 years preceding the company's bankruptcy.

Income and working capital provided by operations were parallel and positive until shortly before the bankruptcy, but cash provided by operations was negative throughout the period except for 2 years when it was slightly plus. The authors suggest that the persistent cash deficit from operations should have been viewed as an indication of financial distress. The disparity between working capital and cash provided by operations was due to faulty estimates of uncollectible receivables, and obsolete inventory.

There is evidence that financial analysts and the stock market were unaware of the cash deficit from operations. The implications of this study have reinforced the recent emphasis of the FASB on cash flows, but further research is needed before any firm conclusions can be drawn.

INTERPRETING FUNDS FLOW DATA

In preparing Opinion No. 19, the APB was influenced by AICPA Accounting Research Study No. 2, *Cash Flow Analysis and the Funds Statement*, by Perry Mason [1961]. According to Mason:

> In evaluating the securities of a company for investment purposes, the analyst uses "cash flow" as one of his more significant tools. It assists him, for example, in arriving at his judgment as to the probability that the debt retirement commitments can be met without refinancing, that the regular dividend will be maintained in the face of falling earnings, that continued exploration in the case of the extractive industries can be financed without additional capital investment, or that plant and equipment can be modernized, replaced, or expanded without increasing the equity or debt capital.

Mason's arguments seem to support presentation of a cash statement rather than a working capital statement. However, the prevailing opinion at the time was opposed to presentation of a cash statement, because it departed from the accrual basis of accounting. For example, Anton's 1962 study, *Accounting for the Flow of Funds*, emphasized the relationship between the funds statement and the other financial statements:

> It [the funds statement] analyzes certain aspects of the income statement as well as the comparative balance sheets. The funds statement is thus inextricably connected with bases of accounting under which both statements are prepared.
>
> A statement of cash receipts and disbursements ordinarily is not considered an acceptable substitute in the general-purpose case. This arises directly from accountants matching revenues and costs on the accrual rather than on the cash basis.

Much of the controversy regarding proper use of the funds statement relates to the significance of funds from operations. A single figure for funds from operations is of little value in predicting future cash flows. Each year, funds from operations must be compared to funds required for purchases of inventory and plant assets, for repayment of debt, and for dividend distributions. Only after this comparison has been made for a period of years it is sensible to evaluate the results of any one year. This point is made by Jaedicke and Sprouse in their 1965 book, *Accounting Flows: Income, Funds, and Cash.* They observe that:

> . . . it is not sound analysis to assume that cash flow from operations is, in the long run, entirely available for debt repayment and cash dividends. This is true only if capital-equipment expenditures are curtailed. If the vital estimate is made of the cash expenditures required merely to *replace* assets (whether the actual expenditure must be made this particular period is irrelevant) and if this amount is deducted from "cash flow from operations" we have the very thing we are looking for—an estimate of net income! For *long-run* analysis, therefore, the primary problem with cash-flow data is that no estimate has been made of the cash expenditure required to at least replace capital assets where such a replacement is necessary to maintain long-run earning power.

Furthermore, changes in cash flow may be due primarily to technological advances:

> Another important point to consider is that the degree of automation in the United States has increased during the past 10–15 years. Automation implies the substitution of *capital* for other factors of production such as labor, materials, and the like. This being the case, more of the firm's costs appear in the income statement as depreciation. Increasing automation, therefore, will have a tendency to result in increased cash flow per share over time [Jaedicke and Sprouse, 1965].

The problems of accounting for depreciation and providing cash for replacement of plant assets have led to considerable controversy and confusion. Depreciation charges are sometimes considered to be a means of recovering the cost of the depreciating asset, the idea being that total cash flows from depreciation will suffice to replace the asset at the end of its useful life. This approach is an oversimplification of a complex problem:

1. The annual cash flow due to depreciation is equal to the depreciation charge for tax purposes times the tax rate, rather than the financial statement depreciation charge.

2. Because the annual depreciation tax savings can be reinvested, the future amount of these savings at the end of the asset's useful life is substantially greater than the arithmetic sum of the annual savings.

3. Whether the future amount of the depreciation tax savings will suffice to replace the existing asset depends on the reinvestment rates and future replacement costs.

4. It is not necessarily true that it will be desirable to replace the asset at the end of its useful life.

These are just some of the problems involved in evaluating the adequacy of depreciation-related cash flows.

PROPOSED REVISIONS OF THE FUNDS STATEMENT

Recent FASB pronouncements have demonstrated renewed interest in cash flows, in addition to the traditional emphasis on income and working capital:

> Financial reporting should provide information to help present and potential investors and creditors and other users in assessing the amounts, timing, and uncertainty of prospective cash receipts from dividends or interest and the proceeds from the sale, redemption, or maturities of securities or loans. The prospects for those cash receipts are affected by an enterprise's ability to generate enough cash to meet its obligations when due and its other cash operating needs, to reinvest in operations, and to pay cash dividends and may also be affected by perceptions of investors generally about that ability, which affect market prices of the enterprise's securities. Thus, financial reporting should provide information to help investors, creditors, and others assess the amounts, timing, and uncertainty of prospective net cash inflows to the related enterprise [FASB, 1978].

Several recent publications have emphasized the importance of information related to solvency, liquidity, and financial flexibility.

In his 1978 AICPA Accounting Research Monograph, *Financial Reporting and the Evaluation of Solvency,* Lloyd C. Heath points out deficiencies in APB Opinion No. 19, and he suggests means of correcting these deficiencies. Heath defines *profitability* as a company's ability to increase its wealth, and *solvency* as a company's ability to pay its debts when due. Because solvency, rather than profitability, involves direct cash measurements, "any information that provides insight into the amounts, timing, and uncertainty of a company's future cash receipts and payments is, therefore, relevant in evaluating its solvency."

This provides a link between the FASB's approach to financial reporting and the problem of evaluating a company's solvency.

Heath claims that APB Opinion No. 19 failed because it tried to do too many things simultaneously. He proposes replacement of the funds statement by three separate but related statements:

1. A statement of cash receipts and payments, including a supplementary schedule of cash provided by operations. ("Operations" refers to a company's profit-directed activities.)

2. A statement of financing activities, reporting changes in the size and composition of the company's capital structure. (By "capital structure" he means equity financing and negotiated debt financing.)

3. A statement of investing activities, reporting changes in the size and composition of its long-term assets.

In responding to the increased interest in direct cash flow data and the need for information regarding liquidity and financial flexibility, the FASB issued a Discussion Memorandum, *Reporting Funds Flows, Liquidity, and Financial Flexibility,* followed by an Exposure Draft, *Reporting Income, Cash Flows, and Financial Position of Business Enterprises.*

The Exposure Draft makes the following definitions: *Liquidity* is "the amount of time that is expected to elapse until an asset is realized or otherwise converted into cash or until a liability has to be paid" [FASB, 1981, par. 29].

"In the case of assets required for operations and liabilities arising directly from operations, liquidity refers to the timing of cash flow in the normal course of business. In the case of nonoperating assets, liquidity refers to marketability" [FASB, 1981, par. 29].

"The liquidity of the enterprise indicates its probable ability to meet its obligations as they fall due" [FASB, 1981, par. 30].

Instead of using liquidity in two distinct ways, it would be clearer to use some other term, such as solvency, for the liquidity of an enterprise, reserving the term liquidity for a quality of assets and liabilities.

"*Financial flexibility* is the ability of an enterprise to take effective actions to alter the amounts and timing of cash flows so it can respond to unexpected needs and opportunities" [FASB, 1981, par. 25].

"*Operations* normally comprise the provision of goods and services that make up the main business of the enterprise and other activities that have to be undertaken jointly with the provision of goods and services" [FASB, 1981, par. 19].

"*Operating capability* is the ability of an enterprise to maintain a given physical level of operations" [FASB, 1981, par. 32].

Although the Statement based on the Exposure Draft will be part of the FASB's Concepts series, it hints strongly that the board intends to replace the funds statement by a cash flow statement:

> Cash flow statements (together with related notes and supplementary information) should provide information about cash inflows and outflows during a period. That information is useful for assessments of the amounts, timing, and uncertainty of future cash flows. Cash statements also should contribute to the purposes of financial reporting by:
> (a) Distinguishing different sources and uses of cash—cash generated and used in operations, cash obtained by borrowing and used to repay borrowing, cash used for investments in resources and obtained from the disposal of investments, and cash contributed by or distributed to owners. The provision of information about investments may be helpful for assessments of changes in the operating capability of an enterprise.
> (b) Providing feedback to users so that they can assess their previous predictions of cash flows.
> (c) Providing information useful in assessing the liquidity and financial flexibility of the enterprise [FASB, 1981, par. 36].

The Discussion Memorandum surveyed a number of specific proposals that were omitted from the Exposure Draft. Some of these proposals may be included in a future Statement of Financial Accounting Standards superseding APB Opinion No. 19.

BIBLIOGRAPHY

Accounting Principles Board (AICPA), *The Statement of Source and Application of Funds*, Opinion No. 3 (APB, 1963).

————, Reporting Changes in Financial Position, Opinion No. 19 (APB, 1971).

Anton, H. R., Accounting for the Flow of Funds (Houghton Mifflin Company, Boston, 1962).

Arnett, H. E., Proposed Funds Statement for Managers and Investors (National Association of Accountants, New York, 1979).

Backer, M., and M. L. Gosman, Financial Reporting and Business Liquidity (National Association of Accountants, New York, 1978).

Cole, W. M., Accounts: Their Construction and Interpretation (Houghton Mifflin Company, Boston, 1915).

Financial Accounting Standards Board, Objectives of Financial Reporting by Business Enterprises, Statement of Financial Accounting Concepts No. 1 (FASB, 1978).

————, Reporting Funds Flows, Liquidity, and Financial Flexibility, FASB Discussion Memorandum (FASB, 1980).

————, Reporting Income, Cash Flows, and Financial Position of Business Enterprises, FASB Exposure Draft of Proposed Statement of Financial Accounting Concepts (FASB, 1981).

Finney, H. A., "The Statement of Application of Funds," Journal of Accountancy, December 1923, pp. 460–472.

Gregory, H. E., Accounting Reports in Business Management (Ronald Press Company, New York, 1928).

Heath, L. C., Financial Reporting and the Evaluation of Solvency, Accounting Research Monograph No. 3 (AICPA, 1978).

Jaedicke, R. K., and R. T. Sprouse, Accounting Flows: Income, Funds, and Cash (Prentice-Hall, Englewood Cliffs, N.J., 1965).

Kester, R. B., Advanced Accounting (Ronald Press Company, New York, 1946).

Largay, J. A., III, and C. P. Stickney, "Cash Flows, Ratio Analysis and the W. T. Grant Company Bankruptcy," Financial Analysts Journal, July–August 1980, pp. 51–54.

Mason, P., Cash Flow Analysis and the Funds Statement, Accounting Research Study No. 2 (AICPA, 1961).

Paton, W. A., Advanced Accounting (Macmillan Company, New York, 1941).

Paton, W. A., and R. A. Stevenson, Principles of Accounting (Macmillan Company, New York, 1918).

Shohet, J., and R. Rikert (eds.), Accounting Trends and Techniques: Annual Survey of Accounting Practices Followed in 600 Stockholders' Reports (AICPA, 1979 and 1980).

Vatter, W. J., "A Direct Method for the Preparation of Fund Statements," Journal of Accountancy, April 1944, pp. 479–489.

CHAPTER 4

Financial Statement

Analysis

Baruch Lev

*Professor of Accounting, Tel Aviv University and
University of California, Berkeley*

HISTORICAL DEVELOPMENT AND RELATION TO OTHER FIELDS

Financial statement analysis (FSA) is a growing and ever-changing set of systems and procedures designed to provide decision makers with relevant information derived from basic sources of data, such as corporate financial statements and industry and government statistics. The origins of FSA in the United States can be traced to the second half of the nineteenth century, when two major economic developments created the need for a systematic analysis of firms' financial data. The first was the emergence of the corporation as the main organizational form of business enterprises, resulting in a need by owners, separated from day-to-day operations, to evaluate and monitor the activities of managers. The second development was the increasing role of financial institutions (banks, investment and insurance companies, etc.) as major suppliers of capital for investment purposes, requiring a formal evaluation system of borrowers' creditworthiness.[1] Initially FSA constituted the computation of a few financial ratios (e.g., the "current ratio") and the comparison of these ratios with past figures for the same firm and with standards, such as the industry average ratio. The first half of the twentieth century evidenced a marked expansion of ratios to reflect various aspects of performance and financial condition, such as profitability, efficiency, and solvency. Also, extensive industry standards were compiled and provided by credit agencies and financial services, such as Dun & Bradstreet and Robert Morris Associates. During the last two decades, emphasis in the development of FSA switched from the use of individual indicators to the construction of formal models designed to explain and predict important business events, such as corporate bankruptcy and bond rating changes.

Up to the 1960s, developments in FSA were rather alienated from related fields and disciplines, such as economics, finance, and decision theory. In the last decade or so, however, the gap has been narrowed. Modern FSA, and in particular the prediction models used in financial and credit analysis, are generally based on economic and finance theories (e.g., the "portfolio selection" model), and are constructed on the foundations of decision theories, making extensive use of statistical tools and techniques. Moreover, the influence goes also in the opposite direction—FSA models and techniques are beginning to be used by researchers and practitioners in economics, finance, and accounting to test and verify new models and theories, and to clarify controversies of public interest.[2]

The following sections present a discussion of the users of FSA, tools and techniques of financial analysis, and financial models for specific uses.

---

[1]For a detailed history of FSA, see Horrigan [1978].

[2]See, for example, the FSA conducted by Shyam Sunder [1977] in the context of the oil industry profits controversy.

USERS OF FINANCIAL STATEMENT DATA AND ANALYSIS

The number and variety of financial data users has been constantly increasing. The traditional, and still major, groups of users are equity investors (particularly via professional analysts) and lenders. The former are interested mainly in evaluating the performance of the firm and its management and in assessing the future earnings potential of the firm, whereas the latter group of users is generally concerned with the solvency status of the firm. There is considerable empirical evidence indicating that the publication of financial data (particularly earnings figures) is associated with stock price changes.[3] This appears to attest to the ongoing use of financial data by equity investors.

Public regulators are also heavy users of financial data and analysis. Financial analysis, particularly of earnings and assets, is conducted in the rate-setting process for utilities, and generally plays an important role in controversies and lawsuits concerning these rates. Regulators, such as insurance commissioners and bank examiners, have recently been using early warning systems based mainly on financial data to predict future default.

Since the New York City financial crisis, bond analysts have been increasingly conducting financial analysis of municipalities to determine the quality (particularly default risk) of the bonds. Labor unions have been using financial data, mainly on labor productivity changes, in the process of wage negotiations. The periodic waves of mergers and corporate acquisitions have created a need for specialized financial analysis to estimate the value of a business enterprise. Corporate financial data and analysis are used in econometric models designed to predict macroeconomic variables, such as gross national product (GNP) and capital expenditures. Researchers in accounting, finance, and economics also use financial data extensively in the process of model construction and verification.

Finally accounting policy makers, such as the Securities and Exchange Commission (SEC) and the Financial Accounting Standards Board (FASB), have recently been using advanced financial analysis to (1) obtain evidence on the consequences of policy decisions,[4] and (2) verify the assumptions underlying policy decisions. It appears that such use of empirical financial data by policy makers is bound to grow considerably in the future.

TOOLS AND TECHNIQUES OF FINANCIAL ANALYSIS

Ratio Analysis. Ratio analysis is still the basic tool of financial statement analysis. It involves the breakdown of the examined financial reports into compo-

---

[3] For elaboration, see Foster [1983, chap. 11].

[4] See, for example, the study conducted for the FASB on the consequences of the oil and gas statement (FASB Statement No. 19) by Dyckman and Smith [1979].

EXHIBIT 1 An Integrated Ratio Analysis System (numbers in parentheses indicate General Electric's 1980, 1979 ratios, respectively)

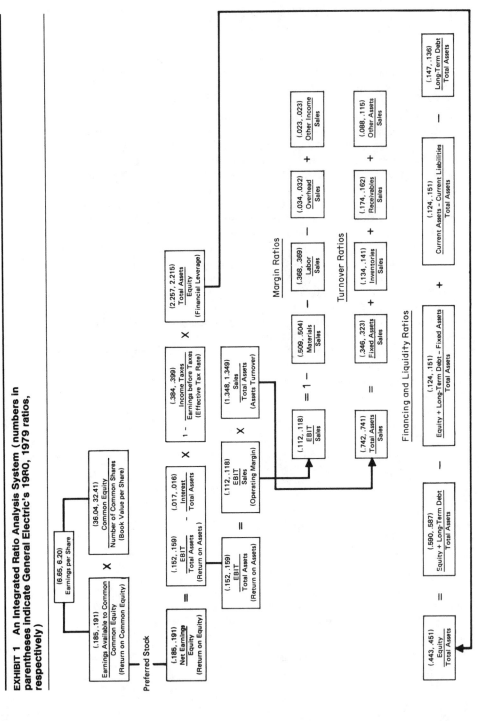

nent parts (e.g., fixed and current assets), which are then evaluated in relation to each other and to exogenous standards. Financial ratios expedite the analysis by reducing the large number of items involved to a relatively small set of readily comprehended and economically meaningful indicators.

Over the years the number of ratios available for financial analysis has proliferated, causing, among other things, a substantial redundancy.[5] Furthermore, given the large number of ratios available, it is difficult to discern the interrelationships among them required for a comprehensive understanding of the entity being analyzed. What is needed is a parsimonious, integrated system of financial ratios, which will incorporate the essential ratios and highlight the interrelationships among them. Such a system is presented in Exhibit 1 and its use in financial analysis is discussed. To facilitate understanding of the computation and interpretation of ratios, the financial reports of the General Electric Company (G.E.), presented in Exhibits 2 and 3, will be used as an example.[6]

Computation and interpretation of ratios—earnings per share. The starting point of the integrated system of ratio analysis presented in Exhibit 1 is the well-known and widely used indicator of the firm's performance—*earnings per share* (EPS). The numerator of this ratio is defined as "net earnings available to common stockholders" (i.e., aftertax earnings minus dividends on preferred stocks), whereas the denominator represents the average number of common shares outstanding.

	1980	1979
EPS computation: Earnings available to common stock (in millions)	$1,514	$1,409
Divided by: Average number of common shares outstanding (in thousands)	227,541	227,173
Yields: Earnings per share	$6.65	$6.20

When the firm has hybrid securities, such as convertible bonds, stock options, or stock warrants, the computation of EPS becomes technically more complex. The computation of EPS in such cases is discussed in Chapter 29 of this handbook.

The interpretation of EPS figures appears to be straightforward. They indicate the profitability of the firm from the shareholders' point of view. Thus, in our example, it appears that G.E.'s profits increased in 1980 relative to the preceding year ($6.65 in 1980 versus $6.20 in 1979). Such a straightforward interpretation of EPS changes is, however, often misleading, as is demonstrated by the following two ratios presented in the second tier of Exhibit 1.

Return on common equity and book value per share. The firm's EPS is determined by two factors: the profitability of the firm's equity, known as the

---

[5]For a comprehensive list and discussion of financial ratios, see Bernstein [1978].

[6]The G.E. ratios reported in Exhibit 1 and discussed throughout this section were computed on the basis of end-of-year balance sheet data. In some cases it is more appropriate to use beginning-of-year data (as in the case of return-on-equity ratios), or average balance sheet data representing the outstanding balance throughout the year (as in the case of turnover and sales-to-assets ratios).

EXHIBIT 2

GENERAL ELECTRIC COMPANY AND CONSOLIDATED AFFILIATES
Balance Sheet
(for the years ended December 31, in millions)

Assets	1980	1979	Equities	1980	1979
Current assets:					
Cash	$ 1,601	$ 1,904	Current liabilities	$ 7,592	$ 6,872
Marketable securities	600	672	Long-term debt	2,719	2,410
Accounts receivable	4,339	3,647	Stockholders' equity[a]	8,200	7,362
Inventories	3,343	3,161			
Total current assets	$ 9,883	$ 9,384			
Property, plant, and equipment—net	5,780	4,613			
Investments and other fixed assets	2,848	2,647			
Total assets	$18,511	$16,644	Total equities	$18,511	$16,644

[a]Average number of shares outstanding (in thousands): 1980—227,541; 1979—227,173.

EXHIBIT 3

GENERAL ELECTRIC COMPANY AND CONSOLIDATED AFFILIATES
Statement of Earnings
(for the years ended December 31, in millions)

	1980	1979
Sales of products and services.	$24,959	$22,461
Operating costs:		
Materials	$12,696	$11,320
Labor	9,196	8,286
Overhead	824	725
Total operating costs	$22,716	$20,331
Operating margin	$ 2,243	$ 2,130
Other income	564	519
Interest and other financial charges	(314)	(258)
Earnings before income taxes	$ 2,493	$ 2,391
Provision for income taxes	(958)	(953)
Minority interest in earnings of consolidated affiliates	(21)	(29)
Net earnings available to common stock	$ 1,514	$ 1,409
Earnings per common share	$ 6.65	$ 6.20

return on common equity (ROCE), and the firm's book value per share (BVPS). The effect of BVPS on EPS results from the fact that firms, in general, retain a portion of earnings (i.e., the dividend payout ratio is smaller than one, and has been on average about one-half for U.S. industrial firms). Such earnings retention, indicated by a change in the BVPS, increases the investment base represented by each share and in general increases the absolute amount of earnings available to common shareholders, thereby increasing EPS. Thus, a change in EPS can be caused by a change in the investment base per share (BVPS) or a change in the earnings power per dollar invested (ROCE), or both.

The hazard in the interpretation of EPS changes is demonstrated in our example. G.E.'s 1980 change in EPS (from $6.20 to $6.65) was caused by the increase in BVPS (from $32.41 to $36.04), namely by, the "earnings retention effect," whereas the profitability of common equity (measured by ROCE) actually *decreased*, from .191 in 1979 to .185 in 1980. Thus, an increase in EPS has masked the decrease in profitability.[7]

What caused the decrease in G.E.'s profitability? To answer this question, we have to continue unmasking the financial picture by descending to lower tiers of Exhibit 1.

The decomposition of return on equity. From examining the return on *common* equity, we move to return on total equity or ROE. This is done by adding to the numerator of the ROCE ratio the preferred dividends paid during the

---

[7]It can still be argued, of course, that G.E.'s earnings applicable to each common share have increased in 1980. Although this is technically true, the *interpretation* of the EPS increase as indicating an increase in the firm's earning power (profitability) can be false.

year, and adding to the denominator the book value of the preferred stock outstanding.[8] The firm's ROE is decomposed in the third tier of Exhibit 1 into three basic factors: return on total assets, effective tax rate, and the firm's capital structure (leverage).

Return on assets. A return on assets (ROA) is a measure of the average profitability of the firm's assets, designed to indicate the efficiency of the total capital employed by the firm. To focus on operational (business) efficiency, as distinct from financial efficiency, the numerator of the ROA ratio is earnings *before* interest and taxes, known as EBIT, thus leaving the financial and tax effects for separate consideration. The exclusion of financing charges from the ROA allows, among other things, a more appropriate interfirm comparison because differences among firms in capital structure, reflected in different interest charges, will not affect the ROA ratio.

	1980	1979
ROA computation: Earnings before interest and taxes (EBIT) (in millions)	$ 2,807	$ 2,649
Divided by: Total assets (in millions)	18,511	16,644
Yields: Return on assets (ROA)	.152	.159

Note that G.E.'s ROA decreased slightly in 1980 (from .159 to .152), whereas interest charges relative to total assets remained practically unchanged (.017 versus .016).

The second component of the ROE decomposition is the effective tax rate, measured as the ratio of the provision for income taxes divided by earnings before taxes. G.E.'s data indicate a decrease in the effective tax rate, from .399 in 1979 to .384 in 1980, positively affecting ROE. The analyst's task in this case is, of course, to identify the reasons for this change and to ascertain whether it is a transitory or a permanent change.

The third factor affecting ROE is the firm's capital structure or degree of leverage. In general, the borrowing rate is lower than the return on the shareholders' equity. Thus, and other things being equal, increases in leverage (i.e., an increase in the share of borrowed capital relative to shareholders' equity) will result in an increase in return on equity, and vice versa. It should be noted, of course, that a return on equity increase due to a leverage change has its cost in the form of a higher degree of *financial risk* associated with the stream of earnings available to common shareholders.[9] Thus, in the case of leverage changes, the analyst should weigh the changes in profitability against the financial risk changes.

There are several alternative ways to measure the degree of leverage: debt to equity; debt to total assets; equity to total assets; and so on. All these alternatives are, of course, equivalent in interpretation. In Exhibit 1, leverage is measured in a nonconventional way as total assets to equity, so that the product

---

[8]G.E. does not have preferred stock outstanding, so ROCE equals ROE.

[9]See Lev [1974, pp. 25–26] for a discussion of financial risk and its relation to capital structure.

of the three components yields the ROE ratio. We note that, for G.E., there was a slight increase during 1980 in leverage; the reciprocal of the total assets-to-equity ratio indicates that whereas equity constituted 45.1 percent of total assets in 1979, it decreased to 44.3 percent in 1980.[10]

Summarizing G.E.'s ROE decomposition, the decrease in the return on equity during 1980 resulted from two conflicting forces: a decrease in the efficiency of using assets (ROA), which was moderated by a decrease in effective tax rate and a leverage increase. We proceed now to identify the causes for the ROA decrease.

The decomposition of return on assets. In the fourth tier of Exhibit 1, the ROA ratio is decomposed into two basic components—operating margin and asset turnover—each of which is further analyzed. Operating margin, measured as EBIT to sales, indicates the average profitability of the firm's sales. Note that for G.E. this average profitability has decreased during 1980, from 11.8 percent to 11.2 percent. Asset turnover, measured as sales to total assets, indicates the extent to which the firm's assets are used to generate sales. Obviously, the higher this measure, the better is the usage of assets in the firm's operations. G.E.'s data indicate stability in this ratio during 1980 at about 1.35.

In the fifth tier of Exhibit 1, the operating margin ratio is analyzed according to the various cost components of the firm's income statement. These indicators are known as "margin ratios." It is evident that the decrease in G.E.'s operating margin was due mainly to an increase in material usage, from .504 in 1979 to .509 in 1980. The other cost components remained essentially unchanged during 1980.

In the sixth tier of Exhibit 1, the assets turnover ratio is analyzed according to the various asset items on the firm's balance sheet.[11] This decomposition yields the well-known "turnover (efficiency) ratios," which indicate management's efficiency in putting to work specific asset items, such as receivables and inventory. G.E.'s assets turnover decomposition indicates that inventory turnover (the reciprocal of the inventories/sales ratio in Exhibit 1) increased in 1980 relative to 1979,[12] whereas the fixed assets and receivables turnover ratios

---

[10]A firm's capital structure, or the consequence of financing decisions, can also be expressed from an income statement point of view. This is the well-known "coverage," or "times interest earned" ratio, which is defined as net earnings before fixed charges on debt (and other fixed commitments, such as noncancelable leases), divided by those fixed charges. The numerator of this ratio is sometimes adjusted for tax benefit received for interest payments (i.e., a charge for the amount of the tax rate times interest payments is deducted from the numerator). Other things being equal, the higher this ratio, the safer are debtholders and the lower is the financial risk of equity holders. G.E.'s "coverage" ratio has decreased from 6.06 in 1979 to 5.44 in 1980 (tax-adjusted).

[11]For arithmetical convenience, the reciprocal of the assets turnover ratio is used on the left-hand side of the sixth tier in Exhibit 1.

[12]Given that inventories are generally valued at cost, it is more appropriate to define the inventory turnover ratio as cost of goods sold divided by average inventory. When a LIFO cost flow assumption is used, the balance sheet values for inventory can be much less than their current costs. For example, in 1980, G.E. reported that if FIFO had been used, balance sheet inventories would have been $2.2 billion (roughly 66 percent) more than the amount, $3.3 billion, actually shown.

decreased in 1980.[13] Again, the analyst's task is to identify the causes of such changes, particularly with respect to inventory and receivables and whether they are transitory or permanent. Such an investigation will provide the analyst with insight regarding management's policies and their implications for future operations.[14]

Financing and liquidity ratios. Discussing thus far profitability and efficiency ratios, we shift attention to the financing aspect of operations. The seventh tier of Exhibit 1 decomposes the leverage ratio (equity over total assets) into various financing ratios. Starting from the left, the "equity and long-term debt over total assets" ratio expresses the firm's capital structure from a nonconventional aspect. Rather than focusing on the relative shares of debt and equity, the dichotomy between long- and short-term financing is stressed here. This dichotomy has obvious implications with respect to the financial stability of the firm (solvency) and the cost of capital employed. This ratio for G.E. remained unchanged (at .59) during 1980. The "equity and long-term debt minus fixed assets divided by total assets" ratio indicates the extent to which fixed assets are financed by long-term capital. Obviously, the higher this ratio, the more stable is the financial composition of the firm. However, stability has its cost. If, for example, equity is larger than fixed assets, it means that a portion of owners' capital is used to finance current assets, usually leading to erosion of capital during inflationary periods. This ratio for G.E. changed during 1980 to .12 from .15 at the end of 1979.

The ratio of "current assets − current liabilities (i.e., working capital) over total assets" is a measure of liquidity.[15] The higher this ratio, the more liquid the firm's situation. Again, high liquidity has its cost, particularly during inflationary periods.[16]

Other ratios. The preceding presentation did not exhaust the set of possible financial ratios, nor was there an intention to do so, given the substantial redundancy in the available ratios.[17] The only exception worth mentioning is the well-known price–earnings (PE) ratio, which is defined as the ratio of the stock market price of a common stock (usually computed as an average price for the

---

[13] A useful extension of the receivables turnover ratio is the "average collection period for credit sales," which is obtained by dividing the number of days in a year, 365, by the receivables turnover ratio. G.E.'s 1980 average collection period is 63.5 days (365/5.75). Changes in this indicator may signal changes in credit terms, changes in the quality of customers to whom credit is extended, or changes in the quality of collection efforts.

[14] It should be noted that both the "margin" and "turnover" ratios can be computed on a finer classification than that presented in Exhibit 1. For example, the materials-to-sales ratio can be broken down into several ratios according to various types of materials, or the receivables-to-sales ratio can be decomposed into different classes of receivables. The fineness of classification will be determined by the objectives of the analysis.

[15] Other measures of liquidity are the current ratio and the quick ratio. For elaboration, see Lev [1974, pp. 22–24].

[16] Increased attention is being paid to cash flow analysis when investigating companies; see, for example, Backer and Gosman [1978].

[17] This redundancy is due mainly to the high correlation between many ratios for the same firm; see Lev [1974, pp. 64–67].

given period) to its EPS. This is a natural extension of the EPS measure, relating the firm's earnings to stock prices in order to answer the question: How much is the investor paying for the EPS? Because stock prices generally reflect investors' expectations regarding *future* earnings of the firm, the PE ratios of companies with prospects of a high earnings growth will be larger (other things, particularly risk, being equal) than those of companies with lower growth prospects. Differences in PE ratios will therefore partially reflect differences in the market's expectations regarding the future earnings growth of firms.[18] This expectation aspect is a unique attribute of the PE ratio as compared with other financial ratios, which are based entirely on historical data.

General Comments on Ratio Analysis

Modes of analysis. Financial ratios are conventionally analyzed in two ways: time series (intrafirm) and cross-sectional (interfirm) analysis. The former is concerned with the behavior of a given ratio over time, whereas the latter involves comparisons between the investigated firm's ratios and those of related firms. The major objective of analyzing the time series of ratios is to search for systematic patterns in the ratios (e.g., constant growth, decline) and to exploit such patterns in predicting future values of the ratios. The objective of the cross-sectional (interfirm) analysis is to derive information by comparing the investigated firm's ratios with exogenous standards or norms, such as the industry mean or median ratios. Data on such standard ratios for a large set of industries are published periodically by Dun & Bradstreet, Robert Morris Associates, and other financial institutions. Both cross-sectional and time series analyses are generally performed simultaneously in the process of ratio analysis.[19]

Inflationary effects. Data presented in conventional financial statements are based on historical costs. During inflationary periods this acounting convention adversely affects the analysis and interpretation of financial data. Thus, for example, profitability ratios, such as earnings over total assets, are biased upward as a result of the fact that the numerator is expressed in current dollars (except for depreciation), whereas the denominator reflects dollars of an earlier vintage having larger purchasing power. Moreover, interfirm comparisons are disrupted because young firms will, other things being equal, have lower profitability measures than older firms, because assets and depreciation figures will be *nominally* higher for the younger firms than for the older ones. More seriously, the effects of inflation on capital erosion and the impact of inflation on current assets versus liabilities (i.e., gains or losses on "monetary items") are not reflected in conventional financial statements.

It is therefore incumbent upon the analyst to adjust for the effects of inflation on the financial data prior to the analysis. This is facilitated by the FASB requirement for large firms to provide supplementary data on the effects of

---

[18]Some doubts about the ability of PE ratios to reflect long-term growth potential are reported in an empirical study by Beaver and Morse [1978].

[19]For elaboration on time series and cross-sectional analysis of ratios, see Foster [1983, chaps. 3–4].

inflation, such as the current cost of inventory, plant, cost of sales, and depreciation, and the gains or losses on items eroded by inflation. For smaller firms, the analyst can use approximate methods for inflationary adjustments.[20]

Accounting and statistical issues. Inflationary adjustments are not the only ones required in financial analysis. It is sometimes necessary to account in the process of ratio analysis for intrafirm changes and interfirm difference in accounting methods (e.g., LIFO versus FIFO inventory methods).[21] Also, the analyst should be aware of the statistical issues involved in the computation and interpretation of ratios and standards.[22] Finally, attention to segmented data is called for in the analysis of diversified companies.[23]

Residual Analysis. The factors affecting a firm's performance can be classified into two groups: *common factors*, which affect the performance of all firms in the economy or the industry, such as inflation, changes in tax policy, or a decrease in the demand for the industry's product; and *specific factors*, which affect the performance of only the investigated firm, such as a managerial policy change, or an advertising campaign for the firm's product. The common factors are to a large extent beyond the control of management, whereas the specific factors are in general under management's control. Accordingly, in evaluating *management's* performance—a major objective of financial analysis—the overall performance (e.g., the firm's profitability) should be decomposed into the part that is under management's control and responsibility (i.e., induced by firm-specific factors) and the part of performance that is beyond management's control. A decomposition of controllable versus uncontrollable factors is a basic tenet of any performance evaluation system.

Such a decomposition can be performed by "residual analysis," which is based on the following regression model:

$$X_{Ft} = a + bX_{Et} + cX_{It} + u_{Ft}$$

where X_{Ft} = performance measure for the investigated firm in period t, such as sales, earnings, return on equity, etc.

X_{Et} = an overall economy measure corresponding to the firm's measure. For example, if X_{Ft} is sales, then X_{Et} can be GNP, or if X_{Ft} is earnings, X_{Et} can be total corporate earnings.

X_{It} = an industry-wide measure corresponding to X_{Ft}. For example, if X_{Ft} is sales, then X_{It} can be total industry sales (excluding, of course, the sales of the investigated firm).

The residual, u_{Ft}, reflects the portion of the total performance, X_{Ft}, that is not accounted for by the economy and industry-wide indices, X_{Et} and X_{It}, namely, that portion of the total performance which is under management's control. By

---

[20]Such an approximate method is illustrated in Davidson and Weil [1975]. See also Ketz [1978] and Fabozzi and Shiffrin [1979].

[21]For elaboration, see Foster [1978, pp. 185–192 and 311–315].

[22]For elaboration, see Lev and Sunder [1979]; also Foster [1983, chap. 6].

[23]For elaboration on segment reporting, see Barefield and Holstrum [1979].

focusing on the sign and change in the residuals, u_{Ft}, the analyst can evaluate the firm's performance attributable to management's actions.[24]

SPECIFIC APPLICATIONS OF FINANCIAL ANALYSIS

The system of ratio analysis described above was aimed at providing the analyst with signals (e.g., return on equity below the industry's median) requiring further investigation to determine their causes and implications. Thus, the purpose of financial statement analysis discussed thus far is to suggest questions or areas for further investigation rather than to provide definite answers. An additional, more advanced use of financial data involves their incorporation in models designed to explain or predict important business events, such as bankruptcy and take-overs.[25] The following discussion outlines briefly the major models and their applications.

Solvency Assessment. Measuring firm solvency for granting credit was the original purpose for which financial statement analysis was developed. It is still an important objective of financial analysis, but both the scope of the objective and the set of users has recently broadened considerably. Models of solvency determination have been extended to include the prediction of corporate bankruptcy and financial distress of municipalities and other not-for-profit organizations. The set of users has been expanded to include, in addition to lenders, (1) *regulatory bodies*, such as state insurance commissioners concerned with protecting policyholders against losses resulting from bankruptcies of insurance companies, or the Federal Deposit Insurance Corporation (FDIC), concerned with minimizing the number of financially distressed banks; (2) *managers and investors*, obviously interested in predicting potential bankruptcy so that action can be taken in advance to avoid the occurrence of this traumatic event (e.g., by a merger) or at least to decrease the costs involved; (3) *auditors*, when issuing an opinion on the financial statement of a corporation, are generally required to render an opinion whether the business will remain as a going concern. Bankruptcy prediction models can aid the auditor in judging the "going-concern" issue.[26]

Attempts to determine solvency or predict bankruptcy generally involve the identification of a statistical relationship (correlation) between various financial indicators and the state of a firm's solvency. Once such a relationship is identified and found to be stable across firms and over time, it can be used to predict bankruptcy. Among the variables found to be useful predictors of bankruptcy

---

[24]For elaboration on, and demonstration of, residual analysis, see Foster [1978, pp. 149–155].

[25]Corporate financial data are also used as inputs to models designed to predict macroeconomic variables, such as GNP and aggregate corporate investment. This use of financial data is beyond the scope of this chapter and will not be discussed further.

[26]See, for example, Altman and McGough [1974].

(or to contribute significantly to the performance of a bankruptcy prediction model) are cash flow to total debt, EBIT over total assets, volatility of earnings, EBIT to interest payments (interest coverage ratio), working capital to total assets, equity over total capital, and firm size.

The technical issues involved in the construction and use of bankruptcy prediction models are beyond the scope of this chapter. For a description of the structure, uses and limitations of such models, see Lev [1974, chap. 9] and Foster [1978, chaps. 14–15]. It should be noted that these models are widely used by lenders and regulatory agencies.

The Prediction of Bond Ratings. Most bond issues in the United States are currently rated by financial agencies, such as Moody's or Standard & Poor's. These debt instruments include industrial, public utility, financial institution, and airline bonds, as well as those of state and local government units and commercial paper of these entities. The bond rating, generally on a nine-point scale, purports to indicate the degree of default risk, as well as some other characteristics of the issue, such as marketability. There is some empirical evidence on the existence of an inverse relationship between the ratings and actual default experience, thus attesting to the credibility of bond ratings.

Models using financial statement indicators (e.g., net income before interest to interest, long-term debt to total assets, etc.), as well as other measures (e.g., the subordination status of the bond and issue size), have been constructed to predict the rating category assigned to corporate or municipal bonds.[27] The performance of these models has been found, in general, to be rather good.

Models designed to predict bond ratings are obviously of interest to rating agencies, because the incorporation of a model into the rating process is one way of reducing inconsistencies between individual ratings. In addition, such models can assist raters in their ongoing activity of reevaluating currently rated bonds, serving as a screening device to signal changing economic conditions of companies or municipalities. Bond rating prediction models are also of interest to investors, particularly in the case of bond issues that are not currently rated (e.g., privately placed bonds), where the model can provide a surrogate for the rating. Managers are also interested in such prediction models: In the case of new issues, the model provides management with an estimate of the prospective rating, and thereby provides a general idea of the cost of capital.[28] In the case of outstanding issues, the model can signal to management the possibility of a change in the rating.

For elaboration on the construction of bond rating prediction models for corporations and municipalities, see Lev [1974, chap. 10], and Foster [1983, chap. 13].[29]

---

[27] In the case of municipal bonds, the financial indicators in the models include, among others, total bonded debt per capita, total revenues per capita, federal and state aid as a percentage of debt services, etc.

[28] A strong inverse relationship was found between the ratings and the market yield on the bonds.

[29] See also Kaplan and Urwitz [1979].

Risk Assessment. A major premise of modern economics and finance theory is that in the performance evaluation of an investment both the risk and return (profitability) factors have to be considered simultaneously. This principle applies to investments in securities as well as to performance evaluation of business enterprises. However, conventional financial statement analysis (ratio analysis) provides measures for the assessment of profitability of operations only, while generally ignoring the riskiness of operations, probably due to lack of adequate risk measures. This situation was remedied in the 1960s with the advent of the portfolio selection and later the capital asset pricing models, which offer a conceptual as well as a practical approach to the assessment of the risk associated with securities. The central risk measure according to this approach is the well-known β which indicates the degree to which a security's rate of return moves (is associated) with the market's average rate of return. In general, a low degree of association, or sensitivity to overall market phenomena, indicates a low risk level, whereas the contrary holds for a high degree of association.[30]

The estimation of a stock's β or other finance-based risk measures is generally made using the stock's history of rates of returns; such estimation is based totally on stock market data. This provides an opportunity to develop risk measures and models, based on financial statement (accounting) data, and compare them with the market-based risk measures. Stated differently, the availability of risk measures determined objectively in the stock market motivated researchers to identify the underlying economic factors determining the firm's risk.

This line of research indicates that indeed some financial statement measures and models are highly correlated with market-based risk measures, and furthermore they can even improve the assessment of a stock's risk.[31] Specifically, financial statement measures, such as the financial leverage (debt over equity), the operating leverage (the ratio of fixed to variable operating costs), the variability of earnings, the covariability of earnings (i.e., the extent of association between the firm's earnings and the average earnings of all firms in the economy), and the dividend payout ratio were found to be highly correlated with the β risk measures and the volatility of stock prices.[32] It can be concluded, therefore, that an assessment of the firm's risk can be made from financial statement data. Such a risk assessment will complete the conventional set of tools available for financial statement analysis. It will be of particular importance in cases of nonpublic companies and business enterprises, where risk cannot be assessed by stock market data.

---

[30]For elaboration on these risk measures and their estimation, see Lev [1974, chap. 12] and Foster [1983, chap. 8]. See also Wallace [1980].

[31]Another implication of modern finance theory is that if capital markets are efficient and prices determined according to the capital assets pricing model, then the major objective of financial statement analysis is the assessment of securities' risk.

[32]For elaboration, see Lev [1974, chap. 13], Foster [1983, chap. 9], and Hill and Stone [1980].

The Prediction of Corporate Acquisition. One clear and undisputed finding emerges from the intensive research on the effects of corporate mergers and acquisitions: The shareholders of the *acquired* firms gain handsomely from such acquisitions.[33] This phenomenon motivated both researchers and practitioners to study the financial characteristics of acquired firms to see if (1) such characteristics differ markedly from the characteristics of nonacquired firms, and (2) such characteristics might be useful in predicting which companies will be acquired.

The published research on the subject appears to suggest that there are differences between the financial characteristics of acquired and nonacquired firms, and that models based on financial data have some ability to discriminate between the two groups of firms. However, results are still inconclusive: Some of the distinguishing financial characteristics change from study to study, and the predictive power of the models is modest. Thus, for example, in one study it was found that acquired firms (relative to nonacquired) were smaller, had lower PE ratios, lower dividend payout, and lower growth in equity [Monroe and Simkowitz, 1971]. However, another study found that neither dividend payout nor the PE ratio seemed to be important discriminatory variables; rather, acquired firms used significantly less debt than did nonacquired firms [Stevens, 1973]. A recent study, pertaining to acquisitions made during the 1970s, reports that the PE ratio and firm size have a strong negative effect on the probability of acquisition; however, the predictive power of the model including these variables is weak [Harris et al., 1981]. It should be noted here, as elsewhere in this section, that the predictability of models based on financial data can probably be improved by adding nonfinancial variables to the model. Thus, for example, in the case of merger prediction, the omission from the models constructed thus far of variables reflecting factors, such as industry concentration and R&D and advertising intensity might explain the modest predictive power of these models.

Summary. The discussion in this section provided examples for the use of financial data in models designed to explain and predict important economic events. Some of the attempts of financial model building were rather successful, leading to the use of such models in practice (e.g., the bankruptcy and credit scoring models), whereas in other cases (e.g., merger prediction), the available models have yet to prove their usefulness. This financial model building endeavor is still in an early stage of development and suffers from various methodological shortcomings,[34] yet it is undoubtedly a most promising avenue for the development of financial statement analysis. Of particular interest is the use of financial (along with nonfinancial) information in stock valuation. This area of research is still in its infancy. For a conceptual discussion, see Beaver

---

[33] For example, in a sample of 161 successful cash tender offers (pertaining to the 1962–1977 period), the bidding firms paid the acquired firms' shareholders an average premium of about 50 percent for the shares they purchased. (This premium is the difference between the price actually paid for the stocks and the market price of the stock prior to the announcement of the cash tender offer.) See Bradley [1980].

[34] See, for example, discussion in Foster [1978, pp. 443–444; 476–480; 510–512].

[1981, chap. 4, particularly pp. 100–110, on the PE ratio]. For examples of valuation models used in practice, see Foster [1978, pp. 301–311], and Hawkins and Campbell [1978].

BIBLIOGRAPHY

Altman, E. I., and T. P. McGough, "The Evaluation of a Company as a Going Concern," *The Journal of Accountancy*, vol. 138, no. 6 (December 1974), pp. 50–57.

Backer M., and M. L. Gosman, *Financial Reporting and Business Liquidity* (National Association of Accountants, New York, 1978).

Barefield, R. M., and G. L. Holstrum, *Disclosure Criteria and Segment Reporting* (University Presses of Florida, Gainesville, 1979).

Beaver, W. H., *Financial Reporting: An Accounting Revolution* (Prentice-Hall, Englewood Cliffs, N.J., 1981).

Beaver, W., and D. Morse, "What Determines Price-Earnings Ratios?," *Financial Analysts Journal*, vol. 34, no. 4 (July–August 1978), pp. 65–76.

Belkaoui, A., "Financial Ratios as Predictors of Canadian Takeovers," *Journal of Business, Finance and Accounting*, vol. 5, no. 1 (Spring 1978), pp. 93–108.

Bernstein, L., "In Defense of Fundamental Investment Analysis," *Financial Analysts Journal*, vol. 31, no. 3 (January/February 1975), pp. 57–61.

———, *Financial Statement Analysis: Theory, Application and Interpretation*, rev. ed. (Richard D. Irwin, Homewood, Ill., 1978).

Bradley, M., "Interfirm Tender Offers and the Market for Corporate Control," *Journal of Business*, vol. 53, no. 4 (October 1980), pp. 345–376.

Davidson, S., and R. L. Weil, "Inflation Accounting: What Will General Price Level Adjusted Income Statements Show?," *Financial Analysts Journal*, vol. 31, no. 1 (January–February 1975), pp. 27–31, 70–84.

Dawson, J. P., P. M. Neupert, and C. P. Stickney, "Restating Financial Statements for Alternative GAAP's: Is It Worth the Effort?" *Financial Analysts Journal*, vol. 36, no. 6 (November–December 1980), pp. 38–46.

Dyckman, T. R., and A. J. Smith, "Financial Accounting and Reporting by Oil and Gas Producing Companies: A Study of Information Effects," *Journal of Accounting and Economics*, vol. 1, no. 1 (Spring 1979), pp. 45–75.

Fabozzi, F. J., and L. M. Shiffrin, "Replacement Cost Accounting: Application to Pharmaceutical Industry," in J. C. McKeown (ed.), *Inflation and Current Value Accounting* (University of Illinois, Urbana, 1979).

Foster, G., *Financial Statement Analysis* (Prentice-Hall, Englewood Cliffs, N.J., 1978).

Harris, R. S., J. F. Stewart, and W. T. Carleton, "The Financial Characteristics of Acquired Firms," paper presented at the Conference on Mergers and Acquisitions: Current Problems in Perspective, January 8–9, 1981, New York University, New York.

Hawkins, D. F., and W. J. Campbell, *Equity Valuation: Models, Analysis and Implications* (Financial Executives Research Foundation, New York, 1978).

Hill, N. C., and B. K. Stone, "Accounting Betas, Systematic Operating Risk and Financial Leverage: A Risk-Composition Approach to the Determinants of Systematic Risk," *Journal of Financial and Quantitative Analysis*, vol. 15 (September 1980), pp. 595–637.

Horrigan, J. O. (ed.), *Financial Ratio Analysis: A Historical Perspective* (Arno Press, New York, 1978).

Kaplan, R. S., and G. Urwitz, "Statistical Models of Bond Ratings: A Methodological Inquiry," *Journal of Business*, vol. 52, no. 2 (1979), pp. 231–261.

Ketz, J. E., "The Validation of Some General Price Level Estimating Models," *The Accounting Review*, vol. 53, no. 4 (October 1978), pp. 952–960.

Langer, R. D., *Accounting as a Variable in Merger* (Arno Press, New York, 1978).

Lasman, D. A., and R. L. Weil, "Adjusting the Debt-Equity Ratio," *Financial Analysts Journal*, vol. 37, no. 1 (September/October 1978), pp. 10ff. and p. 79.

Lev, B. *Financial Statement Analysis: A New Approach* (Prentice-Hall, Englewood Cliffs, N.J., 1974).

Lev, B., and S. Sunder, "Methodological Issues in the Use of Financial Ratios," *Journal of Accounting and Economics*, vol. 1 (December 1979), pp. 187–210.

Monroe, R., and M. Simkowitz, "Investment Characteristics of Conglomerate Targets: A Discriminant Analysis," *Southern Journal of Business*, vol. 6, no. 3 (November 1971), pp. 1–16.

Stevens, D. L., "Financial Characteristics of Merged Firms: A Multivariate Analysis," *Journal of Financial and Quantitative Analysis*, vol. 8 (March 1973), pp. 149–158.

Sunder, S. *Oil Industry Profits* (American Enterprise Institute for Public Policy Research, Washington, D.C., 1977).

Wallace, A., "Is Beta Dead?" *Institutional Investor*, vol. 14, no. 7 (July 1980), pp. 22–30.

CHAPTER 5

Interim Reports

David O. Green

Professor of Accounting and Vice President for Administration, Baruch College, City University of New York

INTRODUCTION

After decades of benign neglect, the decade of the 1970s witnessed widespread accounting interest in the topic of interim reports. For example, the Accounting Principles Board (APB) devoted Opinion No. 28 to the topic; problems concerned with interim reports first appeared on the Uniform CPA Examination; an NAA research study appeared; and a task force of the Financial Accounting Standards Board (FASB) was appointed to study the subject. The task force produced a Discussion Memorandum sufficiently provocative to elicit hundreds of letters of comment and hours of dialogue. For reasons that remain obscure, the FASB decided to disband the task force and table further formal discussion. The expressed hope was that a comprehensive solution to the accounting problems of the annual period would provide solutions to problems associated with the shorter periods reported on by the interim reports.

From one perspective this hope was naive; many accounting procedures and measurements exist because the financial statements cover a period shorter than the life of the organization being described. And if this is true for the annual report, it must be even more true for an accounting report of the shorter period. From this perspective, one could argue that the FASB erred—perhaps blundered—by not devoting resources to the interim report project in the expectation that answers here would yield answers for the annual accounting problems rather than vice versa.

Whatever the merits of the preceding argument, the fact remains that the topic of interim reports is again in a period of benign neglect and the paragraphs that follow are relatively devoid of recent reference to accounting authority such as the FASB and the Securities and Exchange Commission (SEC).

This is not to say that the intellectual aspects of the topic are dead; on the contrary, this territory remains on the frontier. There are great company-to-company variations in the quality and quantity of data reported, in the text that accompanies the accounting reports, even in the number of statements presented. The statement of changes in financial position, for example, is often omitted in an interim report.

One can measure the variety in the format and concepts of interim reports in several ways. An easy measure is, of course, the number of accounting statements included. Another, perhaps, is the number of rows of data in each statement, that is, the extent of summarization. Still another measure might be the ratio of column or square inches given to accounting data versus text, and these individually and/or together to the charts and/or pictures. Repetition and redundancy measures suggest themselves. Curiously, the SEC has contributed to the confusion of variety by permitting the interim balance sheet to be compared to either the one of a year ago or that of the fiscal year-end. We shall say more about this under the problems of seasonality. Still another measure is format (or format and size). Unlike the usual published annual report, the interim report is often the size of a no. 10 envelope for easy mailing and frequently self-mailing. That is, it is designed to receive a mailing label and to be posted as is, even though multipaged. A last aspect of variety is single or multipurpose. The interim financial report can stand alone; it may be intended to accompany a dividend check, indeed to act as a letter of conveyance for the check; it can be an integral part of a mailing that includes the report on the annual meeting.

Consider the first quarter, 1981, report of A. H. Robins, partially reproduced as Exhibit 1, which illustrates some of the points made above. The wraparound cover is printed on 8½″ × 11″ stock folded in thirds; stapled in are two roughly 8½″ × 7½″ sheets both printed on both sides. These provide eight of the nine panels given over to the president's remarks at the annual meeting. On the left two-thirds of Exhibit 1 appear: the only financial statement, a most abbreviated, absolutely SEC minimal, income statement; a highly unusual set of bar charts displaying 5 years of data (a 5-year comparison is also unusual); seldom seen (in interim reports) stock price data for 5 quarters; and a succinct yet complete one-paragraph description of the company. What is the ratio of accounting data to text? Roughly, two-thirds of two separate columns out of ten (or one and one-third out of ten, 13 percent).

In marked contrast with Exhibit 1 is the Harris Corporation first quarter (1981) report reproduced, in part, in Exhibit 2. The exhibit is the "busy" back side of a 9″ × 11½″ sheet, folded in thirds. The income statement is highly abbreviated; the balance sheet, less so; there is no statement of changes; the balance sheet comparison is with a year ago; the ratio of accounting to text is about 50/50 because a panel of text appears overleaf.

The size of the accounting-to-text ratio has little value in predicting the depth of the accounting analysis in an interim report. Consider Exhibit 3; this represents one-sixth, one of three panels of one side of a document printed on both sides, of *Exxon News*. Notice a rather detailed income statement, a balance sheet compared to the fiscal year-end rather than a year ago, a statement of changes, and selected financial and operating data voluntarily provided.

Whatever the variety in presenting interim reports, almost all face one central conceptual problem. The problem would not come into being if each calendar quarter within a year were pretty much alike, that is, with similar amounts of revenue and expense, and so on. When the firm is faced with some sort of recurring seasonal variation in sales or costs, the conceptual problem arises: Should each short period be treated as a mini-fiscal period with the employment of the usual annual procedures, or should it be considered in some other way, that is, as an aid to the reader in predicting the forthcoming annual outcome?

PURPOSE AND LIMITATIONS OF INTERIM REPORTS

Why Have Interim Reports? It seems logical to suppose that interim reports are published because the time between annual reports is too long. Indeed, this was the position of Elijah Watt Sells in an early and eloquent plea for quarterly reports [Sells, 1914]. Sells argued that quarterly reports would "do much to enlighten the public"; he thought they would be a help in achieving "stable markets for negotiable securities." Sells envisioned quarterly balance sheets certified by public accountants, and he reported his view that CPAs "generally are advocates of the quarterly report idea." Subsequent events lead one to

EXHIBIT 1

A. H. Robins Company, Incorporated and Subsidiaries
(In thousands of dollars except per share data)

	Three Months Ended March 31	
	1981	**1980**
Net Sales	**$114,660**	$104,399
Earnings Before Income Taxes and Foreign Exchange Gains (Losses)	**21,778**	16,064
Provision for Income Taxes	**8,681**	6,515
Earnings Before Foreign Gains (Losses)	**13,097**	9,549
Foreign Exchange Gains (Losses)	**(961)**	(623)
Net Earnings	**12,136**	8,926
Per Common Share:		
Earnings Before Foreign Exchange Gains (Losses)	**$.52**	$.37
Net Earnings	**$.48**	$.35
Average Share Outstanding	**25,131**	25,637

Earnings for 1980 have been restated to reflect adoption of the last-in, first-out (LIFO) method of inventory valuation.

The Company is a defendant in various lawsuits alleging injuries resulting from the use of a formerly marketed product. Since the ultimate outcome of the lawsuits cannot presently be determined, no provision for any liability that may result has been made.

Financial Trends (First Three Months)

Net Sales
In Millions of Dollars

'77 74
'78 89
'79 94
'80 104
'81 115

Net Earnings
In Millions of Dollars

'77 6.7
'78 8.9
'79 8.6
'80 8.9
'81 12.1

Earnings per Share
In Dollars

'77 .26
'78 .34
'79 .33
'80 .35
'81 .48

Dividends per Share
In Dollars

'77 .08
'78 .08
'79 .10
'80 .10
'81 .10

Stock Prices*

	High	Low
1981		
First quarter	$14%	$9%
1980		
First quarter	$ 9%	$6%
Second quarter	9	7%
Third quarter	10%	8%
Fourth quarter	12%	9

*Prices are those quoted on the New York Stock Exchange where the common stock of the Company is traded under the ticker symbol of RAH.

The Company

A. H. Robins is a multinational company doing business in more than 100 countries. It is engaged primarily in the manufacture of health care products, most of which are pharmaceutical specialties. These include Dimetapp*, a widely prescribed antihistamine/decongestant, and the Robitussin* family of cough syrups. Through subsidiaries, the Company also manufactures and sells a variety of consumer products. These include the Sergeant's* line of pet care products, Chap Stick* lip balm, the Quencher* line of cosmetics, and Caron* fragrance products.

Forms 10-K and 10-Q

The Form 10-K Annual Report and Form 10-Q Quarterly Report filed with the Securities and Exchange Commission are available without charge on request to the Treasurer, A. H. Robins Company, 1407 Cummings Drive, Richmond, Virginia 23220.

Remarks by E. C. Robins Jr.

I want to begin my remarks by assuring you that the news I have today is much brighter than that contained in our 1980 Annual Report.

No one was more disappointed than I over our earnings for 1980.

However, I am greatly encouraged by several actions taken during 1980 and the first quarter of this year to better position the Company to compete in the marketplace of today and tomorrow.

For example, during 1980 we established a new organizational structure for our Pharmaceutical Division sales force, creating a more responsive organization to meet the needs of our ethical and consumer promoted health care products. We recently announced a further refinement of this structure that will remove a tier of supervision in field management, thereby putting more of our salespeople into direct contact with customers and reducing administrative chores. Our pharmaceutical sales force, often cited by others as one of the best in the industry, thus is being fine-tuned to be even more efficient.

We also took a hard look at the performance of two subsidiaries last year and decided that resources allocated to them could be used more effectively in other areas. This decision led to the sale of the Blair and Wade Divisions of the Chap Stick Company in Lynchburg. We retained that subsidiary's principal product, Chap Stick* lip balm, but divested ourselves of the two extremely labor-intensive operations and the need for initiating costly capital improvements.

Similarly, we concluded the sale of Babcock Swine last year and now are in the process of negotiating a sales agreement for Babcock Poultry Farm, the larger segment of our Babcock Industries subsidiary. It is our view that because of a number of unexpected developments we cannot realize in the near future the earnings we desire from this subsidiary.

Another significant action taken last year was our adoption of the last-in, first-out, or LIFO, method of valuation for substantially

EXHIBIT 2

To Our Shareholders:

Sales, net income orders and backlog all rose in the first quarter ended September 25, 1981 compared with the same period last year.

Sales were $392.3 million, a 13 percent increase over the $347.8 million in the first quarter of fiscal 1981. Net income was $22.2 million, up 7 percent over last year's $20.7 million. Earnings per share were 71 cents compared with 68 cents.

Total orders were up substantially and exceeded shipments. Orders were particularly strong in the Communications and Government Systems Groups. The Information Systems Group also recorded a good increase. Orders were level for the Printing Equipment Group but down significantly for the Semiconductor Group, reflecting the continuing weak demand for digital semiconductor products.

Major orders included contracts totalling more than $40 million from Brunei, Egypt, Kuwait and Venezuela for two-way radio systems, a $5 million contract from Mexico for a Harris power control center, contracts totalling $27 million from the Navy and McDonnell Douglas for computer-based avionic test systems, and a $1.2 million contract from British Telecom for digital microwave transmission systems.

Strong order input overall and increasing sales and profits in the Information Systems, Communications and Government Systems Groups provide a base for continuing growth. However the expected improvement in demand for semiconductor products has not occurred, and the increased value of the U.S. dollar with respect to Euro-currencies has reduced the profitability of our exports to Europe. Until the demand for integrated circuits improves, our profit margins will be depressed and growth in earnings will be limited. An improvement in semiconductor markets will result in a significant increase in earnings.

The annual meeting of shareholders was held October 23 in Melbourne, Florida. A report of the meeting will be mailed to you shortly.

John T. Hartley Jr.
President

Joseph A. Boyd
Chairman

October 26, 1981

Condensed Consolidated Statement of Income

Amounts in thousands except per share

	Quarter Ended	
	September 25 1981	September 26 1980
Net Sales	$392,287	$347,753
Income before Income Taxes	$ 38,139	$ 34,874
Income Taxes	15,894	14,129
Net Income	$ 22,245	$ 20,745
Net Income Per Share	$ 71	$ 68
Average Number of Shares Outstanding	31,240	30,446

Condensed Consolidated Balance Sheet

Dollars in thousands

	Quarter Ended	
	September 25 1981	September 26 1980
Assets		
Cash and Short-Term Securities	$ 114,469	$ 85,854
Trade Receivables	264,896	261,224
Unbilled Costs and Accrued Earnings	140,609	92,584
Inventories	363,511	320,666
Rental Equipment — Net	63,145	58,865
Plant and Equipment — Net	365,590	290,447
Other Assets	51,364	51,549
	$1,363,584	$1,161,189
Liabilities and Shareholders' Equity		
Short-Term Debt	$ 14,742	$ 9,032
Trade Payables and Accrued Expenses	273,364	228,250
Advance Payments by Customers	108,737	97,519
Income Taxes	50,457	61,426
Non-Current Deferred Income Taxes	138,261	86,179
Long-Term Debt	205,539	214,166
Shareholders' Equity	572,484	464,617
	$1,363,584	$1,161,189

The amounts shown above are subject to audit and year-end adjustments.

EXHIBIT 3

Exxon Corporation Consolidated Financial and Operating Data

Financial data are unaudited and expressed in millions except per share amounts. Per share amounts for all periods reflect the two-for-one split, effective May 15, 1981.

INCOME STATEMENT

	Second Quarter 1980	Second Quarter 1981	First Half 1980	First Half 1981
Revenue:				
Sales and other operating revenue	$25,831	$26,959	$52,955	$56,673
Earnings from equity interests and other revenue	392	510	922	1,119
Total revenue	26,223	27,469	53,877	57,792
Costs and other deductions:				
Crude oil and product purchases	14,305	14,771	29,842	32,482
Operating expenses	2,674	3,047	5,192	5,966
Selling, general and administrative expenses	1,327	1,232	2,552	2,477
Depreciation and depletion	570	675	1,140	1,326
Exploration expenses, including dry holes	243	346	460	630
Income, excise and other taxes	5,613	5,810	11,220	11,767
Interest expense	174	183	372	341
Foreign exchange (gain)/loss*	252	(469)	51	(715)
Income applicable to minority interests	35	49	93	93
Total deductions	25,193	25,644	50,922	54,367
Net income	$ 1,030	$ 1,825	$ 2,955	$ 3,425
Net income per share	$ 1.18	$ 2.11	$ 3.38	$ 3.96
*Foreign exchange (gain)/loss related to equity companies included in "Earnings from equity interests and other revenue"	$ 116	$ (119)	$ 3	$ (194)

OTHER SELECTED FINANCIAL DATA

	Second Quarter 1980	Second Quarter 1981	First Half 1980	First Half 1981
Detail of income, excise and other taxes:				
Income taxes	$ 1,375	$ 968	$ 2,819	$ 2,155
Excise taxes	1,272	1,320	2,587	2,577
Other taxes and duties**	2,966	3,522	5,814	7,035
Total taxes	$ 5,613	$ 5,810	$11,220	$11,767
Per dollar of total revenue—cents	21.4	21.2	20.8	20.4
Effective income tax rate—percent***			65.0	43.8
Net income per dollar of total revenue—cents	3.9	6.6	5.5	5.9
Average number of shares (000's)			873,969	864,245
Dividends paid:				
Total	$ 567	$ 648	$ 1,093	$ 1,296
Per share	$ .65	$ .75	$ 1.25	$ 1.50
Shareholders' equity—at June 30			$24,166	$27,546
Capital employed (debt plus equity)—at June 30			$33,150	$37,514
Capital and exploration expenditures	$ 1,683	$ 2,398	$ 3,153	$ 4,593
Energy-related expenditures	$ 1,508	$ 2,100	$ 2,858	$ 4,055
**Includes U.S. "windfall profit" tax	$ 159	$ 582	$ 200	$ 1,166
***Includes 50% of Exxon's share of income taxes paid by equity companies:				
—Aramco (reflects transfer of producing assets to the government, effective April 14, 1980)			$ 2,227	$ 120
—Other companies			$ 441	$ 397

EARNINGS SUMMARY

	Second Quarter 1980	Second Quarter 1981	First Half 1980	First Half 1981
Earnings from operations				
Energy operations:				
Petroleum and natural gas				
United States				
Exploration and production	$ 504	$ 594	$ 1,042	$ 1,209
Refining and marketing	29	50	147	(20)
Foreign				
Exploration and production	431	398	998	974
Refining and marketing	473	220	883	405
International marine	11	15	31	23
Coal mining and development	—	1	3	6
Uranium mining and nuclear fuel fabrication	(5)	(4)	(15)	(8)
Other energy	7	11	13	16
Total energy operations	1,450	1,285	3,102	2,605
Chemical operations:				
United States	33	59	99	78
Foreign	74	37	170	79
Reliance Electric operations	15	10	33	14
Minerals mining and development	(8)	(24)	(14)	(40)
Other operations	(10)	(20)	(15)	(28)
Earnings from operations	1,554	1,347	3,375	2,708
Corporate general and administrative costs	(117)	(114)	(226)	(209)
Corporate interest income	137	87	177	180
Interest expense	(141)	(34)	(224)	(70)
Foreign exchange gain/(loss)	(368)	588	(54)	909
Minority interest	(35)	(49)	(93)	(93)
Net income	$ 1,030	$ 1,825	$ 2,955	$ 3,425

SUMMARY OF FUNDS PROVIDED AND UTILIZED

	First Half 1980	First Half 1981
Funds from operations:		
Net income	$ 2,955	$ 3,425
Depreciation and depletion	1,140	1,326
Other funds from operations	1,610	664
Funds provided from operations	5,705	5,415
Funds from other sources, excluding financing activities (Includes changes in working capital, excluding debt and cash)	(958)	(2,787)
Funds from/(used in) financing activities—long- and short-term debt	102	690
Total funds provided, excluding changes in cash items	4,849	3,318
Utilization of funds:		
Additions to property, plant and equipment	2,482	3,735
Cash dividends to Exxon shareholders	1,093	1,296
Other	284	52
Funds utilized	3,859	5,083
Increase/(decrease) in cash and marketable securities	$ 990	$(1,765)

OPERATING DATA
(Thousands of barrels a day)

	Second Quarter 1980	Second Quarter 1981	First Half 1980	First Half 1981
Net production of crude oil and natural gas liquids by consolidated and equity companies and supplies available under long-term agreements with foreign governments	3,459	3,425	3,562	3,502
Other supplies available under special arrangements	504	400	531	427
Refinery runs	4,114	3,729	4,221	3,875
Petroleum product sales	4,817	4,342	5,081	4,640
Natural gas sales (billions of cubic feet a day)	8.7	8.2	10.1	9.6
Chemical product sales, including transfers to petroleum affiliates (millions of dollars)	$ 2,017	$ 2,204	$ 4,237	$ 4,372

SUMMARIZED BALANCE SHEET

	Dec. 31, 1980	June 30, 1981
Cash	$ 2,762	$ 1,829
Marketable securities	2,164	1,332
Notes and accounts receivable	9,849	9,007
Inventories:		
Crude oil, products and merchandise	5,613	7,398
Materials and supplies	937	1,223
Prepaid taxes and expenses	2,134	3,108
Total current assets	23,459	23,897
Property, plant and equipment—net	30,311	32,439
Investments and other assets	2,807	3,103
Total assets	$56,577	$59,439
Notes and loans payable	$ 1,537	$ 2,093
Accounts payable and accrued liabilities	12,482	12,212
Income taxes payable	2,865	2,441
Total current liabilities	16,884	16,746
Long-term debt	4,717	4,851
Reserves, deferred credits and other liabilities	9,563	10,296
Total liabilities	31,164	31,893
Shareholders' equity	25,413	27,546
Total liabilities and shareholders' equity	$56,577	$59,439

believe that most of Sells' predictions and beliefs were in error. The involvement of the profession with interim reports has been minimal, although this is in the process of change. Few published interim reports have been certified (with the general exception of parts of years included in a prospectus), and subsequent articles have been cautionary on the proposition of enlightenment. Blough [1953, p. 221], for example, wrote: "Accountants know the limitations of quarterly, or other very short-term financial statements, but persons to whom the reports are addressed cannot be depended upon to treat them with adequate caution."

The Special Limitations of Short-Term Financial Statements. As Hatfield [1962, p. 11] once observed, "accountants are asked to perform [a] hopeless task," to take an economic continuum and to chop "it up into arbitrary and meaningless lengths called a year...." Here, of course, Hatfield alludes to the measurement problems inherent with all transactions that originate in one accounting period and terminate in some future accounting period. As the reporting period is shortened from a year to a quarter, it is obvious that the number of incomplete transactions increases. Thus interim reporting shares most if not all of the problems of annual accountings. In addition, it has a few of its own. By "special problems" we mean the attribution of particular revenues, expenses, or losses to a specific calendar quarter, given no problem at all with their attribution to that particular year.

The special problems of interim reports seem to divide into three categories:

1. Unusual or irregular events of the time period
2. The use of accounting measurement methods for the interim report that differ from those used in the annual report
3. Seasonal variations

These special problems exist only if we expect interim reports to articulate in some special way with each other and with the subsequent annual report, or if we expect them to be comparable year to year.

An alternative classification is suggested by Shillinglaw [1961, p. 222]; his factors that "reduce the correlation between the interim statements and the annual statements" are grouped into five categories: (1) seasonal, (2) random, (3) scheduled, (4) cyclical, and (5) nonrecurring. Because, as he observes, cyclical and nonrecurring fluctuations pose no problems unique to interim reporting, only three remain, and these three correspond fairly well with the three listed above.

Articulation and Prediction. We speculate that the surge of interest in interim reports acknowledged at the outset stems from the realization that at least two views obtain about the principal purpose of an interim report. According to APB Opinion No. 28 [1973, pars. 5a, 5b]:

> Some view each interim period as a basic accounting period and conclude that the results of operations for each interim period should be determined in essentially the same manner as if the interim period were an annual accounting period. Under this view deferrals, accruals, and estimations at the end of each interim period are determined by following essentially the same principles and judgments that apply to annual periods.
>
> Others view each interim period primarily as being an integral part of the annual period. Under this view deferrals, accruals, and estimations at the end of each interim period are affected by judgments made at the interim date as to results of operations for the balance of the annual period. Thus, an expense item that might be considered as falling wholly within an annual accounting period (no fiscal year-end accrual or deferral)

could be allocated among interim periods based on estimated time, sales volume, productive activity, or some other basis.

The APB did conclude "that each interim period should be viewed primarily as an integral part of an annual period" [par. 9]. This means that "certain accounting principles and practices followed for annual reporting purposes may require modification at interim reporting dates so that the reported results for the interim period may better relate to the results of operations for the annual periods." Curiously, the FASB task force was not able to come to this conclusion. An early CPA problem (May 1973 Theory, Question 7) effectively illustrates the articulation-prediction-integral part approach to the processing of accounting data. The entire problem (and its unofficial answer) is interesting and relevant, and it goes as follows:

Part a. The unaudited quarterly statements of income issued by many corporations to their stockholders are usually prepared on the same basis as annual statements, the statement for each quarter reflecting the transactions of that quarter.

Required:

1. Why do problems arise in using such quarterly statements to predict the income (before extraordinary items) for the year? Explain.
2. Discuss the ways in which quarterly income can be affected by the behavior of the costs recorded in a Repairs and Maintenance of Factory Machinery account.
3. Do such quarterly statements give management opportunities to manipulate the results of operations for a quarter? If so, explain or give an example.

Part b. The controller of Navar Corporation wants to issue to stockholders quarterly income statements that will be predictive of expected annual results. He proposes to allocate all fixed costs for the year among quarters in proportion to the number of units expected to be sold in each quarter, stating that the annual income can then be predicted through use of the following equation:

Annual Income = Quarterly Income

$$\times \frac{100\%}{\text{Percent of Unit Sales Applicable to Quarter}}$$

Navar expects the following activity for the year (in thousands of dollars):

	Units	Average per unit	Total (000 omitted)
Sales revenue:			
First quarter	500,000	$2.00	$1,000
Second quarter	100,000	1.50	150
Third quarter	200,000	2.00	400
Fourth quarter	200,000	2.00	400
	1,000,000		$1,950

	Units	Average per unit	Total (000 omitted)
Costs to be incurred:			
Variable:			
Manufacturing		$ .70	$ 700
Selling and administrative		.25	250
		$ .95	$ 950
Fixed:			
Manufacturing			$ 380
Selling and administrative			220
			$ 600
Income before income taxes			$ 400

Required (ignore income taxes):

1. Assuming that Navar's activities do not vary from expectations, will the controller's plan achieve his objective? If not, how can it be modified to do so? Explain and give illustrative computations.

2. How should the effect of variations of actual activity from expected activity be treated in Navar's quarterly income statements?

3. What assumption has the controller made in regard to inventories? Discuss.

Answer 7

a. 1. If a corporation's activity could be expected to be the same in all quarters, there would be no problems in using quarterly statements to predict annual results, providing one recognized that the normal activities of any corporation could be disrupted by unforeseen events such as strikes, fires, floods, actions of governmental authorities, and unusual changes in demand for goods or supply of raw materials. Most businesses, however, can be expected to have variations in activity among quarters. Any user of the financial statements who is not also a member of management would probably have great difficulty in making accurate predictions.

A basic cause of fluctuating quarterly activity is seasonality. Sales often show a seasonal pattern. Expenses also may show a seasonal pattern, but the pattern for any expense may differ from the patterns for sales or for the other expenses. Production, expressed in physical units, may show still another pattern. The more product lines a business has, the greater the number of varying seasonal patterns that may be present.

2. Repairs and Maintenance of Factory Machinery is an example of an item which may show substantial variations which are not proportionate to either sales or production. In fact, it would not be unusual for many repair and maintenance projects to be performed during the time when production is lowest, thus causing high unit costs (high costs divided by few units) for the quarter. The effect on income would be spread between the quarter of incurrence and later quarters depending on inventory levels and costing methods. Use of pre-

determined overhead rates would have the same effect (if variances were allocated between inventories and cost of goods sold) or else would confine the effect of the high costs to the current quarter (if variances were included in cost of goods sold). Low costs in periods of high production would result in low unit costs, the effects of which would be spread among quarters as described above.

3. Such quarterly statements do give management opportunities to manipulate the results of operations for a quarter—for instance, through the timing of expenses. Management can defer some expenses in an attempt to make the results of earlier quarters look very profitable, thus delaying discovery of conditions which could reflect on management's performance. On the other hand, management can incur heavy expenses in the earlier quarters in an attempt to show a favorable trend in the later quarters. For example, the time at which maintenance work is undertaken is somewhat discretionary.

b. 1. The controller cannot achieve his objective without modification of his proposal. The basic flaw in his plan arises from allocation of fixed costs in proportion to units sold even though the average sales price per unit varies from time to time. The controller's plan would produce the results ... following ... (in thousands of dollars).

	Quarter				
	First	Second	Third	Fourth	Total
Sales	$1,000	$150	$400	$400	$1,950
Variable costs ($.95 per unit)	475	95	190	190	950
Contribution margin	$ 525	$ 55	$210	$210	$1,000
Fixed costs (50%, 10%, 20%, 20%)	300	60	120	120	600
Income (loss) before income taxes..........	$ 225	$ (5)	$ 90	$ 90	$ 400

In no instance will application of the controller's equation to interim income result in a predicted annual income of $400. Furthermore, the predicted amounts vary significantly as shown below.

Prediction based on	Predicted annual income
First quarter [$225 = 50%]	$450
Second quarter [$(5) = 10%]	(50)
Third quarter [$90 = 20%]	450
First and second quarters [$220 = 60%]	366.7
First, second, and third quarters [$310 = 80%]	387.5

Neither can the controller achieve his objective through allocation of fixed costs in proportion to sales revenue.

Allocation of fixed costs in proportion to contribution margin (sales revenue less variable costs per unit) will achieve the objective as shown in the following schedule.

	Quarter				
	First	Second	Third	Fourth	Total
Contribution margin	$525	$55	$210	$210	$1,000
Fixed costs (52.5%, 5.5%, 21%, 21%)	315	33	126	126	600
Income before income taxes	$210	$22	$ 84	$ 84	$ 400

Prediction based on	Predicted annual income
First quarter [$210 = 52.5%]	$400
Second quarter [$22 = 5.5%]	400
Third quarter [$84 = 21%]	400
First and second quarters [$232 = 58%]	400
First, second, and third quarters [$316 = 79%]	400

For the statements to serve their intended purpose, the relationship of quarterly activity to total expected activity will have to be disclosed.

2. Variations of actual activity from expectations can be included in income for the quarter in which they occur, provided their effect on income is not material.

Variations having a material effect should be handled through allocation to all quarters. Restatement of quarters preceding the most recent quarter would be the most logical presentation. Alternatively, the entire adjustment could be assigned to the latest quarter; if so, only the combined income of all elapsed quarters (rather than the results of each elapsed quarter) could be used to predict annual income.

3. The controller appears to assume that inventories will be stable in both number of units and in total dollar amount. Such could be the case if, for instance, there are stable inventories costed by the LIFO method or if there are no year-end inventories. If the assumption is not valid, the controller's plan will have to be modified.

Notice the practice employed in the solution; it has been called the seasonalized assignment of fixed costs [Green, 1964; see also Moskowitz, 1967]. In this illustration contribution is not invariant and therefore the seasonalized assignment is based on expected contribution rather than expected sales. APB Opinion No. 28 is not explicit on this point and observable practice has, thus far, lagged the implied recommendation of this unofficial answer. Consider some of the other prospective income statements that could be prepared for the first quarter. The discrete or mini-fiscal income statement would appear as follows:

NAVAR CORPORATION
1st Quarter Income Statement Prepared on a Discrete Basis
(in thousands)

Sales		$1,000
Variable costs		475
Contribution		$ 525
One-quarter of expected annual fixed		
manufacturing cost	$95	
One-quarter of expected annual fixed		
selling and administration cost	55	150
Income before income tax		$ 375

This would be misleading because it attributes to the first quarter 93.75 percent of the expected annual profit.

Perhaps a more ordinary solution would attempt to calculate a predetermined indirect (manufacturing) fixed cost rate. Assume that this would be calculated by dividing the budgeted fixed manufacturing costs of $380,000 by the expected activity of 1 million units—a rate of $.38 per unit. Then the normal cost of a unit sold would be $.70 variable plus $.38 fixed, or $1.08. The income statement that would emerge would appear as follows:

NAVAR CORPORATION
1st Quarter Income Statement Prepared on a Discrete Basis with
an Annualization of Fixed Manufacturing Cost
(in thousands)

Sales		$1,000
Cost of goods sold (500,000 × $1.08)		540
Margin		$ 460
Selling and administrative:		
Variable (500,000 × $.25)	$125	
Fixed (¼ of $220,000)	55	180
Income before income tax		$ 280

This reduction in reported income from $375,000 to $280,000, or $95,000, results from the use of the predetermined indirect cost rate. The discrete income statement reports fixed manufacturing costs of $95,000, whereas annualization charges $190,000 (= 500,000 units × $.38) to the first quarter, thereby explaining the difference in reported income of $95,000. The fixed manufacturing cost of $95,000 in the discrete income statement and the difference in income of $95,000 are equal only by coincidence. Notice, then, that the use of a predetermined indirect cost rate tends to operate in the same way as seasonalized fixed cost assignments. Accountants have been reluctant to use similar methods for selling and administrative costs; had there been no such reluctance, then the dilemma of discrete versus integral might never have surfaced because the use of predetermined cost rates is the equivalent of seasonalized cost assignments. For example, if a firm produced in its first quarter entirely for inventory and made no sales, it would expense none of the manufacturing costs incurred—they would all be inventoried.

A subsequent CPA exam (May 1975, Theory, Question 3) extends the articulate-predict approach. Although the unofficial answer again seems ahead of practice in some respects, both the question and answer are reproduced below.

The Anderson Manufacturing Company, a California corporation listed on the Pacific Coast Stock Exchange, budgeted activities for 1975 as follows:

	Amount	Units
Net sales	$6,000,000	1,000,000
Cost of goods sold	3,600,000	1,000,000
Gross margin	$2,400,000	
Selling, general, and administrative expenses	1,400,000	
Operating earnings	$1,000,000	
Nonoperating revenues and expenses	-0-	
Earnings before income taxes	$1,000,000	
Estimated income taxes (current and deferred)	550,000	
Net earnings.................................	$ 450,000	
Earnings per share of common stock..............	$4.50	

Anderson has operated profitably for many years and has experienced a seasonal pattern of sales volume and production similar to the following ones forecasted for 1975. Sales volume is expected to follow a quarterly pattern of 10 percent, 20 percent, 35 percent, 35 percent, respectively, because of the seasonality of the industry. Also, due to production and storage capacity limitations it is expected that production will follow a pattern of 20 percent, 25 percent, 30 percent, 25 percent, per quarter, respectively.

At the conclusion of the first quarter of 1975, the controller of Anderson has prepared and issued the following interim report for public release:

	Amount	Units
Net sales	$ 600,000	100,000
Cost of goods sold	360,000	100,000
Gross margin	$ 240,000	
Selling, general, and administrative expenses	275,000	
Operating loss...............................	$ (35,000)	
Loss from warehouse fire	(175,000)	
Loss before income taxes	$(210,000)	
Estimated income tax	-0-	
Net loss	$(210,000)	
Loss per share of common stock..................	$(2.10)	

The following additional information is available for the first quarter just completed, but was not included in the public information released:

1. The company uses a standard cost system in which standards are set at currently attainable levels on an annual basis. At the end of the first quarter there was underapplied fixed factory overhead (volume variance) of $50,000 that was treated as an asset at the end of the quarter. Production during the quarter was 200,000 units, of which 100,000 were sold.

2. The selling, general, and administrative expenses were budgeted on a basis of $900,000 fixed expenses for the year plus $.50 variable expenses per unit of sales.

3. Assume that the warehouse fire loss met the conditions of an extraordinary loss. The warehouse had an undepreciated cost of $320,000; $145,000 was recovered from insurance on the warehouse. No other gains or losses are anticipated this year from similar events or transactions, nor has Anderson had any similar losses in preceding years; thus, the full loss will be deductible as an ordinary loss for income tax purposes.

4. The effective income tax rate, for federal and state taxes combined, is expected to average 55 percent of earnings before income taxes during 1975. There are no permanent differences between pretax accounting earnings and taxable income.

5. Earnings per share were computed on the basis of 100,000 shares of capital stock outstanding. Anderson has only one class of stock issued, no long-term debt outstanding, and no stock option plan.

Required:

a. Without reference to the specific situation described above, what are the standards of disclosure for interim financial data (published interim financial reports) for publicly traded companies? Explain.

b. Identify the weakness in form and content of Anderson's interim report without reference to the additional information.

c. For each of the five items of additional information, indicate the preferable treatment for each item for interim-reporting purposes and explain why that treatment is preferable.

Answer

a. When publicly traded companies report summarized interim financial information to their securityholders at interim dates, the following data should be reported, as a minimum:

Sales or gross revenues, provision for income taxes, extraordinary items, cumulative effect of a change in accounting principles, and net earnings

Primary and fully diluted earnings per share data for each period presented

Seasonal revenues, costs or expenses, and contingent items

Disposal of a segment of a business and extraordinary, unusual, or infrequently occurring items (including related income tax effects)

Changes in accounting principles or estimates, including significant changes in estimates or provisions for income taxes

Significant changes in financial position

When summarized interim financial data are regularly reported on a quarterly basis, the foregoing information with respect to the current quarter and the current year-to-date or the last twelve-months-to-date should be furnished together with comparable data for the preceding year. When a separate fourth quarter report or disclosure of the fourth quarter results is not included in the annual report, material year-end adjustments, extraordinary items, and disposals of segments of a business should be disclosed in the annual report in a note to the financial statements.

Management should provide commentary relating to the effects of significant events upon the interim financial results, similar to its commentary in annual reports. Published balance sheet and funds flow data at interim dates are desirable, but disclosure of significant changes in financial position or funds flow should be presented as a minimum.

b. There are two general weaknesses in the form and content of presentation of the first quarter information: (1) some information in the statement needs further explanation and (2) additional financial statements or summarized data should be presented and explained as appropriate in the circumstances. (See discussion presented in *a.*)

The major weakness in the first quarter report is that it is misleading because the company is expecting a profit for the year, not a loss as normally would be assumed from the published report alone. Both sales and production were equal to the units budgeted for the first quarter, and if actual activity continues as planned for the rest of the year, Anderson will show a profit of $371,250 {$450,000 − [$175,000 × (1 − .55)]} for 1975. Thus, Anderson should indicate in the interim report that sales, production, and net income (loss) are in line with expectations, as related to budgeted data and first quarters of prior years.

No other weakness in form and content is evident, except as discussed below in *c.*

c. 1. The treatment of underapplied fixed factory overhead as an asset in this situation is the preferred method of accounting. The expected year-end result is that actual production will exactly equal budgeted production upon which the standard was based; thus, no volume variance should exist at year end.

2. The manner in which the selling, general, and administrative expenses were handled in the report is the preferred method. These costs are not inventoriable, they cannot be associated directly with the product, and they have been incurred at expected levels. Thus, they should be expensed as period costs when incurred or be allocated among interim periods based on the estimate of time expired, benefit received, or activity associated with the periods.

3. The warehouse fire loss is an extraordinary item that should be appropriately disclosed in the interim financial report, net of income tax effect. In this situation the $175,000 loss should be reduced by the effective income tax reduction of $96,250. Thus, the loss should reduce net income by $78,750 ($175,000 − $96,250), and the nature of the loss should be appropriately explained in the commentary accompanying the quarterly data.

4. A negative income tax expense (an income tax benefit) should have been included in the interim report. The $35,000 loss from regular operations should have been reduced by $19,250 ($35,000 × 55%), the expected tax reduction to be realized from profitable operations during the remaining three quarters of 1975. The tax effect benefits resulting from losses that arise in the early portion of the year should be recognized only when realization is assured beyond any reasonable doubt. An established seasonal pattern of losses in early interim periods, offset by income in later interim periods, should constitute sufficient evidence that realization is assured beyond reasonable doubt—unless other evidence contradicts this conclusion.

5. Primary and fully diluted earnings per share data for each period presented should be included in the interim report when a company meets the conditions requiring both earnings per share computations. Because Anderson has a simple capital structure, it must show only the primary earnings per share figures. In the situation presented, there should have been a per share amount for the loss, for the extraordinary item, and for the sum of the two.

It is some indication of the rapidity of change in contemporary accounting that some of the answers that would have been acceptable in May 1975 would not be acceptable a year or less later. In particular, the answer to Requirement *a* would be changed as a result of an SEC Release of September 1975. This is discussed in the next section.

INTERIM REPORTS AND THE SECURITIES AND EXCHANGE COMMISSION

Although the Securities Exchange Act of 1934 contained a requirement for "such annual reports ... and such quarterly reports, as the Commission may prescribe," routine quarterly reports of any data were not required until 1945. During this 11-year period, the SEC only required the filing of interim report Form 8-K when some special event occurred during the year.

In 1945, in anticipation of investors' needs for prompt information as the economy changed over from war activities, the SEC required quarterly reports of sales and unfilled orders and separate acknowledgment of sales attributable to war contracts. In addition, immediate reports were required for terminations of war contracts if the uncompleted portion amounted to 20 percent or more of the registrant's previous fiscal year's sales.

In 1946, the SEC acknowledged a continuing interest in quarterly reports and announced a proposal for quarterly operating information to be supplied to it on Form 8-K. The proposal apparently elicited so much adverse comment that the SEC settled for sales reports from companies listed on national securities exchanges indicating quarterly sales. These were to be filed on Form 8-K within 45 days of the end of the quarter. With this requirement, the earlier rule on reporting war-related business was rescinded. Toward the end of 1948, the 8-K requirement was extended to all companies required to file reports pursuant to Section 15 of the Act.

In 1949, the required data reported on Form 8-K was transferred to Form 9-

K. In 1952, the SEC again proposed that sales data be replaced with a quarterly income statement accompanied by a reconciliation of retained earnings and elicited comment on this proposal. Apparently (the file has not been made available for public inspection) much of the comment received was negative, and in early 1953 the SEC announced that the proposal would be dropped. A few months later, the SEC invited comment on a proposal to discontinue Form 9-K; in October of that year, the requirement was rescinded. As a result, there was no longer any SEC requirement for any kind of routine interim report.

In early 1955, the SEC acknowledged that it was considering a new Form 9-K that would require semiannual reports. The Commission stated that:

> it recognizes that preparing profit and loss statements on a quarterly basis may present problems for some issuers and accordingly the proposed report would not constitute a formal profit and loss statement. . . . [Because] interim earnings figures can frequently be arrived at only by the use of reasonable estimates or on the basis of certain assumptions, the proposal provides that reports of such information would not be subject to liability under Section 18 of the Act.

In mid-1955, the Commission adopted the proposed Form 9-K, which called for the following nine items to be received within 45 days of the end of the 6-month period:

1. Gross sales less discounts, returns, and allowances
2. Operating revenues
3. Total of captions 1 and 2
4. Extraordinary items
5. Net income or loss before taxes on income
6. Provision for taxes on income
7. Net income or loss
8. Special items
9. Earned surplus items

Specifically exempted from the 9-K requirements were

1. Banks and bank holding companies
2. Investment companies
3. Insurance companies, other than title insurance
4. Public utilities and common carriers that file financial reports with the Federal Power Commission, Federal Communications Commission, or the Interstate Commerce Commission
5. Companies engaged in the seasonal production and seasonal sale of a single-crop agricultural commodity
6. Companies in the promotional or development stage to which paragraph (b) or (c) of Rule 5A-01 of Article 5A of Regulation S-X is applicable
7. Foreign issuers other than private issuers domiciled in a North American country or Cuba

Of these, however, investment companies and certain real estate companies were required to file quarterly reports.

A study group was appointed in late 1967 "to examine the operations of the disclosure provisions of the [Acts] . . . and Commission rules and regulations thereunder." Their report, prepared under the direction of Commissioner Francis M. Wheat, commented on interim reports as follows [Wheat, 1969]:

> More and more publicly-held corporations are releasing condensed quarterly financial information. Both the New York and American Stock Exchanges require publication of such information by all listed companies, although the standards which they set for such information are minimal. The Study carefully examined a significant sample of quarterly financial reports and releases provided by the two exchanges. It was readily apparent (and acknowledged by representatives of the exchanges) that they varied from extremely useful to extremely poor and uninformative. Conferences were held by the Study with accountants representing both large and small firms throughout the country, with members of a special committee of the Financial Executives Institute, and with the American Society of Corporate Secretaries, regarding the feasibility of condensed quarterly financial reporting. It was the general opinion that such reporting was feasible and that a useful advance in disclosure policy could be achieved by developing standards for such reporting. A special committee of the AICPA greatly assisted the Study in this effort.
>
> The Study proposes that a new form to be designated 10Q be substituted for present Forms 8K and 9K. It would be due 45 days after the close of each fiscal quarter (except that a report of a significant acquisition or disposition of assets would be due 10 days after the execution of a written agreement for such acquisition or disposition). It would consist of two parts. Part I would cover the substance of the present 8K with a number of changes. Part II would consist of condensed, comparative financial information. Part II would not be required for the fourth fiscal quarter. It would not be audited or be subject to the liability provisions of Section 18 of the '34 Act. Quarterly reports to shareholders containing the information required by Part II of Form 10Q could be submitted in lieu of that part of the form.

This proposal for interim reports was accepted and Form 10-Q was required from covered companies effective with the year 1970. In late 1974, the SEC issued its *Notice of Proposals to Increase Disclosure of Interim Results by Registrants* (Release No. 33-5549). And a mighty increase in disclosure was proposed, that is, comparative balance sheets at the end of the quarter, comparative statements of changes in financial position for the year to date, a new narrative analysis of results of operations in addition to less condensed comparative income statements, inclusion of quarterly data in the annual reports, and an increased involvement in the interim reporting procedure by the independent accountant.

The proposed increase in disclosure motivated more than 700 letters of comments; in addition, the Commission held public hearings on the proposals and heard testimony from 14 witnesses. Most of these comments expressed serious concern about the proposals. Nevertheless, the Commission issued Accounting Series Release (ASR) No. 177 in September 1975 and it became effective for Form 10-Q reports covering periods beginning after December 25, 1975. The requirements imposed did not differ importantly from those proposed.

> The new rules require [summarized, i.e., less detailed than required by Regulation S-X] income statements for the most recent quarter, the equiv-

alent calendar quarter in the preceding year and year-to-date data for both years. Condensed funds statements are required on a year-to-date basis for the current and prior year. In addition, registrants are permitted to show income statement data and funds statement data for the twelve month period ending at the interim reporting date for both years if they elect to do so. Balance sheets are required as of the end of the most recent quarter and at the same date in the preceding year.

In addition, the new rules require increased pro forma information in the case of business combinations accounted for as purchases, conformity with the principles of accounting measurement set forth in the Accounting Principles Board opinion on interim financial reports and increased disclosure of accounting changes.

In connection with accounting changes, a letter from the registrant's independent public accountant is required to be filed in which the accountant states whether or not the change is to an alternative principle which in his judgment is preferable under the circumstances.... [In spite of numerous objections, the] rule has ... been adopted as proposed.

In addition to financial statements, a new instruction to Form 10Q requires management to provide a narrative analysis of the results of operations.... The new instruction requires explanation of the reasons for material changes in the amount of revenue and expense items from one quarter to the next (even though the preceding quarter may not be reported as such in the form 10Q), between the most recent quarter and the equivalent quarter in the preceding year, and between the year-to-date data and comparable data for the prior year. While such explanations are to be presented in narrative form, it is expected that they will include quantitative data in explaining the reasons for changes. In addition to requiring an analysis of operations, the new form includes an instruction which permits the registrant to furnish any additional information which management believes will be of significance to registrants [sic; the word probably was meant to be *investors*]. This same instruction requires the registrant to indicate whether a Form 8K was filed during the quarter reporting either unusual charges or credits to income or a change of auditors.

Under the new rules, Form 10Q must be signed by either the chief financial officer or the chief accounting officer of the corporation. This requirement was included in recognition of the fact that the data in the form were primarily financial, and that it was appropriate to emphasize the responsibility of the chief financial or accounting officer for the representations explicit and implicit in the filing. This signature will not relieve other corporate officers of their responsibilities. ...

The financial information included in Form 10Q need not be reviewed prior to filing by an independent public accountant. However, certain registrants will be required to include certain data contained in the form 10Q in an unaudited note to financial statements for the year. Such a note must be reviewed by an independent public accountant in accordance with prescribed professional standards in connection with the annual audit. Since review procedures must be applied to quarterly data in connection with the annual audit of such registrants in any event, the additional cost to these registrants of having a review made on a timely basis should be small, particularly if the annual audit is planned with such a review in mind.

The Commission believes that all registrants would find it useful and prudent to have independent public accountants review quarterly financial data on a timely basis during the year prior to the filing of Form 10Q and it encourages registrants to have such a review made. While such a review does not represent an audit and cannot be relied upon to detect all errors and omissions that might be discovered in a full audit of quarterly data, it will bring the reporting, accounting and analytical expertise of independent professional accountants to bear on financial reports included in Form 10Q and therefore should increase the quality and the reliability of the data therein in a cost-effective way.

Effective for periods after December 15, 1980, *New Interim Financial Information Provisions and Revision of Form 10-Q for Quarterly Reporting* is (the name given to) ASR No. 286. The Commission intended to make the interim reporting rules consistent with those it required for annual reporting. This Release was a part of the Commission's so-called integrated disclosure program. As used here, integrated means the presumption that users of interim reports have read the most recent annual report and that the footnote disclosure there (statements of significant accounting policies and practices, etc.) need not be repeated in the interim report. In other words, interim reports should supplement rather than repeat annual report information. (This seems to be one more, albeit subtle, vote on the side of integral rather than discrete.) Companies are permitted to use their informal or nonstatutory annual and interim reports to satisfy SEC requirements and vice versa. In the main, however, published interim reports fall far short of the 10-Q requirements.

THE PUBLIC ACCOUNTING PROFESSION AND INTERIM REPORTS

Shillinglaw [1961], in what may have been a masterpiece of understatement, pointed out that interim reports "have never received the professional attention that has been devoted to annual statements." This certainly was true until the latter part of 1974, when Coopers & Lybrand indicated a willingness, if not a desire, to get involved in their clients' interim reporting process. They proposed "a limited review that would not be equivalent to an audit." Shortly thereafter, Arthur Andersen & Co. petitioned the SEC, requesting that it prohibit companies from publishing any reports from CPAs based on "limited reviews" of unaudited quarterly data. One other position taken (Price Waterhouse) was that the most beneficial CPA involvement in the quarterly reporting process of clients would be to serve as "formally appointed accounting and reporting consultants to the board of directors...."

> Put simply, our role would be to extend the existing skills of the board by providing special accounting and reporting skills not otherwise available. We would help the directors frame (and answer) the questions they ought to ask, and in fact would ask if possessed of the necessary accounting background, for example: Are the bases of preparation adequate? Consistent with previous quarters? Have generally accepted accounting principles been applied? Any accounting changes in this quarter? If so, are they handled right and reported appropriately? Are significant new financial devel-

opments communicated in the quarterly report? Taken as a whole, is the quarterly report, with its accompanying commentary, an understandable, informative, useful document?

In December 1974, the SEC issued its *Notice of Proposals to Increase Disclosure of Interim Results by Registrants* (Release No. 33-5549) where it considered, in part, the question of increased CPA involvement with quarterly reports. The relevant paragraph reads as follows:

> The Commission also believes that it is useful to investors to have the reporting expertise of independent public accountants drawn upon in the preparation of quarterly reports. In addition, it feels that the involvement of the independent accountant will increase the reliability of such reports even though no audit opinion is issued on the interim financial report. Accordingly, the rules proposed herein encourage this involvement on a timely basis and require an after the fact review of limited interim data at the time of the annual audit by including interim data in the footnotes to the annual financial statements.

Subsequently (April, 1975; Release No. 33-5579), the SEC divulged:

> The proposal which elicited the greatest amount of comment was the proposed amendment to Regulation S-X which would require certain limited quarterly data to be included in a footnote to financial statements for the year. This inclusion would have the effect of involving independent public accountants with quarterly data and it was this effect which was most criticized by commentators.

About this same time (April 15, 1975), the AICPA's Auditing Standards Executive Committee (AudSEC) issued an exposure draft of a proposed statement on auditing standards for *voluntary*, preissuance, limited reviews of unaudited interim financial information. This was not enough to satisfy the SEC, and AudSEC was under pressure to prepare a statement that the SEC would find acceptable. Fortunately, Statement on Auditing Standards No. 10 (SAS No. 10), *Limited Review of Interim Financial Information*, issued in December 1975, did satisfy. SAS No. 10 "describes the nature, timing and extent of procedures that the independent certified public accountant should apply to interim information when the accountant has been engaged to make a *limited review* of that information." A limited review differs from an audit; it does not provide a basis for the expression of an opinion because it does not include many of the procedures ordinarily employed in an audit.

Not unexpectedly, SAS No. 10 was superseded by SAS No. 24 (1979), which was, in turn, superseded by SAS No. 36 (1981). SAS No. 36 (par. 18) provides an example of the accountant's report to accompany the financials; it adroitly summarizes much of the complex language of the Statement. The suggested report is as follows:

> We have made a review of (describe the information or statements reviewed) ABC Company and consolidated subsidiaries as of September 30, 19X1, and for the three-month and nine-month periods then ended, in accordance with standards established by the American Institute of Certified Accountants.

A review of interim financial information consists principally of obtaining an understanding of the system for the preparation of interim financial information, applying analytical review procedures to financial data, and making inquiries of persons responsible for financial and accounting matters. It is substantially less in scope than an examination in accordance with generally accepted auditing standards, the objective of which is the expression of an opinion regarding the financial statements taken as a whole. Accordingly, we do not express such an opinion.

Based on our review, we are not aware of any material modifications that should be made to the accompanying financial (information or statements) for them to be in conformity with generally accepted accounting principles.

THE FASB AND INTERIM REPORTS

As mentioned earlier, the large-scale FASB study has been tabled, but the Board did issue an early statement on one aspect of interim reports.

FASB Statement No. 3 is entitled (and is concerned with) *Reporting Accounting Changes in Interim Financial Statements*, an amendment of APB Opinion No. 28. The statement differentiates changes to LIFO from other accounting changes and also differentiates changes made in the first quarter from those made in other calendar quarters. In brief, for non-LIFO changes:

> If a cumulative effect type accounting change is made during the *first* interim period of an enterprise's fiscal year, the cumulative effect of the change on retained earnings at the *beginning of that fiscal year* shall be included in net income of the first interim period (and in last-twelve-months-to-date financial reports that include that first interim period).

> If a cumulative effect type accounting change is made in *other than the first* interim period of an enterprise's fiscal year, *no* cumulative effect of the change shall be included in net income of the period of change. Instead, financial information for the pre-change interim periods of the fiscal year in which the change is made shall be restated by applying the newly adopted accounting principle to those pre-change interim periods. The cumulative effect of the change on retained earnings at the *beginning of that fiscal year* shall be included in restated net income of the first interim period of the fiscal year in which the change is made (and in any year-to-date or last-twelve-months-to-date financial reports that include the first interim period).

Paragraph 11 details the necessary disclosure to be made in interim reports. Heavily abbreviated, for the non-LIFO changes for the interim period in which the new accounting principle is adopted: (a) explain the nature of and justification for the change, (b) disclose the effect of the change on income of the current period, and (c) disclose the effect of the change on any prior period to which the current period is being compared. Further, "(d) In year-to-date and last-twelve-months-to-date financial reports that include the interim period in which the new accounting principle is adopted, the disclosures specified in . . . (b) . . . and in . . . (c) above shall be made, and (e) in financial reports for a subsequent (post-change) interim period of the fiscal year in which the new accounting principle is adopted, disclosure shall be made of the effect of the change on income...."

Statement No. 3 also provides that:

> When a publicly traded company that regularly reports interim informa-
> tion to its securityholders makes an accounting change during the fourth
> quarter of its fiscal year and does not report the data specified by para-
> graph 30 of *APB Opinion No. 28* in a separate fourth quarter report or in
> its annual report to its securityholders, the disclosures about the effect of
> the accounting change on interim periods that are required by paragraphs
> 23–26 of APB Opinion No. 28 or by paragraphs 9–13 [which are summa-
> rized above] of this Statement, as appropriate, shall be made in a note to
> the annual financial statements for the fiscal year in which the change is
> made.

One aspect of interim reporting that has not, as yet, received careful attention is the accounting for the impact of a significant event whose timing is more or less random. As an example, consider the following paragraphs taken from *The Wall Street Journal*.

> Interlake Inc. said net income from continuing operations for the month
> of August will be increased by $5 million, or $1.40 a share, because of set-
> tlement of a dispute with a supplier of raw material.
>
> The company refused to give more information. A spokesman said Inter-
> lake has an ongoing relationship with the supplier "and it wouldn't be fair
> to get into details."
>
> The diversified steel producer previously reported second quarter net
> profit of $5.5 million, or $1.53 a share, including $1.1 million, or 27 cents a
> share, from income from discontinued operations.

As another example, consider a paragraph from Zenith's quarterly report of June 30, 1978; notice that a deliberate and probably long-run profitable man-agement decision had an adverse impact on dollar sales. We reproduce more than the one-sentence explanation to illustrate an unusual profit-change analysis.

> The reduction in Zenith's dollar sales between the first half of 1977 and
> the first half of 1978 resulted primarily from a decision made by the Com-
> pany to reduce distributor color television inventories and to hold inven-
> tories at levels lower than those of the comparable periods a year ago. Unit
> sales of color television sets to dealers by Zenith distributors during the
> first half of 1978 established an all-time first half record.
>
> The major reasons for the decrease in pretax profit from continuing
> operations are summarized in the following table:

	Second quarter	First 6 months
	(in millions)	
Pretax profit:		
1978	$11	$ 13
1977	15	27
Decrease in pretax profit	$ (4)	$(14)

	Second quarter	First 6 months
	(in millions)	
Reasons for change:		
Price reductions	$ (5)	$(10)
Payroll and material cost increases ...	(7)	(14)
Color TV unit volume, manufacturing efficiencies and other	8	10
Decrease in pretax profit	$ (4)	$(14)

Another aspect that has gone without serious study is the use of the text portion of the interim report as a vehicle for a company or executive forecast. Several examples follow; the first two are from Harris Corporation.

> With our sizeable backlog and continuing favorable order input, we expect to report a substantial increase in sales and profits for the fiscal year ending June 30, 1981.
>
> The company entered the year with a large semiconductor backlog, and this provided a strong sales and profit contribution. However, the industry-wide decline in semiconductor orders, together with the erosion of prices, is expected to cause a significant reduction in Harris semiconductor profits in fiscal 1982. We expect this reduction to be more than offset by good growth in profits from all other business segments during the year.

This was dated April 24; thus only 2 months are being predicted. The next one was dated January 25, 1982; this more than doubles the period being forecast.

> We now assume there will be no significant improvement in business conditions before mid-1982. Under these conditions, we expect a loss for the year in the Semiconductor Group and continued good performance from our other operating groups. This would result in fiscal 1982 earnings on the order of 10 to 15 percent below fiscal 1981 income from operations. This also assumes that we will maintain our strong product development programs in all areas and a carefully controlled capital investment program.
>
> With the expected improvement in business conditions, our new semiconductor products will support an early return to profitability of the Semiconductor Group. A good total backlog and a broad line of new products from all groups, including a major new word processing product line, should result in resumption of normal growth in fiscal 1983.

This is from the Essex Chemical Corporation Second Quarter Report, 1981, dated August 5:

> You may remember that in our Annual Report, we predicted that the first six months of 1981 would be slow but that increasing strength in the second half would result in record sales and earnings for the year. Now, as we report on the highest quarterly and half-year sales and earnings in our history, it's clear that our timetable was slightly off. The upward movement has arrived ahead of schedule. Our optimistic view of the second half has

not changed; therefore, 1981 should truly be a banner year for your company.

Finally, the forecast of January 28, 1982, for the remaining 6-month period of National Medical Enterprises, Inc.:

> The progress we have achieved in the first half of our 1982 fiscal year confirms our expectations for another record year. All the indicators available to us—our sound balance sheet and financial vitality, and our very strong and growing presence in the health care marketplace—re-validate our optimism that there is nothing in the path ahead to impede our forward progress.

QUARTERLY EARNINGS IN THE ANNUAL REPORT

In a 1966 article, Bows recommended that quarterly earnings be shown in the annual report, "particularly if the company is in a seasonal business" [Bows, 1966, p. 24]. According to Bows, "This gives the shareholder the opportunity of understanding the wide fluctuations which may occur within a year for a particular business, and prepares him for seasonal patterns where the quarterly earnings are normally above or below those of a preceding quarter."

Examples of reporting quarterly earnings in the annual report were then rare, but there were increasing numbers of annual reports with such data over the intervening years. In a random sample of 50 annual reports for 1974, 14 companies (28 percent) provided such data on a strictly voluntary basis. ASR No. 177, as noted earlier, *required* certain registrants to include quarterly data in a note to the annual financial statements for years subsequent to 1975.

All of this notwithstanding, shareholders can learn more directly about seasonality from the interim reports of their companies. Consider these two examples:

> The result of operations for the first six months is not necessarily indicative as to the trend for the second half of this fiscal year. We expect profits in the third quarter to be the highest in the Company's history and to *more than offset the losses* for the first six months [from the six months ended October 31, 1981, report of URT Industries, Inc.; emphasis added].

> Since the next six months represent the seasonally strongest part of the Company's fiscal year, earnings are expected to improve during this period, but remain well below last year's level due to soft economic conditions nationally [from the Second Quarter Report for Period Ended September 26, 1981, Boss Manufacturing Company].

THE PRELIMINARY ANNUAL REPORT AND THE FOURTH QUARTER REPORT

An increasing number of companies now furnish shareholders and the financial press with so-called preliminary results, probably because it is such a long time between the end of the reporting year and the appearance of the formal

EXHIBIT 4   Capital Holding Corporation

Financial Statements.

Consolidated Condensed
Statements of Operations

Period Ended December 31 (000's Omitted)	Year 1981	Year 1980	Three Months 1981	Three Months 1980
Revenues:				
Premiums and other considerations	$ 794,054	$382,759	$221,393	$ 97,044
Investment income, net of expenses	207,492	163,676	54,398	41,706
Other income	1,840	2,258	441	94
Total Revenues	1,003,386	548,693	276,232	138,844
Benefits and expenses:				
Benefits paid to policyholders and beneficiaries	410,924	220,687	107,651	56,870
Increase in benefit reserves	175,598	72,565	59,152	15,703
Commissions, net	54,401	44,642	14,322	10,722
General administrative and other expenses, net	102,175	55,206	23,738	14,836
Amortization of deferred acquisition costs, value of insurance in force, and goodwill	87,222	33,575	24,841	8,699
Interest expense	42,279	—	9,971	—
Total Benefits and Expenses	872,599	426,675	239,675	106,830
Gain from Operations before Federal Income Tax	130,787	122,018	36,557	32,014
Provision for federal income tax	31,400	32,500	7,900	8,800
Gain from Operations	99,387	89,518	28,657	23,214
Net realized investment loss	(4,912)	(3,477)	(3,660)	(4,290)
Net Income	$ 94,475	$ 86,041	$ 24,997	$ 18,924
Per share (in dollars):				
Gain from Operations	$ 3.58	$ 3.20	$ 1.04	$ .83
Net realized investment loss	(.18)	(.13)	(.13)	(.16)
Net Income	$ 3.40	$ 3.07	$ .91	$ .67

annual report. If all reports other than the formal annual report are to be known as interim reports, then this is another interim report, and, in a manner of speaking, it could be considered the fourth interim report of the year even though the emphasis is on the year rather than the fourth quarter. In some instances, it consists of a letter that reports the various comparative details of sales and income. In other instances, abbreviated financial statements appear along with rather extensive textual commentary. An example of a combined annual earnings report coupled with a fourth quarter report is shown in Exhibit 4.

BIBLIOGRAPHY

Accounting Principles Board, *Interim Financial Reporting*, Opinion No. 28 (APB, 1973).

Blough, C. G., "Some of the Dangers Inherent in Quarterly Financial Statements," *Journal of Accountancy*, February 1953, pp. 221–222.

Bollom, W. J., and J. J. Weygandt, "An Examination of Some Interim Reporting Theories for a Seasonal Business," *The Accounting Review*, January 1972, pp. 75–84.

Bows, A. J., "Standards for Consistency in Interim Reports," *Financial Executive*, November 1966, pp. 14, 19–20, 22, 24.

Carey, J. L., "The Origins of Modern Financial Reporting," *Journal of Accountancy*, September 1969, pp. 35–48.

Green, D., Jr., "Towards a Theory of Interim Reports," *Journal of Accounting Research*, vol. 2 (Spring 1964), pp. 35–49.

Hatfield, H. R., "An Historical Defense of Bookkeeping," in W. T. Baxter and S. Davidson (eds)., *Studies in Accounting Theory* (Sweet & Maxwell, London, 1962).

Moskowitz, H. D., "Improving Interim Reports of Seasonal Business by Allocation of Fixed Costs," *The New York CPA*, February 1967, pp. 116-123.

Sells, E. W., "Periodical Statement of Corporations Open to Severe Criticism—Quarterly Certified Accountings Inspire Faith among Investory," *The American Banker*, July 11, 1914, pp. 2278-2279.

Shillinglaw, G., "Concepts Underlying Interim Financial Statements," *The Accounting Review*, vol. 36 (April 1961), pp. 222-231.

Wheat, F. M., "Disclosure to Investors—A Reappraisal of Federal Administrative Policies under the '33 and '34 Acts" (SEC, 1969).

CHAPTER 6

Segment

Management

and Reporting

Bryan Carsberg

Arthur Andersen Professor of Accounting, The
London School of Economics and Political
Science, and Director of Research, Institute of
Chartered Accountants in England and Wales

Several factors in recent years have made the divisional form of organization increasingly popular. Mere growth has caused companies to look for some means of breaking their operations into segments of more manageable size. Similar pressures have been exerted by the trend toward diversification, through mergers and acquisitions as well as through the development of new products and new activities within existing companies. Any segmentation of a company's activities carries with it a need for managers to know how each segment is performing; and external users of financial reports have an interest in the performance of different parts of a business. Something more detailed than the measurement of overall corporate performance is required.

This chapter considers the measurement of the performance of segments in two main parts. The first deals with the implications of divisional organization for decisions and control within the enterprise. The main difficulty of a divisional organization is in meeting the challenge of reconciling two partly conflicting aims: the desire to give the division independence of action to obtain the benefits of incentives to divisional managers and of administrative economies; and the desire to ensure that it behaves in the interests of the whole organization. Three sections are devoted to a discussion of the main factors involved—the development of a system for pricing goods and services transferred from one division to another, the allocation of central costs, and the treatment of costs that are not controllable by the division. Finally, the discussion of internal decisions and control deals with the evaluation of the numbers in a divisional income report. The discussion focuses on the usefulness and limitations of two summary indicators, the return on investment and residual income.

The second part of the chapter explains and discusses recent developments in external reporting of the results of segments of an enterprise. During the last few years, both the Securities and Exchange Commission (SEC) and the Financial Accounting Standards Board (FASB) have called for increased disclosure of the results of segments of companies. The discussion includes a review of the rationale of those disclosures and of some research studies that were designed to shed light on the actual usefulness of the disclosures.

DECISIONS AND CONTROL WITHIN THE ENTERPRISE

Divisional Organization. The word *division* has different meanings. Some businesses, organized on functional lines, refer to their "production divisions" or "marketing divisions." This use of the term differs from that widely adopted in the literature and used in this chapter. This chapter uses the word *division* to refer to a segment that has a significant amount of autonomy in decision making and that is assessed on the basis of general measures of performance rather than the implementation of detailed instructions from central managers.

The essence of divisionalization is delegated profit responsibility. Some limits are set by corporate management on what may be done by divisions, but the divisional form of organization allows for greater freedom of action by divisional management precisely because a profit measure of performance is available. This means that detailed instructions about what the division is to do and how it is to proceed can be replaced by broader directives, capped by the general requirement that the division's activities shall result in a satisfactory profit.

Decentralization and agency theory. An enterprise can be organized in many different ways. It can operate as a single unit, managed centrally, or it can be divided into a variable number of divisions, each division being identified with a line of products, a geographical area, and/or some other feature of its operations.

The advantages and disadvantages of divisional organization can be identified within a framework provided by a set of concepts known as *agency theory*. All individuals can be expected to try to improve their own well-being. If they are acting on behalf of someone else (as agents), they will act in the interests of that other person (the principal) to the extent that they have incentives to do so, but they also are likely to pursue personal goals to some extent to the detriment of the interests of the principal.

A business enterprise can be regarded as a complex series of agent-principal relationships. The shareholders are the ultimate principals, and senior managers are their agents; but senior managers have a principal-agent relation with junior managers, and so on. If managers are interested only in money increases in wealth, and if their rewards are related only to increases in wealth obtained for the shareholders, no conflict will arise between the goals of principals and agents. For example, if shareholders desire profit maximization and managers receive a percentage of profits and no other benefits, the managers are likely to act in accordance with the interests of shareholders. In maximizing their own compensation, managers will maximize profits.

In other circumstances, the interests of principals and agents will conflict. If managers are interested in nonpecuniary rewards, they may attempt to obtain them even though the effect is a reduction in profits. For example, managers may seek to obtain luxurious offices and other perquisites, and "leisure on the job." Furthermore, if managers see little connection between their money rewards and profits generated by their efforts, they are likely to limit their efforts in pursuit of profits. (A connection between managers' rewards and profits may be effective as an incentive even though it is remote; for example, a connection may exist if current profits are thought to increase the chances of future promotions.)

Principlals can use various devices to control the behavior of agents, apart from incentives in their compensation scheme. For example, they can employ auditors and supervisors. However, such controls have costs.

The benefits of divisional organization. Creating divisions in an enterprise can involve the following benefits:

1. Creating a division can increase the number of people who can be held accountable for the effect of their actions on the goals of principals. The computation of divisional profit can indicate the extent to which divisional managers have contributed to overall profits.

2. Creating a division can increase the number of people who have incentives to contribute to achieving the goals of principals. Divisional managers can be rewarded on the basis of divisional profits.

3. Creating a division can alter an agent's goals in other ways. For example, the positive motivation associated with the responsibility given to a divisional manager can have the result that the manager gives more weight to the goals of principals and less weight to other factors such as perquisites.

Other advantages claimed for divisional organization include specialization and executive development. Divisional managers can become experts in the field of operations of their division, whereas central managers could not become expert in a wide range of activities undertaken in a diversified company; and experience in managing a division may be good training for top management. Furthermore, the complexity of some organizations makes central management virtually impossible. The cost of the extensive communications that would be involved might well be prohibitive.

Creating divisions does not bring sure benefits in all situations. Benefits are limited partly by the extent to which a division can be established to earn profits independently of the activities of other parts of the enterprise. If that independence is absent, creating a division may be dysfunctional: A manager who improves the profits of a division may reduce the profits of the whole enterprise. This difficulty is examined next.

The independence requirement. Organizing an enterprise into divisions will be successful only if the recording of an increase in profit for a division normally signals an increase in the profits of the whole enterprise. This is the independence requirement. If increases in the profit of a division can be associated with decreases in the profit of the whole firm, the basis for the motivation and control of divisional managers is insecure.

The need for the independence requirement can be illustrated with situations where it does not hold. Independence may be lost when transfers take place between divisions of products and services for which no outside market exists. If the transfers are priced above cost, the producing division will be shown as making profits and yet those profits can be offset when the buying division raises its selling prices to cover the transfer price and hence loses sales. A different difficulty may arise if transfers are priced at total cost. In that case, the effects of inefficiency in the producing division can be passed on to the buying division in the transfer price: The results of both divisions will not fully reflect their performances. The problems associated with transfer pricing will be considered further below.

Another example of lack of independence arises when two divisions are in direct competition for a particular sale. The profit that the successful division makes on the sale will, from the company's point of view, be partly offset by the unsuccessful division's abortive selling expenses and reduced by a low eventual selling price.

Independence does not mean that a division must escape the cost of its activities that arise within the company but outside the division. Independence requires only that external costs charged to the division be limited to costs caused by its activities alone. Thus interdivisional transfers priced at market price or at standard cost could be regarded as preserving independence, whereas transfer prices based on total cost might not.

In practice, few businesses have divisions that meet the criterion of independence completely. Indeed, if they did, questions might arise about the justification for operating the divisions as part of the same company. The company might appear more like an investment company than an operating organization. Minor failures of independence do not destroy the case for divisionalization and can be allowed for in the interpretation of results. However, the existence of major interdependencies among parts of an organization, to the extent that a measurement of the profit of a part would tell little about the success of that part, is normally a signal that divisional organization would not be appropriate.

Measurement of Divisional Performance. Once a choice of divisional organization has been made, the next question that arises concerns the measurement of divisional performance. The measurement has two main interrelated purposes: (1) to motivate divisional managers to behave in a manner that contributes to the achievement of enterprise goals, and (2) to provide a basis for assessing the success of divisional managers.

The primary focus of measuring divisional performance is profitability. It is easy to defend the primary position accorded to such a measure. In the first place, unless a company is profitable, it is unlikely to survive for very long; and if it does not survive, nothing else much matters. Second, profitability, better than any other single index of performance, reflects a great many other ingredients of performance, such as growth, market penetration, product leadership, or productivity. Thus, there is a comprehensive quality to profitability that other performance measures lack.

Relevance for decision purposes should govern performance measurement. If a particular measure of an expense is relevant for a decision—for example, about pricing policy—the same measure should be used for measuring profits. If that approach is not followed, the optimal pricing policy may fail to show the highest profits.

In many cases, the measurement of divisional results follows general accounting practice, without particular complication. For example, a variable cost incurred by a division in purchasing and using goods from an independent organization would be recorded as an expense in the usual way. However, four questions need special attention in the context of measuring divisional performance:

1. The transfer pricing problem. How should products and services transferred from one division to another be measured in computing the revenues of the supplying division and the expenses of the division that acquires them?

2. The cost allocation problem. How should costs incurred centrally for the joint benefit of several divisions be allocated to the divisions (if at all)?

3. The treatment of noncontrollable costs. How should costs that benefit a division but that arise as a result of a central decision be treated?

4. The choice of summary indicator. What measure should be the focus of the system? Should performance be judged on the basis of the absolute amount of profit, the rate of return on investment, or some other measure?

The transfer pricing problem. The foremost problem of divisionalization is the transfer pricing problem: the problem of what price to charge for transfers of goods and services from one division to another. If divisions were entirely independent of each other except in the sense that they were answerable to the same corporate management and body of shareholders and had a common source of supply of capital, the problem would not exist. A valuable aspect of divisionalization would be missing, however, because presumably the corporation benefits from having divisions do business with each other rather than with suppliers and customers outside the corporate family.

The transfer pricing problem arises because, ideally, a divisionalized company must always be seeking two conditions that may conflict. One of these conditions is a substantial degree of decentralization of decision making and freedom for divisional management to follow the courses of action they think best for their divisions. The other condition is maximum attainment of the goals of the corporation as a whole.

The nature of the transfer pricing problem depends on whether the material, component, or product being transferred between divisions can or cannot be bought and sold freely on an outside competitive market. Where such a market exists, theoretically, at least, there is no reason why both of the conditions discussed above should not be secured simultaneously. But the prognosis is not nearly so good where there is no outside market for the transferred item or where there is a market but its prices are affected significantly by the activities of the two divisions themselves. For example, a competitive market may be lacking when a material or product is being transferred in a semiprocessed form (e.g., an unrefined chemical) or is highly specialized to the needs of the receiving division.

Why transfer prices are not neutral. A superficial consideration of transfer pricing might suggest that prices between affiliates are of little importance to the corporation as a whole, so long as neither affiliate has outside shareholders: What comes out of one corporate pocket goes into another, however much money is involved. Such a simplistic view loses sight of the fact that, in a decentralized organization, managers are supposed to react to internal prices in much the same way as to external prices. If a transfer price is higher than it need be and there is no outside market, the buying division may refuse to deal or may buy less than it would take at a lower price. By reacting in this way, it may be doing what is best in terms of its own profitability, but the actions of the two divisions together may not be best for the corporation. The "what comes out of one pocket goes into the other" argument would hold only if divisional behavior were unaffected by the price at which materials and products passed between divisions. Though situations do exist where some variation in price does not affect behavior, this is not the normal state of affairs.

Ideally, transfer prices lead divisions to achieve the same levels of production and sales, looking at their activities as a whole, as would be achieved by a fully integrated, centralized company. The fact of decentralization may cause these activities to be carried out with greater efficiency, but that is not the point at issue here. The nature and scale of the activities ought not to be changed simply because they are divided between two or more divisions. But they will probably be changed, if a buying division has to pay more to increase its supply of a product than the cost to the total corporation. An ill-considered transfer pricing system may have just this effect.

This point is easily illustrated. Suppose that division A, which supplies material to a finishing division, B, charges for the material on a standard cost basis. Its fixed costs are $400 a day, and the variable costs of supplying the material are $1 a unit. Normal capacity is 200 units a day, and standard cost per unit is therefore computed at $2 (= $400/200) for fixed cost plus $1 for variable cost, a standard cost of $3 a unit. This is what division B will have to pay for each unit it takes. B's own profit, ignoring any other activities it may have, will depend on how much of A's material it chooses to convert, and it will probably wish to expand the conversion activity so long as expansion adds to its own profit.

Now suppose that division A and division B are both operating below normal capacity. Division B would incur additional costs of its own of $1.50 for each unit that it converts and it could add $3.40 to its gross revenue for each additional unit sold. If B has to pay A $3 a unit for the material it takes, it can hardly be expected to expand, because it will lose $1.10 (= $3.40 − $3.00 − $1.50) a unit on every unit it sells.

From the corporate point of view, however, B ought to take on the additional business because, looking at the two divisions together, the company would be $.90 a unit better off for each unit that B can sell ($3.40 revenue minus incremental costs of $1 for A and $1.50 for B) until capacity is reached.

This illustration should make clear the nature of the danger that transfer pricing may present. Transfer prices based on a supplying division's average total costs (whether these are actual or standard costs) have the effect of transforming that division's fixed costs into a buying division's variable costs. This is why, when a company's activities are divided between divisions and the divisions are free to deal with each other at arms' length, the aggregate of the divisions' activities may not be the same and may not be so profitable for the company as under centralized direction.

Marginal cost and transfer prices. The above discussion suggests the desirability of a "marginal cost" rule for transfer pricing. A producing division should be prepared to supply other divisions at a price equal to its incremental cost so long as it has unused capacity. If incremental cost is fairly constant over a considerable range of output, the rule as stated above defines the price sufficiently. If incremental cost is different at different levels of output, then the relevant one for transfer pricing purposes is the incremental cost at the margin of actual output. For a division that supplies two or more other divisions, the identification of this number presents practical difficulty. The output margin will be determined by how much is taken by the buying divisions in the aggregate, but this in turn will be determined by the transfer price they have to pay. The transfer price and the output volume then should strictly be determined simultaneously by comparing two schedules, one showing the varying quantities the consuming divisions will take at various prices, and the other the marginal cost of the supplying division at various levels of output. There will be one figure of marginal cost that will equate output with the amount the consuming divisions wish to take. This sets the marginal cost transfer price.

In spite of its theoretical attractiveness, marginal cost is seldom used as a basis for transfer pricing, for reasons to be discussed later. But it is closely related to what is probably the most widely used basis, that is, market price. Where appropriate, market price has everything to commend it as a basis for transfer pricing, both on theoretical and practical grounds. But the circumstances in which it is appropriate and what "market price" means need to be spelled out.

The existence of an outside competitive market for a material or component that is the subject of interdivisional transfers provides an objective basis for pricing transfers, a basis that meets all the requirements of an ideal system. The market price is consistent with the independence criterion. It represents the opportunity cost to the enterprise of using a product internally. Each unit used internally involves a sacrifice equal to the sales proceeds foregone. Internal use should not take place unless it earns more than the market price. Charging the market price to divisions that use the product can be expected to produce conformity to that rule of behavior. Furthermore, this rule does not harm the division that produces the product. The existence of the competitive market implies that the producing division can sell externally any output not required by other divisions.

The benefits of a transfer pricing system based on market prices will be fully realized only if all divisions are free to buy and sell in the market. Whether they actually do so or not does not matter. But freedom of access to the market provides a mechanism whereby each division can seek the maximum satisfaction of its own ends without any danger to the company of suboptimization. A supplying division whose incremental costs per unit are high in relation to the market price may be unable to supply as much as using divisions would like to take (at the market price) without injuring its own profit performance. Its costs may be so high that it is unwilling to supply anything at all. This will not hurt the using divisions if they can go to the market and make up any shortage of internal supply by outside purchases. Conversely, a low-cost supplying division may want to produce more than other divisions are willing to take at the market price. All it has to do is sell its surplus output on the market, after supplying its fellow divisions with what they are willing to buy. Subject to one refinement, to be mentioned shortly, transfers at market price with freedom for divisions to buy and sell outside protect both the company and its divisions from the danger that a profit-maximizing division will harm the whole company.

Access to markets is not free of cost. Costs are incurred to obtain information about prices, terms of trading, and availability of supply; expenses will usually be associated with delivery and receipt of goods; and risks of default must be accepted on delivery and on payment. These costs are usually absent or minimal when affiliates do business with each other. Now suppose that a buying division, faced with the choice of buying from another division or from an outside supplier at the same price, chooses to go outside, and the selling division has to dispose of its output on the outside market; then the company as a whole will probably incur expenses of resorting to the market (twice) that it would save if the transaction took place internally. To encourage divisions to deal with each other, with consequent economies to the company, it is usual to set market-based transfer prices at a level somewhat below the outside market price. The incentive this gives buying divisions to keep their business in the family removes a possible conflict between their own and the company's interests.

A connection exists between the rule, widely used in practice, of basing transfer prices on outside market prices and the incremental or marginal cost rule of transfer pricing. Whether the selling division sells to another division, to the outside market, or to both, at the outside (competitive) price, rational behavior will lead it to sell just that amount which equates its marginal cost with the outside price. At this point, its own profit will be at a maximum. Thus, at the margin of its activities, marginal cost is brought into equality with market price. In this sense, the market price rule for transfer prices can be said to be a special case of the marginal cost rule where competitive markets exist. This explanation does not fit a situation in which a producing division has significant fixed costs and variable (incremental) costs of a constant amount per unit. If market price then equaled incremental cost, divisional income would be negative, suggesting that the division should be abandoned in the interests of the whole enterprise. Competitive markets will not easily exist, however, when fixed costs really are large; in those cases, individual firms will expand to reduce average costs and the market will come to be dominated by one or a few very large firms (subject to any legal restrictions). The situation is different if the fixed costs apply for only a limited range of output. In that case the costs are not genuinely fixed, and average cost will not fall steadily as output expands.

Alternatives to market price. As noted above, market price provides a good basis for transfer pricing only where the price is determined in a reasonably competitive market. When the market is not competitive, or when the market is nonexistent, some other basis is needed. The advantages of incremental (or marginal) cost were illustrated above. That analysis can be extended to deal with an imperfectly competitive market—a market in which sales volume can be increased only by significant reductions in selling price. When an imperfectly competitive market exists, an enterprise that wishes to optimize its profit must expand output to the point at which incremental cost is equal to incremental revenue. Incremental revenue is likely to be less than selling price because of the need to reduce selling prices to dispose of progressively higher levels of output. Incremental revenue and incremental cost equally represent the sacrifice involved in using an extra unit internally rather than selling it, and hence they represent identically appropriate transfer prices for the product.

The above discussion has shown the undesirable results that can follow from the use of average cost as a transfer price. In practice, however, average cost is often preferred over incremental cost as a basis for setting transfer prices. This may be attributable to an unfortunate side effect of adopting incremental cost as a transfer price: If a producing division has large fixed costs, it may be forced to report a loss. Consider again the example of a division with variable costs of $1 per unit, fixed costs of $400 per day, and normal output of 200 units per day. If the division receives a transfer price of $1 per unit (equal to incremental cost), it will report a loss of $400 per day. That result would be undesirable for at least two reasons. First, the loss misrepresents the contribution of the division to the whole enterprise. The division may well be a worthwhile part of the enterprise, perhaps an essential part if no market exists for the intermediate product. Second, reporting a loss may have a detrimental effect on morale in the division. Divisional managers can do little to eliminate the loss, except perhaps to alter methods of production in a manner that increases variable costs while reducing fixed costs; and such a change might have the effect of increasing total costs for the whole enterprise.

The use of average cost in place of incremental cost is, however, not the appropriate solution to the difficulty described. A preferable solution, because it does not provoke suboptimal decisions about the volume of activity, would be to adopt a two-part pricing system. Divisions using the products would pay a fixed sum to the producing division plus an amount per unit equal to variable cost. The fixed sum might be set at a level that would cover fixed costs plus an allowance for a reasonable rate of return on capital employed. This system may be the best available, but it too has its limitations. The fixed sums credited to the producing division and charged to using divisions are bound to be arbitrary to some extent. Consequently, the profit numbers reported by the various divisions will be of limited usefulness as indicators of divisional performance.

Transfer prices under limited capacity. Another situation in which special difficulty attaches to the determination of transfer prices arises when the output of some goods and services is limited by capacity. The producing division may have opportunities for external sales and demands to supply other divisions amounting in aggregate to a volume in excess of what it can produce, at least in the short run. The best result for the whole enterprise will be obtained if each successive unit of the product is put to the most profitable use. The decision process can be visualized as involving a ranking of all available uses of the product concerned in the order of their profitability and application of units of the product in the order given by the ranking until the limit set by capacity is reached.

The difficulty with the decision process described, for a divisionalized organization, is that it requires centralized decision making: Only a centralized system can deal with the ranking of uses of the product—uses that may arise in various divisions. If optimal decisions are to be obtained by divisions, guided by a transfer pricing system, the transfer price must represent the opportunity cost of the scarce product and that is approximately equal to the contribution generated by the product in its marginal use. However, that number can be computed only after all opportunities for use of the product in various divisions have been identified and in conjunction with effective decisions about which opportunities are to be accepted. If more than one resource is scarce, the process may require the analysis of dual prices determined from a mathematical programming formulation of the decision problem.

Summary and implications. The purpose of a transfer pricing system is to establish a set of prices for goods and services transferred between divisions such that the prices motivate divisional managers to make decisions that are optimal from the viewpoint of the whole enterprise. If an external market exists for the goods and services and the market is reasonably competitive, the market price should be used as a transfer price. In that event, divisional profits, computed with reference to the transfer prices, provide a useful basis for the assessment of divisional performance.

Other cases present greater difficulty. If competitive markets do not exist, but incremental costs per unit of output are constant as output expands, a suitable transfer pricing scheme would involve a "two-part tariff," one part fixed and the other part equal to incremental cost. That approach is not applicable when capacity imposes an effective limit on output. If capacity imposes an effective limit on output of the transferred items, or if incremental cost varies with output, the appropriate transfer price can be determined only at the same time as the optimal plan for the whole organization. It may then be thought that divisional organization with decentralized decision making would be unworkable—it would be regarded as a sham. If decisions have been determined centrally, they may as well be implemented centrally and no need arises for transfer prices.

However, many people believe that the motivational benefits of decentralized decision making justify its use even in the circumstances described. An enterprise should, perhaps, publish the transfer prices determined centrally and require their use in decision making in divisions. Centralized information about the decisions implied by the transfer prices would be suppressed. This procedure seems more realistic when the information actually available for decision making is considered. A centralized management would not actually have information about all activities available to divisions, and so it would not be able to determine exactly which activities should be undertaken and on what terms. The best it could do would be to use a generalized model of available business opportunities to obtain estimated transfer prices. Those transfer prices would then be used by divisions to decide on the worthwhileness of actual opportunities as they become known. Actual opportunities should be compared with the assumptions of the model from time to time and adjustments made when the need is revealed.

Difficulties in setting transfer prices are associated with similar difficulties in measuring divisional performance. As noted above, the use of a two-part pricing tariff may produce profit numbers that are unreliable as a guide to divisional performance. A similar difficulty exists in other cases when transfer prices are not equal to prices in a competitive market. The difficulty is that transfer prices aim to reflect the worth of goods or services at the margin—they represent opportunity cost or incremental cost. In the absence of a competitive market, they cannot at the same time reflect the average worth of the amounts of the goods and services transferred. Lump-sum credits and charges can be used to make sure that each division has the opportunity to report a reasonable profit, and that may be important for motivating managers. However, no method exists for measuring the contribution of the division to overall enterprise performance in these circumstances: Overall performance is measurable only as a joint result of the several divisional contributions.

The cost allocation problem. Because common costs are not all alike, classification of them is necessary before a sound accounting treatment can be prescribed. A broad dichotomy can be made between the functions of corporate administration and control on the one hand and the centralized provision of services such as data processing and accounting, product development, process improvement, training, and other personnel services on the other. These services are of a kind that divisions would have to pay for if they were independent businesses, and the quantity of service taken by a division can, to a considerable extent, be determined by decisions taken within the division itself. The same is not true of such corporate activities as the work of the board of directors and top management, internal audit, many treasury functions, some of the work of corporate counsel, and institutional advertising. Pure research of a long-run nature carried out in the corporate research laboratory also belongs in this group, if, as is often the case, it cannot be identified with any existing division.

Central service departments. Surprisingly, many companies treat these two quite different categories of common costs in the same way for allocation purposes. This practice has nothing to commend it except simplicity. Indeed, the grouping of all central services together, let alone combining them with central administration, may still be too crude. The problem of allocating the costs of central service departments is conceptually the same as the problem of establishing a satisfactory transfer pricing system, with the particular difficulty that the quantity of the service transferred is often hard to measure. This perspective indicates that each service should be considered separately for purposes of cost allocation, in the same way as each physical product, at least provided that its costs are significant.

The objectives of transfer pricing are the same for a service as for a physical product. The system aims to ensure that divisions have incentives to use the service efficiently in terms of the objectives of the whole enterprise. If the service can be purchased and sold externally and if the market for the service is reasonably competitive, the market price would represent the appropriate transfer price. In most cases, however, external transactions in services of the kind under discussion will be impracticable or ruled out by strategic considerations. If it is to give good incentives for the production and use of the optimal quantity of a service, the transfer price then should aim to reflect the incremental cost imposed on the enterprise by production and use of a unit of the service. If output is not at the limit of capacity, an appropriate charge per unit can normally be found by dividing total variable costs by the number of units produced. (If capacity is an effective constraint, a higher price may be needed as a rationing device.)

If the service division incurs substantial fixed costs, a two-part pricing tariff is likely to be needed, as discussed above. The pricing system should be based on standard costs rather than actual costs, to ensure that the service department has an incentive to be efficient and cannot simply pass on the results of inefficiencies in the prices it charges.

The greatest difficulty may be to identify an appropriate unit for measuring the transfer of services. Often proxies may need to be used; for example, the costs of a centralized accounting system may need to be priced on the basis of factors such as sales volume, number of customers and suppliers, number of product lines, and so on, because it is not practicable to measure the time spent on the affairs of each division.

Central administrative expenses. The considerations that bear on the treatment of service department costs have no relevance when we turn to corporate administrative expenses. Divisions cannot choose how much of top management's attention they will take up, and there are no make-or-buy decisions to be made. Quite different criteria therefore apply as determinants of methods of allocation to be used. Indeed, the first question to be answered is whether such expenses need to be allocated at all.

One argument for allocation is that it helps divisions to set their selling prices. From a short-run point of view, this argument is not very convincing. To the extent that prices are determined by competitive conditions in the market, the prices will be the same whether corporate expenses are allocated to divisions or not. And to the extent that a division has the power to set or at least to influence its prices, allocations of expenses that are fixed in the short run ought not to affect these prices. It is enough if the division sets its prices so as to optimize its total contribution to central expenses and profit, because whatever prices do this will also optimize the division's net profit after allocations. In the short run, therefore, the question of allocation seems to be irrelevant to the pricing issue.

Furthermore, an allocation of fixed expenses can make an operation look unprofitable, even though it is making a positive contribution to corporate profits. It is unlikely that many people will be misled when looking at the results of a whole division. However, if the practice of allocation is carried down to product lines within divisions, as it often is, the danger of eliminating contribution-making products may be considerably greater.

The following example illustrates the undesirable consequences that may flow from the allocation to divisions of fixed central expenses. The results of a company, with its three divisions, for the first quarter of 19X1 are shown in Exhibit 1. All the costs can be allocated directly to divisions except the central administration expenses, and these, it has been decided, shall be apportioned between divisions in proportion to their sales.

Division A's business falls into two classes, one of them showing a much lower margin of profit than the other. Of the division's total contribution of $300,000, $260,000 is produced by sales of $600,000, whereas the remaining sales of $400,000 contribute only $40,000 to the division's profit. The division would have replaced this part of its business with more profitable lines if it had been able to do so, but in the absence of these the division's management preferred to get a small contribution from the facilities concerned rather than no contribution at all. However, the division's management then realized that so long as corporate management maintained the present method of charging out central administrative expenses, the division could improve its apparent results by liquidating its low-margin business. The result for the company and for the division (assuming that everything else continues as before) is shown in Exhibit

EXHIBIT 1   Operating Statement, First Quarter, 19X1 (thousands omitted)

	Div. A	Div. B	Div. C	Company total
Net sales	$1,000	$500	$500	$2,000
Cost of sales	$ 550	$240	$215	$1,005
Division direct expenses	150	60	85	295
	$ 700	$300	$300	$1,300
Divisional contributions	$ 300	$200	$200	$ 700
Central administration expenses	200	100	100	400
Net profit before taxes	$ 100	$100	$100	$ 300

EXHIBIT 2   Company Results after Division A Liquidates Its Low-Margin Business (thousands omitted)

	Div. A	Div. B	Div. C	Company total
Net sales	$600	$500	$500	$1,600
Cost of sales	$260	$240	$215	$ 715
Division direct expenses	80	60	85	225
	$340	$300	$300	$ 940
Divisional contributions	$260	$200	$200	$ 660
Central administration expenses	150	125	125	400
Net profit before taxes	$110	$ 75	$ 75	$ 260

2. The company is $40,000 a quarter worse off than it was before, whereas division A's profit appears to be $10,000 a quarter better than it was before.

This danger can be avoided if fixed costs of central administration—costs that would not be saved following the closure of the division—are not allocated. Divisional profit should represent the contribution to fixed central expenses and to overall profit.

The above arguments apply only to costs that are strictly fixed, regardless of the existence of a particular division. The assessment of divisional performance requires that, whenever possible, a division should be charged with any cost it inflicts on the company, wherever this may "surface." If an increment of central expenses is attributable to a division, in the sense that central expenses would be smaller by that amount if the division were to close down, that increment is properly chargeable to the division. It has often been noted that, looked at over a period of years, administrative expenses do not exhibit the invariability that they are commonly supposed to have, but in fact creep up more or less at the same pace as the volume of company activity. In that view, it may be reasonable to allocate to divisions all but a hard core of corporate administrative expenses that would be eliminated only if the whole corporation were liquidated.

Bases of allocation for corporate administrative expenses. A wide variety of allocation methods is found in practice. Bases of allocation commonly used include sales, net income before charging allocated expenses or some other profit figure, divisional investment, or total direct expenses. Another widely used base is more complex—the so-called Massachusetts formula, used by several states in determining what proportion of a company's profit shall be subject to state corporate profits tax. When used for allocating corporate expenses to divisions, the formula gives equal weight to sales, assets employed, and amount of payroll. Like many simple formulas, it is arbitrary; but in some circumstances, it may come close to measuring the relative administrative burden a division places on a corporate headquarters, and this is what the sought-for basis is supposed to do.

The treatment of noncontrollable costs. Delegation of authority to divisions is never unconstrained. The extent of divisional autonomy varies from company to company, and so, therefore, must the precise meaning of "divisional performance." In one company, divisional managers may have almost complete control over the setting of selling prices, subject only to an informal requirement to consult with, say, the corporate vice president in charge of marketing before any of a few particularly sensitive prices are changed. At the other extreme, in another company, almost any change in prices or discounts or other conditions of sale may require corporate approval. It is obvious that divisional managers have less genuine responsibility for the results of the division in the second case than in the first.

Variations in the extent of divisional independence are to be found in almost every area of managerial responsibility. In some companies, purchasing is totally decentralized; in others, all important purchases are made centrally; in yet others, certain divisions are given the responsibility for purchasing some bulk items for other divisions as well as for themselves. The extent to which research, advertising, personnel services, data processing, credit and collection, and other services are centralized or decentralized is equally subject to great variation. Thus, divisional performance hardly ever means precisely the same thing in any two companies, even though on the surface they appear to have quite similar organizations.

The variability of divisional autonomy suggests a need to distinguish between the performance of a division and the performance of its managers. The divisional managers can be held responsible for and can take credit for the division's results only to the extent that they control its activities. Managerial performance, then, means performance in this limited area. But corporate management is concerned with more than this when it tries to form judgments about the success and the prospects of the total divisional activity. For this purpose, everything relating to the division is relevant, whether it is the responsibility of divisional or of corporate management. Thus, the cost of research carried out in a corporate research laboratory on a divisional project, at the request of, or at least with the acquiescence of, divisional managers, is properly chargeable in determining the profits earned both by the division and by its managers. If the research were carried out at the instigation of corporate management without consulting the division, then it might be proper to charge the cost of the project to the division as an expense not controllable by its management.

A straightforward example of an expense clearly chargeable to a division but not controllable at divisional level is the divisional general manager's own salary. Corporate administrative expenses charged to divisions may fall into the same category, because divisions have no control over the level of such expenses and will usually have no more than a right to be consulted about the basis on which they are allocated to divisions.

The distinction between divisional profit and controllable profit (which is a part, but only a part, of divisional profit) makes it possible, in a single income statement, to report information by which both the division and its managers may be judged.

The choice of summary indicator. In the present context, a summary indicator is a key number or ratio that is used to judge divisional performance. Just as a financial analyst may use several different indicators to appraise the performance of the whole company, so may central managers use several different indicators of divisional performance. Important among the summary indicators is likely to be a measure of profitability, and the following discussion focuses on the choice of such a measure. Two indicators, in particular, have been the subject of controversy: return on investment and residual income.

The limitations of accounting measures. Both return on investment and residual income are based on a computation of net income, measured in accordance with accounting principles. That number in itself is not an ideal indicator of performance, and its imperfections must be recognized in any system of assessment based on its derivatives.

Specifically, consider two companies having equal capital employed (according to accounting measures) and equal income numbers. Those two companies cannot be said with certainty to have performed equally well. One difficulty may arise because the companies have chosen to use different accounting principles. For example, one company may use a method of accelerated depreciation, the other may use a straight-line method; one may measure cost of goods sold with FIFO (first-in, first-out) flow, another with LIFO (last-in, first-out). Normally, differences of that kind are not serious for purposes of assessment of divisional performance, because a company can require the use of a standard set of accounting principles throughout its divisions. Difficulties may, however, arise where divisional activities are conducted by overseas subsidiaries and legal constraints and cost considerations dictate the use of varying principles. For example, the U.S. operations may use LIFO because of its advantages for tax purposes, whereas the overseas subsidiary may be prevented by law from using LIFO for tax reporting and it may not be considered worthwhile to recompute the measurements for control purposes.

Another, and more pervasive difficulty, comes from distortions associated with differences among the ages and expected lives of assets. Consider an asset purchased for $10,000, expected to have a life of 10 years, and to yield profits of $1,500 per year after deducting depreciation of $1,000 per year. In the first year, the asset will show a rate of return of 15 percent; in the last year, the asset will have been written down to $1,000 and will show a rate of return of 150 percent. The apparent rate of return increases as the asset gets older. (The exact pattern of change depends on the life of the asset and the cash flow profile over its life.) The overall results reported by an enterprise or a division can be regarded as an aggregation of the results of many projects, some using young assets, some using old assets. The overall rate of return will accordingly depend in part on the mix of assets of various ages.

Consequently, enterprises or divisions that earn a constant rate of return on all investments, appraised on a discounted cash flow basis, may report various rates of return on an accounting basis, because:

1. The assets vary in average age.

2. The assets have different lives.

3. New investment varies in amount from year to year (affecting the weighted-average age of assets).

4. Different assets have differing patterns of cash flows over their lives. (For example, a steady decline in annual cash flows will offset the aging effect to some extent.)

5. Different accounting principles are used. (For example, accelerated depreciation will produce a different effect from straight-line depreciation.)

It follows that one division may report a lower accounting rate of return than another division and yet be earning a higher rate of return on a discounted cash flow basis on all its projects. Major distortions of this kind may be rather rare and associated with events such as large expansions. Simulation studies suggest, however, that distortions of one or two percentage points can arise quite frequently.

The effects of changing prices. One further limitation of conventional accounting methods needs particular emphasis because of its topical importance. It concerns the use of historical cost for measuring assets and related expenses. The difficulty can be illustrated with a simple example. Suppose that two divisions each use land carried in their accounts at the (identical) cost prices of $100,000 and equal amounts of other assets; and the two divisions earn the same net income, measured on a historical cost basis. However, one division bought its land in 1981, the other in 1901. The two divisions, almost certainly, are not performing equally well. The land purchased in 1901 presumably could now be sold for a sum greatly in excess of cost, and that current price would better measure the resources being used by divisional managers. Only if such resources are being measured at current prices can assessments of performance obtain some impression about the worthwhileness of keeping the division in existence rather than abandoning it and investing the capital in some other venture.

A second, and related, limitation of historical cost accounting is that it fails to measure the effective cost of using up resources. A divisional manager who is considering the use of raw materials held in inventory needs to weigh the expected sales proceeds against the replacement cost of the materials (assuming that replacement will take place); the original cost of the inventory fails to measure the sacrifice involved in its use. Accordingly, current prices give a better basis than historical prices for the measurement of operating performance.

The timing of purchases may also be an important feature of the performance of divisional managers. Good timing of purchases (or other aspects of buying) may result in important economies of cost. Under historical cost accounting, the results of good buying do not affect income until the resources concerned are realized. The managers responsible for the purchase may then no longer be in charge of the divisional activity. Only if a system of current value accounting (such as current cost accounting) is used can the results of good buying be shown in the period in which they occur; and only then can the results of buying and holding assets be separated from the operating results.

The above arguments indicate that a strong case exists for the use of a system of current value accounting in the assessment of divisional performance. Only then can comparability among divisions be obtained; and other, more general, considerations add weight to the case. This chapter cannot consider all the detailed implications of the use of a system of accounting for the effects of changing prices. However, the Financial Accounting Standards Board has recently called for experimental use by large public companies of a system of current cost accounting in external reporting [FASB Statement No. 33, 1979], and several companies have started to use that system for internal management purposes.

The rate-of-return criterion. Few companies are content to judge divisional performance on the basis of the division's absolute profit, because on this basis the bigger the division, the better its performance will generally appear to be. Undoubtedly, the measure of performance in most general use, either as the sole criterion or as "first among equals," is the rate of return on investment (ROI), that is, divisional net profit as a percentage of divisional capital employed. Both the numerator and denominator in the ROI computation admit of many variations, and we shall look at some of these shortly. But overriding these more detailed questions is the broader issue: Is ROI an appropriate criterion by which to judge the performance of a division, or its managers, or both?

There is a good deal to be said on the positive side. ROI is capable of objective measurement, in spite of the considerable latitude made possible by the variations in accounting method already referred to. It can be used to compare the profitability of units of different size, to the extent that size is adequately represented by the amount of investment. And its use does encourage a manager to economize on capital because, other things being equal, the less capital employed in a division, the higher the ROI. Thus, an incentive is provided for capital-economizing moves such as disposing of redundant assets or choosing a less capital-intensive rather than a more capital-intensive method of expansion.

However, the main objection to the ROI criterion of performance is that it may provide too strong an incentive to economize capital and may discourage investment that ought to take place. A manager who is seeking to show the highest possible rate of return on investment will be reluctant to undertake any investment that will lower the present ROI. The higher the ROI is now, the more restrictive the attitude to expansion is likely to be—even if additional capital is available quite cheaply. From the shareholders' viewpoint, any investment of capital that will show a return in excess of its cost ought to be made. By setting a manager the goal of maintaining the highest possible rate of return on capital, or even of maintaining any rate in excess of the cost of capital, a conflict is created between the interests of the manager and the interests of the company's shareholders.

Residual income as an alternative criterion. If the objection to ROI just advanced is valid, it becomes important to find an alternative criterion that will still relate profitability to size but will not tend to inhibit expansion in the way ROI may do. Such a criterion is available in *residual income*. Like ROI, residual income admits of many variants, but it may broadly be defined as the excess of net income over the cost of capital employed in earning it. It is not a ratio, like ROI, but an absolute number of dollars. An instruction to maximize divisional residual income is an instruction to seek any expansion in the division that will earn more than the cost of the capital required for it. If this instruction is carried out, the division's results should be optimized.

The relationship between ROI and residual income may be brought out by a simple illustration: See Exhibit 3.

Several points of interest emerge from Exhibit 3. First, judged by the ROI

EXHIBIT 3   Comparison of ROI and Residual Income

	Division A	Division B
Capital invested.....................	$1,000	$1,500
Net profit	150	200
ROI................................	15%	13.3%
Residual Income when cost of capital is		
6%	$ 90	$ 110
8%	70	80
10%	50	50
12%	30	20
14%	10	(10)

criterion, division A shows a better performance than B, and this judgment is unaffected by the cost of capital. By the residual income criterion, it is not possible to say which division is performing better until the rate at which capital can be raised has been determined. If capital is relatively cheap, for example, 6 percent, division A's capital costs $60, and its residual income (the excess of net profit over the cost of capital) is $90. Division B's capital costs $90, and its residual income is $110—a superior performance by this criterion. If the cost of capital goes higher, division B's superiority will diminish; and at rates above 10 percent, B will be the inferior division. It is not surprising that a low cost of capital will favor the more highly capitalized division and a high cost of capital will penalize it. The breakeven rate in this example is 10 percent, because this is the ratio of B's extra $50 profit (compared with A's) to its extra investment of $500.

It might be argued that, with half as much capital again at risk as division A, B must show at least half as much profit again as A to be able to claim a comparable performance. But this would be erroneous. The cost of capital already allows for the risks associated with investment, and residual income is what is left after these risks have been compensated for. To take account again of the heavier investment in B would be double counting.

Some people defend the ROI criterion on the ground that divisions do not have control over the level of capital investment in their operations—that capital is fixed as far as the divisions are concerned. If the level of capital employed is fixed, the ROI and residual income criteria do not conflict; conflict arises only because residual income may favor an expansion of capital employed when additional investment can earn more than the cost of capital even though ROI may be reduced—and that possibility does not arise when capital employed is fixed. Moreover, ROI might be preferred in that situation because of its greater familiarity.

However, divisional performance must be distinguished from the performance of divisional managers. Divisions rarely do operate with strictly fixed capital. Major investments in fixed assets often are subject to decisions in the head office, but extra investments that are made by the head office still lead to increases in income and capital employed in the divisions. Furthermore, capital employed usually is affected to a significant extent by the actions of divisional managers. Investment in working capital usually is within their control, as is minor investment in fixed assets. Residual income seems to be a sound basis for the assessment of divisional performance because divisional capital is not fixed. The limited control of divisional managers over some aspects of divisional performance must be recognized in the interpretation of residual income and its components.

The definition of investment. Whether ROI or residual income is used for the assessment of divisional performance, investment in the division will need to be measured, and hence it needs to be defined. In defining investment, we can look at the matter from the "sources" side or the "uses" side. From the sources side, distinctions can be drawn between equity investment, total shareholders' investment (including preferred shares), total long-term investment (including bonds and mortgages), and total investment (including short-term notes and accounts payable). From the uses side, different distinctions are relevant, for example, between total assets and assets employed in the business (i.e., excluding investments in other companies). There is also the question as to how redundant assets (e.g., surplus machinery or idle cash balances) should be dealt with.

Each of several definitions is appropriate to a different purpose, and the immediate task is to choose the investment base most appropriate to the measurement of divisional performance in terms either of ROI or residual income. Because divisions do not generally have separate capital structures (unless they happen to be organized as subsidiary companies), the sources of capital (subject to one reservation to be mentioned shortly) are not relevant to the determination of a division's investment base. The main objective is to encourage the divisional manager to be as economical as possible in the use of capital, and the definition of investment base selected should be designed to serve this purpose; the definition that does this best is assets employed in the business (including redundant assets) minus accounts payable attributable to the division. Redundant assets are included in order to give the division an incentive to dispose of such assets by sale or transfer to another part of the company. Accounts payable are deducted to encourage the division to take full advantage of all the cheap credit it can get from suppliers. This is the one exception, referred to above, to the general rule that the sources of capital are not relevant to the determination of a division's investment base. The exception is made because accounts payable usually are the only source of finance controlled by the division.

A format for reporting divisional profit. Exhibit 4 is a form of divisional income statement that brings together many of the matters discussed above, so as to give not one but several different measures of divisional performance.

The statement distinguishes between the division's external and internal sales and, for the latter, between those made at market prices and those priced on some other basis, such as cost. The purpose of this distinction is to show to what extent the division is dependent on orders from other divisions for its business. It would be relatively simple to carry this distinction further if desired, so as to separate variable profits on external and internal sales. Dependence on other divisions is not so great where an outside market for transferred products exists, because there is a possibility of diverting them to that market.

EXHIBIT 4   Form of Divisional Income Statement Showing Distinction between Controllable and Noncontrollable Items

Sales to outside customers		$xxx	
Transfers to other divisions priced at market value		xxx	
Transfers to other divisions at prices not based on market value		xxx	
			$xxx
Less:			
Variable cost of goods sold or transferred		$xxx	
Variable divisional expenses		xxx	
			xxx
Variable profit			$xxx
Less:			
Controllable divisional overhead		$xxx	
Depreciation on controllable fixed assets		xxx	
Property taxes and insurance on controllable fixed assets		xxx	xxx
Controllable operating profit			$xxx
Add (deduct):			
Nonoperating gains and losses			xxx
			$xxx
Less: Interest on controllable investment			xxx
Controllable residual income before taxes			$xxx
Less:			
Noncontrollable divisional expenses		$xxx	
Central administration expenses charged to division		xxx	
Interest on noncontrollable investment		xxx	xxx
Net residual income before taxes			$xxx
Less: Taxes on income			xxx
Net residual income after taxes			$xxx

It is because of this difference in the degree of dependence that the model statement distinguishes between transfers priced at market prices and those priced on other bases.

The distinction between controllable and noncontrollable items is maintained in the statement, so far as it can be drawn in practice, to give the division's *controllable operating profit*. After bringing in nonoperating gains and losses such as profits and losses upon disposal of fixed assets and deducting interest on controllable investment, the statement shows controllable residual income before taxes. The concept of residual income has already been discussed. Of course, where an ROI criterion rather than residual income is to be used, no charge for interest on divisional investment, whether controllable or noncontrollable, will be made.

   Allocating taxes to divisions. One question remains to be considered, and that is the treatment of income taxes. Unless a division happens to be separately incorporated as a subsidiary company, its income taxes will not be assessed separately; and even where it is separately incorporated, the parent corporation will often file a consolidated return. Where this is the case, or where the division is not separately incorporated, a decision must be made about how, if at all, income tax should be allocated to divisions. Company practices vary, but where taxes are allocated, the allocation is usually made in a somewhat arbitrary manner.

For the purpose of evaluating the performance of a manager, it is before-tax profit that seems to be relevant, because tax is not an expense that is controllable by the manager. But when the results of a division's business are to be evaluated, tax has a different significance. A division may be engaged in a business to which Congress has chosen to give favorable tax treatment. If the results of such a business are to be judged properly, therefore, it is the aftertax profits that are relevant. But this means something more than simply allocating the corporation's total tax bill among divisions in proportion to their profits, unless it so happens that by chance this does reflect their relative susceptibility to tax.

The solution is to allocate the total corporate tax burden among divisions so as to reflect as nearly as possible the tax that each division would pay if it were a separate entity. This treatment will put tax benefits as well as tax burdens where they belong. And if it is aftertax profits that are relevant in evaluating a business, then divisions making losses should, by the same token, get credit for the tax relief they bring to the corporation. To a degree, this goes beyond treating the loss-making division as if it were a separate entity, because if it were, it would not be able directly to recover tax on its losses by offsetting these losses against the profits of other businesses. But the suggested treatment has the merit of rewarding a division for the benefits that it brings to the enterprise as a whole.

Conclusion. The foregoing discussion provides a basis for a conclusion on one of the key questions in the control of divisional performance: Is the use of any summary indicator, such as ROI or residual income, justified? ROI has been seen to have a serious technical failing: Its maximization is not consistent with optimization of overall company performance. However, both measures have been seen to suffer from other defects. If transfer prices are significant in aggregate amount and are not based on prices in competitive markets, the measure of divisional income may fail to reflect the contribution of the division to enterprise performance. If transfer prices reflect marginal costs, a worthwhile division may report losses; a two-part pricing tariff can restore positive income numbers, but it will produce an income number that is essentially arbitrary. Allocations of head office expenses can increase the arbitrary element. The existence of noncontrollable expenses casts doubt on the economic significance of controllable income as a separate number; and distortions introduced by accounting principles also limit the significance that can be attached to the income number.

This impressive list of difficulties suggests that the income number itself should not be given absolute priority in a control system, except, perhaps, in particular cases in which the difficulties can be seen to be of minor importance. A preferable alternative may often be to rely on conventional principles of budgetary control. Under that alternative, divisional managers will be given budgeted targets for all revenues and expenses, and for investment levels, that are within their control. The budget approach and the use of summary indicators are not mutually exclusive. In most cases, both approaches will probably be used, and the amount of weight put on each will depend on the degree of independence of the division. Only for the most independent divisions can great weight be placed on a measure of divisional income.

REPORTS FOR EXTERNAL USERS

In recent years, annual reports of companies in the United States have included more and more information about the results of segments of their operations. This development of reporting practice has corresponded to developments in business organization. Many companies have extended the scope of their operations, often by merger or acquisition, to diversify into different product lines or to become multinational enterprises.

The general rationale for reporting segment results stems from the objectives of financial reporting. These objectives have been described in the conceptual framework project of the Financial Accounting Standards Board (FASB) as involving assistance to users in assessing the amounts, timing, and uncertainty of future cash flows to the enterprise [FASB, 1978]. A step in the assessment of future cash flows is the evaluation of past enterprise performance. Accordingly, the case for reporting segment results rests on the belief that segment reports improve the evaluation of past performance and the assessment of future results. Different segments of a business are affected differently by changes in the environment: Opportunities for growth may differ, the impact of economic recession and recovery may differ, political and economic risks may differ, and so on. If the users of reports have information about likely changes in the environment, their translation of that information into assessments of future results for the whole company is likely to be improved by information about the extent to which current earnings flow from different segments.

The Development of External Reporting. The reporting of some information about segment results has been required for more than 30 years. In 1949, the Securities and Exchange Commission (SEC) required information in the annual Form 10-K report about the relative importance of each line of business that contributed 15 percent or more of gross sales of the enterprise.

Following the SEC action, several organizations issued pronouncements that supported the disclosure of segment results. Notably, among them, the Accounting Principles Board (APB) in 1967 encouraged companies to report segment information voluntarily, although it declined to require such information until research had shown more clearly that it was reliable and useful to users. Other organizations taking a similar position included the Financial Accounting Policy Committee of the Financial Analysts Federation, and the Financial Executives Institute. By the late 1960s, several companies had responded to this climate of opinion. In the 1968 edition of its annual survey of 600 annual reports, *Accounting Trends and Techniques* found that 318 companies reported revenues by segments, although only 69 also reported segment profits.

The SEC started to establish more formal requirements for segment reporting in 1969 when it called for the inclusion of line-of-business information in registration statements. In 1970, those requirements were extended to annual reports filed on Form 10-K, and in October 1974 they were extended to the annual reports of companies that filed with the SEC.

In the early 1970s also, the Federal Trade Commission (FTC) began a program to compile statistics of business results by industry segments. The program involved the collection of special information from large U.S. companies. The commission recognized that the program imposed a cost on industry, but it argued that the merger movement and the continuing trend toward diversification in industry had caused published financial reports to be less informative than previously about the performance of various industries. It believed that the information needed for a free enterprise system to function efficiently was no longer available, but that its collection of information, classified into about 250 industry segments, would remedy the situation. The FTC had a second reason for pressing ahead with the program. It wanted to improve its capability to detect industry-wide infractions of the antitrust laws. When the financial results of one industry become merged with those of another, as they do in the accounts of diversified companies, no clear picture can be obtained of the structure of a particular industry.

The FASB placed the subject of segment reporting on its agenda in April 1973, shortly after the board's formation. A Discussion Memorandum was published in 1974 and drew 144 letters of comment. An Exposure Draft was published in September 1975, and this led to finalization of a standard in December 1976 with the publication of Statement No. 14, *Financial Reporting for Segments of a Business Enterprise*. The SEC adopted and slightly extended the provisions of Statement No. 14 in amendments to its regulation SK, effective March 1978. Minor amendments to FASB Statement No. 14 were made in Statements No. 18, 21, 24, and 30.

Information about segment results is not often required in financial reports in countries outside the United States. A survey of international accounting practices lists fewer than 10 countries in which the disclosure of sales by segments is required. The countries listed include Argentina, Canada, India, Pakistan, and the United Kingdom. The reporting of segment income is even rarer (the Netherlands, Pakistan, South Africa, and the United Kingdom have requirements), and requirements for reporting capital employed in segments are almost unknown. Some companies disclose information about segments on a voluntary basis, but they seem to be a small minority [Fitzgerald et al., 1979].

Various international organizations also have recommended the disclosure of information about the results of segments of multinational corporations. Notable among them have been the United Nations and the Organization for Economic Co-operation and Development (OECD). No doubt these bodies have been mindful of the political implications of the operations of large multinational corporations. OECD, for example, recommended the following main disclosures:

1. The geographic areas in which operations are carried out and the principal activities of the corporation
2. Operating results and sales by geographic area
3. Sales by major lines of business

4. New capital investment by geographic area and, to the extent practicable, by major lines of business

5. Policies followed regarding transfer pricing

Current Disclosure Requirements in the United States. FASB Statement No. 14 (as amended by Statements No. 18 and 21) requires all public enterprises to report information about the results of the operations of segments for fiscal years beginning after December 15, 1976. The requirement applies to annual reports.

Definition of a segment. Enterprises are required to provide information about two main kinds of segment activity: (1) segments defined according to line of business, and (2) segments defined according to geographic area of operation. No hard-and-fast rules are laid down for identifying the boundaries of different segments. The Statement refers to established classification systems such as the Standard Industrial Classification and the Enterprise Standard Industrial Classification, but does not adopt any of them. Instead, the Statement acknowledges the need to leave some flexibility for the application of managerial judgment in selecting a classification system, and it suggests that existing profit centers within the organization may be a good starting point.

Various guidelines are given for determining the number of segments for which reports are to be provided. The basic guidelines comprise a series of "10 percent tests": A line of business or a geographic area is to be the subject of separate reporting if it accounts for 10 percent of at least one of:

1. Revenue (including intersegment transfers)
2. Operating profit or loss
3. Identifiable assets

These basic guidelines are modified in two ways. First, the danger exists that a highly diversified company will escape the segment reporting rules because it has a very large number of segments—or defines its segments in such a way as to create a large number. For example, a company would escape the 10 percent test if it had 11 segments of exactly equal size. To guard against that possibility, the Statement requires segments for which results are reported to account for at least 75 percent of enterprise revenues. If the 75 percent test is not satisfied, smaller segments (below the 10 percent cutoff) must be included in the reporting until the test is satisfied.

An opposite danger is that a highly diversified company may report a very large number of segments and thereby overwhelm users with detailed information, with the result that the costs of using financial reports are greatly increased. That danger also is recognized in Statement No. 14. The board does not give any limit to the number of segments to be reported, but it suggests that a company should avoid a number much above 10 by combining small and closely related segments.

In a vertically integrated business, different stages of vertically related operations need not be treated as different segments. For example, the "upstream" activities of an oil company (exploration, development, and production) need not be separated from the "downstream" activities (refining).

Information to be reported. Information about segments, required to be reported under Statement No. 14, falls into the four categories:

1. Revenue information. Sales to independent customers are to be reported separately from transfers between segments. Transfers between segments are to be priced on the same basis as that adopted for internal purposes, and that basis is to be disclosed.

2. Operating profit or loss. Operating profit or loss is defined as revenue, including transfers to other segments, less operating expenses. Operating expenses that are not traceable directly to a segment are to be allocated on a "reasonable basis," but some expenses are to be excluded from the computation: general corporate expenses, interest expense, and income taxes. Other items to be excluded from the computation of segment operating profit or loss are the results of unconsolidated subsidiaries, gain or loss on discontinued operations, extraordinary items, minority interest, and the effects of changes in accounting principles. An enterprise may present some other measure of profitability, in addition to operating profit or loss, for example, net income. If it does so, it must disclose the basis of the computation.

3. Identifiable assets. Identifiable assets are assets used in a segment, including a portion of assets used jointly by two or more segments. Loans and advances made by one segment to another are not to be included in the assets of a segment unless it is a financial segment—that is, a segment that charges for the supply of financial facilities.

4. Other related disclosures. Other related disclosures include depreciation, depletion, and amortization expense, and capital expenditures (mainly additions to property, plant, and equipment).

Statement No. 14 also requires disclosure of information about export sales and major customers. Export sales are sales made from a domestic segment directly to overseas customers (and not through a foreign segment). They are to be reported separately in aggregate, and analyzed by appropriate geographic areas, when they amount to 10 percent or more of sales to independent customers. The amount of revenue obtained from any single customer also is to be disclosed if it amounts to 10 percent or more of total sales.

The rationale of required disclosures. The board gave as its main reasons for adopting Statement No. 14 the belief that information about the results of segments would be useful to the users of financial reports, in helping them to assess past enterprise performance and to predict future results. This usefulness had to be weighed, however, against two negative factors: possible unreliability of the information and the costs of producing it. Both factors were discussed in an appendix to Statement No. 14, explaining the board's conclusions.

The measurement of the results of the operations of segments for purposes of external reporting is subject to much the same difficulties as measurement for the purposes of internal decisions and control. Choice of a method of transfer pricing can significantly affect the apparent profitability of a segment. It also is important in the motivation of decisions within the enterprise. However, choice of the best transfer pricing system for purposes of motivation may produce misleading numbers for segment profit or loss. For example, as noted above, marginal cost may be an efficient transfer price for purposes of motivation, but its use may force some producing segments to report a loss; the loss can be avoided by use of a two-part transfer pricing system, but that device involves establishing segment profit numbers that are partly arbitrary. The allocation to segments of costs incurred centrally also can be arbitrary to some extent. These arbitrary elements raise questions about the reliability of information about segment results. The board recognized that the reliability of segment information might be less than the reliability of some information included in the consolidated statements. However, it took the view that any lack of complete reliability was insufficient to invalidate the information overall. In essence, it seemed to be saying that the information was highly relevant to users overall, that some parts also were reliable, and that the unreliable parts would not destroy the worth of the more reliable parts.

The costs of the information were considered under two headings. First, the preparation, auditing, disclosure, and use of the information might involve direct additional costs. The board thought that these costs would be slight mainly because reports of segments (or divisions) would be useful for internal purposes and presumably, therefore, prepared already. Second, an indirect cost might be attached to the publication of segment reports: the cost of competitive disadvantage. Some claimed that the disclosures might be helpful to competitors and therefore harmful to their own businesses. This consideration also failed to influence the board. They pointed out that the disclosures would not be in great detail and that they could not be expected to be more harmful than the standard disclosures required of an enterprise that operated in a single industry.

Research into the Usefulness of Segment Reporting. As noted above, segment reporting has been advocated on the grounds that it is likely to be helpful to users of financial reports in assessing future results. Several researchers have investigated this claim. One line of approach has been to develop mathematical models for predicting current earnings (1) using past consolidated earnings and (2) using past segment information. The two sets of predictions are compared with actual earnings to discover whether models based on segment information yield the better predictions. The FASB's recent Statement on the objectives of financial reporting [FASB, 1978] suggests that the users of financial reports ultimately wish to predict future cash flows. However, prediction of earnings can be argued to be an important step toward the prediction of cash flows.

The studies of predictions of earnings have generally found that models based on segment information give better predictions than models based on consolidated information. One study found average errors (mean absolute errors) of 26.41 percent in predictions based on consolidated information. A model based on segment sales and consolidated profit margins had lower error levels of 24.22 percent, and a model based on segment sales and segment profit margins achieved a futher reduction to 22.92 percent [Collins, 1976]. Another study of U.K. data found similar results. The error level in a model based on consolidated data was 25.51 percent. A model using segment sales and consolidated profit margins gave an error level of 22.69 percent; and a model based on segment sales and segment profit margins gave an error level of 22.92 percent [Emmanuel and Pick, 1980]. These studies suggest that segment sales may be the key piece of information. Segment profit margins seem to add little or nothing to predictive ability, possibly a signal that the unreliability of the profit measurements is a matter of some importance. However, the matter cannot be regarded as settled until additional research results are available. The research results depend on the selection by the researchers of a model for predictions. Possibly the models used up to now do not use the full potential of segment information (or, indeed, of consolidated information).

Another approach has been to avoid the specification of predictive models and use financial analysts to make predictions instead. The researchers compared predictions made by analysts who had only consolidated information with predictions made by analysts who had segment information. They found that the analysts' predictions did not improve on the average when segment information was available, but that the consensus among the analysts was greater. In other words, segment information might be viewed as reducing perceived uncertainty [Barefield and Comiskey, 1975]. Somewhat similar conclusions were reached in another study [Ortman, 1975].

Some studies have focused directly on the assessment of risk rather than on the prediction of earnings. Several studies suggest that segment information may be helpful in the assessment of risk [Kinney, 1971; Collins and Simonds, 1979; Ajinkya, 1980], but that conclusion is not undisputed [Horwitz and Kolodny, 1977].

In summary, it seems that research studies undertaken up to now provide a good deal of support for the belief that information about segment results is useful. Exactly what information should be reported is a more difficult question and must await the results of further research.

BIBLIOGRAPHY

Abdel-khalik, A. R., and E. J. Lusk, "Transfer Pricing—A Synthesis," *The Accounting Review*, January 1974, pp. 8–23.

Ajinkya, B. B., "An Empirical Evaluation of Line of Business Reporting," *Journal of Accounting Research*, Autumn 1980, pp. 343–361.

Backer, M., and W. B. McFarland, *External Reporting for Segments of a Business* (National Association of Accountants, New York, 1968).

Barefield, R., and E. Comiskey, "The Impact of the SEC's Line of Business Disclosure Requirement on the Accuracy of Analysts' Forecasts of Earnings per Share," Purdue University Working Paper, March 1975.

Benston, G. J., "The Role of the Firm's Accounting System for Motivation," *The Accounting Review*, April 1963, pp. 347–354.

Collins, D. W., "Predicting Earnings with Subentity Data: Some Further Evidence," *Journal of Accounting Research*, Spring 1976, pp. 163–177.

———, "SEC Line of Business Reporting and Earnings Forecasts," *Journal of Business Research*, May 1976, pp. 117–130.

Collins, D. W., and R. R. Simonds, "SEC Line of Business Disclosure and Market Risk Adjustments," *Journal of Accounting Research*, Autumn 1979, pp. 352–383.

Emmanuel, C. R., and R. H. Pick, "The Predictive Ability of U.K. Segment Reports," *Journal of Business Finance and Accounting*, Summer 1980, pp. 201–218.

Ezzamel, M. A., "Divisional Cost of Capital and the Measurement of Divisional Performance," *Journal of Business Finance and Accounting*, Autumn 1979, pp. 307–319.

Financial Accounting Standards Board, *Financial Reporting for Segments of a Business Enterprise*, Statement of Financial Accounting Standards No. 14 (FASB, 1976).

————, *Objectives of Financial Reporting by Business Enterprises*, Statement of Financial Accounting Concepts No. 1 (FASB, 1978).

————, *Financial Reporting and Changing Prices*, Statement of Financial Accounting Standards No. 33 (FASB, 1979).

Fitzgerald, R. D., A. D. Stickler, and T. R. Watts, *International Survey of Accounting Principles and Reporting Practices* (Price Waterhouse International, New York, 1979).

Hirshleifer, J., "On the Economics of Transfer Pricing," *Journal of Business*, July 1956, pp. 172–184.

————, "Economics of the Divisionalized Firm," *Journal of Business*, April 1957, pp. 96–108.

————, "Internal Pricing and Decentralized Decisions," in C. Bonini, R. Jaedicke, and H. Wagner (eds.), *Management Controls: New Directions in Basic Research* (McGraw-Hill Book Company, New York, 1964), pp. 27–37.

Horwitz, B, and R. Kolodny, "Line of Business Reporting and Security Prices: An Analysis of an SEC Disclosure Rule," *The Bell Journal of Economics*, Spring 1977, pp. 234–249.

————, "Segment Reporting: Hindsight after Ten Years," *Journal of Accounting, Auditing and Finance*, Fall 1980, pp. 20–35.

Jensen, M. C., and W. H. Meckling, "Theory of the Firm: Managerial Behavior, Agency Costs and Ownership Structure," *Journal of Financial Economics*, October 1976, pp. 305–360.

Kinney, W. R., "Predicting Earnings: Entity versus Subentity Data," *Journal of Accounting Research*, Spring 1971, pp. 127–136.

Mautz, R. K., *Financial Reporting by Diversified Companies* (Financial Executives Institute, New York, 1968).

McNally, G. M., "Responsibility Accounting and Organizational Control: Some Perspectives and Prospects," *Journal of Business Finance and Accounting*, Summer 1980, pp. 165–181.

Mepham, M. J., "The Residual Income Debate," *Journal of Business Finance and Accounting*, Summer 1980, pp. 183–199.

Organization for Economic Co-operation and Development, *International Investment and Multinational Enterprises* (OECD, Paris, 1976).

Ortman, R., "Analysis of Alternative Accounting Procedures," *The Accounting Review*, April 1975, pp. 298–304.

Rappaport, A., P. A. Firmin, and E. M. Lerner, *Segment Reporting for Managers and Investors* (National Association of Accountants, New York, 1972).

Reece, J. S., and W. R. Cool, "Measuring Investment Center Performance," *Harvard Business Review*, May/June 1978, pp. 28–46.

Scapens, R. W., "Profit Measurement in Divisionalized Companies," *Journal of Business Finance and Accounting*, Autumn 1979, pp. 281–305.

Securities and Exchange Commission, *Securities Act Release No. 34-9000*, SEC, October 21, 1970, and *Release No. 10591*, January 10, 1974, Accounting Series Release No. 154, 1974, and No. 177, 1975.

Solomons, D., *Divisional Performance: Measurement and Control* (Financial Executives Research Foundation, New York, 1965, and Richard D. Irwin, Homewood, Ill., 1968). This book contains an extensive bibliography relating to the subject matter of this chapter.

Tomkins, C., *Financial Planning in Divisionalized Companies* (Haymarket Publishing, London, 1973).

United Nations, *International Standards of Accounting and Reporting for Transnational Corporations* (United Nations, New York, 1977).

Zimmerman, J. L., "The Costs and Benefits of Cost Allocations," *The Accounting Review*, July 1979, pp. 504–521.

CHAPTER **7**

Financial Forecasts

and Projections*

Robert K. Elliott
Partner, Peat, Marwick, Mitchell & Co.

USE OF PROSPECTIVE FINANCIAL STATEMENTS

Definitions. A *financial forecast*[1] for an entity is an estimate of the most probable financial position, results of operations, and changes in financial position for one or more future periods. *Most probable* means that the assumptions have been evaluated by management and that the forecast is based on management's judgment of the most likely set of conditions and its most likely course of action. Most probable is not used in a mathematical or statistical sense, but is used to mean management's best estimate. An *entity* means any unit, existing or to be formed, for which financial statements could be prepared in conformity with generally accepted accounting principles or another comprehensive basis of accounting. Where an entity is to be formed in the future, management would be the promoters or other individuals responsible for directing the operations of the entity.

A *financial projection*[2] for an entity is an estimate of financial position, results of operations, and changes in financial position for one or more future periods based on assumptions that are not necessarily the most likely. Management may label prospective financial statements a projection for either of two reasons: (1) They have stipulated one or more assumptions rather than using the most probable ones, possibly because of matters beyond their control; or (2) they lack a sufficient level of support or confidence to assert that the presentation is "most probable," that is, their best estimate.

Prospective financial statements is the generic term for financial projections and forecasts.

Purpose of Prospective Financial Statements. The purpose of prospective financial statements is to improve financial decisions. Because the payoffs of

---

[1] Adapted from the AICPA's definition [AICPA, 1980].

[2] Adapted from the AICPA's definition [AICPA, 1980].

financial decisions lie in the future, prospective financial statements are relevant to financial decisions. The usefulness of prospective financial statements is measured not by whether they "come true" but by whether they improve the financial decision being made. Because it may not be possible to measure whether use of prospective financial statements improved any one specific decision, usefulness should be thought of as a long-run concept: Over many decisions, does use of prospective financial statements result in generally better decisions?

The frequent production and use of prospective financial statements suggests that the financial marketplace finds them useful despite the demonstrable fact that they often do not "come true."

Special-purpose prospective financial statements may be prepared for specific business or personal needs, including, but not limited to, the following:

To apply for a certificate of need
To apply for a rate increase
To negotiate a royalty agreement
To plan an estate
To minimize income taxes
To decide whether to buy or lease

In most cases, these special-purpose prospective financial statements are used only by the entity, or by the entity and at most one other party with whom the entity is dealing directly. In these cases, the entity (and the involved party, if any) can decide on whatever type of prospective financial statements they find useful or whatever assumptions they find useful.

If these special-purpose prospective financial statements would not be useful for other purposes (or perhaps even be misleading), they are frequently restricted in distribution and may contain a legend to that effect.

General-purpose prospective financial statements are prepared in such a way that they are expected to be useful for any type of financial decision by any potential user or class of users. General-purpose prospective financial statements are often published for the use of present and potential debt and equity investors.

The preparer cannot establish an individual understanding with each member of the public who may be in possession of the prospective financial statements. Therefore, the most prudent course is to issue either (1) a forecast or (2) a projection that is as close to a forecast as circumstances permit and that includes disclosures of all material departures from a forecast (in particular, a clear identification of any assumptions that are not most probable). In the absence of disclosure to the contrary, a member of the public is entitled to believe that prospective financial statements in his or her possession represent management's best estimate (i.e., are a forecast).

This chapter is applicable to general-purpose financial statements, although much of the information is also relevant to special-purpose prospective financial statements.

When to Publish Prospective Financial Statements. As noted above, prospective financial statements should improve financial decisions, but they also involve costs. As a general rule, prospective financial statements should be published whenever the present value of the benefits exceeds the present value of the costs.

Benefits. Prospective financial statements result in improved financial decisions because they reduce uncertainty about the future. That reduction in uncertainty results in a lower risk premium demanded by capital suppliers, thus resulting in a lower cost of capital. For debt, that translates into a lower interest rate, and for equity, a higher per-share price. Underwriters may speak about the marketability of an issue being higher when prospective financial statements are published; this is a clear indication that prospective buyers would demand a higher return without the prospective financial statements.

Costs. There are several costs associated with publishing prospective financial statements. First is the cost of preparation. (Even if an entity prepares prospective financial statements for its own use, it often incurs additional costs to improve the documentation and disclosure when it plans to publish.) Second is the cost of independent review by a CPA. (Although retaining a CPA to report on prospective financial statements is generally optional, and thus should also meet a cost-benefit test, the association of an independent reviewer is mandatory in some states when prospective financial statements are published in an offering document.) Third is the cost of publication. And fourth is the potential cost of defense should litigation arise over the prospective financial statements. (See "Legal Responsibility of Management" for further discussion of legal risks.)

There are certain circumstances in which it is fairly unlikely that benefits will exceed costs of publishing prospective financial statements. Stable entities for which there is a wealth of information in the public domain are unlikely to publish prospective financial statements. Historical financial statements of a stable company give a reasonable basis for prediction, particularly in light of the other public information, which can be used to adjust expectations based on historical results. Frequently, these entities have publicized their plans and expectations. Given the availability of all this information, the publication of prospective financial statements would provide minimal reduction in uncertainty and therefore minimal reduction in the cost of capital. Market confirmation of this expectation is available: Few, if any, New York Stock Exchange companies publish prospective financial statements.

Conversely, there are other circumstances in which it is fairly likely that the benefits of publishing prospective financial statements will exceed the costs: Those where there is a new entity or a major change in the entity. In these cases, historical financial statements do not exist or are not relevant for making predictions. Prospective financial statements in these cases are useful in reducing investor uncertainty and, therefore, the cost of capital. Market confirmation of this expectation is also available: It is common to include prospective financial statements in offering statements intended to raise funds to construct new capital facilities (or substantially expand existing facilities). Examples include airports, bridges, highways, stadiums, hospitals, hotels, oil drilling ventures, shopping centers, apartment buildings, barge fleets, and drilling rigs.

PREPARATION OF PROSPECTIVE FINANCIAL STATEMENTS

Developing a Model

Identifying key factors. The first step in developing prospective financial statements is to identify the key factors on which the prospective results of the entity will depend. The AICPA [1980] suggests that the consideration of key factors focus on such areas as the following:

1. Availability and cost of resources needed to operate. Principal items usually include raw material, labor, short- and long-term financing, and plant and equipment.
2. The nature and condition of markets in which the entity sells its goods or services, including final consumer markets if the entity sells to intermediate markets.
3. Factors specific to the industry, including competitive conditions, sensitivity to economic conditions, accounting policies, specific regulatory requirements, and technology.
4. Patterns of past performance for the entity or comparable entities, including trends in revenue or costs, turnover of assets, uses and capacities of physical facilities, and management policies.

Relating key factors. Once the key factors affecting the future results of the entity have been identified, they must be related in functional form. These relationships may be thought of as a system of equations and constraints. For example, sales equals units sold times unit price. In this case, productive capacity represents a constraint on unit sales. For a hotel, room rentals may be estimated by the product of the number of rooms, the occupancy rate, and the rental rate. In this case, the constraint is 100 percent occupancy of available rooms.

The relationships among key factors may be quite complex and in some cases reciprocal. For example, in the simple relationship, sales equals quantity times price, quantity may be a function of total demand and the entity's market share. Yet market share will certainly be a function of price. Price will be affected by value, but will also tend to be constrained by cost (few entities being willing to sell consistently below cost). Market share will also be affected by advertising, but the amount of advertising will of necessity be limited by profits. It is readily seen that the entire system of equations for a financial forecast can become complex.

Values. Once a set of relationships has been set up for the key factors, it is necessary to supply values for the variables in the equations. These values will be of four types.

1. Internal facts. If the entity is an existing entity, it has a set of existing conditions at the beginning of the prospective period. These include its existing physical and intangible assets, obligations, executory contracts (for raw material supplies, for sales, for labor, etc.), workforce, patents, and so forth. The values for these items are known or determinable with considerable accuracy. For a new entity, there will be no useful internal facts.

2. Internal assumptions. Internal assumptions represent values for matters that are, to a large extent, under management control. For example, the intended investments in fixed assets, research and development, and advertising during the prospective period are largely under management's control, though constrained by fiscal resources and subject to change. Because these matters are governed by management's intent, they can be estimated with a reasonable degree of assurance.

3. External facts. External facts represent matters that will affect the prospective results that are virtually known for the prospective period. Examples include the tax rates, regulations, and laws that apply to the entity. Although these can change, they are usually not expected to be volatile in the intermediate future. Therefore, they can be estimated with a reasonable degree of assurance.

4. External assumptions. External assumptions are the remaining values that need to be specified, and to a great extent, the real subject of the forecast or projection. They relate to the unknown future actions of suppliers, customers, workers, and the general vagaries of the economy. The estimation of these values is subject to more uncertainty.

Estimating Values for External Assumptions. Estimating the values that relate to external assumptions takes familiarity with the intended business and good business judgment. There are fundamentally two methods, which can be combined as needed in the circumstances: expert consensus and mathematical modeling.

Expert consensus. The expert consensus method involves (1) obtaining predictions, and the rationale for the predictions, from persons expert in the subject matter; (2) feeding all the predictions and rationale back to each of the experts; and (3) obtaining revised predictions and rationale from each. The process is reiterated until the predictions converge and consensus develops. For example, when an entity is trying to estimate future sales, it may elicit the view of certain of the following, all of whom may have expert knowledge of some aspect(s) of the future sales: salespeople, sales managers, sales representatives, distributors, market research personnel, advertising personnel, middle management, and top management. The differing perspectives of these persons are all relevant to the estimation task, and it is expected that the views of each may affect the views of the others as a consensus forecast is reached. By virtue of the different perspectives involved, it is expected that most relevant facts will be brought to bear and a realistic forecast, one that is not too optimistic nor too pessimistic, will result.

Mathematical modeling. The mathematical modeling method involves (1) building mathematical models that incorporate the relevant causal variables, (2) determining the past relationship of these variables to the value to be estimated, and (3) using this model to predict future values. For example, a multiple regression model could be built that expresses sales as a function of consumer demand, number of sales outlets, and marketing efforts. This model could be calibrated on past data and then used to predict future sales based on predicted values for the causal variables. This example assumes a formal model, but the essential benefits can be obtained by less formal methods, such as graphic techniques or ratio and trend analysis.

Forecasting and projecting methods are frequently hybrid methods employing features of both the expert consensus and modeling approaches. The relative weighting of the two approaches varies from case to case.

When estimating future values, it is wise to avoid trying to use methods that operate at too high a level of aggregation. For example, when estimating sales for a diversified company with product lines that are quite different from each other (e.g., sold in different markets), it will generally be appropriate to estimate sales for each product line separately and then aggregate. Individual product line sales predictions may also constitute a better base on which subsequently to estimate costs of sales and expenses, which frequently have a different structure for different product lines.

Prospective Financing Needs. Typically, the development of prospective financial statements focuses on estimating the transaction streams—sales, costs, cash receipts, and cash disbursements. It is necessary, however, to apply these streams to the existing financial structure and to project financial position at future times. There are two reasons to do this:

1. It is necessary to know if the projected operations can be financed. Financing consists of two components: fixed capital, which is usually considered in the prospective statements; and working capital, which is often overlooked in the prospective process. If prospective cash disbursements exceed receipts, financing must be available. If analysis of the prospective balance sheet at the time of the cash need indicates the unlikelihood that cash could be raised, it is necessary to develop more realistic assumptions.

2. One of the elements of cash flow is interest income and expense, which can be estimated only if the net financing position is estimated at various points during the prospective period.

The analysis of interim financial positions during the prospective period should be relatively more frequent during periods of major change in the operation, for example, during a construction and startup period, or when operations are unusually seasonal or cyclical. In some cases, it is advisable to consider financial position on a monthly basis during the prospective period.

Feedback in the Modeling Process. During the course of developing prospective financial statements, there are many occasions when the implications of assumptions made earlier will suggest the advisability of revising those assumptions. Therefore, it is common to revise and refine key assumptions throughout the prospective process. For example, a finding that a facility will not be fully occupied may lead to an adjustment in the proposed size of the facility, a greater assumed marketing effort, or a revised pricing structure. Also, a finding that proposed operations will lead to an untenable debt–equity ratio may lead to a greater assumed equity particiation.

The prospective modeling process can be shown graphically as in Exhibit 1. In box A is the set of assumed values that drive the forecast. Box B contains the set of relationships (equations and constraints) used to predict future events and transactions. Box C contains the predicted events and transactions in quanti-

EXHIBIT 1   Prospective Modeling Process

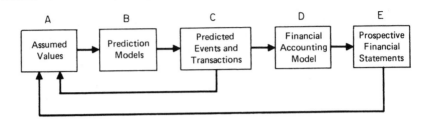

tative terms. These values are then input to box D, which is the financial accounting model. This model converts the predicted events and transactions into a set of prospective financial statements (in box E).

Exhibit 1 shows arrows from boxes C and E back to box A. These arrows mean that the results in boxes C and E may lead to revision of the assumed values in box A. The predicted events and transactions in box C may be inconsistent with management's plans and intentions, resulting in adjustment of the input values in box A. Similarly, the prospective financial statements in box E may demonstrate, for example, that a proposed project will not generate sufficient cash flows to meet the debt service requirements. Therefore, the proposal may be modified (or even abandoned), with consequent revision of the values in box A.

This feedback and revision process is an essential ingredient of the prospective process and frequently results in a revision of plans. In effect, the prospective modeling process becomes a part of management's decision and planning process.

Sensitive Assumptions. Certain assumptions are typically more sensitive than others. An assumption is sensitive if there is a reasonably high probability that the prospective financial results will be materially different due to a different value than that assumed. A variation in any assumption may lead to materially different results, but the probability of material variation is low for some assumptions. This may be for two reasons: (1) Although a relatively small variation would have a material effect, the likelihood of even a small variation is very low (e.g., the federal tax rate or the labor rates as specified in a union contract for the prospective period); or (2) even a large variation would not materially affect the results (e.g., the assumed expense for paper towels in the washrooms).

Typically, there are a few assumptions that are particularly sensitive for a given entity. For example, the occupancy rate for an apartment building or the short-term interest rate for a finance company would be very sensitive assumptions. Management should identify the particularly sensitive assumptions for their entity and devote special attention to developing support for those assumptions and studying their relationship with other assumptions.

Implicit Assumptions. It is not possible to identify all assumptions underlying a prospective presentation. Important assumptions to the prospective results, such as conditions of peace and absence of natural disasters, are rarely identified or studied. Leaving such assumptions in the background is both reasonable and practical as long as there is a reasonable expectation that current conditions will prevail.

Length of Period for Prospective Financial Statements. The time period to be forecasted or projected is governed by the needs of users of the prospective financial statements. The period should be long enough so that users can evaluate the consequences of the decision they are considering.

Where an entity is planning to construct new facilities or substantially expand existing facilities, the prospective statements should generally cover the period through completion of construction and the startup period for use of the facilities and the beginning of the period of normal operations. It is important to cover this entire period, first, to understand how long it will be until normal operations are attained; second, to see the expected normal level of operations as a basis for further projections; and third, to permit evaluation of the adequacy of financing during the construction period.

When a prospective entity is planned as a tax shelter, it is usual to structure the deal to (1) generate losses in early years and profits in later years and (2) convert profits to capital gains to the maximum extent. Thus an understanding of the proposed deal may require prospective statements covering the entire period of losses, then reversal to gains, and finally to sale of the property resulting in the capital gain.

Naturally, as the period covered by the prospective statements lengthens, it becomes more difficult to develop a forecast because well-supported assumptions may not be possible for the distant future. It is therefore common to convert the prospective statements for later years to projections rather than forecasts. Management still should make their best effort to foresee the most likely outcome, but naturally would be reluctant to make a public assertion that it is the most probable outcome. The point at which the presentation is switched from a forecast to a projection is arbitrary, but reflects management's judgment as to the time beyond which their confidence in the outcome drops below the point that they are willing to label the presentation "most probable."

AICPA Guidelines for Preparation. The AICPA has published guidelines for preparation of financial forecasts [AICPA, 1975a]. Although these guidelines do not explicitly cover projections, many of their provisions may be adapted to preparation of projections.

The AICPA states that forecasts are ordinarily prepared as the output of a forecasting system and that their guidelines apply to a "system." However, they go on to state that even informal forecasting efforts may be viewed as a system:

> There may be circumstances in which a financial forecast is prepared without benefit of a formal system—for example, forecasts prepared for a new enterprise or for a very small company. In such situations, a formal

work program and an appropriately constituted forecast project team may be utilized in place of a forecasting system and still conform to these guidelines. The work program must provide for adequate definition of the procedures, methods, and practices to be employed.

The AICPA discusses its guidelines in some detail, but summarizes them as follows:

1. *Single most probable result.* A financial forecasting system should provide a means for management to determine what it considers to be the single most probable forecasted result. In addition, determination of the single most probable result generally should be supplemented by the development of ranges or probabilistic statements.

2. *Accounting principles used.* The financial forecasting system should provide management with the means to prepare financial forecasts using the accounting principles that are expected to be used when the events and transactions envisioned in the forecast occur.

3. *Appropriate care and qualified personnel.* Financial forecasts should be prepared with appropriate care by qualified personnel.

4. *Best information available.* A financial forecasting system should provide for seeking out the best information, from whatever source, reasonably available at the time.

5. *Reflection of plans.* The information used in preparing a financial forecast should reflect the plans of the enterprise.

6. *Reasonable assumptions suitably supported.* The assumptions used in preparing a financial forecast should be reasonable and appropriate and should be suitably supported.

7. *Relative effect of variations.* The financial forecasting system should provide the means to determine the relative effect of variations in the major underlying assumptions.

8. *Adequate documentation.* A financial forecasting system should provide adequate documentation of both the forecast and the forecasting process.

9. *Regular comparison with attained results.* A financial forecasting system should include the regular comparison of the forecast with attained results.

10. *Adequate review and approval.* The preparation of a financial forecast should include adequate review and approval by management at the appropriate levels.

Responsibility for Prospective Financial Statements. Prospective financial statements are the responsibility of the management of the entity for which they are prepared. This must be the case, because only management is in a position to know its intentions and be able to operate the entity to achieve the prospective results. The AICPA has described management's responsibility for a forecast[3] as follows [AICPA, 1980]:

> The forecast including the underlying assumptions is the responsibility of an entity's management. Management cannot guarantee that forecasted

---

[3]The AICPA document did not deal with projections, but the logic and conclusions would be similar.

results will be attained, because achievability depends on many factors that are outside management's control; however, management controls operations by planning, organizing, and directing activities. Management, therefore, is in the best position to develop reasonable assumptions with respect to the key factors upon which financial results depend.

Management may enlist the assistance of outside parties in preparing the forecast. For example, an accountant who is engaged to review and report on the forecast may provide such assistance by helping management identify assumptions, participating in information gathering, or performing the mechanical aspects of preparation.... Regardless of the extent of the accountant's participation, the forecast assumptions remain management's responsibility. The accountant may assist management in the formulation of assumptions, but management must evaluate the assumptions, make key decisions, and present the assumptions as their own.

Legal Responsibility of Management. Management is responsible for prospective financial statements it disseminates. The mere dissemination of prospective statements does not, however, constitute a legal obligation to achieve them. There has been a modest amount of litigation over prospective statements, which can be summed up as follows: If management disseminates prospective statements in good faith and has a reasonable basis for them, the courts will not hold management liable merely for failure to achieve the prospective results.

Under the common law, if a user of the prospective financial statements feels aggrieved and decides to sue management, the burden is on the user to prove that management lacked good faith at the time it disseminated the prospective statements or that it did not have a reasonable basis for them.

If the entity is registered with the Securities and Exchange Commission (SEC), the rules are the same. Although the securities statutes generally provide that the burden of proof is on the issuer; the SEC has adopted a rule for prospective information that places the burden on the user, just as under the common law [SEC, 1979]. The protections of the SEC's "safe harbor" are available only if (1) the prospective financial statements are included in a filing with the commission or in the annual report to shareholders and (2) the registrant's filing of Form 10-K is up to date. The "safe harbor" is denied to investment companies under the Investment Company Act of 1940. It should also be noted that the "safe harbor rule" is only a rule of the SEC, not a law. Its efficacy will be established only by litigation in the future.

PRESENTATION OF PROSPECTIVE FINANCIAL STATEMENTS

Presentation and disclosure of financial forecasts is governed by the AICPA's "Statement of Position 75-4" (SOP 75-4) [AICPA, 1975b]. The AICPA has not yet published presentation and disclosure standards for financial projections, although it plans to do so. The AICPA's requirements for forecasts, however, are generally applicable to projections. Therefore, the following discussion is adapted from SOP 75-4.

Format. Prospective financial statements should preferably be presented in the format of the historical financial statements that would be issued for the period(s) covered. Prospective information presented in the format of historical financial statements facilitates comparison with financial position, results of operations, and changes in financial position of prior periods as well as those actually achieved for the prospective period.

Minimum presentation. At a minimum, the AICPA directs that the following information shall be presented (when applicable):

1. Sales or gross revenues
2. Gross profit
3. Provision for income taxes
4. Disposal of a segment of a business and extraordinary, unusual, or infrequently occurring items
5. Net income
6. Primary and fully diluted earnings per share for each period presented when required for historical financial statements for the period
7. Significant anticipated changes in financial position
8. Summary of significant prospective financial statement assumptions
9. Summary of significant accounting policies

Accounting Principles. Prospective financial statements should be prepared on a basis consistent with the generally accepted accounting principles expected to be used in the historical financial statements to be issued during the prospective period. A summary of the accounting principles used should be disclosed, although if a summary appears elsewhere in the document containing the prospective financial statements (e.g., in the historical financial statements), the disclosure may be done by cross-reference.

Historical financial statements are generally prepared on an accrual basis. Frequently, however, it is desirable for the prospective financial statements to disclose cash flows and cash position. This is often accomplished by preparing accrual-basis prospective statements and then adjusting the net income for noncash items. The advantage of this method is that the historical financial statements of future periods, as they are published, can be compared with the prospective statements to monitor progress toward achievement.

Presentation of Amounts. Amounts in prospective financial statements should be presented as single amounts, although such amounts may be supplemented by the presentation of ranges to emphasize the tentative nature of the amounts and the degree of uncertainty associated with specific amounts.

Assumptions. Management should disclose the assumptions that are most significant to the prospective financial statements. There should be some indication of the basis or rationale for these assumptions and the sources of information used in their development.

It is also desirable to disclose the relative effect on the prospective results of variations in sensitive assumptions.

Identifying the assumptions to be disclosed requires the careful exercise of good-faith judgment by management. The disclosures should include the following:

1. Assumptions as to which there is a reasonable possibility of the occurrence of a variation that may significantly affect the prospective results

2. Assumptions about anticipated conditions that are expected to be significantly different from current conditions, which are not otherwise reasonably apparent

3. Other matters deemed important to the prospective information or to the interpretation of the prospective information

Proprietary information. There is no obligation to disclose information that would be harmful to the entity, such as information that would be of value to competitors or other adverse parties. Although all significant assumptions should be disclosed, they need not be presented in such a manner or in such detail as would adversely affect the interests of the entity.

Assumptions not the most probable. In a projection, one or more assumptions may not be those management deems most probable. These assumptions should be clearly identified and the reasons given for using assumptions other than the most probable. In general-purpose prospective statements, users are entitled to assume that the presentation represents management's best estimate absent information to the contrary.

Caption. Assumptions should be captioned in a manner that best characterizes their nature, such as "Summary of Significant Forecast (or Projection) Assumptions." It should be made clear that the assumptions disclosed are not all-inclusive and that they were based on circumstances as they existed at the date the prospective presentation was prepared. The AICPA recommends a statement such as the following for a forecast:

> This financial forecast is based on management's assumptions concerning future events and circumstances. The assumptions disclosed herein are those which management believes are significant to the forecast or are key factors upon which the financial results of the enterprise depend. Some assumptions inevitably will not materialize and unanticipated events and circumstances may occur subsequent to [date], the date of this forecast. Therefore, the actual results achieved during the forecast period will vary from the forecast and the variations may be material.

Obviously, the foregoing introduction would have to be modified to accompany a projection.

Period to Be Covered. The period covered by the prospective presentation should be governed by the needs of the users. See the discussion under "Length of Period for Prospective Financial Statements."

Correction and Updating. *Correction* of prospective financial statements refers to modification because of subsequent discovery of a flaw that existed at the time they were published. When management discovers that prospective financial statements that are being relied on by others contain a flaw that existed at the time of preparation, they should inform users that the statements should no longer be relied on, and if practicable supply corrected statements. Failure to notify users of a flaw reasonably promptly after its discovery may turn an innocent and defensible error into an intentional and indefensible error.

Updating of prospective financial statements refers to keeping users informed as to the progress in achieving the prospective results as the period expires. When there is regular reporting of historical financial information, it is not generally necessary to update forecasts. It may be prudent, however, to notify users of subsequent developments materially inconsistent with the forecast if publication of historical results that would inform users of the departure is not imminent.

Frequently, management issues prospective financial statements on a one-time basis and has no intention to update. In such cases, management should include that intention in the original disclosure. Following is illustrative language that management could use:

> The following financial forecast was prepared to assist prospective bond-holders in estimating whether the operations of the XYZ Company may be expected to support a $10,000,000 bond issue. Because it is expected that the entire bond issue will be sold within 90 days hereafter, management does not intend to update this forecast to reflect changes in present circumstances or the occurrence of unanticipated events.

The SEC has reminded registrants of their obligation to make prompt disclosure of material facts regarding their financial condition [SEC, 1978]. This would extend, in their view, to situations where management no longer believes that its previously disclosed prospective financial statements have a reasonable basis.

THE CPA'S ASSOCIATION WITH PROSPECTIVE FINANCIAL STATEMENTS

Role of the CPA. Certified Public Accountants offer a range of consulting services relating to prospective financial statements. These services can aid preparers by providing such assistance as the following:

1. Help in identifying sources and reliability of prospective information that can be used in the preparation of prospective statements
2. Help in identifying the key factors affecting prospective results in the preparer's industry
3. Help in formulating assumptions
4. Help in performing the mechanical aspects of preparing the prospective statements, that is, translating the assumptions into a prospective presentation
5. Help in identifying and using computerized prospective models
6. Help in analyzing the sensitivity of assumptions
7. Help in avoiding internal inconsistencies in the prospective statements

8. Help in developing the presentation and disclosure of the prospective presentation so that it will be most understandable and helpful to users

9. Help in dealing with the sometimes intricate process of negotiating and closing debt and equity deals

In addition to the above, CPAs offer a range of services involving public reporting on prospective financial statements. Such reports offer varying degrees of assurance on the prospective reports, including one or more of the following:

1. Assurance that the prospective presentation is mathematically correct and consistent with the stated assumptions

2. Assurance that the prospective presentation is presented in conformity with presentation and disclosure standards of the AICPA

3. Assurance that the assumptions form a reasonable basis for the prospective financial statements

The involvement of a CPA in the prospective process can offer both management and users a degree of assurance that the legal requirements of good faith and a reasonable basis for the forecast are met.

The assurances offered by the CPA do not and cannot cover the following matters, and no CPA would warrant otherwise:

1. The CPA does not make predictions of the outcome of future events nor vouch for the achievability of the prospective results. (This is not only a matter of prudence, but a requirement of the AICPA Code of Professional Ethics, Rule 201-E.)

2. The CPA does not make any representations as to whether the entity publishing prospective financial statements represents a sound investment opportunity.

3. The CPA does not take primary responsibility for prospective financial statements, because only management of the entity, which is in a position to manage the entity to achieve the prospective results, can take such responsibility. Accordingly, the CPA does not assert that he or she "prepared" a prospective presentation, because preparation includes the selection of assumptions and only management is in a position to select the assumptions (the CPA may assist, but management must evaluate the assumptions, make key decisions, and present the assumptions as their own).

The remainder of this section discusses the CPA's role of reporting on prospective financial statements, not various other services offered by CPAs.

Levels of CPA Assurance. There are two basic levels of assurance that CPAs offer on prospective financial statements: compilation and review. "Compilation" of prospective financial statements has not been defined by the AICPA. The term is used here by analogy with the term compilation as used for historical financial statements, because the levels of procedures and reporting are similar. The AICPA is developing compilation standards for prospective financial statements at the time this chapter is being written. "Review" of financial forecasts has been defined by the AICPA [AICPA, 1980]. The AICPA has not defined a service of review of a projection as of the time this chapter is being written, though it is developing policy on the matter. This chapter nevertheless discusses review of a projection on the basis that (1) CPAs are offering such a service and (2) the levels of procedures and reporting are similar to those of a review of a forecast.

The procedures and reporting for both compilation and review are discussed in detail in the next two sections, but a brief comparison is presented here to aid in visualizing the two services:

Objectives	Compilation	Review
1. The prospective financial statements are mathematically accurate.	X	X
2. The prospective financial statements are consistent with the stated assumptions.	X	X
3. The assumptions are internally consistent.	X	X
4. The accounting principles used in the prospective financial statements are appropriate for the entity.	X	X
5. The accounting principles used in the prospective financial statements are consistent with those used by the entity in the past.	X	X
6. The presentation and disclosure of the prospective financial statements are appropriate (e.g., for a forecast, are in conformity with AICPA SOP 75-4).	X	X
7. Although the CPA has not evaluated the assumptions, nothing has come to his or her attention to cause the belief that they are unreasonable.	X	
8. The assumptions form a reasonable basis for the prospective financial statements.		X

As can be readily seen from this comparison, the principal difference between a compilation and a review is in the level of attention the CPA devotes to studying the assumptions and the consequent degree of assurance expressed on them. This difference, however, is critically important, because the assumptions are the essence of the prospective statements, and assurance that they are reasonable is of great importance to the user.

The procedures involved in compiling prospective financial statements are not especially time-consuming and are usually offered by the CPA for a relatively modest fee. However, the procedures involved in studying the assumptions are generally quite time-consuming and thorough and usually entail a substantially higher fee. In some cases, the ratio of fees for a review of a given set of prospective financial statements might be 10 or more times as high as for a compilation.

As defined previously in this chapter, there are two kinds of prospective financial statements (forecasts and projections) and two kinds of reporting services CPAs offer (compilation and review). Exhibit 2 shows schematically how the types of services relate to the types of information.

Exhibit 2 has two axes. The vertical axis represents management's belief in the probability that prospective results will be achieved. By definition, if management believes that a prospective presentation represents the most probable

EXHIBIT 2

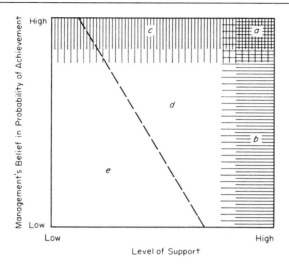

outcome, it is a forecast. Therefore, the shaded area at the top of Exhibit 2 represents forecasts. Management may present prospective statements it does not believe most probable for a number of reasons. For example, it may have made a bid for a material contract that it may not get; nevertheless, management wishes to show the results if the contract is received. Or management may wish to show the level of occupancy at which it would break even, even though it expects to do much better than that. Or, finally, management may wish to present multiple presentations, not all of which can be most probable (e.g., side-by-side presentations of prospective results if a utility is awarded the full rate increase it seeks and if it is denied any increase, where the most probable result may be somewhere in between).

The horizontal axis represents the level of support for the prospective financial statements, that is, the level of rationale and documentation to support the assumptions and relationships underlying the presentation.

The region in Exhibit 2 labeled *a* represents presentations for which management has a high belief in the probability of achievement and has a high level of support for the presentation. This region represents a reviewable forecast under the AICPA's standards for review of a financial forecast [AICPA, 1980]. (This presentation would also be compilable at a lower cost than for a review.)

The region labeled *b* represents less probable but well-supported presentations. An example might be a public utility seeking a rate increase. The company may develop a high level of support for the projections for (1) the full requested increase and (2) no increase. Once the actual increase becomes known, the level of support may permit the presentation to be converted to a forecast with little or no additional support. This region represents a reviewable projection in the view of many CPAs, although the AICPA has not yet established policy in this area. (This presentation would also be compilable at a lower cost than for a review.)

The region labeled c represents presentations for which management has a high degree of belief but a lower level of support. Because of the low level of support, no CPA would issue a review report, but could issue a compilation report. Thus region c represents compilable forecasts. (Often management may elect to label such presentations projections because of their low level of support, notwithstanding their degree of confidence in the outcome.) An example of this type of presentation is where a real estate developer with considerable expertise and experience in projects of the type being contemplated develops a prospective presentation on the strength of his or her knowledge but does not go to the trouble to assemble documentary support for the assumptions on the reasonable basis that personal knowledge is sufficient.

The region labeled d represents presentations that cannot be called forecasts, because management does not believe them most probable, nor can they be reviewed, because of too low a level of support. This region represents compilable projections. An example is a breakeven analysis by a real estate developer based solely on personal knowledge of the real estate business.

The region labeled e represents those presentations with a combination of low probability and low support that would usually lead a CPA to decline to be associated with the presentation. The CPA declines because of a fear that (1) the presentation stands too high a chance of misleading users, and (2) the chances of litigation against the CPA are unacceptably high. Different CPAs will draw the line defining region e at different places, depending on their own philosophies and judgments, but all CPAs will draw such a line somewhere.

Compilation of Prospective Financial Statements. The AICPA has not defined compilation of prospective financial statements, nor has it defined standards for such work, though at the time this chapter is being written, the AICPA is developing such a definition and standards. The following discussion is not based on authoritative pronouncements but is representative of the practice of many CPAs.

Compilation procedures. Following are commonly applied compilation procedures:

1. List or obtain a list of assumptions underlying the prospective financial statements and consider whether assumptions have been made with respect to all key factors on which the prospective results appear to depend.

2. Read the assumptions for possible internal inconsistencies.

3. Inquire about the accounting principles used in the entity's historical financial statements and those expected to be used in the prospective period.

4. Perform or test the computations made to translate the assumptions into prospective financial statements.

5. Read the prospective financial statements, including the disclosures of assumptions, for appropriateness of accounting principles, presentation, and disclosure.

6. Read any available historical financial statements that have been prepared for an expired part of the prospective period for consistency with the prospective results.

7. Based on the above, consider whether any of the assumptions appear to be inappropriate, incomplete, or unsatisfactory for the prospective presentation. If any assumptions do not meet this test, they should be revised.

The above procedures do not provide assurance that the CPA will become aware of all significant matters that would be disclosed by more extensive procedures.

Compilation reporting. When a CPA has completed compilation procedures and has no reason to refuse to be associated with a prospective presentation, he or she may issue a report on the compilation. There are no present standards for such a report, but CPAs' compilation reports must report on the character of work performed and the degree of responsibility they are taking (AICPA Code of Professional Ethics, Interpretation 201-2).

The CPA's report might appear as follows:

> We have compiled the accompanying projected balance sheet, statements of operations, retained earnings, and changes in financial position, and summaries of significant assumptions and accounting policies of XYZ Company as of December 31, 19XX, and for the year then ending. A compilation does not include procedures to evaluate the reasonableness of assumptions as a basis for the projection. We have no responsibility to update this report for events and circumstances occurring after the date of this report.
>
> Because a compilation of projected financial statements is limited as described above, we do not express a conclusion or any form of assurance on the projected financial statements or the underlying assumptions. Furthermore, some assumptions inevitably will not materialize, and unanticipated events and circumstances may occur; therefore, the actual results achieved during the projection period will vary from the projected financial statements and the variations may be material.
>
> [signature of firm]
[date]

Under certain circumstances, CPAs will include a restriction on report distribution in their reports to inform management that the report is limited to a stated distribution and to warn users for whom it is not intended, but who nevertheless obtain it, that they should not rely on it for their purposes. An example of a report restriction is as follows:

> This report is solely for the use of X State Health Authority in considering whether to grant a certificate of need for the proposed project and is not to be distributed to nor used by any other party for any other purpose.

If the CPA has reservations about being associated with the prospective financial statements, and they are not satisfactorily revised, the most prudent course of action for the CPA is to withdraw from the engagement and refuse to issue any report.

Review of Prospective Financial Statements. The AICPA has issued standards for review of financial forecasts [AICPA, 1980] but has not yet developed policy on review of financial projections at the time this chapter is being written. The following discussion, as it relates to forecasts, is consistent with the AICPA pronouncements, and, as it relates to projections, has been adapted from the AICPA's standards for forecasts, as often applied in practice.

Review procedures. The CPA's procedures for review of prospective financial statements include all the procedures listed above for compilation plus the following:

> The CPA should perform those procedures considered necessary in the circumstances to enable him or her to report on whether he or she believes the assumptions provide a reasonable basis for management's forecast.

The CPA can conclude that the assumptions provide a reasonable basis for the prospective financial statements if he or she concludes (1) that management has explicitly identified the factors expected materially to affect the operations of the entity during the prospective period and has developed appropriate assumptions with respect to such factors and (2) that the assumptions are suitably supported.

Although the CPA can reach a conclusion that the assumptions provide a reasonable basis for the prospective financial statements, he or she cannot conclude that any outcome is most probable because (1) realization of the prospective results may depend on management's intentions, which cannot be reviewed; (2) there is substantial inherent uncertainty in forecast assumptions; and (3) some of the information accumulated about an assumption may appear contradictory. Different but similarly reasonable assumptions concerning a particular matter might be derived from common information. However, if the preponderance of information supports each significant assumption, a basis exists for reporting a belief that the assumptions provide a reasonable basis for management's forecast.

The accountant typically concentrates review attention on assumptions that are

Material to the prospective amounts
Especially sensitive to variations
Deviations from historical trends
Especially uncertain

The AICPA discusses support for assumptions as follows [AICPA, 1980]:

> Support for assumptions may include market surveys, engineering studies, general economic indicators, industry statistics, trends and patterns developed from an entity's operating history, and internal data and analyses, accompanied by their supporting logical argument or theory. . . . Support for a forecast can range from information based on informed opinion (such as economists' estimates of the inflation rate) to data that can be tested in traditional ways (such as completed transactions).

The AICPA illustrates six pages of review procedures [AICPA, 1980, pp. 15–20].

Review reporting. When a CPA has completed a review of a financial forecast and is satisfied with the presentation, he or she may issue a review report.

Following is the AICPA's standard report on a financial forecast (which could be adapted for a financial projection):

> The accompanying forecasted balance sheet, statements of income, retained earnings, and changes in financial position, and summary of significant forecast assumptions of XYZ Company as of December 31, 19XX, and for the year then ending, is management's estimate of the most probable financial position, results of operations, and changes in financial position for the forecast period. Accordingly, the forecast reflects management's judgment, based on present circumstances, of the most likely set of conditions and its most likely course of action.
>
> We have made a review of the financial forecast in accordance with applicable guidelines for a review of a financial forecast established by the American Institute of Certified Public Accountants [AICPA Guide for a Review of a Financial Forecast, 1980]. Our review included procedures to evaluate both the assumptions used by management and the preparation and presentation of the forecast. We have no responsibility to update this report for events and circumstances occurring after the date of this report.
>
> Based on our review, we believe that the accompanying financial forecast is presented in conformity with applicable guidelines for presentation of a financial forecast established by the American Institute of Certified Public Accountants [AICPA, SOP 75-4, 1975b]. We believe that the underlying assumptions provide a reasonable basis for management's forecast. However, some assumptions inevitably will not materialize and unanticipated events and circumstances may occur; therefore, the actual results achieved during the forecast period will vary from the forecast, and the variations may be material.
>
> [signature of firm]
[date]

There are two types of report other than the standard report:

1. If the CPA believes that the forecast departs from the requirements of SOP 75-4 or that one or more significant assumptions are unreasonable, he or she will issue an adverse report.

2. If conditions preclude the application of one or more procedures the CPA considers necessary, he or she will issue a scope limitation report that expresses no conclusion on the prospective financial presentation.

The CPA may also expand the report to include other information and comments, to refer to the work of another CPA whose work was relied on, to comment on the responsibility assumed with respect to historical information presented with the forecast, or to emphasize a matter regarding the prospective financial statements.

INTERPRETATION OF PROSPECTIVE FINANCIAL STATEMENTS

Nature of Prospective Financial Information. The user of prospective financial information should always bear in mind that no one can foretell the future and that the purpose of prospective financial information is not to predict the future, but to improve the quality of decisions made in the present. The following quotation from the AICPA should help to keep the interpretation of prospective information in focus [AICPA, 1975a]:

> Forecasts are derived through a combination of judgment and science in which history, plans, reactions, aspirations, constraints and pressures all play a part. Forecasts are based on management's assumptions of future events, some of which assumptions are explicit, but many of which are implicit. The assumptions, in turn, are based on present circumstances and information currently available, including both internal and external data. Forecasts may be affected favorably or unfavorably by many factors such as revenues, costs, employee relations, taxes, governmental controls, and general economic conditions. Accordingly, there is no assurance that the forecasted results will be achieved.
>
> No one can know the future. Predictions are based on information about the past and present. Of necessity, judgment must be applied to estimate when and how conditions are likely to change. These judgments may subsequently prove to be inaccurate; thus, the accuracy and reliability of a forecast can never be guaranteed. Forecasts, by their very nature, are subject to error. When a succession of forecasts is made over a period of time, it is inevitable that at some point a particular forecast will turn out to have been significantly inaccurate. Because of this, forecasts may require updating and revision when conditions significantly change.
>
> Forecast information is substantially less subject to objective verification than historical data. Expected results are often not achieved because of unforeseen occurrences. When working with or using forecast information, it is essential to understand the inherent exposure to inaccuracy involved in any forecast.
>
> The difficulty in making a financial forecast can vary significantly from enterprise to enterprise, from industry to industry, and from time to time. Also, a financial forecast can be especially difficult to prepare in the case of a new venture, where no historical record of performance exists upon which to base a forecast.

With the foregoing in mind, a user who obtains prospective financial statements of an entity in which the user is contemplating a debt or equity investment should ask a number of questions about the statements. A review of this entire chapter will disclose many points that are relevant to interpreting the statements.

Questions to Ask

Management's representations. Does management represent that the presentation is a forecast or a projection? If the presentation is called a forecast, it should represent management's best estimate of future results. In order to make such a representation, management should have a high degree of confidence in the outcome. On the other hand, if the presentation is called a projection, either management lacks confidence in the outcome or has used one or more assumptions that are not the most probable. Try to ascertain which is the reason by scrutinizing the presentation.

Disclosure of assumptions. If the assumptions are not disclosed, disregard the presentation; it is useless. If the assumptions are disclosed, read them carefully to see if they appear realistic and if they appear to be based on a thoughtful analysis of the situation and sound data sources. For example, if projected sales are stated to be 110 percent of the prior year's sales without further rationale, the assumption has little or no substance. But if the sales assumption goes into factors such as projected demand, consumer demographics, competition, marketing effort, sales price, and similar relevant factors, it is probably a more substantive projection.

Time period. What is the period covered by the prospective statements? If the proposed investment contemplates taking advantage of near-term tax losses and long-term capital gains, the period covered should be long enough to assess the entire proposed operation. If the project involves substantial construction, the period covered should include the entire construction period, the startup period, and the beginning of the period of normal operations. In both cases, a shorter period does not provide enough information for the user. At the same time, the user must remember that the further into the future the presentation goes, the less information there is to support the projections and the more likely it is that there will be significant variations.

Dating of presentation. What is the date of the prospective financial statements? If the presentation is undated, it should be approached cautiously, as prospective information tends to go stale with the passage of time. Similarly, if the presentation is dated but the date is not recent, the presentation should be read with caution. What constitutes a current date is a matter of judgment; in rapidly developing circumstances, a 1-month-old presentation may be useless, whereas in more stable circumstances, even a 6-month-old presentation may be useful.

CPA association. Is a CPA associated with the presentation? If so, the presentation should be mathematically accurate, internally consistent, properly presented and disclosed, and not unreasonable on its face. The second question is the degree of responsibility assumed by the CPA. If the CPA has "compiled" the presentation (signified by a report that expresses no assurance on the presentation, or at most, says that it is mathematically accurate), no more than the foregoing may be assumed. However, if the CPA has "reviewed" the presentation (signified by a report that states that the assumptions form a reasonable basis for the prospective financial statements), it may be assumed that the assumptions have been given careful scrutiny and are suitably supported. That does not mean that they are "right," nor that the prospective results will be achieved, but it does mean that the CPA has satisfied him- or herself that they provide a reasonable basis for the prospective financial statements.

Further, if a CPA is associated with the presentation, the CPA's report should be scrutinized for indications of dissatisfaction (e.g., a statement that there is some deficiency in the presentation) or some warning(s) of special uncertainty (e.g., a comment that certain key matters are particularly risky).

Also, if a CPA has reported, the report should be read for a distribution restriction (e.g., a statement that the prospective presentation is solely for the use of [some party other than the present user]). If the user is not the party to whom the report is restricted, the report should be disregarded, because the CPA has concluded that the report may be misleading for other users. In any case, users cannot hold the CPA responsible for the report if they rely on it in the face of such a warning.

After considering all the above points, the user will have formed some impression of the potential usefulness of the prospective financial statements for his or her purpose. Assuming that they have some use, the presentation should be analyzed.

Analysis of Prospective Financial Statements

Challenge assumptions. The user should critically read and challenge all significant assumptions. If the sensitivity of assumptions is not indicated, the user should attempt to identify the particularly sensitive assumptions.

Sensitive assumptions. The user should assess the effect on the prospective results of variations in sensitive assumptions. Where possible, the user should assess the effect on the prospective results of using alternative assumptions that the user deems possible.

After completing the above analyses, the user should combine the results of the analyses with the other available information and consider the investment decision in the light of his or her investment strategies and risk preferences. With the prospective information, the user should be able to make a better investment decision.

Finally, and most important, the user must remember that prospective financial statements are not intended to be predictions. Rather, they are intended to be tools for the more complete analysis of investment decisions. When used in this way, prospective financial statements can substantially enhance investment decisions. However, prospective financial statements are neither intended, nor guaranteed, to "come true."

BIBLIOGRAPHY

American Institute of Certified Public Accountants, *Guidelines for Systems for the Preparation of Financial Forecasts*, Management Advisory Services Guideline Series No. 3 (AICPA, 1975a). This document is reprinted in [AICPA, 1980].
————, *Presentation and Disclosure of Financial Forecasts*, Statement of Position 75-4 (AICPA, 1975b). This document is reprinted in [AICPA, 1980].
————, *Guide for a Review of a Financial Forecast* (AICPA, 1980).
Causey, D. Y., Jr., *Duties and Liabilities of Public Accountants* (Dow Jones-Irwin, Homewood, Ill., 1979). This source includes a discussion of the responsibilities of both CPAs and preparers of prospective financial statements.
Kidd, R. H., *Earnings Forecasts* (Canadian Institute of Chartered Accountants, Toronto, 1976). This book has extensive coverage of virtually all aspects of prospective financial statements.
Securities and Exchange Commission, "Guides for Disclosure of Projections of Future Economic Performance," Release 33-5992 (SEC, 1978). This document is reprinted in [AICPA, 1980].
————, "Safe Harbor Rule for Projections," Release 33-6084 (SEC, 1979). This document is reprinted in [AICPA, 1980].

CHAPTER 8

The Computer and

Modern Accounting

Gordon B. Davis
Professor of Accounting and Honeywell
Professor of Management Information Systems,
University of Minnesota

The computer does not affect accounting principles, because the principles are independent of processing methods, but the enhanced processing capabilities of the computer have improved the capability of organizations to implement advanced management information systems that were not practical using manual processing methods. Therefore, those involved in the accounting and information system of an organization should understand the capabilities of computers and the changes in data processing potential because of the computer. In organizations that use computers for data processing, the accountant needs to understand computer data processing methods and the organization and processing of computer files, because the ability to do analysis, provide meaningful reports, or prepare statements depends, to a great extent, on the existence of appropriate files and processing capabilities. The accountant should also understand quality control for computer processing, because the reliance that should be placed on computer-based records is dependent on the quality of files and accuracy of processing. This chapter provides a basic background summary of the computer data processing system and its planning, development, and operation; the chapter describes the organization and management of computer files, processing methods, and control over quality of processing.

ELEMENTS OF A COMPUTER DATA PROCESSING SYSTEM

There are five basic elements in a computer data processing system. These are the hardware, the generalized software, the applications software, the procedures, and the personnel. Each of these will be described briefly.

Hardware. Hardware for computer data processing consists of equipment that can perform the following functions: data preparation; entry or input to the computer; computation, control, and primary storage; secondary (auxiliary) storage; and output from the computer. Equipment that is connected directly to the computer is termed "on-line," whereas equipment that is used separately and is not connected is called "off-line." The relationship of these equipment functions is shown in Exhibit 1.

The exact selection of equipment in a computer center will depend on the amount and type of processing being performed and the types of equipment available with the computer system being used. In general, an installation will have one or more pieces of equipment for each of the five equipment functions described earlier. The equipment for each of these functions is summarized in

EXHIBIT 1   Functions in a Computer System

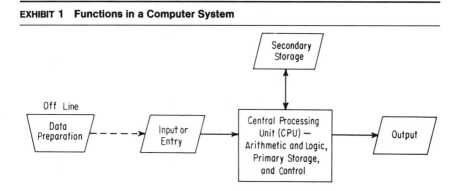

EXHIBIT 2   Type of Equipment for Each Computer Data Processing Function

Function	Type of equipment used
Data preparation	Key-disk system
	Magnetic ink enscriber
	Optical character enscriber
	Key-driven card punch
	Key-driven card verifier
	Paper tape punch
	Data collection devices with keyboard, plastic card sensor, etc., which transcribe onto some machine-readable medium
	Devices to prepare data on magnetic disk, magnetic tape, optical tape, cards, or paper tape as a by-product of another operation
	Conversion devices such as paper tape to magnetic tape
Input or direct entry	Card reader
	Magnetic tape unit
	Paper tape reader
	Magnetic ink character reader
	Optical scanner
	Console typewriter
	On-line data collection devices
	Typewriter terminal
	Visual display terminal
Computation, control, and primary storage	Central processing unit (CPU)
Secondary storage	Storage devices using the following storage media:
	Magnetic tape
	Magnetic disk
	Magnetic drum
	Magnetic core
	Semiconductors
Output	Printer
	Typewriter terminal
	Visual display terminal
	Card punch
	Paper tape punch
	Graphic plotter
	Audio response unit
	Computer output microfilm (COM)

Exhibit 2. Computers used in business data processing are often categorized into three hardware size and capability groupings:

Computer (ranging in size from small to very large)
Minicomputer
Microcomputer (also termed a personal computer)

These three designations are not precise, and the categories overlap. Exhibit 3 shows a medium-scale computer system; Exhibit 4 shows a microcomputer sys-

EXHIBIT 3   Medium-Scale Computer System with Both Magnetic Tape and Magnetic Disk Storage *(Courtesy of International Business Machines Corporation)*

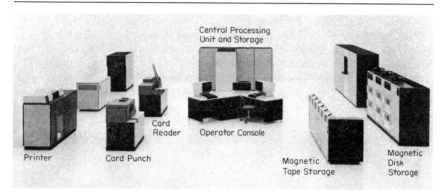

Central Processing Unit and Storage

Card Reader   Operator Console

Printer   Card Punch

Magnetic Tape Storage

Magnetic Disk Storage

EXHIBIT 4   Microcomputer Used for Business Data Processing *(Courtesy of Radio Shack, a Division of Tandy Corporation)*

tem used for business data processing. There is a trend toward the use of micro-computers in a combination of data processing and word processing (storing, editing, and manipulating text in letters, manuscripts, etc.).

Generalized Software. Software consists of computer programs and routines (set of computer instructions) that direct the operation of the computer. Software is as critical to effective use of a computer as hardware. "Software" can refer to generalized routines useful in computer operations or to programs for a specific application (such as payroll). Generalized software provides operating support for individual applications. Generalized software includes computer programs for such tasks as making printouts of machine-readable records, sorting records, organizing and maintaining files, translating programs written in a symbolic language into machine-language instructions, and scheduling jobs through the computer. It is usually obtained from the computer manufacturer or a software vendor.

Applications Software. A complete data processing application usually requires a number of programs. Each of these programs consists of a set of instructions for performing a data processing task. Applications programs are often written by the user installation but are sometimes obtained as prewritten packages from software vendors. Computer manufacturers and independent software vendors offer application programs for common data processing tasks (payroll, accounts receivable, inventory control, etc.).

Procedures. The operation of a data processing system requires procedures for obtaining and preparing data, procedures for operating the computer, and procedures for distributing the output from computer processing. These procedures include control steps such as actions to be taken in the event that there are errors in the data or a malfunctioning of the equipment.

Personnel. Computer data processing requires specialized skills. Three major jobs are found in data processing installations:

Job title	Job description
Systems analyst	Study information needs and data processing requirements. Design a data processing application. Prepare specifications and outline of the application. Prepare procedures for use.
Programmer	Prepare computer programs based on specifications prepared by the systems analyst.
Computer operator	Operate the computer.

Of these jobs, the systems analyst requires the broadest background in terms of education and understanding of organizations. The programmer has to have the specialized skill of designing computer programs and writing program instructions. The computer operator requires less training than the other jobs because the operator function involves well-defined tasks that do not require knowledge of the internal workings of either the equipment or the program. A number of other positions may be found, depending on the size and complexity of the installation. Four important additional control functions are data processing control, library control, data administration, and security. These functions may be staffed by one or more full-time personnel or, in small installations, be assigned as part-time duties for personnel who have responsibilities that are compatible with control activities. The data processing control function establishes control over input, error correction procedures, and distribution of output. The security function establishes and maintains access security for both equipment and data.

THE INFORMATION SYSTEM MASTER PLAN

A computer-based information processing system is complex and therefore needs an overall plan (often called a master development plan) to guide its construction. The plan describes the information system and how it is to be developed. The plan is normally for 3 to 5 years, with more detail for the current year. The master plan, once developed, does not remain constant but is updated as new developments occur.

The information system master plan is part of the organizational planning process. The objectives for the information system should support the accomplishment of organizational objectives, and the information system budget should be integrated with the overall budget for the organization. The master plan has two components—a long-range plan and a short-range plan. The long-range portion provides the general control, and the short-range portion provides a basis for specific accountability as to operational and financial performance.

In general, the master development plan contains four major sections:

1. Organizational goals and objectives
2. Inventory of current capabilities
3. Forecast of developments affecting the plan
4. The specific plan

Each of these sections of the master development plan is described in more detail.

Organizational Goals and Objectives. The first section of the plan might contain the following parts:

1. Organizational objectives
2. External environment
3. Internal organization constraints such as management philosophy
4. Overall objectives for the information system
5. Overall structure for the information system

Within the context of broad organizational goals and organization-wide plans, there should be goals and objectives for the information system. These can be of two types: general and specific operational goals. The general goals provide guidelines for the direction in which the information system effort should be directed. The operational goals are more specific and should be stated so that performance or nonperformance may be measured.

Current Capabilities. The current capabilities section of the plan is a summary of the current status of the computer data processing system. It includes such items as the following:

1. Inventory of
   (a) Equipment
   (b) Generalized software (system software, data management system, etc.)
   (c) Application systems
   (d) Personnel (title, years with firm, experience, etc.)
2. Analysis of
   (a) Expense
   (b) Facilities utilization
3. Status of projects in process
4. Assessment of strengths and weaknesses

Forecast of Developments Affecting the Plan. The impact of technology developments needs to be part of the long-range plan. It is sometimes difficult to estimate future technology, but most developments are announced one or more years before they become generally available to the user. Also, the broad technological changes can be perceived some years before they are implemented.

The Specific Plan. The plan should include schedules for development of new applications and a schedule of the resource requirements. These requirements can be presented as:

1. A hardware and purchased software schedule
2. Application development schedule
3. Schedule of software maintenance and conversion effect
4. Personnel resources required
5. Financial resources required

THE DEVELOPMENT OF A COMPUTER DATA PROCESSING APPLICATION

The decisions as to which applications to develop are reflected in the master plan. Once selected for development, every application needs to go through a development process. The traditional development process for data processing applications has been termed an information system development life cycle. Applications with poorly defined requirements may be developed by a trial-and-error process termed prototyping or heuristic development. The traditional life cycle concept is the most important for accounting applications, so this will be explained in detail. The heuristic development process will receive only a brief explanation.

The steps or phases in the life cycle for information system application development are described differently by different writers, but there is agreement on the basic flow. In order to manage and control the development effort, it is necessary to know what should have been done, what has been done, and what has yet to be accomplished. The phases in the development life cycle provide a basis for this management and control because they define segments of the flow of work that can be identified for managerial purposes and specify the documents to be produced by each phase.

The information system development life cycle consists of three major stages:

1. Definition of the system or application
2. Physical design
3. Implementation

In other words, there is first the process that defines the requirements for a feasible cost-effective system. The requirements are then translated into a physical system of forms, procedures, programs, and so on, by system design, computer programming, and procedure development. The resulting system is tested and put into operation. No system is perfect, so there is always a need for maintenance changes. To complete the cycle, there should be an audit of the system to evaluate how well it performs and how well it meets cost and performance specifications. The three stages of definition, physical design, and implementation can therefore be divided into smaller steps or phases as follows:

Phase in development cycle	Comments
Feasibility assessment	Evaluation of feasibility and cost/benefit of proposed application
Information analysis	Determination of information needed
System design	Design of processing system and preparation of program specifications
Program development	Coding and debugging of computer programs
Procedure development	Design of procedures and writing of user instructions
Conversion	Final test and conversion
Operation and maintenance	Day-to-day operation, modification, and maintenance
Post audit	How well did it turn out?

The eight phases can be organized in terms of the three major stages of information system development:

Stage	Phase
Definition	Feasibility assessment
	Information analysis
Physical design	System design
	Program development
	Procedure development
Implementation	Conversion
	Operation and maintenance
	Post audit

Each phase in the development cycle results in documentation. The sum of the documentation for the phases is the documentation of the application. The amount of detailed analysis and documentation in each phase will depend on the type of application. For example, a large, integrated application will require considerable analysis and documentation at each phase; a report requested by a manager will require little analysis and documentation, but all phases of the cycle are still present.

Note that the information system development life cycle does not include the equipment selection and procurement cycle. The reason is that the selection and procurement of equipment (except for some specialized equipment) is generally related to many systems rather than a single application. If an application requires equipment selection, this will generally take place during the physical design development stage.

The following percentages provide a rough idea of the allocation of effort (say, in hours) in the information system development life cycle from inception until the system is operating properly (i.e., excluding operation and maintenance). These percentages will, of course, vary with each project. The ranges shown are indicative of the variations to be expected.

Stage in life cycle	Phase in life cycle	Rough percentage of effort	Range in percentage of effort
Definition	Feasibility assessment	10	5–15
	Information analysis	15	10–20
Physical design	System design	20	10–30
	Program development	25	20–40
	Procedure development	10	5–15
Implementation	Conversion	15	10–20
	Operation and maintenance	(Not applicable)	
	Post audit	5	2–6
		100	

Definition Stage. During the definition stage the project is proposed, a preliminary survey is prepared, and the feasibility is assessed. A project may be a system module defined by the master development plan, a major maintenance project, or a project allowed but not scheduled in the master plan.

After the project or problem is proposed, the first step is to define the problem. An analyst is assigned to work with the potential users and prepare a proposal report describing the need, rough benefits, and resources to perform a feasibility assessment. The proposal report is reviewed by the department proposing the project, the information system executive, and the information system planning committee. If the project definition is approved, the feasibility study is begun to assess four types of feasibility: technical, economic, operational, and schedule feasibility. A feasibility report is prepared including a proposed development plan. If the project is approved, the next phase is information analysis.

One or more analysts work with users to define the information requirements in detail and to define the information flow. The results of the information analysis phase are as follows:

1. Layouts of the outputs (reports, transaction documents, visual display, etc.)
2. Layouts of inputs (transaction input forms, visual display, etc.)
3. The structure of the data required by the application
4. Specifications regarding items such as a response time, accuracy, frequency of updating, and volume

These specifications complete the definition of what the system is to do; the next step is to design the physical processing system to produce the defined results.

Physical Design Stage. The design of the processing system is divided into three phases—system design, program development, and procedure development. Upon completion of this stage of the life cycle, the processing system will be ready for implementation.

The physical design stage begins with the system design. This is the design of the processing system that will produce the reports specified in the information analysis. It designs the equipment usage, the files to be maintained, the processing method, the file access method, and flow of processing. The results of the system design phase are as follows:

1. File design layout and specifications
2. System flow charts showing, for example, use of equipment, flow of processing, and processing runs
3. A file-building or file-conversion plan
4. Specifications for controls to be implemented in the application
5. Backup and security provisions
6. A system test plan
7. A hardware/software selection schedule (if required)

The programming and procedure development phases can proceed concurrently. The programming phase is described later in the chapter. Procedure development involves the preparation of instructions for the following:

1. Users
2. Clerical personnel providing input
3. Control personnel
4. Operating personnel (computer operator, librarian, data administrator, etc.)

The procedure development phase can also include the preparation of training material to be used in implementation.

Implementation Stage. When the programs and procedures are prepared, the conversion phase can begin. Data is collected, files built, and the overall system tested. There are various methods of testing. One is to test the system under simulated conditions; another is to test under actual conditions, operating in parallel with the existing systems and procedures. It is generally not considered good practice to implement a complex system without one of these full system tests.

After all errors and problems that have been detected in the system test are corrected, the system is put into actual operation. When it appears to be operating without difficulty, it is turned over to the maintenance group in information processing. Any subsequent errors or minor modifications are handled as application maintenance. This is not a trivial activity—from one-third to two-thirds of analyst/programmer effort is devoted to maintenance of existing applications. Because of the importance of maintenance, it is necessary that the system be designed and documented for maintainability.

The last phase of the implementation stage is a post audit. This is a review by an audit task force (composed, e.g., of a user representative, an internal auditor, and a data processing representative). The audit group reviews the objectives and cost/benefit representations made in behalf of the project and compares these to actual performance and actual cost/value. It also reviews the operational characteristics of the system to determine if they are satisfactory.

TOOLS FOR ANALYSIS AND DESIGN OF COMPUTER PROCESSING APPLICATIONS

There are a number of systematic approaches to the task of accumulating requirements and documenting the design of a data processing application. Some basic tools for analysis and design are flow charts, decision tables, and layouts.

Flow Charts. Flow charts can be used to describe a data processing system (often termed a "system flow chart") and also to describe the logic of a computer program (termed a "program flow chart" or "logic flow chart"). Although each person may use whatever flow chart symbols are most meaningful, communication is enhanced if the American National Standard flow chart symbols (also standardized internationally) are used. These are applied to both system and program flow charts (Exhibit 5). It is customary to draw flow charts so that they read from left to right and from top to bottom. If the flow goes in a reverse direction, arrowheads are used. Arrowheads can, of course, be used in normal flow to increase clarity or readability. When it is desirable to identify a symbol for the purpose of referencing it, a notation is placed above the symbol to the left of the vertical bisector or inside the symbol separated by a stripe.

EXHIBIT 5   Summary of Major Flow Chart Symbols *(From Flowchart Symbols and Their Usage in Information Processing, ANSE X3.5-1970, Sec. 5, "Summary of Flowchart Symbols," p. 15)*

Basic Symbols

Input-Output   Process   Annotation

                              Flow Line

Specialized Input-Output Symbols   Specialized Input-Output Symbols

Punched Card   On – Line Storage

Magnetic Tape   Off – Line Storage

                                          Specialized Processing Symbols

Magnetic Disk   Decision

Punched Tape   Predefined Process (Subroutine)

Document   Sort

Manual Input

                                          Auxiliary Operation
Display

Communication Link   Manual Operation

Additional Symbols

Connector   Terminal

Example	Explanation
xxx	Notation at top to left of bisector. Identifies location of other documentation relating to the symbol, for example, a document reference or the page number of a detailed representation of the processing step.
A1	Striping—a line drawn inside the symbol near the top. The identifier inside the stripe references a detailed representation in the same set of flow charts.

The system flow chart describes both computer and noncomputer processing, identifying major computer runs (relatively independent processing segments) by a process symbol (Exhibit 6). There are differences of opinion on the value of program flow charts for detailed analysis and documentation of individual programs. When they are used, each run is documented by one or more program flow charts. A high-level program flow chart can be used to show the overall flow; a detailed program flow chart can document detailed program logic. Alternative charting procedures for analysis and documentation of computer programs consist of hierarchy charts (Exhibit 7) to show the relationship of program modules (set of instructions that perform separate functions required by the program) and HIPO charts, which include hierarchy charts plus input, process, and output diagrams (Exhibit 8).

Decision Tables. This is another method of describing the logic of a procedure or a computer program. Though not as widely used as flow charts, the decision table is useful for describing processing logic for those cases in which there are several sets of conditions leading to different sets of actions.

The decision table is a tabular form divided into four areas:

Decision Rule

Condition Stub	Condition Entries
Action Stub	Action Entries

Conditions and actions are separated by an "if . . . then . . ." relationship. The table can be read: "*if* a set of conditions exists, *then* perform the indicated actions." The stubs describe the conditions or actions and the entries indicate

EXHIBIT 6   Examples of Use of Symbols in System and Program Flow Charts

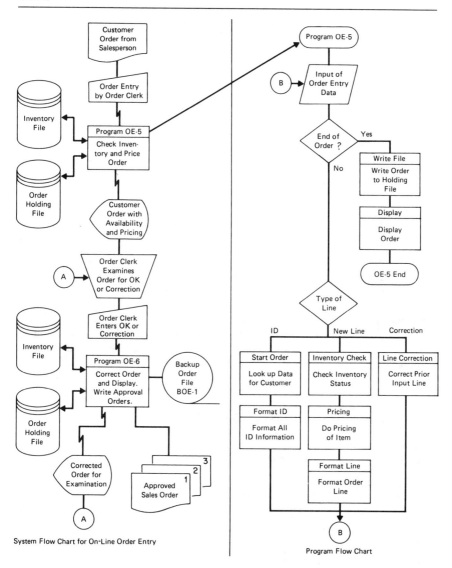

System Flow Chart for On-Line Order Entry

Program Flow Chart

whether or not the element exists; or they may specify other data such as values for the element. The most common approach is a limited entry table with Y used for yes or true as a condition entry and N used for no or false. A dash indicates that either answer is applicable. An X in the action entry specifies that the action is to be taken: a blank indicates that it is not to be taken. Each rule expresses a different set of conditions and actions. A simple decision table

EXHIBIT 7   Hierarchy Chart to Show Program Structure and Module Relationships

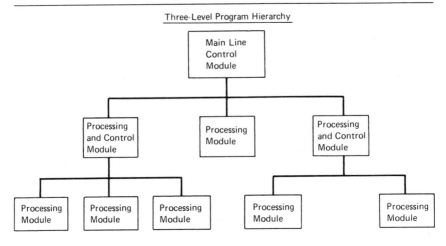

given in Exhibit 9 illustrates a table used to document the logic of the credit-granting decision (say, for department store credit).

Layouts. Layouts are used to show the format of input-output records or the placement of data in storage. Preprinted forms are generally used as a convenience. The major layout forms in use are card layout, tape or disk layout, and printer layout. Card and printer layouts are illustrated in Exhibit 10.

STEPS IN PREPARING A COMPUTER PROGRAM

The computer program development phase of the information system application development life cycle consists of the following general steps:

1. Program planning
2. Coding of computer instructions
3. Compilation (or assembly)
4. Testing and debugging
5. Documentation

The testing, debugging, and documentation activities are carried out concurrently with the first three activities.

Program Planning. The system design phase establishes general program specifications—the input, processing to be accomplished, and output to be provided. The purpose of program planning is to define the structure of the computer programs and to describe the logic to be followed by each routine.

EXHIBIT 8   Example of Input-Process-Output Diagram Used in HIPO Analysis and Documentation Methodology *(Courtesy of International Business Machines Corporation)*

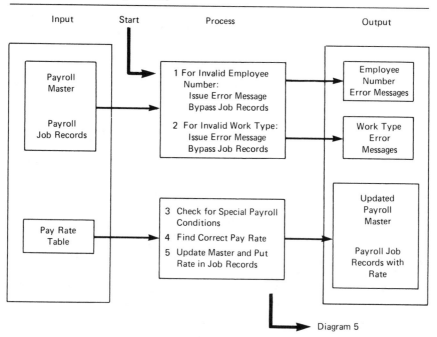

	Extended Description	Routine	Label
1	The program checks for valid employee number. If invalid, job records for that number are bypassed and an error message is printed.	IODNA	DETR
2	A check is made for correct type of work. If invalid, bypass job records and print error message.		
3	Special conditions, such as overtime, shift pay, vacation pay, or holiday pay, are checked to help determine correct rate.		
4	The master record, job records, and pay rate table are all referenced to determine correct pay rate.		
5	When all conditions are checked, payroll job records are rewritten with proper rate and the payroll master is updated.		

EXHIBIT 9   **Example of Decision Table**

				Rules			
Credit Granting Table		1	2	3	4	5	6
Conditions	Held Present Job More Than 1 Year	Y	N	Y	N	N	Y
	Lived at Present Residence More Than 2 Years	–	Y	N	Y	N	Y
	Yearly Income Greater Than $ 7,500	Y	Y	N	N	–	N
Actions	Grant Credit	X	X				
	Refuse Credit			X	X	X	
	Refer to Credit Manager						X

The structure of a computer program is generally a set of modules (also called routines or subroutines) that define independent processing tasks within the program. Major modules may be further subdivided into submodules. For example, a simple program to read data cards, perform computations, and produce a listing might have the following modules:

Input module (to read data)
Validation module (to check input data for valid data)
Processing module (to perform computations on valid data)
Error and control module (to provide error messages on invalid data and to provide control figures)
Output module (to perform output)
Main routine (to direct use of other modules)

The modular approach simplifies the program structure, allows concurrent writing and testing of individual modules, and simplifies changes and maintenance of programs. A significant program planning activity is the definition of the modular structure. The term *structured programming* is used to refer to a disciplined approach to modular design. Top-down design and development of the modules in a program is generally favored. The top, main directing routine is prepared first; other modules in the hierarchy are coded and tested in order from the highest modules down to the lowest-level modules.

The output from the program planning is a hierarchy chart showing the relationship of the program modules, specifications for each of the modules, and description of logic and processing. The traditional method for documenting flow of logic and processing is a program flow chart. A macro chart can be used to show overall logic and micro program flow charts for more detail. An objection to program flow charts is the time required to prepare them and the difficulty of updating them when the program is changed. An alternative design method is the use of a program design language to describe the program logic and flow. The resulting description is English-like but has a structure similar to a program.

Coding of Computer Instructions. Coding is the writing of the actual computer instructions. Although the computer will accept only instructions written in absolute or machine-language form, the programmer typically codes in a symbolic format more suitable for human use. The symbolic instructions must follow rather rigid rules with respect to format, punctuation, and so on. Special coding paper is usually used to assist in following the coding form. The conversion of the symbolic coding to machine-language instructions accepted by the computer is done by the assembly or compilation process.

EXHIBIT 10   Example of Card Layout and Printer Layout for Design of Input and Output Records

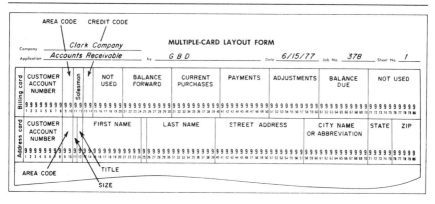

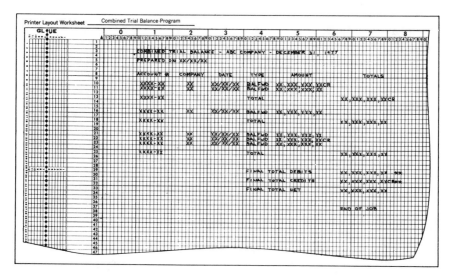

Coding may use a symbolic assembly language that is machine-oriented or a higher-level procedure-oriented language. Most data processing applications are programmed in a procedure-oriented language. Symbolic assembly language coding is used primarily for generalized software and unusual applications requiring attention to machine efficiency.

There are different procedure-oriented languages for different types of problems. The following are the most common:

Type of problem	Language
Data processing	COBOL (COmmon Business-Oriented Language)
	RPG (Report Program Generator)
Mathematical	FORTRAN (FORmula TRANslator)
	BASIC (used primarily in time sharing)
General	PASCAL
	PL/I (Programming Language One)

COBOL is the most common data processing language for all except small business computers, for which RPG is frequently used. The small microcomputers are programmed in BASIC and PASCAL. Exhibit 11 illustrates a simple COBOL program. Note the four divisions of the program: the identification division identifies the program, the environment division describes the machine environment, the data division defines the files and data items in the files, and the procedure division describes the processing procedures. A disciplined approach to programming will use coding structures and coding rules that produce clear, easily maintained programs.

There is a trend toward nonprocedural languages designed for ease of use in specifying problems to be solved (rather than procedures). These languages are especially useful for user-written applications. Examples are languages to prepare budgets, forecasts, and plans.

Compilation or Assembly. Assembly is the translation of a program written in symbolic assembly language instructions into machine-language instructions. Compilation is the term given to the preparation of a machine-language program from a program in a procedure-oriented language. The terms are sometimes used interchangeably, although they do have slightly different meanings. A program written in AUTOCODER, SPS, or BAL (names of symbolic assembly languages) is assembled, whereas a program written in FORTRAN, COBOL, BASIC, and so on, is compiled. In both cases, the assembly or compilation process is carried out by a computer program (assembler or compiler) furnished by the manufacturer or by an independent software vendor. The result is a machine-language program that performs the steps represented by the symbolic coding. Some source programs (especially for microcomputers) are interpreted and executed without being compiled. The interpret and execute mode is especially efficient for programs that are run once or only a few times.

Testing and Debugging. Application development includes a comprehensive test plan. Testing of programs is a continuous process during program devel-

EXHIBIT 11   Example of a Simple COBOL Program

```
IDENTIFICATION DIVISION.
PROGRAM-ID. PAYROLL-REPORT.
*AUTHOR. GORDON B DAVIS.
*SIMPLE COBOL PROGRAM TO READ HOURS-WORKED AND
*    RATE-OF-PAY AND TO COMPUTE REGULAR-PAY, OVERTIME-PAY,
*    AND GROSS-PAY.  OVERTIME-PAY IS ONE-AND-ONE-HALF THE
*    REGULAR RATE FOR HOURS OVER 40.
*
ENVIRONMENT DIVISION.
CONFIGURATION SECTION.
SOURCE-COMPUTER. CYBER.
OBJECT-COMPUTER. CYBER.
INPUT-OUTPUT SECTION.
FILE-CONTROL.
    SELECT PAYROLL-CARD-FILE ASSIGN TO INPUT.
    SELECT PAYROLL-REPORT-FILE ASSIGN TO OUTPUT.
*
DATA DIVISION.
FILE SECTION.
FD  PAYROLL-CARD-FILE LABEL RECORD IS OMITTED
    DATA RECORD IS PAYROLL-CARD.
01  PAYROLL-CARD.
    05  PAYROLL-ID          PICTURE X(5).
    05  HOURS-WORKED        PICTURE 99.
    05  RATE-OF-PAY         PICTURE 9V999.
    05  FILLER              PICTURE X(69).
FD  PAYROLL-REPORT-FILE LABEL RECORD IS OMITTED
    DATA RECORD IS PRINT-PAY-LINE.
01  PRINT-PAY-LINE.
    05  FILLER              PICTURE X(10).
    05  PAYROLL-ID          PICTURE X(5).
    05  HOURS-WORKED        PICTURE ZZ99.
    05  RATE-OF-PAY         PICTURE ZZ.999.
    05  REGULAR-PAY-PRINT   PICTURE $$$$$$9.99.
    05  OVERTIME-PAY-PRINT  PICTURE $$$$$$9.99.
    05  GROSS-PAY-PRINT     PICTURE $$$$$$9.99.
    05  FILLER              PICTURE X(89).
WORKING-STORAGE SECTION.
    77  REGULAR-PAY         PICTURE S999V99.
    77  OVERTIME-PAY        PICTURE S999V99.
    77  GROSS-PAY           PICTURE S999V99.
    77  CARDS-FLAG          PICTURE X(3) VALUE "YES".
*
PROCEDURE DIVISION.
MAINLINE-ROUTINE.
    PERFORM INITIALIZATION.
    PERFORM READ-CALCULATE-PRINT UNTIL CARDS-FLAG EQUAL "NO".
    PERFORM CLOSING.
    STOP RUN.
INITIALIZATION.
    OPEN INPUT PAYROLL-CARD-FILE
         OUTPUT PAYROLL-REPORT-FILE.
READ-CALCULATE-PRINT.
    READ PAYROLL-CARD-FILE AT END MOVE "NO" TO CARDS-FLAG.
    IF CARDS-FLAG EQUAL "YES"
        PERFORM PAY-PROCESSING.
PAY-PROCESSING.
    IF HOURS-WORKED OF PAYROLL-CARD IS GREATER THAN 40
        PERFORM PAY-CALCULATION-WITH-OVERTIME
    ELSE
        PERFORM PAY-CALCULATION-NO-OVERTIME.
    COMPUTE GROSS-PAY = REGULAR-PAY + OVERTIME-PAY.
    PERFORM WRITE-REPORT-LINE.
PAY-CALCULATION-NO-OVERTIME.
    MULTIPLY HOURS-WORKED OF PAYROLL-CARD BY RATE-OF-PAY OF
        PAYROLL-CARD GIVING REGULAR-PAY ROUNDED.
    COMPUTE OVERTIME-PAY = 0.
PAY-CALCULATION-WITH-OVERTIME.
    MULTIPLY RATE-OF-PAY OF PAYROLL-CARD BY 40 GIVING
        REGULAR-PAY ROUNDED.
    COMPUTE OVERTIME-PAY ROUNDED = (HOURS-WORKED OF PAYROLL-CARD
        - 40) * 1.5 * RATE-OF-PAY OF PAYROLL-CARD.
WRITE-REPORT-LINE.
    MOVE SPACES TO PRINT-PAY-LINE.
    MOVE CORRESPONDING PAYROLL-CARD TO PRINT-PAY-LINE.
    MOVE REGULAR-PAY TO REGULAR-PAY-PRINT.
    MOVE OVERTIME-PAY TO OVERTIME-PAY-PRINT.
    MOVE GROSS-PAY TO GROSS-PAY-PRINT.
    WRITE PRINT-PAY-LINE.
CLOSING.
    CLOSE PAYROLL-CARD-FILE, PAYROLL-REPORT-FILE.
```

opment. As each module of a program is coded, it is desk-checked by the programmer, who traces sample transactions through the program module logic. The next checking occurs during translation of the symbolic coding by an assembler or compiler. This process detects language use errors. As each module is completed, it is added to a main-line routine and other completed modules and they are tested by running test transactions with the program. The test transactions should use all of the program logic in order to test all program paths. The expected results of processing the transactions are compared with the computer-produced results to detect errors. During development, other programmers may review the program logic and test data in a formal review process called a *structured walkthrough*. When all modules are completed and tested, the application system is tested in operation, frequently being run in parallel with an existing system until all program errors and operating problems can be corrected.

Documentation. The documentation phase consists of completing parts of the documentation of the program and assembling other documents associated with the program. These are organized as two reports: a run manual and operating instructions. The run manual contains the complete set of documentation for the program. The sections of the run manual are, in general, the following:

Section	Description of contents
Problem definition	A description of the reason why the program was prepared and the program specifications.
System description	A general outline of the program and the related environment or application system in which the program operates. The section contains the system flow charts and record layouts.
Program description	The documentation of the program portion of the application. Contains the hierarchy chart, program listing, and other descriptions that document the contents of the program.
Operating instructions	The instructions required to run the program on the computer.
Summary of controls	A summary of the controls built into the program to detect errors.
Acceptance record	A documentation of steps taken to test the program before acceptance, record of approvals, and a record of subsequent changes.

The documentation in the run manual is kept up to date by recording all changes in it. For example, when a change is made in the program, a change record may be placed in the acceptance record section and a reference noted on the appropriate program description.

The operating instructions furnished to the computer operator provide all information necessary for the operator. This may consist of the operating instructions section of the run manual.

THE BASIC COMPUTER DATA PROCESSING CYCLE

In the computer data processing literature, *data* is used as a singular noun. This usage varies from the plural form used in accounting. The basic cycle for computer data processing consists of six phases:

1. Data capture
2. Data preparation
3. Input or direct entry
4. Data validation (input editing)
5. Processing manipulation
6. Output

The phases in the data processing cycle will be summarized briefly.

Data Capture. Data capture consists of activities for obtaining data and recording it for subsequent processing steps or other use. Data may be:

1. Recorded in a form that requires preparation before it can be input for computer processing
2. Recorded immediately in a machine-readable form, thereby bypassing part of the data preparation phase
3. Input directly into the computer, eliminating all data preparation and input activities (see Input or Direct Entry)

Data capture requiring subsequent transcription into machine-readable form consists of written notes and filled-in documents. Examples are manually prepared new employee records, manually recorded hours worked, and handwritten sales orders.

Data capture in machine-readable form involves the preparation of a machine-readable input. Some types of machine-readable input are as follows:

Handwritten numbers to be read by an optical character reader. An example is handwritten recording of meter reading for an electric utility.

Handwritten marks to be read by an optical reader. An example is a machine-scored examination.

Typewritten documents in a machine-readable font prepared at time of data capture. An example is a credit document typed by a credit interviewer directly onto a machine-readable form.

Data Preparation. There are four types of data preparation activities to make data ready for computer input:

1. Manual review of data documents and possible correction, addition, or deletion of data.
2. Preparation of processing controls such as assembling data into processing batches and making batch control totals.
3. Transcription to machine-readable form. The transcription activities may

also include verification of the correctness of the transcription and checking the validity of some data items.

4. Conversion from one machine-readable form to a storage medium having faster input characteristics.

The manual review of data prior to processing may be used to add codes or other data as well as to make sure the data is complete, legible, and reasonable. The documents need to be assembled in batches for control purposes and control totals prepared. Examples of control totals at this point are transaction record counts, totals of financial data fields such as sales, and hash totals of fields such as account numbers. The control total is written on a control document and attached to the batch.

The batches of documents are then transcribed to a machine-readable form. The transcription process may consist of:

Keying onto disk or tape storage
Punching into cards
Punching into paper tape
Typing onto a document for optical scanning
Hand writing data onto forms for optical scanning

Some of these methods of transcription can be checked by a duplicate verification operation; others require proofreading. In the case of keypunches or keydisk units, the equipment can do a validity check on a code containing a check digit. Keydisk units can also make additional checks on the data fields.

Data transcription (or data capture) utilizing an intelligent terminal (essentially a very small computer with a typewriter or visual display input device) may perform some data validation operations because the terminal can be programmed to do logic tests on the data (such as range tests).

The data preparation activities may utilize a direct-entry methodology in which the data preparation device is connected to the computer. The transcription operation (keying of data) transmits the data directly to the computer, where it is validated and stored. This approach eliminates the input phase.

In cases where data capture or data preparation has resulted in machine-readable data on media that is difficult to read or reading is slow, a data preparation phase activity may be the conversion to a more accessible or faster input speed storage. Examples of such conversion to another storage medium are

Cards to magnetic tape
Paper tape to magnetic tape
Documents read by optical character reader and transferred to magnetic tape
Transfer from keydisk storage to magnetic tape

Input or Direct Entry. The input or direct-entry phase performs the reading of data and stores it for use in program processing. Input may be direct, a transaction at a time, from a transaction input terminal (such as a typewriter or visual display unit), or may be from a batch of input media prepared during the preparation phase. Data validation is generally an integral part of input or direct entry, but will be considered as a separate step because it can be performed separately.

Data Validation. Data validation is the process that examines input data and applies various tests to determine whether or not there are errors. It is sometimes termed "editing." As described earlier, the data validation may be performed in part by a keydisk unit or an intelligent terminal used for data capture or data preparation; however, all data at input should be tested even if prior operations have tested the same data. The tests will be described in more detail later in the chapter. Control totals are also developed during data validation.

Data items that are found to be erroneous by the validation tests are rejected, put into an error file, and sent back to the data originators for correction and reentry. Control totals are adjusted for the rejected items. If there is validation at data preparation, errors may be immediately corrected and the corrected input entered. Direct input to the computer also results in an error message to the entry terminal and a rejection of the data until the error is corrected. The data items that pass the editing test are presumed to be correct and continue into program processing.

Processing Manipulation. There are essentially three major processing operations performed using input data: sequencing, transaction processing, and stored data (file) updating. Sequencing through sorting may be performed prior to transaction processing or file updating; it may also be performed after processing but prior to output in order to have the output in a convenient sequence. Transaction processing operates with input data to produce a transaction document. For example, a sales order input may be used to produce a sales invoice. File updating may involve additions, corrections, and deletions to the file records, as well as updating of stored records with transaction data. A transaction may therefore be used both to prepare a transaction document and to update a master file record. For example, a payroll transaction may result both in a paycheck and also in the updating of the master file record for the employee—for example, updating of wages-to-date, FICA-to-date, and so on.

Output. The output of processing can be output files, direct output to a terminal such as a visual display or typewriter, or a master file or other file to be held for future processing. The output files are generally printed as transaction documents or reports, but other media may be used, such as punched card turnaround document and microfilm.

ORGANIZATION AND MANAGEMENT OF COMPUTER FILES

A file is defined as a collection of related records containing data needed for subsequent data processing. Files are created when the need for a collection of records is recognized. This need may come from the processing requirements in preparing a regular report or from the need to facilitate data retrieval in response to inquiries and requests for special analysis. The organization of computer files is an important factor in computer processing methods. File organization is based on the needs of each application plus the characteristics of the file storage devices.

File Storage Devices. Storage is frequently classified into primary (or internal) storage and secondary (or auxiliary) storage. The programs being executed and the data items being processed are in internal storage; files and programs that need to be available are in auxiliary storage. Virtual storage is the use of hardware and software to segment programs in use so that only part of each need be in primary storage at any one time. Other parts of the program are brought in as they become active and are dropped if they become inactive. This method makes it appear to the user as if there were no internal memory constraints on program size.

The most common internal storage devices are semiconductors and magnetic cores, the most common secondary storage uses magnetic disk or magnetic tape. Data items are stored on a tape or disk by recording patterns of magnetic polarization on small sections of a ferrite-coated surface. Data items are stored in a specific location on the medium; no other data can be stored there without destroying the data already there. However, data can be read without losing the magnetic recording.

Locating data that is stored can be performed serially or directly (also termed randomly). The serial (or sequential) approach to record access on a file is commonly associated with magnetic tape, because the tape is read serially starting from the beginning. The first record must pass under the read/write head before the second record can be accessed; the second before the third; and so on. In order to access the last record on the file, all previous records must have been read. This is similar to a symphony on a tape cassette. In order to get to the last movement of the symphony, all other portions of the symphony must first be played.

In direct access storage, such as disk storage, the storage medium revolves and read/write arms move in and out so that any location is accessed directly by the combination of in or out movement of the arm plus the revolution of the disk. The time to access a record on a disk file consists of the seek time and the rotation time.

1. *Seek time* is the time required to position a movable read/write head over the recording track to be used.

2. *Rotation time* is the rotational delay (also termed latency) to move the disk location underneath the read/write head.

It is normal for several arms to move simultaneously so that a set of storage locations (a cylinder) are active at the same time. Note that locations on a magnetic disk can be read serially if this is desired.

Types of Files. Files are kept for a variety of purposes. Four main types of files are usually identified, as summarized in Exhibit 12. Each record in a file is identified by an identification field. A customer account number, an employee identification number, and a part number are examples of identification items. The identification item, used as the basis for sequencing and searching the file, is frequently called the *record key*. This key can be numeric, such as a social security number, or it can be alphabetic, such as a name. There can be more than one key, and a record may therefore be sequenced on one key in one file and on another key in a second file.

EXHIBIT 12   **Types of Computer Files**

Type	Purpose	Examples
Master file.............	Relatively permanent records containing statistical, identification, and historical information, which is used as a source of reference	Accounts receivable file
Transaction file..........	Also called detail file. Collection of records of transactions used to prepare transaction documents and to update a master file.	Sales invoice file; purchases file; material received file
Report file..............	Records extracted from data in transaction or master files in order to prepare a report.	Report file for taxes withheld; report file for delinquent customer accounts; report file for analysis of employee skills
Sort file................	A working file of records to be sequenced. This may be the original or a copy of a transaction file, a master file, or a report file.	

Employee No.	Name	Street Address	City and State	Gross Wages, etc.
984321	Thomas Grant	115 Crowther	New York, N.Y.	115.55

Key for Record

A record consists of data items that may themselves be formed from two or more items. This process of subdivision can be continued, the last items being termed elementary items. For example, an item DATE may be formed from three elementary items, MONTH, DAY, and YEAR.

Date	10	12	1987
	Month	Day	Year

When the item DATE is specified, the entire item is obtained. MONTH will refer only to the MONTH portion of DATE. The relationship of items in a file thus forms a hierarchical or tree form:

```
                        File
                      /      \
                Record     Record    Record, etc.
               /   |   \
           Item  Item*  Item*
          /   |    \
      Item  Item*  Item*
     /   \
 Item*   Item*                    * Elementary Item
```

In addition to the data items themselves, records in direct access storage may contain cross-referencing items called *pointers*. These establish a relationship between the record, or an item in the record, and other records or items.

Some records may be divided into two parts: a master record and detail or trailer records. For example, a customer accounts receivable record may be divided into the master portion containing the name, address, credit rating, and so on; and several trailer records each containing the data on an unpaid invoice. The trailer records are often termed *detail records* or *repeating records*.

Customer Record

File Management Activities. File management refers to all activities relating to the creation, updating, and use of files. These activities can be classed as:

1. File creation
2. File processing and maintenance
3. Selection (retrieval)
4. Extraction

File creation can refer to the establishing of an entirely new file or to the conversion of an existing file in noncomputer form to a computer file medium. The conversion of existing files is one of the difficult problems of converting to a computer system or from one computer system to another.

File maintenance is the updating of a file to reflect the effects of nonperiodic changes by adding, altering, or deleting data. To maintain a master file, new records are added to the file and obsolete or erroneous records are removed. File processing, on the other hand, is the periodic updating of a master file to reflect the effects of current data (often transaction data) in a detail file.

Selection refers to the retrieval of a record from the file. The retrieval process is straightforward but relatively time-consuming with a sequential file organization; it can become complex but requires less time when using direct access storage organization.

Extraction is the copying of selected records from a file to form a new file for analysis, report preparation, and so on. For example, from the file of all employees, the records of employees with more than 20 years of service may be extracted in order to perform an analysis of the characteristics of these employees.

File Organization. The file organization is the method in which the files are organized for retrieval purposes. The major approaches are sequential and direct access organization, used in data processing; and list organization, used primarily in retrieval applications. The sequential organization means that the records in the file are sequenced in order by a record key such as employee number, customer identification number, social security number, and so on. The record with the lowest number key appears in the first location on the file;

the record with the next higher numbered key appears next; and so on. This organization is very natural for magnetic tape processing but is also used with magnetic disk storage. In the sequential organization, it is not necessary to specify a location address where a record is stored. The records are stored in order, so that as serial processing is performed a record is located when its place in the sequence is found.

The direct organization allows a record to be located without knowing its sequence. Direct access organizations can be implemented in a variety of ways. The two most common are a randomizing procedure and an indexing method. In the randomizing procedure, the record key is manipulated arithmetically to produce a random number that looks like a storage location. This becomes a storage location for that record. If two or more records have the same location using this procedure, one of them is stored in an overflow location and a procedure is established to find the overflow record during processing. The other common direct methodology consists of indexes. An index is established for the file and during processing is searched for the desired record key. When the record key is found in the index, the storage location is indicated. One very common method of organization is indexed sequential, in which records are stored sequentially but can also be located directly through indexes.

List organizations are generally used in retrieval applications where it is desirable to know the relationship among records. List organizations use pointers (data fields containing address of other records) to link records together for retrieval purposes, or use indexes that identify all records having given attributes. There is a trend toward list organizations in order to provide the capability for a variety of user queries.

Data Bases and Data Base Management Systems. Separate applications may utilize separate files having much of the same data. Processing efficiency and improved data control can be achieved by having a common file for all of the applications having common data. Also, lookup and retrieval operations on the data are simplified and improved. However, the common files (termed a data base) require strict control over access to the data and over changes to the data by application programs. This control is achieved by a data administrator responsible for the data and software systems, called data base management systems, to manage all access and updating of the data in the data base.

The data base management system provides data that is requested by an application program and updates data items from data provided by an authorized application program. It in essence removes most of the file access and file update logic from the application program. The data base approach requires direct access files and frequently involves list organizations.

Multiple-Computer Access to Files. An organization may choose to have computers and files at several locations but interconnect the computers via data communication so that any computer in the network may access the files at any location. This is termed a *distributed network*. Another example of multiple access to files are computers that cross company boundaries to access other computers. Airline reservation computers make reservations via data communication directly to connecting airline computers. The networks create a more complex environment, but the basic input-input editing-processing manipulation methods apply.

CLASSIFICATION OF PROCESSING METHODS

Data processing literature frequently refers to only two processing methods: (1) batch processing, and (2) on-line processing. *Batch processing* is used to refer to periodic processing of batches of data, and *on-line processing* refers to immediate processing of individual transactions as they occur. This twofold classification does not take into account the fact that input and input validation may be performed in a different mode than processing manipulation.

A more complete classification of processing methods uses two dimensions: timing of input and input validation, and timing of processing manipulation.

1. *Timing of input and input validation.* Input of data and input validation may be performed either periodically on batches of transactions or immediately on individual transactions as they are entered at a terminal.

2. *Timing of processing manipulation.* Processing manipulation is performed either periodically on batches of transactions or immediately on individual transactions as they are entered via a terminal.

Based on these two dimensions, data processing applications can be classified into three major types of processing:

1. *Batch entry/batch processing:* periodic preparation of batched transaction documents and periodic processing of the batched transactions

2. *Terminal entry/batch processing:* immediate entry of single transactions that are validated and stored for periodic batch processing

3. *On-line entry/on-line processing:* immediate terminal entry of single transactions and immediate processing of single transactions

The three major classifications will now be described in more detail.

Batch Entry/Batch Processing. Processing using batches of input data is the least complex and most common method for data processing applications. The input data is collected into batches and the input, input validation, processing manipulation, and output is performed periodically (say, daily, weekly, or monthly). In a commonly used approach, the master file, which is used with transaction processing and which is updated with transactions or other data, is organized sequentially by a record key (such as employee number). The transactions to be processed (the transaction file) are sorted into the same order as the master file. The master file records are accessed serially. Each record is examined to determine if there is an updating transaction. After updating, the record is written on a new master file (or the record is written without change if there is no updating transaction). The updating process results not only in a new, updated master file, but also preserves the old master file, which is not altered by the "copy old–alter–write new" sequence. The batch of input transactions is assigned a batch number, and all audit trail references are to this batch. A listing of the transactions in each batch is normally prepared for reference purposes. Source documents are usually stored as a batch. The batch sequential mode of processing is illustrated in Exhibit 13.

A variation on the batch entry/batch processing mode is not to sequence the transactions and update file records in place rather than creating a new file by rewriting all records. This method requires the use of a direct access file device. The in-place updating means that, at the end of processing, the old file will have been altered to create the new file. In order to have a backup copy for recovery purposes, the file is copied prior to updating. The original is kept as backup and the copy is updated.

Terminal Entry/Batch Processing. It is possible to have immediate rather than delayed processing of the input. This is often termed direct entry. For example, an application may use terminals through which input data is sent directly to the computer for processing. However, in association with the periodic batch processing method, the only processing that is performed immediately is the input and validation of the data and its collection into batches. All other processing is performed by periodic batch processing runs. In other words, there is immediate data capture by the computer and validation of the input data to detect errors. Error messages are normally sent to the originator of the data so that corrections may be made immediately while the transaction is being prepared and data being entered. The error detection, error reporting, and error correction cycle is therefore substantially reduced. In cases where periodic processing is preferred, such as where the underlying organizational process is periodic, this method retains the advantages of immediate error detection through terminal data entry.

Terminal data validation may use intelligent terminals or may be on-line with access to the relevant computer files. If so, validation can take advantage of a file lookup procedure to examine the master file record associated with each transaction in order to detect any discrepancies between the input data item and the master file record. With this lookup, it is possible to determine whether or not the transaction refers to a valid master record and whether or not it is logically possible for the transaction to apply to the master record. As an example, payment transaction input validation might look up the customer record to see if there is such a customer and if the balance due is reasonable with respect to the payment amount received.

On-Line Entry/On-Line Processing. Immediate on-line processing is the most complex environment for processing (Exhibit 14). In this method of processing, a variety of transactions are accepted from remote input terminals. As each transaction is received, the master record against which it is to be processed is read, the transaction is processed, and the record updated and written back into storage. In other words, direct immediate input is followed by immediate processing of the transaction and immediate updating of the master file record. This is also termed on-line, real-time processing.

The on-line approach has problems, such as the fact that two or more transactions that apply to the same record need to be executed sequentially; otherwise updating might be incomplete. If the two transactions, A and B, arrive at the computer at the same time, the first transaction A reads the master record

EXHIBIT 13   Batch Entry/Batch Processing Using a Sequential File

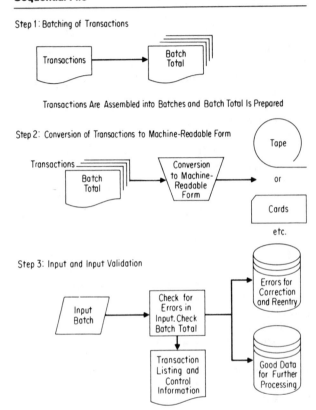

Step 1: Batching of Transactions

Transactions Are Assembled into Batches and Batch Total Is Prepared

Step 2: Conversion of Transactions to Machine-Readable Form

Step 3: Input and Input Validation

and updates it; transaction B simultaneously reads the record and updates it. When transaction A is complete, the master record with updating from A is written back into its storage location. When transaction B is complete, the master record just updated from B is placed back into storage. The updating performed by transaction A is therefore lost because transaction B was processed without knowledge of transaction A. Such "contention" matters can be solved in on-line processing, but they illustrate the additional complexity of the on-line environment.

Because the transactions are being processed on-line in this method, all the advantages of on-line input validation are available, including complete access to the master file for use in detecting errors. The immediate, in-place processing causes some changes with respect to audit trail, backup, and recovery. The input transaction can be assembled and sorted into logical batches. Backup and recovery of the file under this method of processing is performed by copying the file at periodic intervals. For example, it might be copied at the beginning of the day before any processing is performed; or in the case of very active files,

---

**EXHIBIT 13   Batch Entry/Batch Processing Using a
Sequential File (*Continued*)**

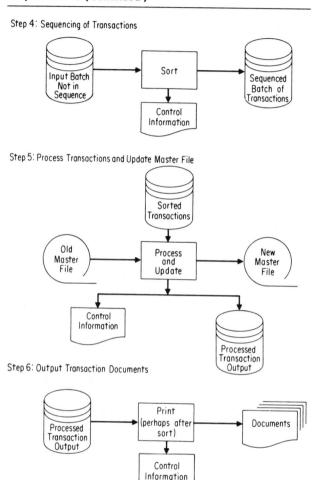

Step 4: Sequencing of Transactions

Step 5: Process Transactions and Update Master File

Step 6: Output Transaction Documents

it might be copied at regular intervals during the day (say, every hour). If there
are any problems with the file, the latest copy is used to restore from that point.

The problems of keeping the file records error-free under on-line processing
and audit trail advantages of batch processing have caused some firms to go to
a modified form of on-line processing with on-line input/editing. The firms
essentially do memo processing during the day to produce immediate
responses, but in the evening all transactions that have been input during the
day are assembled into a batch and are then processed in batch fashion using
a copy of the master file that was maintained for this purpose. The processing
during the day is therefore up to date in the sense of retrieval from the file, but
the file for financial purposes is the one that is processed during the night in a

EXHIBIT 14 On-Line Entry/On-Line Processing

Step 1: Copy Master File for Backup

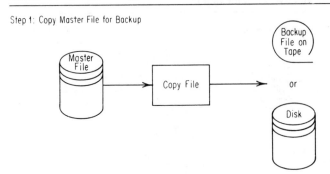

Step 2: Recording, Input, Validation, Logical Batching, and Terminal Output

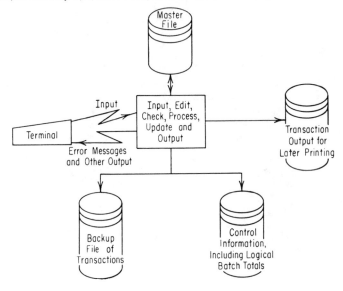

Step 3: Output Printed Transaction Documents

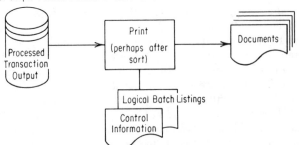

batch processing run. This removes many of the hazards of on-line processing of the file. If there is a processing or hardware problem during the day, it does not affect the quality of the master file but only the memo file.

CONTROL OVER QUALITY OF COMPUTER PROCESSING

Computer processing is all too often carried out with a higher error rate than is desirable. On the other hand, error control is not without cost, and the manager or user who understands the problems of quality control and its methods is able to evaluate the value of tighter control compared to its cost. With computer processing, there are control problems not found in manual data processing, but there are also unique, new control methods because of the capabilities of the computer.

The Organizational Control Framework in a Computer Processing System. There is a hierarchy of control in a computer data processing system. The outer level of control is provided by the company organization management and procedures. Within this framework there operates the organization and management of the data processing activity. A component part of this activity is the control function, which monitors the quality of processing. The computer processing operations are not only subject to departmental control activities but the processing programs also contain control features to detect errors. This hierarchy of control is illustrated in Exhibit 15.

EXHIBIT 15   The Framework of Control in a Computer Data Processing System

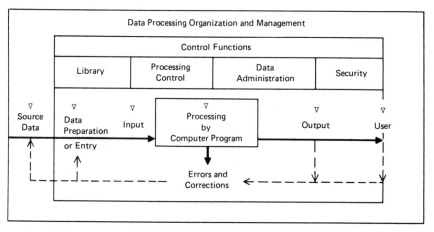

∇ = Control Point

Top management responsibility. Top management has the overall responsibility for data processing. This consists of the following:

Responsibility	Comments
1. Authorization of major systems additions or changes	Each major addition or change should be presented to management as a proposal to be evaluated in terms of its cost and the benefits to be derived from it.
2. Postimplementation review of actual cost and effectiveness of systems projects	Management should follow up on project proposals and evaluate the reasons for deviations from planned cost, planned schedule, and estimated benefit. The assessment of performance on the postimplementation review (also termed a post audit) will aid in evaluating future systems requests.
3. Review of organization and control practices of the data processing functions	Top management has the responsibility for employing competent, adequately trained data processing management personnel and for reviewing the organization and controls they establish. The controls should include computer security, data security, and backup and recovery provisions.
4. Monitoring of performance	Management should require a performance plan or standard and the reporting of deviations from this expected level of performance. The plan and variation reporting should cover four types of performance: (a) Level of processing activity (transactions, reports, etc.) compared to plan (b) Cost of data processing activities compared to planned cost (c) Frequency and duration of delays in meeting processing schedules (d) Error rates for errors detected at various control points

Data processing management responsibility. In the organization of data processing activity, it is desirable both from an operating standpoint and from a control standpoint to separate the three functions of (1) system design and programming, (2) operations, and (3) control. Some installations also separate system design and programming. Control over the storage media containing data files and programs is increased by the use of a separate file librarian. Control over the data in a data base is provided by a data administrator.

Control practices associated with data processing organization and management are as follows:

Standard procedures for application development
Standard operating procedures
Scheduling and supervision of personnel
Provisions for computer system security and data security
Provisions for backup and recovery for computer processing capabilities, data, and software
Enforcement of program documentation and program change documentation
Enforcement of requirements for audit trails
Review of operating statistics, error logs, etc.

The application of management principles to computer data processing operations will typically involve the preparation and use of a systems and procedures manual which describes standard operating procedures. The contents of the manual will usually include:

1. Standard programming procedures
2. Standard computer operating procedures
3. Control procedures
4. Organization and personnel

As with systems and procedures manuals used in other areas of activity, the manual is useful in training, supervision, and evaluation of performance.

The control function. The plan of organization and operating procedures should provide for a control function internal to data processing and for independent, outside controls. The control function internal to data processing can be divided into three parts: processing control, library control, and data base control. The internal processing control is concerned with monitoring the accuracy of processing and ensuring that no data is lost or mishandled within the department during processing. For example, if a detail transaction file is processed with the current master file to produce an updated master file, the sum of the transaction file and the related master file records should equal the total of the records on the updated master file. The person charged with the processing control function is responsible for making or reviewing the results of such a comparison. In a small installation, the data processing manager may perform these control activities; in other installations, a control staff will perform this task.

The activities of the control clerk or control group are specified both in the systems and procedures manual and in the description of control activities for each computer application. The control function will include duties such as the following:

1. Logging of input data and recording of control information
2. Recording progress of work through the department
3. Reconciling computer controls with other control information
4. Supervising distribution of output
5. Scrutiny of console logs and control information in accordance with control instructions
6. Liaison with users regarding errors, logging of correction requests, and recording corrections made
7. Scrutiny of error listings and maintenance of error log or error report

The library function provides for control over programs, data files, and documentation. The data base administrator establishes control over data bases. The security function establishes and monitors access to equipment and data.

Independent outside checks can take several forms but are basically concerned with an independent check of the functioning of the data processing department. This check may be performed by a user department. If the general ledger is, for instance, maintained on the computer, the accounting department may keep a control total of all debits and credits to be posted by the computer. This control can be compared against the debits and credits from the computer run. Another possibility is an independent quality control evaluation group in a user department where the volume of data to be controlled is large. As an example, one large corporation has a payroll processing control group responsible for evaluating the payroll data produced by the computer.

The Control Points for Computer Processing. Computer data processing requires new controls for detecting and controlling errors, but it also provides new methods of control that substitute for human controls. In a manual system, internal control relies on such factors as human alertness, care, acceptance of responsibility, and division of duties. By concentrating the data processing activity, many controls based on human judgment or division of duties are no longer available. However, the computer program provides an alternative for many manual checks. For example, the lowest-level clerk will normally react when receiving a shipping document on which to insert prices if the item cannot be found on the price list. In a computer operation, a nonmatch such as this must be programmed. Once programmed, however, it will be executed faithfully. In most instances, computer checks can be more extensive than those performed manually.

The control points at which specific data processing controls are applied to prevent or detect errors are (1) original document preparation, (2) conversion to machine-readable form, (3) input or direct entry into processing, (4) computer processing, (5) distribution of output, and (6) users of the output. It is noteworthy that only two of these control points involve machine errors or program errors. This illustrates the fact that data processing controls must include controls over human errors in source data preparation, conversion, output, and use as well as controls over the operation of the equipment and programs. The system designer should consider the entire set of controls that apply to an application and the organizational and management environment in which they are applied rather than viewing individual controls in isolation. For the purpose of this chapter, these control points will be discussed as control over input and output and programmed control over processing. An additional control problem—the protection of computer records and files—will also be covered. Hardware controls, which protect against undetected equipment malfunctions, are very reliable and normally satisfactory. Therefore, they will not be covered in this chapter.

Control over Input and Output. Input data is the weakest link in the chain of data processing events. The input data for a program may be in error for one of four general reasons: (1) It may be incorrectly recorded at the point of inception; (2) it may be incorrectly converted to machine-readable form; (3) it may be incorrectly read or otherwise entered into the computer; or (4) it may be lost in handling. Input controls should therefore be established at the point of data creation and conversion to machine-readable form, at the point the data enters the computer, and at points where the data is handled, moved, or transmitted in the organization. As with manual data processing, there should be established procedures for authorization of transactions. The authorization may take the form of signatures or initials on documents from which the input is prepared. If input data may be introduced directly into the computer system without the preparation of documents, there must be alternative means for authorization, such as some form of physical control over access to the input devices or access to the means by which they can be activated.

Before data items are used in updating files or other processing, they are usually tested for errors to the extent possible or appropriate in the light of the consequences of input errors. If errors are detected on data entered at a terminal, the transaction is not accepted and error messages are provided to assist in immediate correction. In batch processing, the erroneous transaction or record found to contain an error is shunted aside rather than stopping the computer to make corrections. It will usually be written on a temporary file to be examined later. There will thus usually be a file of rejects and an error listing indicating the reason for rejection. Items that are rejected by the input editing run should be carefully controlled to make sure that they are corrected and reentered at a later run.

Exhibit 16 presents an inventory of methods from which the system designer selects in order to achieve the level of input data error control required for an application. Each of these methods will be described briefly.

Procedural controls, data review, and input echo. Standard clerical practices and well-designed data forms impose procedural controls on the creation of data. For example, if a part number is to be written on a document, boxes

---

EXHIBIT 16   Methods for Input Data Error Control

At point data is created and converted to machine-readable form	At point data is first input to the computer or input to a terminal with checking capabilities	At point data is handled, moved, or transmitted
Procedural controls	File label (internal)	Transmittal controls
Data review	Tests for validity:	Route slip
Extended input echo	Code	Control total
Verification	Character	External file labels
Check digit	Field	
	Transaction	
	Combination of fields	
	Missing data	
	Check digit	
	Sequence	
	Limit or reasonableness test	
	Control total	

may be printed that contain the exact number of spaces required for the part number. Any clerk writing a part number containing less or more digits than the required number of characters will notice the error. Where direct input devices are used, templates over the keys, identification cards, and other procedural aids help to reduce input errors. Terminals provide instructions and format guides for input.

Some installations make a review examination of input data (especially codes that identify part numbers, product, etc.) before conversion to machine-readable form. This checking may be performed in connection with the addition of information, or it may be an entirely separate step. When data items such as codes are entered at a terminal, the terminal not only displays (echos) the input data but can provide an extended echo by displaying additional data related to the input. For example, if a part code is entered, the input echo can include a short description to aid visual verification.

Verification of conversion to machine-readable form. When data items are punched into cards or keyed onto a keydisk device, the accuracy of the data conversion can be tested by verifying the original keying operation. Punched cards are being dropped from most business data processing and replaced by terminal entry or keydisk encoding. If used, however, the data is first punched by a keypunch operator. The punched cards and original data are then given to a verifier operator, who inserts the punched card into the verifier and rekeys the punches using the original source documents. The verifier does not punch but instead compares the data keyed into the verifier with the punches already in the card. Similar verification is used with a keydisk encoder where data is recorded directly on a magnetic disk. The same device is used (at separate times) both to record data and to verify it. The verification process includes the correction of errors.

Verification is a duplicate operation and therefore doubles the cost of data conversion. Various methods are used to reduce the amount of verifying. One method is to verify only part of the data. Some data fields are not critical and an error will not affect further processing. Examples are descriptive fields containing vendor name, part description, and so on, which under most circumstances are not critical. The use of prepunched cards, prepunched stubs, and duplication of constant data during key entry may allow verification to be restricted to the variable information added by the data preparation step. A second approach used with statistical data is to verify only if the input error rate is above an acceptable level. Each operator's work is checked on a sample basis. If the operator's error rate is acceptable, no verification is made; if not, there is complete verification. Other control procedures (to be explained) may be substituted for verification such as a check digit on an account number, a batch control total, and so on.

Check digit. In most applications involving an identification number, the identification number may be verified for accuracy by a check digit. A check digit is determined by performing arithmetic operations on the code number. The arithmetic operations are performed in such a way that the typical errors encountered in transcribing a number will be detected. There are many possible procedures. All involve the use of digit weights and a modulus. For example, a simple check digit procedure might be as follows:

1. Start with a number without the check digit.
2. Multiply each digit by a weight assigned to the digit position. For example, the weights might be 1, 3, 5, 7, and 9.
3. Sum the digits in the resulting products.
4. Divide the sum by the modulus (usually 10 or 11) and keep the remainder as the check digit.
5. Add check digit to number (at end or elsewhere).

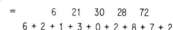

= 6 21 30 28 72

6 + 2 + 1 + 3 + 0 + 2 + 8 + 7 + 2

= 31

31 ÷ 10 = 1

676481

A check digit procedure is not completely error proof, but depending on the weights and modulus used, check digits will detect 90 to 100 percent of transposition and transcription errors and about 90 percent of random errors. The check digit does not guard against assignment of an incorrect but valid code, as for example, the assignment of a wrong but valid identification code to a customer.

The checking of the code number for the check digit either may be performed by the input device or it may be programmed into the computer. The use of the check digit as part of the input device has the advantage that an incorrect code is detected before it enters the computer process and a field checked by a check digit does not need to be verified. Example of uses are charge account numbers, employee pay numbers, and bank account numbers.

Internal file label. A file label is a record at the beginning and also possibly at the end of the file that records identification and control information. File labels are used to ensure that the proper transaction or master file is used and that the entire file has been processed. The label at the beginning is the header label, which identifies the file. Typical header label contents are as follows:

Name of file
Creation date
Purge date
Identification number
Reel number (for magnetic tape)

The trailer label is the last record and summarizes record counts, and so on, for the file.

Tests for valid data. Data items can be subjected to programmed tests by the computer or intelligent terminal to establish that the items are within the limits established for valid data. Some examples of checking that can be done are as follows:

1. Valid code. If there is only a limited number of valid codes, say, for coding expenses, the code being read may be checked to see if it is one of the valid codes.

2. Valid character. If only certain characters are allowed in a data field, the computer can test the field to determine that no invalid characters are used.

3. Valid field size, sign, and composition. If a code number should be a specified number of characters in length, the computer may be programmed to test that the field size is as specified. If the sign of a numeric field must always be positive or must always be negative, then a test may be made to ensure that there is not an incorrect sign. If the field should contain only numerics or only alphabetics, then a test may be made to determine that the field does indeed contain a proper composition of characters.

4. Valid transaction. There is typically a relatively small number of valid transactions that are processed with a particular file. There is a limited number, for example, of transaction codes that can apply to accounts receivable file updating.

5. Valid combinations of field. In addition to each of the individual fields being tested, combinations may be tested for validity. For example, if a sales-person's code may be associated with only a few territory codes, the correspondence can be checked.

6. Missing data test. The program may check the data fields to make sure that all data fields necessary to code a transaction have data in them.

7. Check digit. The check digit is verified on identification fields having this control feature.

8. Sequence test. In batch processing, the data to be processed must be arranged in a sequence that is the same as the sequence of the file. Both the master file and the transaction file may be tested to ensure that they are in proper sequence, ascending or descending as the case may be. The sequence check can also be used to account for all documents, if these are numbered sequentially.

9. Limit or reasonableness test. The limit or reasonableness test is a basic test for data processing accuracy. Input data should usually fall within certain limits. For example, hours worked should not be less than zero and should not be more than, say, 50 hours. The upper limit may be established from the experience of the particular firm. Input data may be compared against this limit to ensure that no input error has occurred or at least no input error exceeding certain preestablished limits. Examples are the following:

> The total amount of a customer order may be compared with the average order amount for the customer. If this order exceeds, say, three times the amount of the average order, then an exception notice may be printed.
>
> A material receipt that exceeds two times the economic order quantity established for the particular item might be subject to question.
>
> A receiving report amount may be compared with the amount requested on the purchase order. If there is more than a small percentage variance, then there is an assumption of an error in the input data.
>
> In a utility billing, consumption is checked against prior periods to detect possible errors or trouble in the customer's installation.

Control totals. Control totals are a basic method of error control to determine whether or not all items in a batch have been received and processed. The control total procedure requires that a control figure be developed by some previous independent processing and that the current data processing recompute this amount, comparing the resultant total with the previous total. Control totals are normally obtained for batches of data. The batches are kept to a reasonable size so that errors can be easily isolated. For example, the sales slips to be processed by computer are first added on an adding machine to arrive at a control total for the sales in the batch. A control total for payroll might be the number of employees for which checks should be prepared. There are three types of control figures: financial totals, hash totals, and document or record counts.

1. Financial totals. Financial totals are totals such as sales, payroll amounts, inventory dollar amounts, and so on, which are normally added together in order to provide financial summaries.

2. Hash totals. Hash totals are totals of data fields that are typically not added. The total has meaning only as a control and is not used in any other way in data processing. To determine that all inventory items are processed, a control total might be developed of the inventory item numbers and this control total would be compared with the sum of the item numbers obtained during the processing run.

3. Document or record count. In many cases, rather than obtaining a financial total or hash total, it may be sufficient merely to obtain a count to ensure that all documents or records have been received and processed.

Control totals prepared prior to computer processing are furnished to computer processing as an input data item. The computer is then programmed to accumulate control totals internally and make a comparison. A message confirming the comparison should be printed out even if the comparison did not disclose an error. These messages are then subject to review by the control staff. In immediate processing of individual transactions, the batch total concept may still be used. During processing, each transaction is classified into one or more logical batches and at the end of the period (such as a day), the logical batch listings with totals are prepared for review and/or comparison with physical control totals such as documents entered, cash receipts, and so on.

Movement and handling controls. Transmittal controls, route slips, control totals, and external file labels are examples of controls over the internal handling and movements of data documents and files. Control totals have already been explained, and external file labels are described in connection with file safeguards. The transmittal controls and route slips are discussed in this section.

When records move about through an organization, there is always a possibility that they may be lost or otherwise diverted from the proper processing channels. To ensure proper identification of documents as they move through the company, and more especially as data moves through the data processing steps, it is customary to use some form of status identification. As they enter the data processing center, batches of data may be logged on a listing showing the data received. As each batch passes a data processing station, it is registered, recording the fact that the batch has been processed. The batch itself usually carries a route slip that indicates the path of processing it should follow and a record of processing performed.

Output controls. The distribution of output should be controlled to ensure that only those authorized to receive reports receive them. The output should be reviewed for completeness and agreement with controls and screened for obvious errors. Persons receiving the output are an important error-detection control point, and provisions should be made in application system design for error feedback from recipients of output.

Programmed Control over Processing. The types of program controls that test the computer processing are the limit and reasonableness test, the cross-footing or cross-testing check, and control figures.

As with input data, a control over processing can be exercised by program steps that test the results of processing by comparing them with predetermined limits or by comparison with flexible limits that test the reasonableness of the results. In a payroll application, the net pay can be checked against an upper limit. The upper limit is an amount such that any paycheck exceeding the limit is probably in error. In a billing operation for a relatively homogeneous product, such as steel bars and plates, the weight of the shipment may be divided into the billing order to develop a price per pound. If the price per pound exceeds the average by more than a predetermined percentage, a message will be written for subsequent follow-up to determine if the billing is in error.

It is frequently possible to check computer data processing in a manner similar to the manual method of cross-footing. Individual items are totaled independently and then a cross-footing total developed from the totals. For example, in a payroll application the totals are developed for gross pay, for each of the deduction items, and for net pay. The total for net pay is then obtained independently by taking the total for gross pay and deducting the totals for each of the deduction items. If this cross-footing does not yield identical figures, then there has been some error in the program or processing.

Control figures developed in a manner similar to the input control totals can be used for testing the data processing within the machine. For example, the number of items to be invoiced in a billing run may be used as a control total and compared with the number of items billed on invoices.

Protection of Computer Records and Files. A data processing installation should establish and follow procedures that safeguard the program and data files from loss or accidental destruction. If loss or destruction does occur, advance provisions should have been made for reconstruction of the records. The protection of computer records and files involves physical safeguards, procedural controls, a retention plan, a reconstruction plan, and insurance.

Physical safeguards. The physical safeguards may be classified as fire and disaster protection, security protection, and off-premises storage. There should be a disaster plan that describes arrangements to be made for disaster recovery, describes what should be done in disaster situations, and defines procedures for recovery using backup facilities, duplicate files, and so on. For fire protection, the computer should be housed in a noncombustible environment. There should be storage of vital records in storage cabinets having a class C rating (1 hour at 1700°F), separate air conditioning and power controls, Halon gas fire extinguishers, and so on. Security protection safeguards both the hardware installation and the data files. For example, when confidential corporate information is kept in a machine-readable format, it should be subject to the same security precautions as are applied to written records. Off-premises storage is used to provide a further safeguard for essential data processing records. Space can be rented in a secure, fireproof location, or another storage location in the same company can be used.

Procedural controls. Procedural controls can be used in the management of a computer center in order to minimize the possibility that an operator error will result in the destruction of a data or program file. Some common methods are external labels, magnetic tape file protection rings, and library procedures.

Files should be clearly labeled so that the operator will know the file contents. Magnetic tape reels and disk packs are labeled with a paper label attached to the tape reel or disk pack. Punched-card files are usually labeled on the top of the deck by use of a felt marking pen.

A physical safeguard used to prevent writing on a magnetic tape and destroying information prior to the release date for the tape is a removable plastic or metal ring, the absence of which will prevent writing on the tape.

Library procedures provide a custodian who maintains a storage area for storage of all tapes, disks, program documentation, and so on. The librarian checks out the tapes and disk packs needed by each processing run and keeps records on use and condition of storage media.

Retention and reconstruction plan. The retention plan of a data processing department provides a means for record or file reconstruction. Source documents are retained at least until the computer file has been proved and balanced with its controls. However, other considerations may require a longer storage period for these documents. Copies of important master files, programs, procedures manuals, forms, and so on, should be maintained in secure storage, preferably off-premises.

A retention plan for files updated by rewriting (i.e., on magnetic tape) usually uses the son-father-grandfather concept. The files retained under this concept on a Wednesday (assuming daily processing) would be

Wednesday's file	(son)
Tuesday's file	(father)
Monday's file	(grandfather)

If, during processing on Thursday, the Wednesday tape was destroyed, Tuesday's tape should be processed again with Wednesday's transactions to re-create Wednesday's master tape. If no other processing or retention considerations require keeping the tape longer, the old grandfather can be released when a new one is produced.

File processing with in-place updating of records (usually using disk storage) does not automatically produce a duplicate, updated copy of the file. To provide for reconstruction, the disk must be duplicated to provide a reference point and all transactions saved until the next reference file copy is made. The reference copy can be put onto another disk or a magnetic tape.

Insurance and Bonding. Insurance should be part of the protection plan of a data processing installation. The major risk is fire, unless work is performed for others, in which case there should be liability insurance for errors or omissions in doing the work. The ordinary fire insurance policy is limited in its coverage of risks associated with losses connected with data processing. Therefore, many organizations take special data processing insurance coverage.

Although the number of losses arising from the dishonesty of data processing employees is apparently quite small, the amount of each loss has tended to be larger than under manual processing. The risks associated with the concentration of the data processing function in a relatively small number of people suggest that bonding (fidelity insurance) of data processing employees is a desirable practice.

PROCESSING REFERENCE TRAIL FOR COMPUTER APPLICATIONS

A significant consideration in the design of computer processing applications is provision for a processing reference trail. This is a trail of document references, processing references, documentation of processing steps, and so on, which allows an investigator to trace data on a source document through processing to its appearance in transaction document outputs or reports or to trace data items on output documents or reports back to the source data or source documents that were processed to produce the result. Although it is termed an "audit trail" and is necessary for auditing, the processing trail is primarily a management trail for internal company investigation. To illustrate the processing trail in a periodic or batch processing environment, the references might be as follows:

1. Source documents stored as a batch with a reference number.
2. Transaction or journal listing by batch. Transaction listing may be in the same order as the batch of documents or may be sorted for easier reference use.
3. Batch reference on all processing of input batch.
4. Summary postings to ledgers contain batch reference.

When documents are not batched or where no documents are prepared, such as in direct input, the computer assigns reference numbers and prepares logical batches of transactions that are sorted and stored or printed for reference use. For example, various transactions may be input by different operators through an input terminal. The computer maintains a record of the operator, terminal, time, and so on, for each transaction. References and control batches are prepared by sorting and printing logical groupings of the transactions. A logical batch might be all transactions of a given type for a day, all transactions by an operator for a day, and so on. The logical batch listings form a source reference for the transactions.

In complex processing environments, the intermediate listings and references are often not found. However, the processing trail from source transaction record to output record must still be maintained. This may be done by a combination of document and processing references and processing documentation.

BIBLIOGRAPHY

American Institute of Certified Public Accountants, Audit and Accounting Guide, *The Auditor's Study and Evaluation of Internal Control in EDP Systems* (AICPA, New York, 1977a).

———, Computer Services Guidelines, *Management, Control and Audit of Advanced EDP Systems* (AICPA, New York, 1977b).

———, "The Effects of EDP on the Auditor's Study and Evaluation of Internal Control," *Codification of Statements on Auditing Standards, Section 321* (AICPA, New York, 1978).

———, Computer Services Guidelines, *Controls over Using and Changing Computer Programs* (AICPA, New York, 1979).

American National Standards Institute, Inc., *Flowchart Symbols and Their Usage in Information Processing,* ANSI X3.5-1970 (ANSI, New York, 1970).

Canadian Institute of Chartered Accountants, *Computer Audit Guidelines,* distributed in the United States by AICPA, New York, 1975.

———, *Computer Control Guidelines,* distributed in the United States by AICPA, New York, 1975.

Davis, G. B., D. L. Adams, and C. A. Schaller, *Auditing & EDP,* 2d ed. (AICPA, New York, 1983).

Davis, G. B., and M. H. Olson, *Management Information Systems: Conceptual Foundations, Structure, and Development,* 2d ed. (McGraw-Hill Book Company, New York, 1983).

Edpacs: a newsletter on EDP audit, control, and security (Automation Training Center, Reston, Va.).

Institute of Internal Auditors, *Systems Auditability and Control: Control Practices* and *Systems Auditability and Control: Audit Practices* (IIA, Altamonte Springs, Fla., 1977).

Mair, W. C., D. R. Wood, and K. W. Davis, *Computer Control and Audit* (Institute of Internal Auditors, Altamonte Springs, Fla., 1978).

Weber, R., *EDP Auditing: Conceptual Foundations and Practice* (McGraw-Hill Book Company, New York, 1981).

CHAPTER 9

Compound Interest—

Concepts

and Applications

Roman L. Weil
Professor of Accounting, University of Chicago

COMPOUND INTEREST

Compound interest refers to *interest on interest* as well as *interest on principal* or to situations where interest is paid periodically during the term of the loan. *Simple interest* applies to the principal only and is paid only once, at maturity of the loan. Compound interest underlies most contemporary interest applications. To illustrate the difference between compound and simple interest, let B = the principal amount (amount borrowed or loaned) and i = the interest rate.

	Simple interest	Compound interest
Amount after 1 period	$B(1 + i)$	$B(1 + i)$
Amount after 2 periods	$B(1 + 2i)$	$B(1 + i)(1 + i)$
Amount after n periods	$B(1 + ni)$	$B(1 + i)^n$

Thus if B = \$100 and i = 8 percent, after 5 periods the total amount at simple interest would be \$140 [= \$100(1.40)], whereas the amount at compound interest would be \$146.93 [= \$100(1.46933)]. Simple interest was widely used in the past on many types of loan obligations. With the advent of "truth-in-lending" legislation, however, disclosure of the true effective (compound) rate on loans became required. Thus a 2-year loan of \$100 with simple interest of 10 percent would require the borrower to pay \$120 for the loan. Most loans, of course, are paid off in installments, so that the *average* amount borrowed over the 2-year period is approximately \$50. The true effective rate of interest, if monthly payments of \$5 (= \$120/24) each are required, is close to 20 percent. This fact was often not disclosed before truth-in-lending legislation.

Amount of \$1. To what amount F will \$1 grow at interest rate i, after n periods, with compounding once per period? The general formula is

$$F = (1 + i)^n$$

The $(1 + i)^n$ amount need not be calculated for most interest rates. Tables have been prepared to show the amount of $(1 + i)^n$ for various interest rates and time periods. This amount is referred to as the *amount of \$1* or the *future value of \$1*. An accepted shorthand expression for this is $a_{\overline{n}|i}$ (read "small a angle n at i"). An excerpt from such a table appears in Table 1 in the Appendix of this book. When the principal amount differs from \$1, the *amount of \$1* factor is multiplied by the principal amount.

  Example 1. To how much will \$1,200 grow if placed in a savings account for 4 periods at an interest rate of 7.5 percent per period?

$$
\begin{aligned}
F &= \$1,200(1.075)(1.075)(1.075)(1.075) \\
&= \$1,200(1.075)^4 \\
&= \$1,200(1.33547) \\
&= \$1,602.56
\end{aligned}
$$

  Example 2. How many periods n are required for our savings account deposit of \$1,200 to double? The interest rate is 7.5 percent and F = \$2,400.

$$\$2,400 = \$1,200(1.075)^n$$

$$\frac{\$2,400}{\$1,200} = (1.075)^n$$

$$2 = (1.075)^n$$

From a table, we find that $(1.075)^{10} = 2.06103$. Hence, our account will double in slightly less than 10 periods.

Doubling rule of thumb. A useful rule of thumb for computing doubling periods is the following: If the rate of interest is r percent per period, then a sum invested at r per period, compound interest, will double in $69/r + .35$ periods. For example, at 7.5 percent per period, a sum will double in about 9.55 $(= 69/7.5 + .35)$ periods.

Example 3. What must the interest rate on our savings account be if the $1,200 is to triple in 19 periods?

$$\$3,600 = \$1,200(1 + i)^{19}$$

$$\frac{\$3,600}{\$1,200} = (1 + i)^{19}$$

$$3 = (1 + i)^{19}$$

From the table we find that $(1.06)^{19} = 3.02560$. Thus our account will triple in 19 periods if the interest rate is about 6 percent.

Present Value of $1. Present value analysis computes the value *today* of a sum to be received in the *future*, at discount rate i. Present value calculations are the inverse of future value calculations. Our future value calculation showed that $100 will grow to $146.93 after 5 periods with 8 percent compound interest.

$$\$146.93 = \$100(1.08)(1.08)(1.08)(1.08)(1.08)$$

$$= \$100(1.08)^5$$

Alternatively, $146.93 received 5 periods from now, discounted at 8 percent, has a present value of $100.

$$\$100 = \frac{\$146.93}{(1.08)^5}$$

$$= \$146.93 \left(\frac{1}{1.08}\right)^5$$

The $1/(1.08)^5$ is the present value of $1 received after 5 periods, discounted at 8 percent. It is, of course, the inverse of $(1.08)^5$. Tables are usually available showing the present value of $1 received at some time in the future for a variety of discount rates and time periods. An accepted shorthand expression for this is $p_{n|i}$ (read "small p angle n at i"). See Table 2 of the Appendix.

Example 4. What is the present value (P) of $2,500 to be received 3 periods hence, with a discount rate of .06?

$$P = \$2,500(1.06)^{-1}(1.06)^{-1}(1.06)^{-1}$$

$$= \$2,500(1.06)^{-3}$$

$$P = \$2,500(.83962)$$
$$= \$2,099.05$$

Length of the Compounding (Discounting) Period. Our discussion so far has said nothing about the *length* of the interest period. Usually, however, interest will be quoted on an *annual* basis but compounded more than once per year. To find the interest factor for r percent compounded m times per period for t periods, use an interest rate of $i = r/m$ for $m \times t$ periods. If a savings account earns interest at the rate of 6 percent, compounded semiannually, the future value after 5 years results from compounding for 10 periods with interest of 3 percent per period. If the interest is compounded quarterly, a rate of 1.5 (= 6.0/4) percent for 20 (= 4 × 5) periods gives the future value at the end of 5 years. To illustrate determining annual effective interest rates from rates quoted for shorter periods, consider the often-quoted terms of sale "2/10, n(et)/ 30." For example, on a $100 gross invoice price, these terms mean that the interest rate during the period of the loan is 2/98, because if the discount is not taken, then a charge of $2 is levied for the use of $98. The $98 is borrowed for (at most) 20 (= 30 − 10) days, so the number of compounding periods in a year is (at least) 18.25 (= 365/20). The expression for the exact annual rate of interest implied by terms 2/10, n/30 is

$$\left(1 + \frac{2}{98}\right)^{365/20} - 1 = 1.020408^{18.25} - 1 = 44.59\%$$

(The rate is even higher if the invoice is paid after the 10th day but before the 30th day.)

The limiting case of the compounding period length is *continuous compounding*. The future value formula for continuous compounding of $1 at annual interest rate i for n years is e^{in}, where e is the base of the natural logarithms. Similarly, the present value formula for continuous discounting of $1 received n years in the future at interest rate i is e^{-in}. Continuous compounding and discounting factors are also available in tabular form and need not be calculated each time. Selected values of e^{-x} are shown in Exhibit 1 (i.e., $x = in$).

A Note on the Equivalence between Continuous and Discrete Compounding. In general, the shorter the length of the compounding period, the greater will be the accumulation after n periods for a given annual rate. This is because more "interest on interest" is earned. For example, at 12 percent compounded annually, $1 will grow to $1.12 at the end of 1 year. If, however, compounding is *quarterly*, then the same dollar will grow to $(1 + .03)^4$ or $1.12551. Under continuous compounding, the $1 will grow by $e^{.12}$ to $1.12750. A *smaller* nominal interest rate is required to cause $1 to grow to a given amount under continuous compounding than is required under discrete compounding. It can be shown that this smaller nominal interest rate is $\ln(1 + i)$ or the *natural logarithm* of $(1 + i)$. This is shown graphically in Exhibit 2, where n is the number of years and B is the principal amount to be compounded.

EXHIBIT 1   Continuous Discount Factors: e^{-x}

x	e^{-x}	x	e^{-x}	x	e^{-x}
.00	1.0000	.30	.7408	2.30	.1003
.01	.9901	.35	.7047	2.40	.0907
.02	.9802	.40	.6703	2.50	.0821
.03	.9704	.45	.6376	2.60	.0743
.04	.9608	.50	.6065	2.70	.0672
.05	.9512	.55	.5770	2.80	.0608
.06	.9417	.60	.5488	2.90	.0550
.07	.9323	.65	.5220	3.00	.0498
.08	.9231	.70	.4966	3.10	.0450
.09	.9139	.75	.4724	3.20	.0408
.10	.9048	.80	.4493	3.40	.0334
.11	.8958	.85	.4274	3.60	.0273
.12	.8869	.90	.4066	3.80	.0224
.13	.8780	.95	.3867	4.00	.0183
.14	.8693	1.00	.3679	4.20	.0150
.15	.8607	1.05	.3499	4.40	.0123
.16	.8521	1.10	.3329	4.60	.0101
.17	.8437	1.15	.3166	4.80	.0082
.18	.8353	1.20	.3012	5.00	.0067
.19	.8270	1.25	.2865	5.50	.0041
.20	.8187	1.30	.2725	6.00	.0025
.21	.8106	1.40	.2466	7.00	.0009
.22	.8025	1.50	.2231	8.00	.0003
.23	.7945	1.60	.2019	9.00	.0001
.24	.7866	1.70	.1827	10.00	.00005
.25	.7788	1.80	.1653		
.26	.7711	1.90	.1496		
.27	.7634	2.00	.1353		
.28	.7558	2.10	.1225		
.29	.7483	2.20	.1108		

ANNUITIES

An *annuity* is a series of equal payments made at the beginning or end of a series of equal time periods. Bond interest payments, lease payments, and annual payments made to a retired employee under a pension plan are common annuities. An annuity whose payments occur at the *end* of each period is called an *ordinary annuity* or an *annuity in arrears*. Semiannual bond interest payments represent an ordinary annuity because the first interest payment is made *after* the bond has been outstanding for 6 months. An annuity whose payments occur at the *beginning* of each period is called an *annuity due* or an *annuity in advance*. Rent is usually paid in advance, so a series of rental payments represents an annuity due. An annuity whose payments begin at some time

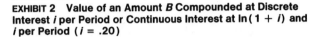

EXHIBIT 2   Value of an Amount *B* Compounded at Discrete Interest *i* per Period or Continuous Interest at ln(1 + *i*) and *i* per Period (*i* = .20)

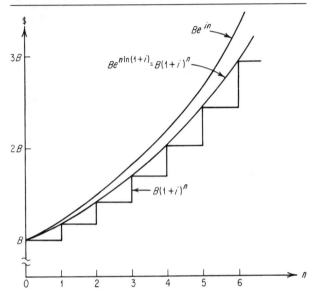

after the end of the first period is called a *deferred annuity*. Prior to retirement age, the annuity payments commencing at retirement represent a deferred annuity. An annuity whose payments continue forever is called a *perpetuity*. The timing of the first payment determines whether a perpetuity is *in arrears* or *in advance*. The British and Canadian governments have, from time to time, issued bonds with no maturity dates. Such bonds are called *consols*; their interest payments represent a *perpetuity in arrears*.

Ordinary Annuities. The formulas for determining the future and present value of ordinary annuities are extensions of the basic compound interest and present value formulas. Consider an ordinary annuity of $1 for 3 periods at 12 percent. The value of the annuity at the end of the third period is calculated as follows:

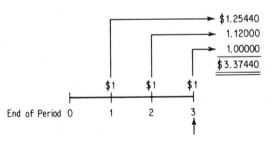

The $1 received at the end of the first period earns interest for 2 periods, so it is worth $1.25440 at the end of period 3. The $1 received at the end of the second period grows to $1.1200 by the end of period 3, and the $1 received at the end of period 3 is, of course, worth $1 at the end of period 3. The entire annuity is worth $3.37440 at the end of period 3.

The formula for the future value (F) of the annuity is

$$F = (1 + i)^2 + (1 + i) + 1$$
$$= \$1.25440 + \$1.12000 + \$1.00000$$
$$= \$3.37440$$

which reduces to

$$F = \frac{(1 + i)^3 - 1}{i}$$
$$= \frac{(1.12)^3 - 1}{.12}$$
$$= \frac{1.40493 - 1}{.12}$$
$$= \$3.37440$$

In general, the formula for the future value of an ordinary annuity of $B compounded at rate i for n periods is

$$F = \frac{B[(1 + i)^n - 1]}{i}$$

A shorthand expression for $[(1 + i)^n - 1]/i$ is $A_{\overline{n}|i}$ ("cap A, angle n at i").

If we wished to find the *present value* of this ordinary annuity of $1 per period for 3 periods, discounted at 12 percent, we would use the calculations shown here:

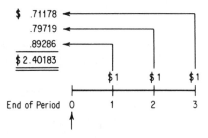

The $1 to be received at the end of period 1 has present value $.89286, the $1 to be received at the end of period 2 has present value $.79719, and the $1 to be received at the end of the third period has present value $.71178. The present value of the annuity is the sum of these individual present values, $2.40183.

The formula for the present value P of the annuity is

$$P = \frac{1}{(1 + i)^3} + \frac{1}{(1 + i)^2} + \frac{1}{1 + i}$$
$$= \$.71178 + \$.79719 + \$.89286$$
$$= \$2.40183$$

which reduces to

$$P = \frac{1 - (1 + i)^{-3}}{i}$$
$$= \frac{1 - .71178}{.12}$$
$$= \$2.40183$$

In general, the formula for the present value of an ordinary annuity of $\$B$ discounted at i percent for n periods is

$$P = \frac{B[1 - (1 + i)^{-n}]}{i}$$

A shorthand expression for $[1 - (1 + i)^{-n}]/i$ is $P_{\overline{n}|i}$ ("cap P, angle n, at i").

The values of $A_{\overline{n}|i}$ and $P_{\overline{n}|i}$ have been tabulated for a variety of interest rates and periods, thus simplifying the calculations in annuity problems. Excerpts from such tables appear in the Appendix: $A_{\overline{n}|i}$ in Table 3 and $P_{n|i}$ in Table 4.

Example 5.[1] The Roberts Dairy Company switched from delivery trucks with gasoline engines to ones with diesel engines. The diesel trucks cost \$2,000 more than the ordinary trucks but \$50 per month less to operate. Assume that the operating costs are saved at the end of each month. If Roberts Dairy Company uses a discount rate of 1 percent per month, how long, at a minimum, must the diesel trucks remain in service for the switch to save money in present value terms?

See Table 4 in the Appendix of this book. The present value of an ordinary annuity of \$1 per period discounted at 1 percent per period is \$40 [= \$2,000/ 50] when the number of annuity periods is between 51 and 52.

Annuities Due. Recall that the basic difference between an ordinary annuity and an annuity due lies in the timing of the *first payment*. With an ordinary annuity, the first payment is received at the *end* of the first period. With an annuity due, the first payment is received at the *beginning* of the first period. Therefore, if tables for the future value and present value of ordinary annuities are available, it is a simple matter to convert these for use in problems involving *annuities due*. A \$1 annuity due for n periods will have a future value equal to the future value of an ordinary annuity for $n + 1$ periods *minus* \$1. We can see this by comparing the payments to be made under an annuity due for 3 periods with an ordinary annuity for 4 periods:

---

[1]This example is taken from Davidson et al. [1980, p. B-23, prob. PB.27].

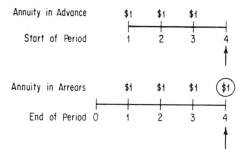

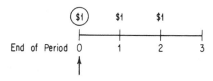

The circled $1 is the $1 that must be subtracted from the 4-*period* annuity in arrears to get the 3-*period* annuity in advance.

Similarly, the present value of an annuity due may be readily computed using the ordinary annuity present value tables. A $1 annuity in advance for n periods has present value equal to the present value of a $1 annuity in arrears for $n - 1$ periods *plus* $1. This can be seen by examining the payments for the present value of an annuity in advance for three periods as shown here:

Notice that except for the first, circled, payment, it looks just like the present value of an ordinary annuity for 2 periods. Therefore, by adding $1 (the circled $1) to the present value of an annuity in arrears for 2 periods, we obtain the present value of an annuity due for 3 periods.

Example 6. What is the present value of rents of $350 to be paid monthly, in advance, for 1 year when the discount rate is 1 percent per month?

The present value will be equal to

$$D = \$350 + \frac{\$350}{1.01} + \frac{\$350}{(1.01)^2} + \cdots + \frac{\$350}{(1.01)^{11}}$$

$$= \$350 \left[1 + \frac{1}{1.01} + \frac{1}{(1.01)^2} + \cdots + \frac{1}{(1.01)^{11}} \right]$$

$$= \$350 + \$350 \left[\frac{1 - (1.01)^{-11}}{.01} \right]$$

$$= \$350 + \$350(10.36763)$$

$$= \$3,978.67$$

The factor 10.3676 is the present value of an *ordinary annuity* of $1, discounted at 1 percent for 11 periods from the appropriate table, Table 4 of the Appendix.

Example 7. Mr. Mason is 62 years old today. He wishes to invest an amount today and equal amounts on his sixty-third, sixty-fourth, and sixty-fifth birthdays so that starting on his sixty-sixth birthday he can withdraw $5,000 on each birthday for 11 years. His investments will earn 8 percent per year. How much should be invested on the sixty-second through sixty-fifth birthdays?

The timing of the payments is

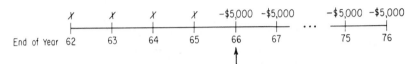

The X's represent the unknown amount of his annual contributions to be made on each of his sixty-second through sixty-fifth birthdays.

For each $1 that Mr. Mason invests on his sixty-second, sixty-third, sixty-fourth, and sixty-fifth birthdays, he will have (see Appendix Table 4) $4.8666 (= $5.86660 − $1) on his sixty-sixth birthday. On his sixty-sixth birthday Mr. Mason needs to have accumulated an amount large enough to fund an 11-year, $5,000 annuity in advance. An 11-year, $1 annuity in advance has present value of $7.71008 (= $6.71008 + $1). Mr. Mason then needs on his sixty-sixth birthday an accumulation of $5,000 × 7.71008 = $38,550.40. Because each $1 deposited on the sixty-second through sixty-fifth birthdays grows to $4.8666, Mr. Mason must deposit $38,550.40/4.8666 = $7,921.42 on each of the sixty-second through sixty-fifth birthdays to accumulate $38,550.40.

Deferred Annuities. When the first payment of an annuity occurs some time after the end of the first period, the annuity is *deferred*. The payment schedule for an ordinary annuity of $1 per period for 4 periods, deferred for 2 periods, is

The arrow marked *P* shows the time for which the present value is calculated; the arrow marked *F* shows when the future value is calculated. The future value is not affected by the deferral and equals the future value of an ordinary annuity for 4 periods.

There are two ways to calculate the present value of a deferred annuity. The first is to calculate the present value of the annuity and then discount the resulting sum from the period of deferral to the present. The second is somewhat simpler and will be illustrated first. The payment schedule of the 4-period annuity deferred 2 periods is as follows:

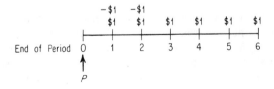

This schedule reflects the present value of an ordinary annuity for 6 periods *minus* the present value of an ordinary annuity for 2 periods. In general, to calculate the present value of an annuity of n payments deferred for d periods, subtract the present value of an annuity for d periods from the present value of an annuity for n + d periods.

    Example 8. What is the present value of Mr. Mason's withdrawals in Example 7? Recall that Mr. Mason is 62 years old, he will receive $5,000 on his sixty-sixth through seventy-sixth birthdays, and his investment earns 8 percent.

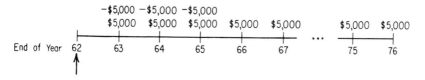

The present value at 8 percent of $5,000 received for 14 years, starting 1 year hence, is $5,000 × 8.24424 = $41,221.20. The present value at age 62 of the $5,000 he will not receive on birthdays 63 through 65 is −$5,000 × 2.57710 = −$12,885.50. The present value of the actual payments to Mr. Mason is $41,221.20 − $12,885.50 = $28,335.70.

    Alternatively, one could discount the present value of an annuity due of $5,000 for 11 periods at 8 percent back to the present. The present value of the 11-period annuity due is $5,000 × (1 + 6.71008) or $38,550.40. Discounting this sum at 8 percent for 4 periods, we have

$$P = \frac{\$38,550.40}{(1.08)^4}$$
$$= \$38,550.40(.73503)$$
$$= \$28,335.70$$

Perpetuities. A periodic payment to be received forever is called a *perpetuity*. Future values of perpetuities are undefined. If $1 is to be received at the end of every period and the discount rate is i percent, then the present value of the perpetuity is $1/i. This expression can be derived with algebra or by observing what happens in the expression for the present value of an ordinary annuity of $B per payment as n, the number of payments, approaches infinity:

$$P = \frac{B[1 - (1 + i)^{-n}]}{i}$$

As n approaches infinity, $(1 + i)^{-n}$ approaches zero, so P approaches B(1/i). If the first payment of the perpetuity occurs now, the present value is B(1 + 1/i).

    Example 9. The Canadian government offers to pay $30 every 6 months forever. What is that promise worth if the discount rate is 12 percent compounded semiannually?

    Twelve percent compounded semiannually is equivalent to 6 percent per 6-month period. If the first payment occurs 6 months from now, the present value is $30/.06 = $500. If the first payment occurs today, the present value is $30 + $500 = $530.

APPLICATIONS IN ACCOUNTING

Compound interest methods have many uses in various kinds of problems in accounting. In the remainder of this chapter, we discuss and illustrate the use of compound interest methods in a representative set of such problems.

Internal Rate of Return or Yield. We are often interested in the effective interest rate implicit in a stream of cash flows. The yield to maturity of a bond and the internal rate of return on a proposed capital investment are examples. This effective interest rate is referred to as either *yield* or *internal rate of return*. It represents *the interest rate required to make the present value of the cash inflows equal to the present value of the cash outflows.* Alternatively, it is the interest rate that makes the net present value of all the cash flows equal to zero.

    Example 10. Investment of $1,000 today will generate 4 equal payments of $302, one each at the end of the next 4 years. To solve for the yield, we set up the following equation:

$$0 = -\$1,000 + \frac{\$302}{1 + i} + \frac{\$302}{(1 + i)^2} + \frac{\$302}{(1 + i)^3} + \frac{\$302}{(1 + i)^4}$$

or

$$\$1,000 = \frac{\$302}{1 + i} + \frac{\$302}{(1 + i)^2} + \frac{\$302}{(1 + i)^3} + \frac{\$302}{(1 + i)^4}$$

The internal rate of return, i, is to be found. In this case, one has an ordinary annuity of $302 for 4 periods and wishes to compute the interest rate that makes the present value of the annuity equal to $1,000.

$$\$1,000 = \$302 P_{\overline{4}|i}$$
$$\frac{\$1,000}{\$302} = P_{\overline{4}|i}$$
$$3.31126 = P_{\overline{4}|i}$$

Scanning the 4-period row in the present value of an ordinary annuity table shows that $P_{\overline{4}|i} = 3.31213$ at $i = 8$ percent. Hence the internal rate of return is about 8 percent.

    The internal rate of return must usually be estimated using trial-and-error procedures. The steps in finding the internal rate of return are as follows:[2]

    1. Make an educated guess, called the "trial rate," at the internal rate of return. You may use zero.

    2. Calculate the present value of all the cash flows after the one occurring at time zero.

---

[2]There are ways to guess the trial rate that will approximate the true rate in fewer iterations than the method described here. If you want to find internal rates of return efficiently with successive trial rates, refer to a mathematical reference book to learn about the "Newton search" method, sometimes called the "method of false position."

3. If the present value of the cash flows is equal to the one at time zero, stop. The current trial rate is the internal rate of return.

4. If the amount found in step 2 is less than the cash flow at time zero, try a larger interest rate as the trial rate and go back to step 2.

5. If the amount found in step 2 is greater than the cash flow at time zero, try a smaller interest rate as the new trial rate and go back to step 2.

Example 11. Find the yield of an investment costing $1,000 that will return $200, $500, and $400 at the end of years 1, 2, and 3, respectively.

$$\$1,000 = \frac{\$200}{1 + i} + \frac{\$500}{(1 + i)^2} + \frac{\$400}{(1 + i)^3}$$

Begin by checking if i is greater than or less than 3 percent. Our investment, evaluated at $i = 3$ percent, has a net present value of

$$\$200(.97087) + \$500(.94260) + \$400(.91514) = \$194.17 + \$471.30 + \$366.06$$
$$= \$1,031.53$$

The net present value is too large, so we increase the trial discount rate.

Now, evaluate the investment at $i = 4$ percent:

$$\$200(.96154) + \$500(.92456) + \$400(.88900) = \$192.31 + \$462.28 + \$355.60$$
$$= \$1,010.19$$

The net present value is still too large, so we now try $i = 4.5$ percent:

$$\$200(.95693) + \$500(.91572) + \$400(.87629) = \$191.39 + \$457.86 + \$350.52$$
$$= \$999.77$$

The yield is slightly less than 4.5 percent per year.

It is important to recognize that the computed yield reflects the assumption that the periodic cash inflows can be reinvested at the *yield rate*. Consequently, the *realized yield* (ex post) may differ from the *computed yield* (ex ante), depending on the actual interest rate earned by the periodic cash inflows.[3]

Most investments are *conventional* investments. That is, they require an initial outflow followed by a series of net inflows. When a stream of cash flows is characterized by alternating inflows and outflows (i.e., a *nonconventional investment*), *multiple yields* may arise. In other words, such streams of cash flows may have *more than one* interest rate that generates a net present value of zero.

Example 12. This example is adapted from one in Bierman and Smidt [1980]. Consider an investment with the following cash flows.

Period	0	1	2
Cash flow	−$72,727	$170,909	−$100,000

---

[3]For an extensive discussion of this problem and a method of investing in coupon bonds to guarantee a rate of return equal to the originally promised yield under realistic assumptions, see Fisher and Weil [1971], and Leibowitz [1980].

The yield of this investment is 10 percent:

$$0 = -\$72,727 + \frac{\$170,909}{1.1} - \frac{\$100,000}{(1.1)^2}$$
$$= -\$72,727 + \$170,909(.90909) - \$100,000(.82644)$$
$$= -\$72,727 + \$155,371 - \$82,644$$

We now show that the yield is also 25 percent per period:

$$0 = -\$72,727 + \frac{\$170,909}{1.25} - \frac{\$100,000}{(1.25)^2}$$
$$= -\$72,727 + \$170,909(.8) - \$100,000(.64)$$
$$= -\$72,727 + \$136,727 - \$64,000$$

The existence of multiple yields on nonconventional investments has implications for the evaluation of capital expenditures. In short, when multiple yields exist and potential investments are being ranked in terms of yield, it becomes difficult to make accept or reject decisions. Hence, one should discount the cash flows with an appropriate discount rate and rank investments in terms of net present value, rather than trying to solve for the yield. Multiple rates of return will not exist, however, when a reinvestment rate is assumed for all cash outflows from an investment. It will always be reasonable to assume a reinvestment rate; therefore, the problem of multiple yields can be avoided.

Interest Imputation. Since APB Opinion No. 21 [1971], one often needs to compute an internal rate of return to impute interest on receivables and payables.

Example 13. The Alexis Company acquires a machine with a cash price of $10,500. It pays for the machine by giving a note promising to make payments equal to 7 percent of the face value, $840, at the end of each of the next 3 years and a single payment of $12,000 in 3 years. What is the implicit interest rate in the loan?

The time line for this problem is

$10,500 −$840   −$840 −$12,840

End of Period   0   1   2   3

The implicit interest rate is r, such that

$$\$10,500 = \frac{\$840}{1 + r} + \frac{\$840}{(1 + r)^2} + \frac{\$12,840}{(1 + r)^3} \tag{1}$$

The internal rate of return is found to the nearest tenth of 1 percent to be 12.2 percent:

Iteration number	Trial rate (%)	Right-hand side of Eq. (1)
1...........	7.0	$12,000
2...........	15.0	9,808
3...........	11.0	10,827
4...........	13.0	10,300
5...........	12.0	10,559
6...........	12.5	10,428
7...........	12.3	10,480
8...........	12.2	10,506
9...........	12.1	10,532

The Alexis Company will make the following journal entries:

Machine	10,500	
Discount on Note Payable	1,500	
Note Payable....................................		12,000
To record acquisition of machine and giving of note.		

At the end of the first year, the company will record:

Interest Expense................................	1,281	
Cash...		840
Discount on Note Payable		441
.122 × ($12,000 − $1,500) = $1,281.		

At the end of the second year, it will record:

Interest Expense................................	1,335	
Cash...		840
Discount on Note Payable		495
.122 × [$12,000 − ($1,500 − $441)] = $1,335.		

At the end of the third year, it will record:

Interest Expense................................	1,404	
Note Payable....................................	12,000	
Cash...		12,840
Discount on Note Payable		564

In the first 2 years, interest expense is found from multiplying the imputed rate by the book value of the loan—the $12,000 face value less the amount in the Discount account. In the last year, interest expense is a "plug," computed to reduce the Discount account to zero. If a more accurate approximation to the internal rate of return is found, then the closer the "plugged" interest expense in the last period will be to the amount derived from multiplying the remaining net book value by the imputed interest rate.

Valuation of Bonds. A bond represents a contract in which the lender acquires the right to a series of interest payments over the life of the bond and to a payment (usually $1,000) at the bond's maturity. Compound interest methods are essential where bonds are concerned. These methods are used to compute bond values (prices) and yields.

Consider a $1,000 face value bond with semiannual coupons totaling 12 percent per year and with 5 years until maturity. The cash flows associated with this bond are

$$BP = \frac{\$60}{1 + i} + \frac{\$60}{(1 + i)^2} + \cdots + \frac{\$60}{(1 + i)^{10}} + \frac{\$1,000}{(1 + i)^{10}}$$

The price of the bond, *BP*, will be equal to the present value of the interest payments ($60 per 6-month period for 10 such periods) plus the present value of the principal payment of $1,000 to be received 5 years (ten 6-month periods) from now. In order to determine the value or price of the bond, we need to know *i*, the current market rate of interest (or yield) on bonds of similar quality and time to maturity. On the other hand, in order to determine the yield to maturity on this bond (or the rate of return investors require to hold the bond), we need to know *BP*, the current market price. Once we know either the current market price or the yield to maturity, we can solve for the other variable. The *yield to maturity* is an *internal rate of return.*

If the yield to maturity on this bond is 10 percent, the price would be

$$
\begin{aligned}
BP &= \frac{\$60}{1.05} + \frac{\$60}{(1.05)^2} + \cdots + \frac{\$60}{(1.05)^{10}} + \frac{\$1,000}{(1.05)^{10}} \\
&= \$60 P_{\overline{10}|.05} + \$1,000 P_{\overline{10}|.05} \\
&= \$60(7.72173) + \$1,000(.61391) \\
&= \$1,077.22
\end{aligned}
$$

Bond tables are available that eliminate the necessity to make tedious bond calculations. Table 6 in the Appendix is an excerpt from a bond table. For 12 percent bonds paying $60 interest semiannually, Table 6 presents various combinations of yield, price, and time to maturity. (Table 5 shows values for 10 percent semiannual coupon bonds.) Observe that bond prices are usually quoted in percentages of par. The price of a $1,000 bond is 10 times the value shown in the table.

If one knows any three of the four important variables—coupon rate, yield, time to maturity, and price—a bond table enables determination of the value of the fourth variable.

To account for serial bonds often requires the computation of an internal rate of return.

Example 14. (Internal rate of return calculation to find effective interest rate on a serial bond issue.) Lexie's Fashionables raises funds through a serial bond issue. Each bond in the issue has $1,000 face amount and carries 10 percent *annual* coupons. Seven bonds are issued as a group: One matures 3 years after the issue date, one matures 4 years after the issue date, and five mature 5 years after the issue date. The market pays 8 percent interest for the 3-year bond (cash price of $1,051.54), 10 percent interest for the 4-year bond, and 12 percent interest for the 5-year bonds (cash price of $4,639.54). What single interest rate can be used in accounting for these bonds with the effective interest method? The time line for this problem is

```
        -$500  -$500  -$ 500  -$ 500  -$5,500
          - 100  - 100  - 100  - 1,100    —
    x     - 100  - 100  - 1,100    —        —
        ├──────┼──────┼──────┼──────┼──────┤
End of Year  0      1      2      3      4      5
```

The bond maturing at the end of year 3 was issued to yield 8 percent:

(Table 4)	$ 100 × 2.57710	= $ 257.71
(Table 2)	1,000 × .79383	= 793.83
Initial proceeds		$1,051.54

The bond maturing at the end
of year 4 was issued to
yield 10% (par) $1,000.00

The bonds maturing at the end of year 5 were issued to yield 12 percent:

(Table 4)	$ 500 × 3.60478	= $1,802.39
(Table 2)	5,000 × .56743	= 2,837.15
Initial proceeds		$4,639.54

The total proceeds are $6,691.08 = $1,051.54 + $1,000.00 + $4,639.54. The effective interest rate on the entire serial bond issue is r such that

$$\$6{,}691.08 = \frac{\$700}{1+r} + \frac{\$700}{(1+r)^2} + \frac{\$1{,}700}{(1+r)^3} + \frac{\$1{,}600}{(1+r)^4} + \frac{\$5{,}500}{(1+r)^5} \qquad (2)$$

The rate appears to be between 10 and 12 percent per year. The trial rates used in finding the internal rate of return resulted in the following steps:

Iteration number	Trial rate (%)	Right-hand side of Eq. (2)
1	10.00	$7,000.00
2	12.00	6,530.74
3	11.00	6,759.74
4	11.50	6,643.88
5	11.25	6,701.46
6	11.40	6,666.83
7	11.30	6,689.89

A rate of 11.3 percent is close enough, as the amortization schedule in Exhibit 3 shows.

EXHIBIT 3   Amortization Schedule for Serial Bond Issue of Annual 10% Coupon Bonds: $1,000 Maturing in 3 Years Issued to Yield 8%; $1,000 Maturing in 4 Years Issued to Yield 10%; $5,000 Maturing in 5 Years Issued to Yield 12%

Proceeds of Initial Issue = $6,691
Effective Annual Interest on Entire Issue = 11.3%

Annual journal entry
Dr. Interest Expense	Amount in column (3)	
Dr. (or Cr.) Bond Liability	Amount in column (5)	
Cr. Cash		Amount in column (4)

Year (1)	Bond liability start of period (2)	Effective interest expense at 11.3% (3)	Interest and serial bond principal payment (4)	Added to (subtracted from) bond liability (5)	Bond liability end of period (6)
0					$6,691
1	$6,691	$756	$ 700	$ 56	6,747
2	6,747	762	700	62	6,809
3	6,809	769	1,700	(931)	5,878
4	5,878	664	1,600	(936)	4,942
5	4,942	558	5,500	(4,942)	0

Relationship between bond prices and yields. The interest payments on a bond are fixed by the contract and normally will not change during the life of the bond. Because the coupon payments are fixed, bond prices are sensitive to changes in market interest rates or yields. Returning to our 12 percent semi-annual 5-year bond, we observed that if the market yield was 10 percent, the bond would sell for $1,077.22. This is a premium of $77.22 above par, or face, value ($1,000). If market yields increase to 12 percent, the bond price would fall to $1,000.00 and the premium disappears. As interest rates fall, bond prices rise, and vice versa. The reason is that a bond pays a fixed amount of cash. If market yields fall, investors will *pay more* for any given bond because the payments will have a larger present value. If market yields rise, investors will *pay less* for any given bond because the fixed amounts of cash will have a lower present value.

Capital Expenditure Analysis. Many firms employ present value techniques in evaluating proposed capital expenditures. Capital expenditures normally have a life spanning several years. Typically, capital expenditures involve the current investment of funds, in return for cash benefits to be received in the future. Knowledge of the time value of money is basic to adjusting the magnitude of future cash inflows to make them comparable to the investment to be made in the present. Predictions of future cash flows are uncertain; changes in demand, technology, selling prices, costs, and general inflation all create uncertainty in future predictions. Nevertheless, the use of present value techniques allows the explicit introduction of the time value of money (which may itself be uncertain) into the analysis; see Hertz [1968].

The mechanics of capital expenditure analysis are straightforward. The general approach is outlined below.

1. Estimate all cash inflows and outflows during the expected life of the investment.

2. Adjust the cash flows for the effects of income and other taxes. Net cash inflows should be reduced by the income taxes paid on those inflows in each period. Noncash expenses, such as depreciation, which are deductible for tax purposes, generate *tax savings* equal to the amount of the noncash deduction times the relevant tax rate. Special tax provisions such as the investment credit and the tax rules dealing with sale or exchange of property must also be considered.

3. Select a discount rate that reflects the aftertax opportunity cost of money to the firm.

4. Discount all cash flows to the present and select those investments that have a positive net present value (i.e., those for which the present value of the inflows exceeds the present value of the outflows). Reject investments having a net present value less than zero.

Several illustrations are given in Chapter 20 of *Handbook of Cost Accounting* [Davidson and Weil, 1978].

LIFE-CONTINGENT ANNUITIES

The principles of compound interest are often applied in situations where future outcomes are uncertain. The annuities discussed above all last for a certain or specified number of payments. Such annuities are sometimes called *certain annuities* to distinguish them from *contingent annuities,* for which the number of payments depends on an event to occur at an uncertain date. For example, businesses often want to know the cost of an annuity (pension) that will be paid only so long as the annuitant (retired employee) lives. Such annuities are called *life-contingent* or *life annuities.* The details of life-annuity calculations are beyond the scope of this handbook, but an unrealistic, hypothetical example is shown below to indicate the subtleties of life annuities.

Ms. Caplan is 65 years old today, and she has an unusual disease. She will die either 1½ years from today or 10½ years from today. Ms. Caplan has no family, and her employer wishes to purchase an ordinary life annuity for Ms. Caplan that will pay her $10,000 on her sixty-sixth birthday and $10,000 on every birthday thereafter on which Ms. Caplan is still alive. Funds invested in the annuity will earn 10 percent per year. How much should Ms. Caplan's life annuity cost?

The Wrong Calculation. Ms. Caplan's life expectancy is 6 years: one-half chance of her living 1½ years plus one-half chance of her living 10½ years. The employer expects that six payments will be made to Ms. Caplan. The present value of an ordinary annuity of $1 for 6 years at 10 percent is $4.35526 (Table 4). Therefore the annuity will cost $43,553.

When a series of payments has uncertain length, the expected value of those payments is *not* the present value of an annuity for the expected life, but is the weighted average of the present values of the separate payments where the weights are the probabilities of the payment's being made.

The Right Calculation. Ms. Caplan will receive 1 payment for certain. The present value of that payment of $10,000 at 10 percent is $9,091 (Table 2). Ms. Caplan will receive 9 further payments if she survives the critical second year. Those 9 payments have present value $52,355, which is equal to the present value of a 9-year ordinary annuity that is deferred for 1 year, $61,446 − $9,091 (Table 4). The probability is one-half that Ms. Caplan will survive to receive those 9 payments. Thus, their *expected* present value is $26,178 (= .5 × $52,355), and the *expected* present value of the entire life annuity is $9,091 + $26,178 = $35,269.

Ms. Caplan's life annuity, calculated correctly, costs only 81 percent as much as is found by the incorrect calculation. Actuaries for insurance companies use mortality tables to estimate probabilities of an annuitant's receiving each payment and, from those data, calculate the expected cost of a life annuity. Different mortality tables have been used for men and women because of the difference in life expectancies.

Mortality Tables. A *mortality table* tracks the life records of a large representative group of individuals. For life insurance calculations (where the conservative assumption is early death with payments soon), the mortality tables used differ from those used for annuity calculations (where the conservative assumption is a long life with many payments). Covering ages ranging from birth, age 0, up to the 100th birthday, a mortality table shows the number of individuals from the original group remaining alive at each age x (l_x) and the number who died in the year between x and $x + 1$ ($d_x = l_x − l_{x+1}$). It is assumed that the number of individuals attaining age 100 is significantly different from zero in most mortality tables (although some annuity tables do not assume death until age 110). From these data, one can write the *probability* that an individual who is alive at age x will live to age $x + n$ as $_np_x = l_{x+n}/l_x$. Similarly, the probability of dying at age x is written $q_x = d_x/l_x$. The probability of dying between age x and age $x + n$ is written $_nq_x = (l_x − l_{x+n})/l_x$.

Mortality tables are generally combined with compound interest tables to construct what are called *commutation tables*.[4] A single commutation table is constructed using a given mortality table and a given interest rate. The terms in commutation tables are called *commutation factors*. These factors provide the following information for a given mortality table/interest rate combination.

---

[4]For more on these matters, see Society of Actuaries [1961].

D_x = the present value of \$1 paid to all individuals of the sample attaining age x. Letting $v^x = (1 + i)^{-x}$, then $D_x = v^x l_x$. (Typically, an annuity-based mortality table is used.)

N_x = the present value of \$1 paid to all individuals attaining age x, plus the present value of \$1 paid to all individuals attaining age $x + 1$ plus ... attaining age 109, or $N_x = \Sigma_{t=x}^{109} D_{xt}$. (Typically, an annuity-based mortality table is used.)

C_x = the present value of \$1 paid in year $x + 1$ to all individuals dying at age x $(C_x = v^{x+1} d_x)$. (Typically, a life insurance-based mortality table is used.)

M_x = the present value of \$1 paid in year $x + 1$ to all individuals dying at age x plus the present value of \$1 paid in year $x + 2$ to all individuals dying at age $x + 1$ plus ... dying at 99, or $M_x = \Sigma_{t=x}^{99} C_{xt}$. (Typically, a life insurance-based mortality table is used.)

A *life annuity* is a series of equal payments beginning at some point and continuing for all or part of the life of the *annuitant*. A *pension plan* is a contractual agreement to pay life annuities to retired employees, subject to various provisions regarding benefit levels and vesting.

Commutation tables are used to compute the amount of pension liability accruing each period. As each year passes, additional future pension liabilities are created. The commutation factors D_x and N_x represent the present value of payments of \$1 to be made to each surviving retired employee. Multiplying these factors by expected benefit levels will give the present value of the current period's pension liability that will be discharged in future years, but that is recorded and, perhaps, funded currently.

Similarly, from the point of view of life insurance contracts, the commutation factors C_x and M_x represent the present value of payments of \$1 to be made to those policyholders who die in future years. This enables life insurance companies to compute net premiums (amounts that must be contributed by living policyholders to pay the claims of policyholders who die) as well as the present value of the companies' future liabilities under the terms of existing policies. The premium charged the policyowner is the net premium plus an overhead factor.

BIBLIOGRAPHY

Accounting Principles Board (AICPA), *Interest on Receivables and Payables*, Opinion No. 21 (APB, 1971).

Ayers, F., Jr., *Mathematics of Finance*, Schaum's Outline Series (McGraw-Hill Book Company, New York, 1963).

Bierman, H., Jr., and S. Smidt, *The Capital Budgeting Decision*, 5th ed. (Macmillan Company, New York, 1980).

Davidson, S., J. S. Schindler, and R. L. Weil, *Fundamentals of Accounting*, 5th ed. (Dryden Press, Hinsdale, Ill., 1981).

Davidson, S., C. P. Stickney, and R. L. Weil, *Accounting: The Language of Business*, 4th ed. (Thomas Horton and Daughters, Glen Ridge, N.J., 1979).

———, *Intermediate Accounting: Concepts, Methods and Uses* (Dryden Press, Hinsdale, Ill., 1980).

Davidson, S., and Weil, R. L., *Handbook of Cost Accounting* (McGraw-Hill Book Company, New York, 1978).

Fisher, L., and R. L. Weil, "Coping with the Risk of Interest Rate Fluctuations: Returns to Bondholders from Naive and Optimal Strategies," *Journal of Business*, vol. 44, no. 4 (October 1971), pp. 408–431.

Hertz, D. B., "Investment Policies That Pay Off," *Harvard Business Review*, January–February 1968, pp. 96–108.

Hummel, P. M., and C. L. Seebeck, Jr., *Mathematics of Finance*, 3d ed. (McGraw-Hill Book Company, New York, 1971).

Leibowitz, M. L., *Pros & Cons of Immunization* (Salomon Brothers, New York, 1980).

Society of Actuaries, *Monetary Tables Based on the 1958 CSO Mortality Table* (Society of Actuaries, Chicago, 1961). (Between 50 and 60 volumes at various dates are currently available.)

CHAPTER 10

Basic Concepts of

Statistical Sampling

for Auditing*

James K. Loebbecke
Professor of Accounting, University of Utah

* The author acknowledges a debt to Robert K. Elliott, who wrote the conceptual chapter on statistical sampling for the second edition of this handbook.

AUDITING AND STATISTICAL SAMPLING

Audit Objectives. All auditors, whether independent public accountants, government auditors, or internal auditors, must reach two important types of conclusions in the course of their audits: (1) whether financial representations are substantially correct and (2) whether systems are operating in accordance with prescribed requirements. Deciding what is a significant error and the acceptable risks of erroneous conclusions may differ according to the purpose of an audit, as may the relative importance of the two types of conclusions. This chapter discusses statistical methods of forming conclusions of these two types from partial (test-basis) examinations.

Because (1) auditors frequently confront enormous masses of data and (2) some level of imprecision can usually be accepted in auditing, nearly all audits are based on partial examinations. The resulting partial (or sample) examination must introduce an element of uncertainty into the conclusions of auditors, who must draw inferences from incomplete information. This is true whether or not auditors use statistical sampling procedures.

The uncertainty resulting from partial examination may frustrate the auditor's desire for correct conclusions in two distinct ways:

1. Financial representations may be correct (or a system may be functioning as prescribed), but the auditor may conclude that they are incorrect (or that the system is not functioning as prescribed).

2. Financial representations may be substantially in error (or a system may be functioning substantially differently from the prescribed method), but the auditor may conclude that they are correct (or that the system is functioning as prescribed).

The auditor who can define what constitutes a substantially wrong conclusion, and what levels of risk (greater than zero) of making the two errors above are acceptable, can then use statistical auditing procedures. In discussing the determination of "substantially erroneous conclusions" and "risk levels" in this chapter, the general objectives of independent public accountants have been explicitly recognized. If these objectives are inappropriate for other types of auditing, the discussion will still apply if the reader substitutes another measure of "substantial error" and "acceptable risk levels."

10-2

Professional Standards. The use of statistical sampling methods by certified public accountants is governed by Statements on Auditing Standards published by the American Institute of Certified Public Accountants (AICPA). All auditors, whether or not certified public accountants, should be familiar with Statement on Auditing Standards (SAS) No. 39, *Audit Sampling*.

This statement of the AICPA makes clear that both statistical and nonstatistical sampling are acceptable approaches to audit sampling when properly applied. The nature of sampling is discussed and guidance is given for proper application of the two approaches.

Substantive versus Compliance Tests. Substantive audit tests (as defined in Section 320.70 of Statement on Auditing Standards No. 1) are those in which the feature of audit interest is the monetary amount of errors that would affect the financial statements being audited, including both unintentional errors and intentional irregularities. By definition, substantive tests are those concerned with reaching conclusions about whether representations of financial amounts are substantially correct. Therefore, statistical substantive tests should normally use statistical methods that result in the estimation of dollar amounts that can be related directly to financial statement impact. These methods include *variables sampling*[1] and *dollar unit sampling*.[2]

Compliance tests (as defined in Section 320.50 of SAS No. 1) are those in which the feature of audit interest is the extent of compliance with a prescribed system. By definition, compliance tests are those concerned with reaching conclusions about whether systems are operating in accordance with prescribed requirements. Therefore, statistical compliance tests normally use *attribute sampling*[3] because the conclusions of attribute sampling are stated in terms of rates of compliance (or noncompliance). These conclusions will be related to the *number* of transactions or the *dollars* of transactions, depending on how the sample is designed (i.e., depending on whether a random sample of physical audit units or dollar units is selected).

---

[1] A *variable* is the quantitative characteristic of a population element, e.g., the amount of an account or the number of days it has been outstanding. *Variables sampling* is statistical sampling designed to estimate or test a population quantity (either total or average) based on the sample.

[2] *Dollar unit sampling* (DUS) is an attribute sampling-based technique (see note 3) where the population is defined in terms of individual dollars. The sample is used to determine a frequency of error rate that is applied to total population dollars to estimate the amount of dollars in error. Other names used for this method of sampling include sampling with probability proportional to size (PPS), cumulative monetary amount (CMA) sampling, and combined attributes-variables (CAV) sampling.

[3] An *attribute* is any qualitative characteristic of a population element, e.g., whether or not a given document was processed in accordance with the prescribed system. *Attribute sampling* is statistical sampling designed to estimate or test a proportion (rate of occurrence) based on the sample.

Cautions in Use of Statistical Sampling. Although the basic concepts in statistical sampling are not difficult to grasp, the application of these concepts may rapidly become complex. Also, the auditor's intuitions in statistical sampling may often prove erroneous. Because of the importance of most audit conclusions and the adverse consequences of erroneous conclusions, it is essential that auditors contemplating the use of statistical sampling techniques be qualified to design and execute valid sampling plans. This chapter is intended as a reference source or refresher in statistical considerations. It should not be used as a self-sufficient guide to statistical auditing for auditors without prior training in statistical auditing.

Statistical sampling is sometimes thought by auditors to reduce the need for, or supplant, judgment in the audit process. That this is not the case is made clear by the following quotation from SAS No. 39 [1981, par. 6].

> Evaluating the competence of evidential matter is solely a matter of auditing judgment and is not determined by the design and evaluation of an audit sample. In a strict sense, the sample evaluation relates only to the likelihood that existing monetary errors or deviations from prescribed procedures are proportionately included in the sample, not to the auditor's treatment of such items. Thus, the choice of nonstatistical or statistical sampling does not directly affect the auditor's decisions about the auditing procedures to be applied, the competence of the evidential matter obtained with respect to individual items in the sample, or the actions that might be taken in light of the nature and cause of particular errors.

As implied in the preceding quotation, auditors should not confuse their evaluation of the strength of audit evidence with the reliability of the statistical statement about that evidence. For example, assume that the auditor takes quite a large sample, sufficient to give 95 percent reliability that the conclusion is accurate within 1 percent of the true value of the population, but applies a very weak procedure (e.g., checking a computer record rather than a source document) to the sample items selected. The apparent strength of the statistical conclusion should not deceive the auditor into believing that the evidence is stronger than it in fact is. The statistical conclusion can be given substantial weight in forming audit conclusions only if the audit procedures performed on each sample item are in fact procedures highly likely to detect those conditions of interest to the auditor.

IMPORTANT STATISTICAL CONCEPTS

Certain statistical concepts that relate to the design of sampling plans and the interpretation of results must be understood in order to use statistical audit tests. They are discussed below.

Population. The results of a sample or test cannot be projected beyond the area from which the sample was drawn. The area from which a sample is drawn is known statistically as the *population* (or, sometimes, *universe* or *field*).

The precise definition of the population in light of the test objective is important. If statistical sampling is applied to an improperly defined or incomplete population, unsatisfactory audit results may result.

The auditor's ultimate objective in any particular audit test may be to draw a conclusion about the correct balance of a given account. The auditor would therefore like to define the population as all of the components making up the correct balance. Normally, however, there is no convenient way to sample the true components of a balance, and the auditor must be satisfied with sampling the recorded components only. Because the population actually sampled is normally the recorded population elements, the statistical conclusion is valid only as to the recorded population (because unrecorded items had no chance of being included in the sample). Conclusions about the recorded population are useful to the auditor in forming an opinion, but are not always sufficient because the unrecorded population elements may be material. Therefore, in every case, the auditor must perform supplemental tests to determine the completeness of the recorded population. Among the common supplemental tests are evaluation of internal control over recording of transactions; sales, purchases, shipping, receiving, and production cutoffs; cash receipts and disbursements cutoffs; and tests for unrecorded liabilities. Only if these tests do not indicate unrecorded amounts can the auditor be satisfied that the population sampled was reasonably complete. If the tests do disclose significant unrecorded amounts, however, such amounts must be evaluated and considered in conjunction with the statistical results to form an overall conclusion about the account being audited.

Importance of conclusions. Once an item has been selected for sampling, the auditor must audit it in one way or another; every selected item must be followed up to some conclusion.[4] If items not easily located for auditing are ignored, then the population sampled consists only of the easily locatable items, and the statistical conclusion would apply only to that population. Such a conclusion would usually have no audit relevance. Failure to audit all selected items would probably bias the sample result as applied to the entire population. This is particularly true in cases where the unlocated items are missing precisely because they are unusual, troublesome, or, worst of all, fictitious.

The necessity of tracking down all selected items may test the auditor's ingenuity; however, there are usually alternative routes to obtaining evidence about a sample item. If, after exhaustive searching, it becomes obvious that *no* evidence can be obtained with respect to a given sample item, then the auditor should estimate the maximum exposure on missing sample items by analysis of related evidence. In the case of an asset, this may require the worst-case assumption that the item is worthless. In the case of a liability, the potential exposure is virtually unlimited, and this makes statistical auditing of liabilities more difficult. In certain cases (e.g., time deposit accounts of a banking institution), it would not normally be possible to estimate the maximum liability for missing sample items; in such cases, statistical variables estimation procedures may be inappropriate.

---

[4]There are statistical methods of relaxing this requirement under certain circumstances, but these methods are generally impracticable for audit use.

Different procedures for different items.   Although all selected items must be audited, it does not follow that the originally contemplated audit procedure must be applied to all items. For example, where the audit procedure is confirmation, some accounts will inevitably fail to confirm. If the auditor can be satisfied as to these nonresponding accounts by means of alternative auditing procedures, the requirement to audit all items can still be met, even though confirmation would have been the preferable procedure. The alternative procedures should be complete, however, not a test within a test. For example, if 100 account balance receivable confirmations are not returned, it would not be adequate to apply alternative tests only to 50 (or even 90) of these accounts, nor to apply alternative procedures to only selected open items within all 100 accounts. All components of the selected items must be audited to some conclusion.

Because every sample item must be audited, *negative confirmation requests cannot be used for statistical variables estimation.* There is no way of identifying whether an unreturned confirmation is a nonresponse or an affirmation. With positive confirmations, all nonresponses must be followed up, so there is no danger of inadvertently considering them to be good responses.

Where it is evident in advance that a population contains some items that may not be verifiable by the proposed audit test, it may not be appropriate to use statistical variables estimation procedures to audit that population. If the items that are not verifiable are known in advance, it may be possible to exclude them from the statistically sampled population and audit them by other means, while applying statistical sampling to the remainder of the population. In such cases, the results of the two separate procedures must be combined to reach an overall conclusion on the account being audited.

It is important to define the population so as to be consistent with the audit objective. For example, if the characteristic being tested is internal control over inventory purchases, it would not make sense to define the population as the voucher register, because the voucher register would include many items unrelated to inventory.

The most important point to remember about the population is that statistical conclusions can relate only to the population from which the sample items were selected. The conclusions cannot be extended to items not in the population, nor can they be applied to individual subpopulations within the population being audited.

Sampling Unit.   A population consists of *sampling units.* The sampling units consist of the individual elements in the population that will be sampled. They may be elements such as documents, account balances, open items, and entries, each comprising one unit in the sample.

More specifically, the sampling unit is the element in the population whose characteristics are to be measured or determined in order to estimate those characteristics for the population.

In a *variables* test, the sampling unit may be any element, provided that the sum of all such elements equals the total value to be estimated. For example, the auditor who wishes to verify the total balance of accounts receivable could select any of the following as the sampling unit: branch store (selected branches would then be verified in total), total customer balance (which is a common method when using confirmations), open invoices (which may be more productive if customers are unable to confirm total balances), line items on open invoices (which may be necessary in the case of very complex invoicing procedures), or any other practical element. The designation of the sampling unit for a *variables* test is solely a matter of convenience, economy, and effectiveness, because sampling units at any level of detail (or aggregation), so long as they are mutually exclusive and exhaust the population, will result in a valid estimate of the total quantity being audited.

However, the definition of the sampling unit for an *attribute* test must be considered in the light of the test objective. For instance, if the objective of the test is to ascertain the frequency with which disbursement vouchers occur without the proper authorizing signature, the voucher itself becomes the sampling unit, and the presence or absence of the signature is the characteristic measured. On the other hand, if the objective is to ascertain that line items on the voucher, of which there may be several, are authorized items, a line item on a voucher becomes the sampling unit, and there may be several sampling units on a single voucher. The objective of the attribute test determines the sampling unit as well as the characteristic of the sampling unit that is to be measured.

Where *dollar unit* sampling is used, the sampling unit is defined as a *population dollar*. This is a dollar contained in an appropriate physical population element as described above for a variables or attribute test. The auditor selects a sample of population dollars and identifies those physical elements containing the selected dollars. These physical elements are audited and the result for each physical element is applied, proportionately, to the sample dollar or dollars it contains. As an example, in a population totaling $1,200,000, dollar 343,712 may be selected and found to be included in voucher No. 7212, which totals $5,870. When this voucher is audited, it is found to be correct; thus, the sampling unit (dollar 343,712) is also deemed to be correct.

Based on this characterization of dollar unit sampling, it can be seen that the population and each sampling unit must have a dollar-magnitude identity for the method to be applicable. Certain accounting populations of interest to auditors, such as shipping records, may not be subject to dollar unit sampling for that reason.

Sampling Error. Whenever the auditor makes a partial (or sample) examination of a population, there is a risk that the sample is not exactly representative of the entire population. This is true even if 999 out of 1,000 items are examined. The *sampling error* is the difference between the estimate of the population value based on the sample and an estimate[5] of the population value that would result from applying the same methods to the entire population. *Sampling error* arises only because the examination does not include all population items. In practice, the true value of a population will never be known (otherwise there would be no need for the statistical sample), so the exact sampling error will

---

[5] If there were no nonsampling error (see below for definition), this estimate would be the true value of the population.

never be known. However, the unique feature of statistical sampling is that the probable magnitude of sampling error can be calculated and, by adjusting the sample size, can be made to conform with audit objectives. Sampling error also exists in judgmental audit samples, but in such samples it cannot be measured.

The way in which probable sampling error is commonly expressed is the *precision interval*. For a hypothetical population, assume that a statistician has computed that 95 percent of all possible sample estimates of a given sample size would be within $10,000 of the true (but unknown) population value. Assume, too, that the statistical estimate of the population total based on one sample of the specified size is $950,000 and that the recorded amount is $1,000,000. The "statistical precision interval" is then $950,000 plus or minus $10,000 at 95 percent reliability. If the true population value were $1,000,000, there is only a 5 percent probability of achieving a statistical estimate as far off as $990,000 or $1,010,000 and a negligible probability of achieving an estimate as far off as $950,000. The auditor is therefore likely to conclude that the true value is not $1,000,000, but is closer to $950,000. In this case, 95 percent is the "reliability" of the estimate, $10,000 is the "precision" of the estimate, $940,000 is the "lower precision limit," $950,000 is the "statistical point estimate," and $960,000 is the "upper precision limit."

Reliability and precision are inversely related; thus, for any given sample size, if the precision limits are made less precise (for example, increased from $10,000 to $15,000), the reliability that the true population value is contained in the precision interval is increased (e.g., from 95 percent to 99.7 percent).

Nonsampling Error. When considering the risks of a statistical audit procedure, the auditor must also recognize the possibility, or even likelihood, that the results obtained may be inaccurate because of mistakes made in inspecting or examining the items in the sample. This is referred to as *nonsampling error.* Human fallibility being what it is, mistakes are likely to occur through fatigue, improper understanding of the assignment, ambiguous documents, or otherwise. Should the fact that a voucher was not correct be overlooked by the auditor, the conclusion drawn from the sampling will be wrong. Similarly, incorrect counts would result in an incorrect inventory valuation.

Unfortunately, the risk in nonsampling error is not generally subject to measurement. However, this same risk would exist even if 100 percent of the data in the entire population were examined. Actually, there may be less nonsampling error in a sample than in a complete examination, because greater pains can be taken to eliminate many of the possibilities of error when the volume of items to be examined is relatively small.

This point is well understood by statisticians. H. V. Roberts says, "A good deal of evidence suggests that non-sampling errors . . . are often more substantial than sampling errors. Since a sample involves a relatively small administrative apparatus as compared with a census (a complete enumeration), it may be possible to reduce the non-sampling errors. . . . One famous example of a sample outperforming a census occurred in the province of Bengal in India, during the late 1930's, when the purpose was to measure the size of the jute harvest. When the true size eventually was ascertained through warehouse records, the census was found to have erred by 20% while the concurrent sample survey came within ½ percent" [Roberts, 1974, p. 30].

The total error inherent in a statistical audit procedure is a composite of the sampling error and the nonsampling error. The probable sampling error can be measured statistically and reduced to a level compatible with the audit objective. Because the nonsampling error cannot be statistically measured and controlled, it is necessary to exercise care to keep it to a minimum so that the audit test produces a valid result. Several precautions are helpful to minimize nonsampling error:

Sampling objectives and the definition of characteristics to be estimated should be stated clearly.

Auditors doing the detail work should be instructed and impressed with the need for careful work.

Detail work should be reviewed.

These precautions should reduce nonsampling error to negligible amounts. The precautions are easier to state, however, than to enforce. Of course, nonsampling error could invalidate any audit work, whether statistical or judgmental; therefore, these same precautions would be applicable to nonstatistical audit work.

Random Sampling. Satisfactory statistical results cannot be achieved unless a random sample is drawn, because only then are the laws of probability, on which statistical mathematics is based, operative. A random sample is one in which each sampling unit has a known, nonzero probability of selection, and each possible sample of a given size has an equal probability of selection. Some examples of random sampling include unrestricted random sampling (all items in the population have an equal probability of selection), stratified random sampling (the population is broken down into mutually exclusive and exhaustive subpopulations called *strata* and unrestricted random sampling is employed in each stratum), and dollar unit sampling (all items have a probability of selection directly proportional to their size and all items of the same size have an equal probability of selection). Mere avoidance of personal subjectivity through haphazard choice of items does not provide a random sample.

Systematic sampling (selecting items at equal intervals after a random start) is not random sampling, although in many cases it may be close enough for practical purposes. Before using such a nonrandom technique as a convenient substitute for unrestricted random selection, the auditor should be satisfied that the population is in random order with respect to the characteristic being measured and that the pattern inherent in the systematic sampling interval does not coincide with any pattern in the population.

Selecting the Sample. After a sampling plan has been designed and the sample size has been computed, it becomes necessary to draw the sample. For the sample to be random, some method of random selection must be devised. This involves selecting random numbers and matching them against the population in such a way that the desired probabilities of selection are achieved.

In principle, it should be easy to select numbers from a random number table, establish some correspondence with the population of audit interest, and draw the items. In practice, however, such manual methods are time-consuming, prone to errors, and generally impracticable for all but very small samples. Any auditor who must repeatedly draw samples should use some form of computerized selection plan to minimize both the cost and the possibility of errors in sample selection.

Many time-sharing vendors have programs available to select random numbers. In any case, the auditor can enter a random-number selection program onto any time-sharing system. Volume VI of the AICPA publication, *An Auditor's Approach to Statistical Sampling*, includes the complete code of a program to select random numbers; this program can easily be entered onto most time-sharing systems.

Many auditors have access to generalized computer audit software that incorporates a random selection feature; such systems can be used effectively where the data to be audited are in machine-readable form.

A third possibility would be for the auditor to program a random selection routine that is used to process auditee data files and select samples. A suitable method of generating random numbers in such programs is the *power residue* method, explained in detail in the publication, *Random Number Generation and Testing*, published by International Business Machines Corporation, Technical Publications Department (document GC20-8011-0).

The process of matching random numbers to sampling units is relatively straightforward for variables and attributes tests. Usually the random number relates directly to a comparable identification number for the sampling unit—for example, voucher number or part number. In other cases, the random number relates to location of the item, such as page number, line number in a journal or subsidiary ledger.

For dollar unit sampling, however, the process is somewhat more complicated, but basically consists of five steps: First, the required number of random numbers are obtained in a range between 1 and the total population dollar value (e.g., between 1 and 1,200,000). Second, these random numbers are sorted in ascending sequence. Third, the population's physical elements are listed in

EXHIBIT 1   Preparing Cumulative Totals for Dollar Unit Sampling

Voucher no.	Recorded amount	Cumulative total	Population dollars contained in voucher
1........	$ 357	$ 357	$ 1–357
2........	1,281	1,638	358–1,638
3........	60	1,698	1,639–1,698
4........	573	2,271	1,699–2,271
5........	691	2,962	2,272–2,962
6........	143	3,105	2,963–3,105

any convenient order, showing the dollar amount of each item. Fourth, the amounts of these items are accumulated. Fifth, the random numbers are matched to the cumulative amounts from step four to determine which elements contain them. Exhibit 1 illustrates this process. Thus, if random number 1,812 were obtained, it would be identified as being contained in voucher no. 4. Note that one physical element of the population can contain more than one selected sample item (dollar) under dollar unit sampling. This requires special consideration in the evaluation stage.

STATISTICAL SUBSTANTIVE TESTS

Sample Design. In designing a substantive sampling plan, the auditor must consider whether the audit objective is (1) to test the reasonableness of a financial representation (e.g., the auditee's purported receivable balance) or (2) to make an independent estimate of some amount (e.g., an estimate of the FIFO inventory when the books are kept at latest invoice price). In the first case the auditor desires to accept the auditee's representation without adjustment if it is reasonably correct, and to propose an adjustment only if it is probable that there might be a material error in the amount as stated by the auditee. In this case, the auditor should use either a *variables hypothesis test* approach to the audit, which statistically discriminates between the hypothesis that the amount as represented is correct and the alternative hypothesis that the amount is materially misstated, or a dollar unit sampling approach, which statistically determines a maximum amount of error that might exist in the population.

On the other hand, when the auditee does not state an amount that purports to be correct (such as when improper accounting principles have been used, or numerous errors are known to exist in the records), the auditor should use a statistical *estimation* approach in order to develop an estimate of the correct account balance. Ordinarily, in such cases the auditor would intend to propose an adjustment to bring the account balance into agreement with the statistical estimate.

It is important to note here that statistical estimation is generally done using variables sampling and *not* dollar unit sampling. Variables sampling estimation is similar to variables hypothesis testing. In fact, design features such as the basis and extent of stratification, the method of selecting and auditing sample items, and the method of computing the statistical point estimate and the standard error of that estimate are identical for both approaches. The major difference is in determining the tolerable magnitude of sampling error and the decision rule to be used.

The next segment of this section deals with hypothesis testing. This is followed by a section on variables estimation and then dollar unit evaluation.

Hypothesis Testing. To apply hypothesis testing, it is necessary to determine the tolerable magnitude of sampling error and relate this to specific decision rules. These are primarily audit considerations and are discussed here. Chapter

11 of this handbook deals with other design considerations, such as stratification, computational methods, and sample size calculations.

Definition of error in substantive test. Because the feature of audit interest in a substantive test is the monetary amount of errors that would affect the financial statements being audited, a sample item is considered to be in error if it contains a monetary error of any amount. A monetary error would include an item recorded at the wrong amount or entered into the wrong account or entered in the wrong period. When sampling from an account, even small errors must be considered, because their effect must be projected to all the items not selected.

If an auditor found an item misclassified between balance sheet accounts, that would be considered a monetary error. On the other hand, if an auditor found an item misclassified between subsidiary accounts (say, individual accounts receivable) but within the correct general ledger account, that would not ordinarily be considered a monetary error because it would have no effect on the financial statement balance. However, the auditor should nevertheless consider the effect such an error would have on the evaluation of internal control.

Valuation approaches. The principal source of entries into books of accounts is the recording of bona fide transactions. Although various accrual and valuation entries are made to convert the basic transaction accounting records to financial statements, the accounting records are essentially transaction-based. The auditor's report attests not merely to the results of transactions, but also to certain economic facts recognized in the financial statements.

For example, an account receivable resulting from a valid transaction may be a legally enforceable receivable based on a valid transaction, but the customer may be bankrupt and unable to pay; therefore, there may be no economic receivable. The auditor can determine the correct net balance of a given asset account in either of two ways:

1. Estimate the net balance directly; or
2. Estimate the gross balance and the required contra or valuation allowance separately.

Although either of the above methods is a valid audit approach, it is important that the statement of statistical objectives identify which is being used. In the first case, the values to be statistically evaluated would be net realizable amounts, whereas in the second, they would be gross amounts. Therefore, different audit procedures would be required. If auditors on the job misunderstand which method is being used, they may invalidate the test by using the wrong amounts in the statistical evaluation, or by mixing the two methods inadvertently.

100 percent stratum. Most auditors, even in judgment sampling, examine all sampling units that are individually significant. Statistically, there are two good reasons to do this: (1) It reduces the variability of the population to be sampled, thus reducing the sample size; and (2) it improves the stability of the standard error of the estimate, thus maintaining the target risk levels of the sampling plan. A useful rule of thumb is to place all sampling units with amounts greater than four or five times the average sampling unit amount into a stratum to be examined 100 percent. (Note that there may be none or very few of such items in many accounting populations.)

Auditors sometimes allocate items to a 100 percent stratum for reasons other than size—for example, items that are old, obsolete, or otherwise attract the auditor's attention. This procedure is perfectly appropriate and statistically valid. The auditor can arbitrarily assign any sampling units to a 100 percent stratum before sampling without introducing statistical bias. However, once the sample has been drawn, it is inappropriate to move items retroactively from the sampled strata to the 100 percent stratum based on sample findings. (Note that selection of high-dollar items is an inherent feature of dollar unit sampling because the probability of selecting an item is proportional to its size. As with variables sampling, however, allocation to a 100 percent stratum on some other basis requires a special effort.)

Normal distribution of sample estimates. The mathematical approaches for variables sampling are all based on the use of sampling techniques that result in normally distributed sample estimates of the standard error. Certain sampling methods do not meet these requirements, either because of characteristics of the underlying populations or because they are based on other mathematical principles. Exhibit 2 summarizes the conditions under which various sampling methods meet these requirements.

The significance of normal theory is that, if it applies, the auditor can use it to make probability statements and draw statistical inferences. For example, assume that an auditor is sampling from accounts receivable with a true value of $1,000,000. (Of course the true value would not be known, otherwise there would be no need to sample.) Assume also that the auditor has taken a sample and computed the standard error of estimate[6] to be $20,000. The auditor who uses estimates that are normally distributed knows that estimates from all possible samples of the type and size being taken are normally distributed about the true value. Further, if the sampling procedure produces a stable estimate of the standard error, then the auditor knows that the normal distribution of sample estimates about the true value will have a standard deviation of about $20,000 ("about" because there is also some sampling error in the estimated standard error). If the true standard deviation of sample results is $20,000, then a sampling procedure producing estimates in the range $19,000 to $21,000 would be reasonably stable, whereas one producing estimates in the range $10,000 to $30,000 would be so unstable as to be unusable.

---

[6]In this chapter, the term "standard error of estimate" is used only in the sense of the standard error of the estimated population *total* value, and is the value computed from the sample that is expected to approximate the standard deviation of the distribution of estimates of total value. This is done because auditors typically consider total errors rather than mean errors; the result is more convenient formulas and calculations. The standard error of the estimated total is obtained from the *standard error of the mean* by multiplying by the number of items in the population. Consider the example given in Chapter 11, Exhibit 8. There the mean estimate is $21.17 and the standard error of the mean estimate is $.976. Both of these figures can be converted to estimates of total population value by multiplying by 100, the number of items in the population. Thus, the estimated population total value is $2,117 (= 100 × $21.17) and the standard error of the estimated total is $97.60 (= 100 × $.976).

EXHIBIT 2   Conditions under Which Normal Theory Applies to Selected Sampling Methods

Name of sampling method	Conditions under which normal theory applies
Mean per unit	Extreme values assigned to 100% stratum
Auxiliary information estimators (ratio, difference, linear regression)	Extreme values assigned to 100% stratum and error rate in population high enough so there is a reasonably large[a] expected number of errors in the sample. If few or no errors are expected (or found), normal theory does not apply.
Dollar unit sampling and attribute sampling	Never. Based on mathematical methods not employing normal theory.

[a]Research by Neter and Loebbecke [1975] indicates that a "reasonably large" number of errors in a sample would be 10%, as long as no more than 75% of the errors are in one direction.

What is the probability, under these conditions, of obtaining a sample estimate of $1,050,000 or greater? In order to find the probability, we must convert these facts into the same units as used in a standard normal table, which we do by computing a Z value.

$$Z = \frac{\$1,050,000 - \$1,000,000}{\$20,000}$$
$$= 2.5$$

The Z value simply expresses the dollar difference as number of standard deviations. We look up 2.5 in a standard normal table (Chapter 11, Exhibit 6) and find that the probability of a sample estimate less than 2.5 standard deviations above the mean ($1,050,000 in this example) is .99379. Conversely, there is only a .00621 probability of a value more than 2.5 standard deviations above the mean ($1,050,000 or greater in the example). If we actually obtained an estimate as high as $1,050,000, therefore, we would probably conclude that we were not sampling from a population whose true value was $1,000,000.

The hypothesis test. The purpose of a hypothesis test is to discriminate between two alternative hypotheses:

1. H_0: The account balance as stated (book value) is correct.
2. H_1: The book value is in error by a material amount.

Unless all items comprising the total book value are examined, there is some risk due to sampling error of accepting H_0 as true when in fact H_1 is true. In other words, there is some risk of accepting as correct a balance that is materially in error; this is defined as the β (beta) risk. There is also the possibility of rejecting H_0 as false when it is true, the risk of rejecting a correct balance. This is defined as the α (alpha) risk.

The following table shows the relationship of the α and β risks:

	Book value	
Audit conclusion	Correct	In error by a material amount
Book value correct	Conclusion correct	β risk
Book value materially in error	α risk	Conclusion correct

To conduct a statistical hypothesis test, it is necessary to specify the amount considered material (M) and the acceptable levels of α and β risks. On the basis of these values, the auditor can compute the target standard error of the estimated total value (SE_T) that must be achieved in the sample to execute the hypothesis test. From that required standard error, the necessary sample size can be estimated using the methods described in Chapter 11.

Required standard error of estimate. Suppose that the book value (BV) is correct, and thus equal to the true value (TV). Any sample estimate of the total value will result in acceptance of the book value if the estimate lies within $\pm A$ (the acceptance range) of the book value; otherwise the book value will be rejected. The distribution of all possible sample estimates drawn from the population can be illustrated as in Exhibit 3.

In other words, of all possible samples, a proportion represented by α will yield an estimate of the total value that is outside the predefined acceptance range of $BV \pm A$. This is the α risk.

Because the sample estimates are normally distributed, the α risk, target standard error, and acceptance range can be related as follows (note that Z_y is the number of standard deviations beyond which an area of y remains in the tail, as computed from a standard normal table):

$$A = Z_{\alpha/2} \times SE_T \qquad (1)$$

EXHIBIT 3   Distribution of Possible Sample Estimates Drawn from Population (BV = Book Value, M = Material Amount, A = Acceptance Range, TV = True Value)

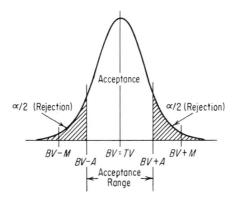

EXHIBIT 4   Distribution of Sample Estimates

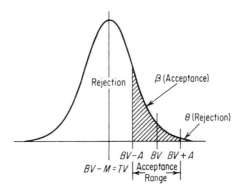

Now suppose that the book value is in error by exactly a material amount M. Again the decision rule will be to accept the book value if the sample estimate is within $\pm A$ of the book value and to reject the book value otherwise. The distribution of sample estimates will now be as shown in Exhibit 4. (Note that Exhibit 4 shows the situation when $TV = BV - M$; the equivalent situation when $TV = BV + M$ is not illustrated because it is just a mirror image of this figure.) Most samples will result in an estimate that lies in the unshaded portion of the distribution, and will therefore result in the proper rejection of the book value.

Of all possible samples, a proportion represented by β will yield an estimate that lies within $\pm A$ of the book value, ignoring the area to the right of $BV + A$, called θ and discussed below. Each of these samples will give rise to an acceptance of the book value even though it is materially in error. This is the β risk.

There is also the remote possibility of a sample result lying in the extreme tail (θ), and such a result would also lead to the rejecting of the book value. However, this possibility is ignored in practice, as θ is negligibly small as long as $\alpha + \beta \leq .60$ (which is typical of most auditing applications).

Again, because the sample estimates are normally distributed, and remembering that θ is negligibly small, the β risk, target standard error, and acceptance range can be related as follows:

$$A = M - Z_\beta \times SE_T \tag{2}$$

By combining Eqs. (1) and (2), we find that the target standard error for a hypothesis test is as follows:

$$SE_T = \frac{M}{Z_{\alpha/2} + Z_\beta}$$

Recall that M is the dollar amount of a material error. Exhibit 5 provides common Z values to assist in making this calculation.

The auditor must select sufficient sample items to be sure that this target standard error is achieved. When the requirement is met, it is possible to decide whether to accept or reject the book value based on whether the statistically estimated total value lies within the acceptance range or not.

The accept/reject decision can be shown diagramatically, assuming that $\alpha = .05$, and $\beta = .05$, by combining Exhibits 3 and 4 into Exhibit 6, top panel. If $\alpha = .05$ and $\beta = .50$, the decision rule would be reflected by the diagram in the lower panel of Exhibit 6.

Thus, based on the auditor's specification of M (the amount considered material), α (the risk of rejecting a correct balance), and β (the risk of accepting a balance materially in error), a statistical hypothesis test can be designed. The following parts of this section deal with considerations in specifying these values.

The hypothesis test described above is a simple alternative hypothesis test, which considers only two absolute amounts of error: zero and exactly a material amount. In reality, the amount of error in an account balance may vary from zero to infinity. The auditor should be aware of the probabilities of accepting as correct account balances in error by various possible amounts. These probabilities can be calculated for any specified sampling plan, and can be plotted as an *operating characteristic curve*. Curves are plotted in Exhibit 7 for the sampling plans $\alpha = .05$, $\beta = .05$ and $\alpha = .05$, $\beta = .50$—two typical audit sampling plans.

From inspection of Exhibit 7, the auditor can compute the probability of accepting book values in error by any amount. A desirable feature of these sampling plans is that the probability of accepting an account balance as correct becomes smaller and smaller as the error in such an account balance becomes larger and larger. For example, even when the auditor uses the sampling plan with $\alpha = .05$ and $\beta = .50$, the probability of accepting the book value as correct is only .05 when the error is 1.84 times the measure of materiality.

Thus it can be seen that even though the auditor specifies acceptance probabilities for only two error levels (zero and M) in designing a hypothesis test,

EXHIBIT 5   Z Values for Computing SE_T, Target Standard Error

α	$Z_{\alpha/2}$	β	Z_β
.05......	1.96	.05	1.65
.10......	1.65	.10	1.28
.15......	1.44	.15	1.04
.20......	1.28	.20	.84
.25......	1.15	.25	.67
.30......	1.04	.30	.52
.35......	.94	.35	.39
.40......	.84	.40	.25
.45......	.76	.45	.13
.50......	.67	.50	.00

the resulting sampling plan is really a continuous range of acceptance probabilities over a continuous range of error magnitudes.

M: **The measure of materiality.** The amount considered material for the audit test must be specified because that measure defines the alternative hypothesis to be tested:

$$H_0: \quad TV = BV$$
$$H_1: \quad TV = BV \pm M$$

Whenever the auditor draws a conclusion about an entire population after examining only a part of it, the conclusion is subject to sampling error, which occurs solely because the entire population was not examined. With statistical sampling, the probable magnitude of sampling error can be measured and, through adjustment of the sample size, controlled. The concept of materiality is therefore important in statistical sampling because it governs the amount of sampling error that can be tolerated in an audit. If, for example, $100,000 is

---

EXHIBIT 6   Accept/Reject Decision as a Function of α and β (top pannel, $\alpha = .05$, $\beta = .05$; bottom panel, $\alpha = .05$, $\beta = .50$)

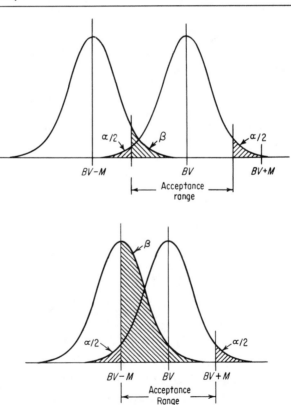

EXHIBIT 7   **Operating Characteristics of Selected Sampling Plans**

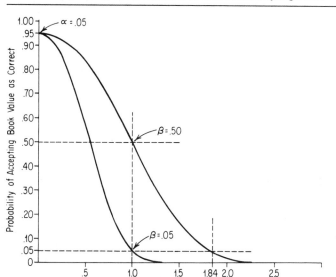

Error in Book Value (measured in multiples of the dollar amount designated as material)

considered material with respect to a set of financial statements, the aggregate sampling error cannot be more than $100,000: Otherwise an error in excess of a material amount could exist in the financial statements with the possibility of not being discovered by the auditor.

This requirement has been recognized in SAS No. 39 [1981, par. 18], which states:

> Evaluation in monetary terms of the results of a sample for a substantive test of details contributes directly to the auditor's purpose, since such an evaluation can be related to his judgment of the monetary amount of errors that would be material. When planning a sample for a substantive test of details, the auditor should consider how much monetary error in the related account balance or class of transactions may exist without causing the financial statements to be materially misstated. This maximum monetary error for the balance or class is called *tolerable* error for the sample. Tolerable error is a planning concept and is related to the auditor's preliminary estimates of materiality levels in such a way that tolerable error, combined for the entire audit plan, does not exceed those estimates.

To perform a statistical variables test, the auditor must specify the measure of materiality for the test. Some auditors may object to the requirement to specify the measure of materiality in advance of performing the test, but it requires no more information than, and is conceptually similar to, evaluating errors after their discovery. The auditor must have some standards for specifying materiality so these standards can be applied in advance to specify a maximum dollar amount of errors that is acceptable. The use of statistical variables sampling necessitates the determination of an amount deemed material.

In general terms, a given fact may be regarded as material if it is significant to a decision maker in the context of the decision to be made. In other words, if the decision maker would reach a different decision if he or she had been aware of the fact in question, then the fact is material. In order to apply this definition to audit decisions about facts, the auditor would have to anticipate what facts would be significant to the user of the audited financial statements. When making judgments, the auditor would have to know: (1) the fact to be considered by the decision maker, (2) who the decision maker is, and (3) the decision process (how the fact is to be used). In practice, the latter two are, at best, dimly known, whereas the first item may become known only if the auditing procedures are sufficient to discover it.

Materiality has somewhat different meanings in accounting and auditing contexts. There are two aspects to *accounting materiality*; the first is *monetary-error materiality* (i.e., by how much could the financial statements be in error without significantly affecting the user?), and the second is *disclosure materiality* (i.e., would the disclosure or nondisclosure of a certain fact significantly affect the user?). Monetary errors would include errors due to (1) the incorrect quantification of accounting information (whether intentional or unintentional), (2) use of accounting principles not generally accepted, and (3) the incorrect classification of data (by description or date). A disclosure error could occur if a material fact is not included or is improperly included in the financial statements (including the footnotes).

On the other hand, *auditing materiality* is related to the sensitivity of the audit to discovering monetary errors of various magnitudes. If audit procedures are such that a $100,000 error might exist without being discovered, then auditing materiality must be at least $100,000. If, for the same company, the measure of monetary-error accounting materiality were $50,000, the auditing materiality would be too large, for a $50,000 to $100,000 error might exist without being discovered, and this, by the definition of accounting materiality, would clearly be significant. Therefore, auditing materiality must not be greater than monetary-error accounting materiality.

The measure of accounting materiality can also be related to the type of audit opinion. If an auditor knows of a certain error in the financial statements but is willing to issue an unqualified accountants' report, then the error must be deemed immaterial. Conversely, if the auditor qualifies the opinion (or gives an adverse opinion), the error must be deemed material. In this sense, the border of materiality is at the point that the auditor decides to issue a qualified opinion rather than an unqualified opinion.

Often the determination of accounting materiality contemplates such factors as net income (or a normal level of net income for such a company), total assets, equity, and other considerations. In consideration of these factors, the auditor should determine the amount to be considered material with respect to the financial statements taken as a whole.

In contract auditing, the auditor may not be interested primarily in the financial statements taken as a whole, but may be more likely to determine the measure of materiality based on the total contract price and other relevant variables.

Allocating materiality to tests. The measure of auditing materiality selected in accordance with the audit objectives would, of course, be the total materiality for the audit as a whole. When selecting the materiality level for a specific statistical test, a lesser figure should be used; otherwise, there would be no margin for error in any other account. For example, if the auditor decided that the overall measure of auditing materiality for the financial statements as a whole was $100,000 and then tested accounts receivables with an auditing materiality of $100,000, there would be no room for error in any other account. Any error in the other accounts in the same direction, added to the possible error of $100,000 in accounts receivable, would exceed the amount specified by the auditor as material for the financial statement as a whole.

It is therefore necessary to allocate the overall measure of auditing materiality to the individual statistical audit tests. A method of doing this among variables hypothesis tests is described in the paragraphs that follow.

Before allocating the overall measure of statistical materiality to the statistical tests, it is necessary to consider the financial statement amounts that are not audited statistically. In determining the materiality for a specific audit test, the auditor should estimate the total uncertainty in the accounts not audited statistically. The auditor should review the potential problem areas and estimate the probable outside limit of possible error for all these accounts. This total must always be less than the overall measure of auditing materiality, or else the work done will be insufficient to warrant an unqualified opinion.

In determining the estimated limit of error in accounts not audited statistically, the auditor should consider the nature of these accounts. If, for example, they were capital stock, additional paid-in capital, and long-term debt, not much allowance for error would ordinarily need to be assigned because each of these accounts could theoretically be audited to achieve an accurate result. On the other hand, if the accounts not audited statistically included receivables, inventories, or accounts payable, a larger allowance for error would ordinarily be assigned.

Having determined the overall measure of materiality and the estimated limit of error in the accounts not audited statistically, the auditor can allocate the difference to the accounts to be statistically audited. The following formula may be used to determine a proper allocation:

$$\sqrt{\Sigma(M_i)^2} \le M_0 - M_{est} \qquad (3)$$

where M_i is the materiality of the ith statistically audited account, M_0 is the total measure of auditing materiality available for allocation, and M_{est} is the materiality allocated to all accounts not audited statistically. An example will illustrate the procedure. Assume the following:

Accounts to Be Audited Statistically—Receivables and Inventory:
M_0: $1,200,000
M_{est}: $ 700,000

In this case, $500,000 is available for allocation to the accounts to be audited statistically ($1,200,000 − $700,000). Then $M_{receivables}$ of $300,000, and $M_{inventory}$ of $400,000 would be a feasible choice, because

$$\sqrt{(\$300,000)^2 + (\$400,000)^2} = \$500,000$$

A whole range of other values would also satisfy this requirement; the allocation is a matter of audit judgment. Note that the sum of all the individual figures ($300,000 for receivables plus $400,000 for inventory plus $700,000 for the nonstatistically audited accounts equals $1,400,000) exceeds the overall measure ($1,200,000) of auditing materiality. This is consistent with the purpose of keeping the probable error within $1,200,000. The reason is that, although accounts receivable could be off by as much as $300,000 statistically, and inventory by as much as $400,000, the probability of a $700,000 error in these two accounts is very remote because it would require both accounts to be off by the maximum amount and in the same direction. The formula given in Eq. (3) adjusts for this to keep the probabilities at a level consistent with audit objectives.

Relation between materiality and sample size. The sample size in a variables test is most heavily influenced by the ratio of the measure of materiality to the balance of the account being tested. If this ratio is less than 1 percent, the sample size is usually large. Furthermore, if the materiality is halved, the sample size is approximately quadrupled. In order to illustrate the effect on sample size of varying the measure of materiality for a statistical test, a hypothetical audit case is given below. The same relationship would hold in all cases.

$$\frac{\text{Material Amount}}{\text{Account Balance}} =$$

Materiality ratio (%)	Approximate sample size (items)
4.0	100
2.0	400
1.0	1,600
.4	10,000

The α risk. The α risk is the probability that the auditor will reject correct financial statement balances. There is, however, little likelihood of actually committing such an error. If the tests point to rejection, the auditor will usually investigate further to ascertain and correct the causes. For statistical purposes, therefore, the risk can be considered as the risk that the auditor will unnecessarily be forced to perform follow-up work when an account balance is erroneously rejected. The costs associated with this risk are only those of this unnecessary audit work. There is a theoretical optimum value in each test for α (between 0 and 1) that will minimize total cost, but it is not practicably possible to solve for this value. It is probable that the optimum value is relatively low, say, .20 or less. Because sample sizes are substantially larger when α is less than .05, a value in the range .05 to .20 appears most practicable. A reasonable approach would be for the auditor to select an acceptable risk level and then use it for all statistical tests as a matter of policy.

The β risk. The β risk is of critical importance to the auditor. When a given audit is complete, the auditor wants to have a great deal of assurance that an unqualified opinion has not been given on materially incorrect financial statements. If the only source of reliance were statistical tests, it is clear that a very low β risk would be required. However, there are other factors in the typical audit.

In carrying out substantive audit tests, the auditor has several sources of reliance for being satisfied that there is no material error condition, or if there is one, that it will be discovered. The auditor must be confident, after considering all sources of reliance, that no material error exists or that any existing material error would come to light. The reliance the auditor places on a statistical test affects the required sample size and is, in turn, influenced by the reliance placed on internal control or on the reliance placed on other (nonstatistical) audit procedures, or both.

The required β risk for a CPA conducting a substantive audit test is discussed in the Appendix to SAS No. 39. The risk that the auditor fails to detect a material error in the financial statements (the ultimate risk) is discussed. This risk is expressed as a combination of various other risks—namely, that (1) a material error occurs in the financial statements, (2) the internal controls fail to detect and correct the error given that it occurred, (3) the auditor's analytical review procedures and other relevant tests fail to detect the error, and (4) the auditor's tests of details (e.g., the statistical tests being performed) fail to detect the error given all the foregoing. Because these risks are conditional, they can be multiplied to give the ultimate risk:

$$UR = EO \times IC \times AR \times TD$$

where UR = ultimate risk
EO = risk of material error occurring
IC = risk of failure of internal control
AR = risk of failure of analytical review and other relevant tests
TD = risk of failure of tests of details

The ultimate risk level desired by the auditor can be set at some reasonable level, and SAS No. 39 illustrates a value of .05 (which is used by many auditors). Because EO is difficult to quantify, it is conservatively assumed by many auditors to equal 1. TD is precisely the β risk as discussed above and can be solved for as follows:

$$\beta(TD) = \frac{UR}{IC \times AR} \qquad (4)$$

It is clear from this formulation that the auditor must evaluate the strength of internal controls and the other (nonstatistical) audit procedures to determine the β risk to use for a given substantive test.

In evaluating internal controls, the auditor need be concerned only with those specific controls to be relied on in selecting a β risk. Once reliance is placed on controls, however, the auditor must test the controls for compliance and effectiveness. Conversely, there is no need for a compliance test when controls are evaluated as nonexistent because, in this case, no reliance will be placed on the controls when selecting a β risk. Furthermore, because the purpose of compliance testing is to permit restriction of other work, it would not be logical to spend more effort on the compliance test than can be saved in the test of financial statement amounts. Before making this decision, the auditor should evaluate which approach will be more efficient. The auditor should remember the purpose of the compliance test and omit it when it is not required or justified.

Even the most effective system of internal control will not prevent deliberate override of the controls by management personnel. Therefore, the auditor must consider the risk of material error through management override of the system of internal control. Although it is impossible to determine with certainty those cases in which management has overridden the internal controls, it should generally be possible to evaluate this risk through consideration of such factors as the type of organization being audited, the susceptibility of the area being examined to misstatement, the requirement for management judgment in computing the amounts in the records, and prior experience in auditing the financial statements of the client. Note that the evaluation is not intended to assess the probability that management is overriding the controls, but merely whether the area being examined presents any significant potential for override.

Whenever the risk of override is deemed to be significant, the auditor should limit reliance on internal control, whether or not there is any evidence or reason to believe that management has overridden the controls. Therefore, the auditor should test at a lower β risk, or, more accurately, should not increase the β risk by relying on internal control.

The other factor the auditor must consider is the nature and effectiveness of other auditing procedures applied in the areas under examination. If the auditor is performing analytic reviews of the ratios and trends or additional detailed audit procedures, or both, reliance on the statistical test is obviously less than it would be in the absence of these other procedures. The auditor can therefore use a higher β risk. It is important to note, however, that in increasing the β risk in reliance on other procedures, the auditor should evaluate any unusual conditions revealed by any of the tests performed. For example, the auditor should not ignore an unusual condition in one test because other tests fail to reveal it. The failure of any single test to reveal a condition of interest is not a positive indication that it does not exist. Unusual circumstances revealed in any test require further investigation regardless of the outcome of other tests.

Other auditing procedures can be classified as to whether they are significantly effective or only moderately effective. A significantly effective additional test would be a test with the relatively high probability of discovering material aggregate error conditions that exist (e.g., most detail tests), whereas a moderately effective test would have a fair probability of discovering material aggregate errors (e.g., many well-designed analytical tests). For example, assume that the audit test in question were a price test of inventory. The following additional tests would ordinarily be significantly effective: comparison of carrying prices with subsequent sales prices as adjusted to exclude normal gross profit, testing to published price quotations, confirmations with vendors, and detailed appraisals. The following tests would ordinarily be moderately effective: analysis of gross profit ratios by product lines, discussions with knowledgeable and reasonably disinterested persons, and analysis of standard cost system and variances.

In order to calculate the β risk by Eq. (4), the auditor must quantify IC and AR after evaluating the strength of internal controls and other audit procedures. Research done so far is inadequate to devise accurate methods of quantifying these risks. In the meantime, auditors faced with the necessity of using some β risk have adopted reasonable and conservative guidelines. A scheme used by some auditors is illustrated in Exhibit 8. This scheme is based on the assumption that risks IC and AR decline exponentially from 1 to .1 (a conservative value) as the strength of internal controls and other audit procedures increase to their maximum values. Note that the guidelines illustrated do not recommend a β risk greater than .50, which is consistent with the values illustrated in SAS No. 39.

EXHIBIT 8   Illustration of Method of Selection of β Risk

Reliance Assigned to Internal Control

If there is a significant risk that management could override the controls in effect over the area being examined, enter 0. Otherwise, evaluate the internal controls in effect over the area being examined.

If the controls are	Enter
Excellent	4
Good	3
Fair	2
Poor	1
Nonexistent	0

Reliance Assigned to Other Audit Procedures

Evaluate the other audit procedures that might detect material errors of the type being tested for by the statistical test. For each significantly effective additional test allow 2 points, and for each moderately effective additional test allow 1 point. Enter the total (not to exceed 4 points).

Total

If the total above is	Use this β risk
0	.05
1	.10
2	.15
3	.30
4	.50
5	.50[a]
6–8	.50[b]

[a] In view of these conditions, the auditor may wish to consider increasing the effectiveness of other auditing procedures and omitting the statistical test.

[b] In view of these conditions, the auditor may wish to consider omitting the statistical test.

In order to demonstrate the value of increasing the β risk to the justifiable maximum, some relative sample sizes follow, based on a hypothetical audit case with $\alpha = .05$ (the same sample size *relationship* would hold in all cases):

β risk	Sample size
.05	340
.10	275
.15	235
.30	160
.50	100

Evaluation of sample results. After designing the sampling plan, selecting the sample, and auditing the sample items, the auditor calculates two values from the sample (using the methods discussed in Chapter 11): the estimated total audit value (AV) of the population and the achieved standard error of the estimate (SE_A).

At this point, the auditor has all the information needed to reach a statistical conclusion, namely:

$$BV = \text{book value of population}$$
$$AV = \text{statistically estimated total audit value of population}$$
$$SE_A = \text{achieved standard error of estimate}$$
$$SE_T = \text{target standard error of estimate}$$
$$M = \text{measure of materiality for test}$$
$$\alpha = \alpha \text{ risk of test}$$
$$\beta = \beta \text{ risk of test}$$
$$n = \text{sample size}$$

The decision process is summarized in Exhibit 9.

The first question the auditor must ask is whether the achieved standard error of estimate is less than or equal to the required standard error of estimate. If not, a hypothesis test cannot be completed using the original values for M, α, and β. Although the auditor could relax the requirements on one or more of these values and possibly complete the test at such new value(s), that is not usually desirable, for presumably the original requirements were selected in such a way as to meet certain audit objectives. To loosen the requirements would then be to fail to meet the audit objectives.

If the target standard error of estimate has not been achieved, an additional sample should be selected and audited. The additional sample size required (ignoring the finite population correction factor discussed in Chapter 11) is $n[(SE_A/SE_T)^2 - 1]$. Many auditors add another 10 to 20 percent to this incremental sample to reduce the possibility of failing to meet the target yet again. After the additional sample items are audited, the auditor should recompute the statistically estimated total audit value and the achieved standard error of estimate and begin the decision procedure again.

After the target standard error of estimate has been achieved, the auditor can test to see whether the book value can be accepted. If $SE_A < SE_T$, then either

EXHIBIT 9 Decision Process for Hypothesis Testing

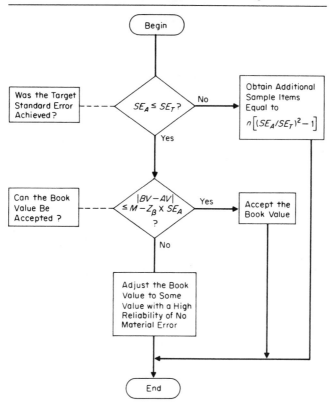

or both of the risk levels can be reduced somewhat (because the sample evidence exceeds the minimum requirements).

If the auditor decides to hold the β risk constant and reduce the α risk, the book value can be accepted if $|BV - AV| \leq M - Z_B \times SE_A$. On the other hand, if the auditor decides to hold the α risk constant and reduce the β risk, the book value can be accepted if $|BV - AV| \geq Z_{\alpha/2} \times SE_A$. Either approach is appropriate (because they are both within the original risk levels specified).

If the test for acceptance of the book value is not met, then it must be rejected as possibly being materially in error. The auditor does not, however, simply qualify the opinion. Rather the auditor needs to know what amount can be accepted as materially correct and then have the client adjust the books to that amount.

In general, the same sample data used to conduct the hypothesis test can be used to make a dollar-value estimate of an account balance. Given the sample data and the amount specified by the auditor as material, it is possible to calculate the reliability that any specified value of the account balance is materially correct.

The β risk used in the hypothesis test may have been greater than .05 because of reliance on internal control or other audit procedures. Once the hypothesis test has rejected the account balance, the auditor has an indication that internal controls or other audit procedures relied on were ineffective. The auditor should therefore adjust the statistical risks so that the risk of the adjusted book value being materially in error is no more than 5 percent.

Therefore the auditor should calculate what value (or range of values) has at least 95 percent reliability of no material error. To achieve at least one point with 95 percent reliability of no material error, the following minimum sample evidence is required:

$$SE_A \leq \frac{M}{1.96}$$

Note that this condition may be more stringent than that required above, and therefore, additional sample evidence may be required in order to achieve at least one point with 95 percent reliability of no material error.

In order to calculate the range into which the book value can be adjusted, we can consider the reliability of no material error if the books are adjusted to the statistically estimated total audit value. The reliability that the estimated total value is materially in error is given by the area in the tails of the normal curve in Exhibit 10.

The reliability that the estimated total value is materially in error can be calculated easily:

$$Z = \frac{M}{SE_A}$$

where Z is the number of standard deviations between the estimated total value and the materiality limits. From a standard normal table, the reliability of the

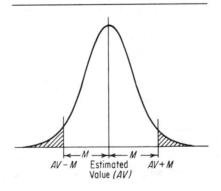

EXHIBIT 10   Reliability That Estimated Curve Value Is Materially in Error Shown in Tails

EXHIBIT 11   Example of Adjustment Range

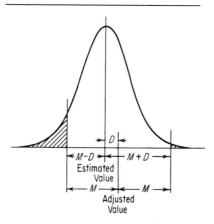

true value lying in the tails of the curve can be obtained. For example, suppose that $M = \$10,000$ and $SE_A = \$5,000$. Then

$$Z = \frac{\$10,000}{\$5,000} = 2$$

From the normal table, the reliability associated with a normal value of 2 is .0228 (the area in one tail). Hence, the reliability of the estimated total value being in error by a material amount is .0456, as both tails (i.e., materially understated and materially overstated) are considered. Conversely, the estimated total value can be accepted with .9544 reliability of being materially correct. This more than meets the required level of 95 percent.

Because the decision logic above requires the achieved standard error to be at most $M/1.96$ before entering this phase, there is always going to be at least one point that can be accepted with 95 percent reliability of no material error. But can a point very near the estimated total value still be acceptable with at least 95 percent reliability of no material error? In other words, is there a range of values within which any point can be accepted with 95 percent reliability of no material error? Consider Exhibit 11. It is desired to find the farthest point to which the adjusted value can be moved and still have at least 95 percent reliability of no material error. The reliability that the adjusted value is materially overstated is given by the shaded area in the left-hand tail, and the reliability of material understatement is given by the area of the right tail. To have 95 percent reliability of no material error, the total area in the two tails must not exceed .05. This can be written as

$$F\left(\frac{M - D}{SE_A}\right) + F\left(\frac{M + D}{SE_A}\right) \leq .05$$

where $F(X)$ is the area in the tail of the normal curve beyond X standard deviations. To find the adjustment range, this equation must be solved for D. This equation can be solved by trial and error (or the table in Exhibit 12 can be used).

When the decision is to reject the book value and adjust it, the auditor should strive to have the auditee adjust it to the statistically estimated total value, as this is the point with the highest reliability of no material error. However, the auditee may, upon finding that there is a problem, reprocess the accounting data and obtain a new book value. In such a case, if the new book value has at least 95 percent reliability of no material error (i.e., is in the adjustment range), the auditor would be satisfied. Also, the auditee may dispute the auditor's statistical estimate, but be willing to adjust to some other value in the adjustment range. The auditor can accept such an adjustment with at least 95 percent reliability of no material error, which is acceptable, even though some other adjustment might have had even higher reliability of no material error.

Although the decision process above seems formidable at first glance, it can easily be reduced to a simple worksheet, as in Exhibit 12. In order to demonstrate the use of this worksheet, Exhibit 13 is filled in assuming the following data:

$$BV = \$10,000,000$$
$$AV = \$9,500,000$$
$$SE_A = \$98,000$$
$$M = \$200,000$$
$$\alpha = .10$$
$$\beta = .35$$
$$n = 300$$

The audit decision resulting from these data is to adjust the book value somewhere into the range of $9,471,580 to $9,528,420 with 95 percent reliability of no material error.

Audit conclusion. After the statistical evaluation has been reached—accept the book value or adjust it—through the analysis in the preceding section, the auditor must not only act on that information, but must also consider whether the sample evidence requires any further action. For example, suppose that the auditor found only one small error in the sample and the statistical decision was to accept the book value, but the item in error was fraudulently misstated. Notwithstanding the favorable statistical decision, the auditor would probably rethink the audit objectives and approach in light of the discovered evidence of fraud.

Alternatively, assume that the auditor found evidence of an improper sales cutoff in the sample. Rather than simply adjusting the books to the statistical estimate, the auditor should consider directing audit attention to all the cutoff procedures and adjusting all errors in light of the sample evidence of improper cutoffs.

The important point to remember is that the statistical "decision" arrived at through the methods of this chapter is not the final audit decision, but is merely evidence the auditor must combine with all other known or discovered facts in reaching a sound audit conclusion. The proper use of the statistical information requires professional audit judgment.

Variables Estimation. The purpose of statistical estimation is to estimate some amount of interest to the auditor, such as the total cost of inventory on hand. This method is generally used when the resulting estimate is to be entered onto the books and records as a substitute for a complete enumeration of the components of an account. When this approach is used, a measure of the precision of the estimate is required so the auditor knows whether the resulting amount is sufficiently precise for the purpose.

To design the sampling plan for a statistical estimate, it is necessary to specify the precision and the reliability required. On the basis of these values, the auditor can compute the target standard error of the estimated total value (SE_T) that must be achieved to obtain the required precision. Using the required standard error, the necessary sample size can be computed using the methods in Chapter 11.

Required standard error of estimate. The relationship between the precision (P), reliability (R), and standard error of estimate (SE_T) can be shown graphically as in Exhibit 14. In words, of all possible samples, a proportion represented by R will yield an estimate of the total value that is within the predefined precision.

Because the sample estimates are normally distributed, P, R, and SE_T can be related as follows:

$$P = Z_{(1-R)/2} \times SE_T$$

and hence

$$SE_T = \frac{P}{Z_{(1-R)/2}}$$

Exhibit 15 provides common Z values to assist in making this calculation.

P : The precision of the estimate. The precision of a statistical estimate should be selected by reference to the sampling objective. If the objective is to estimate the total cost of inventory for presentation in financial statements, for example, the considerations of materiality discussed above would apply. In each case, the use of the financial information containing the statistical estimate must be analyzed to determine the upper limit of precision tolerable for the estimation procedure.

The sample size in variables estimation is most heavily influenced by the ratio of the precision to the total amount being sampled. If this ratio is less than 1 percent, the sample size is usually large. Furthermore, if precision is halved, the sample size is approximately quadrupled. P is dollar amount of precision.

R : The reliability. The reliability is the proportion of times, over the long run, that the precision interval computed from the sample will include the true population value.

Many auditors believe that a reliability of 95 percent is appropriate, in conjunction with a precision equal to the amount considered material for an account, for statistical estimation purposes when the amount is to appear in

EXHIBIT 12 Statistical Decision Procedure—Hypothesis Testing

Enter known data:

Book value .... (1) _____ BV

Statistically estimated total value . (2) _____ AV

Achieved standard error of
estimate .... (3) _____ SE_A

Measure of materiality for test ..... (4) _____ M

Acceptable risk of rejecting
correct balance .... (5) _____ α

Acceptable risk of accepting
materially erroneous balance .... (6) _____ β

Sample size .... (7) _____ n

Step 1: Test for adequacy of sample
evidence

Normal value for (5) (see Table 1
at right) .... (8) _____ $Z_{\alpha/2}$

Normal value for (6) (see Table 2
at right) .... (9) _____ Z_β

Calculate .... (8) + (9) = (10) _____ $Z_{\alpha/2} + Z_\beta$

Enter (10) or 1.96, whichever is
larger .... (11) _____

Calculate .... (4) ÷ (11) = (12) _____ SE_T

If (3) ≤ (12) continue to step 2;
otherwise calculate additional
sample size (13), audit
additional items and restart
evaluation procedure ....

Calculate ... (7) × [((3) ÷ (12))² − 1] = (13) _____ n +

Table 1	
α	$Z_{\alpha/2}$
.05	1.96
.10	1.65
.15	1.44
.20	1.28
.25	1.15
.30	1.04
.35	.94
.40	.84
.45	.76
.50	.67

Table 2	
β	Z_β
.05	1.65
.10	1.28
.15	1.04
.20	.84
.25	.67
.30	.52
.35	.39
.40	.25
.45	.13
.50	.00

For other values, consult standard normal table.

Step 2: Test for acceptance of book value

Calculate .... $③ × ⑨ = ⑭$ $Z_\beta × SE_A$

Maximum estimated error to accept book value ...... $④ − ⑭ = ⑮$ $M − Z_\beta × SE_A$

Estimated error (absolute value) .... $|① − ②| = 16$ $|BV − AV|$

If $⑯ ≤ ⑮$, accept the book value as materially correct; otherwise continue to step 3 ....   Accept/Adjust

Step 3: Calculation of adjustment range

Calculate .... $④ ÷ ③ = ⑰$ M/SE_A

If $⑰ > 2.40$, enter $⑰ − 1.65$; otherwise enter value from Table 3 at right ...... $⑱⑲⑳㉑$

Calculate adjustment range ...... $③ × ⑱ = ⑲$ D/SE_A
D

Lower limit of adjustment range .. $② − ⑲ = ⑳$ $AV − D$

Upper limit of adjustment range .. $② + ⑲ = ㉑$ $AV + D$

Adjust the book value into range $⑳$ to $㉑$ with 95% reliability of no material error.

Table 3

M/SE_A from ⑰	D/SE_A to ⑲
1.96	.00
1.97	.10
1.98	.14
1.99	.18
2.00	.20
2.02	.25
2.04	.29
2.06	.33
2.08	.36
2.10	.39
2.15	.46
2.20	.52
2.25	.58
2.30	.64
2.35	.69
2.40	.75

For intermediate values, interpolate.

EXHIBIT 13 Example of Decision Process

Enter known data:

Book value	①	10,000,000	BV
Statistically estimated total value .	②	9,500,000	AV
Achieved standard error of estimate ...	③	98,000	SE_A
Measure of materiality for test	④	200,000	M
Acceptable risk of rejecting correct balance	⑤	.10	α
Acceptable risk of accepting materially erroneous balance	⑥	.35	β
Sample size	⑦	300	n

Step 1: Test for adequacy of sample evidence

Normal value for ⑤ (see Table 1 at right)	⑧	1.65	$Z_{\alpha/2}$
Normal value for ⑥ (see Table 2 at right)	⑨	.39	Z_β
Calculate .... ⑧ + ⑨ =	⑩	2.04	$Z_{\alpha/2} + Z_\beta$
Enter ⑩ or 1.96, whichever is larger	⑪	2.04	
Calculate .... ④ ÷ ⑪ =	⑫	98,039	SE_T

If ③ ≤ ⑫ continue to step 2; otherwise calculate additional sample size ⑬, audit additional items and restart evaluation procedure

Calculate .... ⑦ × [(③ ÷ ⑫)² − 1] = 13   n +

Table 1			Table 2	
α	$Z_{\alpha/2}$		β	Z_β
.05	1.96		.05	1.65
.10	1.65		.10	1.28
.15	1.44		.15	1.04
.20	1.28		.20	.84
.25	1.15		.25	.67
.30	1.04		.30	.52
.35	.94		.35	.39
.40	.84		.40	.25
.45	.76		.45	.13
.50	.67		.50	.00

For other values, consult standard normal table.

Step 2: Test for acceptance of book value

Calculate 38,220   ③ × ⑨ = ⑭ $Z_\beta \times SE_A$

Maximum estimated error to accept book value 161,780   ④ − ⑭ = ⑮ $M - Z_\beta \times SE_A$

Estimated error (absolute value) .. 500,000 |① − ②| = ⑯ $|BV - AV|$

If ⑯ ≤ ⑮ accept the book value as materially correct; otherwise continue to step 3 ....

Accept/ (Adjust)

Step 3: Calculation of adjustment range

Calculate .... 2.04   ④ ÷ ③ = ⑰ M/SE_A

If ⑰ > 2.40, enter ⑰ − 1.65; otherwise enter value from Table 3 at right .... .29   ⑱ D/SE_A

Calculate adjustment range 28,420   ③ × ⑱ = ⑲ D

Lower limit of adjustment range .. 9,471,580   ② − 19 = ⑳ $AV - D$

Upper limit of adjustment range .. 9,528,420   ② + 19 = ㉑ $AV + D$

Adjust the book value into range ⑳ to ㉑ with 95% reliability of no material error.

Table 3

M/SE from ⑰	D/SE_A to ⑱
1.96	.00
1.97	.10
1.98	.14
1.99	.18
2.00	.20
2.02	.25
2.04	.29
2.06	.33
2.08	.36
2.10	.39
2.15	.46
2.20	.52
2.25	.58
2.30	.64
2.35	.69
2.40	.75

For intermediate values, interpolate.

EXHIBIT 14   Relations among Precision
(P), Reliability (R), and Standard Error
of Estimate (SE_T)

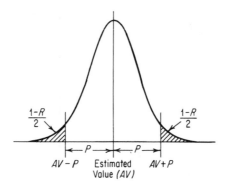

financial statements. Other reliability levels may be appropriate, however, for other statistical estimates, depending on the audit objectives and significance of the information developed.

Evaluation of sample results. After designing the sampling plan, selecting the sample, and auditing the sample items, the auditor calculates two values from the sample (using the methods discussed in Chapter 11): the estimated total audit value (AV) of the population and the achieved standard error of the estimate (SE_A).

The auditor must then ask whether the achieved standard error is less than or equal to the required standard error of estimate. If not, the original precision and reliability requirements cannot be met. In this case, an additional sample should be selected and audited. The additional sample size (ignoring the finite population correction factor) is $n[(SE_A/SE_T)^2 - 1]$, to which many auditors add another 10 to 20 percent to reduce the possibility of failing to meet the target yet again. After the additional items are audited, the auditor should recompute

EXHIBIT 15   *Z* Values for Computing *SE_T*

$$SE_T = \frac{P}{Z_{(1-R)/2}}$$

R	$Z_{(1-R)/2}$
.99	2.58
.95	1.96
.90	1.65
.85	1.44
.80	1.28

the statistically estimated total audit value and the achieved standard error of estimate.

After the target standard error of estimate has been achieved, the auditor can have the books adjusted to the statistically estimated value. The precision of this estimate can be obtained by use of the following formula:

$$P = Z_{(1-R)/2} \times SE_A$$

For example, if the achieved standard error is $40,000, the auditor can have 95 percent reliability that the statistically estimated total value is within $78,400 of the true value (1.96 × $40,000).

Note that it would *not* be appropriate to make a statistical estimate of a population total and, finding the book value somewhere within the precision interval, accept the book value as materially correct. If this type of decision procedure is to be used, the hypothesis testing approach described above should be employed.

Dollar Unit Evaluation. Many of the audit considerations discussed in connection with variables sampling apply when dollar unit sampling is used. These include proper definition of error, valuation approaches, allocating items to a 100 percent stratum, and establishing materiality levels and desired sampling risk. The major differences, in addition to the definition of sampling unit and the method of selection, is in the calculations and format of the sample results.

Attribute-based approach. Whereas variables sampling is based on normal distribution theory, dollar unit sampling (DUS) is an attribute-based approach founded on the *binomial distribution*. This distribution, and its commonly used derivatives—the hypergeometric and the Poisson distributions—deal with the probability of events that have two possible and mutually exclusive outcomes. In the case of auditing with dollar unit (and attribute) sampling, these outcomes are that a sampling unit (recorded population dollar) is either correct or it is wrong. Based on the proportion of sample dollars found to be wrong, the auditor obtains a statistical estimate of the number of population dollars that are wrong using the binomial distribution. This estimate is stated in terms of a reliability or risk level and a maximum error amount. This *upper bound* of error can be compared to the amount of error that is tolerable based on materiality, and the book value accepted or rejected accordingly.

A major advantage of dollar unit sampling is ease of application. The binomial distribution has been compiled in table format to serve use by auditors. Exhibit 16 presents a portion of this type of table.

Simple attributes evaluation. Suppose that the auditor selects a sample of 100 random dollars from a population of vouchers totaling $1,200,000. The corresponding vouchers are audited and no errors are found. Using Exhibit 16, the auditor would conclude that no more than $36,000 (= .03 × $1,200,000) could be in error, with a risk of being wrong of 5 percent.

Now suppose that the sample included one voucher with a recorded value of $500, which the auditor determines should have been recorded as $50. This means that the sample error rate is 1 percent and, using Exhibit 16, the upper error limit is 4.7 percent. Thus, the upper dollar-error bound is $56,400 (.047 × $1,200,000).

EXHIBIT 16   Attribute Sampling Table

Reliability Level 95%[a]

Sample size	0.0	.5	1.0	2.0	3.0	4.0
			Sample error rate			
	Upper limit for error rate in population					
50	5.8			9.1		12.1
100	3.0		4.7	6.2	7.6	8.9
150	2.0			5.1		7.7
200	1.5	2.4	3.1	4.5	5.8	7.1
300	1.0		2.6	3.9	5.2	6.4
400	.7	1.6	2.3	3.6	4.8	6.0

[a]Equivalent to a risk level of 5%.

Note that under simple attributes evaluation it is arbitrarily assumed that all population dollar units deemed to be in error are wrong by their recorded book amount—that is, one dollar—even though sample evidence may include errors of differing amounts.

Combined attributes-variables (CAV) evaluation. A method that recognizes this additional information provided by sample results is CAV evaluation. Under CAV, the portion of population errors represented by pure sampling risk (i.e., before errors are considered) are assumed to be equal to one dollar, but all other estimated errors are given the values of actual errors found in the sample.

Suppose that our above sample of 100 items contains four errors. Exhibit 17 shows the effect of sample errors on the upper-limit error rate.

A common convention applies the increase in the upper error limit to the sample errors in descending order of magnitude, as this provides the most conservative result. Exhibit 18 shows this by continuing the voucher illustration.

Thus, using CAV evaluation, the auditor would conclude, with a 5 percent risk, that the most the vouchers could be wrong (overstated) by is $66,203. Note that if simple attributes evaluation had been used, this amount would be $106,800 (.089 $\times$ $1,200,000), so the use of the additional sample information provided a significant benefit in terms of sampling efficiency.

EXHIBIT 17   Effect of Sample Errors on Upper-Limit Error Rate

---

Number of errors	Upper error limit	Increase in upper error limit resulting from an additional error
0	.03	
1	.047	.017
2	.062	.015
3	.076	.014
4	.089	.013

EXHIBIT 18   Example of Analysis of Errors and Construction of CAV Bound

Errors found in sample			Portion of dollar unit in error
Recorded value	Audited value	Error amount	
$ 500...........	$ 50	$450	.9
750..........	700	50	.067
2,100..........	1,875	225	.107
60..........	30	30	.5

		Construction of CAV bound		
Number of errors	Increase in upper error limit	Population recorded value	Unit error assumption	Error bound portion (columns 2 × 3 × 4)
0.........	.03	$1,200,000	1.0	$36,000
1.........	.017	1,200,000	.9	18,360
2.........	.015	1,200,000	.5	9,000
3.........	.014	1,200,000	.107	1,798
4.........	.013	1,200,000	.067	1,045
Total upper error bound				$66,203

When using CAV evaluation, it is important to note that a separate evaluation is made for both understatement and overstatement errors; thus the term "bound" is used instead of confidence limit. The auditor must take care in computing a bound for understatement errors that sample results do not contradict the one-dollar error-amount assumption, as it is common for understatement errors to exceed the recorded book value by more than 100 percent, whereas this would not be the case for overstatements.

Formulas. The generalized formulas for calculating error bounds for simple attributes and CAV evaluation are shown below. The following symbols are used:

$D(i)$ = maximum total population error bound when i errors are found (D_o for overstatement errors and D_u for understatement errors)

Y = total population recorded dollars

$P_u(i)$ = upper error limit from one-sided attribute table for i errors (e.g., Exhibit 8)

$E(i)$ = amount of a dollar unit error number i [$E_o(i)$ for overstatement error number i, and $E_u(i)$ for understatement error number i]

M = assumed maximum amount of error in any population dollar unit (M_o for overstatement error and M_u for understatement error); e.g., one dollar

Simple Attributes Formula:

$$D(i) = Y \times P_u(i) \times M$$

CAV Evaluation Formula:

$$D(i) = Y \times \{P_u(0) \times M + [P_u(1) - P_u(0)] \times E(1)$$
$$+ [P_u(2) - P_u(1)] \times E(2) + \cdots + [P_u(i) - P_u(i-1)] \times E(i)\}$$

Sample size determination. Sample size determination is a difficult problem with DUS because it is very hard to predict the amounts of errors that will be found, let alone the sample error rate. Most auditors using DUS take a conservative approach of estimating a probable maximum sample error rate and assuming error amounts will equal the maximum amount (e.g., one dollar). Other auditors make less conservative assumptions but prepare to expand sample size if they misestimate sample findings.

Developments in dollar unit sampling. DUS is a relatively new sampling technique that was developed primarily for use by auditors in an effort to overcome some of the shortcomings of more traditional techniques. As a result, it is an area subject to continuing research and improvement. The auditor using DUS should be aware of this and may find it advantageous to acquire more current references for guidance.

STATISTICAL COMPLIANCE TESTS

The auditor undertakes a compliance test to evaluate the extent of compliance with internal controls. Therefore, statistical compliance tests are normally attribute tests, applied to either samples of physical elements or dollar units, because the conclusions of attribute tests are stated in terms of rates of compliance (or noncompliance).

Definition of Error in Compliance Test. Because the auditor's interest in a compliance test is the extent of compliance with internal controls, a sample item is considered to be in error if it does not show evidence of compliance with the control(s) being tested. Evidence of noncompliance with controls not being tested is not considered a compliance deviation for purposes of the compliance test. The reason is that the auditor tests compliance only with those controls on which reliance is placed for the purpose of restricting the extent of substantive tests. Typically, there will be controls that are not to be relied on, and compliance deviations with respect to these controls would not be considered errors in the compliance test. Although other errors (such as monetary errors) located in a compliance test are not considered errors for purposes of evaluating the compliance test of the specific control, they should nevertheless be evaluated as to their nature and cause, their relationship to other phases of the audit, and their potential effect on the financial statements.

Statistical Requirements for Compliance Test. The purpose of a compliance test is to provide a reasonable degree of assurance that the internal control procedures are being applied as understood by the auditor. What constitutes a "reasonable degree of assurance" is a matter of auditing judgment. Although statistical sampling provides one means of carrying out compliance testing, it does not eliminate the need for judgment, because the maximum rate of deviations from prescribed control procedures that would support planned reliance and sampling risk are matters of audit judgment. Paragraphs 31 through 42 of SAS No. 39 discuss audit sampling in compliance tests and give examples of appropriate statistical requirements for compliance testing. These are discussed below.

Sampling risk. Paragraph 36 illustrates sampling risks between 5 percent and 10 percent for audit compliance tests.

Tolerable rate of deviations. Paragraph 33 illustrates that where substantial reliance is to be placed on the control procedures, a rate of 5 percent or possibly less would be reasonable; if less reliance is planned, the auditor may decide that a tolerable rate of 10 percent is reasonable.

In compliance tests, a relatively high tolerable rate for deviations (e.g., .05 as opposed to .01) is acceptable because an item may have a compliance deviation and yet have no monetary error. A compliance deviation does not necessarily result in a monetary error—it means merely that if a monetary error had occurred in the item, the control procedure would not have detected it. In the typical case, most items would be correct even in the absence of internal control; therefore, a control procedure that was applied to at least 95 percent of all items would, if the control were effective at detecting and correcting errors, reduce the monetary error rate to a negligible percentage.

On the other hand, if the feature of interest in an audit test is monetary errors, the upper precision limit on error is related to materiality considerations. Because a potential 5 percent error rate for monetary errors might well be unacceptable in transactions being audited, the acceptable upper precision limit on errors in a dual-purpose test (i.e., a test with both substantive and compliance objectives) might often be lower than if the test were solely for compliance purposes.

Maximum tolerable deviation rates for compliance tests may be illustrated as shown in Exhibit 19. Illustrations are presented for three specific conditions;

EXHIBIT 19   Illustrative Maximum Tolerable Deviation Rates for Compliance Tests

Reliance on internal control	Illustrative maximum tolerable rate
Some reliance, but not a great deal, based on the auditor's conclusions that substantive work will not be substantially reduced in reliance on internal control.	10%
Substantial reliance, based on the auditor's conclusion that substantive work will be substantially reduced in reliance on internal control (e.g., one-half to two-thirds reduction in substantive work). This is a usual situation when controls are good or excellent.	5%
Very great reliance on internal control, based on the auditor's conclusion that the inherent limitations on the planned substantive tests are such that an unusually high amount of reliance must be placed on the internal controls. Such situations, though not rare, would nevertheless be somewhat unusual.	1% (or, rarely, less)

however, in practice different values could be chosen for situations that do not exactly meet these conditions.

Sample Design and Evaluation. Attribute tests can be designed after the reliability and upper precision limit on error are established. Based on these, the sample size can be calculated and the sample drawn (see "Selecting the Sample" above), audited, and evaluated. Sample size calculation and evaluation of results are both done through the use of tables too voluminous to reproduce in this handbook. A good set of tables can be found in *Handbook of Sampling for Auditing and Accounting* by Herbert Arkin [1974].

ANNOTATED BIBLIOGRAPHY

American Institute of Certified Public Accountants, *An Auditor's Approach to Statistical Sampling*, six volumes with supplementary sections. These books are programmed instruction texts on statistical sampling, written in easily understandable style. They include formulas, worksheets, and tables for various types of audit sampling.
———, *Audit Sampling, Statement on Auditing Standards No. 39* (AICPA, 1981). Gives guidance in the use of statistical sampling in auditing.
Arens, A. A., and J. K. Loebbecke, *Applications of Statistical Sampling to Auditing* (Prentice-Hall, Englewood Cliffs, N.J., 1981). A college-level text designed specifically to teach auditors the use of statistical sampling.
Arkin, H., *Handbook of Sampling for Auditing and Accounting*, 2d ed. (McGraw-Hill Book Company, New York, 1974). A basic treatment of statistical audit techniques. Also includes voluminous tables for sample design and evaluation.
Cochran, W. G., *Sampling Techniques*, 3d ed. (John Wiley & Sons, New York, 1980). A standard statistical reference, highly mathematical and technical.
International Business Machines Corporation, *Random Number Generation and Testing* (Document GC20-8011-0) (Technical Publications Department). Explains how to program computers to generate random numbers.
Leslie, D. A., A. D. Teitlebaum, and R. J. Anderson, *Dollar-Unit Sampling—A Practical Guide for Auditors* (Copp, Clark, Pitman, Toronto, Canada, 1979). This is a contemporary, comprehensive text on the theory and use of dollar unit sampling.
Neter, J., and J. K. Loebbecke, *Behavior of Major Statistical Estimators in Sampling Accounting Populations*, Audit Research Monograph No. 2 (AICPA, 1975).
Roberts, D. M., *Statistical Auditing* (AICPA, 1978). Presents a discussion of statistical sampling and its use by auditors for auditors who have a basic knowledge of statistical technology.
Roberts, H. V., *Conversational Statistics* (Hewlett-Packard Company, Cupertino, Calif., 1974). An innovative introduction to statistics, stressing understanding, not technique.

CHAPTER 11

Statistical Methods

for Auditing

and Accounting

Robert S. Kaplan
Professor of Industrial Administration,
Carnegie-Mellon University

INTRODUCTION

Accountants frequently confront masses of data from which they would like to draw systematic and logical conclusions. Perhaps the most frequent occurrence of such a confrontation arises when auditing an account such as accounts receivable or inventory that consists of a large number of individual subaccounts. It would be prohibitively expensive for an auditor to verify each item in such an account. Consequently, a representative sample of the entire population is chosen and this sample checked in detail. Based on the findings from this sample, the auditor attempts to draw conclusions about the entire population. Statistical analysis and, in particular, statistical sampling theory provide a scientific method for drawing reliable and valid conclusions about the properties of an entire population when only a properly chosen sample of the population has been studied in detail.

Although statistical sampling is the most useful statistical technique for many accountants (especially auditors), other statistical techniques are also becoming useful in the practice of modern accountants. Foremost among these is multiple regression analysis, which enables one to detect an underlying relationship among a number of simultaneous and interacting variables. At present, regression analysis is used primarily by management accountants within a firm to determine the cost relations that appear to be operating within a cost center or division. Especially important is the ability of regression analysis to approximate the fixed and variable cost components when the firm is operating within its normal range of activity. But regression analysis is becoming increasingly useful for auditors, too, who can use this technique to guide their audit activities to those areas, branches, or divisions whose operations appear to be significantly different from historical relationships or from the operations of comparable units in the same time period.

This chapter surveys both these statistical techniques, sampling theory and regression analysis. Historically, these statistical techniques were difficult to apply because of the long and tedious calculations that had to be performed. Now, however, the widespread use of computers and time-sharing facilities enables accountants to use these techniques without getting bogged down in a mass of detailed hand computations which, by themselves, often introduced a considerable amount of error into the process. We do not devote much space to computational techniques (e.g., how to compute ordinary least-squares estimates of regression coefficients), because an accountant who wishes to use these techniques can use a computer.

A chapter in a handbook is not the place for a first exposure to statistical analysis. I assume that readers of this chapter have already been exposed to an introductory statistics course. Some introductory business statistics books are referenced at the end of the chapter for anyone who wants to sharpen up or review basic statistical concepts. Although I start with elementary material, this serves mainly to define the notation used. I do not expect that this chapter will constitute a self-contained learning experience for those without formal training in statistics.

BASIC STATISTICAL CONCEPTS

Populations and Distributions. All statistical analysis begins with the basic data to be analyzed. We assume throughout our discussion that we are working with a finite number of items and let N represent the number of items in our population. The population, of course, must be well defined (e.g., the total number of sales invoices, all raw material inventory accounts) so that we can unambiguously decide whether a particular item is included in the population or not. We shall typically be interested in quantitative measures associated with each item such as the dollar value of an account receivable or an inventory item. We denote by X_i the amount or value of the ith item in the population, $i = 1, \ldots, N$.

As an illustration that we carry throughout our analysis, consider a hypothetical population of 100 invoices as shown in Exhibit 1.[1] For this example, $N = 100$, and $X_1 = \$11.87$, $X_2 = \$11.18, \ldots, X_{100} = \$1.65$.

In some circumstances, an auditor may be interested in a qualitative characteristic of each item in the population, such as whether each invoice itemized in Exhibit 1 was properly authorized. In this case, we can let $X_i = 1$ if the ith item has the desired characteristic and $X_i = 0$ if it does not. When auditors examine qualitative characteristics of the population as above, they are interested in estimating the proportion of items that have (or do not have) the desired characteristic. Sampling to estimate proportions is called *attribute sampling*. Sampling to estimate the total value of a population is called *variables sampling*.

One way of displaying the information contained in all the X_i values in a population is to list the value for each item as we did in Exhibit 1. Most populations of interest, however, will contain far too many items for this to be a convenient or even useful practice. The most common alternative to listing all the items in a population is to construct a histogram or frequency diagram to summarize the distribution of values. If the number of possible values that each item can assume is sufficiently small, we would tabulate each possible value and the number of items in the population at this value. For most populations, including the one shown in Exhibit 1, this would not be an interesting way to summarize information because there may be as many different values as there are items in the population. We therefore group the data into a number of somewhat arbitrary ranges and count the number of items whose value falls into each range. Exhibit 2 is a frequency table for the population of invoices shown

---

[1]This exhibit and subsequent ones were taken from Cyert and Davidson [1962].

EXHIBIT 1   Hypothetical Population of 100 Invoices[a]

Invoice number	Invoice value	Invoice number	Invoice value	Invoice number	Invoice value	Invoice number	Invoice value
01	$11.87	26	$21.06	51	$14.54	76	$17.94
02	11.18	27	23.38	52	15.12	77	19.93
03	11.32	28	16.32	53	20.57	78	15.98
04	10.16	29	21.54	54	18.36	79	22.50
05	4.15	30	3.65	55	21.27	80	13.98
06	12.35	31	17.69	56	23.57	81	16.36
07	7.89	32	27.14	57	24.40	82	24.27
08	12.74	33	21.60	58	25.08	83	24.52
09	6.86	34	25.30	59	17.48	84	27.20
10	5.08	35	22.34	60	8.95	85	18.77
11	21.18	36	19.88	61	26.89	86	19.33
12	21.90	37	21.84	62	18.59	87	24.05
13	19.98	38	25.00	63	26.68	88	18.27
14	23.23	39	22.28	64	18.70	89	24.40
15	23.60	40	13.18	65	27.58	90	13.69
16	19.04	41	18.85	66	18.86	91	31.01
17	23.33	42	21.04	67	26.96	92	32.08
18	22.06	43	20.56	68	24.45	93	27.63
19	17.84	44	25.38	69	16.76	94	29.41
20	11.74	45	24.20	70	11.90	95	33.68
21	16.64	46	22.26	71	22.04	96	31.96
22	16.63	47	23.85	72	24.62	97	28.36
23	24.25	48	18.50	73	25.78	98	33.41
24	21.76	49	19.97	74	16.01	99	28.40
25	16.01	50	12.52	75	19.28	100	1.65

[a]Total value of 100 invoices: $1,995.34. Average value of 100 invoices: $19.95.

EXHIBIT 2   Frequency Table: Invoice Population of Exhibit 1

Cell interval	Number of invoices with values falling in listed interval
$ 0.00–4.99	3
5.00–9.99	4
10.00–14.99	13
15.00–19.99	28
20.00–24.99	32
25.00–29.99	15
30.00–34.99	5
Total	100

EXHIBIT 3   Histogram

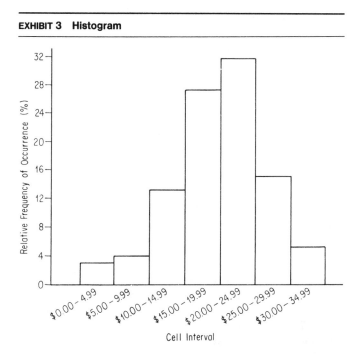

Cell Interval

in Exhibit 1. In this case, because $N = 100$, the number of items in each cell interval equals the percentage of all items in the cell interval. For populations for which N does not equal 100, the numbers tabulated in Exhibit 2 would be divided by N and multiplied by 100 (to yield a percentage between 0 and 100) to compute a relative frequency table. A relative frequency table or distribution for a population displays the percentage of items in the population whose values fall within each cell interval.

It is frequently desirable to display this data graphically. Exhibit 3 is a graphic representation of the data in Exhibit 2 and is called a *histogram, bar chart,* or *relative frequency diagram.* Aggregating the basic data into a frequency table or histogram involves some loss of detail, because we lose sight of individual values. Nevertheless, we typically get a much better picture about the distribution of values in the population by aggregating into cell intervals. In fact, we shall usually want an even further aggregation of the individual items into perhaps two summary measures that characterize the population:

1. A measure of central tendency; an average or typical value for an item in the population

2. A measure of dispersion or variation of the items in the population; how far away might an invoice be from the measure of central tendency

We discuss typical measures of central tendency and dispersion in the next two sections.

Measures of Central Tendency

Median. The median of a population is that value for which half the values in the population are above and half are below it. In effect, the median divides the population into two equal sizes. Strictly speaking, a population has a middle item only when it has an odd number of items. For a population with an even number of items, the median can be defined as the average of the two middle numbers. One can check that the 50th and 51st largest values in Exhibit 1 are $20.57 and $21.04, respectively, so that the median for this population is the average of these two or about $20.80. Although the median of a population is rarely used in statistical inference, it is a valuable summary measure for highly dispersed populations because it is not affected by the particular values assumed by extreme observations. It therefore provides a reasonable representation as to what value a typical item in the population is likely to be near.

Mode. The mode of a population is that value which occurs most frequently. The mode is typically computed on an aggregated frequency table or diagram (Exhibit 2 or 3) rather than the distribution of individual items as shown in Exhibit 1. The modal cell interval for these data is $20.00–$24.99, which contains 32 percent of all the invoices. The mode represents the most typical or most likely set of values in the population.

Arithmetic mean. The most common measure of central tendency is the arithmetic mean, sometimes called the *average* or simply the *mean* of the population. The arithmetic mean is computed by summing the values of all the items in the population and dividing by the number of items. Symbolically, letting $\overline{X}$ be the mean of the population,

$$\overline{X} = \frac{\sum_{1}^{N} X_i}{N}$$

For the data in Exhibit 1, $\overline{X} = \$19.95$. If the X_i's are 0–1 variables, as in attribute sampling, $\overline{X}$ would be the fraction of the population that have the attribute being investigated. Although the mean is probably the most useful measure of central tendency in a population, as we shall see, it does have the disadvantage of being strongly influenced by extremely high or extremely low observations. Therefore it may not be representative of the typical or most common item in the population.

Most frequency diagrams or histograms are unimodal; that is, the height of the curve increases until the mode (highest point) is reached, and decreases for values in excess of the mode. If the histogram or frequency diagram is symmetric, as shown in diagram (a) of Exhibit 4, the median, mode, and mean all occur at the same point. If the distribution is skewed to the left [diagram (b)] the mean, being more influenced by the extreme lower values, is less than the median which, in turn, is less than the mode. If the distribution is skewed to the right [diagram (c)], the opposite order holds for the three measures of central tendency; the mode is less than the median and the median is less than the mean.

EXHIBIT 4   Frequency Distributions

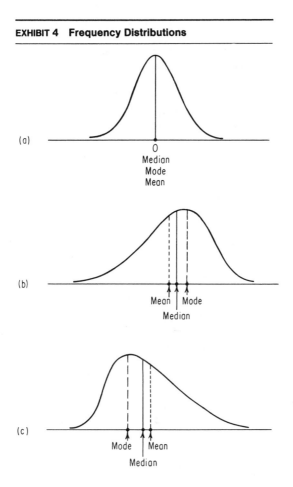

Measures of Dispersion

Range. The simplest measure of dispersion is the range, the difference between the largest and the smallest item in the population. For example, a weather report will usually report the high and low temperature for the day as a measure of the daily fluctuation in temperature. (Unfortunately, some people average the high and low temperatures of the day and incorrectly report this as the day's "average" temperature.) For the data in Exhibit 1, the largest value is $33.68 (invoice 95) and the smallest value is 1.65 (invoice 100), so the range is $32.03. The range is typically used in quality control applications because of its easy computation. It is not too valuable in sampling studies because it is obviously very sensitive to extreme observations and it is also dependent on sample size. The range statistic will generally increase and certainly never decrease as we increase the sample size.

Interquartile range. In order to reduce the dependence of the range statistic on extreme observations and to obtain a statistic that is relatively stable with sample size, a more useful measure is the interval that contains the middle 50 percent of observations. This measure is obtained by identifying Q_{25}, the item value that separates the lowest 25 percent of observations from the upper 75 percent, and Q_{75}, the item value that separates the upper 25 percent of observations from the lower 75 percent. The interquartile range is then computed as $Q_{75} - Q_{25}$. For the data in Exhibit 1, Q_{25} = \$16.34 (average of the 25th smallest invoice, \$16.32, and the 26th smallest, \$16.23) and Q_{75} = \$24.34 (average of \$24.27 and \$24.40). So the interquartile range is \$24.34 $-$ \$16.34 = \$8.00. Although this statistic is a useful summary measure of dispersion for long-tailed and/or highly skewed populations, it is not convenient to work with algebraically and hence does not play a central role in statistical sampling or estimation theory.

Average deviation. The average or mean deviation is the average of the absolute deviations of each item from the arithmetic mean. Symbolically, it can be written as

$$AD = \frac{\Sigma |X_i - \overline{X}|}{N}$$

where the vertical bars refer to the absolute value operation; that is, $|-2|$ = $|+2|$ = $+2$. The deviations are averaged as if they were all positive. The average deviation indicates how far "on average" an item will deviate from the mean. It is an intuitively appealing measure of dispersion, but it too is difficult to work with algebraically. The average deviation for the data in Exhibit 1 is \$5.11.

Standard deviation. The most commonly used measure of dispersion is the standard deviation, σ, of a population. This is defined as

$$\sigma = \left[\frac{\sum_{1}^{N} (X_i - \overline{X})^2}{N} \right]^{1/2}$$

Sometimes, a very similar measure, S, is used to denote the standard deviation of the population, where

$$S = \left[\frac{\sum_{1}^{N} (X_i - \overline{X})^2}{N - 1} \right]^{1/2}$$

The square of the standard deviation, either σ^2 or S^2, is called the variance of the population. The standard deviation, with the square-root formula, is more useful than the variance because it is measured in the same units as the individual items in the population and the mean. For computational ease, the above formulas are frequently rewritten in the equivalent form

$$\sigma = \left[\frac{\sum_{1}^{N} X_i^2}{N} - \frac{\left(\sum_{1}^{N} X_i \right)^2}{N^2} \right]^{1/2}$$

so that the mean and standard deviation can be computed with only one pass through the data. The standard deviation of the data in Exhibit 1 can be calculated as $6.53.

The standard deviation is the easiest measure to work with algebraically and is especially useful when the population is well approximated by a normal or bell-shaped distribution. It is least useful when the population has only a small number of items or when the population is highly skewed, that is, has a long tail. In these situations, the standard deviation is highly sensitive to values of extreme observations.

Coefficient of variation. All of the above measures of dispersion are expressed in the unit of measurement of the individual invoice items, for example, dollars. In comparing two populations, it is useful to have a measure of dispersion that is independent of the units used to measure the individual items or even the average magnitude of items. The coefficient of variation, $\sigma/\overline{X}$, which is the ratio of the standard deviation to the mean, gives a measure of the degree of variation in the population that is independent of the average magnitude of items or units used to measure these items. For the data in Exhibit 1, this measure is .327, implying an average dispersion of about 33 percent about the mean for individual items.

Skewness. Skewness refers to the degree of asymmetry or lopsidedness of a distribution. A simple measure of skewness, Sk, is a function of the spread between the arithmetic mean and the median,

$$Sk = \frac{3(\overline{X} - \text{Median})}{S}$$

where S is the standard deviation previously defined. If the distribution is skewed to the right, the mean is greater than the median, as previously illustrated in Exhibit 4, and the measure is positive. If the distribution is skewed to the left, the measure is negative. For the data in Exhibit 1,

$$Sk = \frac{3(\$19.95 - \$20.80)}{\$6.53} = -.39$$

indicating a slight degree of negative skewness. Examining Exhibit 3, we see that the left-hand tail of the distribution is somewhat longer than the right-hand tail, which confirms this effect.

Many accounting populations are highly skewed. A typical population would have a large number of small-valued items and a relatively few high-valued items accounting for a significant portion of the total dollar value in the population. A population whose skewness measure exceeds 1 would be considered highly skewed.

Another measure of skewness, which is more difficult to compute, is given by G_1, where

$$G_1 = \frac{\sum_i (X_i - \overline{X})^3}{N\sigma^3}$$

G_1 is zero for symmetric distributions; it is positive for distributions skewed to the right.

THE NORMAL DISTRIBUTION

The normal distribution, illustrated in Exhibit 5, is by far the most useful distribution in statistics. The normal distribution is symmetric and is completely characterized by its mean and standard deviation. Although it is possible to express the normal density function (the bell-shaped curve) both mathematically, via an equation, and in tabular form, it is far more convenient to work with the normal distribution function. This function, illustrated and tabulated in Exhibit 6, enables us to compute the probability that an item drawn from a normal distribution with $\overline{X} = 0$ and $\sigma = 1$ will have a value less than or equal to an arbitrary number x. From Exhibit 6, we can see that the probability that an item drawn from a zero-mean, unit-standard-deviation population is less than or equal to 1 is .8413. Although Exhibit 6 tabulates the normal distribution function only for values of x greater than or equal to 0, values for negative values of x can be obtained by exploiting the symmetric properties of the normal distribution; for example, the probability that X is less than -1 must equal the probability that X is greater than $+1$ or

$$\Pr\{X < -1\} = \Pr\{X > +1\}$$

EXHIBIT 5   Graph of the General Normal Density Function

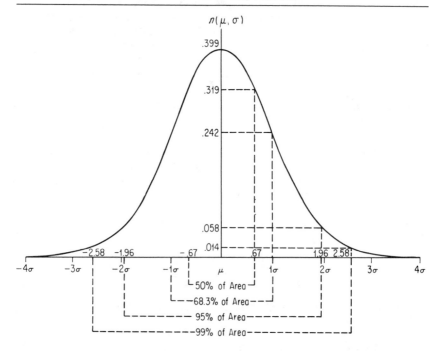

But because $Pr\{X \leq +1\} + Pr\{X > +1\} = 1$, we have

$$Pr\{X < -1\} = 1 - Pr\{X \leq +1\} = 1 - .8413 = .1587$$

A similar analysis can be performed for all negative values of x.

It may appear unduly restrictive to have a table for a single normal distribution—the one with mean zero and standard deviation equal to 1. Fortunately we can always transform any normal distribution with arbitrary mean and standard deviation into a zero-mean, unit-standard-deviation one. Consider an item, X, drawn from a normal distribution with arbitrary mean $\overline{X}$, and standard deviation σ. If we are interested in the probability that X is less than or equal to an arbitrary amount, x, we perform the following series of steps:

$$Pr\{X \leq x\} = Pr\{X - \overline{X} \leq x - \overline{X}\} = Pr\left\{\frac{X - \overline{X}}{\sigma} \leq \frac{x - \overline{X}}{\sigma}\right\}$$

The variable $Z = (X - \overline{X})/\sigma$ also has a normal distribution, but it can be shown that the mean of Z is zero and its standard deviation is 1. Therefore the probability that $X \leq x$ can be obtained from the table in Exhibit 6 for the value associated with $(x - \overline{X})/\sigma$.

For example, assume that X comes from a normal distribution with mean 200 and standard deviation 100. The probability that X is less than or equal to 250 is the probability that a zero-mean, unit-standard-deviation normally distributed variable is less than or equal to

$$\frac{250 - 200}{100} = .5$$

Therefore, $Pr\{X \leq 250\} = Pr\{Z \leq .5\} = .6915$, where Z is the standard notation for a normally distributed random variable with zero mean and unit standard deviation. For any point, X, from a normal distribution, the standard normal deviate $Z [= (X - \overline{X})/\sigma]$ represents the number of standard deviation units the random variable X is above or below the mean.

Using the above analysis, one can verify that for a normal distribution:

68.3 percent of the area is within 1σ of the mean, $\overline{X}$;
95.5 percent of the area is within 2σ of $\overline{X}$; and
99.7 percent of the area is within 3σ of $\overline{X}$.

SIMPLE RANDOM SAMPLING

In order to estimate the mean of an accounting population, the auditor chooses a sample of items. The population mean can be estimated from the mean value of items that were selected in the sample. In simple random sampling, the sample is selected at random from the population as a whole. In order to do valid statistical inference, it is vital that each item in the population have a specified probability of being included in the sample. In the simplest case, we assign each item in the population an equal probability of being selected. We accomplish this goal by resorting to a random number table. Many computerized systems have programmed random number generators, but for illustrative purposes we shall use a table of 700 random numbers shown in Exhibit 7. These

EXHIBIT 6 The Standardized Normal Distribution Function, $F(x)$

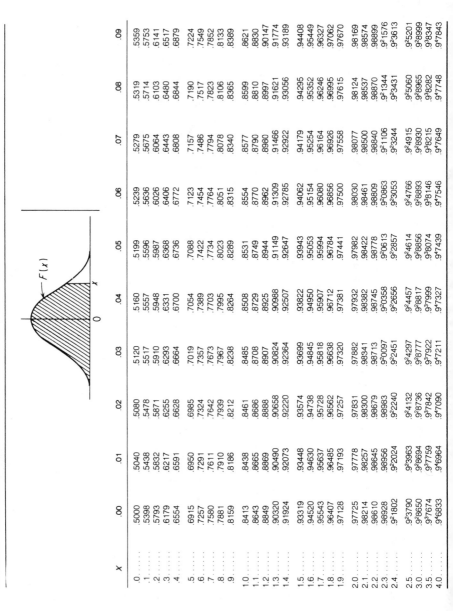

x	.00	.01	.02	.03	.04	.05	.06	.07	.08	.09
0.0	.5000	.5040	.5080	.5120	.5160	.5199	.5239	.5279	.5319	.5359
.1	.5398	.5438	.5478	.5517	.5557	.5596	.5636	.5675	.5714	.5753
.2	.5793	.5832	.5871	.5910	.5948	.5987	.6026	.6064	.6103	.6141
.3	.6179	.6217	.6255	.6293	.6331	.6368	.6406	.6443	.6480	.6517
.4	.6554	.6591	.6628	.6664	.6700	.6736	.6772	.6808	.6844	.6879
.5	.6915	.6950	.6985	.7019	.7054	.7088	.7123	.7157	.7190	.7224
.6	.7257	.7291	.7324	.7357	.7389	.7422	.7454	.7486	.7517	.7549
.7	.7580	.7611	.7642	.7673	.7703	.7734	.7764	.7794	.7823	.7852
.8	.7881	.7910	.7939	.7967	.7995	.8023	.8051	.8078	.8106	.8133
.9	.8159	.8186	.8212	.8238	.8264	.8289	.8315	.8340	.8365	.8389
1.0	.8413	.8438	.8461	.8485	.8508	.8531	.8554	.8577	.8599	.8621
1.1	.8643	.8665	.8686	.8708	.8729	.8749	.8770	.8790	.8810	.8830
1.2	.8849	.8869	.8888	.8907	.8925	.8944	.8962	.8980	.8997	.90147
1.3	.90320	.90490	.90658	.90824	.90988	.91149	.91309	.91466	.91621	.91774
1.4	.91924	.92073	.92220	.92364	.92507	.92647	.92785	.92922	.93056	.93189
1.5	.93319	.93448	.93574	.93699	.93822	.93943	.94062	.94179	.94295	.94408
1.6	.94520	.94630	.94738	.94845	.94950	.95053	.95154	.95254	.95352	.95449
1.7	.95543	.95637	.95728	.95818	.95907	.95994	.96080	.96164	.96246	.96327
1.8	.96407	.96485	.96562	.96638	.96712	.96784	.96856	.96926	.96995	.97062
1.9	.97128	.97193	.97257	.97320	.97381	.97441	.97500	.97558	.97615	.97670
2.0	.97725	.97778	.97831	.97882	.97932	.97982	.98030	.98077	.98124	.98169
2.1	.98214	.98257	.98300	.98341	.98382	.98422	.98461	.98500	.98537	.98574
2.2	.98610	.98645	.98679	.98713	.98745	.98778	.98809	.98840	.98870	.98899
2.3	.98928	.98956	.98983	$.9^2 0097$	$.9^2 0358$	$.9^2 0613$	$.9^2 0863$	$.9^2 1106$	$.9^2 1344$	$.9^2 1576$
2.4	$.9^2 1802$	$.9^2 2024$	$.9^2 2240$	$.9^2 2451$	$.9^2 2656$	$.9^2 2857$	$.9^2 3053$	$.9^2 3244$	$.9^2 3431$	$.9^2 3613$
2.5	$.9^2 3790$	$.9^2 3963$	$.9^2 4132$	$.9^2 4297$	$.9^2 4457$	$.9^2 4614$	$.9^2 4766$	$.9^2 4915$	$.9^2 5060$	$.9^2 5201$
3.0	$.9^3 8650$	$.9^3 8694$	$.9^3 8736$	$.9^3 8777$	$.9^3 8817$	$.9^3 8856$	$.9^3 8893$	$.9^3 8930$	$.9^3 8965$	$.9^3 8999$
3.5	$.9^3 7674$	$.9^3 7759$	$.9^3 7842$	$.9^3 7922$	$.9^3 7999$	$.9^3 8074$	$.9^3 8146$	$.9^3 8215$	$.9^3 8282$	$.9^3 8347$
4.0	$.9^4 6833$	$.9^4 6964$	$.9^4 7090$	$.9^4 7211$	$.9^4 7327$	$.9^4 7439$	$.9^4 7546$	$.9^4 7649$	$.9^4 7748$	$.9^4 7843$

EXHIBIT 7   Random Numbers

Col.	(1)	(2)	(3)	(4)	(5)	(6)	(7)	(8)	(9)	(10)	(11)	(12)	(13)	(14)
1	10480	15011	01536	02011	81647	91646	69179	14194	62590	36207	20969	99570	91291	90700
2	22368	46573	25595	85393	30995	89198	27982	53402	93965	34095	52666	19174	39615	99505
3	24130	48360	22527	97265	76393	64809	15179	24830	49340	32081	30680	19655	63348	58629
4	42167	93093	06243	61680	07856	16376	39440	53537	71341	57004	00849	74917	97758	16379
5	37570	39975	81837	16656	06121	91782	60468	81305	49684	60672	14110	06927	01263	54613
6	77921	06907	11008	42751	27756	53498	18602	70659	90655	15053	21916	81825	44394	42880
7	99562	72905	56420	69994	98872	31016	71194	18738	44013	48840	63213	21069	10634	12952
8	96301	91977	05463	07972	18876	20922	94595	56869	69014	60045	18425	84903	42508	32307
9	89579	14342	63661	10281	17453	18103	57740	84378	25331	12566	58678	44947	05585	56941
10	85475	36857	43342	53988	53060	59533	38867	62300	08158	17983	16439	11458	18593	64952
11	28918	69578	88231	33276	70997	79936	56865	05859	90106	31595	01547	85590	91610	78188
12	63553	40961	48235	03427	49626	69445	18663	72695	52180	20847	12234	90511	33703	90322
13	09429	93969	52636	92737	88974	33488	36320	17617	30015	08272	84115	27156	30613	74952
14	10365	61129	87529	85689	48237	52267	67689	93394	01511	26358	85104	20285	29975	89868
15	07119	97336	71048	08178	77233	13916	47564	81056	97735	85977	29372	74461	28551	90707
16	51085	12765	51821	51259	77452	16308	60756	92144	49442	53900	70960	63990	75601	40719
17	02368	21382	52404	60268	89368	19885	55322	44819	01188	65255	64835	44919	05944	55157
18	01011	54092	33362	94904	31273	04146	18594	29852	71585	85030	51132	01915	92747	64951
19	52162	53916	46369	58586	23216	14513	83149	98736	23495	64350	94738	17752	35156	35749
20	07056	97628	33787	09998	42698	06691	76988	13602	51851	46104	88916	19509	25625	58104
21	48663	91245	85828	14346	09172	30168	90229	04734	59193	22178	30421	61666	99904	32812
22	54164	58492	22421	74103	47070	25306	76468	26384	58151	06646	21524	15227	96909	44592
23	32639	32363	05597	24200	13363	38005	94342	28728	35806	06912	17012	64161	18296	22851
24	29334	27001	87637	87308	58731	00256	45834	15398	46557	41135	10367	07684	36188	18510
25	02488	33062	28834	07351	19731	92420	60952	61280	50001	67658	32586	86679	50720	94953
26	81525	72295	04839	96423	24878	82651	66566	14778	76797	14780	13300	87074	79666	95725
27	29676	20591	68086	26432	46901	20849	89768	81536	86645	12659	92259	57102	80428	25280
28	00742	57392	39064	66432	84673	40027	32832	61362	98947	96067	64760	64584	96096	98253
29	05366	04213	25669	26422	44407	44048	37937	63904	45766	66134	75470	66520	34693	90449
30	91921	26418	64117	94305	26766	25940	39972	22209	71500	64568	91402	42416	07844	69618
31	00582	04711	87917	77341	42206	35126	74087	99547	81817	42607	43808	76655	62028	76630
32	00725	69884	62797	56170	86324	88072	76222	36086	84637	93161	76038	65855	77919	88006
33	69011	65797	95876	55293	18988	27354	26575	08625	40801	59920	29841	80150	12777	48501
34	25976	57948	29888	88604	67917	48708	18912	82271	65424	69774	33611	54262	85963	03547
35	09763	83473	73577	12908	30883	18317	28290	35797	05998	41688	34952	37888	38917	88050
36	91567	42595	27958	30134	04024	86385	29880	99730	55536	84855	29080	09250	79656	73211
37	17955	56349	90999	49127	20044	59931	06115	20542	18059	02008	73708	83517	36103	42791
38	46503	18584	18845	49618	02304	51038	20655	58727	28168	15475	56942	53389	20562	87338
39	92157	89634	94824	78171	84610	82834	09922	25417	44137	48413	25555	21246	35509	20468
40	14577	62765	35605	81263	39667	47358	56873	56307	61607	49518	89656	20103	77490	18062
41	98427	07523	33362	64270	01638	92477	66969	98420	04880	45585	46565	04102	46880	45709
42	34914	63976	88720	82765	34476	17032	87589	40836	32427	70002	70663	88863	77775	69348
43	70060	28277	39475	46473	23219	53416	94970	25832	69975	94884	19661	72828	00102	66794
44	53976	54914	06990	67245	68350	82948	11398	42878	80287	88267	47363	46634	06541	97809
45	76072	29515	40980	07391	58745	25774	22987	80059	39911	96189	41151	14222	60697	59583
46	90725	52210	83974	29992	65831	38857	50490	83765	55657	14361	31720	57375	56228	41546
47	64364	67412	33339	31926	14883	24413	59744	92351	97473	89286	35931	04110	23726	51900
48	08962	00358	31662	25388	61642	34072	81249	35648	56891	69352	48373	45578	78547	81788
49	95012	68379	93526	70765	10593	04542	76463	54328	02349	17247	28865	14777	62730	92277
50	15664	10493	20492	38391	91132	21999	59516	81652	27195	48223	46751	22923	32261	85653

numbers, between 0 and 99999, have been selected and arranged in a random fashion but grouped, for convenience, into rows of 5 and 14 columns. Suppose that we wish to select a random sample of 30 invoices from Exhibit 1. We must first decide how to relate a random number chosen from the table in Exhibit 7 to a particular invoice in Exhibit 1. For this example, such a correspondence is easy. There are exactly 100 invoices in Exhibit 1. Therefore, we can use the first two digits (or the last two or two in the middle, for that matter) of each five-digit number to identify a particular invoice. (We adopt the convention that if the two digits turn out to be 00, we shall choose invoice number 100.)

In general, we would need to adopt a slightly more complex scheme for identifying random numbers with invoices. For example, if we are dealing with a population of 5,300 invoices, we would use the first four digits of each five-digit number from a table as in Exhibit 7 but ignore all numbers we select whose first four digits exceed 5,300. If the population had more than 99,999 invoices, we could group two five-digit numbers to form a ten-digit number and use as many digits as we need to cover the population. The important thing with simple random sampling is that each invoice in the population must have an equal chance of being selected by the random number process.

After establishing the correspondence between random numbers and population items, we select a procedure for choosing a sequence of random numbers from the table. Usually we go down a column or across a row once a starting number has been selected. A random starting number can be chosen by closing our eyes and pointing to a number on the page with a pencil, for example, the number in column 5 row 22: 47070. We can then use this number to give us a random start, such as the number in row 47, column 7, which is 59744. Starting from this number, we move down successive columns until 30 invoices have been selected as shown in Exhibit 8. If a random number turns up an invoice that has already been selected, we ignore it and choose another number until 30 different invoices have been selected. Once the random sample of 30 invoices has been drawn, we can estimate the mean of the 100 invoices in the population by the average of the sample we have chosen. In this example, we chose a sample whose mean value equaled $21.17. Therefore, we would estimate the average value of all invoices in the population as $21.17. Of course, we know that the true value of the arithmetic mean is $19.95. But for any population we encountered in practice, we would have no way of knowing this $19.95 figure without examining the entire population. The whole idea of sampling is to draw a small random sample and hope that we can come close to estimating the true figure by examining only this much smaller sample.

Distribution of sample estimates. Following the procedure just outlined gives us an estimate of the population mean. This estimate is not very useful, however, unless we have some idea of how close this estimate is to the true mean value. Naturally, the true mean is unobservable (unless we sample the entire population), so we shall never know for sure exactly how close we are to the true mean. The remarkable aspect about statistical inference is that we can use the data in our sample to infer a likely interval within which we expect the true mean to be. The principal vehicle that allows us to make this inference is the *central limit theorem*, which states that, for large sample sizes (typically,

EXHIBIT 8   A Random Sample of 30 Invoices

Random number	Invoice number	Invoice value	Random number	Invoice number	Invoice value
59744........	59	$17.48	92144........	92	$32.08
81249........	81	16.36	44819........	44	25.38
76463........	76	17.94	29852........	29	21.54
59516........	59	(already selected)	98736........	98	33.41
14194........	14	23.23	13602........	13	19.98
53402........	53	20.57	04734........	04	10.16
24830........	24	21.76	26384........	26	21.06
53537........	53	(already selected)	28728........	28	16.32
81305........	81	(already selected)	15398........	15	23.60
70659........	70	11.90	61280........	61	26.89
18738........	18	22.06	14778........	14	(already selected)
56869........	56	23.57	81536........	81	(already selected)
84378........	84	27.20	61362........	61	(already selected)
62300........	62	18.59	63904........	63	26.68
05859........	05	4.15	22209........	22	16.63
72695........	72	24.62	99547........	99	28.40
17617........	17	23.33	36086........	36	19.88
93394........	93	27.63	08625........	08	12.74
81056........	81	(already selected)			

50 is a reasonable lower bound), the distribution of sample means tends to be normally distributed, almost independently of the shape of the original population. The fact that sample means from an arbitrary distribution converge to a normal distribution is the reason why the normal distribution plays such a central role in statistical sampling theory.

We can demonstrate the central limit theorem by choosing additional random samples of 30 invoices, that is, replicating the process that we used to generate Exhibit 8. Exhibit 9 shows the results of choosing 100 random samples of size 30 and computing the mean for each one. The grand mean of all these 100 means is $19.95, which also turns out to be the true value, but there is no guarantee that these two numbers will always be the same. The standard deviation of these 100 means is $1.07. If these sample means were distributed exactly in the form of a normal distribution with mean $19.95 and standard deviation $1.07, we would get a distribution as shown in Exhibit 10. The actual distribution of the 100 sample means is plotted in Exhibit 11. We can see, by inspection, that the actual distribution is approximately the same as the normal distribution. If we had plotted more than 100 samples, the distribution would have converged closer to the normal distribution.

If we accept (as we should) the assertion of the central limit theorem that sample means converge to a normal distribution, we still need to know to which normal distribution they converge; that is, what is the mean and standard deviation of the distribution of sample means. The following statements give us the information we need to characterize the distribution of sample means.

EXHIBIT 9   Average Invoice Value from 100 Samples of 30 Invoices

Sample number	Sample average	Sample number	Sample average	Sample number	Sample average	Sample number	Sample average
1	$20.22	26	$20.99	51	$20.69	76	$20.49
2	20.19	27	20.85	52	20.66	77	17.54
3	19.59	28	18.60	53	21.54	78	18.96
4	18.96	29	19.83	54	19.72	79	21.50
5	19.08	30	21.98	55	19.06	80	20.66
6	20.01	31	21.67	56	19.89	81	18.84
7	19.76	32	19.32	57	20.30	82	19.49
8	21.83	33	21.79	58	19.37	83	20.95
9	20.49	34	20.60	59	20.75	84	21.34
10	19.14	35	20.12	60	22.42	85	18.99
11	18.08	36	20.30	61	18.63	86	19.98
12	19.11	37	19.01	62	20.02	87	19.70
13	20.72	38	17.48	63	20.33	88	20.21
14	18.86	39	21.07	64	18.87	89	18.29
15	20.60	40	20.83	65	19.65	90	18.95
16	19.89	41	19.06	66	20.11	91	20.02
17	19.13	42	20.54	67	19.29	92	19.72
18	21.68	43	18.88	68	18.78	93	20.63
19	18.76	44	20.19	69	19.93	94	22.80
20	20.09	45	19.64	70	18.59	95	21.71
21	19.73	46	20.77	71	18.66	96	20.32
22	19.43	47	20.69	72	20.26	97	21.49
23	19.73	48	18.14	73	20.09	98	19.11
24	21.52	49	18.02	74	18.59	99	19.85
25	19.61	50	19.24	75	20.76	100	20.99

Suppose that we have a population of N items with mean $\overline{X}$ and standard deviation σ. If we take a sample of n items ($n \leq N$), the sample mean, $\overline{x}$, is normally distributed with mean $\overline{X}$ and standard deviation equal to

$$\sigma_{\overline{x}} = \sqrt{1 - \frac{n}{N}} \frac{\sigma}{\sqrt{n}}$$

The first term in the standard deviation formula, $1 - n/N$, is called the finite population correction factor. It is included whenever we sample without replacement, as we are doing here (by not allowing the same invoice to enter the population more than once), and indicates that as the sample size n approaches the population size N, there is almost no error in estimating the population mean. The second item in the formula, $\sigma/\sqrt{n}$, is by far the more important one and shows that the uncertainty in estimating the population mean decreases as the sample size increases. The square root of n that appears in the denominator indicates that increasing the sample size by a factor of 4 decreases the standard deviation of the mean estimate by a factor of 2.

In our example we know that the standard deviation σ of the population is

EXHIBIT 10   Normal Distribution of Sample Means

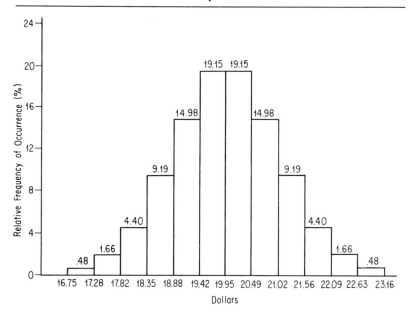

EXHIBIT 11   Actual Distribution of Sample Means

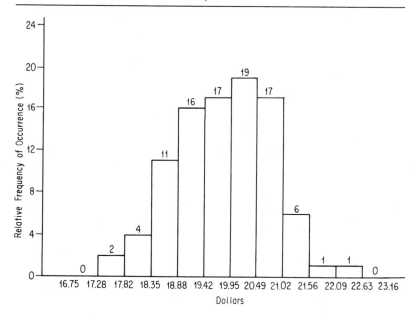

$6.53. Therefore, if we draw a sample of size 30, the standard error of the mean is given by

$$\sqrt{1 - \frac{30}{100}}\frac{6.53}{\sqrt{30}} = .997$$

In practice the standard deviation of the population, σ, will not be known. Fortunately, it can be estimated by the standard deviation of the sample, which will be known. If we sample n items and obtain values $x_1, x_2, \ldots, x_n$, we would first compute the sample mean $\bar{x}$ as

$$\bar{x} = \sum_{i=1}^{n} \frac{x_i}{n}$$

and then compute the sample standard deviation s as

$$s = \left[\frac{\Sigma(x_i - \bar{x})^2}{n-1}\right]^{1/2}$$

or, equivalently, as

$$s = \left(\frac{\Sigma x_i^2 - n\bar{x}^2}{n-1}\right)^{1/2}$$

For the random sample drawn in Exhibit 8, we find that $s = 6.39$. We would therefore estimate that the mean estimate of $21.17 has a standard error of $\sqrt{1 - 30/100}(6.39/\sqrt{30}) = .976$. We expect that in repeated samples of size 30, the average estimated standard error would converge to the true value of .997.

Confidence Intervals. Now that we have an estimate of the population mean as well as an estimate of the uncertainty in this measure, how can we use this information to infer a range of values within which the true population mean is likely to lie? We use the previously cited result that the sample mean is normally distributed about the true mean $\bar{X}$. Therefore, using the normal distribution and our estimate of the standard deviation, we can construct a confidence interval that will likely contain the true mean value. If we construct confidence intervals within 1σ of the mean, this will contain the true mean value about 68 percent of the time. A 2σ-wide confidence interval will contain the true value 95.5 percent of the time, and a 3σ-wide interval will contain the true value 99.7 percent of the time. Although one may think that it would be fine to construct an interval that will contain the true value such a high percentage of the time, in fact a 3σ confidence interval will be so wide that we shall not have restricted the location of the true value very much. In practice a 95 percent confidence interval is typically chosen by using an interval 1.96σ wide.

The width of a confidence interval is usually referred to as the *precision* of the estimate. The percentage figure associated with a given confidence interval (e.g., 95 percent) is called the *reliability* of the estimate. Frequently, people abuse the language when talking about the construction of a confidence interval. They make statements like "the probability is .95 that the true value lies within the confidence interval." Although such a statement may be appropriate for a Bayesian under certain circumstances, it is more accurate to say that "95 percent of the confidence intervals chosen in this manner will contain the true value." For any given confidence interval, the probability is either 0 or 1 that it contains the true value. Because we do not know the true value, we use a procedure such that if a large number of samples of a given size are drawn and a confidence interval 1.96σ wide is constructed as described above, 95 percent of these intervals will include the true population mean. With our numerical example, our 95 percent confidence interval is $\bar{x} \pm 1.96\sigma_x$ or $21.17 \pm 1.96 \times$ (.976) or [19.26, 23.08]. In this case, the 95 percent confidence interval contained the true value. If we repeated the experiment 100 times, about five such intervals would not contain the true mean.

Choosing the appropriate sample size. In the example discussed so far, we have assumed an arbitrary sample size of 30. The auditor, however, must choose an appropriate sample size so that the sampling procedure yields a conclusion consistent with the objective of the overall audit. Usually, the auditor is concerned with detecting a material error if one exists in the population. Therefore a common procedure is to attempt to construct a confidence interval whose width on either side of the means equals the material amount. Let us denote by A the desired precision or confidence interval width of the sample estimate. Because it is meaningless to think of a confidence interval width or precision without specifying the reliability of the test, the auditor must also specify the desired reliability, too. We continue to assume that the auditor specifies a 95 percent reliability figure.

The auditor therefore wants to choose a sample size n such that 1.96 times the standard error of the sample mean $(\sigma_{\bar{x}})$ equals the desired precision figure A. Mathematically,

$$1.96 \sqrt{1 - \frac{n}{N}} \frac{\sigma}{\sqrt{n}} = A$$

Strictly speaking, σ refers to the standard deviation of the distribution of true item values. In practice, however, we may use the standard deviation of the recorded (unaudited) item values in the above equation. Unless large errors are encountered in the sample, the two figures will be quite close to each other. The auditor can thus estimate σ from the list of recorded book values. If such a list is not available, the auditor must estimate σ based on prior judgment, past experience, or even from a preliminary random sample of the account. The above equation is then solved for the sample size n that will yield the desired precision.

If we let $K = 1.96\sigma/A$, we can solve the above equation for n as

$$n = \frac{K^2 N}{K^2 + N}$$

If n is much smaller than N, so that the finite population correction factor can be ignored, we get

$$n = K^2 = \left(\frac{1.96\sigma}{A}\right)^2$$

In our example of 100 invoices, if we want a 95 percent confidence interval that is ±$2 wide about the sample mean (a total of $4 wide, in all), we first compute K,

$$K = \frac{(1.96)(\sigma)}{2} = .98\sigma$$

and then solve for n.

If we interpret Exhibit 1 as a list of recorded values from which the auditor will select a sample to verify, then we may use the standard deviation of this population, which equals 6.53, as an estimate of the standard deviation of the distribution of true (audited) amounts. In this case we have $K = .92(6.53) = 6.0$ and

$$n = \frac{(6)^2(100)}{(6)^2 + 100} = 26.5$$

Therefore, for this population, a sample size of 27 should be adequate to generate a 95 percent confidence interval that is ±$2 wide. Notice that without the finite population correction factor the required sample size would have been $(6)^2$ or 36.

Depending on the particular items that do get selected and the true (audited) values of these items, the actual confidence interval may be wider or narrower than what was originally intended. For example, in our sample size of 30, the 95 percent confidence interval turned out to be equal to ±1.91. If the ex post confidence interval is wider than the originally desired precision, it may be necessary to choose additional items to sample. To avoid this inconvenience, of having to resample, an auditor may choose to be conservative and increase the indicated sample size by some arbitrary amount, say, 10 percent, to be more confident of obtaining the desired precision.

Ex post analysis and statistical inference. Once the sample size has been selected, the sample drawn, and the mean and standard error of the mean estimated, we construct a confidence interval based on the desired precision and reliability requirements. If the recorded book value mean falls within the confidence interval, we conclude that the account is essentially correct, containing no material misstatements. If the confidence interval does not contain the recorded book value mean, we conclude that the account is materially misstated. At this point, we have the option of using the mean per unit estimate from our sample as the new estimated value for this account. Alternatively, we can choose a larger sample to verify this finding and perhaps get a more precise estimate of the true value of this account.

ADVANCED SAMPLING TECHNIQUES

The simple random sampling approach we have outlined forms the basis of more sophisticated plans, but is rarely adequate by itself for any large-scale application. The principal problem is that the sample sizes required to meet an auditor's materiality objective are prohibitively large when only simple random sampling is used. Whereas our simple example was based on a population of 100 items so that a sample size of between 25 and 30 seemed to be adequate, most interesting auditing populations will contain many thousands of items. With such populations, sample sizes of a thousand or more would not be unusual with simple random sampling. These large sample sizes are caused by two factors: First, accounting populations are likely to be widely dispersed and highly skewed. Therefore the underlying standard deviation, σ, of the population will be large. Second, the auditor's requirement for precision in sampling an account will probably be extremely fine. Although sample surveys in political or social science may be content with confidence intervals whose widths are 5 percent of the value being estimated, auditors may require much more precision in their estimates.

Auditors typically audit balance sheet accounts such as inventory or accounts receivable. As mentioned before, the precision requirement is determined by the materiality percentage. Materiality is usually expressed as a percentage of net income, say, 5 to 10 percent of net income. Because many balance sheet accounts are much larger than the income figure, a material error in these accounts must be a lower percentage than the net income percentage. This occurs because any error in these accounts may directly affect the net income figure; for example, if accounts receivable is three times net income, a 5 percent write-down of accounts receivable is a 15 percent write-down of net income (before taxes). In addition, the overall materiality percentage on net income must be allocated across all balance sheet accounts to ensure that errors of less than a material amount in each account will not build up to produce an overall material error for the entire balance sheet. For these reasons, an auditor could be auditing an account with a precision factor of 1 percent or less. Because the sample size goes up with the square of the inverse of the precision figure A [recall that for a 95 percent reliability and ignoring the finite population factor, $n = (1.96\sigma/A)^2$], a reduction in A from 5 percent to 1 percent causes the sample size to increase by a factor of 25. Combining this result with the intrinsically high value of σ in accounting populations, we can see that sizes of random samples in realistic problems can become enormous. We now consider two techniques that are useful in reducing these large sample sizes in practice: stratification and auxiliary information estimators.

Stratified Random Sampling. If a population is heterogeneous but can be divided into segments or strata that are relatively homogeneous, we can use stratified sampling techniques to reduce the sample sizes required to achieve a given level of precision and reliability. As an extreme example, consider a population that consists of two categories of items. All items in a category have the same value. If we were to take a simple random sample of items from the entire population, we would get an estimate of the mean and some established sampling error. But if we were to group all items into the two categories and take a single sample from each category, we would know the total dollar value of the account with no sampling error at all, even though we drew only the two sample items. Although this example is obviously artificial, it does illustrate that if we can stratify the population into groups that are relatively homogeneous, we can sample separately from each group and thereby achieve greater accuracy in our sampling procedure. Accounting populations may not always segregate into natural groupings, but techniques do exist for computing good strata boundaries even in a continuously distributed population.

Assume that the population has been divided into M strata. We shall use the following notation:

X_{ij} = value of item i in stratum j ($j = 1, \ldots, M$)

N_j = number of items in stratum j

$$\overline{X}_j = \sum_{i=1}^{N_j} \frac{X_{ij}}{N_j} = \text{average value of items in stratum } j$$

$$S_j = \sqrt{\sum \frac{(X_{ij} - \overline{X}_j)^2}{N_j}} = \text{standard deviation of items in stratum } j$$

$$N = \sum_{j=1}^{M} N_j = \text{total number of items in the population}$$

$$W_j = \frac{N_j}{N} = \text{proportion of items in stratum } j$$

$$\overline{X} = \sum_j \frac{N_j \overline{X}_j}{N} = \text{average value of all items in the population}$$

Similar notation is used for *sample* values but with lowercase letters substituted for capital letters; for example, x_{ij} is the value of the ith item sampled in stratum j and n_j is the number of samples taken in stratum j. With this notation, the formula for estimating the population mean $\widehat{\overline{X}}$ is given by

$$\widehat{\overline{X}} = \sum_{j=1}^{M} W_j x_j$$

where x_j is the sample mean computed in stratum j. To measure the accuracy of a stratified estimate, we must estimate the standard errors of the mean estimate in each stratum and combine these into an overall standard error. The estimated standard error in stratum j, $s_{\overline{x}_j}$, is given by

$$s_{\overline{x}_j} = \frac{s_j}{\sqrt{n_j}} \sqrt{1 - \frac{n_j}{N_j}}$$

where s_j is the estimated standard deviation of stratum j,

$$s_j = \left[\frac{\sum_{i=1}^{n_j} (x_{ij} - \overline{x}_j)^2}{n_j - 1} \right]^{1/2}$$

The factor $\sqrt{1 - n_j/N_j}$ in the formula for $s_{\overline{x}_j}$ is the finite population correction factor in stratum j, which can be ignored if the sample size n_j in stratum j is a small fraction of the total number of items in stratum j.

The standard error of the overall mean estimate, $s_{\bar{x}}$, is

$$s_{\bar{x}} = \sqrt{\sum_j W_j^2 s_{\bar{x}_j}^2}$$

a weighted sum of the estimated variances in each stratum.

A simple example should help to illustrate the use of stratified random sampling. Suppose that we have a group of invoices that we divide into two strata—a high and a low dollar-value group. The first stratum has 1,000 invoices and we sample 100 of these. The second stratum has 2,000 invoices and we sample 500 of these. These numbers and the sampling statistics are shown in Exhibit 12. The estimate of the population mean is

$$\hat{\bar{X}} = \Sigma W_j \bar{x}_j = \frac{1}{3}(\$10{,}000) + \frac{2}{3}(\$5{,}000) = \$6{,}667$$

The standard errors of the mean estimate in each stratum are

$$s_{\bar{x}_1} = \frac{1{,}000}{\sqrt{100}} \sqrt{1 - \frac{100}{1{,}000}} = \sqrt{9{,}000}$$

$$s_{\bar{x}_2} = \frac{500}{\sqrt{500}} \sqrt{1 - \frac{500}{2{,}000}} = \sqrt{375}$$

Therefore, the standard error for the population mean is

$$s_{\bar{x}} = \sqrt{\sum_j W_j^2 s_{\bar{x}_j}^2} = \sqrt{\frac{1}{9}(9{,}000) + \frac{4}{9}(375)} = \sqrt{1{,}167}$$
$$= 34$$

It can be shown that a simple random sample of 600 items from the same population would have yielded a standard error close to 100. Thus a simple two-way stratification was able to increase the accuracy of the estimate by a factor of almost 3 in this example.

Sample size allocation. The allocations of sample sizes in the above example (100 to stratum 1 and 500 to stratum 2) were arbitrary. One of the design issues in stratified sampling is how to allocate a given sample size among the

EXHIBIT 12   Stratified Sample of Invoices

Stratum number, j	Items in stratum, N_j	Weight of stratum, W_j	Items in sample, n_j	Mean value of sampled invoices in stratum, $\bar{x}_j$	Standard deviation of sampled items in stratum, s_j
1	1,000	⅓	100	$10,000	1,000
2	2,000	⅔	500	5,000	500

various strata. A simple but not optimal method is to use a proportional allocation. In proportional sampling, the proportion of total sampled items allocated to stratum j is equal to the proportion of the number of items in stratum j to the total number of items in the population; for example,

$$\frac{n_j}{n} = W_j \quad \text{for} \quad j = 1, \ldots, M$$

In the above example, a proportional allocation would have 200 sample items in stratum 1 and 400 sample items in stratum 2. Note that if we had used this allocation in the example and obtained the same estimates of stratum mean $\bar{x}_j$ and stratum standard deviation s_j, the standard errors in each stratum would be

$$s_{x_1} = \sqrt{4{,}500} \quad \text{and} \quad s_{x_2} = \sqrt{469}$$

and

$$s_{\bar{x}} = \frac{1}{3} \sqrt{4{,}500 + 1{,}876} = 26.6$$

a considerable improvement over the standard error of 34 achieved with the arbitrary (100, 500) allocation. Proportional allocation is useful when either the variability within strata is constant (the S_j's are approximately equal) or else little is known about the variability within each stratum so that one cannot take advantage of prior knowledge of S_j.

If we have prior knowledge about the variability in each stratum, we can compute an optimal allocation of the total sample size to each stratum.

For the optimal allocation, we allocate samples to stratum proportional to the product of the number of items in the stratum and the standard deviation within the stratum.

$$\frac{n_j}{n} = \frac{N_j S_j}{\sum_{k=1}^{M} N_k S_k}$$

Strictly speaking, this allocation is optimal only if there is an equal cost of sampling in each stratum. If there is a cost C_j of sampling each unit in stratum j, then an allocation that has lowest cost for a given precision level or, conversely, has highest precision for a given total sampling cost would allocate proportional to $N_j S_j / \sqrt{C_j}$.

With the optimal allocation, we take a larger sample in a stratum if the stratum itself is larger or has more internal variability than other strata or both. To apply the optimal allocation method to our numerical example, we compute the products $N_j S_j$ for strata 1 and 2, assuming that the population standard deviation in each stratum approximately equals the sample standard deviation:

$$N_1 S_1 = N_2 S_2 = 1{,}000{,}000$$

In this case the two product terms are equal, so we would allocate 300 samples to each stratum. Again assuming the same sample results, we estimate the standard errors of the mean estimate in each stratum as

$$s_{\bar{x}_1} = \frac{1,000}{\sqrt{300}} \sqrt{1 - \frac{300}{1,000}} = \sqrt{2,333}$$

$$s_{\bar{x}_2} = \frac{500}{\sqrt{300}} \sqrt{1 - \frac{300}{2,000}} = \sqrt{708.3}$$

and the standard error for the population mean is

$$s_{\bar{x}} = \frac{1}{3} \sqrt{2,333 + 4(708.3)} = 24$$

The estimated standard error of 24 is below that achieved by proportional allocation (27) and the arbitrary allocation (34).

Total sample size computation. Although we have now given the formulas for the fraction of the total sample size to be allocated to each stratum under both proportional and optimal allocation methods, we still need to compute the total sample size that is required to achieve a given reliability level and precision. With proportional sampling,

$$s_{\bar{x}_j} = \frac{S_j}{\sqrt{n_j}} \sqrt{1 - \frac{n_j}{N_j}} = \frac{S_j}{\sqrt{nW_j}} \sqrt{1 - \frac{n}{N}}$$

and hence,

$$s_{\bar{x}} = \sqrt{\Sigma W_j^2 s_{\bar{x}_j}^2} = \frac{\sqrt{1 - n/N}}{\sqrt{n}} \sqrt{\Sigma W_j S_j^2}$$

With the optimal allocation, substitution yields

$$s_{\bar{x}} = \left[\frac{(\Sigma W_j S_j)^2}{n} - \frac{\Sigma W_j S_j^2}{N} \right]^{1/2}$$

If we ignore the effects of the finite population correction factor, which has the conservative effect of increasing the required sample size, we obtain the following simpler results.

Simple random sampling: $s_{\bar{x}}^2 = S^2/n$
Proportional stratified sampling: $s_{\bar{x}}^2 = \Sigma N_j S_j^2/nN$
Optimal stratified sampling: $s_{\bar{x}}^2 = (\Sigma N_j S_j)^2/nN^2$

These formulas give the standard deviation or variance of the mean estimate as a function of known parameters and the total sample size n. We then solve for the n that gives the desired reliability and precision for the audit test.

Basis of stratification. Obvious questions in this entire development are on what basis the strata are formed for the auditor and how the auditor knows in advance the standard deviation S_j in each stratum so that an optimal allocation can be used. We assume that the auditor has a complete list of the recorded book values in the account to be sampled. These book values are the basis on which strata are formed and the standard deviation of each stratum is estimated. The auditor is, of course, interested in estimating the true dollar value in the account. In the great majority of cases, however, the book values will either equal or be close to the true (audited) values and, hence, they provide an excellent basis for stratification and prior estimation of strata variance.

It is even possible to use the close dependence between book and audited values to compute strata boundaries that result in minimal sample sizes for given precision and reliability. This technique, which should be especially useful for the highly skewed populations frequently encountered by auditors, is described in Section 5A.6 (pp. 128–133) of Cochran [1963]. A related question is how many strata should be used in a stratified sampling plan. Although it is difficult to be definitive on this issue, there is an inherent uncertainty in the sampling process that limits the value of a very large number of strata. One problem is that the estimate of the standard error in each stratum can become highly variable if there are only a few samples allocated to each stratum. Rules of thumb indicate that between 6 and 10 strata are reasonable upper limits. These rules, however, have been developed on populations in which the auxiliary variable, forming the basis of stratification, is not as closely related to the measured variable as the book value is to the audited value in accounting populations. Therefore it is possible that future research may show that more than 10 strata are useful in the auditing context.

Limitations of mean per unit estimation. Stratification improves the precision of estimates in auditing but, by itself, may still not provide enough precision to satisfy the auditor's materiality requirements. In addition, a peculiar situation may occasionally develop that would seriously question the validity of the statistical sampling procedure. Recall that with a 95 percent reliability level, 5 percent of the time we shall construct a confidence interval that will not contain the true mean value. Thus, 5 percent of the time we shall get a sample that, because of sampling variation inherent in the process, will cause us to conclude that an essentially correct population contains material errors. Suppose now that we happen to draw such a sample of book values; that is, the estimate of the book value mean and the standard deviation of this estimate result in a 95 percent confidence interval that does not contain the overall book value mean. We, of course, shall know the book value or recorded mean of all the items in the population, because we assume that the auditor has the list of these items before starting the sampling process. In this situation, even if every item that has been selected for audit turns out to be absolutely correct (audited value equals recorded book value for every item sampled), we shall construct a confidence interval that does not contain the overall book value mean and, hence, conclude that material errors exist. It would certainly be peculiar to conclude that a population has material misstatements when none of the items audited was in error.

This circumstance arises because of sampling fluctuation in the book values selected for audit. One way to avoid this is always to be sure that the mean book value of items selected for audit equals the overall book value mean. But this is impossible to guarantee when items are selected for audit on a random basis. Another possibility is to keep sampling, past the minimum required sample size, until the sampled book value mean happens to about equal the overall mean. This method, however, may result in much larger sample sizes than are required for the test at given reliability and precision levels. A compromise solution is to sample until at least the confidence interval created by the sample of book values contains the overall mean. This procedure may still require excessive sample sizes. Also, if a few trivial errors turn up in those samples for which the confidence interval just includes the overall mean, the confidence interval based on audited values will not contain the overall mean and the population will be rejected. Those same trivial errors, however, will hardly affect the statistical conclusion of a sample whose book value approximately equals the overall mean.

It seems that a better statistical procedure is needed to eliminate the difficulties that arise because of the whimsical fluctuation in the book value means of the randomly selected sample. Fortunately, such a procedure is available when we use ratio, or regression, estimates of the true population mean.

Auxiliary Information Estimators. We have already mentioned how the auditor can use the list of recorded book values as a basis for stratification. The auditor can also use the information available in the recorded book values of the population in constructing ratio or regression estimators. These estimators are widely used in surveys when extensive information is available on another variable that is correlated with the variable actually being measured by the survey. For example, to estimate consumer spending on leisure, we could use an auxiliary variable of disposable income. This latter figure should be correlated with leisure spending and may be known, in aggregate, for a community from census data. Upon sampling a number of households, we would determine not only the spending figure but also the disposable income for each household. Then the ratio, or regression coefficient, between spending and income is estimated for the households sampled and applied to the mean disposable income of the entire community to arrive at an overall estimate of community leisure spending. This estimate will be more precise than a simple mean per unit estimate, computed from the sampled households, if there is a reasonably high correlation between spending and income. Using an auxiliary variable controls for the sampling variation that would normally occur in the disposable incomes of families that were sampled. A mean per unit estimate of spending would underestimate the true figure if one happened to choose a sample of households whose disposable incomes were below the community average. In the auditing application, mean per unit estimates do not control for the sampling variation in book values of items selected for the sample, as discussed in the previous section.

In applications where auxiliary information estimators are used, the auxiliary information is either a variable that is correlated with the variable being measured (as in the above example) or a rough estimate of the main variable of interest (e.g., an estimate of crop yield on the basis of airplane or photographic surveys). In either case the auxiliary variable is not a perfect surrogate for the variable being estimated. The auditing environment is quite different. The auxiliary variable, the recorded book value of each item in the population, is not just strongly correlated with the main variable, the true (audited) value of each item. In most instances, it is precisely equal to the true value. This condition could lead to greatly reduced sample sizes because the standard error of the estimate is a decreasing function of the correlation between the auxiliary and main variables. Unfortunately, this unique relationship of equality between the two variables can lead to distributional problems in interpreting the standard error of our estimates, as we shall see subsequently.

Notation. Assume that we have an unstratified population. Let

X_i = recorded dollar value of item i $(i = 1, \ldots, N)$

Y_i = true audited value of item i

$\overline{X} = \Sigma \dfrac{X_i}{N}$ = mean recorded value

$\overline{Y} = \Sigma \dfrac{Y_i}{N}$ = mean true value

$S_x^2 = \Sigma \dfrac{(X_i - \overline{X})^2}{N - 1}$ = population variance of recorded dollar values

$S_y^2 = \Sigma \dfrac{(Y_i - \overline{Y})^2}{N - 1}$ = population variance of true dollar values

$R = \dfrac{\overline{Y}}{\overline{X}}$ = ratio of true to recorded dollar values

$\rho = \Sigma \dfrac{(Y_i - \overline{Y})(X_i - \overline{X})}{(NS_yS_x)}$ = finite population correlation coefficient

$B = \dfrac{\rho S_y}{S_x}$ = finite population regression coefficient

As before, sample values are denoted by lowercase versions of the above symbols. The statistical problem is to estimate the true mean value of the population, $\overline{X}$, from our knowledge of $X_1, X_2, \ldots, X_n$, and (x_j, y_j) for $j = 1, \ldots, n$, the items we have sampled. We also need to obtain an estimate of the standard deviation of our mean dollar value estimate that can be used to construct a confidence interval about the mean estimate.

A class of estimators. Almost all auxiliary information estimators of interest are special cases of the general estimator

$$\widehat{\overline{Y}} = \overline{y} + z(\overline{X} - \overline{x})$$

where Y is the estimate of the true mean value and z is either a constant or a function of sample values (x_j, y_j). For a mean per unit estimate, the only type considered up to now, simply set $z = 0$. If we set $z = \overline{y}/\overline{x} = r$, the sample estimator of the population ratio, R, we obtain the ratio estimator $(\overline{y}/\overline{x})X$. If we set $z = b$, the sample regression coefficient, where

$$b = \frac{\Sigma(x_i - \overline{x})(y_i - \overline{y})}{\Sigma(x_i - \overline{x})^2}$$

we obtain the regression estimator. A difference estimator is obtained by setting $z = 1$, which yields

$$\widehat{\overline{Y}} = \overline{X} + (\overline{y} - \overline{x})$$

the mean book value adjusted for the difference between sampled audited and book values.

Estimators for which z is computed from sample data, as in ratio and regression estimators, are biased, which implies that the average of sample estimates made from repeated samples from the same population may not converge to the true population parameter. The bias decreases with sample size, however, and has never been reported to be important with the large sample sizes (in excess of 50) typically used in auditing.

With ratio, regression, and difference estimators, a sample in which no errors are found ($y_j = x_j$ for $j = 1, \ldots, n$) will result in a value of z equal to 1. In this case, the estimated true mean value will always equal the recorded mean value $\overline{X}$ (because $z = 1$ and $\overline{y} = \overline{x}$). Thus we shall never have the situation that arises with mean per unit estimators in which no errors are found in the sample but the true mean value is estimated as being different from the recorded book value mean. The use of the auxiliary information controls for the sampling variation in book values selected for audit.

Variance of auxiliary information estimators. The variance of auxiliary information estimators is estimated from the sample as

$$s_{\overline{y}}^2 = \frac{1 - n/N}{n}(s_y^2 - 2z\hat{\rho}s_y s_x + z^2 s_x^2)$$

where the terms in parentheses are sample estimates of the corresponding population parameters; for example, suppose $\hat{\rho}$ = sample correlation coefficient = $\Sigma(x_i - \overline{x})(y_i - \overline{y})/(n - 1)s_y s_x$. Results for the particular estimators we have described are presented in Exhibit 13. One can verify that the regression estimator will have the lowest estimated variance of all the auxiliary information estimators. In practice, for low-error-rate populations in which $y_i = x_i$ for almost all items, there is not much difference in the variance of the ratio, regression, and difference estimators.

Once we have chosen a particular auxiliary information estimator, we estimate the true mean value, $\overset{\approx}{Y}$, and compute the standard deviation of this estimate using the formulas in Exhibit 13. The next step usually assumes that the central limit theorem holds for mean estimates computed using auxiliary information estimators. Therefore, normal distribution theory can be applied to construct confidence intervals about the estimated mean as we did in a previous section, and see if the recorded mean value is included in such an interval.

Although such a procedure may provide satisfactory results in many circumstances, it is unlikely that the statistical inferences from this procedure will be correct if we are working with a low-error-rate population. As an extreme case,

---

EXHIBIT 13 Auxiliary Information Estimators and Their Variances

$$\overline{Y} = \overline{y} + z(\overline{X} - \overline{x})$$

Name of estimator	z	$ns_{\overline{y}}^2/(1 - n/N)$
Mean per unit	0	s_y^2
Difference	1	$s_y^2 - 2\hat{\rho}s_y s_x + s_x^2$
Ratio	$r = \overline{y}/\overline{x}$	$s_y^2 - 2r\hat{\rho}s_y s_x + r^2 s_x^2$
Regression	$b = \hat{\rho}s_y/s_x$	$s_y^2(1 - \hat{\rho}^2)$

Note: $\hat{\rho} = \Sigma(y_i - \overline{y})(x_i - \overline{x})/ns_y s_x$.

if no errors are found in the sample, then s_y will equal s_x, $\hat{\rho}$ will equal 1, and the standard deviation will be estimated to be zero. If only a few errors are found in the population, the standard errors will be underestimated and confidence intervals will be narrower than they should be. Therefore, instead of 95 percent of the confidence intervals that are $\pm 1.96\sigma_{\bar{y}}$ wide, containing the true mean value, perhaps only 90 percent or 80 percent of the intervals so constructed will contain the true mean value.

Thus, ratio and regression estimators, although avoiding the problem of estimating a true mean value different from the recorded value when no errors are found in the sample, lead to statistical inference problems in low-error-rate situations. This area is still being explored and investigated. One compromise solution is to use the ratio or regression estimate as the estimate of the true mean but to use the stratified mean per unit standard deviation estimate. This standard deviation estimate is an upper bound on the true standard deviation of the ratio or regression estimate and hence will not produce confidence intervals that are too narrow. The difficulty with this procedure is that we are forced to use a sample size that is larger than is really needed given that we are using a ratio or regression estimate of the mean.

An additional possibility is to use stratified ratio or regression estimates to get the combined advantage of both stratification and auxiliary information estimators. Readers interested in this possibility should consult a text in sampling theory such as Cochran [1963].

Dollar Unit Sampling. The most efficient procedure for sampling from a zero- or low-error-rate population is dollar unit sampling (DUS). The DUS procedure has been explored extensively during the past 10 years.

To select an appropriate sample size, we first need an estimate of J, the number of errors we expect to find in the sample while still not rejecting the book value. Typically, this number will be either 0 or 1, because DUS is applied best to populations where the expected error rate is very low. We also need to specify the maximum probability β of accepting a population that contains a material error, and M, the magnitude of a material error. A sample size factor, F, based on β and J, is selected from the table in Exhibit 14. For example, if $\beta = .05$ and we still wish to accept the population if there is one error in the sample ($J = 1$), the factor F equals 4.74. The sample size n is then computed as

EXHIBIT 14   Selection of Dollar Unit Sampling Factor F

		β		
J	.01	.05	.10	.25
0	4.61	3.00	2.30	1.39
1	6.64	4.74	3.89	2.69
2	8.41	6.30	5.32	3.92
3	10.00	7.75	6.68	5.11

$$n = \frac{(F)(BV)}{M} = \frac{F}{m}$$

where BV = book value of the population, and $m = M/BV$ = materiality expressed as a fraction of the book value. If materiality for the account is 2 percent of the book value of the account ($m = .02$), the appropriate sample size is

$$n = \frac{4.74}{.02} = 237$$

To illustrate the technique on the population of invoices in Exhibit 1, it will be simpler to work with a smaller sample size (especially because we have a total of only 100 invoices anyway). Therefore, choose $\beta = .10$ and $J = 0$ so that $F = 2.30$. Then, if the materiality percentage is 5 percent ($m = .05$), the sample size is

$$n = \frac{F}{m} = \frac{2.30}{.05} = 46$$

The total book value of the invoices in Exhibit 1 is $1,995.34. A sample size of 46 implies that we select a sampling interval I determined by

$$I = \frac{BV}{n} = \frac{1,995.34}{46} = 43.38$$

With dollar unit sampling, every Ith dollar is sampled. This is accomplished by choosing a random start between zero and I and then selecting the account containing every Ith dollar thereafter until the end of the population is reached. For example, with the five-digit random number table in Exhibit 7, we select numbers until we obtain one whose first four digits are less than 4,338. This will give us a random start between zero and $I = 43.38$. Following the sequence of random numbers we used in Exhibit 8, we wait until the fifth random number, equal to 14,194, to obtain the random start.

Now, we sum the cumulative amount of each invoice to provide the basis of the dollar unit sampling plan. The procedure is illustrated in Exhibit 15 using the first 20 invoices from Exhibit 1. The invoice containing the 14.19th dollar is number 2, so this is the first invoice selected by the sampling plan. Now we successively add the sampling interval of $43.38 to the random start of $14.19 to select the remainder of the sample, as in Exhibit 16. The selected invoices are noted with an asterisk in Exhibit 15. The process illustrated in Exhibits 15 and 16 is continued until the end of the population of invoices is reached. The 46th, or last, invoice selected will be the one containing the cumulative dollar amount equal to

$$\$14.19 + (45)(\$43.38) = \$1,959.09$$

(Working backwards from the population book value of $1,995.34, we learn that this corresponds to invoice number 98.)

Note that with the DUS procedure, invoices are selected with a probability proportional to their magnitude. Small invoices have a relatively low probability of being selected, whereas invoices containing a large number of dollars

EXHIBIT 15   Cumulative Total of Invoices

Invoice number	Invoice value	Cumulative invoice value
1	$11.87	$11.87
2	11.18	23.05*
3	11.32	34.37
4	10.16	44.53
5	4.15	48.68
6	12.35	61.03*
7	7.89	68.92
8	12.74	81.66
9	6.86	88.52
10	5.08	93.60
11	21.18	114.78*
12	21.90	136.68
13	19.98	156.66*
14	23.23	179.89
15	23.60	203.49*
16	19.04	222.53
17	23.33	245.86*
18	22.06	267.92
19	17.84	285.76*
20	11.74	297.50

have a high probability of being selected. Any invoice that is larger than the sampling interval I is certain to be selected, so the sampling plan cannot miss choosing any large dollar-value item. It is this feature of selecting invoices proportional to their size that causes the high efficiency of the DUS procedure. Also, the DUS plan will have the greatest efficiency gains when the distribution of invoice values is highly dispersed, with a mixture of very large and small items.

EXHIBIT 16   Selection of Dollar Unit Sample

Cumulative value of account to be sampled	Invoice number
14.19	2
57.57	6
100.95	11
144.33	13
187.71	15
231.09	17
274.47	19
⋮	⋮

After the sample of invoices is selected, the items are verified. If the number of errors found is less than or equal to *J*, the specified permissible number of errors, then the population book value can be accepted with the property that the probability is less than or equal to β of the population being in error by more than the material amount *M*. A more complicated evaluation procedure is required if an invoice is found to be partially in error; that is, if invoice number 6 is found to equal $11.35 instead of its recorded book value of $12.35, the invoice is only partially in error in the context of a variables sampling plan. An evaluation procedure for these partial errors is described in an article by Anderson and Teitlebaum [1973].

HYPOTHESIS TESTING

The discussion in the preceding sections has concentrated on *estimating* the true value of a parameter and developing statistical confidence intervals within which the true value of the parameter is likely to lie. Most of the traditional literature applying statistical sampling to variables estimation in auditing has advocated the use of this estimation approach. Some authors, however (see Elliott and Rogers [1972]), have expressed the position that auditors should be more concerned with tests of hypotheses about the parameters of populations rather than estimating these parameters. Although in a certain sense estimation and hypothesis testing can be viewed as being equivalent, the prior specification of the degree of precision or risk may be much easier or more natural for auditors with hypothesis testing than with interval estimation.

Hypothesis testing is most useful when we have some prior feelings about the value of a parameter (such as the mean) of a population. After drawing a random sample of observations from this population, we would wish to test whether this sample is consistent with our prior feelings about the parameter. Typically we test in such a way so that we can conclude either (1) that the sample is inconsistent with our prior feelings so that we reject the hypothesis that the sample could have come from a population with our prespecified value of the parameter; or (2) that the sample is consistent with our prior feelings so that we cannot reject our initial hypothesis about the value of this parameter. This second conclusion is frequently referred to as "accepting our initial hypothesis," but it is more correct to say that "we did not reject it."

To be more specific, let us return to the population of invoices in Exhibit 1 and the random sample of 30 invoices drawn from this population as shown in Exhibit 8. Suppose that we wish to test the hypothesis that these 30 invoices came from a population whose mean equaled $19.95 (the recorded value for the 100 invoices in Exhibit 1). Recall that the sample mean was $21.17 and the sample standard deviation was $6.39. The question we must now ask is: If the true mean of the population were really $19.95, how likely is it that we would draw a random sample of 30 items and find the mean value of the sample to be as high as $21.17, or even higher? In other words, what is the probability that the sample mean could deviate from the true mean by $1.22 just by chance alone. If this probability is sufficiently small, we reject our initial hypothesis (commonly called the *null hypothesis*). If the probability is high enough, we conclude that we cannot reject the null hypothesis.

To test the hypothesis, we use the previously computed standard error of the mean of .976. Thus, the sample mean is 1.22/.976 = 1.25 standard errors away from the assumed mean. Remembering the implication of the central limit theorem that sample means will be normally distributed, we want to know the probability that a normally distributed random variable could be more than 1.25 standard errors away from its mean. Referring to the normal distribution function tabulated in Exhibit 6, we see that there is a probability of $1 - .8944$ = .1056 of getting such a high observation. Allowing for random fluctuations in both directions (both high and low deviations of at least 1.25σ), we see that there is a probability greater than 1 in 5 of getting a sample mean that is more than 1.25σ from the hypothesized mean. We shall likely conclude that this occurrence is sufficiently common that we would not wish to reject our initial or null hypothesis. If the sample mean had turned out to be \$23.00 with a standard deviation of the mean equal to \$1.00, then the sample mean would have been 3.05 standard errors from the assumed mean. The probability of getting such a large deviation by chance alone would be about .002. We would conclude in this case that it was extremely unlikely that the sample came from a population whose mean equaled \$19.95 and hence reject the null hypothesis.

Type I and Type II Errors. Understandably, the question can be raised: What critical value should we select for the probability of getting an observed difference from our null hypothesis by chance, above which we should accept the hypothesis and below which we should reject it? This value is called the *critical probability* or *level of significance,* and is denoted α (alpha). Naturally, the answer to this question is not simple.

Only four possible things can happen when we test a hypothesis. We may be wrong because we:

1. Reject a hypothesis that is really true (a type I error); or
2. Accept a hypothesis that is false (a type II error).

Or we may be right because we:

3. Accept a true hypothesis; or
4. Reject a false hypothesis.

The types of errors noted as possibilities 1 and 2 above are known either as type I and type II errors or as errors of the first kind and errors of the second kind.

Type I errors. In a long run of cases in which the hypothesis is in fact *true* (although we do not know it is true, for otherwise there would be no need to test it), we shall necessarily either be wrong as in 1 or right as in 3. That is, if we make an error, it will have to be type I. Suppose that we adopt 5 percent as the critical probability, accepting the hypothesis when the probability of getting the observed difference by chance exceeds 5 percent and rejecting the hypothesis when this probability proves to be less than 5 percent. This amounts to the decision to accept the hypothesis when the discrepancy of the sample mean is less than 1.96 standard errors and to reject the hypothesis when the discrepancy is more than 1.96 standard errors. Using this value as the critical probability, we would expect to make a type I error 5 percent of the time. This is because even when the hypothesis is true, 5 percent of all possible sample means still lie farther away than 1.96 standard errors. And whenever by chance we get one of these, and the hypothesis is true, we would make the mistake of rejecting a true hypothesis.

Or, we might choose 1 percent as the critical probability, which would correspond to a discrepancy between hypothesis and sample mean equal to 2.58 standard errors. When the hypothesis is in fact true, only 1 percent of all possible sample means would lie farther away than 2.58 standard errors. We would make a type I error only when by chance alone we happened to draw one of these. That is, we would now make an error of the first kind only 1 percent of the time.

Type II errors. So far we have concerned ourselves only with the first kind of error. But there is also the second kind—the possible error of accepting a false hypothesis. The lower the value we set for the critical probability, in general, the fewer the hypotheses we shall reject. But the chances are then increased of accepting more hypotheses that are false. For a fixed sample size we can buy safety in one direction only at the expense of danger in the other.

Unfortunately, it is impossible to predict in general the percentage of times we should expect to commit an error of the second kind on the basis of any particular value adopted for the critical probability. The reason for this is that the chance of accepting a false hypothesis also depends on how far away from the true value the particular hypothesis happens to be. Remember that sample means tend to cluster around the true means of the populations from which they are drawn. If the hypothetical mean is far away from the true mean, it is unlikely that a sample mean will be drawn that appears consistent with the hypothesis. If the hypothetical mean is false but not far from the mark, an error of the second kind is much more likely to be made.

For example, in our population of invoices, if the true mean happened to be $20.50, we would be unlikely to reject the null hypothesis of $19.95 and we would make a type II error almost all the time. If the true mean were $30, however, we would be correctly rejecting the null hypothesis almost always and, hence, rarely making a type II error.

In a long run of instances in which hypotheses are actually false, some will be farther from the true mean than others. Therefore, it is impossible to predict in general the probability of accepting false hypotheses. We can appreciate, however, that the chances of accepting false hypotheses are increased as fewer null hypotheses are rejected due to the use of a lower value for the critical probability.

Balancing type I against type II errors. In testing hypotheses we thus face two dangers: either rejecting a true hypothesis (type I error) or not rejecting a false hypothesis (type II error). The danger of committing a type I error can be made as low as we wish by reducing the value chosen for the critical probability α. This can be done, however, only by increasing the probability of committing a type II error.

In the auditing context, a type I error corresponds to rejecting perfectly correct financial statements. A type II error occurs when the auditor accepts financial statements that contain material errors. Although most applications of hypothesis testing are more concerned with making type I errors than type II errors, we can see that the auditor will be most concerned with making a type II error. The auditor who makes a type I error, by rejecting a correct financial statement balance, will usually investigate further to determine the causes of the errors. Thus the costs associated with this risk arise from the unnecessary follow-up work the auditor subsequently performs. The risk of accepting materially incorrect financial statements, however, is of critical importance to the auditor. Therefore, the auditor wishes to set the probability of making a type II error very low. In fact, being able to control explicitly for type II errors is the principal reason why hypothesis testing may be preferred to interval estimation by auditors.

So long as a given sample size is assumed, the risk of one type of error can be reduced only by increasing the probability of making the other type of error. By taking a larger sample size, however, we can reduce the probability of making either or both types of errors. As the sample size is increased, the sample mean will tend to become closer to the true mean and the estimate of the standard error of the mean will be reduced. If we hold the probability of making a type I error constant, an increase in sample size will enable us to reduce the probability of making a type II error. In summary, the probability of a type II error decreases as each of the following items increases:

1. The critical probability α of a type I error
2. The difference in parameter values (e.g., mean values) between the null hypothesis and the alternative hypothesis
3. The sample size

Given prespecified values of the permissible values of making type I and type II errors, and the amount considered material (which determines the alternative hypothesis), the auditor can estimate what sample size is required to meet these audit requirements with the population being investigated and the characteristics of the statistical procedure being used.

MULTIPLE REGRESSION ANALYSIS

Introduction. Statistical analysis is frequently used to estimate the relation among a number of simultaneous variables. In the most common application for accountants, regression analysis is used to estimate how costs vary with the level of activity of a process or an entire department. Typically a linear relationship is assumed and the fixed and variable components of costs estimated from historical data. These can then be used for product planning and cost control by predicting the expected level of costs at a variety of output volumes.

Although cost estimation has been the most widespread application of regression analysis for accountants, some accountants are increasingly seeing the value of this technique in financial audits. At a given time, the many similar branches or divisions of a large organization (e.g., branch banks, retail outlets) can be compared simultaneously to determine if the cost or profit performance of any of these units is unusual when compared to the normal performance of the great majority of units. Systematic differences among the units such as size or location can be controlled for in the statistical analysis so that any large deviations from normal performance would be attributable initially to unexplained factors. Units with such unexplained deviations then become prime candidates for special attention in the audit process.

Simple Regression. Regression analysis starts with a mathematical model that expresses the analyst's beliefs as to how the dependent variable, say, cost, varies with the level of one or more independent variables, such as measures of output. For example, let Y = monthly overhead cost in a department that produces nothing but widgets, and let X_1 be the number of widgets produced in a month. Then we may postulate a linear relation in which

$$Y = \beta_0 + \beta_1 X_1 + \epsilon$$

where β_0 and β_1 are unknown coefficients to be estimated and ϵ is an error term that represents the effects of omitted and transitory random factors that may occur in a month (excessive sickness, variations in worker morale or machine efficiency, etc.). It would be rare for all the observations on output and cost to have an exact linear relationship. The error term, ϵ, attempts to capture the departures from strict linearity.

In the linear relationship, β_0 represents the fixed overhead costs associated with producing widgets and β_1 represents the variable component of overhead costs. That is, if output X_1 goes up by 1 widget, we expect overhead costs to increase by β_1 dollars. The linear relation implies that if X_1 goes up by 100 widgets, expected overhead costs will increase, proportionately, by $100\beta_1$ dollars.

As a simple example, consider the data in Exhibit 17, which represents the monthly output of widgets and overhead costs in a 12-month period. The first step in any analysis is to plot the data to see if a linear relationship is a reasonable one to postulate. (See Exhibit 18.) In this case, the data do appear to be

EXHIBIT 17

Month	No. of widgets produced, X_1	Overhead cost, Y
1.........	9,000	$390,000
2.........	10,500	410,000
3.........	13,000	435,000
4.........	11,000	410,000
5.........	11,800	431,000
6.........	15,000	440,000
7.........	12,000	420,000
8.........	14,000	434,000
9.........	16,500	470,000
10.........	10,000	410,000
11.........	12,500	430,000
12.........	14,500	450,000

EXHIBIT 18

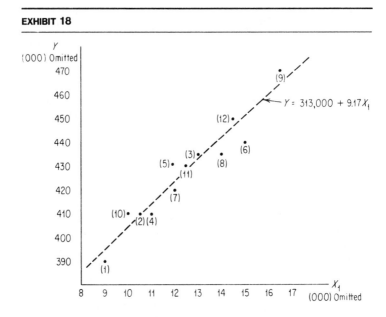

scattered about a straight line, and we can proceed with the analysis. If the relationship between costs and output appears to be nonlinear, then more complex models need to be estimated.

A number of heuristic techniques exist for fitting a line to the data, including the time-tested ones of eyeballing and trial and error. Regression analysis provides a way of computing a unique line that minimizes the sum of the squares of the vertical distances (the least-squares criterion) from each observation point to the estimated line. Although this line may be close to ones that would be fitted using less sophisticated procedures, the regression analysis can be easily extended to handle nonlinear functions and also to allow more than one variable to explain the variation in costs. Consider, for example, a department that produced more than one product or that had strong seasonal components in its cost behavior. Regression analysis also provides a measure of the goodness of fit of the assumed linear relationship and enables us to determine statistical confidence limits for the estimated line.

Many texts describe the formulas used to compute regression coefficients and associated statistical measures. In practice, one would always use a preprogrammed regression routine on a computer to perform the necessary calculations. Therefore, I shall not describe the detailed calculations involved but just indicate the results for our numerical example. For the data in Exhibit 17, the least-squares regression line is

$$Y = \$313,000 + \$9.17X_1$$

Thus, when $X_1 = 10,000$ units, departmental overhead costs are estimated at $\$313,000 + \$91,700 = \$404,700$. When $X_1 = 15,000$ units, overhead costs are estimated as $450,550. The regression line is drawn on Exhibit 18, and one can see that the estimated line does provide a reasonable fit to the data.

A widely used measure of goodness of fit of the regression line is called the *coefficient of determination*, or R^2. With raw data on only the dependent variable (cost in this case), all we observe, initially, is the variation or variance of this variable about its mean; for example, $V(Y) = \Sigma(Y_i - Y)^2/(n - 1)$. Without observing any other variables but this one, we would be able to conclude only that this variable—departmental overhead cost—was highly variable over time, ranging from a low of $390,000 in month 1 to a high of $470,000 in month 9. (One can check that the standard deviation of Y is $21,250.) Most of this variation, however, can be explained by the dependence of overhead cost on output and the actual variation of output throughout the year. That is, if there had been less variation in output, there would have been less variation in overhead cost. The statistic R^2 measures how much of the variation in the dependent variable, cost, can be explained by the variation of the independent variable, output. In this case, the linear fit is very good: $R^2 = .91$, implying that 91 percent of the variation of departmental overhead costs is explained by the regression equation linking cost to output. Therefore, only 9 percent of the variation in departmental costs is nonassignable and due to random, unexplained factors. Such a fit is quite good. One should not always expect that simple linear models will be able to explain complex empirical data so well. Many times we must settle for equations whose R^2 equals 0.5 or less, in which case there is still a considerable amount of scatter of data points about the regression line.

Additional statistics are also available from the regression analysis. It is common to assume that the error term, ϵ, is normally distributed with zero mean and constant variance, regardless of the value of the independent variable X_1. With these assumptions, it is possible to show that the actual values of the dependent variable will be normally distributed about its expected value as estimated from the regression equation. We can then use normal distribution theory to calculate a confidence interval for the predicted level of future overhead costs given an estimate as to what future output will be.

The normality assumption also allows us to construct confidence intervals or test hypotheses about the coefficients of the regression equation. In the above example, the estimated variable overhead coefficient is $9.17 per widget. The standard error of this estimate turns out to be .87. Thus, a confidence interval $\pm 2\sigma$ wide about the estimate would imply that the true value of this coefficient is highly likely to be between $7.43 and $10.91. Alternatively, we frequently want to test whether a given regression coefficient is statistically different from zero. If there is no relation between the dependent and independent variable, the coefficient of the independent variable should be zero. Even if this were the case, sampling fluctuations would cause an estimated coefficient to be different from zero. We would then test whether such an estimate could occur if the true value were zero. A rough rule of thumb in such circumstances is to accept a coefficient as statistically significant if it is at least twice its standard error. In our numerical example (Exhibit 17), the variable cost coefficient is more than 10 times its standard error, and we are confident that the relation between overhead cost and output is statistically significant.

EXHIBIT 19   Cost and Output Data for Three Types of Widgets

Month	Widget type			Total, ΣX_i	Departmental costs, Y
	X_1	X_2	X_3		
1........	8,000	1,600	2,400	12,000	$450,000
2........	7,760	1,720	2,440	11,920	445,000
3........	7,080	1,160	2,440	10,680	425,000
4........	7,240	1,560	2,320	11,120	430,000
5........	7,800	1,520	2,520	11,840	445,000
6........	7,440	1,840	2,480	11,760	438,000
7........	7,400	1,520	2,320	11,240	434,000
8........	7,520	1,680	2,280	11,480	438,000
9........	7,280	1,560	2,560	11,400	433,000
10........	7,440	1,760	2,320	11,520	437,000

Multiple Regression. The discussion so far has assumed that changes in overhead cost are a function of only a single independent variable (output of widgets) and a random error term. In most departments, however, more than one product or type of service is produced, so it may be difficult to arrive at a single measure of output. Sometimes a measure of input such as direct labor hours, direct labor dollars, or machine hours is used as a proxy variable for output, as in classical flexible budgeting. This technique may not be satisfactory if the different products or services use differing amounts of inputs so that no single measure captures the aggregate level of activity in a department.

Multiple regression analysis enables us to estimate simultaneously the effects on overall departmental costs of all the different activities that are performed in a department. To continue our example, let us consider a department that produces three types of widgets. Let X_i = output of widget type i (i = 1, 2, 3) in a period. Exhibit 19 shows, for a 10-month period, the output of widgets and total departmental costs for each month. A simple linear regression of departmental costs versus total output in widgets yields the following estimated relationship:

$$Y = \$235,000 + \$17.61 \; \Sigma \; X_i \qquad R^2 = .91$$
$$(1.98)$$

where the standard error of the coefficient of total output appears in parentheses. The fit is quite good, and we might normally be satisfied with this estimated relationship. Nevertheless, if we believe that there are significant differences in the variable costs of producing the three types of widgets, we might try to estimate the variable cost of each type of widget separately. Because many accounts are only accumulated on a department-wide basis, we cannot get a finer breakdown that would enable us to estimate the variable cost of each widget type without a statistical analysis. We therefore estimate a relation of the form

$$Y = \beta_0 + \beta_1 X_1 + \beta_2 X_2 + \beta_3 X_3 + \epsilon$$

where β_i is the variable cost of producing widget i, $i = 1, 2, 3$. This equation assumes that the extra cost of producing another widget of type 1 is β_1 and this increase in cost is independent of the level of production of the other widgets (types 2 and 3) as well as the current level of production of widget type 1. If we are not happy with these assumptions, then we may need to estimate a more complex model involving interactions among the widgets or nonlinear costs for each widget separately. (Of course, we are already pushing the limits of our data even with our relatively simple linear model when we estimate four coefficients from only 10 data points.)

When the data in Exhibit 19 are used to estimate the above multiple regression model, we get

$$Y = \$228,727 + \$24.60X_1 + \$6.18X_2 + \$5.99X_3 \qquad R^2 = .99$$
$$\qquad\qquad\quad (.39) \qquad\quad (.59) \qquad (1.05)$$

We see, from this estimated relation, that widget type 1 apparently costs about four times as much to produce as either widget type 2 or 3. We have also succeeded in explaining almost all the variation in departmental cost over these 10 periods by the variation in production of the three types of widgets. Before performing the statistical analysis, we would know only that departmental cost over these 10 periods had a mean of $437,500 and a standard deviation of $7,560. We might assume that this standard deviation of about 2 percent of the mean is attributable to normal random fluctuations. In fact, however, almost all of the fluctuation in cost is caused by variations in production levels of the three types of widgets. Again, we should not expect to be able to find such an excellent fit when working with actual data.

A possible next step would be to establish a flexible budgeting scheme for the department in which costs are budgeted to fluctuate not on the basis of total output but on the basis of output of the different types of widgets produced in that department, that is, a flexible budget equation of the form

$$\text{Budgeted Cost} = \$228,700 + \$24.60X_1 + \$6.18X_2 + \$5.99X_3$$

In addition, the standard errors of the regression can be used to construct confidence limits about this regression line to detect when an actual cost is significantly (in a statistical sense) different from the expected level of cost given how much was produced that period.

A Warning. The above discussion only touches on the basic mechanics of using simple regression techniques for cost analysis. In fact, many subtle problems arise and must be dealt with before one can competently use regression analysis. Issues such as adjusting for inflation when using past cost data, changes in operations or technology over time, and a variety of statistical problems not discussed here frequently arise in applications. Techniques for dealing with these issues do exist but require a considerable amount of sophistication on the part of the user. One of the dangers of having regression routines so widely available on time-shared computers is that regression analysis may be used by individuals not familiar with the pitfalls of this technique, and they may attribute more faith in the relationships uncovered by this technique than may actually be warranted. Conversely, interesting statistical relationships may actually exist in a set of data, which do not get discovered because only the most casual analysis is performed. Chapters 2-4 in Kaplan [1982] provide an extensive discussion of the opportunities and problems that regression analysis holds for accountants. Statistical procedures provide valuable tools for accountants, but misuse of these tools is easy without adequate training and experience.

BIBLIOGRAPHY

Anderson, R., and A. D. Teitlebaum, "Dollar-Unit Sampling," *CA Magazine* (April 1973), pp. 30–39.

Cochran, W. G., *Sampling Techniques*, 2d ed. (John Wiley & Sons, New York, 1963).

Cyert, R. M., and H. J. Davidson, *Statistical Sampling for Accounting Information* (Prentice-Hall, Englewood Cliffs, N.J., 1962).

Elliott, R. K., and J. R. Rogers, "Relating Statistical Sampling to Audit Objectives," *Journal of Accountancy* (July 1972), pp. 46–55.

Kaplan, R. S., "Statistical Sampling in Auditing with Auxiliary Information Estimators," *Journal of Accounting Research*, vol. 11 (Autumn 1973), pp. 238–258.

———, "Sample Size Computations for Dollar-Unit Sampling," *Studies on Statistical Methodology in Auditing*, Supplement to *Journal of Accounting Research*, vol. 13 (1975), pp. 126–133.

———, *Advanced Management Accounting* (Prentice-Hall, Englewood Cliffs, N.J., 1982).

Neter, J., and J. K. Loebbecke, *Behavior of Major Statistical Estimates in Sampling Accounting Populations: An Empirical Study* (AICPA, 1975).

Spurr, W. A., and C. P. Bonini, *Statistical Analysis for Business Decisions*, rev. ed. (Richard D. Irwin, Homewood, Ill., 1973).

CHAPTER **12**

Revenue

Recognition

Arthur L. Thomas
Arthur Young Professor of Accounting,
University of Kansas

Virginia Erdwien Jones
University of Kansas

Revenue is both one of the main goals of business enterprises and one of the major concepts of accounting. This chapter, which discusses the revenue concept and its reflection in financial statements, is confined to:

1. Recognition of revenues on general-purpose financial statements (rather than on internal reports, special reports to creditors, tax returns, and the like).
2. Profit-seeking firms that prepare financial statements in accordance with generally accepted accounting principles (GAAP). However, the principles discussed are also followed by many not-for-profit and regulated entities.

DEFINITION OF REVENUE

It is convenient to distinguish the concept of revenue from the rules for measuring it. The word "revenue" came into English from the French; the related French word, *revenir*, essentially means "to come back, to return." The basic notion of revenue is likewise of a *return*: The firm invests resources in its operations; eventually that investment comes back (increased, one hopes, by profit). Whatever comes back is the revenue.

Often, this is expressed by saying that a firm's costs reflect its efforts, whereas its revenues reflect its accomplishments. But what will count as an accomplishment? What should return? The firm's efforts almost always are monetary ones: It pays cash for inputs, or incurs liabilities to pay cash. The parallel rule is that revenue should also be monetary—either cash itself or a right to receive cash (a receivable).

But not all receipts of monetary assets generate revenues, because not all receipts are returns on the firm's efforts to provide goods and services. For example, additional shareholder investment results in an addition to capital, not in revenue, and a loan does not result in revenue, only debt. Instead, firms obtain revenues only by providing goods or services to other entities. Two complications often occur in business practice:

1. Some firms receive the return before they make the effort—they collect in advance. Any company that receives payment for its products or services before providing them fits this description. Until it has done what it has been paid to do, it should report a liability. Once it has extinguished that liability by delivering the product or performing the service, it should report a revenue. Thus, as a rough definition, accountants recognize a revenue whenever a firm exchanges its goods or services for cash, a right to receive cash, or an extinguishment of a liability.

2. The same firm may provide various different goods and services. Some are clearly its customary ones that it is in business to provide; we may call the related revenues "operating" ones. Other, "nonoperating," revenues result from receipts of rent, royalties, interest, and dividends and from incidental sales of used assets (land, buildings, or equipment that are not the firm's regular stock in trade).

Presentation of Nonoperating Gains and Losses. Firms usually report sales of products and services gross: Their revenues equal the full amount of assets received or liabilities extinguished. Costs of assets and services deemed to have been expended to obtain these revenues are then reported separately as expenses. In contrast, firms usually report nonoperating gains and losses net of such costs.

Example. ABC Company purchased a plot of land for $100,000 in 19X1. On 2/10/X9, it sold this land for $173,000.

Case 1. ABC Company is a real estate company whose ordinary operations involve dealing in land. Under this assumption, the transaction is an operating one and revenue would be recorded gross, by entries such as the following:

Cash	173,000	
Land Sales		173,000
To record the sale at its gross amount.		

Cost of Land Sold	100,000	
Land Inventory		100,000
To record the cost of the plot of land sold.		

Case 2. ABC Company is a manufacturer. Under this assumption, the transaction is a nonoperating one and revenue would be recorded net of the cost of the land:

Cash	173,000	
Gain on Sale of Land		73,000
Land		100,000
To record the net revenue.		

Apparently, the main reasons for this difference in treatment are that a firm's nonoperating gains and losses often are of little significance in their own rights or they occur sporadically enough that data about them are of little use for investor predictions and decisions, or both. Accordingly, it is judged appropriate to report the minimum possible amount of detail concerning them.

Some accountants have wished to go further than mere net reporting of nonoperating gains and losses—and have wished to exclude many of them altogether from net income calculations, instead reporting them as direct credits and charges to retained earnings. APB Opinions No. 9, 20, and 30, and FASB Statement No. 16, prohibit this treatment except in certain rare instances of prior period adjustments. FASB Statement No. 16 narrowly defines items that may be accounted for as prior period adjustments:

1. Corrections of certain unintentional, material errors that were made in prior years' financial statements:

> . . . mathematical mistakes, mistakes in the application of accounting principles, or oversight or misuse of facts that existed at the time the financial statements were prepared [APB Opinion No. 20, par. 13].

2. Adjustments resulting from the realization of tax benefits of preacquisition operating-loss carry-forwards of purchased subsidiaries.

FASB Statement No. 16 provides for limited prior period adjustment treatment for adjustments relating to prior interim periods of the current fiscal year.

Finally, certain other unusual and infrequent nonoperating gains and losses, called "extraordinary items," are to be reported separately on the income statement, just above the figure for net income:

> Extraordinary items are events and transactions that are distinguished by their unusual nature *and* by the infrequency of their occurrence. Thus, *both* of the following criteria should be met to classify an event or transaction as an extraordinary item:
>
> a. *Unusual nature*—the underlying event or transaction should possess a high degree of abnormality and be of a type clearly unrelated to, or only incidentally related to, the ordinary and typical activities of the entity, taking into account the environment in which the entity operates. . . .
>
> b. *Infrequency of occurrence*—the underlying event or transaction should be of a type that would not reasonably be expected to recur in the forseeable future, taking into account the environment in which the entity operates [APB Opinion No. 30, par. 20].

Examples of events that might result in reporting extraordinary items include expropriation or prohibition of a firm's activities by a government, earthquakes, and the like. In addition, the provisions of APB Opinion No. 26 and FASB Statement No. 4 indicate that most gains and losses from extinguishment of debt should be reported as extraordinary items.

Accounting for Decentralized Operations. The accountant's concept of revenue pertains mostly to matters discussed in general-purpose published financial statements. But it is natural to extend the use of this concept to certain internal reports for managerial purposes. One such extension occurs when the company has decentralized into separate divisions or branches with a measure of local autonomy or when the company has departmentalized its records.

When this happens, management often wishes divisional, branch, or departmental income statements prepared, as discussed in Chapter 6.

To the extent that the subunits' transactions are with outsiders, these reports present no special problems. But when divisions, branches, or departments engage in intracompany transactions, there can be serious problems in defining and calculating subunit revenues. These problems resemble the problems of parent–subsidiary revenues discussed in Chapter 34. The main difficulty with subunit revenues is that the amounts employed are rarely determined by impersonal market forces (as is the case with ordinary revenues). Instead, they are determined by a process of intracompany bargaining and may be arbitrary.

In any case, such subunit revenues should be excluded from general-purpose financial statements. Revenue results from the provision of goods or services to other entities. A company should not recognize revenue from providing goods or services to itself.

Capital from Donations and Treasury Stock. Two other kinds of receipts remain to be discussed:

1. Occasionally a company will receive a donation of land or buildings as an inducement to conduct its business in a particular locality. Under present accounting rules, such donations are regarded as capital contributions and are not reflected in revenue. Instead, they are credited directly to a special capital account.

2. Occasionally, after a series of transactions in its own treasury stock, a company emerges with more net assets per share than it began with. Once again, the excess is not reflected as revenue but, instead, is credited directly to a special capital account.

In both of these cases it can be argued that the enhancement in asset values resulted from activities far removed from the company's usual efforts and accomplishments and that accordingly their reflection in revenue is inappropriate. With treasury stock transactions, it is additionally urged that a company should not seek to profit from transactions with its owners; therefore, reflection in revenue is doubly inappropriate. Counterarguments could be offered to either of these claims, but the point remains that neither kind of asset increase is currently reflected in revenue.

Holding Gains (and Losses). Just as not all receipts of monetary assets generate revenues, not all revenue recognition issues involve actual receipts of monetary assets. One significant such exception is holding gains and losses. Often the market value of an asset will change during the period that a firm owns it: Land bought in the 1930s may now command a price far greater than its cost. Such a difference between an asset's current market value and its cost (as appropriately adjusted for depreciation or depletion in instances other than land) is called a "holding" gain or loss. FASB Statement No. 33 requires that certain large corporations disclose information on the effect of changing prices. Doing so can result in *supplementary* reporting of gains or losses resulting from unrealized changes in market values. Nonetheless, accountants do not report holding *gains* in the bodies of their financial statements until the firm actually sells the related assets.

Holding losses are much more often recognized. When there has been a material, apparently permanent decline in the current market value of an asset held for resale, accountants recognize a loss despite the asset's not yet being sold—a common example is the rule of reporting inventories at the lower of cost or market. The usual rationale for this practice is conservatism. It seems fair to say, however, that this treatment of holding losses is inconsistent with the one given holding gains. Finally, FASB Statement No. 12 requires a complex form of lower-of-cost-or-market revenue recognition for portfolios of current marketable equity securities, under which recognition of holding losses and a form of holding gains can occur (see Chapter 14).

Theoretical Issues. Several other questions concerning both holding gains and losses and revenue recognition generally are reflected in American Accounting Association studies and committee reports and in various AICPA releases. The appropriate timing of revenue recognition is theoretically puzzling. Any firm's revenues are the joint products of all of its activities over its life to date. For example, a manufacturer's current-year revenues result in part from prior years' product and sales organization development, prior years' advertising and habituation of customers to buy its products, and so forth. In turn, this year's sales and other activities will profoundly affect future years' revenues. *This makes arbitrary any division of the firm's lifetime revenues into revenues reported for individual years*—for the same reason that assignment of the cost of a joint process to individual joint products is arbitrary.

Many authors have suggested alternatives to GAAP revenue recognition rules—different divisions of the lifetime revenues—that, in effect, recognize holding gains and losses prior to sale on *all* the firm's nonmonetary assets (not just ones held for resale that have declined in value). Readers who are interested in pursuing these matters further may wish to consult Chapter 31 and the works by Hendriksen [1977], Sprouse and Moonitz [1962], Sterling [1970], and Thomas [1975] listed in the bibliography of this chapter.

Tax Accounting. Besides preparing financial statements, accountants also prepare tax returns. One would hope to use the same figures for both sets of reports. Tax accounting, however, may be designed to fulfill purposes other than reporting results of enterprise effort, because tax laws serve a variety of other economic and regulatory goals.

Accordingly, there frequently are differences between financial accounting and tax accounting as to when revenues should be recognized, and occasionally there are even differences as to what revenue is. Because of this, for financial accounting purposes, it is best to ignore tax rules when deciding when to recognize revenue.

Summary—Final Definition of Revenue. The previous discussion leads to the following summary definition of revenue. It should be repeated that this definition is intended only as a description of present practices. A revenue results when an asset (usually cash or a claim to receive cash) is received, or a liability is extinguished, as a result of a company's providing goods or services to another entity. There are two main kinds of revenues:

1. Operating revenues result from the company's providing its main products or services to its customers—those products or services that it is in business to provide. They are reported gross.

2. Nonoperating revenues are incidental gains, such as those that result from sales of noncurrent assets and from retirements of noncurrent liabilities. They are reported net.

The dividing line between operating and nonoperating revenues is not distinct. There often are difficulties in determining which products or services provided by a company are main ones and which are incidental. In particular, it currently is acceptable to treat minor revenues from rents, royalties, interest, and dividends as either operating or nonoperating.

TIMING AND MEASUREMENT OF REVENUE

Revenue is recognized when three tests are met:

1. The revenue is captured.
2. The revenue is measurable.
3. The revenue is earned.

The Revenue Is Captured. Either the company is certain to retain the related inflows of assets, or the portion that might be lost is small and susceptible to estimation. Ordinarily, amounts resulting from an acquisition of accounts receivable are captured; uncollectibles may be estimated and the amount calculated either used to reduce the amount of revenues recognized or recorded as an expense.

In contrast, holding gains typically are not captured until the related asset is sold; this is one reason why accountants refuse to recognize holding gains as revenues prior to such sale. For example, site land owned by a company may have doubled in market value since it was purchased. But land values fluctuate. The market value may fall again before the company sells the property. Because there is no way to capture the holding gain except by selling the land, the accountant refuses to recognize revenue until the time of sale.

To be captured, the revenue must also be severable. The company must be able to do whatever it will with the related asset inflow. Holding gains on plant assets often violate this requirement. To use the previous example, site land owned by the company may have doubled in market value since it was purchased. But if this is the land on which the company's plant rests, it is impossible to sell it (unless the company decides to move).

The Revenue Is Measurable. The accountant must have no serious difficulty in valuing the assets received. Cash presents no valuation problem whatever. The problems involved in valuing receivables are manageable:

1. It usually is possible to make estimates of uncollectible accounts receivable.

2. Because of the time period elapsing before they are due, non-interest-bearing receivables are not worth quite as much as cash, even when there is no question of their collectibility. With ordinary trade receivables, this difference is not material and the accountant ignores it. APB Opinion No. 21 specifies that material, long-lived non-interest-bearing receivables should be discounted to their present values.

3. There are various minor problems. For example, any company offering discounts for prompt payment knows that some of its customers will not take their discounts; this also may create a need for estimates.

Accountants are content to make any necessary estimates in measuring revenue; however, there are limits to this tolerance. Some unusual transactions involve exchanges of assets for plant assets, or for the capital stock of another company. If the exchange is for a readily marketable security, it may not be too difficult to measure the amount of asset inflow (and thereby measure the revenue). But sometimes the securities received are not readily marketable. In such cases accountants may find it impossible to value the inflow. If so, they will record the new assets at whatever dollar figure was associated with the assets given up and may refuse to recognize a revenue.

Example. ABC Company, a manufacturer, purchased a plot of industrial site land in 19X1 for $100,000. On 2/10/X9, it sold this land.

Case 1. The land was exchanged for $173,000 cash. There is no problem in valuing the asset inflow. The company would recognize revenue:

Cash	173,000	
Land		100,000
Gain on Sale of Land		73,000
To record the net revenue.		

Case 2. The land was exchanged for General Motors Corporation common stock. The stock had a market value of $173,000 at the time of sale. Once again there are no serious problems in valuing the inflow of assets. The company would recognize revenue:

Investments	173,000	
Land		100,000
Gain on Sale of Land		73,000
To record the net revenue.		

Case 3. Same as Case 2, except that the land was exchanged for DEF Company common stock. DEF Company stock is infrequently traded. Here, reliable valuation of the asset inflow may be impossible. If the accountants believe that they can determine the fair market value of the DEF Company stock, their entry will resemble that in Case 2. If they believe that they can determine a fair value for the land, they may use that figure instead for recognizing revenue. If *all* such possibilities fail, accountants will not recognize revenue. APB Opinion No. 29 says (par. 26): "If neither the fair value of a nonmonetary asset trans-

ferred nor the fair value of a nonmonetary asset received in exchange is determinable within reasonable limits, the recorded amount of the nonmonetary asset transferred from the enterprise may be the only available measure of the transaction." In the example the entry would be

```
Investments ....................................   100,000
   Land ........................................             100,000
   To record the exchange of assets.
```

APB Opinion No. 29 also excludes from revenue recognition exchanges that are largely nominal in nature in that assets of a similar nature are exchanged. Paragraph 21 of the Opinion says:

> If the exchange is not essentially the culmination of an earning process, accounting for an exchange of a nonmonetary asset between an enterprise and another entity should be based on the recorded amount (after reduction, if appropriate, for an indicated impairment of value) of the nonmonetary assets relinquished. The Board believes that the following two types of nonmonetary exchange transactions do not culminate an earning process:
>   a. An exchange of a product or property held for sale in the ordinary course of business for a product or property to be sold in the same line of business to facilitate sales to customers other than the parties to the exchange, and
>   b. An exchange of a productive asset not held for sale in the ordinary course of business for a similar productive asset or an equivalent interest in the same or similar productive asset. . . .

Journal entries for recording these types of exchanges are illustrated in Chapter 19.

The Revenue Is Earned. No significant activities remain to be performed for the customer being provided with the related product or service. At the time financial statements are prepared, it often happens that a revenue is captured and measurable but only partly earned. In such cases, the accountant often allocates part of the total revenue to the current period (in proportion to the relative extent to which it has been earned).

Example. On July 1, 19X1, GHI Company acquired a $10,000 note receivable from JKL Company. Principal and interest at 12 percent are due on July 1, 19X3. GHI Company prepares annual financial statements every December 31.

The total revenue for the services that GHI Company is providing to JKL Company will be $10,000 $\times$ 12% $\times$ 2 = $2,400. This revenue is measurable. Assuming that GHI Company makes suitable estimates of uncollectibles, it is captured, too; it is guaranteed by a firm contract. But, as of 12/31/X1, only one-quarter of the related services has been performed. Only one-quarter of the total revenue has been earned. The accountant allocates one-quarter of the total revenue to the 19X1 income statement:

```
Interest Receivable .............................   600
   Interest Revenue .............................             600
   To record the accrued revenue.
```

Aftercosts. Some vendors of products undergo substantial aftercosts for such things as service contracts and warranties. Where aftercosts are significant, it can be argued that only part of the revenue-earning process has been completed at the time of sale and that an allocation of total revenue is necessary.

Example. MNO Company sells a product that requires considerable servicing. The company guarantees servicing for 2 years after the customer purchases the product. During 19X1, the company's sales of the product totaled $1,000,000. Cost of goods sold was $700,000. 19X1 servicing costs resulting from 19X1 sales were $20,000. The company estimates that over the next 2 years there will be a total of $80,000 more servicing costs resulting from 19X1 sales.

The company could estimate that the total costs of these sales will be $700,000 + $20,000 + $80,000 = $800,000, and allocate $1,000,000/$800,000 = $1.25 of revenue to every dollar of cost incurred. This would result in its making entries similar to the following for 19X1:

Cost of Product Sold	700,000	
Finished Product		700,000
To record the product cost.		
Accounts Receivable	1,000,000	
Sales ($1.25 × $700,000)		875,000
Estimated Service Warranties (a Liability)		125,000
To record 19X1 sales of product and service guarantees, with revenue allocated to the two different activities.		
Service Warranties Expense	20,000	
Various		20,000
To record the 19X1 cost of fulfilling service guarantees on 19X1 sales.		
Estimated Service Warranties	25,000	
Service Revenues		25,000
To record 19X1 revenues resulting from fulfilling service guarantees on 19X1 sales: $1.25 × $20,000 = $25,000.		

Suppose that in 19X2 servicing costs resulting from 19X1 sales were $48,000. Then $48,000 × $1.25 = $60,000 of service revenues would be recognized:

Service Warranties Expense	48,000	
Various		48,000
To record the 19X2 cost of fulfilling service guarantees on 19X1 sales.		
Estimated Service Warranties	60,000	
Service Revenues		60,000
To record 19X2 revenues resulting from fulfilling service guarantees on 19X1 sales.		

As is evident from the example, this approach allocates the revenue to both sales and service. Most companies instead prefer to recognize the entire revenue at the time of sale, and recognize any estimated aftercosts as additional expenses of the year of sale. From the standpoint of theory, it can be argued that this treatment is not as appropriate as an allocation that would allow all major company activities to generate a normal profit margin. But recognition of all revenue at the time of sale is the method customarily followed.

Example. MNO Company normally would recognize the entire $200,000 profit at the time the product was sold. The 19X1 and 19X2 entries would be as follows:

19X1	Cost of Product Sold	700,000	
	Finished Product		700,000
	To record the product cost.		
	Service Warranties Expense	100,000	
	Estimated Service Warranties		100,000
	To record the estimated cost of service guarantees on 19X1 sales.		
	Accounts Receivable	1,000,000	
	Sales		1,000,000
	To record 19X1 sales of product and service, with revenues *not* allocated to the two different activities.		
	Estimated Service Warranties	20,000	
	Various		20,000
	To record the 19X1 cost of fulfilling service guarantees on 19X1 sales.		
19X2	Estimated Service Warranties	48,000	
	Various		48,000
	To record the 19X2 cost of fulfilling service guarantees on 19X1 sales.		

The Spectrum of Revenue Recognition Possibilities. Accountants recognize revenue at the earliest point at which, in their estimation, it is captured, measurable, and earned. There are three main possible points at which revenue might be recognized:

1. At the time a product or service is produced
2. At the time of sale
3. At the time cash is collected

These possibilities form a spectrum over time of possible points of revenue recognition. These three possibilities are discussed successively in the three sections that follow.

To assist comparison of these methods, each section begins with a parallel example (of the activities of the imaginary "Simplified Company"). These Simplified Company examples are designed for the reader who desires a quick overview of the revenue recognition possibilities; they omit many complexities. Subsequent examples in each section examine the individual revenue recognition approaches in greater detail.

THE PRODUCTION BASIS

Revenue may be recognized at the time of production of the related product or service. As we saw in an earlier example, this is the essence of what happens when interest revenue is recognized on an accrual basis. In that example, GHI Company provided one-quarter of its total services as a lender in 19X1. So, it accrued one-quarter of the total related interest revenues during 19X1, on a service production basis. Similar accruals are made of revenues relating to rental services and other contractual services that function by the passage of time. In such cases the rate at which revenue is earned is fully determined in advance by the contract, and therefore is both measurable and captured.

Use of the production basis requires that the total revenue be substantially assured (captured) and measurable and that it be possible to estimate the extent to which revenue has been earned. In some unusual situations this will be the case when goods are being manufactured under firm purchase commitments.

Example. On 3/1/X1, Simplified Company obtained a firm contract to manufacture 500,000 units of product for a total contract price of $5,000,000, or $10 a unit. The company is to make delivery in 100,000-unit batches and is entitled to bill 95 percent of the unit selling price upon delivery. The remaining 5 percent is to be retained by the buyer until satisfactory completion of the entire contract. The product costs Simplified Company $6 per unit to manufacture. During 19X1, the company manufactured 370,000 units at a cost of $2,220,000 and delivered 300,000 units. There is much variety in the account titles used by companies following the production basis of revenue recognition; journal entries under the production basis, using some customary account titles, would be as follows:

Finished Product—At Cost	2,220,000	
Work in Process		2,220,000
To record the cost of manufacturing 370,000 units of product @ $6.		
Product Expense—Long-Term Contract	2,220,000	
Finished Product—At Cost		2,220,000
To record product expense on a production basis. (This entry is similar to a cost of goods sold entry—370,000 units produced @ $6.)		
Finished Product—At Contract Price	3,700,000	
Revenue on Long-Term Contract		3,700,000
To record revenue on a production basis—370,000 units produced @ $10.		
Accounts Receivable—Billed	2,850,000	
Accounts Receivable—Retained Percentage	150,000	
Finished Product—At Contract Price		3,000,000
To record delivery of 300,000 units @ $10 and billing of 95% of contract price, with a retained percentage of 5%.		

The two Finished Product accounts and the two Accounts Receivable accounts are assets; Product Expense—Long-Term Contract is an expense account corresponding to the ordinary Cost of Goods Sold account.

In this case use of the production basis involves matching revenues with costs, instead of the (usual) other way around. Reporting revenues at the full contract price (instead of 95 percent of the full contract price) is justified if there appear to be no obstacles to satisfactory completion of the contract.

Long-Term Construction Contracts. A similar use of the production basis is made with long-term construction contracts where a failure to accrue revenue during the life of the contract could lead to considerable, erratic fluctuations in reported revenues from one year to the next.

Example. Simplified Company is a contractor. On 3/1/X1, the company obtained a firm contract to build a building, at a total contract price of $5,000,000. The company is authorized to bill the purchaser for a total of 95 percent of the contract price at various stages during the building's construction; the remaining 5 percent is retained pending satisfactory completion of the contract. Simplified Company estimates that this building will cost $3,000,000 to build. During 19X1, the company's construction costs were $2,220,000 (74 percent of the $3,000,000 total). Bills were submitted for $3,325,000, representing 70 percent completion of the project ($5,000,000 × 70% × 95% = $3,325,000). Appropriate journal entries are shown below. Once again, account titles vary widely in actual practice.

Construction in Process—At Cost	2,220,000	
Various		2,220,000
To record the costs of 74% completion of the project.		
Construction Expense—Long-Term Contract	2,220,000	
Construction in Process—At Cost		2,220,000
To record construction expense on a production basis (similar to a cost of goods sold entry).		
Unbilled Construction in Process—At Contract Price	3,700,000	
Revenues on Long-Term Contract		3,700,000
To record revenues on a production basis at 74% completion ($5,000,000 × 74% = $3,700,000).		
Accounts Receivable—Billed	3,325,000	
Accounts Receivable—Retained Percentage	175,000	
Unbilled Construction in Process—At Contract Price		3,500,000
To record billing on a 70% completion basis.		

Construction in Process—at Cost and Unbilled Construction in Process—at Contract Price are both asset accounts. Construction Expense—Long-Term Contract is an expense account corresponding to the ordinary Cost of Goods Sold account.

In the previous illustration, revenue was recorded gross of costs of construction. Often, instead, it is reported net of these costs. (Instead of reporting the revenue from construction activities, the accountant reports the gross margin, after subtracting construction costs.) Using such net recording, the corresponding entries for Simplified Company would be as follows:

Construction in Process	2,220,000	
Various		2,220,000
To record the costs of 74% completion of the project.		

Construction in Process	1,480,000	
Gross Margin on Long-Term Contracts		1,480,000
To convert the figure for construction in process to the amount that eventually will be billed, and to record gross margin on a production basis.		

Accounts Receivable—Billed	3,325,000	
Accounts Receivable—Retained Percentage	175,000	
Construction in Process		3,500,000
To record billing on a 70% completion basis.		

Both the gross and the net approaches to accounting for long-term construction contracts are acceptable. The alternative to use of the production method here would be the "completed contract" method, delaying revenue recognition until the contract was completed.

Occasionally the production basis is also employed by companies manufacturing readily marketable extractive or agricultural products when the market price is known and substantially assured. The production basis is widely employed with cost-plus-fixed-fee contracts; here the net approach is common, with only the fee itself being recognized as revenue.

Some Complications. Certain factors often complicate accounting for long-term construction contracts. The most common form of the production basis for contractors is the "percentage-of-completion" method. Under this method, the accountant calculates the revenue to be recognized in any period by first estimating the extent to which completion of the contract has been advanced during that period. Then a proportionate share of the total revenue from the contract is allocated to the period concerned. The extent of completion may be estimated in terms of subtasks to be performed by the contractor. Frequently, as in the following example, it is instead estimated in terms of the relationship between estimated total costs of the contract and costs incurred to date.

Example. PQR Company is a contractor. On May 15, 19X1, the company signed a contract with STU Company to construct an office building. PQR Company estimated that costs traceable to this contract would total $7,500,000. The total contract price was $10,000,000, which was intended to cover traceable costs, various untraceable overheads, and PQR Company's profit. STU Company agreed to an escalator clause whereby it would absorb all increases in labor wage rates as additions to the contract price. The contract specified that payments were to be made by STU Company at 20, 40, 60, and 80 percent of completion, with 10 percent retained until final approval of the completed building by STU Company's architect. PQR Company employs the gross form of the percentage-of-completion method of revenue recognition. The degree of completion of any contract is estimated by comparing total traceable costs incurred to date with the total currently estimated traceable costs of the completed contract. Any costs covered by escalator clauses are excluded from degree-of-completion calculations. During 19X1, the following events occurred under this contract:

1. The company used materials with a total cost of $2,000,000. Because of an unexpected increase in materials prices, the total cost of materials will be $120,000 higher than originally estimated. There is no indication that material usage will vary from the original estimate.

2. Labor costs were $1,500,000. Total labor costs on this contract are now estimated to be $3,600,000, or $350,000 higher than originally anticipated. Of this difference, $320,000 is due to an increase in labor wage rates, which is to begin on 1/1/X2. The remaining $30,000 resulted from extra hours being worked during 19X1.

3. The original contract specified that certain parts of the construction were to be subcontracted. Costs of subcontracted activities were originally estimated at $280,000. During 19X1, subcontractors charged $50,000. PQR Company now estimates that subcontracting costs will total only $265,000.

4. Miscellaneous traceable costs totaled $100,100. Estimates of these costs remain unchanged.

5. After construction had begun, PQR Company and STU Company agreed to install special interior partitions costing an additional $300,000. The contract price (exclusive of payments to be made under escalator clauses) was increased to $10,400,000. No expenditures have yet been made relating to these partitions.

6. PQR Company has submitted bills based on 40 percent completion. These bills have been approved, but payments totaling only $1,872,000 have been received to date.

Calculation of Degree of Completion. The first step in calculating the degree of completion is to determine the total currently estimated traceable cost of the completed contract, exclusive of costs covered by escalator clauses:

Original estimate of total cost		$7,500,000
Additional costs of materials		120,000
Additional costs of labor	$350,000	
Less: Portion covered by escalator clause	320,000	30,000
Additional costs of special partitions		300,000
Subtotal		$7,950,000
Less: Decrease in estimated subcontracting costs		15,000
Total currently estimated traceable costs of contract		$7,935,000

Next, determine the total traceable costs incurred to date (exclusive of costs covered by escalator clauses, of which there happened to be none in 19X1):

Materials	$2,000,000
Labor	1,500,000
Subcontracting costs	50,000
Miscellaneous costs	100,100
Total incurred to date	$3,650,100

The degree of completion may then be calculated by dividing the total currently estimated cost into the total costs incurred to date:

$$\text{Degree of Completion} = \frac{\$3,650,100}{\$7,935,000} = 46\%$$

Total revenues on this contract (exclusive of payments under escalator clauses) will be $10,400,000. Of these, $10,400,000 × 46% = $4,784,000 should be allocated to 19X1 operations. Bills submitted should total $10,400,000 × 40% × 90% = $3,744,000. The appropriate journal entries are shown below:

Construction in Process—At Cost	3,650,100	
Materials and Supplies		2,000,000
Payrolls		1,500,000
Accounts Payable to Subcontractors		50,000
Various		100,100
To record costs incurred in 19X1.		
Unbilled Construction in Process—At Contract Price	4,784,000	
Revenues on Long-Term Contract		4,784,000
To record revenues on a percentage-of-completion production basis.		
Construction Expense—Long-Term Contract	3,650,100	
Construction in Process—At Cost		3,650,100
To record construction expense on a production basis (similar to a cost of goods sold entry).		
Accounts Receivable—Billed	3,744,000	
Accounts Receivable—Retained Percentage	416,000	
Unbilled Construction in Process—At Contract Price		4,160,000
To record submission of bills on the basis of 40% completion: $10,400,000 × 40% = $4,160,000.		
Cash	1,872,000	
Accounts Receivable—Billed		1,872,000
To record cash collections from STU Company.		

In 19X2, the same basic procedures would be followed to compute the further degree of completion and to record 19X2 construction costs. However, revenues recognized and bills submitted for 19X2 must be adjusted for the amounts already recorded in 19X1.

Changes in Estimated Costs. The amount of costs actually incurred on a contract may turn out to be either more or less than originally anticipated. If this occurs, estimates of total income, or profit, from the contract will be incorrect. The question arises as to whether prior years' financial statements should be corrected to reflect the revised cost information or whether a "catch-up" correction should be reflected in the current year's financial statements. APB Opinion No. 20 treats revisions in estimated costs and profits under long-term contracts as a *change in accounting estimate*. Such changes cannot be corrected retroactively. They must be corrected in the current period. The procedures in this case can be summarized as follows:

1. Compute the percentage of completion for the job to date.

2. Compute the new profit figure to be recognized for the entire job as total receipts less total costs. If the amount is negative, all of the loss must be recognized by the end of the current period. If there is a profit on the entire job, the profit or loss for the current period is found in the next two steps.

3. Compute profit to be recognized through the end of the current period as the product of the percentage found in step 1 multiplied by the total profit found in step 2.

4. Subtract the profit already recognized prior to the current period from the amount found in step 3.

   (a) If the amount is positive, it is to be reported as profit this period.

   (b) If the amount is negative, it is to be recognized as a loss for the current period.

By-products and Scrap. The accountant's treatment of by-products and scrap sometimes offers an example of an indirect use of the production basis of revenue recognition. From an economic standpoint, by-products and scrap are as valid a part of a manufacturer's total output as any of its other outputs. But the dollar amounts often are minor, and it is hard to determine what by-product outputs cost. This has resulted in there being two main treatments of these assets and the related revenues:

1. Sometimes an asset is recognized, at an amount equal to its selling price less costs to complete and sell. Production costs are relieved by an amount sufficient to accomplish this. The effect is to reduce costs of manufactured inventories and eventually costs of goods sold, and to increase reported net income, by the by-product's or scrap's selling price, whether or not the by-product or scrap has been sold.

2. Sometimes no asset is recognized. Instead, revenues from the sales of by-products and scrap either are reported gross of any costs, or else offset against costs of manufactured inventories.

Both treatments are currently acceptable.

THE SALES BASIS

Most revenue recognition occurs at the time that the company's products or services are sold. Indeed, it never would occur to many accountants that they use any other basis of revenue recognition.

Example. Simplified Company is a manufacturer. During 19X1, the company manufactured 370,000 units of product and sold 332,500 units. All sales were made on account at a price of $10 per unit. 19X1 collections on these sales totaled $2,850,000. The product cost Simplified Company $6 per unit to manufacture. Appropriate journal entries under the sales basis are as follows:

Finished Goods	2,220,000	
Work in Process		2,220,000
To record the cost of manufacturing 370,000 units of product @ $6.		

Cost of Goods Sold	1,995,000	
Finished Goods		1,995,000
To record product expense on a sales basis: 332,500 units sold @ $6.		
Accounts Receivable	3,325,000	
Sales		3,325,000
To record revenues on a sales basis: 332,500 units sold @ $10.		
Cash.......................................	2,850,000	
Accounts Receivable		2,850,000
To record collections on account.		

Although the sales basis is simple and familiar, it leads to certain difficult problems, too. We already have discussed the problem of aftercosts. Other problems arise with sales cutoffs:

1. The exact point at which a sale occurs involves complicated legal questions. Most accountants cut through this problem by expediently treating the point of sale as the point at which delivery is made to the customer (or to a common carrier). So long as some consistent policy is followed from one year to the next, this can be done without serious distortion resulting. However, the details of establishing a good sales cutoff can be quite complicated.

2. Whatever cutoff method is used for sales, a parallel method must be adopted for a cost-of-goods-sold cutoff. Otherwise there will be product expense without any related revenue in some years, and revenues without expenses in other years.

The Realization and Historical Cost Rules. The rule that revenues should be recognized at the time the company's product or services are sold is often called the realization rule, and it often is asserted that revenues are not realized until the point of sale. The sales basis of revenue recognition has the effect of preserving the magnitudes reported for products (and other nonmonetary assets) at their historical purchase prices until such assets are sold. (With depreciable assets, the magnitude reported is a depreciated historical purchase price.) So, the realization rule is also a historical cost rule: Nonmonetary assets are to be reported at their historical costs; holding gains are not to be recognized until nonmonetary assets are sold. Of course, as we already have seen, most practicing accountants make two main exceptions to the historical cost/realization rule:

1. They employ a form of the production basis for interest, rent, and other time-based contractual revenues.

2. They recognize certain holding losses (and subsequent gains, if any, under some circumstances) prior to the time of sale (as when they report inventories and marketable equity securities at the lower of cost or market).

Some Complications. The sales basis of revenue recognition often will be more complicated than the previous example would suggest. It is assumed in what follows that the company makes all of its sales on account.

The amount shown on a company's sales invoice does not necessarily equal the amount of revenue that it should recognize at the time of sale. There are several reasons why the invoice amount may overstate the revenue.

1. The invoice price may be gross of discounts that the customer is expected to take.

2. Often, a portion of what is furnished customers will be wholly or partly unsatisfactory, resulting in subsequent returns or allowances.

3. Certain accounts receivable may prove to be uncollectible.

Each of these conditions may necessitate adjustment or correction of the amounts recognized as revenue. These revenue adjustments are discussed in detail below. The basic principle involved in all these adjustments is simple: A revenue never should be recognized for an amount greater than what will ultimately be collected from customers. But, as will be seen, in practice this principle is occasionally violated.

Discounts. There are four main reasons for giving discounts to customers:

1. *Trade discounts.* In many industries it is common for manufacturers to write their invoices at figures equal to list prices—the intended selling prices of products to their final customers. The manufacturer then allows trade discounts off list prices to wholesalers, retailers, and other entities involved in distributing these products. When such trade discounts are employed, revenue always should be recognized for the actual net amount sought by the manufacturer from the entity with which it deals. This net amount is all that the manufacturer expects to collect, so it is all that the related revenues are worth. The amount paid by the final customer is irrelevant, except when the company itself sells to these final customers.

Example. VWX Company is a manufacturer. The company sells to retail dealers, allowing a 40 percent trade discount off list. During 19X1 the company's sales totaled $3,500,000 at list prices.

In this example, revenues should be recognized only for the amount that customers are expected to pay—60 percent of the list price ($3,500,000 × 60% = $2,100,000):

Accounts Receivable	2,100,000	
Sales		2,100,000
To record sales at the net amount expected to be received		
by VWX Company.		

2. *Employee discounts.* Similarly, many retail establishments allow their employees to make purchases at prices less than the ordinary retail price. When the discount is of minor amount, such sales should also be recorded net. When large discounts are involved, it becomes possible to argue that a form of supplemental employee compensation is present; in such cases actual accounting practice allows the revenue either to be recorded net or to be recorded gross with the discount reported as an expense. If the discount reduces the price below the product's cost, there is much to be said for treating at least part of the discount as an expense.

3. *Cash discounts.* Some companies (mostly retail establishments) allow customers to pay a lesser amount for a cash purchase than they would if they bought on credit, or allow them to pay less if they do not require delivery services. As before, revenue should be recognized equal to the actual amounts received; revenue should be recognized net of cash discounts.

4. *Discounts for prompt payment.* Other companies allow their customers to take a discount if they pay within a set period of time after billing (or after receipt of the goods). The company intends that such discounts be taken by all customers; the discount rate is set high enough to encourage prompt payment. Therefore, in theory, revenue should be recognized net of these discounts. In practice, though, many companies have found it expedient to record such sales at the gross figure. When this gross approach is used, discounts actually taken should be recorded as downward adjustments of this gross revenue figure, rather than as expenses.

Example. YZA Company is a manufacturer. The company allows a 3 percent discount for payment of accounts within 45 days. All sales are on account. During 19X1, the company's sales totaled $2,100,000. Discounts of $51,000 were taken on $1,649,000 payments of accounts totaling $1,700,000 gross. Discounts of $600 lapsed on accounts totaling $20,000 gross, which were paid late. At 12/31/X1, accounts totaling $380,000 gross are still unpaid. The company expects that discounts of $10,500 will be taken on accounts totaling $350,000 gross and that discounts of $900 will lapse on accounts totaling $30,000 gross.

Under the net method, ordinary sales revenue would be recognized at an amount net of the 3 percent discount for prompt payment. There will also be a special revenue, relatively minor in amount, from lapsed sales discounts—the excess over the net price paid by customers who pay late. In theory, this special revenue might be reported separately; in practice, it rarely is. Both versions of the net method are discussed below.

Net method—in theory

Accounts Receivable	2,037,000	
Sales		2,037,000
To record sales with a gross price of $2,100,000.		

Cash	1,669,000	
Accounts Receivable		1,668,400
Lapsed Sales Discounts		600
To record collections of $1,649,000 + $20,000 = $1,669,000, on net accounts totaling ($1,700,000 + $20,000) × 97% = $1,668,400.		

Accounts Receivable—Estimated Lapsed Sales Discounts	900	
Lapsed Sales Discounts		900
Adjusting entry at year-end to correct accounts receivable for estimated discounts that will not be taken on year-end accounts.		

Net method—in practice. In practice the final $900 accrual entry would almost always be omitted as immaterial; lapsed sales discounts would not be recognized until late payment was actually received. When late payment was received (as in the $600 entry), the credit would usually be either to some miscellaneous revenues account or to Sales.

A similar gap between theory and practice exists under the gross method. In what follows, Sales Discounts is a contra to Sales, not an expense.

Gross method—in theory

Accounts Receivable	2,100,000	
Sales		2,100,000
To record sales with a gross price of $2,100,000.		

Cash	1,669,000	
Sales Discounts	51,600	
Accounts Receivable		1,720,000
Lapsed Sales Discounts		600
To record cash collections of $1,669,000. The *total* sales discounts is 3% of the total accounts receivable involved: $1,720,000 × 3% = $51,600.		

In theory, an entry similar to the final entry shown for the net method might be made:

Sales Discounts	10,500	
Accounts Receivable—Estimated Sales Discounts		10,500
To record sales discounts that are estimated will be taken on accounts totaling $350,000 gross.		

Gross method—in practice. Almost always, the $600 Lapsed Sales Discount would be netted into the Sales Discounts figure, and the final $10,500 accrual omitted (even though the result of this omission is to report Accounts Receivable at an amount $10,500 higher than anticipated collections on account):

Accounts Receivable	2,100,000	
Sales		2,100,000
To record sales with a gross price of $2,100,000.		

Cash	1,669,000	
Sales Discounts	51,000	
Accounts Receivable		1,720,000
To record cash collections of $1,669,000.		

Revenue Recognition When There Is a Right of Return. In some industries, customers have the right to return goods to the seller under a variety of circumstances. If the customer is the ultimate user, there may be a right of return if the goods are unsatisfactory. If the customer ordinarily resells the product, a right of return may exist if the goods are not resold to another customer. In the publishing and phonograph record industries, for example, retail stores have had the right to return large quantities of books or records to the publisher. Prior to recent accounting pronouncements incorporated into FASB Statement No. 48 (1981), these sales were accounted for in one of several ways:

1. No sale was recognized until the product was unconditionally accepted, delaying revenue until returns are no longer possible.
2. Sales were recognized as made, but an allowance for returns was provided, reducing revenue in the period of sale.
3. Sales and returns were recognized in the periods they occur, resulting in a decrease in income in the period of return, rather than in the period of sale.

FASB Statement No. 48 provides that when the buyer has the right to return the product, revenue is not to be recognized in the period of sale unless *all* of the following conditions are met (in addition to the usual conditions for recognizing revenue):

1. The seller's price to the buyer is substantially fixed or determinable at the date of sale.
2. The buyer has paid the seller or the buyer is obligated to pay the seller and the obligation is not contingent on resale of the product.
3. The buyer's obligation to the seller would not be changed in the event of theft or physical destruction or damage of the product.
4. The buyer acquiring the product for resale has economic substance apart from that provided by the seller [footnote omitted].
5. The seller does not have significant obligations for future performance to bring about resale of the product by the buyer.
6. The amount of future returns can be reasonably estimated [FASB Statement No. 48, par. 6, footnote omitted].

If product returns are significant for an enterprise, then gross sales and related accounting policies must be disclosed.

Two possible situations may occur when goods or services prove unsatisfactory and customers are allowed refunds:

1. The customer does not return the goods. In this case the customer is said to receive an allowance.
2. The customer returns goods. Sometimes these goods are taken back into the company's inventory, sometimes not. These are instances of returns.

As with discounts and uncollectibles, if material returns or allowances are anticipated on current-year sales, an estimated adjustment could be made at year-end. However, it is rare for the adjustment involved to be material, and such year-end adjustments for expected returns and allowances are uncommon.

Example. BCD Company is a manufacturer. The company does not provide discounts and does not have uncollectible accounts receivable (except in connection with returns and allowances). All sales are made on account. During 19X1, the company's sales totaled $2,100,000. The related cost of goods sold was $1,400,000. (The company employs a consistent markup of 50 percent over cost.) During 19X1, goods that had sold for $90,000 were returned. Allowances totaling $16,000 were granted to other dissatisfied customers who kept the related goods. Of the goods returned, items that had cost BCD Company $22,500 could be salvaged for resale. Appropriate summary entries are shown below. Account titles employed have not been standardized and vary from company to company. Sales Returns and Sales Allowances are contra-accounts to Sales and are not expenses.

Accounts Receivable	2,100,000	
Sales		2,100,000
To record 19X1 sales, before adjustments.		

Cost of Goods Sold	1,400,000	
Finished Goods		1,400,000
To record 19X1 cost of goods sold, before adjustments.		

Sales Allowances	16,000	
Accounts Receivable		16,000
To record actual 19X1 allowances granted, and to cancel the related sales.		

Sales Returns	90,000	
Accounts Receivable		90,000
To record actual 19X1 returns allowed, and to cancel the related sales.		

Returned Goods	22,500	
Loss on Returns	37,500	
Cost of Goods Sold		60,000
To record the salvage value of goods returned, and to cancel the related cost of goods sold ($90,000/1.5 = $60,000). The loss on returns reflects the damage or other deterioration to these returned goods.		

Often this last entry is simplified to the following, especially when the amount of the loss is not material:

Returned Goods	22,500	
Cost of Goods Sold		22,500

Uncollectibles. Adjustments must also be made for uncollectible accounts receivable. Whenever uncollectibles are frequent, it is customary to estimate them in advance. Such estimates may either be in the form of a percentage of the company's credit sales or may be made by an examination of the individual accounts. In theory, the estimate of uncollectibles should lead to a revenue adjustment. In practice, however, estimated uncollectibles usually are reported as an expense.

Example. EFG Company is a manufacturer. The company's 19X1 sales total $2,100,000, all on account. The company does not offer discounts and has no returns or allowances. It estimates that 2 percent of its sales will prove uncollectible. Appropriate entries would be as follows. "Sales—Uncollectibles" is a contra-account to Sales, not an expense:

Accounts Receivable	2,100,000	
Sales		2,100,000
To record 19X1 sales, before adjustments.		

Sales—Uncollectibles	42,000	
Accounts Receivable—Estimated Uncollectibles		42,000

To record estimated uncollectibles on 19X1 sales. Often the debit in this entry would be to an account called "Bad Debts Expense."

Discounts, returns, and allowances are not ordinarily recorded until actually taken by customers; in contrast, it is customary to estimate uncollectibles in advance, as above. When an actual default by a customer occurs, no revenue adjustment need then be made (or expense be recognized).

During 19X2, $41,000 of EFG Company's 19X1 accounts receivable proved actually uncollectible. The appropriate entry would be

Accounts Receivable—Estimated Uncollectibles	41,000	
Accounts Receivable		41,000

To record 19X1 accounts receivable that actually proved uncollectible in 19X2.

The proper treatment of amounts left over in any of the several accounts receivable contra-accounts discussed above is described in Chapter 15.

Consignment Sales. Some manufacturers ship their products to dealers on consignment, retaining ownership until the dealer actually sells them. In such cases there is no sale until the goods have been purchased by the final customers. A special version of the sales basis of revenue recognition has been developed for consignment sales.

Example. Simplified Company is a manufacturer. During 19X1, the company manufactured 370,000 units of product and shipped 300,000 units to dealers on consignment. This product sells for $10 per unit and costs the company $6 per unit to manufacture. (There are also dealer commissions and costs of shipping these goods to dealers, but for simplicity such costs are ignored.) During 19X1, dealers reported sales of 285,000 units and remitted a total of $2,500,000. The following journal entries would be appropriate. (Once again, there is little standardization in actual account titles.)

Finished Goods	2,220,000	
Work in Process		2,220,000

To record the cost of manufacturing 370,000 units of product @ $6.

Finished Goods on Consignment...................	1,800,000	
Finished Goods		1,800,000

To record shipment on consignment of 300,000 units @ $6.

Cost of Goods Sold	1,710,000	
Finished Goods on Consignment.................		1,710,000

To record product expenses on a consignment sales basis: 285,000 units sold to final customers @ $6.

```
Accounts Receivable  . . . . . . . . . . . . . . . . . . . . . . . . . . . . . . . .    2,850,000
    Sales  . . . . . . . . . . . . . . . . . . . . . . . . . . . . . . . . . . . . . .                  2,850,000
To record sales reported by consignment dealers:
285,000 units sold to final customers @ $10.


Cash. . . . . . . . . . . . . . . . . . . . . . . . . . . . . . . . . . . . . . . . . .    2,500,000
    Accounts Receivable  . . . . . . . . . . . . . . . . . . . . . . . . . .                  2,500,000
To record collections from consignment dealers.
```

THE COLLECTION BASIS

The collection basis of revenue recognition involves waiting until cash is actually collected from one's customers before recognizing revenue. The method is widely used by individuals and small service and professional organizations; it has little theoretical merit for companies preparing annual reports unless the assets received for the company's products or services are so hard to value that revenue recognition itself becomes inappropriate. Occasionally, this is true in retailing. An example of recording retail sales on the collection basis is the installment method of revenue recognition whereby revenue is allocated to each installment payment made by an installment purchaser of the company's products. In Opinion No. 10, the Accounting Principles Board specified that the sales method of revenue recognition should be used for such installment sales, except when "there is no reasonable basis for determining the degree of collectibility," and therefore no way to establish allowances for uncollectible accounts. In cases of extreme uncertainty, recognition of any profit at all may be delayed until the entire cost of the product sold is recovered.

Example. Simplified Company is a manufacturer. During 19X1, the company manufactured 370,000 units of product and sold 300,000 units. All sales were made on account at a price of $10 per unit. 19X1 collections on these sales totaled $1,000,000. The remaining $2,000,000 is receivable in installments over the next 2 years. The product costs the company $6 per unit to manufacture. (Most installment sales require the customer to pay finance charges, but for simplicity such charges are omitted from this example; finance charges and other complicating factors are discussed in subsequent examples.) Ordinarily, the sales basis would be appropriate here, with suitable estimates of uncollectible installment accounts. Assuming, though, that there is no reasonable way to make such estimates, the appropriate entries under one form of the installment method might be as shown below. The particular recording approach shown here has been chosen to parallel the Simplified Company examples under the production and sales bases (see the examples at the beginning of those sections).

Installment method—gross

```
Finished Goods . . . . . . . . . . . . . . . . . . . . . . . . . . . . . . . . . . .    2,220,000
    Work in Process  . . . . . . . . . . . . . . . . . . . . . . . . . . . . . . .                  2,220,000
To record the cost of manufacturing 370,000 units of
product @ $6.
```

Installment Contracts Receivable	3,000,000	
Deferred Revenues on Installment Sales		3,000,000

A self-balancing memorandum entry to record the total amount owed Simplified Company by installment customers.

Goods Delivered under Installment Contracts	1,800,000	
Finished Goods		1,800,000

To record delivery of 300,000 units of product to install-ment customers, @ $6 per unit.

Cash...	1,000,000	
Installment Contracts Receivable		1,000,000

To record collection of installments for one-third of total 19X1 sales.

Deferred Revenues on Installment Sales	1,000,000	
Installment Sales.............................		1,000,000

To record revenues equal to cash collection of one-third of total 19X1 sales.

Cost of Goods Sold	600,000	
Goods Delivered under Installment Contracts		600,000

To record product expense on a collection basis—one-third of total cost of goods delivered to 19X1 installment customers.

Goods Delivered under Installment Contracts is an asset account; Deferred Revenues on Installment Sales is an asset contra-account.

In the event that collection was so uncertain that no profit should be recognized until the entire cost of product sold was recovered, the final entry would instead be

Cost of Goods Sold	1,000,000	
Goods Delivered under Installment Contracts ....:....		1,000,000

There would be no entry debiting Deferred Revenue on Installment Sales and crediting Installment Sales; otherwise, the entries would be the same.

In the previous illustration, revenue was recorded gross of cost of goods sold. Usually, though, it is recorded net of these costs. This exactly parallels the alternative treatment of revenue discussed earlier in accounting for long-term construction contracts. (Instead of reporting the revenue from installment sales, the accountant may report the gross margin, after subtracting cost of goods sold.) Under such net recording, corresponding entries for Simplified Company might be as follows:

Installment method—net

Finished Goods	2,220,000	
Work in Process		2,220,000

To record the cost of manufacturing 370,000 units of product @ $6.

Installment Contracts Receivable	3,000,000	
Installment Sales		3,000,000

To record the total amount of installment sales: 300,000 units of product @ $10. (The apparent recognition of revenue here is canceled in the fourth entry.)

Cost of Installment Sales	1,800,000	
Finished Goods		1,800,000

To record the total product cost of installment sales: 300,000 units of product @ $6. (The apparent recognition of expense is also canceled in the fourth entry.)

Installment Sales	3,000,000	
Cost of Installment Sales		1,800,000
Deferred Gross Margin on Installment Sales		1,200,000

To defer recognition of revenue and expense on installment sales until cash is collected.

Cash	1,000,000	
Installment Contracts Receivable		1,000,000

To record collection of installments for one-third of total 19X1 sales.

Deferred Gross Margin on Installment Sales	400,000	
Gross Margin on Installment Sales		400,000

To record recognition of one-third of total deferred gross profits on 19X1 installment sales: $1,200,000 $\times$ ⅓ = $400,000.

The account Deferred Gross Margin on Installment Sales is frequently shown on the equities side of the balance sheet. However, conceptually it is better viewed as a contra-account to Installment Contracts Receivable. Since revenues are not recognized until collection, it is logical to report accounts receivable at product cost, which would be the effect of such a contra treatment.

This series of entries can be simplified if the company does not wish to record memorandum information about sales and cost of goods sold. The second, third, and fourth entries may be combined into

Installment Contracts Receivable	3,000,000	
Finished Goods		1,800,000
Deferred Gross Margin on Installment Sales		1,200,000

Any of the methods discussed in this subsection is acceptable.

Some Complications. Three main complications are apt to develop in accounting for installment sales:

1. Gross profit rates often change somewhat from year to year; this complicates the calculation of cost of goods sold (or of deferred profit recognized) when installment payments are received.

2. Most installment contracts charge interest. Some way must be found to allocate portions of installment payments received to the contract principal, and portions to interest revenue.

EXHIBIT 1   Data for Illustration of Installment Sales

	19X1	19X2
Cost of goods sold on the installment plan	$ 675,000	$ 960,000
Gross margin on installment sales	825,000	1,040,000
Selling price of goods sold on the installment plan	$1,500,000	$2,000,000
Down payment collected (10% of selling price)	150,000	200,000
Balance of selling price	$1,350,000	$1,800,000
Finance charges (21% of total installment contracts receivable) . . .	358,861	478,481
Total installment contracts receivable	$1,708,861	$2,278,481
Collections of 19X1 installment contracts receivable	$ 460,000	$ 970,000
Collections of 19X2 installment contracts receivable		620,000

3. Defaults and repossessions must be accounted for. (For clarity, the example given below makes the unrealistic assumption of only one default and repossession over a 2-year period; in an actual installment sales situation, they would, of course, be much more common.)

Example. HIJ Company is a retailer. The company sells its goods on the installment plan and recognizes revenue on the installment sales basis, using the net approach. A 10 percent down payment is collected at the time of purchase. The balance, plus finance charges, is to be paid in 20 equal monthly installments. Finance charges are calculated as a uniform 21 percent of the total amount of installment contracts receivable. The details of the company's 19X1 and 19X2 installment sales are given in Exhibit 1.

The 19X1 gross margin is $825,000/$1,500,000 = 55 percent of the 19X1 selling price; the 19X2 gross margin is $1,040,000/$2,000,000 = 52 percent of the 19X2 selling price. Finance charges are 21 percent of total installment contracts. For example, in 19X1 they are $1,708,861 × 21% = $358,861. It is acceptable to recognize interest revenue according to several different methods. Most of these involve relatively complicated compound interest calculations. The simplest method is a straight-line one that regards 21 percent of all installment payments collected as pertaining to finance charges. This method is used in this example. Under the straight-line method of recognizing interest revenue, the calculations may be made as shown in Exhibit 2.

Appropriate journal entries for the company's 19X1 and 19X2 installment sales activities would be as follows:

19X1	Cash (see Exhibit 1)	150,000	
	Installment Contracts Receivable—19X1 (see Exhibit 1)	1,708,861	
	Finished Goods (see Exhibit 1)		675,000
	Gross Margin on Installment Sales		82,500
	Deferred 19X1 Profits on Installment Sales . . .		1,101,361
	To record 19X1 installment sales and receipts of down payments.		

Gross margin on balance of selling price:
$1,350,000 × 55% .... $ 742,500
Finance charges...........................   358,861
Deferred 19X1 profits on installment sales ...... $ 1,101,361

In this entry, gross margin is recognized on the $150,000 of down payments received: $150,000 × 55% = $82,500. The remaining profits on these contracts are deferred until cash is received:

Cash (see Exhibit 1)	460,000	
Installment Contracts Receivable—19X1		460,000
To record collections of 19X1 contracts in 19X1.		
Deferred 19X1 Profits on Installment Sales	296,470	
Gross Margin on Installment Sales (see Exhibit 2)		199,870
Interest Revenue (see Exhibit 2)		96,600
To recognize revenue on 19X1 contracts on a collection basis.		

19X2	Cash (see Exhibit 1)	200,000	
	Installment Contracts Receivable—19X2 (see Exhibit 1)	2,278,481	
	Finished Goods (see Exhibit 1)		960,000
	Gross Margin on Installment Sales ($200,000 × 52%)		104,000
	Deferred 19X2 Profits on Installment Sales ...		1,414,481
	To record 19X2 installment sales and receipts of down payments.		
	Cash (see Exhibit 1)	970,000	
	Installment Contracts Receivable—19X1		970,000
	To record collections of 19X1 contracts in 19X2.		
	Deferred 19X1 Profits on Installments Sales	625,165	
	Gross Margin on Installment Sales (see Exhibit 2)		421,465
	Interest Revenue (see Exhibit 2)		203,700

EXHIBIT 2   Straight-Line Method of Recognizing Interest Revenue on Installment Sales

	19X1 contracts		19X2 contracts
	19X1 collections	19X2 collections	19X2 collections
Amount collected	$460,000	$970,000	$620,000
Interest revenue recognized (21%)	96,600	203,700	130,200
Installment sales recognized	$363,400	$766,300	$489,800
Ratio of gross margin to sales.........	55%	55%	52%
Gross margin recognized.............	$199,870	$421,465	$254,696

To record revenue on 19X1 contracts on a collection basis.

Cash (see Exhibit 1)	620,000	
Installment Contracts Receivable—19X2		620,000
To record collection of 19X2 contracts in 19X2.		

Deferred 19X2 Profits on Installment Sales	384,896	
Gross Margin on Installment Sales (see Exhibit 2)		254,696
Interest Revenue (see Exhibit 2)		130,200
To record revenue on 19X2 contracts on a collection basis.		

Defaults. Suppose that in addition to the amounts given above, early in 19X1 a customer made a $15,800 purchase (of goods that had cost HIJ Company $7,110). The customer paid his 10 percent down payment of $1,580. His installment contract was for $18,000. He made 5 payments of $900, then defaulted. Upon repossession, his goods were worth only $4,000. No further recovery is possible.

Up to the time of default, the entries to record these transactions parallel the entries given earlier:

Cash	1,580	
Installment Contracts Receivable—19X1	18,000	
Finished Goods		7,110
Gross Margin on Installment Sales ($1,580 × 55%)		869
Deferred 19X1 Profits on Installment Sales ...		11,601
To record the sale and receipt of down payment.		

Cash ($900 × 5)	4,500	
Installment Contracts Receivable—19X1		4,500
Deferred 19X1 Profits on Installment Sales ($11,601 × 5/20)	2,900*	
Gross Margin on Installment Sales...........		1,955
Interest Revenue ($4,500 × 21%)		945
To record the five collections.		
*Rounded.		

Upon default, the remaining balances in the installments receivable and deferred profits accounts should be reversed, and the loss on returned goods recorded:

Repossessed Goods	4,000	
Loss on Repossession	799	
Deferred 19X1 Profits on Installment Sales ($11,601 − $2,900)	8,701	
Installment Contracts Receivable—19X1 ($18,000 − $4,500)		13,500
To record the default and repossession.		

Conditional Sales. With most sales of products, a period of time will elapse between the moment the buyer receives the goods and the time they are paid for. Some sales contracts attempt to protect the seller by retaining title to the goods in the seller until some or all of the price has been paid.

Whenever reasonable estimates of uncollectible accounts can be made, present accounting practice is to ignore technical details of transfer of title and simply record a sale. However, in cases of serious uncertainty, such conditional sales would be recorded on the collection basis.

Sales on approval usually are tentative enough that no sale should be recorded until the purchaser accepts the goods. If such acceptance is accompanied by cash payment, a form of the collection basis would be appropriate. Otherwise, an approach similar to the consignment sales method would be appropriate.

Summary—The Various Methods Compared. We can summarize the different revenue recognition methods discussed by observing their similarities:

1. All these methods recognize revenue at some one specific point of time: the time of earning or production (under the production basis), the time of sale (under the sales basis), the time of cash collection (under the collection basis).

2. Over the long run, the total amount of revenue recognized under all of these methods will be the same except where a net approach is employed. Even under a net approach, the total gross margin recognized eventually will be the same under all methods. The differences are only ones of timing—although, of course, such timing differences are very important.

3. All these methods (not just the sales basis) are acceptable under current rules if the circumstances warrant. Also, under any one set of circumstances, current rules usually specify the use of one, and only one, of these methods.

Finally, there are revenue recognition aspects to various technical topics discussed elsewhere in this handbook and in specialized AICPA and FASB releases. In particular, see Chapters 5, 6, 14, 15, 19, 35, 36, 37, and 38 in this handbook, Accounting Research Study No. 11 (extractive industries' reports), the various AICPA Industry Audit Guides, APB Opinions No. 9, 20, and 30 (extraordinary items, etc.), 18 (the equity method), 21 (use of the effective interest method in reporting interest revenue), 22 (disclosure of accounting policies), 26 (gains and losses on early extinguishment of debt), 28 (interim reports), 29 (swap and barter transactions), and FASB Statements of Financial Accounting Standards No. 4 (extinguishment of debt), 12 (marketable securities), 13 (leases), 16 (prior period adjustments), 33 (financial reporting and changing prices), and 48 (revenue recognition when right of return exists).

BIBLIOGRAPHY

Accounting Principles Board (AICPA), *Reporting the Results of Operations*, Opinion No. 9 (APB, 1966).
———, *Omnibus Opinion—1966*, Opinion No. 10 (APB, 1966).
———, *Basic Concepts and Accounting Principles underlying Financial Statements of Business Enterprises*, Statement No. 4, chaps. 6 and 7 (APB, 1970).
———, *The Equity Method of Accounting for Investments in Common Stock*, Opinion No. 18 (APB, 1971).

————, *Accounting Changes*, Opinion No. 20 (APB, 1971).

————, *Interest on Receivables and Payables*, Opinion No. 21 (APB, 1971).

————, *Disclosure of Accounting Policies*, Opinion No. 22 (APB, 1972).

————, *Early Extinguishment of Debt*, Opinion No. 26 (APB, 1972).

————, *Interim Financial Reporting*, Opinion No. 28 (APB, 1973).

————, *Accounting for Nonmonetary Transactions*, Opinion No. 29 (APB, 1973).

————, *Reporting the Results of Operations . . .* , Opinion No. 30 (APB, 1973).

Committee on Accounting Procedure (AICPA), *Cost-Plus-Fixed-Fee Contracts*, Accounting Research Bulletin No. 43, chap. 11A (CAP, 1953).

————, *Long-Term Construction-Type Contracts*, Accounting Research Bulletin No. 45 (CAP, 1955).

Financial Accounting Standards Board, *Reporting Gains and Losses from Extinguishment of Debt*, Statement of Financial Accounting Standards No. 4 (FASB, 1975).

————, *Accounting for Certain Marketable Securities*, Statement of Financial Accounting Standards No. 12 (FASB, 1975).

————, *Accounting for Leases*, Statement of Financial Accounting Standards No. 13 (FASB, 1976).

————, *Prior Period Adjustments*, Statement of Financial Accounting Standards No. 16 (FASB, 1977).

————, *Financial Reporting and Changing Prices*, Statement of Financial Accounting Standards No. 33 (FASB, 1979).

————, *Revenue Recognition When the Right of Return Exists*, Statement of Financial Accounting Standards No. 48 (FASB, 1981).

Hendriksen, E. S., *Accounting Theory*, 3d ed. (Richard D. Irwin, Homewood, Ill., 1977), chaps. 5–7.

Sprouse, R. T., and M. Moonitz, *A Tentative Set of Broad Accounting Principles for Business Enterprises*, Accounting Research Study No. 3 (AICPA, 1962).

Sterling, R. R., *Theory of the Measurement of Enterprise Income* (University Press of Kansas, Lawrence, 1970).

Thomas, A. L., *The Allocation Problem, Part Two*, Studies in Accounting Research No. 9 (American Accounting Association, Sarasota, Fla., 1975).

CHAPTER 13

Cash*

Yuji Ijiri
*Robert M. Trueblood Professor of Accounting
and Economics, Carnegie-Mellon University*

---

*The first four sections of this chapter, through "Control of Cash," are taken from Chapter 13 of the second edition of this handbook. That chapter was written by Williard E. Stone of the University of Florida.

CASH ITEMS AND REPORTING

A business enterprise is in many ways a living organism, and cash flow is its life stream because few transactions take place that do not begin or end with cash. It is the task of management to assure sufficient cash to meet all needs. Profitable ventures fail because of insufficient cash, but unprofitable ones have been known to continue for long periods if sufficient cash is somehow pumped into the system. Managing and accounting for cash, then, is of the greatest importance to the financial health of the organization. Cash must be monitored carefully through accounting for cash transactions and supplying management with cash reports, cash flow statements, and cash budgets.

Definition of Cash. Cash is any medium of exchange that is immediately negotiable. It must be free of restriction for any business purpose. Prime requirements are general acceptability and availability for instant use in purchasing and payment of debt. Acceptability to a bank for deposit is a common test applied to cash items.

Composition of Cash. The item "cash" includes coins, paper currency, demand deposits with banks, and timely checks of others, which are orders on banks to supply funds immediately. Other negotiable cash instruments include the following.

A *cashier's check* is a check drawn by a bank and signed by its cashier. A *certified check* is a depositor's check guaranteed by the bank, which certifies on its face that cash has been restricted for immediate payment. A *bank draft* is a cash instrument prepared by one bank instructing another, in which it has deposits (a correspondent bank), to make payment of cash upon demand. A *money order* is a form of check calling for payment upon presentation at a post office (postal money orders) or at an express company (express money orders). *Traveler's checks* are issued by banks or express companies in even dollar amounts. Signed by the purchaser at time of purchase, they must be countersigned to become negotiable. This feature and guaranteed replacement, if lost or fraudulently endorsed, make them a safe currency for travelers.

Letters of credit are authorizations by banks to draw upon them, or upon designated correspondent banks, for funds as needed up to a specified amount. One type, generally used by travelers, requires payment in advance to the issuing bank and is cash to the value of the unused amount. Another type is a formal commitment by a bank to make a loan of funds up to a specified amount within a designated period of time, when and as required by the borrower. The open amount of this type of letter of credit is not cash. It is merely a promise to lend money and is not recognized in accounting records until exercised.

Items that are not counted as cash include postage stamps, IOUs, advances to officers and employees for travel or other purposes, and marketable securities such as U.S. notes. Postdated checks of customers are included as open accounts receivable until the date the check becomes current. Sometimes checks are returned by the maker's bank as uncollectible because the maker has instructed his or her bank to stop payment or because he or she has insufficient funds in the account to meet the amount of the check (an NSF check). Such checks should be removed from the cash account and carried as open accounts. Often, after contacting the maker, NSF checks may be redeposited and included in cash, if reasonable assurance has been received that they will be honored when presented at the maker's bank.

Amounts in savings accounts are not usually included as cash because they are not intended for operating cash use. Banks may require written notice in advance of withdrawals from such accounts. This restriction, except in times of extreme financial uncertainty, is rarely enforced, however, and if the business has a cash purpose for such funds, they may be designated as cash. Certificates of deposit are issued by banks for amounts of savings (usually in multiples of $100) on which a higher rate of interest is paid in return for the depositor's contracting not to withdraw for a specified period of time. The restriction on withdrawal of these savings removes them from the classification of cash.

Foreign currency on hand and on deposit in foreign banks should be converted to U.S. dollars at the current rate of exchange and included as cash unless restricted. Some foreign countries have regulations that prohibit the free exchange of their money into that of other countries, and their currency cannot be counted as cash. Others, whose currency is exchangeable, have restrictions on the removal of funds from the country. Either type should be labeled Restricted Deposits in Foreign Banks and not included as cash.

Funds. The term *fund* means a sum restricted for a specific purpose. Funds usually consist of cash but may also include marketable securities. *Change funds* are amounts set aside for the specific purpose of providing coins and currency to cash checks or make change. *Payroll funds* are usually amounts deposited in special bank accounts for paychecks drawn. If employees are paid in cash, however, the payroll fund may be a sum of coins and currency turned over to the paymaster for this purpose. Special bank accounts are also set up as *dividend funds* for dividend payments to shareholders. *Petty cash funds* are established to provide currency for minor business expenditures that are inconvenient to pay by check. At times, petty cash funds consist of coins, currency, undeposited checks cashed from the fund, and paid vouchers for sums expended.

Sinking funds are established for long-term purposes such as repayment of bonds at their maturity date. Typically, the resources of the sinking fund are used to acquire the bonds (or occasionally the preferred stock) of the issue for which the sinking fund was established. Sometimes the sinking fund contains investments in U.S. bonds or other securities. Other purposes of sinking funds include purchasing new building, payment of pensions to retired employees, repurchase of preferred stock, and contract performance guarantees.

Cash and Funds on the Statement of Financial Position. Cash on hand and on demand deposit in a bank is usually classified under the simple heading of *Cash*. Change funds and petty cash funds, when relatively insignificant in amount and for current operating purposes, are usually also included as cash. Although these items may be grouped together for statement purposes, for effective internal control the accounting system should provide separate accounts for each fund and bank account.

Sometimes, under the terms of a loan agreement, *maintenance of a minimum balance* is required in a demand deposit account. If the loan that requires this restriction is a current liability, the minimum balance is included as a current asset under a title such as Cash Restricted by Contract but, in any case, it should not be listed as Cash. Cash restricted for other reasons, such as funds in escrow[1] for the purchase of property, savings account balances for nonoperating purposes, certificates of deposit, and restricted funds of significant size such as sinking funds, are separately designated by descriptive titles and are included as current assets only if they are to become available within 1 year to pay current debt. Otherwise, they are classified as investments. Cash in closed banks and deposits in foreign banks in countries with currency restrictions are classified as noncurrent, or other, assets.

Bank overdrafts result when checks are issued in an amount greater than the balance in the demand deposit account; they are shown in the current liability section of the statement of financial position. Overdrafts, if material in amount, should not be offset by positive balances in other bank accounts.

IMPREST PETTY CASH FUND

A sound system of internal control of cash requires that expenditures be made by check. Under this system, it is necessary to have an amount of actual cash available for emergency use or for expenditures so minor in amount that drawing a check is impractical. Although the amount of such a fund is usually not large, it is readily available and the flow through the fund over the year may be a significant amount. Sound accounting is required; this is offered by the imprest system. *Imprest* means that a specific amount is established for the fund and placed in the custody of a petty cashier who is accountable for that precise sum, made up of paid petty cash vouchers and remaining cash. The amount selected is determined by the demands on the fund and should usually be sufficient for about 1 month's needs. Customarily, even amounts such as $50, $100, but usually not exceeding $200, are chosen.

The imprest fund, once established, requires periodic reimbursement. The entry upon reimbursement debits the various expense accounts according to the summarized paid petty cash vouchers to that date. The amount of reimbursement (and credit to Cash) is always the total of the summarized petty cash expenditures for the period between reimbursement dates. No entry is made in the petty cash account, which remains at its original amount unless the imprest sum of the fund is increased or decreased.

---

[1]Escrow funds are amounts restricted for a specified purpose by parties to an agreement. They are usually placed in the custody of a third party, frequently a trust company, and are released only by the joint instructions of both parties to the contract.

BANK RECONCILIATION

At regular intervals, usually on a certain day each month, the bank returns the canceled checks and a statement of the depositor's account. If the balance of the bank statement does not agree with the business's Cash account balance, a reconciliation is prepared. The balance shown on the bank statement will rarely correspond to the balance of the Cash in Bank account. The two basic causes of the difference are time lag and errors. In the normal flow of data, some items will have been recorded by either the bank or the firm without having reached the recording point on the other set of records, hence a *time lag* difference. Causes of such differences include: checks outstanding (i.e., checks recorded in the check register of the firm, but not yet received by the bank on which they were drawn), deposits made just before the bank statement date which do not appear on the bank statement, and transactions (such as service charges, collections of notes or drafts, and the like) that have not yet been recorded on the firm's books. The other basic difference is caused by errors in record keeping by either the firm or the bank. The process of comparing the bank statement with the books is known as *reconciling* the bank account, and the schedule that is prepared to demonstrate the results of the comparing is called a *bank reconciliation*.

The steps of this process include:

1. Compare canceled checks with bank statement.
2. Sort checks into numerical order.
3. Verify that outstanding items of last reconciliation (checks and deposits) have been received by the bank.
4. Compare canceled checks to cash disbursement entries, noting errors and outstanding checks.
5. Compare deposits on bank statement with cash receipts entries, noting differences.
6. List other items on statement not recorded by the business and items in the business records not on the bank statement.
7. Prepare a bank reconciliation (Exhibit 1).

Items on the "bank" side must either be corrected by the bank or will automatically be adjusted when the transaction reaches the bank. They do not require journal entries by the business. The deposit in transit has been sent to the bank too late to be recorded on this statement. A bank error has charged Shoreland Realty Co. with a check drawn by Shore Bros.; this must be corrected by the bank on its records. The outstanding checks have been drawn by Shoreland Realty Co. but have not yet been presented to the bank for payment.

On the "company" side are items commonly found in a bank reconciliation. Notes and interest are frequently collected for a business by the bank because it is convenient and pressures the maker to meet the note when due. The December 15 deposit was understated by $9 because of an error in the total of cash sales. The bank has made a charge of $4 to collect the note and $11.60 for servicing the Shoreland Realty Co. account. A check for $282.70 from Cox Co. was deposited, but when presented to Cox Co.'s bank, there were insufficient funds. It was returned to the bank, which deducted the amount and a protest

EXHIBIT 1   Shoreland Realty Co.—Bank Reconciliation, December 17, 19X0

Bank		Company	
Balance per bank statement	$2,350.70	Balance per cash account.	$2,051.96
Add:		Add:	
Deposit in transit	1,355.20	Note collected (G. Sims)	1,000.00
Check of Shore Bros. deducted in		Interest on note	60.00
error	51.75	Error in Dec. 15 deposit.	9.00
Total	$3,757.65	Total	$3,120.96
Less:		Less:	
Outstanding checks		Note collection fee . . . $ 4.00	
#4321 . . . . $627.30		Service charge 11.60	
#4326 . . . . 111.19		NSF check (Cox Co.) 282.70	
#4350 . . . . 246.50		Protest fee 2.50	
#4351 . . . . 52.50 1,037.49		Counter check 100.00 400.80	
Adjusted bank balance	$2,720.16	Correct cash balance	$2,720.16

fee (for formal legal protest of the nonpayment) from Shoreland Realty Co.'s account. The counter check was secured at the bank by an officer of the company and cashed for travel funds without notifying the bookkeeper.

Adjusting Entries from Bank Reconciliations. Entries must be made for all differences between the book balance of Cash and the corrected cash balance shown on the reconciliation. "Company" items require journal entries as follows:

Cash	1,069.00	
Notes Receivable (G. Sims)		1,000.00
Interest Revenue		60.00
Cash Sales		9.00
Bank Charge Expense	15.60	
Accounts Receivable (Cox Co.)	285.20*	
Travel Expense	100.00	
Cash		400.80

*Note that Cox Co. is charged for the protest fee.

CONTROL OF CASH

The basic objectives of a system of internal control, listed in order of importance, are as follows:

1. To promote efficiency in all business operations
2. To assist accuracy and the timely correction of errors
3. To deter fraud and provide for its early detection

Designing a system of internal control for cash includes establishing a sound business organization, formulating policies, setting up operating procedures for cash transactions, and providing for effective internal audit.

Organization is the designation of clearly defined areas of responsibility and delegation of authority to individuals accountable for each area. *Policies* are overall guides for the control of operations involving business cash. These include establishing maximum and minimum limits for the amount of cash balance, for the method of paying employees by cash or check, for credit terms offered customers, for the rigor of follow-up on collections, requiring daily deposits of total amount of all collections, bonding all employees handling cash, using a voucher system with disbursement by check, and establishing an imprest petty cash fund.

Procedures implement policies by making rules to govern repetitive action. At the heart of the internal control of cash are the procedures set down (usually in an operations manual) to be followed by all who handle cash. These procedures establish an efficient flow of cash, cash documents, and the recording of cash transactions. The *internal audit division*, through surprise examinations, aids in deterring and in the early detection of fraud and errors involving cash. It also makes frequent checks to determine that the system of internal control is adequate as designed and is being followed.

Internal Control Charts. Charting is often used in the design of a system of internal control and in disclosing how it is expected to operate. Auditors also use charts in their examination of the system. Exhibits 2 and 3 chart a system of internal control for cash in a large company. The organization is indicated by the departments and sections, each of which is an area of responsibility with a supervisor accountable for the efficient operation of an assigned portion of the cash function. Cash documents are named and their flow indicated by a solid line. The flow of cash is shown by a dashed line.

Separation of Functions. Although the cash charts presented above are largely self-explanatory, some of the special features are worthy of comment. Note that no employee has responsibility for more than a part of either the cash receipts or the cash disbursements function. No employee who has access to the cash may record cash transactions. Where cash is received and a basic accounting document prepared, special care is taken to maintain good control. For instance, in Exhibit 2, the salesclerk both receives cash from the customer and prepares the cash register tape that is the basis for the accounting entry. The cash register aids in proper recording of the transaction by flashing the amount of the sale for the customer to see and by providing a receipt for the customer. Strict procedural rules for salesclerks further strengthen this control.

1. All clerks have a separate cash drawer, opened only by their own register key (A, B, C, etc.), and all clerks are individually responsible for their own cash.

2. All sales must be recorded on the cash register, and the drawer must be closed between sales.

3. Money taken from a customer is placed on the cash register shelf (not in the cash drawer) and a statement is made to customer, "$1.65 out of $10." After

EXHIBIT 2   Procedural Chart—Cash Receipts Function

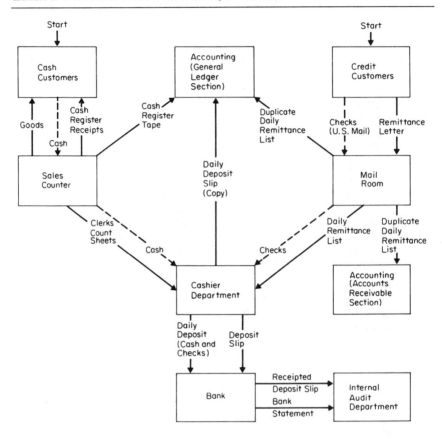

change is counted out to the customer, the $10 bill is placed in the proper compartment and the drawer closed.

4. A cash register receipt must be given to every customer. (Some firms offer an inducement to customers to obtain a receipt, such as stating that a purchase is free if a receipt is not offered or if the receipt contains a red star.)

5. When the cash in a clerk's drawer reaches a certain specified amount, the excess amount is deposited with the supervisor, who issues a receipt.

6. At close of shift, supervisor and clerk prepare a count sheet for money collected by the clerk. With a special key, the supervisor then determines the clerk's register total and determines the cash-over-or-short position.

7. An individual record is maintained of daily cash differences. Excessive amount of overs and shorts are an indication of carelessness or possible fraud.

Mail Receipts.   Another subfunction where both cash and basic recording documents are involved is mail receipt of checks from credit customers. If only

---

EXHIBIT 3   Procedural Chart—Cash Disbursements Function

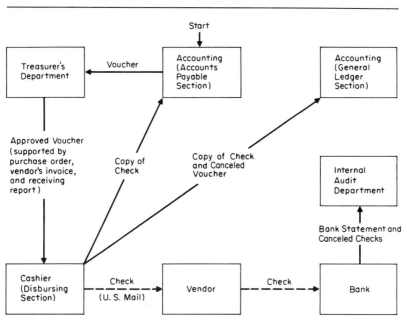

Start

| Treasurer's Department | ← Voucher | Accounting (Accounts Payable Section) | | Accounting (General Ledger Section) |

Approved Voucher (supported by purchase order, vendor's invoice, and receiving report)

Copy of Check

Copy of Check and Canceled Voucher

Internal Audit Department

Bank Statement and Canceled Checks

| Cashier (Disbursing Section) | Check ---- (U. S. Mail) → | Vendor | Check ---- → | Bank |

checks are received, it is generally sufficient to require that the mail clerk prepare a remittance list showing amount and customer's name. The cashier receives the original with the checks, one duplicate copy is sent to the general ledger department, and a different copy is sent to the accounts receivable department.

Firms should discourage remittances in currency and coins. If, however, currency and coins are received by mail, greater precautions must be taken. One clerk opens mail and calls out the name and amount of cash; a second prepares a listing of the transactions. Cash is deposited immediately in a locked compartment. Clerks working together should be rotated frequently to discourage collusion. A careful analysis of complaints of nondelivery of goods by customers will give warning of trouble.

Document Control. Automatic cross-checks of one subfunction on another are built into the system wherever possible. Prenumbered documents are an excellent device for this purpose. For instance, in Exhibit 3, the general ledger section maintains a register by check number in which all checks must be accounted for, even voids, and a missing check is investigated immediately. Each check disbursement is posted against its authorizing voucher, and a check that cannot be so matched is immediately investigated. Vouchers are heavily canceled or perforated and filed out of the control of the cashier so that they cannot be reused to support disbursements. Note that separate copies of the check are sent to the general ledger section, which maintains the control account, and to the accounts payable section, which has the vendors' subsidiary accounts. Monthly reconciliation of the total of the control account with the total of subsidiary accounts ensures a high degree of accuracy in the recording of cash (and also accounts payable).

In addition to many such automatic cross-checks, the internal audit department makes examinations of all subfunctions to determine that prescribed procedures are being followed and that the system results in efficient operations.

CASH REPORTS

Cash balances and cash transactions are summarized and reported in various forms of cash reports.

In designing a cash report, several dimensions of cash balances and transactions should be evaluated before they are included in the report. A single report can incorporate one or two dimensions comfortably, because a table has its natural two (row and column) dimensions. A report could incorporate three or four dimensions by the use of subheadings that are repeated under each main heading. However, beyond four dimensions the report becomes too cluttered and difficult to grasp. A complex set of data having many dimensions to be reported should be divided into a number of reports, each containing a few, preferably not more than two, dimensions.

Several dimensions of cash data may be important in designing a report. These will be considered below.

1. *Time periods.* Cash data may have to be reported on a daily, weekly, monthly, quarterly, or annual basis, showing not only the current period data but also data for one or more past periods for the sake of highlighting unusual items or trends. If the report covers more than one period, the time dimension is frequently spread over columns, either the current period on the right-most column following past periods or on the left-most column followed by past periods in the reverse order of time.

2. *Budget versus actual.* A report may contrast the budgeted amount and the actual amount of a given type of cash balance or transaction. Deviation of the actual from the budget is also normally included in this dimension.

3. *Controlling units.* Cash accounts may be controlled by the headquarters, branches, factories, or other subunits of a company. A cash report may provide details of cash balances and transactions classified by such controlling units.

4. *Types of accounts.* A company normally has a number of cash accounts, such as cash on hand, including a petty cash fund, checking accounts, savings accounts, time deposits, and so on. Balances and transactions may be reported for each such account.

5. *Currencies.* Cash accounts may be classified by currencies in which the account is denominated, especially in the case of multinational corporations, showing the aggregate amount of cash holdings in each currency or each group

of currencies. Currencies that are considered to fluctuate together may be grouped and reported together.

6. *Geographical.* Accounts may also be classified geographically, in particular, classified into domestic and foreign accounts, the latter being classified in further detail based on the countries or regions of the world in which the account or the controlling unit is located. In many cases this classification coincides with the currency classification, but it need not be so. For example, a German subsidiary may hold cash accounts not only in marks but also in pounds, francs, and lire.

7. *Payers and recipients.* Data may be needed showing the amounts of receipts and/or disbursements classified by payers and/or recipients. A need may arise to know the aggregate amount received from or paid to a given entity (an individual, a company, a governmental unit, or internal units of the company), regardless of the types of transactions. Intercompany cash transfers are also highlighted in this dimension.

8. *Nature of receipts and disbursements.* Cash transactions are normally classified first into receipts and disbursements and then further by the nature of the receipts or disbursements. Netting of receipts and disbursements is normally avoided, though exceptions may be observed, for example, in the case of a receipt or a disbursement to cancel an earlier disbursement or receipt made in error. The nature of receipts and disbursements may be represented by the contra-account in the journal entry for the transaction, but frequently a more detailed description of the nature of transactions is given.

A useful classification of cash receipts and disbursements from the standpoint of cash flow evaluation is to classify transactions into (1) operating cash flows (cash generated from operations), (2) financing cash flows (cash inflows from borrowings and other financing activities), and (3) investment cash flows (cash outflows from capital expenditures and other investment activities). This classification will be discussed in more detail below.

OPERATING, FINANCING, AND INVESTMENT CASH FLOWS

When cash transactions and the resulting cash flows are classified into operating, financing, and investment cash flows, data on cash flows highlight an aspect of cash flows that has not been demonstrated in conventional cash reports centered on the receipts-disbursements classification.

To understand this three-way classification, it is useful to start with the dichotomy of investment and financing cash flows in a decentralized organization. When the headquarters supply cash for expansion at a subsidiary, this is an investment cash flow from the headquarters standpoint but is a financing cash flow from the subsidiary's standpoint. When the subsidiary sends cash to a factory for its expansion, this becomes an investment cash flow from the subsidiary's standpoint and a financing cash flow from the factory's standpoint.

An investment cash flow is thus defined as "a cash outflow in anticipation of future cash inflows," whereas a financing cash flow is defined as "a cash inflow to be followed by future cash outflows." When the anticipated future cash flows occur, it is called a recovery (related to a past investment cash flow) or a repayment (related to a past financing cash flow). Thus, the investment-financing classification is related to the conventional receipts-disbursements classification as in Exhibit 4.

In other words, cash receipts and disbursements are further divided into these four categories so as to relate cash flows over time, a recovery being matched with an earlier investment or a repayment being matched with an earlier financing.

What about operating cash flows? They represent cash inflows and outflows from day-to-day operations. When inflows and outflows are netted, the net operating cash flow becomes a recovery that is matched with an earlier investment under which the operation started. Operating cash flows are cash receipts for goods or services rendered or cash payments for materials, labor, or other services received.

For example, a company started with a financing cash flow of $10 million received from shareholders or creditors or its parent company and invested $8 million in a retail store, saving $2 million for future projects. During the year, the store had operating cash inflows of $20 million and operating cash outflows of $17 million, resulting in a net operating cash flow (recovery) of $3 million. Retaining $1 million in the company, it paid $2 million to repay its financing to shareholders, creditors, or its parent company, in the form of dividends, interest, or partial refunding of loans.

A method of reporting operating, financing, and investment cash flows may be observed in the statement of changes in financial position. However, in this statement the concept of cash flow is often extended to include all current assets and current liabilities (net working capital) and all other "financial resources" according to Accounting Principles Board Opinion No. 19, issued in 1971.

The statement of changes in financial position, commonly known as the "funds statement," starts with net income and adds back depreciation and other noncash charges less credits to arrive at funds from operations, which corresponds to net operating cash flows (or recovery) in the above discussion. Other sources of funds are then added to these funds from operations to arrive at total sources of funds. This is followed by a listing of all uses of funds, and all sources and uses are reconciled to net change in funds.

The same approach may be used in a cash flow statement. The first section

EXHIBIT 4   Investment and Financing Cash Flows

	Cash receipts	Cash disbursements
Investment activities	Recovery	Investment
Financing activities	Financing	Repayment

EXHIBIT 5

X COMPANY
Cash Flow Statement
For the Year Ending December 31, 19X0

Operating cash receipts		
Cash sales............................	$ 10,251	
Collection from customers	481,253	
Other	10,976	$ 502,480
Operating cash disbursements		
Payments to suppliers....................	$– 187,501	
Wages and salaries paid	– 232,305	
Other cash expenses	– 41,982	
Income taxes paid......................	– 15,311	–477,099
Net operating cash flows		$ 25,381
Financing cash flows		
Issuance of common stock................	$ 51,215	
New borrowing	210,500	
Debt refunding........................	– 120,600	
Interest paid..........................	– 41,857	
Dividends paid........................	– 62,618	
Investment cash flows.....................		36,640
Capital expenditures: Project X	$– 30,728	
Project Y	– 15,981	
Other	– 17,560	
Recovery from disposal of Plant Z..........	4,826	–59,443
Net cash increase		$ 2,578
Cash balance at beginning		5,101
Cash balance at end..................		$ 7,679

summarizes all operating cash flows, showing the net cash flows from operations. The second section summarizes all financing cash flows, showing the net cash flows from financing (new financing less repayment). These two sections provide the sources of cash. The third section summarizes all investment cash flows, showing the net cash flows from investment (capital expenditures less proceed from disposals). Exhibit 5 is an example.

CASH FLOW EVALUATION

Evaluation of cash flows is often difficult because it is not clear whether a greater amount of cash flows is preferred to less or vice versa. In evaluating sales or net income, it is generally true that more is preferred to less. The same need not be true in cash flows, because the matter depends very much on what was accomplished by the cash outflow or what was given up in return for the cash inflow.

Nevertheless, several techniques may be helpful in digesting cash flow data. Used intelligently, these techniques can highlight the financial health of the company, because virtually all activities of a business will sooner or later show up in cash flows.

1. *Variance analysis.* An evaluation of the variance of actual cash flow from budget or from cash flow in the same period last year highlights unusual cash flows. The effectiveness of variance analysis depends on how well the budget was prepared and how stable the business environment is. When interest rates are volatile and, in the case of multinational corporations, when exchange rates fluctuate widely, there may be numerous cash transactions that were not anticipated or did not occur in previous periods, making the analysis difficult. Variance analysis is also ineffective if the period is short relative to the stability of the business environment. In a discount store where all sales are made in cash, daily cash sales may be meaningfully compared with budget. In a construction company, on the other hand, even annual cash receipts from customers may be difficult to compare with budget in a meaningful way when significant delays in construction are normal.

A cash report that highlights variances should be organized in such a way that recurring cash flows, for which variances are meaningful, are grouped together and presented first, followed by nonrecurring cash flows such as those from a bond issue or for a major plant expansion.

2. *Time series analysis.* Whereas variance analysis is limited to comparing cash flows in the current period with cash flows in the budget or in another period, time series analysis compares cash flows over several or more periods. If the length of period is less than a year, say, a month, seasonality of cash flows may be observed by dividing the monthly cash flows by the annual total. The result shows the percentage of annual cash flows that occur in a given month. By comparing these percentages with those in past years, changes in the seasonal pattern of cash flows may be observed for the given cash flow type. Seasonally adjusted, annualized cash flows may be obtained by dividing actual cash flows by a standard percentage for the month determined based on, say, past such percentages or a future forecast. Seasonal patterns often exist in many types of cash flows, and they offer a helpful basis for predicting future cash flow needs.

For annual cash flows or annualized cash flows, trend analysis may be used to predict future cash flows or to detect unusual deviations from the trend line. The trend line may be obtained in a variety of ways, from a simple free-hand drawing to the least-squares method.

3. *Composition analysis.* Although both of the above techniques are applied to one type of cash flow, composition analysis (sometimes called percentage analysis) is applied to a number of cash flow types to find their percentage in the total cash inflows or outflows. This is to highlight any change in the weight of each source or use of cash relative to total sources or uses of cash. For this analysis, it is better to exclude nonrecurring cash flows from the total in computing percentages, because they often unnecessarily disturb the weights of recurring cash flows.

4. *Ratio analysis.* Analyses discussed earlier all deal with cash flow data only. Ratio analysis, on the other hand, relates cash flow data to data in other financial statement accounts. A ratio is taken between average cash balance and such accounts as sales, purchases, or cash expenses (expenses excluding noncash items such as depreciation), in order to compute, for example, the level of minimum cash balance that may need to be maintained. Average cash balance may also be compared with interest income to evaluate the yield of cash invested in time deposits and other interest-earning cash accounts.

5. *Cash recovery rate.* A newer approach to evaluating cash flows, called the "cash recovery rate," relates operating cash flows (recovery) with gross investments. Other techniques for evaluating cash flows discussed above are aimed at highlighting abnormal items, but are otherwise silent on whether the abnormal items are good or bad. The cash recovery rate highlights abnormal phenomena on cash flows but also is somewhat more susceptible to the better-or-worse interpretation than other techniques. It can also be used to incorporate the time value of money. Because of many aspects of cash recovery rate that need to be discussed, it will be elaborated on in the next section.

CASH RECOVERY RATE

Simply stated, the cash recovery rate is annual recovery divided by gross investment. Recovery means net operating cash flows, normally aftertax; in a broader sense, however, it also includes (aftertax) nonoperating recovery, such as recovery based on disposals of investments. If recovery is limited to net operating cash flows, the resulting cash recovery rate may be called "operating cash recovery rate."

Gross investment is the sum of all investment cash flows to projects that are currently still operating. Investments to terminated projects or to projects that have not reached the operating stage are excluded. Gross investment should be stated at the gross amount; that is, it should not be reduced by depreciation or other similar items. Although the rate may be computed and analyzed strictly on the net basis, the gross basis offers a basis of cash flow evaluation more universal than the net basis, which depends on, among other things, the depreciation method of the company.

The cash recovery rate indicates how many cents per dollar of gross investment the company was able to recover during the year. It is sometimes called "payback reciprocal," because it is the reciprocal of the payback period, namely, the time needed to recover the original investment in a project. Because the payback period is commonly used with a project and rarely with a division or a corporation as a whole, a newer term is used here instead of "payback reciprocal."

Although the cash recovery rate does not directly represent profitability of a company, in many cases it can say something about the long-run profitability of the underlying business, because quite often the rate is reasonably stable over time and, if it is stable, a meaningful profitability measure (corporate DCF rate, which will be discussed below) can be derived.

To show this, suppose that a company has net operating cash flow of $3 million each year on original investment of $10 million. Then (operating) cash recovery rate is 30 percent a year. If the company is expected to last for 20 years before the investment is to be replaced or discontinued, how profitable is the company?

In 20 years, the company is expected to earn $60 million (= $3 million × 20), whereas the cost is $10 million, leaving $50 million profit, or $2.5 million a year on gross investment of $10 million. Hence, under the conventional return on investment (ROI) computation, ROI is 25 percent which is sometimes called "gross return."

Unfortunately, this method does not take into account time value of money, for cash flows in year 1 or year 2 are counted equally, dollar for dollar, as cash flows in later years. In order to incorporate the time value of money, normally the company's cost of capital needs to be specified. The cost of capital is usually derived as a weighted average of cost of debt capital and cost of equity capital, using a target debt-to-equity ratio as weights. Cost of debt capital is determined by the market rate of interest on long-term borrowings by a company of a comparable financial position, and the rate is normally stated on an aftertax basis, reducing the market interest rate by the percentage of marginal income tax rate. Cost of equity capital is usually computed by dividend yield plus expected annual growth rate in dividends.

For example, if the market rate of interest is 15 percent and the marginal income tax rate (tax rate applicable to one more dollar of income) is 40 percent, then the aftertax cost of debt is 15% × (1.0 − .4) = 9%. If the stock price is $20 and dividends are $1 per share, dividend yield is 5 percent. If it is estimated that the current price of $20 is based on investors' expectation that dividends will grow in the future at the rate of 12 percent a year, then cost of equity capital is 5% + 12% = 17%. If the company's debt–equity ratio is expected to stay at the current 1-to-3 ratio ($1 of debt and $3 of equity), the aftertax cost of capital of the company is estimated as 9%(.25) + 17%(.75) = 15%. Annual aftertax operating recovery of $3 million for the next 20 years must then be adjusted for the time value of money at the aftertax rate of 15 percent a year.

The present value at 15 percent of $3 million a year for 20 years is $18.8 million, as will be computed below, which is far above the initial investment of $10 million, leaving $8.8 million as profit after capital charge on the investment (at 15 percent a year), or 88 percent of the $10 million investment in this 20-year project.

Although such a ratio of present value to initial investment can indicate the degree of profitability to some extent, a more popular rate is called the DCF (discounted cash flow) rate (also called internal rate of return) of the project, which may be defined as the maximum cost of capital that the company can pay and still expect to have the project break even. The $10 million, 20-year project with annual cash recovery of $3 million has a DCF rate of 29.8 percent, as will be discussed in more detail later. (See Chapter 8 for computation of this rate.)

A cash recovery rate of 30 percent ($3 million divided by $10 million) is related to the DCF rate in the sense that the recovery rate gives the upper bound of the DCF rate when cash flows in each year are assumed to be constant throughout the project's life. The reason may be seen in the following manner.

Suppose that the annual $3 million cash flows lasts not just for 20 years but to infinity. This is called a "perpetuity." What is the present value of a perpetuity of $3 million a year when the interest rate is, say, 15 percent? The answer is simply $3 million divided by .15, or $20 million, because if the interest rate is 15 percent and if a company has $20 million, it can deposit the money and keep enjoying $3 million a year of interest forever. At an interest rate of 30 percent, a perpetuity of $3 million is worth $3/.30 = $10 million, which is exactly equal to the initial investment; hence at this rate the project breaks even; namely, it is the DCF rate if the recovery is to last forever.

But the project's cash recovery lasts only for 20 years. Having a cash flow stream of a finite duration (called an "annuity") at the rate of $3 million a year for 20 years is the same thing as having a perpetuity of $3 million a year but relinquishing it 20 years later. At an interest rate of 15 percent, the perpetuity is worth $20 million now, as stated above. But it is also worth $20 million 20 years from now, by virtue of the fact that the cash flow is still coming in forever. Thus, having a cash flow stream of $3 million a year for 20 years has the same benefit as getting free use of $3 million for 20 years. What is the value of this free loan? Twenty million dollars to be paid 20 years from now is worth only $20/1.15^{20} = $1.2 when discounted at the rate of 15 percent a year compounded annually. Hence, the value of the free loan is $20 − $20/1.5^{20} = $18.8, which is also the value of the annuity. This explains the rationale behind the formula for an annuity of C dollars a year for n years at interest r given by $(C/r) − (C/r)/(1 + r)^n$, where C/r shows the equivalent amount of the free loan ($20 million) and the second factor shows the present value of the loan to be paid n years from now ($1.2 million).

When the above expression is equated with the initial investment I ($10 million) and solved for r, namely, $I = (C/r) − (C/r)/(1 + r)^n$, the DCF rate is obtained. It may be easily seen that as n approaches infinity, the second term on the right side of the equation (the present value of the loan to be paid) approaches 0. Hence, $I = C/r$ or $r = C/I$, meaning that the DCF rate r equals the recovery rate C/I. For a project with a finite life, the second factor $(C/r)/(1 + r)^n$ is positive, reducing the value of the cash recovery stream. Thus the DCF rate r has to be less than the recovery rate C/I. Because a portion of the recovery C must be set aside for reduction of the initial investment I, the project cannot afford to pay as high a rate r as it could have if it had an infinite life.

The extent to which the DCF rate is lower than the recovery rate depends on the length of the project's life and the level of recovery rate. Generally, the longer the project life, the closer is the DCF rate to the recovery rate; and also the greater the recovery rate, the closer is the DCF rate to the recovery rate. Therefore, a sizable error in estimating the project life may be tolerated in such cases, because its effect on the estimated DCF rate is relatively minor.

Exhibit 6 shows the relationship between the recovery rate and the DCF rate.

The DCF rate computed from cash flow data incorporates the time value of money and, unlike such profitability measures as return on investment, which

EXHIBIT 6   Cash Recovery Rate and DCF Rate

Cash recovery rate (%) at: life (years)	DCF rate (%)				
	10	15	20	25	30
2	−22.00	−12.28	−7.49	−4.75	−3.02
4	−13.93	−5.80	−2.04	0	1.22
6	−8.35	−1.29	1.80	3.40	4.31
8	−3.86	2.37	4.96	6.24	6.93
10	0	5.56	7.75	8.78	9.31
12	3.46	8.44	10.32	11.15	11.55
14	6.64	11.12	12.72	13.40	13.70
16	9.61	13.65	15.03	15.57	15.80
18	12.41	16.08	17.25	17.69	17.87
20	15.10	18.42	19.43	19.78	19.91

is based on the net income figure, it can be compared directly with the cost of capital of the company. If the company's DCF rate is below its cost of capital, the company is performing poorly, and even if the income statement shows positive net income, the company is not generating enough returns to be provided to the investors.

All of the above argument hinges on the assumption that the cash recovery rate is reasonably stable over time. Unlike net income or return on investment, the DCF rate is not an annual rate but is a rate that is supposed to indicate the long-run profitability of a project or a company. Hence, if the recovery rate fluctuates widely, it is difficult to get any sense of profitability from cash flow data. (Even net income may lose meaning as a profitability measure if the company is in a highly volatile environment.)

Stability of the cash recovery rate may be obtained by (1) carefully segregating nonrecurring cash flows so as to evaluate them separately from recurring cash flows, and (2) by aggregating cash flows over time or across projects, divisions, subsidiaries, and other accounting entities. Quarterly recovery rates are more stable than monthly rates; annual rates are more stable than quarterly rates. Divisional recovery rates are more stable than project recovery rates, subsidiary rates are more stable than divisional rates, and consolidated entity's rates are more stable than subsidiary rates. The law of large numbers assures that as cash flows are aggregated, the chances of yielding stable recovery rates are increased.

EXTENDING THE CASH FLOW CONCEPT

The concept of cash has been extended to many levels, starting with (1) currency and deposits, (2) currency, deposits, and marketable securities, (3) current monetary assets (quick assets) less current liabilities, and (4) working capital (current assets less current liabilities). The last item is more frequently called "funds" rather than cash, but the term "cash flow" has been commonly used to designate the flow of working capital in some capital budgeting procedures. Funds from operations obtained by adding back noncash charges less credits to net income is sometimes called "cash income" or "cash earnings," even though it is based on the working capital concept of funds.

Theoretically, the cash recovery rate and the DCF rate derived from it do not depend on the particular cash concept adopted. The rates will vary depending on the definition of cash, but different standards can be established depending on the definition, and analysis can be carried out consistently.

With this flexibility in mind, the cash recovery rate and corporate DCF rates were calculated and are shown in Exhibit 7 for selected major corporations (mostly those included in the Dow Jones industrial average), using the working capital notion of cash. Cash recovery is defined as the sum of (1) funds from operations, (2) interest expense (added back to measure investment performance unaffected by the capital structure), (3) proceeds from disposal of long-term assets (a nonoperating component of recovery), and (4) decrease in current assets (to retain symmetry with long-term assets). This sum is then divided by gross investment (total assets, adding back accumulated depreciation), averaging its beginning and ending balances. The resulting recovery rates over a 7-year span, 1972–1978, are listed in Exhibit 7 along with their averages. Corporate DCF rate is then calculated from this average recovery rate using 20 years as the estimated average life of all projects undertaken by the corporation. This is shown on the next-to-last column. This is followed by corporate payback period, which is simply the reciprocal of the average recovery rate.

Project life is likely to vary from corporation to corporation, and the uniform use of 20 years may distort the true profitability of the corporation to some extent. However, whether it is 20 or 25 or 50 makes only a small difference in the DCF rate for most corporations listed here, the point mentioned earlier, although it can make a sizable difference for corporations with recovery rates significantly lower than 10 percent.

A striking point that may be observed from this table is the stability of recovery rate over the 7-year period for most corporations, giving credibility to the DCF rate derived from it.

If the past is not stable in some respect, no projections into the future can be reliable. The cash flow evaluation technique using recovery rates is aimed at finding such stability in cash flow data and using it as a basis for making reliable projections on the long-run profitability of an enterprise.

BIBLIOGRAPHY

Accounting Principles Board, *Reporting Changes in Financial Position*, Opinion No. 19 (APB, 1971).

Archer, S. H., "A Model for the Determination of Firm Cash Balances," *Journal of Financial and Quantitative Analysis*, vol. 1, no. 1 (March 1966), pp. 1–11.

Baumol, W. J., 'The Transactions Demand for Cash: An Inventory Theoretical Approach," *Quarterly Journal of Economics*, November 1952.

EXHIBIT 7 Corporate Cash Recovery Rates[a]

	1972	1973	1974	1975	1976	1977	1978	Avg.	Corp. DCF rate	Corp. payback period
Alcoa	8.2%	7.8%	9.2%	6.4%	8.4%	8.4%	10.4%	8.4%	5.6%	11.9 yr
American Brands	10.2	10.8	11.4	10.5	9.3	10.5	11.1	10.5	8.4	9.5
American Can	6.5	8.0	8.5	8.1	8.4	8.6	8.1	8.0	5.0	12.5
Bethlehem Steel	6.3	7.2	9.0	8.1	7.2	2.4	8.4	6.9	3.3	14.5
Chrysler	9.1	9.6	4.9	2.8	11.3	6.3	9.7	7.7	4.5	13.0
DuPont	10.8	12.7	10.2	9.1	11.3	11.9	12.7	11.2	9.3	8.9
Esmark	8.6	9.5	11.6	11.2	13.9	12.1	11.2	11.2	9.3	8.9
General Electric	9.9	10.1	10.4	10.8	10.7	10.5	11.2	10.5	8.4	9.5
General Foods	12.1	10.8	10.7	11.3	11.2	11.7	9.8	11.1	9.2	9.0
General Motors	14.6	15.2	9.9	12.0	16.1	15.8	16.7	14.3	13.1	7.0
Goodyear	8.4	8.1	7.8	7.1	7.3	8.7	8.7	8.0	5.0	12.5
Gulf Oil	10.7	13.3	12.9	10.5	11.5	8.9	9.8	11.1	9.2	9.0
IBM	18.2	19.0	18.8	18.3	18.7	19.5	19.9	18.9	18.2	5.3
Int'l. Harvester	6.8	7.0	8.1	8.6	9.4	10.4	6.9	8.2	5.3	12.2
Int'l. Paper	8.4	10.5	12.3	13.3	12.0	11.4	11.4	11.3	9.4	8.8
RCA	14.0	13.9	12.0	10.3	13.7	15.1	15.6	13.5	12.1	7.4
Texaco	9.7	12.6	14.2	6.0	8.1	9.9	9.6	10.0	7.8	10.0
United Technology	7.1	6.7	8.9	8.6	13.0	9.3	9.1	9.0	6.4	11.1
U.S. Steel	4.3	6.3	9.5	7.4	6.4	4.8	5.0	6.2	2.1	16.1
Westinghouse	7.7	8.1	6.4	6.7	6.9	6.6	7.3	7.1	3.6	14.1

[a]From Ijiri [1980].

Eppen G. D., and E. F. Fama, "Cash Balance and Simple Dynamic Portfolio Problems with Proportional Costs," *International Economic Review*, vol. 10, no. 2 (June 1969), pp. 119–133.

Ijiri, Y., "Cash Flow Accounting and Its Structure," *Journal of Accounting, Auditing, and Finance*, Summer 1978, pp. 331–348.

———, "Recovery Rate and Cash Flow Accounting," *Financial Executive*, March 1980, pp. 54–60.

Miller, M. H., and D. Orr, "A Model of the Demand for Money by Firms," *Quarterly Journal of Economics*, August 1966.

Orr, D., *Management and the Demand for Money* (Praeger Publishers, New York, 1971).

Sastry, A. S. R., "The Effect of Credit on Transactions Demand for Cash," *Journal of Finance*, September 1970.

CHAPTER **14**

Marketable

Securities and

Investments

Thomas F. Keller
R. J. Reynolds Industries Professor of Business Administration and Dean of The Fuqua School of Business, Duke University

GENERAL CONSIDERATIONS

Firms invest resources in securities issued by governments and other firms for essentially two reasons: (1) to satisfy precautionary desires for liquidity and (2) to obtain economic benefits beyond the scope of the investing firm's operating activities. Securities that are held primarily for precautionary reasons are generally considered to be temporary investments and as such are normally reported as current assets by the owning firm. Securities that are held for purposes of gaining economic benefits are normally considered to be long-term investments, more in the nature of plant assets.

This chapter reviews: (1) fundamental investment characteristics of securities; (2) accounting considerations of acquisition, holding, and disposition of securities; (3) essential accounting aspects of special-purpose funds; and (4) problems of disclosure related to marketable securities and investments.

Investment Media. The securities that are available for investment can be broadly classified into three groups: (1) contractual, (2) equity, and (3) hybrid. The characteristics of these three broad types are fairly distinct, but there are cases in which the distinctions become blurred as the issuing firm attempts to take advantage of its particular strengths or to capitalize on market conditions at specific times.

Contractual Securities. The rights and obligations of the parties to the contract are specified. The investor has the right to receive specific sums of cash at specified times. The issuer is obligated to make specified payments and may be subjected to various restrictive provisions. These contracts are drawn to minimize the potential interruption of cash flow from the issuer to the investor. The investor is normally interested in appraising the financial solvency of the issuer.

Equity Securities. Equity securities represent residual ownership in the assets of the firm. Owners of these securities are the beneficiaries of the profitable operations of the enterprise. The rights of the equity investor are normally limited to voting rights at annual shareholders' meetings and to receiving dividends as declared by the directors. The equity security holder obtains a return of capital by selling the security in the marketplace. The owner of equity securities is normally concerned with assessing the future profitability of the issuing organization.

Hybrid Securities. Preferred stock is a hybrid security because, although a dividend rate is set by contract and specific provisions are included relative to the investor's rights in the event of nonpayment, there is seldom a maturity date. In some cases a maturity date may be a part of the preferred stock contract. The Securities and Exchange Commission (SEC) requires that preferred stock with stated maturity be excluded from the equity section of the balance sheet. The passing of a preferred stock dividend does not trigger a default situation, as is usually the case with nonpayment of bond interest.

Convertible securities are hybrid securities because, although they may contain all the features of a bond or preferred stock contract, they also permit the investor to exchange the contract for an equity security. The convertible security is in fact two securities: (1) a bond or a preferred stock and (2) a stock option or warrant. The income bond is a third, but extremely rare, type of hybrid security. The income bond differs from preferred stock in that it has a specific maturity date, but the periodic payments to the investor are dependent on the reported profits of the firm and in some cases the action of the board of directors.

Investment Objectives and Security Selection. The objectives to be achieved from the temporary investment of cash and from the expansion of the economic base of the firm are quite different and thus normally dictate investment in different types of securities.

Marketable Securities. The objective of the firm concerned with investing cash for precautionary or specific purposes is twofold: (1) to increase the return on total resources held; and (2) to maintain the availability of a specific amount of cash for planned or unplanned purposes with a minimum risk of loss. In selecting the investment medium, management must decide whether protection of the number of dollars or the purchasing power of the dollars is most important. The decision has often been in favor of number of dollars. Current return on the investment appears to be a secondary consideration. Although there are many issues of common stock that may be readily sold if the number of shares held is not large in relation to normal trading activity, there is normally much greater fluctuation in common stock prices than in prices of bond contracts with near-term maturity dates.

Long-Term Investments. Long-term investments are usually made with the intention of gaining some degree of influence over the operations of the firm in which the investment is made. The benefits to a firm from holding an investment interest in a competing, supplying, or buying firm can be many and varied; the objective is normally greater profits for the investing firm. Because the benefit expected is derived from the exertion of influence on operations over time as well as the profitability of the firm whose securities are acquired, these investments are seldom made with the intention of selling the securities until the potential for benefit ceases to exist. Because the common shareholders usually elect the board of directors, it is natural to expect that most long-term investments will comprise shares of common stock. The criteria of ready marketability and immediate return on investment through dividends are of only secondary consideration in the selection of securities to be held as long-term investments.

The accounting procedures for recording transactions in securities, whether held as marketable securities or as long-term investments, are identical.

Acquisition Cost. Securities, like other assets acquired by a firm, are initially recorded at cost. Cost is generally considered to be the cash or market value of other assets given in exchange for the asset acquired. All costs incident to the acquisition as well as the price of the asset are aggregated to determine the cost of the asset.

Elements of cost. The cost of an investment in securities is the market price, brokerage fees, taxes, and other expenditures necessary to complete the transaction. In the event that securities are acquired in exchange for other assets, the accountant must rely on evidence of fair values of the assets exchanged or on an independent appraisal if there are no known market values. Accounting Principles Board Opinion No. 29 [1973, par. 29] says, "Fair value of a nonmonetary asset transferred to or from an enterprise in a nonmonetary transaction should be determined by referring to estimated realizable values in cash transactions of the same or similar assets, quoted market prices, independent appraisals, estimated fair values of assets or services received in exchange or other available evidence."

Basket purchase. When more than one type of security is acquired for a single price, the accountant is faced with the problem of allocating the acquisition price among the securities. If the market values of the securities are known, the cost is prorated on the basis of relative market price at the date of acquisition. If the current price of only one security is known, normally a portion of the cost equal to the market price will be allocated to that security and the remainder will be considered the cost of the other securities. In the event that two or more securities have no market price, the accountant must delay allocation of the cost until a market is established, or must rely on experts for an independent appraisal of value. These delayed market prices or appraisals are then used to allocate the joint cost among the securities acquired. An illustrative journal entry to record a joint purchase of securities is presented for the following situation:

XYZ Corporation purchased 1,000 units of a new offering of securities by ABC Company for $110,000. Each unit is comprised of one share of $50-par-value 10 percent preferred stock and two shares of $10-par-value common stock. The common stock was traded on an organized exchange on the day of purchase at $31 per share. The preferred stock is a new security that has never been traded. Brokerage commissions were paid by the issuing company.

Investment in ABC—Common Stock	62,000	
Investment in ABC—Preferred Stock	48,000	
Cash		110,000

Exchange and conversions. Determination of the acquisition cost of securities acquired by an exchange or conversion of securities acquired at an earlier date is a controversial matter. The controversy concerns whether the original cost of the securities exchanged or converted should become the carrying value of the securities acquired in the exchange or whether the market value of the securities acquired by exchange or conversion should be used as the carrying value of the new securities. The question is this: Has a gain or loss been realized on the securities being exchanged or converted? If the answer is yes, then the market value should be considered the carrying value of the new securities. If the answer is no, then the new securities take the basis of the securities exchanged.

The common practice is to record the new securities at the cost of those exchanged or converted. The argument cited in support of this position is that, in the case of convertible securities especially, the investor makes only one investment. The gain or loss resulting from changes in market price should not be recognized until the investment position is reduced or eliminated by sale. This position also gains support from tax laws, which permit the deferral of tax on most gains until the investment position is reduced or eliminated by sale.

On the other hand, advocates of the alternative method argue rather convincingly that the presence of a quoted market value at the date of exchange provides the objective evidence needed to allow recognition of the market value at the date of exchange. They argue further that this is a significant event in which the investor has participated, and is not the same as annual recognition of market appreciation or loss on securities held.

Cost Identification. Cost identification of securities becomes a problem only if there are two or more purchases of identical items at different prices. The cost of a particular share of stock or bond is important in the determination, at the date of sale, of the realized gain or loss from holding the security.

The cost may be determined specifically by reference to the certificate number, assuming that the record of the acquisition is maintained in this manner. An alternative is to assume a pattern or flow of securities through the investment account. The most common assumption appears to be the first-in, first-out (FIFO) pattern.

The argument in favor of specific identification of the securities sold is that this method permits an accurate measure of profit derived from a specific investment. The argument against the use of the specific identification method is that the method permits the selection by management of the specific certificate being sold. In this way management may be able to influence the reported profit for a particular period of time. For this reason and for recording simplicity, the FIFO method is commonly used.

Valuation of Securities. The carrying value of investments, both marketable and long-term, like investments in current assets, should generally be the lower of cost or market.

Cost. The acquisition price of an asset represents the resources required to obtain it. Accountants argue that until the asset is disposed of or consumed, it should be valued at acquisition price. It is only then that the gain or loss can be objectively determined. Some accountants find this position difficult to support when current market quotations are readily available for the securities held and disposition can be easily accomplished. Some reevaluation of the cost principle has been mandated for marketable securities by Financial Accounting Standards Board (FASB) Statement No. 12 [1975], as discussed below.

Market. The market value of securities held is usually considered to be the current quote less the brokerage and other costs of disposing of the securities. The market price of securities that are being considered for possible acquisition is the market quote plus brokerage and other acquisition costs. Accountants have continually argued that revenue is realized only when there is an exchange between buyer and seller. Procedures that reflect changes in the market price of assets held have generally not been accepted unless the procedures result in the recognition of a diminution of value. For example, Accounting Research Bulletin No. 43 [CAP, 1953, chap. 3A, par. 9] says of current assets: "Where market value is less than cost by a substantial amount and it is evident that the decline in market value is not due to a mere temporary condition, the amount to be included as a current asset should not exceed the market value." The Bulletin also recognized the importance of market price increases and concluded: "It is important that the amounts at which current assets are stated be supplemented by information which reveals, for temporary investments, their market value . . . ."

In recent years increasing consideration has been given to recognizing changes in the market value of securities. During public hearings held in 1971 on accounting for equity securities, which preceded issuance of Accounting Principles Board (APB) Opinion No. 18, *The Equity Method of Accounting for Investments in Common Stock* [1971], a number of alternatives were considered. The question of timing the recognition of income was of primary concern. Does an enterprise have to enter into a transaction in order to recognize revenue, or is revenue earned by a change in the market value of an asset?

This dilemma was never resolved. The APB reasoned: "Reporting of investments in common stock at market value . . . is considered to meet most closely the objective of reporting the economic consequences of holding the investment. However, the market value method is now used only in special circumstances. While the Board believes the market value method provides the best presentation of investments in some situations, it concludes that further study is necessary before the market value method is extended beyond current practice" [APB Opinion No. 18, 1971, par. 9].

Lower of cost or market. The lower-of-cost-or-market rule is based on a conservative interpretation of the realization principle. The argument supporting the rule is that the market price of an asset reflects the expected earning potential of an asset. If the market price declines, then there must be evidence to support a reduction in expected earning capacity. This loss of earning potential represents an economic loss, which is no less real than if the asset had been physically damaged. To carry the asset at a dollar amount that exceeds this market valuation of future usefulness would be misleading to those relying on financial statements; therefore, price declines must be recognized by a write-down in the carrying value of the asset. This rationale for write-downs applies both to marketable securities reported as current assets and to securities carried as investments where the equity method (see below) is not used.

In applying the lower-of-cost-or market valuation basis to marketable securities, it is logical to apply it to each security individually rather than to the securities as a group. Each security is a distinct item; the portfolio does not consist of a homogeneous group, so the usual arguments for basing the valuation on market value of the aggregate group as compared with the cost of the group do not apply. However, FASB Statement No. 12 requires that the valuation be applied to the portfolio as a whole. Indeed, the statement requires different treatment depending on whether the portfolio is classified as a current asset or a noncurrent asset. Because FASB Statement No. 12 applies solely to equity securities, the specific provisions are discussed on page 14-22.

Equity. The equity basis of valuation requires that securities be recorded initially at acquisition cost and then the carrying value be increased or decreased to reflect the owning company's share of the annual profits or losses of the company whose securities are owned. This valuation method is applicable only to securities that represent a residual claim against assets. All dividends are accounted for as a reduction of the carrying value of the securities. When the equity method is adopted, revenue is recognized in the period in which profits are reported by the owned company; if the cost method were used, revenue would be recognized only when dividends are declared.

The equity method of accounting for investments in equity securities was adopted for domestic, nonconsolidated subsidiaries in 1966 as a part of APB Opinion No. 10. In 1971 a more extensive consideration of the proper method of accounting for equity securities led to an extension of the position adopted in 1966. Specifically, " . . . the Board now extends this conclusion of APB Opinion No. 10 to investments in common stock of all unconsolidated subsidiaries (foreign as well as domestic) in consolidated financial statements" [APB Opinion No. 18, 1971, par. 14].

As was the pattern with APB Opinions, the Board also specified when the equity method was considered appropriate. "The Board concludes that the equity method of accounting for an investment in common stock should also be followed by an investor whose investment in voting stock gives it the ability to exercise significant influence over operating and financial policies of an investee even though the investor holds 50% or less of the voting stock. . . . The Board recognizes that determining the ability of an investor to exercise such influence is not always clear, and applying judgment is necessary to assess the status of each investment. In order to achieve a reasonable degree of uniformity in application, the Board concludes that an investment of 20% or more of the voting stock of an investee should lead to a presumption that in the absence of evidence to the contrary an investor has the ability to exercise significant influence over an investee" [APB Opinion No. 18, 1971, par. 17].

The FASB, in Interpretation No. 35 [1981, par. 4], indicated several types of situations where the presumption of "ability to exercise significant influence" could be overcome even though the investor owned 20 percent or more of the voting stock of the investee. Examples cited were as follows:

1. Opposition by the investee, such as litigation or complaints to governmental regulatory authorities.

2. The investor and investee sign an agreement under which the investor surrenders significant rights as a shareholder.

3. Majority ownership of the investee is concentrated among a small group of shareholders, who operate the investee without regard to the views of the investor.

4. The investor needs or wants more financial information to apply the equity method than is available to the investee's other shareholders, tries to obtain that information, and fails.

5. The investor tries and fails to obtain representation on the investee's board of directors.

The APB stated that the equity method should be applied as if the investee were included in consolidated financial statements (except when the cumulative share of losses exceeds the investment). It further indicated that the difference between the equity method and consolidated financial statements is limited to the details found in the financial statements. The net income for the period and the shareholders' equity at year-end are the same if a subsidiary is consolidated or accounted for as an unconsolidated subsidiary when the equity method is used. The situation is not sufficient justification for excluding a subsidiary from consolidation if the circumstances would normally require consolidation.

INVESTMENTS IN CONTRACTUAL SECURITIES

The value of investments in contractual securities is dependent on changes in the financial stability of the company and changes in the general structure of interest rates. These securities are characterized by a constant dollar cash flow as determined by contract; therefore, they are subject to maximum exposure to purchasing power gains and losses.

Appraisal of Value. The current price of a security that includes contractual provisions for the payment of stated sums of money at specific dates is a function of time and the interest rate required to attract the needed investment. The time to maturity is specified in the contract, and the required yield is related to the supply of investment money—investors' willingness to invest—and the demand for funds by borrowers.

Structure of Interest Rates. In a normative sense, interest is the payment to the provider of capital for the use of the capital for a specified time period, as rent is payment to the provider of space or other facilities. As there is no such thing as the rental rate, so there is no such thing as the interest rate. Instead there is a structure of interest rates beginning with the lowest, which is the rate for the use of money for very short periods of time by borrowers who are considered to present an extremely low probability of financial loss to the lender—the risk-free rate.

The level of interest rates at different times is functionally related to the supply of lendable funds offered by investors and the demand for funds by borrowers. The supply of and demand for funds are influenced in important ways by the level of current economic activity and the expected future level. The expected rate of inflation in the economy is also an extremely important aspect of the decision of both the lender and the borrower. Because, at the present time, substantially all contractual securities provide for the transfer of a specific number of dollars without regard to the purchasing power of those dollars, investors try to protect themselves against the loss in purchasing power by reducing the supply of money placed in contractual investments. Borrowers, to the contrary, find it extremely desirable to be able to buy real goods with dollars of current purchasing power and to repay the loans at a future date with dollars of a lower purchasing power.

The structure of interest rates is further influenced by the length of time elapsing between the time of commitment of money and the date of repayment. The lengthening of the term of the contractual agreement is associated with an increased risk on the part of the lender and the desire for greater flexibility by the borrower.

Finally, the element of financial risk for each borrower adds further to the multiplicity of interest rates found in the market. The selection of a required rate of return by the investor is a complex matter; nevertheless, it is an important part of the investment decision. Contractual security prices are the result of the clearinghouse function of the market. Market rates of interest for various types of contracts thus emerge. The decision to invest is resolved for a single investor by comparing the required rate of return and degree of acceptable risk with the market rate for comparable risk.

Interest Rates and Bond Prices. Bond contracts embody two distinct obligations: (1) to pay interest periodically, as specified in the contract, until maturity; and (2) to pay the face amount of the bond at maturity. The price of the contract is obtained by discounting each expected receipt (promised payment) at the prevailing market rate of interest (16 percent) and summing them.

For purposes of illustration, assume that ABC purchases one XYZ, 12 percent, 10-year, $1,000 bond when the prevailing rate for securities of that particular risk class is 16 percent per year. The market price of this security ($803.59) is calculated as follows:

Present value of the maturity amount due in 20 periods or 10 years:

$$PV_m = \$1{,}000 \left[\frac{1}{(1 + .08)^{20}} \right] = \$214.50$$

Present value of the semiannual interest payment of $60 per period for 20 periods:

$$PV_r = \$60 \left[\frac{1 - 1/(1 + .08)^{20}}{.08} \right] = \$589.09$$

Present value of the contract:

$$PV_m + PV_r = \$214.50 + \$589.09 = \$803.59$$

Interest tables are available for easily ascertaining the decimal equivalents of the fractions contained in brackets.

The purchase of this bond contract would be recorded as follows:

Investment in XYZ Bonds..........................	803.59	
Cash		803.59

Serial Bonds. Serial bonds are issued when the borrowing firm needs money for differing lengths of time or in order to meet the demands of investors. They are frequently issued by municipalities because of their particular needs and occasionally by firms in lieu of bonds requiring the accumulation of a sinking fund. Serial bonds can be thought of as a series of individual contracts; however, we frequently view them as one contract because there is normally only one instrument that specifies serial maturity.

The following example will illustrate how a serial contract may be viewed as two separate contracts:

M Company is offering 9 percent bonds in the face amount of $200,000 with interest payable semiannually and maturity being $100,000 at the end of year 9 and $100,000 at the end of year 10. T Company wishes to earn 10 percent before taxes on its investment and accordingly offers $187,923.10 for the bond issue. The offering price (OP_c) is computed as follows:

9-year portion	10-year portion

$$PV_f = \$100{,}000 \left[\frac{1}{(1 + .05)^{18}} \right] \qquad = \$100{,}000 \left[\frac{1}{(1 + .05)^{20}} \right]$$

$$= \$41{,}550 \qquad\qquad\qquad = \$37{,}690$$

$$PV_r = \$4{,}500 \left[\frac{1 - 1/(1 + .05)^{18}}{.05} \right] \qquad = \$4{,}500 \left[\frac{1 - 1/(1 + .05)^{20}}{.05} \right]$$

$$= \$52{,}603.20 \qquad\qquad\qquad = \$56{,}079.90$$

$$PV_f + PV_r = \$94{,}153.20 \qquad\qquad\qquad = \$93{,}769.90$$

$$OP_c = \$94{,}153.20 + \$93{,}769.90 = \$187{,}923.10$$

The purchase of the serial bond, assuming that all brokerage and other issue costs were paid by M Company, would be recorded as follows:

Investment in M Company Serial Bonds..............	187,923.10	
Cash.......................................		187,923.10

Bond Discount or Premium. The difference between the market price of a bond contract and the face amount—the discount or premium—is the result of the difference between the interest rate stated in the contract and the market rate for comparable contracts. The discount or premium is an adjustment of the interest revenue earned over the life of the contract, because the bond will be redeemed at face value at maturity, barring financial insolvency of the issuer. The discount or premium is accumulated or amortized over the life of the contract to reflect more accurately the interest earned for each time period during which the bond is owned. In the absence of such procedures, the difference between the acquisition price and the face value will be reported as a gain or loss in the year of maturity, a circumstance that does not reflect the economic activity. There are two methods of accumulating the discount or amortizing the premium: (1) straight-line and (2) effective yield.

Straight-line method. The straight-line method of discount accumulation or premium amortization assigns an equal proportion of the discount or premium to each time period. The result is that in the case of a discount, the apparent rate of return on the investment will be greater than the market rate in the early years of the contract and less in the later years. In the case of a premium, the apparent rate of return will be less than the market rate in the early years and greater in the later years. The straight-line method has, as its primary virtue, ease of application. The entry to record the semiannual interest income for the investment in XYZ Company in the earlier illustration would be as follows:

Cash..	60.00	
Investment in XYZ Company Bonds	9.82	
Interest Revenue		69.82
To record semiannual interest income on XYZ Company		
bonds with the discount accumulated using the straight-		
line method [($1,000 − $803.59) / 20 = $9.82].		

This same entry would be repeated each interest period for 20 periods, or 10 years.

Effective yield method. The effective yield method of discount accumulation and premium amortization employs the concept of compound interest calculation used in determining the price of the contractual security. The method produces a return on the investment equal to the market rate of interest prevailing at the date the investment is made. The rate of return is constant over the period from acquisition to maturity. The effective yield method is illustrated for two periods, using the example of the ABC Company investment in XYZ Company bonds:

Cash..	60.00	
Investment in XYZ Company Bonds	4.29	
Interest Revenue		64.29
To record semiannual interest income on XYZ Company		
bonds with the discount accumulated using the effective		
yield method ($803.59 × .08 = $64.29).		

The investment at the beginning of the second interest period is now $807.88 (= $803.59 + $4.29). The entry to record the interest revenue for the second period is

Cash	60.00	
Investment in XYZ Company Bonds	4.63	
Interest Revenue		64.63

To record semiannual interest income on XYZ Company bonds with the discount accumulated using the effective yield method ($807.88 × .08 = $64.63).

Special problems of serial bonds. The discount or premium on serial bonds can be accumulated or amortized for each maturity using either a straight-line or an effective yield method. The effective yield method can be applied to the serial bond as a unit or to each individual component without altering the results. A slight modification of the straight-line method is necessary if each segment cannot be separated. This method, known as the *bonds outstanding* method, is discussed later.

Both the straight-line and the effective yield methods are illustrated for the first interest period of the M Company bonds applied to each segment separately.

9-year segment:
1. Straight-line method:

Cash	4,500.00	
Investment in M Company serial bonds	324.82	
Interest revenue		4,824.82
Market value at date of acquisition	$ 94,153.20	
Maturity amount	100,000.00	
Discount	$ 5,846.80	

Semiannual accumulation of discount

$$\left(\frac{\$5,846.80}{18} = \$324.82 \right)$$

2. Effective yield method:

Cash	4,500.00	
Investment in M Company serial bonds	207.66	
Interest revenue		4,707.66
Market value at date of acquisition	$ 94,153.20	
Effective semiannual interest rate	× .05	
Semiannual interest revenue	$ 4,707.66	

10-year segment:
1. Straight-line method:

Cash	4,500.00	
Investment in M Company serial bonds	311.51	
Interest revenue		4,811.51
Market value at date of acquisition	$ 93,769.90	
Maturity amount	100,000.00	
Discount	$ 6,230.10	

Semiannual accumulation of discount

$$\left(\frac{\$6,230.10}{20} = \$311.51 \right)$$

2. Effective yield method:

Cash		4,500.00
Investment in M Company serial bonds		188.50
Interest revenue		4,688.50
Market value at date of acquisition	$ 93,769.90	
Effective semiannual interest rate	×.05	
Semiannual interest revenue	$ 4,688.50	

The combined discount accumulation for both segments of the serial bond is $636.33 under the straight-line method and $396.16 under the effective yield method. The discount accumulation of each segment, using the effective yield method, will be larger each period as the carrying value of each segment increases, whereas the accumulation using the straight-line method will remain constant for the first 18 periods and then drop to $311.51 per period for the tenth year. The effective yield method applied to the investment in serial bonds as a total will yield the same results as if it were applied to individual segments: $187,923.10 × .05 = $9,396.16.

In serial bond investments, a variation of the straight-line method, the bonds outstanding method, is often used. The amortization of bond premium or accumulation of bond discount for a period using this method is determined by computing the percentage relationship of the bonds outstanding during the period (B_i) to the sum of the bonds outstanding during each period of the bond contract. The percentage so computed is the portion of the total premium (B_p) or discount (B_d) that should be amortized or accumulated during the period (B_i).

This relationship can be expressed as follows:

$$\left(\frac{B_i}{\sum_{i=1}^{n} B_i} \right) (B_d) = B_{di}$$

Referring to the example of the M Company, there is $200,000 of bonds outstanding in each of the first 9 years and $100,000 in the tenth year. The total bond years outstanding is $1,900,000 [= ($200,000 × 9) + $100,000]. The discount accumulation for the first year is thus $1,271.25, computed as follows:

$$\frac{\$200,000}{\$1,900,000} \times \$12,076.90 = \$1,271.25$$

The complete tabulation of the annual accumulation of the discount is presented in Exhibit 1.

The bonds outstanding method approximates the discount accumulation obtained under the straight-line method by considering each portion of the serial contract separately. During the first 9 years the discount accumulation using the separate calculation is $1,271.25; it is $635.63 for the tenth year.

Marketable securities. Frequently the discount or premium on bond investments that are considered temporary will not be accumulated or amortized. The reason given for the failure to handle the discount or premium in the manner suggested is that the holding period is uncertain or will be so short as to make the accumulation or amortization unnecessary.

EXHIBIT 1 Bonds Outstanding Method of Recognizing Revenue on Serial Bond Issue

Year	Bonds outstanding at maturity value	Fraction of total outstanding	Accumulation of discount	Cash receipts	Interest revenue
1......	$ 200,000	2/19	$ 1,271.25	$ 18,000	$ 19,271.25
2......	200,000	2/19	1,271.25	18,000	19,271.25
3......	200,000	2/19	1,271.25	18,000	19,271.25
4......	200,000	2/19	1,271.25	18,000	19,271.25
5......	200,000	2/19	1,271.25	18,000	19,271.25
6......	200,000	2/19	1,271.25	18,000	19,271.25
7......	200,000	2/19	1,271.25	18,000	19,271.25
8......	200,000	2/19	1,271.25	18,000	19,271.25
9......	200,000	2/19	1,271.25	18,000	19,271.25
10......	100,000	1/19	635.63	9,000	9,635.63
	$1,900,000	19/19	$12,076.88	$171,000	$183,076.88

Sale of Bond Investments Prior to Maturity. Gains or losses frequently result from the sale, prior to maturity, of bond investments. These gains and losses are often attributable to changes in the level of interest rates which, as was discussed earlier, are related to the supply of and demand for money. The gain or loss is the difference between the proceeds derived from the sale of the investment and the carrying value, purchase price plus accumulation of discount or amortization of premium, to the date of sale.

To illustrate the procedure, assume that the XYZ Company bond is sold 1 year after the date of purchase for $875.00. The discount is accumulated in accordance with the effective yield method, as illustrated earlier. The carrying value is $812.51 (= $803.59 + $4.29 + $4.63). The entry to record the sale and recognize the gain is

```
Cash .........................................    875.00
    Investment in XYZ Company Bonds ................          812.51
    Gain on Sale of Bonds .........................           62.49
```

This entry assumes that the interest for the two intervening interest periods has been accrued and that the discount has been accumulated correctly. If for any reason the discount had not been accumulated, the investment account would have to be adjusted before the sale could be recorded.

Acquisition or Sale between Interest Dates. Interest, being the payment made to investors for the use of their money for specific time periods, is considered an asset separate and apart from the bond contract. The price of a bond is, as discussed previously, the present value of future receipts by the investor. It is the practice in the bond market for bonds to trade at the present value of the future interest and principal receipts less the portion of the next interest receipt earned by the present holder since the date of the most recent interest receipt. The buyer of the bond acquires two assets—a pure bond value and a receivable for the interest earned since the most recent interest date.

Price determination. The market value between interest dates of the contractual security is determined using the principles of present value as illustrated in the discussion of acquisition on an interest date. The following example illustrates the method:

Assume that Larson Company 12 percent bonds due in 3 years and 9 months, principal amount $100,000, are being considered for purchase. The market rate of interest is 10 percent. The present value of bonds 4 years prior to maturity is

$$PV_f^4 = \$100,000 \left[\frac{1}{(1.05)^8} \right] = \$67,680.00$$

$$PV_r^4 = \$6,000 \left[\frac{1 - 1/(1.05)^8}{.05} \right] = \$38,779.20$$

Present value 4 years prior to maturity.	$106,459.20
Add: Growth at 10% for 3 months ($106,459.20 × .025)	2,661.48
Value of bond and accrued interest at 3 years 9 months	109,120.68
Less: Accrued interest for 3 months: ($100,000 × .030)	3,000.00
Value of bond at 3 years 9 months	106,120.68

The journal entry to record the purchase of the Larson Company bonds is

Investment in Larson Company Bonds	106,120.68	
Accrued Interest Receivable	3,000.00	
Cash		109,120.68
To record purchase of bonds plus accrued interest.		

Interest accrual. The interest received on the investment in Larson Company bonds at 3 years and 6 months is recorded as follows (using the effective yield method):

Cash	6,000.00	
Investment in Larson Company Bonds		338.52
Accrued Interest Receivable		3,000.00
Interest Revenue		2,661.48

The interest revenue is computed using the investment value at the beginning of the interest period and the market rate at the date of acquisition. Because the bonds were held only 3 months of the interest period, only one-half of the total revenue for the period is considered earned by the investor ($2,661.48 = ¼ × $106,459.20 × .10). The premium amortization ($338.52) is the difference between the cash receipt for 3 months interest ($3,000) and the interest revenue ($2,661.48). The other $3,000 cash received is repayment of the accrued interest purchased at the date the bonds were acquired.

Sale between interest dates. The carrying value of a contractual security must be adjusted for the amortization of premium or accumulation of discount before sale if one is to separate price change due to approaching maturity from that due to market forces. If the effective yield method is used, the premium amortization or discount accumulation is allocated on a straight-line basis within the interest period. If the Larson Company bonds are sold 2 years and 8 months before maturity for $107,500 plus accrued interest and if the interest receipt and premium amortization have been recorded using the effective yield method up to the 3-year point, the entries to adjust the accounts and record the sale are

Accrued Interest Receivable	4,000.00	
Investment in Larson Company Bonds		482.24
Interest Revenue		3,517.76
To accrue interest for 4 months.		

Carrying value of investment was $105,527.55 at the beginning of the period.

Cash	111,500.00	
Accrued Interest Receivable		4,000.00
Investment in Larson Company Bonds		105,527.55
Gain on Sale of Securities		1,972.45

The gain on the sale of securities indicates that interest rates have fallen from the 10 percent rate that was effective when the bonds were purchased a little over a year ago. If there had been a loss on the sale, it would be a sign that interest rates had increased in that interval.

The illustrations of interest accrual and sale between interest dates are both presented using the effective yield method. The straight-line method of premium amortization might also be used. The concepts and procedures are the same; the only difference is the periodic amount of the premium amortization and the resulting carrying value of the investment. The final gain on the sale of securities would be different, because the carrying value of the securities would be changed.

INVESTMENTS IN EQUITY SECURITIES

Equity securities represent the residual ownership of the assets of the firm. All assets that are not required to satisfy the priority claims of the investors holding preference securities provide the economic basis of the value of equity securities. There are three primary problems in accounting for and reporting the results of transactions related to investments in equity securities: (1) determining and reporting carrying value at date of acquisition and subsequently, (2) measuring and reporting income during the holding period, and (3) measuring and reporting the gain or loss occurring during the holding period, traditionally recognized at the time of disposition.

Determining and Reporting Carrying Value. The problems of determining and reporting the carrying value of equity securities are similar to those for other securities, which have been discussed earlier in this chapter. The most commonly used methods of valuation are the cost-or-market and equity methods, combined with parenthetical or footnote disclosure of market or cost value. Market values are typically reported as the carrying value of equity securities only when the circumstances exist for the application of the lower-of-cost-or-market valuation, as discussed in FASB Statement No. 12.

The equity investor is frequently in the position of acquiring additional shares of common stock by means other than direct purchase in the market. For example, shares may be received (1) as a pro rata distribution, requiring no payment by the investor from the owned corporation (stock dividend), and (2) by exercise of stock purchase rights that have been acquired as a pro rata distribution, by purchase, or as compensation for services rendered. The determination of acquisition cost in such cases is somewhat more complex than in the case of an outright purchase. These problems are therefore discussed in some detail in this section.

Stock Dividends. Investors occasionally receive shares of common stock as a pro rata distribution from corporations whose common shares they hold as investments. These shares, stock splits and stock dividends, are received without any requirement for the investor to make any payment to the issuing corporation. The investor merely maintains a proportionate interest in the firm. The total equity of the firm whose shares are held, although represented by more shares after the stock dividend or split, does not change as a result of this distribution. The receipt of shares does not increase the assets of the investor or represent income to him or her. The investor, therefore, needs only to note that the investment is represented by a large number of shares. The carrying value per share is reduced for purposes of determining gains and losses upon the sale of any shares.

Accounting Research Bulletin No. 43 supports the opinion that stock dividends and splits do not constitute income to the investor. The Bulletin argues as follows [CAP, 1953, chap. 7B, par. 6]:

> Under conventional accounting concepts, the shareholder has no income solely as a result of the fact that the corporation has income; the increase in his equity through undistributed earnings is no more than potential income to him. It is true that income earned by the corporation may result in an enhancement in the market value of the shares, but until there is a distribution, division, or severance of corporate assets, the shareholder has no income.... In the case of a stock dividend or split-up there is no distribution, division, or severance of corporate assets. Moreover, there is nothing resulting therefrom that the shareholder can realize without parting with some of his proportionate interest in the corporation.

With respect to unconsolidated domestic subsidiaries, the APB has revised its position as to when income should be recognized by a corporate shareholder; however, this change in no way affects the Bulletin's conclusion that the receipt of stock dividends and splits does not constitute income to the investor, because neither the stock dividend nor the stock split is associated with either the distribution of assets or the earning of income by an unconsolidated domestic subsidiary.

The Internal Revenue Code of 1954, as amended, in general exempts stock dividends and splits from taxation except where the stock distribution is in lieu of cash. The stock distribution reduces the per-share cost of the shares held, as discussed earlier.

Share Purchase Arrangements. The terms "right" and "warrant" are used almost interchangeably in reference to instruments that permit the holder to acquire shares of stock of the issuing firm at a stated price. The instrument specifies the price at which a new share may be purchased, how many shares the holder is entitled to acquire at that price, and the period during which the right to purchase may be exercised. The confusion results because: (1) one form of purchase arrangement (stock right) is normally received by existing shareholders without cost and it conveys to them the privilege of acquiring new shares at a stated price in proportion to the number of shares held at the time of receipt; (2) the other form of instrument (stock warrant) is normally purchased by the investor. The period during which the stock right can be exercised is normally limited to 3 or 4 weeks, whereas the period during which the purchased warrant may be exercised is normally quite long and may run for many years. The warrant holder may exercise the warrant (purchase the stipulated number of shares within the specified time period at the stated price) or may sell the warrant, if it is transferable.

The familiar stock option is also a form of a stock warrant, with provisions quite similar to the other forms discussed. It is received in lieu of cash salary by selected employees. The exercise period may range up to 5 years. However, the beginning of the exercise period may be delayed or may be contingent on specific events. The stock option differs from other forms of stock warrants primarily in that it is normally not transferable and is, therefore, seldom held by corporate investors.

Stock Rights. Stock rights are received by existing shareholders in proportion to their holding of common stock—a single right for each share held. The rights received as a distribution represent a portion of the investor's interest in the corporation. The carrying value of the investment must, therefore, be allocated between the rights and the shares held at the time of the distribution on the basis of relative market price. For purposes of illustration, assume that Stelzer Company owns 10,000 shares of Eastern Corporation acquired for $160,000. Stelzer accounts for the investment on the cost basis. On June 1, Stelzer receives 10,000 stock rights. Five rights and $20 are required to acquire one new share from Eastern. The market price of Eastern Corporation stock trading ex-rights was $30 and the market price of a right was $2. (The price of a share including the right was $32.) The carrying value of the 10,000 shares is allocated between the old shares and the rights as follows:

$$\left(\frac{\$2 \times 10,000}{\$32 \times 10,000} \right) (\$160,000) = \$10,000$$

The required journal entry is

Investment in Eastern Corp. Stock Rights	10,000	
Investment in Eastern Corp. Common Stock		10,000
To record portion of the cost allocable to the stock rights.		

When the stock rights are exercised, the cost assigned to the rights plus the cash paid to acquire the new shares is the cost of the new shares. The entry to record the exercise of one-half of the right is

Investment in Eastern Corp. Common Stock	25,000	
Investment in Eastern Corp. Stock Rights		5,000
Cash		20,000
To record acquisition of 1,000 shares of common stock		
at $20 per share and by exercising 5,000 stock rights.		

If 4,500 of the remaining rights are sold for $2.10 each and the remaining 500 are allowed to lapse, the journal entries to record these facts are as follows:

Cash	9,450	
Investment in Eastern Corp. Stock Rights		4,500
Gain on Sale of Stock Rights		4,950
To record sale of 4,500 rights at $2.10 each.		

Loss upon Expiration of Stock Rights.	500	
Investment in Eastern Corp. Stock Rights		500
To record the loss suffered by the expiration of stock		
rights.		

In situations where an investor needs an approximation of the theoretical market value of the stock after a rights offering, an estimate can be made by summing the present market price of the shares that must be held to permit the acquisition of one new share and the cash payment required to acquire one new share; then this total is divided by the number of shares existing after exercise of the right. The difference between the existing price of a share of stock and the theoretical price ex-right is, of course, the theoretical value of the right distributed to present shareholders. This relationship can be expressed as

$$\frac{P(m/n) + C}{(m/n) + 1} = P - nR \quad \text{or} \quad P - nR = C + mR$$

where P = market price of a share, rights on (i.e., before the issue of the rights)
m = number of rights required to acquire one new share
n = number of rights received for each share held
C = cash payment required to acquire one new share upon exercise of m rights
R = market price of one right

Accounting for stock warrants. When stock warrants are acquired by purchase, whether from the issuing company or from shareholders who wish to sell rights received through preemptive provisions, the acquisition is recorded as an investment in stock purchase rights. As an illustration, M Company acquires a warrant for the purchase of 100 shares of R Company common stock at the option of the holder for 5 years at a price of $30 per share. The cost of the warrant is $1,000. The journal entry to record the purchase is

```
Investment in R Company  . . . . . . . . . . . . . . . . . . . . . . . . .      1,000
    Cash . . . . . . . . . . . . . . . . . . . . . . . . . . . . . . . . . . . . . . . . . .              1,000
    To record purchase of warrant for 100 shares of R com-
    mon stock at $30 a share. The warrant may be exercised
    any time within 5 years.
```

At the time the warrant is exercised, the following entry is made:

```
Investment in R Company Common Stock . . . . . . . . . . . . .      4,000
    Investment in R Company Warrant . . . . . . . . . . . . . . . .              1,000
    Cash . . . . . . . . . . . . . . . . . . . . . . . . . . . . . . . . . . . . . . . . .              3,000
    To record acquisition of 100 shares of R Company com-
    mon stock for $30 per share and exercise of warrant pur-
    chased for $1,000.
```

The securities acquired by the exercise of stock warrants are accounted for in accordance with the same principles used for securities acquired without benefit of warrants. Acquisition cost must merely be redefined to include the cost assigned to or paid for the warrant.

Measuring and Reporting Income.   Timing the recognition of revenue derived from investments in common stock is related directly to the method used to value the asset. When the *cost* method is used, revenue derived from the investment for a period is equal to the claims against the assets of the investee arising from the declaration of dividends during that period. Receipt of assets (cash or physical items) may not occur within the period during which the right to receive the asset arises. There are four dates commonly associated with the declaration and receipt of dividends on common stock: (1) date of declaration, (2) ex-dividend date, (3) date of record, and (4) date of receipt. The dividend obligation becomes a liability of the enterprise on the date declared and attaches to the stock as a definite receivable at that time. A strict application of the principles of accrual accounting would require that the revenue and the receivable be recognized on the date of declaration. On the ex-dividend date, the stock trades without the right to receive the dividend even though the date of record normally occurs 3 days later. The day of receipt is insignificant in timing the recognition of revenue. In cases where two accounting periods are involved, the dividend revenue should be recognized on the date of declaration and the receivable transferred with the security in the event of sale before the ex-dividend date.

If the *market* method were to be used, the revenue derived from a common stock investment would be the dividend revenue as discussed above plus or minus the change in the market value of the investment during the period under consideration.

Lower of cost or market.   FASB Statement No. 12, *Accounting for Certain Marketable Securities*, requires that marketable equity securities be carried at the lower of aggregate cost or market determined at the balance sheet date.

Applicable securities. FASB Statement No. 12 applies only to marketable equity securities, a category that includes ownership shares (common, preferred, and other capital stock) and rights to acquire or dispose of ownership shares at fixed or determinable prices (warrants, rights, put and call options). Securities excluded are treasury shares, preferred stock that must be redeemed by the issuer or is redeemable at the option of the investor, convertible bonds, restricted stock, and investments of marketable securities accounted for under the equity method.

Exempt industries. FASB Statement No. 12 does not apply to nonprofit organizations, mutual life insurance companies, and employee benefit plans, but it does apply to mutual savings banks and other profit-seeking mutual enterprises. In addition, companies in industries with specialized industry accounting practices for marketable securities, such as investment companies, broker-dealers, stock life insurance companies, and casualty insurance companies, may continue to follow the specialized accounting practices, which typically involve carrying marketable securities at market and reflecting unrealized gains or losses in the owners' equity section of the balance sheet.

Current versus noncurrent securities. In comparing cost with market, securities are grouped into two portfolios: securities classified as current assets and securities classified as noncurrent assets. (In unclassified balance sheets, the entire portfolio is considered noncurrent.) The classification of a given security as current or noncurrent may change and the accounting for that change is discussed later. "Cost" of each of these two portfolios is the aggregate acquisition cost, as discussed in the preceding section, of all securities in the portfolio. "Market" is the aggregate market value of all securities in the portfolio. The "lower of cost or market" is the lower of these two aggregates.

Effects on income and owners' equity. When the aggregate market value of either of the two portfolios is below its aggregate cost (or if the securities have been held for more than one accounting period, book value), then an asset contra account, called a valuation allowance, is credited to reduce book value to aggregate market value. The debit is either (1) to a loss account shown in the income statement for the current asset portfolio, or (2) to an owners' equity contra account (unrealized holding losses) for the noncurrent asset portfolio. If, later, the aggregate market value increases above book value, then the valuation allowance is debited and the credit is (1) to income for current assets or (2) to owners' equity for noncurrent assets. In no case, however, is the valuation allowance allowed to have a debit balance; aggregate market increases are recognized only to the extent of previously recognized decreases. The effect of this treatment is to recognize some changes in market value of current assets in income but not to recognize any income effect for changes in market value of noncurrent assets except for the special case considered next.

Permanent declines in market value of the noncurrent portfolio. If it is judged that a decline in market value of an individual security in the noncurrent portfolio is "permanent" rather than "temporary," then the current market value of that security becomes the new "cost" basis for that security and a loss is recognized currently on the income statement. Subsequent increases in aggregate market value do not increase the cost basis. Little guidance is available in deciding whether or not a decline should be judged temporary or permanent. In a slightly different context, however, the Staff of the Auditing Standards Division of the AICPA has issued an interpretation on this question. See the *Journal of Accountancy*, April 1975, pp. 69–70. The interpretation contains the following sentence: "When the market decline is attributable to specific adverse conditions for a particular security, stocks or bonds, a [permanent] write-down in carrying amount is necessary unless persuasive evidence exists to support the [current] carrying amount." This sentence and the subsequent discussion appear to indicate that only company-specific events will usually lead to the conclusion that the decline is permanent. Cyclical declines in general stock market prices would not of themselves be judged evidence of permanent declines. Write-downs of this type are rare.

Transfer between current and noncurrent classification. The current versus noncurrent classification of a security may be changed subsequent to its acquisition. At the time of reclassification, the current market value becomes the new cost basis, if that amount is less than acquisition cost. The total difference between the old and the new cost bases must be reflected as a loss in the income statement for the period of reclassification.

Deferred income taxes. Unrealized losses (and later gains, if they occur) are timing differences, as defined in APB Opinion No. 11 and discussed in Chapter 36. Thus the income statement amounts for unrealized holding losses of the period on the current portfolio and the balance sheet amounts of unrealized holding losses on both portfolios should be adjusted for future income tax effects when an offset of the loss with a future taxable gain is assured beyond any reasonable doubt.

Equity method. The Accounting Principles Board, in Opinion No. 18, stated that the equity method should be used in accounting for investments when the investor has the ability to exercise control over the investee. The Board concluded that a holding of 20 percent or more of the voting stock of the investee leads to a presumption of control in the absence of evidence to the contrary. The Board held conversely that a holding of less than 20 percent was presumed to be inadequate to exercise control. When this method is used, the revenue recognized is the proportionate part of the earnings of the subsidiary recognized for the period under consideration. The distribution of dividends is considered to be a reduction in the investment when the equity method is used. The procedure is to recognize the receivable and reduce the investment account of the investor on the ex-dividend date.

In Opinion No. 18, the Board also held that the equity method should be applied so as to achieve results identical with consolidation. The difference between consolidation and the equity method is limited to details; however, in discussing the application of the equity method, the Board listed the following points [APB, 1971, par. 19]:

> a. Intercompany profits and losses should be eliminated until realized by the investor or investee as if the investee company were consolidated. A question arose as to whether 100 percent of the intercompany profit should be eliminated or only the ownership percentage. In an interpretation dated November 1971 the Board recommends that since the equity method is a one-line consolidation that intercompany profits are eliminated only on assets remaining in the accounts of the investee or investor.

The Board also recommends that if the transaction is not at "arm's length" then the intercompany profit or loss should be eliminated 100 percent. If the transaction is at "arm's length," then only the investor's interest in the transaction should be eliminated.

b. A difference between the cost of an investment and the amount of the underlying equity in net assets of an investee should be accounted for as if the investee were a consolidated subsidiary. This implies amortization in accordance with Opinion No. 17 if the difference is considered to be goodwill.

c. The investment in common stock should be shown in the balance sheet as a single amount, and the investor's share of earnings or losses of an investee should be shown in the income statement as a single amount except for extraordinary items.

d. The investor's share of extraordinary items and its share of prior period adjustments reported in the financial statements of the investee should be classified in a similar manner unless they are immaterial in relation to the investor.

e. Transactions of investees of a capital nature that affect the investor's share of stockholder's equity of the investee should be accounted for as if the investee were a consolidated subsidiary.

f. Sales of stock of an investee by an investor should be accounted for as gains or losses equal to the difference between the selling price and the carrying amount of the stock sold.

g. If financial statements of investees are not sufficiently timely for an investor to apply the equity method currently, the investor should record its share of the earnings or losses from the most recent available financial statements. Lags in reporting should be consistent from period to period.

h. A loss in value of an investment which is other than a temporary decline should be recognized as are similar losses of other long-term assets. Evidence of a loss might include the inability to recover the carrying value of the investment, inability of the investee to sustain an earnings level that would justify the carrying value, or a decline in quoted market price which appears to be more than temporary.

i. If the carrying value of the investment is reduced to zero due to recognition of the investor's share of the investee's losses, then the investor should discontinue the use of the equity method unless (1) the investor is contingently liable for the investee's obligations or (2) is committed to provide further financial support for the investee. If the investee subsequently reports net income, the investor should resume applying the equity method only after its share of that net income equals the share of net losses not recognized during the period the equity method was suspended.

j. In determining income tax expense, the undistributed earnings of a subsidiary included in consolidated income should be accounted for as a timing difference unless there is evidence to show that the earnings will be remitted in a tax-free liquidation. Income taxes attributable to timing differences in reporting undistributed earnings of a subsidiary should be accounted for in accordance with the concept of comprehensive tax allocation.

k. When the investee has outstanding cumulative preferred stock, an investor should compute its share of earnings after deducting the preferred dividends whether declared or not.

l. When an investor's percentages of ownership falls below that which would justify the use of the equity method, the investor should discontinue accruing its share of the investee's earnings. The investment account should not be adjusted retroactively.

m. When an investor's percentage of ownership increases to a level requiring the use of the equity method, the investor should adopt it. The investment, results of operations, and retained earnings should be adjusted retroactively in a manner consistent with the step-by-step acquisition of a subsidiary.

n. Any difference that exists between the carrying value of the investment and the underlying equity in the net assets of the investee resulting from the step-by-step procedure should be related to specific accounts of the investee if possible; however, if this is not possible, the difference should be considered to be goodwill and amortized over a period not to exceed 40 years.

Liquidating dividends. Occasionally corporations find themselves in a position of having accumulated large sums of cash for which there appears to be no sufficiently productive use. In such cases, a dividend may be declared and paid that exceeds the profits of the firm for the particular accounting period. The legal interpretation of such distributions is that if the corporation has reinvested earnings that are greater than the dividend, then the distribution constitutes income to the shareholder.

In some cases the dividend received may exceed the earnings reinvested since the stock was acquired by the present holder. The investor may argue that the proper economic interpretation is that the portion of the dividend that exceeds the reinvested earnings is a return *of* capital rather than a return *on* capital. The legal interpretation, however, is that a new investor steps into the shoes of the prior investor with respect to the distinction between dividend income and return of capital. In other words, the law views distributions from the point of view of the corporation and not that of the investor.

Measuring and Reporting Gain or Loss on Disposition. If accountants report the carrying value of securities as the current market price, changes in the market price would be recorded as revenue in the period in which the change occurs. In such cases, the gain or loss in the period in which sale or liquidation takes place would be limited to the price change occurring since the most recent revaluation of the holding.

Under presently accepted accounting principles, the gain or loss derived from holding securities is measured by the difference between the carrying value and the net selling price or liquidation proceeds. The carrying value is most often the acquisition cost of the securities as adjusted for subsequent receipt of shares related to prior investments or such adjusted acquisition cost modified by recognition of the investors' share of reported income of the owned company. The reported gain or loss may represent not the price change occurring during the period in which sale or liquidation is accomplished, but rather the total price change during the entire holding period. The total pretax revenue derived from a specific investment is not changed by the particular accounting procedures adopted; however, the revenue for any one period may be significantly different, depending on the accounting method used and the behavior of market prices between acquisition and sale.

INVESTMENTS IN HYBRIDS

Securities that are classified as hybrids are those that have some characteristics of both contractual and equity securities. The accounting treatment, therefore, must encompass some aspects of both types of investments.

Preferred Stocks. Preferred stocks have the characteristic of a specified cash receipt in the form of periodic dividends. The sanctions against the issuing firm for nonpayment of dividends are not so strong in most cases as those found in bond contracts. The major difference, however, is found in the fact that most preferred stock contracts do not specify a maturity date. This lack of a maturity date implies that the same periodic dividend will be received indefinitely.

In recent years preferred stock contracts have been written that include a maturity date. In these situations the value of a preferred stock is determined using the same method as applied to bond contracts. The value of the security is equal to the sum of the present value of the interest payments over the term of the contract plus the present value of the maturity amount at the end of the contract.

Valuation of a preferred stock. The valuation of a normal preferred stock, that does not have a maturity date differs from the valuation of a typical bond in that there is only one stream of cash receipts to be discounted; there is no maturity value to discount. The formula for the valuation of a preferred stock can thus be written as

$$PV_r = D \left[\frac{1 - 1/(1 + i)^\infty}{i} \right] \Rightarrow D \left[\frac{1}{i} \right]$$

where PV_r = present value of future dividends discounted at the market rate of interest i

D = periodic receipt

The fraction $1/(1 + i)^\infty$ goes to zero as the number of periods approaches infinity. For this reason the market value of a preferred stock (or perpetual bond) approximates the periodic receipt divided by the market rate of interest.

Premium or discount. Preferred stock prices behave quite similarly to bond prices in that as interest rates rise, the prices of the securities decline and as interest rates fall, prices rise. This phenomenon implies that in some instances the prices of preferred stocks are either above or below the face amount or par value of the security. What should be the accounting disposition by the investor of this premium or discount?

Amortization of premium or accumulation of discount. The premium or discount on investments in preferred securities is seldom amortized or accumulated if the contract does not state a specific maturity date. Where a maturity date is included, the premium or discount is normally amortized over the life of the contract in the same manner as for bond contracts. The purpose of premium accumulation or discount amortization is to recognize revenue in the proper period and to value the asset at market if the conditions at date of acquisition persist throughout the holding period.

FASB Statement No. 12 does not apply to the valuation of preferred stock with a stated maturity date. This position is based on the concept that such contracts are not equity contracts, which is consistent with the position taken by the SEC in Accounting Series Release No. 268.

Preferred stock may be redeemable at the option of the issuer. In the event of redemption, the cash proceeds are recorded, the carrying value of the investment is written off, and the difference is reflected as a gain or loss upon redemption. Except in cases where a maturity date is established by the contract, par value or face value is significant only when the contract provides for dividend payments expressed as a percentage of par value or in the event of liquidation.

Timing income receipts. Preferred stock dividends are declared periodically by the board of directors of the issuing corporation. In this sense the periodic distribution is more akin to that of common stock than to that of bonds. If the dividend is not declared, it is not paid. In many cases, preferred stock dividends are cumulative, which means that if the dividend is not declared when due, it accumulates and normally must be paid before any distribution can be made to common stock investors. Because preferred stock dividends are not paid automatically, the investors do not accrue the dividend as they do interest. Instead they should record the dividend as they do common stock dividends. The preferred dividend should be recorded as a receivable and the revenue recognized on the declaration date.

Convertible Securities—Bonds and Preferreds. There is a group of securities broadly referred to as "convertibles." These are basically fixed-income securities (bonds and preferred stocks) with common stock purchase privileges attached. The stock purchase right is normally not detachable from the fixed-income security. The investment characteristics of these securities are such that the investor gets both the advantage of priority of claim, of participation in growth and increased profitability, and the advantage of limited protection against unforeseen disasters that severely hamper future growth prospects.

The value of a convertible security may be determined by computing the value of the fixed-income portion and of the purchase right as separate securities. In effect the investor is making a basket purchase, but determination of the separate values of the two components is complex.

Accounting procedure. Historically, acquisitions of convertible securities have been recorded at acquisition price without recognition of the basket purchase features. Any discount or premium was not accumulated or amortized because the deviation from maturity value was more often attributable to fluctuations in common stock prices than to a reflection of market adjustment for differences in interest rates. Further, because conversion is the normal expectation, maturity value will probably never be a significant quantity except in those cases in which the price of the common stock has declined to such an extent that conversion is not justified. In such cases the investor receives protection because of the fixed-income provisions so long as the company is financially sound. In some cases convertibles are viewed as merely a stopgap on the way to acquisition of common stock.

In December 1966, the APB issued Opinion No. 10, *Omnibus Opinion—1966*. Among other topics, this Opinion included two paragraphs that deal with accounting problems of the issuers of convertible securities, but its recommendations could have been important to the investor as well. The first paragraph of this section of the Opinion states [APB, 1966, par. 8]:

> A portion of the proceeds received for bonds or other debt obligations which are convertible into stock, or which are issued with warrants to purchase stock, is ordinarily attributable to the conversion privilege or to the warrants, a factor that is usually reflected in the stated interest rate. In substance, the acquirer of the debt obligation receives a "call" on the stock. Accordingly, the portion of the proceeds attributable to the conversion feature or the warrants should be accounted for as paid-in capital . . . ; however, as the liability under the debt obligation is not reduced by such attribution, the corresponding charge should be to debt discount.

The implications of the Opinion for the investor would have been that two investment accounts, rather than one, need to be debited when the securities are acquired. The discount or reduced premium on the bond portion of the investment would be accumulated or amortized as in the case of regular bond investments. The following example will serve to illustrate some of the major accounting changes implied by Opinion No. 10 as related to investments in convertible securities. Assume that Northern, Inc., buys for $1,000 a 7 percent convertible bond, $1,000 face value, which matures 5 years after date of acquisition. The prevailing market rate of interest for nonconvertible securities of a similar risk class is 8 percent at the date of acquisition. Each bond is convertible into 50 shares of common stock, currently selling for $18 per share, at the option of the investor at any time before maturity. This acquisition would have been recorded as follows, using the ideas expressed in Opinion No. 10.

Investment in Bonds	959.44	
Investment in Conversion Privilege	40.56	
Cash		1,000.00
To record acquisition of 7 percent convertible bond. The cost is allocated as follows:		

Cash		1,000.00
Market value of 7 percent, 5-year bond:		

$$\text{Principal} \; - \; (\$1{,}000) \left[\frac{1}{(1 + .04)^{10}} \right] = \$675.56$$

$$\text{Interest} \; - \; (\$35) \left[\frac{1 - 1/(1 + .04)^{10}}{.04} \right] = \underline{283.88} \; \dots \qquad 959.44$$

Market value of conversion privilege 40.56

The subsequent accounting for this investment on the first interest date would be as follows, assuming the use of the effective yield method of discount accumulation:

Cash	35.00	
Investment in Bonds	3.38	
Interest Revenue		38.38
To record interest for 6 months.		

The entry to record the conversion, assuming that conversion takes place immediately after receipt of the interest for the first 6 months and that we assume conversion should be recorded at the carrying value of the investment rather than market value of the common stock, is as follows:

Investment in Common Stock	1,003.38	
Investment in Bonds		962.82
Investment in Conversion Privilege		40.56
To record conversion of bonds into common stock.		

If the conventional method of accounting for convertible securities had been followed, the interest revenue would have been only $35, and the carrying value of the investment would have been $1,000; accordingly, the investment cost of the common stock would have been $1,000. The difference of $3.38 in the carrying value of the investment will eventually enter into the income stream when the common stock is sold. The question is this: When is the revenue realized and when should it be recognized?

In March 1969 the APB issued Opinion No. 14, which attempts to distinguish between convertible debt that must be surrendered to convert it into common stock and debt that has detachable warrants entitling the holder to buy a specified number of shares of common stock at a stated price. In this Opinion the Board attached considerable significance to the inseparability of the debt and the conversion option. The Board concluded that when the debt instrument must be surrendered to obtain common stock, no element of common equity had been sold at the time of issuance of the debt. On the other hand, if debt were sold with detachable warrants, there was evidence that equity had been sold at the date of issuance. Throughout this Opinion the Board refers only to the issuer; however, as discussed earlier, because the investor is a party to the transaction under discussion, there are implications for the investor as well. Accordingly, if the investment is in convertible debt with detachable warrants, the method illustrated above is appropriate. On the other hand, if the debt must be surrendered to acquire common stock, the investor should record the total investment as an investment in corporate bonds. The impact of this procedure is primarily on the interest revenue recorded during the period that the bonds are held and, to the extent that the discount would have been amortized, on the carrying value of the common stock investment if conversion takes place later.

In this opinion the Board has been accused by some of placing form before substance in the establishment of accounting principles.

Income Bonds. Income bonds are extremely rare instruments of finance in today's world; perhaps the need for income bonds has been supplanted by convertible securities. Income bonds typically have a maturity date and a face value that is paid to the holder at maturity. The unique feature of this instrument is that the periodic receipt, for the use of funds invested, varies depending on the profits of the firm.

Valuation. The problems of valuation of income bonds are found primarily in the estimates of periodic receipts that the investor will receive. If these estimates can be made, then valuation becomes another calculation of the present value of future receipts.

Discount accumulation and premium amortization. Because income bonds generally have definite maturity dates, any discount or premium should be accumulated or amortized. With a definite life, the discount or premium can be accumulated or amortized on the straight-line basis with little difficulty. If the investor makes estimates of future receipts in preparation of making the decision to invest in income bonds, it seems reasonable to argue that these estimates might be used to apply the techniques of the effective yield method as well. The effective yield method would be employed by computing the present value of expected future receipts at the end of each period. The change in the present value of the receipts would be the appropriate amortization or accumulation of premium or discount.

The interest revenue from these bonds could be accrued if a formula were included in the contract specifying how the distribution would be determined. In cases where the distribution of cash is dependent on the action of the board of directors and is related to common stock dividends, the revenue from these bonds would have to be timed in the same manner as dividends on common stock are timed. The receivable would arise on the date of declaration. The adjustment of the investment would complete the revenue recognition entry.

INVESTMENTS IN SPECIAL-PURPOSE FUNDS

Firms occasionally deposit cash in special-purpose funds as a means of providing cash for desired purposes at specific later points in time or as a means of satisfying specific provisions of contracts between the firm and other parties. The funds required because of specific contract provision are usually administered by trustees who are independent of the firm's management. The voluntary funds created for special purposes at the discretion of management are normally administered by the management of the firm. The cash deposited in either of these types of funds is usually invested in securities so that it will be productive during the holding period. Because in many cases these funds are created to provide specific sums of money at a specified time, the investment medium is usually bonds with maturity dates near the time payment is required. With the obligation to be satisfied stated in dollars, the risk of purchasing power loss present in fixed-dollar securities is not important. On the other hand, the risk of capital loss by large market fluctuations associated with common stock may be extremely important.

Accounting for Funds. The accounting records related to the activities of any fund depend to some extent on the purpose of the fund and legal considerations related to the fund.

Funds are created, voluntarily or in accordance with contractual provisions, (1) to accumulate resources for the purpose of satisfying specific obligations of the firm, or (2) to accumulate resources for the purpose of satisfying obligations for a separate entity, the fund, but with the firm under contract to make specific periodic deposits in the fund and in some cases being contingently liable for the obligations of the fund. The essential distinction between funds created for these two purposes is that for funds created to satisfy specific obligations of the firm, the obligation rests on the firm whether the fund has adequate resources or not. When the obligation is that of the fund, if the firm has fulfilled its contractual requirements of making periodic deposits, then the liability of the firm has been satisfied regardless of whether the fund accumulated is adequate for its purpose or not, except in those specific cases in which the firm is contingently liable for the obligations of the fund.

When the purpose of the fund is to satisfy obligations of the firm, the fund balance is an asset of the firm, and the revenues and expenses relating to the fund should be included in the determination of periodic net income. The transaction information is for purposes of satisfying accountability requirements. Securities held in such funds are accounted for as though they were being held as temporary or long-term investments. The accounting records should include information about (1) transfer of assets to the fund, (2) investment transactions, especially in company-managed funds, (3) revenues derived from investment operations and expenses of administration, and (4) use of the resources of the fund.

One of the duties of a trustee is to submit periodic reports to the interested parties. The report to the corporation responsible for making payments to the fund includes a report of investment activity, revenues derived from the portfolio and expenses of management. The firm then records these data either in the general ledger accounts or in a subsidiary ledger for which the investment account is the control.

For funds whose purpose it is to satisfy obligations of the fund, the firm's obligation extends merely to the deposit of cash in the fund in accordance with contractual provisions and possible contingent liability. No records are necessary for the firm except those necessary to report the expense—usually limited to the required deposit—associated with the contract between the firm and the outside party. Funds of this latter type are most often created for the benefit of employees through a contract made between the firm and a union, the most common type being a pension fund.

Periodic Deposits. Funds created by contract, such as a pension fund, for the benefit of employees usually specify how the amount of periodic deposit is determined and at what dates deposits must be made. Deposits are usually related to the payroll of covered employees. Deposits to funds, contractual or voluntary, whose purpose it is to accumulate a specific sum of money for corporate purposes, are frequently specified as to dollar amount and date of deposit. In some cases the contract provides for minimum balances to be accumulated in the fund by stipulated dates. Regardless of whether the periodic deposit is stated in the contract or determined by the firm to meet specified interim levels, the procedure for determining the amount is usually the same.

The deposit may vary each period based on the investment results of the fund, or stated assumptions may be made that permit the calculation of a uniform deposit for each period. The uniform deposit to be made at the beginning of each period can be computed in accordance with the following formula:[1]

$$A_n = R \left[\frac{(1 + i)^n - 1}{i} \right] \quad \text{or} \quad R = A_n \left\{ \frac{1}{[(1 + i)^n - 1]/i} \right\}$$

where A_n = amount desired in the fund at the end of n periods
   R = periodic deposit to be made at the beginning of each period
   i = estimated return, net of management expense, on the assets held by the fund
   n = number of deposits to be made or number of periods until amount needs to be on hand

The use of this formula is illustrated with the following example. X Company is about to issue a $100,000 bond that requires a periodic deposit with a trustee. The trustee is to hold all funds for the benefit of the bondholder. Ten years from the date of issue, the fund is to contain no less than $100,000. The first deposit is to be made at the beginning of the second year after issue of the bond. X Company estimates that the funds can be invested to yield an average of 11 percent and that the management expenses will average approximately 1 percent of the funds held. The company proposes to make nine equal periodic payments at the beginning of each year, starting with year 2. A final payment will be made at the end of the tenth year to bring the cash on deposit to $100,000. If more than $100,000 has been accumulated, the excess will be returned to the firm by the trustee. The uniform periodic deposit can be computed as follows:

$$R = A_n \left\{ \frac{1}{[(1 + i)^n - 1]/i} \right\}$$
$$= \$100,000 \left\{ \frac{1}{[(1 + .10)^9 - 1]/.10} \right\}$$
$$= \$100,000 \left(\frac{1}{13.5795} \right)$$
$$= \$7,364.04$$

The recording procedures for the first year of operations of the fund, assuming that interest earned is $810 and management expenses are $140, are illustrated below:

Investment in Sinking Fund	7,364.04	
Cash		7,364.04
To record first annual deposit with trustee at the beginning of year 2.		

---

[1]Compound interest tables are published that will permit the immediate evaluation of $[(1 + i)^n - 1]/i$. These tables are titled in various ways, but in essence they provide the user with the amount to which $1 deposited at the beginning of each period for n periods will accumulate, if invested to yield i rate of return. (See the Appendix.)

Sinking Fund Expense	140.00	
Investment in Sinking Fund	670.00	
Sinking Fund Revenue		810.00

To record earnings of the fund and expenses of management for year 2.

Assume that after the deposit at the beginning of year 10, the fund balance is $89,000. The interest earned during year 10 is $8,500 and the expenses of management are $900. At the end of year 10, the adjusting deposit is made and the bonds are retired.

Sinking Fund Expense	900.00	
Investment in Sinking Fund	7,600.00	
Sinking Fund Revenue		8,500.00

To record earnings of the fund and expenses of management for the tenth year since issuance of the bond or the ninth year of the fund accumulation.

Investment in Sinking Fund	3,400.00	
Cash		3,400.00

To record final deposit in the fund to obtain the required balance. The net earnings of the fund were inadequate by $200.

Bonds Payable	100,000.00	
Investment in Sinking Fund		100,000.00

To record payment of the bond obligation by the trustee.

In this illustration, individual transactions involving acquisition, revenue collection, and disposition of securities have been assumed to be recorded by the trustee and no separate records relating to these matters are maintained by the firm.

Cash Surrender Value of Life Insurance. A firm will occasionally purchase a life insurance policy on the life of a principal officer or owner of the firm with the firm named as beneficiary. The proceeds of the policy are expected to be used to purchase the deceased owner's interest from his estate or to help absorb the extra expense of operating for a short time following the loss of the key executive. The firm has the option of buying either term insurance, which is strictly insurance against loss of life, or permanent insurance, which practically always includes, in addition to the insurance, a savings plan. The accumulated savings in the permanent plan are referred to as the "cash surrender value" of the policy. Permanent insurance policies normally permit the policy owner, in the present case the firm, to borrow an amount equal to the cash surrender value of the policy at the next premium date discounted to the date of the borrowing at the interest rate charged the borrower.

Term insurance. Term insurance presents few accounting problems. The cash outlay is made at the beginning of the insurance period. If the insurance period covers parts of more than one accounting period, the expense must be allocated between the accounting periods on the basis of time covered by the insurance policy in each accounting period. If the insurance is acquired from a mutual insurance company, a dividend may be paid at the end of the policy year that reflects the underwriting and investment success of the insurance company during the particular year. If the insurance is acquired from a stock company, there is no dividend or refund at the end of the year, but the premium outlay is normally less.

The accounting problems presented here are two: (1) how to record the insurance expense when the policy is purchased from a mutual company, and (2) allocation of the net cost between accounting periods when the policy year does not coincide with the business year. The practical solution is to use the insurance company's estimate of the dividend to determine the net cost of the insurance. Any adjustment necessary because the actual dividend was not equal to the estimate can be reflected in the expense of the second period. The amount of the difference is likely to be so small as to be insignificant. The second problem is usually resolved by allocating the net outlay for the insurance coverage on the basis of the time for which coverage is provided in each accounting period.

Permanent insurance. Permanent insurance may be purchased from a stock company or a mutual company as in the case of term insurance. The treatment accorded the dividend, where applicable, should be the same as that followed for term insurance. There is the additional problem of accounting for the cash surrender value, which accumulates with most permanent life policies, whether issued by stock or mutual companies.

The cash surrender value is an asset to the firm. At the option of management, the policy may be canceled and an amount of cash equal to the cash surrender value of the policy may be obtained from the insurance company. This asset can also be used as collateral for borrowing from the insurance company. Cash surrender values increase at the end of each policy year.

In many cases both the dividends and the cash surrender values have been treated as reductions of premiums in the year following their accrual. Such a procedure results in insurance expense of the early years that is too high. Most insurance companies provide the buyer with a schedule of guaranteed cash surrender values and an estimate of dividends to be paid on the policy, assuming that the current year's experience is repeated each year. With such data, it seems quite possible to obtain substantially correct figures for each accounting period, with possible small adjustments being made when necessary because of variations in estimated and actual dividend payments.

This approach to the problem of accounting for a permanent plan of insurance purchase from a mutual company is illustrated with the following hypothetical data:

Year	Annual gross premium	Estimated dividend at end of year	Guaranteed cash value increase at end of year
1......	$3,000	$420	$ 100
2......	3,000	450	700
3......	3,000	475	2,500
4......	3,000	510	2,550
5......	3,000	530	2,600

Assume that the policy year is July 1 to June 30 and that the accounting period ends on December 31. The actual dividend experience is as estimated except for year 4, when the actual dividend paid at the end of year 4 is $525. Selected journal entries for years 19X1, 19X2, 19X4, and 19X5 are as follows:

7/1/X1	Prepaid Insurance	3,000	
	Cash		3,000
	To record payment of annual premium.		

12/31/X1	Insurance Expense	1,240	
	Cash Surrender Value	50	
	Prepaid Insurance		1,290
	To record insurance expense and accrual of CSV for the first 6 months including estimate of dividend to be received as a reduction of insurance expense.		

6/30/X2	Dividend Receivable	420	
	Insurance Expense	1,240	
	Cash Surrender Value	50	
	Prepaid Insurance		1,710
	To record insurance expense and accrual of CSV for second 6 months.		

7/1/X2	Prepaid Insurance	3,000	
	Cash		2,580
	Dividend Receivable		420

7/1/X4	Prepaid Insurance	3,000	
	Cash		2,525
	Dividend Receivable		475
	To record payment of fourth annual premium.		

12/31/X4	Cash Surrender Value	1,275	
	Prepaid Insurance		1,245
	Excess of Appreciation over Outlay on Insurance		30
	To record increase in cash surrender value and amortization of prepaid insurance account. Cash surrender value increases by more than premium expectation.		

6/30/X5	Dividend Receivable	525	
	Cash Surrender Value	1,275	
	Prepaid Insurance		1,755
	Excess of Appreciation over Outlay on Insurance		45
	To record increase in cash surrender value, amortization of prepaid insurance, and correction of estimated dividend.		

7/1/X5	Prepaid Insurance	3,000	
	Cash		2,475
	Dividend Receivable		525
	To record payment of fifth annual premium.		

The Excess of Appreciation over Outlay on Insurance account is a revenue or other income account and would be closed out each year in the same way as insurance expense.

If the insured should die during the time that the life insurance policy is in effect, the prepaid insurance balance, adjusted for short-term cancellation provisions and the cash surrender value accrued to date of death, would be converted into cash. The difference between the carrying value of these assets and the total cash collected would be credited to an account such as Proceeds from Life Insurance Policy.

FINANCIAL STATEMENT PRESENTATION

The accounting data accumulated relative to investments in securities and special-purpose cash funds must be reported in the three primary financial statements: (1) balance sheet, (2) income statement, and (3) statement of changes in financial position.

Balance Sheet. The balance sheet classification and presentation of securities can be subdivided into three parts: (1) marketable securities, (2) investments in affiliated companies, and (3) investments in special-purpose funds. Although many of the problems are common to each category, there are some unique areas of interest that will be viewed individually. There is the underlying assumption in accounting that all assets should be recorded at cost. Under certain conditions, loss of economic potential may be reflected in the accounts and the financial statements; however, increases in economic potential should not be reported until verified by transactions with disinterested parties. There is also the general prohibition against offset reasserted in APB Opinion No. 10 [1966, par. 7] that:

> It is a general principle of accounting that the offsetting of assets and liabilities in the balance sheet is improper except where a right of setoff exists. Accordingly, the offset of cash or other assets against the tax liability or other amounts owing to governmental bodies is not acceptable except ... when it is clear that a purchase of securities (acceptable for the payment of taxes) is in substance an advance payment of taxes that will be payable in the relatively near future, so that in the special circumstances the purchase is tantamount to the prepayment of taxes.

Marketable securities. Accountants generally agree that marketable securities are in fact merely an extension of the cash balance. In many cases the two amounts are combined and reported as cash and marketable securities. FASB Statement No. 12 [1975, p. 32.12] requires that the following information with respect to marketable equity securities be disclosed either in the body of the financial statements or in the accompanying notes:

> The aggregate cost and market value of each portfolio with clear identification of carrying amount

For each portfolio—the gross unrealized gains and gross unrealized losses of the marketable equity securities contained in the portfolio

The net realized gain or loss included in the determination of net income

The basis of cost determination used in computing the gain or loss (i.e., average or other method)

The change in valuation allowance included in the equity section and in determination of net income

Long-term investments. Long-term investments are generally described as holdings of securities that cannot be readily sold without impairing intercorporate relationships. These investments are typically classified as noncurrent assets; however, if the amount is small relative to other assets in the category, the investments may follow noncurrent assets in a category frequently labeled "other assets."

APB Opinion No. 18 includes disclosure requirements for investments that qualify for accounting treatment using the equity method. The required information may be disclosed parenthetically, in notes to financial statements, or in separate statements and schedules. The information that must be disclosed includes [APB, 1971, par. 20]:

1. The name of each investee and percentage of ownership of common stock.

2. The accounting policies of the investor with respect to investments in common stock.

3. The difference between the amount at which the investment is carried and the amount of underlying equity in net assets and the accounting treatment of the difference.

4. Where a quoted market price is available, the aggregate value of each identified investment should usually be disclosed.

5. When investments are in the aggregate material, summarized information about the assets, liabilities, and results of operations of the investees should be presented in the notes or separate statements either individually or in groups.

6. Material effect of possible conversions, exercises, or contingent issuances should be disclosed in notes to the financial statements of an investor.

Investments in special-purpose funds. Investments in special-purpose funds are reported along with investments in securities as noncurrent assets or as other assets following the noncurrent asset section. It is important to recognize that the rule pertaining to the offsetting of assets against liabilities applies to special-purpose funds and related obligations of the firm.

Income Statement. The items to be reported on the income statement in this category can be classified as (1) interest or dividend income, (2) share of earnings of unconsolidated subsidiary or affiliate companies, (3) gains and losses upon the sale of investments, and (4) unrealized holding gains and losses on the current asset portfolio of marketable securities. The trend in recent years has been to prepare a single-step income statement instead of the once more popular multistep statement. This means that interest and dividend income is now more often found included among the revenue items before any deductions. In multiple-step statements these items are normally included in a section of non-operating revenues and expenses.

The requirements for reporting deposits to special-purpose funds, the revenue earned, and the management expenses differ depending on the purposes for which the fund is established. If the fund is established to liquidate a recognized obligation of the firm, the annual deposit to the fund represents the increase in one asset and the decrease of another. No expense is recognized. The revenue earned and expenses of management must be reported in the same way that revenues derived from and expenses associated with security investments are reported. If the deposit is to a fund whose purpose is to pay claims against the assets of the fund and there is no recognized liability on the part of the firm, then the deposit itself is an expense that must be reported, for example, pension expenses. The revenues and expenses associated with the operation of these independent funds are not a part of the activities of the firm and should not be included in the financial reports of the firm.

Where the equity basis is used, the amount representing the owning firm's share of unconsolidated subsidiary and affiliate profits and losses is normally reported as a separate item of revenue. The APB, in Opinion No. 18 [1971, par. 19], states: "The investor's share of earnings or losses of investees should ordinarily be shown in the income statement as a single amount except for the extraordinary items ... which should be classified" as such on the investor's income statement. Of course, if the investment is carried on the equity basis, there is no dividend income to be reported.

The third item, gains and losses on the sale of investments, is the difference between the selling price and the carrying amount at the date of sale. This amount is shown as a determinant of net income rather than as an extraordinary item. Unrealized holding gains and losses are disclosed as described above.

Statement of Changes in Financial Position. The definition of funds assumed in this discussion is that of net working capital. The problem of reporting activities related to marketable securities and investments in this statement must be examined in terms of the particular format adopted for the statement itself (see Chapter 2). If we view net income as a source without enumeration of the components, then as far as revenues and expenses are concerned we need concern ourselves only with whether or not to modify the income figure. Of course, all interest and dividend revenue, whether derived from marketable securities or long-term investments, represents an inflow of funds. Although the excess of increases in cash surrender value over net insurance premium payments is not an inflow of funds in the normal use of the term, the cash paid for the premium is a use of funds. Similarly, the net revenue earned on cash deposited in a special-purpose fund is not a source of funds in the strict use of the term. The periodic deposit is, of course, a use of funds. In the case of permanent-plan insurance policies and special-purpose funds, if we report the total increase in the noncurrent asset as a use of funds, then the net revenue or expense reported in the income statement need not be eliminated in cases where net income is reported as a source of funds.

When the equity method is used to account for investments in common stock, the owning company's share of the affiliated company's net income is included in net income. This income does not produce working capital for the investor company, except to the extent that the affiliated company distributes dividends. The investor's share of the undistributed earnings of the affiliate appears on the balance sheet as an increase in the nonworking capital item, Investments in Affiliates. That increase in the carrying value of Investment in Affiliates should appear in the operating section of the statement of changes in financial position as a deduction from net income in arriving at funds from operations. If the affiliate suffers a loss, then the investor's portion of the loss that served to reduce the investor's net income must be added to net income in determining funds from operations.

The remaining problem, that of gains and losses resulting from the sale of securities, must be divided into two parts: (1) If the securities are classified as current assets and as such are a part of working capital, a gain or loss on the sale of a security represents an increase or decrease in working capital. (2) On the other hand, gains and losses may not be handled in the same way when they result from the sale of securities held as long-term investments. The total proceeds of the sale of long-term investments, not merely the gain, represent an increase in funds. Similarly, a loss does not mean a decrease in funds if the loss results from the sale of securities held as long-term investments. A loss in this case merely means that the proceeds were less than the carrying value by an amount equal to the reported loss. Net income included in the funds statement must therefore be adjusted to eliminate the gains and losses arising from the sale of long-term investments. The proceeds from such sales are included as sources of funds.

Finally, any funds used to expand the holding of securities as long-term investments must be reported as a use of funds. Of course, securities purchased as marketable securities are included in working capital; therefore, cash expended to acquire such securities is not reported in the statement of changes in financial position.

BIBLIOGRAPHY

Accounting Principles Board (AICPA), *Omnibus Opinion—1966*, Opinion No. 10 (APB, 1966).

———, *The Equity Method of Accounting for Investments in Common Stock*, Opinion No. 18 (APB, 1971).

———, *Accounting for Nonmonetary Transactions*, Opinion No. 29 (APB, 1973).

Beaver, W. H., "Reporting Rules for Marketable Equity Securities," *Journal of Accountancy*, October 1971, pp. 57–61.

———, "Accounting for Marketable Equity Securities," *Journal of Accountancy*, December 1973, pp. 58–64.

Coda, B. A., and W. J. Morris, "Valuation of Equity Securities," *Journal of Accountancy*, January 1973, pp. 48–54.

Committee on Accounting Procedure (AICPA), *Restatement and Revision of Accounting Research Bulletins*, Accounting Research Bulletin No. 43 (CAP, 1953).

Douglas, P. P., "Accounting for Equity Securities," *Journal of Accountancy*, November 1972, pp. 66–70.

Ernst & Whinney, "Accounting for Certain Marketable Securities," Retrieval No. 38408, Cleveland, 1976.

Financial Accounting Standards Board, *Accounting for Certain Marketable Securities*, Statement of Financial Accounting Standards No. 12 (FASB, 1975).

———, *Criteria for Applying the Equity Method of Accounting for Investments in Common Stock*, Interpretation No. 35 (FASB, 1981).

Hamre, J. C., and M. C. O'Connor, "Alternate Methods of Accounting for Long Term Non-Subsidiary Intercorporate Investments in Common Stock," *The Accounting Review*, January 1972, pp. 308-319.

Imdieke, L. F., and J. J. Weygandt, "Accounting for That Imputed Discount Factor," *Journal of Accountancy*, June 1970, pp. 54-58.

Kieso, D. E., and J. J. Weygandt, *Intermediate Accounting* (John Wiley & Sons, New York, 1980).

Loyd, B. M., and J. J. Weygandt, "Market Value Information for Non-Subsidiary Investments," *The Accounting Review*, October 1971, pp. 756-764.

McCullers, L. D., "An Alternative to APB Opinion No. 14," *Journal of Accounting Research*, Spring 1971, pp. 160-164.

Pacter, P., "Applying APB Opinion No. 18—Equity Method," *Journal of Accountancy*, September 1971, pp. 54-62.

Perlow, M. R., "Accounting Recognition of Holding Gains and Losses on Marketable Securities," *New York Certified Public Accountant* (CPA Journal), February 1969, pp. 95-100.

———, "Several Comments on APB No. 18: The Equity Method of Accounting for Investments in Common Stock," *CPA Journal*, October 1971, pp. 751-773.

———, "Statement on Auditing Procedure No. 51: Long Term Investments," *Journal of Accountancy*, September 1972, pp. 80-82.

Stephens, M. J., "Inseparability and the Valuation of Convertible Bonds," *Journal of Accountancy*, August 1971, pp. 54-62.

Weil, R. L., "Reciprocal or Mutual Holdings: Allocating Earnings and Selecting the Accounting Method," *The Accounting Review*, October 1973, pp. 749-758.

Welsch, G. A., C. T. Zlatkovich, and J. A. White, *Intermediate Accounting* (Richard D. Irwin, Homewood, Ill., 1972), p. 239.

CHAPTER 15

Receivables

Ronald J. Huefner
**Professor of Accounting, State University of
New York at Buffalo**

INTRODUCTION

Definition. *Receivables* are claims of various types held by an entity for the future receipt of cash, goods, or services. Most commonly, receivables are claims for the receipt of cash, which arise from normal trade or other types of transactions.

Transactions giving rise to receivables, and the descriptive titles commonly employed, are as follows:

1. Sale of goods or services to customers (Trade Accounts Receivable; Trade Notes Receivable, if a written promise to pay exists; Installment Receivables, if payments are to be made over several periods of time)

2. Loans made to individuals or other entities (Loans Receivable; Notes Receivable; Advances to Subsidiaries; Advances to Employees; Officer and Employee Receivables; etc.)

3. Leasing property to others (Lease Contracts Receivable)

4. Other revenue transactions (Interest Receivable; Dividends Receivable; Rent Receivable; Commissions Receivable; etc.)

5. Deposits of various kinds, to guarantee performance or payment (Deposits Receivable; Utility Deposits; Contract Retainages; etc.)

6. Claims in insurance, tax, litigation, and other proceedings (Claims Receivable; Tax Refund Receivable; Damage Claims Receivable; etc.)

7. Subscriptions from investors for the purchase of stock (Stock Subscriptions Receivable).

In addition to these fairly general types of transactions, specialized transactions may exist for a particular entity giving rise to differently titled receivable accounts (e.g., Franchise Fees Receivable of a franchisor, or Taxes Receivable of a municipality). The accounting, financial reporting, and control of most of these specialized receivables, however, does not differ from the general types listed above.

Significance of Receivables. The majority of the revenue of almost every business entity results from the credit sale of goods and services to customers. In recent years, while investment in inventory has often decreased due to advances in control systems, investment in receivables has often increased as a result of expansion of credit. Thus, receivables are likely to be a significant asset for many business entities. In addition, because the use of accrual accounting by government and nonprofit organizations has increased, receivables are an important asset for many of these entities.

As is the case with most areas of accounting, the important questions concerning receivables center around recognition, measurement, disclosure, and information required for management uses. The chapter is structured around these topics.

ACCOUNTING FOR RECEIVABLES

Trade Accounts Receivable. Trade accounts receivable arise in the course of sales of goods and services to customers. Records of open-account sales provide the evidence underlying these claims; written instruments (such as notes) do not exist for these receivables.

Recognition. The recognition of trade accounts receivable involves the accounting issues of timing (when shall the receivable be recognized?) and measurement (how much shall initially be recorded?).

The timing of recognition is linked to the question of the recognition of revenue. Various bases for the recognition of revenue are discussed in Chapter 11, and thus will not be extensively discussed here. We shall summarize the effect of the different recognition bases on the timing and nature of receivable recognition.

Revenue is most commonly recognized under the *sales (or delivery) basis*. Under this procedure, accounts receivable are recognized at the time of the exchange of goods or services between seller and buyer. This timing corresponds to the creation of a legal claim for payment from the buyer. The recognition of the receivable occurs simultaneously with the recognition of revenue.

Revenue may be recognized under the *production (or percentage-of-completion) basis*. This method may be appropriate when goods or services are being supplied under a firm contract, such as in the case of long-term construction. Because revenue recognition may occur prior to billing and delivery, no simultaneous claim for payment need be created. The parties to the transaction may, of course, have agreed that payments will occur at various times during production. Nevertheless, the recognition of revenue gives rise to an entry to an asset account such as "Finished Product—At Contract Price" or "Unbilled Construction in Progress—At Contract Price." Because delivery has not yet occurred, title to the goods involved continues to rest with the seller. Hence the accounts debited are in the nature of inventory accounts rather than receivables. Only when delivery of the finished product occurs (or when percentage-of-completion billings are made pursuant to contractual agreement) is a receivable (i.e., a legal claim for payment) created. Thus, under the production basis for revenue recognition, the recognition of the legal account receivable often occurs *after* the recognition of revenue.

When progress billings are made, under either the sales or production basis, recognition of a receivable may precede the recognition of revenue. An asset account, such as Work in Progress, or a liability account, such as Customer Advances, is credited.

A third possibility for the recognition of revenue is the *collection (or cash) basis*. Under this approach, revenue is recognized only when cash is actually collected, either in a single payment or in several payments (installments). This method is appropriate only under the special circumstance when, at the time of sale, collectibility is highly uncertain. Under simple cash basis accounting, no recognition of accounts receivable ever occurs. The exchange of goods or services, and the resulting claim for payment, remain unrecorded until payment occurs. Such accounting most frequently occurs in connection with the sale of services, where the complication of the timing of recognizing an inventory change is not present. Under installment basis accounting, however, recognition of the receivable occurs at time of sale, with a corresponding credit to inventory and to deferred gross margin. Formal recognition of the sale is necessary so that the inventory decrease can also be recorded. As collections occur, appropriate amounts of revenue or income are recognized. More extensive discussion of installment receivables is presented in a subsequent section. Thus, under the collection basis, the recognition of accounts receivable may occur prior to the recognition of revenue, or may not occur at all.

Measurement of receivables. Under most circumstances, the *amount* to be recognized is the exchange price between the parties to the transaction. Two factors may complicate the measurement of this exchange price: the availability of discounts, and the intervening length of time between sale and due date of payment.

The problem of discounts centers around those offered for prompt payment. Other types of discounts, such as trade discounts or quantity discounts, are commonly viewed as factors in the determination of the true selling price. Thus, revenues and receivables are recorded net of these amounts. Prompt-payment discounts (commonly called cash discounts), however, are subject to alternative interpretations.

One interpretation (the "gross price method") views the amount before discount as the true selling price, and therefore the amount of the receivable to be recognized. Any discounts subsequently earned by customers are treated as adjustments to gross sales revenue (or as an expense). Because the recognition of the discount occurs at time of payment, the receivable is unaffected. The only exception is at the end of the reporting period, when potential discounts may be considered in the valuation of outstanding accounts. This topic is discussed in the following section.

The alternative interpretation (the "net price method") views the amount net of discount as the correct measure of the selling price and thereby of the receivable. Additional amounts received from customers whose discount period has lapsed are treated as additional revenue, and are normally recorded when received. Again, at the end of the reporting period the valuation of the outstanding receivables may be adjusted to reflect the increase due to lapsed discounts.

The net price method would appear to have greater theoretical support. Revenues and receivables should be recorded at present value—the cash equivalent amount at the time the sale occurs. Certainly, in the case of sales subject to a cash discount, this amount is the net price. Any additional amount received is properly viewed as a financing charge—an amount earned for extending credit—rather than a payment for the goods or services transferred. Moreover, treatment under the net price method is consistent with the treatment of a sale where no cash discount is allowed but a specific interest charge is made for late payment.

A second issue in determining the amount to be recognized involves the intervening length of time between the creation of the receivable and the due date of payment. Ideally, interest should be recognized in determining the amount of the receivable to be recorded (its "present value"). If the terms of payment include specification of interest at a reasonable rate, then the face amount of the receivable should be recorded. If no provision for interest is included in the terms of payment, then the payments ideally should be discounted to a present value which should be recorded. As a practical matter for trade accounts receivable, the question of interest is usually disregarded unless the due date is quite far removed from the date of sale—say, a year or more. The question of the recognition of interest arises more frequently in the context of notes receivable. Thus, this topic, and the associated APB Opinion No. 21, will be discussed at length in the "Notes Receivable" section of this chapter.

Valuation. After the original transaction has been recognized and recorded, the question of valuation of trade accounts receivable arises in connection with their presentation on a statement of financial position (balance sheet). Adjustments to the initially recorded amount may be appropriate to reflect accumulation of interest, or estimated allowances for future discounts, returns, and uncollectible accounts.

If the terms of sale specify interest charges when payment is not made by a given due date, any accumulation of interest should be recognized in arriving at the financial statement figures. Such interest may be considered as an increase in the trade accounts receivable balance or, if material, should be separately classified as interest receivable. If the receivable had initially been recorded at a discounted present value, the accumulation of interest must be recognized in determining the balance at the financial statement date. This procedure will be discussed more fully in the section on "Notes Receivable."

End-of-period valuation for estimated cash discounts depends on the manner of original recording. Under the gross price method, discounts available to customers as of the reporting date may be recognized if the amount is material. An "allowance for outstanding discounts" is created to reduce the receivables balance to an expected realizable value basis (with a corresponding offset to sales revenue). Under the net price method, on the other hand, the receivables balance must be increased by the amount of any discounts that have lapsed. The principle of valuing receivables at expected realizable value also dictates that allowance be made for expected returns, price adjustments, or other allowances against the recorded amount due. An "allowance for expected returns and allowances" would be recognized, with a corresponding offset to sales revenue. Such "allowances" are contra-accounts to the receivable to which they relate.

The major problem in arriving at expected realizable value, however, lies in the determination of the allowance for uncollectible accounts (or "bad debts"). There are two general approaches to the treatment of uncollectible accounts— the "direct write-off" method and the "allowance" method.

The direct write-off method in effect ignores the need to reflect the possibility of uncollectibility in the valuation of accounts receivable. Under this approach, no recognition of uncollectibility occurs until a specific account is found to be uncollectible, and that account is then written off. Thus, accounts receivable are presented at full face value on the balance sheet, and the income statement reflects the loss on accounts actually written off during the period. The direct write-off approach lacks authoritative support as a means of accounting for uncollectibles. It is likely to produce overvalued asset figures, by presenting the face value, rather than the expected realizable value, of accounts receivable. Also, this method is inconsistent with the accrual basis of income measurement, in that the uncollectibility adjustment is not matched with the period in which the revenues originated.

The preferred method of accounting for uncollectibles is the allowance method. Under this approach, an estimate of future uncollectibles is made each period, under one of several possible computational procedures. The estimate may be based on (1) a percentage of credit sales for the period, (2) a percentage of accounts receivable outstanding at the end of the period, (3) different percentages applied to each of several age categories of accounts receivable outstanding at the end of the period, or (4) probability-of-collection analysis of individual accounts or groups of accounts.

If the estimate is based on a percentage of credit sales, that percentage times the credit sales for the period results in the amount to be debited to the provision for uncollectible accounts (the revenue contra, sometimes treated as an expense) for the period. The percentage to be used is normally based on the company's past loss experience. This implicitly assumes that economic conditions and the company's credit and collection policies have not changed over time. If this assumption is not valid, the percentages used may be modified on a subjective basis, although such modification may be difficult to justify to auditors or tax examiners. If the ratio of credit sales to total sales is relatively constant, a percentage of total sales may be used to estimate the provision for uncollectibles. This approach offers some convenience, as the total sales figure may be more readily available than the credit sales figure.

If the estimate is based on outstanding accounts receivable (whether determined by percentage or specific analysis), the entry results in the required credit balance in the allowance for uncollectible accounts (balance sheet figure). Again, consideration must be given to the assumptions that underlie any relationships based on past experience.

Although approaches based on sales and on outstanding accounts receivable are both widely used, the latter seem preferable. The outstanding accounts approach is based on balances actually outstanding at year-end, and thus uses the latest data available. The percentage-of-sales approach, on the other hand, is based on sales for the entire period, with little if any regard for actual collections. Advocates of this approach argue that a better matching of costs and revenues is obtained. The percentage-of-sales approach, however, does not provide a clear mechanism for correcting past misestimates. The outstanding accounts approach corrects past estimates in arriving at the expense for the current year.

For illustrations of the calculation of the allowance for uncollectibles under the various approaches cited above, see any intermediate accounting textbook [e.g., Davidson et al., 1982, chap. 7].

Disposition. The normal disposition of trade accounts receivable is via *collection*. Accounts receivable are credited for the amount previously recorded as a receivable. The recorded amount may differ from the amount received as a result of discounts taken, late charges, returns, and so forth. Such differences are charged or credited to appropriate accounts. If collection is in the form of a banker's acceptance (a deferred but guaranteed payment),[1] accounts receiv-

---

[1] For additional discussion of bankers' acceptances as related to accounts receivable, see Folson [1977].

able should be credited and bankers' acceptances (or a similar account) debited to show the receipt of this new asset.

Disposition of accounts receivable balances may also be achieved by *write-off* of uncollectible accounts. If an allowance method is used, the charge is made against the allowance for uncollectible accounts. If a collection is made on an account that has previously been written off, the account should be reestablished in the amount of the collection (possibly in the entire amount written off, if collection in full can now be expected). The entries to debit the customer's account and to reflect the subsequent collection are made to show that the customer has attempted to reestablish creditworthiness by the payment. When the customer's account is debited, the credit is normally made to the allowance account. If recoveries are unusually large, a separate "other revenue" account (Bad Debts Recovered) may be used.

Finally, receivables may be disposed of by sale to third parties, commonly known as *factoring*. The accounting procedure is the same as in the case of collection, except that disclosure may be required for any contingent liability to the purchaser. This topic is discussed further in later sections.

Notes Receivable. Notes receivable may arise in the course of sales of goods and services to customers (trade notes receivable), or in the course of other transactions, such as loans (to employees, subsidiaries, etc.) or sales of fixed assets. They are evidenced by formal, written instruments, and typically have a longer maturity than accounts receivable.

Under the Uniform Commercial Code, "a negotiable promissory note is an unconditional promise in writing made by one person to another, signed by the maker, engaging to pay on demand, or at a particular time, a sum certain in money to order or to bearer."

Recognition. As in the case of trade accounts receivable, the recognition of notes receivable involves the issues of timing and measurement.

Trade notes receivable may arise directly from a sales transaction, or from the conversion of existing accounts receivable. Nontrade notes may arise from cash loans, nontrade sales, or settlements of indebtedness. In all cases, recognition occurs as of the date of execution of the note.

The amount to be recognized is subject to several factors, as specified by APB Opinion No. 21 [1971]. Depending on the circumstances, a note may be recorded at its face value, or at the fair value of the goods or services exchanged, or at a discounted present value.

APB Opinion No. 21 is applicable in general to receivables that represent a contractual right to receive money on fixed or determinable dates, whether or not a stated provision for interest exists. Although such receivables are loosely referred to as "notes," accounts receivable and other forms of receivables may also fall under the definition. The Opinion specifically excludes from its provisions the following six categories of receivables:

1. Receivables arising from transactions with customers in the normal course of business that are due in customary trade terms not exceeding approximately 1 year

2. Receivables that will not result in future cash collections, but rather will be applied to the purchase price of property, goods, or services (e.g., advance payments for materials)

3. Receivables intended to provide security for one party to an agreement (e.g., retainages on contracts, or security deposits)

4. Receivables arising from the cash lending activities of financial institutions whose primary business is lending money

5. Receivables arising from transactions where interest rates are affected by tax attributes or legal restrictions prescribed by a governmental agency (e.g., income tax settlements, or government-guaranteed obligations)

6. Receivables arising from transactions between parent and subsidiary companies, or between subsidiaries of a common parent

In these cases, the face amount of the note normally serves as the amount to be recognized. In other cases, the "present value" of the note should be used as the basis for recognition.

A note received solely in exchange for cash is presumed to have a present value (at time of issue) equal to the amount of cash exchanged. If, however, other "rights or privileges" are involved in the transaction, these must be recognized. In such a case, the effective rate of interest on the note, which may differ from the stated rate, is used to determine the present value of the note. The difference between the present value so determined and the cash exchanged would be recorded as a premium or discount. For example, a professional athlete may negotiate a contract that includes a 5-year interest-free loan. The present value of this loan should be determined by appropriate discounting, and the resulting premium (cash exchanged less present value) considered as part of the deferred compensation of the athlete over the term of the contract.

In the case of a note received in exchange for property, goods, or services, arising out of a bargained, arms'-length transaction, it is generally presumed that the interest rate specified by the parties to the transaction represents fair and adequate compensation for the use of funds. The economic substance of the transaction, however, must be considered. Under APB Opinion No. 21, the presumption that the stated interest rate is satisfactory as a basis for recording the transaction should be rejected if (1) no interest rate is specified, (2) the stated interest rate is unreasonably high or low, (3) the face amount of the note is materially different from the market value of the note (at the date of the transaction), or (4) the face amount of the note is materially different from the current cash sales price of the property, goods, or services. In any of these circumstances, it is inappropriate to use the face amount of the note as its present value and hence as the basis for recording the transaction. Rather, the present value of the note should be viewed as either (1) the fair market value of the property, goods, or services exchanged for the note, or (2) the fair market value of the note, whichever is more determinable.

In the case of notes that do not specify a rate of interest, or that specify an unreasonable rate, it is possible that established exchange prices for the property, goods, or services, and also evidence of the note's market value, may both be lacking. In such a circumstance, the present value of the note is to be determined by discounting its future cash flow at an appropriate rate of interest. According to APB Opinion No. 21 [1971, par. 13], in selecting a rate

> ... the objective is to approximate the rate which would have resulted if an independent borrower and an independent lender had negotiated a similar transaction under comparable terms and conditions with the option to pay the cash price upon purchase or to give a note for the amount of the purchase which bears the prevailing rates of interest to maturity.

In summary, the amount to be recognized in recording a note receivable may be its face value, its market value, the fair value of the property, goods, or services exchanged, or the discounted value of its future cash flows. Whichever of these amounts represents the note's "present value," in light of the facts of the case and the rules of APB Opinion No. 21, serves as the basis for recording the note.

Valuation. Following the initial recognition, the main concern in ongoing valuation of the note centers around the amortization of any premium or discount. In any case where the present value of the note (the amount originally recorded) differs from the face value, a premium or discount is created, which must be amortized over the life of the note.

Present value amortization (also known as the effective interest method) is generally regarded as preferable to straight-line amortization, although the latter may be used if it does not have a materially different effect. Under present value amortization, the note continues to be valued at present value using the interest rate in effect at the date the note was received. For example, assume that a company receives a "non-interest-bearing" note with face value of $100,000 and maturity of 5 years. Assume further that, under the provisions of APB Opinion No. 21, the note is discounted to a present value using an interest rate of 10 percent. This yields a present value (and the amount initially recorded for the note) of $62,092. The resulting discount of $37,908 is to be recognized as interest revenue over the 5-year period. Straight-line amortization would result in the recognition of $7,581.60 each year. Present value amortization results in increasing amounts recognized each year, as the present value

---

EXHIBIT 1 Amortization of "Non-Interest-Bearing" Note with $100,000 Face Value over 5 Years with Interest at 10%

Transaction date	Amortization of discount (and interest revenue)	Note balance (present value)
End of year 0		$ 62,092
1	$ 6,209	68,301
2	6,830	75,131
3	7,513	82,644
4	8,264	90,908
5	9,092 (rounded)	100,000
	$37,908	

of the note increases. Each year, 10 percent of the beginning-of-year present value is recognized as revenue, as shown in Exhibit 1.

In cases where periodic interest payments exist, but the present value of the note differs from its face value (i.e., the discount rate differs from the nominal interest rate), a similar process is used to amortize any premium or discount. For example, suppose that the note in the above illustration bore interest at 3 percent per annum, but again 10 percent was considered an appropriate rate for the determination of present value. The present value of this note (see Tables 2 and 4 in the Appendix) would be as follows:

Face value times present value of $1 for 5 years at 10% ($100,000 × .62092)	$62,092
Annual interest payment times present value of annuity of $1 for 5 years at 10% ($3,000 × 3.79079)	11,372
Present value of note	$73,464

The discount of $26,536 would be amortized as shown in Exhibit 2.

Other aspects of valuation discussed under trade accounts receivable are normally not applicable to notes receivable. For example, an allowance for uncollectibles is typically not determined unless a substantial number of trade notes exist.

Income tax aspects. The requirements of APB Opinion No. 21 may create a timing difference between book income and taxable income. Section 483 of the Internal Revenue Code requires that interest be imputed in certain deferred-payment situations. The rules apply only to sales eligible for capital gain treatment, where the selling price is $3,000 or more, and payments extend beyond 1 year. If the note fails to provide for interest of at least 9 percent per year (simple interest), then interest is to be imputed at a rate of 10 percent, compounded semiannually (these rates are subject to change from time to time). APB Opinion No. 21, on the other hand, would require use of a rate reflecting borrowing-lending conditions, which may be well above 10 percent.

Thus, if the note provides a face interest rate that is less than an appropriate rate, interest for financial reporting purposes might be imputed at, say, 18 per-

---

EXHIBIT 2   Amortization Schedule for 5-Year Note with Stated Interest at 3%; Effective Interest Is 10%

Transaction date	Interest earned	Interest collected	Amortization of discount	Note balance (present value)
End of year 0				$ 73,464
1	$ 7,346	$ 3,000	$ 4,346	77,810
2	7,781	3,000	4,781	82,591
3	8,259	3,000	5,259	87,850
4	8,785	3,000	5,785	93,635
5	9,365	3,000	6,365	100,000
	$41,536	$15,000	$26,536	

cent, whereas interest for tax purposes would be imputed at 10 percent. This would create timing differences in the recognition of the gain on the transaction and the periodic recognition of interest. The timing difference is a complex one, in that an initial lower book sales revenue or gain is offset by subsequent higher book interest revenue. Initially there would be a deferred tax debit, which would be reduced at every interest-recognition date.

A timing difference may also be created if the face interest rate is greater than an appropriate rate. APB Opinion No. 21 would require that the appropriate rate be used, whereas tax law would require the face rate. Again, a timing difference involving gain and periodic interest would be created. For extensive illustration of the calculation of, and accounting for, deferred taxes under these conditions, see papers by Wharton [1972] and Pacter [1972].

Disposition. Disposition of a note may take the form of collection, write-off, or sale. Collection and write-off are accounted for in the same manner as accounts receivable. Any unamortized premium or discount should be taken into income in the year of disposition.

Sale of a note may occur with or without recourse in the event of nonpayment. A sale without recourse may be accounted for as a collection. The difference between the face value of the note and the proceeds from its sale is often debited to collection expense. A sale with recourse may be accounted for by leaving the Notes Receivable account unaffected, and crediting an offsetting account, Notes Receivable Discounted. When settlement of the note has been completed, both the Notes Receivable and Notes Receivable Discounted balances would be eliminated. If the note is dishonored, the seller's entry for reimbursement of the buyer will eliminate the Notes Receivable Discounted account. The Notes Receivable balance remains. In view of the dishonoring of the note, however, the balance is often reclassified to Accounts Receivable, frequently with a notation that the amount is past due. For illustrative entries relating to the discounting of notes, see any intermediate accounting textbook.

Installment Receivables. An installment sale is characterized by periodic payments over a designated period of time. Such sales occur frequently in retail transactions, as well as in the sale of equipment and land. Typically, the transaction will involve a down payment, with the balance due in equal amounts.

Accounting for installment receivables. In dealing with installment receivables, we may distinguish two methods of revenue recognition: the usual accrual basis, and the installment (i.e., cash collection) basis. APB Opinion No. 10 [1966, par. 12] states:

> Chapter 1A of ARB No. 43, paragraph 1, states that "Profit is deemed to be realized when a sale in the ordinary course of business is effected, unless the circumstances are such that the collection of the sale price is not reasonably assured." The Board reaffirms this statement; it believes that revenues should ordinarily be accounted for at the time a transaction is completed, with appropriate provision for uncollectible accounts. Accordingly, it concludes that, in the absence of the circumstances referred to above, the installment method of recognizing revenue is not acceptable.

A footnote to this paragraph adds the following [APB Opinion No. 10, 1966, par. 12, fn. 8]:

The Board recognizes that there are exceptional cases where receivables are collectible over an extended period of time and, because of the terms of the transactions or other conditions, there is no reasonable basis for estimating the degree of collectibility. When such circumstances exist, and as long as they exist, either the installment method or the cost recovery method of accounting may be used.

Thus, under most circumstances, revenue on installment sales will be recognized at the time of sale. The resulting receivables will be treated in the same manner as trade accounts receivable, described above. Installment receivables arising from sales in the normal course of operations are usually classified as current assets, on the ground that the collection period constitutes an operating cycle. Installment receivables arising from nonoperating sales (such as the sale of a fixed asset) should be classified as current only to the extent of payments due within 1 year.

With respect to the treatment of interest charges, usual practice is to record the receivable at selling price, and recognize interest as earned. If the receivable is recorded at gross (selling price plus total finance charges), the unearned charges should be shown as a contra-account, analogous to the discount on notes receivable.

Installment sales properly accountable for by the installment method of revenue recognition involve somewhat different accounting. The receivable is recorded at time of sale, inventory is reduced, and gross margin on the transaction is determined. The gross margin (gross profit) is initially recorded as a contra to the receivable or as a deferred credit ("Deferred Gross Profit"), and then is taken into income proportionately as cash is received. The receivable, however, is accounted for in similar fashion as in the case of accrual recognition described above. Further discussion may be found in Chapter 11.

Income tax aspects. In spite of its general nonacceptability for accounting and financial reporting purposes, the installment method is acceptable for tax purposes. Firms that regularly make installment sales may elect to recognize gross profit proportionately as cash is received for tax purposes. This same treatment is also widely available for gains from the installment sale of fixed assets. Because the present value of tax payments is reduced by such an election, it is a sound management policy to elect the use of the installment method for tax purposes in almost all cases where it is available.

Use of the installment method for tax purposes and the accrual method for financial reporting purposes creates a timing difference, and thus requires the use of interperiod tax allocation.

Foreign Receivables. Transactions with foreign customers present the additional problem of currency translation. Chapter 35 presents a comprehensive coverage of this topic. Thus, our coverage here is limited to a brief summary.

Sales to a foreign customer will specify payment either in domestic currency or foreign currency. If domestic currency is specified, the seller faces no different accounting and reporting problems than in the case of sales to domestic customers. If payment is to be in foreign currency, the seller must initially record the receivable by translating the foreign currency into dollars at the appropriate exchange rate. Both "free" and "official" exchange rates may exist;

the one that is expected to be applicable to the settlement of the account should be used.

The exchange rate may change between the time of recording the receivable and the time of collection. On accounts due in foreign currency, this means that a "currency exchange gain or loss" will occur, as the seller receives a greater or lesser amount of domestic currency upon settlement. Normally, the currency exchange gain or loss is recognized at time of collection. However, at the end of the reporting period, outstanding receivables balances (due in foreign currency) should be expressed in terms of the current exchange rate, thereby recognizing any gain or loss at that date.

The seller may hedge against exchange rate fluctuations by simultaneously entering into a currency futures contract. Suppose that on January 10, goods are sold to a foreign customer with payment due in foreign currency in 90 days. The seller could also enter into a contract for the future sale (in 90 days) of the amount of foreign currency involved. The seller would thereby be guaranteed the present (January 10) exchange rate (less transaction costs). The seller, after receiving payment 90 days later, would deliver the foreign currency to satisfy the futures contract, and would be unaffected by any change that might have occurred in the exchange rate.

Further considerations involving foreign receivables, including dealings with foreign branches and subsidiaries, may be found in Chapter 35.

Lease Receivables. Brief mention may be given to the receivables arising under the lease transactions of a lessor. More extensive discussion of accounting for leases is found in Chapter 24.

Statement of Financial Accounting Standards No. 13 specifies the conditions under which leases are classified as operating, direct financing, or sales-type leases. For operating leases, the lessor recognizes rental revenue and, hence, records receivables only as payments accrue.

For direct financing leases, the receivable (usually referred to as the "net investment in the lease") is the difference between the gross investment (minimum lease payments plus residual value) and unearned income. Unearned income is initially defined as the gross investment minus the cost of the leased property; it is generally amortized by the effective interest method, as described earlier for notes receivable.

For sales-type leases, made by a manufacturer of, or dealer in, the property leased, the receivable is generally recorded at the present value of the lease payments (including residual value), and accounted for in a similar manner as long-term notes receivable. Complex provisions exist to deal with the many variations in lease terms; these are discussed in Chapter 24.

FINANCIAL REPORTING

Statement Presentation. Receivables are classified on the balance sheet according to current and noncurrent categories (discussed below), and according to the major types of receivables. Typical items that, if material in amount, would be separately disclosed are

Trade Accounts Receivable
Notes Receivable
Installment Notes and Accounts Receivable
Claims for Income Tax Refunds
Due from Officers and Employees

The order of presentation above is based on ranking in decreasing order of liquidity. The specific terms used are likely to vary, because each firm chooses titles descriptive of the particular types of receivables it holds.

Current versus Noncurrent. Reported receivables are classified as current if collection is reasonably expected within 1 year, or within the firm's normal operating cycle (if longer than 1 year).

Use of the normal operating cycle criterion is most common in the case of installment receivables. If a firm is engaged in a business where it is common practice to sell on an installment basis covering more than 1 year, classification of installment receivables as current assets would be appropriate. However, any significant amounts maturing beyond 1 year from the date of the statement should be disclosed. Such disclosure might take the following form:

Installment notes (including installments of
$300,000 due after 1 year) $800,000

Receivables from unconsolidated affiliates may be classified as current if it is the practice of the affiliate to liquidate the accounts periodically, or if there is reasonable assurance that they can be liquidated at an early date. If these conditions are not met, and the receivables are in effect long-term or permanent advances, they should be classified as noncurrent. Receivables from consolidated subsidiaries are eliminated in consolidation.

Allowances. In reporting notes and accounts receivable, the allowance for uncollectible accounts must also be shown. APB Opinion No. 12 requires that all valuation allowances for losses on receivables be deducted from the assets to which they relate, and be appropriately disclosed. Typical presentation takes the following form:

Trade notes and accounts receivable (less
allowance for doubtful accounts of $20,000) $370,000

In addition to the allowance for uncollectible accounts, other allowances reducing the reported valuation of receivables may exist. APB Opinion No. 6 states that unearned discounts (other than cash or quantity discounts), finance charges, and interest included in the face amount of receivables should be deducted from the assets to which they relate. Presentation might be as follows:

Installment notes receivable (less unearned
finance charges of $100,000) $620,000

Similarly, APB Opinion No. 21 requires that the discount (or premium) resulting from the determination of the present value of a receivable be reported as a deduction from (or addition to) the face amount of the receivable. Typical presentation would be (in the case of noncurrent receivables):

> Long-term receivables (less unamortized discount
> based on imputed interest rate of 9.5%,
> $1,740,000) $13,360,000

As suggested by the above illustrations, allowances for finance charges, unamortized discount, and the like are most prevalent in the case of longer-term receivables.

Financed Receivables. Various methods of financing may be used in conjunction with receivables, as discussed later in this chapter. Presentation on the statement of financial position depends on the nature of the financing.

Financing via receivables may be direct (the outright sale of receivables) or indirect (using receivables as security for a loan), with additional possibilities between these two extremes. If receivables are sold, they are eliminated as an asset, and any gain or loss upon disposition is recognized. If receivables are merely pledged, they continue to be treated in the normal manner for accounting purposes, with the addition of disclosure of the pledging in financial statements.

Four alternatives for the reporting of financed receivables are described next [Schaps, 1966].

1. If receivables are sold outright, or assumed without recourse, the buyer assumes the entire risk of collection. These receivables should be eliminated from the statement (because they have in essence been collected).

2. If receivables are sold to a third party with recourse (a guarantee of repurchase in the event of uncollectibility), the receivables again should be eliminated by virtue of collection. However, a contingent liability (to repurchase) remains, which must be disclosed in a footnote. A typical note would read:

> The Company is contingently liable on approximately $1,500,000 of long-term installment notes sold with recourse.

3. If receivables are retained, but rights to the collections are assigned with recourse, statement presentation may show gross receivables, less a deduction for the amount assigned, as follows:

> Notes receivable $450,000
> Less: Notes receivable
>   discounted 300,000 $150,000

More often, footnote disclosure is used to indicate the existence and amount of contingent liability. If a profit results, because the amount received from the third party exceeds the book value of the receivables (because of interest rate differentials), this profit should be recognized over the usual term of the receivables, rather than recognized immediately.

4. If receivables are pledged as security for indebtedness, the statement should show this fact parenthetically, with footnote disclosure of the amount pledged and the details of the indebtedness. For example:

Receivables in the amount of $7,000,000 have been pledged in connection with the bank loan described in Note 5.

MANAGEMENT OF RECEIVABLES

Credit management is an important element of the overall financial and marketing management of the firm. An important function of credit management is to achieve a proper balance between increasing the firm's credit sales and limiting its losses from uncollectible accounts. At one extreme, a company could minimize its uncollectibles by making credit sales only to the most creditworthy firms, but in so doing, it would restrict the size of its potential market or incur large screening costs. At the other extreme, a company could maximize its sales by granting credit to all who request it. In following this course of action, the company would be likely to incur substantial collection costs and losses from uncollectible accounts. An appropriate balance must be achieved between the costs of granting credit and the potential profits foregone by restricting sales.

Efficient credit management benefits the firm in several ways [The Conference Board, 1972, pp. 4–5]:

1. Protection of corporate liquidity. Failure to collect most receivables when due can cause a rapid deterioration in a firm's cash position. Thus, the credit manager must grant credit and achieve collections so as to maintain a regular flow of cash into the firm, thereby minimizing the need for costly short-term financing.

2. Safeguarding the investment in receivables. According to government data, receivables average about 18 percent of the total assets of manufacturing firms. The substantial investment becomes one of high risk, with significant potential for loss, if the receivables include many poor-quality accounts. Efficient credit management will reduce the riskiness of this investment by the initial selection of only good quality accounts, and the pursuit of aggressive collection procedures.

3. Profit enhancement. Efficient credit management contributes to the firm's profitability by achieving a balance between the costs of extending credit and the gains from expanding sales.

4. Sales assistance. The credit manager complements the efforts of the sales force by assisting in negotiating the financial arrangements of a sale, particularly in cases where special financing is required.

Management Policy. Credit management involves decisions concerning the extension of credit to customers, protection of the investment in receivables, achievement of timely collections, and maintenance of records. To accomplish these tasks, management establishes credit policies. Such policies involve the duties and responsibilities of the credit manager, general guidelines as to credit terms, collection and write-off procedures, and so forth. The policies are usually specified in writing as part of the company's internal control procedures.

Decision Analysis. Several components of credit policy are conducive to economic decision analysis, and thus fall within the broad area of management accounting. Numerous studies in this area have appeared in the literature of accounting and related fields. This section will survey some of the findings of this research.

Extending credit. The decision to extend credit to customers involves consideration of the profit to be gained from the sale against the costs of granting credit (time value of money, collection costs, and risk of loss). Numerous models for this decision have been suggested. One, by Soldofsky [1966], requires that the profit from the sale exceed the sum of (1) the cost not recovered because of uncollectible accounts, (2) the cost of financing, and (3) credit costs (such as investigation, billing, and collection). When expressed quantitatively and simplified, the following model results. Sell if:

$$M - \left(b + Ti + \frac{C}{S}\right) \geq 0$$

where M = profit margin expressed as a fraction
    b = probability that a credit sale will become uncollectible
    T = average time that the accounts are outstanding before collection or write-off
    i = interest rate
    C = credit costs per order
    S = order size

It is further suggested that different risk categories be created for credit sales. Some of the above variables (namely, b, T, C, and S) may take on different values in different risk classes.

To illustrate, suppose that a company's profit margin is 20 percent, and that a 12 percent interest rate is applicable. For simplicity, assume that no cash discounts are offered. Four risk classes of customers are established, and the following estimates made:

Risk cláss	b (%)	T	C	S
1	1	25/365	$15	$2,000
2	3	35/365	35	1,500
3	6	50/365	60	1,000
4	10	80/365	70	500

Calculating the relationship presented above, we have

Risk class	$M - (b + Ti + C/S) \geq 0$
1	.20 − (.01 + .008 + .008) = +0.174
2	.20 − (.03 + .012 + .023) = +0.135
3	.20 − (.06 + .016 + .060) = +0.064
4	.20 − (.10 + .026 + .140) = −0.066

The analysis suggests that sales should be made (i.e., credit extended) to risk classes 1, 2, and 3, but that credit should not be granted to customers in risk class 4.

In the decision to extend credit, the amount of potential loss due to uncollectible accounts is typically considered to be the cost of the product sold (often expressed at selling price less profit margin). Manger [1967] has suggested that the amount should be related to the production–marketing situation faced by the firm. If a strong "seller's market" exists, uncollectible accounts should be viewed in terms of selling price. In an average market, selling price less markup (an approximation of full cost) should be used, and in a strong "buyer's market," out-of-pocket cost should be used. These reflect opportunity costs to the firm. In the seller's market, the firm is producing at capacity, and an uncollectible sale comes at the expense of having made that sale to another customer. In a buyer's market, excess capacity exists, and an uncollectible sale costs only the out-of-pocket costs necessary to produce the product. The average market reflects the normal, long-run situation in which a firm must meet its full costs if it is to survive. Thus, refinements to the credit-granting analysis may be made by incorporating capacity and demand considerations.

Credit terms. Decisions involving credit terms include the size of cash discounts, the length of the discount period, the length of the total payment period, interest charges on past-due accounts, return and adjustment policies, and special financing arrangements.

The size of cash discounts, for example, should be viewed in terms of the effect on sales and collections. By offering cash discounts, it is hoped that additional sales will be gained. In this context, a discount is essentially a reduction in selling price, and its potential effect may be analyzed in terms of the price elasticity of sales. Second, it is hoped that the availability of cash discounts will promote quicker collections. The cost of the discount should be related to the expected reduction in the time the accounts are outstanding. It is often pointed out that, from the buyer's viewpoint, foregoing a discount may be very expensive financing. For example, if payment terms are 2/10, n/30, failure to take the discount (and making payment on the 30th day) involves financing at an effective annual rate of more than 40 percent (see Chapter 9). The same analysis applies to the seller. If offering a 2 percent discount accelerates payment by 20 days, the seller is incurring that same 40+ percent effective annual rate. Moreover, Patterson [1970] has suggested that the high cost may encourage purchasers who do not pay within the discount period to delay their payment well beyond the 30-day "net" period. Thus, the typical cash discount formula, with its single, large increase in payment due, is likely to prove quite costly to both seller (if discounts are taken) and buyer (if discounts are not taken). Moreover, the increase in payment due following the discount period may encourage delay in payment, which is not the behavior the credit manager seeks.

In view of these difficulties with the usual cash discount system, an alternative system is sometimes adopted. Such a system would provide that the invoice price is payable by a specific time (say, 30 days). After that time, an interest charge is made on the past-due balance, in proportion to the length of time overdue. Such a system produces interest costs (to the buyer) and interest revenues (to the seller) that may better represent the cost of financing. Consideration should be given to the possibility that the payment behavior of customers will be affected by stating a price at gross with the possibility of discount compared to stating the price at net with penalty for late payment. Generally, firms selling to other firms adopt the former, whereas firms selling to individuals adopt the latter (e.g., utility companies, credit card companies). In recent years, use of interest charges on past-due accounts has increased [Hochberg, 1975].

Whether a discount system or an interest system is employed, consideration must be given to the length of the credit period. In analyzing this decision, it must be recognized that increasing the length of the credit period increases the cost of holding receivables. Funds tied up in receivables are unavailable for other investment uses, and incur an opportunity cost proportionate to the length of time the receivables are outstanding. Brandt [1972] suggests that this decision be analyzed in terms of a "credit-term elasticity," measuring the responsiveness of sales to extension of the credit period. Factors such as the buyer's liquidity position and short-term investment opportunities, and credit terms offered by other sellers, would determine the elasticity. Thus, the behavior of the customer (in terms of likely effect on sales) must be analyzed, and compared to the cost of delaying collections.

Collections. Several decision problems exist with respect to collections. One is the decision to institute formal collection procedures against a delinquent account. The timing of the various steps, and the methods to be used, must be evaluated in light of the chances for successful collection.

Another important aspect is the reduction of collection float—the time from sale until cash is deposited in the company's bank account. Fredman [1981] identifies four aspects of collection float: invoicing float (the time from sale to invoicing), mail float (mail transit time to and from the customer), processing float (the time to process and deposit a collection), and availability float (the time needed for a check to clear the banking system). These are in addition, of course, to the time between the customer's receipt of the invoice and sending of a check. Various banking techniques are available to reduce some of the components of collection float. Lock boxes can be used to establish collection points around the country (reducing mail and processing float). Funds received by the lock box institutions may then be rapidly transferred (e.g., by wire) to the company's primary bank. The use of preauthorized checks (or the paperless version, commonly known as preauthorized debits) reduces invoicing and mail float, as well as eliminating the time between customer receipt of invoice and sending of payment. Preauthorized checks are most commonly used with regular, repetitive payments, such as insurance premiums and loan payments. However, their use is growing with variable payments, such as utility bills.

Protecting the investment. One of the important tasks of the credit manager is the protection of the company's investment in trade receivables. Trade receivables are typically unsecured, but in certain cases achieving a security interest in the items sold may be an important means of protection. In the past, security interests usually took the form of conditional sales contracts (retention by the seller of title to the goods, along with right of repossession upon default, until payment is completed) or chattel mortgages (transfer of title to goods to the creditor as security for the debt). With the adoption of the Uniform Commercial Code, these devices have been largely replaced by the financing statement. A financing statement is a legal document that, when filed, creates a public record of the main points of a security agreement executed between a buyer and a seller. Thus, in carrying out a secured commercial transaction, the parties agree in writing as to the terms of the sale, and provide a detailed description of the collateral. The seller, upon delivery of the goods, files a financing statement with the appropriate state authority, so as to obtain a legally recognized interest in the collateral. The use of financing statements provides an easy means for firms to sell on credit while maintaining a clear and virtually unassailable claim on the collateral (which is often the goods themselves) until payment is received [The Conference Board, 1972, p. 14].

Another approach to the protection of the investment in trade receivables is through the purchase of commercial credit insurance. Although the firm is expected to bear the normal risks of uncollectible amounts, commercial credit insurance serves to protect against large, abnormal losses, such as the bankruptcy of a major customer. Policy premiums depend on the amount of coverage, the amount of the deductible provision, the credit ratings of the accounts, and the like. The firm must weigh the cost of the insurance against expected uncollectible amounts (and the effects of a major loss) in deciding how much, if any, coverage to acquire.

In addition to protection against large credit losses, credit insurance also may provide an effective collection service, as insurers aid in obtaining payment of delinquent accounts, in the hope of minimizing losses. Finally, credit insurance reduces the risk of expanding sales volume by increasing credit lines available to customers [The Conference Board, 1972, p. 15].

Commercial credit insurance applies to losses on business accounts. Thus, it would be acquired by firms such as manufacturers, wholesalers, advertising agencies, and the like, whose customers are other business firms or institutions. This protection is not available for consumer accounts. Only very limited protection from credit losses is available to firms whose customers are individual consumers. For example, credit life insurance protects against credit loss due to the death of the customer, but general loss protection is not generally available.

Commercial credit insurance typically guarantees all accounts to specified classes of customers, and provides reimbursement for losses in excess of normal expectations. The characteristics of the company, its sales, and its customers influence the decision to acquire credit insurance. Westgate [1979] suggests that companies possessing some of the following characteristics are vulnerable to abnormal losses, and hence may utilize credit insurance:

1. The company is highly sensitive to economic slumps.
2. Sales are concentrated in a few customers.
3. Customers are engaged in one line of activity, or are located mainly in one region.
4. The company deals in seasonal or custom products.
5. The company accepts greater risks in order to maintain its sales volume.

Analysis and Control. Analysis is an important task in the ongoing management of trade receivables. Various measures and control procedures exist to assist management in cash planning (by analysis and control of collections), profit planning (by analysis and control of uncollectible account losses), sales planning (by analysis and control of credit granting), and so forth. In any of these areas, performance must be measured, compared with standards, and necessary actions taken where serious deviations from standard exist.[2]

Collections. Collection results are frequently analyzed in terms of ratios. These attempt to relate collections to sales activity and to the passage of time.

Practice varies as to the exact definition of the terms appearing in the following ratios. It seems most appropriate to define "trade receivables" as gross receivables, before deduction of allowances, and to define "credit sales" as gross credit sales less sales returns. Alternatively, both receivables and credit sales could be defined net of allowances for discounts, uncollectible accounts, and so forth.

Days sales outstanding is one such measure. This ratio indicates, as of a given date, the receivables balance in terms of the number of days' sales that it represents. The ratio is

$$\text{Days Sales Outstanding} = \frac{\text{Trade Receivables Balance}}{\text{Average Daily Credit Sales}}$$

The resulting figure may be compared to the company's credit terms. If, for example, credit terms are 30 days, a calculation showing 53 days' sales outstanding indicates that the company frequently fails to achieve collection within the 30-day period. In analyzing this result, care should be taken to verify that the "average daily credit sales" figure is representative of the period in which the receivables arose.

The *turnover of receivables* ratio is intended to measure the frequency with which receivables are collected. This measure covers a period of time, and thus relates sales to the average amount of receivables outstanding. The usual definition is

$$\text{Turnover} = \frac{\text{Credit Sales}}{\text{Average Trade Receivables}}$$

Because the emphasis is on the analysis of *collections*, and because collections may not parallel sales, it is sometimes suggested that the ratio be stated as

$$\text{Turnover} = \frac{\text{Collections}}{\text{Average Trade Receivables}}$$

The first form, however, seems to be more widely used.

The inverse of the turnover ratio, multiplied by 365 days, gives the average collection period:

$$\text{Average Collection Period} = \frac{\text{Average Trade Receivables}}{\text{Credit Sales}} \times 365$$

This ratio presents the same information as the turnover ratio, but may express it in a more understandable way.

Firms offering discounts for prompt payment may wish to determine the frequency with which payment is received during the discount period. One possible measure is the *quality ratio*, defined as

---

[2]As an example of an integrated report form for receivables, see Brennan [1977].

$$\text{Quality Ratio} = \frac{\text{Discounts Taken}}{\text{Discounts Available}}$$

This ratio is most appropriate when all sales offer the same rate of cash discount. When this condition is not met, an alternative measure must be designed.

Uncollectible accounts. A major tool in the analysis of potential uncollectibility of accounts is the aging schedule. This schedule presents outstanding accounts according to their date of origination, or according to "current" and various "past-due" categories. Both dollar amounts and percentages may be presented for each category.

This approach may be extended to consider also the age of accounts at time of collection [Benishay, 1965]. Derivation of such a distribution makes the aging concept a useful tool in planning cash collections.

Operational Control of Receivables. When the number of accounts receivable is large, a variety of problems typically emerge as the result of (1) the volume of transactions, (2) the distribution of work loads, and (3) the requirements peculiar to computers and other equipment used for handling the high volume of data. Generally speaking, these problems are most typical of concerns that deal directly with individual consumers, such as utilities, large retailers, credit card companies, gasoline distribution companies, consumer finance companies, and banks. These organizations, as a result of the number and nature of their customers, customarily demand payment not upon presentation of an invoice, as is typical of industrial enterprises, but rather by presentation of a statement showing transactions over a period of time.

The control of large volumes of accounts concerns itself with four principal goals: first, that all sales are recorded; second, that those sales are recorded against the proper accounts; third, that proper statements are presented on a timely basis for each account; and fourth, that collections are credited to the proper accounts.

Symptoms of control problems. System problems in the processing of high volumes of receivables will usually be indicated by certain key symptoms. Among these are (1) delays in preparation and mailing of statements, (2) large inventory shortages, (3) frequent customer complaints concerning incorrect billings, and (4) recurring difficulties in balancing detail to the general ledger.

As volume grows, the first symptoms will generally relate to the distribution of work load. The record-keeping staff will operate at a leisurely pace for most of the month, but at month-end they will not be able to prepare statements in a timely manner without excessive overtime. Further, customers may complain that their statements are inaccurate because of the nonrecognition on the statements of payments made between the statement cutoff and the delivery of the statement.

Cycle billing. The customary approach to minimizing this problem is the adoption of cycle billing. This is a method of maintaining and billing accounts receivable whereby the accounts are divided into groups, and each of these groups is billed once a month as of a specified cutoff date. The cycle-billing dates are staggered throughout the month to spread the billing load as evenly as possible over all the working days of the period.

When used in a manual- or machine-posted system, the sales media are sorted daily and filed in applicable customers' account files. Because generally only one cycle is billed on any one day, the customers' account files on any given day contain sales, collection, and adjustment documents supporting an average of a half-month's volume of receivables transactions. The existence of these loose, unproved media at the end of monthly accounting periods poses a major control problem in a cycle-billing operation and represents the principal challenge to its success.

There are three distinct types of manual accounts receivable cycle-billing control systems in common use. They are the one-control system, the cycle-control system, and the two-control system.

Under the one-control system, the end-of-month balance of accounts receivable is established by adding to the totals of cycles billed during the month a tabulation of the unposted media, which is arrived at through a physical inventory and valuation of the unposted media. The total of the cycles billed plus this physical inventory of unposted media should agree with the general ledger balance of accounts receivable, which is the control account under this system.

When the cycle-control system is used, the receivables ledger is segregated by individual control accounts for each cycle, which are balanced in total to the general ledger account. The number of controls is often around 20 (one per working day per month), but it may range from just a few up to 100 or more. The objective of the cycle-control system is to establish controls over small segments of the accounts, which will provide for immediate comparisons with the results of the billing of the segments, facilitate the identification of any differences, and allow immediate action to be taken to correct differences. To accomplish this, the daily totals of sales, credits, cash, and other transactions must be broken down by cycles and made available for posting to the individual cycle-control records, as well as for posting the totals to the master control account or to the general ledger. As of the cutoff date for a cycle, the totals of the various transactions and the balance of the cycle are determined. These should agree with the total of the statements after their preparation.

The two-control system establishes controls on the totals of transactions in two areas, the billed and the unbilled portions. Again, each type of receivables media (sales, returns, cash, etc.) is sorted daily into its proper billing cycle. Control totals are also developed each day for the groups of cycles that will be billed before the end of the month and those that will not be billed until the following month. The two totals and the grand total are posted to the two detail controls and to the master control. At month-end, the billing trial balance controls for all cycles billed during the month are added to the balance in the unbilled detail control account, and the result should balance to the master control. At the end of the following month, the billed media that originated in the following month are subtracted from the total media actually billed during the later month to establish the amount of prior-month media included; this amount should agree with the balance in the unbilled control at the end of the prior month.

The major problem under cycle billing is the handling and recording of transfers of amounts between different control accounts. These transfers may be necessary to correct an original misclassification of media either by type of accounting (regular, budget, installment) or by cycle (missorts). The problem exists only if separate control and general ledger accounts are maintained. Missorts may include errors discovered at the time of billing that affect an unbilled cycle, and errors discovered during billing that affect a cycle already billed.

Under the cycle-control system, all types of correction transfers must be recorded. Under the two-control system, only the adjustments between billed and unbilled controls need to be recorded. No adjustments are necessary under the one-control system.

Account numbering. As the number of accounts increases, a need for customer account numbers is apparent. This need will be signaled by a growing frequency in misposted sales and receipts, particularly between individuals with similar names. The assignment of account numbers, by itself, is very simple. The low-order digits can be assigned in the sequence that appears within each ledger control. If desired, the initial assignments can be leapfrogged so that unassigned digits remain available for insertion of new accounts, with retention of both alphabetic and numeric sequence. With a large volume of accounts or where the composition of the accounts turns over rapidly, this dual ordering becomes burdensome and impracticable. Higher-order digits are customarily assigned to code the accounts by cycle date, type of account, credit classification, or location. Blocks of numbers may also be assigned for this purpose, but the coding approach is usually more practicable if computer processing is used. In any event, the size of the blocks of numbers used should provide for expansion, because a reassignment of account numbers can be difficult.

Charge plates. Although the assignment of account numbers is fairly easy, their use presents another major problem: the acquisition of the account number on the sale medium. Wherever sales can be initiated at a variety of points and occur frequently, the solution has been the use of charge plates. This circumstance is found in retail organizations, oil companies, credit card organizations, banks, and even in some large hospitals. The typical charge plate is embossed with the customer's name and account number so that the information may be mechanically inscribed directly on the sale-recording media. The account number may also be printed magnetically for reading by scanning devices. Sometimes the address is also shown, but most concerns have found that the frequency with which people move renders such plates obsolete too rapidly. An expiration date is normally shown on those cards that can be used over a wide geographic area, whereas more localized plates, such as those for department stores, may be valid indefinitely. Because the cards also serve as a credit authorization, most providers also place a limit on the size of a purchase that may be transacted without checking on the total account balance.

The use of account numbers almost always requires the use of charge plates, because the alternatives would allow customers to present wrong numbers or might result in transcription errors.

Automation. Because the processing of receivables typically involves many repetitive transactions, it is an excellent candidate for automation. Throughout the development of data processing systems, from punched-card to fully integrated computer systems, receivables have been a common application. The design and control of such systems for handling receivables are generally the same as the techniques for design and control of other business applications and are therefore outside the scope of this discussion.

Where the account number must be transcribed manually from the sale medium to machine-readable input, the generally accepted control is the use of self-checking digits as part of the account number.

A *self-checking digit* is a numeric digit that is a function of the other digits of the account number. One such formula multiplies the first digit by 2, the second by 1, the third by 2, and so forth for each digit in the account number. Then the products obtained are added together and the last digit of this sum becomes the check digit. Other variations of this formula are used, as well as completely different formulas.

Descriptive billings. Another practice that may be affected by high volume is the technique used to report to customers the nature of the purchases included in the current statement. The traditional approach has been to remit to the customer a copy of the sales record that was originally signed by the customer and usually included a description of the purchase. With high volumes, however, the sorting may be performed within a computer, and the additional sorting and storage of these media until the statement is prepared may become cumbersome. Banks, with their use of magnetic characters on customer checks, have maintained the practice of returning high volumes of media to customers, but many department stores and credit card companies have turned instead to descriptive billings. Descriptive billings provide details on each transaction shown on the statement. As transactions are recorded, detailed descriptive data is also entered. For example, a department store's scanning device will record product codes along with the cost and the customer's account number. Copies of the original sales slip are not needed for receivables processing, and are not included with the customer's statement.

Revolving charge accounts. The emergence of revolving charge accounts has further complicated the task of preparing statements. Revolving accounts are those accounts where full payment monthly is not required, but rather only a percentage of the outstanding balance. Unlike installment accounts, the revolving account may be used for small routine purchases as if it were a 30-day open account. The partial payments generally call for 10 to 25 percent of the outstanding balance, with a minimum payment of $10 to $25. Interest is usually charged on balance unpaid within 30 days at a rate of 1½ to 2 percent per month.

Basically, the control of these accounts is not much different from that of regular 30-day accounts. However, because interest is usually charged only on the balance unpaid after 30 days, no accurate control can be calculated using the total revolving receivables balance in order to verify the sum of the interest charges on the detail accounts. One customer may pay in full 29 days after receiving a statement but another may pay after 31 days have elapsed. In the first case there is not a charge of 29/30ths of a month's finance charge; there is no finance charge at all. On the other hand, the second case is charged for 1 month, but perhaps not for the 1 day over the month. Therefore, the effective interest yield on the balance in revolving receivables will always be a rate less than the equivalent annual rate that would be indicated if the monthly rate were multiplied by 12. Furthermore, it will fluctuate slightly from month to month according to the particular payment response in each month.

Because of the difficulty of predicting control totals on the interest charges and because considerable working capital may be needed to support this type of receivable, revolving accounts are generally found in larger organizations where the receivables function is automated. The automation provides greater reliability than does a manual system in analyzing accurately the receivables and extending the finance charge on the appropriate balances.

Accounting Systems. The importance of sales and collections to the success of the firm, and the large number of transactions that are frequently involved, require that effective accounting systems be maintained for receivables. The systems should serve the following objectives:

1. All transactions must be recorded.
2. An account must be established for each customer.
3. Entries to customer accounts must be made promptly and accurately.
4. Periodic statements should be provided to the customer, and appropriate reports provided to management.

The specific details of an accounting system may vary from company to company, depending on the nature and size of the business, the number of customers, the use of computerized processing, and other factors. Whatever the details, the system will typically include credit histories, customer account records, collection records, and provision for customer statements.

Maintaining customer accounts. The process of transferring information from the sales invoice to the customer account may take various forms. The three major methods are posting via the sales journal, direct posting, and ledgerless bookkeeping.

In posting via the sales journal, invoices are posted individually, usually daily, to the sales journal. Customer accounts are then posted, usually daily, from the sales journal. At the end of the period, customer accounts are balanced to the sales journal and customer statements prepared. This double-posting processing approach is seldom used unless the volume of transactions is small.

Various mechanical devices can be used to streamline this basic posting approach. A device commonly used is the pegboard. Using carbon paper and a pegboard for aligning forms, one writing can be used to post both the sales journal and the customer account. Other mechanical filing and indexing devices can also aid in locating accounts for posting.

Direct posting covers a variety of procedures whereby customer accounts are updated directly from sales media. In a manual system, direct posting often operates as follows: Invoices are batched, batch totals are computed, and totals are posted to the sales journal. Individual invoices are posted directly to customer accounts, and postings are proved to batch totals. The frequency and size of invoice batching may vary. At one extreme, invoices may be processed daily in small batches of 50 to 100. At the other extreme, invoices may be processed only once a month. Posting in small batches improves control by facilitating the location of posting errors. Posting in large batches improves processing efficiency by decreasing setup operations, such as locating and refiling the customer ledger card.

In a computerized system, direct posting involves point-of-sale entry into the accounting system. Terminals and scanning devices are common means of data entry.

As the name implies, in a ledgerless bookkeeping system, customer ledgers are not maintained. The detailed customer ledger is replaced by a file of unpaid customer invoices. The following processing steps illustrate the principles of ledgerless bookkeeping:

1. Serially numbered invoices are received in batches with control totals.
2. Batch totals are posted to accounts receivable control.
3. Individual invoices in each batch are filed alphabetically by customer name or numerically by customer account number.
4. Remittance advices are received in batches with control totals.
5. Invoices are pulled from the file when cash is to be applied. Fully paid invoices are stamped "paid," or partially paid invoices are stamped "partial payment." Partial payments are entered on the invoices and new balances computed. The "partial payment" invoices are duplicated.
6. Payments on both paid and partially paid invoices are balanced to batch totals. The batch remittance total is posted to accounts receivable control.
7. Paid invoices and copies of partially paid invoices are filed by batch.

With this procedure, the file of unpaid and partially paid invoices constitutes the detailed customer ledger at any time.

When ledgerless bookkeeping is used, a balance-only statement is often prepared at the end of the period.

Statement formats. A statement of account is a written record of the amount owed by or owing to a customer as of a specific date. Statements are prepared principally to remind customers that payment is due and to aid customers in their accounting. A third reason—customer and trade practices—reinforces the widespread use of statements.

The detailed information that supports the amount owed or owing shown in the statement varies by type of statement. Principal kinds of statements include unit (or running balance), balance-only, and open-item.

The unit (running balance) statement shows (1) the balance of the customer account at the beginning of the period, (2) charges during the period, (3) credits during the period, and (4) the balance at the end of the period. Each charge and credit transaction is posted separately. The balance after each transaction may not be, but often is, posted.

The unit statement is normally used by businesses that sell direct to a final consumer. Typically, the final consumer pays on the basis of the statement, not individual invoices. The purchaser may, however, make partial payments frequently. Examples of businesses using unit statements are mail-order houses, public utilities, gasoline companies, and department stores.

There are two variations of the unit statement. One variation, "country club" billing, lists balances, charges, and credits. Additional information in support of charges and credits on the statement is supplied by copies of sales tickets and credit memoranda sent with the statement. The second variation, "descriptive" billing, omits copies of sales media. Charges and credits are identified by referencing a department or merchandise classification.

The balance-only statement shows nothing but the balance of the customer account at the end of the period, usually a month. It reminds the customer of the amount owed, but provides the customer with no information on the transactions leading to that balance. This simple statement format is not widely used.

An open-item statement shows the balance of the customer account at the end of the period, supported by a listing of unpaid or open invoices. Open-item statements are usually used by companies that sell to other businesses or institutions. Typically, the customer pays on the basis of individual invoices where cash discounts are offered. In some cases, the vendor requires customer payment on a specific-invoice basis. Partial payments must be infrequent for the open-invoice basis to be practicable.

Financing Receivables. The management of receivables includes the important task of converting the receivables into cash. In addition to the usual process of collection, conversion to cash may also be accomplished by either of two financing arrangements. The firm may borrow, using its receivables as collateral (commonly called *discounting, accounts receivable financing,* or *commercial financing*), or it may sell its receivables to a third party (known as *factoring*).

Discounting. Discounting usually signifies a financing arrangement whereby a lender advances funds to a borrower in the form of a loan secured by a pledge of the borrower's open accounts receivable.

Under this arrangement, the firm continues to perform its own credit and collection functions. Interest is charged by the lender on funds advanced, and repayment to the lender occurs when the firm's customers make payments on their account. Such payments are transferred, often in their original form, to the bank or finance company. Customers are normally not notified of the pledge of receivables under discounting arrangements, and so they make payment in normal fashion to the firm. In cases of nonpayment by the customer, the borrowing firm must repay the lender from its other funds (or "replace" the accounts with other, previously unpledged accounts).

Accounts receivable financing is typically a continuing arrangement, rather than a one-time transaction. A financing agreement exists between the borrower and lender, perhaps covering a year, or perhaps covering an unspecified time period. The agreement might provide for the assignment of all accounts receivable (perhaps limited to certain categories) as security, in return for which the lender agrees to advance funds up to a specified percentage (e.g., 80 percent) of the accounts pledged. As mentioned above, repayment occurs by transfer of customer remittances to the lender. Upon collection of individual accounts, the lender potentially receives a greater amount than the funds advanced to the borrower. Some of this difference is consumed by returns, allowances, and discounts on other accounts; additional amounts are consumed by the interest charges on funds advanced. Any remaining difference (known as equity) is either credited against the borrower's account or returned to the borrower.

The term *discounting* is also used to signify the sale of receivables with recourse for noncollection from customers. Although the technical details change, the effect of sale with recourse is essentially the same as the secured borrowing described above. The firm retains the risk of loss from nonpayment by its customers, and retains all other credit and collection functions. Discounting (in the sense of sale with recourse) is more frequently encountered with notes receivables than accounts receivable.

Factoring. Factoring signifies a financing arrangement whereby a third party (a "factor") purchases receivables without recourse for nonpayment. Normally, the customer is notified of the transfer of ownership of the receivable, and the factor assumes all credit and collection functions. In exchange for a commission fee (a percentage of the face value of the factored accounts), the factor assumes the risk of uncollectible account losses. The selling firm receives the amount of the receivables (less the commission fee) upon the account's maturity date (or on the "average due date," where many accounts are involved). If desired, the firm may receive earlier payment, for which an interest charge is made.

Occasionally, factoring is done on a non-notification basis. The selling firm retains the collection function, and its customers are unaware of the transfer of ownership of the receivable. As before, the factor purchases the receivables without recourse, and thus assumes all the risk of uncollectible account losses.

BIBLIOGRAPHY

Accounting Principles Board (AICPA), *Omnibus Opinion—1966*, Opinion No. 10 (APB, 1966).

———, *Interest on Receivables and Payables*, Opinion No. 21 (APB, 1971).

Benishay, H., "Managerial Controls of Accounts Receivable: A Deterministic Approach," *Journal of Accounting Research*, Spring 1965, pp. 114–132.

Block, S., "Accounts Receivable as an Investment," *Credit and Financial Management*, May 1974, pp. 32–40.

Brandt, L. K., *Analysis for Financial Management* (Prentice-Hall, Englewood Cliffs, N.J., 1972), pp. 204–206.

Brennan, J. R., "Accounts Receivable: A Method for Successful Management," *Credit and Financial Management*, vol. 79, no. 1 (January 1977), pp. 15–17.

The Conference Board, *Managing Trade Receivables* (The Conference Board, New York, 1972).

Davidson, S., C. P. Stickney, and R. L. Weil, *Intermediate Accounting: Concepts, Methods and Uses*, 3d ed. (Dryden Press, Hinsdale, Ill., 1982).

Folson, N. B., Jr., "Bankers' Acceptances: Obscure but Relevant," *Credit and Financial Management*, vol. 79, no 10 (November 1977), pp. 10–11.

Fredman, A. J., "Accelerating Collections: Float Reduction Techniques," *Credit and Financial Management*, vol. 83, no. 3 (March 1981), pp. 27–29.

Hochberg, M. J., "Interest Charges: Problem-Child or Prodigy?" *Credit and Financial Management*, vol. 77, no. 7 (August 1975), pp. 10–11.

Manger, C. C., "A Yardstick for Cost of Investment in Accounts Receivable," *Credit and Financial Management*, vol. 69, no. 6 (June 1967), pp. 24–26.

Pacter, P. A., "A Synopsis of APB Opinion No. 21," *Journal of Accountancy*, March 1972, pp. 57–67.

Patterson, H. R., "New Life in the Management of Corporate Receivables," *Credit and Financial Management*, vol. 72, no. 2 (February 1970), pp. 15–18.

Schaps, A. L., "Balance Sheet Treatment of Financed Notes and Accounts Receivable," *The New York Certified Public Accountant*, vol. 36, no. 10 (October 1966), pp. 773–774.

Soldofsky, R. M., "A Model for Accounts Receivable Management," *Management Accounting*, vol. 47, no. 5 (January 1966), pp. 55–58.

Stone, B. K., "The Payments-Pattern Approach to the Forecasting and Control of Accounts Receivable," *Financial Management*, Autumn 1976, pp. 65–82.

Westgate, B. C., "Credit Insurance of Business Receivables," *Cost and Management*, vol. 53, no. 1 (January–February 1979), pp. 36–38.

Wharton, D., "Accounting for Interest on Receivables and Payables: Effects of APB Opinion No. 21," *The Arthur Young Journal*, Spring/Summer 1972, pp. 7–19.

CHAPTER **16**

Inventories

Joseph D. Coughlan
Partner, Price Waterhouse

The subject of inventories is significant from at least three distinct viewpoints: the physical existence of assets owned, the value of the assets as determined for a particular purpose, and the value as a factor in stating the results (net income or loss) from operating a business during a particular period.

PHYSICAL EXISTENCE OF INVENTORIES

When inventories are viewed as the quantity of goods needed to operate a business efficiently, consideration must be given not only to the expenses and losses incident to owning and caring for the goods, but also to such factors as sales forecasting, production scheduling, optimum purchasing, and the effects of carrying excessive (or inadequate) quantities.

The expenses and losses incident to owning and caring for inventories include:

Earnings from alternative investments of the working capital applied (commonly computed at current interest rates or at the average earning rate of the company)

Personal property taxes

Insurance premiums

Storage expense, which may represent additional rental payments or an allocated portion of maintaining a warehouse or storeroom

Employee compensation payments, which are increased because of the handling of excess goods and reduction in efficiency caused by the inconvenience of "working around" the extra bulk

Losses due to deterioration and obsolescence, which are continuing risks inherent in ownership of goods and which tend to be higher with respect to finished goods than to raw materials

Where the excess inventory quantities are a result of a purchasing decision motivated by an anticipated rise in prices, the expenses and losses incident to owning and caring for the goods must be offset against the expected saving from the advance purchases.

Management decisions that take into account such factors as sales forecasting, production scheduling, optimum purchasing, and the effects of carrying excessive (or inadequate) quantities are commonly referred to as an *inventory management system*. Any inventory management system seeks to minimize the expenses associated with the maintenance of the goods, and it must recognize the interaction of inventory decisions with other functions in the company. As indicated by the following examples, the management decisions that must be considered involve all facets of the business.

The marketing department will normally establish sales forecasts by product or product line and the level of service that will enable the company to maintain its competitive position.

The operating department will normally establish the overall production rate in the light of the sales forecast, the plant capacity, and the manpower available, as well as deciding what is to be produced and when and what machines, material, and labor will be used.

The financial department will normally determine whether the working capital can be made available to carry out the plans recommended by those concerned primarily with sales and production.

In larger companies several individuals may be involved in each phase of the operation, whereas in a smaller company the same individual may perform more than one function.

The expenses and losses incident to owning and caring for inventories tend to increase directly with the level of the inventory, whereas the measure of other factors tends to vary inversely with the quantity of goods on hand. Examples of factors that tend to favor higher inventory levels include the following:

Larger inventories of finished goods can be expected to reduce the number of instances when orders cannot be filled promptly, which frequently results in lost sales.

Larger inventories of parts and raw materials can be expected to reduce the number of instances when production must be delayed, which results in operating efficiencies.

Larger inventories permit increasing the quantities covered by purchase orders and production runs, which results in savings through quantity discounts and lower per-unit expense for machine setups, etc.

These factors are more difficult to measure than those that vary directly with the level of inventory, but they nevertheless are a significant portion of the aggregate of the expenses and losses, which are sought to be minimized as the objective of an inventory management system. This objective of an inventory management system is portrayed graphically in Exhibit 1.

Classification of Inventory Items to Determine Appropriate Control Measures. Exhibit 2 depicts the commonly accepted *ABC* concept of the classification of goods included in an inventory for the purpose of establishing the appropriate inventory control procedure.

The distribution of annual dollar usage is established by listing the various items in descending order. In a typical manufacturing inventory, it is found that approximately 70 percent of the items carried account for only 5 percent of the annual dollar usage. These items are referred to as the *C* items. Another 15

EXHIBIT 1   Objective of Inventory Management System

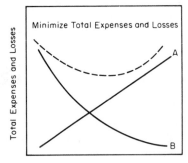

Minimize Total Expenses and Losses

A

B

Working Capital Invested in Inventory

(y-axis) Total Expenses and Losses

A. Factors that vary directly
   with level of inventory:

   Possible earnings from
      alternative investments
   Personal property taxes
   Insurance premiums
   Storage expense
   Added employee payments
   Deterioration and obsolescence

B. Factors that vary inversely
   with level of inventory:

   Lost sales
   Production delays
   Inefficiency of small purchase
      orders and short production
      runs

**EXHIBIT 2   Typical Distribution of Inventory—Manufacturing
Company**

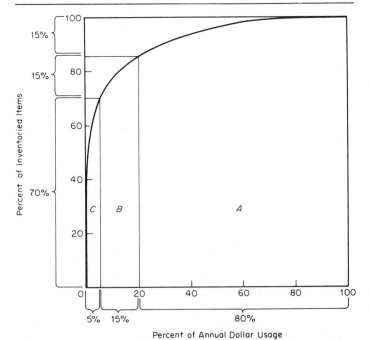

Percent of Inventoried Items

Percent of Annual Dollar Usage

percent of the items may account for 15 percent of the annual dollar usage; they may be referred to as B items. The remaining 15 percent of the items would account for 80 percent of the annual dollar usage and would be referred to as A items.

It is necessary to vary the type of control procedures according to the particular characteristics of the items included in the inventory. No single method of inventory control would be appropriate for all items.

Items classified as A will justify maximum control measures, such as perpetual inventory records, product identification, and precisely determined reorder quantities. In many cases, the economic order quantity (EOQ) will be established by applying an adaptation of the classical EOQ formula, described later.

The control techniques for the B items will be less sophisticated than for the A items. The updating of perpetual inventory records, if maintained for the B items, may not be as frequent; for example, such updating may be on a weekly basis whereas the records for the A items may be maintained on a daily basis.

The primary objective in the control of C items may be to minimize the expense involved in maintaining the control. Some minimum procedures for these items are, however, essential for any inventory control system. Safety stocks for C items can be relatively high, and in many cases a "two-bin" system can be used to eliminate the necessity of maintaining a perpetual inventory record. Items are used out of one of the bins, and the reorder point is identified when the storeroom must go to the reserve stock in the alternate bin to fill an order. When a new shipment is received in the stock room, the reserve stock bin is filled with a quantity equal to the reorder point, and the excess is placed in the primary storage bin.

Formula for Establishing Economic Order Quantity. The principal factors taken into account in establishing the EOQ for a particular item are reflected in Exhibit 3. The minimum point on the total variable cost curve, TVC, is where

---

EXHIBIT 3   Economic Order Quantity

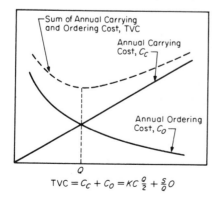

Sum of Annual Carrying and Ordering Cost, TVC

Annual Carrying Cost, C_C

Annual Ordering Cost, C_O

Q

$$TVC = C_C + C_O = KC\frac{Q}{2} + \frac{S}{Q}O$$

Minimun TVC occurs where $C_C = C_O$, giving:

$$Q = \sqrt{\frac{2SO}{KC}}$$

where:

Q = order quantity in units

S = annual demand in units

O = cost per order in dollars

K = annual carrying cost as a percentage

C = unit cost in dollars

the two solid lines intersect or where the annual carrying cost equals the annual ordering cost.

In any particular instance, the basic formula for establishing the economic order quantity must be expanded and modified. For example, Exhibit 4 illustrates a situation in which the material costs vary according to the quantity ordered. In this example, it is assumed that (1) the annual usage is 1,000 units; (2) the ordering cost is $10 per order; and (3) the inventory carrying expenses amount to 15 percent per annum of the working capital tied up in inventory. It is further assumed that for an order under 200 units the cost is $6; this becomes lower as larger quantities are ordered; for example, the per-unit cost is $5.50 if the order is for between 200 and 500 units.

Exhibit 4 reflects the aggregate annual cost and expense curves for the four unit prices examined. The perpendicular lines on the upper portion of the exhibit show how the analyst moves from one curve to the next at points where a new discount takes effect, such as 200, 500, and 1,000 units. It will be noted

EXHIBIT 4   Economic Order Quantity Modified

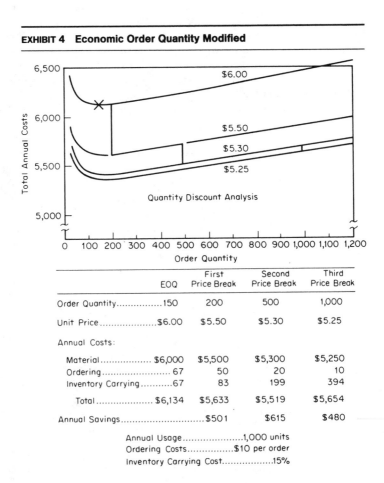

	EOQ	First Price Break	Second Price Break	Third Price Break
Order Quantity.................150		200	500	1,000
Unit Price.....................$6.00		$5.50	$5.30	$5.25
Annual Costs:				
Material.................. $6,000		$5,500	$5,300	$5,250
Ordering........................ 67		50	20	10
Inventory Carrying...........67		83	199	394
Total.................... $6,134		$5,633	$5,519	$5,654
Annual Savings............................$501			$615	$480

Annual Usage......................1,000 units
Ordering Costs................$10 per order
Inventory Carrying Cost..................15%

EXHIBIT 5   General Inventory Decisions

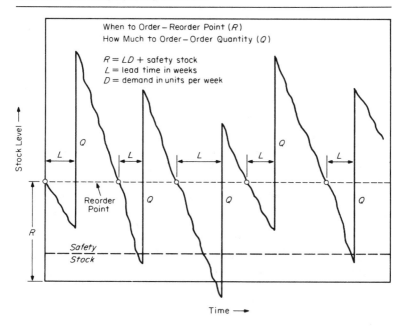

When to Order — Reorder Point (R)
How Much to Order — Order Quantity (Q)

$R = LD +$ safety stock
$L =$ lead time in weeks
$D =$ demand in units per week

Time →

that both the per-unit purchase cost and the per-unit expense decrease as order quantities increase, but that the expense of carrying the inventory increases with the order quantity. The annual savings at the three price breaks relative to the economic order quantity levels are $501, $615, and $480, which means that the indicated optimum order quantity is 500 units.

Timing of Orders. After establishing the optimum quantity of goods to be covered by an order, it is essential to determine when orders should be placed. Exhibit 5 reflects the relationship among stock levels, reorder points, order quantities, lead times, and safety stocks. The reorder point R is defined as (1) the lead time (replenishment time) in days multiplied by the demand per day plus (2) the safety stock. When the stock level reaches the reorder point, action is initiated to issue an order. The lead time L is the elapsed time from the moment the stock level reaches the reorder point until the new order is received. If both the lead time and demand per day were constant, the stock level would reach the safety stock level just as the new order is received. However, both lead times and demand rates represent averages with statistical variations about these averages. If total demand during a lead time period is greater than the average, the stock level will be below that of the total safety stock. The second cycle on the graph shows a case where the demand rate increased above the average and resulted in the stock level being in the safety stock before the new order arrived. The third cycle reflects a stockout situation which came about as a result of an extended lead time.

The size of the safety stock is based on two factors: (1) the likely variability in total demand from the forecast demand during the lead time period, and (2) the acceptable rate of stockouts. If management wants to reduce the number of stockouts, the safety stock must be increased or the variability from forecasted lead time demand must be controlled through improved forecasting of demand and by reducing the number of past-due production or purchase orders.

VALUATION OF INVENTORIES

In accounting literature, the term *valuation* is the one most commonly used in any discussion of inventories. In the majority of instances, however, the amount assigned to a particular inventory for accounting purposes is fundamentally a reflection of cost rather than a determination of value.

There are times when the value of an inventory is of primary significance. For example, where there is to be a forced bulk sale when liquidation of a business is contemplated, the value is the only significant figure. This value will be the amount that a purchaser will pay for all the goods on hand. Value is also significant when a sale of a continuing business is contemplated. For this purpose, the value of the inventory is normally the aggregate of the replacement cost for the individual items on hand that will be useful to the purchaser plus the scrap value of excess quantities and obsolete items.

It may also be necessary to establish the value of an inventory when considering appropriate insurance coverage, the extent to which the inventory will be recognized as collateral for a loan, or the amount on which property tax assessments are based. In these situations, the amount assigned to the inventory in the course of normal accounting procedures may or may not be the answer. For example, in determining the appropriate base for a property tax, primary consideration must be given to the statutory requirements, local practices, and possibly the equalization factors that are part of the assessor's procedures.

Except for additions and revisions necessitated by recognition of the last-in, first-out (LIFO) method, there have been no major changes in the sections pertaining to inventories in the Internal Revenue Code for several decades. The only significant changes in practice are discussed below under "Tax and Other Influences on Overhead Absorption" and "Excess Inventories—*Thor* Decision."

The Internal Revenue Code contains the general requirement that: "Whenever in the opinion of the Secretary or his delegate the use of inventories is necessary in order clearly to determine the income of any taxpayer, inventories shall be taken by such taxpayer. . . ." This section of the law concludes with the requirement that the inventories be taken on the basis that is prescribed by regulations "as conforming as nearly as may be to the best accounting practice in the trade or business and as most clearly reflecting income." The regulations reflect this statutory provision by the conclusions that (1) inventory rules cannot be uniform and (2) an inventory that can be used under the best accounting practice in a balance sheet showing the financial position of the taxpayer can, as a general rule, be regarded as clearly reflecting income.

The federal income tax regulations include only a few general paragraphs to state the meaning of the term "cost." In the case of merchandise on hand at the beginning of the year, cost means the balance sheet valuation of the inventory at the end of the previous year. In the case of merchandise purchased since the beginning of the taxable year, cost means the invoice price less trade or other discounts (except strictly cash discounts approximating a fair interest rate, which may be deducted or not at the option of the taxpayer, provided a consistent course is followed) *plus* transportation or other necessary charges incurred in acquiring possession of the goods. In the case of merchandise produced by the taxpayer since the beginning of the year, the general rule is that cost means the aggregate of [Reg. §1.471-3(c)]

> (1) the cost of raw materials and supplies entering into or consumed in connection with the product, (2) expenditures for direct labor, (3) indirect expenses incident to and necessary for the production of the particular article, including in such indirect expenses a reasonable proportion of management expenses, but not including any cost of selling or return on capital, whether by way of interest or profit.

Use of general language in the income tax regulations is a recognition of the fact that there is no single concept of cost that is appropriate in all businesses.

The Lower of Cost or Market. From the standpoint of modern accounting practice, the concept of value is primarily involved in the principle of stating inventories at the "lower of cost or market." The general rule is that there should be a departure from the cost basis of stating an inventory when the utility of the goods is no longer as great as its cost. The premise is that whether the difference between the cost and the expected utility of the goods is due to physical deterioration, obsolescence, changes in price levels, or other causes, the difference should be recognized as a loss of the period in which the determination of expected utility is made.

As used in the phrase "lower of cost or market," the term "market" means current replacement cost (by purchase or by reproduction, as the case may be) subject to the limitations that (1) market should not exceed the net realizable value, that is, selling price in the ordinary course of business less reasonably predictable cost of completion and disposal; and (2) market should not be less than the net realizable value reduced by an allowance for an approximately normal profit margin. In the statement on "Inventory Pricing" by the Committee on Accounting Procedures of the American Institute of Certified Public Accountants [CAP, 1953, chap. 4, par. 9], this general rule is expanded upon with the following discussion:

> The rule of *cost or market, whichever is lower* is intended to provide a means of measuring the residual usefulness of an inventory expenditure. The term *market* is therefore to be interpreted as indicating utility on the inventory date and may be thought of in terms of the equivalent expenditure which would have to be made in the ordinary course at that date to procure corresponding utility. As a general guide, utility is indicated primarily by the current cost of replacement of the goods as they would be obtained by purchase or reproduction. In applying the rule, however, judgment must always be exercised and no loss should be recognized

unless the evidence indicates clearly that a loss has been sustained. There are therefore exceptions to such a standard. Replacement or reproduction prices would not be appropriate as a measure of utility when the estimated sales values, reduced by the cost of completion and disposal, is lower, in which case the realizable value so determined more appropriately measures utility. Furthermore, where the evidence indicates the cost will be recovered with an approximately normal profit upon sale in the ordinary course of business, no loss should be recognized even though replacement or reproduction costs are lower. This might be true, for example, in the case of production under firm sales contracts at fixed prices, or when a reasonable volume of future orders is assured at stable selling prices.

In many instances, the lower-of-cost-or-market rule for stating inventories will be applied, as a practical rather than a theoretical matter, in accordance with federal income tax regulations. The general rule in the regulations is that, under ordinary circumstances and for normal goods in an inventory, cost is to be compared with replacement cost. The regulations also provide that, whether cost or the lower-of-cost-or-market inventory method is used, the amount assigned to goods that are "unsalable at normal prices or unusable in the normal way because of damage, imperfections, shop wear, changes of style, odd or broken lots, or other similar causes, including second-hand goods taken in exchange" should not exceed net realizable value.

In applying the rule of lower of cost or market, the scrap value of the items included in the inventory constitutes a *minimum* amount.

Federal income tax regulations state that where an inventory is valued on the basis of cost or market, whichever is lower, the market value of each article on hand at the inventory date shall be compared with the cost of the article, and the lower shall be taken as the inventory amount for the article. This may be appropriate in those rare cases where specific identification of individual units of inventory is maintained for costing purposes. When one of the more common cost flow assumptions such as first-in, first-out (FIFO) or LIFO is used, there are many instances in practice where the absolute statement in the regulations is not complied with. There is accounting authority for a broader view of the basis for making comparisons between cost and market.

The purpose of reducing inventory to market is to reflect fairly the income of the accounting period. Although probably the most common practice is to compare cost with market separately for each item in an inventory, there are a number of situations in which the comparison of the aggregate cost with the aggregate value is more significant.

Where a single category of end product is being produced, the reduction of the cost of individual items to market value would ordinarily not be justified if the value to the business of the total inventory less a normal profit margin is in excess of the aggregate cost. This would be particularly true in a case where selling prices are not affected by temporary or relatively small fluctuations in current costs.

When no loss of income is expected to take place as a result of a reduction in cost prices of certain goods because others forming components of the same general category of finished products have a market equally in excess of cost, it is generally held that the components need not be adjusted to market if they are included in the inventory in balanced quantities. If the stock on hand of particular inventory items is excessive in relation to others, clear reflection of income will normally require the direct comparison of cost and value for the excess quantities.

If an item is included in inventory that had been written down to market for purposes of the preceding year's inventory, the comparison should be between the opening inventory value and market at the end of the year. Normally, income should be recognized only from the *disposition* of goods.

In Some Businesses Value May Be an Appropriate Basis for Stating Inventories. Mining companies may inventory gold and silver at current value when there is an effective, viable market. The general rule of modern financial accounting that inventories should not be stated at amounts in excess of cost reflects a practical realization of the uncertainties inherent in doing business in a free competitive economy. Where metals have a fixed monetary value and the sale of the quantities on hand at the end of any particular period at such fixed amounts is practically mechanical, it is appropriate to base the inventory on such value. Any expenditures that will be incurred in the disposition of the inventory should, of course, be taken into account so that the inventory is not stated at an amount in excess of net realizable value. The exception to the general rule sometimes made by mining companies is also justified, at least in part, by the difficulty in establishing the cost for the particular goods in the inventory. The metals may have been extracted from several mines, which have been operated over a long period of time with numerous shutdowns. In this situation, the determination of the provision for depreciation that should be appropriately allocated to any particular production may be subject to a wide range of difference in opinion, to say nothing of the difficulty of establishing the appropriate amount of the provision for depletion.

Agriculture is another industry in which value may be an appropriate basis for stating inventories. As a practical matter, many farmers do not maintain adequate records to establish clearly appropriate costs for the products that may be on hand at the end of a year. For federal income tax purposes, this fact is recognized in the permission granted to farmers to report income on a cash receipts and disbursements basis. Where the farm accounting is placed on an accrual basis for financial reporting, because the units are interchangeable and the immediate marketability at established prices is recognized in the normal course of business, value may be accepted as an appropriate basis for stating inventories without the necessity of establishing costs. The *farm price method* of stating inventories thus provides for a valuation at market price less the estimated direct cost of disposing of the products on hand.

The federal income tax regulations provide that a dealer in securities may use an inventory based on market values as an alternative to stating inventories at either cost or the lower of cost or market. The only requirement in the regulations is that the method used for tax purposes be the same as the method regularly used in the dealer's books of account. A dealer in securities is defined in the federal income tax regulations as a merchant of securities (whether an individual, partnership, or corporation) with an established placed of business, regularly engaged in the purchase of securities and their resale to customers. It is further provided that if such business is simply a branch of the activities carried on by such person, the securities inventoried at market, or at the lower of cost or market, may include only those held for purposes of resale rather than for investment.

AMOUNTS ASSIGNED TO INVENTORIES TO DETERMINE PERIODIC RESULTS FROM BUSINESS OPERATIONS

If the results of operating a business were determined only at the time of completion of a venture, there would be no need for inventory accounting. Modern business, however, is conducted on a "going-concern" basis. With securities being actively traded on established markets, the relationship between the owners and operators of a business is largely impersonal, and there is a constant change in some portion of the owner group. For these reasons, as well as to make possible some degree of management control, it is accepted (quite aside from the requirements of income tax laws) that the income or loss from operating a business should be determined at least annually. The determination of periodic operating results requires the recognition of inventories.

Treatment of Supplies The federal income tax regulations recognize the fact that income cannot be fairly stated without giving proper regard to inventories by inclusion of the following paragraph [Reg. §1.471-1]:

> In order to reflect taxable income correctly, inventories at the beginning and end of each taxable year are necessary in every case in which the production, purchase, or sale of merchandise is an income-producing factor. The inventory should include all finished or partly finished goods and, in the case of raw materials and supplies, only those which have been acquired for sale or which will physically become a part of merchandise intended for sale, in which class fall containers, such as kegs, bottles, and cases, whether returnable or not, if title thereto will pass to the purchaser of the product to be sold therein. Merchandise should be included in the inventory only if title thereto is vested in the taxpaper. Accordingly, the seller should include in his inventory goods under contract for sale but not yet segregated and applied to the contract and goods out upon consignment, but should exclude from inventory goods sold (including containers), title to which has passed to the purchaser. A purchaser should include in inventory merchandise purchased (including containers), title to which has passed to him, although such merchandise is in transit or for other reasons has not been reduced to physical possession, but should not include goods ordered for future delivery, transfer of title to which has not yet been effected.

The foregoing quotation from the current federal income tax regulations is more restrictive than the concept of inventory as reflected in modern accounting practice. Modern accounting practice will include supplies that are to be *consumed* in the production of the goods or services to be sold in the ordinary course of the business. Normally the accounting concept of supplies being part of the inventory is accepted in practice for income tax purposes. In recognition of the fact that the income tax law applies to all businesses, regardless of the size of the operation or the sophistication of its accounting records, the regulations include the following paragraph [Reg. §1.162-3].

> Taxpayers carrying materials and supplies on hand should include in expenses the charges for materials and supplies only in the amount that they are actually consumed and used in operation during the taxable year for which the return is made, provided that the costs of such materials and supplies have not been deducted in determining the net income or loss or taxable income from any previous year. If a taxpayer carries incidental material or supplies on hand for which no record of consumption is kept or of which physical inventories at the beginning and end of the year are not taken, it will be permissible for the taxpayer to include in his expenses and to deduct from gross income the total cost of such supplies and materials as were purchased during the taxable year for which the return is made, provided the taxable income is clearly reflected by this method.

This statement recognizes that for federal income tax purposes supplies on hand are technically conceived of as being deferred charges rather than inventory. It also recognizes that, as a practical matter, smaller businesses may expense all supplies as purchased, and in the case of the larger businesses certain items, if not material in amount, may be so treated.

Measure of Physical Quantities. Regardless of the concept of cost applied in any particular situation, the computations will be premised on a measure of physical quantities. The importance of an auditor being satisfied as to the physical existence of an inventory was reflected in a report entitled "Extensions of Auditing Procedure," which was issued by a Special Committee on Auditing Procedure of the American Institute of Certified Public Accountants and approved by a vote of the membership of the Institute in 1939. This report concluded that, in addition to making auditing tests and checks of the inventory accounts and records, the independent certified public accountant should, wherever practical and reasonable, observe the inventory taking. The report also included the following statement:

> In cases where the concern maintains well-kept and controlled perpetual inventory records supported by (1) a complete physical inventory at a date not coincident with the balance sheet date, or (2) physical inventories of individual items taken from time to time so that the quantity of each item on hand is compared with the inventory record for that item at least once in each year, it will be satisfactory to undertake the procedure outlined at any interim date or dates selected by the auditor, his purpose being to satisfy himself as to the credibility of the perpetual inventory records and whether they may be relied upon to support the inventory totals shown on the balance sheet.

Some companies have developed inventory controls or methods for determining inventories (including statistical sampling) of sufficient reliability to make an annual physical count of each item of inventory unnecessary in certain instances. Even where statistical sampling techniques are used to establish inventory quantities rather than merely to verify the accuracy of perpetual inventory records, the final results are nevertheless premised on a measure of physical quantities.

Assumptions of Movement of Goods. In addition to a difference in the concept of cost in various businesses, there can be a difference in the concept of the assumption applied with respect to identification of the goods on hand. It is only in the most exceptional case that there will be specific identification of the goods. Generally this will be practical and needed for a fair reflection of income only with respect to items of relatively high individual value, such as rare violins, jewels, and valuable paintings. In the operation of a business, identification of particular lots of similar goods is not only impractical but may also distort rather than aid in a fair reflection of income on a going-concern basis. The common practice, therefore, is to reflect in the accounting records average costs, and there is a wide variety of procedures for determining an average. The average may be computed by reference to production or acquisitions during a week, month, or year; or a procedure based on the theory of a moving average may be developed and appropriately applied in particular cases.

In further recognition of the fact that specifically identified costs are not always the most appropriate, an assumption is commonly made that goods move through the business on a FIFO basis, so that the most recent costs can be applied to the quantities on hand at the inventory date. Since approximately 1940, the LIFO assumption as to the movement of goods has been acceptable for federal income tax purposes, and there has been an increasing proportion of business inventories determined on this basis. The mechanics of determining the cost for an inventory on the LIFO basis are described below in some detail.

Another type of assumption as to the movement of goods is reflected in the retail inventory method, which is commonly used in the retail trade and was developed to meet the practical problems inherent in that industry. Inasmuch as the retail method embraces some of the principles of the lower-of-cost-or-market philosophy and does not involve the detailed questions inherent in establishing a cost for a manufacturing concern, this method is specifically considered in the following section.

Retail Inventory Method. Under the retail inventory method, the total of the retail selling price of the goods on hand at the end of the period in each department is reduced by applying a single percentage based on the operations of that department during the period. The determination of this percentage adjustment to the retail value and the mechanics of the computation are illustrated in Exhibit 6.

In the operation of the retail inventory method, it is important that markdowns be based on actual reductions in retail sales prices. The required records to be maintained, with respect to each department, are those showing the aggregate cost and initial retail sales price for all purchases, incoming freight where not included in cost, aggregate sales made, markdowns, discounts allowed to employees and others, and additional markups, if any.

Shortages are recognized as inevitable in retail store operations, so that a provision therefor must be made. These shortages can result from errors in the

EXHIBIT 6   Retail Inventory Method

	Computation approximating					
	Lower of cost or market			Cost		
	Selling price	Inventory		Selling price	Inventory	
		Amount	Percent		Amount	Percent
Opening inventory	$ 10,000	$ 6,000	60.00	$ 10,000	$ 6,000	60.00
Purchases..............	100,000	52,000		100,000	52,000	
Incoming freight, etc.		2,000			2,000	
Additional markups	1,000			1,000		
	$111,000	$60,000	54.05			
Markdowns.............	$ 3,000			(3,000)		
				$108,000	$60,000	55.56
Sales, net	92,000			$ 92,000		
Discounts	1,500			1,500		
Shortages..............	2,500			2,500		
	$ 99,000			$ 96,000		
Closing inventory:						
At retail..............	$ 12,000			$ 12,000		
Amount approximating: Lower of cost or market (54.05% of $12,000)...........		$ 6,486				
Cost (55.56% of $12,000)					$ 6,667	

preparation of sales slips as well as from shoplifting. Frequently, a monthly provision will be made for shortages measured by a fixed percentage of sales during the period as reflected by the experience of each department. Inasmuch as the inventory control records are kept in terms of retail selling prices, the amount of shortage is initially measured at that level.

In order that the inventory determined under the retail method will be stated at an amount that will approximate the lower of cost or market, markdowns are not included in the computation of the adjustment percentage. If the LIFO inventory method is used in conjunction with the retail computation, federal income tax regulations require that retail selling prices be adjusted for markdowns as well as markups in order that the determination will approximate the cost of the goods on hand at the end of the period rather than the lower of cost or market.

Concepts of "Cost" for Manufactured Goods. Just as there are several concepts of value, there are many concepts of cost. For purposes of establishing selling prices, all amounts expended in the conduct of the business must be recovered in the proceeds of sales in order to make a profit. It is unimportant for this purpose whether expenditures are classified as costs or as expenses.

Use of the word "cost" to embrace any and all expenditures can, however, lead to misunderstandings.

Categorizing expenditures is important when the cost of an inventory is being established for the purpose of determining income derived from business operations during a stated period. The basic accounting principle in the measurement of income involves the "matching" of costs and expenses against related revenues. The unabsorbed costs properly chargeable against future sales are carried forward as inventories.

Inclusion of Overhead. Subject to the adoption of an acceptable practice as to the averaging of costs and a stated assumption as to the flow of goods, generally little difficulty is encountered in determining the appropriate amount to be allocated to an inventory for the cost of materials purchased and expenditures for direct labor. Greater differences of opinion exist with respect to overhead.

Expenditures that do not further a productive activity are not part of overhead includable in cost computations; and the extent to which other expenses are included in any particular instance will depend on such factors as the complexity of the organization, the attitude and sophistication of the individuals compiling and using the economic data, and the availability of information. Not every business is equipped to analyze its expenditures to the same degree. Further, costs are computed to meet a particular situation, and no one amount can be said to be "correct" to the exclusion of all others.

There are several viewpoints as to the extent to which the expenses relating to production should be included in cost as a matter of principle. The alternatives for inclusion of overhead in production costs may be grouped broadly in four classes:

1. Prime costing, under which no overhead is included
2. Direct costing, under which expenses that are attributable directly to production and that tend to increase and decrease in proportion to changes in the operating rate are included but no fixed overhead is included
3. Analytical costing, under which overhead expenses attributable to production are included, except for the portion not taken into account because of the production facilities not being fully utilized
4. Full absorption costing, under which all overhead expenses attributable to production are included

Circumstances may make it appropriate and useful to apply procedures falling into any of these four categories in preparing statements and reports for management purposes; and management should understand what procedures have been followed. This is particularly important where the computed costs are utilized in establishing selling prices.

Prime costing has the advantage of simplicity and is applied most frequently where the overhead costs are of little significance. The suitability of this concept of cost for financial statement purposes (in contrast with operating statements prepared for management control purposes) is, however, subject to question. Chapter 4 on "Inventory Pricing" in Accounting Research Bulletin No. 43 specifically states that "the exclusion of *all* [emphasis supplied] overheads from inventory costs does not constitute an accepted accounting procedure."

Direct costing implies that none of the recurring and continuing overhead expenses are to be included in cost of inventories. The major items are frequently depreciation and plant maintenance. The reasoning is that the expenses were incurred as a consequence of decisions that had nothing to do with any particular units of production; that the expenses would have been incurred whether or not any specific units had been produced; and that corresponding amounts of expense will be incurred in subsequent periods regardless of the quantity of the current production. The practice of not including in overhead certain items considered to be period expenses is a partial application of the direct costing principle. Among the items frequently not included in overhead under this concept are research and development, product guarantees, defective parts and rework, pensions, inventory-taking labor, employee training time, downtime, overtime and shift premiums (where abnormal and incurred to effect shipments rather than to produce the goods in the inventory), and plant rearrangement.

Producers of such items as whiskey, wine, and timber normally carry large inventories for long periods of time without guaranteed or contractually fixed selling prices. Storage and similar continuing expenses are frequently not added to the base cost of the particular goods on hand in this situation.

Analytical costing measures the proportion of the recurring and continuing expenses to be included in the computations of cost by comparing the actual rate of activity with a predetermined norm. Expenses for a particular period are included in cost to the extent that available capacity was actually utilized. The portion of the expenses allocable to the unused capacity is considered to represent a loss. This is an economic loss attributable to the lower-than-normal level of production during the period, and is not part of the cost of the units actually produced.

Both the direct costing and analytical costing procedures are premised, in part, on recognition of the fact that, in addition to variable expenses, overhead includes expenses that are recurring and necessary merely to provide the capacity to carry on production activities. The assumption of a certain level of recurring and continuing expenses is essential to being in a position to carry on any activities. During a particular period, however, production may be all or only a part of the total possible with the available capacity. Judgment is exercised in determining how much of the expenses required to provide the existing capacity to produce should be considered part of the cost of the actual production.

Full absorption costing is most frequently applied in smaller enterprises where detailed analyses of the various expense accounts are not available. It may also be appropriate where a plant is consistently operated at capacity or where the aggregate amount of overhead is relatively small. It shares with prime costing the advantage of simplicity; however, special attention must be given to any elements of overhead attributable to events that are not customarily a part of plant operations, and the full absorption costing concept will not be literally applied where the amount of expense resulting from such events can be identified. Examples of events that could justify special recognition in determining the overhead expenses to be included in cost computations are shortages of materials, receipt of defective materials, labor slowdowns and strikes, and interruptions of production caused by a flood, fire, or other casualty. In a business that does not have a regular program for model or product changes, special recognition might also be given to the effect on expenses of disruptions caused by such factors as the introduction of a new product, the training of an expanded labor force, and the realignment of facilities incident to equipping a plant to manufacture a different product.

All the authoritative pronouncements on the subject of accounting for inventories uniformly emphasize that greater weight is to be given to consistency than to the use of any particular method.

Illustration of analytical costing. In applying the analytical costing concept, it is necessary first to establish a normal operating rate or practical capacity. Practical capacity is usually determined by starting with a theoretical capacity and allowing for normal interruptions. Capacity may be measured in terms of tons, pounds, yards, labor hours, machine hours, or any other standard appropriate to the particular operating unit—sometimes a plant, but frequently a department within the plant or other type of "cost center."

The application of this concept may be illustrated on the basis of the following assumptions:

Plant A has a theoretical capacity of 105,000 units per week if operated continuously; however, in determining an annual practical capacity, recognition must be given to the fact that the plant operates on a 5-day week at 8 hours a day. Also, allowances must be made for scheduled holidays, vacation shutdown, and other normal interruptions due to such causes as power failures and shutdowns for repairs. The plant is closed completely for five annual holidays (equivalent to 1 week of operation) and for 2 weeks during the vacation period. In this case, a reasonable allowance for breakdowns is 5 percent.

		Production units
Theoretical capacity (105,000 units for 52 weeks)		5,460,000
Reductions to recognize operations:		
On an 8-hour day ($^{16}/_{24}$ of 5,460,000)	3,640,000	
On a 5-day week ($^{2}/_{7}$ of 1,820,000)	520,000	4,160,000
Capacity on basis of 5-day week at 8 hours per day		1,300,000
Allowances for:		
Scheduled holidays ($^{1}/_{52}$ of 1,300,000)	25,000	
Vacation shutdown ($^{2}/_{52}$ of 1,300,000)	50,000	75,000
Capacity on basis of scheduled operating time		1,225,000
Allowance for normal interruptions (5%)		61,250
Practical capacity		1,163,750

If 1,100,000 units were produced during the year, the basis on which the fixed overhead would be allocated to production would be 1,100,000/1,163,750, or 94.52 percent. All of the variable overhead would also be allocated to production. Assuming that the inventory consisted of 110,000 units and the FIFO convention is applied, 10 percent of the fixed overhead allocated to production would be included in the computed cost for the inventory.

Even if the actual production exceeded 1,163,750 units as a result of favorable operating conditions and not as a result of additions to or improvements made in the facilities that would increase the theoretical capacity, only 100 percent of the fixed overhead would be allocated to production. Allocating more than 100 percent would result in including "phantom dollars" in cost rather than actual expenditures.

For purposes of this simple illustration, the rate of activity has been computed on an annual basis; however, depending on the circumstances, a more significant computation might have been based on the operations during the last month or final quarter in the year during which the particular articles in the inventory are assumed to have been produced.

Tax and Other Influences on Overhead Absorption. The foregoing discussion of the problems in allocating overhead to inventory should be considered fundamental in nature. Emphasized is the fact of differing approaches and the need for judgment as well as the validity of various procedures under differing circumstances. More detailed explanations and analyses of major inventory accounting practices, including diversity of procedures, environmental influences, and continuing questions, are clearly presented in the comprehensive, 1973 AICPA Research Study No. 13, *The Accounting Basis of Inventories*, by Horace G. Barden.

The Cost Accounting Standards Board (CASB) has exerted considerable influence in the costing of inventories of companies engaged in government contracting through its published Standards applicable to accounting techniques and objectives, record keeping, definitions, and methods of overhead allocation and criteria for allowable costs and expenses. For example, specific Standards cover *Consistency in Estimating, Accumulating and Reporting Costs* (401 and 402), *Allocation of Home Office Expense to Segments* (403), and *Use of Standard Costs of Direct Material and Direct Labor* (407). Because many civilian agencies, as well as the U.S. Department of Defense, have adopted the CASB Standards, many smaller contractors have been forced to change their cost accounting and contract reporting practices.

Actual practice seems reflected in the following general conclusions of Paragraph 3.5 of Statement No. 6, issued in 1973 by the Committee on Management Accounting Practice of the National Association of Accountants:

> (a) Where it is practical and meaningful to do so, expenditures for materials, supplies, labor, and services which are necessary for and indirectly associated with producing the goods should be included in the inventories as part of the inventory amount. In some instances it is neither practical nor meaningful to make allocation to the inventory of charges for depreciation, taxes, and certain other classes of expenditures. However, the judgment as to whether or not a particular class of expenditure is included in the amount of inventories should be applied on a consistent basis.
>
> (b) Many companies adopt what they consider a conservative posture in treating as period expenses certain items which might reasonably be asso-

EXHIBIT 7 Analysis of Indirect Production Costs for Full Absorption Purposes

Description of cost	Situation A: Taxpayers using comparable methods of accounting for inventory for tax and financial reporting purposes			Situation B: Taxpayers not using comparable methods of accounting for inventory for tax and financial reporting purposes	
	Category 1: Required to be included in inventory cost	Category 2: Not required to be included in inventory cost	Category 3: Required to be treated same as financial statements	Category 1: Required to be included in inventory cost	Category 2: Not required to be included in inventory cost
Repairs and maintenance	X			X	
Utilities	X			X	
Rent	X			X	
Indirect labor and production supervisory wages, including basic compensation, overtime pay, vacation and holiday pay, sick leave [other than payments pursuant to a wage continuation plan under section 105(d)], shift differential, payroll taxes, and contributions to a supplemental unemployment benefit plan	X			X	
Officers' salary related to business activities as a whole		X			X
Officers' salary related to production			X	X	
Pension contributions representing past service cost		X			X
Pension contributions representing current service cost			X	X	
Profit-sharing contributions			X	X	

Cost item	1	2	3	4	5
Other employee benefit costs, including workmen's compensation expenses, payments under wage continuation plan described in section 105(d), amounts includable in income of an employee under nonqualified pension, profit-sharing, and stock bonus plans, premiums on life and health insurance, and miscellaneous employee benefits ..			X		
Indirect materials and supplies.	X				
Tools and equipment not capitalized.	X			X	X
Cost of quality control and inspection.	X			X	X
Marketing, advertising, and distribution expenses . .		X			X
Interest		X			X
Research and experimental expenses		X			X
Losses under section 165		X			X
Depreciation and depletion reported in financial statements			X	X	
Depreciation and depletion in excess of amount reported in financial statements		X			X
Income tax attributable to income received on sale of inventory.		X			X
Taxes allowable as a deduction under section 164, excluding state, local, and foreign income taxes, attributable to assets incident to production or manufacturing.			X	X	
General and administrative expenses incident to business activities as a whole		X			
Factory administrative expenses			X	X	X
Costs attributable to strikes, rework labor, scrap, and spoilage			X	X	
Insurance incident to production			X	X	

ciated with a product amount, if only rather indirectly. The principal reasons for this attitude given by respondents to an NAA research study on
allocation of indirect charges are:
 a. Method of allocation would be too arbitrary.
 b. Results would be misleading.
 c. Amounts are often insignificant.
Out of 1,200 responses which were included in the tabulation, 671 indicated the firms do not allocate all expenditures indirectly related to production (at least on a broad-brush basis) in preparation of their annual
financial statements (for the general public). For purposes of management
(internal) reporting, 691 companies do not allocate.

In recognition of the complexities in this area and the practical need to rely
on consistent industry accounting practices, in 1973 the U.S. Treasury and
Internal Revenue Service issued so-called full absorption regulations for manufacturers [Reg. §1.471-11(a)] that most practitioners consider "enlightened." In
extending the book/tax conformity objective required for the approval of
changes in the accounting methods, the government made mandatory for most
manufacturers the inclusion of *direct* production costs (Category I), permitted
exclusion of certain indirect costs (Category II), and authorized other indirect
expenses (Category III) to be included or excluded depending on their treatment for financial accounting purposes, provided that the treatment was not
inconsistent with generally accepted accounting principles. For the few taxpayers who do not have comparable methods of determining inventory for both
book and tax purposes, two categories of expenses were mandated: Category I
must be included, whereas Category II may be excluded. A liberal, 2-year
implementation period was established under which the effects on taxable
income were spread over 10 years after giving effect to a specific "pre-1954
adjustment." Special provisions also applied to significant standard cost variances, LIFO computations, and the practical capacity method discussed earlier
in this chapter under "Analytical Costing."

Exhibit 7 illustrates the treatment of typical overhead expenses for manufacturers depending on their particular tax status under these (almost) full absorption regulations.

Excess Inventories—*Thor* Decision. In January 1980, the U.S. Supreme
Court held in *Thor Power Tool Co.* [439 US 522 (1979)] that, even though a
write-down in the carrying value of excessive quantities of inventory is in
accord with generally accepted accounting principles, the tax law does not permit a deduction for this apparent loss in current value. The goods at issue were
in normal condition, the selling prices were not reduced, but the taxpayer had
reason to believe that all the goods would not be sold in the normal business
cycle. The Court distinguished deductible losses from scrapping or market
write-downs relating to reduced selling prices and cases where abnormal goods
were actually disposed of soon after the end of the taxable year.

Because the *Thor* decision had wide application to manufacturing and publishing companies, the Internal Revenue Service provided a standard procedure (Revenue Procedure 80-5, 1980-1 CB 582 and Revenue Ruling 80-60, 1980-
1 CB 97) for reporting the increase in income for the required restoration of

these write-downs over a 10-year period beginning in 1979. Although taxpayers using the first-in, first-out cost flow assumption received some benefit from the 10-year spread in reporting taxable income, those using or adopting LIFO during the spread period must include in taxable income any unreported restoration of the "excess inventory" reserves in order to state LIFO inventories at cost, as noted later with respect to LIFO computations. Firms that adopt LIFO after 1981 may restore these reserves over a 3-year period under Section 472(d).

LIFO

Reasons for Development of the LIFO Assumption as to the Movement of Goods. The acceptance of conventional accounting procedures that recognize cost, or the lower of cost or market, in stating inventories appears to have been a natural consequence of the thought that the principal financial statement is the balance sheet. In reflecting the financial position of a business, it is logical to determine the shareholders' equity by deducting the total of the liabilities from the valuation of the assets.

The development and acceptance of the LIFO inventory method resulted from increasing emphasis being placed on the income statement. Under currently accepted accounting concepts, the statement of financial position is conceived of as reflecting amounts for the assets (other than cash, receivables, and sundry assets from which the maximum cash realization is fixed) that merely represent the unabsorbed portion of expenditures incurred in the past but applicable to the future and to be charged against the revenue of some future period. From this viewpoint, it was logical to develop an accounting convention relative to inventories designed to result in a more appropriate charge being made against current sales for the cost of goods sold. The basic principle of LIFO is that current income is better determined by deducting from the sales of the accounting period the cost of replacing the merchandise used in making the sales; in view of the difficulty of computing the cost for each sale, however, the desired end result is approximated by stating the inventory on a LIFO basis.

The physical quantity of goods may remain constant from year to year, but the number of dollars invested in that inventory may increase or decrease solely as a result of changes in prices. So long as a businessman relies on continuous turnover of inventory to produce income, it is important that the effects of mere changes in prices be distinguished from profits attributable to the sale of merchandise.

If there is on hand at the beginning and end of any year the same physical quantity of goods, but solely as a result of changes in prices the dollar amount attributed to those goods for inventory purposes has increased 10 percent, this 10 percent increase in the dollar amount represents an unrealized inventory profit. This profit cannot be used to pay taxes or wages or dividends but must be retained in the business in order to permit its very continuation by replacing the goods that have been sold. If these unrealized inventory profits continue, the business can be forced to secure additional capital to finance the higher-cost purchases, even though there has been no actual growth.

It is equally significant that a decline in the value of an inventory can, under the FIFO inventory method, depress the operating results; the LIFO method similarly attempts to distinguish this type of charge against income from the normal results of current business operations.

Wherever the quantities in the closing inventory equal or exceed the volume of the opening inventory, the desired result of charging against current income a cost for the goods sold based on contemporary prices is accomplished within reasonable limits. In the event of a reduction in inventory volume, however, the present-day LIFO method departs from the objective of reflecting current replacement costs and yields to the conventional accounting practice of dealing only with accomplished facts.

From the standpoint of those who put primary emphasis on the balance sheet, LIFO is unsatisfactory because the amount assigned to the inventory may have no relationship to current value and may reflect an aggregation of price levels during several unidentified years depending on the number of "layers" considered as being in the inventory. Similarly, from the standpoint of those who believe that true income can be stated only if all the factors of income, costs, and expenses are expressed in terms of a unit with the same monetary value, LIFO is admittedly deficient where there has been a reduction in the volume of goods on hand at the end of the year.

As the result of taxpayer persistence, in the Revenue Act of 1938, Congress authorized the use of LIFO for specified raw materials used by tanners, and the producers and processors of certain nonferrous metals. The following year Congress expanded the use of LIFO and removed the restrictions as to the industries and classes of inventories to which LIFO could be applied. Under the Revenue Act of 1939, any taxpayer could elect the LIFO method with respect to any of the goods in inventory.

The present provisions of the Internal Revenue Code do not permit either (1) the "replacement" of inventories and the restoration of previous costs except upon determination of the Secretary of the Treasury that there has been a "qualified inventory interruption" caused by "an embargo, international boycott or other major foreign trade interruption" or any Department of Energy ruling limiting energy supplies, or (2) the write-down of inventories to market where market is lower than LIFO costs. A write-down to market is permitted by the regulations for financial reporting purposes only.

Timing the Adoption of LIFO. The decision as to when LIFO should be adopted depends on many factors, which will be different in every case. Generally, the principal factors governing the question of "when" include:

1. Rise in prices, because price increases cause paper profits in the inventory

2. High taxes, because a tax saving (or deferment) is the most tangible benefit from electing LIFO

3. Normal inventory quantities, because if there is a substantial increase in inventory quantities during years of inflated prices, the equivalent of such increased quantities may remain indefinitely in the LIFO inventory at the high prices

4. No foreseeable conditions that could cause the liquidation of the inven-

tory during the high-price and high-tax period, because such liquidation would mean that the recognition of income was only temporarily deferred and the income may actually be taxed at a higher rate

After LIFO is once adopted, it will normally be advantageous, so long as high prices continue, to maintain normal inventory quantities and avoid a liquidation at the end of any year. Inventory liquidations at an interim date are immaterial to the LIFO computations, but the necessity to maintain quantities at each year-end may result in the accounting department of a business temporarily directing the volume of purchases and shipments near the close of the year.

Consequences of Cost Reductions. If the LIFO method is applied to the aggregate of the elements of the cost of an inventory of manufactured goods and a procedure is developed for substantially reducing production costs, it may be that the cost savings effected through an improvement in production methods are being offset against the price increases attributable to material in the product. This has prompted some companies to limit the application of the LIFO method to the material content of the inventory. Where the LIFO method is applied to manufacturing costs as well as the material content, the volume of inventoriable production costs is commonly measured in terms of direct labor hours or some other unit in order to preserve the benefits of increased efficiency.

There may also be unforeseen consequences of LIFO in the event of product changes. Such changes can result from using a different raw material on the production of items that had previously been purchased, as well as a distinct change in the finished product. As an illustration, members of the wool industry adopted LIFO and subsequently began to substitute artificial fibers for natural wool. Where the inventory volume is measured in terms of yards and LIFO is applied to one particular type of material, such a change in material means the complete liquidation of the original inventory and the inclusion in income of the entire amount previously deferred through election of the LIFO method. With the passage of time, almost every business may expect that new lines will be added and old ones dropped.

In the case of a business anticipating that it may resort to a different type of raw material, it may be helpful to use the dollar value principle in which the aggregate investment in inventory is considered rather than the quantity of particular items. Where the substituted material has not been the subject of a price increase similar to that of the original material, the dollar value method does not provide a completely satisfactory solution but is of some benefit.

Conditions to the Use of LIFO for Income Tax Purposes. The two principal conditions to be complied with if LIFO is to be used for federal income tax purposes are (1) the filing of appropriate election forms with the federal income tax return covering the year in which the method is first used and (2) the statutory requirement that no other method be used in determining income for the purpose of annual reports to shareholders, creditors, and other interested parties. Of significance is the fact that the LIFO election need not be made until after the close of the year in which the method is to be used for federal income tax purposes. Although state income tax laws do not in all cases provide specifically for an exception to the general rule for securing advance approval of changes in accounting methods, the general practice is to follow substantially the same procedure on state returns as on the federal return.

The requirement in the Internal Revenue Code that no method other than LIFO be used in stating inventories for the purpose of *determining income in annual reports* to shareholders, creditors, and others must be recognized by management and is not a matter of mere detail. Reports to shareholders are frequently prepared before it is necessary to file the federal income tax return and make the final decision as to adoption of the LIFO method for tax purposes. Consequently, it may be necessary to use that method in the annual report going to shareholders even though there is a possibility that the decision will be against the adoption of LIFO for tax purposes.

It is not necessary that the inventory amount as computed for purposes of the financial statements be the same as later used in the tax return. For example, there may be a difference in the classification of the inventory as used in the financial statement computation. The Internal Revenue Code merely requires that no method other than LIFO be used in computing income in financial statements covering a taxable year. The restriction does not apply to interim statements.

Interim Financial Statements and Statements of Product or Departmental Results. Questions naturally arise as to whether, from a practical standpoint, the LIFO principle can be incorporated in a cost accounting system and the commonly used form of statements of product or branch results and of departmental operations. It is reasoned that if the LIFO method results in a better reflection of income, it should be used for all management purposes. In practice, however, LIFO is generally appended to previously used operating statements and cost systems.

In reporting profits of the business as a whole, "ideal" conditions for using LIFO are simple, that is, when closing inventories equal opening inventories and the goods sold are equivalent to the purchases for each accounting period throughout the year. Because such conditions are rarely, if ever, found in practice, the accounting system must provide for reflecting all possible developments.

If at the end of an interim accounting period the inventory of any LIFO group is below the opening inventory for the year, an estimate must be made of the amount of closing inventory for the year. Assuming that at the interim date no reduction is expected for the year, cost of sales for the interim period should be charged with the cost of goods purchased plus an estimated amount to cover the cost that will be incurred in making good the temporary decrease in inventory. An account should be established (ordinarily shown on the balance sheet among current liabilities) for the difference between the estimated replacement cost and the LIFO inventory cost for the quantities liquidated to the interim date.

The opposite situation is where a reduction is expected in the closing inventory as compared with what was on hand at the beginning of the year. Should a substantial difference exist between LIFO cost and current replacement cost and should the major part of the liquidation occur in one month, the charge to cost of sales for the goods liquidated may be abnormally low (or high) and result in a distortion of monthly profits. In some cases this difference is spread over the months remaining from the time such decrease becomes apparent until year-end. In other cases cost of sales is charged with amounts computed by reference to current replacement costs and a special credit (or charge) shown as being attributable to the liquidation of a portion of the beginning LIFO inventory.

Estimates of the year-end inventory volume must also be made when there is an increase in inventory at an interim date. If a decrease or at least no substantial increase is expected for the year as a whole, the temporary increase can be priced at the most easily identified acquisition cost. If an increase is expected for the year, such increase will be reflected in the closing inventory at current-year costs. The difference between the actual acquisition costs at the interim date and the cost at which the increased quantity will be included in the closing LIFO inventory (first-purchase costs for the year, last-purchase costs, or average cost) must be taken into cost of sales during some part of the year. If the amount of such difference is large, care should be used not to reflect it in one period so as to distort profits. If it can be predetermined with reasonable accuracy, this type of difference can appropriately be spread over the remainder of the year because the inventory volume at year-end in excess of the opening inventory is a consequence of the purchasing or production policy followed throughout the year rather than during any particular period.

LIFO Computations Where Quantities Are Determined by Weight or Count. The classification of inventories into groups for LIFO purposes depends primarily on the character of the goods involved and the complexity of the inventories. Although a LIFO computation wherein quantities are determined directly by weight or count is simple and involves the least amount of clerical effort and expense, the chief disadvantage of this procedure is its limited application in a business that has a variety of raw materials and manufactures many types of goods. If the quantity method were adopted in such a business, there would be numerous LIFO groups, and over a period of years, as quantities increased and decreased, there would be a tendency to restore to income some of the inflationary profit that LIFO was designed to eliminate.

The dollar value principle of measuring the volume of goods in a LIFO inventory is usually applied except where the inventory as a whole consists of relatively few raw material commodities or products that can be measured and expressed in units of quantity.

When the LIFO method is first adopted, the opening inventory of the year may have to be adjusted. The goods must be reflected in the beginning inventory at cost and are considered as having been acquired at the same time. In stating the opening inventory at cost, any write-down to market values or provisions for excess quantities (including restoration of write-downs of so-called subnormal goods covered by the LIFO election) with respect to the closing inventory of the preceding year must be restored. Such restorations create additional income or reduce the loss, whichever the case may be, for the preceding year. When the write-down to market and "excess" provisions are restored, the

EXHIBIT 8   LIFO Computations Where Quantities Are Determined by Weight or Count

	LIFO base	Inventories at end of				
		First year	Second year	Third year	Fourth year	Fifth year
1. Inventory quantities	10,000 bu	12,000 bu	11,000 bu	9,000 bu	10,500 bu	10,000 bu
2. Current-year cost per bushel	$2.00	$2.046	$2.107	$2.090	$2.111	$2.143
Inventory on LIFO basis:						
In bushels, attributable to:						
3. Base year	10,000 bu	10,000 bu	10,000 bu	9,000 bu	9,000 bu	9,000 bu
4. First year		2,000	1,000			
5. Fourth year					1,500	1,000
6. Total	10,000 bu	12,000 bu	11,000 bu	9,000 bu	10,500 bu	10,000 bu
At LIFO cost, attributable to:						
7. Base year (3 × $2.00)	$20,000	$20,000	$20,000	$18,000	$18,000	$18,000
8. First year (4 × $2.046)		4,092	2,046			
9. Fourth year (5 × $2.111)					3,167	2,111
10. Total LIFO inventory cost	$20,000	$24,092	$22,046	$18,000	$21,167	$20,111
11. Inventory on current cost basis (1 × 2)		24,552	23,177	18,810	22,166	21,430
12. Cumulative inventory effect from use of LIFO method (10 − 11)		$ (460)	$ (1,131)	$ (810)	$ (999)	$ (1,319)

cost of the goods in the opening inventory will be the cost determined by the method previously used, that is, the cost determined by reference to specific invoices, by the assumption of FIFO, by the use of an average of the opening inventory and purchases during the year, or by any other procedure consistently followed by the company under the lower-of-cost-or-market rule.

The opening inventory for the first LIFO year is the basic "layer." At the close of the year the quantity on hand is compared with the quantity at the beginning. If there is no increase in quantity, the average cost of the basic layer is applied to the quantity on hand at the end of the year to obtain the inventory amount. If there is an increase in quantity, a current-year's cost must be established. The methods commonly used to establish the current-year's cost are generally described as first-purchase costs, last-purchase costs, or the average cost for the year. Many companies that elect to price quantity increments by reference to the actual cost of goods most recently acquired, or by reference to the actual cost of goods acquired during the taxable year in the order of acquisition, determine an average cost for each month during which acquisitions are made, the aggregate of which equals or exceeds the increase in inventory, and then treat the quantity acquired and average cost as a single "layer" for inventory pricing.

Decreases in quantities are taken from the most recent year's acquisitions.

An illustration of LIFO inventory computations where bushels are the unit for measuring the quantity of goods on hand is set forth in Exhibit 8.

LIFO Computations Where Relative Quantities Are Determined by the Retail Inventory Method. The procedures for applying the LIFO concept to the determination of amounts to be assigned to retail department store inventories were developed to meet a specific business need. To superimpose the LIFO principle on the retail method, price fluctuations are adjusted by application of a series of nationwide price indexes to the total dollar value of each departmental inventory.

The LIFO problem peculiar to retailers arises from the fact that because of the nature of the business there is rarely a record of the specific identity of individual inventory items. The retail method consists of accumulating the aggregate retail value of all items in a department at the inventory date and reducing this departmental total by applying an adjustment representing the average gross markup on that department's goods.

The series of inventory price indexes approved by the Treasury Department for federal income tax purposes is based on data furnished by the Bureau of Labor Statistics (BLS) exclusively for the use of retail stores. Because the tabulations published by the Bureau of Labor Statistics use either January or July 1941 as 100 percent, department stores electing LIFO as of later dates compute their own accumulative percentage of price change. To aid in these computations, the government statistics show the percentage of price change during each year.

A form of worksheet for the computation of departmental LIFO inventories is illustrated by Exhibit 9. It will be noted that the BLS index is applied to the retail value of the inventory rather than to the cost.

EXHIBIT 9 LIFO Computations Where Relative Quantities Are Determined by the Retail Inventory Method

Department: _____
No.: _____

		Inventories at end of				
	LIFO base	First year	Second year	Third year	Fourth year	Fifth year
Conversion factors:						
1. Percentage change in BLS index during the year.		2.30%	3.00%	(0.80)%	1.00%	1.50%
2. Index of price-level change from LIFO base.	100.00%	102.30	105.34	104.50	105.55	107.13
Percentage of cost to retail value:						
3. As of base year.	60.00					
4. As of current year.		59.56	59.80	61.00	59.20	60.70
5. Inventory at retail value.	$10,000	$12,000	$11,000	$9,000	$10,500	$10,000
6. Inventory at base-year price (5 ÷ 2).	10,000	11,730	10,442	8,612	9,948	9,334
Inventory on LIFO basis:						
At base-year price level, attributable to:						
7. Base year.	$10,000	$10,000	$10,000	$8,612	$8,612	$8,612
8. First year.		1,730	442			
9. Fourth year.					1,336	722
10. Total.	$10,000	$11,730	$10,442	$8,612	$9,948	$9,334
At LIFO cost, attributable to:						
11. Base year (7 × 60.00%).	$6,000	$6,000	$6,000	$5,167	$5,167	$5,167
12. First year (8 × 102.30% × 59.56%).		1,054	269			
13. Fourth year (9 × 105.55% × 59.20%).					835	451
14. Total LIFO inventory cost.	$6,000	$7,054	$6,269	$5,167	$6,002	$5,618
15. Inventory on current cost basis (5 × 4).		7,147	6,578	5,490	6,216	6,070
16. Cumulative inventory effect from use of LIFO method (14 − 15).		($ 93)	($ 309)	($ 323)	($ 214)	($ 452)

LIFO Computations Where Relative Quantities Are Determined by the Dollar Value Principle. The dollar value principle is that the volume of the goods in annual inventories can be measured in terms of total dollars reflecting cost levels for the inventory items as of a particular year. The appropriate unit of measure for the various items may be yards, tons, gallons, or any combination of these and similar measures, but the common denominator for determining the total volume of goods in the inventories from year to year is dollars.

The term "base-year cost" is the aggregate of the cost (determined as of the beginning of the year for which the LIFO method is first adopted) for all items in the inventory, and the term "base-year units costs" refers to the individual costs as of that date for the various items. Liquidations and increments for a particular LIFO inventory are reflected only in terms of a net liquidation or increment for the inventory as a whole. Fluctuations will occur in quantities of items within the inventory. New items may be added and discontinued items may be dropped without necessarily effecting a change in the dollar value of the inventory as a whole.

In the case of a manufacturer or processor, the entire inventory which is considered to relate to a "natural business unit" is commonly reflected in a single LIFO computation. Where an enterprise is composed of more than one business unit, a separate inventory must be recognized for each. What constitutes a natural business unit is considered in the following excerpt from the federal income tax regulations [Reg. §1.472-8(b)(2)(i)]:

> Whether an enterprise is composed of more than one natural business unit is a matter of fact to be determined from all the circumstances. The natural business divisions adopted by the taxpayer for internal management purposes, the existence of separate and distinct production facilities and processes, and the maintenance of separate profit and loss records with respect to separate operations are important considerations in determining what is a business unit, unless such divisions, facilities, or accounting records are set up merely because of differences in geographical location. In the case of a manufacturer or processor, a natural business unit ordinarily consists of the entire productive activity of the enterprise within one product line or within two or more related product lines including (to the extent engaged in by the enterprise) the obtaining of materials, the processing of materials, and the selling of manufactured or processed goods. Thus, in the case of a manufacturer or processor, the maintenance and operation of a raw material warehouse does not generally constitute, of itself, a natural business unit. If the taxpayer maintains and operates a supplier unit the production of which is both sold to others and transferred to a different unit of the taxpayer to be used as a component part of another product, the supplier unit will ordinarily constitute a separate and distinct natural business unit. Ordinarily, a processing plant would not in itself be considered a natural business unit if the production of the plant, although saleable at this stage, is not sold to others, but is transferred to another plant of the enterprise, not operated as a separate division, for further processing or incorporation into another product. On the other hand, if the production of a manufacturing or processing plant is transferred to a separate and distinct division of the taxpayer, which constitutes a natural business unit, the supplier unit itself will ordinarily be considered a natural business unit. However, the mere fact that a portion of the production of a manufacturing

or processing plant may be sold to others at a certain stage of processing with the remainder of the production being further processed or incorporated into another product will not of itself be determinative that the activities devoted to the production of the portion sold constitute a separate business unit. Where a manufacturer or processor is also engaged in the wholesaling or retailing of goods purchased from others, the wholesaling or retailing operations with respect to such purchased goods shall not be considered a part of any manufacturing or processing unit.

Inventories of wholesalers, retailers, jobbers, and distributors are classified for the purpose of LIFO computations by major lines, types, or classes of goods. Customary business classifications of the particular trade generally provide a satisfactory basis for determining the extent to which items can be combined into a single inventory pool by application of the dollar-value principle. In some cases operations of other than a manufacturer or processor may constitute a single natural business unit.

A wide variety of procedures have been developed for determining an appropriate index to be used in dollar value LIFO inventory computations. As a general rule, however, a "double-extension method" is used for computing the base-year and current-year cost. Under this method, the quantity of each item in the inventory at the close of the year is extended at both its base-year unit cost and the current-year unit cost. The comparison of the relative volume of the opening and closing inventories, as reflected by the totals of the extensions at the base-year unit costs, indicates whether there has been an increment or liquidation for the year. The relationship between the totals of the extensions of the closing inventory at the current-year unit costs and at the base-year unit costs can be used as the factor to be applied in converting an increment from base-year cost to current-year cost. This conversion factor may be measured by whichever procedure was selected for costing increments, that is, on the basis of the earliest acquisitions during the year, the most recent acquisitions, or an average for the entire year.

Under the double-extension method, a base-year unit cost must be established for each new item. In many instances it is most practicable to use the earliest actual cost recorded for the item, but a base-year unit cost may be constructed. For an item that was in existence, the base-year unit cost should be the price that would have been paid by the company had the item been used. Where the new item is a product or raw material not in existence in the base year, an amount should be constructed that represents what the cost would have been in the base year had the item been in existence. Frequently the base-year unit cost for a new item is computed by applying to the current-year cost of such item the percentage relationship between the base-year unit cost and current-year unit cost for an item sufficiently similar in physical characteristics to justify an assumption that the changes in unit cost would have been comparable.

With the passage of time, the proportion of the items in an inventory that were not included in the base-year inventory will increase. In recognition of the facts that the base-year unit costs established for LIFO inventory computation purposes can often be utilized for management control purposes and that reasonably current costs are more significant and accurate than reconstructed costs, the double-extension method of applying the dollar value principle is frequently modified to permit the use of a substitute base year. The updating of the base-year costs does not change the LIFO cost for the inventory, but merely permits the use of the more current and reliable unit costs for purposes of measuring the relative volume of the goods included in the inventories.

Exhibit 10 illustrates LIFO inventory computations where the volume of goods is measured by the dollar value principle.[1]

Link Chain. In recognition of the reliability and practicality afforded by the comparison of current costs to costs of the immediately preceding year, many companies, especially those with changing products, adopt the "link chain" method of determining an annual index. The overall change in cost levels is determined by multiplying the last previously determined cumulative index by the most recent annual index, as illustrated in Exhibit 11 using the same assumption as in Exhibit 10. This procedure, which produces slightly different results from the base-year double-extension method, is also used in compiling the BLS indexes for the computation of LIFO inventories by retail stores.

Use of Government Price Indexes. On March 16, 1982, the Treasury Department followed a directive in the Economic Recovery Tax Act of 1981 (ERTA) to permit taxpayers to use certain government price indexes in the computation of LIFO inventories. Mainly for the benefit of smaller companies in simplifying calculations, this alternative sanctions the use of producer (PPI) or consumer indexes (CPI) published by the Bureau of Labor Statistics.

Manufacturers, processors, wholesalers, jobbers, and distributors may use only PPI (converted cost) price indexes. Retailers may use either PPI or CPI indexes with appropriate adjustment and limitation based on the inventory method used (retail or cost) and types of goods covered.

In general, pools follow the categories provided by the respective published indexes: 11 consumer goods and 15 producer categories. Within each pool, inventory items comprising 10 percent or more of the total inventory must be placed in separate categories to which the most detailed index is applied. This procedure is repeated until all items are included in any index category except possibly goods representing less than 10 percent of the total inventory value, which are placed in a miscellaneous category to which a weighted-average index is applied based on previously classified items in the same pool. Furthermore, inventory *pools* (usually in a separate index category) that comprise less than 5 percent of total inventory may be combined with the largest inventory *pool*.

Consistent with another small business provision in ERTA (Sec. 474) under which a company may use a single LIFO pool if its average annual gross receipts do not exceed $2,000,000 for the 3-year period ending with the current taxable year, a qualifying small firm may use 100 percent of the change indicated in the CPI or PPI indexes. The allowable percentage in LIFO calculations of all other taxpayers shall be 80 percent of the published change in the appro-

---

[1]Further illustration can generally be found in intermediate accounting text books. See, for example, chap. 10 in Davidson et al. [1982].

EXHIBIT 10 LIFO Computations Where Relative Quantities Are Determined by the Dollar Value Principle

	LIFO base	First year	Second year	Third year	Fourth year	Fifth year
			Inventories at end of			
Conversion factors:						
Inventory extended at:						
1. Current-year unit costs	$100,000	$120,000	$110,000	$90,000	$105,000	$100,000
2. Base-year unit costs	100,000	117,300	104,420	86,120	99,480	93,340
3. Percentage of total base-year cost to total current-year cost (2 ÷ 1)	100.00%	97.75%	94.93%	95.69%	94.74%	94.34%
Inventory on LIFO basis:						
At base-year costs, attributable to:						
4. Base year	$100,000	$100,000	$100,000	$86,120	$86,120	$86,120
5. First year		17,300	4,420			
6. Fourth year					13,360	7,220
7. Total	$100,000	$117,300	$104,420	$86,120	$99,480	$93,340
At LIFO cost, attributable to:						
8. Base year (4 × 100.00%)	$100,000	$100,000	$100,000	$86,120	$86,120	$86,120
9. First year (5 ÷ 97.75%)		17,698	4,522			
10. Fourth year (6 ÷ 94.74%)					14,102	7,621
11. Total LIFO inventory cost	$100,000	$117,698	$104,522	$86,120	$100,222	$93,741
12. Inventory on current cost basis (line 1)	$100,000	120,000	110,000	90,000	105,000	100,000
13. Cumulative inventory effect from use of LIFO method (11 − 12)		$ (2,302)	$ (5,478)	$ (3,880)	$ (4,778)	$ (6,259)

EXHIBIT 11 LIFO Computations Where Annual Index Is Determined by the Link Chain Method

			Inventories at end of			
	LIFO base	First year	Second year	Third year	Fourth year	Fifth year
Conversion factors:						
Inventory extended at:						
1. End of current-year unit costs	$100,000	$120,000	$110,000	$ 90,000	$105,000	$100,000
2. Beginning of current-year unit costs	100,000	117,300	106,832	90,729	103,961	98,520
3. Percentage of total beginning of current-year costs to total end of current-year costs (2 ÷ 1)		97.75%	97.12%	100.81%	9.01%	98.52%
4. Cumulative index (previous year's cumulative × current index)	100.00%	97.75%	94.93%	95.70%5	94.75%	93.35%
5. Ending inventory at base-year cost (1 × 4)	$100,000	$117,300	$104,423	$ 83,130	$ 99,488	$ 93,350
Inventory on LIFO basis:						
At base-year costs, attributable to:						
6. Base year	$100,000	$100,000	$100,000	$ 86,130	$ 86,130	$86,130
7. First year		17,300	4,423			7,220
8. Fourth year					13,358	
9. Total	$100,000	$117,300	$104,423	$ 86,130	$ 99,488	$ 93,350
At LIFO cost, attributable to:						
10. Base year (6 ÷ 100%)	$100,000	$100,000	$100,000	$ 86,130	$ 86,130	$ 86,130
11. First year (7 ÷ 97.75%)		17,698	4,525			7,620
12. Fourth year (8 ÷ 94.75%)					14,098	
13. Total LIFO inventory cost	$100,000	$117,698	$104,525	$ 86,130	$100,228	$ 93,750
14. Inventory on current cost basis		120,000	110,000	90,000	105,000	100,000
15. Cumulative inventory effect from use of LIFO method (13 − 14)		$ (2,302)	$ (5,475)	$ (3,870)	$ (4,772)	$ (6,250)

EXHIBIT 12   LIFO Computations Using Government Indexes

	LIFO base	First year	Second year	Third year	Fourth year	Fifth year
Calculation of inventory price index:						
1. Producer (or consumer) price index	100.00%	10.00%	10.00%	(7.50%)	5.00%	5.00%
2. Cumulative producer (or consumer) price index		110.00%	121.00%	111.93%	117.53%	123.41%
3. Cumulative change in producer (or consumer) price index		10.00%	21.00%	11.93%	17.53%	23.41%
4. Cumulative inventory price index = (3) × 80% added to base index	100.00%	108.00%	116.80%	109.54%	114.02%	118.73%
5. Current-year cost	$100,000	$120,000	$110,000	$90,000	$105,000	$100,000
6. Base-year cost = (5)/(4)	$100,000	$111,111	$ 94,178	$82,162	$ 92,089	$ 84,224
Inventory on a LIFO basis:						
At base-year costs, attributable to:						
8. Base year	$100,000	$100,000	$ 94,178	$82,162	$ 82,162	$ 82,162
9. First year		11,111				2,062
10. Fourth year					9,927	
Total	$100,000	$111,111	$ 94,178	$82,162	$ 92,089	$ 84,224
At LIFO cost, attributable to:						
11. Base year	$100,000	$100,000	$ 94,178	$82,162	$ 82,162	$ 82,162
12. First year = (9) × 108%		12,000				2,351
13. Fourth year = (10) × 114.02					11,319	
14. Total LIFO inventory cost	$100,000	$112,000	$ 94,178	$82,162	$ 93,481	$ 84,513
15. Inventory on current cost basis = (5)	100,000	120,000	110,000	90,000	105,000	100,000
16. Cumulative inventory effect from use of LIFO method = (14) − (15)		($ 8,000)	($15,822)	($ 7,838)	($ 11,519)	($15,487)

16-36

priate price indexes. For example, for a pool in a larger company whose published index indicates an annual change of 10 percent, an 8 percent factor should be used in the actual LIFO calculations. The Administration decided that if it were separately computed, the taxpayer's own inflation rate might be overstated when compared to the national average.

Exhibit 12 illustrates the use of (80) government indexes similar to an application under the retail method based on Store Inventory Price Indexes published by the Bureau of Labor Statistics, which must be used by eligible department and specialty stores.

The extent to which large companies presently on LIFO will adopt government indexes rather than continue to compute their own and the acceptability of this alternative for financial accounting purposes are questions to be resolved in the future by each affected company. Recent developments under which a few companies' inventories are costed on a product-line basis in financial statements but on a "natural business unit" for tax purposes seem to project a greater spread in LIFO results even though both reflect only the last-in, first-out method and meet the conformity requirements discussed below.

Disclosures in Published Financial Statements. Prior to the release on January 22, 1981, of amended Treasury Regulation Section 1.472-2, the Internal Revenue Service had taken extremely restrictive positions in interpreting the statute that prohibits the reporting of income on any basis other than LIFO in reports to shareholders, partners, creditors, and so on. In summary, the IRS permitted disclosure in financial reports of the effects of LIFO on income, earnings per share, and financial position in accordance with the requirements of Opinion No. 20 of the Accounting Principles Board solely for the year the LIFO method was *adopted*. Under the less restrictive conformity requirements of the amended regulations, additional information on the effect of LIFO in subsequent years may be supplied providing that such information merely supplements or explains the taxpayer's *primary* presentation of financial income on the LIFO basis. Thus, appropriate footnote disclosure of balance sheet inventory amounts and even the effect on income is permitted as long as the appended material is clearly identified as a supplement or explanation to the primary presentation of income on the face of the taxpayer's income statement. The basic conformity requirement of "LIFO only" does not apply to internal management reports or interim periods aggregating less than any full year.

Companies should keep abreast of changing disclosure requirements of the SEC, FASB, Internal Revenue Service, and other regulatory bodies. An inappropriate presentation of the effect of LIFO on income might afford a basis for the Internal Revenue Service to terminate a company's LIFO election if the financial statement conformity requirements were considered violated.

BIBLIOGRAPHY

Barden, H. G., *The Accounting Basis of Inventories*, Accounting Research Study No. 13 (AICPA, 1973).

Committee on Accounting Procedure, *Restatement and Revision of Accounting Research Bulletins*, Accounting Research Bulletin No. 43 (CAP, 1953).

Cost Accounting Standards Board, *Published and Proposed Standards* (CASB, Washington, D.C.).

Davidson, S., C. P. Stickney, and R. L. Weil, *Intermediate Accounting: Concepts, Methods and Uses,* 3d ed. (The Dryden Press, Hinsdale, Ill., 1982).

General Services Administration, *The Economic Order Quantity Principle and Applications,* Federal Stock No. 7610-543-6765 (GSA, Washington, D.C., 1966).

Hoffman R. A., and H. Gunders, *Inventories—Control, Costing and Effect on Income and Taxes* (Ronald Press, New York, 1970).

James, C. P., C. H. Poedtke, and D. R. Zeigler, *Financing and Accounting for Inventories* (John Wiley & Sons, New York, 1980).

National Association of Accountants, *Guidelines for Inventory Management,* No. 6 on Management Accounting Practices (NAA, New York, 1973).

Plosal, G. W., and O. W. Wight, *Production and Inventory Control* (Prentice-Hall, Englewood Cliffs, N.J., 1967).

U.S. Internal Revenue Code provisions with respect to inventories and related regulations: Code §471 and 472 and Reg. §1.471 and 1.472.

CHAPTER **17**

Land

Morton B. Solomon
Partner, Main Hurdman

INTRODUCTION

Land is a measured area of the surface of the earth that includes the soil, the mineral content beneath the surface, and the space above the surface. Land may be considered for accounting purposes as a variety of rights inherent in its ownership and related to the function it serves. For example, land may be used:

1. As physical support for a structure
2. As a road or other means of passage, involving rights of occupation or easements or rights of way, which rights may be surface, subterranean, or air space
3. As a source of water, oil, gas, mineral deposits, or timber, using diversion, extraction, or severance rights
4. As a medium for the raising or taking of animals or fish, involving rights of grazing and pasture, or hunting and fishing
5. As a medium for the growth of trees, crops, or shrubs, indicating cultivation and severance rights.

Each of these rights has value; each may be purchased, sold, leased, or licensed. Thus, accounting for land may involve accounting for several rights, each of which may be considered an asset.

Types of Legal Interest. The legal interest in land rights varies. Where ownership is perpetual and includes all land rights, title is said to be in fee simple. An individual may have a life estate, granting land usage rights for his or her lifetime. The life estate may include mineral rights, cutting rights or water rights, and so on. An important variation is the interest of the remainderman, who owns a parcel of land subject to either an existing life interest or beneficial interest on the part of another person for a specified term of years.

Limited Interests. Some situations involve ownership of only a limited interest in land. For example, an easement may grant a perpetual right or a right for a limited period to traverse land with a road or a pipeline. Although a limited interest, such as an easement, is not ordinarily characterized as land for accounting purposes (the preference being to use a more descriptive title, such as easements), nonetheless, the procedures used in accounting for land also apply to such limited interests in land.

Leases. An interest in land may be owned through a lease. A lease is generally evidenced by a legal document that confers all, or a portion, of the rights to use and enjoyment of land to a person or other entity for a fixed or determinable period of time in consideration of the payment of rent or royalties. A mineral lease allows the lessee to extract the mineral content of the land, usually subject to certain rights retained by the owner of the land.

Liens and Encumbrances. Land often is purchased subject to a lien or encumbrance in the form of a mortgage. A mortgage is generally given to secure an unpaid purchase price or to secure repayment of money advanced as a loan. It represents a security interest that carries with it the right to foreclosure, generally upon nonpayment or nontimely payment of related debt.

BALANCE SHEET PRESENTATION

The purpose for which land is acquired and held determines how it is presented in the balance sheet and what additional disclosures are to be made.

Land as a Part of Property, Plant, and Equipment. Land, which by conventional criteria has asset status because of its use in productive operations, is generally classified as a part of property, plant, and equipment. Thus land is typically a plant asset. However, land held for a future plant site, land held for speculation, or land held as inventory is not so classified.

Land as a Potential Future Plant Site. Land held as a future plant site may be classified either as a long-term investment or among other assets. To the extent practicable in the circumstances, such land should be described as accurately as possible by a caption ("land held for future plant sites").

Land as an Investment. Land has long been a favorite medium for investment. When land is acquired for investment purposes, it should be classified as a long-term investment until the facts of an individual case suggest that it may be classified as a current asset. It may be desirable in certain situations for an entity to disclose in some supplementary fashion the current value of land held as an investment.

Land as Inventory. A significant exception to the general presumption against including land among current assets is the classification of land as inventory by companies whose business includes the sale of land to others. Land is the stock-in-trade of land developers or subdividers; in this case, it should be considered as inventory. Some of the accounting problems peculiar to land developers are considered in a later section, "Retail Land Sales."

Impairment of Economic Usefulness. Regardless of prior classification, if certain land is currently held for sale as a result of adverse factors that evidence impairment of its economic usefulness, such land should be segregated in the balance sheet from other properties held for continuing business advantage. Pending sale, it should be carried forward at recoverable cost if the latter is estimated to be lower than acquisition cost. A current loss provision should be made for that portion of cost deemed to have become "nonrecoverable."

Land Encumbered by a Mortgage. When land encumbered by a mortgage is acquired, the acquirer should record a liability for any unpaid balance of the original debt secured by the mortgage, when the debt covered by the mortgage is assumed by the buyer. The existence of the lien should be disclosed in the financial statements, usually in a footnote.

Carrying Value. All expenditures made to acquire land and place it in condition for the purpose intended should be considered part of the cost of land. Interest [FASB, 1979b, pars. .09–.11], real estate taxes, and other similar costs incurred during a holding period between the time of purchase and the time when land is placed in condition for use should be similarly considered part of the cost of land only during periods in which the land is undergoing activities necessary to get it ready for its intended use [Accounting Standards Division, 1980]. Thus, the cost of land includes any land option costs; any obligations assumed or payments made to discharge taxes, interest, and other expenses accrued at the time of purchase; obligations or outlays to discharge mortgages and other liens and encumbrances existing at the time of acquisition; finders' fees, attorneys' fees, and title insurance and title search costs; costs of necessary land grading, filling, clearing, or draining; costs of demolition of existing structures (unless the land was acquired with the intent of using such structures); and other costs necessary to gain access to the land, take possession of the land, and put the land to the use intended.

When land has been acquired for the purpose of supporting a building, all costs incurred up to the point of excavation for the building are generally considered land cost. The cost of excavation for a building is part of the building cost. However, if excavation is undertaken for purposes of contouring land for a golf course or terracing land for farming, such excavation costs would be capitalizable as a component of total land cost.

Appreciation. Valuation of cost (unless reduced to a lower estimated remaining useful cost due to impairment) has long been the rule in financial statement presentation.[1] Accounting Principles Board (APB) Opinion No. 6 [1965] states in this connection that " . . . property, plant and equipment should not be written up by an entity to reflect appraisal, market or current values which are above cost to the entity."

Depletion and Amortization. Costs attributable to land rights that lose value with use (such as the right to extract mineral content) are recognized through systematic charges (called depletion) against income, but only if there is a practicable basis for measuring or estimating relative periodic utilization of mineral or other content. Although depletion is generally associated with the extraction of mineral resources and severance of timber, there may be cases that justify reflection of depletion for the loss of value of other land rights. For example, the loss of soil fertility (where crop rotation and soil conservation practices were not carried out or when certain natural events have caused abnormal erosion) might give rise to the recognition of depletion.

Costs attributable to land rights that expire with the passage of time are recovered through systematic charges against income called amortization. Thus, costs to acquire a lease are amortized over the term of the lease. Similarly, costs to acquire an easement that expires at the end of a period of time are amortized over the term of the easement.

Costs attributable to land rights that do not diminish in value either with the passage of time or through use of the land are not amortized or depleted. For example, costs of land purchased to support a structure or a road across the surface ordinarily are not amortized or depleted. Similarly, the residual value of land used for mining purposes should remain unamortized even after exhaustion of the mineral or other content for which the land was originally purchased.

Salvage Proceeds. Proceeds from transactions incidental to preparing land for agricultural or commercial use, such as the sale of timber or crops cleared from the land or the sale of scrap from demolished structures, usually are treated as a reduction of land cost. In theory, the negotiated price reflects such anticipated proceeds.

Income and Costs during a Holding Period. Often land is acquired as an investment or for a specific future use, which contemplates the passage of time between the purchase date and the later date of sale or placement of the land to a specific use. Until the FASB issued Statement No. 34, *Capitalization of Interest Cost*, in 1979, and the AICPA issued Statement of Position (SOP) 80-3, *Accounting for Real Estate Acquisitions, Development, and Construction Costs*, in 1980, there was little guidance concerning the treatment of income and costs during this holding period, except for retail sales (see later section). FASB Statement No. 34 requires that interest be capitalized on land only during the

---

[1]See Principle C-2 and discussion under the heading "Property Stated on Cost Basis," in Grady [1965, pp. 252–253].

periods in which the land is undergoing activities necessary to get it ready for its intended use. If these activities are suspended voluntarily (except for brief interruptions caused by external factors), capitalization should stop until the activities are resumed. Interest incurred after the land is ready for use should be charged to expense as incurred. SOP 80-3 adopts the same criteria for capitalization of other costs (such as real estate taxes and maintenance charges) as the FASB did for interest. Because the costs to be incurred during this holding period entered into the decision to acquire the land, these costs logically may be considered a part of the total investment in the land, unless it is likely that a portion of costs so capitalized may not be recoverable; that is, a prospective future loss on disposition is foreseeable.

Any excess of incremental income over incremental costs from incidental operations during the holding period (such as income from ground rents or crops) should reduce total land cost. An excess of incremental costs over incremental income should be charged to expense as incurred.

Alternatively, when there is a regularly recurring and material source of income from land during a rather prolonged holding period, both revenue and expense may be reflected currently, particularly if the use of the land is considered an integral part of operations. In that event, the allocation of costs between land and depreciable assets may be necessary.

Land Option Costs. The cost of an option to acquire land is part of the cost of land. When an option is allowed to expire, expense should be recognized in that period. Under certain circumstances, however, if options are obtained on alternative parcels of land, one of which is eventually acquired for the stated purpose, the costs of the expired options as well as the cost of the exercised option may be added to the cost of the parcel of land acquired.

Land Improvements. The cost of land improvements (such as paving and sidewalks) that deteriorate with use or the passage of time should ordinarily be capitalized and depreciated over their estimated useful lives. However, the cost of improvements that do not deteriorate with use or passage of time (such as landscaping) ordinarily is not depreciated. Because these improvements are not depreciated, there is little need to distinguish their cost from the cost of land. Therefore, their cost is often capitalized directly as part of the cost of land.

Soil or Water Conservation Costs. Costs incurred to protect land from wind or water erosion should be capitalized, because the land is made suitable for the use intended. If, on the other hand, costs are incurred regularly to maintain land in its existing condition and thereby enable its continued use, these costs should be charged to expense currently. An important exception may occur during a "holding period," when even the maintenance costs may be considered as additional costs of land.

Allocation of Cost of "Basket Purchases." Often the purchase of a parcel of land is an inseparable part of a "basket purchase" of assets or net assets of a going concern. In such cases, the measurement of total cost or consideration is the lump sump paid, plus any liabilities assumed. The basket purchase price should then be allocated among the assets and liabilities acquired, in accordance with APB Opinion No. 16 [1970a].

The fair market value of each tangible asset purchased is, for the most part, the basis for allocating cost among the various assets. If the basket purchase includes intangible assets, the fair market value of the tangible assets, including land, originally is considered to be their cost, and any residual portion of the total basket purchase cost is then attributed to intangible assets.

The determination of fair market value is a problem that must be solved by reference to all the facts and circumstances in each individual case. Use of a qualified independent appraiser is recommended as the best practice; in some cases, however, appraisals are made by the board of directors. Other methods used to estimate fair market value include:

Recent sales prices for comparable land parcels, which may be used to determine the amount of cost attributable to the land. The remaining portion of the basket purchase price may be deemed to represent the cost of other tangible or intangible assets.

Cost of the land to the predecessor owner, which may indicate fair market value if it is known that such cost represents a recently bargained purchase price.

Replacement cost of other tangible assets, which sometimes can be estimated. This replacement cost, reduced by an allowance for depreciation when appropriate (the amount depending on the age, type of construction, and state of repair of the buildings and improvements), can be attributed to the other tangible assets and the remainder attributed to the land (or possibly, in part, to intangibles).

Assessed value of land for property tax purposes, which usually is not a reliable indicator of fair market value; however, if the assessed value can be demonstrated to be in constant ratio to the fair value, it may assist in estimating fair market value.

Future ability of the land to produce income, which is sometimes an accepted indicator of fair market value, although its estimation is not subject to exact computation. Probable future income from the land should be considered, however, as a test of the reasonableness of fair market values derived by other means.

Noncash Acquisitions

Exchange of nonmonetary assets for land. The basic principle expressed in APB Opinion No. 29 [1973] is that accounting for nonmonetary transactions should be based on the fair values of the assets involved, except for those transactions in which fair value is not determinable or the earnings process is not complete. Thus, an exchange of nonmonetary assets generally should be accounted for at the fair value of the nonmonetary asset surrendered or received, whichever is more clearly evident. Any gain or loss on the exchange should be recognized—except that when "similar" assets are involved, gain will not be recognized currently (unless some cash is received by the party trading in—a rare case). For transactions in which fair value is not measurable, accounting should be based on the recorded amount of the nonmonetary asset relinquished.

Issuance of a corporation's own securities. Issuance of a corporation's own securities for land is a frequent transaction. In general, the fair market value of the securities issued in exchange is considered to be the cost of the land when there is a reliable and readily ascertainable market value for the securities. This procedure usually is appropriate for companies whose securities are traded actively and in sufficient volume to establish a fair market value. When corporate bonds are issued, the problem of establishing the cost of land acquired is less difficult, because bonds specify coupon and principal payments at certain dates. These represent legally enforceable debt obligations ultimately payable in cash. Discounting at a rate reflecting current interest cost for a firm of this risk class values the bonds and, indirectly, the land. The par value or stated value of the securities issued is not a reliable indicator of the value of the land purchased in exchange for these securities. If the securities issued have no reliable and readily ascertainable market value, land valuation will have to be estimated by the methods described in the previous section on "basket purchases."

Donated Land. When a parcel of land is acquired by donation (nonreciprocal transfer with nonowner, under provisions of APB Opinion No. 29 [1973]), the land should be recorded at its fair value at the time the gift becomes effective. Donation of land results in an increase in capital (donated capital or capital contributed in excess of par value) and ordinarily does not result in income.

Land donated subject to continuing restrictions or conditions as to use (such as endowment) may be given asset status at the effective date of the gift, with disclosure of the continuing restrictions clearly indicated. If the unfulfilled conditions preclude reflecting the donated land as an asset until the conditions are met, the contingent nature of the asset and the unfulfilled conditions should be disclosed.

Land Costs Contingent on Future Events. Sometimes land is purchased for an amount that is dependent on future events; thus, its total cost is uncertain. The extent of this uncertainty determines the accounting treatment. For example, if the purchase contract provides for periodic payments during the seller's lifetime, the buyer may record the estimated land cost and the related liability based on the present discounted value of a life-contingent annuity for someone of the seller's age. Similarly, if land that produces a contractual income (e.g., fixed ground rents for a definite term of years) is acquired by promising periodic payments of a percentage of the rentals, an estimated cost can be based on the present value of the prospective payments. On the other hand, if the purchase contract provides for payments in the future dependent on income to be earned from the land that cannot be reasonably estimated, the buyer would not reflect the contingent cost until paid but would disclose the terms of purchase. Future income cannot be considered to be subject to reasonable estimate. Thus, no entry would be made at the date of purchase with regard to the contingent payments. Each period thereafter as payments are made, the land account would be debited [APB Opinion No. 16, 1970a].

Vested Remainderman Interest in Land. Acquisition of land subject to an intervening life estate may pose special valuation or cost measurement problems. Unless the land is acquired for cash, it will be necessary to estimate the present fair market value and then discount that amount by the use of life expectancy tables and an appropriate interest rate. This remainderman interest in land should be classified as an investment or among other assets, rather than as property, plant, and equipment. Financial statements should disclose the deferred nature of this claim.

Contribution of Land to a Venture. Land acquired by a venture as a part of its contributed capital raises special problems. For federal income tax purposes, the basis of the land to the venture usually is the basis to the contributing venturor. For financial reporting purposes, however, such land is properly reflected on the venture's financial statements at its fair market value at the date of acquisition.

The whole issue of accounting for ventures (and in particular real estate and construction ventures) has received considerable attention in recent years. The AICPA, in 1978, issued SOP 78-9, *Accounting for Investments in Real Estate Ventures* [Accounting Standards Division, 1978c], and in 1981 a revised *Audit and Accounting Guide for Construction Contractors* [Construction Contractor Guide Committee, 1981].

SALE OF LAND

For many years the accounting practices and principles governing recognition of profit on sales of land were based on the concept expressed in Chapter 1A of Accounting Research Bulletin (ARB) No. 43 [CAP, 1953]: "Profit is deemed to be realized when a sale in the ordinary course of business is effected, unless the circumstances are such that the collection of the sales price is not reasonably assured." Thus, subject to evaluation of the consideration received in the transaction, profit should be recognized at the time of sale if a bona fide sale had occurred. This concept was reaffirmed in APB Opinion No. 10 [1967], which stated: "Revenues should ordinarily be accounted for at the time a transaction is completed with appropriate provision for uncollectible accounts." This opinion provided for revenue recognition on the installment and cost recovery methods only in instances when there was no reasonable basis for estimating the degree of collectibility of the sales price. These concepts served as generally accepted accounting principles for specifying the time when revenue should be recognized until the issuance of APB Statement No. 4 [1970b], which promulgated, in part, more comprehensive principles of revenue recognition. Statement No. 4 defines revenue as "a gross increase in assets or decrease in liabilities . . . that result from those types of profit-directed activities of an enterprise that can change owners' equity. Revenue ... is derived from three general activities: (a) selling products, (b) rendering services ... and (c) disposing of resources other than products. ..." The statement held that realization is the measurement principle on which revenue recognition is based, and set forth this principle as follows.

Realization. Revenue is generally recognized when both of the following conditions are met: (1) The earnings process is complete or virtually complete, and (2) an exchange has taken place.

Inasmuch as these concepts were broad in nature and did not specifically address themselves to the real estate industry, the AICPA issued two industry accounting guides: *Accounting for Retail Land Sales* [Committee on Land Development Companies, 1973] and *Accounting for Profit Recognition on Sales of Real Estate* [Committee on Accounting for Real Estate Transactions, 1973]. The latter accounting guide on real estate specifies the two elements that are most important in timing of profit recognition: (1) the extent of the buyer's initial and continuing investment in the property; and (2) the continuing involvement of the seller with the property sold.

Two subsequent AICPA Statements of Position expand upon the original guide: SOP 75-6, *Questions Concerning Profit Recognition on Sales of Real Estate* [Accounting Standards Division, 1975], and SOP 78-4, *Application of the Deposit, Installment, and Cost Recovery Methods in Accounting for Sales of Real Estate* [Accounting Standards Division, 1978b].

GENERAL PRINCIPLES OF PROFIT RECOGNITION UPON SALE OF REAL ESTATE

Timing of Revenue (and Profit) Recognition. In conventional transactions, revenue can be recognized at the time land is sold, provided that two interdependent conditions exist: (1) The amount of revenue is measurable and the collection of the sales price is reasonably assured; and (2) the earnings process is complete or virtually complete and the seller is not involved in significant postsale activities. The installment method or the cost recovery method of accounting must generally be used if collectibility of sales price is not reasonably assured. The deposit method may, however, be appropriate if uncertainty as to collectibility exists. Under the deposit method, the date of recognition of the sale is deferred, and no revenue is recognized before the sale is considered to be effective. All cash received before the sale is considered to be effective is accounted for as a deposit on the sales price, and credited to a liability account.

Substance over Form. The economic substance of a transaction should govern the accounting rather than the legal form. Some transactions that are a legal sale may actually be a construction or service contract, a lease, a joint venture, a deposit, or an option. For a transaction to be accounted for as a sale it should: (1) transfer from the seller to the buyer the usual risks and rewards of ownership; and (2) limit the seller's risk to that of a secured creditor.

Sales Must Be Consummated. If a profit is to be recognized for a period, a sale must be consummated before the end of the period. Consummation occurs when parties are bound by the contract terms, all considerations are exchanged, and all conditions precedent to closing are performed.

Buyer's Investment. Because of the uncertainty as to collectibility of receivables that may be present in a sale of real estate, there must be some additional assurance that the sales price will be collected before profit can be recognized. This additional assurance can be obtained by a significant buyer investment (both initial and continuing) that adequately demonstrates a commitment to pay for the property.

Initial Investment. Factors to be evaluated in deciding whether the buyer's initial investment (down payment) is sufficient to indicate a reasonable assurance of collecting the receivable are (1) the relative size of the buyer's down payment compared to the sales value; and (2) the composition of the down payment.

If full profit is to be recognized, the down payment must be equal to the major part of the difference between the sales value of the property and the usual loan limits of an established lending institution. Reasonable down payments are set forth in Exhibit A of the industry guide [Committee on Accounting for Real Estate Transactions, 1973]; these range from 5 percent for a single-family house to 25 percent for land that is to be developed after 2 years and for certain startup situations. Because property appraisals occasionally differ and specific properties may not fall within the established limits of the industry accounting guide, a sale can also be recognized if the down payment is equal to or greater than the amount by which the sales value exceeds 115 percent of either (1) the permanent loan or (2) the permanent loan commitment established by an independent lending institution.

To assure collectibility of the receivable, the percentage requirement of the minimum down payment must generally consist of cash or notes supported by irrevocable letters of credit. The buyer may also make payments to third parties to reduce previously existing debt, may pay the seller points or a management fee, or may make other payments that in substance represent a financial investment in the property.

Continuing Investment. If profit is to be recognized at the time of sale, the buyer must, in addition to making the requisite down payment, be "required to continue to increase his investment (that is, reduce indebtedness) in the property each year" [Committee on Accounting for Real Estate Transactions, 1973]. Such payments must be in amounts at least equal to the level annual payments that would be required over the customary term of a first mortgage, or over 20 years on a land sale. If this continuing investment on the buyer's part is not met, the seller should recognize a reduced profit. Such reduction is determined by applying an appropriate discount rate to reduce the receivable to its present value of the lowest level of annual payments over the customary term (20 years for land). In this situation, the buyer's payments must equal the annual level of payments of principal and interest on the maximum first-lien indebtedness available on the property, plus interest at an appropriate rate on the excess of aggregate actual indebtedness.

The initial and continued investment test of the buyer should be applied cumulatively each year. If the above requirements are not met, the installment or cost recovery method of recognition should be applied.

Receivables Subject to Subordination. Because of the difficulties in evaluating collectibility of receivables subject to future subordination, profit should be limited to amounts computed under the cost recovery method if the receivable is subject to later subordination. This would not apply to a receivable subordinate to a primary lien on the property existing at the time of sale or to a future loan whose proceeds are used to pay the seller's receivable.

Seller's Continued Involvement. The third key element determining timing of profit recognition is that of the seller's continued involvement with the property after its sale. This continued involvement may include the seller's arranging financing; managing, developing, or constructing the property; guaranteeing a return to the buyer; initiating and supporting operations after the property is sold; or participating in a real estate syndication.

Each type of continued seller involvement will have to be evaluated separately (as to substance) to determine appropriate accounting treatment. To the extent that the seller has substantial obligations to perform after the sale, profit should not be recognized until such performance has been accomplished. Additionally, a sales contract should not be accounted for as a sale when the seller retains most of the risks of ownership.

The following summarizes types of seller involvement and the appropriate accounting treatment covered by the industry accounting guide:

1. *Seller will participate in future profits without the risk of loss.* Full profit can be recognized.

2. *Seller is responsible for obtaining or providing permanent financing.* Permanent financing must be arranged before the transaction is accounted for as a sale.

3. *Seller is to provide management services without compensation (or at less than prevailing rates for the service required).* Compensation should be imputed at prevailing rates and its discounted present value deducted from the sales price in measuring profit at time of sale and recognized over the term of management contract.

4. *Seller is obligated to develop property in the future, to construct facilities on the land, or to provide offsite improvements.* Where costs of future required work can be reliably estimated, profit should be recognized on a percentage-of-completion basis. In a situation where total cost cannot be estimated, profit should be recognized on the completed-contract method when all work is completed.

5. *Seller is to initiate or support operations of property for a specific time period, or is to provide for a return on the investment to the buyer.* The sub-

stance of the transaction determines whether an actual sale has occurred. Accounting treatment should follow substance.

6. *A sales contract may, in substance, be a pure financing, leasing, or profit-sharing arrangement, rather than a sale.* No sale is recognized and payments should be accounted for as funds loaned, rental payments, or transfers required for proper division of profits as the substance of transaction indicates.

Sale-and-Leaseback Transactions. In the absence of exceptional circumstances, usual sale-and-leaseback transactions involving land should not result in the immediate recognition of income.

In Statement No. 28 [FASB, 1979a], the Financial Accounting Standards Board stated: Any (usually recognized) profit or loss on the sale shall be deferred and amortized in proportion to the related gross rental charged to expense over the lease term, unless the seller-lessee relinquishes the right to substantially all of the remaining use of the land or retains only a minor portion of the use. In the latter situations, varying proportions of profit may be recognized. Because of the complexities and individual nature of each transaction, FASB Statement No. 28 [1979a] and Statement No. 13, as amended [FASB, 1980], should be consulted for specific guidance.

Sale of Air Rights, Easements, Mineral Interests, or Other Partial Rights to the Land. When a sale is made of one, or a few, of the rights to a parcel of land, the computation of the amount of the gain or loss from the sale depends on the allocation made of costs attributable to the interest sold. In many cases, a useful and meaningful allocation of costs can be made by obtaining an estimate of the fair market value of the land immediately before and immediately after the partial interest in the land has been sold. The percentage by which the fair market value has declined after the sale is considered to be the percentage of total land costs attributable to the interest sold. Sometimes assessed valuations are used as a basis for allocation.

Distribution of Land to Shareholders. Occasionally, land may be distributed to shareholders as a dividend, particularly in closely held companies. This type of transaction is provided for as a nonreciprocal transfer with owners in APB Opinion No. 29 [1973]. It should be recorded at the fair value of the asset transferred. Gain or loss (if any) should be recognized upon the disposition of that asset.

RETAIL LAND SALES

Land sales companies typically engage in the purchase, development, and resale of land. The land is purchased in one or more large tracts that are subdivided into smaller parcels (lots) on the basis of a master plan. This plan may call for certain offsite improvements and amenities to provide basic recreational and community facilities. The land sales company may complete all development and construction for the entire project. Often, however, the company will complete only certain land improvements (directly or by contract), such as streets and sewers, and then sell portions of the tract to other developers or builders for completion. A purchaser of an individual lot typically makes a small down payment and pays the balance of the land sales contract over a number of years.

The industry accounting guide pertaining to retail land sales [Committee on Land Development Companies, 1973] applies to retail lot sales on a volume basis, with down payments that are too small to permit evaluation of eventual collectibility of sales proceeds. The guide specifies accounting under the accrual and installment methods.

Timing of Revenue and Income Recognition. The realization concept, as discussed under "Sale of Land," and the time when realization occurs determine the accounting period when revenue and expenses should be matched to determine the income or loss of a business activity. Accordingly, costs should be accrued and deferred until the related revenue is recognized to measure periodic income properly. Because of an extended earnings process in land sales, it is difficult to ascertain the period in which realization is said to occur. Some of the special features of this situation are discussed below.

Accounting Considerations. A sale transaction involving retail land should not be viewed as giving rise to revenue until conditions indicate that (1) the customer seriously intends to complete the contract; and (2) the company is capable of fulfilling its obligations under the contract so that customers cannot later demand and be entitled to receive refunds for failure to deliver. Each of the following three conditions must be satisfied before a contract can be recorded as a sale:

1. The customer has made a down payment and all regularly required subsequent payments until the period during which cancellation with refund is permitted has expired.

2. The aggregate customer payments (including interest) are equal to or greater than 10 percent of the contract sales price.

3. Based on current circumstances and knowledge, it is apparent that the selling company has the capabilities (currently and prospectively) (a) to provide the land improvements and offsite facilities included in the contract; and (b) to meet any other representations it has made.

Funds collected prior to satisfying all these conditions are credited to an account similar to the one usually called "Advances from Customers."

Accounting Methods. The industry accounting guide specifies that the method of accounting (accrual, installment, or deposit) for income depends on the evaluation of collectibility of the receivable resulting from the sale and the seller's experience with previous projects.

The accrual method should be used on a project-by-project basis when there is reasonable evidence that the receivable will be collected and all of the following conditions are met:

1. The properties clearly will be useful for residential or recreational purposes when the normal payment period is complete. There must be a reasonable expectation that the land can be developed for its intended purposes.

2. The project's improvements have progressed beyond preliminary stages, and there is evidence that the work will be completed according to plan.

3. The receivable is not subject to subordination to new loans on the property, except for home construction purposes.

4. The company's collection experience on this project indicates with reasonable predictability that the receivable will be collected and that 90 percent of the contracts in force 6 months after sales are recorded will be collected in full. The "contracts in force" requirement may be measured either in dollars (principal amount) or numbers of contracts, provided that consistency is maintained.

Absence of any of the above conditions requires use of the installment method for recording sales. If, because of existing uncertainties, the sale is recorded on the installment method but these uncertainties are subsequently resolved, thereby fulfilling the above conditions, the accrual method should be adopted. This change should be accounted for as a change in an accounting estimate (without retroactive adjustment of retained earnings), in accordance with Paragraphs 31–33 of APB Opinion No. 20 [1971].

Accrual Method. When the above conditions for recording income under the accrual method are met, the following procedures should be applied:

1. Gross sales (the contract price) should be recorded before deducting any discount applicable for valuation of the receivable ("Interest Rate," discussed below) or for revenue to be earned from improvement work to be performed in the future ("Future Performance," discussed below). The portion applicable to future improvements should be classified as deferred revenue and recognized as work is performed.

2. A contract recorded as a sale and subsequently canceled in the same reporting period should be included in and then separately deducted from gross sales or should have other appropriate disclosure.

3. Gross sales should be reduced by those sales that are not expected to be collected due to cancellations in subsequent periods, along with any related discount and deferred revenue to arrive at net sales. A matching credit to an allowance for contract cancellations (a contra to receivables) would be made. When a contract is deemed to be canceled, the receivable balance should be charged to the allowance for contract cancellations.

4. The computation of cost of sales, such as land and improvement costs incurred and carrying costs, should be based entirely on the net sales thus recorded.

5. On the balance sheet, receivables should be reduced by the unamortized valuation discount and the allowance for contract cancellations.

Delinquency and cancellation. Criteria have been set forth in the industry audit guide for deciding when delinquent receivables are presumed to be uncollectible. A representative sample of historical data should be selected to determine the company's delinquency experience; such experience should be used to evaluate the adequacy of the allowance for contract cancellations. The industry accounting guide establishes guidelines for deciding when contracts should be considered canceled [Committee on Land Development Companies, 1973]:

> If receivables in the sample are past due at the end of the period of time selected ... the receivables should be considered uncollectible and the contracts presumed to be cancelled (for this purpose) if regular payments due are unpaid for the following delinquency periods.

Percent of contract price paid	Delinquency period (days)
Less than 25%	90
25% but less than 50%	120
50% and over	150

These periods may be extended in certain extenuating circumstances if it can be ascertained that the purchaser has the ability to complete payment in accordance with the contract and plans to do so.

Interest rate. The guide recognizes that contract receivables would have to be discounted to reflect higher interest rates when the stated rate is less than the prevailing rate for an obligation with similar terms, security, and risk. In discussing the initial measure of consideration, the guide states: "Generally the credit ratings of retail land purchasers approximate those of users of retail consumer installment credit provided by commercial banks and established retail organizations." It goes on to conclude that "the effective annual yield on the receivable without a reduction for deferred revenue (attributable to future services such as site improvements or deferred income tax) should not be less than the minimum annual rate charged locally by commercial banks and established retail organizations to borrowers financing purchases of customer personal property with installment credit" [Committee on Land Development Companies, 1973].

Future performance. The earnings process may be incomplete at the time the sale is recorded if the seller has an obligation to complete improvements, amenities, and other facilities applicable to lots sold. This causes certain problems in ascertaining the amount of revenue to be recognized upon performance of such obligations. The guide concludes: "The amount of revenue recognized (discounted contract price) at the time a sale is recorded should be based on the stage of completion of the required performance." This stage (percentage) of completion is computed from the ratio of project cost incurred to date to estimated total project costs (including selling costs). Thus, to the extent that the earnings process is complete, total revenue will be recognized; to the extent that there exists an element of future performance, revenue will be deferred and matched against those future expenses.

Installment Method. The installment method must be applied to those sales that do not qualify for the accrual method under the above-mentioned criteria. The installment method requires application of the following procedures:

1. The entire contract price applicable to the installment sale, without reduction for discounts or cancellations, should be reported as revenue in the year the sale is recorded.

2. The applicable expenses (cost of sales, selling, general and administrative, provision for future improvement costs) related to the revenue recorded in procedure 1 should be currently charged to income.

3. The difference between procedures 1 and 2 (gross profit less selling costs directly associated with the project) should be treated as deferred profit and recognized in income as customer payments are received. The unamortized portion of this deferred profit should be shown on the balance sheet as a deduction from contracts receivable.

4. Interest income at the stated contract rate should be recorded as income when payment is received.

5. If both the accrual and installment methods are being used, the portion of receivables and sales applicable to the installment method should be disclosed.

6. If contracts are canceled, all applicable receivables, liabilities, and deferred profit should be reduced; recoverable land and improvement costs should be restored; and any remaining costs should be treated as a loss in the period of cancellation.

Deposit Method. Until a contract qualifies as a sale under the accrual or installment method, funds collected (including interest) should be recorded by crediting an account similar to Advances from Customers. This is necessitated by the high rate of customer default prevailing in the industry and the inability to predict the likelihood that a customer will fulfill the contract. Project selling costs should be deferred until the sale is recorded, at which time they should be charged to expense. Upon cancellation of a contract, unrecovered deferred selling costs should be charged against income and deposits forfeited should be credited to income.

Capitalizable costs. All costs related specifically to inventories of unimproved land or to additional construction necessary to bring such land to a salable condition should be capitalized and carried at a cost not exceeding net realizable value. Examples of such costs are qualified interest and real estate taxes. As discussed earlier in the section on income and costs during a holding period, FASB Statement No. 34 [1979b] establishes standards for interest capitalization and requires that interest be capitalized on land only during the periods in which the land is undergoing activities necessary to get it ready for its intended use (i.e., to be sold as developed lots).

Amenities. Costs of amenities (such as golf courses, club houses, lakes, parks, and utilities) should be evaluated in light of their estimated useful lives, their anticipated return, their effectiveness as selling aids, and expected selling date for the entire project. Unrecoverable costs should be charged to the cost of home sales on a pro rata basis. If these amenities prove to be productive selling aids, their costs can be depreciated over their useful lives or over the period in which lots are projected to be sold, whichever is shorter.

Cost allocation. Capitalized costs (many of which are joint costs) can be allocated to projects and parcels on any reasonably consistent method that will fairly match such costs with related revenues. The various methods used for this allocation include: (1) area methods (square footage, acres, frontage, or some other measure); (2) value methods (mortgage release prices, estimated selling prices, or appraisals); (3) specific identification methods; or (4) hybrid methods having some element of the other three methods.

Disclosures. The following additional disclosures are required in financial statements of retail land companies:

1. A statement of changes in financial position, presented for all periods in which earnings information is reported. The statement should be prepared on the basis of sources and uses of cash, rather than changes in working capital.

2. The method of income recognition and the interest rate(s) used for discounting.

3. Receivables, with the following related information: (a) 5-year receivable maturities; (b) cancellation policy; (c) method of identifying and computing the amount of delinquent accounts; (d) weighted average and range of stated interest rates; (e) amount of contracts not recorded as sales and related receipts.

4. Land and improvement inventories, classified as to: (a) unimproved land, (b) land being improved, (c) fully improved land, and (d) land subject to unrecorded sales contracts. The capitalization policy of costs and the allocation method of amenities and carrying charges should also be disclosed.

5. Future improvements, as follows: (a) estimated costs of future improvements (in total and for each of the next 5 years) and the methods of determining these estimates, (b) improvements behind schedule, and (c) amount of deferred profit.

6. Others, including (a) long-term debt maturities for each of the next 5 years [FASB, 1979c] and the weighted average and range of interest rates, (b) liabilities restricted to specific assets, and (c) certain information regarding the composition of the sources (and related costs) of income.

Valuing repossessed properties. When repossessions occur, they are valued either at the lower of (1) original cost, (2) fair value (net realizable value on resale), or (3) the uncollected installment receivable plus refunds, if any, to the defaulting purchasers. When repossession occurs in the same period as the sale, the practice, almost universally, is to value the lot at original cost.

FASB DEVELOPMENTS

The FASB has extracted the specialized accounting and reporting principles contained in the various AICPA real estate and related Guides and SOPs into two Statements of Financial Accounting Standards (SFASs). The Board did not change the basic principles discussed in this chapter. The FASB and AICPA documents involved are identified in the Bibliography.

Original AICPA Document	New FASB Statement
Accounting for Profit Recognition on Sales of Real Estate (Accounting Guide)	*Accounting for Sales of Real Estate*
SOP 75-6, *Questions Concerning Profit Recognition on Sales of Real Estate*	
SOP 78-4, *Application of the Deposit, Installment, and Cost Recovery Methods in Accounting for Sales of Real Estate*	
Accounting for Retail Land Sales (Accounting Guide)	
SOP 78-3, *Accounting for Costs to Sell and Rent, and Initial Rental Operations of Real Estate Projects*	*Accounting for Costs and Initial Rental Operations of Real Estate Projects*
SOP 80-3, *Accounting for Real Estate Acquisitions, Development, and Construction Costs*	

BIBLIOGRAPHY

Accounting Principles Board (AICPA), *Status of Accounting Research Bulletins*, Opinion No. 6 (APB, 1965).

———, *Omnibus Opinion—1966*, Opinion No. 10 (APB, 1967).

———, *Business Combinations*, Opinion No. 16 (APB, 1970a).

———, *Basic Concepts and Accounting Principles Underlying Financial Statements of Business Enterprises*, Statement No. 4 (APB, 1970b).

———, *Accounting Changes*, Opinion No. 20 (APB, 1971).

———, *Accounting for Nonmonetary Transactions*, Opinion No. 29 (APB, 1973).

Accounting Standards Division (AICPA), *Questions Concerning Profit Recognition on Sales of Real Estate*, Statement of Position 75-6 (AICPA, 1975).

———, *Accounting for Costs to Sell and Rent, and Initial Rental Operations of Real Estate Projects*, Statement of Position 78-3 (AICPA, 1978a).

———, *Application of the Deposit, Installment, and Cost Recovery Methods in Accounting for Sales of Real Estate*, Statement of Position 78-4 (AICPA, 1978b).

———, *Accounting for Investments in Real Estate Ventures*, Statement of Position 78-9 (AICPA, 1978c).

———, *Accounting for Real Estate Acquisitions, Development, and Construction Costs*, Statement of Position 80-3 (AICPA, 1980).

Cerf, A. R. "Accounting for Retail Land Sales," *The Accounting Review*, vol. 50, no. 3 (July 1975), pp. 451–465.

Committee on Accounting Procedure (AICPA), *Restatement and Revision of Accounting Research Bulletins*, Accounting Research Bulletin No. 43 (CAP, 1953).

Committee on Accounting for Real Estate Transactions (AICPA), *Accounting for Profit Recognition on Sales of Real Estate*, Industry Accounting Guide (AICPA, 1973).

Committee on Land Development Companies (AICPA), *Accounting for Retail Land Sales*, Industry Accounting Guide (AICPA, 1973).

Construction Contractor Guide Committee, Accounting Standards Division (AICPA), *Audit and Accounting Guide for Construction Contractors* (AICPA, 1981).

Financial Accounting Standards Board, *Accounting for Sales with Leasebacks, an Amendment of FASB Statement No. 13*, Statement of Financial Accounting Standards No. 28 (FASB, 1979a).

————, *Capitalization of Interest Cost*, Statement of Financial Accounting Standards No. 34 (FASB, 1979b).

————, *Disclosure of Long-Term Obligations*, Statement of Financial Accounting Standards No. 47 (FASB, 1979c).

————, *Accounting for Leases—Financial Accounting Standards Board Statement No. 13 as Amended and Interpreted through May 1980* (FASB, 1980).

————, *Accounting for Sales of Real Estate*, Statement of Financial Accounting Standards No. 66 (FASB, 1982a).

————, *Accounting for Costs and Initial Rental Operations of Real Estate*, Statement of Financial Accounting Standards No. 67 (FASB, 1982b).

Grady, P., *Inventory of Generally Accepted Accounting Principles for Business Enterprises*, Accounting Research Study No. 7 (AICPA, 1965).

Klink, J. J., *Real Estate Accounting and Reporting—A Guide for Developers, Investors and Lenders* (John Wiley & Sons, New York, 1980).

Paton, W. A., and W. A. Paton, Jr., *Assets—Accounting and Administration* (Roberts & Roehl, Detroit, 1971).

CHAPTER **18**

Natural Resources

Horace R. Brock
Director, Extractive Industries Accounting
Research Institute, North Texas State University

CHARACTERISTICS OF NATURAL RESOURCE PRODUCERS

Natural Resources Defined. Natural resources, sometimes called *wasting assets*, are those irreplaceable assets created primarily by the work of nature. For accounting purposes, the definition is usually sharply limited to "products" that are extracted or removed directly from the earth or sea. Thus, although the surface area of land is in the broad sense a natural resource, it is not normally extracted, removed, or produced, and it is not included in this definition.

Based on the methods employed to extract or remove the product, natural resources may be conveniently classified in three categories. These recovery methods, which largely determine the accounting problems involved, are as follows:

1. Production through wells drilled below the earth's surface. The principal minerals produced by this means are oil and gas and sometimes sulfur.

2. Extraction through mining from either open pit or shaft mines. Most metals such as copper, iron, lead, silver, and gold, along with minerals such as coal, salt, potash, and limestone, are included in this category. Sand, gravel, clay, stone, and similar products are likewise extracted from mines or quarries.

3. Harvesting of growing products. Standing timber has historically been considered a wasting asset because until a very few years ago, "cut" forests were not replaced with seedlings but were left barren, to be reforested only by nature—if at all. The practices of planting trees as a crop, selective cutting, and reforestation have now become so widespread that the timber industry has many more of the characteristics of agricultural farming than of an extractive industry. For this reason, only a brief description of accounting for standing timber is included at the end of this chapter.

The third category could be further extended to include orchards, fisheries, and similar activities closely related to nature, but these, too, are more akin to farming than to natural resource extraction.

The definition of natural resources emphasizes two factors: (1) the removal or extinguishment of the asset, and (2) replacement of the resource only by action of nature, if at all. Diminution of a mineral or ore deposit by production is referred to as *depletion* of the resource. The contrast with a "depreciable" asset, such as a building, machine, or item of equipment—which is used as a whole until its retirement from service—is obvious.

Physical Activities in Natural Resource Industries. Physical activities involved in finding, acquiring, developing, and producing natural resources can be classified into four functions.

1. Exploration. Historically the preliminary activities carried out to locate potential deposits of natural resources has been referred to as *prospecting*. Subsequent activities to determine if the resource does exist in commercially recoverable quantities has been called *exploration*. Today the latter term is commonly used to describe work performed at both stages. Exploration may

entail the use of a myriad of sophisticated equipment and techniques, such as gravity meters, magnetic meters, seismographs, aerial photography, chemical analysis of soil and rocks, and drilling of test wells.

2. Acquiring legal rights to extract and dispose of the resources found. In the early days of mining, prospectors merely "staked a claim" giving them the right to produce and sell minerals or ores. Today, title is usually obtained through *mineral leases* or outright purchase. Some exploration activities may be carried out before the mineral rights are acquired, whereas others can be conducted only after the rights are secured.

3. "Developing" the property. After a deposit has been found, some means must be developed to permit the contents to be extracted. This may require merely the removal of the overlying layers of earth in order to reach the mineral or ore. Frequently, however, underground tunnels or shafts must be constructed to obtain access to the deposit. In still other cases, most notably in producing oil and gas, holes must be drilled deep below the earth's surface to tap and extract the mineral. Wells that were drilled initially to find the oil and gas reserves may also be used to produce the minerals found.

4. Extraction of the resource. Once deposits have been found and facilities constructed to remove the product, actual production, which may continue over many years, is begun.

Sources of Accounting Problems. Most accounting problems peculiar to the extractive industries result from two factors:

1. Very large capital outlays are necessary to find and develop natural resource deposits.

2. A high degree of uncertainty or risk is associated with many of these capital investments, because the properties to which they apply often prove commercially unproductive. In this respect, the search for natural resources is like the search for patentable drugs and other fruits of research expenditures. Additionally, there may be a long period between the time that expenditures are incurred and the time when it is known if they have resulted in productive assets.

These two factors have combined to produce a rather complicated and inconsistent application of generally accepted accounting principles, a situation abetted by federal tax laws permitting companies engaged in extractive activities to compute taxable income by methods unacceptable for financial accounting purposes. One result of large capital investments, the high degree of uncertainty, and special tax laws has been the development of many unusual contracts and legal arrangements for risk sharing that create unique accounting problems. In addition, federal and state regulation of the oil and gas industry has led to attempts to prescribe accounting methods to be followed by companies in the industry, causing further confusion over appropriate financial accounting principles.

To facilitate the analysis of accounting in the extractive industries, the discussion will center around three industry segments:

The oil and gas industry
The mining industry
The timber industry

THE OIL AND GAS INDUSTRY

During the last decade, the question of what accounting and reporting standards should be required for oil and gas producing companies has been controversial and widely debated in the accounting profession.

Development of Accounting and Reporting Requirements. Before 1960, most oil and gas producing companies followed some variation of what has come to be known as *successful efforts accounting*. The central idea of successful efforts accounting is that costs incurred in finding, acquiring, and developing minerals are properly capitalized to the extent that they can be directly related to specific reserves, whereas costs of activities that cannot be related to specific reserves are charged to expense.

Even though the general concept of successful efforts accounting was followed by almost all companies, there were many different interpretations and applications of the idea. For example, some companies concluded that geological and geophysical expenditures inherently are not associated with specific reserves and that all such costs should be charged to expense, whereas other companies attempted to relate a part of exploration costs to minerals found, and still other companies capitalized all exploration costs. There were also divergences in accounting for the costs of dry holes. In addition, some entities charged the costs of unproved leases to expense only when leases were surrendered or expired, whereas others amortized the cost of unproved leaseholds during the period they were expected to be held. Thus, there evolved many variations of successful efforts accounting.

In the late 1950s a new approach to accounting for oil and gas exploration, acquisition and development, known as *full costing*, emerged. Under this concept, *all* costs incurred in searching for, acquiring, and developing oil and gas reserves in a *cost center* were capitalized, regardless of whether or not the specific activities were successful. The capitalized costs were subsequently amortized as the reserves in that center were produced. Some companies treated their entire worldwide activities as being in a single cost center, some considered the continent or the individual nation as an appropriate cost center, and still others viewed "basins" or other geological areas as cost centers. Thus, under full costing as well as under successful efforts accounting, there were variations between applications of the concept by different companies. Since its inception, the full cost method has been widely adopted by small companies, so that today more than half of all publicly held oil and gas companies use full costing.

By the mid-1960s many accountants, financial analysts, and others were urging the Accounting Principles Board (APB) to narrow the diversity of accounting methods being used in the industry. In 1964 the APB commissioned Robert E. Field to conduct a research study into financial accounting and reporting in the extractive industries. In his report, Accounting Research Study No. 11 (ARS No. 11), published in 1969, Field concluded that the successful efforts method of accounting was appropriate and that, in effect, the full cost method should be eliminated as an acceptable method. Shortly thereafter, in 1969, the APB appointed a committee to develop and recommend rules of accounting to be adopted in an authoritative Opinion for the oil and gas industry. The efforts of this committee were controversial, and despite considerable attention devoted to this question, the APB was not able to issue an Opinion on this subject before its demise in 1973. The newly organized FASB decided in 1973 that it would not include a project on oil and gas accounting in its initial agenda.

The Arab oil embargo later in 1973 focused public attention on the nation's energy problems, and in 1975 the U.S. Congress passed the Energy Policy and Conservation Act (EPCA), which, among other things, called for establishment of a national energy data base, including financial and statistical data about the industry. The act required the Securities and Exchange Commission (SEC) to develop within 2 years accounting practices to be followed by all oil and gas producers in reports to be filed with the Department of Energy (DOE). The act, however, permitted the SEC to rely on accounting practices developed by the FASB if the SEC deemed that those practices were acceptable. Just prior to the passage of EPCA, the FASB added to its agenda a project entitled "Financial Accounting and Reporting in the Extractive Industries."

The FASB's project resulted in the issuance, in December 1977, of Statement of Financial Accounting Standards No. 19, *Financial Accounting and Reporting by Oil and Gas Producing Companies* (SFAS No. 19). SFAS No. 19 required that oil and gas companies follow a prescribed method of successful efforts accounting and prohibited use of the full cost concept. The Statement also contained principles of accounting for mineral property conveyances and required comprehensive deferred income tax allocation. In addition, the Statement required disclosures of certain costs related to mineral activities as well as quantities of proved reserves of oil and gas owned or controlled by reporting entities.

As a result of widespread protests by small producers, by members of Congress, by regulatory agencies, and by others against SFAS No. 19, the SEC decided to hold public hearings to determine whether the Statement should be adopted for use in reports to be filed with the DOE and also in reports filed with the SEC. Most of the individuals appearing at the hearings or responding in writing opposed the proposed rules on the basis that they would make it difficult for small, relatively new companies to raise capital because of the adverse impact on earnings and on shareholders' equity resulting from successful efforts accounting.

In August 1978, the Commission issued Accounting Series Release No. 253 (ASR No. 253). It concluded that *neither* successful efforts accounting *nor* full cost accounting satisfactorily portrays the operating results or financial position of an oil and gas producing company, because neither method adequately reflects (1) the results of a company's primary activity (searching for proved reserves of oil and gas) or (2) the most important asset (oil and gas reserves) of an oil and gas company. The Commission announced that it would develop a more appropriate accounting method, to be known as *reserve recognition accounting* (RRA), which would assign a value (discounted present value of future net cash flows) to proved reserves of oil and gas and would reflect in an earnings summary the changes in "value" of proved reserves. In addition, the Commission announced that it would require the presentation of a great deal of information about oil and gas activities to assist statement users in assessing the profitability and financial condition of companies.

The SEC concluded, however, that because of certain problems, especially the lack of highly reliable methods for estimating reserve quantities and values, it was not immediately feasible to require RRA as a replacement for historical cost-based methods in the primary statements. Thus the Commission stated that for an indefinite period (3 years was mentioned as a likely period), reporting companies could base their primary statements either on the successful efforts method (essentially that called for by the FASB in SFAS No. 19) or on a full cost method to be prescribed by the SEC. (The SEC's accounting rules for oil and gas producing companies are summarized later in this chapter.) The Commission specified that no matter which method was used in the primary statements during the period while RRA was being perfected, supplementary statements based on RRA must be included. The Commission stated that after the period of experimentation with and development of RRA, the method would replace the historical cost methods in the primary statements.

After the SEC announced that it would allow publicly held companies to use either the full cost or the successful efforts method, the FASB issued SFAS No. 25 in February 1979 suspending indefinitely the effective date of the successful efforts requirements of SFAS No. 19. However, SFAS No. 25 specified that the provisions of Statements relating to deferred income taxes and those relating to disclosures would become effective as scheduled.

In February 1981, the SEC issued ASR No. 300. It concluded that RRA has shortcomings that make it inappropriate as the primary basis of accounting and stated that plans to replace historical cost methods with RRA as the basis for the primary statements were being abandoned. At the same time, the Commission announced that the FASB would undertake a project to develop a set of comprehensive supplemental disclosure requirements for oil and gas companies that would likely be adopted by the Commission. The Commission stated that such disclosures would, it hoped, include "values" of oil and gas reserves, and that if the FASB's requirements did not include such values, the Commission would, nevertheless, probably require value disclosures. The SEC also commented that it had no preconception as to whether an *operating statement* based on value changes should be required. The Commission made it clear that the FASB's project would deal only with supplemental disclosures, and that for the foreseeable future both successful efforts accounting and full costing would continue to be viewed as acceptable methods by the Commission.

The FASB issued SFAS No. 69 in November 1982, which is applicable only to publicly held companies. SFAS No. 69 requires disclosure of the present value of proved reserves, but does not call for an operating statement based on value changes.

The accounting rules issued by the SEC and the FASB for publicly held oil and gas producing companies will be examined in the following order:

1. Successful efforts accounting
2. The full costing concept

3. Mineral conveyances
4. Disclosure requirements

The SEC's rules are found in the *Code of Federal Regulations*, Sec. 210.4-10 (Reg. SX 4-10). Because of the suspension of SFAS No. 19 and the fact that SFAS No. 69 does not apply to nonpublicly held companies, there are no specifically prescribed rules to account for oil and gas producing activities of nonpublic companies.

Successful Efforts Accounting. The rules developed by the FASB in SFAS No. 19 (and subsequently suspended by SFAS No. 25) were adopted by the SEC for public companies electing to use the successful efforts method of accounting. The most important of those rules govern which costs are to be capitalized and how capitalized costs are to be subsequently charged to expense. Costs are classified by Reg. SX 4-10 into five categories: acquisition costs, exploration costs, development costs, production costs, and support facilities and equipment.

Capitalization of costs incurred. The capitalization rules of Reg. SX 4-10 are based primarily on the nature of the costs incurred.

Mineral rights costs. In the petroleum industry, most "operating rights" in minerals take the form of leaseholds; fee interests are far less frequently acquired. In addition to operating rights that place on their owners the responsibility for drilling wells and developing and producing the minerals, there are several types of nonoperating rights whose owners do not have the responsibility and obligations to develop and operate the property. Nonoperating rights include a royalty interest or an overriding royalty interest that gives its owners the right to receive a specified fractional share of gross production, a net profits interest entitling its owner to receive a specified portion of net profit from the property involved, and a production payment that entitles the holder to receive a specified number of units or dollars from production.

The entire purchase price of fee interests in minerals, including incidental acquisition costs such as abstracts, attorney's charges, commissions, and stamp taxes, should be capitalized to the Unproved Properties account. The total purchase price should be allocated between the surface and mineral rights in proportion to their relative values. Where the value of either type of property (surface rights or mineral rights) can be readily ascertained, while the value of the other right is not, common practice assigns this portion of the purchase price to the property whose value is known and allocates the remaining cost to the other property element.

Mineral leases are secured for a *primary term*, regardless of whether mineral production is obtained, and for a secondary term for as "long thereafter as minerals are produced in commercial quantities." A *bonus* is paid at the time of signing the lease. This bonus must be capitalized as a cost of the mineral rights and charged to unproved properties. Similarly, costs of options to acquire leases, and miscellaneous acquisition costs such as attorney fees and stamp taxes, should be capitalized as part of the leasehold cost.

Delay rentals are paid each year after the first year until production is secured or the lease is surrendered. (The lessee may terminate the lease at any time during the primary term simply by failing to pay rentals. If oil or gas is not found in a well whose drilling was begun during the primary term, the lease expires. Once oil or gas is found, the lease continues in force for as long as there is production.) Rentals are included in "carrying costs," which are treated in Reg. SX 4-10 as exploration costs by companies using the successful efforts method.

When mineral properties are acquired by lease, the lessor retains a *royalty interest*, under which a specified percentage or fractional part (usually one-eighth, but frequently greater) of the gross value of all minerals produced will be paid to the royalty owner. The lessor or royalty owner usually bears none of the development or production expenses except the production taxes and windfall profit taxes on the royalty's share of output. The royalty owner's share of reserves and production are ignored by the operator in accounting entries and computations. More complex contracts involving special property interests in leased mineral rights are examined later in this chapter.

When developed properties are acquired, it is customary to allocate to the tangible equipment an amount equal to its market value, with the balance of cost assigned to mineral rights acquired.

Exploration costs. All costs incurred in (1) identifying areas that may warrant detailed examination and (2) examining specific areas that are identified as possibly containing oil or gas reserves are classified as exploration activities. These include such items as:

1. Aerial photography, magnetic measurements, gravimetric measurements, soil analysis, seismic tests, core drilling, chemical analysis of soil and rock, and many other geological and geophysical (G&G) methods used to locate reservoirs that may contain oil and gas deposits.

2. Costs of drilling and equipping exploratory wells. (Exploratory wells are all wells drilled except those drilled to gain access to, and produce, oil and gas reserves classified as "proved reserves.") These costs include both "intangible drilling and development costs" (IDC) that in themselves have no tangible physical existence or salvage value and "tangible equipment costs" that do have a physical existence.

3. Costs of drilling exploratory-type stratigraphic test wells. Stratigraphic test wells are wells drilled primarily to gain geological information and not intended to be used to produce oil or gas if it is found. They are sometimes referred to as "slim holes."

4. Costs of carrying and retaining undeveloped, unproved properties, such as delay rentals, ad valorem taxes on properties, legal costs for title defense, and the maintenance of land and lease records.

5. Drilling contributions—contributions to others to help defray part of their cost in drilling wells, in return for geological information.

Under the successful efforts method in Reg. SX 4-10, *all* exploration costs, except the costs of exploratory wells and stratigraphic-type exploratory test wells that result in proved reserves, are charged to expense as they are incurred. Thus, costs of geological and geophysical exploration activities, test well contributions, lease rentals, and so on, are never capitalized under this method.

Historically, many companies using the successful efforts method have capitalized all or part of geological and geophysical (G&G) exploration costs. The FASB justified its requirement that all exploration costs except the cost of successful wells be expensed on several bases. First, these costs are much like research costs, which must be expensed. To a large extent, G&G costs are incurred before any properties are acquired, and in the majority of cases the acreage surveyed is either never acquired or, if acquired, is abandoned or surrendered. Finally, it is difficult to relate G&G work with a specific discovery made years later. Thus, the Board decided all such costs should be charged to expense when incurred.

Under Reg. SX 4-10, costs of exploratory drilling are deferred as part of the company's uncompleted wells, equipment, and facilities until the outcome of the well is known. Then, if the well finds proved reserves of oil or gas, the deferred costs are capitalized as part of the company's wells and related equipment and facilities accounts. On the other hand, if the exploratory well does not find proved reserves, all deferred costs of the well are charged to expense.

A major problem for companies using the successful efforts method is in deciding how long to defer costs that apply to an exploratory well that has been drilled, but whose outcome is not yet known. In making this decision, Reg. SX 4-10 provides guidelines for two basic situations.

An exploratory well may have found oil or gas reserves, but classification of those reserves as "proved" depends on whether a major capital expenditure, such as a trunk pipeline, can be justified, which, in turn, depends on whether additional exploratory wells find a sufficient quantity of additional reserves. In such cases, the cost of the discovery well can continue to be deferred only if (1) the well has found a sufficient quantity of reserves to justify its completion as a producer if the additional required capital outlay is made, *and* (2) drilling of additional exploratory wells is underway or firmly planned for the near future. Both of these tests must be met; otherwise the exploratory well will be deemed to be "impaired" and the accumulated costs charged to expense. Similar tests are applied for stratigraphic-type exploratory wells that find oil or gas reserves.

The costs of other exploratory wells that may have found oil and gas reserves, but not reserves that can be classified as proved, shall not be deferred as an asset for more than 1 year following the completion of drilling. If after 1 year it cannot be decided that proved reserves have been found, the exploratory well will be deemed to have been impaired and the deferred costs charged to expense.

In deciding that an exploratory well is dry, "hindsight" must be used. If a well whose drilling has been completed by year-end but whose outcome is unknown at that time is subsequently found to be dry before financial statements are issued, the well is deemed to have been impaired as of year-end and the accumulated costs must be charged to expense as of that date.

In Interpretation No. 36 [1981], the FASB extended this concept to an incomplete well that is in progress at year-end but is found to be dry before the financial statements are issued. In that event, the costs incurred prior to year-end are to be treated as expense of the year in which they were incurred, whereas costs incurred subsequent to the balance sheet date are charged to expense in the following year.

Development costs. Development costs are incurred to gain access to proved reserves and to provide facilities for extracting, treating, gathering, and storing the oil and gas. They include costs incurred to drill and equip development wells, development-type stratigraphic test wells, and service wells. They also include costs of acquiring, constructing, and installing production facilities such as flow lines, separators, treaters, headers, heaters, and improved recovery systems. Proved reserves are those reserves that geological and engineering data demonstrate with reasonable certainty to be recoverable from known reservoirs under existing economic and operating conditions.

Under Reg. SX 4-10, companies using the successful efforts method capitalize all development costs, including the cost of wells that prove dry. Because dry exploratory wells are charged to expense whereas dry development wells are capitalized, the definitions of exploratory wells and development wells become extremely important. Development wells and development-type stratigraphic test wells are limited to those drilled within the proved area of an oil or gas reservoir to the depth of a stratigraphic horizon known to be productive. All other wells are classified as exploratory wells.

Production costs. Production involves lifting the oil and gas to the surface and gathering, treating, processing, and storing them in the field. Typical production costs are labor, repair and maintenance, fuel, materials and supplies, taxes and insurance on property, severance and production taxes, and the windfall profit tax. Under Reg. SX 4-10, depreciation and depletion of capitalized exploration, acquisition, and development costs are not classified as production costs.

Production costs (along with depreciation and depletion of capitalized exploration, acquisition, and development costs) become part of the cost of oil and gas produced. In practice, however, these costs are often charged to expense at the time they are incurred.

Support facilities and equipment. Support facilities and equipment serve one or more of the functions described above. They include such assets as field service units, warehouses, camp facilities, and trucks. Costs of owning and operating these assets are allocated to the functions served.

Disposition of capitalized costs. Regulation SX 4-10 contains specific rules to be followed in disposing of capitalized costs.

Unproved properties. Unproved properties must be assessed periodically—at least annually—to ascertain if their values have been "impaired." If impairment has occurred, a loss is recognized and an allowance account is established to reflect the decrease in value. Impairment is not defined in Reg. SX 4-10, although that statement does suggest that impairment has likely occurred if, for example, a dry hole has been drilled on a property and the company has no plans for further drilling. Also, the likelihood of partial or total impairment of a property increases as the expiration of the lease term approaches and if drilling has not commenced on the property or nearby properties. Presumably, "impairment" means that the property's value is less than its recorded cost.

Impairment may be recorded in one of two ways. If costs associated with an individual property are significant, impairment must be assessed on that property individually. The term "significant" is not defined in Reg. SX 4-10. Individual impairment may also be recorded on properties that are not individually significant, but this is not required.

Unproved properties that are not individually significant may be combined in one or more groups and impairment measured and recorded on the basis of the total group. The valuation allowance needed to provide for impairment on properties in a group is determined by amortizing the properties' costs on the basis of the experience of the entity in similar situations and other factors such as the primary lease terms of the properties, the average holding period of unproved properties, and the relative proportion of unproved properties that have been proved in the past. Some companies merely maintain an allowance account at some predetermined percentage of the unproved properties account.

The method used to record impairment determines how the cost of abandoned leases and the cost of leases transferred to proved properties will be recorded. If impairment is recorded on an individual lease, a property's net book value (cost less impairment allowance) is charged as a loss if the lease is surrendered. Similarly, if individual impairment has been recorded on a property, when the lease becomes proved the net book value is transferred to "proved properties" to be amortized through depletion as the reserves are produced.

On the other hand, if group amortization is applied, when a property becomes proved its original capitalized cost is transferred from the Unproved Properties account to the Proved Properties account to be amortized as the reserves are produced. Under the group method of impairment, when an unproved property is surrendered, its cost is credited to the Unproved Properties account and charged to Allowance for Impairment.

Proved properties. Two categories of capitalized costs are associated with proved properties: (1) mineral acquisition costs and (2) wells and related equipment and facilities. Both types of costs are normally amortized on the unit-of-production basis as the related reserves are produced. The reserves related to each type of cost may differ—acquisition costs are amortized over all *proved* reserves, whereas wells and related equipment and facilities costs are amortized over *proved, developed* reserves only. Amortization may be computed separately for each property, or may be computed on the basis of some reasonable aggregation of properties with a common geological structural feature or stratigraphic condition (e.g., a reservoir or a field). As discussed later, if both oil and gas are found on a property or group of properties, the unit cost should generally be calculated on the basis of the total estimated equivalent units of proved oil and gas reserves. Amortization for the period is determined by multiplying the cost per unit by the number of units produced during the period.

Mineral acquisition costs. Mineral acquisition costs for proved properties consist of the amounts transferred from unproved properties when proved reserves are found or the cost assigned to mineral rights when proved properties are purchased.

The amortization (depletion) per unit for mineral acquisition costs is computed by dividing the unamortized costs at the end of the period by the *total proved reserves* attributed to the property or group of properties at the beginning of the period.

If the enterprise has a relatively large number of royalty interests whose acquisition costs are not individually significant, they may be aggregated in computing amortization, without regard to whether they are in a common geological structure. In some cases, it may be impossible to obtain information about estimated reserve quantities related to royalty interests owned; in this event, a method other than the unit-of-production method (e.g., straight-line amortization over some reasonable period) may be used to amortize their acquisition costs.

Wells and related equipment and facilities. The costs of successful exploratory wells, along with all development costs, make up an enterprise's wells and related equipment and facilities. Amortization (depreciation) per unit on wells and equipment costs for a property or appropriate group of properties is computed on the basis of total estimated units of *proved developed reserves* related to that property or group of properties. Future development costs are never to be anticipated and included in the computation of the amortization rate under the successful efforts method.

In some cases significant development costs may be incurred in connection with planned development wells before all of the wells have been drilled. For example, a costly off-shore drilling platform may be constructed from which will be drilled 20 or more development wells, but at the end of the current fiscal period only a small number of the wells may have been drilled. In this case it will be necessary to exclude a portion of these development costs in determining the unit-of-production rate until the additional wells have been drilled. On the other hand, in cases where proved developed reserves can be produced only after significant additional development costs are incurred—for example, where improved recovery systems are to be installed—those proved reserves should be excluded in making the computation.

Joint production of oil and gas. In most cases both oil and gas are produced from a property or from a group of properties with common cost. In these cases, both the oil and gas reserves and the oil and gas produced generally must be converted into a common unit of measure based on their approximate relative energy content. (Most companies use the generalization that 1 barrel of oil contains approximately six times as much energy as does 1,000 cubic feet of gas.)

Regulation SX 4-10 provides, however, two major exceptions to this common unit-of-measure requirement. First, if the relative proportion of oil and gas extracted in the current year is approximately the same as the proportion of oil and gas in the proved reserves, the unit-of-production amortization may be based on only one of the two minerals. Second, if either oil or gas clearly dominates both the current production and the reserves (in terms of energy content), unit-of-production amortization may be based on the dominant mineral alone. No guide is given as to the meaning of "clearly dominates."

Dismantlement and removal costs. Regulation SX 4-10 specifies that dismantlement, restoration, and abandonment costs, along with estimated residual salvage values, are to be considered in determining amortization and depreciation rates. As a matter of practice, for routine on-shore operations most operators merely assume a net salvage value (residual salvage, less dismantlement and removal costs) of zero, and thus altogether ignore salvage value in the depreciation computation. In many cases, such as off-shore activities and operations on the North Slope of Alaska, removal and reclamation costs far exceed residual salvage value, so that a negative salvage value must be considered.

Although a case can be presented for treating the estimated negative salvage (or its present value) at the time of acquisition as a liability and as part of the assets' cost, this practice is not followed. Instead, the estimated negative salvage value is commonly accrued on a unit-of-production basis and recorded each period by a charge either to depreciation expense or to estimated reclamation expense, with a corresponding credit to either accumulated depreciation or to an accrued liability account. The latter approach appears preferable; otherwise, the accumulated depreciation account will eventually exceed the related asset account. In addition, the accumulated amount clearly represents an estimated liability. In accruing this liability, in spite of its long-term nature, amounts are not generally discounted and accumulated over time at interest. Such discounting would be acceptable.

Revision of estimated reserves. Unit-of-production amortization rates are to be revised whenever new information becomes available, but must be reviewed at least once a year and revised if appropriate. Because of the inherent subjectivity of reserve estimates, revisions are common. Revisions are to be accounted for on a prospective basis as called for in APB Opinion No. 20 [1970]. Questions have been raised as to the effects of revisions in the latter part of a year when quarterly statements have been issued earlier in the year. In practice, most enterprises either treat the quarter as the fiscal period and give effect to the revisions as of the first day of the quarter in which the revision is made, or they give effect to the revision as of the first day of the fiscal year, but do not revise quarterly statements previously issued. Under the latter practice, the "catchup" adjustment will be reflected in the quarter in which the revision is made.

The Full Costing Concept. In August 1978, the SEC refused to accept the successful efforts method of SFAS No. 19 as the sole allowable method of accounting for oil and gas operations, and announced that it would subsequently prescribe rules for companies electing to use the full cost method. Those rules, now a part of Reg. SX 4-10, were contained in ASR No. 257. The key elements of the requirements are summarized below.

The cost center. Each country in which the entity conducts operations is treated as a cost center. In other words, all capitalizable costs incurred in a country are to be matched against all reserves in that center. Individual properties within a country lose their identities for most accounting purposes.

Costs to be capitalized. All property acquisition costs, exploration costs, and development costs within a cost center are capitalized. Costs related to production, general corporate overhead, and similar activities are to be charged to expense as incurred.

Amortization of costs to be capitalized. Capitalized costs within a cost center are to be amortized on the unit-of-production basis, with one exception, using proved oil and gas reserves in the cost center as the base over which the capitalized costs are to be spread. Oil and gas are converted to a common measure of energy content, based on the assumption that one barrel of oil is equivalent to 6,000 cubic feet of gas.

The one exception to unit-of-production amortization arises when, because of the effects of price regulation, the use of units of revenue is a more appropriate basis for computing amortization. In that case, amortization is to be computed on the basis of current *gross* revenues from production in proportion to future gross revenues from proved reserves. The computation of future gross revenues shall include consideration of changes in existing prices only to the extent that they are provided in contractual arrangements. The effect of a significant price increase during the year on estimated future gross revenues shall be reflected in the amortization provision only for the *period after* the price increase occurs.

The costs to be included in the amortization base include (1) all related capitalized costs (other than certain omitted costs described below), less accumulated amortization; (2) the estimated future expenditures (at current cost levels) to be incurred in developing proved reserves; and (3) estimated net dismantlement and abandonment costs.

The costs of investments in unproved properties, along with related exploration costs, may be excluded from the amortization calculation if the costs related to such properties are unusually significant in relation to the aggregate costs to be amortized. Regulation SX 4-10 gives as an example the costs of acquiring major off-shore leases. These costs are excluded from the amortization-computation until it is found whether or not there are proved reserves attributable to the properties. During the period such costs are excluded, the properties must be periodically assessed to see if they are impaired. Any impairment must be added to the amortization base.

In addition, costs of major development projects may be excluded from the amortization base if unusually significant development costs are to be incurred prior to ascertaining the quantities of proved reserves attributable to the properties under development. Examples given in Reg. SX 4-10 are the installation of an off-shore drilling platform from which wells are to be drilled into reserves whose quantities have not yet been ascertained, and the installation of improved recovery programs, and similar major projects undertaken in the expectation of significant additions to proved reserves. In such cases, a portion of the costs may be excluded from the amortization base until the proved reserves resulting from them have been determined, or until impairment occurs.

Under full costing, amortization computations are made on a consolidated basis, including investees accounted for on a proportionate consolidation basis. However, investees accounted for by the equity method are not included in the calculations.

Limitations on capitalized costs. Under full costing, all acquisition, exploration, and development costs are capitalized. Therefore, there is a danger that capitalized costs in a cost center may exceed the "value" of the mineral-related assets in that center. Thus, Reg. SX 4-10 provides that a "ceiling" is to be placed on the net carrying value. For each cost center, capitalized costs, less accumulated amortization and deferred income taxes, are limited to the sum of (1) the present value of future net revenues (future gross revenues, less future costs to develop and produce the proved reserves, with revenues and costs being based on current price and cost levels, discounted at a rate of 10 percent) from proved reserves in the cost center, plus (2) the cost of unproved properties not being amortized because they are unusually significant, plus (3) the lower of cost or estimated fair value of unproved properties included in the amortization base, less (4) income tax effects related to difference between the value computed above and the tax bases of the properties involved, also giving consideration to future investment tax credits, percentage depletion, and so on. Any amount by which unamortized capitalized costs in a cost center, less related recorded deferred income taxes, exceed the cost ceiling for that center is to be charged to expense.

Conveyances of Mineral Interests. An unusual characteristic of the oil and gas industry is its almost unlimited variety of contracts under which the owner or lessee of mineral rights conveys a portion of those rights to other parties. Because of their unusual characteristics, these contracts have been accounted for in many different ways by both transferors and transferees of interests. In SFAS No. 19, the Financial Accounting Standards Board developed broad guidelines to be used in accounting for such transactions and gave a limited number of illustrations of how the guidelines would apply to the most common conveyances. These rules were adopted by the SEC and in general apply to both successful efforts companies and full cost companies, although full cost companies are subject to additional rules, examined later. The rules describe cases in which neither gain nor loss is to be recognized, cases in which loss but not gain is to be recognized, transactions in which gain or loss is generally recognized, and transactions in which the interest retained or transferred is to be treated as a monetary payable or receivable.

Transactions in which neither gain nor loss is recognized. Four situations are described in which no gain or loss is to be recognized at the time of mineral conveyances. These include transactions that are treated essentially as poolings of assets, transactions that represent exchanges of productive assets, transactions in which cash proceeds are treated as recovery of cost because of the high risk involved, and transactions where the seller has a substantial obligation for future performance.

Poolings of assets. Some transactions represent the pooling of assets by two or more entities to carry out a common activity. For example, if the lessee assigns the operating interest in an unproved property with retention of a non-operating interest in return for drilling, development, and operation of the property by the assignee, a pooling of assets has occurred. The assignor records no gain or loss, but assigns the cost of the original interest to the interest retained. The assignee likewise has no gain or loss from the transaction and treats all costs incurred in the normal way.

Similarly, if part of an operating interest in an unproved property is assigned in exchange for a "free well" with provision for joint ownership and operation, no gain or loss is recognized by either party. The assignee assigns no cost to the mineral interest acquired, and the assignor assigns no cost to wells and equipment.

A third example of the pooling-of-assets concept is a "carried interest" under which the assignee agrees to defray all costs to drill, develop, and operate the property and is to receive all revenues from the property until the assignee's costs have been recovered. The assignor (carried party) makes no accounting for any costs or revenue until after the carrying party has recovered all costs ("payout" is reached). During this time the carrying party records all revenues and costs. Subsequent to payout, each party accounts for its share of costs and revenues.

The essence of the pooling-of-assets concept is that the cost or carrying value of the original mineral interest is deemed to apply to the interest retained by the assignor.

Exchange of productive assets. Transactions treated as exchanges of similar productive assets are almost identical in character to those considered to be poolings of assets. For example, a part of an operating interest owned by one party may be exchanged for part of an operating interest owned by another party. No gain or loss is recognized by either party. Another exchange of productive assets takes place when all the interest owners in a producing area agree to form a single operating unit, transferring their interests in the individual properties and receiving in turn an undivided interest in the entire unit. In such cases, the fractional mineral interest received is usually in proportion to estimated reserves of oil or gas contributed to the unit. Because properties contributed are not at the same stage of development, some participants may have to pay cash and others will receive cash to "equalize" the contributions of wells and equipment. Cash paid is treated as an additional investment, whereas cash received is considered to be a recovery of costs. Only if cash received exceeds the carrying value of the property contributed is a gain to be recognized.

Transactions where high risk is involved. Transactions in which no gain is recognized because of the high risk associated with an interest retained usually involve unproved properties. In a conveyance in which only part of the mineral rights in an unproved property is transferred and some type of interest is retained, no gain is generally recognized. Gain is recognized if the proceeds from the partial interest transferred exceeds the entire carrying amount of the property when the property is subject to individual impairment, or if the proceeds exceed the original cost and in a case where the property is part of a group on which amortization is being recorded. Losses may be recognized on high-risk transactions.

Substantial obligation for future performance. In situations where a part of an interest is sold but the seller has an obligation to drill a well or to operate the property without proportional reimbursement for that portion of the drilling or operating costs applicable to the interest sold, no income is recognized at the time of sale because the seller has a substantial obligation for future performance.

Other transactions. Most other conveyances for which cash consideration is received give rise to recognized gain or loss under the successful efforts method. For example, if the entire interest in an unproved property is sold, gain or loss is recognized if impairment was assessed individually on the property. If an unproved property is part of a group on which impairment is recorded, no gain or loss is recorded on its sale unless the sales price exceeds the original cost of the property, in which case the excess is treated as a gain.

The sale of an entire interest in a proved property that constitutes a separate amortization base, or the sale of part or all of a proved property constituting a part of a group amortization base, is treated as a sale on which gain or loss is recognized. In the latter case, the unamortized cost of the property or group of properties, a part of which is sold, is apportioned to the interest sold and the interest retained on the basis of the fair value of those interests. Similarly, the sale of the operating interest in a proved property for cash, with retention of a nonoperating mineral interest, is treated as a sale and gain or loss is recognized. The seller allocates the unamortized cost of the proved property to the interests sold and retained on the basis of their fair values.

Although abandonments of assets associated with proved properties are not conveyances in the normal sense, they do have similarities. Normally, no gain or loss is to be recognized (1) if a single item of equipment or an individual well is abandoned or (2) if a lease or other part of a group of proved properties constituting the amortization base is abandoned or retired when the remainder of the property or group of properties continues to produce oil or gas. Instead, the cost of the asset retired or abandoned is to be charged to accumulated depreciation, depletion, or amortization. Only when the *last* well on the property (or group of properties) ceases to produce and the entire property or property group is abandoned is gain or loss recognized. However, if an abnormal abandonment or retirement occurs—for example, in a natural catastrophe—gain or loss is recognized.

Interests treated as payables and receivables. "Production payments" call for the holder to receive a specified physical quantity of product or a specific dollar amount, to be paid out of a specified fractional share of the working interest share of production "when, if, and as" oil or gas is produced. These payments may be "carved out," in which case the lessee retains the working interest in the property, transferring the production payment rights to another party for cash, or they may be "retained." In a retained transaction the working interest owner conveys the working interest in the property, retaining a production payment.

Prior to the issuance of SFAS No. 19, many different approaches were used to account for payments out of oil or gas. SFAS No. 19 contained guides for treatment of payments, and those rules were made effective by SFAS No. 25. Under these rules, certain production payments are viewed as being monetary payables or receivables. In all cases where the payment is secured by the borrower's general credit, the transaction is to be treated as a loan. Similarly, a payment payable from a proved property that calls for the holder to be paid a specified amount of cash out of production from the property is a monetary item if the amount involved is reasonably assured of payment. On the other hand, an unsecured production payment out of an unproved property, or from a proved property if realization is not reasonably assured, is treated as a mineral interest (an overriding royalty).

Special conveyance rules for full cost companies. The general rules for conveyances specified in Reg. SX 4-10, apply both to companies using successful efforts accounting and to those using full costing. Additional rules apply to the latter. In general, no gain or loss is recognized on property conveyances under full costing, unless treating proceeds as a recovery of cost would result in a significant change in the amortization rate.

Special rules were laid down in Reg. SX 4-10 for the treatment of "drilling arrangements" by companies using full costing. These rules were clarified and explained in SEC *Staff Accounting Bulletin No. 47* [1982]. In general, income or loss is recognized from participation in various forms of drilling arrangements only if the properties involved were originally acquired with the specific purpose of reselling them or conveying them in drilling arrangements, and they have been accounted for separately. Even then, gain may be recognized only if the cash consideration received exceeds the total cost of the properties involved in the conveyance, plus any exploration and development costs to be incurred subsequently. Income from management activities may be recognized only if the cash compensation represents reimbursements for amounts currently charged to expense.

Supplemental Disclosures. Since 1976 the accounting profession and the petroleum industry have been confronted with constantly changing requirements for "disclosures" in financial reports of oil and gas producing companies. Both the FASB and the SEC have issued pronouncements mandating disclosures not previously required and then subsequently have changed those disclosure requirements. The SEC, in particular, has frequently modified the content and format of supplemental disclosures it requires. In addition, the Commission has on different occasions postponed or suspended the requirements that certain data be included in the scope of independent auditors' reports. Although the SEC's requirements apply only to publicly held companies required to file reports with the SEC, the promulgations of the FASB have in the past applied to *all audited entities,* both those that are publicly held and those that are not publicly held. SFAS No. 69 [FASB, 1982], however, which gives the FASB's present disclosure rules, applies only to publicly held companies. Thus, nonpublic companies have no special disclosure requirements other than that the method of accounting (full costing or successful efforts accounting) be disclosed in the statements, as is required of all oil and gas producing companies by SFAS No. 69.

FASB requirements. SFAS No. 19 lists certain "supplemental data" to be included in financial reports of oil and gas producing companies. Although SFAS No. 25 indefinitely suspended the effective date of most of the accounting provisions of SFAS No. 19, the supplemental disclosure requirements were not suspended. Those requirements, continued in SFAS No. 69 for publicly held companies, may be grouped into three categories: (1) mineral reserve quantities, (2) capitalized costs, and (3) costs incurred.

Mineral reserve quantities. The FASB's requirements for mineral reserve quantities include disclosure of net quantities of an enterprise's interest in proved reserves and proved developed reserves of (1) crude oil (including condensate and natural gas liquids) and (2) natural gas. Reserve quantities are reported as of the beginning and the end of each year. The beginning and ending figures are to be reconciled, with changes resulting from each of the following to be shown separately: (1) revisions of previous estimates; (2) improved recovery; (3) purchases of minerals-in-place; (4) extensions, discoveries, and other additions [including additions to an enterprise's proved reserves that result from (a) extention of the proved acreage of previously discovered (old) reservoirs through additional drilling in periods subsequent to discovery and

(b) discovery of new fields with proved reserves or of new reservoirs of proved reserves in old fields]; (5) production; and (6) sales of minerals-in-place.

In addition, proved *developed* reserves in each geographical area as of the balance sheet date are to be disclosed. If some or all of its reserves are located in foreign countries, the disclosures of net quantities of reserves of oil and of gas and changes in them are to be reported separately for (1) the enterprise's home country and (2) each foreign geographic area in which significant reserves are located.

The quantity disclosures above do not include oil or gas subject to purchase under long-term supply, purchase, or similar agreements and contracts, including such agreements with governments or authorities. However, quantities subject to such agreements with governments or authorities as of the end of the year and the net quantity of oil or gas received under the agreements during each such year shall be separately disclosed if the enterprise participates in the operation of the properties in which the oil or gas is located.

Exhibit 1 shows the reserve quantity disclosures taken from the annual report of The Superior Oil Company for 1980.

Capitalized costs. Aggregate capitalized costs and the related accumulated DD&A related to mineral assets must be reported as of the end of each period for which financial statements are presented.

Costs incurred. Total costs incurred, both those capitalized and those charged to expense during the year, categorized by functions, must be disclosed.

Segment operating results. A new requirement added by SFAS No. 69 is a statement of results of operations from oil and gas producing activities, showing for each geographical area revenues from (1) sales to outside parties and (2) intracompany transfers of oil and gas valued at time of transfer from the producing property. All expenses of the oil and gas producing segment are to be deducted; however, there is no deduction for general and administrative overhead nor for financing costs. Income taxes related to the results of the segment's operations are to be deducted.

Other information. The entity must disclose the method of accounting (full costing or successful efforts accounting) for costs incurred in oil and gas activities as well as the manner of disposing of capitalized costs brought into the activities. These disclosure requirements were added by SFAS No. 25 at the time of suspension of SFAS No. 19, and SFAS No. 69 continues this requirement for all companies, both publicly and privately held.

Regulation SX 4-10 extended the FASB's reserve quantity disclosures by requiring an additional disclosure of the estimated future net revenues (gross expected production value based on current prices, minus estimated future expenditures, based on current costs) to be incurred in developing and producing proved reserves. The expected net revenues for each of the first 3 succeeding years was required to be shown, and the remainder for subsequent years was to be shown in a single amount. This disclosure was not adopted by the FASB in SFAS No. 69.

Value disclosures. One of the most controversial accounting pronouncements of the SEC in recent years was its proposal to replace historical cost methods of accounting for oil and gas reserves with a "value"-based method

EXHIBIT 1

THE SUPERIOR OIL COMPANY AND SUBSIDIARY COMPANIES

Crude oil and natural gas liquids

(thousands of barrels)	United States	Canada	United Kingdom	Indonesia	Gulf of Suez	Other foreign	Total
Proved reserves at December 31, 1977	137,529	141,103	510			5,124	284,266
Increases (decreases) due to:							
Revisions of previous estimates	12,146	2,693	(255)			1,503	16,087
Purchases of minerals in place	13,734			2,847			16,581
Extensions, discoveries, or other additions	12,237	1,248	30		12,834	162	26,511
Current-year production	(20,332)	(9,862)	(44)	(340)	(1,343)	(2)	(31,923)
Proved reserves at December 31, 1978	155,314	135,182	241	2,507	11,491	6,787	311,522
Increases (decreases) due to:							
Revisions of previous estimates	(11,933)	4,175	2	89		(252)	(7,919)
Extensions, discoveries, or other additions	7,881	6,601		1,524		208	16,214
Expropriation by foreign government					(5,314)		(5,314)
Current-year production	(19,738)	(10,471)	(42)	(466)	(6,177)	(318)	(37,192)
Proved reserves at December 31, 1979	131,524	135,487	201	3,654		6,425	277,311
Increases (decreases) due to:							
Revisions of previous estimates	1,001	(1,844)	33	(163)		(97)	(1,070)
Extensions, discoveries, or other additions	13,579	2,940		743		2,011	19,273
Current-year production	(18,799)	(9,484)	(40)	(360)		(711)	(29,394)
Proved reserves at December 31, 1980	127,305	127,099	194	3,874		7,628	266,120
Proved developed reserves at December 31,							
1977	123,912	118,041	510				242,463
1978	139,078	132,513	238	2,507	10,726	6,722	291,784
1979	120,043	132,435	198	3,674		6,425	262,775
1980	115,569	125,573	191	3,894		6,650	251,877

Natural gas

(billions of cubic feet)	United States	Canada	United Kingdom	Indonesia	Other foreign	Total
Proved reserves at December 31, 1977	2,047	1,495	146		45	3,733
Increases (decreases) due to:						
Revisions of previous estimates	(173)	8	7		(4)	(162)
Purchases of minerals in place	99			226		325
Extensions, discoveries, or other additions.	398	59	34		32	523
Current-year production.	(274)	(52)	(23)	(12)		(361)
Proved reserves at December 31, 1978	2,097	1,510	164	214	73	4,058
Increases (decreases) due to:						
Revisions of previous estimates	(142)	(28)	(4)	34	(16)	(156)
Extensions, discoveries, or other additions.	249	89		124	6	468
Current-year production.	(313)	(56)	(22)	(14)		(405)
Proved reserves at December 31, 1979	1,891	1,515	138	358	63	3,965
Increases (decreases) due to:						
Revisions of previous estimates	1	136	6	7	1	151
Extensions, discoveries, or other additions.	316	73		84	41	514
Current-year production.	(296)	(50)	(25)	(14)	(2)	(387)
Proved reserves at December 31, 1980	1,912	1,674	119	435	103	4,243
Proved developed reserves at December 31,						
1977	1,664	1,161	146			2,971
1978	1,760	1,201	162	214	11	3,348
1979	1,555	1,141	136	358	11	3,201
1980	1,579	1,257	116	435	43	3,430

known as *reserve recognition accounting* (RRA). In February 1981 the SEC announced its conclusion that RRA is not appropriate for use as the primary basis of accounting and that the FASB was undertaking a project to develop a comprehensive set of disclosure requirements. In SFAS No. 69, the culmination of that project, the FASB adopted essentially the SEC's requirements for the disclosure of discounted present value of proved reserves. Presumably the SEC will adopt SFAS No. 69 to replace the disclosure requirements found in Reg. SX 4-10 prior to the issuance of SFAS No. 69.

In announcing its intent to develop RRA as the primary basis of accounting for oil and gas producing activities, the SEC stressed the need for oil and gas reserves to be reflected at their "value" in the balance sheet and for the results of the most important activity of an oil and gas company, finding proved reserves, to be reflected in the earnings statement. Three disclosure requirements were designed to provide this information:

1. Present value of estimated future net reserves at year-end
2. Summary of oil and gas producing activities
3. Summary of changes in present value

In SFAS No. 69 the FASB adopted the first of these, rejected the second, and accepted in modified form the third.

Present value of future net revenues. Regulation SX 4-10 requires that the present value of estimated future net revenues, based on a discount rate of 10 percent, be shown as of the end of each fiscal year for which an income statement is required. The SEC's original requirement ignored income taxes in computing the discounted present value of reserves. The calculation required by SFAS No. 69, however, does reflect the effects of income taxes. The format suggested in SFAS No. 69 for the disclosure of the present value of future cash flows from proved reserves is shown in Exhibit 2.

Summary of oil and gas producing activities. The summary of oil and gas producing activities (which the SEC stated that it would not insist on being included in the FASB's Statement on disclosure, and which is not included in SFAS No. 69) is designed to provide a measure of "earnings" based on the current year's additions to the present value of proved reserves and the costs associated with the additions and revisions, together with all costs determined to be nonproductive during the period. Separate identification must be made of certain items reflecting those changes.

1. Value changes resulting from exploration and development activities. The value added is determined by applying year-end prices to estimated future production of oil and gas reserves added during the year and discounting the result at a rate of 10 percent. Estimated future development and production costs may either be deducted in determining additions, or they may be reported separately as deductions of the current period.

2. Revisions of estimates of value of proved reserves at the beginning of the year. Revisions resulting from changes in price must be shown separately from other revisions. Other revisions may be due to changes in cost factors, expected time of production, quantity of reserves, or other factors. These may be com-

EXHIBIT 2   Standardized Measure of Discounted Future Net Cash Flows Relating to Proved Oil and Gas Reserve Quantities

	Total	United States	Foreign geographic area A	Foreign geographic area B	Other foreign geographic areas
Future cash inflows . . .	$ X	$ X	$ X	$ X	$ X
Future production and development costs . .	(X)	(X)	(X)	(X)	(X)
Future income tax expenses	(X)	(X)	(X)	(X)	(X)
Future net cash flows .	$ X	$ X	$ X	$ X	$ X
10% annual discount for estimated timing of cash flows	(X)	(X)	(X)	(X)	(X)
Standardized measure of discounted future net cash flows	$ X	$ X	$ X	$ X	$ X
Enterprise's share of equity method investees' standardized measure of discounted future net cash flows	$ X	$ X	$ X	$ X	$ X

bined. In addition, significant gains on sales of reserves-in-place must be disclosed.

3. Accretion of interest. The carrying value of beginning reserves will increase by 10 percent (the discount rate) as a result of the passage of 1 year. This is a major source of "income" under RRA.

4. Expired costs. The expired costs of the period include acquisition costs of properties that have been either proved or impaired during the period. Costs of exploratory wells determined to be either dry or to have found proved reserves, exploration and carrying costs, development costs associated with current extension and discoveries, those found to be nonproductive, and certain other costs.

5. Production costs.

6. Estimated future development and production costs. The present value of these costs may either be deducted from the gross additions and extensions, or may be reported separately as expenses of the current period.

7. Income tax provisions. Income taxes for the period are computed by applying the current statutory rate to the future taxable income from the proved reserves, deducting the deferred tax at the beginning of the year, and adding the current tax provision for oil and gas producing activities.

As previously pointed out, SFAS No. 69 does not require this disclosure. Nevertheless, because of the importance of this requirement in the development of oil and gas accounting standards, the summary of oil and gas producing activities for Sun Company, Inc., taken from its 1980 annual report, is shown in Exhibit 3.

Changes in present value. The SEC's original requirements in Reg. SX 4-10 called for a reconciliation between beginning and ending RRA values of proved reserves. Certain factors causing changes were to be shown separately. These included:

1. The total additions, revisions, and accretion of discount, less related future development and production costs
2. Purchases of minerals in place
3. Previously estimated future development costs incurred during the year
4. Sales of oil and gas and value of intracompany transfers, net of production costs
5. Proceeds from sales of minerals in place

SFAS No. 69 does not require a reconciliation of beginning and ending present values of proved oil and gas reserves. Instead, it suggests that, if significant, the change during the year resulting from each of the following factors should be disclosed:

Sales and transfers of oil and gas produced, net of production costs
Net changes in prices and production costs
Extensions, discoveries, and improved recovery, less related costs

---

EXHIBIT 3

SUN COMPANY, INC.
Summary of Oil and Gas Producing Activities on the Basis of Reserve Recognition Accounting

	1980	1979
	(millions of dollars)	
Additions and revisions to estimated proved oil and gas reserves:		
Present value of additions, gross	$ 806	$ 544
Revisions to estimates of proved reserves:		
Changes in prices	6,242	2,897
Other[a]	(4,197)	(688)
Interest factor	666	461
	$3,517	$3,214
Deductions for costs of oil and gas producing activities:		
Costs incurred, including impairments	$ 546	$ 356
Present value of estimated future costs	311	150
	$ 857	$ 506
Additions and revisions, net of deductions	$2,660	$2,708
Provision for income taxes	1,267	1,436
Results of oil and gas producing activities on the basis of reserve recognition accounting	$1,393	$1,272

[a]Primarily windfall profits tax in 1980 and increases in estimated costs in 1979.

Development costs incurred during the period
Revisions of previous quantity estimates
Accretion of discount
Net change in income taxes
Other

THE MINING INDUSTRY

The basic activities in mining are similar to those in the oil and gas industry. These include prospecting, property acquisition, exploration, development, and production. The basic principles followed by most companies in accounting for their mining activities are also similar to those required of the SEC for oil and gas companies electing to use the successful efforts method. Few mining companies use the full cost method.

Prospecting. Prospecting is made up of those activities undertaken to locate mineral or ore deposits. These costs are not significant in most cases, and are usually charged to expense at the time they are incurred.

Acquisition. In most mining activities, property rights are acquired by mineral lease. Variations of the lease contract may be referred to as concessions or permits. However, in many cases outright fee interest in the land and minerals may be purchased. There are still limited cases in which mining rights may be obtained on public lands by "staking a claim." Acquisition costs should be capitalized. These costs include lease bonus payments, lease options, option renewals, abstract costs, recording fees, attorney's fees, and similar costs. If fee rights in property are acquired, the acquisition costs should be pro rated between the mineral or ore deposit and the land surface rights.

Exploration. In mining, exploration involves proving the existence, location, quantity, and quality of reserves. It may be necessary to open a mine, remove overburden, or otherwise gain physical access to the deposit in order to test the quality and quantity of the ore or mineral present. The exploration stage also involves analysis of potential methods and approaches to developing the deposit. Costs of geological and geophysical studies, core drilling, hydrological testing, mapping, and feasibility studies are typical exploration costs.

Mining exploration costs are usually charged to expense as incurred. However, some mining companies defer exploration costs at the time they are incurred; if the area to which the costs are related is later abandoned, the costs are charged to expense at the time of abandonment. If commercial reserves are developed, the costs are capitalized and amortized as the reserves are produced. Other companies achieve the same result by initially expensing exploration costs, but "reversing" the costs and capitalizing them if commercial reserves are subsequently found to be present, even when the reversal occurs in a subsequent accounting period.

Development. The development stage is the period during which preparation is made for sustained production, but before commercial production actually begins. Development activities involve gaining access to the deposit and constructing facilities to handle the ore or mineral produced. Costs for such activities and functions as acquiring licenses and construction permits, compiling environmental impact information, constructing access roads, sinking shafts, driving tunnels, removing initial overburden, constructing slopes, installing processing equipment, building storage facilities, testing of facilities, and building dikes are treated as development costs.

In many cases it is difficult to distinguish clearly between exploration activities and development activities or between exploration activities and production activities. For example, production may expose additional reserves requiring new development outlays.

Development costs should be capitalized and amortized to expense as the reserves are produced from the deposit. However, some mining companies charge development costs to expense at the time they are incurred.

One accounting method found in some mining activities is the "receding face cost" method. Under this method, *additional* facilities such as wiring, tracks for ore cars, substation equipment, air shafts, mine cars, and so on, needed to maintain the productive capacity of the mine are charged directly to expense when they are incurred. This method is, in many respects, like *replacement, retirement, betterment* (RRB) accounting, used by many railroads.

Reclamation Costs. It is generally agreed that estimated costs of restoring mined properties should be charged to expense as the reserves in the mine are produced. Reclamation costs include such items as costs of performance bonds, removal and storing of top soil, grading, control of erosion, revegetation, maintenance of revegetation, open pit refill, and shutdown and removal of facilities.

Many companies accrue the estimated costs during the productive life of the deposit. However, other companies expense such costs on a pay-as-you-go basis, because reclamation is substantially concurrent with production. This is particularly common in strip mining activities, where refill and revegetation work follows closely behind ore removal.

Depletion and Amortization. Amortization of capitalized acquisition, exploration, and development costs are centered around the property unit. The "mineral deposit" (a geological area with mineral deposits) is normally treated as the property unit. The individual mine location and seams of ore within a mine location are also sometimes treated as the property unit. Some companies use general areas, such as a county or state, for making the amortization calculations.

Conceptually, amortization of all costs should be based on the unit-of-production method, unless a physical asset has a life shorter than the expected period of production. In this event, the asset's cost should be amortized (depreciated) over the life of the asset.

Unit-of-production amortization is often difficult in mining, because there may be several different metals or minerals in the ore, the quality may vary from one part of the mine to another, and changing reserve estimates frequently may be necessary. The amortization rate may be based on cost per unit of ore, or on cost per unit of the metal or minerals. In general, basing the rate on the quantity of mineral or metals is preferable, because the mineral content of ore can vary greatly. Amortization is computed by dividing the capitalized costs by the recoverable units and then multiplying the rate per unit by the production for the period. Changes in estimated reserves are treated prospectively, in accordance with APB Opinion No. 20.

Disclosure Requirements. The Financial Accounting Standards Board issued SFAS No. 39 in October 1980, extending the current cost disclosure requirements of SFAS No. 33 to the mineral resource assets of mining enterprises. In addition, the Statement requires disclosure of information about quantities, production, and selling prices of mineral resources other than oil and gas.

THE TIMBER INDUSTRY

In many ways the accounting problems encountered in the timber industry are identical to those in mining and mineral extraction. The basic problems are (1) deciding which costs are to be capitalized, and (2) computing depletion for the timber cut during the year.

Acquisition and Development of Timber Resources. In the early decades of this century, most Americans considered timber to be an inexhaustible resource. Lumber companies purchased, cut, and milled timber without giving consideration to selective cutting or replanting seedlings. Now, however, lumber companies, paper pulp producers, and other timber users have found it necessary to purchase lands and grow timber for their own use.

As in the case of mineral and ore properties, all acquisition costs relating to the timber should be capitalized. When standing timber and land are purchased, a portion of the purchase price representing the fair value of the surface rights should be charged to the Land account.

Carrying costs of timber being raised, including such items as clearing underbrush, reseeding, fire protection, treatment for insects and disease, and insurance protection, should be capitalized. This is especially appropriate in view of the extremely long period of development that may be required before revenues are generated from the particular tract and the fact that growth of timber increases the value of the property. Even after the cutting has begun, those carrying costs that apply to future production should be capitalized. In actual practice, however, nearly all companies treat these development costs, regardless of whether incurred before or after cutting begins, as current expense.

Other development costs not specifically related to the growing of timber—such as construction of roads, drainage canals, and so on—should logically be capitalized, either as part of the timber cost or in separate accounts to be amortized or depreciated over their useful lives.

Depletion of Timber Costs. The depletion charge for timber cut during the year is computed on a unit-of-production basis. The net book value of the timber block at the end of the year is divided by the number of units available for cutting (the units on hand at the end of the year, plus the units cut during the year) in order to arrive at a depletion rate per unit. (Timber is usually measured in board feet.) The unit rate is then applied to the number of units cut to compute the total depletion for the year. This procedure is followed for both financial accounting and tax purposes. (There is no percentage depletion allowance for timber.)

To illustrate the depletion computation, assume that the remaining book value of a timber block on January 1 was $56,000. During the year additional costs of $4,000 were capitalized and 80,000 board feet were produced from the property. On December 31, estimated remaining standing timber was 520,000 board feet. The depletion rate is thus $.10 (= $60,000/600,000 feet) per board foot, and the depletion charge for the year is $8,000 (= 80,000 feet $\times$ $.10 per foot).

The remaining reserves of timber can be estimated with far greater accuracy than the reserves of most mineral and ore deposits. As a result, the depletion charge is more precise and meaningful. It is not unusual for the depletion rate to decrease from year to year because of an increase in estimated "reserves" from the growth of timber.

As previously noted, most timber producing companies charge all carrying costs of growing timber to current expense, so that blocks which were acquired not as standing forests but as almost barren lands subsequently planted with seedlings will have little, if any, capitalized depletable cost. This, plus the fact that cutting is normally done on a selective basis, with only a part of the standing timber harvested each year, makes many timber operations essentially farming enterprises.

Recording Accretion. Some accountants argue that the increase in value (accretion) resulting from growth of standing timber should be recognized in the accounts each year because the value can be reliably measured and verified. It is argued that the key factor in income production is the growth of the timber, and that this should be reflected in the accounts. Recognition of accretion might be accomplished by a debit to the asset account and a credit to either an income or an unearned income account. Accretion is seldom recorded in practice, however, because of adherence to the realization principle in accounting and the uncertainty about the price at which the product will ultimately be marketed.

In November 1980, the FASB issued SFAS No. 40, *Financial Reporting and Changing Prices: Specialized Assets—Timberlands and Growing Timber*, establishing for the timber industry rather complex special disclosure requirements to reflect the impact of inflation. Under the Statement, large companies are required to combine measures of timber lands, growing timber, and related expenses at either historical cost/constant dollar amounts or at current cost amounts with the current cost measurement of other assets and expenses. Different approaches may be used in measuring current cost. If current cost is estimated on the basis of a specific price index, the historical "cost" to be adjusted may be deemed to be either the historical cost of timber as shown in the balance sheet or it may be a historical cost figure adjusted to include reforestation and management costs.

BIBLIOGRAPHY

Accounting Principles Board (AICPA), *Accounting Changes,* Opinion No. 20 (APB, 1970).

Accounting Principles Board Committee on the Extractive Industries (AICPA), *Accounting and Reporting Practices in the Oil and Gas Industry* (APB, 1973).

Adkerson, R. C., "Can Reserve Recognition Work?" *Journal of Accountancy,* vol. 148, no. 3 (September 1979), pp. 72–81.

Bierman, H., R. E. Dukes, and T. R. Dyckman, "Financial Reporting in the Petroleum Industry," *Journal of Accountancy,* vol. 138, no. 4 (October 1974), pp. 58–64.

Brock, H. R., J. P. Klingstedt, and D. M. Jones, *Accounting for Oil and Gas Producing Companies* (Professional Development Institute, Denton, Tex., 1981).

Connor, J. E., "Discovery Value—The Oil Industry's Untried Method," *Journal of Accountancy,* vol. 139, no. 5 (May 1975), pp. 54–63.

Field, R. E., *Financial Reporting in the Extractive Industries,* Accounting Research Study No. 11 (AICPA, 1969).

Financial Accounting Standards Board, *Financial Accounting and Reporting by Oil and Gas Producing Companies,* Statement of Financial Accounting Standards No. 19 (FASB, 1977).

———, *Suspension of Certain Accounting Requirements for Oil and Gas Producing Companies,* Statement of Financial Accounting Standards No. 25 (FASB, 1979).

———, *Financial Reporting and Changing Prices: Specialized Assets—Mining and Oil and Gas,* Statement of Financial Accounting Standards No. 39 (FASB, 1980a).

———, *Financial Reporting and Changing Prices: Specialized Assets—Timberlands and Growing Timber,* Statement of Financial Accounting Standards No. 40 (FASB, 1980b).

———, *Accounting for Exploratory Wells in Progress at the End of a Period,* Interpretation No. 36 (FASB, 1981).

———, *Disclosure about Oil and Gas Producing Activities,* Statement of Financial Accounting Standards No. 69 (FASB, 1982).

Janson, E. C., S. Knup, and D. Wright, *Financial Reporting and Tax Practices in Nonferrous Mining* (Coopers and Lybrand, New York, 1979).

Meyers, J. H., *Full Cost vs Successful Efforts in the Petroleum Accounting, An Empirical Approach* (John Meyers, Bloomington, Ind., 1974).

National Coal Association Accounting Committee, *Results of 1980 Survey of Accounting Practices in the Coal Industry* (NCA, Washington, D.C., 1980).

Porter, S., *Petroleum Accounting Practices* (McGraw-Hill Book Company, New York, 1965).

Securities and Exchange Commission, *Requirements for Financial Accounting and Reporting Practices for Oil and Gas Producing Activities,* Accounting Series Release No. 257 (SEC, 1978).

———, *Oil and Gas Producers—Supplemental Disclosures on the Basis of Reserve Recognition Accounting,* Accounting Series Release No. 269 (SEC, 1979).

———, *Staff Accounting Bulletin No. 47* (SEC, 1982).

Sunder, S., "Full Costing and Successful Efforts Costing in the Petroleum Industry," *The Accounting Review,* vol. 51, no. 1 (January 1976), pp. 1–18.

U.S. Department of Energy, Federal Energy Regulatory Commission, Comments before the United States Securities and Exchange Commission, Accounting Practices—Oil and Gas Producers—Financial Accounting Standards File 57-715, April 1978.

U.S. Government, *Code of Federal Regulations,* SEC. 210.4-10 (U.S. Government Printing Office, Washington, D.C.).

CHAPTER 19

Buildings and

Equipment

John Leslie Livingstone
Vice President, Management Analysis Center, Inc.,
Dallas, Texas

CHARACTERISTICS OF BUILDINGS AND EQUIPMENT

Classification of Fixed Assets. Buildings and equipment constitute a subclass of the fixed asset category. Fixed assets consist of long-lived assets not intended for resale in the regular business of the enterprise. Fixed assets are usually classed as either tangible or intangible. Tangible fixed assets are characterized by physical existence; they include land, wasting assets, property improvements, buildings, and equipment. Intangible fixed assets lack physical substance; they include items such as patents, copyrights, organization costs, and goodwill.

Within the class of tangible fixed assets, buildings are normally regarded as construction used to house the activities of people and equipment, and for storage. Buildings are distinguished from construction that does not house operations. For example, roads, railroad tracks, bridges, paving, tunnels, piers, canals, and similar items are usually not regarded as buildings but rather as property improvements.

Equipment comprises industrial and office machinery and tools, transportation equipment (such as automobiles, aircraft, barges, and reusable containers such as barrels and drums), furniture and fixtures, and farm animals.

The distinction between buildings and equipment is not always clear-cut. Items such as elevators, ductwork, power lines and wiring, piping, built-in appliances, sinks and toilets, and other structural fixtures may be classed either with buildings or with equipment.

Nature of Buildings and Equipment. Hendriksen [1977, p. 357] lists the following five distinguishing characteristics of buildings and equipment:

1. These assets are physical goods used for facilitating the output of commodities or to furnish services to the enterprise or its customers in the normal course of business.

2. They all have a finite life, at the termination of which they have to be abandoned, substituted for, or replaced. This life may be a given period of years based on wear and tear in use, or it may be variable according to the level of use and the quality of maintenance.

3. Their value derives from the ability to exclude others in exercising the legal property rights in their use, rather than from enforcement of contractual obligations.

4. They are of nonmonetary nature in that benefits tend to flow from use or sale of their services instead of from their conversion directly into sums of money.

5. Usually the benefits are received over a period greater than a single year or the operating cycle of the enterprise. A few exceptions to this rule occur. For instance, some items such as tools may have a useful life shorter than the operating cycle of the entity.

By reason of these characteristics, notably the long-lived nature and repeated use of the services of buildings and equipment, they merit treatment as a separate class of assets for accounting purposes. This grouping provides relevant information to users of accounting statements regarding the tangible capital investment of the enterprise.

Importance of Buildings and Equipment. The relation of the investment in buildings and equipment to total assets or revenues naturally varies from one enterprise to another. In general, it may be relatively slight in service industries (such as retailing and insurance) and very substantial in industries such as heavy manufacturing and transportation. For the investor-owned electric utility industry as a whole, net utility plant amounts to more than 90 percent of total assets, and represents more than 4 years' operating revenues.

U.S. Department of Commerce statistics for a recent year show nongovernment expenditures on new plant and equipment amounting to approximately 10 percent of GNP. The magnitude of these expenditures, coupled with the obvious observation that virtually all enterprises make use of buildings and equipment, are ample evidence of the economic importance of this class of assets.

PLANNING CAPITAL EXPENDITURES

Long-Range Planning of Capital Expenditures. The results of decisions regarding capital expenditures are generally far-reaching and of significant effect on the success or failure of an enterprise. It may not be possible to dispose of ill-advised capital additions without substantial loss. The incurrence of indebtedness to finance capital expenditures commits future earnings. If sufficiently increased earnings fail to result from capital additions, the ability of the enterprise to service its financial obligations could be seriously impaired and may be economically disastrous. By the same token, failure to engage in desirable capital expenditure programs could deprive an enterprise of valuable opportunities for profitable growth.

Planning capital expenditures for expected growth. Long-range planning should be related to the present programs and activities of the enterprise. In effect, it provides the bridge between the current situation and longer-term objectives. The integration of short- and long-term goals is necessary to provide for orderly growth in the planned directions. By this means, guideposts can be established to compare actual with intended progress, given a time schedule of planned objectives. Therefore, short-term capital expenditure plans represent the immediate time segment (usually 1 or 2 years ahead) of the long-term plan.

Balancing capital facilities. Attention should be given to careful balancing of various types of productive capacity at successive stages of the operations and manufacturing processes of the enterprise. This is necessary to avoid facility bottlenecks resulting from unbalanced expansion and the accompanying excess costs and delays. It also protects against uneconomically idle equipment, excessive work in process inventories, and the burden of extra depreciation, insurance, and interest expense.

Well-balanced capital investment is likely to stem from relating capital facilities to anticipated volume of output derived from careful analysis of sales and operating budgets. The productive capacity of each process should be coordinated with the requirements of successive operations, allowing for breakdowns, retooling, spoilage, and other interruptions in production. Capital additions should be planned to maintain or improve the existing balance of facilities.

Evaluation of Projects. An enterprise is likely to have a number of necessary or potentially profitable projects in which to invest funds. The efficiency with which these investment opportunities are analyzed, acted upon, and executed directly influences the future attainment of enterprise objectives such as profitability and maintenance of competitive position. Because the amounts involved are often large and the investments are frequently long-lasting, capital expenditure decisions are one of the most important of all management tasks.

The process of selecting projects is extremely complex. Many important considerations are neither quantifiable nor certain and can be dealt with only by means of intuitive judgment. For example, investment in equipment to reduce air or water pollution may have cost effects amenable to estimation or measurement. The benefits are difficult to quantify, however, as they may consist primarily of avoiding unfavorable publicity and compliance with legal requirements.

Although these difficulties must be borne in mind, capital expenditure proposals should be supported by quantitative analysis and compared by means of quantitative criteria as far as reasonably possible. The main methods for these purposes are briefly described below.[1]

---

[1]For a more comprehensive treatment, see Bierman and Smidt [1980].

Cost of funds. In strict theory, enterprises should continue to raise and invest funds to the point where the incremental cost of capital funds required equals the incremental return on investment. In practice, however, there are reasons that usually prevent enterprises from approaching this point. For instance, available management talent may be insufficient to plan and control so rapid a rate of growth; the risk involved in certain investments may deter their acceptance although the expected return equals or exceeds the cost of capital; or certain possible projects may lie outside the area of operation desired by (or permissible under antitrust and other laws to) the enterprise.

Therefore, the cost of funds may not provide a sufficiently strict criterion to distinguish acceptable from unacceptable investment proposals. Project evaluation may employ a minimum acceptable rate of return (or cutoff rate) in excess of the cost of capital, or rate of return may not even be used as one of the project selection criteria.

Payback period. This criterion for project evaluation does not employ a rate of return concept. The payback period is the length of time required for cash inflows of an investment project to equal the original cash outlay. For instance, a proposed investment requires a present outlay of $1,000 and has expected cash inflows of $200 at the end of 1 year and $400 at the end of each succeeding year for the next 4 years. The payback period will be 3 years in this case.

Note that this method does not consider the time value of money; that is, it treats all dollars as being equal in value regardless of the time when they are expected to flow in or out. For example, if our illustration were changed to have the first cash inflow consist of $1,000 at the end of 3 years, the payback period is unaltered although there is postponement of cash inflows of $200 for 2 years and $400 for 1 year. In addition, the method ignores investment profitability by neglecting cash flows subsequent to the payback period. As an extreme instance, it shows no discrimination between our original example and one exactly alike except for a cash inflow of $100,000 rather than $400 in the final year. There is little in favor of the payback method except its extreme simplicity and ease in application. Where liquidity is an overriding factor, however, its importance is increased. Also, where alternative investment projects are alike or indistinguishable in all other respects, the project with the shortest payback period may be preferred, on the grounds of the lesser degree of future uncertainty involved by a faster recovery of invested funds.

If a payback period is used, many accountants would prefer the *discounted payback period*, which is the shortest length of time required for the aggregate *present value* of the future cash flows to equal or exceed the initial cash outlay. The rate of discount normally applied in this case is the firm's cost of capital. Although the discounted payback period does recognize the time value of money, it fails to consider inflows occurring after the end of the discounted payback period.

A method that takes into account the cash recovery from a project that is aborted prior to completion of its expected life is the *bailout* or *discounted bailout* period. The bailout period is the length of time during which the initial outlay remains recoverable from cash flows plus the salvage value of the project's assets. The discounted bailout period is the length of time that the initial outlay can still be recovered from discounted cash flows and salvage values.

Accounting rate of return. There are variations in this method, but the most common approach is computation of average net income (= cash flows less depreciation) per year divided by average net book value of the assets over the project life. Alternative rate of return computation methods include use of the first year's cash inflow in place of the average for the numerator, and use of gross rather than net asset book value for the denominator. As an illustration, consider the original example cited under the payback period heading.

Straight-line depreciation for the $1,000 investment over its 5-year life is $200 a year, assuming no salvage value. Cash flows after depreciation are zero in year 1 and $200 in each of the next 4 years, or an average of ⅕($0 + $800) = $160 a year. The average net book value of the assets at year-end is ⅕($800 + $600 + $400 + $200 + $0) = $400. The accounting rate of return is 160/400 = 40 percent on net book value, if taxes are ignored.

Because the method treats dollar flows in different periods as equivalent, it ignores the time value of money. For instance, if the $200 cash inflow of year 1 took place in year 5 instead and the $400 cash inflow of year 5 were switched to year 1, there would be no change in the accounting rate of return. Another limitation of this technique is that results are dependent on the method of depreciation used. Use of accelerated depreciation, rather than straight-line, could materially alter the average earnings and asset book values computed for the project and hence produce a different rate of return. A possible advantage of this method, though, is its consistency with the effect of the project on accounting reports in the future, so that the method of project evaluation before investment takes place is a means of projecting future reported operating results. However, the effect on future accounting reports is not necessarily the best or only criterion for selection of capital expenditure projects.

Internal rate of return. The internal rate of return technique, sometimes referred to as the "investor's method," is based explicitly on the time value of money. In fact, its purpose is to determine a time-adjusted rate of return for any project. This is done by finding a rate of return that, when applied to all cash flows, makes net outflows equal to net inflows.

Again using the previous example, plus a set of present value tables, we find a rate of return at which the present values of cash inflows and outflows are equal.

At a 25 percent rate of return, the discount factors from present value tables and the cash inflows are

Value at end of year 1 of $400 a year for years 2–5 = 2.362 × $400	$ 944.80
Add cash inflow, year 1	200.00
	$1,144.80
Present value at beginning of year 1 = 0.8 × $1,144.80	$ 915.84

Because $915.84 is less than the $1,000 present cash outlay, the internal rate of return on the project is not 25 percent but a lower rate. At 20 percent the results are

Value at end of year 1 of $400 a year for years 2–5 = 2.589 × $400	$1,035.60
Add cash inflow, year 1	200.00
	$1,235.60
Present value at beginning of year 1 = 0.833 × $1,235.6	$1,029.25

Because $1,029.25 is slightly larger than $1,000, the rate of return is slightly above 20 percent. The precise rate can be found by further trial and error.

This method does take into account both the profitability of the project and the time value of money. However, its drawbacks are as follows:

1. When there are net cash *outflows* in years of project life after the first year, there may be several internal rates of return, all of which are applicable. For instance, a project may have internal rates of return of 20, 30, and 50 percent. In such cases there is no uniquely "correct" rate, or any method of selecting one of the multiple rates as "truly representative" of the project's profitability.

2. The technique assumes reinvestment of all cash inflows at the *same* internal rate of return as that of the project. Where this is not the case, the method is not applicable without modification.

3. If internal rate of return is used to rank a number of projects in order of desirability, the ranking is not reliable unless all projects have both identical initial cash outlays and identical lives.

For these reasons, the internal rate of return method should be used only in circumstances where these limitations are not present.

Present value methods. Present value methods avoid the problem of possible multiple rates of return involved in the internal rate of return method. The approach is to discount future cash flows at a preselected rate, usually the minimum acceptable or cutoff rate of return.

Again using our example, assume a 15 percent cutoff rate of return. At this rate, the present value of the future cash flows is

Value at end of year 1 of $400 a year for years 2–5 = 2.855 × $400	$1,142
Add cash inflow, year 1	200
	$1,342
Present value at beginning of year 1 = 0.87 × $1,342	$1,168

From this point two alternative techniques may be used. The *net present value* method ranks projects on the excess of the present value over the immediate outlay. In the example above this would be ($1,168 − $1,000) = $168. The greater this excess, the more desirable in general is the project.

The *present value index* method is based on the ratio of the present value of future cash flows to the immediate outlay required. In the example this would be (1,168/1,000) = 1.168. The larger the value of this ratio, or index, the more desirable the project according to the net present value method.

The present value index may give incorrect decisions when projects are mutually exclusive. Correct decisions will result from selecting the projects with positive net present values as between mutually exclusive projects, choose the one with the largest excess present value [Davidson et al., 1975, p. 767].

A detailed comparison and evaluation of these two present value methods would far exceed both the space and scope of this chapter. Many complex factors are involved, and the concerned reader is referred to specialized works. Specialized works should also be consulted for methods and problems not mentioned explicitly above: for example, income tax considerations in capital investment; buy-or-lease questions; dealing with risk and uncertainty; treatment of complementary, independent, and mutually exclusive projects; the implications of the cost of capital and capital rationing; and estimation of the expected rate of return on reinvested funds.

Control of Capital Expenditures. "Control" in the context of capital expenditures does not mean simple downward pressure or minimization of expenditures. Rather it means maintaining a detailed check on all phases of capital expenditure—from inception to completion of each project—to ensure that management plans are executed as nearly as possible. Furthermore, control means coordination of capital expenditure planning with related plans such as cash and operating expense budgets.

Plant and equipment budget procedures. The budgeting process for plant and equipment, while differing from one organization to another, generally includes the following procedures. Periodic requests, typically once a year, are usually made by the head office to the departments and operating units of an enterprise for capital expenditure proposals. Frequently this timetable parallels that of the operating budget cycle.

The managers of departments and operating units submit these proposals to the budget director (or the controller or other official performing these functions, according to the organization of the particular enterprise concerned). The budget director reviews the proposals and makes a critical analysis of the information on which the proposals are based. Care is taken to ensure, so far as possible, that predictions such as sales volume and prices, engineering, production, administrative and distribution costs, and working capital requirements are the result of thorough study and realistic estimation. Techniques used for this purpose by the budget director usually include reference to historical records of similar projects, products, or processes, comparison with available industry information relevant to the respective proposals, and discussion and reexamination with the persons responsible for preparing and submitting the various proposals.

There are many technical aspects of proposals that accountants will not be able to check, especially in cases involving engineering and other specialized areas. However, it can be ensured that these technical aspects have been studied carefully by qualified personnel and are reflected in reliable estimates. A careful review by the budget director's office can be the source of major revisions and improvements of proposals; further, it provides a safeguard against the late discovery of costly errors of estimate in projects to which funds have already been committed. Also, the process of reviewing proposals may suggest alternative courses of action that might be superior to those considered.

Plant and equipment budgets. After projects have been reviewed by the budget director and revised where necessary, it is usual for top management to formulate a long-term capital expenditure budget. Examples are shown in Exhibits 1 and 2.

Normally, a long-term capital expenditure budget is divided into two classes of items. One class consists of major projects where each one requires a large amount of funds: for instance, buildings, ships, and big items. Capital expenditures of such a nature often involve both construction and outlays extending beyond a single year. It can be seen in Exhibit 1 that all individual designated projects have this characteristic.

The other class of projects covers minor capital expenditures, which may not be planned in detail as far ahead as major projects. These consist of lesser-cost equipment, additions and improvements to buildings, and other smaller items. Items of this type would not usually be considered individually in long-range capital expenditure planning. Normally an aggregate sum is allowed to cover these expenditures, as in Exhibit 1 where the heading "undesignated" is used for this purpose.

The long-term capital expenditure budget segments expenditures by years. This segmentation is required for coordination with the annual, or short-term, capital expenditure budget. An example of an annual capital budget is shown in Exhibit 3.

Inclusion of a project in the annual capital budget does not necessarily provide automatic authorization to spend funds or incur financial obligations with respect to that project. Controls are generally exercised at three stages: inclusion in the budget, approval of the appropriation of funds, and authorization of expenditures. These controls serve several purposes, one of which is to maintain flexibility in changing the annual capital budget if unforeseen circumstances so require. For this reason, projects may be classified by priority groups, such as essential, profitable, and desirable. In Exhibit 3 it can be seen that there is a category for "expansion and growth" and another category entitled "replacements." The second category is further divided into "absolutely essential," "competitively necessary," "economics basis" (i.e., profitable), and "other." Note that there is also a contingency allowance. This would allow for some variation between budgeted and actual expenditures and, if so desired, the later addition of one or more projects not presently in the budget.

Cash management. The annual capital expenditure budget must be coordinated with the cash budget in order to assure compatibility between budgeted capital outlays and availability of funds. Unless these respective budgets are carefully dovetailed, there is danger of being unable to carry out capital expenditures as planned, or of siphoning off cash required for working capital into capital expenditures, thus hampering the ability of the enterprise to meet its current financial obligations.

In order to integrate the cash and capital expenditure budgets fully, the timing of capital expenditures should be planned explicitly by month and by quarter of the year. This detailed breakdown allows short-term cash budgeting to be carried out properly.

Appropriations. The setting up of an appropriation for a project in the annual capital budget usually signifies management's firm decision to commit funds to that project. Woods [1967] states that appropriation provides a means of:

1. Identifying the project specifically so that transactions related to it can be separately recorded
2. Restricting the scope of the project to its approved form
3. Limiting the cost of the project to the budgeted amount, within a given tolerance (commonly plus or minus 10 percent)
4. Recording evidence that the project is consistent with the capital expenditure budget

EXHIBIT 1 Long-Range Capital Expenditures Budget[a]

THE XYZ CORPORATION—Long-Range Plan
Capital Expenditure Budget—Summary by Product and Years
For the Period January 1, 19X3 through 19X7
(in thousands of dollars)

Description of projects	Reference for detail	Budgeted Date	Budgeted Amount	Amount authorized to January 1, 19X3	Amount subject to authorization	Amount spent to January 1, 19X3	Unexpended balance of appropriation	19X3[b]	19X4	19X5	19X6	19X7	Subsequent years
Approved projects													
Regular:													
Project A, etc.	A-1	19X1	$1,000	$800	$ 200	$700	$100	$150	$ 75	$ 50	$ 25		
Special:													
Project E, etc.	E-1	19X2	500	200	300	180	20	220	70	30			
Total approved													
Budgeted projects[b]													
Regular:													
Project H, etc.	H-1	19X3	800		800			100	150	250	200	$ 75	$ 25
Special:													
Project M, etc.													
Undesignated[c]		19X3	270					50	50	50	60	60	
Total budgeted—19X3													
Total regular													
Total special													
Grand total													
For information only													
Projects under study:													
Project X, etc.	X-1	19X4	1,700		1,700				200	350	500	400	250
Total special													
Total—all projects													

Year of expenditure—cash requirements

[a] Adopted from Welsch [1976, p. 359].
[b] Detailed in 19X3 profit plan.
[c] To take care of minor capital additions; see annual profit plan for 19X3 departmental appropriations.

EXHIBIT 2 Long-Term Capital Expenditures Budget (Adapted from The Babcock and Wilcox Company, internal documents)

FORM 1

THE BABCOCK & WILCOX COMPANY

DIVISION OR SUBSIDIARY DIAMOND POWER SPECIALTY CORPORATION (CONSOLIDATED)

ESTIMATE OF CAPITAL REQUIREMENTS
FOR THE FIVE-YEAR PERIOD
JANUARY 1, 1941 TO DECEMBER 31, 1945

DATE ___JULY 1, 1940___

PROJECT DESCRIPTION	DEPARTMENT OR WORKS	ESTIMATED FUTURE CAPITAL REQUIREMENTS			ESTIMATED DATE OF SUBMISSION TO PRESIDENT FOR CONSIDERATION		1941				PERIOD OF ESTIMATED EXPENDITURES									CAPITAL ITEMS UNDER $1,000
		REPLACEMENT	NEW CAPACITY	TOTAL	QUARTER	YEAR	1ST QUARTER	2ND QUARTER	3RD QUARTER	4TH QUARTER	1942 1ST HALF	2ND HALF	1943 1ST HALF	2ND HALF	1944	1945				
D.P.S.C. (U.S.A.)																				
Mechanical (Incl. Engr.)	Lancaster																			
1941																				
Factory Addition			275,000	275,000	Fourth	1940	137,500	137,500												14,700
Parking Lot			25,000	25,000	"	"	25,000	25,000												6,000
City Utilities			20,000	20,000	"	"	20,000													4,100
500 KVA Sub Station			25,000	25,000	"	"	25,000													1,500
Coupling Machine			15,000	15,000	"	"	15,000													
Heat Treating Facility		35,000		35,000	"	"			35,000				* Items to be capitalized less than							
20 Ft. Press Brake		34,000		34,000	"	"	34,000						$2,500 not included in totals							
Hydraulic Shear		4,500		4,500	"	"		4,500					1941	60,800						
3-Axis Measuring Mach.		21,000		21,000	"	"	21,000						1942	41,100						
W-Diehoff		30,000		30,000	"	"				30,000			1943	41,800						
Precision Indexing Head 1,200 Sq. Ft. Band Base Bldg.		3,000		3,000	"	"	6,000			3,000			1944	39,400						
Vertical Checking Fixture		6,000		6,000	"	"	9,000						1945	36,600						
MIG Spot Welder		5,000		5,000	"	"	5,000						Total	219,700						
14 WIG Turret Lathe		7,000		7,000	"	"	7,000													
#2 Turret Lathe		39,000		39,000	"	"		17,000		39,000										
Tracer Lathe		17,000		17,000	"	"														
Calorizing Furnace		17,000		20,000	"	"	17,000			20,000										
1941 Total		93,000	505,500	598,500			287,500	184,000		68,000										14,700
1942 Total		124,000	166,500	466,500	Fourth	1941					228,000	238,500								6,000
1943 Total		89,500	290,000	179,500	"	1942							79,500	300,000						4,100
1944 Total		90,000	170,000	220,000	"	1943									220,000					1,500
1945 Total		80,000	15,000	95,000	"	1944										95,000				
Total Mechanical		506,500	1,253,000	1,759,500			287,500	184,000		68,000	228,000	238,500	79,500	300,000	220,000	95,000				26,300
Electronics	Lancaster																			
1941		1,000	370,000	371,000	Fourth	1941					373,000									82,100
1942																				13,100
1943																				13,700
1944																				13,900
1945																				10,600
Total Electronics		3,000	370,000	373,000							373,000									71,400
Acquisitions																				
1941 - Process or Pollution Control		-	1,500,000	1,500,000	First	1941		500,000	500,000	500,000	750,000	750,000								
1942 - Japan - Joint Venture		-	350,000	350,000	"	"		350,000			750,000	750,000								
1942 - Electronic Product		-	500,000	500,000	Fourth	"			500,000	500,000										
Total Acquisitions		-	350,000	350,000				850,000	500,000	500,000	750,000	750,000								
Total D.P.S.C. (U.S.A.)		509,500	973,000	481,500			287,500	1,034,000	500,000	568,000	351,000	988,500	79,500	300,000	220,000	95,000				99,700
D.P.S. LTD. (U.K.)		-	344,000	344,000			100,000	34,000			104,000		29,000		67,000	8,000				120,000
TOTAL CONSOLIDATED		509,500	1,317,000	826,500			369,500	1,068,000	500,000	568,000	455,000	988,500	128,500	300,000	287,000	103,000				219,700

GD-8888A

EXHIBIT 3 Annual Capital Budget[a]

THE ALLAN COMPANY
Annual Capital Budget Request—19X3
(in thousands of dollars)

| | | Appropriations | | | | | | Schedule of capital expenditures | | | | |
| | | New | | | | Return on investment (DCF) | Total commitments | | | | | |
Description	Prior years	First quarter	Second quarter	Last half	19X3			19X2 and prior	19X3	19X4	Later years	Total
Expansion and growth												
Naphthalene plant				$ 8,650	$ 8,650	22.3	$ 8,650		$ 2,130	$ 3,890	$2,630	$ 8,650
Butadiene recovery system				3,100	3,100	19.2	3,100		2,200	900		3,100
Hydrogen plant	$2,600					14.2	2,600	$2,310	290			2,600
Sulfur recovery system	1,900					8.7	1,900	1,500	400			1,900
Alkylate plant			$12,300		12,300	17.6	12,300		6,000	6,300		12,300
Isocracker		$25,000			25,000	23.8	25,000		6,500	17,300	1,200	25,000
Total expansion	$4,500	$25,000	$12,300	$11,750	$49,050		$53,550	$3,810	$17,520	$28,390	$3,830	$53,550
Replacements												
Absolutely essential:												
Fitzpatrick grinder	$ 590						$ 590	$ 400	$ 190			$ 590
Pneumatic tube system		$ 390			$ 390		390		390			390
"R" plant conveyor			$ 800		800		800		400	$ 400		800
Rosin crushers	210						210	190	20			210
"X" air pollution catcher				$ 1,020	1,020		1,020		300	720		1,020
Other	20	10	10	30	50		70	15	55			70
	$ 820	$ 400	$ 810	$ 1,050	$ 2,260		$ 3,080	$ 605	$ 1,355	$ 1,120		$ 3,080

Competitively necessary:												
"L" quality control lab	$ 300						$ 300	$ 200	$ 100			$ 300
Fine screening plant			$ 670		$ 670		670		240	$ 430		670
Color retention process				$ 2,300	2,300		2,300		870	1,430		2,300
Other	20	$ 20	10	20	50		70	10	60			70
	$ 320	$ 20	$ 680	$ 2,320	$ 3,020		$ 3,340	$ 210	$ 1,270	$ 1,860		$ 3,340
Economics basis:												
Urea system		$ 800			$ 800	20.0	$ 800		$ 800			$ 800
Drum dumpers			$ 200		200	16.4	200		200			200
Lift trucks				$ 100	100	12.3	100		100			100
		$ 800	$ 200	$ 100	$ 1,100		$ 1,100		$ 1,100			$ 1,100
Other:												
Roof—North plant			$ 70		$ 70		$ 70		$ 70			$ 70
Toledo landscaping				$ 15	15		15		15			15
Miscellaneous	$ 40	$ 5	10	10	25		65	$ 35	30			65
	$ 40	$ 5	$ 80	$ 25	$ 110		$ 150	$ 35	$ 115			$ 150
Total replacement	$1,180	$ 1,225	$ 1,770	$ 3,495	$ 6,490		$ 7,670	$ 850	$ 3,840	$ 2,980		$ 7,670
Contingency	$ 300	$ 2,000	$ 700		$ 2,700		$ 3,000	$ 300	$ 1,000	$ 1,700		$ 3,000
Grand total	$5,980	$28,225	$14,770	$15,245	$58,240		$64,220	$4,960	$22,360	$33,070	$3,830	$64,220

[a]Reproduced by permission from Heckert and Willson [1967].

5. Recording evidence of approval by the proper authority for the commitment of funds to the project

Exhibit 4 shows an appropriation request form covering a single cost-reduction project. Appropriations should be made in advance of any significant expenditures on a project.

EXHIBIT 4   Appropriation Request[a]

Authorization for capital expenditure

AFE No.   605

Date ___6/27/XX___

Western division   Los Angeles plant

This request for authorization of a capital expenditure is made necessary by:

☐ Normal replacement   ☒ Cost reduction
☐ Change in manufacturing method   ☐ New business—product
☐ Change in quality control requirements   ☐ Increased volume of business
☐ Change in styling

Title: Automatic Packaging Equipment

Description and Justification:

Bagomatic to be used in packaging "R" chemical at Smead Avenue warehouse. Cost of container will be reduced by $0.50. Present usage 36,000 per year. See attached study on packaging operation.

(Use added sheets if necessary)

Estimated cost		Return on investment	
Materials	$ 800	(Discounted cash flow method)	40.1%
Purchases	21,600		
Labor	—	Payout period	2.61 yr
Total	$22,400	Estimated useful life of equipment	6 yr
Contingency 5%	1,100	Time to construct	—
Total cost	$23,500	Salvage value	$500

Controller's comments and recommendations:

	Accounting Dept.	
	No.	Amount
Cash flow appears realistic		
Return is above minimum of 16%	Capital Account 19-790	$23,500
Approval recommended		
	Expense	

	Date		
Approvals and authorization:	Approval	Rejection	Reason for rejection:
Requested by _____	_____	_____	
Approved by _____	_____	_____	
Department head _____	_____	_____	
Executive committee _____	_____	_____	
Board of directors, per _____	_____	_____	

[a]Reproduced by permission from Heckert and Willson [1967].

Expenditure authorization. After the establishment of an appropriation, individual expenditure requests are usually required to authorize the placing of orders or letting of contracts for goods and services required for the project. Expenditure requests must be approved by the designated official. In large enterprises this authority is often delegated according to the amount involved. In one major manufacturing corporation, the following limits are applied.

Management level	Maximum approval authority
President	$300,000
Executive vice presidents (3)	100,000
Vice presidents (10)	50,000
General managers	25,000
General superintendents, regional sales managers, etc.	70,000
District managers	1,000

Because practice varies quite widely, these example limits are illustrative only, and not necessarily descriptive on any broad basis.

Control reports. Regular reports should be prepared that compare actual expenditures and commitments with the appropriated amounts. Exhibit 5 is an illustration of this type of report. Not only are such reports useful in the control of capital expenditures, they also facilitate updating of cash budgets.

Even where careful control of capital expenditures is exercised, some projects may exceed their time or money limits. When it appears likely that a project's expenditures will exceed its appropriation, this should be reported to management as soon as possible. Excess expenditures may signal inefficiency, unpredicted cost increases, or even changes in scope. An early review is desirable, because it may be possible to take action to mitigate or avoid further cost increases if no time is lost. To ensure thorough review, the overexpenditure should be subject to a supplemental appropriation, applying the same requirements for approval as in the case of the original appropriation. The supplemental appropriation should, in turn, be watched carefully for early warning of any further excessive expenditures.

It is more difficult to control time overruns. Nevertheless, significant delays beyond the original time estimate should be reported to management as soon as they are observed. The presence of delay may be a symptom of errors in project planning or changes in scope. Delay may indicate that increased costs may be incurred, because delay is seldom costless, or that future earnings from the project will not be received in accordance with previous expectations of timing or amount. In any case, a thorough review is desirable.

Most companies set up blanket appropriations to cover minor capital expenditures required in the normal course of operations. Normally, an upper limit is set on the amount of any single purchase. It is desirable to exercise careful control over expenditures charged to blanket authorizations, so that temptation to "beat the system" is minimized. Possible temptations include purchase of items over the ceiling limit by means of two or more seemingly separate expenditure requests, and the designation of expenditures related to specific appropriations as pertaining to blanket appropriations (sometimes to avoid showing

EXHIBIT 5   Appropriation Status Report[a]

MONROE MANUFACTURING COMPANY
Appropriation Status Report
As of August 31, 19X0

Appropriation no.	Description	Work order no.	Amount appropriated	Actual completion date	Original estimate	Outstanding commitments	Actual expenditures to date	Estimated cost to complete	Indicated total cost	(Over) or under original estimate
24	Ottawa Avenue Plant		$ 750,000							
	Buildings and equipment	241			$670,796.52	$286,672.84	$384,123.68		$670,796.52	
	Site clearance	242			13,552.86		13,552.86		13,552.86	
	Total appropriation 24				$684,349.38	$286,672.84	$397,676.54		$684,349.38	
25	Modifications of Overhead		35,000							
	Conveyor	251								
	Installation Y building				$ 28,353.00	$ 14,533.05	$ 236.39	$13,583.56	$ 28,353.00	
	Others completed as of 7/31/X0				2,990.00		4,645.55		4,645.55	($1,655.55)
	Total appropriation 25				$ 31,343.00	$ 14,533.05	$ 4,881.94	$13,583.56	$ 32,998.55	($1,655.55)
26	Miscellaneous Improvements		183,400							
	Magnesium pilot line	261		7/31	$ 8,910.00		$ 8,551.48		$ 8,551.48	$ 358.52
	Wrapping equipment	262		2/28	16,900.00	$ 6.50	14,122.52		14,129.02	2,770.98

Item	Description	Date	Appropriation						
	Roll mill—design and install—								
263	A.C. plant			11,680.00	8,944.00	154.00	$ 2,582.00	11,680.00	
264	Intercommunication system			24,974.00	4,794.57	20,179.43		24,974.00	
265	Move hydraulic press and install in Y building	5/31		1,155.50	79.15	926.68		1,005.83	149.67
266	Design and install air conditioning unit in Y building			9,725.00	750.00	8,626.84	348.16	9,725.00	
267	Changes and modifications in paint room	5/31		30,115.00	29.89	26,664.06		26,693.95	3,421.05
268	Buggy scales			11,275.00	212.20	10,158.39	904.41	11,275.00	
269	Tote boxes—A.C. plant	7/31		3,597.00	340.57	3,198.86		3,539.43	57.57
270	Prepare annealing oven for production use			7,700.00	1,290.03	6,202.29	207.68	7,700.00	
271	Move electric furnaces to A.C. plant			3,585.00	2,989.20		595.80	3,585.00	
272	Lift truck with oxide batteries and battery charger			30,486.00	21,670.19	2,737.83	6,077.98	30,486.00	
273	Purchase and install 100-HP motor in Y building	7/31		4,692.00	424.00	3,701.97		4,125.97	566.03
	Others completed as of 7/31/X0			3,701.00		2,482.18		2,482.18	1,218.82
	Total appropriation 26			$168,495.50	$ 41,530.30	$107,706.53	$10,716.03	$159,952.86	$8,542.64
29	Aluminum Experimental Unit Construction of unit		50,000	$ 50,000.00	$ 5,533.34	$ 15,385.04	$29,081.62	$ 50,000.00	
291									
	Total appropriation 29			$ 50,000.00	$ 5,533.34	$ 15,385.04	$29,081.62	$ 50,000.00	
	Grand total		$1,018,400	$934,187.88	$348,269.53	$525,650.05	$53,381.21	$927,300.79	$6,887.09

aReproduced by permission from Heckert and Willson [1967].

EXHIBIT 6 Postevaluation Report[a]

CAPITAL EXPENDITURE PERFORMANCE REPORT
(Actual Versus Justification)

DEPARTMENT __Naphthalene__ TITLE __Install Turbogenerator__

AUTHORIZATION NO. __12345__ DATE APPROVED __6/20/X1__ AMOUNT __$1,200,000__ MONTH OPERATION BEGAN __April 19X2__

REPORT OF STATUS AS OF 12/31/X5

(000's omitted)	Original authorization justification to date	Actual to date	Actual over (+) or under (−) justification	
			Dollars	Percent
Expenditure charged to auth. A/C-plant	$ 800	$ 900	$+100	+13 (1)
Expense	350	200	−150	−43 (2)
Investment	50	75	+25	+50 (3)
Total	1,200	1,175	−25	−21
Other balance sheet charges— inventory, equipment, etc.	100	225	+125	+125 (4)
Total	1,300	1,400	+100	+8
Net cash income (before F.I.T.):				
For year 19X5	400	450	+50	+12 (5)
For all prior years	1,700	1,550	−150	−10 (6)
Total	2,100	2,000	−100	− 5
Evaluation:				
Cumulative cash position	+800	+600	−200	
Cumulative book income	757	1,065	+308	
Rate of return				
Rate of return (approved method)	19%	22%		
Rate of return (approved method)	Original authorization justification life of project	30%		

ANALYSIS OF DIFFERENCES BETWEEN ACTUAL AND JUSTIFICATION

(1) Price rise in materials and labor

(2) Lower cost of site clearance

(4) Increase in inventories

(5) Higher sales price

(6) Slower startup of 9 months accounted for lower income of $125

cost excesses) or vice versa (sometimes to conceal cost savings). There may also be temptation to spend on nonessentials to use up any excess in the blanket appropriation and to avoid possible future reductions in this appropriation.

When it is ascertained that a project is complete, the appropriation is closed. At this point it is desirable to have an inventory taken of the project. For large or complex projects, this requires considerable labor and effort. In the case of so-called turnkey contracts, where no detailed listing may be supplied by the contractor, the task is even more burdensome. However, the more complicated and extensive the project, the more necessary is the inventory. The inventory provides the evidence for closing the appropriation and forms the basis for the transfers to the fixed asset accounts. Therefore, its accuracy is important. A completion report should be filed.

After closing of the appropriation, it is possible that late charges may arise. Any late charge in excess of a reasonable minimum (possibly $5,000 in the case of larger projects) should require a special appropriation, approved under the same guidelines as supplemental appropriations. The purpose is not simply to penalize lateness. After an appropriation is closed and a project has been inventoried, there is no longer any authority for further expenditures on it. Therefore precautions are required against hidden or unanticipated overexpenditures and possible omissions in the inventory.

Postcompletion evaluation. An important part of a sound capital expenditure control system is the postcompletion evaluation or performance audit. The main purposes are (1) to detect areas where action can be taken to improve future performance of the project, and (2) to gain information that will help improve planning and budgeting techniques for future projects.

The scope of postcompletion evaluation procedures varies with individual enterprises and projects. Some firms limit the evaluation to major projects over $1 million in cost. Exhibit 6 shows a specimen evaluation report in brief summary form.

The timing of evaluation is important. It should take place as soon as operating results are no longer significantly affected by startup problems.

On large projects, such as a new plant, several evaluations are desirable. The initial one might be undertaken during construction, to provide information on progress and revised estimates of cost. A second report should be made upon completion of construction, giving an almost-final estimate of construction costs and an updated forecast of output capability. Finally, after the breaking-in period, the actual postcompletion evaluation can be made.

For performance of the postcompletion evaluation, Woods suggests the following steps:

1. A careful physical inspection of the facilities and comparison with the plans and estimates and physical performance data

2. Identification of the specific asset items from the detailed accounting records of work in progress or fixed asset accounts

3. A check of actual operating results regarding income, expense, and working capital with project budget estimates, followed by preparation of revised estimates

4. Comparison of the revised estimates with the budgeted projections and analysis and explanation of any significant differences

5. Submission of a report covering the above-mentioned steps to management

ACCOUNTING FOR ACQUISITIONS

The Cost Principle. It is generally accepted practice to record and report buildings and equipment at their historical cost. Cost means the amount of the purchase consideration in cash or its equivalent at the time of asset acquisition. Included are all outlays incurred to put the asset into condition and location for use, such as charges for freight and installation.

The cost principle is that assets are to be recorded initially at cost and kept at cost until realization takes place. In the case of fixed assets, depreciation is recognized in the accounts but is based on historical cost. Cost less depreciation is the valuation basis generally adhered to throughout the life of each asset.

Generally accepted accounting principles do not specifically require disclosure of the basis of valuation of property, plant, and equipment in the financial statements. Most companies, however, voluntarily provide this information. Companies whose securities are registered with the Securities and Exchange Commission are required to make such disclosures under Regulation S-X.

Reasons for use. There are several alternative methods for the valuation of tangible fixed assets. These methods include not only historical cost but also historical cost adjusted for changes in the general price level. Other bases of valuation are current net resale price (either in a forced or an orderly liquidation) and current cost of replacement of asset services by later-model, non-identical equipment. Thus historical cost is only one of a number of possible bases of tangible fixed asset valuation.

Departures from the cost principle raise serious problems. As the basis of *initial* valuation, cost is a most reasonable choice. Normally, asset acquisition results from a market transaction at arms' length by two parties, each presumed to act rationally in his or her own self-interest. This establishes a strong likelihood that cost is the best measure of value at the time of acquisition.

At subsequent dates, as circumstances have time to change, it can be argued that historical cost and value may no longer be the same. Nevertheless, the cost principle remains the most widely accepted and most often used rule. It has the advantage of being based on an *actual* market transaction, whereas alternative methods of valuation usually postulate *hypothetical* transactions (such as an imaginary sale or replacement of the asset).

In addition, whereas historical cost is usually easy to verify by following well-established procedures, the alternative valuation methods incorporate few if any standard procedures and can result in widely varying amounts. It has frequently been said that historical cost is objective, whereas other valuation methods are subjective in nature.

Variations from cost. Sometimes it may be evident, even at the time of acquisition, that there is a significant difference between cost and market value. If cost is in excess of market value, this may be the result of defects in judgment, major changes made during construction of plant, excessive delays in completing a building, or other adverse factors. In such cases most authorities agree that recorded cost should not exceed that which would have been incurred under normal circumstances. Hendriksen [1977, pp. 362, 363] states:

> Only those costs that would normally be paid for property by reasonably prudent management should be included in prudent costs. This concept has been used by public utility regulators as a method of placing the public interest ahead of the interests of promoters, management, and stockholders. But the prudent cost concept is also applicable to the general valuation of plant and equipment. The costs to be allocated to the services of future periods should not include excessive costs representing costs of inefficiency and other losses incurred in the period of acquisition.

In practice this concept may not be easy to apply, because it can be difficult to distinguish between costs that are prudent and costs that are excessive. As a rule, the costs agreed to by management at the time of the initial commitment are assumed to be prudent in the absence of evidence to the contrary. Additional costs incurred afterward could be regarded as excessive, because evidence is lacking that management would initially have been willing to accept these extra costs.

It is possible for assets to be acquired at a bargain price, perhaps in a distress sale. In this event, authorities differ as to whether actual cost should be written up to market value. Because accounting practices tend toward conservatism in ambiguous cases, most accountants would not favor writing up in this situation.

"Original" cost. As used in public utility regulation, "original" cost means the cost of property when first put into public service. Any excess paid over original cost less accumulated depreciation by a subsequent purchaser is not allowed as an expense of operation by most regulatory agencies. This rule attempted to protect consumers from financial manipulation (often by holding companies) in an earlier era. At that time there was temptation for a holding company to reap a profit by selling an asset to a subsidiary at an enhanced price, at the same time inflating the subsidiary's rate base and hence its allowable earnings under regulation.

Although there is (or was) merit in this rule for regulatory purposes, it has little application in nonregulated business where earnings are the determinant of asset value, rather than the converse, which applies in the regulated sector.

Methods of Acquisition. It is generally accepted that the cost of a fixed asset should include all expenses of transporting the asset to the proper location and placing it in the condition necessary for its intended service. Although this broad principle provides the basic accounting guidelines, questions of interpretation arise. The way in which such questions are treated affects not only the initial asset valuation but also the charges to expense in the acquisition period and the amount of depreciation in subsequent periods.

New or used assets, acquired in completed form. When an individual asset requiring no further construction is purchased, cost is the aggregate outlay incurred to bring the asset into its intended use. For instance, if a drill press is purchased from a manufacturing firm, f.o.b. its Syracuse plant, for use in a Los

Angeles factory, the cost to the acquiring firm is the invoice price, less all cash discounts offered, plus freight from Syracuse to Los Angeles and cartage to the Los Angeles factory, plus costs to install the press and to test and adjust it in order to have it operate according to specifications. Cash discounts available but not taken by the purchaser should, strictly speaking, be treated as an expense rather than as a part of the cost of the asset. In practice this procedure is not always followed.

According to the National Association of Accountants [1972, p. 10], the costs to be capitalized for equipment include:

1. Original invoice or contract price
2. Freight, drayage and cartage in, import duties, handling and storage charges payable
3. Specific in-transit insurance
4. Sales, use, and other taxes related directly to the purchased equipment
5. Preparation of foundations and other costs of a proper operating site for the equipment
6. Installation costs, including any applicable company overhead on the same basis as it is charged to inventory
7. Charges for testing and preparation for use
8. Reconditioning, if used equipment is purchased

Equipment used in research and development presents problems of accounting treatment. Where the equipment is of special or single-purpose type, its usefulness may be inherently limited to a specific research or development project. Therefore its ultimate worth may be indeterminate, just as the life, success or failure of the research project may be indeterminate. In these circumstances, there is justification for expensing rather than capitalizing the cost of such equipment. Similarly, research equipment may be subjected to damaging stress, such as testing with corrosive gases or radioactivity, or drastic experimental modification, or "cannibalization" (i.e., assimilation into other pieces of equipment). These possibilities require careful consideration in determining whether specific items of research and development equipment should be given normal capitalization treatment or written off as current research and development expense. In general, the Financial Accounting Standards Board has required by its Statement No. 2 [1974] that research and development expenditures should be expensed and not capitalized.

FASB Interpretation No. 4 [1975] deals with the applicability of FASB Statement No. 2 to business combinations accounted for by the purchase method. It includes the following statement:

> The subsequent accounting by the combined enterprise for the costs allocated to assets[1] to be used in research and development activities shall be determined by reference to Statement No. 2. Paragraph 12 of Statement No. 2 requires that costs identified with research and development activities shall be charged to expense when incurred unless the test of alternative future use in paragraph 11 (a) or 11 (c) is met. That requirement also applies in a business combination accounted for by the purchase method. Accordingly, costs assigned to assets to be used in a particular research and

development project and that have no alternative future use shall be charged to expense at the date of consummation of the combination. Therefore, the accounting for the cost of an item to be used in research and development activities is the same under paragraphs 11 and 12 of Statement No. 2, whether the item is purchased singly, or as part of a group of assets, or as part of an entire enterprise in a business combination accounted for by the purchase method.

---

[1]In this regard, paragraph 69 of APB Opinion No. 16 states in part that: "The nature of an asset and not the manner of its acquisition determines an acquirer's subsequent accounting for the cost of that asset.")

A purchase agreement may provide for interest-free installment payments or a series of non-interest-bearing notes covering the purchase consideration. In such a case, the interest charges are implicit and should be ascertained and excluded from the cost recorded for the asset. The amount of the implicit interest may be ascertained by deducting the spot-cash price from the actual price paid. If no spot-cash price can be determined (because the seller may sell only on installment terms), an estimated interest rate can be applied. This procedure, however, is not always followed in practice.

Examples of items in addition to the contract price that may be included in the cost of an existing building are

1. Architects' plans for remodeling
2. Fees and charges of brokers, agents, notaries, attorneys, title companies, inspectors, county clerks, and recorders
3. Initial remodeling, including permanently attached floor coverings and similar items
4. Permits and privileges
5. Payments made to former tenants to cancel leases
6. Property taxes to date of purchase assumed by the purchaser

The National Association of Accountants [1972, p. 11] states that the following items should not be capitalized:

1. Extraordinary costs associated with construction, such as those due to strike, flood, fire, or other casualty. However, anticipated costs such as rock blasting, piling, or relocating the channel of an underground stream *should* be capitalized.
2. Costs of abandoned construction.
3. Bonus payments to contractors, temporary construction because of shortages of material for permanent construction, and similar costs incurred for the purpose of hastening completion.

Contract construction. Fixed assets constructed under contract are usually not entered into the fixed asset records until completion. If, as frequently occurs, the contract calls for advance and partial payments before completion, these payments are normally recorded as advances. By making such payments while construction continues, the payer does not acquire ownership of the fixed assets, but rather has a claim against the contractor. This claim is liquidated by the contractor's delivery of the completed asset. Upon completion, the asset or assets are entered as such in the accounting records.

Self-construction. When an enterprise constructs its own buildings or equipment, there is no single purchase price or contract amount representing the cost of the new assets. Under these circumstances, problems can arise as to what should be included or excluded in determining asset cost.

One problem relates to the treatment of indirect overhead and its apportionment between the construction activity and the normal production operations. Three alternatives are generally recognized. The first is to assign no indirect overhead to the construction cost of the fixed asset. The reasons given to support this approach are the following:

1. Indirect overhead tends to be fixed in nature and is not increased by irregular construction activity.

2. Work on self-constructed assets tends to be done in slack periods, and absorption of indirect overhead into fixed asset costs results in an arbitrary overstatement of current net income.

3. If normal operations are not curtailed by the construction activity, there is no indication that management would have been willing to incur any greater cost on the construction than the direct charges.

These reasons are based on the assumption that fixed asset self-construction is an irregular rather than a continuing activity.

A second alternative is to assign indirect overhead to construction cost on the same basis as used for the assignment to normal production. The reasons advanced for this approach are the following:

1. It avoids special treatment or exemptions of self-constructed assets from a fair share of overhead costs.

2. It avoids the overcosting of normal production with respect to indirect overhead.

Where firms (such as public utilities and railroads) tend to engage in continuous self-construction, these reasons constitute an appropriate case for full costing.

The third possibility is to allocate indirect overhead to the extent that it would have been assigned to the production that is curtailed because of the construction activity. This proposal is appealing in theory, but it may be difficult to apply because it depends on "what otherwise might have been."

Dyckman [1967] suggests that the alternative methods depend on different circumstances. He generally favors the direct cost approach in being reluctant to charge to construction any overhead that does not appear to have resulted directly by reason of the undertaking of construction activity.

On the other hand, Kieso and Weygandt [1980, p. 476] prefer the full costing approach. But these authors add that if the allocated overhead causes construction costs to be in excess of their business usefulness, or in excess of what would be charged by an independent outside contractor, then the excess overhead should be expensed as a period loss rather than capitalized.

Interest as Cost. Whether construction of plant and equipment is contracted out or not, the question of including interest charges in cost arises if the assets require a period of time to get them ready for their intended use. The Financial Accounting Standards Board established applicable standards in Statement No. 34, *Capitalization of Interest Cost* [1979]:

> The historical cost of acquiring an asset includes the costs necessarily incurred to bring it to the condition and location necessary for its intended use. If an asset requires a period of time in which to carry out the activities necessary to bring it to that condition and location, the interest cost incurred during that period as a result of expenditures for the asset is a part of the historical cost of acquiring the asset.

This treatment is based on the theory that, if not for the asset construction, interest costs would be avoided. The Statement does not require interest capitalization in cases where the difference between interest capitalization and the policy of charging interest expense when incurred is not material. In addition, interest cannot be capitalized for inventories that are routinely manufactured or otherwise produced in large quantities on a repetitive basis.

Capitalization is permitted during periods in which all three of the following factors are met:

Expenditures for the asset have been made.
Activities to ready the asset for its intended use are in progress.
Interest costs are being incurred.

If the enterprise suspends substantially all activities related to acquisition of the asset, interest capitalization should cease until the activities are resumed.

The amount of interest that should be capitalized is computed by applying an interest rate (the capitalization rate) to the average amount of accumulated expenditures for the asset during the period. The capitalization rate should be based on the rates applicable to borrowings outstanding during the period. If a specific new borrowing is undertaken to finance the assets construction, the enterprise may use the rate on that borrowing as the capitalization rate.

The rules adopted by the FASB differ from those adopted by some other regulatory agencies. The Federal Energy Regulatory Commission allows electric and gas utility companies to charge to construction the cost of all funds employed, whether or not they are separably identifiable. Funds employed include equity as well as borrowed capital. The rate of interest prescribed is the net cost of borrowed funds and a reasonable rate on other funds used. The Interstate Commerce Commission does not allow the imputed cost of equity capital, but it is allowed by the Federal Communications Commission. The Cost Accounting Standards Board allows the cost of borrowed funds only.

Donation or gift. When assets are obtained by way of gift or donation, the cost principle of valuation is not applied. Instead, the fair value of the assets (either the applicable market price or an appraisal in the absence of an available market price) is used. The offsetting credit should be to a proprietorship (paid-in capital) account, separately labeled as "donated capital." This credit should be reduced by an amount equal to any costs incurred in acceptance of the donation, such as legal fees or transportation and installation charges.

It is sometimes argued that donated assets should be excluded from the accounts because no cost was incurred to acquire them. This argument has little support, because it results in ignoring values committed to the enterprise and future depreciation charges to operations.

Sometimes gifts are conditional upon performance of certain requirements by the receiver. For instance, local governments may offer a free site and perhaps a building to any firm that agrees to employ a given minimum number of local residents for a certain time period. Regardless of such conditions, the entries should still be made as recommended above. In addition, the accounting records and statements should (usually by means of a note) indicate the contingency and state that clear title has not been obtained.

Other methods of acquisition. Assets may be acquired by means of leasing and through pooling of interests. These methods are dealt with in Chapters 24 and 34.

Basket purchases. "Basket purchases" refers to the acquisition of a group of assets for a single lump-sum price. In the purchaser's accounting records, it is necessary to allocate the cost to the different types of assets acquired. Although accountants are not usually expert in appraising property values, it is an accounting responsibility to see that valuation appraisals made by others seem reasonable and are adequately supported by evidence. This is more easily done before completion of the transaction than after the fact. Therefore, if the accountant knows of a contemplated basket purchase, he or she should inform management of the importance of careful apportionment of the total cost and request that a sound determination be made.

In the absence of a prior apportionment, the following points should be considered: When current assets are included in the basket purchase, their reasonable value is often not difficult to establish. Inventories of finished goods, work in process, and raw materials can usually be valued at replacement costs. Items sold off may be recorded at the net proceeds of disposal.

Most difficult to appraise are intangibles, such as goodwill, patents, trademarks, and similar items. Frequently, any excess of the total purchase price over the valuation of the tangible assets is assigned as the value of intangible assets.

With respect to buildings and equipment, the joint purchase cost may be allocated in proportion to the relative values of the respective assets. Appraisals made for insurance purposes may be used to determine relative values. This information may be incomplete, however, because portions of buildings such as foundations, excavations, and underground conduits are not usually insured against fire and other casualty loss.

Assessed valuations made for property tax purposes may be available. Such information has an objective nature (i.e., third-party impartiality), but it may be neither up to date nor based on diligent investigation. Although it is the most costly method, independent professional appraisal may be required. For major acquisitions its use is probably well advised.

Net book values of the former owner may be ascertainable with little cost or effort. Their use in apportionment of value in a basket purchase, however, is of dubious worth unless all the assets involved were acquired recently. Book values for older assets are not usually claimed to represent good approximations of relative asset values.

There is a definite necessity for supportability of the results of allocating a lump sum to the different types of assets required. The matter is most significant for income tax purposes, as well as financial reporting purposes. Its importance is underscored by the issue of APB Opinions No. 16 and 17. These Opinions set forth criteria for determining the cost of individual assets, while also urging that judgment be used in view of the complexity and imprecise nature of the factors involved. Concerned readers should consult Chapter 34.

Methods of Payment. When assets are acquired by means of payment other than cash outlays, direct cost valuation tends to be difficult or impossible. This is especially the case when the method of payment involves the issue of securities or an exchange of assets.

Issue of securities. Assets may be acquired against the issue of stocks or bonds. The par or nominal value of these securities is not a reliable indicator of their worth or of the value of the assets acquired.

Where the securities are actively traded by numerous parties, their current market value is the basis that should be used for asset valuation. When trading is not active or is confined to only a few large holders, it is necessary to estimate the value of the acquired assets, preferably by means of independent appraisal.

Exchange and trade-in. Where buildings or equipment are acquired in a barter transaction, the market value of the assets given up is usually the most satisfactory basis for valuation. In some cases, as with used automobiles or trucks, such market values may be readily available. Occasionally, there may be more reliable evidence of the value of the new asset being acquired than of the asset being given up, for example, if there are many sales of like-new assets for cash. If so, the current cash price of the new asset would be used for valuation. In general, the goal is to use the most reliable indication of market value available for valuing the new asset.

If there is a cash payment (or receipt) in addition to the trade-in, the amount should be added to (or subtracted from) the market value of the assets given up to determine the valuation of the assets received.

If old equipment is traded in, it is common for the dealer to allow more in trade than the current value of the old asset. This is in lieu of a price concession on the new asset. To avoid overstatement of the cost of the new asset and of current income, the accountant should examine the evidence carefully, including, where obtainable, the realistic market values of the old and new assets. If inflation of the trade-in allowance is found, its amount should be deducted from both the cost of the new asset and the amount shown as being received from the disposal of the old asset.

Davidson et al. [1982, p. 61] give the following useful rules for accounting for trade-in transactions:

> The accounting for a trade-in depends upon whether or not the asset received is "similar" to the asset traded in and whether the accounting is for *financial statements* or for *income tax* returns. Assume an old asset cost

$5,000, has $3,000 of *accumulated depreciation* (after recording depreciation to the date of the trade-in), and hence has a *book value* of $2,000. The old asset appears to have a market value of $1,500, according to price quotations in used-asset markets. The old asset is traded-in on a new asset with a list price of $10,000. The old asset and $5,500 cash *(boot)* are given for the new asset. The generic entry for the trade-in transaction is:

New Asset	A		
Accumulated Depreciation (Old Asset)	3,000		
Adjustment on Exchange of Asset	B	or	B
Old Asset			5,000
Cash			5,500

(1) The *list-price* method of accounting for trade-ins rests on the assumption that the list price of the new asset closely approximates its market value. The new asset is recorded at its list price (A = $10,000 in the example); B is a *plug* (= $2,500 credit in the example). If B requires a *debit* plug, the Adjustment on Exchange of Asset is a *loss*; if a *credit* plug is required (as in the example), the adjustment is a gain.

(2) Another theoretically sound method of accounting for trade-ins rests on the assumption that the price quotation from used-asset markets give a more reliable measure of the market value of the old asset than is the list price a reliable measure of the market value of the new asset. This method uses the *fair market value* of the old asset, $1,500 in the example, to determine B (= $2,000 book value − $1,500 assumed proceeds on disposition = $500 debit or loss). The exchange results in a loss if the book value of the old asset exceeds its market value and in a gain if the market value exceeds the book value. The new asset is recorded on the books by plugging for A (= $7,000 in the example).

(3) For income tax reporting, no gain or loss may be recognized on the trade-in. Thus the new asset is recorded on the books by assuming B is zero and plugging for A (= $7,500 in the example). In practice, firms that wish to recognize the loss currently will sell the old asset directly, rather than trading it in, and acquire the new asset entirely for cash.

(4) *Generally accepted accounting principles* (APB Opinion No. 29) require a variant of these methods. The basic method is (1) or (2), depending upon whether the list price of the new asset (1) or the quotation of the old asset's market value (2) is the more reliable indication of market value. If, when applying the basic method, a debit entry, or loss, is required for the Adjustment on Exchange of Asset, then the trade-in is recorded as described in (1) or (2) and the full amount of the loss is recognized currently. If, however, a credit entry, or gain, is required for the Adjustment on Exchange of Asset, then the amount of gain recognized currently depends upon whether or not the old asset and the new asset are "similar." If the assets are not similar, then the entire gain is recognized currently. If the assets are similar and cash is not received by the party trading in, then no gain is recognized and the treatment is like that in (3); i.e., B = 0, plug for A. If the assets are similar and cash is received by the party trading in—a rare case—then a portion of the gain is recognized currently. The portion of the gain recognized currently is the fraction *cash received/market value of old asset*. [When the list-price method, (1), is used, the market value of the old asset is assumed to be the list price of the new asset plus the amount of cash received by the party trading in.]

The results of applying GAAP to the example in case (4) can be summarized as follows:

	Old asset compared with new asset	
More reliable information	Similar	Not similar
New asset list price	A = $7,500	A = $10,000
	B = 0	B = 2,500 gain
Old asset market price	A = $7,000	A = $ 7,000
	B = 500 loss	B = 500 loss

Installment contracts. When assets are acquired by means of installment contracts, title to the property may not pass to the purchaser until payment is completed. Nevertheless, it is generally regarded as proper to record the asset cost at the date of delivery (net of explicit or implicit interest charges) and to recognize the total amount due in payments as a liability.

Accounting Records. It is difficult to exaggerate the importance of maintaining adequate records for effective control and reliable accounting in regard to plant and equipment. The purpose served by these records are as follows:

1. To form the basis for necessary management reports and financial statements
2. To supply the information in sufficient detail for normal internal control procedures, primarily the audit and inventory of tangible fixed assets
3. To provide the required information for preparation of insurance claims for assets that have been damaged or destroyed
4. To show the location and, to some extent, support the valuation of assets for the purposes of real and personal property tax assessments

The importance of adequate accounting records is further emphasized by the provisions of the Foreign Corrupt Practices Act of 1977. The Act includes a requirement that all issuers of securities registered with the SEC "make and keep books, records and accounts, which, in reasonable detail, accurately and fairly reflect the transactions and dispositions of the assets of the issuer."

The SEC has responsibility for the administration of certain aspects of the Foreign Corrupt Practices Act and has issued rules that further amplify the requirements of the Act in relation to the books, records, accounts, and safeguarding of assets.

Chart of accounts. The costs and other details of buildings and equipment should be classified according to a logical property chart of accounts. Exhibit 7 shows an illustrative property chart of accounts, which classifies assets by depreciation type and rate, function or use, life, location, cost center, date of acquisition, real and personal property tax group, and amount capitalized.

Uniform charts of accounts, for assets and other items, are prescribed by many regulatory agencies and are recommended for member use by numerous trade associations.

Plant ledger. The plant ledger contains detailed plant and equipment records and functions as a subsidiary ledger controlled by the general ledger. The plant ledger consists of individual cards for separate assets or asset groups. The

EXHIBIT 7   Property Chart of Accounts[a]

Coding key to property cards

CARD POSITION 1
Type of Depreciation—   Code #
Old or regular depreciation   1
New or double declining   2

CARD POSITION 2
Rate of Depreciation—   Code #
4 year life   25%   1
5 year life   20%   2
25 year life   4%   3
10 year life   10%   4
15 year life   6.7%   5
20 year life   5%   6
33.3 year life   3.3%   7
40 year life   2.5%   8
50 year life   2%   9

CARD POSITIONS 4–8
Property Tag Number
   (Positions 4 and 5 signify year of acquisition.)

CARD POSITIONS 9–10

Assets—Real Property	Code # (Class)	Life (Yr)	Code # (Depr.)
Land	00		
Land improvements	01	10	
Columbus plant—bldgs.	02	50	
Worthington warehouse	03	40	
Viking Engraving	04	50	
Restaurant and canteens	05	33.3	
Century Tank (chrome plating)	06	10	
California plant—bldgs.	07	20	
	08		
Rental property	09	10	4
Shop fixtures—real	10	5	2
Machinery foundations	11	15	5
Heating and ventilating	12	15	5
Electric power and light	13	15	5
Steam, water, and sewer	14	15	5
Elevators and conveyors	15	15	5
Storage tanks	16	15	5
	17	15	5
Automatic sprinklers	18	15	5
Dry rooms and dryers	19	15	5
Deep wells	20	15	5
Boiler house equipment	21	15	5
Water fountains	22	15	5
Pneumatic tubes	23	15	5
Electric transformers	24	15	5

EXHIBIT 7   Property Chart of Accounts[a]   (Cont.)

CARD POSITIONS 9-10

Assets—Personal Property		*Code #* *(Class)*	*Life* *(Yr)*	*Code #* *(Depr.)*
Machinery and equipment		50	15	5
Shop fixtures—*personal*		70	5	2
Copper print rolls		72	15	5
Steel rolls—emb.		75	15	5
Paper rolls		76	15	5
Steel plates—emb.		77	15	5
Motor vehicles—trucks		88	4-6	
Motor vehicles—automobile		89	3	
Furniture and fixtures—Columbus		90	10	4
Furniture and fixtures—Worthington		91	10	4
		92		
		93		
Furniture and fixtures—Atlanta		94	10	4
Furniture and fixtures—Burlingame		95	10	4
Furniture and fixtures—Detroit		96	5	2
Furniture and fixtures—Newark		97	10	4
		98		
Furniture and fixtures—New York		99	10	4

CARD POSITIONS 11-13
Cost Center (Dept. #)   101-999

CARD POSITIONS 14-15
Month of Acquisition   01-12

CARD POSITIONS 16-17
Year of Acquisition   (19)32-present

CARD POSITION 18
Tax Group

Personal property—Columbus	1
Personal property—Worthington	2
Real property—Columbus	3
Personal property—New York	4
Real property—Newark	5
Personal property—Detroit	6
Personal property—Newark	7
Personal property—Atlanta	8
Personal property—Burlingame	9

CARD POSITIONS 19-24
Amount Capitalized

CARD POSITIONS 25-60
Description of Asset

[a]Reproduced by courtesy of The Borden Company.

property cards described in Exhibit 7 are representative examples. In fully computerized systems, these cards may be replaced with equivalent electronic records on magnetic tapes, disks, drums, or similar devices.

The cards are usually prepared from property acquisition reports. Such reports usually provide for physical control procedures by requiring tagging of assets with a serial number for identification. The serial number is noted on the property card (see Exhibit 7 for an example) for future inventory purposes.

Unit detail. A separate property card is kept for each unit of property. But how should a "unit" be defined? The property record manual of a major manufacturing company makes the following classifications:

III. CLASSIFICATION OF PLANT ASSETS

For purposes of the property records for purchases after January 1, 19X7, plant assets shall be divided into three classes, with a somewhat different method of handling the records for each class, as follows:

CLASS I. INDIVIDUALLY IDENTIFIABLE UNITS—This class shall include assets which can readily be identified as individual physical units. Most of the productive machinery falls into this class. A separate property record sheet shall be kept for each asset of this class, or, in cases where there are a large number of items of exactly the same type (for example, a group of machine tools of the same type and year of manufacture), a single sheet may be used for the entire group. When assets in this class are sold or discarded, there will be no difficulty in determining from the property record sheets the gross value, accrued depreciation, and residual value of each item.

CLASS II. MAJOR GROUP EQUIPMENT—This class shall include group assets such as lighting systems, water and sewerage systems, plumbing and heating installations, power wiring, shafting, steam piping, yard improvements, etc., the various parts of which cannot readily be identified as separate units. (Landscaping will not be capitalized.) When all or a part of an asset unit in this group is discarded, and adjustment in the plant accounts is required under the rule stated in section IV, paragraph 2-(b), the accounting department shall review the details with plant management, and an estimate shall be made of the cost and accrued depreciation on the portion removed. In order to facilitate the preparation of such estimates, assets in this class shall be broken down, as far as practicable, into groups or sections, either on the basis of the nature of the items involved or on the basis of physical location, and a separate property record sheet shall be set up for each group or section—for example, separate sheets may be set up for plumbing installations in each building, for the shafting and wiring in each major department, etc. Such a breakdown should not be carried beyond the point necessary to make proper adjustment for removals.

CLASS III. MINOR GROUP EQUIPMENT—This class shall include assets which cannot be readily identified except as a relatively small part of a major group. Examples of assets which fall in this class are: office desks and chairs, lockers, bins, etc.; this class should not include any significant items, such as large scales, office machines, etc., which it is possible to identify and put in Class I. For purposes of the property record, items in this class shall be grouped under major headings such as those suggested above; and a single property record sheet shall be maintained for each year's additions in each group, provided that further breakdown may be made by departments or burden centers if desired for purposes of cost or expense allocation.

No attempt shall be made to identify assets in this class which are discarded or to adjust the accounts therefor; the proceeds from any sale of such assets shall be credited to the plant account so that no profit or loss will be shown. As each year's additions in each group become fully depreciated, the entire value thereof shall be credited to the plant account and charged against the reserve, and depreciation thereon shall cease.

The possible degree of detail is almost infinite: a separate record could be kept for each hammer, pencil, or chair, if expense was of no concern. Clearly this is unthinkable, and the question is one of where to draw the line for the ultimate unit.

In some cases, it may be advisable to go within a single asset item. For instance, with expensive trucks or buses, the engine and tires may be segregated, principally because of different expected service lives. The same procedure is followed with aircraft engines. For buildings, the ultimate units may be structural components (such as roof, elevators, flooring, etc.) or materials used (such as plumbing, carpentry, glazing, etc.).

For continuous structures such as railroad tracks, water mains, and power lines, the unit could be each individual stretch by date of installation (or expected replacement or retirement) and location. A more detailed alternative would be each major element in a stretch, such as rails, ties, or ballast.

The choice of ultimate units that are too small and numerous leads to records too cumbersome to be kept up without exorbitant cost and effort. Although a reasonable degree of detail is desirable, a balance between practicality and detail must be found.

MAINTENANCE AND REPAIRS

Cooper and Ijiri [1983] define *maintenance* as "the keeping of property at a standard of operating condition" and *repair* as "the restoration of a capital asset to its full productive capacity after damage, accident, or prolonged use, without increase in the previously estimated service life or capacity."

Although in theory maintenance and repairs do not extend prior estimates of service life or capacity, in practice this principle can be difficult to apply unequivocally. A relatively low level of expenditure on maintenance and repairs may significantly curtail asset service life or capacity, whereas a relatively large expenditure may accomplish the opposite. Therefore, any estimate of expected service life or capacity assumes a given level of maintenance and repairs. For this reason, a distinction is usually made between ordinary repairs (charged to revenue as an expense) and extraordinary repairs debited to an asset account or to accumulated depreciation.

Capitalization or Expense. Repairs frequently involve replacement of parts of equipment. This factor is a consideration in designating the ultimate property unit for accounting purposes. Where replacement of an entire property unit takes place, the proper procedure is to record a retirement of the old unit and the capitalization of the new unit. For instance, if the engines of trucks are treated as separate property units distinct from the remaining parts of the trucks, the engines will be written off when replaced. If, however, the entire truck is the property unit, then replacement of engines is normally treated as a repair expense.

An advantage of setting up property units for individual components of single assets is to avoid many of the problems of whether or not to capitalize major repairs. Where individual components constitute more homogeneous groups than do the whole asset units and where the amounts involved justify the expense, it is worthwhile to establish major components as ultimate property units.

In the absence of suitable replacement property units, repairs are usually expensed. Grady [1965, p. 156] states that "Alterations which merely modernize, rather than improve, buildings or equipment are also expensed as incurred, unless the program is so extensive as to warrant reconsideration of the estimated life of the asset."

Accounting Treatment. In addition to the direct expensing of maintenance and repairs, several alternative accounting methods exist. These are as follows:

Budget allowances. It is sometimes desired to spread the expense of maintenance and repairs evenly over the year (or other operating cycle) rather than have monthly (or other short-period) operating results fluctuate because of varying amounts of maintenance and repair expense. For this purpose a budgetary allowance may be set up. The usual method is to divide the year's budgeted maintenance and repair expense by 12, to charge one-twelfth to operations each month, and to credit a budget (allowance) account. Actual maintenance and repair expenses are then debited to the budget account and the balance is carried forward. Any net balance in the budget allowance account at the end of the year should be treated as an adjustment to operations expenses for the year.

Instead of allowing an equal twelfth for each month, the budget allowance is sometimes set up on the basis of sales, manufacturing volume, direct labor hours or dollars, or some other measure of activity.

Charge to "reserve." The monthly budget allowance method is sometimes extended beyond individual fiscal periods to encompass estimated maintenance and repairs over the entire life of the asset. Equal annual charges are made to expense, and actual expenditures are charged against the allowance, formerly called a "reserve." The balance in the allowance account is not written off at the end of each year but is carried forward to the following year so long as the asset is in service. The purpose is to equalize annual charges for estimated maintenance and repairs over the life of the asset. This procedure has been criticized on several grounds. Reliable estimates of future maintenance and repair expenditures are extremely difficult to make. The nature of the credit balance in the allowance is ambiguous. It is not a liability, nor a proprietorship account, nor an asset contra.

Charge to accumulated depreciation. Extraordinary repairs, which increase the service life or capacity of an asset, are sometimes charged to the accumulated depreciation account. The justification offered for this method is that the extension of service life has caused a recovery of part of the accumulated depreciation. Where extraordinary repairs have increased the capacity or productivity of an asset but have not lengthened its service life, the justification above does not seem to apply.

This method has been criticized on the grounds that it fails to consider that accumulated depreciation may be less than the cost of asset replacement. Also, it allows the cost of parts replaced to remain in the asset account. Continuing extraordinary repairs may extend asset service life by a considerable period, yet the accounts would not reflect the actual cost of the asset if the prices of replaced parts fluctuated over time.

Control of maintenance. In order to develop sound records and to control maintenance expenditures effectively, careful accounting procedures are required. It is useful to keep a maintenance and repair history record for each major piece of equipment. Exhibit 8 shows a specimen record.

The systems manual of a leading manufacturing corporation covers the following sets of procedures and document flows for plant maintenance:

A. Emergency repair system
B. Minor service order system
C. Preventive maintenance job order system
D. Routine job order system
E. Maintenance job order system
F. Job order system
G. Maintenance service contract system
H. Budget control system
I. Procurement of material system

Section H, the budget control system shown as Exhibit 9, serves not only as an illustration of a particular system, but also as a model of part of a carefully written systems manual dealing with maintenance and repair accounting procedures.

ADDITIONS AND IMPROVEMENTS

According to Finney and Miller [Johnson and Gentry, 1974, p. 392], an addition is not a simple replacement, but includes new units and extensions, expansions, and enlargements of old units. Additions may comprise entirely separate assets such as a new building, or, for example, extra rooms or wings added to an existing (previously acquired) building, or the installation of two-way radios in a fleet of delivery vehicles.

EXHIBIT 8   Maintenance Record *(Reproduced by permission of The Jeffrey Manufacturing Company)*

P-M DATA CARD			OUT	OUT	OUT	MACH. NO.
ITEM	MANUFACTURER					
SIZE	MODEL NO.	SERIAL NO.		TYPE		DEPT. NO.
INST. DATE	PURCH. COST	INST. COST	P. O.		BLDG. NO.	
SPAN	BRIDGE SPEED	TROLLY SPEED	HOIST SPEED			
				PURCHASED FROM		

ELECTRICAL DATA

FUNCTION						
MAKE						
H. P.						
R. P. M.						
VOLTAGE						
PHASE						
AMPS						
FRAME						
SER. NO.						

SPECIAL INFORMATION:

CODE:	A · ANNUAL	B · SEMI · ANNUAL	C · QUARTERLY	D · MONTHLY	E · SEMI · MONTHLY	F · WEEKLY

PREVENTIVE MAINTENANCE SCHEDULE

MISC	LUB	ELECT	MECH	WEEK	
				RED	BLUE
				1	27
				2	28
				3	29
				4	30
				5	31
				6	32
				7	33
				8	34
				9	35
				10	36
				11	37
				12	38
				13	39
				14	40
				15	41
				16	42
				17	43
				18	44
				19	45
				20	46
				21	47
				22	48
				23	49
				24	50
				25	51
				26	52

SPARE PARTS ON HAND

PART NO.	DESCRIPTION	LOC.	PART NO.	DESCRIPTION	LOC.

"VISIrecord"
PL 12986

THE JEFFREY MFG. CO.
COLUMBUS, OHIO

8X10   232   .75
v + 1

EXHIBIT 9   Budget Control System: Work Flow

Responsible person and department	Operation

Department 43
Plant maintenance controls
Supervisor & budget analyst
	1. Prior to the beginning of each fiscal year, department 43 develops a proposed plant maintenance fiscal budget. The forecast dollars are furnished in three (3) major categories as follows:
	    Labor
	    Material and purchased services
	    Supplies and expenses

2. After approval, the budget is distributed into five (5) major categories for each of three (3) departments, 41, 42 and 43 as follows:

	41	42	43	Total
Administration labor	X	X	X	X
Trades labor	X	X	X	X
Materials	X	X	X	X
Purchased services	X	X	X	X
Supplies & expenses	X	X	X	X
Total	X̄	X̄	X̄	X̄

3. The trades labor, material, and purchased services forecast is further distributed within each department by eight (8) separate work categories, and thirteen (13) separate labor, material, and purchased service accounts.

4. Fiscal labor, material, and purchased service estimates are then developed for each individual job order within each separate work category.

5. The day-to-day and routine job order estimates are routed for signature approval and distributed to maintenance supervision for daily use in charging labor, material, and purchased service, and to accounting for entry of fiscal estimates in the maintenance cost reports. Exceptions are maintenance job orders (M.J.O.'s) which are written on an "as required" basis throughout the year and require individual approval.

6. Each month department 43 submits a monthly budget to department 68 for each of the three maintenance departments (41, 42, 43). This monthly budget is based on the fiscal forecast; but during the year the monthly budgets may be adjusted, depending on the total business trend. However, any change from the fiscal forecast is initiated by department 68.

7. Each month the total actuals for all maintenance expenditures are reported on the overhead summary for all three maintenance departments. The actuals on the overhead summary are from the maintenance cost reports. These actuals are summarized by major category.

8. During the fiscal year, twelve (12) separate budget control charts are utilized by the maintenance manager to compare and control actual monthly costs in relation to budget forecasts.

EXHIBIT 9   Budget Control System: Work Flow (Cont.)

Responsible person and department	Operation

9. Plant maintenance cost reports—at the present time, the maintenance department receives six (6) data processing reports for the purposes of (1) controlling maintenance expenditures, (2) recording cost information, and (3) forecasting maintenance budgets.

These reports have enabled maintenance administration to develop a high quality in cost control of maintenance expenditures and provide a fast means of collecting cost information of maintenance operations.

(a) *Maintenance cost report no. 1*—monthly—by job order number, account, department by, benefiting department, etc.

Purpose: (1) Used monthly to record final job costs on all burden MJO's (1000–3849) Navy requirement on all maintenance and repair of USN facilities.

(2) Used monthly to audit and control actual maintenance expenditures vs. estimated on recurring job orders (1–999).

(3) Used monthly by department 68 to collect data in performance rating of departments 41 and 42.

(b) *Maintenance cost report no. 2*—monthly—by account, benefiting department, department by, job order category, etc.

Purpose: (1) Used monthly to develop actual maintenance expenditure information by benefiting departments or divisions as requested by management or department heads.

(2) Used annually to forecast fiscal maintenance expenditures by divisions. (Manufacturing, material, engineering, etc.)

(c) *Maintenance cost report no. 3*—monthly—by department, by account, PE code, job order category, etc.

Purpose: (1) Used, as required, to develop maintenance expenditure information by PE codes. (Paved surfaces, roofs, floors, etc.)

(d) *Maintenance cost report no. 4*—monthly—by department, by account, job order category, etc.

Purpose: (1) Used monthly to analyze and control maintenance expenditures by job categories.

(2) Used annually to forecast maintenance expenditures by job order categories.

(e) *Maintenance cost report no. 5*—quarterly—by account, PE code, department by, and benefiting department.

Purpose: (1) Used to develop semiannual cost reports on actual and estimated maintenance expenditures for class 3 and 4 facilities.

(2) Used to develop other maintenance cost information by PE codes.

(f) *Maintenance cost report no. 6*—monthly—job orders completed during month with cost expenditures.

Purpose: (1) Used by department 68 in performance rating of departments 41 and 42.

(2) Used by department 43 for a review of actual vs. estimated costs on completed job orders (1000–9999).

Improvements or, synonymously, betterments are distinguished from additions. Finney and Miller [Johnson and Gentry, 1974, p. 392] state that an addition is merely an increase in quantity, whereas an improvement is a substitution with an increase only in quality. Cooper and Ijiri [1983] define a betterment as:

> . . . an expenditure having the effect of extending the useful life of an existing fixed asset, increasing its normal rate of output, lowering its operating cost, increasing rather than merely maintaining efficiency or otherwise adding to the worth of benefits it can yield. The cost of adapting a fixed asset to a new use is not ordinarily capitalized unless at least one of the foregoing tests is met. A betterment is distinguished from an item of *repair* or *maintenance* in that the latter have the effect merely of keeping the asset in its customary state of operating efficiency without the expectation of added future benefits.

Examples of improvements are substitution of a tile roof for wooden shingles, replacement of pine flooring by hardwood, or the installation of a more powerful motor in a commercial fishing boat. Minor improvements might include the substitution of locking for nonlocking gasoline tank caps on vehicles and the replacement of conventional rearview vehicle mirrors by nonglare mirrors.

In principle, when additions consist of an entirely new unit, the expenditure is of a capital nature and should be charged to an asset account. In the recording of additions that pertain to existing assets and of improvements, it is theoretically correct to charge the new property to an asset account and eliminate the cost of items replaced or removed from the asset accounts.

Minimum Capitalization Amount. In practice, strict observance of capitalization principles would require intolerable attention to detail in regard to minor items, such as the substitution of a 75-watt light bulb in place of a 50-watt bulb.

To avoid this problem, most organizations establish a minimum capitalization amount. Individual expenditures below this minimum are expensed rather than capitalized. The accounting manual of one major midwestern manufacturing corporation states that no item with a total cost less than $500 shall be capitalized.

Leasehold Improvements. Improvements to leased property usually revert to the owner of the property upon termination of the lease, unless the lease agreement specifies otherwise. The cost of improvements made by the lessee should be capitalized in his records with the description of "leasehold improvements." These assets should be amortized or depreciated over the remaining term of the lease or their expected service life, whichever is shorter. Renewal options in the lease agreement are usually ignored in determining its remaining term, since renewal cannot be predicted with certainty.

Alteration and Rearrangement. Alteration is a term usually applied to the modification of buildings and structures. Included are the cutting of new entry and exit openings, closing old ones, erecting new walls, windows, and partitions, and removing old ones.

Rearrangement refers normally to machinery, involving the removal, shifting, and reinstallation of units, and reconnecting of units in possibly new configurations. Expenditures on alterations and rearrangements should be analyzed carefully in order to determine the amounts that strictly represent improvements. The latter should be capitalized. Sometimes the capitalization treatment used is not a debit to the appropriate fixed asset amount, but rather a debit to an improvement account, to be amortized over the ensuing periods benefiting from the improvements.

It may be difficult to make a clear segregation of improvement expenditures between those to be capitalized and those to be charged to expense. Estimation and judgment may be needed, in which case consideration should be given to the possibility that the new book value, net of accumulated depreciation, may exceed the market cost of a new unit of similar remaining service potential. If this is so, capitalization of improvement expenditures should be limited to an amount that will not cause the new book value to exceed replacement cost.

With respect to reinstallation costs, Finney and Miller [Johnson and Gentry, 1974, p. 394] state:

> Presumably the cost of one installation will already have been charged to the machinery account. Theoretically, therefore, the cost, or the undepreciated remainder of the cost, of the first installation should be removed from the accounts, and the reinstallation cost should be capitalized by charge to the machinery account.

It may be impracticable to determine original installation costs in the necessary detail, in which case they are often estimated, or ignored if minor.

In the case of building alterations, it may be decided to remove walls between new and old portions of the building or to modify load-bearing structural components. Although in principle the asset accounts should be relieved of the old costs, practical considerations often prevent the breaking down of the cost of the building to determine the amount applicable to a relatively minor portion thereof.

In the case of buildings, capitalization for unduly long periods of the costs of successive alteration and remodeling should be avoided. Rented buildings may often be adapted or converted to the different requirements of successive tenants, and it is not reasonable to capitalize all these successive outlays subject to amortization over the life of the structure as a whole. Alterations for an individual tenant should be capitalized in a special account and written off over the term of that particular lease. Although the lease may be renewed or the alterations may have utility for the next tenant, such eventualities cannot be relied upon.

Rebuilding. Alterations of buildings and equipment may be so major that virtually a new building or piece of equipment is the result. The term "rebuilding" is used in this sense. For example, the rebuilding of a truck engine may involve replacement of all valves, pistons, rings, connecting rods, bearings, cylinder walls, and so on, preserving few of the previous components apart from the engine block.

If the rebuilding is very extensive, the transaction may reasonably be treated as a replacement. The book value of the old unit should be closed out, after allowing for parts to be retained in the rebuilt unit. The costs of rebuilding plus the allowance for the retained parts, should be entered in the records as a new unit of property.

A justification for treating the rebuilt unit as a new asset is that its service life after rebuilding is likely to be quite different from the remaining portion of the originally estimated life.

Care should be taken to avoid unwarranted inflation of the book value of the rebuilt asset. Removal costs should not be capitalized, and neither should excessive costs of installation or erection. A rebuilt asset may not be the ideal structure or piece of equipment. Even if the rebuilding expenditure is well justified, the asset may be too large or too small in capacity, or relatively expensive in operation, or less productive than alternative equipment. The rebuilt property should not be carried in the accounts at a cost exceeding the current price of a new unit of equivalent efficiency and capacity, less an allowance reflecting the secondhand nature of the components preserved from the old unit.

Restoration and Rehabilitation. When buildings or equipment are acquired in a condition requiring expenditures on restoration or rehabilitation, these expenditures should be capitalized. Because it is reasonable to expect that such expenditures, together with any costs of removal and demolition, were considered in arriving at the purchase price, they should be charged to the cost of the asset.

On the other hand, restoration or rehabilitation expenditures incurred on assets not recently acquired fall into a different category. The costs of restoring and rehabilitating property that has been owned for a considerable time should generally not be capitalized, except where they clearly can be classified as improvements. In the latter case, capitalization, at least in part, would be required if the old book value of the dilapidated property understates the reasonable cost of the improved property. Such a situation may arise with assets acquired in a serious state of disrepair, even if considerable time elapses until rehabilitation occurs.

Accounting Records. The property ledger cards should include provision for details of additions and improvements. Procedures should be set up to ensure that these records are promptly updated whenever necessitated by addition and improvement expenditures, and that adequate descriptive information is recorded.

Control and Review. Proposals for additions and improvements should be subject to the same control and review procedures as regular capital expenditure projects. Usually there is no reason not to follow the system of proposal, evaluation, approval, authorization, budgeting, appropriation, and postcompletion audit. Addition and improvement expenditures of relatively smaller amounts may be dealt with under blanket appropriations.

RELOCATION, REPLACEMENT, RETIREMENT, AND DISPOSAL

"Relocation," as the term implies, is simply a change in physical location. "Replacement" involves a substitution of a new asset or a new part for an old asset or an old part. Replacements classified as minor are usually expensed; for instance, new spark plugs for an engine would almost certainly be written off as an expense. Major replacements should be capitalized.

Replacements are distinguished from improvements by the type of substitution made. Substitution in kind, for example, of a new machine identical except in age and condition, is a replacement but not an improvement. Substitution of a superior new machine for an old one is a replacement not in kind, and also an improvement.

Cooper and Ijiri [1983] give as the principal definition of retirement: "The removal of a fixed asset from service, following its sale or the end of its productive life, accompanied by the necessary adjustment of fixed asset and depreciation-reserve accounts."

Elimination of Expired Costs. Paton and Paton [1971, p. 252] point out that replacement is a combination of two distinct transactions: (1) the elimination of the old unit and (2) the acquisition of the new unit.

Although the acquisition transaction presents no accounting difficulty, the elimination (or retirement) transaction may not be so easily handled. Where the property record units are such that the old unit is separately identifiable and the book value and accumulated depreciation of the eliminated unit are shown, no problems arise. This is not always possible; however, in the case of discrete, individual items of property such as a building, a ship, a truck, a boiler, and so on, it can be done. But when items are not discrete in nature, as in the case of railroad tracks, power lines, water mains, or other unsegmented, continuous structures, the selection of a property record unit is necessarily arbitrary. This makes it difficult to distinguish between repairs and replacements and, in turn, between proper charges to capital and to revenue.

In order to assure uniformity in accounting under these conditions in regulated industries, regulatory agencies such as the ICC, the FPC, and state public service commissions have prescribed the use of specified retirement units. Generally it is required that replacements involving entire units be capitalized, whereas replacements of fractional units are to be charged to expense. The prescribed units are usually allowed to be further subdivided into smaller components, but not to be combined or modified so as to result in units larger than those prescribed.

It is sometimes suggested that it is expedient to treat some replacements as a single transaction rather than two distinct (elimination and acquisition) transactions. This occurs when the cost of a replacement is charged to the depreciation allowance, and no elimination transaction is recognized. Paton and Paton [1971, pp. 252–253] say of this practice:

> Whatever arrangement of entries is employed the practice of charging the cost of the new unit to the allowance for depreciation should be avoided. Even for replacements in kind this treatment is improper. The cost of the

property acquired seldom equals that of the asset eliminated; moreover, the depreciation accrued to date on the old asset will almost certainly not equal the expenditures for replacement. The result, accordingly, is misstatement of both plant cost and depreciation allowance. The practice of crediting the amount recovered through salvage or otherwise to the depreciation allowance is also objectionable. Instead there should be a closing out of the cost of plant removed and the accrued depreciation applicable, coupled with clear-cut recognition of removal cost, amount recovered, and retirement loss or gain.

Removal and Reinstallation Costs. As stated previously, removal costs should be capitalized when property is acquired with the intention of modifying it, and, for this purpose, removal of some existing components is necessary. Except in these circumstances, costs of removal, demolition, and the like should generally not be capitalized but should be expensed when incurred. The new unit replacing the old should not have removal charges included in its cost.

Where a replacement involves removal and reinstallation of old parts, reinstallation costs should not be capitalized without elimination of the original installation costs. To do otherwise would result in the double counting of both the costs of the original and reinstallation events.

Salvage Recovery. The proceeds from materials recovered as salvage should be applied to offset the costs chargeable against depreciation allowances. These proceeds may take the form of cash or materials that are reusable by the enterprise. In the latter event, the materials placed in stores should be valued at estimated current cost, with appropriate adjustment for their secondhand condition.

Where salvage is very large, the use of market price valuation may imply indirect recognition of unrealized appreciation.

When retired units are traded in as a part payment on new acquisitions, salvage consists of the allowance made by the vendor. Because the stated amount of the allowance often exceeds actual market value, it may be necessary to substitute an estimate of market value for the stated allowance in order to account properly for the retirement and for the cost of the new asset. See the section on "Exchange and Trade-In" above.

Idle, Reserve, and Standby Capacity. Sometimes fixed assets are retired from active service but are not disposed of or even removed from their previous locations. If they are retained as standby or reserve capacity, Finney and Miller [Johnson and Gentry, 1974, p. 400] recommend that no accounting entries be made. However, if their usefulness as operating assets is at an end, these authors suggest that the asset and accumulated depreciation accounts be relieved, that estimated salvage value be recorded in an abandoned property account, and that the estimated loss or gain be recognized.

Extraordinary Obsolescence. Extraordinary obsolescence may result from sudden style changes, new inventions, or unforeseen cessation of demand. Most accountants would agree to immediate recording of any loss, even though it is unrealized and even though they would be cautious about recognizing unrealized appreciation. Some accountants, influenced perhaps by the practical difficulty of estimating realizable values, would defer recognition of loss until actual disposal or abandonment occurred.

Gains or Losses upon Disposal. When a unit of property is retired, the proper accounting treatment is (1) to complete the recording of depreciation up to the date of retirement, and (2) to relieve the accounts of all amounts pertaining to the retired asset. Whether the retired asset is to be replaced or not has no bearing on these procedures. Likewise the cause of retirement, whatever the reason, is not relevant in this regard. What is essential is to ensure that the retirement is recorded properly so that future accounting statements do not show misleading amounts for fixed assets and for depreciation expense. In addition, proper recording of retirements enables insurance coverage to be adjusted when necessary and also facilitates elimination of retired assets from property tax rolls. The existence of inadequate property records is a severe impediment to the proper treatment of retirements.

To illustrate the recording of a retirement, assume that a machine costing $11,000 has been depreciated at an annual rate of 10 percent for 6 years, based on an estimated final salvage value of $2,000. In the middle of the seventh year it is sold for $4,000. The entries to be made are

(1)	Depreciation Expense	450	
	Accumulated Depreciation of Equipment		450
	To record depreciation at 10% for 6 months on machine #—, costing $11,000 with estimated salvage value of $2,000, sold June 30, 19X9.		
(2)	Cash	4,000	
	Accumulated Depreciation of Equipment	5,850	
	Loss on Sale of Equipment	1,150	
	Equipment		11,000
	To record sale of machine #—.		

If the machine had been sold for $6,000, there would have been a gain of $850 upon sale rather than a loss of $1,150.

The example above was based on the procedure of computing depreciation on acquisitions from the date of acquisition until the date of disposal. Sometimes different procedures are employed, such as computing depreciation on every acquisition and disposal for half a year, regardless of the actual dates of acquisition and disposal; or no depreciation may be taken in the year of acquisition, and a full year's depreciation may be taken in the year of disposal, or vice versa. Whichever procedure is adopted, it should be followed consistently.

Gains or losses on disposal of depreciable assets should be treated as income statement items, and, if material in amount, are usually separately disclosed. This treatment is stated in APB Opinion No. 30. [1973]. If the "operations of a segment of a business" are sold, abandoned, spun off, or otherwise disposed of, Opinion No. 30 states that the results of "continuing operations" should be reported separately from "discontinued operations." Also, any gain or loss from disposal of the segment should be reported in conjunction with the related results of discontinued operations and not as an extraordinary item.

Involuntary Conversion and Coinsurance. Asset services may be lost through fire, casualty, condemnation, or other involuntary events. Gains and losses resulting from involuntary conversion should be treated for accounting purposes no differently than those arising from voluntary disposals. The FASB, in Interpretation No. 30 [1979] said: "Involuntary conversions of nonmonetary assets to monetary assets are monetary transactions for which gain or loss shall be recognized even though an enterprise reinvests or is obligated to reinvest the monetary assets in replacement nonmonetary assets." The Board added: "Gain or loss resulting from an involuntary conversion . . . that is not recognized for income tax reporting purposes in the same period in which the gain or loss is recognized for financial reporting purposes is a timing difference for which comprehensive interperiod tax allocation . . . is required."

Federal income tax rules on involuntary conversion specify in most cases that no gain need be recognized at the time of disposal if the owner of the property uses the funds received to replace the involuntarily converted asset.

Property insurance contracts may include a coinsurance clause stipulating that if insurance coverage is below the required minimum, the insured party absorbs a portion of any loss. Because recovery of loss is usually based on fair market value, rather than book value, of the assets lost, insurance settlements may result in either a loss or gain on involuntary conversion due to insured risks.

Tools, Dies, and Other Small Items. It is not unusual for enterprises to have a significant investment in small assets such as tools, dies, drawings, patterns, jigs, templates, scientific instruments, eating utensils, and bed and table linens. Detailed accounting for these is difficult by virtue of their high mobility, generally short life, and usually low unit cost. Relocations and retirements can seldom be made subject to reliable reporting for record purposes.

Smaller items of relatively high value or relatively long service life may be charged to an appropriate asset account and depreciated at a composite rate sufficiently rapid to allow for the difficulty in maintaining control over them. It is desirable for periodic inventories to be taken so that the records can be verified or adjusted, as the case may be.

Often such items are not capitalized, and the minimum capitalization amount may be set to achieve such a result. However, where the investment in small items is considerable, such a procedure can materially understate reported assets and income.

Frequently, small items are charged to an asset account, and their periodic value and associated depreciation are determined by taking inventory at the close of the fiscal period. Because those on hand can be expected to vary in age and condition, averaging perhaps 50 percent depreciation from their cost, they may be valued at 50 percent of their average cost new.

An alternative practice is to recognize the original expenditures on such items as an asset and, in lieu of depreciation, to charge all subsequent expenditures to expense. If subsequent expenditures represent replacements only, this procedure may be adequate. However, growth and expansion of these expenditures or increases in replacement prices cause this practice to understate assets and income.

Control of the costs of small items may be facilitated by charging them to user departments, if departmental supervision is thereby motivated to be more cost conscious in respect to these items.

Some degree of physical control may be exercised by charging personnel for items issued to them, and requiring return of those no longer usable before issuing replacements.

Containers. Concerns that deliver goods in returnable containers, such as barrels, drums, carboys, bottles, and metal cylinders, face problems of accounting for this class of equipment.

If container deposits are not billed to customers and nonreturns are considerable, the container costs may be expensed as operating supplies, with the amount being determined by periodic inventories. If carried as fixed assets in these circumstances, the periodic inventory method should be used to determine the asset balance, allowing for depreciation of containers on hand.

Where customers are billed for containers, it may be advisable to keep separate records of balances receivable from customers in cash and balances to be settled by return of containers.

Some containers, even when cash deposits are collected on them, may not be returned because of breakage, negligence, or other causes. In these cases, periodic adjusting entries are required to diminish the asset account for containers (and the deposit liability to customers). Where deposits exceed the cost of the containers, this excess should be credited to income and not to the asset account.

Transfer Reports and Control. Proper asset control requires authorization and reporting of all relocations, replacements, retirements, and disposals. For this reason well-managed enterprises usually institute and maintain carefully designed procedures to secure adequate control. As an illustration, an excerpt from the property procedure manual of a major manufacturing concern is reproduced below.

IV. PLANT ADDITIONS, REMOVALS, AND TRANSFERS

1. *Authorization Necessary*—No plant assets shall be purchased or removed, and no charges or credits to plant accounts shall be made, unless authorized in advance by the president's office. The procedure for such authorization shall be as follows:

(a) *Authorization for Additions*—Proposals for expenditures for land, building, machinery, and equipment shall be submitted by the Works Manager or Office Manager on the prescribed "Mechanical Equipment Approval" form. When a "Mechanical Equipment Approval" has been approved by the president's office, the Cost Department shall issue a plant order to which all expenditures against the authorization shall be charged; no order covering plant expenditures shall be authoritative unless supported by an approved "Mechanical Equipment Approval." The amount appropriated on any "Mechanical Equipment Approval" shall be available for the specific purpose of that authorization only, and no part thereof may be transferred to any other authorization or used for any other purpose.

(b) *Authorization for Removals*—Proposals for sales or removals of plant assets shall be submitted on the prescribed "Capital Removal Authorization" form. The authorization request shall include information as to the cost and depreciated value of the assets to be removed, the proposed selling price or salvage value, and the gain or loss to be recorded in the accounts as a result of the removal. The approval and procedure for capital removal authorizations shall be the same as described in the preceding paragraph for capital expenditure authorizations.

(c) *Sundry Addition and Removal Authorizations*—In order to reduce the work involved in handling of authorizations for small routine additions or removals, the president's office may issue a "Sundry Authorization" for an amount not exceeding $1,000. These authorizations will not specify any particular work or item.

The Works Manager may assign to a sundry authorization routine additions or removals of items having a gross value of $1,000 or less.

When the total value of the assets added or removed on any sundry authorization approaches the total authorized, a new sundry authorization should be requested, the request being accompanied by a statement of the expenditures or removals applied against the previous sundry authorization.

The purpose of these sundry authorizations is to facilitate the handling of small routine expenditures and emergency needs; it is not intended that they shall be used for all expenditures under the $1,000 limit. Expenditures for additions or improvements (as distinguished from routine replacements) or for wholesale replacements of office equipment, etc., or unusual expenditure of any kind, particularly if over $500 in amount, should be covered by separate authorizations.

An additional reason in favor of a strict system of procedures is that it may be tempting for employees to misappropriate the salvage proceeds from asset disposals. Adequate authorization and reporting requirements for relocations and retirements form part of an efficient internal control system that includes the safeguarding of salvage proceeds.

FINANCIAL STATEMENTS

Balance Sheet Disclosure.   The annual surveys of corporate financial reports made by the AICPA *(Accounting Trends and Techniques)* show current examples of the disclosure of property, plant, and equipment.

APB Opinion No. 12 [1967] contains this statement:

> ... the following disclosures should be made in the financial statements or in notes thereto:
> a) Depreciation expense for the period,
> b) Balances of major classes of depreciable assets, by nature or function, at the balance-sheet date,

   c) Accumulated depreciation, either by major classes of depreciable
   assets or in total, at the balance-sheet date, and

   d) A general description of the method or methods used in computing
   depreciation with respect to major classes of depreciable assets.

Liens, pledges, and other encumbrances. The nature and extent of hypoth-
ecated or pledged fixed assets should be shown. The borrowing should be
shown as a liability and the amount of any category of fixed assets serving as
security should be stated. Retention of protective title by creditors or third parties should also be disclosed. In many cases the description of the liability, for
instance "first mortgage bonds," is sufficient disclosure that there is a mortgage
lien on all fixed assets and no additional notations of this fact are deemed necessary in the fixed asset section of the balance sheet. However, when the prior
claims are unusual or more complex than normal, further disclosure, usually
by footnote, is desirable. This may be the case if prior claims restrict the freedom of operation by management, for instance, with respect to the declaration
of dividends or the financing of asset expansion or replacement.

Revaluation. Assets may be revalued for numerous reasons. The question
arises as to whether, and in which circumstances, the cost basis may be
departed from in the financial statements. Revaluation has long been a permissible procedure in exceptional circumstances, but it is not a standard procedure in general use. A major issue exists as to whether it should become a
standard procedure. For a complete treatment of the controversy, see Chapter
32.

In the rare case where buildings or equipment are stated as appraised
amounts instead of cost, the balance sheet should clearly indicate this fact. It is
also desirable to indicate the date and basis of the appraisal. Furthermore, it
should be disclosed whether the appraisal was made by independent appraisers or by company officers or employees, because the same degree of impartial
objectivity may not be attributable to these respective parties.

Fair value. The term "fair value" has a special meaning in public utility regulation. It refers to the valuation of the rate base (principally utility plant) on
which the investors are entitled to earn a reasonable return. Court decisions
have held that the determination of fair value should encompass all relevant
factors, including the prudent historical costs and costs of reproduction. In
practice, fair value has usually turned out to be a weighted average of historical
cost and reproduction cost of the rate base. It is therefore not a specific basis of
fixed asset valuation that can be applied to financial statements in general.
Rather it is a composite of two different valuation bases determined by regulatory agencies for the special purpose of setting permissible rates of return.

Quasi-reorganization. A quasi-reorganization takes place when a corporation, usually in difficult financial circumstances, voluntarily readjusts its paid-
in capital without legal action by its creditors and without coming under the
supervision of the courts. Normally there is a write-down of overstated asset
values, which not only exhausts any balance in the Retained Earnings account
but also requires a reduction of additional paid-in capital. Thus Retained Earnings is set at zero to provide a fresh starting point from which to record future
accumulated earnings on the new basis of accountability.

Despite the effect of obscuring historically significant information through the write-down of asset values and the elimination of a deficit, the procedure is generally accepted because it results in more relevant asset valuation. In addition, a quasi-reorganization allows a corporation to make a fresh start as a profitable concern, freed from the stigma of a large deficit, recurring operating losses, and incapability of declaring cash dividends.

Accounting Research Bulletin No. 43 [1953] includes the following statement referring to quasi-reorganization:

> A write-down of assets below amounts which are likely to be realized thereafter, though it may result in conservatism in the balance sheet at the readjustment date, may also result in overstatement of earnings or of earned surplus when the assets are subsequently realized. Therefore, in general, assets should be carried forward as of the date of readjustment at fair and not unduly conservative amounts, determined with due regard for the accounting to be employed by the company thereafter.

Segment Reporting. Diversified, multinational companies have grown widespread in recent years. Because of the large array of product lines these companies manufacture and sell, and the different markets in which they operate, traditional consolidated financial disclosures were deemed inadequate by some users of financial statements. To enable these users to assess better an enterprise's past performance and future prospects, the FASB issued Statement of Financial Accounting Standards No. 14, *Financial Reporting for Segments of a Business Enterprise*, in 1976. This Statement, as amended by Statements No. 21 and 24, requires certain segment information from *public* companies relating to operations in different industries, foreign operations, export sales, and major customers.

The disclosure requirements in this Statement are applicable if segments meet certain size tests. If any of these size requirements are met, the company must disclose the aggregate carrying amount of the identifiable assets and certain revenue, profitability, and other disclosures set forth in the Statement. There are also SEC requirements for disclosure of industry segment information. Further discussion of segment information is found in Chapter 6 of this handbook.

BIBLIOGRAPHY

Accounting Principles Board (AICPA), *Omnibus Opinion—1967*, Opinion No. 12 (APB, 1967).

———, *Reporting the Results of Operations*, Opinion No. 30 (APB, 1973).

Bierman, H., Jr., and S. Smidt, *The Capital Budgeting Decision*, 5th ed. (Macmillan Company, New York, 1980).

Committee on Accounting Procedure (AICPA), *Restatement and Revision of Accounting Research Bulletins*, Accounting Research Bulletin No. 43 (CAP, 1953).

Cooper, W. W., and Y. Ijiri (eds.), *Kohler's Dictionary for Accountants*, 6th ed. (Prentice-Hall, Englewood Cliffs, N.J., 1983).

Davidson, S., J. S. Schindler, and R. L. Weil, *Fundamentals of Accounting*, 5th ed. (Dryden Press, Hinsdale, Ill., 1975).

Davidson, S., C. P. Stickney, and R. L. Weil, *Financial Accounting: An Introduction to Concepts, Methods and Uses* (Dryden Press, Hinsdale, Ill., 1976).

———, *Accounting: The Language of Business*, 5th ed. (Thomas Horton and Daughters, Glen Ridge, N.J., 1982).

Dyckman, T. R., *Long-Lived Assets* (Wadsworth Publishing Company, Belmont, Calif., 1967).

Financial Accounting Standards Board, *Accounting for Research and Development Costs*, Statement of Financial Accounting Standards No. 2 (FASB, 1974).

———, *Applicability of FASB Statement No. 2 to Business Combinations Accounted for by the Purchase Method*, FASB Interpretation No. 4 (FASB, 1975).

———, *Financial Reporting for Segments of a Business Enterprise*, Statement of Financial Accounting Standards No. 14 (FASB, 1976).

———, *Accounting for Involuntary Conversions of Nonmonetary Assets to Monetary Assets*, Interpretation No. 30 (FASB, 1979).

———, *Capitalization of Interest Cost*, Statement of Financial Accounting Standards No. 34 (FASB, 1979).

Grady, P., *Inventory of Generally Accepted Accounting Principles for Business Enterprises*, Accounting Research Study No. 7 (AICPA, 1965).

Heckert, J. B., and J. D. Willson, *Business Budgeting and Control*, 3d ed. (Ronald Press Company, New York, 1967).

Hendriksen, E. S., *Accounting Theory*, 3d ed. (Richard D. Irwin, Homewood, Ill., 1977).

Johnson, G. L., and J. A. Gentry, Jr., *Finney and Miller's Principles of Accounting: Intermediate*, 7th ed. (Prentice-Hall, Englewood Cliffs, N.J., 1974).

Kieso, D. E., and J. J. Weygandt, *Intermediate Accounting*, 3d ed. (John Wiley & Sons, New York, 1980).

National Association of Accountants, *Fixed Asset Accounting: The Capitalization of Costs*, Statement No. 4 on Management Accounting Practices (NAA, 1972).

Paton, W. A., and W. A. Paton, Jr., *Assets—Accounting and Administration* (Roberts and Roehl, Warren, Mich., 1971).

Quirin, G. D., *The Capital Expenditure Decision* (Richard D. Irwin, Homewood, Ill., 1967).

Suelflow, J. E., *Public Utility Accounting* (Institute of Public Utilities, Michigan State University, East Lansing, Mich., 1973), chap. 8.

Welsch, G. A., *Budgeting: Profit Planning and Control*, 4th ed. (Prentice-Hall, Englewood Cliffs, N.J., 1976).

Woods, L. M., *Accounting for Capital, Construction, and Maintenance Expenditures* (Prentice-Hall, Englewood Cliffs, N.J., 1967).

CHAPTER 20

Depreciation

Sidney Davidson
Arthur Young Professor of Accounting,
University of Chicago

THE MEANING OF DEPRECIATION

Depreciation is one of the most discussed and most disputed terms in all of accounting. A half-century ago, Henry Rand Hatfield, one of the giants in accounting history, wrote an interesting essay describing 36 different approaches or procedures used in dealing with depreciation questions. The years that have passed have resulted in an expansion, rather than a contraction, in the number of approaches to depreciation questions, so the topic remains one of controversy and dispute in the accounting literature.

Definition of Depreciation. In an effort to deal with this problem, the committee on terminology of the AICPA offered the following definition of depreciation accounting in 1953. "Depreciation accounting is a system of accounting which aims to distribute the cost or other basic value of tangible capital assets, less salvage (if any), over the estimated useful life of the unit (which may be a group of assets) in a systematic and rational manner. It is a process of allocation, not of valuation" [AICPA, 1953].

The investment in a depreciating asset is the price paid for a series of future services. The asset account may well be considered as a prepayment, similar in many respects to prepaid rent or insurance—a payment in advance for services to be received. As the asset is used in each accounting period, an appropriate portion of the investment in the asset is treated as the cost of the service received and is recognized as an expense of the period or as part of the cost of goods produced during the period. This cost of service used is described as depreciation.

However defined, it must be recognized that depreciation is a joint cost. It is joint with respect to the several time periods during which a plant asset is used.

20-2

It is joint with respect to the products that are turned out from any piece of equipment. It is joint with respect to the individual units of production that are manufactured during any given time period. Economic theory suggests that joint costs cannot be allocated satisfactorily. Yet in a variety of circumstances we are faced with the problem of allocating these joint costs of depreciation—costs that are joint to an extent unmatched by almost any other kind of cost.

The Causes of Depreciation. The causes of depreciation are the causes of decline in an asset's service-rendering potential and of its ultimate retirement. The services or benefits provided by land do not ordinarily diminish over time, so land is not depreciated. Many factors lead to the retirement of assets from service, but the causes of decline in service potential can be classified as either *physical* or *functional*. The physical factors include such things as ordinary wear and tear from use, chemical action such as rust, and the effects of wind and rain. The most important functional or nonphysical cause is *obsolescence*. Inventions, for example, may result in new equipment, the use of which reduces the unit cost of production to the point where continued operation of the old asset is not economical, even though the asset may be relatively unimpaired physically. Retail stores often replace display cases and storefronts long before they are worn out in order to keep the appearance of the store as attractive as their competitors'. Changed economic conditions may also become functional causes of depreciation, such as when an old airport becomes inadequate and must be abandoned, and a new, larger one is built to meet the requirements of heavier traffic.

Identifying the specific causes of depreciation is not essential for considering the fundamental problem of its measurement. It is enough to know that almost any physical asset will eventually have to be retired from service and that in some cases the retirement will become necessary at a time when physical deterioration is negligible. The specific causes do become important, however, when the attempt is made to estimate the useful life of an asset.

Depreciation as a Decline in Value. Depreciation is frequently used in ordinary conversation to mean a decline in value. Such an interpretation may be fundamentally sound when applied to the entire service life of a plant asset—there certainly is a decline in the value of an asset from the time it is acquired until it is retired from service. A decline in asset values is not, however, an appropriate description of the charge made to the operations of each accounting period. One incorrect inference from such a description is that if, in a given period of time, there has been an increase in the market value of an asset, such as an increase arising from increasing prices for the asset, then there has been no depreciation during that period. Rather, there have been two partially offsetting processes: (1) an unrealized holding gain on the asset, which usually is not recognized in historical cost accounting, and (2) depreciation of the asset's historical cost. As Chapter 31 indicates, a holding gain is an increase in the market price of an asset since the time the asset was acquired or last revalued.

Further, the word *value* has so many uses and connotations that it is not a serviceable term for a definition. (The noun *value* should seldom be used in accounting without a qualifying adjective.) "Decline in value" is not entirely inappropriate in describing an element of depreciation, but is not helpful in isolating its essence.

Summary of Depreciation Concepts. Depreciation, as it is used in accounting, is a process of cost allocation, not one of valuation. This chapter discusses the problems of *allocating* an asset's cost to the periods of benefit. A depreciation problem will exist whenever (1) capital is invested in services to be rendered by a plant asset, and (2) at some reasonably predictable date in the future the asset will have to be retired from service with a residual value less than its acquisition cost. The problem is to interpret and account satisfactorily for the diminution from acquisition cost to residual value.

Note that replacing the asset is *not* essential to the existence of depreciation. Depreciation is the expiration or disappearance of service potential from the time the plant asset is put into use until the time it is retired from service. Whether or not the asset is replaced does not affect the amount or treatment of its depreciation.

THE DEPRECIATION CALCULATION

There are three principal accounting problems in allocating the cost of an asset over time:

1. Ascertaining the depreciation basis of the asset
2. Estimating its useful service life
3. Deciding on the pattern of expiration of services over the useful service life

Whenever feasible, depreciation should be computed for individual items such as a single building, machine, or truck. Where many similar items are in use and each one has a relatively small cost, individual calculations may be impracticable and the depreciation charge is usually calculated for the group as a whole. Furniture and fixtures, tools, and telephone poles are examples of assets that are usually depreciated in groups. Depreciation of individual assets, sometimes described as "unit depreciation," is described first. Depreciation of groups of assets, referred to as "group or composite depreciation," is then described.

DEPRECIATION BASIS OF PLANT ASSETS

Depreciation charges are usually based on the acquisition cost of the asset less (except for declining-balance methods described later) the estimated salvage value—the amount to be received when the asset is retired from service. As inflation has become recognized as a major economic problem, there has been increasing recognition that basing depreciation charges on acquisition costs will not in most cases charge to expense amounts sufficient to maintain the productive capacity of the business. Basing depreciation on acquisition costs will enable a business to provide for maintenance of its financial position measured in dollars, but not of its physical productive capacity in periods of rising prices.

Inflation Adjustments to Basis. Financial Accounting Standards Board Statement No. 33 [1979] requires large firms to report as supplementary data depreciation charges on both a constant dollar and current cost basis. In order to calculate depreciation on these bases, almost all firms will find it necessary to compute the constant dollar and current cost basis of their plant assets. The Statement requires a disclosure in the supplementary data of the current cost of property, plant, and equipment, net of accumulated depreciation. The procedures for calculating basis and depreciation charges under the constant dollar and current cost approaches are described in Chapter 31. The formal financial statements continue to use the acquisition cost basis for depreciation.

Estimating Salvage Value. The total depreciation of an asset over its life is the difference between its acquisition cost and the amount that can be received for the asset when it is retired from service, either in a cash sale or as a trade-in allowance. The amount received is described as the asset's *salvage value* or *residual value*. Estimates of salvage value are necessary for making the depreciation calculations. (The terms "salvage value" and "residual value" refer to the estimated proceeds on disposition of an asset less all removal and selling costs. Salvage value must be an estimate at any time before the asset is retired. Hence, before retirement, the terms "salvage value" and "estimated salvage value" are synonymous.)

For buildings, common practice assumes a zero salvage value. This treatment rests on the assumption that the cost to be incurred in tearing down the building will approximate the sales value of the scrap materials recovered. For other assets, however, the salvage value may be substantial, and should be estimated and taken into account in making the periodic depreciation charge. This is particularly true where it is planned to retire an asset while it still has substantial value. For example, a car rental firm will replace its automobiles at a time when other owners can use the cars for several more years. The rental firm will be able to realize a substantial part of acquisition cost from the sale of used cars.[1] Past experience usually forms the best basis for estimating salvage value.

Salvage values can be negative. (Consider, for example, the expected "decommissioning" costs of a nuclear power generating plant. At the time the plant is constructed, the expected costs for safe dismantling at retirement are substantially larger than the expected salvage proceeds.) *Negative salvage values* are generally treated arithmetically just the opposite of positive salvage values. The amount of salvage value is subtracted from cost (in the case of negative salvage value, the expected net cost of removal is added to cost) to derive the amount to be depreciated.

Estimates of salvage value are necessarily subjective. Disputes over estimated salvage value in the past led to many disagreements between Internal Revenue Service agents and taxpayers. Partly to reduce such controversy, the

---

[1]See *Hertz Corporation v. United States* (364 U.S. 122), 1960.

Internal Revenue Code was amended to provide that, starting in 1962, salvage value of up to 10 percent of the cost of assets such as machinery and equipment may be ignored in depreciation calculations for tax purposes. The Internal Revenue Code was amended again in 1971 to provide that salvage value may be ignored entirely in calculating depreciation if a procedure known in the Code as the *asset depreciation range* (ADR) system was used. The *accelerated cost recovery system* instituted in 1981 permits taxpayers to ignore salvage value entirely in calculating cost recovery. Despite the tax provisions, the illustrations in this chapter assume that the entire salvage value is to be taken into account in calculating depreciation unless explicit contrary statements are made.

ESTIMATING SERVICE LIFE

The second factor in the depreciation calculation is the estimated economic service life of the asset. In making the estimate, both the physical and the functional causes of depreciation must be taken into account. Experience with similar assets, corrected for differences in the planned intensity of use or alterations in maintenance policy, is usually the best guide for this estimate.

In 1962, the Internal Revenue Service published guidelines of useful lives suggested for tax reporting [Revenue Procedure 62-21]. The guidelines provided estimated useful lives based on categories of assets by broad classes. In 1972 [Revenue Procedure 72-10], the Internal Revenue Service ruled that the guideline lives need not be strictly followed. Rather, the IRS said that taxpayers may use a life anywhere in the range from 80 to 120 percent of the guideline life. Such ranges were called *asset depreciation ranges.*

The Economic Recovery Tax Act of 1981 abandons the use of the term "depreciation" entirely in calculating taxable income and provides instead for an *accelerated cost recovery system* (ACRS). The "cost recovery" charge is exactly comparable to depreciation, but it provides for an accelerated write-off of the depreciable asset. Service lives of 3 years for automobiles and other light vehicles and 5 years for almost all other equipment are prescribed for ACRS; service lives of 10 or 15 years are prescribed for various types of buildings. A taxpayer may elect to use longer service lives, but such elections are rare.

The lives prescribed in ACRS are in most cases shorter, and in many cases much shorter, than the likely economic service life of the assets. Congress was aware of this difference, but it established the shorter service lives for tax purposes in an effort to stimulate investment in depreciable assets and thus to speed up technological advances. The difference between depreciable lives for tax purposes and estimated economic service lives is so great that the AICPA has indicated that most firms should make separate calculations of cost recovery for tax purposes and depreciation for financial reporting purposes, using different service lives for each. This difference adds to the deferred tax problem discussed in Chapter 36.

Despite the abundance of data from experience, estimating of service lives is the most difficult task in the entire depreciation calculation. Making proper allowances for obsolescence is particularly difficult, because obsolescence results for the most part from forces external to the firm. Unless the estimator possesses prophetic powers, it is likely that the estimates will prove to be incorrect. For this reason, the estimates of useful service life of important assets or groups of assets should be reconsidered every few years. Estimating the "true" economic life of an asset with a long life, as required for financial reporting, is hard. Many firms have used for financial reporting the depreciable lives permitted by the IRS for tax reporting. As discussed above, these lives tend to be shorter than economic lives. Therefore, the depreciable lives used by many firms for financial reporting are, in practice, shorter than economic lives.

PATTERN OF EXPIRATION OF SERVICES

Once the acquisition cost has been calculated and both salvage value and service life have been estimated, the total of depreciation charges for the whole estimated life of the asset has been determined. There then remains the problem of selecting the pattern for allocating those charges to the specific years of the life. There are five basic patterns for such allocations. They are labeled E, A, S, D, and N in Exhibit 1.

If salvage value is assumed to be zero, then, of course, the salvage value line coincides with the horizontal axis and the entire acquisition cost is depreciated.

The patterns are discussed in more detail in the next section. A represents *accelerated* depreciation; S, *uniform* or *straight-line* depreciation; and D, *decelerated* depreciation. (Understanding the terms "accelerated" and "decelerated" is easier if you compare the depreciation charges in the early years to straight-line depreciation, as in Exhibit 1.) Patterns A and S are much more commonly used than D. Pattern E, of course, represents immediate expensing of the item. All costs are charged to the period when the cost is incurred. The immediate expensing of research and development expenditures is an example of this pattern. Pattern N represents the situation, such as for land, where there are no periodic depreciation charges. The asset is shown on the books at acquisition cost until it is sold or otherwise retired.

Exhibit 1 illustrates the book value of the asset during various periods of its life. The pattern of depreciation charges can also be depicted by showing the annual depreciation charges over the life of the asset. The same five patterns illustrated in Exhibit 1 are shown in Exhibit 2. The areas under each of the five curves in Exhibit 2 are equal. All are equal to acquisition cost less estimated salvage value.

DEPRECIATION METHODS

All depreciation methods seek to allocate the basis of an asset to its periods of use. Accounting Research Bulletin No. 43, Chapter 9 (1953), states that the allocation must be "systematic and rational." A variety of methods, described in the following paragraphs, meet these criteria and are thus encompassed within generally accepted accounting principles. A systematic allocation involves the use of a formula, without judgment. For example, a method not considered systematic is the annual appraisal method. This involves expert opinion as to the

EXHIBIT 1 Patterns of Depreciation: Book Value over Life of Asset

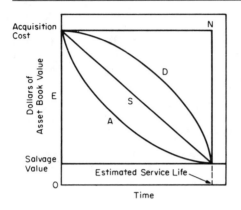

E – Expense Immediately

Capitalize and Then Use:

A – Accelerated Depreciation
S – Straight-Line Depreciation
D – Decelerated Depreciation
N – No Depreciation

physical and economic efficiency of the asset and an amount at which the asset should be reported. The diminution in this amount is the depreciation charge for the period.

The permitted depreciation allocations can be made either on the basis of use or on the basis of time. The use basis, also known as the "production basis," is conceptually superior if obsolescence is not a primary factor in causing retirement. However, because estimating the likely number of units of use of a plant asset is usually even more difficult than estimating its likely service life, the great majority of plant assets are depreciated on a time basis.

The use basis is almost always applied by a straight-line method; that is, each unit of use is assigned an equal charge. When a time basis is used, any of sev-

EXHIBIT 2 Patterns of Annual Depreciation: Charge over Life of Asset

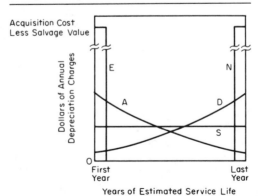

eral methods may be employed. The time bases discussed here are the following:

1. Straight-line method (pattern S in Exhibits 1 and 2)
2. Declining-balance method (pattern A in Exhibits 1 and 2)
3. Sum-of-the-years'-digits method (pattern A in Exhibits 1 and 2)
4. Compound interest method (pattern D in Exhibits 1 and 2).

Three methods are used for calculating depreciation in the years of acquisition and retirement:

1. Depreciation may be charged only for that portion of the period during which the asset is used.
2. Depreciation may be charged for one-half of a year in the year of acquisition and one-half of a year in the year in which the asset is retired. This approach is called the "half-year convention" and is required for income tax reporting under accelerated cost recovery.
3. A full year's depreciation may be taken in the first year for assets acquired in the first half of the year, and no depreciation may be taken in the first year on assets acquired in the second half of the year; for assets retired in the first half of the year, no depreciation is taken in the retirement year, but if retirement occurs in the second half of the year, a full year's depreciation is taken.

Any of these methods is acceptable, but the chosen method should be followed consistently.

Production or Use Method. Many assets are not used uniformly over time. Manufacturing plants often have seasonal variations in operation, so that certain machines may be used 24 hours a day at one time and 8 hours a day or less at another time of year. Trucks are not likely to receive the same amount of use in each month or year of their lives. The time methods of depreciation may, then, result in depreciation charges for such assets that do not reflect usage patterns.

When the rate of usage varies from period to period and when the total usage of an asset over its life can be estimated reliably, a depreciation charge based on actual usage during the period may be justified. For example, depreciation of a truck for a period could be based on the ratio of miles driven during the period to total miles expected to be driven over the truck's life. The depreciation cost per unit (mile) of use is

$$\text{Depreciation Cost per Unit} = \frac{\text{Acquisition Cost} - \text{Estimated Salvage Value}}{\text{Estimated Number of Units}}$$

The calculation is simple, but it requires a special record of the units of operation of each asset or of the number of units produced. If a truck that costs $36,000 and has an estimated salvage value of $2,400 is expected to be driven 200,000 miles before it is retired from service, then the depreciation per mile is $.168 [= ($36,000 − $2,400)/200,000]. Then, if the truck is operated 2,000 miles in a given month, the depreciation charge for the month is 2,000 × $.168 = $336.

If the production method is used, depreciation becomes a variable cost of output. Total depreciation cost for the period will vary with output, but depreciation cost per unit will be fixed. If the straight-line (time) method is used, the total depreciation cost for the period is fixed, but the cost per unit varies.

The argument against the use method is that it is more difficult to estimate the life of an asset in terms of use than in terms of time. Furthermore, if the life of the asset is ended because of obsolescence rather than because of physical deterioration, the first step must be to estimate life in years before it becomes obsolete, followed by an estimate of the number of hours of use during this period of time.

The Straight-Line (Time) Method. The allocation method that is used most commonly for financial reporting is the straight-line method. It was used almost exclusively until 1954, when the income tax laws were revised to recognize other depreciation methods for general use. Under the straight-line method, the cost of the asset, less any estimated salvage value, is divided by the number of years of its expected life in order to arrive at the annual depreciation:

$$\text{Annual Depreciation} = \frac{\text{Acquisition Cost} - \text{Estimated Salvage Value}}{\text{Estimated Life in Years}}$$

For example, if a machine costs $12,000, has an estimated salvage value of $1,000, and has an expected useful life of 5 years, the annual depreciation will be $2,200 [= ($12,000 − $1,000)/5]. Occasionally, instead of a positive salvage value, the cost of removal exceeds the gross proceeds upon disposition. This excess of removal costs over gross proceeds should be added to the cost of the asset in making the calculation. Thus, if a building is constructed for $370,000, and it is estimated that it will cost $50,000 to remove it at the end of 25 years, the annual depreciation would be $16,800 [= ($370,000 + $50,000)/25].

A common practice when the salvage value is assumed to be zero is to apply an appropriate percentage, known as the depreciation rate, to the *acquisition cost* in order to calculate the annual charge. The rate is chosen so that it will charge the entire acquisition cost off over the estimated life. A rate of 5 percent will write off the cost of an asset in 20 years, a rate of 25 percent in 4 years, and so on.

Accelerated Depreciation. The efficiency and earning power of many plant assets decline as the assets grow older. Cutting tools lose some of their precision; printing presses are shut down more frequently for repairs; rentals in an old office building are lower than those in its gleaming new neighbor. Some assets tend to provide more and better services in the early years of their lives while requiring increasing amounts of maintenance as they grow older. Where this is the case, methods that recognize progressively smaller depreciation charges in successive periods may be justified. Such methods are referred to as *accelerated depreciation* methods because the depreciation charges in the early years of the asset's life are larger than in later years. Accelerated depreciation leads to a pattern such as A in Exhibits 1 and 2. For convenience, the depreciation charges for a year, however they are determined, are allocated on a straight-line basis to periods *within* the year.

EXHIBIT 3   Double-Declining-Balance Depreciation Asset with 5-Year Life, $5,000 Cost, and Zero Estimated Salvage Value

Year	Acquisition cost (1)	Accumulated depreciation as of Jan. 1 (2)	Net book value as of Jan. 1 (1) − (2) (3)	Depreciation rate (4)	Depreciation charge for the year = (3) × (4) (5)
19X0	$5,000	$ 0	$5,000	.40	$2,000
19X1	5,000	2,000	3,000	.40	1,200
19X2	5,000	3,200	1,800	.40	720
19X3	5,000	3,920	1,080[a]	.40	432
19X4	5,000	4,352	648	.40	259
19X5	5,000	4,611	389		

[a]If the asset had a zero salvage value, the firm would switch to straight-line write-off of the remaining life, or $540 (= $1,080/2) a year for the last 2 years.

Declining-Balance Methods. The *declining-balance method* is one accelerated depreciation method. In this method, the depreciation charge is calculated by multiplying the *net book value* of the asset (acquisition cost less accumulated depreciation) at the start of each period by a fixed rate. The estimated salvage value is not subtracted from the cost in making the depreciation calculation, as is the case with other depreciation methods. Because the net book value declines from period to period, the result is a declining periodic charge for depreciation throughout the life of the asset.[2] The rate most commonly used is the maximum one formerly permitted for income tax purposes, which ordinarily is twice the straight-line rate. When this rate is used, the method is called the *double-declining-balance* method. Thus, for example, an asset with an estimated 10-year life would be depreciated at a rate of 20 percent (= 2 × ⅒) per year of the book value at the start of the year. To take another example, if a machine costing $5,000 is purchased on January 1, 19X0, and it is estimated to have a 5-year life, a 40 percent (= ⅕ × 2) rate would be used. The depreciation charges would be calculated as shown in Exhibit 3.

[2]Under the declining-balance method, as strictly applied, the fixed depreciation rate used is one that will charge the cost less salvage value of the asset over its service life. The formula for computing the rate is

$$\text{Depreciation Rate} = 1 - \sqrt[n]{\frac{s}{c}} = 1 - \left(\frac{s}{c}\right)^{1/n}$$

In this formula n = estimated periods of service life, s = estimated salvage value, and c = cost.

Estimates of salvage value have a profound effect on the rate. Unless a positive salvage value is assumed, the rate is 100 percent—that is, all depreciation is charged in the first period. For an asset costing $10,000, with an estimated life of 5 years, the depreciation rate is 40 percent per period if salvage value is $778, but it is 60 percent if salvage value is $102.

The effect of small changes in salvage value on the rate and the seeming mathematical complexity of the formula have resulted in widespread use of approximations or rules of thumb instead of the formula.

The undepreciated cost as of December 31, 19X4, as shown in Exhibit 3, is $389 (= $648 − $259). This amount is unlikely to equal the salvage value at that time. The problem is usually anticipated and solved by adjusting the depreciation charge in one or more of the later years. If the salvage value is large, the asset is likely to be depreciated to that value before the end of the estimated service life and the last period(s) will have no depreciation charges. If the salvage value is small, the firm can switch in the last years of asset life to writing off the undepreciated cost minus salvage value in straight-line fashion over the remaining life.

Refer again to Exhibit 3. If the asset had an estimated salvage value of $200, the depreciation charges in 19X3 and 19X4 would be $440 a year (net book value at January 1, 19X3, of $1,080 less the estimated salvage value of $200 divided by the 2 years of remaining life). In general, the switch to the straight-line method for the remaining life is made when the switch will produce a greater depreciation charge than the one resulting from continued application of the double-declining-balance method. For assets with zero salvage value, this ordinarily occurs in the period following the midpoint of the service life.

If the asset were acquired at mid-year, depreciation in 19X0 would be $1,000 (= ½ × .40 × $5,000). Depreciation in 19X1 would be based on the book value at January 1, 19X1, of $4,000 and would be $1,600 (= .40 × $4,000). Similar calculations would be made for each following year.

Sum-of-the-Years'-Digits Method. Another accelerated depreciation method is the *sum-of-the-years'-digits method*. Under this method, the depreciation charge is computed by applying a fraction, which diminishes from year to year, to the acquisition cost less estimated salvage value of the asset. The numerator of the fraction is the number of periods of remaining life at the beginning of the year for which the depreciation calculation is being made. The denominator is the sum of all such numbers, one for each year of estimated service life; if the service life is n years, the denominator for the sum-of-the-years'-digits method is $1 + 2 + \cdots + n$.[3]

The method is illustrated by again considering an asset costing $5,000 purchased January 1, 19X0, which has an estimated service life of 5 years and an estimated salvage value of $200. The sum of the years' digits is 15 (= 1 + 2 + 3 + 4 + 5).[4] The depreciation charges are calculated in Exhibit 4.

If the asset were acquired at mid-year, depreciation in 19X0 would be $800 (= ½ × 5/15 × $4,800). Depreciation in 19X1 would be made up of two parts, the remaining half of the first year's charge and the first half of the second year's charge. The amount would be $1,440 [= (½ × 5/15 × $4,800) + (½ × 4/15 × $4,800)]. Similar computations would be made for each of the following years.

---

[3]A useful formula for summing the numbers 1 through n is $1 + 2 + \cdots + n = n(n + 1)/2 = (n^2 + n)/2$.

[4]That is, according to the formula given in the previous footnote: $1 + 2 + 3 + 4 + 5 = (5 \times 6)/2 = 15$.

EXHIBIT 4   Sum-of-the-Years'-Digits Depreciation: Asset with 5-year Life, $5,000 Cost, and $200 Estimated Salvage Value

Year	Acquisition cost less salvage value (1)	Remaining life in years (2)	Fraction = (2)/15 (3)	Depreciation charge for the year = (3) × (1) (4)
19X0	$4,800	5	5/15	$1,600
19X1	4,800	4	4/15	1,280
19X2	4,800	3	3/15	960
19X3	4,800	2	2/15	640
19X4	4,800	1	1/15	320
				$4,800

Compound Interest Methods. Compound interest methods of depreciation are not widely used in financial accounting, but they are theoretically sound for many management decisions. For plant assets producing equal annual net inflows of cash, compound interest depreciation leads to a pattern like D in Exhibits 1 and 2. The straight-line and accelerated methods described earlier in this chapter are both simpler than the compound interest methods, but they do have one flaw, discussed next, that the compound interest method is designed to correct.

Rate of return on investment. To illustrate both the compound interest method and the flaws in the other methods, consider an asset that costs $11,400 and has an estimated service life of 5 years with no salvage value. Assume further that it was estimated when this asset was acquired that it would increase cash flows (increase revenues or decrease operating expenses other than depreciation) by $3,000 per year. A plant asset costing $11,400 and yielding an annuity of $3,000 per year for 5 years has an internal rate of return of approximately 10 percent per year.[5] (See the discussion in Chapter 9.) In this context, the internal rate of return is called the "earning rate."

The depreciation charge each year under the compound interest method is found from the following formula:

Compound Interest Depreciation for Year = Cash Flow for the Year
— (Earning Rate × Undepreciated Balance at Beginning of Year)

Management is often evaluated on the rate of return on investment (ROI) it produces. The rate of return on investment is defined to be net income for the period divided by the book value of assets for the period. Ordinarily, some average of the entire year's assets is used in the denominator. To keep the example that follows simple, the book value of assets at the beginning of the

---

[5] $11,400/$3,000 = 3.80. See Appendix Table 4, 5-period row, for the amount closest to 3.80. At 10 percent, the factor is 3.79079, so the implicit rate is slightly less than 10 percent.

EXHIBIT 5   Illustration of Rate-of-Return Calculation for 5-Year Asset Costing $11,400 with $3,000 Annual Cash Flow

Year (1)	Book value at start of year = cost − accumulated depreciation (2)	Net cash flow given (3)	Depreciation charge (calculated) (4)[a]	Income = (3) − (4) (5)	Percentage rate of return = [(5)/(2)] × 100 (6)
		For year			
		Straight-line method			
19X0	$11,400	$3,000	$2,280	$ 720	6.3
19X1	9,120	3,000	2,280	720	7.9
19X2	6,840	3,000	2,280	720	10.5
19X3	4,560	3,000	2,280	720	15.8
19X4	2,280	3,000	2,280	720	31.6
		Sum-of-the-years'-digits method			
19X0	$11,400	$3,000	$3,800	(800)	−7.0
19X1	7,600	3,000	3,040	(40)	−0.5
19X2	4,560	3,000	2,280	720	15.8
19X3	2,280	3,000	1,520	1,480	64.9
19X4	760	3,000	760	2,240	294.7
		Compound interest method (rate of return = 10%)			
19X0	$11,400	$3,000	$1,860	$1,140	10.0
19X1	9,540	3,000	2,046	954	10.0
19X2	7,494	3,000	2,251	749	10.0
19X3	5,243	3,000	2,476	524	10.0
19X4	2,767	3,000	2,723[b]	277	10.0

[a]See text for descriptions of calculations for column (4).
[b]Rounding error. If an earning rate of 9.905% were used, then the rounding error would be eliminated.

year is used for the denominator. Exhibit 5 shows the rate-of-return calculation for an asset when depreciation is calculated with the straight-line, the sum-of-the-years'-digits, and the compound interest methods.

Note that when the straight-line method is used in the example, the rates of return range from 6.3 percent in 19X0 to 31.6 percent in 19X4. The increases in the rate of return implied by the sum-of-the-years'-digits method are even more severe in this assumed case of equal annual cash inflows. A flaw in the straight-line and accelerated methods is that they show increasing rates of return on the investment in the plant asset as time passes. If cash flows from the asset decline over time (more down time, lower rents, higher repair costs, etc.), this flaw in those methods becomes less significant but rarely disappears. The compound interest method is designed to give *equal rates* of return each year of the asset's life; see column (6).

Pattern of charges. As the example illustrates, when equal annual cash flows are assumed, the compound interest method results in increasing depreciation charges over time. The depreciation charge of $1,860 in 19X0 is calculated by deducting from the cash flow of $3,000 the earning rate times the book value of the asset at the start of the year; $1,860 = $3,000 − .10 × $11,400. The depreciation charge for 19X1 is calculated as $3,000 − [.10 × ($11,400 − $1,860)] = $2,046.

If cash flows from the asset decline over time, then the increases in depreciation charges year by year under this method diminish and there may even be decreasing depreciation charges if the cash flows decline rapidly enough. If, in the example, total cash flows remain at $15,000, but are $5,000, $4,000, $3,000, $2,000, and $1,000 from the first to fifth years, respectively, depreciation charges would decline each year as shown in Exhibit 6.

The compound interest method illustrated here is sometimes called the *sinking fund method*. Another compound interest method, described as the *annuity method*, shows the *same net expense* each year but recognizes larger depreciation charges offset by interest income.

The compound interest methods produce equal rates of return on investment each year. They can be justified on theoretical grounds as follows.

An asset is acquired because of its future benefits. Amortization traces the reduction in the asset's book value as the future benefits are used up. The compound interest method of depreciation writes off the asset's cost for a period in direct proportion to the present value dollars of benefit from the asset that have been received during the period. A little experimentation with the examples should convince you that compound interest depreciation writes off an asset's cost in exact "straight-line" proportion to the number of present value dollars of benefit that have been generated by the asset during the period.

To use the compound interest method requires estimates of cash flows for each year of the asset's life. Accurate estimates are hard to make, but management can use the same estimates for calculating depreciation that were used to make the decision to acquire the asset in the first place. Despite its logical advantages, the compound interest method is found in practice only in rare public utility situations. It is the least conservative method of recording depreciation. Most accountants would say that it is not in accord with generally accepted accounting principles.

EXHIBIT 6   Illustration of Compound Interest Method with Declining Cash Flows

Year (1)	Book value at start of year (2)	Net cash flow (given) (3)	Income (calculated) (4)[a]	Depreciation charges (3) − (4) (5)	Percentage rate of return[b] [(4)/(2)] × 100 (6)
19X0	$11,400	$5,000	$1,482	$3,518	13.0
19X1	7,882	4,000	1,025	2,975	13.0
19X2	4,907	3,000	638	2,362	13.0
19X3	2,545	2,000	331	1,669	13.0
19X4	876	1,000	114	886[c]	13.0

[a]Column (4) = column (3) − column (2) × .13.
[b]Calculation of the 13% internal rate of return requires a trial-and-error procedure illustrated in Chapter 9.
[c]Rounding error of $10 (= $886 − $876). Exact earnings rate is slightly less than 13.03%.

FACTORS TO CONSIDER IN CHOOSING
THE DEPRECIATION METHOD

To the individual firm, depreciation is a factor in the calculation of income reported on the financial statements as well as a deduction from otherwise taxable income on tax returns. The firm need not choose the same depreciation method for both financial and tax reporting purposes (and probably should not).

Financial Reporting. The goal in financial reporting for long-lived assets is to seek a statement of income that realistically measures the expiration of those assets. The only difficulty is that no one knows, in any satisfactory sense, just what portion of the service potential of a long-lived asset expires in any one period. All that can be said is that financial statements should report depreciation charges based on reasonable estimates of asset expirations so that the goal of fair presentation can more nearly be achieved.

A recent issue of *Accounting Trends and Techniques*, the AICPA's annual survey of the accounting practices of 600 large corporations, shows that the straight-line method was used for financial reporting purposes by almost 75 percent of the firms.

Tax Reporting. It seems clear that the goal of the firm in selecting a depreciation method for tax purposes should be to maximize the present value of the reductions in tax payments from claiming depreciation. When tax rates remain constant over time and there is a flat tax rate (for example, income is taxed at a 46 percent rate), this goal can usually be achieved by maximizing the present value of the depreciation deductions from otherwise taxable income. That is, for tax purposes the asset should be written off as quickly as possible. Of course, a firm can deduct only the acquisition cost, less salvage value, from otherwise taxable income over the life of the asset. Earlier deductions are, however, worth more than later ones, because a dollar of taxes saved today is worth more than a dollar of taxes saved tomorrow. In deciding between alternative methods of claiming deductions for the determination of taxable income, it seems clear that the firm should choose that alternative which meets the general goal of paying the least amount of tax, as late as possible, within the law. This goal is sometimes called the *least and latest rule.*

Management has an obligation in a competitive economy to carry on operations so as to minimize all costs—that is, to minimize the present value of those costs over the long run. Failure to minimize costs hinders the attempt of the competitive market economy to allocate resources efficiently. Management's obligation to reduce costs applies to taxes as well as to other costs, and, in most circumstances, the present value of taxes is minimized by taking depreciation as rapidly as is legally possible. This usually means taking the maximum deductions permitted under ACRS. For machinery and equipment, ACRS provides for a 5-year write-off under a 150 percent declining-balance method using a half-year convention in the year of acquisition. (For totally unexplained reasons, the percentage write-offs in the 5 years are 15, 22, 21, 21, and 21 percent.) The Economic Recovery Tax Act of 1981 called for the rates to be increased in later years to a 175 percent and then to a 200 percent declining-balance method, but the Tax Equity and Fiscal Responsibility Act of 1982 canceled those promised increases, so the deductions under the 150 percent method will continue.

DEPRECIATION DISCLOSURES

Information about depreciation practices and amounts has always been of prime interest to financial statement readers. The Accounting Principles Board recognized this in Opinion No. 12 [1967] by saying:

> Because of the significant effects on financial position and results of operations of the depreciation method or methods used, the following disclosures should be made in the financial statements or in notes thereto:
> a. Depreciation expense for the period,
> b. Balances of major classes of depreciable assets, by nature or function, at the balance-sheet date,
> c. Accumulated depreciation, either by major classes of depreciable assets or in total, at the balance-sheet date, and
> d. A general description of the method or methods used in computing depreciation with respect to major classes of depreciable assets.

APB Opinion No. 22, *Disclosure of Accounting Policies* [1972], cites depreciation methods as an example of disclosure commonly required to be made.

FASB Statement No. 33 [1979] requires supplementary disclosure by large firms of depreciation on both a constant dollar basis and on a current cost basis. In addition, the current cost of the plant "assets' remaining service potential" must be included in the supplementary disclosure.

SPECIAL DEPRECIATION
ACCOUNTING PROBLEMS

Correction of Misestimates of Service Life or Salvage Value. The first step in the depreciation process as described in the previous sections is the estimation of service life and salvage value. All of the previous discussion of depreciation methods assumes that the initial estimates will prove to be correct. The probability of this being true is small.

Misestimates of the useful life of an asset may become apparent at any time during its life. It is usually possible to improve the degree of accuracy of the estimates as the time of retirement approaches. If it appears that the misestimate will be relatively minor, an adjustment usually is not made. If the misestimate appears to be material, corrective action must be taken if the effect of the previous estimation error is to be kept at a minimum. The generally accepted procedure for treating revisions of estimates is prescribed in APB Opinion No. 20 [1971] and reaffirmed in FASB Statement No. 16 [1977]. The procedure makes no adjustment for the past misestimate, but spreads the remaining undepreciated balance less the revised estimate of salvage value over the new estimate of remaining service life of the asset. To illustrate the accounting for changes in periodic depreciation, assume the following facts. An office machine was purchased on January 1, 19X0 for $74,000. It was estimated that the machine would be operated for 8 years, with a salvage value of $2,000. On December 31, 19X3, before the books are closed for the year, it is found that in the light of presently available evidence, a total useful life of 12 years, with the same salvage value of $2,000, would be a more reasonable estimate. The depreciation charge recorded for each of the years from 19X0 through 19X2 under the straight-line method would have been $9,000 [= ($74,000 − $2,000)/ 8].

If the revised estimate of service life were ignored, the original annual depreciation charge of $9,000 would be continued through 19X7. The next 4 years would receive no charge to operations for the use of the machine. The Accumulated Depreciation account would remain undisturbed for those years until the machine was retired from service. Thus, during the last 4 years that the machine was in service, no charge would be made for depreciation.

The accepted procedure for recognizing this substantial increase in service life is to revise the future depreciation so that the correct total will presumably be accumulated in the Accumulated Depreciation account at the end of the revised service life. In our example, the total amount of acquisition cost yet to be depreciated before the 19X3 adjustments is $45,000 [= $74,000 − $2,000 − (3 × $9,000)]. The new estimate of the *remaining* life is 9 years, so the new annual depreciation charge is $5,000 (= $45,000/9). The only change in the accounting procedure is to substitute the new amount of $5,000 for the former annual depreciation of $9,000. The depreciation entry on December 31, 19X3, and each year thereafter, would be

Depreciation Expense	5,000	
Accumulated Depreciation		5,000
To record depreciation on a revised basis.		

Repairs and Replacements. As Chapter 19 indicated, it is frequently difficult to distinguish between repairs, which are charged to expense, and replacements and improvements, which are capitalized. Whether an item is treated as a repair or a replacement frequently depends on the detail of the recording of plant assets. If plant assets are defined in terms of complete units, such as an airplane or a building, the cost of a new engine or of a new roof is treated as a repair. On the other hand, if plant assets are recorded in greater detail in terms of structural elements subject to separate depreciation, then the cost of replacing such items is not treated as a repair but is capitalized in the plant asset accounts.

If an item is treated as a replacement, the depreciation accounts are affected. The preferred treatment is to retire the old asset by a credit to a plant account, a debit to Accumulated Depreciation, a debit to an asset account for the proceeds of retirement, if any, and a debit or credit to Gain or Loss on Retirement. Then the cost of the new element is recognized by a debit to a plant account for the amount paid, or to be paid, for the new element. The new amount in the plant account forms the basis for subsequent depreciation charges.

An alternative treatment for replacements results in the cost of the new element being debited to Accumulated Depreciation (with a credit to Cash or other means of payment), and no other entry is made. This approach is likely to be followed when there is a replacement that extends the estimated service life of the asset. It is viewed as a recovery of past depreciation charges. This approach has little conceptual justification, because even if the replacement element were fully depreciated, the changing cost of elements of plant makes it most unlikely that the new cost would equal past depreciation. This approach may, however, be a practicable way of accounting for the replacement if the accumulated depreciation on the item replaced is not known.

Catch-up Depreciation in Current Cost Accounting. Because accountants usually want to show both original cost and accumulated depreciation for plant assets, the accounting for them on a current cost basis presents some problems that do not arise in current cost accounting for inventories or other assets. These problems are sometimes described as problems of "catch-up depreciation" or "backlog depreciation." The problem can be seen more clearly by use of an example.

Assume that the Victoria Corporation has an asset that was purchased on January 1, 19X0, for $25,000, with an estimated service life of 10 years and no salvage value. At December 31, 19X2, the asset is 30 percent depreciated and its replacement cost is $40,000; at December 31, 19X3, it is 40 percent depreciated and its replacement cost is $46,000. Accumulated depreciation on a current cost basis at December 31, 19X2, is $12,000 (= .30 × $40,000), and at December 31, 19X3, is $18,400 (= .40 × $46,000). Exhibit 7 shows the balance sheet data with regard to the asset. The accumulated depreciation on a current cost basis grows by $6,400 during 19X3 (= $18,400 − $12,000). Yet the entry to record depreciation charges for the year on a current cost basis, with depreciation based on average replacement cost during the year as required by FASB Statement No. 33, is $4,300. The entry would be

Depreciation Based on Historical Cost................	2,500	
Additional Depreciation Based on Current Cost	1,800	
Accumulated Depreciation		4,300

Current cost depreciation is 10% of $43,000, or $4,300, which is $1,800 greater than historical cost depreciation.

EXHIBIT 7

VICTORIA CORPORATION
Assumed Data for Catch-up Depreciation

	Dec. 31, 19X2, 30% depreciated		Dec. 31, 19X3, 40% depreciated	
	Historical cost	Current cost	Historical cost	Current cost
Plant asset	$25,000	$40,000	$25,000	$46,000
Accumulated depreciation	7,500	12,000	10,000	18,400
Net plant	$17,500	$28,000	$15,000	$27,600

The difference between the $6,400 increase in the Accumulated Depreciation account and the $4,300 credit to that account for the year, or $2,100, represents the amount of catch-up depreciation.

The catch-up depreciation is treated as an offset to the unrealized holding gain on the asset. The replacement cost increased by $6,000 (= $46,000 − $40,000) during the year, but the unrealized holding gain recognized is only $3,900 (= $6,000 − $2,100). If an entry were made, it would be

Plant Asset	6,000	
Accumulated Depreciation		2,100
Unrealized Holding Gain		3,900

To recognize increase in replacement cost of asset and record catch-up depreciation, leaving a net unrealized holding gain of $3,900.

Part of the unrealized holding gain is realized during the year in an amount equal to the excess of replacement cost depreciation over historical cost depreciation, $1,800 in the example. If an entry were made, it would be

Unrealized Holding Gain	1,800	
Realized Holding Gain		1,800

An alternative treatment for catch-up depreciation would be to include it in depreciation charges for the year. If that were done, the depreciation entry in the example would become

Depreciation Based on Historical Cost	2,500	
Additional Depreciation on a Current Cost Basis	3,900	
Accumulated Depreciation		6,400

This procedure was followed in France in the 1950s when assets were revalued (a process described as "revalorization"), but it is not permitted under the terms of FASB Statement No. 33.

GROUP AND COMPOSITE DEPRECIATION

The previous sections discussed depreciation calculated on individual assets, the "unit basis." Many companies, however, find it advantageous to account for certain kinds of assets on a group or composite basis. *Group basis* and *group method* refer to depreciation of a collection of assets that are similar in nature, such as sewing machines in a shoe factory; *composite method* refers to depreciation of a collection of assets that are dissimilar, such as all equipment used in manufacturing shoes. From an accounting standpoint there is no distinction between the group and composite methods. The same procedures are followed and the same entries are made for both. The Internal Revenue Service permits the use of the group and composite basis as well as the unit basis.

Calculation of Group and Composite Depreciation Rates. The procedures for both group and composite depreciation are generally the same. First, find a group depreciation rate. Second, in each year, multiply that rate by the acquisition cost of the assets remaining in the group to find the depreciation charge for the year. When an asset is retired from the group, remove its cost from the asset account and remove sufficient amounts from the Accumulated Depreciation account so that there is no gain or loss upon retirement of the asset.

Three methods of finding the group depreciation rate are described and then illustrated. An additional method is permitted in the tax law; the rate is the reciprocal of the longest-lived asset in the group. This rate would yield results that are so "nonconservative" that the method is generally held to be not in conformity with generally accepted accounting principles; it is used for tax purposes extremely rarely in cases where the taxpayer wishes to reduce the amount of depreciation expense allowed. The three methods of finding the ratio are to:

1. Compute the group depreciation rate as the reciprocal of the unweighted average life of assets in the group. This method can be used for groups of assets with similar lives.

2. Compute a depreciation rate as the ratio of the sum of each asset's annual depreciation charge divided by the acquisition cost of the entire group. This method is most often used in practice. It is somewhat simpler than the third method, below, and more accurate than the first method.

3. Compute a weighted-average depreciation rate for the group taking into account, for each asset, both its cost and its life.

All of these methods work similarly when the assets have the same life. To the degree that the lives of the assets in the group differ, the methods give different results. Only the third method will yield no gain or loss upon retirement of the last asset when asset retirements exactly match the original estimates.

Exhibit 8 illustrates the three methods of finding the group depreciation rate. We assume a group of assets costing $75,000 acquired on January 1. Estimated salvage value of the individual assets sum to $4,800, so the amount to be depreciated is $70,200.

In general, the group need not survive intact from the day it is acquired until the day it is retired. Assets can be added to the group or retired from the group at any time. The dollar amount of the depreciation charge will change as the assets in the group change, but the depreciation rate, once found, is generally used throughout the life of the group. It should be recomputed if the composition of the group changes substantially.[6]

---

[6]Note that the procedure for calculating depreciation on a straight-line basis under the composite method differs in one important way from that used in the unit method. In the unit method, the service life of the asset being depreciated is estimated. The depreciation rate is the reciprocal of the service life. The depreciation charge for the year is found as this rate multiplied by the *depreciable basis* (= acquisition cost less salvage value). In the composite method, the depreciation rate is calculated and applied to *acquisition cost*, not the depreciable basis.

EXHIBIT 8   Three Methods of Computing the Group Depreciation Rate

| | | Assumptions | | | |
| | Acquisition | Estimated salvage | Amount to be | Estimated service life | Annual straight-line |
Machine number	cost	value	depreciated	in years	depreciation
101	$15,000	$1,800	$13,200	8	$1,650
102	22,500	1,500	21,000	10	2,100
103	28,500	1,500	27,000	12	2,250
104	9,000	0	9,000	5	1,800
Totals	$75,000	$4,800	$70,200		$7,800

1. From average life of items

$$\text{Group Depreciation Rate} = \frac{1}{(8 + 10 + 12 + 5)/4} = 11.4\% \text{ per Year}$$

2. From ratio of sum of individual depreciation charges to cost of assets in group

$$\text{Group Depreciation Rate} = \frac{\$1,650 + \$2,100 + \$2,250 + \$1,800}{\$15,000 + \$22,500 + \$28,500 + \$9,000}$$

$$= \frac{\$7,800}{\$75,000} = 10.4\% \text{ per Year}$$

3. From weighted-average cost and life for each asset

Year of group's life	Cost of machines in use during year
1...	$ 75,000[a]
2...	75,000
3...	75,000
4...	75,000
5...	75,000
6...	66,000[b]
7...	66,000
8...	66,000
9...	51,000[c]
10..	51,000
11..	28,500[d]
12..	28,500
	$732,000

$$\text{Group Depreciation Rate} = \frac{\text{Costs to Be Depreciated}}{\text{Cost of Assets in Use, Summed over All Years of Group's Life}}$$

$$= \frac{\$70,200}{\$732,000} = 9.6\% \text{ per Year}$$

[a]Cost of machines 101, 102, 103, and 104.
[b]Cost of machines 101, 102, and 103.
[c]Cost of machines 102 and 103.
[d]Cost of machine 103.

Recording Group and Composite Depreciation. The year's depreciation charge is calculated as either (1) some fraction of the acquisition cost of the assets in the group (if the straight-line method is used), or (2) some fraction of the book value of the assets in the group (if the declining-balance method is used). The depreciation charge can never be larger than the current book value of the assets in the group.

The major difference between group (or composite) depreciation and unit methods is the treatment of asset retirements. The group method assumes, in effect, that although items have the same expected service life, some individual items will be retired earlier than average and others will remain in use longer than average. Items retired from a group are assumed to be sold, or otherwise disposed of, at *book value*. Consequently, a gain or loss is not recognized upon retiring assets from a group until either (1) the last item in the group has been retired, (2) the group has a book value of zero, or (3) accumulated depreciation after acquisition date becomes zero as a result of dispositions, whichever of these three comes first. There is not uniform agreement on criterion (3) for recognizing a loss. Some would debit the Accumulated Depreciation account with the cost less proceeds of disposition, thereby creating a debit balance in the Accumulated Depreciation account. Following this procedure, recognition of loss would be deferred until one of the first two criteria was met.

Composite Depreciation Journal Entries. Journal entries for the first 3 years of life of the group of assets assumed in Exhibit 8 are illustrated below. The group is assumed to have been acquired January 1, 19X0. We use the second method of finding the depreciation charge, 10.4 percent, in this example. Machine 104 is sold at December 31, 19X1, yielding cash proceeds of $4,000. A new machine costing $12,000 is acquired and added to the composite group at that date. New acquisitions for a given group do not alter the depreciation rate under the composite method for that group, so no information on the estimated service life of the new machine is needed. The example assumes that all depreciation charges are product costs.

Dec. 31, 19X0	Work-in-Process Inventory	7,800	
	Accumulated Depreciation		7,800
Dec. 31, 19X1	Work-in-Process Inventory	7,800	
	Accumulated Depreciation		7,800
	Cash	4,000	
	Accumulated Depreciation	5,000	
	Machinery and Equipment		9,000
	Machine 104 is retired. The debit to Accumulated Depreciation is the amount that will result in no gain or loss on retirement being recognized.		
	Machinery and Equipment	12,000	
	Cash and Payables		12,000
	Machine 105 is acquired.		

Dec. 31, 19X2	Work-in-Process Inventory	8,112	
	Accumulated Depreciation		8,112

Depreciation at 10.4% on new cost of
$78,000 (= $75,000 − $9,000 +
$12,000).

Flow assumption for retirements. In the preceding example, the specific asset retired was identified and removed from the composite account. Group depreciation generally assumes that the items in the group are so sufficiently alike that the time-saving method of group depreciation is warranted. Therefore, the burdensome task of determining which particular assets have been retired and their original cost is not necessary. Rather, a flow assumption can be made, much the same as the flow assumption made in valuing inventories.

The easiest flow assumption to implement in group depreciation, and the one most consistent with the theory of group depreciation, is the weighted-average flow assumption. Thus, for example, assume that a group consists of 1,000 telephone poles, which were purchased at many different times and together originally cost $160,000. If 150 poles are retired during a period, the weighted-average flow assumption would imply that $24,000 (= $160,000 × 150/1,000) of acquisition costs are retired.

When the group consists of relatively unlike items, such as a group of all office furniture and equipment, then a FIFO (first-in, first-out) flow assumption is easier to implement. For example, as typewriters are retired, we assume that the first typewriter purchased is the first retired, and so on.

RETIREMENT AND REPLACEMENT SYSTEMS

The depreciation methods considered thus far assign the depreciable basis to the periods benefited by the asset in a systematic and rational manner. Two alternative methods recognize expense, not by period of use, but only when the asset is retired. These two methods are the retirement method and the replacement method. These alternatives are frequently called "depreciation methods," although strictly speaking, they do not "allocate cost to periods of benefit" and are not, therefore, depreciation methods. The Internal Revenue Code, for example, calls them depreciation methods.

The retirement method charges the cost of the asset retired, less any salvage proceeds, to expense in the period of retirement. The replacement method charges the acquisition cost of the asset that replaces the retired asset, less the salvage proceeds of the retired asset, to expense in the period the replacement asset is acquired. In neither case is any depreciation recognized during the periods of use of the plant asset. Under the replacement method, the book value of the asset account at all times is equal to the full acquisition cost of the first units of property of each type acquired. Under the retirement method, the book value of the asset account for all periods after the replacement occurs is equal to the full cost of the replacement assets less the salvage proceeds of the assets retired. The retirement method corresponds to line N in Exhibits 1 and

2. Under the replacement method, whenever an asset is replaced, the cost of the replacement asset is charged to expense, which corresponds to line E in those exhibits.

The retirement and replacement methods are sometimes used in public utility and railroad accounting, where large numbers of interrelated, relatively low-cost items must be accounted for, such as telephone poles or railroad tracks and ties. These methods are also frequently used for low-cost items such as hand tools. As an example, if 10 telephone poles are acquired in 19X0 for $60 each and are replaced in 19X5 for $100 each when the salvage value of the old poles is $5 each, the accounting would be as follows:

Retirement Method

Plant Assets	600	
Cash		600
To acquire assets in 19X0.		

Retirement Expense	550	
Salvage Receivable	50	
Plant Assets		600
To record retirement and expense in 19X5.		

Plant Assets	1,000	
Cash		1,000
To record acquisition of new assets in 19X5.		

Replacement Method

Plant Assets	600	
Cash		600
To acquire assets in 19X0.		

Replacement Expense	950	
Salvage Receivable	50	
Cash		1,000
To record replacement expense on old assets in amount quantified by net cost of replacement in year 19X5.		

The retirement method is like FIFO in that the cost of the first assets is recorded as expense, and the cost of the second assets is put on the balance sheet. The replacement method is like LIFO (last-in, first-out) in that the cost of the second assets determines the expense and the cost of the first assets remains on the balance sheet.

DEPRECIATION AND CASH FLOWS

Chapter 3 noted that, in the statement of changes in financial position, depreciation is added back to net income in calculating funds provided by operations. It is an expense that does not use funds currently. Because it is added back to net income, the financial press often defines funds from operations as net income plus depreciation. This leads some financial writers to describe depreciation as a "source of funds." Such a description is clearly and unquestionably wrong. Funds from operations come from revenues from customers, not by making accounting entries. In fact, depreciation expense results from an outflow of funds in an earlier period that is only now being recognized as an operating expense. The following example illustrates the fact that depreciation does not produce funds. Assume first that the Jonathan Manufacturing Company has net income in 19X0 of $20,000, resulting from revenues of $125,000, expenses other than depreciation of $95,000, and $10,000 of depreciation. Now assume that depreciation increases to $25,000 while other expenses and revenues are unchanged; net income is $5,000. (Ignore income taxes in both examples.) Exhibit 9 shows that changes in depreciation do not affect funds from operations; funds from operations would be the same, $30,000 in both examples.

Depreciation does help determine cash flow, however, by its effect on the measurement of taxable income and thus tax expense. The more rapid the rate of depreciation charges for tax purposes, the slower the rate of tax payments. For this reason, accelerating depreciation for tax purposes stimulates acquisition of depreciable assets and is viewed as significant in increasing the rate of capital formation. In the United States in the last third of a century, as well as in most other Western countries, there has been much tinkering with the depreciation provisions (sometimes called "capital consumption allowances" or "cost recovery systems") of the tax laws to stimulate new investment and to speed up the rate of economic growth.

EXHIBIT 9   Impact of Depreciation on Funds from Operations

JONATHAN MANUFACTURING COMPANY
Year 19X0

Income statement		Funds from operations	
		Depreciation $10,000	
Revenues.	$125,000	Net income	$20,000
Expenses except		Add back expenses	
depreciation.	(95,000)	not using working	
	$ 30,000	capital:	
Depreciation expense	(10,000)	Depreciation	10,000
Net income	$ 20,000	Total funds from	
		operations	$30,000
		Depreciation $25,000	
Revenues.	$125,000	Net income	$ 5,000
Expenses except		Add back expenses	
depreciation.	(95,000)	not using working	
	$ 30,000	capital:	
Depreciation expense	(25,000)	Depreciation	25,000
Net income	$ 5,000	Total funds from	
		operations	$30,000

BIBLIOGRAPHY

American Institute of Certified Public Accountants, *Accounting Terminology Bulletin No. 1* (AICPA, 1953).

Accounting Principles Board (AICPA), *Omnibus Opinion—1967*, Opinion No. 12 (APB, 1967).

——, *Accounting Changes*, Opinion No. 20 (APB, 1971).

——, *Disclosure of Accounting Policies*, Opinion No. 22 (APB, 1972).

Anton, H. R., "Depreciation, Cost Allocation and Investment Decisions," *Accounting Research*, vol. 7 (April 1956), pp. 117–134.

Davidson, S., and D. F. Drake, "Capital Budgeting and the 'Best' Tax Depreciation Method," *Journal of Business*, vol. 34 (October 1961), pp. 442–452.

——, "The 'Best' Tax Depreciation Method—1964," *Journal of Business*, vol. 37 (July 1964), pp. 258–260.

Financial Accounting Standards Board, *Prior Period Adjustments*, Statement of Financial Accounting Standards No. 16 (FASB, 1977).

——, *Financial Reporting and Changing Prices*, Statement of Financial Accounting Standards No. 33 (FASB, 1979).

Reynolds, I. N., "Selecting the Proper Depreciation Method," *The Accounting Review*, vol. 36 (April 1961), pp. 239–248.

Terborgh, G., *Realistic Depreciation Policy* (Machinery and Allied Products Institute, Washington, D.C., 1954).

Thomas, A. L., *Allocation Problem in Financial Accounting*, Studies in Accounting Research No. 3 (American Accounting Association, 1969); and Studies in Accounting Research No. 9 (American Accounting Association, 1974).

U.S. Treasury Department, *Depreciation Guidelines and Rules* (Washington, D.C., 1964).

Vancil, R. F., and R. L. Weil, "Current Replacement Cost Accounting, Depreciable Assets, and Distributable Income," *Financial Analysts Journal*, July–August 1976, pp. 38–45.

Wright, F. K., "Towards a General Theory of Depreciation," *Journal of Accounting Research*, vol. 2 (Spring 1964), pp. 80–90.

CHAPTER **21**

Goodwill and

Other Intangibles

Dennis R. Beresford
Partner, Ernst & Whinney

Richard H. Moseley
Manager, Ernst & Whinney

INTRODUCTION

Because there is no generally accepted definition, intangibles are frequently defined by example. As Hatfield noted more than 50 years ago:

> Intangible assets are defined as meaning patents, copyrights, secret processes and formulas, goodwill, trademarks, trade brands, franchises, and other like property. The phrase is not particularly appropriate and, except by enumeration, the separation between tangible and intangible assets is not easily made. Accounts receivable are considered tangible assets, although literally there is nothing tangible about them. Real estate is considered typically tangible, a franchise intangible. But there is no real difference between them as regards tangibility, materiality, or realness.... While the term intangible assets is without etymological significance, it is still of use as a collective term, in general embracing the items given in the definition just quoted [Hatfield, 1927, p. 111].

This description is as accurate today as when it was written. Since then, however, a vast amount of time and resources have been devoted to discussions of intangible assets, particularly goodwill.

This chapter comprises three major sections. The first section discusses the various conceptual arguments that have generated much of the controversy in accounting for goodwill. It concludes with the accounting requirements for goodwill as they exist under generally accepted accounting principles (GAAP). The second section discusses aspects of intangibles (other than goodwill), including detailed discussions of specific intangible assets (e.g., patents, copyrights). The last section discusses a number of items that are common to both goodwill and other intangibles (e.g., amortization, income tax treatment, and financial statement presentation).

Partnership goodwill is discussed in Chapter 30. This chapter concentrates on corporate goodwill. Leaseholds, which are often considered intangible, are discussed in Chapter 24.

GOODWILL

The Financial Accounting Standards Board (FASB) has identified a number of common characteristics of goodwill:

> 1. Goodwill relates to a business as a whole and, accordingly, is incapable of separate existence and of being sold apart from the identifiable assets of the business.
> 2. Individual factors that may contribute to goodwill are not susceptible to independent valuation by any method or formula. Their values can be determined only as an aggregate in relation to a business as a whole.
> 3. The future benefits of goodwill recognized in a combination may have no relationship to the costs incurred in the development of that goodwill.

Goodwill may exist in the absence of specific costs to develop it [FASB Discussion Memorandum, 1976, p. 47].[1]

Nature. Because there is no precise, accepted definition of goodwill, many articles focus on the different aspects of its nature. A brief examination of the nature of goodwill will thus help to provide insight into the problems of defining this important intangible asset.

Master valuation account. The master valuation account concept results from combining two earlier views of goodwill, the going value and the unrecorded assets concepts.

Going value. According to the going value concept, goodwill is not a separate producing asset per se (i.e., like cash or inventory), but a special valuation account representing the excess of the value of the combined assets of the entity over the sum of their individual values ("the whole is greater than the sum of its parts").

Unrecorded assets. According to the unrecorded assets theory, goodwill is a measure of unrecorded assets, such as a favorable line of credit, superior management, loyal customers, or a favorable location. These unrecorded assets may result from a variety of factors—advertising costs, a reputation for proper business conduct, or acceptance of product differentiation in the marketplace.

The master valuation account concept developed because of the inability to measure or allocate the value of goodwill to its various individual components (i.e., going value component and unrecorded asset component). The master valuation account concept implies that goodwill is a common or joint value that cannot be properly allocated to individual categories of assets. This view is reflected in Canning's [1929, p. 39] observation: "Elementary components of goodwill are interesting to speculate about but only the mass resultant, in any given enterprise, is capable of statistical generalization."

Excess earnings. Under the excess earnings concept, goodwill is the present value of the excess future earnings of the business. Proponents of this view believe that the going value and unrecorded assets concepts of goodwill are evidence of an entity's ability to generate excess future earnings. Catlett and Olson [1968, p. 12] expressed this opinion:

> In today's business environment the earning power concept of goodwill is the most relevant. The sales and purchases of business enterprises as a whole are motivated primarily by the expectation of future profits. Further, the value established for a business in a sale-purchase transaction reflects evaluations as to the earning power of the business. To the extent the value of the business as a whole exceeds the value of its separable resources and property rights, the earning power of the business evident in the transaction must relate to other attributes. Goodwill thereby becomes associated

---

[1]This and all subsequent citations from the FASB are copyrighted by the Financial Accounting Standards Board, High Ridge Park, Stamford, Connecticut 06905, and are reprinted with permission. Copies of the complete documents are available from the FASB.

with the variety of interrelated intangible attributes which in the aggregate derive value from an evaluation of future earning potentialities of the business enterprise.

The Internal Revenue Service endorses this concept in Revenue Ruling 59-60 [26 CFR 20.2031-2], which defines goodwill as the expectation of excess earnings above a fair return on the capital invested in the means of production.

Valuation. One of the basic concepts of accounting is that assets should be valued initially at their acquisition cost. Therefore, only goodwill that is acquired (i.e., purchased goodwill) is recorded in the accounting records of an entity. This concept simplifies a number of the valuation problems surrounding goodwill. For example, although an entity's superior management ability might be one of its most valuable assets, it would not be recorded as goodwill because it is nearly impossible to assign a verifiable cost to management ability.

The recording issue becomes less clear when advertising expenditures are examined. Creating a favorable customer reaction that will convince people to keep returning is often the primary purpose for advertising expenditures. These are not, however, recorded as goodwill. This presents a conceptual problem: Expenditures to acquire one of the basic types of goodwill are not recognized as a purchase of goodwill. It is the measurement problem that makes the capitalization of these types of expenditures impracticable. How much goodwill was created by the expenditure? What period will be benefited by the expenditure? Having no basis for answering these questions objectively, accountants have taken a conservative view and immediately recognized advertising and other goodwill-creating expenditures as expenses.

Thus hampered by measurement limitations, accounting assumes that goodwill is purchased and recorded as part of the consolidation process. Therefore, the discussion that follows concentrates on consolidated goodwill only.

Consolidated goodwill is valued in two ways, by the direct method and by the residual method.

Direct method. Under the direct method of valuing goodwill, which is closely related to the excess earnings concept, goodwill is considered to be a separate, distinct, and productive asset of the company. Therefore, its fair value must be determined separately.

Excess earnings generally are regarded as the earnings over and above those of similar businesses. "Similar businesses" are those in the same industry facing the same elements of risk and uncertainty. The earnings of similar businesses may be in excess of the earnings that would accrue to the individual assets if they were used independent of an organized business. To measure such excess earnings, accountants would have to adjust for different accounting procedures and for different financial structures, so that both earnings and risks would be comparable among the similar businesses. In this sense, the excess earnings, which reflect goodwill, are relative. Suppose, for example, that other businesses within an industry were to increase earnings, whereas the earnings of one company in the industry with goodwill remained unchanged. This company's goodwill would decrease in value merely because of the relative increase in the earnings of competitors in similar businesses.

Because the price to be paid for goodwill is a payment for anticipated future excess earnings, there has to be a way to reduce these future excess profits to their present value. The basic formula for the computation of such goodwill is

$$G = \frac{D - rC}{j}$$

where D = expected future annual earnings
r = constant annual rate of return typically earned in the industry
C = amount of the capital of the business
j = goodwill capitalization rate (i.e., the annual rate of return to be earned on the goodwill)

For example, assume that a company's expected future earnings are $80,000. The company has capital of $400,000, capitalizes goodwill at a rate of 15 percent, and operates in an industry whose typical rate of return is 12 percent a year. Goodwill is computed as follows:

$$G = \frac{D - rC}{j} = \frac{\$80,000 - .12(\$400,000)}{.15} = \frac{\$32,000}{.15} = \$213,333$$

This method is consistent with the "formula" approach described by the Internal Revenue Service in Revenue Ruling 68-609 [26 CFR 1.1001-1] for determining the fair market value of the intangible assets of a business.

Clearly, computing goodwill by the direct method depends on the values assigned to D, r, C, and j—which may be subject to considerable differences in opinion.

Modifications of the basic formula may, however, provide a somewhat more realistic estimate of the value of goodwill. For example, goodwill may be measured as the present value of the average of the high and low estimates of D, r, C, and j by years for various possible lives of the business. Assigning goodwill a range of values, whether or not supported by probability measures of each value, is a more realistic measure than such frequently used methods as multiplying excess earnings by an arbitrary number of years (typically 3 to 5). It is still, however, a subjective estimate.

Proponents of the direct method argue that goodwill, like any other enterprise asset, must be valued independently. Using any other valuation method, they believe, violates this basic concept.

Residual method. The residual valuation method is related to the master valuation account concept of goodwill. All the individual tangible assets and liabilities, and identifiable intangible assets, are assigned current values. The difference between the purchase price and the current values of the net assets is identified as the cost of goodwill.

For example, assume that a company acquires 100 percent of another company's stock for $1 million in cash. After all assets and liabilities have been assigned their current value, the acquired company has net assets of $925,000. Goodwill recognized from this acquisition is $75,000 (= $1,000,000 − $925,000). Computing the value of goodwill by the residual method obviously depends on the reliability of the various estimates of current value.

Proponents of the residual method argue that it is more objective than the direct method because it involves fewer variables. They argue that the uncertainties involved in the direct valuation of goodwill preclude any reasonably objective measure.

An example contrasting the two valuation methods will help clarify the differences between them. Assume that Company X purchases 100 percent of the stock of Company Y for $600,000 in cash. Company Y's assets and liabilities at historical cost and current value are presented in columns 1 and 2 of Exhibit 1. Company Y's expected annual earnings are $60,000, the average rate of return for its industry is 10 percent, and goodwill is capitalized at a rate of 20 percent. The direct valuation of goodwill, using the formula approach discussed previously, is computed as follows:

$$ G = \frac{D - rC}{j} = \frac{\$60,000 - .10(\$500,000)}{.20} = \frac{\$10,000}{.20} = \$50,000 $$

Thus, the direct valuation of goodwill equals $50,000. The current value of Company Y's net assets, including the direct valuation of goodwill, totals $575,000 (column 3). But Company X is purchasing the net assets for $600,000. What happens to the $25,000 difference between the current value of the net assets, including the direct value of goodwill ($575,000), and the acquisition cost ($600,000)? This excess normally is allocated on a pro rata basis to the individual nonmonetary items (including goodwill) of the acquired company (see column 4). Under the direct method, total goodwill recognized in this business combination is $52,016 (column 5).

EXHIBIT 1   Methods of Valuing Goodwill

	Historical cost (1)	Current value (2)	Direct method Current value (3)	Direct method Allocation of excess (4)	Direct method Total (5)	Residual method (6)
			Assets			
Cash	$150,000	$150,000	$150,000	$ -0-	$150,000	$150,000
Inventory	150,000	152,500	152,500	6,149[a]	158,649	152,500
Property, plant, and equipment	400,000	415,000	415,000	16,734	431,734	415,000
Identifiable intangibles	-0-	2,500	2,500	101	2,601	2,500
Goodwill.	-0-	-0-	50,000	2,016	52,016	75,000
	$700,000	$720,000	$770,000	$25,000	$795,000	$795,000
			Liabilities			
Debt	200,000	195,000	195,000	-0-	195,000	195,000
Net assets	$500,000	$525,000	$575,000	$25,000	$600,000	$600,000

[a]Computed as follows:

Total Assets ($770,000) − Monetary Assets ($150,000) = Base ($620,000)

($152,500/$620,000) × $25,000 = $6,149

Amounts allocated to other nonmonetary assets are determined in a similar manner.

The residual method of valuing goodwill (i.e., purchase price less current value of net assets acquired) results in total goodwill of $75,000 ($600,000 − $525,000), as shown in column 6.

Measuring current value. The current values assigned to the assets and liabilities of the acquired company are critical in computing the amount of goodwill resulting from a business combination. Using different assumptions to determine current values can result in wide fluctuations in the amount assigned. There are two basic approaches to estimating the current value of nonmonetary assets, current entry value and current exit value.

Current entry value. The current entry valuation approach assigns values to assets based on the current cost of obtaining them. This cost can be measured by reproduction cost or replacement cost. Reproduction cost refers to the cost of replacing the asset with an identical asset. Replacement cost, on the other hand, focuses on replacing the asset with one of equivalent capacity rather than an identical asset.

Current exit value. The current exit valuation concept assigns values to assets based on the amounts that could be received by selling the assets in an orderly liquidation. Quoted market prices for sales of similar assets normally are used as the basis for the current costs—for example, reliable quoted market values for used computer equipment.

Valuing monetary assets and liabilities. The current value of monetary assets and liabilities is assigned based on the present value of the cash inflows or outflows using a current discount rate. Determining the current discount rate is critical for this measurement.

Accounting. Once the amount of goodwill has been computed, one of three approaches can be used to record the goodwill: (1) Recognize an asset, (2) reduce shareholders' equity, or (3) recognize an immediate charge to income.

Recognize as an asset. Much of the discussion in this area has centered around the various definitions of assets. In 1980 the FASB stated that an asset has the following three essential characteristics:

(a) It embodies a probable future benefit that involves a capacity, singly or in combination with other assets, to contribute directly or indirectly to future net cash inflows,

(b) A particular enterprise can obtain the benefit and control others' access to it, and

(c) The transaction or other event giving rise to the enterprise's right to or control of the benefit has already occurred [FASB Concepts Statement No. 3, 1980, p. 9].

Criteria (b) and (c) pose no particular problems for recognizing goodwill as an asset. The event giving rise to the recording of goodwill (the business combination) has already taken place; and control of access to the goodwill is accomplished by not divesting the acquired entity. Criterion (a), however, will not silence the debate on whether goodwill qualifies as an asset.

Most previous definitions have emphasized that an asset was an economic resource with future benefits. The various arguments for recording goodwill as an asset followed these same lines, depending on which of the two major concepts of goodwill was adopted:

Excess earnings. Because goodwill represents excess earnings, it will ultimately either increase cash inflows or reduce cash outflows, or both. Goodwill should thus be treated as an asset.

Valuation account. Intangible resources are used in the generation of income just as tangible assets are. Therefore, goodwill represents future benefits to the company and should be classified as an asset.

These two general arguments still prevail under criterion (a). The future benefits from goodwill may be relatively certain or considerably uncertain. Depending on how the phrase "probable future benefit" is interpreted, goodwill may or may not qualify as an asset. In the final analysis, the FASB's asset definition probably will change few minds regarding the recording of goodwill as an asset.

Reduce shareholders' equity. The supporters of reducing shareholders' equity by the amount of goodwill argue that payments for goodwill represent disbursements for anticipated future earnings. That is, the payment for goodwill is in reality a distribution of anticipated future earnings and should, like any distribution of earnings, be treated as a reduction of shareholders' equity. Catlett and Olson [1968, p. 90] support this position:

> Thus, amounts paid for goodwill in a business combination represent disbursements of a portion of a company's resources . . . in anticipation of future earnings. The disbursement of resources reduces the stockholders' equity in a company's separable resources and property rights by a corresponding amount, and accounting for purchased goodwill as a reduction in stockholders' equity evidences that fact.

Two proposals have been advanced for treating goodwill as a reduction of shareholders' equity. Under the first, an immediate write-off to a shareholders' equity account, goodwill would not appear in the balance sheet. Under the second, goodwill would be shown as a continuing deduction from shareholders' equity in the balance sheet, much like treasury stock. Some favor amortizing this deduction, and others believe it should remain on the balance sheet indefinitely.

Immediate charge to income. Proponents of this method argue that because one cannot objectively associate goodwill with specific future benefits, it should be charged to income immediately. They also point out that this approach would enhance comparability between those companies that have financed growth internally and those companies that have grown through acquisition.

Negative Goodwill. During periods of inflation, the increase in current values of the net assets of an entity often outstrips the fair market value of its stock. Even when a premium is paid to purchase the stock, the current value of the net assets acquired may be in excess of the aggregate cost to acquire the entity. There are two primary means of recording this difference: (1) Recognize it as negative goodwill, and (2) recognize it as a valuation adjustment.

Recognize as negative goodwill. Supporters of this view contend that the excess of net assets over cost is the opposite of positive goodwill and should be accounted for accordingly. Possibilities for recording negative goodwill are exactly the opposite of those previously discussed for positive goodwill, that is, record as a liability, recognize as an addition to shareholders' equity, and immediately add to income. The rationale supporting these three approaches parallels that for positive goodwill.

Recognize as a valuation adjustment. This view of the excess is based on the assertion that in the vast majority of cases, negative goodwill does not exist. Instead, the difference is attributable to an overvaluation of the acquired company's net assets. Others base their support of this concept on the historical cost premise (i.e., the values recorded in the accounting records cannot exceed aggregate cost). There are two alternatives for recording this valuation adjustment. Some favor adjusting the values assigned to the identifiable assets and liabilities; others believe the difference should be recorded as a separate line item in the balance sheet, which is essentially the same treatment afforded negative goodwill.

Generally Accepted Accounting Principles for Goodwill. The discussion of goodwill thus far has centered on the various positions that have generated much debate and controversy in the accounting profession. With Opinions No. 16 and 17, issued in 1970, the Accounting Principles Board (APB) resolved the issues (although not the controversy) by establishing generally accepted accounting principles for the initial recording of and subsequent accounting for goodwill.

Nature of goodwill. APB Opinion No. 16 established GAAP for accounting for purchased goodwill. Under the pooling-of-interests method, goodwill is not recorded; it can result only from a combination recorded under the purchase method. "A difference between the sum of the assigned costs of the tangible and identifiable intangible assets acquired less liabilities assumed and the cost of the group is evidence of unspecified intangible values" [APB Opinion No. 16, 1970, par. 68]. The APB thus viewed goodwill in the master valuation account sense rather than as excess future earnings.

Valuation of goodwill. The APB endorsed the residual method of valuing goodwill (i.e., purchase price less current value of net assets acquired equals goodwill). It stated that " ... the excess of the cost of the acquired company over the sum of the amounts assigned to identifiable assets acquired less liabilities assumed should be recorded as goodwill" [APB Opinion No. 16, 1970, par. 87]. It also specifies how fair values are to be measured in a number of instances:

Marketable securities at net realizable value.
Receivables at the present value of inflows using a current discount rate.
Inventories at estimated selling price (current exit value) less costs to complete, costs of disposal, and a reasonable profit allowance.
Plant and equipment at current replacement cost.
Other assets, including identifiable intangibles, at appraised values. Presumably current entry or current exit values could be used in determining appraised values.
Liabilities at the present value of outflows based on a current discount rate.

Accounting for goodwill. APB Opinion No. 17 [1970, par. 09] states: " . . . a company should record as assets the costs of intangible assets acquired from others, including goodwill acquired in a business combination." Thus, reducing income by an immediate charge and reducing shareholders' equity are not acceptable methods of accounting for goodwill.

Negative goodwill. In Opinion No. 16 [1970, par. 91], the APB endorsed the valuation adjustment concept of accounting for the excess of net assets over acquisition cost:

> The value assigned to net assets acquired should not exceed the cost of an acquired company because the general presumption in historical-cost based accounting is that net assets acquired should be recorded at not more than cost. . . . An excess over cost should be allocated to reduce proportionately the values assigned to noncurrent assets (except long-term investments in marketable securities) in determining their fair values (paragraph 87). If the allocation reduces the noncurrent assets to zero value, the remainder of the excess over cost should be classified as a deferred credit and should be amortized systematically to income. . . .

Future Prospects. In August 1976, the FASB issued a Discussion Memorandum (DM) "to determine appropriate financial accounting and reporting standards for business combinations and purchased intangibles within the existing framework of historical-cost-based financial statements" (p. 1).

The DM opened a "Pandora's box" that had been nearly closed since the APB issued Opinions No. 16 and 17. Although accountants were not necessarily satisfied with the treatment afforded business combinations and intangibles in the APB Opinions, they had learned to live with it.

From the time the Board issued the Discussion Memorandum until early 1981, the project remained on the FASB's agenda, with no news of an exposure date for an impending Standard. In early 1981 the FASB removed the project from its agenda, and indicated that it is prepared to deal with practice problems by issuing Interpretations or Technical Bulletins, if necessary. Thus the debate on goodwill is likely to continue into the foreseeable future.

OTHER INTANGIBLES

Much of the controversy surrounding goodwill extends to other intangibles. However, except in the area of amortization versus nonamortization, the arguments are somewhat less fervent.

Valuation

Purchased intangibles. A company may purchase intangibles from others or develop them internally. Purchased intangibles are recorded as assets; internally developed intangibles are not. This position is supported by the APB in Opinion No. 17 [1970, par. 24], which states " . . . a company should record as assets the cost of intangible assets acquired from other enterprises or individuals. Costs of developing, maintaining, or restoring intangible assets which are not specifically identifiable, have indeterminate lives, or are inherent in a continuing business and related to an enterprise as a whole—such as goodwill—should be deducted from income when incurred."

The primary reason for not recording internally developed intangibles is because no objective determination of the amount and future periods benefited can be made for internally developed intangibles. Therefore, such costs are expensed as incurred.

At one time, the treatment of research and development costs was an exception to this general rule. However, in one of its first pronouncements, the FASB prohibited the capitalization of research and development expenditures. The FASB considered four methods of accounting for research and development costs:

(a) Charge all costs to expense when incurred.
(b) Capitalize all costs when incurred.
(c) Capitalize costs when incurred if specified conditions are fulfilled and charge all other costs to expense.
(d) Accumulate all costs in a special category until the existence of future benefits can be determined [FASB Statement No. 2, 1974, par. 37].

The Board selected method (a), citing the uncertainty of future benefits, the lack of relationship between expenditures and benefits, and the difficulty of objectively measuring future benefits. The Board said that no useful purpose is served by allocating the expenses to several accounting periods.

The Discussion Memorandum that preceded issuance of the Exposure Draft and Statement No. 2 included research and development and "similar" costs. The FASB decided not to address "similar" costs in Statement No. 2, and this aspect of the project has been shelved indefinitely.

However, the FASB continued to support the inclusion of purchased intangibles in the asset category. In the same pronouncement, the FASB was careful to make this distinction:

> The costs of intangibles that are purchased from others for use in research and development activities and that have alternative future uses (in research and development projects or otherwise) shall be capitalized and amortized as intangible assets in accordance with *APB Opinion No. 17.* . . .
> However, the costs of intangibles that are purchased from others for a particular research and development project and that have no alternative future uses (in other research and development projects or otherwise) and therefore no separate economic values are research and development costs at the time the costs are incurred [FASB Statement No. 2, 1974, par. 11].

Because purchased intangibles are included as assets, whereas nonpurchased intangibles usually are not, there is a double standard for asset recognition. This makes comparisons among companies difficult. For example, assume that Company A has developed a patent as a result of its own research efforts. The patent would not be shown as an asset in Company A's accounting records (except for any direct costs associated with obtaining the patent). However, were Company A to sell the patent to Company B for $100,000, Company B would record the patent as an asset at its $100,000 cost. Even though the patent remains unchanged, its transfer from the original owner to a new owner for consideration gives rise to the recognition of an asset.

Cost deferral. The cost deferral concept emphasizes income determination and is related directly to the accepted definition of accounting income. The calculation of accounting income is based on the process of matching costs with the revenues to which they relate. When costs are incurred that are expected to benefit revenues of future periods, they may be deferred until the time when they may be "matched" with the related revenues to determine income. The asset classification of the balance sheet can thus be viewed as an array of costs awaiting final disposition through periodic charges against revenues, rather than as an inventory of resources owned by a company.

The relationship between the costs of activities that may be classified as intangibles and the subsequent production of revenues is not always clear-cut, however. With items such as merchandise, it may be possible to trace the accumulation of costs through to the ultimate production of revenues. But activities such as research and development provide merely an increased potential for earning revenue, with no assurance of any favorable results. By issuing Statement No. 2 the FASB, in effect, stated that research and development expenditures could not be properly deferred.

As a part of its conceptual framework project, the FASB is reevaluating the entire recognition process. One of the major areas to be addressed is the matching concept and related cost deferrals.

Determination of cost. If cost is to be used as the basis for recording intangible assets, the cost of these items must be determined. At first it might seem that this would be a simple matter—the cost of an item is the amount paid to acquire it, which should be readily determinable. In the case of intangibles, however, several complexities can arise.

In Accounting Research Study No. 7, Paul Grady [1965, p. 261] states:

> All expenditures incident to the acquisition of an intangible asset are part of its cost. In addition to the price paid to a seller, cost of an intangible may include government fees, attorneys' fees and expenses, experiment and development costs, assignment costs (where royalty and license agreements have been assigned for a consideration) and other expenditures directly identifiable with their acquisition. For example, legal and other expenses of successfully defending against an interference suit in Patent Office proceedings are part of the cost of acquiring a patent.

Special problems could arise when allocating costs of intangible assets acquired in a business combination or as a part of a group of resources. APB Opinion No. 16 [1970] requires that all tangible assets and liabilities and identifiable intangible assets be valued at their current value before the amount of goodwill recorded in a business combination is determined.

Determining the value of some intangible assets may be relatively easy. For example, the values of certain franchises and licenses that are regularly sold may be based on the current market prices of similar intangible assets. Valuing intangible assets using this market value approach is essentially the current entry value concept of valuation.

Other intangible assets are expected to be sold in the near future. In that case, assigning a value based on the expected sales price (current exit value) is acceptable; an example is the contract of a professional athlete.

Frequently, however, intangible assets are unique, and there are no readily available market values. The value of these intangibles can be approximated by estimating the present value of the future cash streams (in the form of revenues or expense savings) that the asset is expected to generate. The appropriate discount rate used to determine the present value should reflect the time value of money, as well as the risk and uncertainty connected with this stream.

Suppose, for example, that a patent is expected to produce royalty income over a 10-year period as shown in the first two columns of Exhibit 2. The royalty income of each year would be multiplied by the present value factor, $(1 + r)^{-n}$, where n is the number of years until the income will be received and r is the discount rate. These factors may be found in tables of present values. Assuming a discount rate of 20 percent to reflect the time value of money as well as the inherent risk in holding this asset, the present value of the stream of royalty income would be calculated as shown in Exhibit 2.

This process is similar in concept to the direct valuation method for goodwill. Again, the validity of the estimate depends on the accuracy of the estimate of royalty income to be received as well as the discount rate selected. It might also be appropriate to estimate a range of royalty income (i.e., high, expected, low), discount each estimate, and determine the average.

Occasionally it is important to establish the value of intangibles after the date of acquisition. For instance, APB Opinion No. 17 [1970] states that the value of future benefits from an intangible may indicate that the unamortized cost should be reduced. This valuation technique may be useful to ascertain if such a write-down is necessary.

EXHIBIT 2   Calculation of Present Value of Royalties[a]

Year (1)	Royalty Income (2)	$(1.20)^{-n}$ (3)	Present value (4)
1..........	$ 8,000	.833	$ 6,664
2..........	18,000	.694	12,492
3..........	25,000	.579	14,475
4..........	30,000	.482	14,460
5..........	34,000	.402	13,668
6..........	43,000	.335	14,405
7..........	44,000	.279	12,276
8..........	39,000	.233	9,087
9..........	27,000	.194	5,238
10..........	12,000	.162	1,944
Present value.			$104,709

[a]Columns 1 and 2, assumed. Column 3, see Table 2 in the Appendix. Column 4 = column 2 X column 3.

Research and Development. FASB Statement No. 2 requires that all research and development costs be charged to expense when incurred. Deciding what constitutes research and development costs may require some judgment, however. In this regard, the FASB has defined research and development as follows:

> (a) *Research* is planned search or critical investigation aimed at discovery of new knowledge with the hope that such knowledge will be useful in developing a new product or service ... or a new process or technique ... or in bringing about a significant improvement to an existing product or process.
>
> (b) *Development* is the translation of research findings or other knowledge into a plan or design for a new product or process or for a significant improvement to an existing product or process whether intended for sale or use. It includes the conceptual formulation, design, and testing of product alternatives, construction of prototypes, and operation of pilot plants. It does not include routine or periodic alterations to existing products, production lines, manufacturing processes, and other on-going operations even though those alterations may represent improvements and it does not include market research or market testing activities [FASB Statement No. 2, 1974, par. 8].

FASB Statement No. 2 provides examples of activities that typically would and would not be included in research and development. The Statement is effective for fiscal years beginning on or after January 1, 1975, but it was retroactive: All research and development costs recognized as assets previous to that date had to be charged to expense.

After the issuance of Statement No. 2, one aspect of research and development costs, computer software, continued to raise certain questions. Therefore, the FASB issued Interpretation No. 6 [1975]. This Interpretation clarifies the accounting treatment afforded the various aspects of computer software. Costs to purchase computer software generally are not considered research and development costs unless the computer software is used solely for research and development purposes with no alternative future use. Costs of purchased research and development software with no alternative use, and research and development costs of internally developed software regardless of its use (e.g., to be marketed or used internally for research and development), should be treated as research and development expenditures and charged to expense when incurred.

Specific Intangibles. The previous discussion applies to most items that can be classified as intangible assets. Some specific items are treated differently. These are discussed below.

Patents. A patent is a legal device giving the holder the exclusive right to use or control an invention. Patents are granted for a period of 17 years, but several factors could make the useful life much shorter.

Although a patent may allow the holder to exclude others from using the process, it does not ensure any economic benefit. If the process is not useful, the patent may have little or no economic value. A patent can also become obsolete by the development of another process that is more economical or otherwise advantageous. If the patent pertains to a product that does not gain consumer acceptance, the patent will be similarly short-lived. Finally, by issuing the patent, the U.S. Patent Office merely indicates its own approval; this grant could be withdrawn through litigation. The cost of a patent should be amortized over the legal life or the economic life, whichever is shorter.

The cost of a patent is not limited to the price paid to the seller. It should also include government fees, attorneys' fees and expenses, and other costs associated with its acquisition. The successful defense of an interference suit should be capitalized as part of the patent cost, whereas the cost of unsuccessful legal suits should be charged to expense.

Because there may not be any connection between the cost of a patent and its value, the unamortized cost should be examined periodically to make sure that it does not exceed the current value. If a patent has lost its commercial value for any reason, its unamortized cost should be written down.

Copyrights. A copyright gives the holder certain rights to published material. In some instances, a copyright does not entitle the holder to the exclusive use of a work, but merely to receive royalty payments from others for public performances.

A copyright is granted to a corporation for a period of 75 years. In some cases (e.g., "classic" songs, books), the work may be expected to have economic value during the entire 75-year period of legal protection. These cases are rare, however, and in most instances the commercial life of a copyright is relatively short. A copyright is granted to an individual for life plus 50 years.

The same factors that determine patent valuations affect the valuations of copyrights as well.

Trademarks and trade names. A trademark is a designation used to identify a particular commercial product or service. Such marks can be registered to provide added legal protection, but common law confers ownership on the earliest continuous user for a class of products in a geographic area. A trade name or brand may similarly be used to designate the products of a particular company.

The economic value of a trademark or trade name stems from its ability to give the user superior earning power. This superior earning power is sometimes ascribed to goodwill. However, whereas goodwill can relate to the excess earning potential of the organization as a whole, a trademark or trade name can presumably be separately identified and possibly transferred to another organization while the original organization continues in existence.

If a trademark or trade name is purchased, its acquisition cost includes the purchase price plus any additional costs of registration, legal fees, and so on. Often, however, valuable trademarks and trade names are developed through years of advertising and customer satisfaction. In such cases, the advertising costs are not included as a cost of the trademarks or trade names but are charged to expense as incurred. Although some future benefits may be obtained from advertising in the form of a valuable trade name, it is extremely difficult to ascertain the relationship between expenditures for advertising and the value of the resultant asset.

Although trademarks and trade names have indefinite useful lives, their economic potency can eventually expire. If customer acceptance wanes or if a company must increase expenditures for advertising to maintain brand loyalty, the trademarks and trade names of a product could have little or no value. In addition, the legal status of these rights may be lost if the company fails to continue their use, if another user successfully challenges them, or if the name becomes the generic term for the product. Thus, the acquisition cost of trademarks and trade names is often amortized over relatively short periods.

For federal income tax purposes, a distinction is made between trademarks and trade names and "trademarks and trade name expenditures." Because trademarks and trade names have indeterminate lives, the direct consideration paid in acquiring such assets cannot be amortized. However, special treatment is afforded trademark and trade name expenditures. Such expenditures may be treated as an asset and amortized over a period of not less than 60 months.

Organization costs. The costs of organizing a corporation are frequently included in intangible assets. These costs include legal fees and other costs of obtaining the corporate charter, raising initial capital, and promoting the enterprise. Some accountants argue that reasonably anticipated losses from operations during the first few years also should be included in organization costs. This viewpoint is not generally accepted, however.

Organization costs may be regarded as having perpetual life, benefiting all the years of corporate existence. For federal income tax purposes, however, such costs of newly formed corporations may be amortized over a period of not less than 60 months. This also is the normal treatment afforded organization costs for financial reporting.

AMORTIZATION AND OTHER MATTERS

Amortization. Once the value of goodwill or other intangibles is recorded, another basic accounting question arises. Should the value be written off or maintained in the accounting records indefinitely? In ARB No. 43 [1953, chap. 5, par. 2], intangible assets were classified for accounting purposes into two categories:

> (a) Those having a term of existence limited by law, regulation, or agreement, or by their nature (such as patents, copyrights, leases, licenses, franchises for a fixed term, and goodwill as to which there is evidence of limited duration);
> (b) Those having no such limited term of existence and as to which there is, at the time of acquisition, no indication of limited life (such as goodwill generally, going value, trade names, secret processes, subscription lists, perpetual franchises, and organization costs).

Although the cost of type (a) intangibles was amortized over the period benefited, type (b) intangibles were not amortized unless it became evident that their term of existence was indeed limited—that they had, in effect, become type (a).

In APB Opinion No. 17 [1970, par. 27], the APB reversed this position for type (b) intangibles, ruling "that the value of intangible assets at any one date eventually disappears and that the recorded costs of intangible assets should be amortized by systematic charges to income over the periods estimated to be benefited." Thus, all intangible assets are regarded as having limited lives, and their costs must be amortized over some relevant period.

Many have argued that a distinction should be made between intangibles with a limited life and intangibles with indeterminate or unlimited lives. Although there seems to be general agreement that intangibles with limited lives should be amortized over the periods benefited, intangibles with indeterminate or unlimited lives have been the subject of much controversy.

Those favoring indefinite maintenance of goodwill base their argument on the premise that because goodwill is not consumed in the operations of the entity, it should not be reduced unless its value definitely decreases. They believe that because goodwill generally has no predictable life, and measurement after the business combination is very subjective, amortization would be arbitrary. They also argue that the results of operations among companies are more comparable when goodwill is not amortized.

Proponents for nonamortization of other intangibles argue that these intangibles should be maintained at cost unless their future benefits diminish below cost. They believe that mandatory amortization is arbitrary and should not apply to intangibles, some of which are increasing in value.

Others believe that goodwill should be amortized in all cases. If goodwill is viewed as a measure of excess earnings, then goodwill is a cost associated with them and should be amortized accordingly. Another argument supporting amortization of goodwill and other intangibles is that because of technological obsolesence and changing economic conditions, all intangibles are likely to decline in value. Therefore, they should be amortized over their estimated useful lives.

When the FASB began reexamining purchased intangibles in 1976, the motor carrier and broadcasting industries commented that motor carrier operating rights and broadcasting licenses were different from other intangibles. These industries made strong cases that their intangibles actually increased in value over time, and therefore should not be amortized. The increase in value can be related to the oligopolistic benefits conferred on them by various governmental licensing agencies.

The Motor Carrier Act of 1980 raised doubts as to the future benefits of motor carriers' interstate operating rights. The Act essentially made it easier to enter into the industry and to expand existing routes. In December 1980, the FASB issued Statement No. 44, which requires the write-off of unamortized costs relating to interstate operating rights.

The newspaper industry presented similar comments to the FASB dealing with goodwill recorded as a result of business combinations. One comment letter indicated that a survey of recent business combinations revealed that approximately 75 percent of the purchase price was allocated to goodwill. The industry strongly believes that the value of these intangible resources increases over time, and therefore amortization of goodwill is not appropriate.

Amortization period. By nature, intangibles' useful lives are subject to great uncertainty. But because APB Opinion No. 17 requires amortization of intangibles over the periods estimated to be benefited, estimating those periods is critical.

The APB suggested that companies determine the period of amortization by considering these and other "pertinent factors":

 a. Legal, regulatory, or contractual provisions may limit the maximum useful life.
 b. Provisions for renewal or extension may alter a specified limit on useful life.
 c. Effects of obsolescence, demand, competition, and other economic factors may reduce a useful life.
 d. A useful life may parallel the service life expectancies of individuals or groups of employees.
 e. Expected actions of competitors and others may restrict present competitive advantages.
 f. An apparently unlimited useful life may in fact be indefinite and benefits cannot be reasonably projected.
 g. An intangible asset may be a composite of many individual factors with varying effective lives [APB Opinion No. 17, 1970, par. 27].

Many intangibles have a maximum life prescribed by law. A patent, for example, is granted for a period of 17 years and may not be renewed. Copyrights are issued to corporations for 75 years. From an economic standpoint, however, it is relatively rare for an intangible asset to maintain its value during the entire period of its legal existence. For example, a patent may be made obsolete by a new development that supersedes it. A copyright may not provide any revenues after the first year or two of its existence. For these reasons, the useful life of an intangible asset should be regarded as the shorter of the legal or economic life.

But there is an upper limit on the amortization period. The APB stated that: "The period of amortization should not, however, exceed forty years. Analysis at the time of acquisition may indicate that the indeterminate lives of some intangible assets are likely to exceed forty years and the cost of those assets should be amortized over the maximum period of forty years, not an arbitrary shorter period" [APB Opinion No. 17, 1970, par. 29].

Estimating the number of future periods to benefit from goodwill requires judgment. APB Opinion No. 17 provides the only guidance in the authoritative literature on the selection of an amortization period for goodwill. As a result, companies normally amortize goodwill over the maximum allowable period, 40 years. They are required, however, to evaluate this amortization period continually to ensure that the life has not been shortened by events occurring subsequent to the acquisition date. On the other hand, negative goodwill generally is amortized over a relatively short period (e.g., 5 to 10 years). Opinion No. 17 applies only to intangibles acquired after its effective date, October 31, 1970. Therefore, many companies amortize goodwill and other intangibles with an unlimited life recognized after October 31, 1970, but not those intangibles recognized earlier.

Amortization procedure. Once an amortization period has been established, the cost of the intangible asset may be amortized over this period by any systematic method. The APB, however, concluded "that the straight-line method of amortization—equal annual amounts—should be applied unless a company demonstrates that another systematic method is more appropriate" [APB Opinion No. 17, 1970, par. 30]. Unlike depreciation of tangible assets, the amortization of intangibles is generally recorded through a direct credit to the asset account, rather than to a contra account. Use of a contra account, though allowed, is rarely seen in practice. The financial statements should disclose the method and period of amortization.

Write-down or write-off. APB Opinion No. 17 [1970, par. 31] states:

> A company should evaluate the periods of amortization continually to determine whether later events and circumstances warrant revised estimates of useful lives. If estimates are changed, the unamortized cost should be allocated to the increased or reduced number of remaining periods in the revised useful life but not to exceed forty years after acquisition. Estimation of value and future benefits of an intangible asset may indicate that the unamortized cost should be reduced significantly by a deduction in determining net income.... However, a single loss year or even a few loss years together do not necessarily justify an extraordinary charge to income for all or a large part of the unamortized cost of intangible assets.

This Opinion does not prohibit a complete write-off of the unamortized cost of an intangible asset, provided that the company can show a reasonable basis for such action.

APB Opinion No. 17 permitted a special write-down or write-off of an intangible to be treated as an "extraordinary item" in the income statement if the amount involved was material. However, APB Opinion No. 30 [1973] tightened the criteria for determining extraordinary items, and specifically excluded extraordinary status for write-offs of intangibles.

Income Tax Treatment. The income tax treatment of intangibles seems to have affected the accounting treatment accorded these items, even though there is no conformity requirement. Intangible property can be depreciated for tax purposes if its use in business is of definitely limited duration. Such items include patents, copyrights, leaseholds, licenses, and franchises. Items that have been held not to be depreciable because of the indefinite duration of their usefulness include goodwill, trade names, trademarks, brands, and formulas. Because intangibles that are not depreciable for federal income tax purposes must nevertheless be amortized over a period of 40 years or less in financial statements, holding such assets will result in taxable income exceeding reported income. This excess is treated as a permanent difference, rather than a timing difference, and does not require interperiod allocation of income taxes.

Intangibles are considered "capital assets" in the hands of a purchaser, but not when held by the inventor or developer. Thus the sale of a patent or copyright by a firm that has purchased the right would qualify for capital gain or loss treatment for income tax purposes. On the other hand, the gain on a sale of such a right by the inventor or author would be taxed as ordinary income.

Financial Statement Presentation. Intangible assets (including goodwill) are shown on the balance sheet, net of amortization, and are separately described in the noncurrent asset section. Many companies simply include them with "other assets," making no separate disclosure of these items when they are not individually material. APB Opinion No. 17 requires companies to disclose the method and period of amortization for intangibles. This disclosure is normally made in the financial statement footnotes.

BIBLIOGRAPHY

Accounting Principles Board (AICPA), *Accounting for Business Combinations*, Opinion No. 16 (APB, 1970).
———, *Accounting for Intangible Assets*, Opinion No. 17 (APB, 1970).
———, *Reporting the Results of Operations*, Opinion No. 30 (APB, 1973).
Canning, J. B., *The Economics of Accountancy* (Ronald Press Company, New York, 1929).
Catlett, G. R., and N. O. Olson, *Accounting for Goodwill*, Accounting Research Study No. 10 (AICPA, 1968).
Committee on Accounting Procedure (AICPA), *Restatement and Revision of Accounting Research Bulletins*, Accounting Research Bulletin No. 43 (CAP, 1953).
Financial Accounting Standards Board, *Accounting for Research and Development Costs*, Statement of Financial Accounting Standards No. 2 (FASB, 1974).
———, *Applicability of FASB Statement No. 2 to Computer Software: An Interpretation of FASB Statement No. 2*, Interpretation No. 6 (FASB, 1975).
———, *An Analysis of Issues Related to Accounting for Business Combinations and Purchased Intangibles*, FASB Discussion Memorandum (FASB, 1976).
———, *Elements of Financial Statements of Business Enterprises*, Statement of Financial Accounting Concepts No. 3 (FASB, 1980).
———, *Accounting for Intangible Assets of Motor Carriers*, Statement of Financial Accounting Standards No. 44 (FASB, 1980).
Gellein, O. S., and M. S. Newman, *Accounting for Research and Development Expenditures*, Accounting Research Study No. 14 (AICPA, 1973).
Grady, P., *Inventory of Generally Accepted Accounting Principles for Business Enterprises*, Accounting Research Study No. 7 (AICPA, 1965).
Hatfield, H. R., *Accounting: Its Principles and Problems* (D. Appleton and Company, New York, 1927).
Internal Revenue Service, 26 CFR 20.2031-2, *Valuation of Stocks and Bonds*, Rev. Rul. 59–60.
———, 26 CFR 1.1001-1, *Computation of Gain or Loss*, Rev. Rul. 68–609.
Yang, J. M., *Goodwill and Other Intangibles* (Ronald Press Company, New York, 1927).

CHAPTER 22

Current

Liabilities

Thomas R. Dyckman
Professor of Accounting, Cornell University

LIABILITIES

Liabilities represent obligations of a debtor to pay cash, other assets, or to render services in the future. Typically these obligations arise from past activities but, in the case of accrued liabilities, they may not have been recorded by the end of the accounting period. Accrued income taxes payable are an example. The obligations must involve specific monetary amounts or be subject to reasonable estimation based on written or verbal contracts.

Liabilities and Uncertainty. In Statement of Financial Accounting Concepts No. 3 [1980], the Financial Accounting Standards Board defines liabilities as probable future sacrifices of economic benefits arising from present obligations of a particular entity to transfer assets or provide services to other entities in the future as a result of past transactions or events. The existence and amounts need not be certain for an item to qualify as a liability; estimations and approximations will often be required.

The Board's definition does not include a statement of the degree of probability required, nor does it require conservatism. These are measurement considerations. Recognition or measurement considerations stemming from uncertainty may result in not recognizing liabilities that qualify as such under the definitions or in postponing recognition until their existence becomes more probable or their measures become more reliable.

Current Liabilities. Current liabilities are debtor obligations payable within 1 year of the balance sheet date. However, if a firm's operating cycle exceeds a year, as it would in shipbuilding, current liabilities are those payable within the next cycle. The SEC follows these practices as well. However, it permits the exclusion of certain items from current liabilities, including customer deposits and deferred income, provided that an appropriate explanation of the circumstances is made (SEC Accounting Series Release No. 148 [1973]).

In Accounting Research Bulletin No. 43 [1953, chap. 3A], the Committee on Accounting Procedure of the AICPA defined current liabilities as follows:

The term current liabilities is used principally to designate obligations whose liquidation is reasonably expected to require the use of existing resources properly classifiable as current assets, or the creation of other current liabilities.

The Committee elaborated on this definition as follows:

As a balance sheet category, the classification is intended to include obligations for items which have entered into the operating cycle, such as payables incurred in the acquisition of materials and supplies to be used in the production of goods or in providing services to be offered for sale; collections received in advance of the delivery of goods or performance of services; and debts which arise from operations directly related to the operating cycle, such as accruals for wages, salaries, commissions, rentals, royalties, and income and other taxes. Other liabilities whose regular and ordinary liquidation is expected to occur within a relatively short period of time, usually twelve months, are also intended for inclusion, such as short-term debts arising from the acquisition of capital assets, serial maturities of long-term obligations, amounts required to be expended within one year under sinking fund provisions, and agency obligations arising from the collection or acceptance of cash or other assets for the account of third persons.

Although all legal liabilities are considered accounting liabilities, not all accounting liabilities are recognized as legal debts. Current accounting liabilities also include credit balances representing estimated future outlays that will be made in the next operating cycle, even though no immediate legally enforceable contract exists. The Committee on Accounting Procedure went on to cover such situations:

This concept of current liabilities would include estimated or accrued amounts which are expected to be required to cover expenditures within the year for known obligations (a) the amount of which can be determined only approximately (as in the case of provisions for accruing bonus payments) or (b) where the specific person or persons to whom the payment will be made cannot as yet be designated (as in the case of estimated costs to be incurred in connection with guaranteed servicing or repair of products already sold).

The specific amount payable or the specific identification of the payee need not be known before a liability may be classified as current. Payables of estimated amounts such as those for taxes, and payables to unknown persons, such as those for guarantees or product warranties, should be listed as current if the time of payment appears reasonably certain to fall within the next operating cycle.

Measurement of Current Liabilities. Liabilities should be measured by the present value of all required future cash flows or cash flow equivalents in the case of services and related liabilities. The recording of interest-bearing notes at face value provides an example where this practice is followed. However, with regard to open accounts payable and most other short-term liabilities where interest is not explicitly written into the contract, the discount factor is not calculated. This practice is based primarily on materiality considerations and to a lessor extent on the difficulties inherent to selecting an appropriate interest rate. The APB recognized the problem explicitly and excluded short-term payables arising from transactions with suppliers in the normal course of operations from those requiring the application of present value techniques in APB Opinion No. 21 [1971, par. 3].

Although the amount of a current liability is usually clear, there are rare situations in which the precise amount cannot be established and a reasonable estimate is not available. Such obligations should be disclosed by footnotes where they are potentially material.

FINANCIAL STATEMENT PRESENTATION

Detail of Disclosure. Most of the detail concerning the company's liabilities need not be included in the reported financial statements. Although current liabilities must be recorded in the books of account in sufficient detail to facilitate their payment and ensure control over their incurrence, this same amount of detail would be unnecessarily cumbersome if included in the balance sheet. The detail that should be shown in the balance sheet depends on the type of organization reporting and the nature of its current liabilities.

The principal types of current liabilities include accounts payable, short-term notes payable, advances from customers (such as subscription and rent payments), accrued payables (including wages, salaries, bonus payments, commissions, rentals, royalties, interest, and taxes), and other obligations to be paid out of short-term assets (currently maturing long-term debt, for example).

Certain liabilities are important by their nature and should be shown separately even when the amounts are relatively small. Examples include any debt owed to an organization by its officers or other closely associated individuals, and current obligations with prior claims to assets or claims on noncurrent assets.

Although consistency in account titles for statement purposes is desirable, the changing nature of a company's liabilities precludes precise uniformity over time.

Order of Presentation. The most common method of presenting current liabilities is in accordance with the nature of the liability, such as accounts payable, notes payable, and taxes payable, with special items indicated by a descriptive title. These categories are occasionally placed in the balance sheet in order of maturity, with the earliest maturing item first. In other statements the size of the amount is used, with the largest item listed first. The nature of any security associated with the creditor's claim is rarely used as a basis for ordering the presentation, except in a Statement of Affairs prepared for a liquidating company or one in receivership.

Practical problems arise when liabilities are arranged in order of maturity. The major problem occurs because the timing of payment is not uniform, such as in accounts payable where accounts with 30-day terms, 90-day terms, and even 6-month terms are included in the same category. For this reason an arrangement based on maturity is difficult to apply in practice and seldom used. (Bank overdrafts, however, are usually listed first among current liabilities, in deference to their priority of maturity.) A listing of current liabilities according to size adds little to the data being presented, especially because the amounts change from period to period and inconsistencies in arrangement between accounting periods result.

Amounts that are immaterial can be combined with other categories, or a miscellaneous classification may be used. Care should be given to communicating the nature of substantive specific amounts. Noninformative captions, such as "Deferred Credits," should not be used.

Estimated Liabilities. An estimated liability exists when the amount payable cannot be ascertained with reasonable certainty on the balance sheet date. In such cases the amount must be estimated as accurately as possible, and this amount is then reported in the balance sheet. Many liabilities cannot be known with certainty and must therefore be estimated because the exact amount depends on future events. Federal income tax liability, for example, depends on the final assessment by the Internal Revenue Service. Liabilities for product guarantees depend on the number of units of product that ultimately need repair or replacement. Liabilities for tokens, tickets, and gift certificates outstanding depend on the number eventually submitted by customers for redemption.

Liabilities that are subject to reasonably accurate estimation should be reported in the main body of the balance sheet rather than by footnote. The amount should be estimated on the basis of all information available, and the account title should then indicate that the amount is estimated.

Offsets against Assets. Generally accepted accounting principles do not permit the offset of an asset against a liability so that only the net amount appears in the statements. Such treatment implies an association that seldom exists. The balance sheet is based on a reflection of total properties employed, matched by the total equities on those properties. Offsetting a liability against a specific asset, even though the asset is pledged as security for that debt, would destroy the overall portrayal of properties and equities. Footnotes or parenthetical expressions are employed to reflect a specific relationship between an asset and a liability.

An example of inappropriate offsetting would be deducting an account receivable of one customer from an overpayment to another customer. The first should be shown as a current receivable and the second as a current liability.

Two exceptions exist to the general rule prohibiting offsets. The first is when a legal right of offset exists and the creditor has a debt payable to the company as well as a receivable. Thus, a company may offset an overdraft in a bank account against its balance in another account at the same bank. Offsetting between two different banks, however, is not permissible.

The second exception to the general rule against offsets exists for a few government securities that represent an advance payment of taxes. APB Opinion No. 10 [1966, par. 7] describes the limited amount of offsetting permitted in this way:

1. It is a general principle of accounting that the offsetting of assets and liabilities in the balance sheet is improper except where a right of setoff exists. Accordingly, the offset of cash or other assets against the tax liability or other amounts owing to governmental bodies is not acceptable except in the circumstances described in paragraph 3 below.

2. Most securities now issued by governments are not by their terms designed specifically for the payment of taxes and, accordingly, should not be deducted from taxes payable on the balance sheet.

3. The only exception to this general principle occurs when it is clear that a purchase of securities (acceptable for the payment of taxes) is in substance an advance payment of taxes that will be payable in the relatively near future, so that in the special circumstances the purchase is tantamount to the prepayment of taxes. This occurs at times, for example, as an accommodation to a local government and in some instances when governments issue securities that are specifically designated as being acceptable for the payment of taxes of those governments.

Valuation accounts, such as those for accumulated depreciation and allowances for doubtful accounts, may not properly appear in the liabilities section of the balance sheet. These valuation accounts must be subtracted from their related asset accounts. The general rule against offsets is not violated by subtraction of valuation accounts from assets, because the valuation account was established primarily to prevent direct credits to the asset itself and, as a contra-account, is in reality a part of the asset account.

Conversion of Foreign Balances. When consolidated financial statements are being prepared for two or more companies, one of which is a foreign company with money amounts stated in foreign currency, the current liabilities should be converted for consolidation purposes into dollars, using the current rate of exchange [FASB Statement of Financial Accounting Standards (SFAS) No. 52, 1981]. One exception to this general rule is that deferred income is translated at the historical rate.

LIABILITIES WITH SPECIFIC VALUES

Current liabilities can be categorized into two main groups based on the means by which their values are determined. These groups include: (1) liabilities with specific values usually determined from contracts and (2) liabilities whose values must be estimated. The nature and special problems associated with specific-valued current liabilities are discussed next.

Accounts Payable. Trade accounts payable are debts owed to trade creditors. They normally arise from the purchase of goods or services. Such debts exist in the form of open accounts and should be distinguished from debts evidenced by promissory notes. Particular care must be exercised at the end of the fiscal period to ensure that all trade payables arising from the purchase of goods and services are recorded. A liability is considered to exist at the time title passes. When goods are received near the end of the period or shipped f.o.b. shipping point but an invoice has not arrived, a liability nevertheless exists and should appear in the statements.

Accounts payable to trade creditors may be recorded either at the gross invoice price or at the net invoice price (i.e., less cash discounts). Showing the invoice at gross is the more common practice, primarily because it is more expedient. If this method is followed and cash discounts are material in amount, the discounts available on unpaid accounts should be recognized at the end of the period and subtracted from the liability account. The balancing entry reduces inventories or purchases. On the other hand, if the accounts payable to trade creditors are recorded at the net amount, any discounts not to be taken must be added back to the amount payable on the balance sheet date. The balancing entry should be made to a loss account, because such lapsed discounts involve very high interest rates and indicate poor financial management.

Notes Payable. Although trade notes payable may arise from the same sources as trade accounts payable, they are evidenced by negotiable instruments and therefore should be reported separately if they are material in amount. The maturity date of these notes may extend from a few days to a year, and they may be either interest-bearing or non-interest-bearing. It is normally customary to record trade notes at their face value and to accrue interest on the interest-bearing notes, using a separate Interest Payable account. If interest is included in the face value of the note, making it for all practical purposes a non-interest-bearing note, the full face value of the instrument, if it matures within a year, may be recorded in the Notes Payable account without segregation of the interest portion. Any interest included in the face value of the note, however, should be recorded separately as interest expense and not as part of the cost of the goods or services acquired when the note was given. Even though no interest rate was stated at the time the note was issued, implicit interest is nevertheless included in the face amount of the note. This implicit interest should be removed from the cost of the asset or service acquired at the time of issuance of the note. An estimated interest rate normal to the firm and industry may be used for this purpose.

Interest is sometimes subtracted from the face value of a note when funds are borrowed from a financial institution. This is called *discounting* the note, and the discount is the difference between the face value of the note payable and the proceeds from the loan. The discount is recorded in a debit account titled Discount on Notes Payable and is amortized to interest expense over the life of the note. Any balance in the discount account would be subtracted from the face value of the note payable on the balance sheet so that the liability is reflected at its present value.

Interest Payable. Interest payable is typically the result of an accrual and is recorded at the end of each accounting period. Interest payable on trade notes, notes payable to banks, installment contracts, and other types of interest-bearing documents is usually reported as a single item. In the absence of significant legal differences in the nature or status of the interest, the amounts can be combined. Interest in default on bonds is an example of an item sufficiently important to warrant separate reporting. Interest payable on noncurrent liabilities, such as long-term debt, should be listed as a current liability, because the interest is payable within the next operating cycle.

The interest portion of any current installment contract payment need not be separated from the principal amount for reporting purpose.

Wages and Salaries Payable. A liability for unpaid wages and salaries is created when employees are paid at fixed intervals that do not coincide with the balance sheet date. Such amounts frequently include related items such as unpaid bonuses and commissions. These latter amounts should be stated separately if they are either unusual in nature or significant in amount.

Unclaimed wages that have not been paid to employees because of failure to claim their earnings should be included in salaries and wages payable. If payroll checks that are long outstanding have been removed from the books and returned to cash, a liability exists for at least a period of several years, or until the statute of limitations removes the contingency. In some jurisdictions, such unclaimed amounts revert to the state under the applicable escheat law.

In most cases, wages and salaries payable appear in gross amount. Payroll taxes or other related withholdings are not segregated. A difficult problem is frequently encountered in the determination of the amount of wages and salaries payable on the balance sheet date. Calculation of the amount payable for a portion of a pay period can be a laborious process, especially when employees are paid on an hourly basis. An estimate of the liability can be accomplished by estimating the wage cost per day and projecting this daily cost for the number of days' unpaid wages. Unpaid commissions, fees, and similar types of employee compensation may also be estimated in the same way.

Compensated absences. Firms may agree to pay employees for absences such as vacations, illness, and holidays. A liability is accrued if the following conditions are met [SFAS No. 43, 1980, pars. 6-7]:

1. The employer's obligation relating to employees' rights to receive compensation for future absences is attributable to employee services already rendered.

2. The obligation relates to rights that vest (payment is required even if employment is terminated) or accumulate.

3. Payment of the compensation is probable.

4. The amount can be reasonably estimated.

An employer is not, however, required to accrue a liability for nonvesting accumulating rights to receive sick pay benefits, because the amounts are generally not sufficiently large to justify the cost of computation.

Employee Withholdings Payable. Withholdings from employees' wages include Old Age and Survivors' Insurance, federal income taxes, and a host of miscellaneous deductions. Some of the deductions, such as those for hospitalization insurance, are frequently required by the employer, whereas others, such as union dues and savings bonds, are either optional or are required by contracts with labor unions. The liabilities for withholdings are frequently recorded at the same time as wage expense, as illustrated below:

Wage and Salary Expense	17,593.42	
Federal Old Age Benefits Payable		639.22
Federal Income Tax Withholding Payable		1,952.11
Union Dues Withholding Payable		156.00
Employees Savings Bond Withholding Payable		240.00
Group Hospitalization Withholding Payable		312.68
Wages and Salaries Payable		14,293.41

The organization is acting as the employees' agent in withholding these sums, and the liability accounts are debited directly when monies are forwarded to the appropriate payee. Although separate accounts are used for the various withholdings, they are usually combined in the balance sheet.

Old Age and Survivors' Insurance withholding. Old age and survivors' benefits are authorized by the Federal Insurance Contributions Act and provide for the withholding of a percentage of the earnings of all covered employees. The employer matches the amount withheld from employees, and the two amounts are forwarded to the appropriate agency of the federal government. This deduction from employees' wages is often referred to as "the social security tax," although in reality the social security tax includes both the state and federal unemployment compensation insurance paid by the employer.

Both the rate and base earnings on which this tax is based have been changed frequently since the withholding was first authorized. Thus it is important to check current requirements before accruing these amounts.

This withholding is sometimes labeled OASI tax (Old Age and Survivors' Insurance), FOAB (Federal Old Age Benefits), or FICA (Federal Insurance Contributions Act). The tax applies to employers of one or more persons, with certain limited exceptions. The amount withheld from employees, plus the matching amount paid by the employer, must be remitted regularly to an authorized bank. If the combined amount withheld from employees and assessed against the employer is more than $100 in any one month, the payment is made monthly, even though the reports are filed quarterly. If an employee changes employers during the calendar year, the new employer does not consider any withholdings made by the previous employer in computing the wages subject to withholdings.

Income taxes withheld. Income tax withholdings from an employee's wages are affected both by the number of personal exemptions and by the earnings for the period. The amounts withheld are payable to the governmental agency at the same time as the Old Age and Survivors' Insurance payments. The amount to be withheld in any given period is computed either by formula or may be read from tables prepared and furnished by the government. These tables are constructed for varying combinations of earnings, pay-period intervals, and number of dependents.

Other employee withholdings. When withholdings are made from employees' pay for such things as union dues, hospitalization premiums, or savings bonds, the amounts are normally credited directly to liability accounts at the time withheld. A later remittance to the labor union or the insuring company, or the purchase and distribution of savings bonds to employees, relieves the company of its liability for the amounts withheld. The employer is acting as the employee's agent in making the withholdings, and the amounts are considered held in trust for the employee.

Unemployment Compensation Insurance Payable. In addition to the matching amounts that employers must pay for FICA taxes, they are also subject to taxes for federal unemployment compensation insurance and state unemployment compensation insurance. Both types of unemployment compensation insurance were made mandatory by the Federal Insurance Contributions Act. State employment compensation tax is computed as a percentage of the employee's earnings, but the percentage is established by state regulatory bodies, even though the tax is required by federal law. The Federal Insurance Contributions Act made a state plan for unemployment compensation mandatory.

The frequency with which reports must be filed depends on the regulations of the individual state, but reports are usually required on a quarterly basis. Quarterly returns must indicate the earnings of each employee, as well as the tax payable for that quarter. In some states employees must also contribute to the unemployment program through payroll withholdings.

The employer's contribution for the federal portion of the unemployment compensation is a fixed percentage of a defined amount earned by each employee during each calendar year with each employer. Payments are made annually to the federal government, and the annual report accompanying payment must be submitted no later than 1 month following the end of the calendar year. Unemployment benefits are paid to individuals only out of the various state unemployment funds; the federal unemployment contributions of employers are used in case a state should have insufficient funds to cover its unemployed workers.

Property Taxes Payable. The liability for property taxes is normally based on the assessed valuation of the properties as of a given date, using the currently approved tax rate. The date at which the assessed valuation is rendered usually differs from the balance sheet date. Accounting treatment has, in general, held that taxes accrue ratably over a tax year rather than occurring instantaneously as of the assessment date. The Committee on Accounting Procedure of the AICPA, in Accounting Research Bulletin No. 43 [1953, chap. 10A, par. 14], states: "Generally the most acceptable basis of providing for property taxes is monthly accrual on the taxpayer's books during the fiscal period of the taxing authority for which the taxes are levied." The Committee indicates, however, that consistency of application from year to year is the important consideration, and because special circumstances may suggest an alternative accrual period, selection of other accrual periods is acceptable.

The legal view is that taxes on real property are the liabilities of a given business as of the date on which the taxes become a property lien, usually the date of the assessment. Accountants, however, maintain that accrual on a straight-line basis provides a better measure of net income and financial position.

Sales and Excise Taxes Payable. Federal and state laws typically require businesses to act as agents for the government in the collection of sales and excise taxes. Generally, the sales taxes collected from customers are recorded separately at the time of collection, and the current sales tax liability represents taxes collected that have not yet been remitted to the appropriate governmental organization. Frequently, the collecting company is permitted to retain a small percentage of the collections to offset the clerical costs incurred in making and remitting the tax. The total collections from customers may not exactly equal the amount that must be remitted, especially if the remittance is computed as a percentage of total sales. The balance sheet should reflect only the amount payable to the governmental organization and should not include any portions to be retained by the company.

Bonuses Payable. Many employment contracts provide for the payment of a bonus to officers or other employees, or for the distribution of a share of profits. The bonus is treated as an operating expense in the income statement, and any unpaid portion must be recorded as a current liability pending its payment. In some cases, the bonus calculation is based on aftertax income, even though the bonus itself is an expense entering into the determination of taxable net income. To illustrate, suppose that a company subject to a 40 percent tax rate agrees to pay a bonus of 20 percent of aftertax net income, and the income before taxes or bonus is $100,000. The computation requires the simultaneous solution of two equations:

$$\text{Bonus} = .20 \times (\$100,000 - \text{Tax})$$
$$\text{Tax} = .40 \times (\$100,000 - \text{Bonus})$$

Substituting the expression for tax into the equation for the bonus produces an equation that can be solved to determine the bonus:

$$\text{Bonus} = .20 \times [\$100,000 - .40(\$100,000 - \text{Bonus})]$$
$$= .2(\$60,000 + .4 \times \text{Bonus})$$
$$= \$12,000 + .08 \times \text{Bonus}$$
$$.92 \times \text{Bonus} = \$12,000$$
$$\text{Bonus} = \$13,043$$

Dividends Payable. Dividends become legal liabilities when formally declared by the board of directors. Dividends to be paid in cash should be reported as liabilities whenever declared before the end of the balance sheet period, even though the date of record[1] or the date of payment falls in the subsequent accounting period. The courts have held that after a dividend has been declared and made public, it may not be revoked and has the same legal force as any other unsecured debt. Unpaid dividends, if material in amount, should be shown separately on the balance sheet.

If there are dividends in arrears on cumulative preferred stock, the arrearages are not shown as liabilities on the balance sheet, even though the company has sufficient cash to pay the arrearage. However, a footnote should be used to reflect this information. Preferred stock specifies a periodic dividend, usually

---

[1]The date of record is the date on which the holders of the equity securities entitled to receive the dividend are determined.

a percentage of par value. Such dividends need not be paid, however, and are not accrued. Preferred dividends may be cumulative or not. Where they are cumulative, all preferred dividends in arrears must be paid before a dividend can be declared on common equity. Noncumulative preferred stock dividends, once passed, are permanently lost to preferred stockholders.

A stock dividend is not shown as a liability. A stock dividend does not require a payment or distribution of assets and represents nothing more than a transfer from the retained earnings account to the contributed capital account(s). Dividends payable in stock are properly shown with the capital stock in the owners' equity section of the balance sheet.

Current Portion of Long-Term Debt. Current liabilities usually include that portion of long-term debt which becomes payable within the next year. The maturing portion of a serial bond issue, for example, would be classified as a current liability under most conditions, even though the remainder of the bonds payable is classified as long-term debt. If payment is to be made on the maturing portion of the serial bond issue from cash in a special sinking fund shown as a current asset on the balance sheet, the bonds due to be retired must appear as a current liability. On the other hand, when an entire issue of bonds or other debt becomes payable within the 12-month period, its inclusion in current liabilities implies that payment will be made with current assets. If payment is in fact to be made from a sinking fund that appears in another category of assets, the maturing issue should not be listed as a current liability if it is material in amount. When an entire issue of bonds payable is to be retired in the next year and assets for payment are held in a special sinking fund, neither the bonds payable nor the sinking fund should appear as a current liability or a current asset.

Debt to Be Refinanced. Sometimes debts that have maturity dates within the next accounting cycle are expected to be refinanced and consequently will not require an outlay of current assets. Commercial paper, construction loans, and the maturing portion of long-term debt provide examples. FASB Statement No. 6 specifies that this debt should not be classified as current if payment is to be made from a sinking fund or the cash is obtained from noncurrent sources. Furthermore, the current portion of long-term debt should be excluded from current liabilities if [SFAS No. 6, 1975, par. 11]:

> The enterprise's intent to refinance the short-term obligation on a long-term basis is supported by an ability to consummate the refinancing demonstrated in either of the following ways:
> (a) After the date of an enterprise's balance sheet but before the balance sheet is issued, a long-term obligation or equity securities have been issued for the purpose of refinancing the short-term obligation on a long-term basis; or
> (b) Before the balance sheet is issued, the enterprise has entered into a financing agreement that clearly permits the enterprise to refinance the short-term obligation on a long-term basis on terms that are readily determinable, and all of the following conditions are met:

(i) The agreement does not expire within one year (or operating cycle) from the date of the enterprise's balance sheet and during the period the agreement is not cancelable by the lender or investor (and obligations incurred under the agreement are not callable during the period) except for violation of a provision with which compliance is objectively determinable or measurable.

(ii) No violation of any provision in the financing agreement exists at the balance-sheet date and no available information indicates a violation has occurred thereafter but prior to the issuance of the balance sheet, or, if one exists at the balance-sheet date or has occurred thereafter, a waiver has been obtained.

The lender or the prospective lender or investor with which the enterprise has entered into the financing agreement is expected to be financially capable of honoring the agreement.

Pension and Retirement Plans. Pension plans may be fully or partially funded, and the funding may be self-administered or trustee-administered, usually by an insurance company. When the pension or retirement plan is fully funded with an insurance company, the premiums that are payable annually represent the total cost to the company. In such cases, current liabilities must include all premiums payable within the next operating cycle that relate to employee services already performed, whether these amounts are for past service benefits or for current service benefits. If the past service portion of the pension agreement is to be paid to the insurance company over a stipulated period of time, such as 10 years, only the current installment appears as a current liability.

Advances from Customers. Monies received in advance from customers create a liability for the future delivery of goods or services. Tuition fees received by a school and subscriptions received in advance by a magazine publisher are representative. The advances are initially recorded as liabilities and are then transferred from the liability account to revenue when the goods or services are delivered.

Advance receipts from customers for the performance of services or for future delivery of goods are current liabilities only if the performance or delivery is to be completed within the time period included in the definition of current liabilities. Advance collections on ticket sales would be considered current liabilities, whereas deposits received on a contract to be completed in 2 years would be a noncurrent liability.

Receipts from customers become earned revenues upon delivery of the goods and services, and thus these amounts contain the eventual profit. The eventual profit should remain in the liability account, and no distinctions between the cost and profit elements should be undertaken until the revenues are earned.

Deposits received on containers are recorded in the same way as customer advances, that is, as current liabilities, if there is a reasonable expectation that the deposit will be refunded within the next accounting period. In some cases, customer deposits may not be listed as current liabilities because their return is not normally contemplated within the time period used to define current liabilities. Utility companies, for example, sometimes require a deposit to offset possible nonpayment of billings. Because there is no intent to refund the deposits to customers within the current operating cycle, these amounts may be shown more properly as a noncurrent liability.

Sometimes a separate liability category entitled "Deferred Credits," "Deferred Revenues," or "Deferred Liabilities" appears in the balance sheet, usually between current liabilities and owners' equity. These amounts arise either as a result of company policy in the recognition of revenue, such as on installment receivables, or because some doubt exists that income will ultimately be realized. Welsch et al. [1979, p. 313] describe four types of items commonly found in this classification:

1. Revenues collected in advance (sometimes called unearned revenue or, less descriptively, deferred revenue), such as prepaid interest or rent, and advances received for services yet to be rendered. These items require that obligations, benefits, or services be rendered in the future before income is realized.

2. Credits arising through external transactions, that are difficult to classify. Examples are unearned deposit on royalties and deferred income on installment sales.

3. Credits arising through certain internal transactions. Examples are deferred repairs, allowance for rearrangement costs and equities of minority interests (on consolidated statements).

4. Credits arising from income tax allocation procedures (deferred income taxes).

The failure to classify each of these items as a current liability, long-term debt, or owners' equity is a possible source of misinterpretation. Use of a labeled deferred credit, deferred liabilities, or deferred receivable should be avoided. The term "unearned revenue" should also be avoided. Revenue is a measure of service rendered, and thus "unearned" revenue is a self-contradictory term.

LIABILITIES WITH ESTIMATED VALUES

Estimated liabilities occur when either (1) a legal obligation of uncertain amount has a specific due date or (2) future events are relevant in establishing a legal obligation of uncertain amount. Income taxes are an example of the first type of estimated liability, and endorsement of notes represents an example of the second. If sufficiently objective data are available to make reasonably accurate estimates of the amount, the debt should be reflected in the liability section of the balance sheet. If the probable maturity date, or time in which cash, goods, or service will be provided occur within the firm's operating cycle, the amount is classified as a current liability. Liabilities for product guarantees or for estimated federal income taxes are current liabilities even though the amounts are not precisely determinable on the balance sheet date.

Liabilities that depend on future events are often referred to as *contingent liabilities.* Contingent liabilities arise from assigned accounts receivable, accommodation endorsements, purchase commitments, pending lawsuits, and discounted notes.

Two classes of items are sometimes described as contingent liabilities, differing in their degree of uncertainty. The first class is made up of items where it is probable that an asset has been impaired or a liability has been incurred at the date of the financial statements. The FASB [SFAS No. 5, 1975, par. 8] has ruled that such items must be recognized as losses with a corresponding credit to a liability or an asset if the amount of the loss can be reasonably estimated.

If only a range can be estimated for the loss, then either the most probable amount within that range should be accrued or, if there is no such single value, the minimum value of the range is used. The nature of the contingency must be disclosed, together with the extent of any additional exposure to loss [FASB Interpretation No. 14, 1976, par. 3].

Disclosure, but not accrual, is also required if there is a reasonable possibility that a loss may have been sustained by the balance sheet date. Disclosure is also in order if knowledge of the existence of such a liability occurs after the balance sheet date but before issuance of the financial statements [SFAS No. 5, 1976, par. 11].

Certain loss contingencies should be disclosed even if the possibility of loss may be remote. Such contingencies are characterized by a right to proceed against an outside party if the guarantor is called upon to satisfy a guarantee. Examples include guarantees of indebtedness, obligations of commercial banks under "standby letters of credit," and guarantees to repurchase receivables [SFAS No. 5, 1976, par. 12].

Adequate disclosure can be achieved in any of the following ways:

1. By parenthetical comment in the main body of the financial statement
2. By a footnote to the financial statement
3. By showing the contingency with other liabilities by extending the amount "short," so that it is not included in the dollar amount of payables
4. By an appropriation of retained earnings

Only the last of these four methods entails an entry in the books of account. Because of the possibility of misinterpretation, this method is not frequently used. Appropriations of retained earnings must be shown within the shareholders' equity section of the balance sheet and clearly identified as appropriations.

Federal Income Taxes Payable. Business units organized as proprietorships or partnerships are not taxable entities, and liabilities for federal income taxes normally do not appear on their financial statements. Corporations, however, are subject to the federal income tax. Determination of the exact income tax liability is a complex task, and taxable income usually differs from the corporation's reported pretax financial income. Differences are produced by income not subject to tax, expenses that are not tax deductible, and items taxed or deducted for tax pur₊oses in one period but affecting reported financial income in another period. The tax return contains a schedule that requires the reconciliation of reported financial net income with the taxable income appearing on the income tax return.

The income tax liability usually appears under the heading of "Federal Income Taxes Payable" or "Estimated Federal Income Taxes Payable." It is an estimation because the final tax assessment is made by the federal government, and the submission of a tax return is required in order to furnish the information that permits the Internal Revenue Bureau to assess the tax. If the regulations are interpreted properly, the tax as computed by the corporation will be correct, but when errors or omissions occur, additional tax assessments are made or excess taxes paid are refunded.

In many cases, the tax liability cannot be computed precisely because of uncertainties in interpretation of the law, the fact that certain transactions are not covered by any established rule, or because the taxing authorities have either not established clear boundaries or have allowed inconsistent interpretations. Thus, additional assessments or refunds are common. Both the tax liability for the current year and any additional assessments for prior years are current liabilities. These two taxes need not be separately reported in the body of the statement. However, footnotes that adequately explain a material additional assessment may be appropriate.

Deferred Income Taxes. In those cases where the company's reported net income and its taxable net income differ, an interperiod allocation of income taxes may be necessary. A company engaged in long-term construction projects, for example, may measure its reported income on the basis of construction in progress but pay taxes only when its contracts are completed. Generally accepted accounting principles indicate that the tax expense appearing on the income statement should, in general, be computed by applying the current tax rates to the reported net income; consequently, a difference may remain.

The classification of the deferred income tax credit as either current or noncurrent will be based on either (1) the expected reversal date of the specific timing difference or (2) by the nature of the item producing the tax difference. The latter approach is used for deferred taxes resulting from timing differences related to an asset or liability that gave rise to the timing difference. The former is used for (1) tax loss carry-forwards and carry-backs and when the deferred tax item is not related to an asset or liability because (a) there is no associated asset or liability or (b) reduction of an associated asset or liability will not cause the timing difference to reverse [SFAS No. 37, 1980, par. 4].

Thus, if installment receivables are a current asset, the deferred credits representing the tax effects of uncollected installment sales should be a current item; if an estimated provision for warranties is a current liability, the deferred charge representing the tax effect of such provision should be a current item.

Refunds of past taxes or offsets to future taxes arising from recognition of the tax effects of operating loss carry-backs or carry-forwards should be classified either as current or noncurrent. The current portion should be determined by the extent to which realization is expected to occur during the current operating cycle.

Guarantee and Warranty Liabilities. Guarantee and warranty liabilities are created when a company agrees to provide repair services or furnish parts to replace those found to be defective. Under these circumstances, a more accurate matching of current costs and revenues is effected by estimating the future costs to be incurred as a result of current sales. Recording these future costs necessitates the recording of an estimated liability.

In some cases, the customer pays a special fee for future service or replacement guarantees covering a specified period of time. These fees must be accounted for in the same way as customer advances. They are recorded as a liability at the time received and recognized as revenue over the period covered by the warranty contract. If the customer's payment is not intended to cover the full cost of servicing the unit over a specified contract period, the full amount should be recorded as a liability and not just the amount received. The balancing debit is to a current expense.

In some cases, the expenses and costs incurred in providing services or replacement parts are debited in full to expense accounts, whereas the earned portion of fees received from customers is recorded in a separate revenue account, so that costs and revenues are not directly offset in the accounts. In other cases, the actual costs or expenses incurred are debited directly against the credits recorded at the time the customer's fees were received.

The contract with the customer may contain a stipulation wherein the company agrees to perform a specified service at some designated time. For example, a company may agree to restore the surface of a property that is being mined at the termination of the mining contract, or to restore property to its original condition before returning it to a lessor. Such liabilities should be accumulated over the life of the contract by debits to current expense accounts and credits to an appropriate liability account. The liability would be considered current only if payment is contemplated, or if costs are to be incurred, during the next operating cycle.

Trading Stamps and Premiums. A liability does not necessarily exist when a retailer gives customer trading stamps to be redeemed by an outside company. A retailer who pays a fixed price for the stamps transfers the obligation to the trading stamp company. The cost of trading stamps given to customers is simply a part of the retailer's operating expense. The trading stamp company, however, will have a liability for the stamps issued to retailers that have not as yet been redeemed.

Many companies offer their customers a variety of personal properties as premiums for the return of a specified number of wrappers, box tops, stamps, or certificates. The estimated costs of the premiums that will be given to customers in return for the wrappers or certificates during the next 12 months should be recorded as a current liability.

Endorsements. Contingent liabilities arise from accommodation endorsements on legal instruments and from assigning accounts receivable with recourse. The event on which the contingency rests is the payment of the debt by the maker of the instrument or the customer, and should timely payment not be made, the contingent liability becomes a full legal liability. Footnotes are used for this contingency, because the amounts are usually difficult to establish and the probability of payment is remote.

Lawsuits Pending. Lawsuits pending is a type of contingent liability that results from unresolved legal action against the organization. The outcome of legal action is often difficult to predict, and may be contingent on the findings of a court or the verdict of a jury. Even in those cases where the evidence may not be favorable to the defendant company, there is strong pressure not to include specific dollar liabilities in the financial statements, because their use may unfavorably influence the position of the defendant company. For this reason footnotes are used almost exclusively for this type of contingent liability.

Purchase Commitments. Purchase commitments for future delivery of materials or services are a normal part of the operation of a business, and the contingent liability thus created is not recognized in the accounts under normal conditions. The contingent asset to be received is presumed to offset the contingent liability for its payment, and thus no accounting entry or disclosure is deemed necessary. However, a different situation exists when a material decline in the market price of the goods or services ordered occurs, while the company is committed to pay the previously agreed amount. In such cases, a loss has occurred that should be recorded in the current period, because it was in that period that the price decline occurred. The recording of such a loss necessitates the reflection in the accounts of the corresponding liability.

A distinction must be maintained between losses on purchase commitments that can be measured realistically and those contingent losses that might occur at some future date. The latter may be disclosed by means of a footnote. The former, however, should be recognized with a debit to a current loss account and a credit to a current liability if the receipt and payment of the goods or services are to be made within the next operating cycle. At the time of receipt of the goods or services, they are recorded in the books at an amount equal to their current market value and not at the amount paid for them in accordance with the terms of the purchase commitment. The balancing debit is made to the liability account for the estimated loss.

BIBLIOGRAPHY

Accounting Principles Board (AICPA), *Offsetting Securities against Taxes Payable*, Opinion No. 10 (APB, 1966).

———, *Interest on Receivables and Payables*, Opinion No. 21 (APB, 1971).

Committee on Accounting Procedure (AICPA), *Restatement and Revision of Accounting Research Bulletins*, Accounting Research Bulletin No. 43, chaps. 3A and 10A (CAP, 1953).

Financial Accounting Standards Board, *Accounting for Contingencies*, Statement of Financial Accounting Standards No. 5 (FASB, 1975).

———, *Classification of Short-Term Obligations Expected to Be Refinanced*, Statement of Financial Accounting Standards No. 6 (FASB, 1975).

———, *Accounting for the Translation of Foreign Currency Transactions and Foreign Currency Financial Statements*, Statement of Financial Accounting Standards No. 8 (FASB, 1975).

————, *Reasonable Estimation of the Amount of a Loss: An Interpretation of FASB Statement No. 5*, Interpretation No. 14 (FASB, 1976).

————, *Balance Sheet Classification of Deferred Income Taxes*, Statement of Financial Accounting Standards No. 37 (FASB, 1980).

————, *Accounting for Compensated Absences*, Statement of Financial Accounting Standards No. 43 (FASB, 1980).

————, *Elements of Financial Statements of Business Enterprises*, Statement of Financial Accounting Concepts No. 3 (FASB, 1980).

————, *Foreign Currency Translation*, Statement of Financial Accounting Standards No. 52 (FASB, 1981).

Securities and Exchange Commission, *Amendments to Regulations S-X and Related Interpretations and Guidelines Regarding the Disclosure of Compensating Balances and Short-Term Borrowing Arrangements*, Accounting Series Release No. 148 (SEC, 1973).

Welsch, G. A., C. T. Zlatkovich, and W. T. Harrison, *Intermediate Accounting* (Richard D. Irwin, Homewood, Ill., 1979).

CHAPTER 23

Long-Term Liabilities

Theodore M. Asner
Partner, Alexander Grant & Company

Barry Jay Epstein
Blackman, Kallick and Company, Ltd.

THE GENERAL CHARACTER OF LONG-TERM LIABILITIES

Long-term liabilities are those liabilities that are not current in nature—that is, those that have maturities beyond one operating cycle (or year) from the balance sheet date. When long-term liabilities have mixed maturities, a portion being due within one operating cycle or year and another portion being due later, proper financial statement presentation requires that the earlier maturities be shown as current and the later maturities as long-term, with disclosure of the relationship between the two.

All liabilities—current and long-term—represent obligations to perform services for or to distribute resources to parties external to the reporting entity at some point in the future. However, some liabilities are more determinate than others: Estimated liabilities (such as warranty claims) are less certain as to ultimate amount and identity of the obligee, whereas contingent liabilities may not even result in an economic sacrifice if some prerequisite event does not first occur. Current generally accepted accounting principles require that liabilities that are at least probable and subject to reasonable estimation—which includes virtually all estimated liabilities and some contingent ones—be presented in the balance sheet of the obligor.

Statement of Financial Accounting Concepts No. 3 of the Financial Accounting Standards Board, *Elements of Financial Statements of Business Enterprises* [1980] lists three essential characteristics of all liabilities: (1) a present duty to provide a future transfer or use of assets, (2) the existence of little or no discretion to avoid the future sacrifice, and (3) the *past* occurrence of the event or transaction that gave rise to the obligation. The last of these points relates to accounting's traditional reluctance to recognize executory contracts—contracts in which neither party has yet performed its obligations—in the accounting records. Thus, liabilities presented in the financial statements represent obligations of the reporting entity to other entities that have already performed their contractual duties.

THE TIME VALUE OF MONEY AND LIABILITIES

Long-term liabilities result from delay in payment or other aspects of performance. This element of delay, which may extend for decades in the case of bonds or debentures, makes it imperative that the time value of money (the "price of delay" in the words of Concepts Statement No. 3) be recognized explicitly. For this reason, long-term liabilities are normally recorded at their present discounted value, and interest is recognized over the period of time between the incurrence of an obligation and its ultimate discharge. Examples of liabilities subject to such accounting treatment include bonds, notes, and lease obligations.

The most accurate and the only generally accepted method for discounting long-term liabilities to present value utilizes compound interest computations. The present value of a future amount is given by the expression

$$Pv = Fv \times \frac{1}{(1 + i)^n}$$

where Pv = present value
Fv = future value or amount due
i = periodic interest or discount rate
n = number of periods

For example, if a non-interest-bearing note of $50,000 is due at the end of 5 years, and the appropriate discount rate (based on the rate implicit in the borrowing or on the best estimate of alternative borrowing sources) is 16 percent, then the present value of the obligation at the date the debt is incurred is

$$\$50,000 \times \frac{1}{(1 + .16)^5} = \frac{\$50,000}{2.10034} = \$23,805.65$$

As an example of the application of this approach to an actual transaction, if a parcel of land is acquired in exchange for the above-described note, it would *not* be appropriate to record the land and the note for $50,000. Rather, the actual value of the land would be inferred from the present value of the obligation (barring the existence of other information indicative of the real value of the land), and thus both the land and the note would be recorded at $23,805.65. In each period subsequent to this, until the maturity of the note, interest expense would be recognized, with the matching credit being an increase in the amount of the liability. At maturity, the full $50,000 face value of the obligation would have been reflected in the accounts.

The difference between the face and present value ($50,000 − 23,805.65 = $26,194.35) would not be amortized in equal installments (i.e., interest would *not* be recognized at the rate of $5,238.87 per year), as this would not properly reflect interest *compounding* as the recorded value of the obligation increased from the original discounted present value to the face amount. The correct approach—assuming here for simplicity that the compounding period corresponds with the entity's fiscal year—would result in the following interest charges and liabilities:

Year-end	Interest expense for year	Liability at year-end
1	$23,805.65 × .16 = $3,808.90	$27,614.55
2	$27,614.55 × .16 = $4,418.34	$32,032.89
3	$32,032.89 × .16 = $5,125.26	$37,158.15
4	$37,158.15 × .16 = $5,945.30	$43,103.45
5	$43,103.45 × .16 = $6,896.55	$50,000.00

This example is illustrative of the possible, but rather unusual, situation of a single lump-sum payment due at a future date. More commonly, there will be a series of payments over the course of time until the obligation is retired. These payments may contain an explicit interest element or, as in the case above, the interest component may be implicit, or there may be a combination of explicit and implicit components.

A series of equal payments made at regular intervals is referred to as an *annuity*. Mathematically, the present value of an ordinary annuity is given as

$$Pv = R \times \frac{1 - 1/(1 + i)^n}{i}$$

where R = the periodic payments or rent
   i = the periodic interest rate
   n = the number of payment periods

As an example, consider the purchase of a parcel of land in exchange for an agreement to pay $10,000 at the end of each of the next 6 years. (A series of payments at the end of each period is known as an *ordinary* annuity; payments at the beginning of each period result in an *annuity due*.) Also, assume that the implied interest rate in this arrangement is 16 percent. Using the above formula, the present value of this series of payments is

$$\$10,000 \times \frac{1 - 1/(1 + i)^n}{i}$$

$$= 10,000 \times \frac{1 - 1/(1.16)^6}{.16}$$

$$= 10,000 \times 3.684736 = \$36,847.36$$

As the payments are made at subsequent year-ends, interest expense will be recorded as a function of the declining principal balance of the obligation using the "effective interest rate" method. The amortization schedule of this loan would be as follows:

Year	Payment	Principal	Interest	Year-end loan balance
1	$10,000	$4,104.42	$5,895.58	$32,742.94
2	10,000	4,761.13	5,238.87	27,981.81
3	10,000	5,522.91	4,477.09	22,458.90
4	10,000	6,406.58	3,593.42	16,052.32
5	10,000	7,431.63	2,568.37	8,620.69
6	10,000	8,620.69	1,379.31	0.00

Interim conversion factors. Interest rates are sometimes expressed as nominal percentages per year, compounded for shorter intervals. Interest at 16 percent compounded or payable semiannually is not really the same as 16 percent per year, because the payment intervals are shorter. Interest being paid more frequently than once a year makes the effective rate somewhat higher. For example, 16 percent per year compounded semiannually does not represent a conversion factor of 1.16 per year, but 1.08 per half-year, and the accumulation effect over 1 year is (1.08)(1.08), or 1.16640. Similarly, 16 percent per year compounded quarterly has an accumulation effect (conversion factor) of 1.16986 per year.

This increase in growth effect from more rapid compounding does not, however, grow proportionately to the shortening of the payment interval; "16 percent compounded monthly" represents a conversion factor of 1.17227 per year. Daily compounding produces a conversion effect of only 1.17347 per year. The limit to this increase of interest effect by faster conversion is, of course, instantaneous or "continuous compounding." For 16 percent per year, continuous compounding produces a conversion effect of 1.17351.

It is possible to compute interest over a longer period than the payment interval. This arises when payments are made, say, semiannually, but the interest rate is specified as 16 percent compounded annually. If such a series of payments is to be dealt with, the effective rate of interest must be expressed in terms of a conversion period that coincides with the payment interval. For example, if payments are to be made semiannually, when the rate of interest is specified at 16 percent per year with no shorter compounding period, the effect of interest must be stated in semiannual terms. A 16 percent per year effective rate is the result of compounding for two payment intervals of 6 months each, and the effective interest per payment interval is

$$1.16 = (1 + x)^2$$
$$1 + x = \sqrt{1.16}$$
$$1 + x = 1.07703$$

BORROWING AS A SOURCE OF FUNDS

It is not possible to state whether borrowing as a source of funds is preferable to the sale of equity. Of course, for some businesses at all times—such as small businesses that are unable to sell stock or whose owners refuse to consider the possibility of diluting their ownership interests—and for most other businesses at certain times—as when it appears that equity markets are, for varied reasons, unreceptive to new stock offerings—debt may be the only source of funds. In general, however, the relative attractiveness of borrowing or issuing equity interests will vary due to a number of factors. The decision to raise capital by one or another method may not even be based on economic reasoning.

Traditionally, the arguments in favor of debt financing focus on the retention of control by the preexisting ownership group; the tax deductibility of interest on debt contrasted to the double taxation of earnings distributed as dividends on preferred and common stock; and the possible benefits of "leveraging" or "trading on equity" as these accrue to shareholders. The last-noted point refers to the fact that, if the borrowed funds are invested at a return greater than their cost, the excess earnings are allocated to the residual owners—that is, the common shareholders—who thus benefit without investing additional capital.

The differential tax treatment accorded to debt and equity may play a major role in choosing a financing strategy. For example, assume that a corporation has the option of issuing a new debt at an interest cost of 17 percent or preferred stock with a dividend rate of 12 percent. Without considering the impact of income taxes, it appears that the preferred stock financing would be less costly. With income taxes at a 46 percent rate, however, the net, or aftertax, cost of the debt is only $(1.00 - .46) \times 17$ percent = 9.18 percent, whereas the preferred stock, the dividend on which is nondeductible, remains at a now less advantageous 12 percent. At least at a superficial level, debt financing now appears to be the more desirable course for the company.

Before embarking on debt financing, however, several additional factors must be considered. First, the debt will have to be repaid (or refinanced, possibly at a higher rate) at some future date, perhaps even retired with a sinking fund or serial retirement feature, thus reducing the average amount of funds provided to the company. (For example, a $10 million bond offering due serially at the rate of $500,000 per year over 20 years will only provide, on the average, $5 million of funds to the obligor.) Preferred stock generally will not have to be repaid, although in recent years some preferred stocks having mandatory retirement provisions have been issued, raising the question whether these are not in actuality debt.

Second, using the example above, although the debt issue may have an economic advantage over equity at the current 46 percent tax rate, this could change if (1) the statutory rates decline—with the breakeven point in this case being 29.4 percent; or (2) if the level of future earnings lowers so that a lower tax rate applies; or (3) if the tax laws are changed so that preferred (or common) dividends become tax deductible, as has been proposed a number of times in recent years. Once the company has committed to a course of action, any change could make the decision taken seem unfortunate in retrospect. For this reason, an economic decision such as this should consider not merely present conditions but, to the extent possible, expected future conditions as well.

Third, the immediate or short-term financing need should not be seen as totally divorced from the entity's long-range financing strategy. If the additional debt incurred at this time makes the corporation "fully leveraged" in the eyes of investors and analysts, future financing options may be severely limited, possibly only to internal (retained earnings) financing. On the other hand, equity financing, even if more costly in the short run, may allow the company to borrow more funds in the near-term future.

In reality, of course, financing alternatives are rarely limited to such simple options as straight debt or equity issues. In fact, particularly for smaller or closely held businesses, financing alternatives have become more and more complex, involving such combination vehicles as convertible debentures and debt instruments with stock purchase warrants attached. These are substantially more difficult to analyze in purely economic terms, because one must consider such factors as the likelihood and timing of conversion or exercise of stock purchase options. In general, small business owners have resisted the idea of stock issuances or combination debt and stock (including warrants or conversion features) offerings, on the grounds that the potential dilution of ownership would be a major disadvantage. For various reasons, including the unprecedented inflation rates of recent years, investors in smaller businesses, such as SBICs and venture capitalists, have been increasingly demanding equity participation in companies to which they advance funds.

Conventional wisdom has held that in times of rising general price levels, an entity should seek to maximize its borrowing, because repayment will occur with depreciated dollars. This logic holds only if lenders permit borrowers to take advantage of them. Because interest rates include a component (the largest component, in recent years) for *anticipated* inflation, borrowers can benefit at the expense of lenders only if their estimates of the course of future inflation are both greater and more accurate than their lenders'. In the long run, this is unlikely to be the case. With 15 percent annual inflation, borrowers will indeed pay back their loans with "cheaper" dollars, but this does not in and of itself justify borrowing at 23 percent interest rates.

Finally, there is the matter of a business enterprise's overall cost of capital. Logically, management should attempt to minimize the average cost of capital, all things being equal (such as the question of retaining flexibility for future financings, as noted above). The theory of finance is, however, filled with controversy over how this goal can be achieved. One view, which is usually described as the traditional view, holds that there is an optimum mix of stocks and bonds that will minimize the firm's cost of capital. This view holds that by issuing securities with differing degrees of risk, the firm can appeal to the preferences of different groups of investors, and, by the right combination, minimize its cost of capital. The other view holds that the cost of capital is independent of the financing instruments used. Although debt may be issued at a lower rate than the presently prevailing cost for common stock, the effect of the issuance of debt is to increase the risk of the residual equity (common stock) and thus to increase its cost. The overall cost of capital, made up of the lower-rate debt and the now higher-cost common stock, will be unaffected.

ACCOUNTING FOR NOTES, LOANS, AND BONDS

Accounting for Notes. The simplest case of long-term borrowing is the single-payment note. In the case of an equipment purchase, the purchase price may be settled by a single note for, say, $100,000, payable after 3 years "without interest." Although the note apparently is non-interest-bearing, the postponement of payment is certainly not free. The amount of the interest charge may frequently be established by the discount that could have been had for immediate payment. Suppose that the cash price were $75,000; the rate of discount may be found by observing that the present worth of the note is .75 of the face amount due 3 years hence. Entering an appropriate present value table (or using a suitable calculator), the present worth factors for 3-year terms at various interest rates may be compared with the .75 specified. In the 10 percent rate column will be found the factor .75131, almost the same as the actual discount effect. The rate of interest is thus very close to 10 percent per year. The note should be recorded:

Equipment Cost...............................	75,000	
Long-Term Notes Payable		75,000

It is more common to record the note at the face amount with a contra-account for the discount of $25,000. However, this adds no real information; the obligation at the time of incurrence is that amount which would have settled the debt then, not 3 years afterward.

In accounting for this loan, interest would be computed at the 10 percent rate, even though no payment is required until the end of the 3 years. The first year's interest charge is $7,500, which would be charged as an expense and credited to Long-Term Notes Payable (or to the discount account, if one were used). The second-year interest charge is based on the carrying value of $82,500 (original $75,000 plus unpaid interest of $7,500) and would be $8,250.

The third year's interest charge, based on a carrying amount of $90,750, would be $9,075; this would bring the carrying amount to $99,825. The difference of $175 arises from the fact that the rate of interest was not exactly 10 percent per year. This difference (too small to be material) would simply increase the last year's interest charge to $9,250. The history of the obligation would thus be

Balance beginning of year	Interest added to debt	Balance end of year
$75,000	$7,500	$ 82,500
82,500	8,250	90,750
90,750	9,250	100,000

The accumulation could have been made on a straight-line basis at $8,333.33 per year, and for practical purposes this might be satisfactory. But in such a case, the effective rate of interest in each year would be different (11.11, 10.00, and 9.09 percent) even though the 3-year total of interest would be the same; this is because of the increase in the carrying amount for each year.

Installment Loans. The payment of an obligation may be handled in installments; the $100,000 equipment purchase may have been made payable in three equal payments "without interest." Such an arrangement combines interest and principal, but the effect of interest may be measured. At a cash price of $75,131, the rate of interest is considerably higher than 10 percent because the payments are due earlier than before. To see how high the rate is, we inquire what rate of interest will make $75,131 the present worth of three annual $33,333 payments. Using an annuity table, the three payments at 10 percent are worth $82,900; at 15 percent the present value is $76,107, and at 20 percent it is $70,217. Evidently, the correct rate of interest in this plan is between 15 and 20 percent; using a linear interpolation (approximation), the rate may be estimated at 15 percent plus 977/5,890 of the 5 percent difference in rates, which is about 15.8 percent.

Amortized Loans. Loans may be repaid according to an amortization schedule at some specified rate of interest, the payments to include interest at that rate, plus repayment of the principal over the term. This form of loan is common practice in residential real estate finance. The payments are computed by setting the initial principal as equal to an annuity of $x for the given rate and time:

$$\$75{,}131 = R \times \frac{1 - 1/(1 + i)^n}{i}$$

At 10 percent this becomes

$$\$75{,}131 = R(2.48685)$$
$$R = \$30{,}211$$

The way in which this payment serves to amortize the $75,131 principal may be seen in an amortization table, as shown in Exhibit 1.

EXHIBIT 1   Three-Year Amortization of $75,131 Loan at 10%

Year	(a) Balance at beginning of year	(b) Interest on (a)	(c) Total (a) + (b)	(d) Payment made at end of year	(e) Balance forward (c) − (d)
1	$75,131	$7,513	$82,644	$30,211	$52,433
2	52,433	5,243	57,676	30,211	27,465
3	27,465	2,746	30,211	30,211	0

Bonds Payable. Actually, a bond issue is an aggregation of many certificates of indebtedness formalized through legal procedures; it is often handled through a trust company, a marketing syndicate, or a group that sells those certificates in the investment market. The bonds are typically printed in denominations of thousands of dollars and are sold at whatever price the market will bear. The bond issue really arises from a contract called the bond or trust "indenture," executed by the corporation and a designated trustee. In the indenture various details are specified, such as the pledge of property or other protection for the loan, and the various rights and obligations of the corporation, as well as the dates, amounts of payment, and other details.

For accounting purposes, bonds are a specific kind of debt for which the accounting issues involved are more or less spelled out in the indenture. However, all bonds have certain features in common, which determine the major accounting procedures that are required.

Overall nature of bond obligations. A bond is usually a promise to pay (1) a principal sum at its maturity date, and (2) a series of interest payments that offset the accumulation of the principal. When a bond sells at its face value (principal amount to be repaid at the end of the term), the interest payments are exactly equal to the interest accumulations. A 14 percent 20-year bond which is issued at par carries interest payments of 14 percent per year; however, traditionally bond interest is paid semiannually, which means that the effective rate is 14 percent compounded semiannually, or 7 percent each 6 months. The principal to be repaid is thus discounted for 40 periods at 7 percent (the P_v factor is .06678) and the principal (say, $1 million face value) thus has a present worth of $66,780. The interest annuity consists of 40 payments of $70,000, payable semiannually. The present value of an annuity factor at 7 percent is 13.3317, and the entire series of interest payments is thus worth $933,220. The sum of the present worth of principal repayment ($66,780) and the interest annuity ($933,220) is $1,000,000. This relationship is of significance in determining the price of a bond issue.

Kinds of bonds. There are various classes of bonds with different combinations of features, some of which are mentioned here. Some bonds have coupons attached to the major certificate, one for each interest payment. Such coupons are on their due dates presented for payment (through the banking system) to the trustee who has received the money to pay those amounts from the corporation. But other bonds are registered; that is, the trustee keeps a record of the bondholders' names and addresses and mails a check for the proper amount to each bondholder on the due date. Thus the trustee serves as a disbursing agent for the debtor corporation.

Nearly all bonds carry a specific rate of interest as part of the borrowing agreement. This is called the coupon rate, because it is usually printed on the coupons, when these are used. The coupon rate, fixed in the indenture, only roughly indicates interest cost or yield on the issue, because bonds are sold in the open market where the price may or may not be the face or maturity amount.

Some bonds, however, have variable rates of return. Occasionally, "income" bonds pay interest only if the company earns it, but in no event more than a specified rate. In this situation, it is not easy to distinguish income bonds and preferred stocks, both of which may be cumulative, with various other contingencies and arrangements.

Some bonds (an increasing number in recent years) are made convertible into common stock. Until so converted, however, these are treated as bond liabilities; conversion requires retirement of the bonds and replacement by shares of stock, as specified in the trust indenture.

The impression persists that bonds are "secured" obligations; that is, the payment of interest, principal, or both is guaranteed by the pledge of specific property. This is not without truth, but the various kinds and degrees of security cover a wide range; it would be difficult if not impossible for a balance sheet or even the footnotes thereto to cover all the details that could be involved. Seldom if ever is there any reference to specific properties pledged against bond issues within going-concern balance sheets. The reader is presumed to be aware of the need to establish the specific features of bonds by reference to financial manuals or other sources of information.

Mention should be made, however, of one specific kind of unsecured bond—debentures. Holders of debenture bonds simply rank as general creditors with other unsecured creditors. The risk involved in such securities varies with the financial strength of the debtor. Such issues are commonly protected by various requirements to limit dividends, to maintain working capital, or by other financial restrictions. Here, too, is good reason for the accountant to examine carefully the trust indenture.

ISSUANCE PROCEDURES FOR BONDS

Marketing Arrangements. Bonds may be issued directly by the debtor corporation; this sometimes happens in the case of new, small, or closely held companies, where the market for capital is so local and so restricted as to make direct sale the easiest course. But most bond issues are marketed through investment bankers, often operating as syndicates to combine effort and minimize risk of loss. "Underwriting" an issue (assuring the debtor corporation of a certain amount of funds from its sale) entails the risk of price fluctuations; often additional service and advice are entailed. But securities are thus "sold" at wholesale to investment bankers, who resell those securities to their customers. There are a number of legal procedures, filing of reports with the Securities and Exchange Commission or state corporation control offices, which are beyond the scope of this chapter. No corporation should embark on any extensive financing campaign without competent advice on the legal and institutional pitfalls that may be involved.

Bond Authorization. Bond issuance, like the issuance of other securities, has a legal basis. In the case of a corporation, the issue of bonds is based on action of the board of directors pursuant to shareholder authorization in some form. Bonds are sometimes authorized in an amount greater than the immediately expected issue. In such case, double-entry record may be made of this action:

Unissued 15% 20-Year Bonds	5,000,000	
15% 20-Year Bonds Authorized		5,000,000

This entry is really only a memorandum, as there is no actual transaction involving assets, liabilities, or shareholders' equity; the amounts are mere face values, which may have little relevance to the actual issue price. If the bonds are then offered for subscription (as might be the case in a smaller corporation or under certain restrictions of the corporate charter or bylaws), suitable entries might record these in a fashion similar to that used for stock subscriptions:

Subscriptions Receivable, 15% 20-Year Bonds	1,975,000	
15% 20-Year Bonds Subscribed...................		1,975,000

This entry, unlike the preceding one, records a real claim for payment and an obligation to issue bonds at a stated price; but the bonds would probably not be issued unless paid for in full. When this occurs, collection of cash and issuance of bonds would be recorded:

Cash..	1,975,000	
20-Year Bonds Subscribed	1,975,000	
Discount on Bonds Payable........................	25,000	
Subscriptions Receivable, 15% 20-Year Bonds		1,975,000
Unissued 15% 20-Year Bonds		2,000,000

This entry assumes the authorization entry to have been made. If the authorization was not regarded as an accountable transaction (for reasons already hinted at), the credit (above) to Unissued 15% Bonds would have been made to the account 15% 20-Year Bonds Payable. It will be noted that, conventionally, the face amount of the bonds is separated from the premium or discount recognized in the subscription price. Computation and treatment of these premium or discount amounts are discussed in the following paragraphs.

Bond Prices. Bonds, like other investment securities, are traded in markets where prices are established by competition between buyers and sellers. Bonds may be issued at any price, but the price reflects the market interpretation of the investment value of the promises contained in the bond and its indenture. It has been observed that a bond is a promise to pay some face or maturity value and a series of interest payments on specified future dates. The present worth of those payments, calculated at the current yield rate (which reflects the market appraisal of risk and desirability of the bond), is the price of the bond.

However, when bond prices are determined by bargaining rather than direct computation from given yield rates, the relationship between price and yield rate may be only approximate. The stated price of the bond issue recorded immediately above implies a yield rate of about 7.6 percent each 6 months (15.2 percent compounded semiannually), as shown in the computation:

Principal: $2,000,000 (.053396).................	$ 106,792	
"Interest" ($150,000 each 6 months for 20 years):		
$150,000 × 12.45532......................	1,868,297	
Computed price	$1,975,089	

The price as computed is only a little more than the actual recorded one; this suggests that the yield rate of 7.6 percent each 6 months is only a little too low. The difference of $89 between the actual and the computed price is not of great consequence over 20 years on a $1,975,000 amount. Note that the $89 difference is viewed not as a result of decimal rounding but of the impossibility of computing and using the exact rate without the assistance of a computer.

It is the market (real, negotiated) rate of interest—or *yield*—that is the effective rate used in all bond valuations and pricing. The coupon or nominal rate, which determines merely how many dollars will be paid each 6 months, is not the effective rate, except in the rather uncommon case when the bond sells precisely at par in the market. This fact is here emphasized by the use of "interest" (in quotation marks) to designate coupon rates or the promised "interest" payments; interest (without quotation marks) means interest cost of the effective (market) rate established by the price of the bond.

Direct calculation of bond price. Bond prices may be established for given maturities and coupon rates, as related to yields, by reference to "bond tables." A partial example is presented in the Appendix of this handbook. There, it may be seen that a bond viewed from 20 years before its maturity, with a coupon rate of 15 percent (7½ percent each 6 months) and a required yield of 7.6 percent (15.2 percent compounded semiannually), would sell at a price of 98.754 percent of par. This is almost precisely the same as was computed above; $1,975,089/$2,000,000 = 98.75445.

Price derived from par and yield. Another way to calculate the price of a bond is to compare it with one that would sell at par in the 15.2 percent market. Such a $1,000 bond would have to have 40 coupons of $76, payable each 6 months, to sell at par. The bond here under consideration carries $1 lower "interest" payments, and therefore sells at a discount, the amount of which is the present worth of an annuity of $1 for 40 periods at 7.6 percent. $1 $\times$ 12.45532 would be $12.5, the discount for one $1,000 bond; the discount for the whole issue would be about 2,000 times this, or $25,000, the same as indicated above.

Ancillary issuance costs. The issue prices for bonds are presumed to be net of all costs of issue. Legal fees, commissions, printing, and other costs of issue are deducted from the bond proceeds. This has the effect of amortizing such costs over the life of the issue as a part of the premium or discount involved.

Interim Interest. Bonds may be issued or acquired on dates different from those on which "interest" is payable. The complexities of this situation are usually resolved by accumulating the "interest" at the coupon rate for whatever period is necessary. Thus, an issue whose certificates were dated October 1 (interest dates April 1 and October 1) was actually sold and delivered on October 10; these bonds would have added to their price the accrued (simple) coupon interest. The issuer or seller would merely credit this extra amount to Interest Charges, thus partially offsetting the later payment of the regularly specified "interest." The inaccuracy thus introduced is seldom significant.

ACCOUNTING FOR OUTSTANDING BONDS

Interest Accruals. The accounting related to an outstanding bond issue involves not only the payments specified by the bond indenture, but also an appropriate method of matching interest charges with the fiscal period of the issuer. Because most bond issues involve the use of an intermediary trustee or disbursing agent, the entries for payments would be made when such funds are transferred to the trustee or interest disbursing agent as an "advance." This advance would be "expensed" when the report of final payment to bondholders was received. But when interest dates do not correspond to fiscal closing dates, an accrual entry must take up interest charges for reporting purposes. This requires not only a proration of cash "interest," but also that something be done about whatever premium or discount may have resulted from the issue.

Discount and Premium Amortization. Premium or discount is a part of the issue price of bonds, and it represents adjustments to "interest" cost. It has been observed that only a bond selling at par or face value has a yield rate equal to the coupon rate. If the bond sells at some other price, the difference (premium or discount) reflects the difference between the "interest" payments at the coupon rate and the effective yield rate.

Straight-line amortization. The simplest way to carry premium or discount into the periodic interest charge is to apply a straight-line (equal annual charge or credit) amortization of premium or discount. Thus, a 20-year 15 percent bond issue sold for $1,975,000 would require amortization of discount, $\frac{1}{40} \times \$75,000$ = $1,875 each semiannual period. Interest cost for each half-year would be recorded:

Interest Charges	151,875	
Discount on Bonds Payable		1,875
Interest Payable		150,000
$75,000/40 = $1,875.		

If the bond had been sold at a premium, for example, at a price of $101.95 or $2,039,000 total, the first semiannual accrual entry would be

Interest Charges	149,025	
Premium on Bonds Payable	975	
Interest Payable		150,000
$39,000/40 = $975.		

In such a case, the difference between the issue price and par is spread over 40 periods, each 6 months. The carrying amount would thus decrease to par (the redemption amount) at the maturity date.

Using straight-line amortization, the equal annual amounts charged to interest will not produce the same apparent percentage interest rate in each year. Amortization of premium causes the liability to decrease from year to year; an equal number of dollars charged each year for interest produces an increasing annual rate for successive years. Similarly, equal annual charges that include amortization of discount will appear as declining percentages of the increasing principal.

Accounting Principles Board Opinion No. 21 [1971] specifies that discount or premium should be "amortized as interest expense . . . over the life of the note [bond] in such a way as to result in a constant rate of interest when applied to the amount outstanding at the beginning of any given period." This would seem to rule out the straight-line amortization method, but the Opinion goes on to add: "However, other methods of amortization may be used if the results obtained are not materially different from those which would result from the 'interest' method." The "however" clause serves as a basis for continued acceptability of the straight-line method, although the interest (or more properly the "effective yield") method is preferred.

Interest or effective yield amortization of premium. The interest or effective yield method results in an interest charge that is a constant percentage of the effective bond liability at the beginning of each period. The discount amortization is the excess of this interest charge over the interest payable. For the 20-year, 15 percent bond sold for $1,975,000, the first 6 months' interest accrual would by this method be based on the yield rate (calculated above at 15.2 percent compounded semiannually):

Interest Charges	150,100	
Discount on Bonds Payable		100
Interest Payable		150,000
.076 × $1,975,000 = $150,100.		

The interest charge is 7.6 percent of $1,975,000; because the cash paid for this period is $100 less than the calculated interest cost, that amount is viewed as an increment of principal via the discount account. For the second 6 months, the carrying amount of the bonds would be $100 larger or $1,975,100, and interest charges in the second period would then be 7.6 percent of this new carrying amount. The interest accrual for the second 6-month period would require the following entry:

Interest Charges	150,108	
Discount on Bonds Payable		108
Interest Payable		150,000
.076 × $1,975,100 = $150,108.		

It will be observed that the discount amortization is a little larger in each successive period, but that the *ratio* of interest charges to the carrying amount (face and unamortized premium) remains constant at 7.6 percent. This scheme of amortization will write off the discount precisely over the term, but with somewhat different interest charges in the individual years than would be the case with the straight-line procedure.

Accumulation of Premium. If the issue had been sold at a premium (15 percent coupons and 20-year maturity, but a price of $2,051,523), the market yield rate is 14.6 percent (7.3 percent per half-year). The first 6 months' interest cost would be 7.3 percent of $2,051,523, and the interest accrual entry would appear:

Interest Charges	149,761	
Premium on Bonds Payable........................	239	
Interest Payable		150,000

.073 × $2,051,523 = $149,761.

For the second 6-month period, the carrying amount of the liability would decrease by $239 to $2,051,284, and the second 6-month accrual entry would be

Interest Charges	149,744	
Premium on Bonds Payable........................	256	
Interest Payable		150,000

.073 × $2,051,284 = $149,744.

Interest calculations, interim dates. The bond year does not always coincide with the fiscal year of the company. This means that the amortizations as presented above must be realigned to fit the company reporting period. Suppose that the bond "interest" payment dates are April 1 and October 1, and the company reports cover the calendar year. Bonds issued on April 1 will, at December 31, have accrued 9 months of interest. This would have included the entry given above for the first 6 months (ended September 30). The entry at December 31 would accrue one-half of the *second* 6 months' interest charges and amortization. The accrual entry at March 31 would take up the other half. This serves to meet the needs of financial statements without undue disturbance to the regular patterns of discount or premium amortization.

Changes in Market Rates after Issue. Obviously, market prices change, and the current market yield rate on outstanding bonds changes with them. The question arises as to whether this has any effect on the accounting for interest cost of that bond issue. If one accepts the proposition that reports and accounts should reflect current conditions and current prices, there would seem to be some reason to recognize changes in the cost of capital as they would appear by changes in actual bond prices and yields. But practice has not recognized this because the contract with the bondholders is not a currently alterable arrangement. A low price for a bond in the market does give opportunity for a company to reacquire its bonds at that price with some advantage, but this opportunity is not always of much significance because only a few bonds may be offered. More important, if the company has a profitable use for the borrowed capital, there is no point in paying it out. When bond prices rise sufficiently (and yields decline), there may be reason for the company's refunding the earlier issue; but that depends on whether bondholders will give up their higher-than-current-market yield by selling their bonds. As long as the bonds are outstanding, conventional accounting statements do not reflect the changes in yield rates and bond prices; the yield rate in the interest expense calculations continues to be set by the initial issue price and the terms of the indenture. This is, of course, in accord with the principles of historical cost-based accounting.

RETIREMENT OF BONDS

Sinking Funds

Providing the cash for repayment—sinking funds. In some cases, and especially in quasi-public operations, it may be essential to make advance provisions for payment of the maturity amount when due. In order to be reasonably
sure that such commitments will be met, borrowers may be required to establish funds for the purpose to which systematic contributions will be made over
the term of the borrowing contract. These funds, called sinking funds, are
invested to produce a desired return, and will accumulate the amount required
to pay off the obligation at maturity. Sinking funds are provided to add security
to an issue and thus may make it easier to market.

The trustee's function in sinking fund procedure. The sinking fund is an
example of a way in which an intermediary trustee can be useful. Obviously
the funds are no protection to the bondholder unless removed from the direct
control of the borrower. The trustee receives the sinking fund contribution,
invests the available funds in appropriate ways, and uses the accumulated
amount to pay off the bonds. In this situation, the intermediary acts for the benefit of the bondholders: a trustee's duties and activities are prescribed by the
trust indenture, in which the trustee represents the bondholders as a group.

Contribution amounts. The periodic fund contributions are usually required
by the indenture to be paid at certain times and in specified amounts. Obviously
a voluntary contribution made at merely convenient times would not be of
much use in systematic debt retirement, nor would it afford much protection
for bondholders. The amounts and payment dates are fixed by calculation,
which involves annuity tables. The terminal value of an annuity is the total
accumulation of the specific rents over n payment intervals with interest at
some specified rate. There are also tables of the reciprocals of corresponding
terminal value factors. Such tables show the ratio of the periodic payment or
rent to the principal repayable at maturity, on the express assumption that the
entire accumulation will be invested at the specified rate of interest. A $2 mil-
lion maturity value may be accumulated over 40 interest periods by making
semiannual contributions of $10,018 if the fund can be invested to earn 7 per-
cent (14 percent compounded semiannually). The rate expected to be earned
in the fund does not bear any necessary relation to either the coupon or yield
rate on the bond issue; it is merely what is expected to be earned by the fund
as invested by the trustee. Obviously, the rate applicable to the fund may be
(and usually is) less than the rate on the bond issue. This is a disadvantage to
the borrower, because the funds might (and probably would) earn more if used
in the business for which they were borrowed. But like other costs, the difference in interest earnings on the fund and the borrowing rate may be worth
incurring.

Relation of borrower to sinking fund. It may be worthwhile to stress that the
borrower does not control the fund; it is really "bondholders'" money in the
hands of the trustee. Yet the fund does serve to offset the borrower's obligations
and is therefore an accountable item, even though it is not an asset to the borrower. The trustee will periodically report to the corporation the status of the

fund, so that the proper accounting may be maintained for correct costs and financial position. Trustees may also report to bondholders, but such reports are rare and of limited content. The borrower's payment to the trustee will be occasion for the entry:

Bond Sinking Fund	10,018	
Cash		10,018

When the trustee makes investments, there is no need to record these on the borrower's books, but income or loss will be reported periodically. Usually the trustee will report the position of the fund in detail as well as the related income and expense data per semiannum—certainly not less often than once a year. Typically these data will be received by the borrower in time for his own annual report; often, the reporting period coincides with that of the borrower.

Taking up fund income and expense. The borrower seldom has reason to bring details of retirement fund transactions into his records. Usually, the only entry required on the books of the borrower is to take up the income (or loss) from the trustees' operations. This is

Bond Sinking Fund	xxx	
Bond Interest Charges		xxx

By this entry, the sinking fund income merely reduces the interest charges on that bond issue. (Obviously, the accounting for several issues is kept separate.) If desired, the credit in the entry above might be made to Sinking Fund Income to preserve this detail; however, the net effect is not income to the borrower but only a reduction in his cost of borrowing. The fund belongs to the bondholders, and its assets and income merely offset the borrower's obligations and costs.

Income from sinking funds rarely necessitates allocation to fit the amounts into the borrower's fiscal period. Many trustees' reports are on a cash basis. If needed to prevent serious distortions, the trustee's reporting date could be synchronized with the corporate fiscal period.

Combining interest and retirement fund contributions. If the trustee who handles the retirement fund is also the disbursing agent for the interest on the bonds, the payment for both purposes may be combined.

The sinking fund contribution should generally be computed separately, as outlined above, and the amount required for interest *payments* added as a separate amount. This is applied to the case just described, a $2 million, 15 percent bond to be retired by semiannual contributions to a sinking fund that is expected to earn 7 percent semiannually. The amount required for each semiannual payment to cover principal and interest would be $10,018, plus $150,000 for "interest," a total of $160,018.

Perhaps it is worth noting that a sinking fund invested at the coupon rate is mathematically equal to an amortized mortgage loan. Any compound interest calculation assumes that every dollar in the computation grows at exactly the same rate; that is, there is automatic reinvestment implicit in the accumulation of receipts and payments over time, unless the calculations specifically make it otherwise. If the rate of interest earned by the fund is equal to the coupon rate on the bonds and the bonds are to be retired at par, the sinking fund is mathematically no different from an amortized mortgage in which each payment combines interest and principal to retire the debt over the term.

Sinking funds invested in bonds of the same issue. The question may well be asked: Why is the sinking fund not used to acquire bonds of the issue it is supposed to retire? The answer is, of course, that this is indeed a good use of such funds, not only because it serves the intended purpose of the fund (to pay off bonds of that issue), but also because the rate of return may be higher than that of other investment opportunities for the trustee's investment.

But it must be recognized that investment in bonds of the same issue that the fund is supposed to pay off is really retirement of those bonds. In the absence of specific provisions to permit resale of those bonds, they must be regarded as effectively retired when they come into the hands of the trustee. Hence it is not acceptable to treat such bonds as outstanding and to show interest cost to the borrower (corresponding to income to the fund), when the bonds are actually held by the trustee, even though the trustee may consider them to be "live" investments of the fund.

When bonds of the issue are acquired by the trustee and reported to the corporation, the amount of bonds, the remaining unamortized premium or discount, and any premium, discount, or cost involved in the reacquisition by the trustee should be written off.

To illustrate, suppose that $5,000 face value of bonds (15 percent, 20-year, $2 million issue, originally sold for $1,975,000) are acquired by the trustee 17 months after the issue date. The bonds then have a carrying amount of $4,941.93 on a straight-line basis (original issue price $4,937.50, plus 17 months' amortization at $.26 per month). Assuming that the trustee acquired these bonds at 99 (plus 5 months' accrued coupon "interest" at 15 percent per year), his cost was $5,262.50 ($4,950 + $312.50 "interest"). The trustee's report would (on a cash basis) show only the $5,262.50 payment. The borrower's books, however, would record:

Interest Charges	312.50	
Bonds Payable	5,000.00	
Loss on Retirement of Bonds	8.07	
Discount on Bonds Payable		58.07
Bond Sinking Fund		5,262.50

Thereafter, this $5,000 face value of bonds would be ignored in the borrower's records, even though the trustee would continue to be paid the cash "interest" and to report "income from investments" of this amount. The simplest treatment would of course be to cancel the bonds entirely, if necessary adjusting the sinking fund contribution to make up for the change in investment income. (The amount of this adjustment would of course be small, because the retirement amount is reduced by the reacquisition.) But most sinking fund indentures do not provide for this, because the requirements of the indenture are satisfied only by payment of specified amounts, the cash transfers for interest will continue, with corresponding offsets of interest charges against sinking fund income. Any subsequent accruals or amortizations in the trustee's records and reports concerning these reacquired bonds would of course be ignored by the borrower in his own financial statements.

FASB Statement of Financial Accounting Standards No. 4 [1975] requires that the loss (or analogous gain) on bond retirement be shown as an extraordinary item net of tax effects, if the amount is material. If, however, the bond indenture *requires* periodic sinking fund retirements of the bonds, then the loss (or gain) is not extraordinary.

REFUNDING

At Maturity. At the maturity date, it may be desirable to continue borrowing, even though the old issue must be settled. Refunding is the process of setting up a new issue of bonds sufficiently large to retire the old issue; sometimes the new issue is larger, when growth requires additional capital and the market makes such additional borrowing advantageous. Refunding at maturity date is accounted for as a new issue of bonds, of which some or all of the proceeds are applied to payment of the predecessor obligation. This raises no particular problems, because the two contracts are legally separable.

Before Maturity. When market yield rates have fallen, it may be desirable to replace an outstanding obligation with one that can be marketed at a lower rate of yield. Many bond issues are made callable, to permit the borrower to refinance in this way; the bonds may, under the indenture, be redeemed before maturity at the borrower's option. To compensate the bondholder for what may be for him a disadvantageous repayment, a "call premium" is paid. Usually these vary with the remaining life of the bond. The call privilege raises questions as to the method of accounting for the call premium and other costs of the refunding, as well as the disposition of unamortized premium or discount on the old issue.

Call premiums. The call premium may be viewed as the extra cost of getting rid of the old issue, but it may also be considered as the cost of obtaining the lower rate or other advantages of the new issue. There is no really clear answer to this in most cases, and there has been a variety of practice regarding it in the past. Generally the amount is too large to warrant its absorption as mere interest cost of the period in which the call privilege is exercised. There are, conceivably, several ways to deal with the situation. One is to charge the call premium as a special item of the period of refunding. By this approach, no part of the call premium is charged against the new issue.

Alternatively, one might view the call premium as exclusively the cost of advantageous refunding, and the call premium may be subtracted from the proceeds of the new issue, thus being absorbed into the future interest charges via amortization of premium or discount. By this approach the call premium is not separately reported, except as ancillary information.

A third approach might be to amortize the call premium over the remaining life of the old issue, on the ground that the premium was paid to reduce interest in that interval of overlap.

Premium or discount on the retired issue. When a bond issue is retired before maturity, there is likely to be some amount of unamortized premium or discount. The unamortized balances must be dealt with. They present the same sort of problem as the disposition of the call premium and have been dealt with in the same variety of ways.

The problem was resolved by the Accounting Principles Board in Opinion No. 26 [1972], where it held that "a difference between the reacquisition price including call premiums, if any, and the net carrying amount of the extinguished debt should be recognized currently in income of the period of extinguishment as losses or gains and identified as a separate item." Subsequently, the Financial Accounting Standards Board, in Statement No. 4 [1975], required that such gains or losses be reported as extraordinary items on the income statement.

Establishing discount or premium on the new issue. When the old issue is paid off from proceeds of the new issue, there is not much question of what price was realized and how much discount or premium applies to the new issue. But when the new bonds are exchanged for the old ones, which are then canceled and retired (before maturity), it may not be easy to establish the premium or discount on the new issue.

If some of the refunding bonds are sold in the market, their price may be used to establish the premium or discount on the entire refunding. A market price of 102 suggests a premium of 2 percent on the whole new issue to be amortized over its term.

OTHER RETIREMENT SITUATIONS

Troubled Debt Restructurings. Occasionally, an existing long-term obligation may be discharged or restructured under circumstances that in effect grant an advantage to the debtor company. These so-called troubled debt restructurings are characterized by debtors unable to obtain normal refinancing and unlikely to be able to repay the existing obligations without being forced into liquidation or some other drastic action. In such a situation, the creditor(s) may conclude that a compromise settlement—which may involve reduction of the principal amount owed, stretching out of the maturities of the repayments, reduction or forgiveness of interest charges, or the exchange of the debt for assets or equity interests in the debtor—would be preferable to the uncertain outcome of a forced liquidation.

FASB Statement No. 15 [1977] provides that, under certain conditions, troubled debt restructuring will give rise to the recognition of a gain by the debtor and a loss by the creditor. This will occur if the obligation is settled by the transfer from the debtor to the creditor of assets having a fair value lower than the carrying value of the debt owed. A gain will also be recognized by the debtor if it issues equity securities having a fair value lower than the carrying value of the debt discharged. In either case, in the period of the troubled debt restructuring, full disclosure of the transaction must be made in the financial statements, and the gain on the restructuring (if any is realized) must be reported as an extraordinary item, net of income taxes, if it is material.

Other types of debt restructurings do not result in the recognition of gains and losses. If the restructuring involves a change in either the amounts or timing of future principal or interest payments—that is, a stretching out or reduction of these future payments—there will generally be no gain recognition by the debtor. Instead, the restructuring is accounted for prospectively, as future payments are made. The only exception is where future payments for principal and interest are less than the recorded carrying value of the obligation. In this case, the carrying value must be written down, and a gain recognized for the amount of this reduction.

For example, consider a debtor that had issued a $500,000 note bearing 15 percent interest due in 5 years. After a period of losses and other difficulties, the debtor has negotiated a restructuring with its creditor. The new arrangement reduces the amount owed to $200,000, and also reduces the interest rate to 10 percent. The resulting debt is to be paid in 10 equal installments every 6 months. Consulting an annuity table (or by use of a calculator), we find that this will require semiannual payments of $25,900.

In this case, gain will be recognized by the debtor at the time of the restructuring, because the total of the future interest and principal payments ($25,900 × 10 = $259,000) is lower than the recorded value of the obligation that has been restructured ($500,000). Therefore a gain of $500,000 − $259,000 = $241,000 is recognized. All future payments will then be treated as reductions of the revised principal value of the debt, with no interest component. Note that the original interest rate (15 percent in this case) plays no role in computing the gain to be recognized in this restructuring.

If the foregoing example were altered so that the revision of the loan agreement called for a new principal amount of $400,000, again with 10 percent interest and semiannual repayments, no gain would be recognized on the restructuring. This is because total future payments for interest and principal equal $518,000 (approximately), which exceeds the recorded amount of the old obligation. The restructuring would be recognized prospectively, however, in this manner: The future semiannual payments would be treated as having an interest component of approximately .65 percent per (semiannual) period, or about 1.30 percent per annum, which is the rate necessary to equate an annuity of $51,800 for 10 semiannual periods to a present value of $500,000. Again, the original 15 percent interest rate is irrelevant.

Finally, if a restructuring involved a combination of asset transfer (or equity issuance) and alteration of the terms of the original debt (a stretch-out or reduction of principal or interest), a gain may or may not arise. FASB Statement No. 15 [1977] specifies that the asset swap (or equity issuance) must be applied dollar for dollar against the old obligation, with no gain recognition; but that the accompanying modification of terms be compared to the remaining face value of the old debt as illustrated above, with the possible recognition of a gain if the future interest and principal payments are lower than this residual. For example, if the $500,000 15 percent obligation above were restructured so that assets having a fair value of $200,000 were transferred immediately to the creditor, who also agreed that the remaining obligation would be settled by semi-annual payments of $25,900 as in the above example, then a gain of $41,000 would be recognized by the debtor, computed as follows:

Original obligation	$500,000
Less: Fair value of assets transferred	200,000
Residual obligation	$300,000
10 year, 10% semiannual annuity series, giving	
semiannual payments of $25,900	
Times number of payments . . . . $\times$ 10	
Total payments under new agreement	259,000
Gain on restructuring	$ 41,000

If the foregoing arrangement had called for the transfer of the same property plus a reduction of the remaining loan to $250,000 (a nominal $50,000 loan forgiveness) with interest at 10 percent (again, a nominal reduction from the original 15 percent rate), with semiannual repayments over 5 years, *no* gain would have accrued, as shown below:

Original obligation	$500,000
Less: Fair value of assets transferred	200,000
Residual obligation	$300,000
New obligation: $250,000 plus 10% interest, due	
semiannually, yielding annuity payments	
of $32,376	
Times payments . . . . $\times$ 10	
Total cash payments due	323,760
Excess of future payments over residual	
obligation.	$ 23,760

As long as the total of future interest and principal payments exceeds the recorded value of the existing obligation (reduced, if appropriate, by the fair value of assets transferred or equity interests given in partial settlement thereof), no gain on the troubled debt restructuring will be recognized. Benefits of the restructuring (lower future payments) will thus be recognized only—implicitly—as future payments are made.

ADDITIONAL RETIREMENT SITUATIONS

Purchase in the Market by the Borrower. A borrower who has funds that are not needed for operations may well view the market quotations on outstanding bonds as an opportunity for savings. The decision to purchase bonds in this way is based on an analysis much like that just described in refunding. But the alternatives are somewhat different. The amount that would be required to pay off some existing debt would alternatively be invested in various ways.

The effective interest rate in such an analysis is not that of the bonds (either coupon or yield rate), because the bond purchase is not an investment but debt retirement. The effective interest rate in this situation is the *highest* comparable yield that could be had from investing elsewhere that amount needed to retire the bonds. Any lower yield is less desirable unless it is accompanied by lower risk or other offsetting features. But the investment term must be the same as the remaining life of the bonds.

Discounting the maturity amount and the "interest" payments at the "highest comparable yield" should produce a lower figure than the current market price of the bonds, if retirement is advantageous. This lower figure measures the cost of retiring the issue (the earning rate if invested elsewhere). If the cost of retiring the issue is less than the cost of continuing it, the bonds should be purchased and retired.

When bonds are reacquired, they are retired, even if not canceled. The par amount is carried as treasury bonds, offset against outstanding face amounts on the balance sheet. Premiums and discounts arising from purchase, as well as those amounts remaining unamortized from the original issue, are written off as gain or loss on bond retirement. If reissued, the bonds may, for practical reasons, be restated at the carrying value of the other bonds of that issue. This avoids the complication of tracing the discount or premium separately for the reissued bonds.

Purchase by Sinking Fund Trustee. This has already been mentioned above. The essential point is that in the reports of the borrower, bonds held by a sinking fund trustee are treated as effectively retired, even though cash may still be transferred to the sinking fund to cover "interest" on the bonds so held, in keeping with fund calculations.

General Offers to Repurchase Bonds. Sometimes in an effort to retire debt that is not callable, borrowers may make general public offers to purchase such securities. Any such purchases would be accounted for in the same way as detailed above; amounts in excess of or less than par, and any unamortized premium or discount, would appear as (extraordinary) gain or loss on retirement of bonds.

Conversion. Some bonds carry the privilege of conversion into other securities, and this may serve as a means of retiring the debt. The conversion privilege is usually restricted to certain periods, and there is a specified conversion price or ratio, such as "at a price of $68 per common share" or in the ratio of "20 shares for each $1,000 principal amount (par) of bonds." All that is required to record such conversion is to transfer the book equity of the bonds (par plus or minus unamortized premium or discount) to appropriate stock equity accounts. But it should be stressed that the conversion should transfer the pro rata amount of all bond premiums or discounts and other costs that may be involved, against the credits to various paid-in capital accounts.

Some accountants would favor crediting the stock or paid-in capital accounts with the market value of the shares issued on conversion, showing the difference between this amount and the related bond equities retired as a gain or loss on conversion. This is in keeping with the view of market price as the opportunity cost of issuing shares to other parties or the amount that bondholders could realize by selling the shares immediately after conversion. However, it must also be recognized that convertible bonds are issued with full recognition of the possibility of conversion; the change in investment position is thus inherently assumed in the original issue. The weakness in using the market price of the stock issued on conversion is not only that the book value of the debt includes the expected value of the conversion privilege, but also that it results in a gain or loss to the corporation when only securities are exchanged. An advantage or disadvantage to other shareholders is not a gain or loss to the entity.

Reorganizations and compositions. Bonds are frequently involved in recapitalizations, reorganizations, and compositions in which securities may be exchanged to give priority or to rearrange the financial structure generally. Bonds may be exchanged for other bonds, or for preferred or common stock in various ways. Because such arrangements generally involve a scaling down of equities carried over to the new structure, the principal issue is to be sure that all the elements of exchanged, retired, or canceled obligations are written off along with the major equities involved. Because the details of this are generally spelled out in the negotiations, the accountant needs only to be sure that the negotiations do in fact cover all the necessary angles and that the resulting pattern of equities and interest will accomplish the desired results.

FINANCIAL STATEMENT PRESENTATION OF BONDS

Each issue separately shown and labeled. The borrower will, of course, identify and separate the accounting for each bond issue in the balance sheet or the notes thereto. For each issue, the general nature of the obligation should be revealed, as by caption, "15 percent 20-year second mortgage bonds," even though it may not be possible to indicate to what property the second mortgage applies and what else may be involved in the bondholder's position. The caption must identify the issue, even though it cannot completely explain its provisions.

Authorization amounts disclosed. The authorized amount of each issue should be given, especially where there are authorized but unissued bonds, and additional bonds may be issued upon management's decision to do so. Any part of the issue that matures at a date different from the rest of the issue should be segregated and reported separately, especially if the earlier maturity makes that portion of the bond a current liability.

Discounts or premiums. Discounts or premiums on issue should be amortized by an accepted method, and the balances subtracted from, or added to, the par or face amount of the liability. Bond discount formerly was frequently treated as an asset and bond premium as a liability separate from the par amount. Accounting Principles Board Opinion No. 21 [1971] ruled out such practice by holding that "The discount or premium . . . is not an asset or liability separable from the note [bond] which gives rise to it. Therefore the discount or premium should be reported in the balance sheet as a direct deduction from or addition to the face amount of the note [bond]. It should not be classified as a deferred charge or deferred credit."

Other offsets—sinking fund balances. Bond retirement funds or sinking funds should appear as deductions from the current amount of the outstanding debt, to reflect the net liability on the issue. It will be noted that this will serve to reduce the net liability by the amount of any reacquired bonds held alive by the trustee. Obviously, any bonds treated as effectively retired would have been subtracted from the par, discount, or premium accounts by those entries. "Reserves" for sinking funds are misnomers; when there is appropriation of retained earnings, it should be so labeled.

Treasury bonds. Occasionally a borrowing company may acquire some of its own bonds, which it may hold as "treasury" bonds. If such bonds cannot be resold under the terms of the bond indenture, they should be canceled with appropriate entries, to retire face, unamortized issue premium or discount, and any other costs or savings from reacquisition. If the bonds can be resold by the borrower, there is no objection to carrying them at cost, so long as that cost is not in excess of reasonably recoverable amounts. Any such excess is a loss from reacquisition of bonds. According to FASB Statement No. 4 [1975], material losses, net of tax effects, on acquisition of such treasury bonds are extraordinary. When such bonds are resold, their accounting status should be made the same as the other bonds of that issue at that time, to avoid the need for separate premium or discount calculations related to probably immaterial amounts.

When treasury bonds do appear on the balance sheet, the amount should be subtracted from the bond liability that remains after deduction of sinking fund balances.

SERIAL BONDS

Current portion. When portions of long-term obligations, such as bonds payable, are due within one operating cycle (usually defined as 1 year) from the balance sheet date, that portion should be presented as a current liability, appropriately identified as being related to the long-term portion of that debt. An analogous situation arises when an item customarily treated as a short-term liability is *not* going to be extinguished within one operating cycle—that is, when it is not going to require the use of current assets to settle the obligation. In such a case, it may be inappropriate to present the liability in the current section of the balance sheet.

FASB Statement No. 6 [1975] provides that when a short-term obligation (which could include the current portion of a long-term debt issue) is the object of an intention to refinance on the part of the obligor, and when the obligor can demonstrate the ability to consummate this refinancing, the liability should be presented in the noncurrent section of the balance sheet. Essentially, the ability to consummate the intended refinancing must be demonstrated either by the actual post-balance sheet date issuance of long-term obligations or equity securities, or by the existence of a valid financing agreement entered into *before* the balance sheet date.

Sinking or bond retirement funds have the advantage of systematizing the repayment of bonds, but there are disadvantages. These arise from the fact that there is no assurance of obtaining a return on the sinking fund investment equal to the yield rate on the bonds, nor any certain way to retire a part of the issue before maturity. These disadvantages may be avoided by substituting an arrangement that calls for specific retirements on definite dates. Some of these arrangements are structured quite systematically in patterns of serial maturities. That is, bonds of a given issue covered by a single indenture may have maturity dates of 5, 10, 15, and 20 years, for example, one-fourth of the issue being due on each of the maturity dates, as specified on its face.

Such a serial bond issue is like any other issue, except that the several retirement dates complicate the computation of yield rates for the issue as a whole and thus make the accounting for discounts or premiums a somewhat complex matter. This is not to say that there is no yield percentage that can be applied to the issue, for the average rate could indeed be computed. But this calculation would be a tedious one, and it is doubtful that such an "average" rate (for that is what it would be) really makes complete sense. A bond that matures early obviously has a yield different from one that matures later, for the length of term affects the yield substantially. There has been much written on this topic of the term structure of interest rates. Differences between two compared proposals may be *relatively* much larger or smaller than the absolute figures suggest. A 50-year term is 10 years longer, and 1¼ times as long as a 40-year term; but a 15-year term, 10 years longer than a 5-year term, is three times as long! To be precise in dealing with yields on serial bonds, we ought to compute a yield for each maturity block and account for each block's premiums or discounts separately; this is not easy, for example, when there are 20 blocks, with maturity dates 2 years apart.

The simplest way to handle discount or premium on a serial bond issue is to use the *bonds outstanding method.* This prorates the bond discount or premium so that each $1,000 unit bears the same dollar charge or credit per time period; the interest charges are thereby kept reasonably consistent. The method will be clear from the following example. Suppose that a $1 million, 8 percent bond issue matures in amounts of $200,000 each year, beginning at the end of the fifth year after issue. There will be $1 million of bonds outstanding in the first 5 years, $800,000 during the sixth, $600,000 in the seventh, $400,000 in the eighth, and $200,000 in the ninth year, a total of $7 million "dollar years."

If the entire issue was sold for $1,014,000, the premium of $14,000 divided by the $7 million dollar year total gives a rate of premium amortization per dollar of bonds outstanding per year. The figure is $2/1,000 = .002$. The premium amortization, cash interest, and total interest charges may be seen in Exhibit 2. This apparently gives the same charge for each dollar of bonds outstanding per year and is a reasonable solution to the problem. But it is, after all, a "straight-line" solution of the problem, which does not show the true rate of interest in the individual years. The apparent rate of interest (7.8 percent) is a linear average rate but not the correct yield rate, because the correct yield rate should discount all the future payments to the issue price.

Single yield rate for the entire issue. The basic problem in using the compound interest amortization with a single rate for the entire serial bond issue is to calculate the correct yield rate. This requires a trial-and-error approach. For example, the bonds outstanding calculation just presented gives an apparent

---

EXHIBIT 2   Illustration of "Bonds Outstanding" Method

Year	Outstanding bonds	Coupon "interest"	Premium amortized	Net interest cost
1	$1,000,000	$ 80,000	$ 2,000	$ 78,000
2	1,000,000	80,000	2,000	78,000
3	1,000,000	80,000	2,000	78,000
4	1,000,000	80,000	2,000	78,000
5	1,000,000	80,000	2,000	78,000
6	800,000	64,000	1,600	62,400
7	600,000	48,000	1,200	46,800
8	400,000	32,000	800	31,200
9	200,000	16,000	400	15,600
Totals......	$7,000,000	$560,000	$14,000	$546,000

---

rate of 7.8 percent (3.9 percent semiannually). If this rate is applied to discount the payments involved, the present worth is approximately $1,010,545. The smaller premium suggests that the rate of 3.9 percent is slightly too high; trial of, say, 3.8 percent might indicate that the correct rate is between these, and the approximation could continue to any desired level of precision. Use of that rate would follow the compound interest yield procedure described earlier. Applying the yield rate to the carrying amount gives the initial charge for that period; the difference between the interest charge and the cash "interest" for that period is the amortization of premium or discount.

Separate rates for different maturities. This approach treats each block of bonds as a separate issue and establishes a yield rate for each block. The compound interest procedure will thus give appropriate charges and amortization amounts. This procedure is most useful when specific prices are established for each block of bonds—which is not uncommon. But if the entire issue is sold at a single price, there is no satisfactory way to prorate the discount or premium to separate blocks so as to establish a yield for each block.

OTHER LONG-TERM LIABILITIES

The long-term liabilities that have been discussed in this chapter have their origin in borrowing transactions. Repayments of loans due after 1 year have been shown at their present worths using interest rates specified in the contracts or inferred from them. Liabilities arising from other transactions are subject to somewhat different treatment.

Deferred Revenue Obligations. When customers pay for goods or services in advance of delivery, these payments represent an obligation to complete the transaction, for revenue is not "earned" until then. This obligation may run for only a short period, and in such case is a current liability; but if the interval between the transfer of cash and delivery is longer than a year, the obligation is considered of long-term nature. An example is prepayment for magazine subscriptions. Receipts would be credited to a deferred revenue account, transferred to income as deliveries are made; at the end of each year the balance would be divided into short- and long-term maturities. Because the rate charged for long-term subscriptions is lower per issue, amortization on a straight-line basis would leave the liability at a kind of "present worth" that, though not explicitly determined, is implied in the contract.

Similar items arise from the receipt by fire and casualty insurance companies of premiums for 3 or 5 years in advance. Financial position for insurance companies is not judged in the same way as that for commercial and industrial ones, and the distinction between current and long-term liabilities is not maintained in their financial reports.

There may be other long-term liabilities in the form of advances on long-term construction contracts; these are really deferred revenue, typically shown at the amounts received—not discounted. Such items are specifically exempted from the need for discounting in Accounting Principles Board Opinion No. 21 [1971].

Product Warranties. When a vendor company has agreed to make repairs or replacements of defective parts over a period of years, a liability is created for the estimated cost of making such repairs or replacements. Otherwise, the period of sale would not show part of the expense attributable to the revenues recognized in that period. Determination of such costs entails estimation, for their incidence is uncertain. Experience data provide a basis for such estimates; or laboratory testing will indicate likely failure rates for various parts and assemblies. Assume that over a 5-year period for one such item these failure rates may be 1, 2, 2, 4, and 5 percent. The expected cost of making this replacement being $35 per unit, the current year's sale of 100,000 units implies costs to be incurred in the first year after sale of $35,000, and the other years should show $70,000, $70,000, $140,000, and $175,000, respectively. In the year of sale, the total estimated warranty expense of $490,000 is debited with a credit to Estimated Liability, Product Warranties. The outlays made during that year are charged against Estimated Liability; if these are $32,000, the balance of $458,000 will appear as $73,000 current liability and $385,000 long-term liability.

This procedure serves to match costs against sales revenue unless the failure rates are incorrect. Adjustment may be made whenever the error becomes apparent. To be strictly logical, however, the liability should be shown discounted to present worth; the company has the use of the customers' money to cover these costs until they are incurred. And unless the expected costs of replacement are estimated in terms of the prices that will prevail when replacements occur, the liability is not stated precisely. In a period of rising prices these two errors may tend to offset each other.

Outstanding Tickets, Coupons, and Trading Stamps. The obligation to honor tickets, coupons, or trading stamps is a liability unless limited by an expiration date. These obligations may involve refunds or the delivery of goods or services, and sometimes the period over which they extend may be long. Identifying the issue date of such obligations (by serial number, code markings, or otherwise) provides a basis for experience data to be collected, matching issues with redemptions over a time. Because some items may be entirely unredeemed, there may be no way to check the outstanding obligation, and/or to identify windfall income from unredeemed items. Reasonableness is the only test that can be applied. As in the case of product warranties, discounting and anticipated price changes are ignored.

Pension Liabilities. Obligations to provide some form of retirement income for superannuated employees or for those disabled by accidents constitute a class of long-term liabilities. Accounting for these will depend on the way in which the situation is handled. A part of this group of obligations is covered by government agencies, and some firms have merely made specified contributions to a pension trust fund or to an insurance company to transfer the pension liability. In such cases, the accounting liability of the employer is merely the amount owed to the trust fund or the insurance company. But if, as has become increasingly the case, the company recognizes the entire liability in its accounting, the actuarially computed amount is the discounted net probable future payments to retired employees. There are a number of complex issues involved in accounting for pension costs, and they are discussed in Chapter 25.

Leases. Many leases that cover more than a relatively short lease term are, in economic substance, transfers of substantial ownership interests in the underlying property. Such leases, which are referred to as *capital leases,* are properly accounted for (in accordance with FASB Statement No. 13 [1976]) as purchases of assets and as long-term obligations by the lessee, and as sales of property and the creation of receivables by the lessor. As with most other long-term liabilities, generally accepted accounting principles require that these obligations be presented at the discounted present value of the future payments—the appropriate discount rate generally being related to either the rate implicit in the lease agreement or the so-called incremental borrowing rate of the lessee. Also in common with other long-term debt obligations, the current portion, if any, is presented as a current liability in the balance sheet. Lease accounting is discussed in greater detail in Chapter 24.

Deferred Tax Liabilities. One of the most complex areas of accounting theory and practice involves interperiod income tax allocation, or deferred tax accounting. Briefly, because the federal income tax laws and regulations in many cases permit or require income or expense items to be included in taxable income in periods other than are required by generally accepted accounting principles, there will arise so-called timing differences in computing income tax expense for financial reporting purposes. As one consequence, deferred tax benefits (assets) or deferred tax credits (liabilities), or both, may appear on the balance sheet.

Although APB Opinion No. 11 [1971] refers to these items as deferred tax credits, they are usually treated as long-term liabilities. Unlike most other long-term liabilities, deferred tax liabilities are *not* presented at the net present value of future outflows, but rather are presented at the amounts computed (in accordance with APB Opinion No. 11) on the timing differences at the time those differences originated. This will not necessarily be the amount that ultimately must be paid—and, in fact, in periods when the statutory tax rates have changed, as they have several times in recent years, the reported deferred tax liability may differ substantially from the estimated obligation for future taxes upon the reversal of the timing differences.

Whether a deferred tax liability (or, for that matter, a deferred tax benefit) should be presented as a current or a noncurrent item in the balance sheet depends not on when it is expected to result in a cash outflow—as would generally be the criterion—but on which liability or asset the tax account is related to. For example, if an entity utilized accelerated cost recovery methods for tax reporting purposes, but straight-line depreciation for financial statement purposes, a deferred tax liability will result, part of which may be "short-term" insofar as expected reversal is concerned. Nonetheless, because this item is related to plant assets, which are noncurrent, the resulting deferred tax account will also be shown as a noncurrent item.

In a few cases, a deferred tax liability may not be traceable directly to a specific asset or liability account on the balance sheet, and thus it may be difficult to identify it as current or noncurrent in nature. In such instances, using the guidance provided by FASB Statement No. 37 [1980], the traditional accounting criterion, expected timing of the settlement of the obligation, is appropriate.

For a more complete discussion of this topic, see Chapter 36.

Miscellaneous Other Debts. Whenever there exists a legal or equitable requirement to pay money or deliver services to outsiders at some determinable future time for benefits received currently, a liability should be recorded, even if the amount can only be estimated. For example, agreements to replace topsoil removed for strip mining or similar operations, to make improvements such as landscaping a real estate subdivision, or to restore leased property to its condition at the inception of the lease entail charges to expense and recognition of the liability thus recognized. The cost of future performance should be estimated and accumulated by systematic accrual over the term of the agreement to assign the future costs on the basis of benefits received.

Suppose that a development contract will require outlays estimated to be $15,000 at the end of 2 years, and also $25,000, $40,000, and $50,000 at the end of successive years, a total expenditure of $130,000. This cost might be assigned on the basis of annual sales in units in the 5 years, expected to be 8,000, 6,000, 7,000, 4,000, and 2,000 in order. The expense charges credited to a long-term liability account would then be $38,518, $28,889, $33,704, $19,259, and $9,630 in the successive years; the outlays when made would extinguish the liability at the end of the term, if the estimates were correct. The costs would have been recognized as expense in the years when benefits (as measured by sales) were received.

Although this treatment is conventionally accepted, it ignores the timing of events and payments; only a small part of the liability would be paid by the end of the third year, for example. This can be taken into account by compound interest methods to achieve a better allocation of costs with respect to timing and the interest cost.

The present worth of future outlays at 10 percent is $15,000(1.1)^{-2}$ + $25,000(1.1)^{-3}$ + $40,000(1.1)^{-4}$ + $50,000(1.1)^{-5}$. Using a present value table, these reduce to $12,397 + $18,784 + $27,320 + $31,046; the total present worth is $89,547.

EXHIBIT 3   Compound Interest and Cost Allocation

Year	(1) Beginning balance	(2) Interest at 10%	(3) Expense charge	(4) Actual payments
1	0	0	$ 33,374	0
2	$33,374	$ 3,337	25,031	$ 15,000
3	46,742	4,674	29,203	25,000
4	55,619	5,562	16,687	40,000
5	37,868	3,787	8,344	50,000
Totals.		$17,360	$112,639	$130,000

The benefit series would also be discounted: $8,000(1.1)^{-1} + $6,000(1.1)^{-2} + $7,000(1.1)^{-3} + $4,000(1.1)^{-4} + $2,000(1.1)^{-5}$, which would work out to $7,272 + $4,959 + $5,259 + $2,732 + $1,242, a total of $21,464.

Dividing the present worth of future payments by the present worth of future benefits, we get $4.1718 as the unit relationship of cost to benefits. This unit cost applied to the sales volumes of individual years gives expense charges of $33,374, $25,031, $29,203, $16,687, and $2,344. This totals to only $112,639, because interest has not been computed on the difference between expense charges and payments in the individual years. This can be worked out in an amortization table, as shown in Exhibit 3. Beginning balance (1) is the remainder of the preceding line, which is (1) + (2) + (3) − (4). These calculations assume that interest is charged at the end of each year; more refined computations assuming shorter periods would be somewhat more "accurate," but the net effect of this would not be substantial. The total of the "beginning balance" column is meaningless—an average computed from this total would not be correct unless based on an abstruse calculation that included compound interest effects.

Expense charges would then be the sums of interest and expense: $33,374, $28,368, $33,876, $22,249, and $12,131. This allocation is preferable to conventional procedure on logical grounds, but is not often followed in practice.

CONTINGENT LIABILITIES

Accounting Principles Board Statement No. 4 [1970] states in Paragraph 133:

> The *financial position* of an enterprise at a particular time comprises its assets, liabilities, and owners' equity and the relationship among them, plus those contingencies, commitments, and other financial matters that pertain to the enterprise at that time. . . .

FASB Statement No. 5 [1975] defines a loss contingency as an existing condition, situation, or set of circumstances involving uncertainty as to possible loss to an enterprise that will ultimately be resolved when one or more future events occur or fail to occur. These may then confirm the impairment of an asset or the incurrence of a liability.

In general, loss contingencies are to be either accrued and presented as a liability in the balance sheet or disclosed in the notes; the precise treatment depends on the degree of precision with which the liability may be estimated and the likelihood with which the ultimate impairment or incurrence is anticipated. Statement No. 5 establishes three such degrees of likelihood: probable, reasonably possible, and remote. Loss contingencies that are judged to be probable, and that can be reasonably estimated as to the amount of loss, are to be accrued—that is, the loss is to be charged against income currently, and the liability is to be reflected in the balance sheet. FASB Interpretation No. 14 [1976] explains that when "the reasonable estimate of the loss is a range," the most likely estimate within the range is the amount of the loss to be recognized. If no amount within the range is thought to be more likely than any other, then the amount at the lower end of the range is recognized.

Probable losses that cannot be reasonably estimated as to amount, and loss contingencies that are deemed to be "reasonably possible" in likelihood, are to be disclosed as footnote-type items, but will not affect the financial statement amounts directly. Remote loss contingencies either are not disclosed at all or are simply presented in footnotes, depending partially on tradition (e.g., certain guarantees of indebtedness, which give rise to only a remote loss contingency, are generally disclosed).

The practice, common at one time, of setting up a "reserve for general contingencies" through charges against earnings is no longer permissible. It is still acceptable to appropriate part of the retained earnings account and label this as being reserved for general contingencies, but this is now rarely done. No actual losses may be charged against this reserve. Actual losses, when they occur, must be charged against income in the period they occur or, if earlier deemed to be probable and subject to reasonable estimation, in such earlier period.

BIBLIOGRAPHY

Accounting Principles Board (AICPA), *Interest on Receivables and Payables*, Opinion No. 11 (APB, 1971).

———, *Interest on Receivables and Payables*, Opinion No. 21 (APB, 1971).

———, *Early Extinguishment of Debt*, Opinion No. 26 (APB, 1972).

Davidson, S., J. S. Schindler, and R. L. Weil, *Fundamentals of Accounting*, 5th ed. (Dryden Press, Hinsdale, Ill., 1975), chap. 15.

Financial Accounting Standards Board, *Reporting Gains and Losses from Extinguishment of Debt*, Statement of Financial Accounting Standards No. 4 (FASB, 1975).

———, *Accounting for Contingencies*, Statement of Financial Accounting Standards No. 5 (FASB, 1975).

———, *Classification of Short-Term Obligations Expected to Be Refinanced*, Statement of Financial Accounting Standards No. 6 (FASB, 1975).

———, *Accounting for Leases*, Statement of Financial Accounting Standards No. 13 (FASB, 1976).

———, *Reasonable Estimation of the Amount of a Loss*, Interpretation No. 14 (FASB, 1976).

———, *Accounting for Debtors and Creditors for Troubled Debt Restructurings*, Statement of Financial Accounting Standards No. 15 (FASB, 1977).

————, *Balance Sheet Classification of Deferred Income Taxes,* Statement of Financial Accounting Standards No. 37 (FASB, 1980).

————, *Elements of Financial Statements of Business Enterprises,* Statement of Financial Accounting Concepts No. 3 (FASB, 1980).

————, *Extinguishments of Debt Made to Satisfy Sinking Fund Requirements,* Statement of Financial Accounting Standards No. 64 (FASB, 1982).

Kieso, D. E., and J. J. Weygandt, *Intermediate Accounting* (John Wiley & Sons, New York, 1980), chap. 14.

Meigs, W. B., *Intermediate Accounting,* 4th ed. (McGraw-Hill Book Company, New York, 1978), chap. 18.

Simons, H., *Intermediate Accounting,* Comprehensive Volume (Southwestern Publishing, Cincinnati, Ohio, 1972), chap. 18.

Welsh, G. A., C. T. Zlatkovich, and W. T. Harrison, Jr., *Intermediate Accounting,* 5th ed. (Richard D. Irwin, Homewood, Ill., 1979), chap. 17.

CHAPTER 24

Leases

Dennis W. Monson
Partner, Peat, Marwick, Mitchell & Co.

INTRODUCTION

A lease is a contract that conveys the right to use property, generally for a specified period of time. Leases have been used for centuries as a device for transferring to a user of property less than full ownership rights in that property. The user or lessee receives a leasehold interest in the property that is defined by the terms of the lease agreement and protected by the principles of contract law.

Until relatively recently, leasing was confined primarily to real property. Since the end of World War II, however, leasing has become increasingly popular as a means of financing the acquisition of personal property as well.

Among the economic considerations that have contributed to the growing popularity of leasing as a financing alternative are the following:

1. Leasing makes it possible to transfer the significant tax benefits derived from ownership of property from the user of that property to another party. Thus, a lessee with a low marginal income tax rate may be able to obtain a significantly reduced borrowing cost by arranging to lease the capital equipment from a lessor having a higher marginal income tax rate. This transfer of tax benefits is usually a significant economic factor in leveraged leasing.

2. Leasing generally has provided lessees with "off-balance-sheet" financing of production facilities and equipment. By not recording leased assets and corresponding lease liabilities on their balance sheets, lessees have been able to improve balance sheet ratios and change the timing of reported earnings in a generally favorable way.

3. Leasing can provide lessees with significant protection against losses resulting from technological obsolescence. This feature accounts for much of the popularity of leasing in many high-technology markets including, most notably, computer hardware and electronics. (One presumes, however, that rational lessors take potential obsolesence into account in negotiating lease terms.)

4. Leasing usually results in a lower cash outflow for the lessee during the early years of a lease than would be required through a purchase with conventional financing.

5. Leasing is often the only financing method available to thinly capitalized companies and companies with weak credit ratings. Most leases require only a nominal cash investment from the lessee at the beginning of the lease. Thus, a lessee who could not accumulate the down payment required for a conventional secured loan may be able to obtain the use of an asset that would not be otherwise affordable. At the same time, the lessor of such an asset retains a security interest in the asset that is superior to that of a secured lender. In the event of default or bankruptcy, it is generally easier to regain control of leased property than to foreclose on a lien or mortgage.

6. Leasing may provide lessors some protection against interest rate fluctuations and inflation. As the owner of the leased asset, a lessor can realize significant appreciation in the value of an asset at the end of the lease. For example, in recent years the market value of some jet aircraft at the end of an initial 15-year lease has proved to be greater than the original cost of the aircraft. Thus,

whereas mortgage lenders are just beginning to experiment with "shared appreciation mortgages" for real estate loans, leasing companies have, in effect, been making such loans on personal property for years in the form of financing leases.

Leasing has proved to be a versatile and flexible vehicle for financing the acquisition of capital goods. It has adapted easily to changes in tax laws and accounting standards. There is every reason to believe that it will continue to play an important role in financing business expansion and improvements.

Accounting for leases has been a major topic of discussion within the accounting profession for more than 30 years. In 1949, the Committee on Accounting Procedure of the American Institute of Accountants issued the first authoritative pronouncement on the subject, entitled *Disclosure of Long-Term Leases in Financial Statements of Lessees*. In early 1960, the newly formed Accounting Principles Board (APB) of the American Institute of Certified Public Accountants sponsored a research project that culminated in the publication, in 1962, of *Reporting of Leases in Financial Statements*, Accounting Research Study No. 4. Subsequently, the APB issued four opinions addressing various aspects of lease accounting.

Accounting for leases was one of the first topics placed on the agenda of the Financial Standards Accounting Board (FASB) in 1973 when it assumed responsibility for accounting standard setting from the APB. During its existence, the FASB has spent more time on this topic than any other accounting issue with which it has dealt. Beginning with the issuance of *Accounting for Leases*, Statement of Financial Accounting Standards (SFAS) No. 13 in November 1976, the FASB has issued more than a score of Statements of Financial Accounting Standards, Interpretations, and FASB Technical Bulletins on the subject, as well as several exposure drafts of proposed standards that were never adopted.

The Securities and Exchange Commission (SEC) has also played a prominent part in the development of lease accounting principles. The SEC adopted Accounting Series Release (ASR) No. 147 in October 1975. ASR No. 147 required public company lessees to disclose the present value of obligations relating to "financing" leases (as defined by the SEC) as well as the impact on net earnings that would have resulted if those leases had been capitalized. However, the SEC has rescinded ASR No. 147 for companies that comply with SFAS No. 13.

ACCOUNTING METHODS

The lease accounting standards adopted by the FASB identify two basic methods of accounting for leases: the financing method and the operating method.

Under the financing method, the lessor records a long-term receivable and recognizes interest income over the term of the lease based on his declining investment in the leased property. The lessee records a capital asset in property, plant, and equipment, called a "leasehold," and amortizes it. In addition, the lessee records a liability equal to the present value of the lease payments.

The lessee prorates each lease payment between interest expense and reduction of this liability according to an amortization schedule, as is done for other long-term liabilities.

From the standpoint of the lessee, the FASB refers to all leases accounted for by the financing method as "capital leases." From the standpoint of the lessor, however, there are three different kinds of financing leases: (1) sales-type leases, (2) direct financing leases, and (3) leveraged leases. The accounting entries prescribed for each of these three lease types represent different applications of the basic financing method of accounting.

Under the operating method, the lessor records the leased property as part of property, plant, and equipment and depreciates it based on the usual considerations that determine depreciation. Operating lease revenue is recognized over the term of the lease, as the periodic rentals become receivable. The lessee records no asset or liability. Rental expense is recorded during the term of the lease, usually as the rentals become payable.

The financing method accelerates the recognition of income for the lessor as compared to the operating method. The theoretical justification for accelerating income is the fact that in a financing lease, substantially all of the risks of owning the leased property are covered by the lessee's commitment to make lease payments. When a substantial portion of the risks of owning the property have been assumed by the lessee, the transaction takes on the characteristics of a financing arrangement for a sale and the lessor's income is recognized accordingly.

Likewise, the financing method accelerates the recognition of expense for the lessee as compared to the operating method. Whereas expense under the operating method is generally level throughout the term of the lease, expense under the financing method consists of a depreciation charge that is level (assuming that the straight-line method is used) and an interest charge that is higher in the earlier periods and lower in the later periods as the lease obligation is reduced.

Because of these differences, plus the off-balance-sheet treatment afforded lessees under the operating method, lessees generally prefer to use the operating method and lessors generally prefer to use some form of the financing method.

CHOICE OF ACCOUNTING METHOD

Introduction. Prior to SFAS No. 13, lessees often used the operating method to account for a lease that was recorded under the financing method by the lessor. This asymmetrical accounting treatment was criticized for inconsistency and was viewed as a major defect in the lease accounting principles developed by the APB. In SFAS No. 13, the FASB adopted a single set of lease classification criteria for both lessees and lessors in an attempt to remedy this problem.

The lease classification criteria in SFAS No. 13 are based on the theory "that a lease that transfers substantially all of the benefits and risks incident to the ownership of property should be accounted for as the acquisition of an asset and incurrence of an obligation by the lessee and as a sale or financing by the lessor. All other leases should be accounted for as operating leases" [FASB, 1976, par. 60].

Definition of Terms. For purposes of applying the criteria, the following terms are specifically defined by SFAS No. 13:

Lease term: The period during which the lessee can be required or is expected to make lease payments including (1) the non-cancelable term of the lease, plus (2) any periods for which failure to renew the lease results in a penalty to the lessee in an amount such that, at the inception of the lease, it is reasonable to assume that the lease will be renewed, plus (3) any periods subject to a bargain renewal option or preceding the date that a bargain purchase option becomes exercisable, plus (4) any periods during which the lease may be renewed or extended at the option of the lessor. Under this definition, the lease term for accounting purposes may be different from the term specified in the lease agreement.

Bargain option: An option permitting the lessee to renew the lease or purchase the leased property for an amount that is sufficiently below expected future market value at the date the option becomes exercisable so that exercise of the option appears, at the inception of the lease, to be reasonably assured.

Estimated economic life of leased property: The estimated remaining period during which the property is expected to be economically usable for the purpose for which it was intended at the inception of the lease.

Fair value: The price at which the property could be sold in an arms'-length transaction. For a manufacturer or dealer, fair value would be the normal selling price for this product. For other lessors, fair value usually would be cost or book value. However, fair value may be different from book value if the lessor has owned the property for some period prior to the inception of the lease.

Minimum lease payments: The sum of (1) those payments that the lessee can be required or is expected to make during the lease term (other than amounts representing taxes, maintenance, insurance and other executory costs included in the lease payments and paid by the lessor), plus (2) any penalties that the lessee must pay for failure to renew or extend the lease beyond the lease term, plus (3) amounts that the lessee or a party related to the lessee guarantees to be realizable from sale or release of the property at the end of the lease term, plus, for lessors only, (4) amounts that an unrelated third party guarantees to be realizable from sale or release of the property at the end of the lease term.

Inception of the lease: The date that the principal provisions of the lease are committed to in writing by the parties.

Unguaranteed residual value: The expected fair value of the leased property at the end of the lease term excluding the amount of any guarantees included in the minimum lease payments.

Interest rate implicit in the lease: That discount rate that equates the present value of the minimum lease payments plus the unguaranteed residual value to the fair value of the leased property at the inception of the lease less any investment tax credit retained and expected to be realized by the lessor.

Lessee's incremental borrowing rate: The rate of interest that the lessee would have had to pay at the inception of the lease to borrow the funds to purchase the leased property under similar terms.

The Classification Criteria. A lease that meets any of the following criteria should be classified as a financing lease:

1. The lease transfers ownership of the property to the lessee by the end of the lease term.
2. The lease contains a bargain purchase option.
3. The lease term is equal to 75 percent or more of the estimated economic life of the leased property.
4. The present value at the beginning of the lease term of the minimum lease payments equals or exceeds 90 percent of the excess of the fair value of the leased property to the lessor at the inception of the lease over any related investment tax credit retained by the lessor and expected to be realized by him.

All other leases are operating leases. However, notwithstanding the above, leases commencing within the last 25 percent of the total economic life of the leased property are always classified as operating leases unless they transfer ownership to the lessee during or at the end of the lease term.

The discount rate used by the lessor to compute the present value of the minimum lease payments for the fourth criterion is the interest rate implicit in the lease. The lessee should use the lower of his incremental borrowing rate or, if it can be ascertained, the interest rate implicit in the lease.

By adopting the first two criteria, the FASB reaffirmed the principle, first stated in APB Opinion No. 5, that a lease that is, in substance, an installment purchase contract should be capitalized by the lessee. Thus, a lease that transfers title to the lessee during the lease or through operation of a bargain purchase option is always a financing lease.

The only subjective judgment required to apply the first two criteria is to determine if, at the inception of the lease, a purchase option constitutes a "bargain" as defined above. A "nominal value" purchase option clearly is a bargain. A "fair market value" option clearly is not a bargain. All other purchase options must be evaluated on their individual merits.

In general, to qualify as a bargain, an option would have to be at a fixed price or at a stated percentage (e.g., 50 percent) of fair market value. However, a fixed price option that appears to be a bargain only if one assumes that the cost or value of similar property will increase during the lease term is not generally viewed as a bargain for purposes of lease classification.

By adopting the third and fourth criteria, the FASB reaffirmed existing principles related to lessor classification as stated in APB Opinions No. 7 and 27. However, the FASB incorporated into its criteria specific quantitative guidelines for determining when a lease should be treated as a financing lease. By comparison, the APB opinions cited the "transference of risks of ownership" concept, but provided little guidance as to how that concept was to be applied to individual leases.

By adopting these two criteria for lessees as well as lessors, the FASB extended the "transference of risks of ownership" concept to lessee classification. As a result, for the first time lessees are now required to capitalize many leases that are not installment purchases. This was clearly one of the primary objectives of the FASB in issuing SFAS No. 13.

The third criterion, the "economic life test," is more subjective than the fourth criterion. Economic life may be difficult to estimate. Therefore, the criterion is not generally effective. A lessee who does not wish to capitalize a lease can often support an estimated economic life such that the lease will qualify as an operating lease under this guideline. However, it would generally not be acceptable to assume an economic life that is greater than the estimated useful life used by the lessee to depreciate similar owned property.

The fourth criterion, the "recovery of investment test," provides a more objective measure of the extent to which the risks of ownership have been transferred to the lessee. This criterion provides the basis for capitalizing most financing leases other than those that are, in substance, purchase contracts.

The "recovery of investment test" tends to favor capitalization by the lessee. In computing the present value of the minimum lease payments, the lessee uses the lower of the incremental borrowing rate or the interest rate implicit in the lease (if it can be ascertained). The lower the discount rate used to compute the present value of the minimum lease payments, the higher will be their computed present value. The higher the computed present value, the more likely is the lease to be classified as a capital lease.

If the estimated residual value at the end of the lease when discounted to the present is more than 10/90 of the present value of the lease payments, the lease does not meet the "recovery of investment" test. Thus, the tendency of lessors to estimate high residual values for leased property, and thereby increase income on the financing lease transaction, is restrained.

The examples that follow illustrate the application of the fourth criterion to the lease described in Exhibit 1.

The first step in applying the fourth criterion is to compute the interest rate implicit in the lease (i.e., the discount rate that equates the present value of the rental payments plus the present value of the residual value to the fair value of the leased property less investment tax credit retained by the lessor). This can be accomplished most easily using a computer program that solves for the rate of return on a stream of unequal payments.

The interest rate implicit in the lease can also be computed manually by trial and error. This method is illustrated in Exhibit 2 for the example lease.

The first trial, using an interest rate of 16 percent, produces a combined present value that is below the adjusted fair value. Therefore, 16 percent is too high.

EXHIBIT 1   Example Lease

Terms and assumptions	Lessor	Lessee
Lease term	7 yr	7 yr
Annual rental, due in advance	$10,000	$10,000
Fair value of leased property	$58,000	$58,000
Purchase option at end of lease term		Fair market value
Renewal option at end of lease term		None
Estimated residual value percentage	20%	
Lessee's incremental borrowing rate		16%
Investment tax credit to lessor	10%	
Executory costs paid by lessor	None	

EXHIBIT 2   Finding the Interest Rate Implicit in the Lease

	First trial 16%	Second trial 14%	Third trial 15%
Fair value	$ 58,000	$ 58,000	$ 58,000
Less: Investment tax credit	(5,800)	(5,800)	(5,800)
Adjusted fair value	$ 52,200	$ 52,200	$ 52,000
Annual rental	$10,000	$ 10,000	$ 10,000
Discount factor (present value of $1 per year for 7 years, due in advance)[a]	X 4.6847	X 4.8887	X 4.7845
Present value of rentals	$ 46,847	$ 48,887	$ 47,845
Gross residual value (20% of fair value)	$ 11,600	$ 11,600	$ 11,600
Discount factor (present value of $1 due in 7 years[b])	X .3538	X .3996	X .3759
Present value of residual value	$ 4,104	$ 4,635	$ 4,360
Combined present value	$ 50,951	$ 53,522	$ 52,205
Adjusted fair value	(52,200)	(52,200)	(52,200)
Difference	$ (1,249)	$ 1,322	$ 5

[a]Computed by the formula $PV = 1 + [1 - (1 + i)^{-(n-1)}]/i$, where PV = present value, n = number of rental periods, and i = interest rate.
[b]Computed by the formula $PV = (1 + i)^{-n}$.

The second trial, using 14 percent, produces a combined present value that is above the adjusted fair value. Therefore, 14 percent is too low.

The results of the first two trials prove that the actual implicit rate is somewhere between 14 and 16 percent. Furthermore, the fact that the differences computed in these two trials are almost equal in magnitude and opposite in sign suggests that the actual implicit rate is approximately halfway between 14 and 16 percent. As shown by the negligible difference computed in the third trial, the interest rate implicit in this lease is, in fact, almost exactly 15 percent.

The next step in applying the fourth criterion is to compute the present value of the minimum lease payments and compare them to the fair value of the leased property less investment tax credit retained by the lessor. If the present value of the minimum lease payments is more than 90 percent of the adjusted fair value, the lease is a financing lease. The calculations are illustrated for the example lease in Exhibit 3.

Using the interest rate implicit in the lease, this lease is a financing lease because the present value of the lease payments exceeds 90 percent of adjusted fair value. Using the lessee's incremental borrowing rate, however, this lease would be classified as an operating lease.

According to SFAS No. 13, the lessor must use the implicit rate to perform the recovery of investment test. The lessee need use this rate, however, only if it is "practicable for him to learn the implicit rate computed by the lessor and the implicit rate computed by the lessor is less than the lessee's incremental borrowing rate" [FASB, 1976, par. 7(d)]. Otherwise the lessee must use the incremental borrowing rate.

EXHIBIT 3   Illustration of the "Recovery of Investment" Test

	Using implicit interest rate (15%)	Using incremental borrowing rate (16%)
Annual rent	$10,000	$10,000
Discount factor (see Exhibit 2 for derivation)	× 4.7845	× 4.6847
Present value of lease payments	$47,845	$46,847
Adjusted fair value (see Exhibit 2)	÷ $52,200	÷ $52,200
	91.7%	89.8%

It is often not practicable for the lessee to learn the implicit rate computed by the lessor. The lessee who knows the lessor's estimate of the residual value can make the calculation in the manner illustrated in Exhibit 2. The FASB has no authority to compel lessors to disclose their residual value estimates to their customers. At one point the FASB proposed requiring the lessee to estimate the lessor's residual value if he could not ascertain the lessor's estimate. This proposal was withdrawn, however, after being exposed for public comment. As a result, lessees retain some flexibility in choosing a discount rate for applying the fourth criterion. This flexibility may result in asymmetrical lease classifications between lessor and lessee for leases that are near to the 90 percent cutoff point of the fourth criterion.

The application of the "recovery of investment test" to a complex lease transaction may involve numerous judgments, estimates, and assumptions. For example, the presence of renewal or extension options, purchase options, guarantees of the residual value, or penalties for failure to renew may affect the measure of minimum lease payments. The lessee may not know the lessor's cost for the leased property and may therefore have to estimate fair value. The lessee's incremental borrowing rate and the value of the property at the end of the lease are not precisely measurable. Thus, although the fourth criterion provides a more objective standard than previously existed for classifying leases, it does not eliminate the need for the judgments and estimates that are common to many significant accounting issues.

A lease that meets any one of the four criteria is a capital lease to the lessee. To qualify as a financing lease to the lessor, however, a lease must not only meet one of the four criteria but must also satisfy *both* of the following conditions:

1. Collectibility of the minimum lease payments must be reasonably predictable.

2. There must be no important uncertainties as to the amount of unreimbursed costs to be incurred by the lessor in the future Examples of such costs include guarantees that are more extensive than normal warranties or that have the effect of protecting the lessee from technological obsolescence [paraphrased from FASB, 1976, par. 8].

If these two conditions are not met, the lessor must account for the lease as an operating lease.

ACCOUNTING ENTRIES—LESSEE

Capital Leases. At the commencement of a capital lease, the lessee records as an asset and obligation the present value of the minimum lease payments (excluding amounts, if any, to cover maintenance, property taxes, and insurance provided by the lessor). The discount rate is the rate that was or would have been used to classify the lease under the fourth classification criterion— the lower of the lessee's incremental borrowing rate or the rate implicit in the lease, when this rate can be estimated. If, however, the present value of the minimum lease payments using this discount rate exceeds the cost or fair value of the property, then the lessee must use a higher rate that reduces the present value of those cash payments to fair value. The procedure for computing such a rate is similar to that illustrated in Exhibit 2.

An asset acquired via a capital lease is depreciated like any other depreciable asset. If the lease meets either of the first two classification criteria, it should be depreciated over its total estimated useful life (which may be different from the lease term) to its estimated salvage value. If, however, the lease is a capital lease only because it meets either of the last two classification criteria, then the property should be depreciated over the lease term to the value, if any, accruing to the lessee at the end of the lease.

The lease payments comprise interest expense and reduction of the obligation recorded at lease commencement. The interest charge should be based on a constant periodic rate of interest applied to the declining balance of the obligation. The interest rate is the discount rate used to compute the initial liability (which is equal to the initial capitalized value of the leased property).

The entries required to record the example lease from Exhibit 1 as a capital lease using a discount rate of 15 percent are as follows:

Leased Property under Capital Lease	47,845	
Obligations under Capital Lease		47,845
To record capital lease at present value of lease payments.		
Obligations under Capital Lease	10,000	
Cash		10,000
To record initial payment at lease commencement.		

At the end of the first year, the entries, assuming straight-line depreciation, are

Depreciation Expense	6,835	
Accumulated Depreciation: Leased Property		6,835
To record annual depreciation on leased property.		

Interest Expense	5,677	
Interest Payable		5,677

To record annual interest at 15 percent: .15 × ($47,845 − $10,000).

At the beginning of the second year, the rental payment is recorded as follows:

Interest Payable	5,677	
Obligations under Capital Lease	4,323	
Cash		10,000

To record second annual payment.

Note that the combined depreciation and interest expense for the first year totaled $12,512, compared to the $10,000 rental payment called for by the lease.

Entries for depreciation in subsequent years are the same as for the first year. Entries for interest expense are for the amounts shown in Exhibit 4.

If a capital lease is renewed or extended beyond the original lease term, the lessee must classify the renewal or extension according to the four classification criteria. If the renewal or extension is a capital lease, then the present value of the additional rentals should be recorded as an addition to the asset and obligation already on the books. The present value should be computed using the same discount rate that was used to record the original lease. If the renewal or extension is an operating lease, then no entries are required until the renewal period begins. At that time the entries required are those pertaining to an operating lease.

If a capital lease is terminated before the end of the lease term, then the asset and obligation should be removed from the books and a gain or loss, including any termination penalties, should be recognized in the period of the termination. For example, if the Exhibit 1 lease were terminated without penalty at the end of the third year, the entry to record the termination would be

---

EXHIBIT 4 Amortization Schedule of Seven Payments in Advance

	Interest (at 15%) (1)	Reduction of obligation (2)	Remaining obligation (3)
Original obligation			$47,845
First payment, in advance		$10,000	37,845
Second payment	$5,677	4,323	33,522
Third payment	5,028	4,972	28,550
Fourth payment	4,282	5,718	22,832
Fifth payment	3,425	6,575	16,257
Sixth payment	2,439	7,561	8,696
Seventh payment	1,304	8,696	-0-

(1) = .15 × (3), preceding period.
(2) = $10,000 − (1).
(3) = (3) preceding period − (2).

Interest Payable	4,282	
Obligations under Capital Lease	28,550	
Leased Property under Capital Lease		27,340
Gain on Termination of Capital Lease		5,492
To record gain on early termination of capital lease.		

The $5,492 gain from early termination is a plugged figure in this journal entry, but is equal to the amount of expense recorded during the first 3 years of the lease in excess of the expenses that would have been recorded under the operating method of accounting for leases.

Some leases contain provisions that result in increases or decreases in the basic rental amounts based on a formula that is contingent on events whose outcome cannot be known at the inception of the lease. These increases or decreases are called "contingent rentals" in SFAS No. 13. Examples of contingent rentals include fluctuations based on changes in the prime interest rate, rentals based on sales volume, and rentals based on mileage or usage of the leased asset.

Contingent rentals are specifically excluded from the definition of minimum lease payments in SFAS No. 13. Therefore, a lease with rentals tied to the prime interest rate should be classified and, if appropriate, capitalized, based on the assumption that the prime interest rate will remain constant throughout the lease term.

When a capital lease contains provisions that give rise to contingent rentals, such rentals should be recorded as additional rental expense of the period in which they accrue or, if negative, as a reduction of interest expense.

Operating Leases. The lessee records rental expense associated with an operating lease based on the passage of time. SFAS No. 13 requires that rental expense be recognized straight-line over the term of the lease unless another systematic method produces a result that more closely parallels the use benefit derived from the property. Examples of alternatives to the straight-line expense pattern include methods based on miles driven, hours used in production, or units produced.

For a level-payment lease, rental expense generally will coincide with the lease payments. For a non-level-payment lease, the straight-line expense method will result in an asset or liability on the balance sheet equal to the difference between expense recognized and payments made.

If lease payments are due in advance, all or a portion of the most recent payment will represent a prepaid rental. For leases with semiannual or annual payments, the amount of prepayments could be significant.

The lessee makes no entries to record the property or lease obligation related to an operating lease. This is the off-balance-sheet feature that continues to make the operating method the preferred method of accounting among lessees. A lessee who purchases the leased property from the lessor during or at the end of the operating lease term should record the purchase and depreciate the property based on acquisition cost.

The lessee unable to determine the interest rate implicit in the lease described in Exhibit 1 would classify the lease as an operating lease and record the following entries (assume that the lease commences on July 1, 198X, and the lessee has a calendar year-end):

Prepaid Rent	10,000	
Cash		10,000
To record first lease payment due in advance.		

At December 31, 198X, the entry to record 6 months of rental expense would be

Rental Expense	5,000	
Prepaid Rent		5,000
To record 6 months of expense on operating lease.		

Subsequent rental payments could be charged directly to expense with the remaining prepaid balance being amortized to expense in the last 6 months of the lease term. As with capital leases, contingent rentals are charged to expense as they accrue.

ACCOUNTING ENTRIES—LESSOR

The FASB has identified three types of lessor financing leases: direct financing leases, sales-type leases, and leverage leases. In order to account properly for a financing lease, therefore, the lessor must decide which of the three types of lease has been entered into.

Direct Financing Leases. All financing leases that do not qualify as sales-type or leverage leases are direct financing leases. The lessor would make the following entries at the beginning of the direct financing lease described in Exhibit 1.

Equipment	58,000	
Cash		58,000
To record purchase of property.		

Minimum Lease Payments Receivable	70,000	
Unguaranteed Residual Value	11,600	
Equipment		58,000
Unearned Lease Income		23,600
To record commencement of direct financing lease.		

Cash	10,000	
Minimum Lease Payments Receivable		10,000
To record initial payment in advance.		

Typically, a financing lessor will incur various front-end costs related to negotiating, documenting, and consummating a lease agreement. These costs are referred to in SFAS No. 13 as "initial direct costs" and are to be expensed in the period incurred. Included in the definition of initial direct costs are (1) outside legal and professional fees, (2) sales commissions, (3) costs of evaluating and documentating the lessee's creditworthiness, and (4) costs of preparing and processing documents for new leases. In addition, initial direct costs include an allocation of the salaries of personnel who worked directly on negotiating and documenting a lease. However, they do not include allocations of rent, supervisory expenses, general administrative expenses or other indirect expense [paraphrased from FASB, 1977, par. 8].

At the commencement of a direct financing lease, the lessor recognizes as finance lease income a portion of the unearned lease income equal to initial direct costs associated with the lease. The initial direct costs incurred should be charged to expense in the same period.

The remainder of the unearned lease income is amortized over the term of the lease so as to yield a constant periodic rate of return on the lessor's net investment in the lease. The net investment in the lease at any time consists of the remaining lease payments receivable plus the unguaranteed residual value reduced by the remaining unearned lease income.

To compute the interest rate that amortizes the remaining unearned lease income, the lessor must use the same trial-and-error approach illustrated in Exhibit 2. Instead of solving for the discount rate that produces a combined present value equal to the fair value less investment tax credit, however, the lessor now must solve for the discount rate that produces a combined present value equal to the original net investment in the lease. The original net investment in the lease is the cost of the property plus the initial direct costs related to the lease.

Assuming that initial direct costs total $1,000 for the lease described in Exhibit 1, the lessor would compute an approximate interest rate of 10.3 percent as shown in Exhibit 5. More iterations yield a more precise calculation of 10.3077 percent.

EXHIBIT 5   Calculation of Interest Rate

Net investment in the lease:	
Minimum lease payments at commencement	$70,000
Unguaranteed residual value . . . . :	11,600
Less: Unearned lease income at commencement, net of initial direct costs . . .	(22,600)
Net investment at commencement	$59,000
Present value analysis:	
Annual rental	$10,000
Discount factor (present value of $1 per year for 7 years at 10.3%, due in advance)[a]	× 5.3172
Present value of minimum lease payments	$53,172
Gross residual value	$11,600
Discount factor (present value of $1 due in 7 years at 10.3%)[a]	× .5035
Present value of residual	$ 5,840
Combined present value . . . .,	$59,012

[a]See Exhibit 2 for derivation of discount factors.

The entries to amortize unearned lease income for the first year are as follows:

Unearned Lease Income	1,000	
Finance Lease Revenue		1,000
To recognize unearned lease income to offset initial direct costs.		

Unearned Lease Income	5,051	
Finance Lease Revenue		5,051
To record income from first year of lease.		

At the end of year 1, the net investment in the lease would be $54,051, computed as follows:

Minimum lease payments remaining	$60,000
Unguaranteed residual value	11,600
Less: Unearned lease income	(17,549)
	$54,051

The entries to record payments in subsequent years are identical to the first-year entry. Entries to amortize the remaining unearned lease income in subsequent years would be identical to the entry in year 1 using the amounts computed in Exhibit 6. Contingent rentals, if any, should be recorded as revenue as they accrue according to the provisions of the lease.

At the end of year 7, all payments will have been received and all unearned lease income will have been amortized. The remaining net investment in the lease will be exactly equal to the unguaranteed residual value. Entries subsequent to year 7 related to this residual value depend on how the lessor chooses

---

EXHIBIT 6   Amortization Schedule for Seven Payments in Advance

	Net investment in the lease (beginning balance)	Amortization of unearned income at 10.3077%	Reduction in minimum lease payments receivable	Net investment in the lease (ending balance)
Lease commencement	$58,000	$ 1,000[a]	$10,000	$49,000
First year (second payment)	49,000	5,051	10,000	44,051
Second year........	44,051	4,541	10,000	38,592
Third year..........	38,592	3,978	10,000	32,570
Fourth year........	32,570	3,357	10,000	25,927
Fifth year	25,927	2,672	10,000	18,599
Sixth year..........	18,599	1,917	10,000	10,516
Seventh year	10,516	1,084		11,600
		$23,600	$70,000	

[a]Represents revenue recognized at commencement to offset initial direct costs.

to use or dispose of the leased property. If the property is sold, this balance would be used to compute the gain or loss on sale. If the property is leased, this value would be the book value for computing certain accounting entries, but it would probably not be the fair value to be used for classifying the new lease.

The lessor must review estimates of residual value at least annually to see if they are still appropriate. A lessor who concludes that recovery will be less than the original estimate must recompute the net investment in the lease as though the new estimate had been used in the first place. Then the lessor records an entry to adjust downward the unguaranteed residual value account and the unearned lease income account to the newly computed values and records a loss (part of current income) equal to the decline in net investment resulting from the revised estimate. An upward adjustment of the original residual value estimate is prohibited by SFAS No. 13.

An amendment or modification of a direct financing lease that changes the amount of the remaining minimum lease payments should be reflected in the accounts in the period when the new agreement is executed. If the revised payments still constitute a direct financing lease, the lessor should adjust the unearned lease income account by the amount of the increase or decrease in the minimum lease payments. The revised unearned lease income balance should be amortized over the remaining lease term so as to produce a constant periodic rate of return on the net investment in the lease.

If the revised payments constitute an operating lease, or if the lease is terminated altogether, the lessor should adjust the accounts making up the net investment in the lease to zero. The lessor records the leased property as an asset at the lowest of (1) current book value, (2) current fair value, or (3) original cost, with any net adjustment being charged as a loss in the period of the change in the status of the lease.

If the lease is renewed or extended prior to the end of the original term, then the lessor must classify the renewal or extension separately as an operating or financing lease. To do so, the lessor must estimate, as of the inception of the renewal or extension, the fair value of the leased property at both the beginning and the end of the renewal or extension period.

If the renewal or extension is classified as an operating lease, no entries are required until the new lease term begins. At that time, the renewal or extension is accounted for as an operating lease using the balance in the residual value account as the initial book value of the property.

However, if the renewal or extension is a financing lease, the minimum lease payments receivable and unearned lease income accounts should be increased by the amount of the payments due during the renewal or extension period. The revised unearned lease income is then amortized at the appropriate interest rate over the remaining lease term, including the additional period.

Sales-Type Leases. A sales-type lease is distinguished from a direct financing lease by the fact that the fair value of the leased property at the inception of the lease differs from the cost or book value of the property to the lessor. Most sales-type leases involve a manufacturer or dealer who uses leasing as a marketing tool to sell the product. However, a lessor who is not a manufacturer or

EXHIBIT 7   Example Leases

Data for Illustrations in Exhibits 8 and 9

	Lease A	Lease B
Fair value of leased property	$55,000	$55,000
Lessor cost of leased property	40,000	40,000
Lease term	7 yr	7 yr
Annual rental, due in advance	$10,000	$10,836
Investment tax credit retained by lessor	4,000	
Estimated unguaranteed residual value	8,393	8,393
Initial direct costs	1,000	1,000
Implicit interest rate	15%	15%

dealer can also enter into a sales-type lease if the fair value of the leased asset is different from its book value.

At the commencement of a sale-type lease, the lessor records as sales revenue the present value of the minimum lease payments, discounted at the interest rate implicit in the lease. The cost of sales equals the cost or carrying value for the leased property, reduced by the present value of the unguaranteed residual value, also discounted at the interest rate implicit in the lease. Initial direct costs are charged to expense in the same period as the sale is recognized.

After the sale is recorded, the lessor accounts for the lease as if it were a direct financing lease of property having a cost equal to the combined present value of the minimum lease payments and the unguaranteed residual value. However, no unearned lease income is recognized at commencement to offset initial direct costs. The entire unearned lease income balance is amortized over the lease term using the interest rate implicit in the lease.

Exhibit 7 illustrates the key provisions and assumptions of two sales-type leases. Lease A assumes that the investment tax credit is retained by the lessor, whereas lease B assumes that the investment tax credit is transferred to the lessee in exchange for a higher rental.

The interest rate implicit in each of these leases is 15 percent, and both leases qualify as financing leases under the "recovery of investment" criterion as illustrated in Exhibit 8.

The entries to record lease A are as follows:

Leased Property	51,000	
Cost of Sales	36,845	
Sales		47,845
Inventory		40,000
To record sale of inventory under sales-type lease.		
Minimum Lease Payments Receivable	70,000	
Unguaranteed Residual Value	8,393	
Unearned Lease Income		27,393
Leased Property		51,000
To record commencement of sales-type lease.		

EXHIBIT 8   Example: Sales-Type Leases

	Lease A	Lease B
Fair value	$55,000	$55,000
Less: Investment tax credit retained by lessor	(4,000)	
Adjusted fair value	$51,000	$55,000
Annual rentals................................	$10,000	$10,836
Discount factor (see Exhibit 2)	× 4.7845	× 4.7845
Present value of rentals	$47,845	$51,845
Unguaranteed residual value	$ 8,393	$ 8,393
Discount factor (see Exhibit 2)	× .3759	× .3759
Present value of residual value	$ 3,155	$ 3,155
Combined present value	$51,000	$55,000
Present value of rentals	$47,845	$51,845
Adjusted fair value	÷ 51,000	÷ 55,000
	93.8%	94.35%

In addition, the lessor will recognize $4,000 of investment tax credit reducing the tax provision. This credit would properly be recognized in proportion to the amortization of unearned lease income over the life of the lease. The flow-through method is, however, also acceptable for lessors using it for investment tax credits.

The entries to record lease B are as follows:

```
Leased Property .................................    55,000
Cost of Sales.....................................    36,845
    Sales ........................................              51,845
    Inventory ....................................              40,000
To record sale of inventory under sales-type lease.

Minimum Lease Payments Receivable ...............    75,852
Unguaranteed Residual Value .....................     8,393
    Unearned Lease Income........................              29,245
    Leased Property .............................              55,000
To record commencement of sales-type lease.
```

The entries to record the annual rental payments and contingent rentals are the same as for a direct financing lease.

The amortization of unearned lease income is computed in the manner illustrated in Exhibit 9 using the interest rate implicit in the lease. The entries to record lease income are identical to those for a direct financing lease. The annual revenue figures and net investment balance for each year are shown for both leases A and B in Exhibit 9. Note that the final net investment balance is the unguaranteed residual value.

The entries to record the effect of amendments, renewals, and extensions of a sales-type lease are identical to those for a direct financing lease. The sales-type lessor is also required to evaluate the adequacy of residual value estimates

EXHIBIT 9   Amortization Schedule for Seven Payments in Advance

	Lease A		Lease B	
	Lease revenue	Net investment	Lease revenue	Net investment
Commencement		$41,000		$44,164
First year (second payment)	$ 6,150	37,150	$ 6,625	39,953
Second year	5,573	32,723	5,993	35,110
Third year	4,908	27,631	5,266	29,540
Fourth year	4,145	21,776	4,431	23,135
Fifth year	3,266	15,042	3,470	15,769
Sixth year	2,256	7,298	2,365	7,298
Seventh year	1,095	8,393	1,095	8,393
	$27,393		$29,245	

at least annually and to follow the accounting procedures described for direct financing leases if a permanent decline in value has occurred. Upward revisions of the residual value estimate are not permitted.

Leverage Leases. A leverage lease is a lease having all of the following characteristics:

1. If it were not a leverage lease, it would be classified as a direct financing lease.

2. It involves three parties, an investor/lessor, a lessee, and a long-term lender.

3. The financing provided by the lender is nonrecourse to the general credit of the lessor and is sufficient to provide "substantial leverage" in the transaction (however, the lender may retain a security interest in the leased property and the unremitted rentals due in the future from the lessee).

4. The lessor's net investment in the lease declines during the early years of the lease followed by an increase in subsequent years, a pattern that may be repeated more than once [paraphrased from FASB, 1976, par. 42].

A lessor who uses the flow-through method to account for the investment tax credit arising from leased property may not use the leverage lease method to account for the related lease, even though it has all of these characteristics, but must use the direct financing method instead.

The lessor records the investment in a leverage lease net of principal and interest on the nonrecourse debt. This offsetting of asset and liability departs from previous authoritative accounting literature.

The method of recognizing income is unique in the accounting principles. The lessor is required at the beginning of the lease to prepare a schedule of aftertax cash flows for the entire lease term. This schedule defines the lessor's net cash investment in the lease at the end of each accounting period during the lease term.

In a typical leveraged lease, the lessor's net cash investment will be negative during the middle years of the lease because of temporary cash inflows derived from the tax effects of accelerated depreciation. This cash flow in excess of the original investment will be paid back in later years as the depreciation timing differences reverse.

The total aftertax income generated during the entire lease is allocated to those periods during which the lessor's net investment is positive, so as to produce a constant aftertax rate of return on the net investment during the years that it is positive. No income is allocated to periods when the investment is negative.

The individual components of aftertax income (i.e., pretax income, income tax expense, and investment tax credit) are recognized in the same proportion that the net income allocated to an accounting period bears to total net income from the lease. For example, in order to recognize 15 percent of the total net income from the lease in a given period, the lessor would recognize 15 percent of the pretax income, 15 percent of the estimated income tax expense, and 15 percent of the investment tax credit generated over the term of the lease.

Initial direct costs are charged directly against the original unearned lease income balance, thus reducing the amount of pretax income recognized over the lease term. As a result, initial direct costs associated with a leverage lease are never recorded explicitly in the lessor's income statement.

The net investment in a leverage lease is defined as the algebraic sum of the following balances:

1. Gross rentals receivable less the portion representing principal and interest on the nonrecourse debt
2. Investment tax credit receivable
3. Unguaranteed residual value
4. Unearned and deferred income consisting of the portions of the pretax income and investment tax credit not yet recognized
5. Deferred taxes arising from differences between pretax accounting income and taxable income

This definition also represents a departure from previous accounting practices because for the first time, deferred taxes will actually affect the amount of pretax income recognized for accounting purposes.

The aftertax rate of return for a leverage lease is computed by trial and error. For a procedure, see Shanno and Weil [1976]. Because change in the amount of income allocated to a period changes the net investment at the end of the period and vice versa, it is virtually impossible to compute the rate of return for a complex leverage lease without the aid of a computer.

Appendix E to SFAS No. 13 contains detailed illustrations of the cash flow and income allocation schedules required to account for a leverage lease. Readers interested in a more comprehensive treatment of the details of leverage lease accounting should refer to that appendix.

The leverage lessor is required to review key assumptions and estimates that affect the amount of income to be recognized over the term of the lease at least annually. Examples of such assumptions and estimates include the residual value, the income tax rate, the realization of investment tax credit, and the amount and timing of tax benefits and charges. An upward revision in the estimate of residual value is not permitted.

If any of the assumptions or estimates are changed, the lessor must recompute the rate of return from the inception of the lease using the new assumptions and estimates. Then the accounts making up the net investment in the lease are adjusted to the balances that would have resulted from applying the new rate of return from inception. Any gain or loss would be recognized in the period of the revision.

Operating Leases. The lessor records revenue associated with an operating lease based on the passage of time. SFAS No. 13 requires that rental revenue be recognized straight-line over the term of the lease unless another systematic method produces a result that more closely parallels the use benefit accruing to the lessee. Examples of alternatives to straight-line revenue recognition include methods based on units of production, hours used in production, or miles driven.

For a level-payment lease, rental income generally will coincide with the lease payments. For a non-level-payment lease, the straight-line method of revenue recognition will result in a deferred receivable or deposit representing the difference between income recorded and payments received. Appropriate accruals are required if the payments are due on a date other than the end of the accounting period.

Property subject to an operating lease should be depreciated over its estimated useful life to its estimated salvage value. The method of depreciation (e.g., straight-line, sum-of-the-years' digits, or declining-balance) should generally be consistent with the method of recognizing rental revenue. Thus, if units of production were appropriate for revenue recognition, it would also be the most appropriate depreciation method.

The entries to record an operating lease are as follows:

Rental Property	xxx	
Cash		xxx
To record purchase of rental property.		
Cash	xxx	
Rental Income		xxx
To record rental income under lease.		
Depreciation Expense	xxx	
Accumulated Depreciation		xxx
To record depreciation on property subject to operating lease.		

Some leases require the lessor to pay executory costs such as property taxes, maintenance, and insurance. These costs should be accrued and charged to expense with the passage of time or as related services are provided.

The remaining payments due on an operating lease are generally not sufficient to ensure recovery of the remaining book value of the leased property. Therefore, an operating lessor should perform a review, at least annually, to see if projected future rentals and sales proceeds, after deducting projected marketing and administrative expenses associated with leasing operations, are sufficient to recover the remaining net book value of property subject to operating leases. Whenever projected future revenues are found to be insufficient to recover the net book value of rental property, the lessor should record additional depreciation expense in the current period to reduce the carrying value of the property to a level that can be recovered.

FINANCIAL STATEMENT PRESENTATION AND DISCLOSURE

Lessee Presentation. A lease is a means of obtaining the use of revenue-producing assets. It is also a claim on the future resources of a business. Therefore, in order to evaluate the performance of an enterprise and assess its prospects for the future, a reader of financial statements needs to know the impact of leasing on a company's operating results and the extent of a company's future lease commitments. If this information is not provided directly in the basic financial statements, it must be disclosed in footnotes.

For capital leases, the balance sheet automatically reflects the capitalized asset and the long-term obligation. Therefore, the additional disclosure requirements for capital leases are designed to provide information comparable to that provided for other depreciable assets and long-term debt. SFAS No. 13 requires that the lessee disclose in the financial statements or related footnotes the following with respect to capital leases:

1. The gross amount of assets recorded under capital leases by major type and the accumulated amortization thereon
2. Future minimum lease payments due in total and for each of the next 5 fiscal years, with separate identification of those portions representing executory costs and interest imputed on the long-term obligation
3. Total minimum sublease rentals to be received in the future from noncancelable subleases
4. Total contingent rental expense included in each income statement presented
5. The amount of amortization expense relating to capital leases included in each income statement presented, unless such expense is included with depreciation expense and that fact is disclosed

For operating leases having initial or remaining noncancelable lease terms in excess of 1 year, the lessee should disclose:

1. Future rental payments due, in the aggregate and for each of the next 5 years subsequent to the latest balance sheet presented
2. The aggregate rentals to be received in the future from noncancelable subleases

In addition, the operating lessee should disclose the amounts of fixed rental expense, contingent rental expense, and sublease revenues included in each income statement presented. The lessee also provides a general description of the leasing agreements, including, for example, dividend or borrowing restrictions, renewal or purchase options, rent escalation clauses, and contingent rental provisions.

The following footnotes from the 1980 annual report of Safeway Stores, Incorporated, illustrate the application of SFAS No. 13 disclosure requirements by a company that uses leasing extensively to finance its operations:

NOTE A—SUMMARY OF SIGNIFICANT ACCOUNTING POLICIES

Property and Depreciation

Property is stated at historical cost. Depreciation is computed for financial reporting purposes on the straight-line method. The following are the principal rates of depreciation used during the year:

Stores and other buildings	2½ to 5%
Fixtures and equipment	5 to 20%
Transport equipment	12½ to 16⅔%

Leasehold improvements include buildings constructed on leased land and improvements to leased buildings. Buildings and major improvements are amortized over the shorter of the remaining period of the lease or the estimated useful lives of the assets, while minor improvements are amortized over the shorter of the remaining period of the lease or six years.

Property under capital leases is amortized over the terms of the leases. Accumulated amortization of property under capital leases was $469,532,000, $447,938,000 and $421,735,000 at year-ends 1980, 1979, and 1978, respectively.

Capitalization of Leases

The wide fluctuations in interest rates in 1980 and the increasing residual values of underlying properties have made it impracticable to determine the interest rates implicit in the leases as defined by Statement of Financial Accounting Standards No. 13. Therefore, beginning in 1980, the Company is using its incremental borrowing rate for capitalization of leases. The effect has been to substantially decrease the number of leases capitalized.

NOTE F—LEASE OBLIGATIONS

The Company and its subsidiaries occupy primarily leased premises, which were covered by 3,470 leases at year-end 1980. Of these leases 1,904 are considered capital under Statement of Financial Accounting Standards No. 13. The remainder are operating leases.

Most leases have renewal options with terms and conditions similar to the original lease. Of all the leases, 1,585 can be cancelled by the Company by offer to purchase the properties at original cost less amortization, with purchase obligatory upon acceptance of the offer by the lessor.

The Company owns most of its fixtures and equipment.

The following is a schedule by years of future minimum rental payments required under capital leases and under operating leases that have initial or remaining non-cancellable lease terms in excess of one year as of year-end 1980 (in thousands):

	Capital leases	Operating leases
1981	$ 118,491	$ 79,802
1982	115,996	79,204
1983	112,945	76,800
1984	110,235	73,738
1985	106,613	69,363
Later years	1,058,880	714,788
Total minimum lease payments	$1,623,160	$1,093,695
Less executory costs	24,829	
Net minimum lease payments	$1,598,331	
Less amount representing interest	709,465	
Present value of net minimum lease payments	$ 888,866	
Less current obligations	44,855	
Long-term obligations	$ 844,011	

In addition to minimum lease payments, contingent rentals may be paid under certain store leases on the basis of the stores' sales in excess of stipulated amounts. Contingent rentals on capital leases amounted to $7,887,000 in 1980, $7,667,000 in 1979, and $8,598,000 in 1978.

The following schedule shows the composition of total rental expense for all operating leases (in thousands):

	1980	1979	1978
Property leases:			
Minimum rentals	$ 97,484	$78,151	$72,824
Contingent rentals	7,972	8,006	6,863
Less rentals from subleases	(6,036)	(5,619)	(5,065)
	$ 99,420	$80,538	$74,622
Equipment leases	19,182	15,631	14,054
	$118,602	$96,169	$88,676

Lessor Presentation. The reader of a lessor company's financial statements would typically be interested in ascertaining the extent to which the lessor has retained economic risks associated with the leased property and the lessor's cash flow prospects, particularly with respect to the immediate future.

The presentation and disclosure requirements of SFAS No. 13 are intended to facilitate these types of analyses. The disclosure requirements are applicable only to companies for which leasing activities are significant to the revenues, net income, or assets of the enterprise.

For financing leases, the lessor must disclose on the face of the balance sheet or in a note to the financial statements the components of the net investment in each type of financing lease. A common format for presenting this information is to include a single line item on the balance sheet (e.g., "Net investment in direct-financing leases" or Net investment in leveraged lease") and provide the detail of individual components in a note.

Other disclosures required for sales-type and direct financing leases include:

1. Future minimum lease payments to be received in each of the 5 years succeeding the date of the latest balance sheet presented.

2. The amount of unearned income recognized to offset initial direct costs in each period for which an income statement is presented (for direct financing leases only).

3. The amount of contingent rentals included in each income statement presented.

4. A general description of the lessor's leasing arrangements. Disclosures under this provision might include, if significant, the type and amount of residual value guarantees, the basis on which contingent rentals are determined, the original cost, by major type, of property for which residual values are recorded, and the existence and terms of renewal and extension options held by lessees.

For operating leases the lessor should provide the following information:

1. The cost or carrying value of property on operating lease or held for lease by major type or functional class of property and the amount of accumulated depreciation in total as of the latest balance sheet presented

2. Depreciable lives, salvage value assumptions, and depreciation methods for each major class of property

3. Total minimum lease payments due on noncancelable leases as of the date of the latest balance sheet presented, in the aggregate and for each of the next 5 fiscal years

4. Total contingent rentals included in income for each period for which an income statement is presented

5. A general description of leasing arrangements

The financial statements and footnotes of a company with significant leasing operations might contain disclosures similar to those in Exhibit 10.

OTHER SPECIALIZED AREAS

The FASB recognized that the general lease accounting and disclosure requirements above did not cover adequately certain special types of lease-related transactions. Therefore, the Board included a number of separate sections in SFAS No. 13 for the purpose of standardizing accounting treatment of such transactions. These sections are summarized briefly below.

Participation by Third Parties. A lessor who sells or assigns a financing lease or property subject to a financing lease should leave the original lease accounting intact, remove the net carrying value of the lease at date of sale from the books, and record a gain or loss from the sale, as appropriate. However, if the buyer has recourse to the seller in the event of a lessee default under the lease,

---

EXHIBIT 10 **Illustrative Disclosure for Lessor**

ABC COMPANY
Balance Sheet
December 31, 1984 and 1983

Assets	1984	1983
	\(in thousands\)	
Net investment in sales-type and direct financing leases (note D)	$46,917	$39,109
Investment in leveraged leases (note D)	7,498	5,622
Rental property at cost, net of accumulated depreciation (note D)	80,143	76,214

Note D—Investment in Leases. Net investment in sales-type and direct financing leases at December 31, 1984, consists of the following (in thousands):

Total minimum lease payments receivable	$ 75,541
Less: Amounts representing executory costs	(1,654)
Minimum lease payments receivable	$ 73,887
Less: Allowance for doubtful lease payments	(3,861)
Net minimum lease payments receivable	$ 70,026
Unguaranteed residual values of leased property	8,104
Less: Unearned lease income	(31,213)
	$ 46,917

Future minimum sales-type and direct financing lease payments receivable for each of the next 5 years are, respectively, $12,087,000, $10,329,000, $9,643,000, $8,127,000 and $7,846,000.

Finance lease revenue includes $1,170,000 and $943,000 for the years ended December 31, 1984 and 1983, respectively, recognized to offset initial direct costs incurred in negotiating and consummating direct financing leases. Also included in finance lease revenue are contingent rentals of $426,000 and $378,000 for the years ended December 31, 1984 and 1983, respectively.

Net investment in leveraged leases at December 31, 1984, consists of the following:

Rentals receivable (net of principal and interest on nonrecourse debt) .	$ 3,711,000
Unguaranteed residual values of lease property	5,286,000
Less: Unearned and deferred income	(1,499,000)
Investment in leveraged leases	$ 7,498,000
Less: Deferred taxes arising from leveraged leases	(5,026,000)
Net investment in leveraged leases	$ 2,472,000

Residual values represent management's estimates of the proceeds to be received from future dispositions of leased property subsequent to the expiration of the original lease terms. Minimum lease payments includes $3,749,000 representing residual value amounts guaranteed as to recovery by lessees and independent third parties. The original cost or fair value of leased property, summarized by major type, for which residual values have been recorded are summarized as follows:

		Recorded residual values	
Type of property	Original cost or fair value	Guaranteed	Unguaranteed
		(in thousands)	
Commercial jet aircraft	$ 41,319		$ 6,280
Machine tools	23,741	$ 518	2,802
Railroad rolling stock	15,493	621	2,478
Computers	20,952	2,457	684
Other	12,990	153	1,146
	$114,495	$3,749	$13,390

Rental property consists of equipment leased or held for lease to others under operating leases. The cost, accumulated depreciation, depreciable lives, and estimated salvage values of such property by major type at December 31, 1984, are as follows:

Property type	Cost (in thousands)	Depreciable lives (yr)	Estimated salvage values (%)
Railroad rolling stock	$ 47,926	20–30	15
Trucks and trailors	28,413	10–15	10
Computer peripherals	19,106	5–7	10
Automobiles	16,361	3–5	10
Other	9,789	5–10	10
	$121,592		
Less: Accumulated depreciation	(41,449)		
	$ 80,143		

Rentals receivable under noncancelable operating leases total $83,792,000 in the aggregate and $15,246,000, $14,819,000, $12,198,000, $11,721,000, and $11,114,000 during 1985 through 1988, respectively. Included in rental income for the years ended December 31, 1984 and 1983, are contingent rentals of $2,498,000 and $2,105,000.

the gain or loss must be deferred and amortized over the lease term in a systematic manner.

A borrowing of the present value of all future minimum lease payments in exchange for a promissory note is in substance a sale, provided that the holder of the promissory note does not have recourse to the general credit of the seller in the event of a lessee default. Such notes are usually secured by an assignment of the lease payments and a security interest in the leased property.

If a lessor sells property subject to an operating lease or if an owner of property sells it to a buyer who intends to lease it under an operating lease and the seller agrees to retain any of the market risks usually associated with ownership of the property, then the seller should not record the transaction as a sale. Instead the sales proceeds are credited to a liability account as a loan and the transaction is accounted for as if the seller were the owner/lessor of property subject to an operating lease. Examples of the types of agreements that a seller may not enter into and record a transaction as a sale include:

1. A commitment to reacquire the property in the event of a default or early termination by the lessee

2. A guarantee of a specified minimum rate of return on the investment

3. An agreement to remarket the equipment upon the termination of the initial or subsequent operating leases unless such agreement provides appropriate compensation for the effort expended in remarketing and does not require the seller to give any type of priority to the buyer's property over similar property owned and marketed by the seller

4. Extended or unusual warrantees that effectively protect the buyer from risk of loss resulting from technological obsolescence

Leases Involving Real Property. Real estate transactions traditionally have been subject to special accounting rules and conventions, and real estate leases are no exception. The specific rules applicable to leases involving real property result from the fact that such leases often involve only a portion of a property or they involve land. Usually, land is not a depreciable fixed asset.

The FASB identified the following four categories of leases involving real property:

1. Leases involving land only
2. Leases involving land and buildings
3. Leases involving only part of a building
4. Leases involving both real and personal property

Leases involving land only. A lease involving land only is always an operating lease for the lessee unless the lessee obtains title to the property as part of the lease or obtains the right to purchase the property during or at the end of the lease at a bargain price. A lease that transfers title to the lessee or contains a bargain purchase option is a capital lease. However, the capitalized asset normally would not be amortized.

A land-only lease that is a capital lease to the lessee is a financing lease to the lessor if collectibility of the lease payments is reasonably assured and no important uncertainties exist with respect to the amount of future costs to be incurred by the lessor.

A lease that otherwise would be classified as a sales-type lease must nevertheless be accounted for as an operating lease unless, at the beginning of the lease term, the transaction also complies with the requirements for sales treatment under the Statement of Financial Accounting Standards No. 66, *Accounting for Sales of Real Estate*. SFAS No. 66 prohibits profit recognition on sales of real property unless there is an adequate initial and continuing investment in the property on the part of the buyer. The definition of an adequate investment differs depending on the type of property (primary residential, recreational, commercial, etc.). SFAS No. 66 provides specific minimum guidelines for each type. See Chapter 17.

SFAS No. 66 also prohibits profit recognition if the seller/lessor agrees to guarantee a minimum return on the buyer's investment or otherwise to retain a significant continuing involvement in the property. It would generally be true, however, that a lease that transfers sufficient risk of ownership to the lessee to qualify as a sales-type lease would also satisfy the requirements in this area.

Leases involving land and buildings. If a lease involving land and a building transfers title to the lessee or contains a bargin purchase option, it is a capital lease to the lessee. The capitalized value must be apportioned between the land and building based on their relative fair values. The building portion should be depreciated over its estimated total economic life, just as any building would be. The land normally would not be depreciated.

If a lease involving land and a building contains neither a bargain purchase option nor a transfer of title, then the lessee must apportion the fair value between the land and building before applying the economic-life and recovery-of-investment tests. If land represents less than 25 percent of the total fair value, the land and building should be viewed as a single asset for classification purposes. Otherwise the land and building must be classified separately.

Whenever land constitutes 25 percent or more of the total fair value of the leased property the lessee and lessor must allocate a portion of the rent to the land and account for it using the operating method. The amount of the rent assigned to the land must be computed by multiplying the fair market value of the land times the lessee's incremental borrowing rate. The remainder of the rent, after deducting executory costs, if any, should be assigned to the building for purposes of applying the recovery of investment test.

If a lease of a building (where land is 25 percent or more of the total fair value) or of land and a building (where land is less than 25 percent of the total fair value) meets the economic-life or recovery-of-investment test, then the lessee should capitalize the lease and account for it like any other capital lease. The lessor should account for such a lease as a direct financing or sales-type lease. A sales-type lease, however, must also meet the SFAS No. 66 guidelines described above relating to profit recognition on sales of real estate. Otherwise it must be treated as an operating lease.

Leases involving only part of a building. The lessee's accounting for a lease covering only part of a building depends on the lessee's ability to ascertain the fair value of the leased property. If fair value can be measured objectively, the lessee should follow the accounting prescribed for leases involving land and buildings. If fair value cannot be measured objectively, then the recovery-of-investment test cannot be applied. The lessee should classify the lease as an operating lease unless the lease term equals or exceeds 75 percent of the leased asset's estimated economic life. To capitalize such a lease, the lessee must use the incremental borrowing rate, because the interest rate implicit in the lease cannot be measured.

The lessor's accounting for a lease involving only a part of a building depends on the lessor's ability to ascertain both the fair value and cost of the leased property. If either of these amounts cannot be measured objectively, the lease must be accounted for as an operating lease.

Leases involving both real and personal property. If both real and personal property are included on the same lease, the rent applicable to the personal property must be measured in a reasonable and systematic manner. The classification criteria should be applied separately to the real and personal property as if there were two separate leases. The accounting for the personal property should follow the general lease accounting rules, whereas the accounting for the real property should follow the special rules applicable to leases of real estate.

Sale-Leaseback Transactions. The sale-leaseback transaction has been used for many years in real estate financing. However, sale-leaseback transactions involving equipment have become more common in recent years.

In a typical sale-leaseback, a company constructs a facility. Upon completion it sells the facility to another company and then leases it back for a specified period. The sale of the property usually involves a gain or loss to the seller. However, this gain or loss generally has not been recognized at the time of the transaction. When the seller simultaneously agrees to lease the asset being sold, the sale price may not reflect the value that could be obtained in an arms'-

length negotiation with a buyer who did not intend to lease the property back to the seller.

The FASB reaffirmed the established accounting principles relating to sale-leaseback transactions in SFAS No. 13. Gains or losses must generally be deferred and amortized in parallel with the lessee's pattern of recognizing expense relating to the lease. If the lease is a capital lease, the deferred gain or loss should be amortized in proportion to the amortization of the capitalized asset. If the lease is an operating lease, the gain or loss should be recognized in proportion to lease expense over the period of the lease.

However, the FASB has identified three exceptions under which part or all of the gain or loss need not be deferred:

1. A seller who leases back only a minor portion of the remaining use value of the property must recognize the gain or loss at the time of sale. For example, if the present value of the lessee's required lease payments is less than 10 percent of fair value of the property, it is reasonable to conclude that the risks of ownership have been substantially assumed by the buyer and that immediate recognition of a gain or loss is appropriate. If the rentals called for during the term of the leaseback are unreasonable in relation to market conditions existing at the inception of the lease, then an appropriate amount of the gain or loss must be deferred or accrued to be amortized ratably over the period of the lease.

2. The seller who retains more than a minor portion, but less than substantially all of an asset through a leaseback, may recognize an immediate profit on the sale to the extent that the profit from the sale exceeds (a) the present value of the noncancelable lease payments (assuming that the lease is an operating lease) or (b) the capitalized value of the leased asset (assuming that the lease is a capital lease). In applying this provision to an operating lease, the discount rate to be used is the lower of the lessee's incremental borrowing rate and the interest rate implicit in the lease.

3. If the fair value of the property at the time of sale is less than the book value of the property on the seller's books, the seller must recognize an immediate loss in the amount of the difference between these two values.

The above exceptions notwithstanding, no gain should be recognized on a sale-leaseback transaction involving real estate unless it satisfies the requirements of SFAS No. 66 *Accounting for Sales of Real Estate* [FASB, 1982].

The special rules governing sale-leaseback transactions apply only to lessees. The purchasor/lessor in such a transaction should account for the transaction as for any other lease transaction involving similar property.

Subleases. Many leases give the lessee the right to sublease the leased property to another party. SFAS No. 13 provides the following guidelines for the lessee/sublessor's accounting for such transactions:

1. If the original lease was classified at inception as a capital lease because it transfers ownership to the lessee or contains a bargain purchase option, the sublease should be classified according to the four classification criteria and, if appropriate, accounted for as a financing lease. If the new transaction satisfies the requirements of a financing lease, the unamortized book value of the original capital lease should be used as the sublessor's cost for purposes of recording the new lease.

2. If the original lease was classified at inception as a capital lease because it met the requirements of the economic-life or recovery-of-investment test, usually only the economic-life test should be used to classify the sublease. If the sublease does not meet this test, it should be treated as an operating lease by the sublessor. However, SFAS No. 13 provides an exception to this general rule in those instances where the timing and other circumstances surrounding the negotiation of a sublease suggest that the sublessor is acting only as an intermediary between the lessor and the sublessee. If this condition is present, the sublessor should also apply the recovery-of-investment test to classify the sublease. In applying the recovery-of-investment test, the sublessor's fair value of the leased property should be the same fair value used by the original lessor at the inception of the original lease.

3. If the original lease is an operating lease to the lessee/sublessor, the sublease will always be an operating lease.

The accounting of the original lessor is not affected by a sublease unless the lessor enters into an agreement that modifies the rights and obligations under the original lease. The new sublessee should classify the sublease in the same way as any other similar lease, without regard to the fact that it is a sublease.

Leasehold Improvements. Leasehold improvements are additions to the property made by the lessee. They become the property of the lessor when affixed to the property. If the leasehold improvement has a life longer than the current fiscal year, it is proper for the lessee to spread its cost over its useful life as with any depreciable asset. Useful life to the lessee cannot be longer than the remaining life of the lease unless the lessee has a right to renew the lease. If the lessee has the right to renew and is likely to do so, then the useful life of the improvement is limited by the renewal terms of the lease. If the lease expires before the physical usefulness is gone, the remaining usefulness belongs to the lessor. The lessee should record the cost of the improvement in an account bearing a title descriptive of the asset and containing terms to identify it as a leasehold improvement. The balance should be amortized regularly as if it were an owned asset being depreciated.

The lessor typically makes no entry for leasehold improvements. A lessee is not likely to make improvements that will have substantial value beyond the original term or the guaranteed renewal term of his leases. Therefore, there is little likelihood that the leasehold improvement will prove valuable to the lessor. If there is likely to be value, it is also likely that the lessee would try to get the lessor to share in the cost. To the extent that the lessor shares in the cost, of course, an asset is recorded in the amount of lessor's cost.

FEDERAL INCOME TAXES AND LEASING

The Internal Revenue Service may from time to time use different criteria from those used by the taxpayer for judging whether a lease should be capitalized. Thus, some leases that are not capitalized on the books may be required to be treated as purchases for tax purposes, and vice versa. Differences in accounting for tax purposes and financial reporting purposes may give rise to tax deferrals. Tax deferrals arising from leasing activities should be treated like those arising from any other cause (see Chapter 36).

BIBLIOGRAPHY

Financial Accounting Standards Board, *Accounting for Leases*, Statement of Financial Accounting Standards No. 13 (FASB, 1976).

———, *Accounting for Leases—Initial Direct Costs*, Statement of Financial Accounting Standards No. 17 (FASB, 1977).

———, *Profit Recognition on Sales-Type Leases of Real Estate*, Statement of Financial Accounting Standards No. 26 (FASB, 1979).

———, *Classification of Renewals or Extensions of Existing Sales-Type or Direct Financing Leases*, Statement of Financial Accounting Standards No. 27 (FASB, 1979).

———, *Accounting for Sales with Leasebacks*, Statement of Financial Accounting Standards No. 28 (FASB, 1979).

———, *Determining Contingent Rentals*, Statement of Financial Accounting Standards No. 29 (FASB, 1979).

———, *Accounting for Sales of Real Estate*, Statement of Financial Accounting Stardards No. 66 [FASB, 1982].

Shanno, D., and R. L. Weil, "The Separate Phases Method of Accounting for Leveraged Leases: Properties of the Allocating Rate and an Algorithm for Finding It," *Journal of Accounting Research*, vol. 14, no. 2 (Autumn 1976), pp. 348–356.

CHAPTER 25

Pensions

Katherine Schipper*

Associate Professor of Industrial Administration,
Carnegie-Mellon University

*The author acknowledges a debt to Ernest L. Hicks and René A. Miller, the authors of
the pension chapter in the second edition of this handbook.

INTRODUCTION

The private pension system in the United States has exhibited a pattern of growth that reflects both the expansion of the economy and the adoption of the social objective of providing a measure of economic security for persons retiring from employment. The development of private retirement plans has resulted in large part from the initiative of employers and labor leaders, but public agencies have both encouraged and regulated private plans through tax and labor laws, laws setting standards of fiduciary obligation for trustees, and laws requiring disclosure concerning various aspects of retirement and welfare plans.

In 1974 Congress enacted the Employee Retirement Income Security Act of 1974 (ERISA) to regulate private-sector, single-employer pension plans.[1] ERISA set standards for eligibility, vesting, and funding; established standards of conduct for fiduciaries of employee benefit plans; set reporting and disclosure

---

[1] Subsections (b) and (c) of Section 2 of ERISA state the policy of the act: "(b) . . . to protect interstate commerce and the interests of participants in employee benefit plans and their beneficiaries, by requiring the disclosure and reporting . . . of financial and other information . . . by establishing standards of conduct, responsibility, and obligation for fiduciaries . . . , and by providing for appropriate remedies, sanctions, and ready access to the Federal courts; (c) . . . to protect interstate commerce, the Federal taxing power, and the interests of participants in private pension plans and their beneficiaries by improving the equitable character and the soundness of such plans by requiring them to vest the accrued benefits of employees with significant periods of service, to meet minimum standards of funding, and by requiring plan termination insurance."

25-2

requirements for such plans; liberalized the treatment of plans covering self-employed individuals and shareholder employees of Subchapter S corporations; set limits on contributions and benefits; changed the tax treatment of lump-sum distributions; and allowed persons not covered by employer-sponsored retirement plans to create individual plans. This chapter takes into consideration the aspects of ERISA that affect an employer's accounting for the cost of a pension plan.

The basic operations of a pension plan are simple, but the concepts can be lost in a variety of details and procedures. In a pension plan:

1. The employer sets up a pension plan, specifying the eligibility of employees, the types of promises made to employees, the method of funding, and the pension plan administrator. Typically, the plan's funding agent is a bank or insurance company.

Pension law differentiates between the *plan administrator* (one with fiduciary responsibility for plan) and the *funding agent* (who holds and invests funds). This chapter does not distinguish between these two functions.

2. Each period, the employer computes a pension expense according to some formula. The employer debits Pension Expense for that amount and credits Pension Liability. This process is referred to here as *expensing pension obligations*.

3. The employer transfers cash to the plan each period according to some formula. The employer generally debits Pension Liability and credits Cash. This process is referred to here as *funding pension liabilities*. The amounts expensed each period in Step 2 are *not* necessarily the same as the amounts funded in this step.

The preceding steps comprise the employer's accounting for pensions. The employer is sometimes called the *plan sponsor*. The following steps are carried out for the pension plan by the plan administrator, who maintains the accounting records of the pension plan.

1. The plan receives cash each period from the plan sponsor. In the accounting records of the pension plan, Cash is debited and Pension Liability to Employees is credited.

2. As time passes, payment dates approach. The pension plan debits Interest Expense and credits Pension Liability to Employees for the increase in present value of the pension liability. Meanwhile, the funds received are invested to generate income. The pension plan debits Cash Received from Earnings and credits Investment Revenue. The interest expense and investment income are not part of the employer's (sponsor's) income for the period, but are reported in separate financial statements of the pension plan.

3. The plan makes payments to those entitled to receive them. The plan debits Pension Liability to Employees and credits Cash.

ACCOUNTING PRINCIPLES

From 1966 through the early 1980s, APB Opinion No. 8 [1966] and the FASB's SFAS No. 36 [1980] governed the employer's accounting and reporting for pension plans.[2] In 1982 the FASB indicated that an Exposure Draft of new rules for pension accounting would appear within a few years. At the same time it announced some *Preliminary Views* [FASB, 1982] that provide guidance as to the likely form of the eventual rules. Where pertinent, this chapter is based on the *Preliminary Views*. Because this chapter is devoted to pension accounting concepts and problems rather than to specific accounting procedures, most of the discussion appears unlikely to be made obsolete by the eventual rules, even if they differ from the Preliminary Views.

Since 1980, there have been separate accounting rules for the employer and the pension plan. The discussion in this chapter is based on SFAS No. 36, issued in 1980, and the 1982 *Preliminary Views*.

For purposes of this discussion, private retirement programs are grouped into three categories: (1) deferred-compensation contracts with individual employees, (2) defined-contribution plans, and (3) defined-benefit plans. Most plans in the second and third categories are given effect through formal plans whose provisions are intended to meet the requirements of ERISA and the requirements for qualification imposed under the Internal Revenue Code. If the plan is qualified: (1) The employer's contributions are deductible for federal income tax purposes within specified limits; (2) earnings of trust funds established under the plan are not subject to federal income tax; and (3) employees are taxed only when they receive benefits.

Deferred-Compensation Contracts with Individual Employees. A deferred-compensation contract typically is a contract of employment with an individual executive; it requires the executive to perform specified duties during periods of active employment and establishes the total amount of compensation during that period. The contract provides that the executive also will receive periodic payments (the "deferred compensation") after retirement, either for life or for a specified number of years; it may also provide for payments to a beneficiary when the executive dies. The contract may also specify that, after retirement, the executive (1) will not compete with the employer and (2) will act as a consultant when requested to do so by the employer. The right to receive the deferred payments may be contingent on fulfilling these and other conditions.

---

[2] Until the APB issued Opinion No. 8, employers followed pension accounting principles set forth (although with less specificity) in Accounting Research Bulletins (ARB) No. 36 (1948) and No. 47 (1956) of the Committee on Accounting Procedure of AICPA. ARB No. 36, later incorporated in ARB No. 43, *Restatement and Revision of Accounting Research Bulletins* as Chapter 13(a), dealt mainly with past service cost, recommending allocation of such cost generally to "current and future periods." ARB No. 47 added a preference for systematically accruing current and future service cost during the expected period of active service of covered employees, and accounting for past service cost over some reasonable period (not defined). ARB No. 47 recognized an alternative method "for the present" and "as a minimum." Under the alternative method, financial statements were to "reflect accruals equal to the present worth, actuarially calculated, of pension commitments to employees to the extent that pension rights have vested in the employees, reduced, in the case of the balance sheet, by any accumulated trusteed funds or annuity contracts purchased."

Accounting. In 1967, the Accounting Principles Board issued Opinion No. 12, dealing with, among other matters, "deferred compensation contracts." Paragraph 6 of the Opinion provides that:

> ... deferred compensation contracts should be accounted for individually on an accrual basis. Such contracts customarily include certain requirements such as continued employment for a specified period and availability for consulting services and agreements not to compete after retirement, which, if not complied with, remove the employer's obligations for future payments. The estimated amounts to be paid under each contract should be accrued in a systematic and rational manner over the period of active employment from the time the contract is entered into, unless it is evident that future services expected to be received by the employer are commensurate with the payments or a portion of the payments to be made. If elements of both current and future services are present, only the portion applicable to the current services should be accrued.

In applying this paragraph, an appraisal must be made of the circumstances expected to prevail following the executive's retirement. In general, the excess of the cost of the future payments over the value of any services the executive is expected to perform following retirement should be recognized as an expense during the working lifetime.

Defined-Contribution Plans. Defined-contribution plans provide retirement benefits for retired persons as members of groups, rather than as individual contracting parties. These plans comprise primarily deferred profit-sharing plans and money-purchase plans. Under plans of both types, an employee's benefits are the amounts that can be provided (often by purchase of an annuity) by the sums contributed for that employee.

Deferred profit-sharing plans. The amount of an employer's contribution for a given period under a deferred profit-sharing plan is calculated under a formula specified in the plan; the total amount is in turn allocated among participants using another formula prescribed in the plan. Earnings of the trust fund, and in some instances amounts becoming available because of the withdrawal of other participants, are also so allocated.

Money-purchase plans. A money-purchase plan differs from a deferred profit-sharing plan primarily in the method of determining the employer's contributions. In a money-purchase plan, the contribution is ordinarily determined as a percentage of the compensation of participating employees.

Accounting. Defined-contribution plans do not ordinarily raise difficult accounting questions. The amount contributed for a reporting period (whether or not paid in the period) is the expense for the period.

Defined-Benefit Plans. This chapter is concerned primarily with defined-benefit plans. Such plans state the amount of the benefits, or the method of determining the benefits, to be received by employees after retirement. In some plans, the payment is the same for all retired employees (e.g., $200 per month). In plans for hourly employees, the benefit is typically a specified amount per month (e.g., $20 for each year of credited service). In plans for salaried employees, the benefit is more often related to compensation (e.g., an annual pension equal to a specified percentage, such as 2 percent, of total earnings for the entire period of employment, or a percentage, such as 30 percent, of the average earnings for a specified period, such as 5 years, immediately prior to retirement). In some instances, social security benefits reduce the benefits payable under the employer's pension plan.

The terms of a defined-benefit plan reflect the interaction of many factors. (This is also true of other types of retirement plans, but the impact on the accounting considerations is greater for defined-benefit plans.) Some plans are negotiated (resulting from collective bargaining); others are unilateral (established by an employer without negotiation). As to many aspects of a plan, the standards specified in ERISA are important considerations. Under ERISA, a plan must be *funded* (the employer sets funds aside for future pension benefits by making payments to a funding agency—in an insured plan to an insurance company, in a trust fund plan to a trustee). Some plans are *contributory* (the employees bear part of the cost of the stated benefits or voluntarily make payments in order to increase their benefits); others are noncontributory (the employer bears the entire cost). These differences, together with various eligibility requirements, specified retirement ages, disability options, and levels of benefits, contribute to an almost infinite variety of plans.

Accounting. The principles of accounting for the cost of a defined-benefit pension plan are the primary concern of this chapter.

ACTUARIAL TECHNIQUES

To understand the accounting principles for pension cost, one must know something of the techniques actuaries use in estimating pension cost and be familiar with the specialized terminology. The paragraphs that follow are intended to draw the outlines, from a lay viewpoint, of actuarial techniques;[3] certain specifics will be considered in more detail in later sections.

Actuarial Valuation. Basic to the fabric of pension costing is the process by which actuaries determine the amounts to be used in computing the periodic funding requirements of a pension plan (other than a plan that uses insurance or annuity policies calling for payment of specified premiums). This process is referred to as an *actuarial valuation* of the plan. A valuation is made as of a specific date, which need not coincide with either the beginning or end of the period for which funding is being determined. Valuations are usually made annually, but some employers have them made at less frequent intervals. ERISA contemplates an actuarial valuation at least every 3 years unless required more frequently by regulations in particular cases.

In making valuations, actuaries work with information furnished by the employer, for example, the sex, date of birth, employment date, and compensation of each employee covered by the plan. The calculations are made for a

---

[3] For a more comprehensive discussion of actuarial techniques, see McGill [FASB, 1981a].

specific group—ordinarily, employees presently covered by the plan, former employees having vested rights, and retired employees receiving benefits. It is recognized that subsequent valuations can be expected to produce different results, even in the absence of changes in other factors, because the composition of the group will have changed.

The purpose of an actuarial valuation is to estimate the cost of benefits to be paid over varying periods of time in the future and, in some cases, the cost of payments for expenses of administering a plan or trust. The estimated cost is expressed in terms of the present value, as of the date of the valuation, of the expected future benefit payments. The present value is the amount that, if invested at the date of the valuation at a stated rate of interest, would provide the benefits expected to become payable.[4]

The resulting valuations are estimates, because in making a valuation actuaries must tentatively resolve a number of significant uncertainties concerning future events. In doing so, they use factors called *actuarial assumptions*. Although these assumptions do not affect the actual (ultimate) cost of a plan, they have an important effect on present estimates of the cost.

ACCOUNTING METHODS FOR EXPENSE ATTRIBUTION CONTRASTED WITH ACTUARIAL METHODS DEVELOPED FOR FUNDING[5]

Actuarial cost methods were developed by actuaries to suggest *funding* patterns to assist business in accumulating over long time spans amounts of cash adequate to pay pensions. An emphasis on funding without placing undue burdens on any one year led actuaries to attend to *smoothness* of cash flows in devising the methods. Accounting has not, however, generally allowed smoothness of expenditures to determine expense recognition patterns: To the accountant, a cash expenditure leads to an asset if there is a future benefit; an expense is recognized for the period when the future benefit expires.

An exception to this rule has occurred in the area of pension accounting. Historically, accountants have allowed the actuarial cost methods, developed primarily to aid in funding decisions, to influence the allowable patterns of expense recognition. See, for example, paragraph 5 of Accounting Research Bulletin No. 47 and paragraph 24 of APB Opinion No. 8.

The difference between the funding goals of actuarial cost methods and the expensing goals of accounting, coupled with accounting's historical reliance on actuarial cost methods in devising expense patterns, has given the accounting standard setters some difficulty in sorting out the methods that can and cannot

---

[4]In pension plan valuations, actuaries combine (1) arithmetic probability factors (examples are factors for changes in compensation levels and for mortality) bearing on the amounts of benefits expected to become payable with (2) arithmetic factors representing the accretion of interest. To most actuaries, determining the present value of future pension benefits means applying factors of both types.

[5]The material in this section is adapted from Schipper and Weil [1982]. A good discussion of these issues, but without examples, appears in Skinner [1981].

EXHIBIT 1   Actuarial Cost and Accounting Expense Attribution Terminology[a]

Actuarial cost method (term used by actuaries)	Expense attribution approach (description used by accountants)
Accumulated benefit Accrued benefit Unit credit Single premium Step rate	Accumulated benefits
Projected unit credit Modified accrued benefit	Benefit/years of service or benefit/compensation
Individual level premium Attained age level premium Projected benefit cost Entry age normal	Cost/years of service
Entry age normal Projected benefit cost (with supplemental liability) Frozen initial liability	Cost/compensation
Aggregate	Cost/compensation or cost/years of service

[a]From FASB [1981a, p.69].

be allowed for accounting purposes. The discussion and example in this section are designed to focus on various methods of attributing expenses to accounting periods and to highlight the differences between these methods and certain actuarial cost methods. The phrase *expense attribution*, rather than the more usual phrases, *expense allocation* and *cost allocation*, is used to distinguish between accounting problems and funding problems. Actuaries have for many years used the term *cost allocation method*, where an accountant might use the term *funding pattern*. In the following discussion, the phrase *cost allocation* is used in its historical, actuarial sense of a funding pattern, and the phrase *expense attribution* is used for the accounting problem. This usage follows that introduced by the FASB in its 1981 Discussion Memorandum [FASB, 1981a]. Exhibit 1 shows the correspondence between the terms used by actuaries for their cost methods with the descriptions used by accountants for the expense attribution methods. Later sections explain these methods.

Simplified Pension Example. This section develops the issues of expense attribution and funding patterns by expanding on an example originally developed by the chairman of the Financial Accounting Standards Board [Kirk, 1981] during the 1981 exposure period of the FASB Discussion Memorandum [FASB, 1981a].

Suppose that a firm promises an employee compensation contingent on some period of continuous employment. Specifically, assume that this compensation is equal to 20 percent, multiplied by the number of years of employment, multiplied by the annual salary at the end of the last year of employment. This accounting problem captures the issues associated with pension accounting because it involves compensation to be paid in a subsequent accounting period that is earned over several periods. Furthermore, the amount of compensation is based on salary of a future period whose amount is unknown at the time the agreement is made.

For concreteness, assume an executive earning $100,000 for the first year whose wage is estimated to be $120,000 by the end of the second year and $150,000 by the end of the third year. Throughout, assume an interest rate of 10 percent per year. At the end of the first year the executive is earning $100,000 per year and is believed to be likely to stay employed for 2 years more. The end-of-first-year estimate of the nominal amount of compensation at the end of the third year is $90,000 (= $150,000 × .20 × 3). The next section discusses the various actuarial and accounting treatments of this compensation.

Benefit Allocation Methods Versus Cost Allocation Methods. The taxonomy of actuarial cost methods distinguishes *benefit allocation methods* from *cost allocation methods* (see, e.g., McGill [FASB, 1981a, p. 193]). The FASB has preserved this distinction between benefit allocation and cost allocation methods in its writings about pension-related expenses. In a benefit allocation method, the actuarial present value of a discrete dollar amount of pension benefit is separately computed and assigned to each year of credited service as an amount to be funded. In a cost allocation method, an estimate is first made of the total amount to be paid to the employee at retirement. That cost is then apportioned in some systematic way among the years the employee works. Various methods of allocating costs can be used; methods discussed in the literature include straight-line (equal amounts of cost to each year) and percentage-of-salary (amounts allocated to a year in proportion equal to that year's salary as a fraction of total career earnings). If the costs are computed for an individual, then allocated to that individual's work years before the amounts for a given year are summed over all employees, the method is known as an *individual* method. Costs may also be aggregated across individuals before being allocated to years, in which case the method is known as *aggregate* method.

Benefit Allocation Methods. Benefit allocation methods divide into two classes:

1. Those based on accumulated or accrued benefits, making no projections about the future earnings and employment patterns of the employee
2. Those based on projected or estimated benefits to be earned over the work life of the employee

These methods are illustrated in Exhibit 2.

Accumulated benefit method. At the end of the first year, the employee is earning $100,000 per year and has worked for 1 year. Under the accumulated benefit method, the benefit for the first year is $20,000 (= $100,000 × 1 year × .20) and the obligation at the end of the first year is computed to be $16,529 (= $20,000 × 1.10^{-2}). If accounting recognition is accorded this number, the

EXHIBIT 2   Methods of Attributing Compensation Expense to Periods

$$\text{Lump-Sum Payment} = \frac{\text{Annual Salary Rate End of Third Year}}{} \times \frac{\text{Number of Years of Work}}{} \times .20$$

Salary at End of First Year	= $100,000
Salary Estimate for End of Second Year	= 120,000
Salary Estimate for End of Third Year	= 150,000

	Benefit allocation method based on			Cost allocation method based on	
		Benefits calculated as a function of projected salary and			
	Actual salary (1)	Years of service (2)	Compen-sation (3)	Years of service (4)	Compen-sation (5)
Year 1					
Deferred-compensation expense.....	$16,529[a]	$24,793[f]	$20,103[k]	$27,190[p]	$22,333[s]
Year 2					
Amount equivalent to interest	$ 1,653[b]	$ 2,479[g]	$ 2,010[l]	$ 2,719[q]	$ 2,233[t]
Deferred-compensation expense.....	25,454*	27,273*	26,536[m]	27,190[p]	26,799[u]
Total year 2 expenses	$27,107[c]	$29,752[h]	$28,546	$29,909	$29,032
Year 3					
Amount equivalent to interest	$ 4,364[d]	$ 5,455[i]	$ 4,865[n]	$ 5,710[r]	$ 5,136[v]
Deferred-compensation expense.....	42,000*	30,000*	36,486[o]	27,191[p]	33,499[w]
Total year 3 expenses	$46,364[e]	$35,455[j]	$41,351	$32,901	$38,635
Three-year total expenses	$90,000	$90,000	$90,000	$90,000	$90,000
Summary and reconciliation					
Deferred compensation expense.....	$83,983	$82,066	$83,125	$81,571	$82,631
Amounts equivalent to interest.......	6,017	7,934	6,875	8,429	7,369
Three-year total expenses	$90,000	$90,000	$90,000	$90,000	$90,000

* Indicates a plugged or forced calculation. Other numbers are calculated as indicated in the following notes.

[a] ($100,000 × 1 × .20) × 1.10^{-2}.

[b] .10 × $16,529.

[c] [($120,000 × 2 × .20) × 1.10^{-1}] − $16,529.

[d] .10 × ($16,529 + $27,107).

[e] ($150,000 × 3 × .20) − ($16,529 + $27,107).

[f] ($150,000 × 1 × .20) × 1.10^{-2}.

[g] .10 × $24,793.

[h] [($150,000 × 2 × .20) × 1.10^{-1}] − $24,793.

[i] .10 × ($24,793 + $29,752).

[j] ($150,000 × 3 × .20) − ($24,793 + $29,752).

[k] .243243 × $100,000 × 1.10^{-2}. Note that $\dfrac{(\$150,000 \times 3 \times .20)}{(\$100,000 + \$120,000 + \$150,000)} = .243243$.

[l] .10 × $20,103.

[m] (.243243 × $120,000) × 1.10^{-1}.

[n] .10 × ($20,103 + $28,541).

[o] .243243 × $150,000.

[p] Amount of an ordinary annuity accumulated for 3 years at 10% is $3.31; $90,000/3.31 = $27,190 except in year 3, where it is $1 more to correct for rounding error.

[q] .10 × $27,190.

[r] .10 × ($27,190 + $29,909). Note that if [($100,000P) × 1.10^2] + [($120,000P) × 1.10] + $150,000P = $90,000, then $P = \dfrac{\$90,000}{\$403,000} = .223325$.

[s] $100,000 × .223325.

[t] .10 × $22,333.

[u] $120,000 × .223325.

[v] .10 × ($22,333 + $29,032).

[w] $150,000 × .223325.

amount to be recognized is $16,529, because there is an obligation for $16,529 where there was none at the start of the year. At the end of the second year, the total accumulated benefits amount to $48,000 (= $120,000 × 2 years × .20), so the benefit accumulated during the second year is $28,000 (= $48,000 − $20,000). The present value of this obligation at the end of the second year is $43,636 (= $48,000 × 1.10⁻¹). If the accounting system records these obligations as expenses, the second year's expense will total $27,107 (= $43,636 − $16,529). Part ($1,653 = .10 × $16,529) of this expense is an amount equivalent to interest on the $16,529 obligation from the first year, part reflects the application of the higher salary to the first year's work, and part is attributable to the second year's work. (If the $16,529 were funded at the end of the second year, then the earnings on the fund might be offset against the amount equivalent to interest and the total expense might not be reported; this point is discussed later.) By the end of the third year the accumulated benefit is $90,000 (= $150,000 × 3 years × .20) and the obligation is also $90,000 because the payment is now due. The accounting number to be recognized for the third year is $46,364 (= $90,000 − $43,636).

Exhibit 2 summarizes this approach in the first column as the benefit allocation method based on actual salary. It is sometimes known as a *benefit allocation method based on accrued benefits.*

Salary projection benefit methods. Under the salary projection methods, the benefit for any year is based on expectations about salary. In the example, the benefit for the first year is based on the expected final salary of $150,000. It is computed as $30,000 (= $150,000 × 1 year × .20), so the obligation at the end of the first year is $24,793 (= $30,000 × 1.10⁻²). Note that the "projection" involves wages only, not total years of employment. The number to be recognized in the accounting system for the first year is also $24,793. At the end of the second year, the total benefits accumulated amount to $60,000 (= $150,000 × 2 years × .20), which have a present value of $54,545 (= $60,000 × 1.10⁻¹). If the accounting system recognizes these obligations as expenses, then the expense for the second year is $29,752 (= $54,545 − $24,793). This expense includes an amount equivalent to interest of $2,479 (= $24,793 × .10) on the obligation from the first year and expense for compensation of $27,273 (= $29,752 − $2,479). The second column of Exhibit 2 shows the components of expense for each of the 3 years. The method is known as the *accrual benefit method with salary projection based on years of service;* see Cassel and Kahn [1980]. Each year is given equal weight in computing the benefit for a year. This method has been tentatively chosen by the FASB [1982, par. 11].

Another method, preferred by some, including Cassel and Kahn [1980], is the *accrual benefit method with salary projection based on compensation.* Under this method the annual deferred compensation benefit is assumed to be equal to a fraction of each year's salary that is constant over time. Because the sum of all (estimated) salaries is $370,000 (= $100,000 + $120,000 + $150,000) and the (estimated) deferred payment is $90,000, the benefit attributable to each year is 24.32 percent (= $90,000/$370,000) of each year's salary. The third column of Exhibit 2 shows the components of expense for each of the 3 years under the salary projection method based on compensation.

Cost Allocation Methods. Cost allocation methods allocate to the years of work the total benefit to be paid (estimated at the end of the first year of the example to be $90,000). Cost allocation methods, unlike benefit allocation methods, take into account at each calculation the estimated number of total years to be worked, rather than focusing only on the work done by the end of the period when the calculation is being made. Like the salary projection benefit methods, cost allocation methods also take into account estimates of future wages.

Years of service. When costs are allocated based on expected years of service, equal costs are assigned to each year. An ordinary annuity of $1 in arrears for 3 periods accumulated at 10 percent per period has a future value of $3.31. Thus an annuity of $27,190 (= $90,000/3.31) will accumulate at 10 percent interest to $90,000. See column (4) of Exhibit 2.

Costs proportional to salary. Another method of cost allocation assigns costs to each period in proportion to the salary earned. A factor of proportionality of expected payment to total discounted salaries is solved for. This factor is then multiplied by the salary each period so that the resulting amounts, accumulated at interest, will sum to the total costs to be allocated. The fifth column of Exhibit 2 illustrates this method. The proportionality factor is solved for at note s to that exhibit. The FASB [1982, par. 11] has tentatively concluded that the accrued benefit method with salary projections based on years of service is to be used by employers in their calculations.

Generalizations about the Expense Attribution Methods. If we assume that the accounting system recognizes the obligations incurred by the employer as expenses, then various generalizations can be made about the expense attribution methods and their actuarial cost method analogs.

Total compensation expense is not constant over all methods. Exhibit 2 demonstrates that *total* expense over the life of the compensation plan (of the employer and the plan together) is equal to the cash expenditure of $90,000. Part of the expense each period may be shown as compensation expense and part as an "amount equivalent to interest." The term "amount equivalent to interest" is used because it may not actually appear in any financial statement labeled as interest expense. Consider, for example, the $16,529 reported as compensation expense in the accrued benefit method, column (1) of Exhibit 2, for the first year. If this amount is expensed but not funded, a liability will appear on the balance sheet. Interest of $1,653 will accrue for the second year and will be debited to interest expense and credited to the liability account. If, on the other hand, the $16,529 is funded as it is expensed, with the funding payment made to an outside fiduciary (such as a pension plan or its administrator), then the fund and not the sponsor will report an obligation to the employee. The fund's income statement may report only the net amount of the investment income less the increase in the liability: If the investment earnings rate exceeds 10 percent, there will be an actuarial gain; if the earnings rate falls short of 10 percent, there will be an actuarial loss; only the net may appear. Whereas total expense will equal the cash expenditure, the amount reported as compensation expense differs across methods.

Accumulated benefits approach. The compensation component of annual expense increases more rapidly throughout the employee's career with an accumulated benefits approach without salary projections than under the other methods, projected benefit or cost allocation, because each year the full effect of another year of service and higher wages is recognized. None of this impact has been anticipated.

Benefits approach versus cost allocation approach. Other things being equal, a cost allocation approach implies larger amounts in the early years than does a benefits approach, because it takes into account the estimated total years of work. For any calculation, the cost allocation approach attempts to estimate the total costs to be incurred over the life of the plan and to allocate them to the various periods. The benefit approach uses only the elapsed work history to date in making calculations for a period. Although the benefit approach with salary projections uses estimates of future salary in periodic computations, it does not use estimates of eventual number of years worked.

Years-of-service versus compensation approaches. The years-of-service approach, other things being equal, treats every year equally in assigning costs to years, whereas the compensation approaches assign costs to each year in proportion to that year's salary as a fraction of all salaries expected to be earned. Because salaries generally increase over time, the compensation approaches generally show smaller compensation cost in the early years than do the years-of-service approaches.

No universally applicable generalization can be made comparing cost or expense patterns of projected benefits based on years of service against cost allocation based on compensation. In Exhibit 2, the former, column (2), shows a larger first-year expense than the latter, column (5), but that result is happenstance.

Individual versus group effects. In the simple example, the "work force" of one person ages at the rate of 1 year for every year of elapsed calendar time. Generally, the average age and salary of a group of employees will not increase as rapidly as the average age and salary of a single employee. Thus, differences in the methods across a group of employees will not be as dramatic as in this example for a single employee.

Giving Employees Credit for Years of Service Prior to a Plan Change. The term *plan change* encompasses both a change in an existing plan and the adoption of a new plan. To make this discussion concrete, refer to the example of Exhibit 2, but assume that the plan is not adopted until the executive has been employed for 1 year. At the *end* of the first year, the business makes the same promise as before, to make the deferred compensation payment at the end of the third year. Exhibit 3 shows the extension of the example to illustrate a plan change.

Generally, when a defined-benefit plan is changed and the benefit is partly a function of the number of years of service, the benefit is based on all of a given employee's work years, not merely the years elapsing between the plan change and retirement. Assume that the employee's right to receive the benefit

EXHIBIT 3   Actuarial Cost Method Determines Existence and Amount of Actuarial Accrued Liability

	Benefit allocation method based on		Cost allocation method based on individual years of service	
	Actual salary (1)	Benefits as a function of projected salary and years of service (2)	Entry age normal (3)	Attained age normal[a] (4)
End of year 1				
Actuarial accrued liability created	$16,529[b]	$24,793[g]	$27,190[j]	
Year 2				
Interest on unrecognized actuarial accrued liability	$ 1,653[c]	$ 2,479[h]	$ 2,719[k]	
Amount equivalent to interest on recognized expenses				
Deferred-compensation expense	25,454[b]	27,273[g]	27,190[j]	$42,857[m]
Amortization of actuarial accrued liability	8,265[d]	12,397[d]	13,595[d]	
Total year 2 expenses	$35,372	$42,149	$43,504	$42,857
Year 3				
Interest on unrecognized actuarial accrued liability	$ 827[e]	$ 1,240[j]	$ 1,360[l]	
Amount equivalent to interest on recognized costs	3,537[f]	4,215	4,350	$ 4,286[n]
Deferred-compensation expense	42,000[b]	30,000[g]	27,191[j]	42,857[m]
Amortization of actuarial accrued liability	8,264[d]	12,396[d]	13,595[d]	
Total year 3 expenses	$54,628	$47,851	$46,496	$47,143
Three-year total expenses	$90,000	$90,000	$90,000	$90,000
Summary and reconciliation				
Deferred-compensation expense	$67,454	$57,273	$54,381	$85,714
Amounts equivalent to interest on expenses recognized	3,537	4,215	4,350	4,286
Amortization of actuarial accrued liability	16,529	24,793	27,190	
Interest on unrecognized actuarial accrued liability	2,480	3,719	4,079	
Three-year total expenses	$90,000	$90,000	$90,000	$90,000

[a]Because there is only one employee covered, a column based on the aggregate level dollar cost actuarial method would give the same numbers as in this column. See the discussion in the text.
[b]See Exhibit 1, column (1).
[c].10 × $16,529.
[d]Amortize actuarial accrued liability over 2 years. $16,529/2 = $8,264.50. $24,793/2 = $12,396.50. $27,190/2 = $13,595.
[e].10 × ($16,529 − $8,265).
[f].10 × $35,372.
[g]See Exhibit 1, column (2).
[h].10 × $24,793.
[i].10 × ($24,793 − $12,397).
[j]See Exhibit 1, column (4).
[k].10 × $27,190.
[l].10 × ($27,190 − $13,595).
[m]The future value of a 2-period annuity of $1 in arrears accumulated at 10% per period is $2.10; $90,000/2.10 = $42,857.
[n].10 × $42,857.

is fully *vested*;[6] relaxing this assumption changes the amounts in the calculations, not the concepts. By adopting a plan change that gives credit for prior years of service, the employer incurs an obligation to be discharged later. Accountants' and actuaries' differing emphasis on expensing patterns versus funding patterns may lead to a difference in treatment in recognizing this obligation. Actuaries have used several different names for amounts related to this obligation: *past service liability, prior service liability, supplemental liability, supplemental actuarial value, gross actuarial deficiency, net actuarial deficiency,* and *accrued actuarial value.* Those who set generally accepted accounting principles have tended to use the then-current actuarial term; see, for example, the use of *past service* and *prior service* in APB Opinion No. 8 and *supplemental actuarial value* in FASB SFAS No. 35. The Joint Committee on Pension Terminology [1981] has endorsed the terms *actuarial accrued liability, actuarial liability, accrued liability,* and *actuarial reserve.* The term *actuarial accrued liability* is used in the remainder of this discussion to refer to the funding obligation, if any, incurred by the employer as a result of a plan change.

Funding after a plan change. After a plan change, the actuary selects an actuarial cost method for computing an amount to be funded in *each* time period after the change. The actuary calls the periodic amount the *normal cost* or the *normal actuarial cost.* Under some actuarial cost methods, the sum of all normal cost plus interest accumulating on those amounts will be sufficient to build a fund to pay *all* of the benefits promised by a given plan change, including both benefits associated with work done before the plan change and benefits to be earned after the plan change. Put another way, the present value of normal costs in these cases equals the present value of the benefits promised by the plan change. If so, the actuary says that there is no actuarial accrued liability resulting from the plan change. Column (4) of Exhibit 3 illustrates such an actuarial cost method.

If the present value of the future normal costs resulting from application of a particular actuarial cost method is less than the present value of the benefits generated by the plan change, the shortage is called actuarial accrued liability and is given special treatment in the funding plan. That is, an additional funding series will be generated to cover this shortage in funding from normal costs. The accrued actuarial liability, if any, is a residual resulting from the characteristics of the actuarial cost method used in computing the "normal," periodic costs after the plan change. Columns (1), (2), and (3) of Exhibit 3 illustrate actuarial cost methods that generate actuarial accrued liability. The FASB [1982, par. 11] has tentatively chosen the method in column (2).

Which actuarial cost methods generate actuarial accrued liability? Actuarial cost methods are applied to individuals before being summed for the group or they are applied in aggregate to the entire group. If an individual actuarial cost method is based on the age of the employee at the time of the plan change (the "attained age") rather than the age of the employee when

---

[6]That is, the employee has the right to receive the entire benefit resulting from application of the formula with one input being the actual number of years of work, even though that number is less than 3.

work commenced (the "entry age"), then the actuarial method will spread all the cost of all obligations, including those arising upon plan adoption, over the remaining work life of the employee. If the individual method for computing normal costs is based on the entry age of the employee, then the sum of the normal costs for all years subsequent to the plan change will be insufficient to build the fund to a level to cover the years of work before the plan change. Column (3) of Exhibit 3 illustrates an entry-age calculation. Columns (1) and (2), which are analogous to the first two columns of Exhibit 2 in that they are based on benefit methods rather than cost allocation methods, lead to an actuarial accrued liability at the time of a plan change.

If the actuarial cost method is an aggregate method, then there is no actuarial accrued liability. The periodic "normal" cost for each period subsequent to the plan change is defined and derived so that the present value of future normal costs at the time of the plan change equals the present value of the future benefits to be paid; see McGill [FASB, 1981a, p. 200].

Summary of Exhibit 3. Exhibit 3 is designed to highlight the essential characteristics of actuarial cost methods in the context of a plan change.

1. Total expenses over the life of the plan are independent of the actuarial cost methods, although the allocation of the components of expense among
   (a) Deferred compensation expense,
   (b) Amounts equivalent to interest on deferred compensation expense already recognized,
   (c) Amortization of accrued actuarial liability, and
   (d) Interest on unrecognized actuarial accrued liability
is a function of the actuarial cost method chosen.

2. At the time of the plan change, an actuarial accrued liability arises or not depending on the computation of the amounts to be funded in each of the subsequent periods.

3. If there is an actuarial accrued liability, an amount uncovered by future normal costs, then the amount is a residual, a function of the method of computing the future normal costs.

A major difference between actuarial science and accounting. The difference between the actuary's emphasis on funding and the accountant's emphasis on expense and liability recognition is easy to see in Exhibit 3. The actuary devises a rule for computing a periodic funding amount subsequent to a plan change and calls that amount *normal cost.* If the sum of normal costs and interest equivalents thereon (i.e., the present value of normal costs) is sufficient to accumulate the fund required by the plan change, then there is no actuarial accrued liability. If, on the other hand, the actuary's rule for computing the annual funding amount and interest thereon is insufficient to accumulate the fund required by the plan change, then, and only then, does actuarial accrued liability arise. Furthermore, the amount of the actuarial accrued liability is a residual and a function of the actuarial cost method chosen.

This notion may seem alien to accountants.[7] To an accountant past events and

---

[7]The following procedure seems analogous and is clearly alien to accounting. Consider the following scheme of accounting for a depreciable asset: First, pick a depreciation

future cash flows, not future voluntary funding patterns, determine whether or not a liability exists and its amount. A plan change creates an obligation that has a fixed (though perhaps uncertain) series of future cash flows. One need not know how the future cash flows are to be funded to decide

Whether or not the adoption of a plan change creates an obligation,
Whether or not that obligation deserves to be called an accounting liability, and
The procedure for computing its amount.

That actuaries view the matter as primarily one of funding and believe that the funding pattern determines the amount of actuarial accrued liability seems clear in the following statement by actuaries from an article included in the 1981 FASB Discussion Memorandum: "Regardless of the allocation between [the present value of future normal costs] and [unfunded actuarial liability], the sum of these two . . . is the same. The [unfunded actuarial liability] is simply a by-product of the particular *budgeting* method." (See Gewirtz and Phillips [1978, p. 159], emphasis added.) The FASB [1982], in its *Preliminary Views*, has tentatively rejected the notion that funding patterns determined by actuaries are sufficient to determine accounting expenses.

ACTUARIAL ASSUMPTIONS

In making actuarial determinations, actuaries must assign values to a number of significant uncertainties concerning future events. Although the ultimate cost of a pension plan is not affected by the actuarial assumptions selected, the effect on the cost for specific years can be material. The following brief review may help in understanding the uncertainties.

---

method and a periodic depreciation amount for an asset based on cost and expected service patterns. Then compute and sum the amount of depreciation charges resulting from these choices. If the sum of the depreciation charges is less than the cost of the asset, call the residual *salvage value* and devise a separate accounting procedure for it. If the sum of the depreciation charges equals the cost of the asset, there is no salvage value.

Another apt analogy may be this. Consider a company that borrows $100 million under a long-term zero-coupon bond (or single-payment note), promising to pay $310 million 10 years hence, implying an effective interest rate of about 12 percent per year. The treasurer of the firm works out a scheme for funding the $310 million maturity payment by setting aside in a *voluntary* sinking fund $49 million per year for the last 5 years of the 10-year loan. Five payments of $49 million each will be sufficient to accumulate a fund of $310 million if interest is earned at the rate of 12 percent per year. There would be no supplemental amount to be funded at maturity. If, to take a different pattern for voluntary sinking fund payments, the treasurer were to put aside only $40 million each year for the last 5 years, there would be a shortage of about $55 million. Separate funding consideration will have to be given to raising this $55 million. Most accountants would not let the choice of one of these two methods of accumulating a fund influence the amount of expense recognized in each year nor the amount recorded for the liability at the inception of the loan or any other time.

Interest (Return on Funds Invested). The interest assumption used in an actuarial valuation is an expression of the average rate of earnings expected on the funds invested or to be invested to provide for the future benefits. Investments may include equity securities as well as debt securities, together with investments in real estate or other assets. Accordingly, earnings include dividends and rentals on real estate as well as interest. Realized and (under certain circumstances) unrealized gains or losses on fund investments are also considered by actuaries to be an element of investment return.

Expenses of Administration. In some instances, the expenses of administering a pension plan, for example, fees of attorneys, actuaries, and trustees, and the cost of keeping pension records, are borne directly by the employer. In other cases, such expenses, or some of them, are paid by a trust or insurance company from funds contributed by the employer. In the latter cases, expenses to be incurred in the future must be considered in estimating the employer's pension cost.

Benefits. Several assumptions must be made as to the types and extent of the future benefits whose present value is used in expressing the cost of a pension plan. The principal such assumptions are discussed briefly in the following paragraphs.

Future compensation levels. Benefits under some pension plans depend in part on future compensation levels. For example, the annual retirement benefit may be a stated percentage, for each year of service, of the employee's average compensation for the final 3 or 5 years of employment. Under plans of this type, provision can be made for normal increases arising from the progression of employees through the various earnings categories, based on the employer's experience. Provision is not specifically made, however, for general earnings-level increases, such as those that may result from inflation.

Cost of living. In order to protect the purchasing power of retirement benefits, some plans provide that the benefits otherwise determined will be adjusted from time to time to reflect variations in a specific index, such as the Consumer Price Index of the U.S. Bureau of Labor Statistics. In estimating the cost of such a plan, actuaries make provision for expected changes in the cost-of-living index.

Mortality. The length of time an employee (and a survivor under a joint and survivor annuity option) covered by a pension plan will live is a determining factor in the amount and timing of the benefit payments to be provided. If an employee dies before becoming eligible for pension benefits, no payments are made (although in some plans lump-sum or periodic benefits are paid to beneficiaries). The total amount of pension benefits for employees who reach retirement is determined in large part by how long they (and their survivors) live thereafter. Actuaries rely on mortality tables in estimating future pension payments. A high degree of judgment must be exercised in selecting and using mortality tables, because they are developed from a universe that may not have the same characteristics as the group to which the table is to be applied.

Retirement age. Most plans provide a normal retirement age, but many plans permit employees to work thereafter under certain conditions. Some plans provide for retirement in advance of the normal age in case of disability, and most plans permit early retirement at the employee's option under certain conditions. When there are such provisions, actuaries must estimate their effects on the amount and timing of the benefits that will ultimately be paid.

Turnover (withdrawal). In many plans, an employee who leaves the employer for any reason other than retirement and before completing vesting requirements (see following paragraph) forfeits the right to receive benefits. In estimating the amount of future benefits, actuaries may make allowance for the effect of turnover (withdrawal).

Vesting. An employee's right to receive a pension "vests" when it is no longer contingent on the employee's remaining in the service of the employer. A pension plan covered by ERISA must provide vesting in accordance with standards set forth in the act. Vesting is taken into consideration in estimating the effects of turnover.

Social Security Benefits. For plans that provide that pensions otherwise payable are to be reduced by all or part of social security benefits, it is necessary to estimate future social security benefits. Ordinarily, this estimate is calculated as if the level in effect at the time the valuation is being made would continue.

EFFECT OF INFLATION ON PENSION COSTS

Increases in general prices have two distinct effects on defined-benefit pension plans and the expenses related thereto. First inflation affects the amounts to be paid. Most directly, some plans index benefits to various measures of the cost of living. Indirectly, some plans compute the benefit from a formula involving future wages. The larger the rate of increase in prices, the larger will be the likely future wages, the pension payments based thereon, and the pension expense or liability related to those future payments.

Second, the anticipated rate of inflation affects interest rates, including those used in discounting future pension payments in computing actuarial valuations. The higher the anticipated rate of inflation, the higher the discount rate, the lower the present value of a given future payment, and the smaller is the pension expense or liability related to those future payments.

Although these two effects work in opposing directions, they do not offset each other completely. Skinner [1980, pp. 71-72] points out that

> the interest (discount factor) operates over the whole period between the time the benefits are earned and their payment dates. In a [plan based on future wages] in contrast the escalation of benefits occurs only from the time the benefits are earned to the years before retirement when the final earnings average is being determined. Plan benefits would have to be fully indexed over plan members' lifetimes, both before and after retirement, for the impact of inflation on pension expense to cancel out. . . . Inflation if expected tends to reduce pension expense unless a plan's benefits are fully indexed, because the interest (discount) factor is more powerful than the benefit escalation factor.

Inflation Combined with the Accumulated-Benefit Actuarial Cost Method.
When an actuarial cost method without salary projection is used to compute
pension costs, the effects of future inflation on final wage payments and pension benefits are ignored until the increases in actual wages occur. The anticipated future inflation is, however, reflected in current interest rates. The higher
the anticipated inflation, the lower is current pension expense. Some accountants advocate using a real rate of interest (i.e., an interest rate reduced for the
amount of expected inflation) in computing actuarial valuations when an
accrued benefit method is used. These accountants argue that to use a benefit
method without salary projection, ignoring inflation in future wages, produces
benefit numbers whose present values are unrealistically low because they are
discounted using a nominal interest rate that includes the effects of anticipated
inflation. Skinner [1980, chap. 10] discusses these issues and estimates the size
of the distortions caused by incorporating inflation into the discount rate while
ignoring it in the actuarial cost method.

Effect of ERISA Funding Standards on Accounting.   Some of the accounting
principles in APB Opinion No. 8 pertaining to the minimum and maximum
amounts of pension expenses required or allowed were, in effect, made obsolete by the funding standards of ERISA. Because many companies conform
their pension expenses to amounts of pension funding, the funding requirements of ERISA became binding in the late 1970s. ERISA imposes upper and
lower limits on pension plan contributions. The primary administrative vehicle
for monitoring the minimum funding requirements of ERISA is the "funding
standard account." In addition, there are a "full funding limitation" and an
"alternative minimum funding standard account." Exhibit 4 illustrates, in simplified form, the operation of these funding accounts.

ACTUARIAL GAINS AND LOSSES

As discussed earlier, actuaries must deal with several uncertainties in estimating the cost of a pension plan. These uncertainties relate to interest (return on
funds invested), to expenses of administration, and to the amounts and timing
of benefits to be paid. Actuaries use actuarial assumptions in tentatively resolving these uncertainties.

Accounting principles do not specify the selection of actuarial assumptions.
Rather, they accept the actuarial cost methods described *when the actuarial
assumptions are reasonable*. This allows for the exercise of judgment in the
selection of assumptions. The important consideration is the effect of the
assumptions taken together, rather than the effect of any single assumption.
Unless the assumptions, taken together, appear to be unreasonable, accounting
requirements are probably being met. As an extreme example, if the sole consideration in selecting a set of assumptions had been an intention to develop
the least possible provision for pension cost, the assumptions probably would
be considered unreasonable. ERISA similarly requires that the actuarial
assumptions be "reasonable" in the aggregate and take into account "the experience of the plan and reasonable expectations."

Regardless of the actuary's degree of skill, it is unlikely that actual events will coincide with each of the corresponding assumptions used. As a result, the actuarial assumptions may be changed from time to time as experience and judgment dictate. In addition, whether or not the assumptions as to events in the future are changed, it may be necessary to recognize in the calculations the effects of differences between actual prior experience and the assumptions used in the past. The effects on actuarially calculated pension cost of (1) changes in actuarial assumptions and (2) deviations between actual experience and the actuarial assumptions used are called "actuarial gains and losses." If the new assumptions are more optimistic or if experience has been favorable, the adjustments that result are actuarial gains; if the new assumptions are less optimistic or if experience has been unfavorable, the adjustments are actuarial losses. The net effect of the gains and losses computed in a particular valuation is ordinarily dealt with as a single amount.

INSURED PLANS

Insured plans are pension plans under which a life insurance company provides the funding instrument.

One class of insured plan uses contracts in which premiums and benefits are computed for each covered employee. Under one such arrangement, the insurance company issues an *individual policy or policies* for each employee, usually to a trustee. Another form of arrangement in this class is a *group annuity contract* issued to the employer. (Both individual and group contracts may provide death benefits in addition to retirement benefits.) Each of these types of arrangement specifies the premiums to be paid by the employer and the benefits to be paid to participants.

In the other class of insured arrangement, amounts contributed by the employer are not identified with specific employees until they retire. One such arrangement is called a *deposit administration contract* (or, more explicitly, a *deposit administration group annuity contract*). The insurance company keeps a separate account of the funds contributed by the employer and adds interest at an agreed rate, which is subject to change at intervals (typically 5 years). When an employee retires, the insurance company issues an annuity that will provide the benefits stipulated in the pension plan and transfers the single premium for the annuity from the employer's accumulated contributions. The premium rates for annuities are stated in the deposit administration contract. These rates, like the interest rates, are subject to change at intervals (again, typically 5 years). The insurance company usually makes charges for its expenses only through the annuity premiums. Periodic dividends based on experienced expenses, mortality, and investment earnings are credited to the employer.

A similar type of funding instrument is the *immediate participation guarantee contract*, which differs from a deposit administration contract principally in the treatment of expenses, mortality, and investment earnings. Expenses are charged directly to the employer's account, rather than through annuity premiums as they are under a deposit administration contract; mortality among

EXHIBIT 4   Funding Example under ERISA*

This exhibit illustrates the alternatives available under the Funding Standard account and the Alternative Minimum Funding Standard account. Though not intended to show all the complexities of the funding requirements, the chart traces a single plan through 3 consecutive plan years, including a change from the alternative funding standard to the basic funding standard. Although the Alternative Minimum Funding Standard account has not been widely used under ERISA, this example demonstrates its application to provide a more complete understanding of the funding standards available under the statute.

Briefly stated, the operation of the Funding Standard account develops a series of debits, as described on lines (1) through (5), and a series of credits, as described on lines (7) through (9), which are netted to determine the account balance. When a plan is funded at the minimum required level, the excess of credits over debits on line (11) will be zero. A positive balance in line (11) means that more funding has taken place than is essential to meet minimum standards; for a negative balance, the converse is true.

The plan year beginning January 1, 19X0, generates debits of $77,160 to the Funding Standard account, and (under this standard) the employer must contribute at least this amount during the plan year to avoid a funding deficiency. However, the contribution required under the Alternative Minimum Funding Standard account is smaller, and the employer can elect to comply with the funding standards by using the alternative method and making a contribution of only $75,000. The chart is based on the assumption that the employer makes that election and will now be required to maintain both funding standard accounts.

On January 1, 19X1, the plan is amended to provide increased benefits resulting in an increase in the Unfunded Past Service Liability account as shown in item (C). In addition, the actuarial experience during 19X0 results in a loss of $250,000. These events have a significant impact on the employer's decision to use the alternative or the basic funding standard. Under the alternative standard the excess of the present value of accrued benefits over the market value of assets has increased to $312,300 on January 1, 19X1.

Illustration of the Minimum Funding Standard

	January 1, 19X0	January 1, 19X1	January 1, 19X2
Basic data			
(A) Valuation date			
(B) Unfunded past service liability	$422,800	$420,400[b]	$417,840[b]
(C) Increased unfunded due to plan amendment		150,000	148,260[b]
(D) Experience gain or (loss) from prior years		(250,000)	15,000
Funding standard account			
Debits			
1. Normal cost for year	$ 49,100	$ 59,800	$ 65,800
2. Item (B) amortized over 40 years from 1/1/X0	28,060	28,060	28,060
3. Item (C) amortized over 30 years from 1/1/X1		10,790	10,790
4. Loss in item (D) amortized over 15 years from 1/1/X1		24,980	24,980
5. Excess of debit balance in Funding Standard account over debit balance in Alternative Funding Standard account amortized over 5 years		520	520
6. Total debits [(1) + (2) + (3) + (4) + (5)]	$ 77,160	$124,150	$130,150

EXHIBIT 4   Funding Example under ERISA[a] (*Continued*)

Illustration of the Minimum Funding Standard (*Continued*)

Credits

7. Employer contributions	$75,000[c]	$125,000	$130,000
8. Gain in item (D) amortized over 15 years from 1/1/X2.			1,500
9. Excess (with interest) of debit balance in Funding Standard account over debit balance in Alternative Minimum Funding Standard account		2,300	
10. Total credits [(7) + (8) + (9)] . . .	$75,000	$127,300	$131,500
11. Excess (deficiency) of credits over debits [(10) − (6)]	($ 2,160)	$ 3,150	$ 1,350
12. Credit (debit) balance beginning of year [line (13) from prior year with interest]	0	(2,300)[d]	905[d]
13. Credit (debit) balance	($ 2,160)	$ 850	$ 2,255

If the employer returns to the basic Funding Standard account, any funding deficiency on the standard—developed while using the Alternative Funding Standard account—must be amortized within 5 years of returning to the basic standard. The impact of this catch-up contribution is developed in lines (5) and (9) resulting in the necessary adjustments. In 19X1, the illustrative plan has the choice of continuing with the Alternative Funding Standard and paying $365,800 or returning to the basic Funding Standard and making a contribution of $124,150. In the illustration it is assumed that the employer returns to the basic Funding Standard.

The mechanics of calculation are essentially the same for the plan year beginning January 1, 19X2, except that 19X1 experience produces a gain that is to be amortized over the following 15 years. Whichever account—basic or alternative—is used to determine the minimum funding requirement, the amount so determined cannot exceed the full funding limitation as displayed following the Alternative Minimum Funding Standard account.

Illustration of the Alternative Minimum Funding Standard

Valuation date	January 1, 19X0	January 1, 19X1	January 1, 19X2
Debits			
1. Normal cost[e]	$ 43,200	$ 53,500	$ 59,900
Excess of present value of accrued benefits over market value of assets:			
(a) Accrued benefits	750,100	886,900	993,300
(b) Assets	718,300	574,600	668,700
2. Excess	31,800	312,300	324,600
3. Total debits [(1) + (2)]	75,000	365,800	384,500

Full Funding Limitation

Entry age normal accrued liability	$1,141,100	$1,362,400	$1,453,000
Entry age normal cost	49,100	59,800	65,800
Total	1,190,200	1,422,200	1,518,800
Assets[f]	700,000	574,600	668,700
Limitation.	490,200	847,600	850,100

[a]Example developed by Peat, Marwick, Mitchell & Co., and reproduced with their permission.
[b]Unamortized balance.
[c]Based on Alternative Minimum Funding Standard account.
[d]Brought forward from prior year at 6½%.
[e]Lesser of normal cost under cost method used or unit credit normal cost.
[f]Lesser of assets under actuarial valuation method used or market value.

retired employees affects the employer's cost at shorter intervals; annual investment earnings credits are based on the insurance company's experience, rather than on a guaranteed rate.

FUNDING VEHICLES

Unless specified in the plan, it is necessary to choose the type of *funding instrument* (e.g., a life insurance or annuity contract or a trust agreement) and a specific *funding agency* (e.g., a specific life insurance company or a specific trust fund administered by a corporate or individual trustee). In some cases, two or more types of funding instrument (and, perhaps, two or more funding agencies) are used in combination.

When a life insurance company provides the funding instrument, the pension plan is known as an *insured plan*. Insured plans were discussed in the preceding section.

When the funding instrument is a *trust agreement* and the funding agency a *trust fund*, the pension plan is called a *trust fund plan*. Under this type of arrangement, the employer's payments are made to a trustee. The trustee invests the funds in accordance with the terms of the trust agreement and either pays retirement benefits from the accumulated funds or purchases annuities from such funds for employees who retire. The trustee may be a bank or trust company, or an individual or individuals. Depending on the terms of the trust agreement, the trustee may have sole discretion in investing the trust funds or may be subject to the general direction of the employer in making investments. Ordinarily, the trustee accepts the instructions of the employer as to the identity of the beneficiaries who should receive payments under the plan and as to the amounts of the payments.

INCOME TAXES

As a general rule, the federal income tax consequences of a pension plan depend on whether the plan is a *qualified* one, that is, whether it complies with certain requirements of the Internal Revenue Code and of the Internal Revenue Service. One practical effect of these requirements is that, on a cumulative basis, normal cost plus an amount equivalent to interest on any unfunded actuarial accrued liability must be funded.

REQUIRED DISCLOSURES FOR DEFINED-BENEFIT
PLANS BY EMPLOYERS

SFAS No. 36 requires that the employer make the following disclosures with respect to its defined-benefit plans:

1. A statement that a pension plan exists, identifying or describing the employee groups covered
2. A statement of the firm's accounting and funding policies

3. The pension expense for the period

4. The nature and effect of significant matters affecting comparability for all periods presented, such as changes in actuarial cost methods, amortization of supplemental actuarial value, or treatment of actuarial gains and losses

5. The actuarial present value of vested accumulated plan benefits based on the accrued benefit actuarial cost method

6. The actuarial present value of nonvested accumulated plan benefits based on the accrued benefit actuarial cost method

7. The plan's net assets available for benefits

8. The assumed rates of return used in computing actuarial present values of vested and nonvested accumulated benefits

9. The date as of which the benefit information was computed

Proposed Accounting for Net Pension Liabilities and Assets. The FASB [1982, par. 11] has tentatively concluded that the amounts in disclosures 5 and 6, above, should be computed with an actuarial cost method based on salary projections, contrary to SFAS No. 36. Even more far-reaching in its potential effects on the appearance of financial statements, the FASB [1982, par. 8] has tentatively concluded that the net amount of items 5, 6, and 7 should appear on the balance sheet. If the net assets available for benefits are less than the present value of accumulated benefits, then the net amount (called the "net pension liability") is to appear among noncurrent liabilities.[8] The offsetting debit is to an intangible asset account that is to be amortized to expense each year in proportion to the average remaining work life of the active plan participants. If, for example, the average remaining service period is 20 years, then the amortization for the year is 5 percent (= 1/20). If the net assets available exceed the present value of accumulated benefits, then the net amount is to appear among noncurrent assets. The offsetting credit is to a "deferred pension credits" account to appear with deferred income taxes and deferred investment credits among the noncurrent equities. It will be amortized to income in the same way as the intangible asset is amortized, described above.

GENERALLY ACCEPTED ACCOUNTING PRINCIPLES BY THE PLAN FOR DEFINED-BENEFIT PENSIONS

The pension plan receives the cash paid by the employer/sponsor and invests it until it must be paid to pensioners. The plan keeps its own accounting records and makes disclosures according to rules in FASB Statement No. 35. The major provisions of Statement No. 35 are as follows:

1. The pension fund reports its assets, usually investments of various sorts, at fair market value.

---

[8]So long as the employer is ultimately responsible for shortages in the pension fund (and is entitled to the benefits of any actuarial gains), Skinner [1981, pp. 189–191] argues that this presentation is compelled by accounting theory.

2. The liabilities of the pension fund must be computed using the accrued benefit actuarial cost method.

3. Actuarial gains and losses, including unrealized holding gains and losses on pension fund investments, are included in the net income of the plan each year as they arise.

4. The following information about the pension fund must be disclosed each year in the notes to the financial statements of the plan:

(a) A statement that includes information regarding the net assets available for benefits as of the end of the plan year.

(b) A statement showing the principal reasons for changes in net assets available for benefits during the year, including net appreciation or depreciation in fair value of significant classes of investments, investment income, contributions received from the employer and employees, benefits paid to participants, and administrative expenses.

(c) Information regarding the actuarial present value of plan benefits as of either the beginning or end of the plan year. The beginning-of-the-year valuation date is acceptable because of the time often required to calculate the present value of accumulated benefits.

(d) Information regarding the effects of significant factors affecting the year-to-year changes in actuarial present value of accumulated plan benefits, such as changes in actuarial cost methods, treatment of actuarial gains and losses, and the interest rate used in discounting.

BIBLIOGRAPHY

Accounting Principles Board (AICPA), *Accounting for the Cost of Pension Plans*, Opinion No. 8 (APB, 1966).
————, *Omnibus Opinion—1967*, Opinion No. 12 (APB, 1967).
Cassel, J. M., and D. W. Kahn, "FASB Statement No. 35: Not Enough about the Future?" *Financial Executive*, December 1980, pp. 44–51.
Commerce Clearing House, *Pension Reform Act of 1974—Law and Explanation* (Commerce Clearing House, New York, 1974).
Davidson, S., C. P. Stickney, and R. L. Weil, *Intermediate Accounting*, 3d ed. (Dryden Press, Hinsdale, Ill., 1982).
Financial Accounting Standards Board, *Disclosure of Pension Information*, Statement of Financial Accounting Standards No. 36 (FASB, 1980).
————, *An Analysis of Issues Related to Employers' Accounting for Pensions and Other Postemployment Benefits*, Discussion Memorandum (FASB, 1981a).
————, *Exposure Draft, Accounting for the Cost of Pension Plans and Other Postemployment Benefits by the Employer* (FASB, 1981b).
————, *Preliminary Views on Major Issues Related to Employers' Accounting for Pensions and Other Postemployment Benefits* (FASB, 1982).
Gewirtz, P. A., and R. C. Phillips, "Unfunded Pension Liabilities . . . The New Myth," *Financial Executive*, August 1978, pp. 18–24, reprinted in FASB [1981a], pp. 155–162.
Joint Committee on Pension Terminology, Final Report, July 1, 1981, mimeographed, distributed by the Committee Chairman, Michael J. Tierney, Tillinghast, Nelson & Warren, Inc., 815 S. Main Street, Jacksonville, Fla. 32207.
Kirk, D. J., "Pension Accounting: A Major Theme of the 1980's," address at the University of California, Berkeley, printed and distributed by the Financial Accounting Standards Board, Stamford, Conn., May 14, 1981; reprinted in the *Journal of Accountancy*, vol. 152, no. 4 (October 1981), pp. 92–100.

McGill, D. M., *Fundamentals of Private Pensions* (Richard D. Irwin, Homewood, Ill., 3d ed. 1975, 4th ed. 1979); references are to page numbers in the FASB Discussion Memorandum [1981a].

Schipper, K., and R. L. Weil, "Alternative Accounting Treatments for Pensions," *The Accounting Review*, vol. 57, no. 4 (October 1982), pp. 806–824.

Skinner, R. M. *Pension Accounting: The Problem of Equating Payments Tomorrow with Expenses Today* (Clarkson Gordon, Toronto, 1980).

———, "Research and Standard Setting in Financial Accounting—An Illustrative Case," in S. Basu and J. A. Milburn (eds.), *Research to Support Standard Setting in Financial Accounting: A Canadian Perspective* (Clarkson Gordon Foundation, Toronto, 1981).

Treynor, J. C., P. J. Regan, and W. W. Priest, Jr., *The Financial Reality of Funding Under ERISA* (Dow Jones-Irwin, Homewood, Ill., 1976).

CHAPTER 26

Off-Balance-Sheet
Financing;
Commitments and
Contingencies

David L. Landsittel
Partner, Arthur Andersen & Co.

John E. Stewart
Partner, Arthur Andersen & Co.

The Financial Accounting Standards Board (FASB) has issued several *Statements of Financial Concepts*. There continues, nevertheless, to be no sharp definition for when an obligation of an enterprise becomes a liability requiring accounting recognition. When does an executory contract commitment become an obligation to be recorded as a liability in the balance sheet? When does a contingency become a recordable obligation? When is it appropriate to look through the form of an arrangement and record the substantive obligations it may have created irrespective of whether or not a legal claim has been established?

Until professional standards are sharpened, there will inevitably be transactions and events that create obligations of an enterprise for which the decision of whether or not they represent accounting liabilities is difficult. These are characterized in this chapter as "soft" liabilities.

"Soft" liabilities have emerged in today's environment primarily in connection with financing arrangements—specifically in connection with innovative "off-balance-sheet financing." Accordingly, financing vehicles of this nature are the focal point of the discussion in this chapter. The latter pages of the chapter discuss some accounting considerations relating to other commitments and contingencies.

OFF-BALANCE-SHEET FINANCING

Introduction. For a long time, companies raised new funds by issuing stocks or bonds or by borrowing money from their bankers. More and more frequently, however, corporations are adopting complex and ingenious financing structures under which the resulting obligations do not have to be recorded on the balance sheet. The goal appears to be to arrange long-term financing that has the least impact on the financial statements. *Forbes* summed up the trend as follows: "The basic drives of man are few: to get enough food, to find shelter and to keep debt off the balance sheet" [Greene, Nov. 24, 1980].

This section of the chapter discusses several, but not all, off-balance-sheet financing techniques that are being used today—that is, techniques being used by companies to finance the acquisition of assets without presenting the assets and related obligations in the financial statements. This chapter only briefly mentions leases, which are treated in Chapter 24.

Off-Balance-Sheet Financing Vehicles. Discussed below are several of the more common, as well as more recently developed, off-balance-sheet financing techniques. These techniques can be combined in various ways.

Finance subsidiaries. The accounting literature guiding the preparation of consolidated financial statements (see Chapter 34) helps keep assets and debt off the balance sheet by permitting the nonconsolidation of finance subsidiaries. Accounting Research Bulletin No. 51, *Consolidated Financial Statements* [CAP, 1959] provides guidance on which subsidiaries may not be consolidated on the basis that "presentation of financial information concerning the particular activities of such subsidiaries would be more informative to shareholders and creditors of the parent company than would the inclusion of such subsidiaries in the consolidation." It further states, "for example, separate statements may be required for a subsidiary which is a bank or an insurance company and may be preferable for a finance company where the parent and the other subsidiaries are engaged in manufacturing operations."

The implementation of this language in practice permits nonconsolidation of finance subsidiaries. As a result, companies have increasingly established so-called captive finance companies—that is, subsidiaries set up to own and finance receivables arising from the normal selling activities of the parent company. In many cases, roughly equal amounts of receivables and debt are transferred to the unconsolidated subsidiary and are thereby eliminated from the consolidated balance sheet.

In practice, nonconsolidation is accepted even when the parent company directly or indirectly guarantees the debt of the subsidiary. A common form of indirect guarantee is a fixed-charge-coverage maintenance agreement. Under such an agreement, the parent company agrees to contribute money to the subsidiary if the subsidiary's ratio of income to fixed charges (interest, etc.) falls below a specified figure.

As a result of these accounting practices, the balance sheet of a company with an unconsolidated captive finance subsidiary looks significantly different from a similar company that finances its trade receivables without such a subsidiary, even though the total operations of the two enterprises are economically identical. Some would argue that form has overpowered substance in this case.

Another related technique is the establishment of an operating subsidiary as a subsidiary of the unconsolidated finance subsidiary rather than as a direct subsidiary or division of the operating parent company. The hope is that the gross assets and liabilities (including debt) of the third-tier operating company can be excluded (via nonconsolidation) from the parent's financial statements.

The Accounting Standards Executive Committee (AcSEC) prepared an Issues Paper in 1978 entitled *Reporting Finance Subsidiaries in Consolidated Financial Statements* and forwarded it to the FASB for its consideration. In its advisory conclusions to the FASB, AcSEC indicated that it did not favor a requirement to compel consolidation of all finance subsidiaries, but did favor that criteria be specified for determination of those finance subsidiaries that should be consolidated. No definitive criteria were provided by AcSEC in its advisory conclusions.

In 1982, the FASB added to its agenda a major project on consolidations and the equity method. The project is to develop the concept of an accounting or reporting entity and to apply the concepts to problems that have been identified in practice. The scope of the project encompasses all major aspects of accounting for affiliations between entities and covers Accounting Research Bulletin No. 51, APB Opinion No. 18, *The Equity Method of Accounting for Investments in Common Stock* [1971], as well as other pronouncements and AcSEC issues papers (including that related to unconsolidated finance subsidiaries) that bear on the subject. The FASB's announced timetable does not provide for a final statement before 1985.

While not singling out the unconsolidated finance subsidiary, the FASB has called for improved disclosure of indirect guarantees of indebtedness. In FASB Interpretation No. 34, *Disclosure of Indirect Guarantees of Indebtedness of Oth-*

ers [1981], the Board indicated that the disclosures mandated in FASB Statement No. 5, *Accounting for Contingencies* [1975], applied to fixed-charge and working-capital maintenance agreements. This interpretation will probably have little impact in practice, because such arrangements are already generally disclosed.

Sales of receivables with recourse. Some view sales of receivables with recourse as the same as a secured borrowing—that is, a loan secured by the pledge of accounts receivables. Under this view, the proceeds received are reported as a liability and the receivables remain on the balance sheet. Because the "lender" has recourse to the "seller" of the receivables in case of noncollection, this view has merit to some. Others regard such transactions as sales of receivables, with the proceeds reducing existing borrowings. Following this view, the effect on a consolidated balance sheet is similar to the creation of an unconsolidated finance subsidiary: Receivables *and* liabilities are eliminated from the balance sheet.

Recourse may take the form of a guarantee, a "dealer reserve" (a holdback of a portion of the sales price by the buyer to cover uncollectible accounts), or an obligation to repurchase accounts. It also may take other forms that constitute recourse in substance, such as guarantees by the seller of a "yield" to the buyer on the receivables sold.

The accounting issues become more complex when the "seller" retains the risk for only a portion of the receivables that are "sold"—for example, when the "seller" retains a *limited* amount of recourse (say, 10 percent of the receivable balances), or when the "seller" has transferred credit risk but has retained interest-rate risk.

In 1974, the AICPA issued Statement of Position (SOP) 74-6, *Recognition of Profit on Sales of Receivables with Recourse,* which addresses the income statement issues for such transactions, but reaches no conclusion on the balance sheet treatment. SOP 74-6 acknowledges that these transactions are financings, and holds that even when the sale is reflected as a reduction of the receivable balances, the "differential" (gain or loss arising from the sale) should be deferred and amortized by its two elements—interest income and interest expense—as if the sale had been accounted for as a financing. However, when it is not practicable to divide the differential into the two elements, it is acceptable to amortize the net differential through the effective interest method (or another method if the results are not significantly different) based on the anticipated collections of the receivables. In either case, the seller achieves both off-balance-sheet financing and no immediate loss recognition.

In 1980, AcSEC prepared an Issues Paper entitled *Accounting for Transfers of Receivables with Recourse,* which addressed the balance sheet question for "sales" (transfers) of receivables with recourse. In the paper, which was forwarded to the FASB, AcSEC concluded that (1) transfers of receivables with full recourse should be accounted for as borrowings and (2) certain other recourse arrangements have characteristics for which accounting as a borrowing may also be appropriate, depending on the probability that the debtor will default and thereby cause the risk to remain with the transferor/"seller."

In 1981, the FASB added the project to its agenda. In late 1981, the FASB issued an exposure draft on the subject and, in response to extensive comments received thereon, developed a revised exposure draft in 1982.

The FASB's revised exposure draft specifies that a transferor of receivables with recourse ordinarily would report such a transaction as a sale if (1) the transferor surrenders its control of the future economic benefits relating to the receivables (e.g., the transferor does not have an option to repurchase the receivables at a later date) and (2) the transferee cannot return the receivables to the transferor except pursuant to the recourse provisions. If those conditions do not exist or if the transferor cannot reasonably estimate its obligation under the recourse provisions, the amount of proceeds from the transfer would be reported as a liability. Sales accounting would not be precluded, however, by provisions in the transfer agreement that adjust the sales price based on changes in prevailing interest rates after the date of sale.

Under the exposure draft, when the transfer qualifies as a sale for balance sheet purposes (contemplated to be the usual case), the gain or loss on the transfer, including any provision for bad debt losses, would be handled consistently—that is, recognized at the time of the sale. Subsequent adjustments to the transfer price because of a floating interest rate provision would be considered changes in estimates of the sales price and reported in income in the period of the changes.

Interestingly, the FASB's proposed solution to the issue appears to focus more on the notion of *control* of the asset (a part of the definition of an asset under the FASB's Conceptual Framework) and less on the *risks* of ownership of the asset (bad debts, interest rate, etc.) as recommended by AcSEC. The FASB is likely to finalize its statement in 1983 and, of course, its tentative conclusions are subject to change. If the FASB proceeds along its present path, the conclusions of SOP 74-6 will be superseded, but this form of off-balance-sheet financing would appear to be continued.

The discussion of this off-balance-sheet financing technique will conclude with an interesting footnote. In recent years, a few large *unconsolidated* finance subsidiaries have desired to raise new funds but perhaps have had concerns about the public perception of their *own* debt levels. They have entered into agreements to sell significant amounts of receivables with, at least, limited recourse, and removed those receivables from their balance sheets.

Product financing arrangements. Product financing arrangements are agreements in which a company (the sponsor):

1. Sells inventory (product) to another entity and, in a related transaction, agrees to repurchase the product (or a substantially identical product); or

2. Arranges for another entity to purchase the product on the sponsor's behalf and, in a related transaction, agrees to purchase the product from the other entity.

In each of these cases, the sponsor (1) agrees to purchase the product, or processed goods of which the product is a component, from the other entity at specified prices over specified periods, or (2) guarantees resale prices to third parties in lieu of a more direct purchase commitment.

Other characteristics that commonly exist in product financing arrangements but that are not necessarily present in all arrangements are the following:

1. The entity that purchases the product from the sponsor or purchases it directly from a third party on behalf of the sponsor is established expressly for that purpose or is an existing trust, nonbusiness organization, or credit grantor.

2. The product covered by the financing arrangement is to be used or sold by the sponsor, although a portion may be sold by the other entity directly to third parties.

3. The product covered by the financing arrangement is stored on the sponsor's premises.

4. The debt of the entity that purchases the product being financed is guaranteed by the sponsor.

Prior to late 1978, when the AICPA issued SOP 78-8, *Accounting for Product Financing Arrangements*, transactions described above were often accounted for off-balance-sheet. The sale of the product was recognized (with profit recorded currently or deferred), but with no recognition in the accounts of the agreement to repurchase. The effect was similar to a borrowing with the pledge of inventory, except that neither the borrowing nor the inventory was reported in the balance sheet of the borrower.

SOP 78-8 indicated that sales of product with an agreement to repurchase and similar transactions should be recognized as borrowings rather than as sales when certain specified characteristics were present.

Soon after issuance of SOP 78-8, the staff of the SEC indicated that it also believed arrangements dealt with in the SOP should be included on-balance-sheet. Additionally, in 1981, the FASB issued FASB Statement No. 49, *Accounting for Product Financing Arrangements*, which upheld the conclusions in the SOP and made them mandatory for private as well as publicly held companies.

FASB Statement No. 49 applies to product financing arrangements for products that have been produced by or were originally purchased by a company (the sponsor) or purchased by another entity on behalf of the sponsor and have *both* of the following characteristics:

1. The financing arrangement requires the sponsor to purchase the product, a substantially identical product, or processed goods of which the product is a component, at specified prices. The specified prices are not subject to change except for fluctuations due to finance and holding costs. This characteristic of predetermined prices also is present if any of the following circumstances exists:

   (a) The specified prices in the financing arrangement are in the form of resale price guarantees under which the sponsor agrees to make up any difference between the specified prices and the resale prices for products sold to third parties.

   (b) The sponsor is not required to purchase the product but has an option to purchase the product, the economic effect of which compels the sponsor to purchase the product—for example, an option arrangement that provides for a significant penalty if the sponsor does not exercise the option to purchase.

(c) The sponsor is not required by the agreement to purchase the product, but the other entity has an option whereby it can require the sponsor to purchase the product.

2. The payments that the other entity will receive on the transaction are established by the financing arrangement, and the amounts to be paid by the sponsor will be adjusted, as necessary, to cover substantially all fluctuations in costs incurred by the other entity in purchasing and holding the product (including interest).

The Statement provides that transactions having these characteristics are to be accounted for as borrowings by the sponsor with the inventory reflected on the balance sheet.

Now that specific accounting rules have been set forth, the creative financiers of the world can begin devising financing structures to "get around" the rules. For example, one arrangement that is being explored involves two or more companies (sponsors) forming a corporation or partnership in which each sponsor owns 50 percent or less of the corporation or partnership (the entity). As a result, the entity need not be consolidated by any of the sponsors. Each of the sponsors contributes more than a nominal amount of equity to the entity. The entity purchases inventory and finances it by borrowing money on a basis nonrecourse to the sponsors. Each of the sponsors has the option (not the stated obligation) to purchase inventory from the entity at the entity's FIFO (first-in, first-out) costs plus interest and carrying costs. It is argued that Statement No. 49 does not require the sponsors to reflect the inventory and related debt on their respective financial statements because the sponsors are not *obligated* to purchase (repurchase) the inventory.

Leases. Chapter 24 discusses lease accounting, including the provisions of FASB Statement No. 13, *Accounting for Leases* [1976]. As a result, a common form of off-balance-sheet financing using lease arrangements is dealt with only briefly here.

The objective of FASB Statement No. 13 as described in its Appendix ("Basis for Conclusions") is that "a lease that transfers substantially all of the benefits and risks incident to the ownership of property should be accounted for as the acquisition of an asset and the incurrence of an obligation by the lessee and as a sale or financing by the lessor." In addition, the FASB believed that the Statement "removes most if not all of the conceptual differences in lease classification as between lessors and lessees and that it provides criteria for such classification that are more explicit and less susceptible to varied interpretation than those in previous literature." Thus, one of the major objectives of FASB Statement No. 13 was to provide symmetry in place of the previously existing inconsistencies in accounting by lessors (under APB Opinions No. 7 and 27) and lessees (under APB Opinion No. 5).

To implement these concepts, the FASB developed specific (and, to a great extent, arbitrary) criteria against which lessees and lessors are to test their lease arrangements for purposes of deciding whether or not the lease is a financing arrangement (i.e., a capital lease). In short, the Board took an approach between capitalizing substantially all leases and capitalizing only those when title passes. Implementation required arbitrary rules.

Almost as soon as Statement No. 13 was issued, lessees and lessors began to structure lease arrangements that achieved their diverse accounting objectives (off-balance financing to the lessee and a sale or financing to the lessor). This was possible even though the intent of the FASB was to provide symmetry, because of the arbitrary nature of the FASB's lease classification rules. As the "loopholes" were found, the FASB attempted to deal with them by issuing a stream of interpretations of and amendments to the Statement.

The objectives of FASB Statement No. 13 set forth above have not been fully achieved. In fact, a significant number of long-term leases that pass substantially all the risks and rewards of ownership of property to the lessee continue to be accounted for as operating leases by lessees, resulting in a continuation of this form of off-balance-sheet financing. In addition, although the drafters of new leases may have had to sharpen their pencils a bit (and sometimes give up something of value in the process), it is common to find agreements negotiated that provide a finance lease for the lessor and an operating lease for the lessee. And clearly, given the numerous amendments and interpretations of the Statement, it has not been "more explicit and less susceptible to varied interpretations."

In summary, leasing continues to be a popular off-balance-sheet financing technique. Even though the FASB has publicly indicated its unhappiness with the numerous implementation problems, it is unlikely that the Statement will be reconsidered until completion of the FASB's Conceptual Framework project. The Board has given us, however, a preview of what may happen if and when it gets back to lease accounting. In a FASB *Action Alert* published by the Board in March 1979, it was reported that a majority of the Board expressed "the tentative view that, if Statement No. 13 were to be reconsidered, they would support a property right approach in which all leases are included as 'rights to use property' and as 'lease obligations' in the lessee's balance sheet." Adoption of such a view would, of course, end the use of lease arrangements as an off-balance-sheet financing vehicle.

Take-or-pay contracts and throughput contracts. A take-or-pay contract is an agreement between a purchaser and a seller that provides for the purchaser to pay specified amounts periodically in return for products or services. Most significantly, the purchaser must make specified minimum payments, whether or not it takes delivery of the contracted products or service. In addition, in some cases the purchaser is obligated to make payments even if the seller's facility is not operating. Such arrangements are sometimes negotiated as part of construction of the related facilities and are used as a basis to secure financing for the construction.

For example, a company enters into a take-or-pay contract with the owner of an ammonia plant under which the company is obligated to purchase, say, 50 percent of the planned capacity of the plant each period while the debt used to finance the plant remains outstanding. The monthly payment is designed to equal the sum of 50 percent of raw materials costs, operating expenses, depreciation, interest on the debt used to finance the plant, and a return on the owner's equity investment.

A throughput contract is similar to a take-or-pay contract except that it relates to transportation or processing. Specifically, a throughput contract is an agreement between a shipper (processor) and the owner of a transportation facility (such as an oil or natural gas pipeline or a ship) or a manufacturing facility that provides for the shipper (processor) to pay specified amounts periodically in return for the transportation (processing) of a product. The shipper (processor) is obligated to provide specified minimum quantities to be transported (processed) in each period and is required to make cash payments even if it does not provide the contracted quantities.

The majority of such arrangements are accounted for off-balance-sheet—that is, the purchaser discloses the commitment only in the notes to its financial statements. Some argue that the arrangements are more extensive than the traditional inventory purchase commitment and should, therefore, be reflected as assets and liabilities in the purchaser's balance sheet. In the example above, it is argued that the purchaser has, in effect, assumed substantially all of the risks and rewards of ownership of 50 percent of the plant. Others, however, consider take-or-pay and throughput contracts to result in commitments or contingent liabilities that should not be recognized on balance sheets.

In 1979, AcSEC prepared an Issues Paper, *Accounting for Project Financing Arrangements*, and requested the FASB to consider the subject, including take-or-pay contracts, throughput contracts, and other unconditional purchase obligations typically associated with project financing arrangements.

The FASB responded in 1981 by issuing Statement No. 47, *Disclosure of Long-Term Obligations*. As its title implies, the Statement was an interim measure, requiring additional disclosures only. It does *not* require that any such arrangements be reflected as assets and liabilities. The Board took this interim step pending further work on its Conceptual Framework.

Specifically, FASB Statement No. 47 requires that a company disclose its commitments under unconditional purchase obligations that are associated with suppliers' financing arrangements. For long-term unconditional purchase obligations that are not recognized on the purchasers' balance sheet (the most common situation), the disclosures required include the nature of the obligation, the amount of the fixed and determinable obligation in the aggregate and for each of the next 5 years, a description of any portion of the obligation that is variable, and the purchases in each year for which an income statement is presented.

Joint ventures. In recent years, a number of financing arrangements have been devised for large construction and operating projects. Common among these arrangements is the joint venture.

For example, a joint venture is formed by two or more entities, with no one entity owning more than 50 percent of the venture. It is thinly capitalized and highly leveraged, frequently with the debt guaranteed by the venturers. One venturer may have purchase options for the ownership interests of the other venturer(s). Under current accounting practice, as specified by APB Opinion No. 18, *The Equity Method of Accounting for Investments in Common Stock* [1971], investments in such ventures are accounted for following the "one-line" equity method—that is, the investor's share of the *net* assets of the entity is reflected in one amount, with the result that no portion of the debt of the joint venture is reported in the balance sheet of any venturer. Consolidation of the joint venture is not required, because no venturer owns more than 50 percent.

Thus, the debt is off the balance sheet. (See Chapter 14 for additional discussion of the equity method.)

Some believe that a proportionate consolidation approach, rather than the equity method, better reflects the activities and significance of the joint venture in the financial statements of the venturer. Under such an approach, each venturer records its proportionate share of *each* of the venture's assets, liabilities, revenue, and expense. Others have suggested an "expanded equity method," under which the venturer's share of total current assets, current liabilities, noncurrent assets, and noncurrent liabilities are each presented on a one-line basis, with separate disclosure, in the appropriate sections of the venturer's balance sheet. This approach avoids a weakness of proportionate consolidation under which, say, 50 percent of cash of the venture is added (without separate identification) to the cash of the venturer.

The AICPA has developed two documents in this area. First, it has issued SOP 78-9, *Accounting for Investments in Real Estate Joint Ventures* (1978), which deals with real estate joint ventures and specifies that the equity method be used.

Second, in 1979, AcSEC forwarded to the FASB an Issues Paper, *Joint Venture Accounting*, dealing with joint ventures in the broad sense (i.e., not limited to real estate). The paper indicates that a variety of methods are used in practice, ranging from proportionate consolidation to the one-line equity method. The paper also notes that some companies have used proportionate consolidation in the income statement and the one-line equity method for the same venture in the balance sheet. Consistent with APB Opinion No. 18, the paper recommends the one-line method (except for undivided interests) and that there be symmetry in presentation between the balance sheet and the income statement.

The equity method of accounting for investments was developed to achieve improved recognition of income from the investment and improved reflection of the economic earning capacity of the investor. The FASB's announced project on consolidations and the equity method (mentioned earlier) will need to consider whether the equity method presents a fair view of the investor's balance sheet.

Construction period trusts. The use of a trust or other intermediary to handle the financing of large capital assets during the construction period is another project financing arrangement that is designed to result in the borrowing not being reflected in an entity's balance sheet, at least during construction when the assets are nonearning.

Under this arrangement, which has been commonly used by electric utility companies, the company (sponsor) assigns its interest in property and other contract rights to a construction intermediary, with the latter authorized to obtain funds to finance construction via term loans, bank loans, commercial paper, and other sources. The intermediary's borrowings are generally guaranteed in part by the work in progress, but more significantly, although indirectly, by the obligation of the sponsor to purchase the project upon completion and assume or otherwise settle the borrowings. The sponsor may also be committed to provide any deficiency of funds that the intermediary cannot obtain, and excess funds may be loaned to the sponsor by the intermediary.

This form of off-balance-sheet financing for electric utilities was curbed in

1978. In late 1978, the Securities and Exchange Commission, which appears to be increasingly concerned by the spread of off-balance-sheet financing, issued Staff Accounting Bulletin Release No. 28, which requires electric utility companies to include in their balance sheets the assets and liabilities of construction period trusts.

Limited partnerships and trusts. Increasingly, various transaction forms are arising that have the following characteristics:

1. A sponsoring company sells a portion of its long-term operating assets (e.g., plants, hotels, retail outlets, transportation equipment, natural resources, etc., which may or may not be newly constructed or developed) to a limited partnership or trust (or perhaps even a corporation).

2. The limited partnership interests or trust units are sold to outsiders via a public or private offering. The sponsor may serve as the general partner, with a nominal percentage interest and no equity contribution.

3. The partnership or trust is highly leveraged. The sponsor may guarantee directly or indirectly all or some of the partnership's or trust's debt. An indirect guarantee may be in the form of an operating (noncapital) lease of the property between the sponsor, as lessee, and the partnership or trust, as lessor.

4. The sponsor shares, sometimes in a significant way, in the operating profit and appreciation of the property. This sharing may take the form of a fee charged by the sponsor to the partnership or trust for managing the property. Alternatively, the sponsor may achieve this sharing by retaining the excess of operating profits over operating lease rental payments made by the sponsor to the partnership or trust. Further, the sponsor may have repurchase options on the assets or interests in the entity.

As a result of these arrangements, the investment return to the limited partners or trust unit holders may be limited to a financing return in addition to receiving the tax benefits of property ownership.

Even though the sponsor has retained a significant portion of the rewards (and perhaps risks) of ownership of the property, it is argued that such an arrangement constitutes a sale with the related assets and liabilities being off-balance-sheet. Those who hold this view argue that consolidation is not appropriate because the sponsor does not own more than 50 percent of the trust or limited partnership entity (in fact, he may have made no equity investment), and thus does not control it in an accounting sense.

Others argue that the sponsor should consolidate the entity because the sponsor has retained significant rewards (and risks) of ownership. They view the limited partnership interests to be not unlike preferred stock interests with the sponsor, in fact, controlling the entity through its general partnership interest or otherwise. They note that, practically speaking, the sponsor may make the key operating decisions regarding use of the assets.

The accounting literature dealing with consolidation of noncorporate entities is sparse. SOP 78-9 on real estate joint ventures, which does deal with partnerships, is not free of ambiguity. As a result of this, these transactions are dealt with on a case-by-case basis and often are off-balance-sheet. Off-balance financing is achieved while substantial operating control, profits, and participation in asset appreciation are retained.

Existing accounting literature (specifically, FASB Statement No. 5 and Interpretation No. 34) does provide that, if a guarantee of the partnership's or trust's debt is present, the sponsor should disclose that fact. At the present time, however, the official accounting literature may not require much more, although this may possibly change with the completion of the FASB's project on consolidations and the equity method.

Timber financing. Certain timber financing arrangements have similarities to the arrangements described in the preceding section. For example, an entity sells its standing timber at cost to a newly created thin-equity company whose sole purpose is to handle this transaction. The entity also enters into a timber cutting contract with the newly created company, giving the entity the right to harvest certain quantities over a specified period at specified rates. The entity agrees to make certain payments at future dates should the minimum specified timber harvest not be achieved, unless, perhaps, the timber is damaged by fire or infestation. The newly created thin-equity company finances the purchase of the timber through bank financing secured by the timber and the cutting contracts. The entity removes the timber from its balance sheet and accounts for the payments under the cutting contract as they are made. It does disclose the aggregate commitment under the cutting contract in the notes of its financial statements.

There is little accounting literature on this arrangement.

Research and development partnerships. Of recent vintage are new and innovative arrangements for financing of research and development (R&D) costs. Such arrangements not only have off-balance-sheet features but have off-income-statement considerations as well. The arrangements take a variety of forms, including general partnerships, limited partnerships, and corporate joint ventures, and they are being used principally in high-technology industries to finance the R&D of a variety of new products and services—such as information processing systems, medical technology, experimental drugs, electronics devices, automobiles, and aerospace equipment.

Common characteristics of these R&D financing arrangements are as follows:

1. Frequently, the arrangement is a limited partnership formed to finance the research and development of products or technologies of particular interest to a sponsor. In many such arrangements, the sponsor has conducted preliminary development work on the product or owns the rights to it.

2. The sponsor usually contributes its preliminary development work or rights to the product to the limited partnership in exchange for a general partnership interest. General partners could possibly include officers, directors, or shareholders of the sponsor. Limited partners (who may also include officers, directors, or shareholders of the sponsor) usually contribute cash or notes in exchange for their partnership interests. Limited partners' capital contributions usually provide all or substantially all the partnership's funds.

3. The R&D work is usually performed by the sponsor under a contract with the partnership whereby the partnership usually owns the rights to any resulting product. The sponsor's compensation under the contract commonly is either a fixed fee or reimbursement of direct costs plus a fixed percentage of such costs. The sponsor generally agrees to perform specified R&D work on a best-efforts basis, with no guarantee of either technological or commercial success.

4. The arrangement between the sponsor and the partnership usually con-

templates, but may not require, that the sponsor will produce and market the product (if successfully developed), with the partnership receiving royalties based on product sales.

5. The partnership agreement generally provides that all or substantially all losses will be allocated to limited partners to provide them with income tax deductions that may equal or exceed their contributions to the partnership. Partnership royalty income from sales of the product (which may be taxed as capital gains) is allocated to the limited partners.

6. Under some arrangements, the financial return to the limited partners is limited. For example, an agreement may require or permit the sponsor to acquire the limited partners' interests for a specified amount of cash or stock, or may specify a maximum financial return to the limited partners. In some arrangements, the risk of loss to the limited partners may be limited. For example, an agreement may guarantee minimum royalty payments to the partnership, or may obligate the sponsor to purchase the partnership's rights to the product.

The basic accounting issue is how the sponsor should characterize and account for the substance of the financing arrangement. Some view the R&D partnership as an enterprise apart from the sponsor, and they view the general and limited partners as owners of equity interests in that separate enterprise. Accordingly, they view the R&D activities as activities of the partnership. Under that view, the partners are credited or charged with their proportionate shares of partnership earnings or losses as provided for under the partnership agreement. The sponsor would reflect neither the funds raised by the partnership nor the partnership's R&D expenditures in its financial statements (other than perhaps for its general partnership interest).

Others, however, view the R&D activities of the limited partnership as activities of the sponsor, and they view the limited partners' investments as, in substance, loans to, or some form of equity investment in, the sponsor. Under that view, the funds used to finance the R&D activities are reflected in the balance sheet of the sponsor, and the cost of the R&D effort is charged against the sponsor's earnings when incurred.

Some believe the basic accounting issue turns on the obligations and risks assumed by the sponsor (see characteristic 6), whether or not the general partner has an investment in the entity. When the risks associated with success of the R&D activities are in substance with the partnership, the sponsor need not include the partnership's activities in its financial statements. However, when the risks are those of the sponsor, such as when minimum royalty payments or product repurchases are guaranteed by the sponsor irrespective of the success of the R&D activities, the funds raised by the partnership would be reflected in the sponsor's balance sheet and the R&D expenditures of the partnership would be expensed by the sponsor. Similar accounting might be followed in cases when the limited partners are related parties.

In 1981, AcSEC sent a detailed letter to the FASB identifying the key issues in this area. Subsequently, the FASB added the matter to its agenda and, in 1982, issued FASB Statement No. 68, *Research and Development Arrangements*. The provisions of that statement are generally consistent with the views expressed in the previous paragraph.

Why Remove Debt from the Balance Sheet?[1] What motivates companies to use the various techniques described above? Several different motivations—over and above those that are purely economic—seem to exist to encourage entities to remove liabilities from their balance sheets.

By getting debt off the balance sheet, some believe that the apparent character, or quality, of the balance sheet is improved. Ratios that have stood the test of usefulness for generations will therefore appear more favorable to the borrower. Specifically, the debt-equity ratio is decreased, and such decrease is perceived to be viewed positively by many who evaluate balance sheets. More frequently, the motive is to prevent an adverse ratio from evolving. The entity may be near a danger point in its debt-equity relationship based on historical standards. Additional debt may be perceived to so impair the ratio that it would trigger other, more adverse developments. Credit ratings could be altered, and borrowing costs may increase. Future expansion, replacement, or research plans could be called off. These concerns and motivations obviously call into question whether historical relationships for the debt-equity ratio continue to be useful to evaluate financial liquidity under current financing arrangements.

Loan covenants may pose even more significant stumbling blocks to accounting for financing arrangements. Loan covenants often impose specific restrictions on the amount of additional debt a company can incur. Sometimes they specify a debt-equity ratio that must not be exceeded to prevent an existing loan from being placed in default. Loan covenants that were prepared in times of less complicated financing may not preclude the borrower from incurring additional obligations, such as those arising from leases, captive finance subsidiaries, or any of the project financing vehicles commonly found today. As loan covenant drafters have become more sophisticated, however, they have required that certain types of off-balance-sheet obligations (e.g., leases) be considered the equivalent of balance sheet debt for the purposes of determining compliance with particular loan covenants. Consequently, new and more innovative vehicles are being developed.

Other motivations for off-balance-sheet financing are possible. Corporate planning may indicate a level of borrowing over the next several years that will press projected historical debt-equity ratios. Although a current project may not lead to a critical problem in this area, the goal may be to get the financing for the current project off the balance sheet to provide capacity for future borrowing. Thus, some entities that today appear to have no real debt-equity problems may be using off-balance-sheet methods as part of a longer-range financing strategy.

In addition, interest cost reductions are sometimes a motivation. The use of a trust method by rate-regulated entities for financing projects during the construction period was aimed principally at removing the interest costs from the regulated entity's accounts during the construction period. Because interest incurred and capitalized by an entity is viewed by some analysts with suspicion, the motivation may not be entirely spurious. Similarly, some merchandi-

---

[1]Certain portions of this and following sections have been adapted from Dieter and Wyatt [1980].

sers attempt to eliminate non-interest-bearing receivables and their interest-bearing financing from the balance sheet in order to reduce interest costs and to improve a key ratio in the merchandising industry, the ratio of earnings to fixed charges. In other industries, return on total assets is considered important. Thus, removal of an equal amount of assets and debt is viewed favorably.

Compounding these motivations is the desire on the part of some companies to improve their comparability with competitors. If their competitors use off-balance-sheet financing vehicles, the companies desire their own financial statement ratios to be based on similar facts and accounting techniques.

Credit Rating Agencies and Other Users. When one delves into the area of off-balance-sheet financing, one can ask if it is all worth it. Are the judgments of users of financial statements influenced by such techniques?

The authors of this chapter have not conducted any extensive research to answer this question. However, we have heard the views of some in the credit rating business, clearly important and sophisticated users of financial statements. Several of the views of some who participate in that process are summarized below:

1. They continue to examine closely off-balance-sheet liabilities or potential liabilities. They calculate an adjusted capitalization structure for a company that may include such off-balance-sheet liabilities as take-or-pay contracts, throughput contracts, and leases. But each company is viewed on a case-by-case basis.

2. With regard to consolidation, they have no firm rules. In general, they would prefer more information be disclosed so that they can decide whether or not to consolidate. If a company has a joint venture that is vital to its basic operation, such as a raw material supply that most competitors would own outright, they would likely "consolidate" it in their analysis. They might even consolidate the entire debt, not just the company's share. However, if a joint venture is a minor business that is being leveraged conservatively on a stand-alone basis, they may well not deem it necessary to adjust their analysis to reflect the ventures as if they were consolidated. They would probably consolidate most captive finance companies, but there could be exceptions, especially if the subsidiaries had diversified stand-alone operations—that is, if the primary reason for their existence were *not* to finance or facilitate the sale of the parent's products.

3. They add to the guarantor's debt guarantees of the indebtedness of others if the guaranteed party or affiliate is young or weak.

4. They are aware that some companies are structuring leases that fall just short of the standards for capitalization. They believe financial statement disclosures in the lease area are not entirely adequate for their needs, particularly for operating leases.

5. In general, they attempt to adjust for off-balance-sheet liabilities so that companies that use such techniques can be compared with those that do not.

The FASB sponsored a research study [FASB, 1981] conducted principally by A. Rashad Abdel-khalik on the economic consequences of FASB Statement No. 13 on accounting for leases. The results of this study may also have relevance to the question of whether judgments of financial statement users are influenced by off-balance-sheet arrangements. The results showed an apparent conflict between what some bankers and financial analysts said they did and what they actually might have done. To direct survey questions, the majority answered that they did not downgrade their evaluation of companies that capitalize leases. But when researchers showed them financial statements of two identical companies, differing only in their method of accounting for leases, more than 40 percent of the bankers and analysts considered the company that did not capitalize its leases more profitable. Only about 8 percent considered the other more profitable, and about 50 percent considered the two companies equal. More than 25 percent of the analysts and bankers indicated that the company that kept leases off the balance sheet had a better debt-paying ability.

The FASB study also suggests that managers' beliefs about how investors and creditors use financial information as indicators of a company's performance are likely to influence managers' actions. For example, if a manager of a lessee company believes that readers of financial statements regard the debt–equity ratio or certain reported measures of liquidity as indicators of management performance, the manager may alter perceived adverse effects by taking actions to keep the lease off the balance sheet.

In summary, though the adage "out of sight, out of mind" may be true for some users of financial statements, it apparently is not for all of them.

Why Is Off-Balance-Sheet Financing Increasingly Prevalent? Why has the trend of eliminating debt from the balance sheet become so pronounced? The motivations discussed in the previous pages may provide some of the reasons for off-balance-sheet financing—even though a more thorough analysis of user awareness of the effects of these strategies may lead some to assert that these motives are ill-directed. In any case, these motives probably do not explain completely the increasingly prevalent use of off-balance-sheet financing vehicles. Some of the other potential reasons for the increasing trend are set forth below.

Existing accounting rules have not limited this trend. For example, the existing accounting concepts of a liability are not well defined and thus are not adequate to deal with the increasingly sophisticated financing methods being practiced today. The concept of a liability under historical cost accounting relies much more on legal notions than on economic notions. If the financing arrangement does not result in legal debt to the reporting entity—that is, if the entity is only a guarantor or is only secondarily liable—a strong argument can be made to exclude the financing from the entity's balance sheet.

Further, the existing accounting literature on consolidation is more than 20 years old. Accounting Research Bulletin No. 51 did not contain tight rules in this area and certainly did not contemplate the ingenuity of certain of the financing structures of today nor the degree of diversified operations found in large corporations. FASB Statement No. 13 compounded the "problem" because its arbitrary provisions seem to have inspired the creativity of managements (and their advisors) not only to structure leases that still produce "favorable" financial statement impacts, but also to design other alternative off-balance-sheet financing vehicles.

Another plausible explanation is that off-balance-sheet financing is a consequence of the inability of historical cost accounting to deal with inflation. Under historical cost accounting, the effects of inflation on the economic activities of the enterprise are neither well reported nor well understood. One result is that the balance sheet carrying amounts of many assets are currently far below their current values. For example, many companies have adopted the LIFO (last-in, first-out) method of accounting for inventory costs, both to lower taxes and to eliminate the effect of price fluctuations on "inventory profits." Under LIFO, the carrying amounts for inventories during periods of inflation increasingly diverge from the current values of those inventories. The carrying amount of depreciable property often shows a similar disparity.

As this divergence becomes more pronounced, the pressures for getting new financing arrangements off the balance sheet may also increase. If asset-carrying amounts were reported on their higher, current value basis, a significant portion of the increased basis (generally the amount of increase less perhaps, the related tax effect) would be added to the shareholders' equity on the entity's balance sheet. Consequently, using traditional debt–equity relationships, entities would have additional capacity to carry increased liabilities. Similarly, to the extent that loan covenant restrictions relate to debt–equity relationships, such covenants would be more easily met on a current value basis and would thereby tend to permit companies to embark on new capital replacement or expansion programs by using traditional financing arrangements.

Thus, what we have today under the historical cost accounting basis that underlies current practice is a failure of balance sheets to recognize the current value of assets and a consequent pressure to eliminate from the balance sheet liabilities associated with financing arrangements.

In 1979, the FASB issued Statement No. 33, *Financial Reporting and Changing Prices,* which requires supplemental disclosures by large, publicly held corporations of specified information about the effects of inflation and changing prices on their financial statements. This represents a first step in achieving an awareness of how badly inflation distorts the historical cost balance sheet and indirectly promotes creation of novel financial vehicles.

Summary. In recent years, though certain of the off-balance-sheet financing arrangements described above have been addressed by AcSEC through the issuance of either Statements of Position or Issues Papers, several of the arrangements remain fertile ground for additional work. Even for the selected areas addressed by AcSEC, the issues are not completely (and in several instances are far from) resolved. In addition, although the FASB has agreed to undertake projects dealing with some off-balance-sheet financing vehicles, it has not agreed to undertake a broad-based project to deal with the expanding phenomenon of off-balance-sheet financing.

The FASB has taken some initial steps in its Conceptual Framework that may have a bearing on off-balance-sheet financing by issuing Statement of Financial Concepts No. 3, *Elements of Financial Statements of Business Enterprises* (1980). That document defines liabilities as "probable future sacrifices of economic benefits arising from present obligations of a particular entity to transfer assets or provide services to other entities in the future as a result of past transactions or events." This appears to be a broader definition than one based on legal notions.

However, this broadened accounting definition of liabilities has no immediate impact on accounting practice today for two reasons:

1. The Board is currently working on the "accounting recognition criteria" phase of its Conceptual Framework, which will provide guidance as to when an asset or liability is to be *recorded*. Stated otherwise, even though an arrangement may meet the definition of a liability in Statement of Concepts No. 3, it may not meet the as-yet-undefined recognition criteria. (Resolution of these issues is certainly key to many areas of accounting in addition to those dealt with in this chapter.)

2. FASB Statements of Financial Accounting Concepts do not establish generally accepted accounting principles and are not intended to invoke application of Rule 203 of the Rules of Conduct of the Code of Professional Ethics of the AICPA.[2] Rather, such statements are intended to set forth objectives and fundamentals that will be the basis for development of financial accounting and reporting standards; that is, they will *guide* the Board in developing standards for particular items or events.

Thus, it will probably be some time before we see a broad-based solution to the accounting issues associated with off-balance-sheet financing. In the meantime, there appears to be sufficient motivation to remove debt from the balance sheet to produce a continued proliferation of financing arrangements that accomplish that purpose—even if that motivation is recognized by sophisticated financial statement users.

COMMITMENTS AND CONTINGENCIES

The above discussion has included reference to specific types of commitments (e.g., leases and take-or-pay contracts) and contingencies (e.g., indirect guarantees of debt) that are parts of off-balance-sheet financing arrangements. Other chapters of this book deal with commitments and contingencies that relate to the specific subject matter of a particular chapter—for example, pension and profit-sharing plan commitments, purchase orders for goods and services, product warranties, receivable collectibility, and tax loss carry-forward contingencies.

The purpose of this section is to describe the existing accounting literature in the broad area of commitments and contingencies. FASB Statement No. 5, *Accounting for Contingencies* [1975], is the focal point of that literature.

---

[2]Rule 203 prohibits a member of the American Institute of Certified Public Accountants from expressing an opinion that financial statements conform with generally accepted accounting principles if those statements contain a material departure from an accounting principle promulgated by the Financial Accounting Standards Board, unless the member can demonstrate that because of unusual circumstances the financial statements would otherwise have been misleading.

Contingencies. Statement No. 5 defines a contingency as "an existing condition, situation, or set of circumstances involving uncertainty as to possible gain ... or loss ... to an enterprise that will ultimately be resolved when one or more future events occur or fail to occur." Loss contingencies are those that may result in the incurrence of a liability or the impairment of an asset. Examples are adverse litigation, a breach of contract or law, disputes with taxing and rate-setting authorities, guarantees, threats of expropriation, and uninsured risks. Gain contingencies are those that may result in the acquisition of an asset or reduction of a liability. They arise, for example, from litigation or claims against others, tax carry-forwards, and unrealized appreciation of assets carried at cost.

The accounting process requires the use of estimates. Uncertainties of the estimation process are not, however, considered contingencies for the purpose of this chapter.

The basic financial reporting issues in the area of contingencies relate to the timing of the recognition of the effect of the uncertainties and to their financial statement disclosures.

Loss Contingencies. The treatment of loss contingencies depends on two determinations:

1. Whether the likelihood of the underlying adverse event occurring is "probable," "remote," or "reasonably possible." FASB Statement No. 5 defines these terms as follows:

"*Probable*—The future event or events are likely to occur.

Reasonably possible—The chance of the future event or events occurring is more than remote but less than likely.

Remote—The chance of the future event or events occurring is slight."

2. Whether the amount of loss can be reasonably estimated.

These determinations are frequently difficult to make and require an informed judgment by management based on the best information available before the release of the financial statements. Information to be considered in making these determinations includes the views of legal counsel and other experts, past experiences of the company or others in similar situations, and intentions of the organization (e.g., if an appeal of an adverse court decision will be made).

Loss probable. Under FASB Statement No. 5, when it is "probable" that a loss has been incurred at the balance sheet date, the loss (net of probable recoveries) should be accrued, but only if there is a reasonable basis for estimating it. For example, an actuary's calculation of malpractice losses for an individual hospital might be the best available estimate but, if the statistical degree of accuracy of the estimate is insufficient, the loss should not be deemed to be reasonably estimable.

FASB Interpretation No. 14, *Reasonable Estimation of the Amount of a Loss* [1976], clarifies the fact that the "reasonably estimated" condition does not delay accrual of a loss until only a single amount can be reasonably estimated. If only a range of loss can be determined, the best estimate within the range should be accrued; if none of the estimates within the range is better than another, the lowest amount should be accrued, inasmuch as it is not likely that the ultimate loss will be less than that minimum amount.

Certain unasserted claims against the entity may require accrual. For example, unreported claims for injury and damages against a transportation company for incidents occurring before the balance sheet date should be accrued, provided that experience or other information gives a reasonable basis for estimating the losses. If no basis is available, the fact that there are or may be unreported claims should be disclosed. Similarly, if an enterprise takes a favorable position on a transaction reflected in its tax return, the potential liability should be accrued if it is probable that the enterprise's position will not be sustained and the amount is reasonably estimable.

When a loss contingency has been accrued, the nature of the contingency, the amount of the accrual and, if appropriate, the possibility of further losses should be disclosed if doing so is necessary to prevent the financial statements from being misleading.

When the amount of a probable loss cannot reasonably be estimated (and therefore no accrual can be made), disclosure should be the same as indicated below for "reasonable possible" losses, with notation to the effect that the loss is probable.

Loss reasonably possible. When a loss is "reasonably possible," but not "probable," no accrual should be recorded. However, disclosure should be made of (1) the nature and status of the contingency, and (2) the estimated amount (or range) of the possible loss or a statement that an estimate cannot be made. It is also not uncommon to disclose management's or legal counsel's opinion, if any, on the outcome of the matter and, in some situations, it may be appropriate to present pro forma information giving effect to the possible loss. When the amounts claimed in a lawsuit or other dispute are obviously inflated, such as may be the case in professional negligence and product liability cases, many believe that it is unnecessary and sometimes even misleading to disclose the amount of damages claimed.

Under FASB Statement No. 5, an unasserted claim generally need not be disclosed unless it is considered probable that the claim will be asserted and reasonably possible that a loss will be incurred. If, for example, a company breaches a contract but it is not probable that the other party will file a claim because it has not suffered significant damage, no disclosure is required. But if an enterprise has sold a product that is later proved to have caused significant damage to its users and the enterprise believes that claims will be filed, disclosure (and possible accrual) should be made.

Loss remote. Disclosure generally is not required when the likelihood of loss is "remote." For example, disclosure per se is not required of the fact that tax returns, renegotiation reports, cost reimbursement settlements, and so on, are still subject to review by outside authorities. However, if such open reports include uncertainties involving material amounts, these contingencies should be accrued and/or disclosed in accordance with the preceding paragraphs.

Notwithstanding the above, FASB Statement No. 5 provides that the nature and amounts of material guarantees, letters of credit, and similar arrangements having a characteristic of a guarantee (normally with a right to proceed against an outside party in the event that the guarantor is called on to satisfy the guarantee) should be disclosed even if chances of loss are remote. FASB Interpretation No. 34 clarifies the fact that the above disclosure requirement includes "indirect" guarantees—for example, an agreement to advance funds if a second entity's income, coverage ratio, or working capital falls below a specified minimum.

Care should be exercised to make certain that guarantees are not, in substance, liabilities that should be recorded, especially when they involve related parties. For example, a guarantee of the indebtedness of another company with few resources, or one experiencing significant operating losses, may require accrual of the guaranteed amount. Accrual may be particularly appropriate when the guarantor is likely to provide additional financial support to the other company.

Uninsured risks. Many companies are uninsured or only partially insured for certain risks that may or may not be insurable. This "self-insurance" may take one or more forms: nominal coverage, deductibles, coinsurance, and retrospective premium arrangements under insurance policies. In some cases, the uninsured risks are covered through loss-sharing arrangements with others or by captive insurance companies.

A reasonable application of FASB Statement No. 5 would require that accruals be made for probable losses relating to uninsured risks for incidents occurring on or before the balance sheet date when loss estimates can be made based on experience and other sources. No accruals should be established, however, for losses that apply to events occurring after the balance sheet date, although material losses of this nature should be disclosed.

Disclosure of exposure to uninsured risks depends on the circumstances. When the risk is commonly insured against and when there is a possibility of incurring substantial losses that could have a material effect on the financial statements, many argue that disclosure should be made. The fact that insurance is not available or that its cost is prohibitive often indicates a situation requiring disclosure. If, on the other hand, the risk is not commonly insured against and the likelihood of loss is remote or the impact of a loss occurrence would not be significant, disclosure is probably not required. For example, disclosure is probably not necessary for a company not insuring its inventories if they are located in approximately equal amounts at 100 separate sites.

When disclosure of exposure to uninsured risks is made, it might include:

1. A description of the uninsured risks
2. The amount of insurance coverage when the limits are nominal or low in relation to coverage carried by similar companies in the same industry and, in other circumstances, the deductible, coinsurance, and retrospective premium arrangements
3. A description of the risk-sharing arrangements with others, including the amount of exposure and funding arrangements, if any
4. The accounting treatment followed

Provisions for future expenses and arbitrary or unspecified purposes. An important aspect of FASB Statement No. 5 is its explicit proscription of the practice of accruing for arbitrary or unspecified general contingencies or business risks (including what are sometimes referred to as "catastrophe" or "hidden" reserves or "self-insurance" reserves for events that have not occurred). Such items do not meet the conditions for accrual described earlier in this section.

Many believe, however, that the above-stated proscription does not preclude the accrual of prudent but not excessive amounts for matters that cannot be specifically identified, if the accrual can be reasonably estimated on an overall basis. For example, an accrual for income taxes may well include an amount to cover deficiencies that taxing authorities may assess for matters that, although not specifically identifiable, are likely to arise, based on past experience.

Effect of subsequent data. Information about loss contingencies obtained before the release of the financial statements indicating that a liability was incurred or an asset impaired at the balance sheet date (or that there was a possibility of such incurrence or impairment) should be recognized in the financial statements. If, for example, a lawsuit is filed after the date of the financial statements relating to an event occurring before that date, the potential loss should be accrued and/or disclosed, as appropriate.

On the other hand, no adjustment should be made for events occurring after the balance sheet date that do not indicate that a liability had been incurred or an asset impaired at such date. An uninsured loss of a building due to a fire after year-end, for example, should not be accrued. Significant losses or loss contingencies of this type should be disclosed, however.

Gain Contingencies. Statement No. 5 states that the FASB has not reconsidered the guidance contained in Accounting Research Bulletin No. 50, *Contingencies* (1958), regarding gain contingencies. That Bulletin provides that contingencies that "might result in gains usually are not reflected in the accounts since to do so might be to recognize revenue prior to its realization." In practice this has not precluded recording of gain contingencies that are highly probable of occurrence and can be estimated with a considerable degree of accuracy.

An example of a gain contingency that might be recorded is a favorable settlement of litigation against defendants who are financially able to make payment and have decided not to appeal the decision (or have only a remote chance of being successful if they do appeal). Another example is anticipated insurance recoveries when there is little chance the insurer will not pay the amount accrued.

If the contingency cannot be recorded, the nature, amounts (if estimable), and other facts relating to it should generally be disclosed unless the chance of a favorable resolution is unlikely. FASB Statement No. 5 reiterates a caveat originally articulated in ARB No. 50, emphasizing that care should be taken not to mislead readers with implications about the likelihood of recovery.

Commitments. Commitments are agreements to perform in the future. Contracts to construct facilities or purchase equipment, agreements to lend or borrow funds, accepted sales orders, and agreements to acquire other businesses or make investments are examples of commitments. Stock repurchase agreements and purchase orders for goods and services are other examples.

As a general rule, existing accounting literature and practice provide that executory contracts of this nature do not create a basis for accounting recognition of an asset and liability. The financial reporting problems that do arise in the area of commitments relate primarily to recognition of losses inherent in certain commitments and to their disclosure.

Disclosure should typically be made of any extraordinary commitments that are material to the financial position of an enterprise, including, for example, extraordinary commitments for capital additions.

Disclosure would typically include the nature, amounts, and any unusual terms or uncertainties of the commitment. For capital additions, it is frequently more informative to disclose the total cost of the construction program rather than only the portion covered by commitments. When commitments exceed the current resources of an enterprise, an indication of how they will be financed desirably should be included.

Losses inherent in other unhedged commitments should be accrued if the commitment relates to an item that would have been written down had it been on hand at the balance sheet date. Contingent losses, including those applicable to construction programs that are encountering difficulties, should be treated as indicated in the earlier parts of this section.

Summary. At the present time, FASB Statement No. 5 provides the general authoritative accounting literature for the accrual and/or disclosure of contingencies and commitments. As the FASB moves further into the development of the Conceptual Framework, the issues of accounting recognition of gains and losses, assets and liabilities, contractual rights and obligations will be visited or revisited. This long-term project may ultimately affect the handling of certain of the "soft" liabilities dealt with in this section of the chapter.

BIBLIOGRAPHY

Accounting Principles Board (AICPA), *The Equity Method of Accounting for Investments in Common Stock*, Opinion No. 18 (APB, 1971).

Accounting Standards Executive Committee (AICPA), *Reporting Finance Subsidiaries in Consolidated Financial Statements*, Issues Paper (AcSEC, 1978).

————, *Accounting for Project Financing Arrangements*, Issues Paper (AcSEC, 1979).

————, *Joint Venture Accounting*, Issues Paper (AcSEC, 1979).

————, *Accounting for Transfers of Receivables with Recourse*, Issues Paper (AcSEC, 1980).

American Institute of Certified Public Accountants, *Rules of Conduct of the Code of Professional Ethics of the AICPA*.

————, *Recognition of Profit on Sales of Receivables with Recourse*, Statement of Position 74-6 (AICPA 1974).

————, *Accounting for Product Financing Arrangements*, Statement of Position 78-8 (AICPA, 1978).

————, *Accounting for Investments in Real Estate Joint Ventures*, Statement of Position 78-9 (AICPA, 1978).

Bohan, M. P., "Accounting Developments," *Journal of Accounting, Auditing & Finance,* vol. 4 (Fall 1980), pp. 77–83.

Committee on Accounting Procedure (AICPA), *Contingencies*, Accounting Research Bulletin No. 50 (CAP, 1958).

————, *Consolidated Financial Statements,* Accounting Research Bulletin No. 51 (CAP, 1959).

Dieter, R., and A. R. Wyatt, "Get It Off the Balance Sheet!," *Financial Executive,* vol. 48 (January 1980), pp. 42, 44–48.

Financial Accounting Standards Board, *Accounting for Contingencies,* Statement of Financial Accounting Standards No. 5 (FASB, 1975).

————, *Accounting for Leases,* Statement of Financial Accounting Standards No. 13 (FASB, 1976).

————, *Reasonable Estimation of the Amount of a Loss,* FASB Interpretation No. 14 (FASB, 1976).

————, *Action Alert* (FASB, March 8, 1979).

————, *Financial Reporting and Changing Prices,* Statement of Financial Accounting Standards No. 33 (FASB, 1979).

————, *Elements of Financial Statements of Business Enterprises,* Statement of Financial Concepts No. 3 (FASB, 1980).

————, *Disclosure of Long-Term Obligations,* Statement of Financial Accounting Standards No. 47 (FASB, 1981).

————, *Accounting for Product Financing Arrangements,* Statement of Financial Accounting Standards No. 49 (FASB, 1981).

————, *Disclosure of Indirect Guarantees of Indebtedness of Others,* FASB Interpretation No. 34 (FASB, 1981).

————, *The Economic Effects on Lessees of FASB Statement No. 13, Accounting for Leases,* A. Rashad Abdel-khalik et al. (FASB, 1981).

————, *Research and Development Arrangements,* Statement of Financial Accounting Standards No. 68 (FASB, 1982).

Greene, R., "How to Owe Money without Seeming to," *Forbes,* vol. 125 (May 26, 1980), pp. 54–56.

————, "The Joys of Leasing," *Forbes,* vol. 126 (November 24, 1980), p. 59.

Gurwin, L., "Why Utility CFO's Are Becoming Corporate Heroes," *Institutional Investor,* vol. 13 (May 1979), pp. 141–142, 144, 196.

Hershman, A., with L. Adkins and G. Knecht, "The Creative New Look in Corporate Finance," *Dun's Review,* July 1981.

Securities and Exchange Commission, *Financing by Electric Utility Companies through Use of Construction Intermediaries,* Staff Accounting Bulletin Release No. 28 (SEC, 1978).

CHAPTER 27

Contributed

Capital

Melvin Penner
Partner, Arthur Young & Company

Ernest L. Hicks
Retired Partner, Arthur Young & Company
Adjunct Professor of Accounting,
The Ohio State University

CONTRIBUTED CAPITAL

The equity interest, or owners' interest, in the assets of a business corporation[1] is the residual interest—the amount that remains after deducting the corporation's liabilities from its assets. The amount of the equity interest ordinarily arises from two sources: investments by the owners of the corporation, and earnings retained for use in the corporation's business. Chapter 28 discusses the principles of accounting for retained earnings.

The equity interest may be represented by a single class of security, usually called "common stock." Often, the ownership interest comprises two or more classes of capital stock having different rights—to vote, to participate in distributions of the corporation's assets, and to share in the assets in the event of liquidation. Thus, a corporation may, for instance, have several classes of common stock and preferred stock. As a result of the differences in rights, some owners may bear relatively more of the loss when the corporation is unprofitable or may benefit proportionately more when it is profitable than other owners. Nevertheless, all classes of equity ordinarily depend at least to some extent on profitable operations for distributions of the corporation's assets, and no class of common stock carries an unconditional right to receive future transfers of assets from the corporation except in liquidation, and then only after liabilities have been satisfied.[2]

A corporation's financial statements identify the several classes of its capital stock; show the number of shares of each class that have been authorized, issued, and reserved for issuance; assign amounts to each class; and describe any special rights the owners have. This information may be presented in the corporation's balance sheet, in a separate statement of shareholders' equity, or in notes to the financial statements.

---

[1]This chapter does not discuss the principles of accounting for contributed capital of unincorporated businesses, such as partnerships (see Chapter 30), sole proprietorships, and mutual organizations; enterprises not organized for profit; or companies in regulated industries, such as insurance companies and public utility companies. Also, this chapter does not discuss principles of accounting for contributed capital in connection with business combinations (see Chapter 34).

[2]The foregoing discussion is compatible with and in part has been taken from, FASB SFAC No. 3 (1980, pars. 43, 44, and 46). An introduction to SFAC No. 3 includes the following concerning the Statement's authority "Statements of Financial Accounting Concepts do not establish standards prescribing accounting procedures or disclosure practices for particular items or events, which are issued by the Board as Statements of Financial Accounting Standards. Rather, Statements in this series describe concepts and relations that will underlie future financial accounting standards and practices and in due course serve as a basis for evaluating existing standards and practices."

The total of the amounts assigned to the several divisions constituting the owners' interest section of a corporation's balance sheet is equal to the carrying amount of the corporation's net assets. The net assets, in turn, are stated on various bases, such as cost, partly amortized cost, and estimated net realizable values, which have little relation to the current value of the net assets.[3] Consequently, the amounts at which the equity interests are stated do not represent an allocation or assignment of the current value of the corporation's net assets. For related but somewhat different reasons, these equity amounts also do not represent the values of the ownership interests themselves.

Incorporation and State Laws. Most enterprises are able to choose the state in which they will be incorporated. For companies whose operations are widespread, the state may be chosen because its statutes offer tax advantages or lenient registration or reporting requirements. Other considerations in the selection include the degree of flexibility allowed in a corporation's capital structure, the extent to which liabilities can attach to managers, directors, or shareholders, and the nature of requirements pertaining to shareholder meetings, shareholders' voting rights, and preemptive rights. These and other factors should be reviewed with benefit of legal advice by an enterprise considering incorporation.

The laws of the state in which a corporation is chartered govern the types of ownership interests it may issue and the types of transactions into which it may enter with the owners of the interests. In some instances, these laws prescribe the manner in which such transactions or their results are to be presented in the corporation's financial statements. State laws also govern the procedural steps necessary for incorporating. In most states, the Secretary of State oversees the filing process.

The certificate (articles) of incorporation, once approved by the state, becomes a public document. Typically, state law requires the articles to include the name of the corporation, the address of its corporate and home office, the proposed types of corporate activity, information about the capital structure, a detailed description of each class of securities, and an indication of the corporation's planned life if not perpetual. Changes in the articles often require shareholder approval. Ordinarily such changes meet no resistance from the state.

The affairs of a corporation are conducted pursuant to bylaws—rules drawn up by the incorporators or directors or, occasionally, by shareholders. Unlike a corporation's certificate of incorporation, or charter, its bylaws are not a matter of public record. Bylaws cannot extend the corporation's powers beyond those specified in the charter; most of them deal with such matters as issuing securities, transferring ownership of shares, paying dividends, and holding meetings of directors and shareholders.

---

[3]Pursuant to the provisions of SFAS No. 33, which the FASB issued in 1979, certain corporations present, with their financial statements, supplementary information that shows the effects of changing prices on certain assets, related expenses, and revenues.

CAPITAL STOCK

Common Stock. The common shareholders retain the residual interest in a corporation's net assets, after all obligations and all other interests. Common shareholders alone, among all the investors in and creditors of an enterprise, are not entitled to a specified amount or rate of return. Consequently, they stand to suffer the most from unsuccessful operations and may gain the most from successful operations.

Typically, a corporation has only one class of common stock. In some companies, however, there may be two or more classes of common stock with different voting rights or dividend prospects, or with other special rights or preferences. In some cases, dividend preferences and voting restrictions may give rise to a class of common stock that is more like preferred stock than it is like the usual common stock.

Preferred Stock. Preferred stock is an equity security that is senior to common stock. Preferred stocks usually entitle holders to receive dividends at a stated rate or amount per share before any dividends are paid on the common stock. Some preferred stocks give the holders voting privileges—when dividends are in arrears, for example. In some cases the preferred shareholders are entitled to participate in dividends exceeding a specified level (participating preferred) or to receive dividends in arrears before a dividend is paid to common shareholders (cumulative preferred). The preferred shareholders' claims on the assets of the company are subordinate to the claims of debt holders but are superior to those of common shareholders. It is not unusual for preferred shareholders to have the right to receive in liquidation an amount that is greater than the par value of their shares.

In some instances preferred shareholders are protected against dilution of their interests. The protective provisions may specify, for example, that no new debt and no preferred stock with superior rights may be issued without the consent of a specified majority of the preferred shareholders or may require their collective consent for certain major corporate actions such as the sale of the business or a reorganization.

In order to enable readers of the financial statements to understand the rights and privileges of the holders of preferred stocks, the issuer's statements disclose the important characteristics of each class of preferred: dividend and voting rights, liquidation preferences (if different from par values), conversion privileges, and amounts in arrears if dividends are cumulative.

The features of some preferred stock, for example, those with mandatory redemption provisions, may parallel closely those of debt securities. In these circumstances, consideration may have to be given to whether it is appropriate to treat the preferred stock as an equity security. The Securities and Exchange Commission has addressed some of the issues involving preferred stock with mandatory redemption provisions in *Financial Reporting Release No. 1* [1982], Section 211, and in Staff Accounting Bulletin No. 40. [1981]. (See "Redeemable Preferred Stock" below.)

Par Value and Stated Value. The articles of incorporation state whether the capital stock will have a par value. The original concept was that par value represented an investment level to be maintained for the protection of creditors. This investment level has been variously described as "legal," "statutory," and "stated" capital, and many states prohibit corporations from declaring dividends out of such capital. The par value concept itself, however, has become obsolete. Many companies issue no-par-value, nonassessable stock; this is legal in nearly all states. No-par-value stock usually has a stated value, which simply is specified by the corporation as a part of the selling price.

State laws control a corporation's ability to change its capital shares from par value to no par value or vice versa, or to change the par or stated value. Unless stated capital (the aggregate par or stated value of the shares) changes, no entry is called for in the corporation's books. If stated capital is reduced, the difference is credited to Capital in Excess of Par Value.[4] An increase in par or stated value will increase stated capital if Capital in Excess of Par Value or Retained Earnings is available for transfer to the par or stated value account. Ordinarily, Capital in Excess of Par Value is exhausted before a transfer is made from Retained Earnings.

Private Placements and Public Offerings. Stock may be issued in either a public offering or a private placement, both of which are subject to the laws of the states in which the shares are issued. A private placement ordinarily involves relatively few purchasers who are relatively well informed about the company, whereas in a public offering there are numerous prospective purchasers, many of whom do not know much about the company. Public offerings may have to be registered with the Securities and Exchange Commission. To meet the SEC's requirements, a corporation must provide a comprehensive description of its business, management, and operations. Financial information in both statement and narrative form is required. The financial statements and certain other information must be "certified" by independent accountants (see Chapter 38).

Certain public offerings of securities are exempt from registration with the SEC. One exemption is for offerings of less than a specified amount—at present, $1,500,000. Another exemption is for intrastate offerings. Strict compliance with the SEC's terms for exemption is essential.

Records of Issuance and Transfer of Shares. For a corporation whose securities are not widely held, maintaining shareholder records is relatively simple. Stock certificates are recorded in a stock certificate book, and new issues, cancellations, and transfers are recorded in a stock transfer journal. As the number of shareholders grows, independent registrars and transfer agents, who specialize in providing services for transfers of stock, are usually retained.

The negotiability of stock certificates is governed by the Uniform Stock

---

[4]Or to Capital in Excess of Stated Value, if appropriate. For convenience, in this chapter this substitution will in most instances be assumed rather than mentioned.

Transfer Act and the Uniform Commercial Code. Most stock certificates in use are printed or engraved documents, but some companies use stock "cards" instead of certificates to facilitate data processing.

Issuance of Shares for Cash. When a company issues shares of stock for cash, the proceeds are credited to the contributed capital accounts. If the stock has a par or a stated value, an amount equal to the total such value of the stock issued is credited to the capital stock account and the rest of the proceeds is credited to Capital in Excess of Par Value. In the rare event that stock is issued for cash at a discount—that is, at a price less than par value—the capital stock account is credited for the aggregate par value of the shares and Capital in Excess of Par Value is reduced by the difference between that amount and the proceeds. If the difference exceeds the balance in that account, the excess is debited to Retained Earnings. Some states allow or require a company to set up a separate negative (debit balance) equity account when stock is issued at a discount, rather than to reduce Retained Earnings.

When no-par-value stock without a stated value is issued, it is customary to credit the full amount of the proceeds to the capital stock account. In some instances the board of directors may assign only a portion of the proceeds of such an issue to the capital stock account, with the remainder going to Capital in Excess of Par Value.

SEC Staff Accounting Bulletin No. 40 suggests that when stock is issued in exchange for a promise to pay cash, the receivable should be presented as a deduction from shareholders' equity if payment is not received prior to publication of the issuer's financial statements. (Also, see the discussion under "Subscribed Shares.")

Noncash Share Transactions. When shares are issued for assets other than cash (such as properties, property rights, and intangible assets) or for services, the valuation of the consideration requires the exercise of judgment. The general guideline is that the transaction should be recorded at the fair value of the shares issued or the fair value of the goods or services received, whichever is more clearly evident. For a publicly held corporation, the market value of the shares issued may be the best indicator of the amount of the proceeds. In a closely held corporation, the value of what was acquired may be the best indicator. In most states, the board of directors is empowered to decide the value of consideration received in exchange for shares.

The SEC has adopted certain policies regarding the issuance of shares to promoters in exchange for services and the issuance of shares for nonmonetary assets with no readily determinable value. (See, for exmaple, Staff Accounting Bulletin No. 48 [1982].) The SEC may require that no value be assigned to such proceeds (other than to the extent of cash or other liquid assets received), because the ultimate value of the nonmonetary assets is related directly to the future fortunes of the corporation itself. Also, SEC Staff Accounting Bulletin No. 40 states that deferred compensation that arises from issuance of capital stock to officers and other employees at prices below fair value should be presented in the balance sheet as a deduction from shareholders' equity.

Subscribed Shares. A company may accept subscriptions from potential investors to purchase shares at a later date or on an installment basis. The initial accounting recognition of the subscription agreement is to debit Stock Subscriptions Receivable for the consideration to be paid, and to credit Common (or Preferred) Stock Subscribed for the par or stated value of the subscribed shares and Capital Subscribed in Excess of Par Value for the consideration to be paid in excess of the par or stated value. If the amount of the consideration ultimately received differs from the corresponding amount in the subscriptions receivable account, the difference is debited or credited to Capital in Excess of Par Value.

When the shares are issued, the amount in the stock subscribed account is transferred to Common (or Preferred) Stock. The terms of the agreement determine when the shares are delivered, and, depending on statutory provisions, certificates may be issued before the proceeds are collected in full.

If the subscriber defaults on the subscription obligation, state law may stipulate the procedures to be followed. Generally, one of the following will result: The issuing corporation (1) returns all payments to the subscriber; (2) issues shares corresponding to the amount paid before default; (3) declares all partial payments to be forfeited by the subscriber.

It is usually appropriate in financial statements to show shares subscribed separately from shares issued. Depending on the circumstances, subscriptions receivable may be included on the asset side of the balance sheet (classified as current or noncurrent according to its terms) or as a deduction from the shareholders' equity accounts. The SEC has consistently maintained that receivables for capital stock subscriptions should not be shown as assets unless the receivable has been collected before the financial statements are issued. When the receivable for subscribed shares is treated as a deduction from shareholders' equity, it is usually set forth as a separate item.

Stock Issuance Costs. Issuing stock usually entails some costs. These include statutory filing fees, legal and accounting fees, and printing costs, and in a public offering they may be significant. Some companies have charged the costs to earnings, usually over a period of time, but the more common practice has been to deduct them from the issue proceeds. The SEC allows either method.

Conditional Securities. Conditional securities are contractual arrangements giving the owners the right to acquire a corporation's capital stock in accordance with specified terms. Conditional securities include stock subscription rights, warrants, convertible debt, convertible preferred stock, and stock options.

Stock subscription rights. Stock subscription rights entitle the holder to purchase stock at a stated price, usually during a specified time period and for a price less than the market price of the stock at the time the rights are issued. Such rights are ordinarily issued to holders of the company's stock, and no change in the shareholders' equity accounts results from issuing them. Information about the rights, including the exercise price and the expiration date, is disclosed in the notes to the financial statements. The company records the exercise of stock subscription rights in the same manner as any other issuance of stock for cash.

Warrants. Warrants are similar to stock subscription rights, except that warrants are usually sold, separately or attached to other securities, and the purchasers ordinarily are not shareholders. The stock purchase price specified by warrants may change with the passage of time and is often greater than the market price of the stock at the time the warrants are issued.

If detachable warrants are issued in conjunction with debt, the proceeds of sale are allocated between the debt and the warrants, based on the fair values of each at the time of issuance. The amount allocated to the warrants is credited to Capital in Excess of Par Value. If warrants are issued in conjunction with debt and are not detachable, the proceeds are not segregated for accounting purposes (see APB Opinion No. 14 [1969]).

When warrants are issued with preferred stock, the proceeds are attributed entirely to the stock; allocating a portion of the amount received to the warrants would serve no useful purpose.

Stock options. A corporation may offer stock options to its employees to promote employee stock ownership or to provide additional compensation. Stock options differ from other conditional securities in that they are usually granted only to employees, frequently as part of a compensation plan, and are not transferable.

Accounting for stock options and their effect in computing earnings per share are covered extensively in authoritative literature—in Chapter 13B of ARB No. 43, [1953], in APB Opinions No. 15 [1969] and 25, [1972], and in FASB Interpretations No. 28 [1978] and 31 [1980]. (See Chapter 29 of this handbook.) Generally, stock option plans are categorized as either compensatory or noncompensatory. Noncompensatory options are those that generally are available to all employees and can be exercised only during a relatively limited period. Specific criteria for noncompensatory plans are set forth in Paragraph 7 of APB Opinion No. 25. All other stock option plans are considered compensatory— even though in many circumstances the issuance of compensatory options does not result in a charge to earnings for compensation.

Compensatory stock option plans are of two general types—traditional plans and complex plans. Traditional stock option plans are the "qualified" and "restricted" plans that have been commonly used by corporations for the past 35 years or so. For traditional plans, compensation is measured at the date the option is granted; there is deemed to be compensation to the extent that the market value of the securities exceeds the option price at the grant date. To the extent that such plans involve a measurable amount of compensation, the accounting for such plans is straightforward; compensation is debited to operations or to deferred compensation and credited to Capital in Excess of Par Value.

Complex stock option plans are a more recent phenomenon. Such plans may tie the number of shares or the option price to employee performance or to the company's earnings performance. Complex plans may also provide the employee with alternative stock option packages. These plans may even involve "phantom" securities, that is, rights that base compensation on the change in market price of the corporation's common stock but that do not require the actual issuance of common stock. The general rules are that compensation is recorded in an amount equal to the difference between the "option price" and the fair value of the securities at the measurement date. The measurement date is defined as the date when both the number of shares and the option price are definitely known. The recorded compensation is charged to operations over the period during which the employees perform the related services.

Convertible securities. In order to maintain flexibility in its financial structure, a corporation may attach a "conversion privilege" to its debt or preferred shares. The privilege of converting these securities to common shares at a predetermined rate may have advantages for both the holder and the issuing corporation. The holder is able to become a common shareholder when it becomes economically desirable to do so. On the other hand, the corporation may obtain a wider distribution of the debt or preferred shares or a better price for them by "sweetening" the issue with a conversion right.

When preferred stock is converted, the par or stated value of the converted shares is removed from Preferred Stock; Common Stock is credited for the par or stated value of the common shares issued, and any difference between this amount and the amount removed from Preferred Stock is credited or debited to Capital in Excess of Par Value. Should a debit to Capital in Excess of Par Value exhaust that account, any remaining debit is charged to Retained Earnings. Retained Earnings is not increased as a result of a conversion.

No part of the proceeds from the sale of convertible debt is attributed for accounting purposes to the conversion privilege. Upon conversion, the carrying amount of the converted debt, which is removed from the accounts, is deemed to be the proceeds received upon issuance of the capital stock. No gain or loss is recorded as a result of the conversion. APB Opinion No. 14 discusses the accounting principles and underlying rationale.

Disclosure. Authoritative accounting pronouncements call for broad disclosures relative to conditional securities. Generally, enough information must be given to enable readers of the financial statements to assess the effect exercise or conversion of conditional securities might have on the equity holders' rights. Customary disclosures include:

Number of common shares reserved for issuance on exercise or conversion
The terms and conditions under which conditional securities may be exercised or converted
Exercise or conversion prices
Termination date
Details of exercises or conversions during the period(s) being reported upon
Contingent security agreements

Stock Dividends, Stock Splits, and Reverse Splits. In both a stock dividend and a stock split there is a proportional distribution of shares to holders, and the assets of the company are unaffected. However, the distributions are accounted for differently.

There are various reasons for declaring stock dividends or stock splits. Management may desire to retain undistributed earnings permanently for use in the company; by issuing a stock dividend, retained earnings are transferred to capital and to that extent the legal ability to declare cash dividends is reduced. A stock split may reduce the market price of the shares, and thus may stimulate trading and result in a wider distribution of shares.

A *stock dividend* is described in Chapter 7B of ARB No. 43 as a share distribution "prompted mainly by a desire to give the recipient shareholders some ostensibly separate evidence of a part of their respective interests in accumulated corporate earnings." A distribution of less than 20 to 25 percent of the number of shares previously outstanding is normally considered a stock dividend. When there is a stock dividend, a portion of Retained Earnings is capitalized (transferred to Capital Stock and Capital in Excess of Par Value and thus made part of permanent capital). ARB No. 43 requires that, when specified circumstances exist, the amount of retained earnings capitalized be an amount equal to the fair value of the shares issued.

A *stock split* is a share distribution "prompted mainly by a desire to increase the number of outstanding shares for the purpose of effecting a reduction in their unit market price and, thereby, obtaining a wider distribution and improved marketability of shares." A stock split does not call for a transfer of Retained Earnings to the permanent capital accounts, if the company reduces the per-share par value of outstanding stock in proportion to the amount of stock being issued as a result of the stock split. Alternatively, the company may choose to leave the par values unchanged and account for the stock split by transferring to the Capital Stock account the equivalent of the par value of the shares issued as a result of the stock split. This amount may be transferred either from Capital in Excess of Par Value or from Retained Earnings.

A *reverse stock split* is sometimes referred to as a "share consolidation." The objective is to raise the price of the shares to a level at which they are expected to be more attractive to potential investors. A reverse split usually is accomplished by increasing the per-share par or stated value and reducing the number of shares outstanding.

Reacquired Shares. Companies may acquire their own equity securities for a number of reasons and in a number of ways. Reacquired stock may be canceled and retired or held for subsequent reissue. Several accounting treatments are available to record such transactions. The appropriate treatment may depend on the purpose and specific nature of the transaction. The common thread running through these alternatives goes back to one of the earliest pronouncements of the AICPA: A company should not recognize profit or loss on transactions in its own shares.

Preferred stock. The terms of preferred stock may permit the issuer to "call" the shares at a specific price, which normally exceeds the original issue price. This option provides some flexibility to the corporation. If the terms of the preferred stock become burdensome to management's financial goals, the issue may be called (reacquired and canceled). Other things being equal, callable preferred stock should provide lower proceeds from issuance than noncallable preferred stock.

When preferred stock is called, the par value and any other specific elements of capital related to the issue are removed from the accounts. If there is a call premium (call price exceeds issue price), it ordinarily is debited to Retained Earnings. If the issue is called at an amount less than the issue price, the difference between that price and the call price is credited to Capital in Excess of Par Value. This procedure reflects the accepted notion that a corporation does not credit Retained Earnings in transactions involving its own equity securities. Preferred shares reacquired through the exercise of the call option are usually retired.

Common stock. A company may acquire its own common stock for retirement or for later reissuance. If the stock is retired, the accounting is essentially the same as for preferred stock that is retired.

When a company reacquires shares of its own stock and does not retire them, the stock is referred to as "treasury stock." Treasury stock transactions are often regulated by state laws and by stock exchange rules—which are by no means uniform. State laws usually limit the amount that can be expended for treasury shares either to available amounts in excess of "legal capital" or to unrestricted retained earnings. Also, in most states the amount of retained earnings that is permitted to be distributed as dividends is reduced by the cost of the shares acquired.

Treasury stock ordinarily is recorded at the cost of the reacquired shares and is reported as a deduction from the shareholders' equity accounts (with parenthetical disclosure of the number of shares held in the treasury). This is called the "cost method." Some companies allocate the reduction in shareholders' equity resulting from the acquisition of treasury stock to Common Stock, Capital in Excess of Par Value, and Retained Earnings—thus treating the treasury stock as though it had been retired. This is called the "par value method." The par value method requires specific identification of both the shares acquired and the entries made on original issue of these shares. Consequently, it is not widely used.

Some companies list treasury stock among the noncurrent assets when the shares are purchased for distribution under an employee stock option plan. With proper disclosure, APB Opinion No. 6 [1965] permits treasury stock to be shown as an asset under limited circumstances. Nevertheless, reporting treasury shares as an asset creates the paradoxical situation of a corporation owning part of itself. Also, treasury shares have no value in liquidation proceedings, and voting and dividend rights do not attach to stock certificates held in the treasury.

When treasury stock is sold, no profit or loss is recognized. If the proceeds exceed the carrying amount, Capital in Excess of Par Value is credited. If the proceeds are less than the carrying amount, the difference may be charged to Capital in Excess of Par Value to the extent of previous credits arising from the issuance of the stock, or to Retained Earnings.

When stock prices are depressed, managers may wish to reacquire outstanding shares. In some cases, the objective is to eliminate public ownership; this is sometimes referred to as "going private." When the number of shareholders and outstanding shares is reduced, management may obtain some relief from reporting requirements of the SEC and other governmental agencies. "Going private" is subject to increasing regulation by the SEC.

CAPITAL IN EXCESS
OF PAR (OR STATED) VALUE

Capital in Excess of Par (or Stated) Value is also called "Additional Paid-in Capital" or, less preferably, "Capital Surplus." This account arises most frequently when stock is sold for an amount in excess of its par (or stated) value. Other transactions that may affect Capital in Excess of Par (or Stated) Value include sales of warrants, conversion of debt or preferred stock, stock dividends, treasury stock acquisitions, quasi-reorganizations, business combinations, payments made (or stock plans established) by a principal shareholder for the benefit of the corporation, and realization of income tax benefits from deductions for compensation expenses related to employee stock options to the extent that the amount deducted is different from that recognized for financial reporting purposes.

CAPITAL DONATIONS

Municipalities and other government agencies may grant rights or give property to a corporation in order to promote industrial development or employment. The donation may be made outright, or it may be contingent on the attainment of a goal such as the employment of a specified number of people or occupancy for a specific period of time. APB Opinion No. 29 [1973]provides that such a transaction (which the Opinion would categorize as a "nonreciprocal transfer") is to be recorded at the fair value of the nonmonetary asset received. The financial statements disclose any performance requirements imposed by the donor.

A number of foreign governments have established programs to promote or guide the development of business activities by providing financial assistance to business enterprises, and an increasing number of multinational companies are taking advantage of these programs. Government assistance of this kind usually takes one of three forms:

1. Payments to reimburse, or contribute toward, certain expenses incurred or to be incurred—for example, expenses of training a labor force

2. Payments to supplement sales, past or future—for example, to subsidize exports

3. Payments contributing to the purchase of productive assets—for example, Canada's area development incentive grants

The assistance usually is conditional; for example, a certain kind of expenditure must be incurred, a certain kind of product must be sold, a certain kind of productive asset must be acquired, or the business must maintain an operation in a certain location for a specified period of time.

Assistance of this kind differs from that commonly provided by governments in the United States, which is usually in the form of investment tax credits, property tax abatements, other tax benefits, or low-interest loans. No specific authoritative pronouncement of generally accepted U.S. Accounting Principles other countries, notably Canada and the United Kingdom, authoritative pronouncements have established principles of accounting applicable in those countries to government assistance, and practice in the United States appears to have been influenced by those pronouncements. The following methods have been used in the United States:

1. The capital method—the amount of the assistance is credited to contributed capital.

2. Income methods, which are used by most U.S. companies that receive material amounts of this type of assistance. The amount of the assistance is credited to income in one of three ways:

(a) Revenue is increased or expense is decreased in the period of receipt or accrual.

(b) Income is deferred and recognized over a period of time extending beyond the period of receipt or accrual.

(c) The cost of a depreciable asset is reduced, with consequent reduction of depreciation expense over the life of the asset.

FINANCIAL STATEMENT PRESENTATION

Exhibit 1 illustrates the shareholders' equity section of a hypothetical balance sheet. (This example does not purport to reflect all kinds of capital accounts or related disclosures that might be required in any particular situation.)

There are a number of comments to be made about Exhibit 1. The various accounts have been included in the order most frequently seen in financial

EXHIBIT 1 Illustrative Balance Sheet Presentation of Shareholders' Equity

	December 31	
Shareholders' equity	19X1	19X2
6% cumulative preferred stock, par value $100, authorized 5,000 shares, issued and outstanding, 3,000 shares and 2,000 shares....................	$300,000	$200,000
Convertible $3.50 preference stock, no par value, stated value $50, authorized, issued, and outstanding 1,200 shares at each year-end (involuntary liquidation preference $50,000)...........................	60,000	60,000
Common stock, no par value, stated value $1, authorized 15,000 shares, issued 10,000 and 8,000 shares..................................	10,000	8,000
Capital in excess of stated value..................	200,000	150,000
Retained earnings............................	250,000	190,000
Less treasury stock at cost (500 and 300 shares of common stock)............................	(40,000)	(25,000)
Total shareholders' equity	$780,000	$583,000

statements, beginning with the most senior equity securities and descending to common stock and other paid-in capital accounts. Retained earnings customarily comes after paid-in capital, and treasury stock is most commonly shown (as a deduction) as the final item in the shareholders' equity section. It will be noted that the example includes a number of disclosures regarding the attributes of various equity securities. Although this presentation is common, some companies prefer to disclose these details in notes rather than on the face of the balance sheet—a practice that is acceptable.

The prescribed dividend rates for the senior securities (6 percent for the preferred stock and $3.50 for the preference stock) are stated. Also, the cumulative dividend privileges of the preferred stock are disclosed. With respect to each class of stock, the par or stated value is disclosed along with the numbers of shares authorized, issued, and outstanding. For the convertible preference stock, the amount the holders would receive in case of involuntary liquidation is shown, because it differs significantly from the stated value. Finally, with respect to the treasury stock, the carrying basis (cost) and the number of shares are both disclosed.

There are a number of other disclosures regarding capital accounts that are customarily included in the notes to the financial statements: rights of holders of senior securities (preferred and preference stocks) to participate in earnings and dividends above the stated rate; dividend arrearages; conversion privileges, together with the conversion price, restrictions on conversion, antidilutive provisions, and the number of common shares reserved for conversion; the price and timing of call options; the price and timing of redemptions; and sinking fund requirements.

Disclosure requirements for common stock options are set forth in Paragraph 15 of ARB No. 43, which states:

> In connection with financial statements, disclosures should be made as to the status of the option or plan at the end of the period of report, including the number of shares under option, the option price, and the number of shares as to which options were exercisable. As to options exercised during the period, disclosure should be made of the number of shares involved and the option price thereof.

Disclosures for other conditional securities (warrants, rights, and convertible debt) are similar to those for stock options. In general, the purpose of the disclosures relating to conditional securities is to provide readers with information to assess their potential impact on shareholders' equity.

Information about transactions, events, or conditions that might impact the equity interests of the preferred and common shareholders should also be disclosed. Examples of such information include details of stock repurchase agreements and the circumstances in which common shares are contingently issued or issuable in connection with a business combination.

Redeemable Preferred Stock. Companies subject to SEC reporting requirements that have "redeemable preferred stocks" outstanding (see definition below) must present separately, on balance sheets included in annual reports to shareholders and SEC filings and reports, amounts applicable to the following three general classes of securities: (1) preferred stocks subject to mandatory redemption requirements or whose redemption is outside the control of the issuer (see below); (2) preferred stocks that are not redeemable or are redeemable solely at the option of the issuer; and (3) common stocks. A general heading, "Shareholders' Equity," may not be used by these companies and they may not present a combined total for equity securities, inclusive of redeemable preferred stocks. It is acceptable to combine shareholders' equity items other than redeemable preferred stocks under an appropriately designated caption, such as "Nonredeemable Preferred Stocks, Common Stocks, and Other Shareholders' Equity."

The term "redeemable preferred stocks," as defined by the SEC, means "any stock which (i) the issuer undertakes to redeem at a fixed or determinable price on a fixed or determinable date or dates, whether by operation of a sinking fund or otherwise; (ii) is redeemable at the option of the holder; or (iii) has conditions for redemption which are not solely within the control of the issuer, such as stocks which must be redeemed out of future earnings." Preferred stocks that meet one or more of the above criteria are to be classified as redeemable preferred stocks regardless of their other attributes such as voting rights, dividend rights, or conversion features.

The title, carrying amount, and redemption amount of each issue of redeemable preferred stock must be disclosed on the face of the balance sheet. A separate note captioned "Redeemable Preferred Stocks" must include disclosure of redemption terms, 5-year maturity data, changes in redeemable preferred stocks for each period for which an income statement is presented, and the accounting treatment for the difference, if any, between the carrying value and redemption amount of the redeemable preferred stocks. In aggregating the 5-year maturity data, it is not necessary to include amounts for preferred stocks redeemable at the option of holders of preferred stocks that have conditions for redemption not solely within the control of the issuer, provided that the redemption terms of these issues are described in the footnote.

QUASI-REORGANIZATIONS

A company that has experienced substantial losses may desire to "begin anew," using a procedure termed a "quasi-reorganization." A quasi-reorganization involves the formal adoption of a plan to restate all of the corporation's assets and liabilities at current values and to charge an accumulated deficit to the paid-in capital accounts. The tax basis of the assets and liabilities remains unchanged. The AICPA and the SEC have specified rules relating to a quasi-reorganization in ARB No. 43, Chapter 7A, and SEC *Financial Reporting Release No. 1*, Section 210.

Also, APB Opinion No. 11 [1967] states that future tax benefits that may result from net operating loss and investment tax credit carry-forwards should be recognized as assets in a quasi-reorganization "only if realization is assured beyond a reasonable doubt." If realization is not assured at the quasi-reorganization date, the benefits realized at some future date should be credited to Capital in Excess of Par Value and not recorded as income.

The retained earnings account discloses the date of the quasi-reorganization, in order to indicate that the balance has been accumulated subsequently. SEC Regulation S-X requires that retained earnings be dated for 10 years and that the amount of deficit eliminated be disclosed for 3 years.

BIBLIOGRAPHY

Accounting Principles Board, (AICPA), *Status of Accounting Research Bulletins*, Opinion No. 6 (APB, 1965).

————, *Accounting for Income Taxes*, Opinion No. 11 (APB, 1967).

————, *Accounting for Convertible Debt and Debt Issued with Stock Purchase Warrants*, Opinion No. 14 (APB, 1969).

————, *Earnings per Share*, Opinion No. 15 (APB. 1969).

————, *Accounting for Stock Issued to Employees*, Opinion No. 25 (APB, 1972).

————, *Accounting for Nonmonetary Transactions*, Opinion No. 29 (APB, 1973).

————, *Stockholders' Equity*, Accounting Research Study No. 15 (APB, 1973).

Committee on Accounting Procedure (AICPA), *Restatement and Revision of Accounting Research Bulletins*, Accounting Research Bulletin No. 43 (CAP, 1953).

Davidson, S., C. P. Stickney, and R. L. Weil, *Intermediate Accounting* (Dryden Press, Hinsdale, Ill., 1980/81).

Financial Accounting Standards Board, *Accounting for Stock Appreciation Rights and Other Variable Stock Option or Award Plans*, FASB Interpretation No. 28 (FASB, 1978).

————, *Financial Reporting and Changing Prices*, Statement of Financial Accounting Standards No. 33 (FASB, 1979).

————, *Elements of Financial Statements of Business Enterprises*, Statement of Financial Accounting Concepts No. 3 (FASB, 1980).

————, *Treatment of Stock Compensation Plans in EPS Computations*, FASB Interpretation No. 31 (FASB, 1980).

————, *Determining Whether a Convertible Security Is a Common Stock Equivalent*, Statement of Financial Accounting Standards No. 55 (FASB, 1982).

Kieso, D. E., and J. J. Weygandt, *Intermediate Accounting* (John Wiley & Sons, New York, 1980).

Schattke, R. W., and H. G. Jensen, *Financial Accounting Concepts and Uses* (Allyn and Bacon, Boston, 1978).

Securities and Exchange Commission, *Form and Content of Financial Statements*, Regulation S-X.

————, *Codification of Staff Accounting Bulletins*, Staff Accounting Bulletin No. 40 (SEC, 1981).

————, *Financial Reporting Release No. 1* (SEC, 1982).

————, *Staff Position on Transfer of Assets by Promoters and Shareholders*, Staff Accounting Bulletin No. 48 (SEC, 1982).

CHAPTER 28

Retained Earnings

and Dividends

Oscar S. Gellein
Retired Partner, Deloitte Haskins & Sells
Former Member, Financial Accounting
Standards Board

Michael H. Sutton
Partner, Deloitte Haskins & Sells

Aurora M. Rubin
Partner, Deloitte Haskins & Sells

RETAINED EARNINGS

Definition. The capital of an enterprise is measured by the difference between its assets and its liabilities. Some of that capital represents amounts paid in or contributed by owners, as well as amounts deemed to have been contributed by owners as a result of stock dividends and other transactions with similar effects. That portion of enterprise capital generally is referred to in this chapter as *invested capital*. Another portion of enterprise capital represents accumulated undistributed earnings. For a business enterprise organized as a corporation, that portion of capital often is referred to as *retained earnings*. Balance sheets also may show elements of shareholders' equity other than invested capital and retained earnings. Examples are a valuation allowance for noncurrent marketable equity securities (required by FASB Statement No. 12 [1975]) and, although rarely found, appraisal capital.

Significance. In mathematical terms, retained earnings represents the accumulated net income of a corporation since its inception, reduced by distributions to shareholders and transfers to invested capital accounts, as well as certain charges and credits (some of which are commented upon later). If losses, dividend distributions, transfers, and other charges in the aggregate exceed income and other credits in total, the result is a *deficit*. Retained earnings may be subdivided or "appropriated" to indicate amounts judged to be not available for dividends currently for specified reasons. The absence of an appropriation, however, does not imply that assets equivalent to the retained earnings balance are necessarily available, immediately or otherwise, for distribution to shareholders, because funds derived from earnings may have been reinvested.

A business enterprise invests and deploys assets with the expectation of obtaining a return *of* and *on* its investment. Its capital is considered to have been maintained if the return is equal to or greater than its investment, and if the aggregate distribution to owners is not greater than the cumulative return on enterprise investments. Retained earnings, therefore, provides an ongoing measure of amounts that could be distributed to owners or otherwise diminished without impairing invested capital. (The foregoing comments are not intended to deal with questions of law concerning amounts available for dividends. That matter will be addressed later in this chapter.)

Terminology. Accounting Terminology Bulletin No. 1, issued in 1953 by the Committee on Terminology of the American Institute of Accountants (predecessor of the AICPA), recommended terms intended to show the source of earned capital, suggesting "retained income," "retained earnings," "accumulated earnings," or "earnings retained for use in the business." Terms consistent with that Bulletin are used in most published annual reports. The term "retained earnings" is generally used in this chapter.

Distinction between Retained Earnings and Invested Capital. Separate classification in the balance sheet of the components of shareholders' equity is a well-established reporting practice. For companies that report to the Securities and Exchange Commission, Rule 5-02(31) of Regulation S-X requires that the balance sheet contain separate captions for additional paid-in capital, other additional capital, and retained earnings (classified between appropriated and unappropriated). In addition, Rule 4-08(e) requires disclosure of the undistributed earnings of unconsolidated subsidiaries and 50 percent or less owned companies included in the amount of retained earnings.

Investors, creditors, and other users of financial statements may be interested in the distinction between retained earnings and invested capital for several reasons. Justifying the separate classification of shareholders' equity by source, Hendriksen [1977, p. 500] states:

> ... a description of the sources of capital provides information regarding the historical development and the current position of the corporation. Corporate growth provided through internal sources of funds is relevant information when compared with a firm that has grown entirely through the sale of preferred and common stocks or through the sale of debentures.

Sprouse and Moonitz [1962, p. 42] add:

A distinction between invested capital and retained earnings has relevance to stockholders. For example, when cash dividends are distributed, stockholders are entitled to assurance that they are based on current or past profits and do not constitute merely a return of some of the cash or other assets originally invested in the enterprise or of previous earnings converted into invested capital. The distinction between invested capital and retained earnings is also significant from the viewpoint of creditors. Invested capital constitutes a buffer against enterprise losses. These losses must exceed the amount of retained earnings and stockholders' invested capital before creditors' equities are impaired.

Differing views have been expressed about the relevance of that distinction, however. Welsch et al. [1979, p. 550], for example, maintain that accountants adhere to the concept of classifying capital by source not on theoretical grounds but "primarily to comply with legal requirements which are stated in the laws of the various states in terms of the sources of capital."

Further, it has been observed that when transfers are made from retained earnings to invested capital, the original classification by source is lost. FASB Statement of Financial Accounting Concepts No. 3 [1980, p. 64] notes:

> ... transactions and events such as stock dividends (proportional distributions of an enterprise's own stock accompanied by a transfer of retained or undistributed profit to capital stock and other contributed capital) and reacquisitions and reissues of ownership interests (commonly called treasury stock transactions in corporations) mix the sources and make tracing of sources impossible except by using essentially arbitrary allocations. Thus, categories labeled invested or contributed capital or earned capital may or may not accurately reflect the sources of equity of an enterprise.

As Accounting Research Study No. 15 [Melcher, 1973, p. 93] points out:

> Transfers from retained earnings to capital stock or additional capital obviously lose their original designation. Thus a general classification of capital surplus may include a conglomeration of items applicable to several classes of stock, either presently or previously outstanding. A few corporations describe additional capital as "capital contributed and earnings capitalized in excess of stated value of common stock." That caption, of course, tells something—differing components of equity are combined in one amount—but its only value is to serve as a flag.

It can be argued, however, that the event of committing retained earnings to invested capital establishes the source because it amounts to a distribution to shareholders who, in turn, have made an equivalent investment in the enterprise. Therefore, the original classification by source may not be lost after all.

Accepted departures from a classification based on source are found in financial statements of banks. Banks periodically transfer amounts from retained earnings to invested capital accounts in compliance with statutory requirements, to increase lending limits, or for other purposes. In addition, supervisory agencies frequently direct newly organized banks to transfer a portion of initial invested capital to retained earnings to avoid showing a deficit in retained earnings during their early years. As soon as profitable operations permit, however, the amount so transferred is required to be restored to invested capital.

Transactions Affecting Retained Earnings. Periodic income statements provide the measure of the principal element of retained earnings. Other transactions and events affecting the measure of retained earnings will be considered under the following classifications:

Restatements of prior period financial statements
Dividends and stock splits
Treasury stock transactions
Redemption of preferred stock
Subsidiary and investee transactions
Recapitalizations and reorganizations
Miscellaneous matters

RESTATEMENTS OF PRIOR PERIOD FINANCIAL STATEMENTS

Prior Period Adjustments. FASB Statement No. 16 [1977] eliminated the criteria for prior period adjustments provided in APB Opinion No. 9 [1966]. The Statement limits prior period adjustments to items of profit and loss related to the following:

Correction of an error in the financial statements of a prior period
Adjustments that result from realization of income tax benefits of preacquisition operating loss carry-forwards of purchased subsidiaries

All other items of profit and loss recognized during a discrete accounting period should be included in calculating net income for that period.

FASB Statement No. 16 does not affect the manner of reporting accounting changes required or permitted by existing APB Opinions, FASB Statements, and FASB Interpretations (some of which are discussed in succeeding paragraphs).

APB Opinion No. 20 [1971] defines errors as those accounting changes resulting from "mathematical mistakes, mistakes in the application of accounting principles, or oversight or misuse of facts that existed at the time the financial statements were prepared." A change to an accounting principle that is generally accepted from one that is not is considered to be a correction of an error. Errors do not include changes in accounting estimates that are the result of new information or subsequent developments that bring about better insight or improved judgment. Those changes would be accounted for in the period of change if the change affects that period only, or the period of the change and future periods if the change affects both.

APB Opinion No. 11 [1967] specifies that income tax benefits of preacquisition operating loss carry-forwards of purchased subsidiaries should be recognized as assets at the date of purchase only if their realization is assured beyond any reasonable doubt. Otherwise, they would be recognized only when realized, and would be recorded as retroactive adjustments of the purchase transaction.

Special Changes in Accounting Principle. APB Opinion No. 20 requires that most changes in accounting principle be reported by including the cumulative effect of the change in net income of the period of the change, with no restatement of amounts previously reported. Prior period restatement is limited to:

A change from the LIFO (last-in, first-out) method of inventory valuation to another method

A change in the method of accounting for long-term construction contracts

A change to or from the "full cost" method of accounting, which is used in the extractive industries

A change made when a company first issues its financial statements in connection with an initial public distribution of securities

Change in the Reporting Entity. A change resulting in financial statements that in effect are those of a different reporting entity should be reported by restating the financial statements of all prior periods. APB Opinion No. 20 indicates that this type of change is limited mainly to:

Presenting consolidated or combined statements in place of statements of individual companies

Changing specific subsidiaries comprising the group of companies for which consolidated financial statements are presented

Changing the companies included in combined financial statements

Combining companies in a pooling of interests (for a more detailed discussion of this topic, refer to Chapter 33)

Adoption of Accounting Pronouncements. Authoritative pronouncements of accounting rule-making bodies, including the APB and the FASB, and Accounting and Audit Guides and Statements of Position issued by the AICPA, may require or permit retroactive application by restatement of financial statements presented for prior periods. Examples of such changes are the following:

Accounting for investments in certain affiliated companies under the equity method in accordance with APB Opinion No. 18 [1971]

Deferral of certain fees in accordance with the AICPA Industry Audit Guide, *Audits of Finance Companies* [1973]

Capitalization of certain leases to comply with FASB Statement No. 13 [1976]

Accruals of liabilities for compensated absences in accordance with FASB Statement No. 43 [1980], as illustrated in the following note to the financial statements included in the 1980 annual report of Geo. A. Hormel & Company:

> ... effective October 28, 1979, the Company changed its method of accounting for compensated absences from the cash to the accrual basis to comply with the Financial Accounting Standards Board Statement No. 43. Earnings reinvested in business as of October 28, 1978, have been restated for the cumulative effect of this change on prior years' net earnings. Net earnings for the years ended October 25, 1980, and October 27, 1979, are $794,000 and $642,000 lower, net of tax effect, respectively, as a result of the change.

Exhibit 1 shows the related statement of changes in consolidated shareholders' investment for this change in accounting.

Financial Statement Presentation. If financial statements presented for prior periods are restated, the adjustment for the cumulative effect on prior periods' earnings usually appears in the statement of retained earnings or statement of changes in shareholders' equity as illustrated in Exhibit 1.

A footnote to the financial statements for the year in which the adjustment is made should disclose the effects of the adjustment (both the gross amount and its effect on net income) for all prior periods presented. Similar disclosure is recommended in interim reports issued during the year subsequent to the recording of such adjustment. For corrections of errors, special changes in accounting principles, and changes in the reporting entity discussed previously, disclosure of the effect on income before extraordinary items and earnings per share also is required. In addition, disclosure of the nature of and justification for changes in accounting principle is required. For poolings of interests, special disclosure rules apply (see Chapter 33). Financial statements for years sub-

EXHIBIT 1   Illustration of Statement of Changes in Consolidated Shareholders' Investment

GEO. A. HORMEL & COMPANY AND SUBSIDIARIES

	Common stock	Additional paid-in capital	Earnings reinvested in business
Balance at October 28, 1978, as previously reported	$9,006,109	$2,761,377	$155,102,533
Cumulative effect to October 28, 1978, of accounting change less related taxes of $5,652,107—Note F . . .			(6,123,116)
Balance at October 28, 1978, restated	$9,006,109	$2,761,377	$148,979,417
Net earnings for the year 1979 as previously reported			30,612,215
Effect of accounting change less related taxes of $609,535—Note F			(642,333)
Cash dividends declared— $.74 a share			(7,108,821)
Balance at October 27, 1979, restated	$9,006,109	$2,761,377	$171,840,478
Net earnings for the year			32,758,220
Cash dividends declared— $.84 a share			(8,069,473)
Balance at October 25, 1980.	$9,006,109	$2,761,377	$196,529,225

sequent to the year in which the adjustment is made need not repeat the disclosures.

DIVIDENDS

Nature and Forms. A *dividend* represents a distribution by a corporation to a class of shareholders, proportional to the number of shares held. If the term is used without qualification or other description, there is a presumption that the distribution reduces retained earnings, and is not a return in whole or in part of invested capital or capital arising from a source other than earnings. The distribution may comprise corporate assets (or a claim against corporate assets), or it may consist of stock of the corporation of the same or a different class. The latter type, labeled a stock dividend, in a real sense is not a distribution at all, because it merely results in a transfer from retained earnings to invested capital, with no change in total shareholders' equity. Cash commonly is used to pay dividends other than stock dividends.

A distribution may reduce working capital or other assets, or increase liabilities. The source of a distribution may be retained earnings, hence a distribution of profits, or invested capital, resulting in a return of shareholder investment.

Regardless of source, dividends and any resulting distributions are not expenses and, therefore, do not affect the computation of net income. As noted in FASB Statement of Financial Accounting Concepts No. 3 [1980, p. 6], shareholders expect to be adequately compensated—that is, they expect to receive appropriate returns on their investments commensurate with their risks. From a financial standpoint, corporate management may consider dividends to be part of the overall cost of capital.

Dividend Policy. Major factors influencing a corporation's dividend policy include:

Statutes defining sources for distribution
Governmental regulations
Restrictive covenants in indentures and other contractual limitations
Profitability and stability of profits
Liquidity and resources available for distribution
Rate of growth and plans for business expansion
Access to and status of capital markets
Tax considerations

Apart from limitations imposed by those factors, however, the amount and manner of each dividend distribution generally are determined by the board of directors.

The SEC encourages corporations to disclose their dividend policy in annual reports provided to shareholders and in their annual reports on Form 10-K to the SEC. Accounting Series Release No. 279, issued in 1980, provides that corporations that (1) have not paid dividends despite available earnings and (2) do not intend to pay cash dividends in the foreseeable future are encouraged to state that fact. Also, those with a history of paying dividends are encouraged to indicate whether they expect to continue paying dividends in the future. The 1980 annual report of Merck & Co., Inc., contains the following management discussion relative to the company's dividend policy:

> Maintenance of a strong financial position has permitted the Company to finance growth over the last decade in its capital asset base and dividends to stockholders predominantly from internally generated funds. The trend of sources and applications of funds is:

	Two year (1979–1980)	Five year (1976–1980)	Ten year (1971–1980)
	Sources		
Net income	78%	77%	72%
Depreciation and deferred taxes	20%	21%	19%
Funds from operations	98%	98%	91%
Proceeds from stock options	2%	2%	2%
Long-term debt			7%
Total	100%	100%	100%
	Applications		
Expenditures for property, plant, and equipment	42%	43%	44%
Dividends to stockholders	32%	32%	33%
Purchase of treasury stock	9%	4%	3%
Other, including increase in working capital	17%	21%	20%
Total	100%	100%	100%

> In comparison with the most recent two-year period, no significant change is foreseen for the near future in the trend of sources and applications of funds, except for the increase in the authorized amount of treasury stock purchases in 1981 to $100 million. Purchases of common stock for the treasury in 1980 were $47 million.

Sources of Dividends and Legality. The sources of capital available for dividends are governed by the laws of each state; there is considerable diversity in the laws. Although it is beyond the scope of this chapter to analyze those laws, the following excerpt from Welsch et al. [1979, pp. 582–583] illustrates some of the more typical variations:

> There are at least two provisions which appear uniform—namely, that dividends may not be paid from *legal capital* (usually represented by the capital *stock* accounts) and that unappropriated retained earnings are available for dividends. Aside from these two provisions, there are numerous variations, depending upon the respective state statutes, such as the following:
>
> 1. All contributed capital, other than legal capital, is available for dividends.

2. Specified items of contributed capital, other than legal capital, are available for dividends.

3. Contributed capital, other than legal capital, is available for dividends on preferred stock but not on common stock.

4. Unrealized capital is not available for dividends.

5. Unrealized capital is available for stock dividends only.

6. Debits in the contributed capital accounts and a deficit in Retained Earnings must be restored before payment of any dividends.

7. Dividends from Retained Earnings must not reduce the Retained Earnings balance below the cost of treasury stock held.

The accountant has a responsibility in circumstances where the propriety and legality of dividends are at issue to (a) ensure that such matters are referred to an attorney and (b) ascertain that the financial statements fully disclose all known and material facts concerning such dividends.

A corporation that declares and pays dividends from sources other than retained earnings should disclose the attending circumstances in its financial statements.

PROPERTY DIVIDENDS

Although not a common practice, corporations occasionally distribute assets other than cash as dividends to shareholders. For example, dividends may be paid in shares of stock of another company. Dividends paid in assets other than cash are called *property dividends* or *dividends in kind*. Generally, property dividends are taxable to the recipient on the basis of the fair market value of the property on the date distributed, and the distributing corporation realizes no gain or loss for federal income tax purposes. The accounting treatment may differ, however, from the tax treatment. APB Opinion No. 29 [1973] provides that nonreciprocal transfers of nonmonetary assets to owners "should be accounted for at fair value if the fair value of the nonmonetary asset distributed is objectively measurable and would be clearly realizable to the distributing entity in an outright sale at or near the time of distribution." Exempted from this provision are "distributions to owners of an enterprise in a spin-off or other form of reorganization or liquidation [to be discussed in a subsequent section of this chapter] or in a plan that is in substance the rescission of a prior business combination" and a "pro rata distribution to owners of an enterprise of shares of a subsidiary or other investee company that has been or is being accounted for under the equity method." Also exempted are transfers solely between companies or persons under common control. The recorded amounts of the assets distributed, after giving effect to any impairment of value, are used in accounting for these exempted distributions.

If the fair value of the property dividend is not determinable within reasonable limits, the accounting also should be based on the recorded amount of the assets distributed, and, accordingly, no gain or loss would be recognized. APB Opinion No. 29 provides that fair value should be regarded as not determinable within reasonable limits if there are major uncertainties about the realizability of the fair value that would be assigned. If a property dividend is paid, required disclosures include a statement concerning the nature of the transaction, the basis of accounting for the assets transferred, and any gains or losses recognized.

SCRIP DIVIDENDS

Although rarely done, a corporation may distribute scrip or promissory notes as a dividend. A liability for the scrip or note and a corresponding charge to retained earnings are recorded when the distribution is made. Interest payments are not part of the dividend and, accordingly, should be charged to operations as incurred.

LIQUIDATING DIVIDENDS

Shareholders generally expect to receive income distributions on their investment before any return of their capital. Accordingly, a corporation is expected to exhaust its retained earnings before charging invested capital for a dividend distribution. An exception occurs when a corporation declares liquidating dividends.

A *liquidating dividend* is a special distribution reducing invested capital accounts. As noted in Accounting Research Study No. 7 [Grady, 1965, pp. 200–201], liquidating dividends may be paid to effect a shrinking or dissolution of a corporation:

> Dividends paid with the express intent of reducing the capital of the corporation, and with a view toward partial or complete dissolution, are known as liquidating dividends or distributions of capital. Accounting for these dividends should follow the intent expressed in resolutions of the directors or stockholders. When a liquidating dividend has been declared and all the legal steps taken requisite to the reduction of the stock, but the payments to stockholders have not been made, the balance sheet should show the outstanding stock at its reduced amount and the liquidating dividend as a current liability, adequately described.

Liquidating dividends are not uncommon for companies with wasting assets, such as mining companies. Paton [1941, pp. 385, 394] notes that for these companies, "it is not necessary to deduct the expiring cost of property not subject to replacement in ascertaining the amount legally available for distribution to the stockholders." Thus, "funds may accumulate for return to stockholders representing liquidation of depreciable assets which will not require replacement as well as liquidation of the mineral deposit or similar resource." Further, Simons [1972, p. 742] states that:

> Corporations owning wasting assets may regularly declare dividends that are in part a distribution of earnings and in part a distribution of the corporation's invested capital. Entries on the corporation books for such dividend declarations should reflect the decrease in the two capital elements. This information should be reported to stockholders so that they may recognize dividends as representing in part income and in part a return of investment.

CONSTRUCTIVE DIVIDENDS

Under Section 301 of the Internal Revenue Code, informal distributions to shareholders without board approval are treated as dividends for income tax purposes if made by a corporation "with respect to its stock," unless the distribution is in satisfaction of a shareholder's claim as a creditor. Any difference between the exchange price and the fair value of assets or services transferred in a transaction between a corporation and its shareholders may be treated similarly. Such informal distributions, sometimes called "constructive dividends," include compensation considered excessive by the Internal Revenue Service, reimbursement of a shareholder's personal expenses, and payments to shareholders for rent, interest, and the purchase of assets in excess of the fair value of the consideration received by the corporation.

Although the corporation will not be allowed a tax deduction for a distribution treated as a constructive dividend, it may be appropriate to record the distribution as a charge to income (rather than as a dividend) for accounting purposes. For example, salaries or bonuses paid to shareholder-employees may be considered excessive by the Internal Revenue Service. Those payments should be reflected as an expense if they are deemed to represent compensation, despite the contrary position of the Internal Revenue Service, recognizing that generally there is no objective standard for measuring the value of personal services.

The appropriate accounting treatment of transactions with shareholders in which the exchange price differs from fair value is not clearly defined. In some instances any excess of the exchange price over fair value, based on appraisals or amounts charged or paid to unrelated parties, is treated as a contribution to capital, or as a dividend in the reverse situation. In other instances these transactions are recorded at the exchange prices, and the nature and amounts of these transactions are disclosed in the financial statements. These differing treatments have not been resolved, although this question was the subject of a 1969 exposure draft of an APB Opinion. The Board at that time generally advocated full disclosure without giving accounting recognition to fair values. An Opinion on the subject was never issued.

Before recording a charge to retained earnings for a constructive dividend not distributed to all shareholders in proportion to their respective share ownership, the corporation should ascertain the legal implications of the transaction. A preferential distribution may be illegal in the state of incorporation, and as such may establish a claim against the recipients.

SIGNIFICANT DIVIDEND DATES

Date of Declaration. The formal announcement of the board of directors' intention to issue a cash, property, or scrip dividend establishes a liability, which usually cannot be rescinded without shareholder consent (exceptions include fraudulent or illegal dividends—an attorney should be consulted if in doubt). The dividend liability should be recorded as of the declaration date, even though the payment date may be sometime in the future.

Date of Record. The date of record is generally a few weeks after the date of declaration, and is used to establish the list of shareholders entitled to receive the dividend. If shares are traded between the date of declaration and the date of payment, the holder on the date of record is entitled to receive the dividends. As a practical matter, however, listed stocks are usually traded "ex-dividend" on the fourth business day preceding the record date, so that the list of shareholders eligible for the dividend can be compiled on a timely basis.

Date of Payment. The date of payment generally follows the date of record by a few weeks, and marks the actual distribution of cash, property, or scrip.

STOCK DIVIDENDS AND STOCK SPLITS

Definitions. A *stock dividend* is defined by the Committee on Accounting Procedure of the AICPA in Accounting Research Bulletin No. 43 [1953, chap. 7B] as:

> ... an issuance by a corporation of its own common shares to its common shareholders without consideration and under conditions indicating that such action is prompted mainly by a desire to give the recipient shareholders some ostensibly separate evidence of a part of their respective interests in accumulated corporate earnings without distribution of cash or other property which the board of directors deems necessary or desirable to retain in the business.

The Bulletin defines a *stock split* as:

> ... an issuance by a corporation of its own common shares to its own common shareholders without consideration and under conditions indicating that such action is prompted mainly by a desire to increase the number of outstanding shares for the purpose of effecting a reduction in their unit market price and, thereby, of obtaining wider distribution and improved marketability of the shares.

Thus, the basic distinction for accounting purposes between a stock dividend and a stock split is in the underlying intention of the corporation. If the intention is to transfer part of retained earnings to invested capital (sometimes referred to as a "permanent capitalization of retained earnings"), the transaction should be accounted for as a stock dividend; if the distribution is intended to bring about a reduction of the market price of outstanding shares, the transaction should be accounted for as a stock split. The effect of the transaction, however, must be consistent with the intention. ARB No. 43 indicates that the intended effect of a stock dividend would ordinarily be accomplished if the additional shares issued did not exceed 20 to 25 percent of the number previously outstanding. A greater distribution ordinarily would constitute a stock split.

The New York Stock Exchange rules for listed companies are somewhat more precise. Any share distribution of less than 25 percent is considered to be a stock dividend, whereas distributions of 25 percent or more are considered to be stock splits. The Exchange stipulates, however, that splits of 25 to 100 percent of the previously outstanding shares may require treatment as stock dividends if "in the opinion of the Exchange, such distributions assume the character of stock dividends through repetition under circumstances not consistent with the true intent and purpose of stock split-ups."

The SEC, in Accounting Series Release No. 124, issued in 1972, adopted a policy similar to that of the New York Stock Exchange. That Release provides that distributions of less than 25 percent of the shares outstanding, and those over 25 percent if "part of a program of recurring distributions designed to mislead shareholders," should be accounted for as stock dividends.

Accounting for a Stock Split. The accounting for a stock split recognizes that there is no intention to distribute accumulated earnings. Accordingly, no accounting entries are required if the par or stated value is proportionately reduced in relation to the amount of the stock split. For example, an issue of shares equal to 100 percent of the number of shares previously outstanding is accompanied by a change from a $1 par value stock to a 50 cents par value stock. If the par or stated value is not reduced, or the reduction is not in proportion to the amount of the stock split, transfers from invested capital or retained earnings are necessary. An example of such a transfer is disclosed in the 1980 annual report of R. H. Macy & Co., Inc.:

> On January 22, 1980, the Board of Directors authorized a three-for-two stock split of the common shares, distributed on April 1, 1980. The stock split was accounted for by transferring $20,419,000 from additional paid-in capital to common shares. No change has been made in the assigned value of the common shares.

At times, a stock split is effected in the form of a dividend, and it is difficult to avoid using the term "dividend," either in the announcement of the stock split or in the disclosure of the transaction in the financial statements. In those situations, a description such as "stock split effected in the form of a dividend" is desirable to make the substance of the transaction clear.

Accounting for a Stock Dividend. In accounting for a stock dividend, an amount of retained earnings equivalent to the fair value of the additional shares issued is transferred to invested capital, as exemplified by the following disclosure taken from the 1979 annual report of The Cessna Aircraft Company:

> In November 1979 Cessna paid a 5% common stock dividend and in connection therewith credited paid-in surplus $15,737,119 for the difference between the market value, $16,620,754, charged to earnings reinvested in business, and $883,635 for the par value of the shares issued.

Accounting Research Bulletin No. 43 provides that:

> ... the corporation should in the public interest account for the transaction by transferring from earned surplus to the category of permanent capitalization (represented by the capital stock and capital surplus accounts) an amount equal to the fair value of the additional shares issued. Unless this is done, the amount of earnings which the shareholder may believe to have been distributed to him will be left, except to the extent otherwise dictated

by legal requirements, in earned surplus subject to possible further similar stock issuances or cash distributions.

Fair value often will exceed the legal minimum requirement (usually par or stated value). The most reasonable measure of the fair value would seem to be the market price at or near the date of declaration of the dividend, and in practice this price is the most widely used. However, market prices at other dates, such as date of record or date of issuance, or appropriate average market prices for appropriate periods are used on occasion.

The New York Stock Exchange has developed standards of disclosure which require that, in addition to the required accounting disclosures, the following information should be disclosed in shareholder notices of stock dividends:

The amounts capitalized per share and the aggregate amount thereof

The relation of the aggregate amount to current undistributed earnings

The account or accounts to which the aggregate amount has been charged or credited

The reason for issuing the stock dividend

The fact that the sale of the dividend shares would reduce the shareholders' proportionate equity

Accounting Series Release No. 124 expresses the view of the SEC about the issuance of stock dividends if retained earnings are not sufficient to cover the required transfer to invested capital. Such transactions are considered to be "characteristic of a manipulative scheme." The Release also cautions that if the accounting for the transaction is improper, or disclosure is inadequate, the SEC will deem the transaction to be misleading.

Exceptions. The accounting and disclosure guidelines for stock dividends generally are intended to obviate misconceptions by shareholders as to the effect of a stock dividend distribution on their equity in the issuing company as well as its relation to the company's current earnings. Shareholders of closely held companies may be expected to have an intimate knowledge of their companies' affairs. For those companies, therefore, transfers from retained earnings for stock dividend distributions need not exceed legal requirements.

Banks have customarily accounted for stock dividends by transferring the par value of the shares issued from their surplus account to capital stock (both of which are invested capital accounts). In many cases, an amount is also transferred from their retained earnings to surplus, but not usually in an amount equal to the fair values of the additional stock issued. The exposure draft of the proposed AICPA industry audit guide for banks, issued in 1980, would require conformity with the generally accepted accounting principle prescribed for stock dividends [Banking Committee, 1980, p. 126].

Criticism of Current Accounting Practices. Criticism of the current accounting practices for stock distributions generally centers on the distinction made between stock splits and stock dividends. Arguments against current practice can be summarized as follows (an expanded discussion is presented by Melcher in Accounting Research Study No. 15 [1973, pp. 213–220]):

The dividing line between stock splits and stock dividends of 20 to 25 percent of the currently outstanding stock is arbitrary and has no theoretically or empirically justifiable basis.

There is no difference between a stock split and a stock dividend, in that the only change brought about is in the proportionate ownership of the corporation represented by one share of stock. The proportionate interest of each stockholder is the same before and after the distribution.

The rationale for distinguishing a stock dividend from a stock split espoused by *ARB No. 43* is that "many recipients of stock dividends look upon them as distributions of corporate earnings and usually in an amount equivalent to the fair value of the additional shares received." Thus, while recognizing that in theory there is no effective difference between a stock dividend and a stock split, the *Bulletin* bases its conclusion on an assumption about stockholder reaction.

The effect on retained earnings is misleading. Distribution of a small number of shares may reduce retained earnings more than the distribution of a large number of shares.

Empirical studies [Melcher, 1973, p. 215] indicate that the stock market eventually discounts the effect of a stock dividend, thus invalidating the assertion in the *Bulletin* that, in most cases, stock dividends "do not have any apparent effect upon the share market price and, consequently, the market value of the shares previously held remains substantially unchanged."

Reverse Stock Splits. A *reverse stock split* is a proportional contraction of the number of outstanding shares without a concurrent distribution of assets to shareholders. Like a regular stock split, no accounting entries are required if the par or stated value is increased in proportion to the amount of the reverse split. If the par or stated value is not increased and, accordingly, a reduction of the stated capital account is necessary, the entry would be to increase additional paid-in capital rather than retained earnings.

An example of a reverse stock split is disclosed in the 1979 annual report of Titan Group, Inc.:

Pursuant to the one-for-ten reverse stock split which was approved by the shareholders at the June 28, 1979, Annual Meeting, and which became effective upon the close of business on July 31, 1979, the Company's outstanding shares were pro-rata reduced with minor adjustment for fractional shares and $5,410,000 was reclassified from Common Stock to Additional Paid-in Capital.

Fractional Shares. Stock dividends generally give rise to fractional share interests. For example, an investor holding 75 shares would, after declaration of a 2 percent stock dividend, be entitled to 1½ additional shares. Because only whole shares are usually issued, the fractional share interests are commonly settled by issuing scrip certificates or payments in cash. If immediate cash payment is made, retained earnings are charged for the full share distribution, and the cash portion is accounted for as a cash dividend. Usually, scrip certificates do not carry rights associated with share ownership, have limited life, and may be traded. Often the issuing corporation designates a trustee to purchase and sell scrip certificates on its behalf, and to redeem them for full shares. When scrip is issued, a transfer is made from retained earnings to a fractional share interest account, which is closed to capital stock as the scrip is redeemed for shares. Forfeited amounts may be transferred to additional paid-in capital, if statutes so provide, or returned to retained earnings.

Stock Dividends or Stock Splits—Treasury Stock. Practice varies as to whether any treasury shares participate in the distribution accompanying a stock dividend or stock split. Practice may be influenced by the planned use of the treasury shares. For example, if the treasury shares are intended for issuance in connection with employee stock options, the number of shares under option is usually adjusted for any stock dividends or splits, and the treasury shares, accordingly, may participate in the distribution. Unless there are reasons such as this for doing so, no useful purpose is served by allowing treasury shares to participate in the additional distribution, because they are essentially equivalent to authorized but unissued shares. The legal requirements of some states specifically prohibit considering treasury shares as outstanding when issuing stock dividends.

Date of Recording a Stock Dividend. Welsch et al. [1979, p. 575] describe how the courts view the declaration of stock dividends in relation to the declaration of cash, other property, or scrip dividends:

> ... In the absence of fraud or illegality, the courts have held that formal announcement of the declaration of a cash, property, or liability dividend constitutes an enforceable contract (i.e., an irrevocable declaration) between the corporation and the shareholders. In view of the irrevocability of this action, such dividends are recorded on declaration date. In the case of *stock dividends*, no assets are involved, directly or indirectly, as far as the corporation is concerned; therefore, the courts generally have held that a stock dividend declaration is revocable. Consequently, no entry is made on declaration date in the case of a stock dividend.

Accountants generally recommend the recording of a stock dividend at the date of declaration, but also recognize the acceptability of deferring the recording until the date of issuance, provided that disclosure of the declaration is made in financial statements. Although deferral of the recording could be justified on the grounds that stock dividends, unlike cash dividends, can be rescinded by the company's directors prior to issuance, the SEC prefers the recording of such dividends when declared, because such rescissions are rare. Furthermore, if the stock dividends are declared after the date of the financial statements but before the financial statements are issued, the SEC requires that retroactive effect be given to the change in capital structure as of the date of the financial statements.

Stock dividends declared are commonly presented separately in the balance sheet under common stock at the par or stated value of the shares to be issued, the market value of the dividend having been charged to retained earnings, and any excess of market value over par or stated value credited to additional paid-in capital.

Effect of Stock Dividend or Stock Split on Earnings per Share. APB Opinion No. 15 [1969] states that:

> If the number of common shares outstanding increases as a result of a stock dividend or stock split or decreases as a result of a reverse split, the computations [of earnings per share] should give retroactive recognition to an appropriate equivalent change in capital structure for all periods presented. If changes in common stock resulting from stock dividends or stock splits or reverse splits have been consummated after the close of the period but before completion of the financial report, the per share computations should be based on the new number of shares because the readers' primary interest is presumed to be related to the current capitalization. When per share computations reflect such changes in the number of shares after the close of the period, this fact should be disclosed.

DIVIDENDS ON PREFERRED STOCK

The accounting for cash dividends on preferred stock is similar to the accounting for cash dividends on common stock. The preferred stock may be cumulative or noncumulative. Cumulative preferred stock with a stipulated dividend rate is entitled to receive any arrearage of dividends previously passed plus the amount currently payable before any dividends are paid on common stock. An arrearage in preferred stock dividends ordinarily is not a liability to be reflected in the balance sheet, because the liability for a dividend arises only as a result of the declaration of a dividend by the board of directors. Nonetheless, the amount of dividend arrearage, both per share of preferred stock and in total, should be disclosed for each class of preferred shares.

Some preferred stocks subject to mandatory redemption requirements provide that the redemption price include any accumulated but unpaid dividends ("dividends in arrears"). In those cases, a strong argument can be made for accruing those dividends (by charging retained earnings) over the period that the issue is outstanding. Accrual would be consistent with the objectives of accreting the difference between the carrying value and the mandatory redemption price of the stocks. Those objectives are (1) to have a carrying amount equivalent to the mandatory redemption price at the date of redemption, and (2) to adjust, for purposes of computing earnings per common share, any cash dividends paid during the period the issue is outstanding for the additional payment required on redemption of the preferred stock.

Any accounting for dividends in arrears on redeemable preferred stock should be based on the specific terms of the issue and expectations of payment. In some cases, dividends in arrears may be expected to be paid within a relatively short period of time or at a date prior to redemption. In those circumstances, accrual of an undeclared dividend as a current liability or as a current addition to the carrying value of the preferred stock may be appropriate. In other cases, it may be expected that dividends in arrears will be paid only at redemption, even though future dividends may be expected to be declared and paid currently. In those circumstances, accretion of a dividend in arrears over the remaining period the issue is outstanding, using the interest method (see paragraphs 16 and 17 of APB Opinion No. 12 [1967]), may be appropriate.

If redeemable preferred stocks are in fact debt instruments and, accordingly, presented as liabilities on the balance sheet, related dividends should be accounted for as interest expense.

DIVIDENDS OF COMPANIES WITH SPECIAL TAX STATUS

The dividends of certain companies are often based on the minimum amounts required to be paid to maintain a special tax status. For example, qualifying regulated investment companies and real estate investment trusts pay federal income taxes only on undistributed income if dividends paid are at least 90 percent of their otherwise taxable income. An illustrative disclosure of the tax status and dividend policy of such companies is included in the 1981 annual report of the Adams Express Company:

> No provision has been made for Federal income taxes on net investment income, capital gain or net unrealized appreciation of investments since it is the policy of the Company to comply with the provisions available to investment companies as defined in applicable sections of the Internal Revenue Code and to make distributions of investment income and capital gains sufficient to relieve it from all, or substantially all, Federal income taxes.

"Small business corporations," as defined in Section 1371 of the Internal Revenue Code (Subchapter S corporations), may elect to have their income taxed directly to shareholders, which is similar to the tax treatment of a partnership. As a result, the dividend policy of many Subchapter S corporations is to provide the shareholders with sufficient cash for payment of taxes on their proportionate share of the corporation's taxable income. Other Subchapter S corporations may distribute all, or substantially all, of their income as dividends. The tax status and dividend policy of a Subchapter S corporation and any estimated dividend requirements not declared at the date of the financial statements should be disclosed.

TREASURY STOCK TRANSACTIONS

The acquisition of a corporation's own preferred or common shares, or rights, warrants, or options to purchase such shares may result in reductions of retained earnings in certain circumstances. This matter is dealt with extensively in Chapter 27.

REDEMPTION OF PREFERRED STOCK

The redemption price of a redeemable preferred stock frequently will differ from the proceeds or fair value of the stock at the date of issue. Differences exist, for example, if preferred stock issued at par is redeemable at a premium or discount, or if preferred stock redeemable at par is issued at a premium or discount.

If redemption is not mandatory (for example, if it is callable at the option of the corporation), the preferred stock is generally recorded at the issue price (proceeds or fair value of the consideration received), with any excess of the issue price over par or stated value being credited to some other invested capital account. On redemption, all invested capital balances relating to the shares redeemed are removed from the accounts; any loss is charged to retained earnings; and any gain is credited to another invested capital account, appropriately titled.

On the other hand, preferred stock subject to mandatory redemption requirements may be recorded at the date of issue at either (1) the issue price, with any excess of issue price over par or stated value credited to another invested capital account, as explained above, or (2) the redemption price, with any excess of redemption price over par or stated value being credited to an account described as, for example, "additional amount due on redemption." If a redeemable preferred stock is initially recorded at the redemption price, any excess of the redemption price over the issue price should be recorded in an account described as, for example, "redemption price in excess of issue price." That account is contra to the preferred stock account and would be shown as a deduction from the carrying amount of preferred stock.

If redeemable preferred stock is assigned a value upon issuance that is less than the redemption price, this difference is accreted using the interest method, most often by making periodic charges to retained earnings. The annual accretion should be deducted from net income in computing earnings applicable to common stock. If redeemable preferred stock is assigned a value upon issuance that is greater than the redemption price, alternatives have been used to account for this credit difference. One is to credit the difference initially to an invested capital account applicable to common stock; the other is to amortize it to retained earnings as described above.

The 1981 annual report of Tenneco, Inc., illustrates the difference in financial statement presentation of preferred stock with and without mandatory redemption provisions. As to the stock with mandatory redemption provisions, a note to the company's financial statements states:

> Tenneco, Inc., has recorded the preference stock at its fair value at date of issue (approximately $430 million) and is making periodic accretions of the excess of the redemption value over the fair value at date of issue. Such accretions are included in preference stock dividends as a reduction of net income to arrive at net income to common stock.

On the other hand, the preferred stock without mandatory redemption provisions is extended on the balance sheet at par value, with a note disclosing its redemption value.

SUBSIDIARY AND INVESTEE TRANSACTIONS

Stock Dividends of Subsidiaries. Occasionally, a subsidiary will declare a stock dividend or effect a stock split, thus permanently capitalizing a portion of the subsidiary's retained earnings. This raises the question of whether the transaction should be recorded similarly in the consolidated financial statements. On this point, ARB No. 51 [CAP, 1959] states that:

> This does not require a transfer to capital surplus on consolidation, inasmuch as the retained earnings in the consolidated financial statements should reflect the accumulated earnings of the consolidated group not distributed to the shareholders of, or capitalized by, the parent company.

It is appropriate, where material, to disclose that consolidated retained earnings include specified portions of subsidiary retained earnings that have been permanently capitalized.

Retained Earnings of Subsidiary as Source of Parent's Dividend. As stated in ARB No. 43, the retained earnings of a subsidiary accumulated prior to acquiring the subsidiary are not part of consolidated retained earnings; and any dividends declared and paid to the parent from those earnings should be treated as a return of invested capital by the parent. Earnings accumulated by the subsidiary after acquisition may not be available, of course, for distribution to the parent because of contractual commitments. Any such restrictions causing a material portion of consolidated retained earnings to be unavailable for dividends should be disclosed.

The availability of unremitted subsidiary retained earnings for distribution by a parent is a complicated legal question, which should be resolved through consultation with an attorney. Of course, a parent may be able to avoid this difficulty by having the subsidiary declare and pay a dividend from its unrestricted retained earnings, thus resulting directly in an increase in parent company retained earnings.

Issue of Subsidiary Stock. The accounting for an issue of subsidiary stock generally is determined by whether previously unissued shares are issued by the subsidiary or whether the parent sells some of its holdings. As pointed out by Nemec [1973, p. 214]:

> When the offering takes the form of the subsidiary's direct sale of a number of unissued shares, the resulting change (usually an increase) in the parent's equity in the subsidiary's net assets is shown as additional contributed capital. However, if a portion of the parent's holdings in the subsidiary is sold in a secondary offering, the transaction is reported in the statement of earnings. A combination offering of unissued shares and shares owned by the parent may also be made, in which case the two segments are accounted for separately in the consolidated statements as additional contributed capital and earnings.

The SEC has required that the issuance of a subsidiary's stock that increases the parent's equity in the subsidiary should be treated in consolidated financial statements as an adjustment to invested capital, rather than as a gain.

Treating the issuance of additional shares by the subsidiary as a capital transaction in the consolidated financial statements may be based on the theory that equity financing by a subsidiary results in an infusion of paid-in capital and as such should not give rise to income in the consolidated financial statements, whereas a parent's sale of subsidiary stock results in a partial divestiture requiring gain or loss recognition. In addition, the latter transaction results in a direct cash flow to the parent, whereas the former does not.

On the other hand, some would argue that in consolidated financial statements, a gain or loss is recognizable on a sale of subsidiary stock whether the sale is made by the subsidiary or the parent, just as APB Opinion No. 18 would require with respect to unconsolidated subsidiaries. The FASB has indicated that it will address this matter when it considers the whole issue of consolidation accounting.

Subsidiary Purchase of Parent Company Stock or Its Own Stock. The purchase of parent company stock by a subsidiary is treated in consolidated financial statements as though the parent had acquired its own stock. ARB No. 51 states that "shares of the parent held by a subsidiary should not be treated as outstanding stock in the consolidated balance sheet." Meyer [1973, p. 1019] also notes that "when a subsidiary owns stock of its parent . . . the cost of the subsidiary's investment would be an aggregate deduction from total consolidation net worth . . . [and] individual net worth accounts are reduced in what becomes a modified version of the constructive retirement approach to treasury stock." This approach is also supported by a committee of the American Accounting Association [1955, p. 196]:

> Shares of the controlling company's capital stock owned by a subsidiary before the date of acquisition of control should be treated in consolidation as treasury stock. Any subsequent acquisition or sale by a subsidiary should likewise be treated in the consolidated statements as though it had been the act of the controlling company.

A purchase by a subsidiary of its own stock is treated similarly, except that the usual procedure is to reduce shareholders' equity in consolidated financial statements only to the extent of the parent's equity in the cost of the subsidiary's treasury stock. Literature supports this approach (see Griffin et al. [1980, pp. 414–416] for a detailed presentation of the entries required by the parent and eliminations in consolidation).

Capital Transactions of Investees. APB Opinion No. 18 requires that "a transaction of an investee of a capital nature that affects the investor's share of stockholders' equity of the investee should be accounted for as if the investee were a consolidated subsidiary." Thus, if an unconsolidated subsidiary or qualifying affiliate engages in any of the transactions discussed in this section, appropriate capital adjustments should be made by the investor.

RECAPITALIZATIONS AND REORGANIZATIONS

Increase in Par Value. A recapitalization that increases the par or stated value of shares may require capitalization of retained earnings. For example, assume that a corporation has the following equity accounts:

Capital stock, par value $10, 1,000 shares issued and outstanding	$ 10,000
Additional paid-in capital arising from capital stock issuance	65,000
Retained earnings	150,000

If the corporation decides to increase the par value of its shares to $100, the following entry is made:

Capital Stock, $10 Par Value	10,000	
Additional Paid-in Capital	65,000	
Retained Earnings	25,000	
Capital Stock, $100 Par Value		100,000

A reduction in par value, in contrast, cannot increase retained earnings. Thus, the entire reduction in par or stated value would be transferred to additional paid-in capital.

A recapitalization that is intended to eliminate a deficit is a *quasi-reorganization* and is described in Chapter 27. ARB No. 46 [CAP, 1956] recommended that retained earnings following a quasi-reorganization be dated for at least 10 years. Rule 5-02(31) of Regulation S-X specifies the same time requirement and, in addition, provides that the balance sheet disclose the total amount of deficit eliminated for at least 3 years.

Conversion of Preferred Stock. The conversion of preferred shares to common shares results in a charge to retained earnings if the total paid in for the shares being converted is less than the par or stated value of the shares into which they are converted. For example, assume the following:

Preferred stock, par value $10, issued 500,000 shares, each share convertible into two shares of common stock	$5,000,000
Premium on preferred stock	500,000
Common stock, par value $8, authorized 2,000,000 shares, issued 500,000 shares	4,000,000
Retained earnings	3,000,000

The entry to record the conversion of 200,000 shares of preferred stock into 400,000 shares of common stock would appear as follows:

Preferred Stock (200,000 × $10)	2,000,000	
Premium on Preferred Stock ($500,000 × 200,000/ 500,000)	200,000	
Retained Earnings (Balance of Charge)	1,000,000	
Common Stock (400,000 × $8)		3,200,000

Divisive Reorganizations. Spin-offs, split-offs, and split-ups are described collectively as *divisive reorganizations*. In each case, a segment of the assets of an existing business entity is transferred to a separate entity. A *spin-off* occurs when shares in the segment are distributed to the original entity's shareholders without surrender of their shares. A *split-off* is similar to a spin-off, except that shares of the original entity are exchanged pro rata for shares of the new entity. A *split-up* occurs when all of the operations of the original entity are transferred to two or more new entities, and the original entity ceases to exist [Lembke, 1970, p. 458].

APB Opinion No. 29 [1973] states:

> Accounting for the distribution of nonmonetary assets to owners of an enterprise in a spin-off or other form of reorganization or liquidation or in a plan that is in substance the rescission of a prior business combination should be based on the recorded amount (after reduction, if appropriate, for an indicated impairment of value) of the nonmonetary assets distributed. A prorata distribution to owners of an enterprise of shares of a subsidiary or other investee company that has been or is being consolidated or that has been or is being accounted for under the equity method is to be considered to be equivalent to a spin-off.

Thus, APB Opinion No. 29 precludes gain recognition in accounting for a divisive reorganization. The Opinion is silent, however, on the effects of a reorganization on the retained earnings of the existing entity and whether any retained earnings should be carried forward to the new entity. Powell [1957, p. 56] discusses the subject of starting the new entity with retained earnings and sets forth the following conditions which may justify that accounting:

> The transferee corporation has acquired a sufficiently integrated segment of the corporation's net assets and personnel to form a going business, and has not merely acquired certain assets such as a plant building.
> There is reasonable evidence that the business acquired had contributed to the income of the transferor and that the circumstances and factors responsible for its profitable contribution can be expected to continue after separation.
> Substantially all of the assets and business then acquired had been previously held by the transferor.

An example of a spin-off that carried forward retained earnings to the new entity is Brandywine Sports, Inc. A note to the company's 1978 annual report explains the reorganization, as follows:

> The Company was incorporated by RLC Corp. in May 1977 to acquire all the stock of RLC Corp.'s wholly-owned subsidiary, Brandywine Raceway Association, Inc. In October 1977, RLC Corp. transferred all of the issued and outstanding stock of Brandywine Raceway Association, Inc. to the Company in exchange for 852,920 shares of its common stock. On October 31, 1977, RLC Corp. distributed, on a pro-rata basis, the 852,920 shares of the Company's common stock to the shareholders of RLC Corp. Accordingly, the accompanying consolidated financial statements are presented as if the Company was formed and the reorganization effected on or before October 1, 1976.

The company's consolidated statement of shareholders' equity shows a retained earnings balance at September 30, 1976, of $4,311,000.

At present there are some variations in the accounting for such transactions by transferors. Although income statement presentation of the discontinued operation conforms with APB Opinion No. 30 [1973] (see Chapter 3), there is no general agreement on the manner of recording the diminution of shareholders' equity in the divisive reorganization. One alternative is to show the net cost of the assets spun off as a property dividend. Another is to charge it against retained earnings and additional paid-in capital. Still another approach is to charge consolidated retained earnings for that portion attributable to the operations spun off into the new entity. If the new entity carries forward an equal amount of beginning retained earnings, the original equity classification by source would not be affected by the divisive reorganization. If the operations spun off were originally acquired in a business combination accounted for as a purchase, however, the charge to consolidated retained earnings should not be for an amount greater than the new entity's earnings since acquisition (because earnings prior to acquisition are not included in consolidated retained earnings).

MISCELLANEOUS MATTERS

Change in Reporting Period of a Subsidiary of a Pooled Company. A subsidiary of a company recently acquired in a pooling of interests may have a fiscal year-end that differs from that of other companies in the combination. If it is decided to conform their fiscal year-ends, a direct entry to retained earnings is usually made in the year of the change for the net results of operations for the overlapping period.

As an alternative, the operations of the companies may be included in the statement of operations for the period of the change and the immediately preceding reporting period, with the overlapping result eliminated by a direct charge to retained earnings.

Redemption of Stock Purchase Warrants. The excess of amounts paid to redeem or repurchase stock purchase warrants over amounts assigned to the warrants at issuance is charged to retained earnings.

Board Resolution to Capitalize Permanently a Portion of Retained Earnings. A corporation may, by board resolution, permanently capitalize a part or all of existing retained earnings, if the capitalization is not prohibited by law or contractual agreement.

RESTRICTIONS OF RETAINED EARNINGS

Types. As was noted under "Distinction between Retained Earnings and Invested Capital," the entire balance in retained earnings may not be "available" for dividends because of certain legal or contractual commitments, or because of a need for funds for internal corporate purposes.

Examples of retained earnings restrictions include those imposed by:

Treasury stock requirements
Dividend arrearages on cumulative preferred stock
An excess of involuntary liquidation preference over the par or stated value of preferred stock
Restrictive provisions of a trust indenture or loan agreement
Restrictive provisions of the corporation's articles of incorporation
An order or requirement of a regulatory agency

Treasury Stock Requirements. In some states, dividends issued after a treasury stock acquisition are limited by statute to the excess of the balance of retained earnings over the cost of any treasury shares.

Dividend Arrearages on Cumulative Preferred Stock. Most agreements for the issuance of cumulative preferred stock require that no dividends may be paid to common shareholders as long as there are cumulative unpaid preferred stock dividends. Because such provisions restrict the amount of retained earnings available for distribution to common shareholders, the amount and nature of any material restriction should be disclosed.

Excess of Involuntary Liquidation Preference over Par or Stated Value of Preferred Stock. Preferred stocks requiring or permitting future redemption may require that a premium over par be paid in the event of redemption. If state law restricts retained earnings to the extent of this premium, the restriction should be disclosed.

Restrictive Indenture or Loan Agreement Provisions. It is necessary to disclose restrictions imposed by agreements that limit cash dividend payments to specified amounts or limit the acquisition of treasury stock. Usually, however, there are no restrictions placed on the issuance of stock dividends, because a stock dividend has little effect on creditors, the parties ordinarily intended to be protected by the restrictions.

A covenant frequently included in lending agreements requires the maintenance of a minimum amount of working capital. The question arises whether a working capital covenant should be considered a restriction on retained earnings available for dividends. It could be argued that dividends could be paid from noncurrent assets or from funds obtained through the issuance of long-term debt; although such action would be unlikely, it would not be prevented by a covenant of this type. An answer to the question cannot be provided here, because the determination depends essentially on an interpretation of the pertinent covenant. Even if a working capital covenant of this type is not interpreted to constitute a retained earnings restriction, disclosure of the restriction on working capital itself may be necessary.

An example of restrictive loan agreement provisions is disclosed in the 1980 annual report of Super Food Services, Inc.:

The loan agreements limit the payment of cash dividends and the purchase of any class of capital shares in any one year to the extent of 50% of consolidated net income in the previous fiscal year. In addition, the agreements as amended require that consolidated working capital be not less than $27,000,000, that a current ratio of 1.40 be maintained, that short-term debt be reduced to 20% of consolidated net worth (including redeemable preferred stock) for a period of 45 consecutive days during the fiscal year (this restriction was waived for 1980 and 1979), and contain certain other restrictions with respect to additional borrowings, commitments and guarantees. At August 30, 1980, approximately $1,637,000 of consolidated retained earnings is not restricted under the above limitations.

Restrictive Provisions of the Corporation's Articles of Incorporation. An example of a restriction of this type is disclosed in the 1981 annual report of Texas Power & Light Company:

> The Company's articles of incorporation, the mortgage, as supplemented, and the debenture agreements contain provisions which, under certain conditions, restrict distributions on or acquisitions of its common stock. At December 31, 1981, $32,239,000 of retained earnings was thus restricted as a result of the provisions of the articles of incorporation.
>
> The articles of incorporation restriction provides in effect that the Company shall not pay any common dividend which would reduce retained earnings to less than one and one-half times annual preferred dividend requirements. The mortgage restriction is based primarily on the replacement fund requirements of the mortgage. The restriction contained in the debenture agreements is designed to maintain the aggregate preferred and common stock equity at or above 33⅓% of total capitalization.

Order or Requirement of a Regulatory Agency. State law or certain regulatory agencies may also impose limitations on the payment of dividends. The 1981 annual report of Banc One Corporation discloses that:

> The banking affiliates are subject to various regulatory restrictions as to the amount of dividends that may be paid. Under the national banking laws, surplus in an amount equal to the par value of capital stock is restricted, and not available for dividends. In addition, the Comptroller of the Currency must approve the declaration of dividends by a national bank in any year in an amount in excess of the sum of profits for that year and retained net profits for the preceding two years, less any required transfers to surplus. Ohio banking corporations are subject to Ohio laws which provide that dividends may be declared only if out of undivided profits. Whenever surplus is not equal to or greater than the par value of capital stock, Ohio law requires that 10% of net income be credited to surplus each year until surplus equals capital and that dividends may only be declared from the balance of undivided profits.
>
> At December 31, 1981, total shareholders' equity of the banking affiliates approximated $273,815,000 of which $52,046,000 was available for the payment of dividends without approval by the Comptroller of the Currency.

Restrictions on Consolidated Retained Earnings. As was discussed under "Subsidiary and Investee Transactions," consolidated retained earnings may not represent the amount available for dividends if, among other reasons, a subsidiary's unremitted retained earnings are not available for distribution by the parent. It is customary, therefore, to disclose restrictions on components of consolidated retained earnings because the reader may interpret the balance to represent an amount available to the parent for distribution. Furthermore, Rule 4-08(e) of Regulation S-X extends to the issuer's subsidiaries—consolidated or not—the requirement for disclosing the most significant dividend restrictions. Firstmark Corporation, for example, disclosed in its 1981 annual report that:

> The agreements relating to certain long-term and short-term debt of subsidiary companies contain, among other things, restrictions on the payment of dividends or redemption of capital stock or junior debt, and requirements as to maintenance of certain debt ratios and adjusted net worth (as defined). At December 31, 1981, the Company's domestic consolidated subsidiaries had an aggregate of $1,300,000 of retained earnings which was unrestricted as to payment of cash dividends to the parent.

Voluntary Restrictions. Although rare, dividend restrictions may be imposed by a resolution of the board of directors as a formal expression of financial policy and the administration of retained earnings.

Disclosure in Financial Statements. Any significant contractual or legal restriction should be disclosed. Accounting Research Study No. 7 [Grady, 1965, p. 203] states that:

> Restrictions may be indicated by footnote or parenthetical notation. Restrictions imposed by bond indentures, bank loan agreements, state laws, or charter provisions are examples of those which should be disclosed. The restriction may be based upon the retention of the balance of retained earnings as of a specified date, upon the corporation's ability to observe certain working capital requirements, or upon other considerations. When there is more than one type of restriction, disclosure of the amount of retained earnings, so restricted, may be based on the most restrictive covenants likely to be effective in the immediate future. In other words, restrictions seldom, if ever, pyramid in amount.

Rule 4-08(e) of Regulation S-X also requires disclosure of the most restrictive of any dividend restrictions, with an indication of the source, pertinent provisions, and the amount of retained earnings so restricted or free of such restrictions.

Disclosure may be made in the footnotes to the financial statements or by means of retained earnings appropriations. Although, in certain instances, bond indentures and similar agreements require appropriations, footnote disclosure is currently the most common method in all but a few specialized and regulated industries (such as insurance, banking, and utilities).

APPROPRIATIONS OF RETAINED EARNINGS

Nature. *Appropriations of retained earnings* are the result of an action taken by a company's board of directors to transfer a portion of retained earnings to a separate account for a particular reason. Appropriations are common in some regulated industries, including banking (a portion of the "Reserve for Loan Losses") and insurance ("Mandatory Securities Valuation Reserve"), but are otherwise rarely used. In its 1980 annual report, Appalachian Power Company disclosed the following as to its appropriated retained earnings:

> Pursuant to an order of FERC, the entire balance of amortization reserves relating to hydroelectric project earnings has been reclassified to appropriated retained earnings as of January 1, 1978. Appropriated retained earnings at December 31, 1980 relating to such project earnings amounted to $1,409,000.

FASB Statement No. 5 [1975] adds:

> Some enterprises have classified a portion of retained earnings as "appropriated" for loss contingencies. In some cases, the appropriation has been shown outside the stockholders' equity section of the balance sheet. Appropriation of retained earnings is not prohibited by this Statement provided that it is shown within the stockholders' equity section of the balance sheet and is clearly identified as an appropriation of retained earnings. Costs or losses shall not be charged to an appropriation of retained earnings, and no part of the appropriation shall be transferred to income.

Use of the Term "Reserve."   In 1948, the Committee on Terminology of the American Institute of Accountants recommended that in accounting practice the term "reserve" be limited:

> . . . to indicate that an undivided or unidentified portion of the net assets, in a stated amount, is being held or retained for a special purpose, as in the case of a reserve (a) for betterments or plant extensions, or (b) for excess cost of replacement of property, or (c) for possible future inventory losses, or (d) for general contingencies. In this sense a reserve is frequently referred to as an appropriation of retained income.

RIGHTS TO RETAINED EARNINGS IN LIQUIDATION AND DISSOLUTION

Preferred shareholders may be entitled to payments in liquidation ahead of common shareholders. Frequently, for example, the preferred stock's liquidation preference is considerably greater than par value, and this preference may be greater in voluntary liquidation than in involuntary liquidation. If the preferred stock is cumulative, it may also be entitled to receive unpaid dividends before any distribution is made to common shareholders. Participating preferred stock is sometimes entitled to share with common stock in the distribution of any assets remaining after other preference claims have been settled.

The existence of more than one class of common stock may also create certain preferences in liquidation. In the absence of preferred stock or two-class common stock, each common shareholder has the right to receive, after corporate liabilities have been satisfied, corporate assets in proportion to the number of shares held.

ACCUMULATED EARNINGS TAX

The *accumulated earnings tax* is a penalty imposed on corporations that are deemed to have accumulated earnings purposely to avoid taxes on their shareholders. The key criterion is whether a corporation's earnings have been accumulated beyond the "reasonable needs of the business." For this purpose, the reasonably anticipated future needs of the business are considered in addition to its immediate needs. Common reasons for accumulations of retained earnings include working capital requirements; acquisitions or replacements of property, plant, and equipment; business acquisitions or expansions; and specific business contingencies.

In Audit Guidelines to its agents, the Internal Revenue Service lists the following factors as suggestive of a potential accumulated earnings tax:

1. The business needs for the accumulation are vague and indefinite.
2. The need for working capital can be met from current operations.
3. The corporation has investments of a passive nature which are in nonliquid form.
4. Diversification into an unrelated business is only contemplated.
5. Stock of the corporation is closely held.
6. The corporation has made stock redemptions.
7. The corporation has outstanding loans to stockholders or other businesses of the stockholders.
8. The dividend history of the corporation is unfavorable, such as:
   (a) Nonpayment of cash dividend
   (b) Payment of cash dividends related to stockholders' tax status
   (c) Declaration of stock dividends
9. The corporation is unable to pay dividends because of:
   (a) Restriction on dividend payments
   (b) Lack of liquid funds
10. The corporation has investments in subsidiaries that are not controlled.
11. The corporation has no outstanding debt obligations, or the debts were incurred for nonbusiness reasons.
12. The stockholders are in a high tax bracket.
13. The corporation has a high current asset-current liability ratio.
14. The corporation has a high current asset-working capital ratio.
15. The corporation is aware of the accumulated earnings tax and made a conscious attempt to avoid its application.

The penalty tax (which is in addition to the income tax) is based on the corporation's "accumulated taxable income" at the rate of 27½ percent of the first $100,000 and 38½ percent of the excess. The basis represents the corporation's taxable income minus taxes (and other specified adjustments), dividends paid, and an accumulated earnings credit (principally an amount equal to the earnings and profits of the taxable year retained for the "reasonable needs of the business").

Accumulated earnings tax is not a distribution to shareholders but an additional income tax, and should be treated accordingly.

PRESENTATION OF RETAINED EARNINGS CHANGES

APB Opinion No. 12 [1967] requires that:

> When both financial position and results of operations are presented, disclosure of changes in the separate accounts comprising stockholders' equity (in addition to retained earnings) and of the changes in the number of shares of equity securities during at least the most recent annual fiscal period and any subsequent interim period presented is required to make the financial statements sufficiently informative. Disclosure of such changes may take the form of separate statements or may be made in the basic financial statements or notes thereto.

Rule 11-02 of Regulation S-X further requires that for each class of "other stockholders' equity" shown in the balance sheet (namely, additional paid-in capital, other additional capital, and retained earnings), a summary be given of the following information:

1. *Balance at beginning of period.* State separately the adjustments to the balance at the beginning of the first period of the report for items that were applied retroactively to periods prior to that period.

2. *Net income or loss from income statement.*

3. *Other additions.* State separately any material amounts, indicating clearly the nature of the transactions out of which the items arose.

4. *Dividends.* For each class of shares, state the amount per share and in the aggregate.

    (a) *Cash.*

    (b) *Other.* Specify.

5. *Other deductions.* State separately any material amounts, indicating clearly the nature of the transactions out of which the items arose.

6. *Balance at end of period.* The balance at the end of the most recent period shall agree with the related balance sheet caption.

Recent annual surveys by the AICPA (*Accounting Trends and Techniques*) indicate a trend toward presentation of retained earnings changes in a separate statement. If the only changes in retained earnings are net income and dividends, and there are no changes in other shareholders' equity accounts, a combined statement of income and retained earnings would be the most efficient manner of presentation. If, however, there are several transactions affecting retained earnings and other shareholders' equity accounts, a separate statement summarizing all such changes is generally presented.

BIBLIOGRAPHY

Accounting Principles Board (AICPA), *Reporting the Results of Operations*, Opinion No. 9 (APB, 1966).

————, *Accounting for Income Taxes*, Opinion No. 11 (APB, 1967).

————, *Omnibus Opinion—1967*, Opinion No. 12 (APB, 1967).

————, *Earnings per Share*, Opinion No. 15 (APB, 1969).

————, *The Equity Method of Accounting for Investments in Common Stock*, Opinion No. 18 (APB, 1971).

————, *Accounting Changes*, Opinion No. 20 (APB, 1971).

————, *Accounting for Nonmonetary Transactions*, Opinion No. 29 (APB, 1973).

————, *Reporting the Results of Operations*, Opinion No. 30 (APB, 1973).

American Accounting Association, Committee on Concepts and Standards, Supplementary Statement No. 7, "Consolidated Statements," *The Accounting Review*, April 1955, pp. 194–197.

American Institute of Certified Public Accountants, *Audits of Finance Companies*, Industry Audit Guide (AICPA, 1973).

Bandy, D., "How to Minimize the Threat of the Accumulated Earnings Tax," *The Practical Accountant*, February 1981.

Banking Committee (AICPA), *Audits of Banks*, Exposure Draft of Proposed Audit Guide (AICPA, 1980).

Committee on Accounting Procedure (AICPA), *Restatement and Revision of Accounting Research Bulletins*, Accounting Research Bulletin No. 43 (CAP, 1953).

————, *Discontinuance of Dating Earned Surplus*, Accounting Research Bulletin No. 46 (CAP, 1956).

————, *Consolidated Financial Statements*, Accounting Research Bulletin No. 51 (CAP, 1959).

Committee on Terminology (AIA), *Review and Resume*, Accounting Terminology Bulletin No. 1 (COT, 1953).

Copeland, T. E., "Liquidity Changes Following Stock Splits," *The Journal of Finance*, March 1979, pp. 115–141.

Financial Accounting Standards Board, *Accounting for Contingencies*, Statement of Financial Accounting Standards No. 5 (FASB, 1975).

————, *Accounting for Certain Marketable Securities*, Statement of Financial Accounting Standards No. 12 (FASB, 1975).

————, *Accounting for Leases*, Statement of Financial Accounting Standards No. 13 (FASB, 1976).

————, *Prior Period Adjustments*, Statement of Financial Accounting Standards No. 16 (FASB, 1977).

————, *Elements of Financial Statements of Business Enterprises*, Statement of Financial Accounting Concepts No. 3 (FASB, 1980).

————, *Accounting for Compensated Absences*, Statement of Financial Accounting Standards No. 43 (FASB, 1980).

Grady, P., *Inventory of Generally Accepted Accounting Principles for Business Enterprises*, Accounting Research Study No. 7 (AICPA, 1965).

Griffin, C. H., T. H. Williams, and K. D. Larson, *Advanced Accounting*, 4th ed. (Richard D. Irwin, Homewood, Ill., 1980).

Hendriksen, E. S., *Accounting Theory*, 3d ed. (Richard D. Irwin, Homewood, Ill., 1977).

Lembke, V. C., "Some Considerations in Accounting for Divisive Reorganizations," *The Accounting Review*, July 1970.

Madeo, S. A., "An Empirical Analysis of Tax Court Decisions in Accumulated Earnings Cases," *The Accounting Review*, July 1979.

Melcher, B., *Stockholders' Equity*, Accounting Research Study No. 15 (AICPA, 1973).

Meyer, P. E., "Some Accounting Ramifications of Treasury Stock," *The CPA Journal*, November 1973.

Nemec, M. J., "Reporting in Consolidated Statements the Sale of a Subsidiary's Stock," *The CPA Journal*, March 1973.

Paton, W. A., *Advanced Accounting* (Macmillan Company, New York, 1941).

Powell, W., "Business Separations," *The Journal of Accountancy*, March 1957.

Simons, H., *Intermediate Accounting*, 5th ed. (South-Western Publishing Co., Cincinnati, 1972).

Soter, Dennis S., "The Dividend Controversy—What It Means for Corporate Policy," *Financial Executive*, May 1979.

Sprouse, R. T., and M. Moonitz, *A Tentative Set of Broad Accounting Principles for Business Enterprises*, Accounting Research Study No. 3 (AICPA, 1962).

Welsch, G. A., C. T. Zlatkovich, and W. T. Harrison, Jr., *Intermediate Accounting*, 5th ed. (Richard D. Irwin, Homewood, Ill., 1979).

CHAPTER 29

Earnings

per Share*

Loren A. Nikolai
Professor of Accountancy,
University of Missouri

---

*Adapted from Chapter 30, by Frank T. Weston, of the second edition of this handbook.

INTRODUCTION

As indicated in Chapters 2 and 3, the format for reporting financial data by business corporations emphasizes three basic statements. One of these, the balance sheet or statement of financial condition, shows the financial position of the entity at a particular date. Another, the statement of income—either separately or combined with a statement of retained earnings—shows the results of operations of the entity for one or more periods. Currently, primarily because of the interest of users of financial statements in comparing investment opportunities among various corporations, a ratio that combines certain elements of these two basic financial statements into a single statistic—the earnings per share of common stock—is required to be reported on the income statement. As a result of the increasing investor interest in corporate securities, this ratio has become one of considerable importance not only to the investor, but also to the management of business corporations and to the independent public accountants whose reports accompany the financial statements of business entities.

PURPOSE AND LIMITATIONS OF EARNINGS PER SHARE

Uses of Earnings per Share. Earnings per share is a handy tool to use in comparing the operating results of business entities, either the same entity over one or more periods of time, or two or more entities. For an entity with a simple capital structure, that is, common stock only, earnings per share reduces the two component variables, the common stock of the entity and the net income for the period, into a single figure. The figure so computed may be compared with prior estimates of the earnings per share for the period and also with forecasts of earnings per share, similarly computed for future periods. When the earnings per share for two or more periods for such an entity are compared, the effects of the two variables are combined so that a meaningful comparison can be made. Thus, if there is no change in the capital structure between the two periods, the statistic shows the relative changes in the net income of the entity.

If there are changes in the capital structure during the periods, the per-share data will effectively reflect the changes and produce a figure of net income per common share that is a meaningful measure of the results of the period in terms of the outstanding shares. Thus, the earnings-per-share computation is a valuable device for reducing complex accounting information to a simple statistic.

The resulting figure of earnings per share for an entity can be compared with dividends paid for one or more periods. This comparison gives meaningful information as to the proportion of net income that is paid to shareholders in the form of dividends and the proportion that is retained for corporate use.

A further use of earnings per share is in the evaluation of the shares outstanding. This is usually done by means of price–earnings ratios, which have been developed by analysts as a means of estimating the value of a share of common stock based on the general conditions of the industry and the future prospects of the entity in particular.

Limitations of Earnings per Share. Although earnings per share is a useful tool in the case of a corporation with a simple capital structure, it does have its drawbacks, even in such a case. For example, earnings per share does not disclose significant changes in the nature of the business. Thus, if a company were to shift from manufacturing a product for sale to leasing the product to its customers, the earnings per common share might not change between years but the nature of the business and the risks involved would have changed considerably. Similarly, although "extraordinary items" included in the net income for a period are reflected separately in earnings per share, any unusual items that might significantly affect the amount of net income for the period but that would not qualify for separate disclosure in the earnings-per-share data as extraordinary items (or as discontinued operations, as discussed in a later section) would not be disclosed separately by the earnings per share. In similar vein, significant changes in operating ratios, such as the gross profit percentage or the relationship of administrative expenses to operating profit, would not be disclosed in earnings per share.

If all or a portion of the annual net income is retained for corporate use, the investment per share increases accordingly. Under these conditions, an increase in the amount of earnings per share from year to year may reflect merely the same (unchanged) rate of earnings on a greater investment, rather than an apparent improvement in performance levels, or a rate of growth greater than the real rate after adjustment for the increased investment.

Also, changes in the composition of the capital structure would not be disclosed by the earnings-per-share data. Although the computations themselves would reflect such changes, earnings per share standing alone would not inform the reader as to the substance of the underlying changes, which might significantly affect the status of security holders.

Investors using earnings-per-share data should also appreciate that there are various other shortcomings to the data in addition to those of a purely mechanical nature outlined above. For example, earnings per share usually does not represent the amount available for dividends to the common shareholder. Neither does an increase in the amount of earnings per share from one period to the next indicate that a similar increase in dividends should be expected or is warranted. Furthermore, because the ratio reflects, as indicated above, a combination of financial data of great variety, all of which are themselves subject to estimates and uncertainties as to future developments, the resulting earnings per share carries no more assurance as to future certainty than do the underlying earnings themselves. In addition, when a corporation has a complex capital structure, there is no assurance that an increase or decrease in the absolute amount of earnings in the future will necessarily result in a proportionate increase or decrease in the earnings per common share. Finally, the investor must appreciate that an increase in the amount of earnings per share will not necessarily result in a corresponding increase in the market value of the common stock. A great many other factors also influence that value.

Thus, although earnings per share has the appearance of being a simple, informative, all-inclusive tool for investment analysis and decision, its very simplicity may be deceptive. Accordingly, experienced investors rarely, if ever, use it alone; they combine its use with a careful review of the basic financial statements—the balance sheet, the statement of income, and the statement of changes in financial position—in making a realistic evaluation of the financial accounting aspects of the investment opportunities involved.

The Problem of Complex Capital Structures.   The above discussion as to the purpose and limitations of earnings per share has approached the subject in terms of a simple capital structure consisting only of common stock. When securities other than common stock are outstanding—for example, when there are preferred shares or when convertible securities or options and warrants are outstanding—the computation becomes more complex. Some of the complexities involved are discussed in subsequent sections.

METHODS OF COMPUTATION

Because earnings-per-share information is used in investment decisions to make comparisons within and among corporations, it is essential that computations of earnings per share be made on a consistent basis for all corporations. Accordingly, guidelines have been developed for the computation and reporting of such data. The authoritative source of such guidelines for the public accounting profession is APB Opinion No. 15, issued in 1969. The methods of computation, ranging from the simple situations to those involving complex securities, have as their purpose a meaningful and consistent attribution of the earnings of the entity for a period to the various elements of its capital structure.

Common Stock Outstanding.   When only common stock is outstanding, the computation of earnings per share is simply a matter of dividing the net income by the shares outstanding during the period. Because the number of shares outstanding may fluctuate during the period—as the result of issuance of shares for cash or other considerations, or as the result of the acquisition of shares for the treasury or for retirement—an averaging technique should be used to reflect properly the portions of the year during which the shares were outstanding. Thus, if a corporation issued significant amounts of common stock halfway through the accounting period, these shares should be reflected in the computation of earnings per share only for the period during which they were outstanding. In this case, assuming no other issuances or retirements during the period, the number of shares to be reflected in the computation would be those outstanding at the beginning of the period, weighted for the entire period, plus those outstanding for half the period, weighted for that period. Thus, if 1 million shares were outstanding at the beginning of the period and 400,000 shares were issued halfway through the period for cash, the number of shares to be used in computing earnings per share for the period would be 1.2 million shares. As indicated, the weighting is based on the respective time periods involved. A similar technique would be used in case significant amounts of common shares were acquired for the treasury or for retirement during the period. This weighting technique is also used when common shares are issued on conversion of other securities or upon the exercise of options and warrants.

In applying these techniques in simple capital structure situations, care must be exercised to reflect the substance of the changes in the capital structure and not merely the form. Accordingly, certain exceptions are required to the general rule that issuance or reductions in outstanding common shares are weighted based on the time of occurrence. Two relatively simple exceptions are the issuance of additional shares in stock splits or the reduction of outstanding shares through reverse stock splits, and the issuance of shares in stock dividend transactions. In these cases, there are no proceeds or other considerations involved; there is merely a change in the aggregate number of shares outstanding without any change in the aggregate amount of capital. Therefore, increases and decreases of this nature in the common shares outstanding are reflected for the entire period involved. This is seen to be logical in, for example, the case of a 2-for-1 stock split occurring at the middle of the accounting period. The capital structure at the end of the period consists of double the number of shares outstanding at the beginning of the period. However, investors reviewing financial data, including earnings per share, should be given information expressed in terms of the present capital structure, and the income for the entire period should be related to the present structure. Nothing of economic significance has happened in terms of the aggregate amount of investment available to the corporation to generate earnings. Therefore, changes in the common stock outstanding as a result of this type of transaction are reflected for the entire period, without weighting. Earnings-per-share data for all prior periods presented should be similarly adjusted, retroactively.

Poolings of Interests. Another exception to the use of time periods for weighting common shares outstanding exists in the treatment of shares issued during a period in a business combination accounted for as a pooling of interests. In this case, in accordance with the pooling-of-interests concept that the corporations are considered to have been retroactively combined for a number of periods, the common shares issued in the business combination are likewise considered to have been issued at the beginning of the earliest period being reported on. In computing the number of common shares to be included for the current and prior periods, appropriate recognition should be given not only to the exchange ratio involved in the business combination but also to any significant changes in the outstanding common or other shares of the acquired company whose securities are being exchanged for the common stock of the surviving company.

Reflecting the Effects of Subsequent Events. As is true in the reporting of other significant financial information, it is customary to make additional disclosures affecting earnings-per-share data whenever subsequent events indicate that the information otherwise reported might possibly be subject to misinterpretation or might be inaccurate in terms of current conditions. For example, if significant conversions of securities into common stock occur after the close of the period but before completion of the financial report, it is customary to furnish supplementary disclosure of the earnings per share for the period expressed in terms of the revised capital structure, as if the conversions had occurred at the beginning of the period. Thus, whereas the historical earnings per share would be based on the capital structure during the period, the more meaningful information for investors using the financial data subsequent to the date of its issuance would be the earnings per share expressed in terms of the then-current capital structure.

On the other hand, when changes in common shares outstanding occur as a result of stock splits or reverse splits or stock dividends after the close of the period but before completion of the financial report, it is customary to restate the earnings-per-share data for all periods to reflect such changes. When the historical earnings per share are restated for such changes, the financial statements should contain appropriate disclosure.

Complex Capital Structure—Preferred Stock. When securities other than common stock are outstanding, the computation and reporting of the earnings-per-share data become more complicated. If the additional security is a preferred stock, the computation of earnings per share of common stock reflects the deduction of the amount of earnings attributable to the senior security based on its contractual terms. Thus, if the preferred stock is cumulative, the dividend requirements for the period are deducted from net income in order to determine the balance of earnings attributable to the common shares. If the dividends on preferred stock are not cumulative, then only the amount declared during the period is deducted from net income. When the number of preferred shares outstanding during the period changes because of retirements, conversion, or issuances of additional preferred shares, appropriate recognition should be given to the claims of the preferred shareholders against the earnings in accordance with the provisions of the security.

Because the usual senior preferred stock has a claim on the earnings of the entity of a fixed amount, any attribution of earnings to such a security in excess of the amount to which it is entitled under its terms would be inappropriate. Accordingly, it is not considered proper to report earnings per share for senior preferred stock by dividing net income by the number of preferred shares outstanding. Because investors in such securities are often interested in the number of times or the extent to which the dividend requirements have been met, it is satisfactory to divide the net income by the total annual dividend requirements for such stock and express the result in terms of the number of times the dividend requirements are "covered." This ratio is quite different from earnings per share, and any disclosures of this type should therefore avoid use of the latter term and should be expressed clearly to avoid possible confusion.

Potential Dilution. Many capital structures are more complex in that they contain securities other than common stock and senior preferred stock. Securities such as convertible preferred stock, convertible debt, options, and warrants are not unusual. Furthermore, agreements may exist for the issuance of additional shares of common stock based on the fulfillment of certain conditions in the future. Although the common shares issuable under the terms of these securities and agreements are not outstanding at the present time, it is essential that the investor or potential investor be informed as to the potential reduction that issuance of additional common shares under the terms of these securities would have on earnings per share. Any decrease in earnings per share that such issuances would cause is called *dilution*.

A number of problems occur with respect to the computation and disclosure of the potential dilution that results from the existence of such securities and agreements. In order to have a meaningful base against which to measure the extent of the potential dilution, it is customary to compute the dilution in terms of the current level of earnings. Thus, two earnings-per-share figures, the historical (primary) earnings per share and the fully diluted earnings per share, would be reported on the income statement. This approach permits a comparison of the historical earnings per share for the current period with the fully diluted earnings per share assuming conversion, exercise, or issuance of the additional securities involved for the same period. However, because of the number of variables involved, it would be a rare case in which the computed dilution—measured by the difference between the historical earnings per share and the fully diluted earnings per share at the current earnings level—would in fact result at any other level of earnings. For this reason, the disclosure of potential dilution based on the current earnings level is sometimes criticized as being unrealistic. However, use of data based on the current earnings level does clearly disclose an absolute measure of potential dilution, expressed in close relationship to the current earnings per share—the ratio in which the investor currently has considerable interest.

Critics of the disclosure of dilution in these absolute terms claim that the level of net income would have to be considerably higher before the holders of convertible securities, options, and so on, would exchange their securities for common shares; under these conditions, therefore, the earnings per share on a fully diluted basis might be higher than the historical earnings per common share previously reported. This line of reasoning, however, overlooks the fact that, had the convertible securities not been outstanding and had the common shares not been issued thereunder, the earnings per share would have increased proportionately with the increase in the earnings applicable to the common shares. Dilution would in fact result from the issuance of the shares.

Another method of disclosure of potential dilution has been suggested—the expression of the potential dilution in terms of a percentage of the historical or primary earnings per share. This method, however, appears to have several disadvantages. In the first place, an expression of dilution as a percentage of the primary figure would probably be more confusing to the average investor than disclosure of a second per-share figure from which the absolute potential dilution could readily be computed. Furthermore, use of a percentage might imply that this same percentage of dilution would result at different earnings levels. As indicated above, this would seldom be true.

Although the thrust of the disclosure of potential dilution is protection of the investor or the potential investor, questions are raised as to whether the effect of the issuance of additional shares should not be disclosed in the earnings-per-share figure regardless of whether the effect on earnings per share is dilutive or incremental. Present practice, however, concentrates on the potentially adverse effects of such contingencies and, in large part because of the position taken on this matter by regulatory agencies, incremental effects due to conversions and other potential issuances are rarely disclosed.

Convertible preferred stock. The method of computing the potential dilution varies, depending on the type of security involved. In the case of convertible preferred stock, an assumption is made that the shares were converted at the beginning of the period. In making the computation, therefore, the preferred dividend requirements on these preferred shares are disregarded. The equivalent common shares into which the preferred shares are convertible are added to the common shares outstanding for the period, and the total is divided into the amount of net income. If the resulting amount of earnings per share is less than the earnings per share computed on the historical basis, disclosure of the "fully diluted" or "if converted" amount is required.

Convertible debt. In case the security involving the additional issuance of common stock is a convertible debt issue, a similar assumption of conversion at the beginning of the period is made. In this case, however, the interest expense on the debt, less any applicable income tax effect, is added to net income for the period. This adjusted amount is then divided by the sum of the average number of common shares outstanding and the number of common shares assumed to have been issued in conversion of the debt. If the resulting amount of earnings per share is less than that computed on the historical basis, disclosure of the fully diluted amount is required.

Options and warrants. If the additional common shares that are contingently issuable relate to outstanding options or warrants, a somewhat similar computation of potential dilution is made. In this case, the options and warrants are assumed to have been exercised at the beginning of the period. Because with these securities the assumption of exercise generates assumed proceeds to the entity, some further assumption must be made as to the use to which the proceeds are put. A number of assumptions could be made—the acquisition of shares of the company for its treasury, the investment of the assumed proceeds in investment-grade securities, or the use of the proceeds to retire outstanding debt. The method required assumes that the proceeds are used for the purchase of shares for the treasury. (See APB Opinion No. 15 [1969, pars. 36 and 42].) Under this computation, the assumed proceeds are considered to have been used to purchase shares at the *higher* of the average or ending market price for the period. Any excess of the number of shares assumed to be issued upon exercise over those assumed to have been so purchased is included in the number of shares considered to be outstanding for the entire period (or from date of issuance of the options or warrants if issued during the period) in the computation of fully diluted earnings per share. Because of the method of computation, whenever the market price per share of the stock is less than the exercise price per share under the options and warrants, expressed in equivalent shares, the assumed purchase would result in the acquisition of more shares than would be issued. Because this effect would not be dilutive, the exercise is assumed not to occur. Thus, under this method there is dilution only when the market price is greater than the exercise price; the amount of the computed dilution increases proportionately as the market price rises above the exercise price.

When the number of shares subject to options and warrants is substantial in relation to the common shares outstanding, the use of the "treasury stock method" described above is limited to the purchase of shares equal to 20 percent of the common shares outstanding at the end of the period [APB Opinion No. 15, 1969, pars. 38 and 42]. This approach recognizes that it may be unrealistic to assume that a corporation could purchase a significant number of shares at the current market price. Accordingly, when the shares obtainable under options and warrants are in excess of 20 percent of the outstanding common shares at the end of the period, the proceeds from the assumed exercise of all the options and warrants are applied first to purchase up to 20 percent of the number of outstanding common shares, at the higher of the average or ending market price. Any excess proceeds are then applied first to reduce any outstanding debt and then to invest in U.S. government securities or commercial paper. In the latter cases, net income is adjusted for the reduction of interest expense, less any income tax effect, or for the increase in investment income, less any income tax effect. The effects of these computations are aggregated and, if such effect is dilutive, it is reflected in the fully diluted computation. If the effect is not dilutive, it is not reflected in the fully diluted computation.

Other contingent issuances. When the potential dilution relates to agreements to issue additional shares, similar pro forma computations are made giving effect to the assumed issuance of the shares. If the condition of issuance is an increased level of earnings, the possibility of dilution is computed by assuming an increase in earnings to the specified level and including in the outstanding common shares the number of shares issuable at that level. If the amount so computed is less than the primary earnings per share, disclosure of the dilution is required.

In some cases, the issuance of additional shares is dependent on the market value of the common stock at some future date. Computations of earnings-per-share data should be based on the number of shares issuable based on the market price at the close of the period. No further assumptions are warranted.

A number of other circumstances may exist in which additional shares may be issued or in which the number of shares to be issued may increase or decrease upon the happening of certain events. Thus, securities may be convertible into common stock at increasing or decreasing rates, or the right of conversion may be postponed or terminated. The computations of potential dilution and the presentation of fully diluted earnings-per-share data under these circumstances generally reflect the least advantageous (from the point of view of the issuer of the security) conversion ratio to be in effect during the succeeding 10 years. The latter approach is based on the assumption that the average investor is not significantly influenced by conditions that may exist more than 10 years in the future.

See "Antidilutive Effects" below for further problems in computing dilution.

COMMON STOCK EQUIVALENTS

Occasionally, a capital structure contains securities that are considered to be the substantial equivalent of common stock. These securities are designated as *common stock equivalents.*

The concept that a security other than common stock should be considered the equivalent of common stock for purposes of the computation of earnings per share developed as a result of the issuance of increasingly complex securities containing characteristics of both senior securities and common stock. As indicated previously, the computation of earnings-per-share data attributes the earnings of an entity for a period to the various elements of its capital structure, based on their relative legal or economic relationships, preferences, and privileges. In making this attribution, it is generally recognized that the substance, rather than the form, of the various elements of the capital structure should govern. Accordingly, it is often necessary, in the computation of historical (primary) earnings per share, to reflect certain securities, which are considered to be in substance the equivalent of common shares, as common shares. In evaluating the characteristics of a security which may indicate that it is a common stock equivalent, particular attention must be paid to those terms that give the holder of the security the right to become a common shareholder. Thus, the conversion privilege in a convertible preferred stock or a convertible debt, and the purchase option in the case of options and warrants, may indicate that the security involved is in fact the substantial equivalent of a common stock. The application of this concept to various types of securities is discussed below.

Convertible Preferred Stock and Convertible Debt. Various methods have been suggested to determine whether a particular convertible security is a common stock equivalent. These are generally based on a comparison of the estimated value of the "senior security" characteristics of the security—primarily its fixed yield in terms of interest or dividends—and the market value of the security. In the case of a security that is convertible into common stock, the market value of the security may be based to a significant extent on the option to convert into common stock. For example, if a convertible preferred stock of $100 par value carries a fixed dividend rate of 8 percent based on its par, it would have an investment value as a senior security of approximately $80, based on an assumed required yield of 10 percent and disregarding the conversion feature. If this stock were convertible into, say, two shares of common stock, and if the common stock had a market value of approximately $85 per share, the convertible preferred stock might well have a market value of about $170 per share—more than 200 percent of its investment value. The yield would be less than 5 percent on its market value. In such a situation, the question at issue is whether the convertible preferred stock derives such a substantial portion of its value from its common stock characteristics, as distinguished from its senior security characteristics, that it should be considered as a common stock equivalent in computing earnings per share.

When the market value of the convertible preferred stock is at a very high level so that the yield is very low, it becomes evident that the security is being traded on the basis of its convertibility into common stock and that the fixed dividend yield is of considerably less importance. Because the marketplace evaluates the stock in terms of its common stock convertibility and thus looks in a very significant way to the right of the preferred shareholder to share in the value potential of the common stock, it appears logical that any attribution of earnings of the corporation to the various securities outstanding should also give recognition to this fact. Stated another way, if 1 million shares of common stock are outstanding, along with 200,000 shares of the convertible preferred stock described above, it is clear that the marketplace evaluates the common shares and the preferred shares as the equivalent of 1.4 million common shares. If this is so, then the earnings should be attributed to the aggregate equivalent shares. Under these conditions, to attribute all the earnings of the company after preferred dividends to the 1 million shares of common stock would result in a material overstatement of the earnings per share and a disregard of the economic substance of the provisions of the preferred stock. This is the basis of the concept of common stock equivalents.

Time of Determination. In the application of the above concept, a question arises as to whether the determination of the nature of a convertible security and thus its treatment in the computation of earnings per share should be based on an evaluation of the security's characteristics at the time of its issuance and only then, or whether effect should be given to changes in the relative values of the characteristics at regular, subsequent intervals. Views differ as to which of these approaches results in more meaningful and useful earnings-per-share data for investors.

Although there are arguments in support of each side of this particular question, the view adopted by the Accounting Principles Board requires a decision on the status of a convertible security as a common stock equivalent only at the time of its issuance. (See APB Opinion No. 15 [1969, par. 28].) In other words, subsequent market value changes do not affect the classification of the security as a common stock equivalent for the purpose of computing earnings per share.

In the view of many accountants, the determination of the status of a convertible security as a common stock equivalent only at the date of its issuance does not result in the most meaningful and useful presentation of earnings per share. For example, if the market value of the common stock involved were to increase substantially following issuance of a convertible security, it might well be that the marketplace would evaluate the convertible security as the substantial equivalent of common stock. Many convertible securities are designed for this purpose—that is, their nature changes as the underlying common stock increases in value. It is considered unrealistic to disregard these obvious economic factors in a computation that purports to attribute the earnings of a corporation to the elements of its capital structure based on a meaningful evaluation of their characteristics. Such a current attribution should, in the view of these accountants, be based on present circumstances, and not on those existing at the date of issuance, possibly years previously.

Method of Determination. As indicated above, the methods suggested to determine whether a particular convertible security is a common stock equivalent are generally based on a comparison of the estimated value of its senior security characteristics—its investment value—and its market value. In these determinations there are three variables—the cash yield in interest or dividends, the capitalization factor for the security (based on current conditions of the risk involved and the cost of money) which, when applied to the cash yield, determines the investment value, and the overall market value of the security. As shown in the examples above, the market value of the convertible security is often directly affected or based to a substantial degree on the value of the underlying common stock into which it is convertible.

Given the yield, the capitalization factor, and the overall market value of the security in question, a judgment must be made as to the point at which the common stock characteristics are reflected in the value of the security to such an extent that the security is the substantial equivalent of a common share for purposes of attributing earnings. (It is important to note that common stock equivalency is a notion closely related to economic and market factors concerning investment in equity securities in a going concern. It is not based on, and may even be in conflict with, legal relationships or liquidation preferences.) Of the various methods proposed, one that received widespread use was expressed in terms of the relationship of the market value of the security to its investment value. Thus, whenever the market value of the convertible security was 200 percent or more of its investment value, the security was considered a common stock equivalent. In the example cited, when the market value of the common was $85 per share, the convertible preferred stock would be considered a common stock equivalent because its market value was more than 200 percent of its investment value. Had the market value been $60 per share, the convertible preferred stock would not be considered a common stock equivalent, because its approximate $120 market value would be less than 200 percent of its estimated investment value of $80.

As is evident from the above, the determination of the point at which a convertible security should be considered a common stock equivalent is largely a matter of judgment and convention. If the determination were to be made on a continuing basis, it would doubtless be advisable to establish uniform limits for the initial qualification of a common stock equivalent and for the reversal of this classification. Such limits should be far enough apart so that there would not be a continual shifting of classification based on minor fluctuations in market values. Ranges of 150 to 200 percent for initial qualification and 100 percent for subsequent reversal have been proposed.

One of the disadvantages of the method outlined above is that it requires a determination of investment value for each convertible security. It is often difficult to determine the investment values of such securities, because this requires an estimate of the risk and money cost factors, which vary from company to company and from year to year. For this reason, this method, although theoretically superior, has not been widely supported.

The method adopted by the FASB for the determination of the status of a convertible security is based on the same general approach, but it uses the same capitalization factor for all companies at any particular time of issuance. This is done by using the average Aa corporate bond yield as a benchmark. Thus, this method compares the yield of a convertible security, expressed as a percentage of its market value at date of issuance, with the then-current average Aa corporate bond yield. If the yield is less than 66⅔ percent of the average Aa corporate bond yield, the convertible security is considered a common stock equivalent at the date of its issuance and forever thereafter. (See FASB Statement No. 55 [1982, par. 7].)

Using the example given above and assuming that the average Aa corporate bond yield at date of issuance was 12 percent, the 8 percent, $100-par-value, convertible preferred stock with a market value of $170 would be a common stock equivalent, because its yield of 4.7 percent (= $8/$170) on its market value would be less than 8 percent, which is two-thirds of the bank prime interest rate of 12 percent. Disregarding the difference between the 10 percent capitalization factor used above and the assumed 12 percent average Aa corporate bond yield, this method gives basically the same results as the investment value/market value method at the 150 percent level.

This method has the advantages of simplicity and of consistency of application among companies. However, it disregards risk differentials between companies. Accordingly, it does not differentiate between the securities of a high-risk issuer and those of a low-risk issuer.

Options, Warrants, and Other Securities. Securities other than convertible preferred stocks and convertible debt may also merit classification as common stock equivalents. The most common such securities are options and warrants to purchase common stock. Because these securities generally have no yield, their entire value is derived from the right to obtain common stock and they thus clearly are common stock equivalents in the marketplace. Certain problems arise, however, in determining the *number* of common shares to be reflected in the computation of primary earnings per share under these conditions. (This problem is different from that arising in the computation of potential dilution under outstanding options and warrants, because the latter computation is a pro forma one that assumes the exercise of these securities at the beginning of the accounting period and permits some assumptions as to the pro forma use of proceeds for the period. See the section on "Potential Dilution— Options and Warrants" above.)

One method of determining the number of shares of common stock represented by outstanding options and warrants is based on the relationship of the value of the option or warrant to the market value of the common stock. Thus, if a company has 100,000 warrants outstanding enabling the holders to acquire 100,000 shares of common stock at $40 per share, and if the market value of each of the 100,000 shares of common stock outstanding is $50 per share, the value of each warrant might be approximately $10. The percentage relationship of the market value of the warrant to the market value of the common stock— 20 percent ($10 divided by $50)—would then be applied to the total shares obtainable by the warrant holders (100,000) to determine the number of equivalent common shares, 20,000, to be included in the denominator in the computation of primary earnings per share.

This method is similar in concept to the investment value/market value method of determining the common stock equivalent status of convertible securities described previously, because it is based on the evaluation of security characteristics in the current marketplace. Its primary disadvantage is that a value must be established for each option or warrant for purposes of the calculation. As compared to the methods described below, it has significant appeal because it does not require any adjustment of historical earnings or any assumed attribution of earnings on the assumed proceeds from exercise.

A number of other methods exist for the computation of historical earnings per share when options and warrants are considered to be common stock equivalents. Most of these are similar to those discussed earlier under the potential dilution of options and warrants. Their principal weaknesses are that they require adjustments of historical earnings or unrealistic assumptions as to the use of proceeds, both of which are considered by many accountants to be unsatisfactory in the computation of historical earnings per share.

The method that is generally accepted at present is the treasury stock method. (See APB Opinion No. 15 [1969, par. 36].) When it is used for the computation of historical earnings per share, the proceeds of exercise are assumed to have been used to purchase common stock at the *average* market price during the period. (For the fully diluted computation, the market price at the close of the period is used if it is higher than the average price.) The limitation on the use of the treasury stock method when the shares obtainable under options and warrants exceed 20 percent of the outstanding common shares also applies in the historical computation. Under this method, there is no effect on historical earnings per share unless the exercise price of the option or warrant is less than the average market price of the common stock.

In addition to the securities discussed above, other complex securities may also qualify as common stock equivalents. Certain participating securities, two-class common stocks, and other securities that derive significant portions of their value from their common stock characteristics might require such treatment. In all these cases, it is necessary to evaluate the various preferences and privileges provided by the terms of the security and to reflect the substance of the situation in accordance with the overall concepts governing the computation of earnings per share.

Occasionally, special circumstances exist which require that earnings per share be computed using one of several complex methods. A relatively common example is the computation for real estate investment trusts when options or warrants are outstanding. In this case, the "two-class" method is used. This method first attributes to each type of outstanding security any distribution made to its holders; then the balance of undistributed income is allocated to all the common shares and common stock equivalents outstanding [APB, 1970, pp. 84–87].

Antidilutive Effects. In the application of the concept of common stock equivalents, certain overriding limitations have also been applied. Thus, if the effect on earnings per share as otherwise computed of considering a security as a common stock equivalent resulted in an increased amount of earnings per share, that is, an antidilutive or incremental effect, the common stock equivalent would not be reflected in the computation of historical (primary) earnings per share. This is consistent with the present approach to the computation and disclosure of potential dilution discussed in a preceding section. However, under this approach, a security that is deemed to be a common stock equivalent may enter into the computation of historical earnings per share in one period but not in another, due entirely to its effect on the computed amount.

An interesting computational problem arises when the capital structure contains a number of convertible securities whose effects on primary (or fully diluted) earnings per share must be tested to determine whether they are individually dilutive or antidilutive. The problem is to determine the order in which the computations reflecting assumed conversion should be made. It is generally accepted that the amounts reported as primary and fully diluted earnings per share should reflect the *maximum* dilution or potential dilution and therefore should exclude any securities whose effect would be to increase per-share amounts otherwise computed. The accepted method of determining the proper sequence for the computations is to rank the per-share effect of the conversion of each security in terms of one common share, and then to make successive cumulative computations, starting with the most dilutive issue, until all securities are included or until one security has an antidilutive or incremental effect on earnings per share. At that point, that security is excluded and the prior cumulative amount reflects the maximum dilution [Davidson and Weil, 1975].

Recognition of Common Stock Equivalents in the Financial Statements.
The concept of common stock equivalents outlined above is applied only in the computation of earnings per share. Questions arise as to whether, if certain securities are the substantial equivalent of common stock, the basic financial statements should not also give recognition to this and classify these securities along with common stock as an element of shareholders' equity. Although a consistent application of the concept would seem to require such treatment, it is not generally accepted.

STEPS IN COMPUTATION OF EARNINGS PER SHARE

To this point, the basic computations (weighted-average common shares, stock dividends and splits, preferred dividends, treasury stock method for options and warrants) for the components of earnings per share have been discussed. Included in the discussion of historical (primary) earnings per share were securities classified as common stock equivalents. Also discussed was the potential dilution of historical (primary) earnings per share due to outstanding convertible preferred stock and convertible bonds, as well as stock options and warrants. When a corporation has a complex capital structure—one including convertibles and options and warrants—it is advisable to compute earnings per share in a sequential manner to avoid errors of interpretation or antidilution.

Primary Earnings per Share. For primary earnings per share, the computational steps include the following: (1) Calculate the basic earnings per share [(net income — preferred dividends) ÷ common shares]; (2) include dilutive stock options and warrants and compute a tentative primary earnings per share; (3) for each convertible preferred stock and convertible bond, determine whether it is a common stock equivalent; (4) develop a ranking of the impact of each common stock equivalent (from step 3) on primary earnings per share; (5) include each common stock equivalent in primary earnings per share in a sequential order based on the ranking and compute a new tentative primary earnings per share; and (6) select as the primary earnings per share the lowest computation from step 5 [Nikolai et al., 1983, p. 755].

Fully Diluted Earnings per Share. A similar set of steps should be completed for fully diluted earnings per share, with two exceptions. First, when including dilutive stock options and warrants, the ending market price should be used in the treasury stock method (discussed earlier) when this price is higher than the average market price. Second, instead of a ranking of common stock equivalents, a ranking is developed of the impact of *all* convertible securities on fully diluted earnings per share. These securities are then included sequentially in fully diluted earnings per share until the lowest figure is computed. A useful flow chart approach for computing both primary and fully diluted earnings per share is presented by Matulich et al. [1977] and Stephens [1978].

DISCLOSURE OF EARNINGS-PER-SHARE DATA

As the interests of investors and others in financial statement presentations, and particularly in the reporting of earnings-per-share data, have increased, disclosure practices have developed to such an extent that there are certain generally accepted patterns of disclosure of data related to this type of information. The amount of earnings per share must be disclosed on the face of the income statement of each public enterprise [APB Opinion No. 15, 1969, par. 12]. Nonpublic enterprises are not required to disclose earnings-per-share information in their financial statements [FASB Statement No. 21, 1978, par. 12]. A nonpublic enterprise is defined as "an enterprise other than one (a) whose debt or equity securities trade in a public market on a foreign or domestic stock exchange or in the over-the-counter market (including securities quoted only locally or regionally) or (b) that is required to file financial statements with the Securities and Exchange Commission" [FASB Statement No. 21, 1978, par. 13]. Thus, a subsidiary, corporate joint venture, or other investee that is a nonpublic enterprise need not disclose earnings-per-share information in its complete set of separately issued financial statements [FASB Statement No. 21, 1978, par. 12].

When a company that is a public enterprise discloses its earnings-per-share information, in the case where there are any outstanding securities or agreements that could cause potential dilution, it is generally accepted that the fully diluted earnings per share must also be shown on the face of the statement of income [APB Opinion No. 15, 1969, par. 15]. There should be adequate disclosure of the bases of the various computations involved, and a description of the terms and characteristics that cause certain securities to be considered common stock equivalents in these computations. Furthermore, the financial statements must contain a description of the pertinent preferences and privileges of the various securities outstanding, including such information as conversion rates, liquidation preferences, participation rights, and sinking fund requirements. In certain complicated cases, schedules or reconciliations of the data and methods used in the computations should be provided.

If a company has an investment in another company that is accounted for by consolidation or by use of the equity method of accounting and if the latter company has outstanding securities that are convertible or that are common stock equivalents, certain adjustments may be necessary in computing earnings-per-share data for the parent company [APB Opinion No. 15, 1969, pars. 65-69]. If material, these adjustments should be disclosed.

If extraordinary items are present, earnings-per-share data with and without inclusion of the extraordinary items should be disclosed. Similarly, if the income statement segregates income from continuing operations from the results of discontinued operations, earnings-per-share data for income from continuing operations and for net income should be presented on the face of the income statement [APB Opinion No. 30, 1973, par. 9]. If the income statement includes a caption and an amount for the cumulative effect of an accounting change, the per-share amount of the change should also be shown on the face of the statement of income [APB Opinion No. 20, 1971, par. 20].

As explained earlier, certain supplementary per-share data should also be furnished if subsequent events tend to diminish the relevance of the historical data.

CONCLUSION

The increasing emphasis placed on the computation and presentation of earnings-per-share data is an indication of the dynamic nature of the accounting and reporting process. As a need appears for information derived from financial accounting data, disclosure is provided and related computational guidelines are developed, which become generally accepted. Although some accountants believe that the criteria for the computation of earnings-per-share data are not matters of accounting principle, many other accountants feel that because these data are based on elements of the financial statements and because it is obviously essential that all corporations follow the same general guidelines in the computations, accounting principles should include guidelines for the preparation of this important business ratio.

Although it is agreed that the earnings-per-share ratio does have value, it is essential that all users bear in mind that these data do have many limitations. The careful investor will become fully informed as to the limitations and shortcomings of earnings per share before the investor uses it in investment decisions. Accountants, for their part, have a responsibility to make sure that all computations are made in accordance with the guidelines that are generally accepted in the business community. In this way, the earnings-per-share ratio will prove most meaningful and useful to all concerned.

BIBLIOGRAPHY

Accounting Principles Board (AICPA), *Earnings per Share*, Opinion No. 15 (APB, 1969).
———, *Computing Earnings per Share*, Unofficial Accounting Interpretations of APB Opinion No. 15 (APB, 1970).
———, *Accounting Changes*, Opinion No. 20 (APB, 1971).
———, *Reporting the Results of Operations*, Opinion No. 30 (APB, 1973).
Davidson, S., and R. L. Weil, "A Short-Cut in Computing Earnings per Share," *Journal of Accountancy*, December 1975, pp. 45–47.
Financial Accounting Standards Board, *Suspension of the Reporting of Earnings per Share and Segment Information by Nonpublic Enterprises*, Statement of Financial Accounting Standards No. 21 (FASB, 1978).
———, *Determining Whether a Convertible Security Is a Common Stock Equivalent*, Statement of Financial Accounting Standards No. 55 (FASB, 1982).
Matulich, S., L. A. Nikolai, and S. K. Olson, "Earnings per Share: A Flow Chart Approach to Teaching Concepts and Procedures," *The Accounting Review*, January 1977, pp. 233–247.
Nikolai, L. A., J. D. Bazley, R. G. Schroeder, and I. N. Reynolds, *Intermediate Accounting*, 2d ed. (Kent Publishing Company, Boston, 1983), chap. 18.
Stephens, W. L., "Earnings per Share: A Flow Approach to Teaching Concepts and Procedures: A Comment," *The Accounting Review*, January 1978, pp. 260–262.

CHAPTER 30

Partnership

Accounting

R. Glen Berryman
*Professor of Accounting, University
of Minnesota*

THE PARTNERSHIP FORM OF ORGANIZATION

Attributes. A business or profession may be carried on as a sole proprietorship, general partnership, limited partnership, corporation, joint venture, syndicate, trust, or other form of organization. The owner or owners adopt a form based on their evaluation of the relevant factors surrounding the firm's operations, such as legal and income tax considerations. Businesses frequently begin as sole proprietorships, then change to the partnership form when there are needs for additional capital and owners, and then to the corporate form. The Uniform Partnership Act and the Uniform Limited Partnership Act, adopted in most states, cover the rights and obligations of partners and parties dealing with a partnership.

Section 6 of the Uniform Partnership Act states: "A partnership is an association of two or more persons to carry on as co-owners of a business for profit." A partnership is a separate entity for purposes of accounting. Assets, liabilities, and equities are treated as those of a separate and distinct business unit and are accounted for separately from those belonging to the partners individually.

In the event of financial difficulties, a partnership may be petitioned into bankruptcy. Such petition may place only the partnership in bankruptcy, or it may place the partnership along with one or more of its partners in bankruptcy. Partnership creditors have first claim to partnership assets in a bankruptcy proceeding. Creditors of individual partners in the partnership have first claim to the personal assets of the respective partners. In most jurisdictions, a partnership may hold title to real estate, may sue in the courts, and may be sued in its own name.

In a partnership, each person with an ownership interest has certain rights and responsibilities. These should be defined and set out explicitly by the contract of partnership, sometimes called the "articles of partnership." Essential provisions are reviewed in a later section.

In contrast to the sole proprietorship and partnership (general and limited), the corporation is a legal entity, as noted by Chief Justice Marshall of the U.S. Supreme Court in the following terms: "A corporation is an artificial being, invisible, intangible, and existing only in contemplation of law. Being the mere creature of law, it possesses only those properties which the charter of its creation confers upon it, either expressly or as incidental to its very existence."[1] Exhibit 1 summarizes the key differences between a partnership, a limited partnership, and a corporation.

Alternative Forms. A *joint venture* is usually a temporary partnership organized by two or more parties for the purpose of carrying out a specific business

---

[1] *Dartmouth College v. Woodward*, 4 Wheat. (U. S.)518(1819).

plan. It is typically, though not necessarily, of short duration. A *syndicate* is an association of persons who combine to carry out a financial or industrial project such as the underwriting of a bond, stock, or other security issue. Although a syndicate is typically formed to carry out a single business operation, it may carry out a series of operations such as the purchase and development of a real estate tract. A joint venture, in contrast to a syndicate, usually contemplates a series of business operations. Each partner in a "regular" partnership is an agent of the partnership and has the authority to make binding commitments for the partnership. A member of a joint venture is not necessarily an agent of the other members of the venture and does not automatically have authority to bind the venture in contracts. In a partnership, the death of a partner dissolves the partnership, whereas in a joint venture the death of a venturer does not necessarily dissolve that venture.

Another form of business organization is that of *joint stock company*. This is quite similar to the regular partnership in that it is formed by a contract among the parties, and makes each member of the company assume unlimited liability with respect to obligations incurred by the company while he or she is a member thereof. It differs from a partnership in that its directors, elected by members of the company, are responsible for its business operations. The members are not agents of the company. The shares of the company are transferable without the consent of the other members, and the death of a member does not dissolve the company.

A special type of partnership is the *limited partnership*. This is composed of one or more general partners plus one or more limited partners. In a regular partnership, the organization is formed by contract among the partners. In a limited partnership, it is essential for the organization to be formed on the basis of a specific enabling statute. Further, the limited partners do not assume responsibility for debts of the partnership beyond the capital they have paid in or have agreed to pay in to the partnership. A limited partnership agreement may contain specific provisions for the retirement of a limited partner or provision for him to assign one or more of his rights as a partner. Action in accordance with such provisions does not automatically terminate the partnership or dissolve it.

Each limited partnership must have at least one substantial general partner. Failure to do so could result in the limited partners being classified as general partners. To perfect the position of the limited partners (liability for partnership debts only to the extent of their actual or agreed-upon capital contribution), the certificate stating the name and character of the business, location, names of general partners and of limited partners, and so on, must be filed in the office of the public official designated in the enabling state statute. A limited partner may contribute cash or property but not services. The name of the limited partnership is not to contain the surname of a limited partner unless that surname is also the surname of a general partner.

A *mining partnership*, commonly regulated by specific state statute, is an association of two or more owners of mineral rights who organize for the purpose of obtaining a profit from extraction of the minerals. Generally, mining partners have the right to sell their partnership interests, and the acquirees become members of the partnership. The partnership is not terminated by sale

EXHIBIT 1 A Comparison of General Partnership, Limited Partnership, and Corporate Form of Organization

Aspect	General partnership	Limited partnership	Corporate
Creation	By contract between two or more parties.	By contract between two or more parties, under statutory enabling legislation, with recording of certificate in prescribed office.	Under statutory enabling legislation with charter granted by a governmental entity.
Legal status	Governed by state partnership law, commonly the Uniform Partnership Act or variant thereof. Each partner has authority to bind the partnership when dealing with outsiders in the usual manner.	Governed by state partnership law, commonly the Uniform Limited Partnership Act or variant thereof. Only general partners (not limited partners) deal with outsiders on partnership business.	A legal entity that may carry out all activities authorized by the charter issued by the governmental unit.
Life of organization	Ceases at death, withdrawal, or addition of a partner, or earlier by contractual provision. Business operation may continue by contractual arrangement.	Ceases at death, withdrawal, or addition of general partner, or earlier by contractual provision. Withdrawal or addition of limited partners need not terminate the partnership. When all limited partners cease to be such, partnership is terminated.	Perpetual, unless limited by charter.

Ownership share transferability	Only with consent of all other partners.	General partner interests may be changed only with consent of all partners. Limited partner interests may be assigned; assignees may become substituted limited partners with consent of all other partners or by action of assignor if certificate gives assignor such authority.	Freely transferable, unless limited by a contractual arrangement.
Management	Each partner is entitled to an equal voice unless the partnership agreement provides otherwise.	Only general partners have rights to manage.	Responsibility is vested in the board of directors who commonly employ the chief executive officer.
Status of owners	Each partner is a principal and an agent of the other partners.	Each general partner is principal and agent of the other general partners. Limited partners do not serve as principal or agent for other partners.	Shareholder is neither principal nor agent, but has contractual rights only.
Liability of owners	Unlimited liability for debts of the partnership and torts of partners, unless limited by contract (subject to limitations).	Limited partners not liable to creditors unless they take part in management of the business. General partners have liability similar to that of partners in a general partnership.	Shareholders not liable for debts of corporation.
Additional owners	Creates new partnership. All current partners must consent.	Additional limited partners may be admitted upon filing amendment to original certificate, subject to rights of original partners.	Limited by charter and preemptive rights of current shareholders.

of a partner's interest or death. A member does not automatically become an agent of the partnership; usually one partner is named as manager and only such person has the authority to bind the partnership. All partners do have unlimited liability for partnership debts as do general partners in other partnerships.

Different *classes of partners* may be created by the partnership contract or subsequent amendment thereto. A general partner incurs unlimited liability for the debts incurred in the course of partnership business. A general partner typically is active in the management of the business and known to the public as a principal and an agent of the organization. Limited partners are not liable for debts incurred by the firm beyond their contributed capital unless, in addition to the exercise of their rights and powers as a limited partner, they take part in the management of the business. A silent partner has unlimited liability but takes no part in the conduct of regular partnership business. A secret partner has all the usual obligations and rights of a general partner but the participation in the partnership is not known by the public.

Accounting Records. Accounting records are needed to enable the partnership to report financial information as needed to parties entitled to such data. Periodically statements of operations and financial position and changes in financial position will be prepared from the financial records. The records should include data needed for inclusion in financial reports to partners, tax authorities, management, and other persons to whom such information is given. A major factor for many partnerships in deciding the form and content of accounting records is the data needed to comply with income tax reporting requirements and the data needed for tax planning. Many partnerships, particularly those that primarily provide services to clients or customers, will adopt a cash basis of accounting for tax purposes and for their accounting records. Tax (cash) basis financial statements, though not necessarily conforming to the requirements of generally accepted accounting principles (GAAP), may well be partially or entirely satisfactory for nontax reporting purposes, such as reports to partners. Conversion of tax basis financial statements to GAAP basis financial statements can be accomplished by a worksheet approach if the reconciling data are accumulated in the financial records.

Accounting records that reflect transactions between the partner and the business entity must be maintained. A capital account, reflecting all transactions related to a partner's long-term contribution of funds, must be maintained. The current (drawing) account shows all transactions representing temporary changes in the partner's investment in the partnership, withdrawal of profits, buying from or selling to the business, and so on. For example, a partner might withdraw certain products for personal use although they were owned by the partnership and were held for sale in the ordinary course of business. Such withdrawals would be charged to the partner's current account. Also, partners' shares of earnings are usually credited to their current accounts. Transfers between the current account and the capital account are made periodically as the partners make decisions on the amount of permanent capital needed. Occasionally, the capital and current accounts are merged into a single account. A loan account will be set up if a partner either borrows from or makes a loan to the partnership with the intent that repayment take place at a future date.

Major areas of difference between GAAP basis accounting records and tax (cash) basis accounting records relate to changes in relative partnership interests, admission of new partners, and retirement of existing partners. GAAP/tax account balance differences would relate to

1. Partner capital accounts at organization and in subsequent periods
2. Carrying value for assets contributed by partners
3. Receivables based on services rendered to customers and clients
4. Timing of recognition of certain expenses

Records need to be maintained with respect to all book-tax differences so that either GAAP or tax (cash) basis financial data, including financial statements, can be prepared as needed.

Access to partnership books is covered by Section 19 of the Uniform Partnership Act:

> The partnership books shall be kept, subject to any agreement between the partners, at the principal place of business of the partnership, and every partner shall at all times have access to and may inspect and copy any of them.

Ownership of Assets and Liability for Debts. Section 8, paragraph 3, of the Uniform Partnership Act states: "Any estate in real property may be acquired in the partnership name. Title so acquired can be conveyed only in the partnership name." Real estate used by a partnership can be recorded in the name of one or more partners or a third party instead of in the partnership name. In these cases, a trust relationship exists between the owner of record and the partnership, and the partnership is the equitable owner of the realty.

Equitable title to realty used by a partnership but recorded in a partner's name may be obscure. Questions to raise in determining equitable ownership to realty include the following:

1. Has the income or the proceeds from the sale of the property been treated as partnership funds?
2. Have taxes and other associated expenses been paid by the partnership?
3. Has the property been improved with funds furnished by the partnership?
4. Has the property been recorded on the books and financial statements of the partnership?

As with realty, other assets of the partnership may be held by the partnership in its own name. This applies to inventories, receivables, bank account balances, securities, fixed assets other than realty, and so on. The partnership would have the title to such items, and individual partners acting as agents of the partnership would have the right to convey them to third parties in the ordinary course of business. Further, a partner as agent of the partnership would have the power to encumber the property through a borrowing arrangement.

Prospective, current, and retiring partners are usually concerned with their potential liability for debts of the partnership and debts incurred by other partners as agents of the partnership. The following provisions in the Uniform Partnership Act are related to such concerns:

Section 15 (Nature of Partner's Liability.) All partners are liable.

a) Jointly and severally for everything chargeable to the partnership under sections 13 and 14.

(Partnership Bound by Partner's Breach of Trust.)

b) Jointly for all other debts and obligations of the partnership; but any partner may enter into a separate obligation to perform a partnership contract.

Section 17 (Liability of Incoming Partner.) A person admitted as a partner into an existing partnership is liable for all the obligations of the partnership arising before his admission as though he had been a partner when such obligations were incurred, except that this liability shall be satisfied only out of partnership property.

Section 36 (Effect of Dissolution on Partner's Existing Liability.)

(1) The dissolution of the partnership does not of itself discharge the existing liability of any partner.

(2) A partner is discharged from any existing liability upon dissolution of the partnership by an agreement to that effect between himself, the partnership creditor and the person or partnership continuing the business; . . .

(3) Where a person agrees to assume the existing obligations of a dissolved partnership, the partners whose obligations have been assumed shall be discharged from any liability to any creditor of the partnership who, knowing of the agreements, consents to a material alteration in the nature or time of payment of such obligations.

(4) The individual property of a deceased partner shall be liable for all obligations of the partnership incurred while he was a partner but subject to the prior payment of his separate debts.

Section 40 (Rules for Distribution.)

(h) When partnership property and the individual properties of the partners are in possession of a court for distribution, partnership creditors shall have priority on partnership property and separate creditors on individual property, saving the rights of lien or secured creditors as heretofore.

(i) Where a partner has become bankrupt or his estate is insolvent the claims against his separate property shall rank in the following order:

I. Those owing to separate creditors,

II. Those owing to partnership creditors,

III. Those owing to partners by way of contribution.

Note that a partner does not have unlimited liability with respect to all aspects of partnership business. Under Section 15, for example, the ordinary obligations of a partnership give rise only to a joint liability on the part of the partners. Under Section 17, a new partner does not assume personal responsibility for any debts contracted by a partnership prior to his or her becoming a member of that partnership. Under Section 36, a partner's personal liability to a specific creditor can be eliminated by a specific agreement between that person, the partner, and the partnership continuing a business. Further, Section 40 provides that the personal liability of partners for debts to the partnership does not come into play until the partnership's assets are in the hands of a court for distribution and the partnership property is found to be inadequate to satisfy the claims of creditors. In contrast to the joint liability that partners have for the debts incurred in the ordinary course of business by a partnership, the liabilities of partners for torts committed by a partner or an employee of the partnership are joint and several. A person not a member of a partnership might make a representation to another person that he or she was a member of the partnership or might permit a partner to represent that he or she was a member of the partnership. If another party relied on such representation and was injured, the nonpartner who was represented as a partner could be held liable as though he or she were a member of the partnership.

Life of the Organization. One of the alleged weaknesses of the partnership form of organization is its uncertain life. In those businesses in which long-term commitments are essential, some degree of certainty as to continuity of the organization is highly desirable. Section 27 of the Uniform Partnership Act (Assignment of Partner's Interest) provides:

> (1) A conveyance by a partner of his interest in the partnership does not of itself dissolve the partnership, nor, as against the other partners in the absence of agreement, entitle the assignee, during the continuance of the partnership, to interfere in the management or administration of the partnership business. . . .

The assignment of a partner's interest does not give an assignee the right to partner status, particularly those rights related to management of the business. Section 18 (g) provides: "No person can become a member of a partnership without the consent of all the partners." An individual could become a partner only if accepted as such by all existing partners. Although a partnership can be terminated by one partner, such right can be circumscribed substantially by an appropriate provision in the articles of partnership and/or by a separate agreement among the partners that would establish procedures for changing partnership interests among existing partners, admit new, and/or retire existing partners. Such a provision or agreement could indicate not only the partner's right to withdraw from the business but also a formula for determining the value of the partner's interest and responsibilities to the partnership, and the rate at which withdrawals can be made. Such a provision could help assure an orderly transition of the operation from one set of partners to another set and also minimize the risk of loss to outsiders when one partner retires from the partnership. Another provision might involve a requirement that all partners as of a certain date are required to maintain a certain minimum capital investment for a certain minimum period of time. Buy/sell agreements are frequently helpful in providing for an orderly transition from one set of partners to a subsequent set of partners.

Advantages and Disadvantages of the Partnership Form. The advantages claimed for the partnership form of organization include the following:

1. Ease in formation and dissolution. A simple contract between two or more people can give rise to a partnership. Dissolution can proceed with an oral or written statement by a partner to the other partners. The rights and responsibilities of each partner in the event of a dissolution will be governed by the initial contract and related amendments, or, where they are silent, by the applicable partnership law. This contrasts with the corporation, in which a formal application for a charter from the governmental body must be prepared and filed. When the corporation is dissolved, its charter is surrendered. A limited partnership must have a certificate prepared and filed, but this can be simpler than the preparation of incorporation papers.

2. Relative flexibility in partnership actions. Changes in the capital structure of a partnership can be achieved by mutual agreement among the partners, in contrast to the corporate situation where the issuance of new stock may involve an amendment to the charter, preemptive rights of shareholders, and so on. Major changes in business operations would be the subject of an informal agreement or amendment to the initial partnership contract, whereas in the corporate situation a charter amendment might be required. Though most corporate charters are drawn in very general terms to permit maximum flexibility in conduct of corporate business, it is typically easier to change a partnership agreement.

3. Personal character of the organization. Many persons feel that a partnership retains more of a personal character than does a corporation. Historically, professional groups such as attorneys and doctors, which have public service orientations, have employed the partnership form. More recently, however, many such groups have been organized as or have been converted to professional corporations. Individuals practicing in the corporate form continue to have personal responsibility for their errors of omission or commission.

Disadvantages of the partnership form include the following:

1. Personal liability of partners. Partners are personally responsible for all debts of a partnership, in contrast to the corporate situation in which the owner's possible liability is limited to the capital investment. A general partner may be called upon to contribute substantially more than the initial capital in the event of partnership financial difficulties.

2. Lack of business continuity. Because the partnership is legally dissolved when a partner dies or withdraws, outside parties may feel less assurance in dealing with a partnership than with a corporation. On the other hand, it is possible, as noted above, for business continuity to be provided for in the articles of partnership or a separate agreement among the partners.

3. Transference of ownership. Rights of a partner to the financial benefits of the partnership interest can usually be assigned unless the articles of partnership preclude such a transaction. However, the right to participate in management cannot be assigned without concurrence of all other partners. The sale of a partnership interest or admission of a new partner takes place only with consent of the current partners. This is in contrast to the corporation, where all ownership rights are transferred by a sale of corporate stock, and stock gives rights to manage through its right to vote for members of the board of directors, to propose resolutions at annual meetings, and so on.

4. Difficulty in raising large amounts of capital. No significant difference is likely to arise with respect to raising debt-type capital, because the individual shareholders of a closely held corporation and the partners in a partnership are both likely to be asked by the lender to guarantee a substantial loan. However, equity capital sources are likely to be more available to the corporation as a result of the ease of transferring interests and the absence of personal liability for such capital providers. Limited partnership interests can frequently be negotiated, because such investors can avoid personal liability beyond their agreed-upon investment and can usually assign their interests freely.

Tax factors, both federal and state, must be considered before deciding whether the corporate or partnership form of organization is preferable. The taxes to be levied, including federal and state income taxes, franchise taxes, and property taxes, must be computed with respect to each form of organization. Both current and prospective tax levies should be considered in weighing this factor. Further, because the tax field is not static, tax changes may suggest a periodic reevaluation of the decision to incorporate or to operate as a partnership.

A partnership must file an annual federal income tax return. This is an information return only, because the partnership itself pays no federal income tax. The distributive shares of partnership income are included in the personal tax returns of the partners and retain their character in the partner's personal tax returns. This is in contrast to the corporation, which is a taxable entity. However, under Internal Revenue Code Section 1371 *et seq.*, it is possible for a corporation to elect not to pay corporate tax on its income, but to have its shareholders pay the income taxes on it. Taxable income is computed at the corporate level and is then attributed to the shareholders in proportion to their shareholdings. The character of the corporate income and expense items is generally retained in the shareholder's personal tax returns. Strict limits exist as to which corporations are eligible for this tax status. Requirements for classification as a "Subchapter S corporation" include:

1. The corporation must have no more than one class of stock issued and outstanding.

2. The corporation must have no more than 35 shareholders.

3. The shareholders must all be individuals, except that an estate and certain trusts may be shareholders.

The partnership form is frequently desirable when losses are anticipated, because such losses (ordinary and capital) can be passed through to the individual partners. Losses in excess of the cost of the partnership interest can be passed through if there are certain debts of the partnership outstanding at year-end.

THE PARTNERSHIP FINANCIAL STATEMENTS

The basic classifications for partnership financial statements are the same as those employed for other forms of business organization. However, certain particular subclassifications are commonly used by partnerships, and some disclosures related to the partnership type of organization are necessary. Particular attention must be directed to transactions between the partner and the partnership to be sure that such transactions during the period and the position as of the end of the period have been adequately reflected. Footnote disclosures may be needed to reflect such transactions fully and to report commitments that have been made.

The owners' equity section of a partnership balance sheet will differ significantly from a corporate and from a sole proprietorship balance sheet. Partners' permanent capital accounts and the balance of their current (or drawing) accounts should be shown separately in order to indicate the extent of long-term commitment to the enterprise. The separation serves as a continuing reminder to the reader of the financials of the partners' basic commitment to the partnership in terms of capital. In the event of dissolution, a partner entitled to a distribution will receive payments on loan and current account balances before any return of capital account.

The current account balance shown separately in owners' equity represents the amount due to or from the partnership by the partner, and is the result of (1) withdrawals by the partners, (2) distributive shares of profits, (3) short-term contributions or loans, and (4) any amounts not subject to specific settlement plan. Significant partner loans to or from the business, subordinated to the rights of outside creditors, should not usually be included in the capital account but should be classified as assets or liabilities. Classification of such loans as current or long-term is dependent on the reasonably anticipated settlement date.

With respect to the income statement, salaries paid to partners for personal services and interest on partners' capital account balances should be reflected as expenses of the period, unless otherwise provided in the articles of partnership. Further, a schedule showing the disposition of net income to the various partners should be included in the set of financial statements. In some instances, the income applicable to individual partners for tax return purposes will differ significantly from that determined in accordance with generally accepted accounting principles. In such cases disclosure of the amount and nature of the discrepancy may be desirable. Tax allocation is not required in partnership financial statements, because a partnership is not a taxable entity for income tax purposes. Disclosure in the notes to the financial statements as to the fact that income taxes are the personal responsibility of the partners and that no provision is made for them is appropriate.

Material items involving partners, such as rent paid to a partner, should be reflected specifically in the statements or footnotes. The amount of business done by a partnership with a partner and amounts owing to/from a partner by the partnership should be disclosed. The objective of such disclosures is to assure readers that they will be informed fully of transactions that do not involve arms'-length dealings. Also, it is appropriate to offset a receivable from a partner against an amount due the partner if settlement is to be made on a net basis.

The initial partnership financial statements should be included as a part of the partnership agreement. Such inclusion will establish the specific assets that the partnership is taking over from partners personally or from a predecessor partnership, the valuations of such assets, and the liabilities the partnership is expected to assume.

Financial statements of limited partnerships are frequently prepared on a tax basis only, based on the assumption that the limited partners are investors interested primarily in the tax status of their investments. This approach has been taken in situations where "tax shelters" have been sold to the public. If a registration with the Securities and Exchange Commission (SEC) is required, the presentation must be based on generally accepted accounting principles [SEC, 1974]. Tax basis data may be presented in footnotes or supporting schedules, but they cannot supplant the GAAP basis presentations.

An illustrative set of partnership financial statements is shown as Exhibits 2, 3, and 4.

THE ARTICLES OF PARTNERSHIP

Needed Provisions. The basic agreement among the partners is usually called the "articles of partnership" and should state the purpose of the partnership and the rights and obligations of the parties. In the absence of provisions in the articles, the Uniform Partnership Act or common law rules will be applicable. Legal counsel and advice from accountants are desirable in developing and finalizing the articles so that coverage is complete, unintended outcomes are avoided, and mechanisms are prescribed for resolution of disputes. The articles of partnership should include:

1. Names of partners and name of the partnership.
2. Purpose of the partnership.
3. Business location(s).

EXHIBIT 2

AMES AND FIERS
Balance Sheet (Condensed)
December 31, 19X3

Assets

Current assets:			
Other current assets		$ 90,000	
Advance to Ames		16,000	$106,000
14% 6-year note, due June 30, 19X5, from Fiers			10,000
Property, plant, and equipment (at cost less accumulated depreciation):			
Land (contributed by Ames)		$ 34,000	
Buildings and equipment	$65,000		
Less: Accumulated depreciation	35,000	30,000	64,000
			$180,000

Equities

Current liabilities:			
Other current liabilities		$ 30,000	
Account payable—merchandise purchased from Ames ..		12,000	$ 42,000
Partners' equities:			
Permanent investment (capital account)		$110,000	
Undistributed profits (current account)................		28,000	138,000
			$180,000

EXHIBIT 3

AMES AND FIERS
Schedule of Changes in Partners' Equities
For Year Ended December 31, 19X3

	Ames	Fiers	Total
Permanent investment, Jan. 1, 19X3	$60,000	$40,000	$100,000
Additional cash investment per agreement of June 30, 19X3	-0-	10,000	10,000
Permanent investment, Dec. 31, 19X3	$60,000	$50,000	$110,000
Undistributed profits, Jan. 1, 19X3	$14,000	-0-	$ 14,000
Interest on permanent investment at 15%	9,000	$ 6,750	15,750
Partners' salaries for 19X3	25,000	20,000	45,000
Share of net income for 19X3	35,275	35,275	70,550
	$83,275	$62,025	$145,300
Withdrawals: Salaries	$25,000	$20,000	$ 45,000
Other	40,000	32,300	72,300
	$65,000	$52,300	$117,300
Undistributed profits, Dec. 31, 19X3	$18,275	$ 9,725	$ 28,000

EXHIBIT 4

AMES AND FIERS
Income Statement
Year Ended December 31, 19X3

Sales	$400,000
Cost of goods sold	250,000
Gross margin	$150,000
Operating expenses:	
Selling expense	$ 10,700
Administrative expense	8,000
Partners' salaries	45,000
Interest on partners' permanent investment . . .	15,750
	$ 79,450
Net income for 19X3	$ 70,550

Allocation of Income Statement Items to Partners

	Ames	Fiers	Total
Salary allowance	$25,000	$20,000	$ 45,000
Interest on partners' permanent investment . . .	9,000	6,750	15,750
Net income for 19X3 (50% for Ames and 50% for Fiers)	35,275	35,275	70,550
Total allocation	$69,275	$62,025	$131,300

4. Date of formation and term (if not of indefinite duration).

5. Contributions of each partner, valuations assigned to noncash consideration, and determination of capital account balances.

6. Method(s) of accounting to be employed and the partnership fiscal year.

7. Partner interests in profits and losses, allowances (if any) for interest on capital investments and for salaries for partners. Computational rules for each, including any guarantees.

8. Partner withdrawal and dissolution rights, and partner responsibility for additional contributions.

9. Responsibilities of partners and limitations (if any) on their authority.

10. Procedures for resolving disputes.

Assignment of values to contributed assets, as noted in item 5, is of critical importance because gains or losses subsequent to dates of property contribution to the partnership will be distributed to the partners in accordance with their profit-sharing ratios unless the articles specify otherwise. Gains or losses attributed to periods preceding contribution are applicable 100 percent to the contributing partner. Timing of contribution of cash and noncash assets should be specified as an aid in fixing values and setting the starting date for attributing revenues and expenses to the partnership.

The classes of partners, including any particular provisions with respect to limitations on liability, should be stated explicitly. Any rights of the partners to borrow money from the partnership and the rate of interest to be paid on such loans should be specified. The obligation of a partner to loan money to the partnership, the rate of interest, and other terms of such transactions should be specified to minimize the chance of dispute.

Extreme care should be taken in drafting the articles to ensure a common understanding as to the applicable principles of income measurement, asset valuation, and measurement of liabilities. To minimize disputes as to accounting methods, the articles could specify the use of generally accepted principles of accounting. Further, where accounting alternatives exist, the articles could (1) list the methods selected or (2) specify the procedure for selecting methods or (3) use a combination. Adoption of new standards of accounting promulgated by the Financial Accounting Standards Board, and Releases of the Securities and Exchange Commission could also be specified. Elements such as when to recognize revenue and what year to expense employee bonuses should be considered. Particular care needs to be placed on when to recognize unusual items such as gains on disposal of fixed assets, losses that result from selling a segment of business, and any special partner interests in such profits or losses.

The rights of individual partners to perform certain management functions exclusively, the minimum hours of work required of partners, and the exclusive rights granted to serve as an agent of the partnership should be specified in the articles. Rights of partners in the event of dissolution should be specified. This would include:

1. Responsibilities of the individual partners during a dissolution and liquidating process,

2. Methods to be used in placing values on assets that are to be distributed to partners rather than sold,

3. Plans for distributing cash prior to completion of all liquidation procedures,

4. Provisions for partners to buy out other partners in the event of dispute or death of one of their number, and

5. Methods of calculating goodwill.

Interpretations When Articles of Partnership Are Silent. Carefully drawn articles of partnership can serve as an effective guide to operating relationships and business objectives as well as state procedures for resolving disputes. However, no drafter of articles is likely to foresee all contingencies or avoid all ambiguities; hence guidance must on occasion be obtained by reference to the applicable statute, usually the Uniform Partnership Act, or to common law.

The articles of partnership, unless they contravene one of the provisions of the statutes covering partnerships or are against public policy, determine the rights and duties of partners. Section 18 of the Uniform Partnership Act emphasizes the importance of the articles when it states: "The rights and duties of the partners in relationship to the partnership shall be determined, subject to any agreement between them, by the following rules. . . ."

Differences of opinion with respect to such rights and duties are handled in the same way under common law and the Uniform Partnership Act. The latter provides in Section 18 (h): "Any difference arising as to ordinary matters connected with the partnership business may be decided by a majority of the partners; but no act in contravention of any agreement between the partners may be done rightfully without the consent of all partners." A problem might exist as to what constitutes a majority of the partners if equal numbers voted on each side of an issue. No precise procedure exists in the law for resolving this; as a result, the partnership agreement should normally provide a specific device for settling such differences. As to actions in "contravention of any agreement between the partners," it is necessary to have unanimous agreement among the partners to effect such change. Depending on inclusions in the initial articles of partnership, such actions might include the shifting of business objectives, closing out operations at a specified address, or disposition of a major segment of the partnership's business.

FORMATION OF PARTNERSHIPS

Initial Capital. Cash, property, personal services, business contracts, trademarks, and so on, contributed by partners to a partnership at the outset constitute the initial capital of that partnership. The value of each contribution should be recognized as an asset. Difficulties in valuation of services, noncash assets, and noncash assets subject to debts, liens, or claims frequently exist. For example, a partner might contribute to the partnership the use of a piece of vacant property for a period of 25 years, with the provision that the partnership would be required to pay the property taxes, including special assessments on the property, during that period. The fair market value of the net rentals, discounted to the date of the transfer of the rights to use of the property, should be the measure of the contribution of that partner. Disagreements as to the discount rate, fair market value of rentals at the various dates, and so on, should be resolved by mutual agreement of the parties prior to transfer of the assets.

The amount of the initial contributions of capital by the partners is expected to remain intact, subject only to losses that might decrease the amount or subsequent agreements among the partners that would require further contributions or a reallocation of balances among them.

On occasion, an existing going concern may be contributed to a partnership as one partner's share of the initial capital. In such an instance, it may be appropriate to recognize that the value of the business as a going concern is greater than the book value of the assets or the sum of their individual fair market values. The total going-concern value would be entered in the partner's capital account as the contribution. The difference between the going-concern value and the fair market value of the individual assets might be set up as goodwill (assuming that no specifically identifiable assets exist relative to such amounts) on the initial balance sheet of the partnership.

Partner's interests in capital may not be the same as their profit and loss ratios. Values assigned to partnership assets and liabilities at the onset of the business or at any time a contribution of noncash assets is made are extremely important. Subsequent changes in value become partnership gains and losses and are allocated in accordance with the profit and loss ratios specified in the partnership agreement. If no profit and loss ratios are specified, then the law presumes them to be equal. However, it is possible to have the partnership agreement specify that partners' capital accounts are to be adjusted later relative to gains and/or losses realized on dispositions of named contributed property. Thus, initial valuation must be fairly recorded or provision made for subsequent adjustments if equity and the original agreements among the partners are to be preserved. Equity as to income tax considerations requires the partners to recognize the implications associated with the fact that the tax basis of assets contributed to a partnership does not change at contribution date regardless of the fair market value of the property.

The capital recorded in a partner's capital account, when the records are maintained on the basis of generally accepted accounting principles, will not necessarily equal the tax basis of a partner's interest in the partnership. When the partner pays cash for the interest in the partnership, the tax basis of its interest will be the cash paid. For GAAP purposes, the preliminary balance in that partner's capital account will be the cash contributed. However, under GAAP, such balance could be increased if the partner is given credit for goodwill or a bonus from another partner. It could be decreased if the partner provides a bonus to another partner. If the partner contributes unencumbered property, the tax basis of the property will remain unchanged, regardless of the fair value of the property at date of contribution. For GAAP purposes, fair value of that property would constitute the initial credit to capital. If the property contributed is subject to debt and/or if other debts of the contributing partner are assumed by the partnership, the tax basis of the partner's interest will be the basis of the property contributed less the portion of the debts assumed by the other partners. For GAAP purposes, fair value of the property less the debts transferred to the partnership would constitute the initial credit to capital.

As an example of an initial financial statement, assume that S contributes property with fair value of $100,000, tax basis of $40,000, subject to a mortgage of $30,000, to the SB Partnership, and B contributes cash of $70,000. Each receives a 50 percent interest in the partnership. The initial balance sheets (GAAP basis and tax basis) are shown in Exhibit 5. Note that the mortgage is considered a factor in determining the basis of each partner's interest in the partnership when the tax approach is employed. The assumption by B of one-half or $15,000 of the mortgage on property contributed is considered a distribution of money to S, thereby reducing S's partnership interest basis from $40,000 to $25,000. The assumption by B of one-half or $15,000 of the mortgage is considered a contribution of money by B, so that the basis of B's partnership interest is increased from $70,000 to $85,000.

Some partners may wish to sell assets to "their" partnerships rather than contribute those items, because of such factors as income tax considerations and amounts of contributions by other partners. Such procedure is appropriate, but should be carefully documented to minimize the risk of subsequent controversy.

Changes in Asset Valuation. Assets held for extended periods of time may change greatly in value. So long as the membership of the partnership and the profit and loss ratios remain unchanged, there is no serious problem with respect to the time such incremental value is recognized. However, in many partnerships these factors do change. Prior to changing a profit and loss ratio or membership in the partnership, asset revaluation should be considered. Otherwise gains or losses may be allocated to parties not properly chargeable or creditable with such changes in value.

A new partner must consider not only the fair market value of the assets but also the potential liability for capital gains tax on any fair market value that exceeds the basis of that asset to the partnership. If asset values have declined

---

EXHIBIT 5

SB PARTNERSHIP
Balance Sheet and Statement of Assets and Equities on a GAAP Basis
and on a Tax Basis at Date of Organization

	Basis			Basis	
	GAAP	Tax		GAAP	Tax
Cash	$ 70,000	$ 70,000	Mortgage	$ 30,000	
Property	100,000	40,000	S capital	70,000	
			S partnership interest......		$ 25,000
			B capital	70,000	
			B partnership interest		85,000
	$170,000	$110,000		$170,000	$110,000

below their book value, an incoming partner will be interested in the value of the loss that has not been deducted on tax returns of the other partners. The interest of existing partners in increases or decreases in fair market values in relation to the tax basis of the assets will be opposite to that of incoming partners. Adjustments to asset values, whenever changes in profit and loss ratios take place or when a partner is admitted or retired, should recognize the inherent benefit or cost associated with the difference between the fair market value and the tax basis of the assets held. To illustrate the above:

BLACKMAN AND DORRIS
Balance Sheet
December 31, 19X3

Common stock of Durango Corp. at cost		Blackman, capital	$150
(market value is $1,000)	$300	Dorris, capital	150
	$300		$300

Assume further that Ungerman is interested in becoming a member of the partnership by buying out Dorris's interest entirely and that Blackman is willing to accept Ungerman as a partner. The revaluing of the assets would involve recognition of the increment in market ($700) and the related capital gains tax effect ($140, assuming a 20 percent tax rate), or a net of $560. The journal entries for revaluation and the admission of Ungerman to partnership might be as follows:

1. Revalue the asset:
   Common Stock of Durango—Revaluation
   Increment   700
      Deferred Federal Income Taxes—Unrealized
      Gains   140
      Blackman, Capital   280
      Dorris, Capital   280

2. Transfer Dorris's interest to Ungerman:
   Dorris, Capital   430
      Ungerman, Capital   430

Because partnerships are not subject to federal income tax, nonrecognition of income tax effects related to valuation changes is acceptable. The onus for such knowledge is then placed on the individual partners. In the above illustration, the deferred tax account would then be omitted, the credits to the two capital accounts in the first entry would be $350 each, and the balance transferred to Ungerman would be $500, independent of the amount paid by Ungerman to Dorris.

Disposition of a Partner's Interest. There are three ways for a partner to dispose of a partnership interest: (1) sale to an outside party, (2) sale to other partner(s), and (3) retirement, with partnership assets being distributed, or the partnership issuing notes or equivalent payable to the partner. With (1) and (2), no change in partnership assets takes place. After revaluation, the capital, current, and loan accounts related to the retiring partner are transferred to the new and/or old partner(s). In order to assure equity between the new and/or old partners when relative profit and loss ratios change, revaluation of assets should take place before the admission of the new partner. Because a new partnership results and relative profit and loss ratios are likely to change, it is appropriate for revaluation to take place. An example of a sale to an outside party was given above.

The following example illustrates sale to other partners, with tax effects being disregarded.

DAVID, ESTHER & FRANKLIN
Balance Sheet
December 31, 19X3

Assets, at cost		David, capital	$10,000
[market value of		Esther, capital	15,000
($60,000)]	$45,000	Franklin, capital......	20,000
	$45,000		$45,000

Esther is buying out David and paying $15,000 for David's interest. Profits and losses have been shared equally, and after the buy-out will be allocated 60 percent to Esther and 40 percent to Franklin. Note that in neither situation are profits and losses shared in the capital ratios.

1. A. Revalue the assets:

Assets—Revaluation Increment...............	15,000	
David, Capital..........................		5,000
Esther, Capital		5,000
Franklin, Capital.......................		5,000

2. A. Transfer David's capital to Esther:

David, Capital..........................	15,000	
Esther, Capital		15,000

Failure to revalue the assets would result in Esther being credited with only $9,000 of the gain (60 percent) when the assets were sold, instead of $10,000 as noted above ($5,000 increment applicable to both David's and Esther's capital accounts).

If tax considerations were considered and the asset values in the balance sheet above are equal to their tax basis, and a tax rate of 20 percent were assumed to be applicable, then the following entries would be needed.

1. B. Revalue the assets:

Assets—Revaluation Increment...............	15,000	
Deferred Federal Income Taxes—Unrealized		
Gains		3,000
David, Capital..........................		4,000
Esther, Capital		4,000
Franklin, Capital.......................		4,000

2. B. Transfer David's capital to Esther:

David, Capital	14,000	
Esther, Capital		14,000

The following example illustrates retirement of a partner. Assume the same initial balance sheet as above, the same undervaluation of assets, and that retiring partner David is to be paid in cash by the partnership.

1. C. Revalue the assets (same as 1A above)
2. C. Retire David from the partnership:

David, Capital	15,000	
Cash		15,000

The revised balance sheet would report assets of $45,000, Esther's capital as $20,000, and Franklin's capital as $25,000.

A member of a partnership who retires may be paid more or less than the balance in his or her capital account, after recording the needed asset revaluations. Either a bonus method or goodwill method will have to be used for handling such transactions. To illustrate, assume the same partnership balance sheet shown above and the same asset revaluation. Assume further that David is to retire and receive $20,000 in assets from the partnership. If the bonus method is employed, a charge will be made against Esther's and Franklin's capital accounts. The difference between the carrying value of the assets to be distributed and the balance in David's capital account will be allocated in accordance with the Esther and Franklin profit and loss ratios, as noted below:

David, Capital	15,000	
Esther, Capital	2,500	
Franklin, Capital	2,500	
Assets		20,000

On the other hand, if the goodwill method is employed, recognizing goodwill to the extent that the remaining partners have purchased it, the following entry is needed:

David, Capital	15,000	
Goodwill	5,000	
Assets		20,000

Goodwill might also be recognized to the full extent implied by the transaction. Then the journal entry would be as follows:

David, Capital	15,000	
Goodwill	15,000	
Esther, Capital		5,000
Franklin, Capital		5,000
Assets		20,000

Goodwill is the excess over book value paid to the retiring partner of $5,000 (= $20,000 − $15,000) divided by the retiring partner's profit and loss sharing ratio.

Or David might receive only $8,000 from the partnership, which is less than the balance in his capital account. This amount might be the result of poor bargaining power on the part of David, an overstatement of asset values, a bleak outlook as to future profits, or other reasons. If the bonus method is used and no asset revaluations are needed, the journal entry to record David's withdrawal is as follows:

David, Capital	10,000	
Esther, Capital		1,000
Franklin, Capital		1,000
Assets		8,000

If assets were overvalued, they should be written down to current market values.

Admission of a New Partner. A party can become a partner only with the consent of all the existing partners. However, partners can assign their financial interests in a partnership to another party or parties without the consent of each of the other partners provided that no prohibition on such action is stated in the partnership agreement. Such assignment does not transfer any rights to manage to the purchaser, but will permit a sharing in the partnership profits and losses. If such assignment takes place, the partnership will only note on the assigning partner's accounts that his or her financial interests have been assigned.

The incoming partner can acquire the interest by: (1) purchase of an interest from an existing partner or partners, (2) contribution of assets, or (3) combination of the two methods. The sale of an existing interest to an outside party was illustrated above. When there is a purchase of an interest by contributing assets, the values assigned to assets contributed by the incoming partner are important, because subsequent depreciation, gains or losses on disposition, and so on, will be allocated to the partners on the profit and loss ratios then in place.

The credit to the incoming partner's capital account need not necessarily equal the market values of the items contributed. Goodwill may be recognized when a partner is admitted, with the amount allocated to the old or new partners or both. Or a bonus may be charged and/or credited to the new and/or old partners.

The following sets of assumptions will serve to illustrate alternative accounting methods for recording admission of a partner. The balance sheet for Black and White is shown below:

BLACK AND WHITE
Balance Sheet
December 31, 19X3

Assets at cost (market value of $40,000)	$40,000	Black, capital	$24,000
		White, capital	16,000
	$40,000		$40,000

Assume that profits and losses are shared equally and that Gray, the incoming partner, is to contribute assets with market value of $20,000 and receive a one-third interest in capital. No bonus or goodwill is implied, so Gray's entry to the partnership is recorded as follows:

Assets	20,000	
Gray, Capital		20,000

However, if the fair value of partnership assets is $60,000, tax effects are recognized at a 20 percent tax rate, and Gray is to contribute assets with tax basis and market value of $28,000, the entries would be

1. Revalue the assets and recognize the tax effect:

Assets—Revaluation Increment.	20,000	
Deferred Federal Income Taxes—Unrealized		
Gain.		4,000
Black, Capital		8,000
White, Capital.		8,000

2. Record Gray's contribution:

Assets.	28,000	
Gray, Capital		28,000

An agreement to admit a new partner contributing assets to a partnership should state whether the bonus method or the goodwill method is to be employed to recognize differences arising from the relationship of his or her capital interest to the market value of the assets he or she contributes. If the bonus method is chosen, the bonus may be applicable to either the incoming partner or to the existing partners. The following formula is suggested to ascertain the accounting entries:

$$x = a(b + c)$$

where x = credit to the new partner's capital account
a = percentage of partnership equity applied to the incoming partner
b = contribution of the new partner
c = balance of existing partners' capital accounts

Apply this to the initial balance sheets above, but assume that Gray is to contribute $20,000 and receive a one-quarter interest in capital. Substituting in the equation, note that:

$$x = .25(\$20,000 + \$40,000)$$
$$= \$15,000$$

The difference between Gray's contribution of $20,000 and the credit to Gray's capital account of $15,000 would be split equally between the existing partners because they share profits and losses equally. The entry to record the admission of Gray is as follows:

Assets	20,000	
Black, Capital		2,500
White, Capital		2,500
Gray, Capital		15,000

If the goodwill method was used, an additional unknown would be used, namely:

$$y = \text{Total Capitalization}$$

If goodwill is applicable to the existing partners, the formula employed would be expressed as

$$y = \frac{b}{a}$$

or if goodwill is applicable to the incoming partner,

$$y = \frac{c}{1 - a}$$

Apply this to the illustration above and capitalization may be computed as follows:

$$y = \frac{b}{a}$$

Substituting, $y = \$20,000/.25$, or $\$80,000$. Goodwill is $\$20,000$ [= $\$80,000 - (\$20,000 + \$40,000)$]. The entry to record Gray's admission is as follows:

Assets	20,000	
Goodwill	20,000	
Black, Capital		10,000
White, Capital		10,000
Gray, Capital		20,000

On the other hand, if goodwill is believed to be applicable to the incoming partner, the calculation would proceed as follows:

$$y = \frac{c}{1 - a}$$

Substituting, $y = \$40,000/(1 - .25)$, or a $\$53,333$ total capitalization. Because the assets ($\$20,000$) contributed by the incoming partner, plus the assets of the existing partners ($\$40,000$), total $\$60,000$ and this is greater than the indicated capitalization of $\$53,333$, goodwill of the entering partner is nonexistent. This is obviously not feasible, so the preceding formula in which goodwill is allocated to existing partners must be used.

If the agreement allocates the incoming partner a one-half interest in capital for the $\$20,000$ investment, the second method could be employed. Total capitalization would be $\$80,000$, goodwill would be $\$20,000$, and the new partner's capital account would be credited with $\$40,000$.

Sometimes the credit to the new partner's capital account or total capitalization will be known and one or the other items mentioned will be unknown.

Such a change in the list of knowns and unknowns does not change the formulas.

The goodwill and bonus methods will produce identical results as to partners' equity in the partnership if (1) the incoming partner's share of profits is equal to the initial ratio of the incoming partner's capital to total capital and (2) the existing partners continue to share profits in proportion to their original ratios. In the event that both the above conditions are not met continuously after admission of the new partner, the goodwill and bonus methods will give different results.

PARTNERSHIP NET INCOME

Measurement of Periodic Net Income. Periodic net income for a partnership is usually calculated in the same manner as for other types of business organizations. Timing of revenue and expense recognition is particularly important for a partnership because profit and loss sharing ratios and membership in the partnership may change from period to period. Virtually all items coming to light in the current year are recognized as applicable to this period's income. The principal exceptions to current-year recognition are (1) correction of an error (SFAS No. 16) [FASB, 1982, A35.103], which requires that the item(s) be attributed to the year(s) in which they arose; and (2) special changes in accounting principle (APB Opinion No. 20) [FASB, 1982, A35.114], which require retroactive restatement.

Partnership contracts may contain special provisions with respect to timing, measurement, and allocation of income. Also, special methods for recording transactions between a partner and the partnership may be specified. If one of these conflicts with generally accepted accounting principles, the accountant reporting on the fairness of such statements must indicate the nature of the deviation and its effect.

In the interest of full disclosure, the following types of transactions between a partner and the partnership should be specifically identified and summarized in the financial statements or their related notes: (1) salary, (2) interest on capital investments, (3) interest on loans, (4) margins on sales, and (5) rentals. Revenue and expense attributes of such transactions are customarily treated as affecting partnership income and are not considered as a division of profits. Where applicable, each category should be reported because of its effect on income determination and the resultant portion of profits applicable to each partner. When services are rendered and/or loans made, an appropriate salary and/or interest cost should be recognized as appropriate elements in measuring profitability of the business.

Interest on capital investments might be calculated in any one of the following ways: (1) a percentage of the beginning, ending, or average capital investments; (2) a percentage of capital in excess of a specified dollar amount (with interest being charged any partner whose balance is below a specified minimum); and (3) a percentage of capital balances, in excess or deficiency, based on the proportion required by the partnership agreement. This calculation can be troublesome if the term "capital" is not precisely defined. Distinction should be made in the partnership contract as to whether capital means initial capital contributed, the sum of all capital and current accounts outstanding at the beginning of the year, the average balance of the combined capital and current accounts, or some other definition.

Revenues, expenses, and losses should be recorded in partnership records, and partnership statements should be prepared on a basis that conforms to the accounting practices typical in the industry in which the partnership operates or on a tax basis, depending on the accounting provision of the articles of partnership. Revenue and expense items, whether they arise from transactions with partners or nonpartners, should be handled as though they were expenses or revenues of the partnership and not as distributions of profit.

Allocation of Net Income and Losses. The articles of partnership are critical as to the allocation of profits among the partners. When the articles are drafted, the fiscal year-end should be established and the bases for allocating all elements of revenues, expenses, and losses stated clearly. Not only may the amount of income attributed to partners differ, but also the types of revenue, expense, and loss allocated to each partner may differ. An illustration of allocation of partnership net income was presented as part of Exhibit 4.

If the articles are silent as to profit and loss allocations to partners, they will be allocated in equal amounts to each partner. Section 18 of the Uniform Partnership Act provides:

> The rights and duties of the partners in relation to the partnership shall be determined, subject to any agreement between them, by the following rules: a) Each partner shall ... share equally in the profits and surplus remaining after all liabilities, including those to partners, are satisfied; and must contribute towards the losses, whether of capital or otherwise, sustained by the partnership according to his share in the profits.

Various ways of allocating profits and losses can be specified in the articles of partnership:

1. Equal amounts to each partner
2. Arbitrary ratio
3. Ratio of partners' capitals (beginning, month-end average, ending, etc.)
4. Interest on partner's capitals and/or salaries (bonuses) with the balance allocated equally to each partner or in an arbitrary ratio

Arbitrary ratios are frequently employed for profit distributions. Such ratios normally recognize the anticipated relative contributions of the partners, including special knowledge of an individual partner, hours to be spent, experience, reputation, and so on. Such a ratio might be expressed as 3 to 2 to 1 for a three-person partnership.

Different items of income are sometimes allocated on different bases and may be related to initial asset contributions or tax circumstances of individual partners. For example, a different distribution formula might be employed with respect to dividends and interest received on investments from that used to allocate operating margins realized from trading operations. Or regularly recurring income items might be allocated in one manner but unusual gains and losses, such as those resulting from sale of a segment of a business, might be allocated in another manner. Obviously, great care needs to be taken in drafting the articles of partnership so that ambiguities relative to income allocations are minimized.

Tax Considerations. Internal Revenue Code Section 702 specifies that the following items of partnership income must be set out separately:

1. Short-term capital gains and losses
2. Long-term capital gains and losses
3. Gains and losses from sales or exchanges of Section 1231 property (primarily fixed assets used in a business or profession)
4. Charitable contributions
5. Dividends for which there is an exclusion or dividends for which there is a deduction for dividends received by corporations
6. Taxes paid or accrued to a foreign country and to U.S. possessions
7. Other items of income, gain, loss, deduction, or credit specified by the regulations
8. Taxable income or loss, exclusive of the above items

Illustrative of the items contemplated under item 7 are intangible drilling and development costs in the extractive industries, amounts received on accounts previously written off as bad debts, contributions to a qualified pension plan or a profit-sharing plan, and soil and water conservation expenditures.

Generally, the Internal Revenue Service permits allocations of special items specified by the articles of partnership unless tax avoidance is the principal purpose for such provisions. For instance, an agreement specifying an allocation to reflect the difference between the fair value and the basis of contributed property for purpose of allocating gain or loss on disposition, and depreciation or amortization, would be recognized. For example, a partner might contribute a piece of machinery with a $5,000 basis but a fair market value of $10,000. Depreciation allowable to the partnership is limited to the $5,000 basis, because the contribution was made to the partnership tax-free. Up to 100 percent of the depreciation provision could be allocated to noncontributing partners and up to 100 percent of the first $5,000 gain on disposition could be allocated to the contributing partner.

In deciding on income allocations, consideration should be given to the individual partners' personal tax positions. It might be advantageous, for example, to allocate items subject to capital gains tax to relatively high tax bracket taxpayers and ordinary income items to relatively low tax bracket partners. Compensation for such difference could then be undertaken through the medium of adjusting the profit and loss ratios otherwise decided on. Also, the partners' share of the partnership investment in machinery and equipment is needed for purposes of computing the investment credit applicable to each partner. Again, the partnership agreement might be used to advantage to specify the portions applicable to each partner. To be effective, such allocations must have substantial economic effect.

WINDING UP THE PARTNERSHIP

Dissolution, Termination, and Distribution. The terms dissolution, termination, and distribution should be differentiated. *Dissolution* implies the ending of a specific partnership agreement but not necessarily the ending of the business. Dissolution, for example, takes place at the death of a partner. At that time the estate of the deceased partner becomes entitled to the value of the deceased partner's interest in the business. Thus, a transfer of the deceased partner's interest from the owners' equity category to the liability classification takes place.

Termination of the business involves termination of the business operations, including liquidation of the assets or their transfer to some of the partners and payment of all debts. *Distribution* involves transferring some or all of the assets to creditors and partners.

Termination of a partnership business may result from the same causes that terminate any other going concern, such as inability of a firm to compete effectively, desire of owners to get out of business, and shortage of working capital. Because of the unique character of a partnership, it is often possible for one partner to force termination of the business, if there is no provision in the articles of partnership to prevent it. If the partner requesting termination and the other partners cannot agree on the amount he or she is to receive and when, then in the absence of a provision for resolution of such differences (e.g., by arbitration), a sale of the business as a going concern or liquidation of individual assets and payment of all liabilities will of necessity ensue. During liquidation, gains and losses should be allocated to the partners' current accounts in their profit and loss ratios unless another ratio is specified by the partnership agreement. The partnership agreement is the governing instrument, and it continues to govern the relationships among the partners until the partnership operation is completely terminated.

If certain assets are to be distributed to the partners, their values should be adjusted to market and the differences between carrying value and market should be recorded as gains and losses on liquidation. Tax effects may appropriately be taken into consideration in computing such gains and losses, because such gains and losses will eventually be recognized at the partner level. At distribution the current value of such assets should then be charged against the partners' current accounts. In this way, all partners share in gains or losses on all assets, whether they are distributed to the partners or sold to outsiders.

Various types of accounts between a partner and the partnership may exist, including capital, current, and loan accounts. The rights of partners to partnership funds are always subordinated to those of outside creditors. With respect to partners' claims against the partnership and the partnership claims against the partner, a right of offset exists. Thus, if the partnership owed a partner money on a loan but the partner owed the partnership a current account balance, the debit and credit balances would be offset and settlement in liquidation would be on the basis of a net amount.

Extreme care needs to be taken with respect to distribution of cash or other assets during the liquidation proceedings so that only those parties entitled to a distribution will in fact receive such. Distributions must first go to satisfy creditor claims. Creditors having priorities must be paid before other creditors, and secured creditors have first claim on proceeds from assets to which their lien applies. If all creditor claims cannot be satisfied at a given time and a distribution is to be made, such distribution should be on a pro rata basis for that category of creditors whose claims cannot be paid in full. After outside creditor claims have been satisfied, distributions can be made to partners.

Section 40 (b) of the Uniform Partnership Act states the following rules for making payments in liquidation.

The liabilities of the partnership shall rank in order of payment, as follows:
I. Those owing to creditors other than partners,
II. Those owing to partners other than for capital and profits,
III. Those owing to partners in respect of capital,
IV. Those owing to partners in respect of profits.

Section 40 (d) states:

The partners shall contribute, as provided by section 18 (a), the amount necessary to satisfy the liabilities; but if any, but not all, of the partners are insolvent, or, not being subject to process, refuse to contribute, the other partners shall contribute their share of the liabilities, and, in the relative proportions in which they share the profits, the additional amount necessary to pay the liabilities.

Section 40 (i) states:

Where a partner has become bankrupt or his estate is insolvent the claims against his separate property shall rank in the following order:
I. Those owing to separate creditors,
II. Those owing to partnership creditors,
III. Those owing to partners by way of contribution.

It is clear that the partnership creditors other than partners rank ahead of partners. Because of the right to offset, there is no doubt that the partner as a creditor ranks below all outside creditors. Further, it may be appropriate in some instances to make payment to partners with respect to their capital balances even though other partners have loan balances still outstanding. This condition may exist where the partner with the loan balance has a capital account deficit and the right of offset is applied.

Personal assets of a partner are applied first to payment of claims against that partner personally, as noted under Section 40 (i) above. To the extent that the partner is entitled to funds from the partnership at its liquidation, these are available for the personal creditors. If the partner has more than enough personal assets to pay personal creditors, then the excess could be available for contribution to the partnership to pay otherwise unsatisfied partnership creditors or to settle claims of other partners whose capital accounts have credit balances. Creditors of the partnership must look first to partnership assets. If these prove insufficient to satisfy their claims, creditors may look to an individual

EXHIBIT 6

JASPER AND KRICTON
Partnership Liquidation Statement
Three Months Ended November 30, 19X1

Event or position	Assets		Liabilities		Jasper		Kricton	
	Cash	Other	to others	Loan	Current	Capital	Current	Capital
Profit and loss ratios						60%		40%
Account balances, Sept. 2, 19X1	$ 3,000	$ 97,000	$ 55,000	$15,000	$ 5,000	$ 10,000	$(1,000)	$ 16,000
Realization on other assets and distribution of loss	62,000	(97,000)				(21,000)		(14,000)
Payment of liabilities	(55,000)		(55,000)					
Balances	$ 10,000	-0-	-0-	$15,000	$ 5,000	$(11,000)	$(1,000)	$ 2,000
Apply right of offset				(6,000)	(5,000)	11,000	1,000	(1,000)
Pay partner's loan	(9,000)			(9,000)				
Pay partner's capital account	(1,000)							(1,000)

partner's personal assets, but must recognize that their claims are subordinated to those of the partner's personal creditors.

Lump-Sum Distributions in Complete Liquidation. When sale of assets and payments to all creditors in liquidation have been completed, all gains and losses will be known and should be distributed to the partners' accounts. If any partner's account has a deficit at that point in time, a determination will have to be made as to whether contribution from that partner can be expected. If no contribution is possible, such deficit from the individual partner must be distributed to the remaining partners on the basis of their individual profit and loss ratios. Before any cash is distributed, not only must gains and losses incurred during liquidation be distributed to partners' capital accounts, but also losses due to the inability of the partnership to obtain contribution to cover deficits in partners' capital accounts must be recognized.

The Statement of Partnership Liquidation shown in Exhibit 6 illustrates the process the accountant follows when losses do not produce net debit balances for any partner. Exhibit 7 carries a partnership through a liquidation process in which it is assumed that one partner, Kricton, is personally insolvent and unable to make payment to the partnership for the debit balance in his capital account. The balances on the books would not be closed out because Jasper would continue to have a right against Kricton for contribution. If Kricton should acquire assets at a later date and assuming that he was not discharged from such obligations in a bankruptcy action, Jasper might attempt collection.

Installment Distributions. In Exhibits 6 and 7, all the assets were realized before any distributions to partners took place. Frequently, partners will request that some distribution be made to them prior to complete realization of its assets and incurrence of all liquidating expenses. At such time, total losses are unlikely to be known. The person undertaking the liquidation process must be extremely careful not to make an improper distribution, because he could be held personally liable for losses resulting from such improper distribution. Therefore, it is necessary that payments be made only to those partners who would have net credit balances remaining in their personal accounts after all possible losses have been distributed to those accounts. Such losses would include both losses incurred on disposition of assets and the inability to obtain a contribution from partners with net debit balances in their personal accounts.

Frequently, partners want a plan for distribution for cash or other assets prepared prior to liquidation. This will minimize the need for a calculation of "safe" payments to partners at various times during the liquidation process. Exhibit 8 illustrates an advance plan for cash distribution. Exhibit 9 presents a partnership liquidation statement and a schedule showing the amount to distribute at a time prior to completion of the liquidation process. It is to be noted that in an installment liquidation procedure each distribution is to be made on the assumption that: (1) partners with deficits will not be able to pay amounts owed to the partnership; and (2) no net recovery on remaining assets is possible.

EXHIBIT 7

JASPER AND KRICTON
Partnership Liquidation Statement
Three Months Ended November 30, 19X1

Event or position	Assets		Liabilities to others	Loan	Jasper		Kricton	
	Cash	Other			Current	Capital	Current	Capital
Profit and loss ratios						60%		40%
Account balances, Sept. 2, 19X1 .	$ 3,000	$ 97,000	$55,000	$ 15,000	$ 5,000	$ 20,000	$(1,000)	$ 6,000
Realization on other assets and distribution of loss	62,000	(97,000)				(21,000)		(14,000)
Payment of liabilities	(55,000)		(55,000)					
Balances	$ 10,000	-0-	-0-	$ 15,000	$ 5,000	$ (1,000)	$(1,000)	$ (8,000)
Apply right of offset					(1,000)	1,000		
Pay partner's loan	(10,000)			(10,000)				
Balances[a]	-0-	-0-	-0-	$ 5,000	$ 4,000	-0-	$(1,000)	$ (8,000)

[a]Represents rights of Jasper to contribution from Kricton. Rights are currently unenforceable, because Kricton's personal assets are insufficient to pay personal creditors.

EXHIBIT 8

LUELLA AND MERTON

Calculation of Loss Which Prevents a Partner from Sharing in Cash Distributions

Event or position	Assets		Liabilities	Luella (combined capital, current, and loan accounts)	Merton (combined capital, current, and loan accounts)
	Cash	Other			
Profit and loss ratios				60%	40%
Balances, Oct. 1, 19X1	$3,000	$ 97,000	$55,000	$ 30,000	$ 15,000
Loss to eliminate Merton from sharing in cash distributions . .		(37,500)		(22,500)	(15,000)
Balance	$3,000	$ 59,500	$55,000	$ 7,500	-0-
					$ 8,488

Schedule for cash distributions during liquidation

		Liabilities	Luella	Merton
First $55,000		$55,000	-0-	-0-
Next $7,500		-0-	$7,500	-0-
All over $62,500		-0-	60%	40%

EXHIBIT 9

LUELLA AND MERTON
Partnership Liquidation Statement
Two Months Ended November 30, 19X1

Event or position	Assets Cash	Assets Other	Liabilities to others	Loan	Luella Current	Luella Capital	Merton Current	Merton Capital
Profit and loss ratios						60%		40%
Account balances, Oct. 1, 19X1	$ 3,000	$ 97,000	$ 55,000	$ 15,000	$ 5,000	$ 10,000	$(1,000)	$ 16,000
Realization on other assets and distribution of loss	57,000	(71,000)				(8,400)		(5,600)
Payment of liabilities	(55,000)		(55,000)					
Apply right of offset							1,000	(1,000)
Payment to partner[a]	(5,000)			(5,000)				
Account balances, Nov. 1, 19X1	-0-	$ 26,000	-0-	$ 10,000	$ 5,000	$ 1,600	-0-	$ 9,400
Realization on other assets and distribution of gain	$ 30,000	(26,000)				2,400		1,600
Balances, Nov. 30, 19X1	$ 30,000	-0-	-0-	$ 10,000	$ 5,000	$ 4,000	-0-	$ 11,000
Payments:								
Partner's loan	$ 10,000			$ 10,000				
Partner's current account	5,000				$ 5,000			
Partners' capital accounts	15,000					$ 4,000		$ 11,000
Total payments	$ 30,000	-0-	-0-	$ 10,000	$ 5,000	$ 4,000	-0-	$ 11,000

[a]Calculations of installment payment appropriate as of November 1, 19X1

	Loan	Luella Current	Luella Capital	Merton Current	Merton Capital
Balances as of Nov. 1, 19X1, but before payment to partners	$15,000	$5,000	$ 1,600	$(1,000)	$ 10,400
Distribute possible loss on sale of remaining assets of $26,000			(15,600)		(10,400)
Balances	$15,000	$ 5,000	$(14,000)	$(1,000)	-0-
Apply right of offset	(9,000)	(5,000)	14,000		
Balances	$ 6,000	-0-	-0-	$(1,000)	-0-
Distribute possible loss if Merton were to become personally insolvent	(1,000)			1,000	
Cash to be distributed	$ 5,000	-0-	-0-	-0-	-0-

INCORPORATING A BUSINESS OPERATED AS A PARTNERSHIP

The need to limit liability or make transfer of ownership interests easier may suggest converting from the partnership to the corporate form of organization. The corporation would then take title to the assets and assume the liabilities of the old partnership. The old partnership would be dissolved and the partners become shareholders of the new corporation. Prior to transference of title, the new corporation must obtain a charter from the appropriate governmental entity. A contract between the old partnership and the corporation should be executed covering the specific items to be transferred and the shares of stock to be issued therefor.

EXHIBIT 10

PETER AND KATHRYN
Balance Sheet
January 31, 19X3

Assets

Cash.		$ 6,000
Trade receivables		10,000
Inventories		20,000
Equipment	$25,000	
Less: Accumulated depreciation.	6,000	19,000
		$55,000

Equities

Trade payables	$ 4,000
Bank loan.	15,000
Peter, capital[a]	16,000
Kathryn, capital[b]	20,000
	$55,000

[a]Entitled to 60% of profits.
[b]Entitled to 40% of profits.

Entry 1. Revalue the assets and allocate the net change to the partners

Equipment	4,000	
Accumulated Depreciation	6,000	
Deferred Federal Income Taxes*		2,000
Peter, Capital		4,800
Kathryn, Capital		3,200

*A tax rate of 20% is assumed to be appropriate.

Entry 2. Issue corporate stock to partners:

Peter, Capital	20,800	
Kathryn, Capital	23,200	
Capital Stock (220 shares, $100 par)		22,000
Additional Paid-in Capital		22,000

EXHIBIT 11

Entry 1. Revalue the assets and allocate the net change to the partners:

Equipment	4,000	
Accumulated Depreciation	6,000	
Deferred Federal Income Taxes*		2,000
Peter, Capital		4,800
Kathryn, Capital		3,200

*A tax rate of 20% is assumed to be appropriate.

Entry 2. Receipt of corporate stock for net assets of the partnership:

Corporate Stock	44,000	
Trade Payables	4,000	
Bank Loan	15,000	
Deferred Federal Income Tax	2,000	
Cash		6,000
Trade Receivables		10,000
Inventories		20,000
Equipment		29,000

Entry 3. Distribute corporate stock to partners:

Peter, Capital	20,800	
Kathryn, Capital	23,200	
Corporate Stock (220 shares, $100 par)		22,000
Additional Paid-in Capital		22,000

Prior to transferring assets, they should be placed on the books at current value and the gain or loss on such revaluation calculated and allocated to the partners' accounts in their profit and loss ratios. Though profit and loss will be recorded on the books of the partnership, it is usually possible for incorporation of an existing partnership business to be carried out in a tax-free manner. The values shown on the corporate books following the transfer will not necessarily be the same as their tax basis. It is appropriate to reflect the tax effect of such book-tax differences in the accounts.

One of the decisions facing a partnership to be incorporated is whether to retain its existing set of books or to open a new set of books covering activities of the successor corporation. If the existing partnership books are to be retained, the following procedures should be employed:

1. Revalue the partnership assets and allocate the net change to the partners.
2. Close the partners' accounts and set up the appropriate capital stock and additional paid-in capital accounts.

An illustration of this procedure in a partnership where the partners share profits and losses in a 60–40 ratio is noted in Exhibit 10.

Exhibit 11 presents the entries needed to close out the partnership books when a new set of corporate books is to be opened. All other factors are the same as in Exhibit 10. The procedures needed are as follows:

1. Revalue the partnership assets and allocate the net change to the partners.

2. Record the transfer of the assets and assumption of the liabilities by the corporation in return for its stock.

3. Record the transfer of the stock to the partners in full settlement of their partnership interest.

BIBLIOGRAPHY

American Institute of Certified Public Accountants, *Professional Standards*, vol. 3 (AICPA, 1981).

Beams, F. A., *Advanced Accounting*, 2d ed. (Prentice-Hall, Englewood Cliffs, N.J., 1982), chaps. 16 and 17.

Financial Accounting Standards Board, *Professional Standards, Vol. 2, Current Text as of June 1, 1982* (McGraw-Hill Book Company, New York, 1982).

Griffin, C. H., T. H. Williams, and K. D. Larson, *Advanced Accounting*, 4th ed. (Richard D. Irwin, Homewood, Ill., 1980), chaps. 14–16.

Huefner, R. J., and J. A. Largay III, *Advanced Financial Accounting* (Dryden Press, New York, 1982), chaps. 2 and 3.

Meigs, W. B., A. N. Mosich, and E. J. Larsen, *Modern Advanced Accounting*, 2d ed. (McGraw-Hill Book Company, New York, 1979), chaps. 1 and 2.

Securities and Exchange Commission, *Requirements for Financial Statements of Certain Special Purpose Limited Partnerships in Annual Reports Filed with the Commission*, Accounting Series Release No. 162 (SEC, 1974).

CHAPTER 31

Adjustments

for Changing

Prices

Clyde P. Stickney

Professor of Accounting, The Amos Tuck
School of Business Administration,
Dartmouth College

The most persistent and significant criticism of the conventional accounting model based on a nominal dollar measuring unit and historical, or acquisition, cost valuations is that it ignores the economic facts of life. Throughout the world, a steady and rapid upward movement in prices has been occurring during the last decade. Yet, until 1979, this important economic phenomenon largely went unrecognized under generally accepted accounting principles. Financial Accounting Standards Board Statement of Financial Accounting Standards No. 33, *Financial Reporting and Changing Prices* [FASB, 1979], however, now requires that the conventional financial statements be supplemented with certain information about the impact of changing prices on a firm. This chapter discusses the accounting problems associated with changing prices and illustrates techniques for dealing with them. The discussion and illustrations will be broader than the supplemental disclosures currently required by Statement No. 33.

TYPES OF ADJUSTMENTS

In preparing a set of financial statements, decisions must be made as to (1) the measuring unit to be used, and (2) the valuation method to be employed.

The measuring unit used in preparing conventional financial statements is the nominal, or actual, dollars expended or received at the time transactions are recorded. Use of nominal dollars as the measuring unit rests on the presumption that the purchasing power of the dollar is reasonably stable over time. If this were the case, measurements made at one time (e.g., the measurement of the cost of a machine acquired 5 years ago for $10,000) could be meaningfully related to measurements made at other times (e.g., the measurement of the cost of inventory items acquired 1 week ago for $10,000).

As general price levels change, however, the purchasing power of the dollar, or its command over goods and services, changes. The general purchasing power sacrificed to acquire the machine 5 years ago is not equivalent to the purchasing power sacrificed last week to acquire the merchandise inventory. In terms of general purchasing power, therefore, the dollar does not represent a constant, or uniform, measuring unit through time. The amounts assigned to individual assets in the conventional balance sheet cannot be meaningfully summed to obtain a measure of total assets. Likewise, the portion of the acquisition cost of various assets recognized as an expense of the current period (cost of goods sold, depreciation expense) cannot be meaningfully matched with revenues of the period.

Thus, an alternative to using nominal dollars as the measuring unit is to use "constant" dollars. That is, all transactions and events could be measured in terms of dollars of a constant amount of general purchasing power. These measurements might be made in constant end-of-current-year dollars, constant mid-current-year dollars, or constant dollars at some earlier date.

The valuation method used in preparing conventional financial statements is generally historical, or acquisition, cost. Assets are initially recorded at the amount expended to acquire the assets (i.e., the exchange price). As the services of these assets are consumed, a portion of the acquisition cost is recognized as an expense. Likewise, the issue of bonds is initially recorded at the amount of cash received. The measurement of interest expense over the life of these bonds is generally based on the interest rate implicit in the initial issue proceeds.

The specific prices of individual assets and liabilities, however, are likely to change over time. The current exchange price will therefore differ from the earlier exchange price. Conventional financial statements based on historical cost valuations will not reflect these changing prices, either in the valuation of assets and liabilities or in the measurement of revenues and expenses.

Thus, an alternative to using historical cost valuation is to use a current valuation. As discussed more fully later, the current valuation might be based on current purchase prices (i.e., current entry values), current selling prices (i.e., current exit values), or present values of future cash flows (i.e., current value in use).

The two measuring units (nominal dollars and constant dollars) and two valuation methods (historical cost and current cost[1]) provide four possible combinations of accounting bases:

1. Historical cost/nominal dollar accounting
2. Historical cost/constant dollar accounting
3. Current cost/nominal dollar accounting
4. Current cost/constant dollar accounting

Conventional financial statements are based on historical cost/nominal dollar accounting. Each of the other three accounting bases is designed to provide particular types of information about the effects of changing prices. They should not be viewed as alternative methods of accounting for changing prices. Rather, they should be assessed in terms of the relevance of the particular types of information about changing prices each attempts to convey.

In the sections that follow, each of these three approaches to accounting for changing prices is discussed and illustrated. The specific disclosures required by FASB Statement No. 33 are discussed at the end of the chapter.

---

[1]The term "current cost" is used simply to mean current exchange price. As discussed later in the chapter, FASB Statement No. 33 defines current cost somewhat more restrictively.

HISTORICAL COST/CONSTANT DOLLAR ACCOUNTING

Objective of Constant Dollar Accounting. The attribute measured in conventional financial statements is the historical sacrifice in general purchasing power made at the time assets were acquired or liabilities were incurred. The measuring unit is the nominal number of dollars either received or expended at the time of these transactions. Conventional financial statements are therefore based on historical cost valuations and a nominal dollar measuring unit.

Because dollars received or paid over time represent different amounts of purchasing power, conventional financial statements are not based on a constant, or uniform, measuring unit. The objective of constant dollar accounting is to state all financial statement amounts in dollars of uniform purchasing power, thereby obtaining a common, or uniform, measuring unit. The attribute measured is still the historical sacrifice made when assets were acquired or liabilities were incurred. This historical sacrifice, however, is measured in terms of a uniform measuring unit. The restatement of conventional financial statement amounts for changes in the purchasing power of the measuring unit is referred to as historical cost/constant dollar accounting. The measuring unit used in the conventional financial statements is referred to as a nominal dollar. In constant dollar statements, the unit is a constant dollar. To distinguish constant dollars from nominal dollars, the letter "C" precedes the dollar sign in the constant dollar financial statements (e.g., C$10,000) presented in this chapter.

Selecting the date for the constant measuring unit is an arbitrary choice. Some have suggested that the date ought to be the base year of the price index used for restatement. Others have suggested using the end of the current year. Still others, including the FASB for certain supplementary disclosures, advocate using midyear of the most recent year being reported. The procedures are analogous, whatever date is used.

The general approach is to convert the number of dollars received or expended at various price levels (nominal dollars) to an equivalent number of dollars in terms of the general price level on some common date (constant dollars). For example, assume that two parcels of land are held on December 31, year 10, at which time an index of the general price level is 300.[2] Tract A was acquired during year 2, when a general price index was 160. Tract B was acquired during year 5, when a general price index was 224. The acquisition cost of these parcels of land could be restated in terms of constant dollars of year 2 purchasing power (price index = 160), constant dollars of year 5 purchasing power (price index = 224), or constant dollars of year 10 purchasing power (price index = 300). Exhibit 1 demonstrates the restatement procedure.

The sacrifice in general purchasing power made during year 2 when tract A was acquired for $100,000 is equivalent to sacrificing C$140,000 (= 224/160 × $100,000) in year 5 general purchasing power and to sacrificing C$187,500 (= 300/160 × $100,000) in year 10 general purchasing power. Likewise, the sacri-

---

[2]The values given for price indices throughout this chapter are assumed for illustration purposes; they are not the actual values of indices published by the federal government.

EXHIBIT 1   Illustration of Constant Dollar Restatement of Land

| | | Acquisition cost measured in: | | |
| | | | Constant dollars | |
Item	Nominal dollars	Year 2	Year 5	Year 10
Tract A	$100,000			
$100,000 × 160/160		C$100,000		
$100,000 × 224/160			C$140,000	
$100,000 × 300/160				C$187,500
Tract B	100,000			
$100,000 × 160/224		71,429		
$100,000 × 224/224			100,000	
$100,000 × 300/224				133,929
Total	$200,000	C$171,429	C$240,000	C$321,429

fice in general purchasing power in year 5 when tract B was acquired for $100,000 is equivalent to sacrificing C$71,429 (= 160/224 × $100,000) of year 2 general purchasing power and C$133,929 (= 300/224 × $100,000) of year 10 general purchasing power.

Thus, the three constant dollar measurements of the total acquisition cost of the land are economically equivalent. That is,

$$C\$_{\text{year } 2}171,429 = C\$_{\text{year } 5}240,000 = C\$_{\text{year } 10}321,429$$

The key concept is that both parcels of land are stated in terms of the same measuring unit at each of the three constant dollar dates. Their amounts can therefore be added more meaningfully than if nominal dollars were used. In the illustrations in this chapter, the end of the current year will be used as the constant dollar date. That is, all amounts will be stated in terms of dollars of end-of-current-year general purchasing power.

Two important aspects of the constant dollar restatement procedure illustrated in Exhibit 1 should be noted. First, historical cost is still used as the valuation method. The historical cost amount ($200,000) is merely expressed in terms of different constant measuring units. Second, the amounts shown for constant-dollar restated acquisition costs do not attempt to reflect the current market prices of these two parcels of land. The market prices of the land could have changed in an entirely different direction and pattern from that of the general price-level change. The focus of constant dollar accounting is on making the measuring unit more comparable over time and not on reflecting current market prices of individual assets and equities.

Restatement of Monetary and Nonmonetary Items.   An important distinction is made in the constant dollar restatement procedure between monetary items and nonmonetary items.

Monetary items. A *monetary item* is either cash or a claim receivable or payable in a specified number of dollars or other currency unit, without reference to future prices of goods or services. Examples of monetary items are cash; accounts, notes, and interest receivable; accounts, notes, and interest payable; income taxes payable; and bonds. Claims receivable or payable in a foreign currency as well as deferred income taxes are treated as monetary items by FASB Statement No. 33. As discussed later, however, these items exhibit many of the characteristics of nonmonetary items.

In preparing a constant-dollar restated balance sheet, the valuation of monetary items at the number of dollars due automatically states them in terms of the general purchasing power of the dollar at that time. No restatement is therefore necessary, and the conventionally reported and restated amounts are the same. For example, assume that a firm has $30,000 of cash on hand on December 31, year 10. On the conventionally prepared balance sheet, this item would be stated at $30,000, the amount of cash on hand. On the constant-dollar restated balance sheet, this item would also be reported at C$30,000, representing $30,000 of December 31, year 10, general purchasing power.

Because monetary items are receivable or payable in a specified number of dollars, rather than in terms of a given amount of general purchasing power, holding monetary items over time while the general purchasing power of the dollar changes gives rise to what are called *purchasing power*, or *inflation, gains and losses*. During a period of inflation, a holder of monetary assets loses general purchasing power. For example, a firm with outstanding notes receivable incurs a purchasing power loss, because the dollars loaned had more general purchasing power than the dollars to be received when the note is collected. Likewise, a debtor holding monetary liabilities gains in general purchasing power during periods of inflation, because the dollars required to repay the debt have less purchasing power than the dollars originally borrowed. The gain or loss from holding monetary items is reported in historical cost/constant dollar financial statements but is not included in historical cost/nominal dollar statements.

The nature of purchasing power gain or loss on monetary items. In conventional financial statements, the interest expense is the reported cost of borrowing in nominal dollars. It depends on the interest rate negotiated between the borrower and lender at the time of the loan. That interest rate depends partly on both the lender's and borrower's expectations of the rate of inflation during the term of the loan. Lenders are aware that, when inflation occurs during the term of a loan, they will be repaid with dollars that have less general purchasing power than the dollars loaned. Thus, for a given default risk, lenders will ask a higher interest rate, the more inflation they expect.

Borrowers, on the other hand, are willing to pay a higher interest rate in times of expected inflation because they expect to repay the loan with "cheaper" dollars; that is, they expect the real value of the debt to fall. Thus the interest expense on the borrower's conventional income statement reflects the inflation expected by both the borrower and the lender at the time the debt was issued. But the reported interest expense is partly offset by the reduction in the reported cost of borrowing caused by the general inflation that reduces the value of the dollars to be repaid.

Whether either the borrower or the lender benefits at the other's expense depends on the amount of unexpected inflation during the term of the loan. If the actual rate of inflation during the term of the loan is greater than that expected at the time the loan was made, then the borrower benefits at the expense of the lender. The dollars actually repaid have less general purchasing power than they were expected to have at the time the loan was made.

In any case, the purchasing power gain reported by a borrower (or loss reported by a lender) in times of general price increase is conceptually an offset to reported interest expense (or revenue). The net interest after purchasing power gain (or loss) shows the cost of borrowing (or return to lending) in terms of general purchasing power sacrificed or earned.

Nonmonetary items. A *nonmonetary item* is an asset or equity that does not represent a claim to or for a specified number of dollars or other currency unit. That is, if an item is not a monetary item, then it must be nonmonetary. Examples of nonmonetary items are inventory, land, buildings, equipment, common stock, and retained earnings, including the temporary accounts for revenues and expenses. In conventionally prepared financial statements, nonmonetary items are stated in terms of varying amounts of general purchasing power. The amount depends on the date the nonmonetary assets were acquired or the non-monetary equities arose. As illustrated in Exhibit 1 with the two parcels of land, the conventionally reported amounts of these items are restated to an equivalent number of dollars of constant purchasing power as of the constant dollar date. The amount of this restatement does not represent a gain or loss to be included in historical cost/constant dollar net income, but merely an adjustment to make the measuring unit comparable. One way to understand that the increased number on the balance sheet does not represent a gain is to consider restating an amount shown on a British balance sheet in pounds sterling to U.S. dollars. Suppose that £100 of inventory is restated to $180 of inventory. No gain has occurred, only a translation from one measuring unit to the other. Similarly, plant assets acquired for $100 in an earlier year when the general price index was 100 can be restated as C$180 in a year when the price index is 180 without recognizing a gain. The change in amounts is merely a translation from one measuring unit to another, not a gain.

Constant-Dollar Restatement Procedure. The procedure for restating the conventional financial statements to a constant dollar basis is as follows:

1. The assets and equities on the most recent balance sheet are separated into monetary and nonmonetary items. The monetary items are extended to the constant dollar balance sheet using the same amounts as are reported in the conventional balance sheet. The nonmonetary items are restated from the purchasing power of the dollar when the nonmonetary assets were acquired or nonmonetary equities were incurred to the equivalent number of dollars of purchasing power on the date of the balance sheet. FASB Statement No. 33 requires that the Consumer Price Index for All Urban Consumers be used for the restatement. The restatement involves multiplying the historical amount by a restatement ratio. Assuming that the financial statements are stated in constant end-of-current-year dollars, the numerator of the ratio is the Consumer Price Index for the date of the balance sheet and the denominator is the Consumer Price Index when the asset was acquired or the equity was incurred. If other constant dollars are used, the numerator is changed, accordingly. Because the Consumer Price Index is issued monthly, the index used is for the month that includes the date of the balance sheet and the index for the month that includes the date of acquisition. Restated Retained Earnings is the residual, or "plug," to equate constant dollar assets and constant dollar equities. The "plug" is checked by independent calculations in the next step.

2. Calculate the restated retained earnings amount at the end of the year by restating each of the amounts in the Retained Earnings account during the period. Reconcile the result to that from step 1. This step generally involves three substeps.

(a) Calculate the constant dollar balance in Retained Earnings at the beginning of the period. If constant dollar financial statements were prepared for the preceding period, the constant dollar amount of Retained Earnings at the end of the preceding period is restated to end-of-the-current-period constant dollars. This restatement involves multiplying the constant-dollar beginning retained earnings amount by a ratio. The numerator of the ratio is the Consumer Price Index at the end of the current period and the denominator is the Consumer Price Index at the end of the preceding period. As discussed later, the calculation of the restated beginning amount of retained earnings is more complex in the first year that constant dollar statements are prepared.

(b) Calculate the amount of constant dollar net income for the current period. Each revenue and expense is restated from the purchasing power of the dollar when the measurements underlying the revenues and expenses were initially made to the purchasing power on the date of the balance sheet. In addition, the purchasing power gain or loss for the period on net monetary items is calculated and included in constant dollar net income.

(c) Restate dividends and any other changes in the Retained Earnings account during the period.

If the restatement procedure has been performed correctly, then the amount of restated Retained Earnings at the end of the period as determined in step 2 should be equal to the residual, or "plug," in step 1.

Illustration of the Constant-Dollar Restatement Procedure. Exhibit 2 presents the income statement and Exhibit 3 presents the comparative balance sheet of Sweeney Corporation for year 10 used to illustrate the restatement procedure. Exhibit 4 presents assumed amounts for an index of general price levels for various dates. The amounts shown are based on the average prices for each month. When an index for the end of a month is needed, the average index for the month is generally considered a satisfactory approximation.

Step 1: Restate the end-of-the-period balance sheet. The accounts on the balance sheet on December 31, year 10, are classified into monetary and nonmonetary categories. Each item is then restated as appropriate. Exhibit 5 summarizes these restatements.

EXHIBIT 2   Income Statement for Sweeney Corporation in Nominal Dollars for Year 10

Revenues and gains:	
Product sales	$5,180,000
Maintenance contracts	20,000
Gain on sale of equipment	80,000
Total revenues and gains	$5,280,000
Expenses and losses:	
Cost of goods sold	$3,960,000
Selling, general, and administrative	512,000
Depreciation	248,000
Interest	100,000
Income taxes	200,000
Total expenses and losses	$5,020,000
Net income	$ 260,000
Less preferred stock dividend	(20,000)
Net income to common shareholders	$ 240,000
Earnings per common share (based on 100,000 outstanding shares)	$2.40

Cash and Accounts Receivable. Cash and Accounts Receivable are monetary items. They are either a specified number of dollars or are claims to a specified number of dollars regardless of changes in the price level. They are therefore extended to the constant dollar balance sheet at the same amounts as shown in the nominal dollar balance sheet.

Inventories. Inventories are nonmonetary items, because they are not claims to specific cash amounts. They are stated in the conventional balance sheet in terms of historical acquisition costs. These historical cost amounts must be restated to an equivalent number of constant dollars. To do so requires knowing the dates of acquisition and the historical costs, which presents a special problem. Most firms do not use specific identification in the valuation of their inventories and cost of goods sold. Instead, a cost flow assumption (FIFO, LIFO, weighted average) is used. The constant dollar restatement must be consistent with the assumption used.

Sweeney Corporation uses a FIFO cost flow assumption. The inventory turnover ratio is 3.88 [= $3,960,000/.5($1,000,000 + $1,040,000)]. Thus, the inventory on hand at the end of the year represents about one-fourth of the year's purchases. If inventories are assumed to be acquired more or less continuously throughout the year, then the ending inventory was acquired during the last quarter of the year. The average price index for the last quarter is 223.7 [= (222.3 + 223.9 + 225.0)/3]. The ending inventory on a constant dollar basis is C$1,046,044 (= $1,040,000 × 225.0/223.7).

If a LIFO or weighted-average cost flow assumption had been used, the price index in the denominator of the restatement ratio would be changed to reflect the purchases from which the ending inventory was assumed to come (for example, each LIFO layer).

If the lower-of-cost-or-market valuation had been used and some inventory items had been stated in terms of market prices at the end of the year, no restatement would be required for these items. They would already be stated in terms of end-of-the-year dollars. Although the acquisition cost for an item may be less than market value in the conventional financial statements, its re-

EXHIBIT 3   Comparative Balance Sheet for Sweeney Corporation in Nominal Dollars, December 31, Year 10 and Year 9

	December 31, year 10	December 31, year 9
Assets		
Current assets:		
Cash	$ 280,000	$ 240,000
Accounts receivable (net)	800,000	760,000
Inventories (at first-in, first-out)	1,040,000	1,000,000
Prepayments	80,000	100,000
Total current assets	$2,200,000	$2,100,000
Investment in common stock (at cost, which is less than market)	$ 320,000	$ 320,000
Property, plant, and equipment:		
Land	$ 160,000	$ 160,000
Building (net of accumulated depreciation)	420,000	440,000
Equipment (net of accumulated depreciation)	1,100,000	1,040,000
Total property, plant, and equipment.........	$1,680,000	$1,640,000
Total assets................................	$4,200,000	$4,060,000
Liabilities and shareholders' equity		
Current liabilities:		
Accounts payable	$ 340,000	$ 420,000
Salaries payable	80,000	100,000
Total current liabilities	$ 420,000	$ 520,000
Long-term liabilities:		
Advances on maintenance contracts	$ 40,000	$ 60,000
Bonds payable (10%, semiannual coupons, due January 1, year 24)	1,000,000	1,000,000
Deferred income taxes	40,000	20,000
Total long-term liabilities...................	$1,080,000	$1,080,000
Total liabilities	$1,500,000	$1,600,000
Shareholders' equity:		
Preferred stock (4,000 shares, 5%, $100 par value, $115 redemption value)..............	$ 400,000	$ 400,000
Common stock ($1 par value, 100,000 shares issued and outstanding)	100,000	100,000
Additional paid-in capital	150,000	150,000
Retained earnings	2,050,000	1,810,000
Total shareholders' equity	$2,700,000	$2,460,000
Total liabilities and shareholders' equity	$4,200,000	$4,060,000

EXHIBIT 4   General Price Index for Various Dates

Date	Index[a]	Date	Index[a]
January year 1 (when corporation was formed and land was acquired)	104.3	October year 9 (when preferred stock was issued)	198.2
		November year 9	199.3
Average for year 2 (when building was constructed)	106.5	December year 9	201.6
		January year 10	202.3
February year 4 (when intercorporate investment was acquired)	132.6	February year 10	204.6
		March year 10	206.9
		April year 10	209.2
October year 4 (when equipment was acquired)	137.5	May year 10	211.5
July year 5 (when equipment was acquired)	150.7	June year 10 (when equipment was sold)	214.1
April year 6 (when equipment was acquired)	162.4	July year 10 (when equipment was acquired)	216.6
		August year 10	218.4
November year 7 (when equipment was acquired)	178.5	September year 10	220.6
		October year 10	222.3
October year 8 (when maintenance contracts were sold)	184.9	November year 10	223.9
		December year 10	225.0
		Average year 10	214.6

[a]These are hypothetical index numbers, not actual ones for any particular time period.

stated acquisition cost for the constant dollar financial statements may exceed its market value. In this case, the lower market value is used. Thus, some items may be reported at market value in constant dollar financial statements even though they are stated at acquisition cost in the conventional, nominal dollar financial statements.

Prepayments. Prepayments are measured in terms of the nominal dollars expended and are therefore nonmonetary assets. As such, they must be restated from the number of dollars expended in making the prepayment to an equivalent number of constant dollars. Prepayments on the balance sheet of Sweeney Corporation on December 31, year 10, represent prepaid rent. The prepayment was made October 15, year 10. The restatement ratio to convert Prepayments to dollars of December 31, year 10, purchasing power uses the price index for October in the denominator. Restated Prepayments are C$80,972 (= $80,000 × 225.0/222.3).

Investment in Common Stock. The Investment in Common Stock account represents a holding of 10 percent of the common stock of a major supplier. The amount shown in the nominal dollar balance sheet is the acquisition cost of the investment. The investment is a nonmonetary item. Internal records indicate that the investment was acquired 6 years ago. The price index then was 132.6. The investment restated to December 31, year 10, purchasing power is C$542,986 (= $320,000 × 225.0/132.6). As long as the market value of the common stock exceeds $542,986, the investment would be stated at this amount. Otherwise, the investment must be stated at the lower market value under the lower-of-cost-or-market method. In applying lower of cost or market to a port-

EXHIBIT 5   Restatement of Balance Sheet from Nominal to Constant Dollars for Sweeney Corporation, December 31, Year 10

	Nominal dollars	Restatement ratio	Constant December year 10 dollars
Assets			
Current assets:			
Cash	$ 280,000	225.0/225.0	C$ 280,000
Accounts receivable (net)	800,000	225.0/225.0	800,000
Inventories (at first-in, first-out)	1,040,000	225.0/223.7	1,046,044
Prepayments	80,000	225.0/222.3	80,972
Total current assets	$2,200,000		C$2,207,016
Investment in common stock (at cost, which is less than marked)	$ 320,000	225.0/132.6	C$ 542,986
Property, plant, and equipment:			
Land................................	$ 160,000	225.0/104.3	C$ 345,158
Building (net of accumulated depreciation) .	420,000	225.0/106.5	887,324
Equipment (net of accumulated depreciation)	1,100,000	See Exhibit 6	1,448,650
Total property, plant, and equipment......	$1,680,000		C$2,681,132
Total assets	$4,200,000		C$5,431,134
Liabilities and shareholders' equity			
Current liabilities:			
Accounts payable	$ 340,000	225.0/225.0	C$ 340,000
Salaries payable	80,000	225.0/225.0	80,000
Total current liabilities	$ 420,000		C$ 420,000
Long-term liabilities:			
Advances on maintenance contracts	$ 40,000	225.0/184.9	C$ 48,675
Bonds payable (10%)	1,000,000	225.0/225.0	1,000,000
Deferred income taxes	40,000	225.0/225.0	40,000
Total long-term liabilities	$1,080,000		C$1,088,675
Total liabilities	$1,500,000		C$1,508,675
Shareholders' equity:			
Preferred shareholders' equity (4,000 shares, 5%, $100 par value, $115 redemption value)	$ 400,000	225.0/198.2	C$ 454,087
Common stock ($1 par value, 100,000 shares issued and outstanding)	100,000	225.0/104.3	215,724
Additional paid-in capital...............	150,000	225.0/104.3	323,586
Retained earnings	2,050,000	PLUG	2,929,062
Total shareholders' equity	$2,700,000		C$3,922,459
Total liabilities and shareholders' equity......	$4,200,000		C$5,431,134

folio of investments measured in constant dollars, restate the acquisition cost of each item remaining in the portfolio to end-of-current-period constant dollars. Then, compare the sum of the restated costs to the current market value of the portfolio. If the current market value is less than the restated acquisition cost amount, then create the proper credit balance in the Allowance account.

If the equity method is used for an affiliate or unconsolidated subsidiary, the balance sheet of the affiliate or subsidiary must be restated to a constant dollar basis. The investor, or parent, will then report in its constant dollar balance sheet its equity in the restated common shareholders' equity of the affiliate or subsidiary.

Property, plant, and equipment. Constant dollar restatements of property, plant, and equipment are straightforward. But because large numbers of items and an equally large number of acquisition dates are involved, the initial restatement process can be tedious.

Sweeney Corporation acquired the land when the corporation was formed in year 1. The price index at this time was 104.3. Land is therefore restated to C$345,158 (= $160,000 × 225.0/104.3). Note that the restatement is for the *cumulative* inflation since the land was acquired.

The building was constructed during year 2 at a cost of $580,000 when the average price index was 106.5. The building was occupied at the beginning of year 3. It is being depreciated using the straight-line method over a 28-year period. Estimated salvage value is $20,000. The restatement is as follows:

Acquisition cost: $580,000 × 225.0/106.5	C$1,225,352
Accumulated depreciation: $160,000 × 225.0/106.5	338,028
Net book value: $420,000	C$ 887,324

The equipment held by Sweeney Corporation on December 31, year 10, consists of items acquired over several years as shown in Exhibit 6. By applying the appropriate restatement ratio, the constant dollar equipment amount on December 31, year 10, net of accumulated depreciation, is C$1,448,650.

EXHIBIT 6   Restatement of Sweeney Corporation's Equipment Account as of December 31, Year 10

Year acquired	Stated in nominal dollars			Stated in constant December 31, year 10, dollars	
	Acquisition cost	Accumulated depreciation	Restatement ratio	Acquisition cost	Accumulated depreciation
Year 4	$ 520,000	$ 299,000	225.0/137.5	C$ 850,909	C$ 489,273
Year 6	940,000	611,000	225.0/162.4	1,302,340	846,521
Year 7	480,000	210,000	225.0/178.5	605,042	264,706
Year 10	320,000	40,000	225.0/216.6	332,410	41,551
Total	$2,260,000	$1,160,000		C$3,090,701	C$1,642,051
Net book value	$1,100,000			C$1,448,650	

Current liabilities. Accounts Payable and Salaries Payable are both monetary items and are extended to the constant dollar statements at the same amount as shown in the nominal dollar balance sheet.

Advances on Maintenance Contracts. In some businesses, payments are received from customers before goods are provided or services are rendered. These advances represent obligations requiring settlement in goods or services. In nominal dollar statements, these obligations are stated at the amount of cash received, not at the future expected outlays required to discharge them. The advances are nonmonetary liabilities because settlement does not require a fixed, known cash amount. The amount shown on the December 31, year 10, balance sheet is for advances received during year 8, when the price index was 184.9. The restated amount of Advances on Maintenance Contracts is C$48,675 (= $40,000 × 225.0/184.9).

Bonds Payable. Bonds are stated in terms of the present value of the number of dollars payable on the bond (using the market interest rate on the date the bonds were issued as the discount rate). As such, bonds are monetary items and do not require restatement on December 31, year 10. A premium or discount account is also a monetary item, because these amounts are adjunct or contra-accounts to a monetary account.

Deferred Income Taxes. The classification of Deferred Income Taxes as a monetary or a nonmonetary item is more complex than for most other accounts.

There are two methods of interperiod tax allocation. Under the *liability method,* deferred taxes are a measure of the number of dollars to be paid in the future when timing differences reverse. Under the liability method, deferred taxes are monetary items. Under the *deferral method,* deferred taxes are a measure of the tax savings realized in the current and prior periods from timing differences. Because these tax savings are based on past transactions and events, they would appear to be nonmonetary items.

FASB Statement No. 33 recognizes the theoretical rationale in support of treating deferred taxes as nonmonetary items, but, for practical reasons, requires that they be treated as monetary items. If deferred taxes were to be treated as nonmonetary, it would be necessary to identify the amount and timing of each deferred tax provision that comprises the Deferred Income Taxes account on the balance sheet. Because portions of the Deferred Income Taxes account are the result of offsetting timing differences, some of which periodically reverse themselves, such specific identification is usually difficult.

By treating Deferred Income Taxes as a monetary item, they are stated at $40,000 on the nominal dollar balance sheet and C$40,000 on the constant dollar balance sheet on December 31, year 10.

Preferred Stock. The Preferred Stock account is stated at the number of dollars received when the stock was issued in October, year 9. Preferred Stock is therefore a nonmonetary item. The price index at the time of issue was 198.2. The restated amount for Preferred Stock is C$454,087 (= $400,000 × 225.0/198.2).

Preferred Stock may not be stated on the constant dollar balance sheet at an amount greater than the redemption price of $460,000 (= 4,000 shares × $115). Once the restated amount equals the redemption price, the Preferred Stock becomes a monetary item stated in terms of the number of dollars required to redeem the stock. Thus, Preferred Stock may be either a monetary or a non-monetary item, depending on both the amount of cumulative inflation since the stock was issued and its redemption price.

Common Stock and Additional Paid-in Capital. These accounts are stated at the number of dollars received when the common stock was issued and are therefore nonmonetary items. The price index at the time of issue in year 1 was 104.3. The restated amounts are as follows:

Common Stock	$100,000 × 225.0/104.3 = C$215,724
Additional Paid-in Capital	$150,000 × 225.0/104.3 = C$323,586

Retained earnings. Restated Retained Earnings is the amount necessary to equate restated assets and restated equities. Exhibit 5, which presents the nominal dollar and constant dollar balance sheets as of December 31, year 10, shows that the constant dollar balance in Retained Earnings is C$2,929,062.

Step 2: Reconcile to end-of-the-period retained earnings. The second step is to trace the changes in the Retained Earnings account in order to reconcile to the ending balance in restated Retained Earnings of C$2,929,062.

Restate beginning balance in Retained Earnings. We begin by calculating the restated beginning balance in Retained Earnings. In the first year that constant dollar financial statements are prepared, this step requires that the entire balance sheet at the beginning of the period be restated to the price level as of the beginning of the period; restated Retained Earnings must then be rolled forward to the price level at the end of the period. Exhibit 7 demonstrates this initial restatement and then roll-forward of the balance sheet amounts on December 31, year 9. The restatement process in the first three columns of Exhibit 7 is identical to that in Exhibit 5 except that all beginning-of-the-period amounts are stated in terms of the general price level on December 31, year 9. Exhibit 8 shows the restatement of the Equipment account. The roll-foward of the restated amounts in the last two columns of Exhibit 7 results in a balance in Retained Earnings at the beginning of year 10 but restated to constant dollars of December 31, year 10, purchasing power of C$2,854,940.

In subsequent years, the restatements in the first three columns of Exhibit 7 are not necessary. The restated beginning balance in Retained Earnings will be the same as the restated ending balance of the preceding period. All that is required is that the restated beginning balance be rolled forward to the purchasing power of the dollar at the end of the period.

Restate income before purchasing power gain or loss. The next step is to restate the revenues and expenses in the income statement. Exhibit 9 summarizes the restatements.

The measurements of product sales, interest, and income taxes were made evenly over the year. Thus, their restatement is based on the average price index for year 10 of 214.6.

The maintenance contract revenue is based on advances received from customers in year 8 when the price index was 184.9. Thus, they are restated to C$24,337 (= $20,000 × 225.0/184.9).

EXHIBIT 7 Restatement of Balance Sheet from Nominal to Constant Dollars for Sweeney Corporation, December 31, Year 9

	Nominal dollars	Restatement ratio	Constant December 31, year 9, dollars	Restatement ratio	Constant December 31, year 10, dollars
Assets					
Current assets:					
Cash	$ 240,000	201.6/201.6	C$ 240,000	225.0/201.6	C$ 267,857
Accounts receivable (net)	760,000	201.6/201.6	760,000	225.0/201.6	848,214
Inventories	1,000,000	201.6/199.7	1,009,514	225.0/201.6	1,126,690
Prepayments	100,000	201.6/197.9	101,870	225.0/201.6	113,694
Total current assets	$2,100,000		C$2,111,384		C$2,356,455
Investment in common stock	$ 320,000	201.6/132.6	C$ 486,516	225.0/201.6	C$ 542,986
Property, plant, and equipment:					
Land	$ 160,000	201.6/104.3	C$ 309,262	225.0/201.6	C$ 345,158
Building (net)	440,000	201.6/106.5	832,901	225.0/201.6	929,577
Equipment (net)	1,040,000	See Exhibit 8	1,313,466	225.0/201.6	1,465,922
Total property, plant, and equipment	$1,640,000		C$2,455,629		C$2,740,657
Total assets	$4,060,000		C$5,053,529		C$5,640,098
Liabilities and shareholders' equity					
Current liabilities:					
Accounts payable	$ 420,000	201.6/201.6	C$ 420,000	225.0/201.6	C$ 468,750
Salaries payable	100,000	201.6/201.6	100,000	225.0/201.6	111,607
Total current liabilities	$ 520,000		C$ 520,000		C$ 580,357
Long-term liabilities:					
Advances on maintenance contracts	$ 60,000	201.6/184.9	C$ 65,419	225.0/201.6	C$ 73,012
Bonds payable (10%)	1,000,000	201.6/201.6	1,000,000	225.0/201.6	1,116,071
Deferred income taxes	20,000	201.6/201.6	20,000	225.0/201.6	22,321
Total long-term liabilities	$1,080,000		C$1,085,419		C$1,211,404
Total liabilities	$1,600,000		C$1,605,419		C$1,791,761
Shareholders' equity:					
Preferred stock	$ 400,000	201.6/198.2	C$ 406,861	225.0/201.6	C$ 454,087
Common stock	100,000	201.6/104.3	193,289	225.0/201.6	215,724
Additional paid-in capital	150,000	201.6/104.3	289,933	225.0/201.6	323,586
Retained earnings	1,810,000	PLUG	2,558,027		2,854,940
Total shareholders' equity	$2,460,000		C$3,448,110		C$3,848,337
Total liabilities and shareholders' equity	$4,060,000		C$5,053,529		C$5,640,098

EXHIBIT 8 Restatement of Sweeney Corporation's Equipment Account from Nominal Dollars to Constant Dollars as of December 31, Year 9

Year acquired	Stated in nominal dollars			Stated in constant December 31, year 9, dollars	
	Acquisition cost	Accumulated depreciation	Restatement ratio	Acquisition cost	Accumulated depreciation
Year 4	$ 520,000	$ 273,000	201.6/137.5	C$ 762,415	C$ 400,268
Year 5	160,000	120,000	201.6/150.7	214,041	160,531
Year 6	940,000	517,000	201.6/162.4	1,166,896	641,793
Year 7	480,000	150,000	201.6/178.5	542,118	169,412
Total	$2,100,000	$1,060,000		C$2,685,470	C$1,372,004
Net book value	$1,040,000			C$1,313,466	

EXHIBIT 9 Restatement of Income Statement for Sweeney Corporation from Nominal Dollars to Constant Dollars for Year 10

	Nominal dollars	Restatement ratio	Constant December 31, year 10, dollars
Revenue and gains:			
Product sales	$5,180,000	225.0/214.6	C$5,431,034
Maintenance contracts	20,000	225.0/184.9	24,337
Gain on sale of equipment	80,000	See text	69,925
Total revenues and gains	$5,280,000		C$5,525,296
Expenses and losses:			
Cost of goods sold	$3,960,000	Exhibit 10	C$4,274,495
Selling, general, and administrative	{ 100,000	{ 225.0/197.9	{ 113,694
	{ 412,000	{ 225.0/214.6	{ 431,967
Depreciation	248,000	Exhibit 13	344,158
Interest.	100,000	225.0/214.6	104,846
Income taxes	200,000	225.0/214.6	209,692
Total expenses and losses.	$5,020,000		C$5,478,852
Income before purchasing power gain or loss . . .			C$ 46,444
Purchasing power gain on net monetary position (see Exhibit 14)			48,187
Net income	$ 260,000		C$ 94,631
Less preferred dividend: First 6 months	(10,000)	225.0/214.1	(10,509)
Second 6 months	(10,000)	225.0/225.0	(10,000)
Net income to common	$ 240,000		C$ 74,122
Earnings per common share (based on 100,000 shares outstanding)	$ 2.40		C$ .74

Calculating the constant dollar gain on the sale of equipment is made easier by reconstructing the journal entry made in nominal dollars. The equipment sold had been acquired for $160,000 in year 5. Accumulated depreciation up to the time of sale in June, year 10, was $128,000. The equipment was sold for $112,000. The nominal dollar journal entry to record the sale is

Cash...	112,000	
Accumulated Depreciation.........................	128,000	
Equipment.......................................		160,000
Gain on Sale....................................		80,000

The constant dollar gain is calculated as follows:

Selling price: $112,000 × 225.0/214.1.........................	C$117,702
Less book value: ($160,000 − $128,000) × 225.0/150.7........	47,777
Constant dollar gain on sale...............................	C$ 69,925

Note that the selling price, book value, and gain are all stated in terms of constant December 31, year 10, dollars.

Exhibit 10 shows the calculation of constant dollar cost of goods sold for year 10. Here, too, it is useful to begin with the nominal dollar amounts. The inventory at the beginning and end of year 10 is obtained from Exhibit 3 and the cost of goods sold is obtained from Exhibit 2. Purchases for the period are then derived from the inventory equation:

$$\text{Purchases} = \frac{\text{Cost of}}{\text{Goods Sold}} + \frac{\text{Ending}}{\text{Inventory}} - \frac{\text{Beginning}}{\text{Inventory}}$$

The restatement of both the beginning and ending inventories is based on a FIFO cost flow assumption. Because the inventory turnover is approximately four times each year, the inventories were acquired during the last quarter of their respective years. Purchases are assumed to occur evenly over each year, so that the average price index for year 10 is used in the denominator of the restatement ratio. Constant dollar cost of goods sold on a FIFO basis is

---

EXHIBIT 10   Calculation of Constant Dollar Cost of Goods Sold for Sweeney Corporation for Year 10

	Nominal dollars	Restatement ratio	Constant December 31, year 10, dollars
Beginning inventory...........	$1,000,000	225.0/199.7	C$1,126,690
Purchases..................	4,000,000	225.0/214.6	4,193,849
Available for sale............	$5,000,000		C$5,320,539
Less ending inventory.........	(1,040,000)	225.0/223.7	1,046,044
Cost of goods sold...........	$3,960,000		C$4,274,495

EXHIBIT 11   Illustration of Fractions of Year's Price Change Used in Price-Level Adjustments of Cost of Goods Sold Assuming FIFO Cost Flow

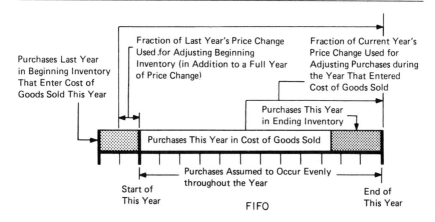

C$4,274,495. Exhibit 11 shows graphically the restatement of FIFO nominal dollar amounts to a constant dollar basis. Exhibit 12 shows the corresponding process for a LIFO cost flow assumption.

Selling, General, and Administrative Expenses is restated as follows:

Expiration of prepayments: $100,000 × 225.0/197.9	C$113,694
Costs incurred evenly during year 10: $412,000 × 225.0/214.6 . .	431,967
Total	C$545,661

Exhibit 13 presents the restatement of Depreciation Expense. Note that depreciation is restated for the *cumulative* inflation since the depreciable assets were acquired. Constant dollar depreciation for year 10 is C$344,158, compared

EXHIBIT 12   Illustration of Fraction of Year's Price Change Used in Price-Level Adjustments of Cost of Goods Sold Assuming LIFO Cost Flow

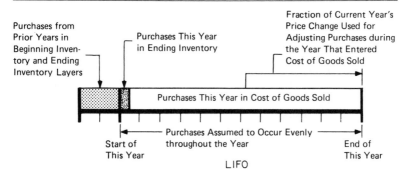

EXHIBIT 13   Calculation of Constant Dollar
Depreciation Expense

Year acquired	Nominal dollars	Restatement ratio	Constant December 31, year 10, dollars
Building:			
Year 2.........	$ 20,000	225.0/106.5	C$ 42,254
Equipment:			
Year 4.........	26,000	225.0/137.5	42,545
Year 5.........	8,000	225.0/150.7	11,944
Year 6.........	94,000	225.0/162.4	130,234
Year 7.........	60,000	225.0/178.5	75,630
Year 10........	40,000	225.0/216.6	41,551
Total	$248,000		C$344,158

to $248,000 in nominal dollars. The restatement of depreciation is the major reason why constant dollar net income is less than nominal dollar net income for most firms. For Sweeney Corporation for year 10, constant dollar income before the purchasing power gain or loss is C$46,444 compared to $260,000 on a nominal dollar basis.

Calculate the purchasing power gain or loss. Purchasing power gains and losses are recognized when financial statements are based on a constant dollar measuring unit. The reported gain or loss arises from holding monetary assets and monetary liabilities over time while the general purchasing power of the dollar changes. Exhibit 14 presents the calculations for Sweeney Corporation for year 10. Two steps are involved in the calculations:

1. Prepare an analysis of the net changes in monetary accounts during the year in nominal dollars. That is, starting with the net monetary asset or net monetary equity position at the beginning of the year, add all transactions causing monetary assets to increase or monetary equities to decrease (net debit changes in monetary accounts), subtract all transactions causing monetary assets to decrease or monetary equities to increase (net credit changes in monetary accounts); the result is the ending net monetary asset or net monetary equity position. This step is perhaps the most time-consuming in the constant dollar restatement process, because an analysis of changes in monetary accounts is not routinely prepared as part of the usual accounting process each period. (The analysis is analogous to a statement of changes in financial position in which funds are defined as net monetary assets and equities.) If the beginning balance plus (or minus) the transactions identified as affecting monetary accounts during the period do not reconcile to the actual ending balance in net monetary accounts as shown on the balance sheet, then some transactions have been overlooked.

2. Restate the beginning balance and each transaction affecting a monetary account from the nominal dollars when the measurements were made to the

dollars of constant purchasing power at the end of the period. Note in this step that sales revenue, interest expense, income tax expense, and so on, are not being restated. These restatements were made in calculating constant dollar income before the purchasing power gain or loss in Exhibit 9. The restatement in Exhibit 14 is for the other half of the journal entry (debit to Accounts Receivable, credit to Cash or Accounts Payable). The constant dollar, net monetary liability position on December 31, year 10, is C$428,187. Because the actual net liability position is only $380,000, Sweeney Corporation had a purchasing power gain of C$48,187 (= C$428,187 − $380,000) during the year. The major cause of this gain is the long-term debt outstanding. The debt will be paid at maturity with dollars of smaller purchasing power than the dollars initially received when the debt was issued. A portion of this total gain is recognized each period under constant dollar accounting. The recognition of a purchasing power gain on long-term debt is one of the most important reasons why constant dollar net income (including the purchasing power gain) exceeds nominal dollar net income for some firms in some years.

Restate other transactions affecting retained earnings. The final step is to restate any other transactions affecting the Retained Earnings account other than net income for the period. For Sweeney Corporation, only the preferred

---

EXHIBIT 14   Calculation of Purchasing Power Gain or Loss for Sweeney Corporation for the Year 10

	Nominal dollars	Restatement ratio	Constant December 31, year 10, dollars
Net monetary asset (equity) position, January 1, year 10	$ (540,000)	225.0/201.6	C$ (602,678)
Add increases in net monetary assets:			
From product sales........................	5,180,000	225.0/214.6	5,431,034
From sale of equipment	112,000	225.0/214.1	117,702
Less decreases in net monetary assets:			
From purchase of merchandise	(4,000,000)	225.0/214.6	(4,193,849)
From selling and administrative costs	(412,000)	225.0/214.6	(431,967)
From interest costs	(100,000)	225.0/214.6	(104,846)
From prepayments	(80,000)	225.0/222.3	(80,972)
From income taxes........................	(200,000)	225.0/214.6	(209,692)
From dividends: First 6 months	(10,000)	225.0/214.1	(10,509)
Second 6 months	(10,000)	225.0/225.0	(10,000)
From equipment purchased	(320,000)	225.0/216.6	(332,410)
Actual net monetary asset (equity) position, December 31, year 10	$ (380,000)		
Constant dollar net monetary asset (equity) position, December 31, year 10			C$ (428,187)
Purchasing power gain: C$428,187 − C$380,000 .			C$ 48,187

EXHIBIT 15   Reconciliation of Constant Dollar Retained Earnings for Year 10

	Nominal dollars	Restatement ratio	Constant December 31, year 10, dollars
Balance, January 1, year 10	$1,810,000	See Exhibit 7	C$2,854,940
Plus: Net income	260,000	See Exhibit 9	94,631
	(10,000)	225.0/214.1	(10,509)
Less: Preferred dividends	(10,000)	225.0/225.0	(10,000)
Balance, December 31, year 10	$2,050,000		C$2,929,062

stock dividends require restatement. Exhibit 15 shows the restatement of dividends, as well as the reconciliation of constant dollar retained earnings to an ending balance of C$2,929,062. Because this amount is the same as the amount treated as a "plug" to Retained Earnings in Exhibit 5, the restatement process has been carried out correctly.

Constant dollar date other than current year-end. Not all constant dollar financial statements use the purchasing power of the dollar at the end of the current year as the measuring unit. Some use the purchasing power for the base year of the price index. That is, the year when the price index is 100 is used, 1967 in the case of the CPI. The advantage of a base-year constant dollar measure is that the numbers in old annual reports and new annual reports are the same. The year 5 numbers are the same in the year 10 report or in the year 9 report. The numbers in old annual reports are not "rolled forward" each year to be restated in end-of-current-year dollars.

The FASB requires supplementary disclosure using as the measuring unit the purchasing power of mid-current-year dollars in some cases. The advantage of this otherwise-awkward date is that many income statement accounts in nominal dollars are already stated in units of mid-year purchasing power. Any revenue or expense occurring evenly throughout the year is so stated. Typically, cost of goods sold and depreciation expense are the only major items not spread evenly throughout the current year. Thus restatement is usually required in the income statement for only those two items when a mid-current-year unit is used.

In this chapter, we restate all items to end-of-current-year purchasing power. Once all items are stated in end-of-current-year constant dollars, a further restatement to some other constant dollar unit is mechanical. For example, assume that the price index for the base year is 100.0, for the middle of the current year is 214.6, and for the end of the current year is 225.0. To restate all items to base-year constant dollars, multiply end-of-current-year measurements by $100.0/225.0 = 0.444$. To restate to middle-of-current-year constant dollars, multiply all end-of-current-year measurements by $214.6/225.0 = 0.954$.

Constant Dollar Accounting—The Statement of Changes in Financial Position. FASB Statement No. 33 does not require the disclosure of information from a constant dollar statement of changes in financial position. There may be important differences, however, between the nominal dollar amount and the constant dollar amount for several items in this statement, particularly in the amount of working capital provided by operations. The procedures for restating the statement of changes in financial position are described in this section. As is the case in preparing the statement of changes in financial position in nominal dollars, the constant dollar statement is most easily prepared after the restated balance sheet and income statement have been prepared. The nominal dollar statement of changes in financial position of Sweeney Corporation is shown in the first column of Exhibit 16.

EXHIBIT 16   Statement of Changes in Financial Position for Sweeney Corporation for the Year Ended December 31, Year 10

	Nominal dollars	Constant December 31, year 10, dollars
Sources of working capital:		
Net income	$ 260,000	C$ 94,631
Add:		
Depreciation expense	248,000	344,158
Deferred income taxes	20,000	20,969
Subtract:		
Decrease in advances on maintenance contracts	(20,000)	(24,337)
Gain on sale of equipment	(80,000)	(69,925)
Purchasing power gain on noncurrent bonds payable		(116,071)
Purchasing power gain on noncurrent deferred income		
taxes		(3,290)
Working capital provided by operations	$ 428,000	C$ 246,135
Sale of equipment	112,000	117,702
Total sources	$ 540,000	C$ 363,887
Uses of working capital:		
Preferred dividends	$ 20,000	C$ 20,509
Purchase of equipment	320,000	332,410
Total uses.	$ 340,000	C$ 352,919
Increase in working capital	$ 200,000	C$ 10,918

Analysis of increase (decrease) in working capital		
Cash	$ 40,000	C$ 12,143
Accounts receivable	40,000	(48,214)
Inventories	40,000	(80,646)
Prepayments	(20,000)	(32,722)
Accounts payable	80,000	128,750
Salaries payable	20,000	31,607
Increase in working capital	$ 200,000	C$ 10,918

Working capital provided by operations. The calculation of working capital provided by operations begins with the net income amount from the constant dollar income statement. Constant dollar net income for Sweeney Corporation, as shown in Exhibit 9, is $94,631.

Several additions to and subtractions from net income are required to compute working capital provided by operations. The depreciation charge for the period is usually the most significant add-back. For Sweeney Corporation, the nominal dollar depreciation charge of $248,000 is restated to C$344,158, as shown in Exhibit 13. Similarly, an add-back to net income is required for the increase in deferred taxes during the period. The add-back for Sweeney Corporation of $20,969 is calculated as follows:

$$\$20,000 \times \frac{225.0}{214.6} = \$20,969$$

This add-back amount is also equal to the change in the constant dollar deferred income taxes account for the period. Add-backs of this type would also be made for depletion, amortization of goodwill and other intangible assets, amortization of discount on noncurrent debt, and the minority interest in earnings if these items appear in the conventional income statement. The constant dollar amounts for these add-backs can generally be obtained from the constant dollar income statement.

A subtraction from net income is required for the maintenance contract revenues in calculating working capital provided by operations. The revenue recognized from maintenance contracts during year 10 arose from the sale of maintenance contracts in year 8. Because Advances on Maintenance Contracts is treated as a long-term liability, the recognition of maintenance contract revenue in year 10 did not result in a corresponding increase in working capital; thus, a subtraction from net income is required in computing working capital provided by operations.

A subtraction is also required for the gain on sale of equipment. The entire proceeds from sales of noncurrent assets are usually classified as nonoperating sources of working capital rather than having the gain included among operating sources.

Two other subtractions, which appear in the constant dollar statement but do not appear on the nominal dollar statement, relate to the purchasing power gains on long-term debt and deferred income taxes. The purchasing power gains on these two items are included in constant dollar net income but do not provide working capital. They must therefore be subtracted in computing working capital provided by operations. The purchasing power gain on long-term debt is C$116,071 [= ($1,000,000 × 225.0/201.6) − $1,000,000]. The purchasing power gain on noncurrent deferred income taxes is calculated as follows:

Deferred income taxes balance, January year 10:	
[($20,000 × 225.0/201.6) − $20,000]	C$2,321
Increase in deferred income taxes for year 10:	
[($20,000 × 225.0/214.6) − $20,000]	969
Total	C$3,290

Working capital provided by operations on a constant dollar basis of C$246,135 is considerably less than the $428,000 provided on a nominal dollar basis. The lower amount relates primarily to a larger constant dollar reduction in inventories when goods were sold.

Other sources of working capital. The sale of equipment resulted in an increase in working capital of $112,000 in nominal dollars. This amount is restated as follows:

$$\$112,000 \times 225.0/214.1 \ldots \ldots \quad \text{C}\$117,702$$

Similar adjustments must be made for working capital provided by issuing non-current debt and capital stock.

Other uses of working capital. The working capital used for preferred stock dividends is restated as follows:

$10,000 × 225.0/214.1	C$10,509
$10,000 × 225.0/225.0	10,000
Total	C$20,509

The working capital used in acquiring equipment must also be restated.

$$\$320,000 \times 225.0/216.0 \ldots \ldots \quad \text{C}\$332,410$$

Similar adjustments would be made for working capital used in redeeming bonds and acquiring treasury stock.

Analysis of changes in working capital accounts. The change in each working capital account shown in the lower portion of Exhibit 16 is obtained from the constant dollar comparative balance sheet in Exhibits 5 and 7.

Constant Dollar Accounting—Special Problems

Manufactured inventories. The illustration assumed that all inventories were purchased. For manufacturing companies, the restatement procedure is bound to be somewhat more complicated. It may be convenient to restate manufacturing companies' inventories according to the three components as they would appear in a statement of cost of goods manufactured: materials, labor, and overhead.

The materials component can be restated in the manner described for Sweeney Corporation's cost of goods sold. Restatement of the labor component is simpler because there are no beginning and ending inventories of labor. If we assume that production is spread evenly throughout the year, labor cost can be restated using the average index for the year.

Restatements of overhead costs are likely to be the most difficult, and they may also be the most significant. Many overhead costs involve current cash outlays (e.g., utilities, indirect labor, general and administrative salaries). These overhead costs can generally be restated in the same manner as direct labor. Other overhead costs involve amortization of previous cash outlays (e.g., depreciation of building and equipment). The restatement of depreciation charges on buildings and equipment for a manufacturing firm is no different from the restatement of depreciation expense described in the illustration for a non-manufacturing firm. Here, as in other cases, the crucial data are the date of expenditure and the price-level index applicable to that date.

Some inventory items may be stated at the standard cost of manufacturing the items. If the cost standards used in valuing the inventory reflect end-of-the-period prices, then the items are already stated in current dollars and no restatement is required. If, however, the cost standards used are significantly out of date or if manufacturing cost variances are partially allocated to units in ending inventory, then the valuation of the units is probably closer to acquisition cost in nominal dollars. In this case, constant dollar restatements of the ending inventory are required.

Measurements based on current market prices. Monetary assets are not necessarily the only accounts that are automatically stated in current dollars and therefore require no restatement. Investments held by a mutual fund are typically stated at their market values on the date of the balance sheet. These investments are already stated in terms of current dollars and do not require restatement. On a comparative balance sheet, the investments at the beginning of the period, shown at beginning-of-the-period market prices, will have to be restated to the general price level at the end of the period. The gain or loss recognized from market price changes in nominal dollars will not usually be the same as the constant dollar gain or loss. The nominal and constant dollar gain or loss will only be the same if the weighted-average change in market price for the portfolio of investments is equal to the change in the general price level.

Some inventory items may be stated at net realizable value (i.e., the number of dollars expected to be received upon the sale of the inventories). For example, certain products in agricultural and natural resource industries are frequently measured at their net realizable values rather than their historical costs. Because these inventory items are already stated in terms of current prices, no constant dollar restatement is necessary. If, instead, these items are stated at acquisition cost, a constant dollar restatement will be necessary. The need for constant dollar restatements, therefore, is determined by the measurement unit used rather than by the inherent nature of the item itself.

Even though constant dollar restatements are not required for assets stated at current market prices or net realizable values, it is important to distinguish such assets from monetary assets. Monetary assets represent claims to a fixed number of dollars; therefore holding them necessarily gives rise to measurable purchasing power gains (deflation) and losses (inflation). Whether gains or losses result from holding nonmonetary assets, however they may be measured, depends on the movement of the prices of those specific assets relative to changes in the general price level.

Estimated liabilities. Estimated liabilities arising from warranty, premium, and some pension plans are nonmonetary in that they represent obligations to provide goods or services whose prices may fluctuate. As with other nonmonetary items, these items must be restated to the general purchasing power of the dollar on the most recent balance sheet date.

In some cases, the nominal dollar amount of the estimated liability is already stated in current dollars and needs no restatement. For example, the amount shown for estimated warranty claims is often reassessed at the end of each period in light of changing material prices, wage rates, and rate of customers' claims. The end-of-the-period balance in the liability account is increased or decreased to reflect the estimated future costs of the warranty plan. Under these circumstances, the estimated liability would not need to be adjusted for price-level changes. As was the case with inventory items stated at market prices, estimated liabilities stated at end-of-the-year prices are not monetary items. The estimated liability does not represent an obligation to pay a fixed number of dollars. The amount to be paid in the future depends on changes in the prices of specific goods and services.

Consolidation of foreign subsidiaries. Two possible methods exist for consolidating foreign subsidiaries in constant dollar financial statements: (1) the accounts of foreign subsidiaries can be restated in terms of constant units of the foreign currency using a price-level index for the foreign country and then the restated amounts can be translated into U.S. dollars (restate-translate sequence); or (2) the accounts of foreign subsidiaries can be translated into U.S. dollars and then the translated amounts can be restated in terms of constant U.S. dollars using a price-level index for the United States (translate-restate sequence). If exchange rates between the foreign currency and the U.S. dollar changed continuously and precisely to reflect changes in the relative general purchasing powers of the monetary unit of the two countries involved, then the restate-translate approach and the translate-restate approach method would produce virtually identical results. Because exchange rates do not always change precisely to reflect changes in relative purchasing powers, the two methods can produce different results. An example may serve to clarify the differences.

Assume that U.S. Domestic Company established a whollly owned Foreign Subsidiary on January 1, year 1, with an investment of $100,000. The investment was immediately converted into 500,000 units of local currency (LC), the exchange rate being $.20 per LC, or LC5 to $1. Foreign Subsidiary immediately purchased land for LC800,000, paying LC300,000 in cash and signing a long-term mortgage note for LC500,000. During year 1, Foreign Subsidiary had no other transactions. The U.S. general price level increased 10 percent and the general price level in the foreign country increased 25 percent during year 1. At the end of year 1, however, the exchange rate remained unchanged at $.20 per LC (LC5 to $1). Balance sheets under both methods are shown in Exhibit 17.

In preparing financial statements by the restate-translate approach, price-level-adjusted statements in terms of December 31, year 1, LC are first constructed using a general price-level index for that country. Those price-level-adjusted statements are then translated from foreign monetary units to dollars at the current exchange rate, in the example at the rate of $.20 per LC (LC5 to $1). In preparing financial statements under the translate-restate method, the nominal dollar amounts in the foreign subsidiary's accounts are first translated using appropriate exchange rates. In general, current exchange rates are used for monetary items and the exchange rates in effect at the historical dates are used for nonmonetary items. The resulting nominal dollar amounts are then restated for changes in the U.S. price level since those historical dates.

EXHIBIT 17   Restatement of Foreign Currency Accounts

FOREIGN SUBSIDIARY
Balance Sheet
December 31, Year 1

	Restate—translate				Translate—restate		
	Historical LC	Restated dollars (25% inflation)	Translated, dollars ($.20 per LC)		Historical LC	Translated, dollars ($.20 per LC)	Restated dollars (10% inflation)
Cash	200,000	200,000	$ 40,000		200,000	$ 40,000	$ 40,000
Land	800,000	1,000,000	200,000		800,000	160,000	176,000
	1,000,000	1,200,000	$240,000		1,000,000	$200,000	$216,000
Long-term debt	500,000	500,000	$100,000		500,000	$100,000	$100,000
Shareholders' equity	500,000	700,000	140,000		500,000	100,000	116,000
Total	1,000,000	1,200,000	$240,000		1,000,000	$200,000	$216,000

Statement of income and shareholders' equity for the year ended December 31, year 1

Purchasing power loss on net monetary working capital (.25 × LC200,000)	LC(50,000)	$ (10,000)	(.10 × $40,000)	$ (4,000)
Purchasing power gain on long-term debt (.25 × LC500,000)	125,000	25,000	(.10 × $100,000)	10,000
Net income	LC 75,000	$ 15,000		$ 6,000
Shareholders' equity, Jan. 1—LC500,000	LC625,000	125,000	LC500,000 $100,000	110,000
Shareholders' equity, Dec. 31	LC700,000	$140,000		$116,000

Each of the two methods has its advantages and disadvantages. The choice should depend on the primary informational objectives to be served. For example, in the restate-translate balance sheet, land is reported at $200,000. That is the current U.S. dollar equivalent of the historical amount of foreign purchasing power that was invested in foreign land. It would take 200,000 December 31, year 1, dollars to duplicate the *foreign purchasing power* invested in land. In the translate-restate balance sheet, land is reported at $176,000. That is the current U.S. dollar equivalent of the historical amount of *U.S. purchasing power* that was invested in foreign land. The $176,000 understates the amount of foreign purchasing power invested in the land and the $200,000 overstates the amount of U.S. purchasing power invested in the land. This phenomenon is the direct result of the failure of exchange rates to equate the purchasing power of the monetary units in question.

If the primary goal is the consistent reporting of financial statement amounts in terms of constant U.S. dollars, the translate-restate procedure would seem preferable. On the other hand, if the primary purpose is to reflect the performance of foreign investments in the unique economic environment in which they operate, the restate-translate procedure would be preferable. As this book goes to press, the FASB has this topic under consideration, but has not issued a final pronouncement.

Evaluation of Constant Dollar Accounting. The procedures for restating financial statements to a constant dollar basis can be traced back to before 1920 [Middleditch, 1918]. Yet it was not until 1979 that disclosure of constant dollar information became a part of generally accepted accounting principles. The usefulness of constant dollar information has been, and continues to be, controversial.

The case for constant dollar accounting. Proponents of constant dollar accounting offer the following arguments:

1. Constant dollar accounting makes the results of arithmetic operations more meaningful. If the measuring unit (the dollar) varies over time because of changes in the general purchasing power of the dollar, then additions and subtractions of recorded amounts cannot be made meaningfully.

2. Constant dollar accounting makes interperiod comparisons more meaningful. Changes in the amount of an item (sales, cost of goods sold) are difficult to interpret if the measuring unit used is not the same over time.

3. Constant dollar accounting provides useful information about the comparative impact of inflation across firms. Inflation affects firms differently, depending on the age and composition of their assets and equities. Heavily capital-intensive firms are likely to report significantly larger constant dollar depreciation expense than nominal dollar depreciation expense. Highly leveraged firms will report a larger purchasing power gain during periods of increasing prices than firms that use relatively little debt. Constant dollar accounting reports these differing effects of inflation across firms.

4. Constant dollar accounting improves the meaning and measurement of net income. Revenues and expenses are matched in terms of a constant measuring unit. Also, a gain or loss is explicitly recognized for the change in the general purchasing power of monetary assets and liabilities held. Income before the purchasing power gain or loss must exceed any loss of purchasing power of monetary assets and equities if the purchasing power of the monetary, or financial, capital of the firm is to be maintained.

5. Government policy makers are accustomed to using real, not nominal, dollar measuring units. To report corporate accounting data in nominal, rather than real, terms may disadvantage corporations in government policy decisions.

The case against constant dollar accounting. Opponents of constant dollar accounting argue that it fails to measure the economically significant effects of changing prices on a firm. They argue as follows:

1. With respect to nonmonetary items, the strategies that firms follow in coping with inflation focus on changes in the prices of the specific goods and services that the firm normally acquires and not on changes in the prices of a broad market basket of consumer goods and services. Raw materials are purchased early in anticipation of increased acquisition costs. A capital-intensive plant is constructed in anticipation of increased labor costs. Yet, under constant dollar accounting, the results of these decisions are judged against a standard based on changes in the general purchasing power of the dollar.

2. With respect to monetary items, the purchasing power gain or loss is based on an inappropriate index of purchasing power. Users of financial statements are interested in a firm's ability to maintain the purchasing power of its monetary assets for the particular kinds of goods and services that it normally purchases.

Users must recognize that constant dollar financial statements are not designed to provide information about the effects of changes in specific prices on the performance and financial position of a firm. An educational effort is required to inform statement users as to the kinds of interpretations that should and should not be made from constant dollar financial statements. FASB Statement No. 33 requires that only certain constant dollar information be disclosed (discussed later in this chapter). These limited disclosures provide an opportunity for studying the costs of preparing constant dollar financial statements as well as for educating statement users as to the potential value of the information disclosed.

CURRENT VALUE ACCOUNTING

Objectives of Current Value Accounting. The objective of current value accounting is to report the effects of specific price changes on the operating performance and financial position of a firm. It provides measurements of an attribute, current value, thought more relevant to decision making than the attribute, historical acquisition cost. There are, however, different approaches to calculating current values, each of which provides different information about the impact of changing prices. Three valuation methods are discussed below.

1. Current cost of replacing the service potential embodied in the specific assets of a firm. This measure, often referred to as replacement cost, current cost, or current entry value, is equal to the amount a firm would have to pay currently to replace the service potential embodied in its specific assets. It takes into account the inherent technological capabilities and levels of obsolescence of the existing assets. For example, if a firm owned a 2-year-old automobile, it would base its current replacement cost valuation on the price of similar 2-year-old automobiles in the used car market. If replacement cost amounts for identical, used assets were not available, then the replacement cost of new assets with similar service potential would be used. The replacement cost of the new asset must be adjusted downward, however, for both the used condition of the existing asset and any technological changes that have occurred.

The fact that the firm would probably not acquire a similar 2-year-old automobile if replacement were made is not considered important in this approach to measuring current replacement cost. FASB Statement No. 33 uses this measure of current value and refers to it as current cost. Income each period on a current cost basis is composed of two elements: (a) an operating margin equal to the difference between sales revenue and the current cost of replacing the service potential of the specific assets consumed in generating revenues, and (b) holding gains and losses equal to the changes in the current replacement costs of the firm's particular assets. FASB Statement No. 33 uses the term "income from continuing operations" to refer to operating margin (a) and the term "increases in current cost amounts" to refer to holding gains (b).

2. Current price at which existing assets could be sold. This measure, often referred to as *net realizable value* or *current exit value*, is equal to the net cash amount that a firm would receive if it sold its existing assets after subtracting any costs of disposal. Income each period is composed of two elements: (a) a purchasing margin equal to the difference between the net realizable, or exit, value of an asset at the time it is acquired and the acquisition cost of the asset, and (b) a holding gain or loss equal to changes in the net realizable value of assets while they are held. FASB Statement No. 33 prescribes that assets expected to be sold (e.g., inventories) should be stated at net realizable value if the amount is less than the current cost (measure 1 above) of the specific assets.

3. Present value of future cash flows. This measure is equal to the present, or discounted, value of the net cash flows expected to be generated from an asset. Income each period under this valuation method is composed of three elements: (a) a purchasing margin equal to the difference between the present value of the net future cash flows from an asset at the time of acquisition and the acquisition cost of an asset, (b) interest revenue each period as cash flows become nearer, and (c) a holding gain or loss arising either from changes in the amounts of future cash flows (due to changing prices, competition, or other factors) or from changes in the discount rate used. FASB Statement No. 33 prescribes that assets expected to be used instead of sold (e.g., depreciable assets) should be stated at the present value of the future cash flows if this amount is less than the current cost (measure 1 above) of the specific assets.

As a basis for providing information about the effects of changes in specific prices on a firm, Statement No. 33 requires that the current cost of existing assets (measure 1) be used in almost all cases. This valuation basis reports the cost of replacing the specific productive capacity that the firm has chosen to use. These current costs are matched against sales revenue to provide information on a firm's ability to cope with the specific price changes faced by the firm.

The use of net realizable values can be criticized in that changes in the exit values of assets that firms intend to use instead of sell, such as depreciable assets, are usually not considered in management's actions to cope with specific price changes. The approach of using net present values can be criticized in that changes in the valuation of assets may be due to factors other than specific price changes (e.g., change in the discount rate, change in the pattern of cash flows). Thus, although each of the three valuation methods has strengths and weaknesses with respect to asset valuation and income measurement, the approach of using the current cost of existing assets best captures the separate effects of changes in specific prices on a firm.

Financial Statements Based on Current Costs. The accounting procedures for preparing financial statements that reflect changes in specific prices are similar, regardless of which of the three valuation methods is used. In this section and the next, the procedures for preparing financial statements based on the current cost of existing assets are discussed and illustrated. As with constant dollar restatements, the restatements for changes in replacement costs can be most easily performed after the conventional financial statements have been prepared. Formal journal entries to restate historical cost amounts for either general or specific price changes are not necessary.

FASB Statement No. 33 requires restatement to current costs of selected asset and expense items only. In the discussion and illustration that follow, consideration is given to changing the valuation basis to current costs for all items in the financial statements. The more limited measurements and disclosures required by Statement No. 33 are discussed later.

Restatements of assets. Cash and accounts receivable are normally stated on the balance sheet at their current cash or cash equivalent value, and therefore do not require restatement for specific price changes. Most other assets will be recorded at unadjusted or adjusted acquisition costs, which differ from current cost. The current costs of marketable securities and investments in securities can usually be calculated from quoted market prices on organized securities exchanges. The current cost of inventories can be found in current invoices, in vendors' price lists, from standard manufacturing costs that reflect current costs, or by revising historical costs using price indices for the specific goods and services measured. The current cost of property, plant, and equipment can be found directly through current invoice prices or prices quoted in active markets for land and used plant and equipment. Alternatively, historical cost amounts may be restated using price indices for the particular items of property, plant, and equipment. Chapter 32 describes more fully techniques for computing current costs.

Restatement of liabilities. As with cash and accounts receivable, most current liabilities are stated at their current cash equivalent value and do not require restatement. On the other hand, the book value of long-term debt, based on the market rate of interest at the time of issue, will likely differ from the current market price of the debt based on current market rates of interest. The current cost of debt can be found by referring to quoted market prices for the outstanding debt obligation. Similar comments apply to preferred stock. The excess of the current cost of assets over the current cost of liabilities and preferred stock is the equity of the common shareholders. Any further breakdown of the common shareholders' equity into the current cost of the contributed capital and current cost of retained earnings is of questionable usefulness.

Restatement of revenues and expenses. Sales revenues and most operating expenses (except cost of goods sold and depreciation) are likely to be stated at amounts close to their current costs, and no restatement is usually necessary. Cost of goods sold must be restated to the current costs of goods at the time they were sold. Under most circumstances, LIFO perpetual cost of goods sold is virtually the same as replacement cost and LIFO periodic cost of goods sold is almost the same. As with inventories on the balance sheet, current invoice prices or vendors' price lists usually provide the basis for calculating the current cost of goods sold.

The calculation of depreciation expense is more controversial. One view holds that the net change in value is reported either as appreciation (net increase in value) or as depreciation (net decrease in value). By the time the asset has been retired, its historical cost will have been written off. The increases and decreases in value that occur will be reported each period.

Others argue that a change in value of a long-term asset consists of a "using up" of service potential and a value change or holding gain on what is left. The value change in the remaining service potential can exceed the value of the service used up, so the value at the end of the year is greater than at the beginning. Still, to separate the decline caused by the "using up" from the more-than-offsetting value change provides information useful to understanding the current operating performance of the business.

Statement No. 33 requires that the decline in current value caused by "using up" service potential be separated from the increase in current value arising from holding gains (or holding loss contributing to further declines in value). Depreciation in current cost accounting should attempt to measure as expense the current cost of the service potential used up, even when value changes in remaining service potential offset this expense.

The procedure to calculate current cost depreciation starts with a determination of the current cost of depreciable assets in use during a period. A portion of this cost must then be allocated to expense to match as closely as possible the current cost of replacing the services of the specific assets consumed during the period. Selecting a depreciation method that will accomplish this allocation can be difficult. The firm's regular depreciation method may be inappropriate if it was chosen partly to allow for expected cost increases (e.g., as when an accelerated depreciation method is used).

The calculation of income tax expense on a current cost basis is controversial. Some accountants argue that income tax expense should be based on pretax current cost income. The total income from the acquisition and sale of any asset is the difference between the amount of cash received at the time of sale and the amount of cash expended at the time of acquisition. Current cost accounting merely affects the period in which the income is recognized (through increased expenses and/or holding gains and losses). The differences between current cost amounts and historical cost amounts are therefore timing differences for which deferred income taxes should be provided in the usual fashion. Other accountants argue that differences between current cost and historical cost amounts are permanent differences. Income tax expense in the current cost income statement should, according to their view, be based on pretax historical cost income. FASB Statement No. 33 requires that the latter treatment be followed.

Income in current cost statements. To an economist, income is a measure of the amount that can be consumed during a period and still be as well off at the end of the period as at the beginning:

$$\text{Income} = \text{Ending Wealth} - \text{Beginning Wealth} + \text{Dividends}$$

But the economist's definition of income does not indicate explicitly how "well-offness" or wealth is to be measured. Two bases are discussed in the accounting literature: financial capital and physical capital. Financial capital measures "well-offness" in terms of units of purchasing power. The firm has income for a period to the extent that the dollar value of its assets (or the purchasing power embodied in its assets) at the end of the period exceeds their amounts at the beginning of the period (plus consumption, or dividends, less any new capital contributions). In the financial capital view, all holding gains are labeled as part of income. Physical capital measures "well-offness" in units of productive capacity. The firm has income for a period to the extent that the productive capacity of its existing assets has increased (plus consumption, or dividends, less any new capital contributions). In the physical capital view, holding gains on existing assets are not considered an element of income. Rather, they are increases in dollar value not accompanied by increases in productive capacity. The assets are indeed written up (with debits), but credits are made directly to owners' equity rather than to an income account.

FASB Statement No. 33 did not express a preference for one view or the other. In the illustrations in this section, we take a financial capital viewpoint, including holding gains and losses in income.

Illustration of Financial Statements Based on Current Costs. Exhibit 18 presents selected financial statement data for Sweeney Corporation, discussed earlier in the chapter, on both a historical cost and a current cost basis. For balance sheet and income statement amounts not shown, it is assumed that the historical cost and current cost amounts are the same.

Current cost income statement. The current cost income statement is divided into two main sections: (1) the operating margin, equal to the difference between revenues and expenses measured in terms of current costs, and (2) holding gains and losses. The holding gains and losses section is further divided into realized holding gains and losses and unrealized holding gains and losses. An example may be helpful in understanding the calculations involved.

Example. A company acquired two items of inventory on November 1, year 1, for $10 each. On December 31, year 1, these items had a current cost of $12 each. On July 1, year 2, one of the two items was sold for $18 at a time when its current cost was $15. On December 31, year 2, the current cost of the item remaining in inventory was $17. A current cost income statement appears in Exhibit 19. The operating margin is equal to the difference between the selling

EXHIBIT 18   Historical and Current Cost Data for Sweeney Corporation for Year 10

	December 31, year 10		December 31, year 9	
	Historical cost	Current cost	Historical cost	Current cost
Balance sheet				
Inventories	$1,040,000	$1,060,000	$1,000,000	$1,015,000
Investment in common stock	320,000	430,000	320,000	450,000
Land	160,000	210,000	160,000	200,000
Building (net)	420,000	625,000	440,000	630,000
Equipment (net)	1,100,000	1,750,000	1,040,000	1,620,000
Bonds Payable	1,000,000	865,938	1,000,000	862,352

	For the year ended December 31, year 10	
	Historical cost	Current cost
Income statement		
Cost of goods sold	$3,960,000	$4,030,000
Depreciation	248,000	410,000
Interest	100,000	103,586
Gain on sale of equipment	80,000	1,000

EXHIBIT 19   Current Cost Income Statement for a Company for Year 2

Sales	$ 18		
Current cost of goods sold	(15)		
Operating margin		$ 3	
Realized holding gain:			
Current cost of goods sold	$ 15		
Historical cost of goods sold	(10)		5
Conventional gross margin		$ 8	
Unrealized holding gain for year 2:			
Cumulative unrealized holding gain, December 31, year 2:			
Ending inventory at current cost	$ 17		
Ending inventory at historical cost	(10)	$ 7	
Cumulative unrealized holding gain, December 31, year 1:			
Beginning inventory at current cost	$ 24		
Beginning inventory at historical cost	(20)	(4)	3[a]
Net income on current cost basis			$11

[a]The $3 unrealized holding gain for year 2 is the net of (1) an unrealized holding gain of $5 (= $17 − $12) on item 2 and (2) a reclassification from unrealized to realized of the $2 ($12 − $10) holding gain on item 1 recognized in year 1.

price of the item sold and its current cost at the time of sale on July 1, year 2 ($3 = $18 − $15). The operating margin indicates a firm's success in setting selling prices to cover the current costs of assets consumed. The realized holding gain is the difference between the current cost and the historical cost of the item sold ($5 = $15 − $10). This holding gain represents the increase in the cost of the item from the time it was acquired until the time it was sold. The operating margin of $3 plus the realized holding gain of $5 is equal to net income as reported in the conventional financial statements based on historical costs ($8 = $18 − $10). In the current cost income statement, net income is segregated into two components, operating margin and realized holding gain or loss. The unrealized holding gain for year 2 is the difference between the cumulative unrealized holding gain on inventory at the end of the year and the cumulative unrealized holding gain on inventory at the beginning of the year ($3 = $7 − $4). This unrealized holding gain will become realized when the inventory item is sold. Until then, the cumulative unrealized holding gain is reflected in the valuation of inventory on the balance sheet. In general, separating realized from unrealized holding gains and losses requires a cost flow assumption. For example, assume instead of the above information that item 1 was acquired in October, year 1, for $8 and item 2 was acquired in December, year 1, for $12. The acquisition cost of goods available for sale is still $20 and the total holding gain is still $8. But whether the holding gain is $7 (= $15 − $8) realized and $1 [= ($17 − $12) − ($24 − $20)] unrealized or $3 (= $15 − $12) realized and $5 [= ($17 − $8) − ($24 − $20)] unrealized depends on whether we assume that item 1 or item 2 was sold.

Controversy exists as to whether holding gains and losses should be considered as elements of income. A firm that purchases early in anticipation of increasing prices (thereby realizing holding gains) may in fact be better off than a firm that purchases later at the higher price. The firm cannot pay dividends equal to the holding gain, however, without impairing its ability to replace the productive capacity, or service potential, of its assets.

The current cost income statement for Sweeney Corporation for year 10 using the format described above, is shown in Exhibit 20, with the calculation of unrealized holding gains and losses shown in Exhibit 21.

Revenues and gains. Revenues from product sales and from maintenance are assumed to be the same under historical cost and current cost systems. The gain on sale of equipment of $80,000 under a historical cost system is equal to the difference between the selling price of $112,000 and the book value of $32,000 (= $160,000 − $128,000). Under a current cost system, the gain is equal to the difference between the selling price and the current cost of replacing the asset. Sweeney Corporation determines that the current cost of replacing the equipment sold is $111,000. In markets with no transaction costs, the selling price and current cost should be the same and no gain or loss would be recognized. In real markets with transaction costs, there is a difference in the price at which Sweeney Corporation could sell the equipment and the price at which it could be purchased. The gain on sale is $1,000 (= $112,000 − $111,000).

Expenses and losses. Cost of Goods Sold and Depreciation Expense are stated at the current cost of the items sold or services used during the period.

Selling, General, and Administrative Expenses are assumed to be the same on a historical cost and a current cost basis. Historical cost interest of $100,000 on Bonds Payable is equal to the historical market rate of 10 percent times the face value of the bonds of $1,000,000. Because these bonds are stated at their face value on the balance sheet, they were apparently issued at par value (i.e., coupon rate equaled market rate at the time of issuance). At the beginning of year 10, we ascertain that the bonds have a current cost, or market price, of $862,352. A check of internal records shows that these bonds pay interest semiannually and are due on January 1, year 24. Thus, at the beginning of year 10, these bonds have a 15-year term to maturity. To calculate the market yield (current cost) at the beginning of year 10, it is necessary to ascertain the interest rate that will discount the $50,000 semiannual interest payments and the $1,000,000 principal back 15 years so that it has a present value of $862,352. That discount rate is 12 percent [($1,000,000 × .17411) + ($50,000 × 13.76483) = $862,352]. Following a similar procedure at the end of the year, we ascertain that the current market price of the bonds is $865,938. The interest rate that will discount the interest and principal payments back 14 years to a present value of $865,938 is also 12 percent. Thus, the market rate throughout year 10 was apparently 12 percent. Interest expense on a current cost basis is

First 6 months: .06 × $862,352	$ 51,741
Second 6 months: .06 × ($862,352 + $1,741)	51,845
Total interest expense	$103,586

Income Taxes are assumed to be the same on a historical cost and a current cost basis.

The operating margin of a negative $54,586 indicates that selling prices were inadequate to cover the current cost of assets consumed in operations.

Realized holding gains. The realized holding gains are equal to the difference between the current cost and historical cost amounts for various expenses and gains. Note that virtually all of the gain on sale of the equipment is a holding gain. Under a current cost system, this gain would have been recognized piecemeal over the life of the equipment as prices for the equipment increased. Under a historical cost system, all of the gain is recognized in the period of sale.

Note that, of the $260,000 conventional net income amount, $314,586 represents a realized holding gain netted against a loss of $54,586 on operating margin. A firm that generates a large portion of its income from realized holding gains instead of from operating margins is not likely to replace its assets as they wear out and remain in business without significant inflows of new capital.

Unrealized holding gains and losses. The unrealized holding gain or loss for year 10 on various assets and liabilities is the *incremental* unrealized amount for the year. The incremental gain or loss is calculated by subtracting the cumulative unrealized gain or loss at the beginning of the year from the *cumulative* unrealized gain or loss at the end of the year. Incremental holding gains are recognized on the inventories, land, building, and equipment. An incremental loss is recognized on the investment in common stock and the bonds payable (see Exhibit 21).

**EXHIBIT 20   Income Statement Based on Historical and Current Cost
for Sweeney Corporation for the Year 10**

	Historical cost	Current cost
Revenues and gains:		
Product sales..	$5,180,000	$5,180,000
Earned on maintenance contracts	20,000	20,000
Gain on sale of equipment	80,000	1,000
Total revenues and gains	$5,280,000	$5,201,000
Expenses and losses:		
Cost of goods sold	$3,960,000	$4,030,000
Selling, general, and administrative	512,000	512,000
Depreciation	248,000	410,000
Interest..	100,000	103,586
Income taxes...	200,000	200,000
Total expenses and losses............................	$5,020,000	$5,255,586
Operating margin..		$ (54,586)
Realized holding gains:		
Inventory sold ($4,030,000 − $3,960,000)...................		$ 70,000
Depreciable assets used ($410,000 − $248,000)		162,000
Fixed assets sold ($111,000 − $32,000)....................		79,000
Interest expense ($103,586 − $100,000)...................		3,586
Total holding gains and losses		$ 314,586
Conventional net income.................................	$ 260,000	
Operating margin plus realized holding gains		$ 260,000
Unrealized holding gains and losses (calculations shown below):		
Inventories		$ 5,000
Investment in common stock		(20,000)
Land...		10,000
Building		15,000
Equipment		70,000
Bonds		(3.586)
Total unrealized holding gain or loss		$ 76,414
Current cost net income		$ 336,414

Current cost balance sheet. The balance sheet based on current costs is
shown in Exhibit 22. Retained Earnings is the amount necessary to equate
assets and equities.

Journal Entries to Convert to Current Costs. Current cost financial statements can be prepared by restating the amounts in the historical cost financial
statements. It is not necessary that the firm's accounting system formally incorporate current costs. An examination of the journal entries made if current
costs are incorporated into the formal accounting system, however, helps in
understanding current cost adjustments.

The following entries would be made to restate revenues and expenses based

EXHIBIT 21 Calculation of Unrealized Holding Gains and Losses for Sweeney Corporation for Year 10

	Cumulative unrealized holding gain or loss		Increase (decrease) in unrealized gain or loss for year 10
	End of period	Beginning of period	
Inventories......	$1,060,000 – $1,040,000 = $20,000	$1,015,000 – $1,000,000 = $15,000	$ 5,000
Investment......	$430,000 – $320,000 = $110,000	$450,000 – $320,000 = $130,000	(20,000)
Land	$210,000 – $160,000 = $50,000	$200,000 – $160,000 = $40,000	10,000
Building........	$625,000 – $420,000 = $205,000	$630,000 – $440,000 = $190,000	15,000
Equipment......	$1,750,000 – $1,100,000 = $650,000	$1,620,000 – $1,040,000 = $580,000	70,000
Bonds	$865,938 – $1,000,000 = ($134,062)	$862,352 – $1,000,000 = ($137,648)	(3,586)

EXHIBIT 22   Comparative Balance Sheet for Sweeney Corporation in Current Costs, December 31, Year 10 and Year 9

	December 31, year 10	December 31, year 9
Assets		
Current assets:		
Cash.................................	$ 280,000	$ 240,000
Accounts receivable (net)	800,000	760,000
Inventories	1,060,000	1,015,000
Prepayments	80,000	100,000
Total current assets...................	$2,220,000	$2,115,000
Investment in common stock...............	$ 430,000	$ 450,000
Property, plant, and equipment:		
Land................................	$ 210,000	$ 200,000
Building (net of accumulated depreciation)....	625,000	630,000
Equipment (net of accumulated depreciation) .	1,750,000	1,620,000
Total property, plant, and equipment	$2,585,000	$2,450,000
Total assets	$5,235,000	$5,015,000
Liabilities and shareholders' equity		
Current liabilities:		
Accounts payable	$ 340,000	$ 420,000
Salaries payable	80,000	100,000
Total current liabilities.................	$ 420,000	$ 520,000
Long-term liabilities:		
Advances on maintenance contracts	$ 40,000	$ 60,000
Bonds payable (10%, semiannual interest due January 1, year 24)...................	865,938	862,352
Deferred income taxes	40,000	20,000
Total long-term liabilities	$ 945,938	$ 942,352
Total liabilities	$1,365,938	$1,462,352
Shareholders' equity:		
Preferred stock (4,000 shares, 5%, $100 par value, $115 redemption value)	$ 400,000	$ 400,000
Common stock ($1 par value, 100,000 shares issued and outstanding)................	100,000[a]	100,000[a]
Additional paid-in capital	150,000[a]	150,000[a]
Retained earnings	3,219,062[a]	2,902,648[a]
Total shareholders' equity..............	$3,869,062	$3,552,648
Total liabilities and shareholders' equity	$5,235,000	$5,015,000

[a]Common shareholders' equity on a current cost basis is equal to the difference between assets at current cost and liabilities plus preferred shareholders' equity at current cost. It is not meaningful to separate common shareholders' equity into the portions attributable to contributed capital and retained earnings. It is done here, however, so that Exhibit 23 can reconcile retained earnings on a historical cost to a current cost basis.

on historical cost to a current cost basis and to record the *realized* holding gain or loss.

(1) Current Cost of Goods Sold	4,030,000	
Historical Cost of Goods Sold		3,960,000
Realized Holding Gain on Inventories		70,000
(2) Current Cost Depreciation Expense	410,000	
Historical Cost Depreciation Expense		248,000
Realized Holding Gain on Depreciable Assets		162,000
(3) Current Cost Interest Expense	103,586	
Historical Cost Interest Expense		100,000
Realized Holding Gain on Bonds		3,586
(4) Gain on Sale of Equipment (historical cost)	80,000	
Gain on Sale of Equipment (current cost)		1,000
Realized Holding Gain on Equipment Sold		79,000

The following entries would be made to restate assets and liabilities at the end of year 10 to a current cost basis and to record unrealized holding gains and losses. The credit to Retained Earnings in each entry is for the cumulative unrealized holding gain or loss that would have been recognized in prior years on a current cost basis (see Exhibit 21).

(5) Inventories	20,000	
Retained Earnings		15,000
Unrealized Holding Gain on Inventories		5,000
(6) Investment in Common Stock	110,000	
Unrealized Holding Loss on Investments	20,000	
Retained Earnings		130,000
(7) Land	50,000	
Retained Earnings		40,000
Unrealized Holding Gain on Land		10,000
(8) Building (net)	205,000	
Retained Earnings		190,000
Unrealized Holding Gain on Building		15,000
(9) Equipment (net)	650,000	
Retained Earnings		580,000
Unrealized Holding Gain on Equipment		70,000
(10) Bonds Payable	134,062	
Unrealized Holding Loss on Bonds	3,586	
Retained Earnings		137,648
To record unrealized holding gain on Bonds Payable through beginning of year and to recognize an unrealized holding loss for the year.		

Exhibit 23 presents a reconciliation of retained earnings from a historical cost basis to a current cost basis for year 10. Cumulative unrealized holding gains

---

EXHIBIT 23   Reconciliation of Common Shareholder's Equity for Sweeney Corporation to a Current Cost Basis for the Year 10

Retained earnings, January 1, year 10, on historical cost basis		$1,810,000
Plus cumulative unrealized holding gains and loss of prior years:		
Inventories	$ 15,000	
Investment in common stock	130,000	
Land	40,000	
Building	190,000	
Equipment	580,000	
Bonds payable	137,648	1,092,648
Retained earnings, January 1, year 10, on current cost basis		$2,902,648
Plus net income for year 10 on current cost basis		336,414
Less preferred stock dividends		(20,000)
Retained earnings, December 31, year 10, on current cost basis		$3,219,062

---

and losses of prior years are adjustments of Retained Earnings at the beginning of year 10. The amounts shown for Retained Earnings in Exhibit 23 are the same as the amounts determined by "plugging" in Exhibit 22.

Evaluation of Current Cost Accounting. As with constant dollar accounting, current cost accounting continues to be controversial.

The case for current cost accounting. Advocates of current cost accounting offer the following arguments.

1. Management's actions to cope with changing prices are based on expected changes in the prices of the particular goods and services normally acquired by a firm. Current cost financial statements provide a consistent basis on which to evaluate management's actions and performance.

2. Current cost income is separated into operating margins and holding gains and losses, permitting statement users to assess the impact of changing prices on the profitability of the firm.

3. Current cost balance sheets provide a more realistic indication of the current economic value of assets and liabilities than do the balance sheets based on historical costs.

The case against current cost accounting. Opponents of current cost accounting offer the following arguments:

1. Current cost amounts are often difficult to calculate, particularly for specialized used assets, raising questions about the reliability and comparability of current cost data between firms.

2. Current cost accounting in nominal dollars fails to recognize that the measuring unit used to calculate current cost amounts is not of the same dimension over time. Changes in the general purchasing power of the dollar make current cost amounts on the balance sheet at the beginning and end of the period non-comparable. Likewise, net income amounts over time using current costs are not based on a constant measuring unit.

3. Changes in current costs relative to changes in the general price level are not considered in measuring holding gains and losses under nominal dollar, current cost accounting. A holding gain on a tract of land of 8 percent on a current cost basis has one meaning when the general price level increases 6 percent and another meaning when general prices increase by 10 percent.

4. Current cost accounting fails to recognize purchasing power, or inflation, gains or losses on monetary items. As discussed earlier in this chapter, monetary items gain or lose purchasing power as they are held over time. These gains and losses are often equally as important as holding gains and losses on inventories, depreciable assets, and similar items.

CONSTANT DOLLAR AND CURRENT COST ACCOUNTING

A careful study of the arguments for and against constant dollar accounting and current cost accounting reveals that most of the criticisms of these two approaches to accounting for changing prices could be overcome by combining the two methodologies. Because constant dollar accounting deals with the measuring unit and current cost accounting deals with the attribute measured, there are no theoretical obstacles to combining the two approaches.

Example. Refer to the earlier example for Sweeney Corporation. The equipment sold during year 10 for $112,000 had been acquired during year 5 for $160,000 at a time when a general price index was 150.7. The equipment was sold during year 10 when its book value was $32,000 (= $160,000 − $128,000), its current cost was $111,000, and a general price index was 214.1. The index at the end of year 10 was 225.0. Exhibit 24 shows the calculation of the gain on the sale of equipment under (1) historical costs in nominal dollars, (2) historical costs stated in constant dollars, (3) current costs in nominal dollars, and (4) current costs stated in constant dollars.

The gain in column (1) matches the selling price measured in nominal dollars at the time of sale with the book value of equipment measured in the nominal dollars expended 5 years ago (adjusted for depreciation to date of sale). The gain in column (2) is based on a constant measuring unit, in that both the selling price and book value are stated in terms of dollars of December 31, year 10, purchasing power. The total gain in column (3) of $80,000 is identical to the gain in column (1). In column (3), however, the gain is separated into a gain from the sale and a gain from holding the equipment while its current cost increased. [Note in column (3) that there would be a decrease of $79,000 (= $111,000 − $32,000) in the *unrealized* holding gain for the portion of the realized holding gain resulting from changes in current costs in prior years while the equipment was held. In this case, all of the realized gain was an unrealized holding gain of a previous period.] The amounts in column (3) are not stated in dollars of constant purchasing power. The gain on sale is stated in terms of dollars of purchasing power at the time of sale, whereas the realized holding gain is stated in terms of dollars both at the time of sale (the $111,000 current cost) and at the time the equipment was acquired in year 5 (the $32,000 book value). In column (4), these differences in the measuring unit are removed. Both the gain on sale and the holding gain are stated in terms of December 31, year 10, purchasing power.

EXHIBIT 24   Calculation of Gain on Sale of Equipment for Sweeney Corporation

	(1) Historical cost/ nominal dollars	(2) Historical cost/ constant dollars	(3) Current cost/ nominal dollars	(4) Current cost/ constant dollars
Selling price:				
Nominal price	$112,000		$112,000	
Constant dollar price, $112,000 × 225.0/ 214.1		C$117,702		C$117,702
Less adjusted cost:				
Historical/nominal	32,000			
Historical/constant, $32,000 × 225.0/ 150.7		47,777		
Current/nominal			111,000	
Current/constant, $111,000 × 225.0/ 214.1				116,651
Gain on sale	$ 80,000	C$ 69,925	$ 1,000	C$ 1,051
Plus realized holding gain:				
Current/nominal, $111,000 − $32,000 . .			79,000	
Current/constant, ($111,000 × 225.0/ 214.1) − ($32,000 × 225.0/ 150.7)				68,874
Total gain	$ 80,000	C$ 69,925	$ 80,000	C$ 69,925

Example. Refer again to the data for Sweeney Corporation. Exhibit 20 indicates that an unrealized holding gain of $10,000 was recognized on the land. The calculation of this unrealized holding gain is based on a mixture of dollars of various purchasing powers. To restate the unrealized holding gain to a constant dollar basis, the following adjustments are necessary:

Current cost at end of year in December 31, year 10, dollars	C$ 210,000
Historical cost at end of year in December 31, year 10, dollars, $160,000 × 225.0/ 104.3	(345,158)
Unrealized holding gain (loss) at end of year	C$(135,158)
Current cost at beginning of year in December 31, year 10, dollars, $200,000 × 225.0/201.6	C$ 223,214
Historical cost at beginning of year in December 31, year 10, dollars, $160,000 × 225.0/ 104.3	(345,158)
Unrealized holding gain (loss) at beginning of year	C$(121,944)
Incremental holding gain (loss) for the year	C$ (13,214)

Each amount is stated in terms of constant December 31, year 10 dollars. The $10,000 unrealized holding gain on a current cost basis measured in nominal dollars is restated to an unrealized holding loss on a constant dollar, current cost basis. Thus it can be seen that increases in the current cost of land have not kept pace with changes in the general price level. The incremental holding loss of C$13,214 is the holding loss net of general price inflation.

REQUIRED DISCLOSURES OF THE EFFECTS OF CHANGING PRICES

Given the need for experimentation with various techniques of accounting for changing prices, FASB Statement No. 33 does not require the presentation of a full set of financial statements based on historical cost/constant dollars, current cost/nominal dollars, and current cost/constant dollars. Instead, only certain supplementary information need be disclosed. The minimum disclosures listed below are required to be made by public enterprises with either (1) inventories and property, plant, and equipment (before deducting accumulated depreciation, depletion, and amortization) amounting in aggregate to more than $125 million; or (2) total assets amounting to more than $1 billion (after deducting accumulated depreciation). FASB Statement No. 54 [1982] excludes investment companies from these disclosures.

1. Income from continuing operations for the current fiscal year on a historical cost/constant dollar basis.
2. The purchasing power gain or loss on net monetary items for the current fiscal year.
3. Income from continuing operations for the current fiscal year on a current cost basis.
4. Current cost of inventory and property, plant, and equipment at the end of the current fiscal year.
5. Increases or decreases for the current fiscal year in the current cost amounts of inventory and property, plant, and equipment (referred to as *holding gains and losses* in this chapter), net of inflation (i.e., stated on a constant dollar basis).
6. For the 5 most recent fiscal years, the following items must be disclosed:
   (a) Net sales and other operating revenue
   (b) Historical cost/constant dollar information:

   Income from continuing operations
   Income per common share from continuing operations
   Purchasing power gain or loss on monetary items
   Net assets at fiscal year-end

   (c) Current cost information:

   Income from continuing operations
   Income per common share from continuing operations

Increases or decreases in current cost amounts of inventory and property, plant, and equipment, net of inflation

Net assets at fiscal year-end

(d) Other information in constant dollars:

Cash dividends declared per common share

Market price per common share at fiscal year end

SEC Accounting Series Release No. 279 requires firms to include a narrative discussion of the effects of changing prices on the firm. This narrative discussion is included either in the note containing the above disclosures or in management's discussion and analysis of financial conditions and results of operations.

Statement No. 33, when originally issued, excluded certain specialized assets from its current cost disclosure requirements. The FASB wished to study these specialized assets more fully to assess the applicability of current cost disclosures. Four additional pronouncements now extend, with some modification, the requirements of Statement No. 33 to these assets.

1. Statement No. 39—mining and oil and gas assets. Current cost information as prescribed by Statement No. 33 must now be disclosed for mineral resource assets. Because of difficulties in measuring the current cost of finding mineral resource assets, Statement No. 39 permits firms to measure current cost by restating historical cost amounts with specific price indices. Because some firms use successful-efforts costing while other firms use full costing, the resulting current cost amounts are not comparable among firms. Statement No. 39 also requires the disclosure of information about the quantities of proved mineral reserves.

2. Statement No. 40—timberlands and growing timber assets. These assets and related expenses may be stated at either their historical cost/constant dollar amounts or at their current cost amounts. Because of difficulties in measuring the current cost for growing timber, the FASB permits firms to use either approach to measuring the effect of changing prices. The FASB's position in this case seems questionable. Constant dollar accounting and current cost accounting are designed to solve different problems (i.e., a measuring unit problem versus a valuation problem). Permitting either method to be used reduces comparability among firms and could confuse financial statement users.

3. Statement No. 41—income-producing real estate assets. These assets and related expenses may also be stated either at their historical cost/constant dollar amounts or at their current cost amounts. The FASB's requirements in this case, as with timberlands and growing timber, may be viewed as a compromise position. Respondents to an earlier Exposure Draft argued that current cost is largely irrelevant in the case of income-producing real estate. Future cash flows from rentals and current market (exit) values of real estate properties are the relevant items of information about changing prices. The FASB, however, felt that these two items of information were not measurable with sufficient reliability for inclusion in financial reports. Firms that feel that current cost amounts are irrelevant in the case of income-producing real estate will likely report only historical cost/constant dollar information. Therefore, no information about the effects of changes in specific prices will be disclosed.

4. Statement No. 46—motion picture films. As with timberlands and growing timber assets, motion picture films can be stated at either their historical cost/constant dollar amounts or their current cost amounts.

These four pronouncements reflect the political nature of the standard-setting process. Much of the criticism of the Exposure Draft of Statement No. 33 came from firms with mineral resource, timber, income-producing real estate, and motion picture films as assets. The FASB excluded these assets from the current-cost requirements of Statement No. 33. The positions finally taken on these assets in Statements No. 39, 40, 41, and 46 reflect the compromises required in order to obtain majority agreement on a position within the FASB.

SUMMARY

Accounting for changing prices is currently in a period of transition and experimentation. Financial statement preparers and users have recognized for many years that changing prices, either in general or for specific goods and services, bring to question the validity and meaningfulness of conventional financial statements based on historical cost and nominal dollars. The pronouncements by the Financial Accounting Standards Board provide firms considerable flexibility in the way changing prices are accounted for and disclosed. Whether constant dollar accounting, current cost accounting, or some other approach replaces or regularly supplements the historical cost/nominal dollars financial statements will depend on the benefits of the disclosures as perceived by users relative to the cost of generating the necessary data. It is as yet too early to evaluate effectively these benefits and costs.

BIBLIOGRAPHY

Beaver, W. H., "Accounting for Inflation in an Efficient Market," *The Impact of Inflation on Accounting: A Global View, The International Journal of Accounting,* 1979, pp. 21–42.

Chambers, R. J., *Accounting, Evaluation, and Economic Behavior* (Prentice-Hall, Englewood Cliffs, N.J., 1966).

Davidson, S., C. P. Stickney, and R. L. Weil, *Inflation Accounting* (McGraw-Hill Book Company, New York, 1976).

Edwards, E. O., and P. W. Bell, *The Theory and Measurement of Business Income* (University of California Press, Berkeley, 1961).

Financial Accounting Standards Board, *Reporting the Effects of General Price-Level Changes in Financial Statements,* Discussion Memorandum (FASB, 1974).

———, *Financial Reporting and Changing Prices,* Statement of Financial Accounting Standards No. 33 (FASB, 1979).

———, *Foreign Currency Translation,* Statement of Financial Accounting Standards No. 52 (FASB, 1981).

———, *Financial Reporting and Changing Prices: Investment Companies,* Statement of Financial Accounting Standards No. 54 (FASB, 1982).

Middleditch, L., "Should Accounts Reflect the Changing Value of the Dollar?," *Journal of Accountancy*, February 1918, pp. 114–120; reprinted in *Asset Appreciation, Business Income and Price-Level Accounting*, S. A. Zeff, Ed. (Arno Press, New York, 1976).

Staff of the Accounting Research Division, *Reporting the Financial Effects of Price-Level Changes*, Accounting Research Study No. 6 (AICPA, 1963).

Sterling, R. K., "Relevant Financial Reporting in an Age of Price Changes," *Journal of Accountancy*, February 1974, pp. 42–51.

Sweeney, H. W., *Stabilized Accounting* (reissued) (Holt, Rinehart and Winston, New York, 1964).

CHAPTER **32**

Uses of

Current Cost

Data

Terence E. McClary
Vice President, Corporate Financial
Administration, General Electric Company

INTRODUCTION

Inflation and changing prices have significantly diminished the usefulness of traditional financial statements for most businesses. When reported profits do not include provisions for replacing the inventories sold and the plant and equipment used up, these profits do not represent a reasonable measure of operating performance for a going concern. This becomes apparent as reported profits continue to increase while the cash generated from operations is insufficient to replace the inventories and the worn-out equipment, let alone finance business growth.

Not only are profits misstated, but investment, which is shown on the balance sheet at book value, often bears little relationship to its current value. Consequently, because conventional accounting methods usually overstate profit and understate investment, the reported return on investment (and return on equity) is overstated.

The major distortions are caused by changing prices and can be largely eliminated by adjusting profit and investment to reflect the current cost of inventories and plant and equipment. Although the methods used to calculate the current cost adjustments necessarily involve some estimates and judgments, this shortfall in precision is insignificant when compared with the alternative of using historical cost data to measure performance. It is better to base decisions on data approximating reality rather than on precise data misrepresenting the performance and financial condition of the business.

This chapter describes some of the uses of current cost data for analyzing actual or forecasted results and for making operating and investment decisions. It assumes that the reader is familiar with the basic definitions and calculations of current cost data.

REAL PROFITABILITY AND GROWTH

Current cost income is a more realistic measure of profit than historical cost income because current dollar revenues are matched against current dollar costs. Similarly, current cost investment is a better measure of net asset value. Once income and investment have been restated to a current cost basis, conventional profitability measurements can be calculated; then these measurements more nearly represent real performance.

The basic information that should be prepared and analyzed for each business segment or product line is shown in Exhibit 1. For illustration purposes, only 4 years are shown; a more comprehensive analysis will include additional years of actual and forecast data. Key financial data are shown "as reported" on traditional financial statements and adjusted to a current cost basis. The current cost adjustments represent the differences between reported amounts and current cost amounts. In the example shown, the business segment appeared to be earning a 10 percent return on sales and a 20 percent return on investment. On a real basis, returns are lower and are declining.

EXHIBIT 1   Operating Results Adjusted for Major Effects of Changing Prices and Inflation[a]

Actual			Forecast	
1979	1980		1981	1982
		Net sales billed		
$10,000	$11,000	As reported	$12,000	$13,000
12,489	12,100	Constant dollar	12,000	11,818
		Net income		
1,000	1,100	As reported	1,200	1,300
		Cost of goods sold adjustment—		
100	120	current cost	140	160
250	280	Underdepreciation—current cost	320	360
650	700	Current cost	740	780
812	770	Current cost/constant dollar	740	709
		Average investment		
5,000	5,500	As reported	6,000	6,500
10	15	Inventory adjustment—current cost	20	25
		Plant and equipment adjustment—		
1,250	1,400	current cost	1,500	1,600
6,260	6,915	Current cost	7,520	8,125
7,818	7,607	Current cost/constant dollar	7,520	7,386
		Percent net income to net sales billed		
10.0%	10.0%	As reported	10.0%	10.0%
6.5	6.4	Current cost	6.2	6.0
		Percent return on investment		
20.0	20.0	As reported	20.0	20.0
10.4	10.1	Current cost	9.8	9.6

1979–1980		1981–1982
	Average annual growth rates	
	Net sales billed	
10.0%	As reported	8.3%
3.1[b]	Constant dollar	1.5[b]
	Net income	
10.0	As reported	8.3
5.2[b]	Current cost/constant dollar	4.2[b]

[a]Constant dollars represent dollars of average year 1981 purchasing power.
[b]Denotes negative.

Real Return on Investment.   Return on investment is one of the best measures of profitability because it is the product of operating performance (return on sales) and asset management (investment turnover). It is important that management know what real returns are and also what they should be.

Various surveys of industrial companies that reported current cost data in 1979 disclosed that the composite "as reported" return on investment in the 16 percent to 17 percent range dropped to the 5 percent to 8 percent range when adjusted to a current cost basis. From this information, it is reasonable to assume that an 8 percent real return on investment is average to above average for an average-risk business. Higher-risk businesses demand higher real returns. A real positive return at any rate is certainly more attractive than the negative 2 percent real return that results from investment in interest-bearing securities earning 15 percent before tax when inflation is 10 percent. (Assuming a 46 percent tax rate, the aftertax return is only 8 percent before adjusting for inflation.)

Although it is unwise to make decisions or draw conclusions on a single measurement, the current cost return on investment is certainly the key measure of real profitability. In addition, the current cost return on investment approximates the real economic return. The relationship of current cost return on investment with the internal or economic rate of return will be discussed later in this chapter.

Real Growth. Inflation creates an illusion of growth; even current cost data will not fully dispel this illusion. For more meaningful comparisons with other periods, current cost results must be expressed in dollars of equivalent purchasing power. For example, 1979 current cost income of $650,000 shown on Exhibit 1 is equivalent to $812,000 in terms of 1981 purchasing power. These amounts are defined as current cost/constant dollar and are used to calculate real growth rates. As Exhibit 1 shows, what was reported to be 10 percent growth in 1980 over 1979 was actually a reduction in real earnings.

FASB Statement of Financial Accounting Standards No. 33 requires that the Consumer Price Index for All Urban Consumers (CPI-U) be used for the constant dollar restatement. Although there may be disagreement as to whether this restatement should be based on the CPI-U, GNP deflator, or some other measure of inflation, an adjustment for general inflation is necessary to measure real growth.

IMPROVING RESULTS

An understanding of real costs—current costs—should lead to actions that improve results. In some cases, appropriate action would have been taken anyway, even without current cost data. In other instances, the problems may not surface until long after the damage has been done. Regular reporting and analysis of current cost results should identify problems more quickly.

Exhibit 2 shows the relationship of current cost data to historical cost income using Exhibit 1 amounts. It can be seen that the current cost adjustments are taking an increasing share of reported profit. Further analysis of these adjustments can lead to actions that will improve real results.

Cost of Goods Sold Adjustment. The example business, like many industrial companies, uses the first-in, first-out (FIFO) cost flow assumption for inventories. Because most businesses face increasing replacement costs, those using FIFO will have a substantial adjustment to reported cost of goods sold; however, the adjustment is not deductible for tax purposes. By switching to last-in,

EXHIBIT 2   Current Cost Data: Relationships to Historical Cost Data

	1979	1980	1981	1982
Historical cost income	100.0%	100.0%	100.0%	100.0%
Cost of goods sold adjustment	10.0	10.9	11.7	12.3
Underdepreciation	25.0	25.5	26.7	27.7
Current cost income	65.0%	63.6%	61.6%	60.0%

first-out (LIFO), this adjustment can be substantially eliminated. More important, taxes will be reduced—a real cash saving.

Even a business using LIFO will find historical cost of goods sold less than current cost of goods sold when a dip into inventory layers occurs. An adjustment to historical LIFO cost of goods sold is necessary because the decrease in inventory was charged to cost of goods sold at prices from earlier periods. When the inventory is replaced at current costs, the tax deferral on the difference between the current cost and cost on a LIFO basis is lost. It may have been optimal to reduce inventories, but the tax effect should be considered when making temporary reductions.

Depreciation Adjustment. The depreciation adjustment requires extensive analysis. The size of adjustment reflects to some extent the capital intensity of the business and the age of equipment. Reported income for each year in the example decreased by approximately 25 percent as a result of this adjustment. However, because the percentage impact is dependent on reported earnings, which could fluctuate significantly, the analysis shown in Exhibit 2 should be used primarily for reviewing long-term trends. Another useful analysis is the comparison of underdepreciation with historical cost depreciation, as shown in Exhibit 3. The relationship is affected by the average age of plant and equipment and changes in current replacement costs. The reasons for year-to-year changes in this ratio should be understood.

It is not always desirable to replace buildings and equipment. Although replacement will result in investment tax credit and additional tax benefits from higher depreciation, many additional factors bear on the capital investment decision. The adjustment relating to buildings should be analyzed separately from that relating to machinery and equipment.

EXHIBIT 3   Current Cost Data: Relationships to Historical Cost Data

	1979	1980	1981	1982
Historical cost depreciation	100.0%	100.0%	100.0%	100.0%
Current cost depreciation	150.0	151.0	153.0	154.0
Underdepreciation	50.0%	51.0%	53.0%	54.0%

If plant buildings are adequate for the next 10 to 20 years, replacement would be unnecessary even though the gap between historical cost depreciation and current cost depreciation would widen as building costs escalate. The adjustment should continue to be made, however, to show whether a real return is earned on the value of investment. If that return is inadequate, consideration should be given to alternative uses or sale of plant facilities and land that could lead to higher returns.

A detailed analysis of the current cost adjustment for machinery and equipment is likely to result in opportunities to improve real profits and offers a systematic approach to reviewing productivity of machinery and equipment. Such an analysis will not provide specific answers as to what equipment should be replaced, but because the analysis focuses on older equipment, it should stimulate discussions leading to profit-improvement opportunities.

Because current cost depreciation is based on estimates, it is important that the method used to calculate the current cost of depreciable assets be appropriate for the business being measured. There are two basic methods: the reproduction cost approach and the replacement cost approach. The reproduction cost approach results in an estimate of the current cost of replacing assets identical to those owned. This is the simplest method and is generally done by applying suitable price indexes to the historical cost of the assets. The replacement cost approach results in an estimate of the current cost of replacing the same service potential of the assets owned. This method reflects changes in technology and should be used when it is anticipated that most assets will in fact be replaced by technologically superior assets. It is also necessary to be able to obtain consistency from year to year. Comparisons with other businesses in the industry may not be meaningful if methods differ.

RANKING BUSINESS SEGMENTS

Business segments are generally categorized for planning and resource allocation purposes. One approach, shown on Exhibit 4, is to position each business segment in a nine-block diagram. The vertical axis represents business strengths and the horizontal axis represents industry attractiveness. Those busi-

---

EXHIBIT 4   Planning and Resource Allocation Matrix

Factors influencing business strength	Industry attractiveness	Factors influencing industry attractiveness
• Market share • Competitive position • Relative profitability	Business strength Most ... Least Most Least	• Size • Cyclicality • Growth • World scope • Profitability • Inflation recovery

EXHIBIT 5   Ranking Business Segments

Business segment	As reported		Current cost	
	ROI	Rank	ROI	Rank
A	30%	1	2%	5
B........	24	2	6	4
C	22	3	7	3
D	18	4	10	2
E........	17	5	11	1

ness segments positioned toward the upper left are given investment priority for growth, whereas business segments positioned toward the lower right become candidates for harvesting or disposition. Business segments between the extremes are given selective reinvestment strategies.

Some of the factors used to assess industry attractiveness are shown in the exhibit. Most are beyond the scope of this chapter; however, inflation recovery is closely related. Inflation recovery represents the ability of the industry or business segment to recover cost inflation through selling prices and productivity in order to maintain or improve operating margin rates.

Profitability of the business segment as well as the profitability of the industry is one of the key variables for positioning. Current cost return on investment will generally result in a more realistic ranking and may result in an entirely different order than would result using historical cost return on investment (ROI). Exhibit 5 shows how the ranking changed for five business segments of a manufacturing company. Business A reported a 30 percent ROI based on historical cost data but dropped to 2 percent on a current cost basis. Its rank changed from first to fifth. Business E, which ranked fifth on a historical cost basis, jumped to first on a current cost basis. Further analysis showed that, although both businesses were capital-intensive, business A had relatively older facilities (and thus relatively higher underdepreciation) and lower operating margins (resulting in a larger percentage impact).

The analysis does not necessarily mean that business A should be abandoned, but investment strategies will be made with the knowledge that real profitability is 2 percent, not 30 percent. Management of the manufacturing company found that current cost ROI was more consistent with the ranking achieved using other criteria, whereas previously, historical cost ROI was sometimes inconsistent with the other data.

MAINTENANCE OF PRODUCTIVE CAPACITY

The ratio of investment expenditures to depreciation is sometimes used as a rough measure of changes in physical capacity. However, because of significant increases in the replacement costs of assets, historical cost depreciation may not be a reasonable measure of productive capacity consumed, and the ratio can be misleading.

EXHIBIT 6   Maintenance of Productive Capacity

Business segment	Reported			Current cost	
	Depreciation	Plant and equipment additions	Additions as percent of depreciation	Depreciation	Additions as percent of depreciation
A	$ 33	$ 52	157%	$ 70	74%
B	38	56	146	70	80
C	111	146	132	181	81
D	53	80	150	80	100
E	99	178	180	120	148

Current cost depreciation is a better measure of real capacity consumed and can be compared with plant and equipment expenditures to measure whether or not physical capacity has been maintained. Expenditures in excess of real depreciation indicate growth, whereas lower expenditures indicate failure to maintain capacity. Exhibit 6 shows five business segments, all of which appear to be investing at rates exceeding reported depreciation and thus giving the impression that they are expanding capacity. But, when additions are compared with current cost depreciation, only one is expanding, whereas three may be losing capacity.

This simple analysis is, of course, only a starting point for measuring the adequacy of investment spending and, because equipment replacement patterns may be irregular, the cumulative effect over several years is a better measure than any single year. Also, for some business segments, reducing capacity may even be an appropriate strategy; but for a growth business, investments should generally outpace current cost depreciation.

REAL RETURNS ON NEW INVESTMENT

The financial evaluation of capital investment projects should be based primarily on discounted cash flows. If the net present value is positive, when discounted by the firm's cost of capital, the investment is financially acceptable. An alternative method is to compute the internal rate of return or IRR (the interest rate that results in a net present value of zero). The project is acceptable as long as the internal rate of return exceeds the cost of capital. Because the cost of capital is generally calculated for the firm as a whole, hurdle rates should be raised for projects having higher risks.

Although the cost of capital is the standard of comparison for new investment projects, it is not immune from the effects of inflation. An acceptable project returning 10 percent in an economy with low inflation rates becomes unacceptable in an economy with double-digit inflation. To avoid frequent updating of hurdle rates, and to facilitate comparison of projects in different economies and time periods, the real internal rate of return on investment should be the key financial measurement.

EXHIBIT 7   Calculation of Internal Rate of Return on Nominal and Inflation-Adjusted Cash Flows

	End of year				
	0	1	2	3	IRR
Cash flows	$1,000[a]	$400	$500	$600	21.7%
General inflation index	1.00	1.10	1.18	1.25	
Adjusted cash flows	$1,000[a]	$364	$424	$480	12.3%

[a]Denotes negative.

The first step is to calculate the internal rate of return based on the cash flows over the life of the project. It is essential that the project cash flows include anticipated changes in selling prices and cost inflation because, in most cases, these elements of cash flow will be affected differently (i.e., labor costs may be expected to increase greater than selling prices). Because inflation affects cash flow elements differently, the real return cannot be calculated by holding price and cost levels constant.

The second step is to adjust the current dollar cash flows for general inflation and compute the real IRR. Because general inflation may vary by year, each year's cash flow should be restated separately.

An example with different inflation assumptions each year is shown on Exhibit 7. An investment of $1,000 results in cash inflows for the next 3 years. The top line includes the effects of specific price and cost level changes and results in an internal rate of return of 21.7 percent. The center line represents the general inflation index (with beginning of year 1 equal to 1.00). The bottom line shows the inflation-adjusted cash flows used to calculate the real internal rate of return of 12.3 percent.

It is difficult to compare the internal rate of return with IRRs of other companies and industries to determine if the project return is adequate and appropriate. An internal rate of return is a measurement used for internal business purposes and is not normally made available externally. One way that this benchmark problem can be circumvented is to make the comparison using ROI, which companies publish on both historical and real bases. ROI, an accounting concept, and IRR, an economic concept based on timing of cash flows, are closely related. When ROI is adjusted to a current cost basis, it approximates the real economic return over a period of time. It is important to note, however, that it is erroneous to compare the internal return on a new project with the historical cost return on investment for the business that has experienced various inflation effects over time.

SELLING PRICES

Selling prices are seldom set on the basis of current costs because selling prices are generally determined by market forces. However, it is essential to know whether or not selling prices are adequate to cover all costs, including the costs of replacing inventories sold and equipment used up. If selling prices cannot be raised and are too low to recover real costs and provide an adequate return, consideration must be given to discontinuing the product line. Although many businesses have recognized the need to recover the costs of replacing inventories, the higher cost of replacing plant and equipment (underdepreciation) is often overlooked. Because current cost data can be calculated for most businesses, there is little excuse for disregarding real costs.

DIVIDENDS

Current cost income can aid in establishing dividend policy. Management should be aware of the real payout rate—based on current cost earnings—to help ensure that funds will be available to support replacement needs as well as planned investment growth. Also, directors should be aware of the effect of dividend payments on the purchasing power of shareholders.

OPPORTUNITIES

Industries that can recover current costs and still generate satisfactory profits are obviously more attractive than those that cannot. In general, those segments with relatively small current cost adjustments, such as service businesses, have the least difficulty coping with inflation. Although one could argue that service businesses are also affected severely by inflation, it appears that because their reported costs are much closer to current costs, it is easier to establish price levels that result in real profits. High-technology businesses are also more attractive because they offer products with unique characteristics that can usually be priced to yield excellent real returns. In addition, these products often provide cost-reduction opportunities for customers, resulting in even higher demand during inflationary periods.

CONCLUSION

Net income, if it is real, should generally approximate the amount of funds available for dividends and expansion. In addition, the net worth of a business should be reflected in the balance sheet. For most businesses, however, reported income and net worth based on historical costs fall far short of these objectives. This misrepresentation is caused principally by changing prices and inflation. Current cost information, though not perfect, eliminates much of the distortion and more closely meets the above objectives. Use and understanding of current cost data will improve measurement of the real performance of the business and should help management to make more effective operating and investment decisions.

CHAPTER **33**

Mergers,

Acquisitions,

and Poolings

of Interests

Arthur R. Wyatt
Partner, Arthur Andersen & Co.

INTRODUCTION

Growth has been a way of life for American business virtually from the day business activity began in colonial times. Growth can be accomplished either from forces within the business unit or through combination with other business units. Combinations of one type or another have been effected ever since colonial times, including a few periods of relatively intensified activity around 1900 and again in the 1920s. In the period subsequent to World War II, however, growth by combination accelerated markedly, so that during the 1950s and 1960s business combinations increased at a rapid rate and have become a common phenomenon on the American business scene.

Definition of Terms. Various terms have been used to describe business combinations, and the passage of time has blunted the precise meaning once associated with many of the terms. A *merger* is a business combination in which two or more entities join together with one being fused into the other. A *consolidation* is a combination in which two or more entities join together and go forward under a new name or a new legal form. An *acquisition* (or a *purchase*) is a combination in which little or no effort is made to continue in existence the identity of the acquired company. An acquisition can take the form of a merger or of a consolidation. A *pooling of interests* is a combination in which two or more entities join together, "marry," or pool their interests and go forward as one entity (and in some respects as if they had always been one entity). A pooling of interests may also take the form of a merger or of a consolidation.

The terms identified above all have rather well-defined technical meanings, but over the years they have come to be used interchangeably to a considerable extent. The term *business combination* is used as the broader generic term to describe a business transaction in which two or more entities join together. This term encompasses all those identified above and is used throughout this chapter except when the more specific technical meaning implicit in the other terms is intended.

The business combination event embraces numerous complexities requiring careful consideration prior to consummation; legal, taxation, financial, marketing, production, personnel, and other matters all require careful attention before final terms are agreed upon. Likewise, accounting for a combination requires advance consideration. Not uncommonly the accounting consequences of a combination will affect the terms of the combination. The accounting aspect of combinations is complicated by the fact that two generally accepted methods of accounting for business combinations exist in practice. These two methods may be equally applicable to some combinations, with the results flowing from the application of each producing quite different balance sheets upon consummation of the combination, quite different income statements in periods subsequent to the combination, and even quite different income statements on a retroactive basis for periods prior the combination.

Historical Development. Prior to the mid-1940s, most business combinations were accounted for as purchases. The acquiring company recorded the transaction at the fair value of the consideration it gave in the combination transaction. For many combinations the fair value of this consideration was easy to measure, because it involved either cash or a combination of cash and notes payable over a relatively short period of time. If a lump-sum price were paid for the acquired company, a common situation, the amount paid was allocated among the several specific resources and property rights acquired. For some combinations a portion of the consideration was allocated to an intangible, goodwill. Generally, the goodwill value was recognized when the allocation of the purchase price to the several specific resources and property rights did not absorb all of the purchase price. Any excess of the purchase price over the fair values of the specific resources and property rights was charged to goodwill.

Combinations effected for common stock prior to the mid-1940s were accounted for in a similar manner. The fair value of the stock issued (generally based on market values at the time of the transaction) became the measure of the consideration given. Goodwill might be recognized in combinations effected by stock, in a manner similar to that noted for cash acquisitions. However, at this time common stocks were selling at relatively low multiples of earnings, with the result that stock prices per share were relatively much closer to the fair values of the underlying specific resources and property rights than was true in the years following World War II.

Various changes in economic circumstances during the postwar period led business managements and their accountants to seek alternative methods to account for business combinations. Many began to challenge the continued applicability of the capitalization-amortization pattern of accounting for goodwill recommended by the bulletins of the American Institute of Certified Public Accountants (AICPA) and supported by the Securities and Exchange Commission (SEC). The amortization pattern adopted was often based on arbitrary assumptions and, of course, acted to lower reported net income below what would be reported in the absence of amortization. Further, the income tax laws did not permit goodwill amortization to be deducted in determining taxable income. Many found within these tax laws a practical basis for challenging the amortization through income of the cost of goodwill.

Tax Arrangements. At the same time, other provisions of the Internal Revenue Code specified that certain types of business combinations could qualify as corporate reorganizations that would be "tax-free." Corporate reorganizations that so qualified were tax-free in the sense that the selling company (or its shareholders) did not generate any income or gain subject to tax in the reorganization (combination) transaction. In reality, the transaction was tax-deferred rather than tax-free, because the securities received by the seller in the reorganization transaction assumed the same tax basis possessed by the securities or assets conveyed to the buying corporation. Any tax incurrence was delayed until the securities newly received by the seller were sold or otherwise disposed of. Although a number of technical considerations must be met for a combination to be tax-free, a characteristic of certain types of tax-free reorganizations is that the seller must receive all, or substantially all (i.e., no less than 80 percent) of the consideration in the form of voting stock. Thus, the tax law provided a stimulus for some business combinations to be effected by the use of voting securities rather than by cash or other assets.

Effect on Earnings per Share. Other forces in the economy provided added impetus to the use of stock. For some companies desiring to grow externally, cash was not readily available, and no other source of assets could be developed on a timely or economical basis. Use of unissued stock was the convenient substitute. At the same time came the recognition that the statistic of earnings per share (one measure by which the success of an enterprise was measured) might be improved by an acquisition for stock. Thus, a company whose earnings multiple was, say, 40 (stock price of $80 when earnings were $2 per share) could acquire a company whose multiple was, say, 10 and thereby produce an increase in earnings per share.

For example, assume the following:

	Company A	Company B
Reported earnings	$10,000,000	$2,000,000
Shares outstanding	5,000,000	250,000
Earnings per share	2	8
Market price per share (average)	80	80

If a combination were effected on a share-for-share basis, the resulting company would have (assuming that other conditions remaining unchanged) earnings of $12 million and shares outstanding of 5.25 million. Thus, earnings per share would increase from $2 to $2.29 (= $12,000,000/5,250,000). If the earnings multiple of 40 remained unchanged, the price of Company A stock would increase from $80 to more than $91 per share. Company A could even offer Company B a premium, offering, say, two shares for one. Here the Company B shareholders would receive two shares of stock valued at $80 each for each $80 share of their Company B stock. Even here the resulting company earnings per share would increase from $2 to $2.19 (= $12,000,000/5,500,000) and an earnings multiple of 40 would produce a price per share of more than $87. Results of this nature, of course, provided encouragement for others to attempt similar combinations.

American business prosperity in the period after World War II through much of the 1950s and 1960s led to increased earnings per share for American corporations and was accompanied by generally higher multiples attached by the investment community to corporate earnings. As an increasing portion of business combinations came to be effected by use of stock, the fair value of the shares exchanged by the acquiring company (generally as measured by the market price at or near the combination date) commonly exceeded the book value or the net assets of the acquired companies. Often the amount of the excess was substantial. Accountants had traditionally classified all or a portion of an excess arising in this manner as goodwill. The substantial amounts of goodwill thus generated in an accounting environment that supported amortization by charges to income, as noted above, caused many to challenge this aspect of accounting for goodwill. The result was to develop a new concept of accounting for those business combinations effected by means of voting stock. This concept is known as "pooling of interests," and its widespread acceptance has been fostered in part by the opportunity to bypass the recognition and subsequent accounting for goodwill at a time when the economic environment encouraged growth in business via the combination route.

The Basic Concepts. Conceptually, business combinations came to be classified in two categories: purchases and poolings of interests. A purchase combination exists when one company clearly acquires or purchases the other so that the acquired company is absorbed, in a business sense if not legally, into the acquiring company. In a purchase combination the ownership and management interests of the acquired company either disappear or are clearly subordinated after the combination. Thus, a purchase combination is viewed much like any purchase. What was once owned by one party is now owned by another, and the former owners retain no particular financial or business interest in the property sold.

A pooling of interests, however, has a quite different concept. A pooling-of-interests combination exists when the various interests in the combination fuse their divergent parts into one enterprise. Neither is buying out the other. Rather, the interests are joining together, as in a marriage, to go forward as one united enterprise. The combination is viewed as one in which the interests of the various constituents continue in somewhat the same roles as existed prior to combination. All the former shareholders continue as shareholders, the former managements retain their managerial responsibilities, and all that really happens in a business sense is a change in legal designations of what formerly were separate corporations.

ACCOUNTING RESEARCH BULLETINS

Accounting Research Bulletin No. 40. The Committee on Accounting Procedure of the AICPA issued Accounting Research Bulletin No. 40 in 1950. In this Bulletin the Committee indicated the nature of the accounting treatment for each type of combination and concluded that the accounting treatment would be presumed to rest upon the nature of the transaction, the attendant circumstances, and not upon legal distinctions. The attendant circumstances of a pooling of interests included a continuation in the surviving company of all or substantially all the equity interests in the combining companies. Likewise, continuity of management or of the power to control management was contemplated. The combining companies would normally be expected to be of relatively the same size and would be in business activities that were similar or complementary.

A purchase, on the other hand, would exist when the ownership interests after the combination were substantially altered, when management continuity was not affected, when the relative size of the constituents was disproportionate, and when the constituent companies had been engaged in dissimilar or noncomplementary activities. No one of the criteria was considered to be determinative, and the accountant was expected to review all the characteristics of the combination to determine its proper classification. One clear differentiation did exist, however, and that was that any substantial amount of cash in the transaction would be presumptive of a purchase combination.

The accounting differences contemplated by this Bulletin can be summarized briefly: In a purchase the assets acquired are accounted for at their fair values at the date of acquisition, generally as measured by the cash paid or value of other assets paid or stock issued, whereas in a pooling of interests the assets of the combining companies are merged together at existing book values. Thus, in a pooling of interests the fair values of the considerations exchanged are not relevant; only book values have significance. No goodwill arises in a pooling of interests, as existing asset book values are carried forward, although certain adjustments are permitted to conform the accounting practices of the combining entities. In a purchase the purchase price is allocated among the various resources and property rights acquired, and to the extent that an excess exists after the allocation, an amount of goodwill is recognized in the transaction.

Accounting Research Bulletin No. 43. The distinctions between purchases and poolings of interests as set forth in ARB No. 40 were largely continued in ARB No. 43 (as Chapter 7c), issued in 1953. ARB No. 43 was primarily a restatement and revision of the preceding 42 Bulletins, and because practice under ARB No. 40 was not extensive prior to the preparation of ARB No. 43, no significant revision was made.

Accounting Research Bulletin No. 48. The AICPA issued as ARB No. 48 a more thoroughgoing revision of the guidelines for accounting for business combinations in 1957. To some extent this Bulletin reflected changes in practice that had developed subsequent to the issuance of ARB No. 40, and to some extent it developed the pooling-of-interests concept more fully in areas not previously dealt with to any extent. The various attendant circumstances were again discussed. Thus, continuity of ownership interests, continuity of voting rights, continuity of operations, continuity of management, and similarity in size continued to be the criteria by which a business combination was to be evaluated for purposes of determining the appropriate accounting treatment.

ARB No. 48 did attempt to establish the extremes for the similarity of size criterion at about 90 to 95 percent for any single constituent. That is, the relative share interests subsequent to the combination were expected to be in a ratio of 19 to 1 or less if the combination were to qualify as a pooling of interests for accounting purposes. Any size disparity greater than 19 to 1 was to be indicative of a purchase combination. However, this size criterion proved to be ineffective over the years following issuance of ARB No. 48, so that for practical purposes similarity of size became virtually insignificant in evaluating business combinations.

ARB No. 48 recognized one aspect of the pooling concept that had evolved in practice—that the retained earnings of the constituents in a business combination should be pooled or merged together in accounting for the pooling of interests. Some hesitancy had existed to pool the retained earnings accounts in earlier applications of the pooling concept, possibly because of doubts as to legal consequences and because of an earlier AICPA position that a company could not increase its retained earnings by the acquisition of another company. As a pooling of interests came to be better understood as a business event quite different from an acquisition, a joining together of retained earnings accounts was not considered to fall under the earlier prohibition. Likewise, retained earnings came more and more to be viewed in an accounting sense as the aggregation of the reported earnings over a company's life, less amounts distributed as dividends or otherwise adjusted by transactions affecting the capital accounts. Legal status as to availability for dividend distribution assumed lesser significance.

Another extension of the pooling concept recognized in ARB No. 48 concerned the use of pooling accounting when one of the constituents in the combination remained legally in existence as a subsidiary of another constituent. To some accountants this position appeared to be in clear violation of the pooling-of-interests concept. On the other hand, however, many combinations that otherwise would qualify for pooling accounting contained valid business reasons for continuing one entity as a subsidiary. If such a combination met the pooling criteria in other respects, the subsidiary status appeared insufficient in substance to warrant purchase accounting.

Finally, ARB No. 48 clarified certain reporting aspects of business combinations. Under the pooling concept the constituents were viewed as if they had always been one business unit; for example, assets were carried forward at book values and retained earnings accounts were combined. Under this concept the operating results for the constituents in the year of combination would be presented on a combined basis from the start of the year, as if the companies had been pooled for the entire period. Under purchase accounting, on the other hand, operating results of the constituents would be combined only for the period following the effective date of the combination. Further, ARB No. 48 recommended that presentations of historical data on operating results should be restated after a pooling to include the data of the pooled company for the prior periods. At times, combining the operating results for the entire year or presenting restated historical data might result in changes that would be immaterial, and if so the Bulletin indicated that restatement would not be necessary.

ACCOUNTING PRINCIPLES BOARD OPINIONS

Accounting Principles Board Opinions No. 6 and 10. Opinions No. 6 and 10 of the Accounting Principles Board, issued in 1965 and 1966, respectively, contained sections to clarify the pooling concept. Thus, Opinion No. 6 strengthened the recommended positions of ARB No. 48 as to reporting combined operating results of a combination after a pooling of interests from the start of the period of combination and as to the presentation of restated historical operating data. Under the Opinion the recommended reporting and restatement were to be followed in all poolings of interests unless the results thereof would be immaterial, in which case disclosure of the fact of immateriality would be necessary. Opinion No. 10 recognized a practice that had evolved of effecting business combinations that qualified as poolings of interests after the end of a fiscal year, with the inclusion of the pooled companies and their operating results as if the combination had been effected prior to the end of the fiscal year. Opinion No. 10 attempted to limit such "post-year-end poolings" to those effected within a reasonable period after the end of the year.

Accounting Principles Board Opinion No. 16. In 1970 the APB superseded all existing authoritative literature on accounting for business combinations by issuing Opinion No. 16. Opinion No. 16 continued to recognize the purchase and the pooling-of-interests methods, but it specified new criteria by which to determine the method appropriate for a given combination. The two methods were not to be alternatives from which a selection could be made. Either the specified criteria existed, and the combination was to be accounted for as a pooling of interests, or one or more of the criteria was absent, and the combination was a purchase. In addition, a given business combination could no longer be accounted for partially as a purchase and partially as a pooling.

Certain of the previous criteria for distinguishing a purchase from a pooling were no longer viewed as necessary. Thus, the relative size of the combining companies was no longer considered relevant, a recognition that a "size test" had proved to be unworkable in practical application. Likewise, the concepts of continuity of management and continuity of ownership were no longer specified as necessary. These criteria were replaced by a more elaborate set of conditions that had to be present if the combination were to be viewed as a pooling of interests.

Certain of the criteria merit additional comment. The combining companies must be autonomous (not a part of another entity) and independent of each other. The combination must be effected within 1 year after its initiation and can involve only the issuance of common stock in exchange for the common stock interest of other combining companies. No special voting or dividend-sharing arrangements are permitted. Each combining company must refrain from changing its equity interests or from acquiring its own shares for a period of 2 years prior to the combination, and no contingent share issuance arrangements to former shareholders of a combining company can exist at the date a combination is consummated. Finally, the combined corporation cannot agree to reacquire any stock issued, cannot enter into any financial arrangements for the benefit of former shareholders, and cannot intend or plan to dispose of a significant part of the assets of the combining companies until 2 years after the combination.

The principal aim of these criteria is to assure that the formerly separate shareholder groups "pool their interests" on a mutual risk-sharing basis in the combination. Certain of the criteria were also aimed at preventing, or precluding, various alleged abuses of the criteria for pooling under ARB No. 48. Despite the rather elaborate set of criteria, a substantial number of "interpretations" of Opinion No. 16 were found necessary in the first few years after its adoption. In addition, on several occasions, the SEC issued Accounting Series Releases that, in effect, amended the criteria of Opinion No. 16. For example, ASR No. 135 specified that certain shareholders ("affiliates") could not dispose of shares received in a pooling combination for a specified period following the combination, and ASR No. 146A established new standards for the reacquisition of shares (treasury stock) by a combining company in the 2-year period prior to a combination and for a "reasonable" period following a combination.

Accounting Principles Board Opinion No. 17. Coincident with the issuance of Opinion No. 16, the APB also issued Opinion No. 17, *Intangible Assets* [1970]. The principal conclusion of that Opinion, that the cost of intangibles (including goodwill) should be amortized by charges to income over a period not to exceed 40 years, altered existing practice in accounting for goodwill. Although the conclusions of Opinion No. 17 do not affect the determination of whether a business combination is a purchase or a pooling of interests, the conclusions often have a significant effect on the postcombination results of a business combination accounted for as a purchase.

ACCOUNTING FOR A BUSINESS COMBINATION

The distinctions between a purchase and a pooling of interests may be sharpened through the example in Exhibit 1. The example will focus on two accounting aspects of a business combination: the accounting for the combination transaction itself, and the consequences of that accounting in fiscal periods subsequent to the combination.

Assumption one. First, assume that the managements of A Company and B Company negotiate to consummate a combination in which A Company buys all the common stock of B Company for $16 million.

Because cash is the consideration, purchase accounting is appropriate; pooling accounting would not be acceptable. A Company gives up $16 million in cash and receives in return all the B Company stock, which entitles it to B Company's receivables, inventories, and plant and equipment (assuming that B Company will use its cash to liquidate its current payables).

The initial accounting problem for A Company involves the allocation of the $16 million cash to the various assets acquired, assuming for the moment that

EXHIBIT 1   Financial and Operating Data for A Company
and B Company

	A Company	B Company
Cash	$ 28,800,000	$ 800,000
Receivables (net)	36,600,000	3,000,000
Finished goods, raw materials, etc.	50,400,000	3,600,000
Plant and equipment	72,600,000	4,200,000
Other assets	3,200,000	—
Goodwill	1,600,000	—
	$193,200,000	$11,600,000
Current payables	$ 43,800,000	$ 800,000
Long-term liabilities	48,000,000	—
Common stock:		
A (6,000,000 shares at $10 par)	60,000,000	
B (60,000 shares)		6,000,000
Capital in excess of par	18,900,000	—
Retained earnings	22,500,000	4,800,000
	$193,200,000	$11,600,000
Sales	$206,800,000	$12,600,000
Cost of sales	136,000,000	7,100,000
Gross margin on sales	$ 70,800,000	$ 5,500,000
Other operating expenses	42,000,000	3,388,000
Income before taxes	$ 28,800,000	$ 2,112,000
Federal income tax (assume 50%)	14,400,000	1,056,000
Net income	$ 14,400,000	$ 1,056,000
Earnings per share	$2.40	$17.60
Market price range, past 3 months	$28–$52	[a]

[a]Limited market. Only sale in last 3 months between two existing shareholders for 200 shares at $340 per share.

B Company is to be dissolved. The book value of the assets acquired (also the book value of B Company's stock) is $10.8 million. Thus, the price paid exceeds the book value of the assets acquired by $5.2 million. The question is, what accounting disposition should be made of the $5.2 million?

A common answer to this question is to label the $5.2 million as goodwill. This answer is frequently merely an expedient one, because in concept goodwill is the appropriate label only if that amount represents the cost of acquiring excess earning power possessed by the acquired company. (See Chapter 21 for a more complete discussion on goodwill.) More commonly, one would expect all or part of the $5.2 million to be attributable to various of the specific resources or property rights possessed by B Company.

Thus, for example, B Company may have provided more than adequate allowances for uncollectible receivables, may have undervalued its inventories by establishing unneeded obsolescence or shrinkage reserves, may have written down its plant and equipment through depreciation entries at a more rapid rate than they were actually depreciating, or may possess valuable secret processes or patent rights that have not been recorded.

The main principle is that careful study should be made of B Company to determine as closely as possible the fair values of the various resources and property rights that it owned prior to the combination. In fact, such study would normally be an integral part of the negotiation process preliminary to reaching the final combination terms. Only the difference that remains after determining the fair values of the separable resources and property rights acquired in comparison to the purchase price should be labeled goodwill.

Assume that careful review of B Company's records, discussions with appropriate officials, and access to other sources of information revealed the following fair values for B Company's assets:

Receivables	$3,000,000
Inventories	4,800,000
Plant and Equipment	6,000,000
Patents	700,000

These values should be recorded for the acquisition, and because the sum of these values ($14.5 million) is $1.5 million less than the purchase price, goodwill of $1.5 million would also be recorded.

If B Company were to be dissolved as a separate company, the accounting entry for the acquisition would be as follows on the books of A Company:

Receivables	3,000,000	
Finished Goods, Raw Materials, etc.	4,800,000	
Plant and Equipment	6,000,000	
Patents	700,000	
Goodwill	1,500,000	
Cash		16,000,000

If B Company were to be operated as a subsidiary company and maintain its own accounting system, A Company would make the following entry for the combination:

Investment in B Company	16,000,000	
Cash		16,000,000

The values for the specific assets, as indicated in the preceding entry, would become embodied in A Company's financial statements at year-end through the process of preparing consolidated financial statements. The "Investment in B Company" would be replaced in the consolidated statements by the assets as shown in the first entry.

If the combination were effected by issuance of 320,000 shares of common stock having a fair value of $16 million and one or more of the criteria for a pooling of interests were not met, the combination would be accounted for as a purchase. The only change in the two entries above would be a credit to Common Stock for $3.2 million and a credit to Capital in Excess of Par for $12.8 million rather than a credit to Cash.

Assumption two. Now, assume that the negotiations between A Company and B Company lead to an agreement to combine in which A Company agrees to exchange 320,000 shares of its stock for all 60,000 shares of B Company stock outstanding. The A Company board of directors establishes $50 per share as the fair value of the common stock conveyed in the combination. Because common stock is the consideration involved here, and assuming that all the criteria specified in APB Opinion No. 16 are met, the combination will be accounted for as a pooling of interests.

The essence of the pooling concept is that the combination event is different from an exchange transaction that possesses real economic substance. As a corollary, pooling accounting leaves the relationships existing prior to combination basically undisturbed. Thus, the basis of accountability for the assets of both companies remains the book value of those assets at the time of combination. Minor adjustments are sometimes made to the account balances of the pooled company (B Company in this case) in order to conform the accounting practices of the constituents. In general, however, the fair value of the shares issued to effect the combination is of no consequence to the accounting entries.

Under the pooling concept, and again assuming that B company retains its cash and current payables, the entry to account for the combination would be as follows if B Company were dissolved as a separate company:

Receivables	3,000,000	
Finished Goods, Raw Materials, etc.	3,600,000	
Plant and Equipment	4,200,000	
Common Stock (320,000 shares at $10)		3,200,000
Capital in Excess of Par		2,800,000
Retained Earnings		4,800,000

All these values appeared in B Company's books prior to combination, except for the credits to Common Stock and Capital in Excess of Par. Because par value per share of A Company common stock is $10, only $3.2 million can be credited to Common Stock, even though $6 million appeared as common stock for B Company. The difference becomes additional paid-in capital. At times the par or stated value of the shares issued exceeds the related capital stock and paid-in capital of the pooled company. In such a situation, any paid-in capital in excess of par on the books of the other company could be used to absorb the excess, or the retained earnings of the pooled company could be reduced to permit recording of the appropriate amount of paid-in capital. Thus, under pooling accounting the book values of the several assets are carried forward, and the retained earnings of the pooled company are likewise carried forward except for any portion needed to achieve appropriate balances for the paid-in capital accounts.

If B Company were to be operated as a subsidiary company and thus maintain its own accounting system, A Company would make the following entry to record the combination:

Investment in B Company	10,800,000	
Common Stock		10,800,000

In the year-end accounting process of preparing consolidated financial statements, the various balances in B Company's asset accounts would replace "Investment in B Company," and the amounts as shown in the previous entry for Common Stock, Capital in Excess of Par, and Retained Earnings would replace the credit above to Common Stock. The end result in the consolidated statements would be identical to that resulting from the previous entry.

Summary of Accounting Alternatives. These illustrative assumptions, while simplified in nature, lead to the following observations:

1. A business combination effected for cash (or notes) is considered to be a purchase combination and is accounted for accordingly.

2. A business combination effected for stock is considered to be a pooling of interests if all criteria of APB Opinion No. 16 are met. If any one of the criteria is not met, the combination is considered to be a purchase, and the accounting would be based on the fair values exchanged.

3. For a purchase combination:

(a) The fair values of the resources and property rights acquired or the fair value of the consideration given, whichever is more clearly evident, provide the basis for future accountability.

(b) The retained earnings of the acquired company are not carried forward as such after the combination but become capitalized, in effect, in the combination entry.

4. For a pooling-of-interests combination:

(a) The book values of the resources and property rights of the pooled company provide the basis for future accountability.

(b) The retained earnings of the pooled company are carried forward in the combined entity, except to the extent necessary to effect adjustments to paid in capital.

5. No real accounting significance attaches to whether the purchased or pooled company (B Company, above) loses its legal existence or continues as a subsidiary company.

Postcombination Effects. Of greater significance than the distinctions in the accounting entries to give effect to the combination are the differences in the effects on financial presentations in subsequent periods resulting from these entries. Virtually all asset values (including goodwill) become charges against revenue in future income statements. This means that if B Company had not entered into a combination with A Company, its assets (except cash) of $10.8 million would have been charged against future revenues in some manner, either directly through depreciation charges or as cost of sales, or indirectly through collection of receivables and use of the proceeds of collection for operating expenses, inventory acquisitions, or plant asset additions or replacements.

If A Company acquires these assets in a purchase combination at a price of $16 million, its future revenues may be charged with $16 million for these same assets. If revenues are not affected by whether A Company or B Company owns and operates the assets, future net income of the two companies combined into a single, consolidated entity would be $5.2 million less over the same period than the sum of the net incomes of the two companies operating and reporting independently, disregarding any related income tax effects.

If, on the other hand, the combination of A Company and B Company is considered to be a pooling of interests and the assets of B Company are carried forward after the combination at $10.8 million, regardless of the fair values exchanged in the combination, the combined entity will report the same net income from the operation of these assets as B Company would have operating them separately, assuming no variation in revenues or changes in operating conditions, and so on.

Exhibit 2 summarizes the postcombination effects on net income of the three assumed sets of facts presented above. In addition to the assumed fair values previously set forth, also assume that:

1. Inventory turns over rapidly in the combined entity, so that all the B Company inventory at the combination date was sold within the next operating period. Thus, the $1.2 million difference between book value and fair value of B Company inventory is charged to cost of sales in the period after combination.

2. Plant and equipment and patent costs are amortized over a 10-year period, with the amortization included in operating expenses.

3. Goodwill on the A Company balance sheet at combination date is not amortized. Goodwill arising in the combination is amortized over 5 years and is not deductible for income tax purposes.

4. The purchase combination involving an exchange of stock does not meet the requirements of a tax-free reorganization.

The first column reports what one might expect from a cash acquisition—an increase in earnings per share (from $2.40 for A Company prior to combination to $2.41 on a combined basis). However, the increase in this example is nominal

EXHIBIT 2 Operating Results of A Company and B Company (Combined): Year after Combination

	Purchase for cash	Purchase for stock	Pooling for stock
Sales	$219,400,000	$219,400,000	$219,400,000
Cost of sales	$144,300,000	$144,300,000	$143,100,000
Operating expenses	45,638,000	45,638,000	45,388,000
Goodwill amortization	300,000	300,000	—
Total.	$190,238,000	$190,238,000	$188,488,000
Income before taxes	$ 29,162,000	$ 29,162,000	$ 30,912,000
Federal income tax	14,731,000	14,731,000	15,456,000
Net income	$ 14,431,000	$ 14,431,000	$ 15,456,000
Shares outstanding	6,000,000	6,320,000	6,320,000
Earnings per share	$2.41	$2.28	$2.45

and less than one might expect from a cash acquisition. The new values assigned to the assets of B Company acquired resulted in increased charges to income as compared with B Company's previous operating results. In fact, an increase in reported earnings does not always result from a cash acquisition, particularly when the purchase price indicates a wide disparity in the fair values of the acquired company's assets as compared to the book values of those assets.

Furthermore, the above example does not make provision for the cost of the $16 million in cash used to acquire B Company. Assuming a 12 percent interest rate, the cost would be $960,000 (after taxes at a combined 50 percent rate), or 16 cents per share. Thus, earnings per share would actually fall to $2.25.

The second column indicates that if the purchase of B Company were effected in exchange for stock, earnings per share would decline to $2.28 from $2.40 prior to the combination, assuming the conditions cited in the example. The increase in net income was less than proportionate to the increase in the number of shares outstanding as a result of the combination. A similar observation to that made in reference to the data in the first column is appropriate to this assumption also; reported earnings are affected by the disparity between the fair values of the assets acquired and their book values.

The data in the third column indicate the results of the combination if stock were used and if the combination met all the criteria to be accounted for as a pooling of interests. The net income reported is substantially higher ($15,456,000 compared with $14,431,000) than under the two other assumptions. This result can be attributed to the fact that book values are brought forward for the assets of B Company in a pooling of interests, whereas current fair values are brought forward in a purchase. When the book values are lower than current values, lower charges to revenues, and thus a higher net income, will result. Similarly, no goodwill is recognized in the combination transaction, so that future income does not have to bear any charge for goodwill amortization. The result is that earnings per share of $2.45 can be projected for the combined business, as compared with $2.28 under a purchase for stock or $2.41 ($2.25 after adjustment for the cost of money) under a cash purchase.

The facts assumed in the illustration are admittedly oversimplified to highlight the main issues. On the other hand, the facts assumed are not unreasonable; certainly during periods of inflation one would expect the fair values of the assets of a company to be in excess of their book values. Under these conditions, and with continuing emphasis on earnings per share as a measure of enterprise success, the pooling-of-interests method of accounting has become widely accepted. The terms and attendant circumstances of many business combinations were structured in such a way that pooling-of-interests accounting was appropriate.

The Negative Goodwill Situation. Under different circumstances, on the other hand, purchase accounting might be preferred for a combination effected by an exchange of stock. Even though Opinion No. 16 eliminated the option that previously existed as to choice of accounting method for a business combination, purchase accounting remains applicable to almost any business combination because of the relative ease with which one or more of the pooling criteria can be violated. Assume that in the above illustration the book value of B Company's net assets was $16 million and the agreed-upon purchase price was $10.8 million. Under pooling accounting A Company would be accountable for $16 million, the book value of assets acquired, even though the fair value of the consideration given was $5.2 million less than this. Apparently some factors exist so that the assets of B Company are overvalued, a circumstance that makes accounting for the book value undesirable after the combination because such book values would become charges to income in succeeding periods.

Under purchase accounting, on the other hand, the difference of $5.2 million, or the excess of book value over fair value of the consideration in the combination (sometimes denoted "negative goodwill" in accounting jargon) will be allocated to particular assets to state them at fair value or will be allocated to long-lived assets if an excess remains after fair values have been recognized. The reduction in the carrying amounts of the assets will reduce charges to income in future periods. Under these conditions accounting for the combination as a purchase would result in a higher earnings per share than would result from accounting for the combination as a pooling of interests.

Summary. A few generalizations on the accounting aspects of business combinations are appropriate, even though exceptions may be found as circumstances vary. Combinations effected for cash are considered to be purchases, so that the fair values of the assets acquired become the basis of accountability for those assets. Earnings per share after a combination effected for cash will frequently be higher than they were previously, although as the gap widens between the fair values and book values of assets subject to charge in future income statements, the increase in earnings per share diminishes and may become a decrease in some cases. In making comparisons between precombination and postcombination earnings, one should take care to consider the cost of the capital used to effect the combination.

Combinations effected for stock will merit classification as a pooling of interests when all of the criteria specified in Opinion No. 16 are met. If one or more of the specified criteria is not met, the combination will be accounted for as a purchase. Generally, if the fair value of the stock issued in the combination exceeds the book values of the assets of the company to be absorbed, efforts will be made to see that all of the specified criteria are met so that pooling-of-interests accounting can be used. The book values then become the basis of accounting for these assets. The earnings brought forward by the absorbed company will generally be higher in relation to the combined postcombination earnings than the shares issued in the combination are in relation to postcombination shares outstanding, thus increasing postcombination reported earnings per share. On the other hand, if the fair value of the stock issued in the combination is less than the book value of the assets of the company to be absorbed, purchase accounting will be desirable and efforts will be made to see that one or more of the specified criteria for pooling-of-interests accounting is not met. The fair value of the stock issued then becomes the basis of accounting for the assets, and the reduction in book values for the assets of the absorbed company will enhance reported earnings in future years as the assets are amortized.

PRACTICAL ASPECTS AND DEVELOPMENTS IN ACCOUNTING FOR BUSINESS COMBINATIONS

As business combination activity evolved and expanded in the 1960s, many new and innovative characteristics were utilized in combination transactions. These innovations involved the use of a variety of new and somewhat unique securities, the use of two or more different securities or assets in a given combination, and forms of combination arrangements that satisfied the pre-Opinion No. 16 criteria for use of pooling-of-interests accounting. Many of these innovations created dilemmas in an accounting sense and led accountants to modify or alter existing concepts and practices in order to give effect to the intent of the transactions. Many also were responsible for certain of the criteria included in Opinion No. 16 in an effort to eliminate what some viewed as "abuses" of the pooling concept. Several examples of these practical developments are considered in the following paragraphs.

Use of Convertible Securities. During the 1960s, convertible preferred stock was used increasingly to effect combinations, whereas previously this type of security was rarely used. Had such a security been used in earlier years, it would have been strongly suggestive of a purchase transaction. As the pooling concept evolved, however, securities that were voting when issued and that were convertible into common shares gradually became encompassed within the concept. Convertible securities were particularly useful to companies that desired eventual equity financing but at a price higher than market price at the time of the combination. The convertible securities issued really became a deferred issuance of common stock at a price higher than existed for the common at the time the securities were issued.

The convertible preferred securities were attractive to many companies for several reasons. First, they enabled the shareholders of the selling company to receive dividends after the combination at least equal to those received prior to combination. Not uncommonly the shareholders of the selling company were receiving proportionately greater dividends at the time of combination than shareholders of the buying company. An issuance of common stock sufficient to provide the shareholders of the selling company with dividends at least equal to those previously received would mean that the buying company would either have to issue an excessive number of common shares or increase the dividend payout on all common shares. At times a significant increase would be necessary. The preferred shares permitted a higher dividend payment on those shares without also increasing the payment on the common shares. In addition, by making the preferred shares convertible into common at a conversion price higher than that at which the common was selling at the time of combination, the buying company could achieve the combination with the issuance of fewer shares of common than if the common were issued at the transaction date.

The criterion in Opinion No. 16 that specified that only common stock could be exchanged if the combination were to be a pooling of interests effectively reduced the use of convertible securities to effect a combination.

Use of Treasury Stock. On the surface the use of treasury stock rather than previously unissued stock appears to be an insignificant difference in evaluating a combination for accounting purposes. In either case, shares of common stock are issued, and if other criteria are met, pooling-of-interests accounting would appear to be appropriate. However, assume the following situation: A Company desires to acquire B Company and desires to pay cash to consummate the transaction; B Company shareholders prefer to receive common stock; in addition, A Company desires to follow pooling accounting in order to avoid the recognition of the excess of the current fair values of B Company's resources over their book values. A Company might decide to enter the marketplace to acquire approximately the number of shares of its own stock needed to effect the combination. Although careful planning is necessary to prevent any upsetting effect on the market price of the stock, for larger companies whose shares are widely traded this generally poses no problem. After obtaining the shares (now treasury shares), A Company could consummate the combination by an exchange of shares, using either the treasury shares or previously unissued shares. The result is a combination effected for stock, but with no increase in total shares outstanding because the shares issued to bring about the combination had been acquired for that purpose. In substance, A Company effected the combination for cash, but because the form of the combination event involved stock, accountants argued that pooling accounting was appropriate. Opinion No. 16 (as supplemented by Accounting Series Release No. 146A) created certain barriers to the use of pooling accounting when treasury shares have been acquired in the 2 years prior to initiation of the combination.

Part Purchase, Part Pooling. Another unusual accounting result was achieved in combinations accounted for in part as a purchase and in part as a pooling. Assume A Company owns, say, a 35 percent interest in B Company, which was acquired for cash several years ago. If all or substantially all of the remaining 65 percent interest in B Company is obtained by issuance of common stock, the resultant combination would likely have been considered a 35 percent purchase and a 65 percent pooling prior to issuance of Opinion No. 16. Thus, the goodwill associated with the 35 percent purchase would appear in the postcombination financial statement, whereas no goodwill would be associated with the 65 percent pooling. Retained earnings applicable to the 65 percent portion would be carried forward as retained earnings in the postcombination statements, whereas the retained earnings applicable to the 35 percent portion would be eliminated for statement presentation.

The part-purchase, part-pooling approach to accounting for a combination was somewhat inconsistent with the pooling concept of accounting for two merged companies as if they had always been one company. This approach is no longer permissible under Opinion No. 16.

Contingent Payments. Combinations that involve contingent payments generally arise from a disagreement among the parties as to the appropriate values of the companies involved. For example, the sellers may demand a price for excess earning capacity that the buyers feel is unsupportable. As a compromise, the terms agreed upon might include a provision for a fixed number of shares, say, 200,000, with an additional provision for a contingent payment of up to 50,000 additional shares within the following 5 years. Generally, the operating results of the selling company during the 5-year period will determine what portion of the additional 50,000 shares will be paid.

In some instances payment of the additional shares is contingent upon the market action of the buyer's stock in the forward period. For example, the buyers may argue that whereas the 200,000 shares are worth only $10 million at today's prices, these shares can be projected to be worth $20 million within 5 years because of the growth characteristics of the company that the market recognizes. Compromise terms may include provision for up to 50,000 additional shares to be issued, depending on the actual market performance of the buyer's stock.

With either of the above examples, prior to issuance of Opinion No. 16 a combination effected entirely for stock would have qualified for pooling accounting. Because the value of the consideration issued to bring about the combination is not significant to accounting for a pooling, the contingent aspect of part of the shares would have little effect on the accounting. The issuance of any of the contingent shares would result only in an entry increasing capital stock and reducing capital in excess of par of the buying company. The issuance of the contingent shares would not affect in any way the amounts recorded for the assets and properties taken over in the combination if it were accounted for as a pooling. On the other hand, under purchase accounting the fair value of the contingent shares issued would generally result in the recording of an additional amount of goodwill. Contingent payments, whether related to future earnings or future market prices, preclude pooling accounting under Opinion No. 16.

Continuity of Ownership. One of the criteria by which proposed accounting for a business combination has been judged is the continuity of ownership. Thus, a combination effected by stock results in a continuing of ownership interests, whereas a combination effected for cash results in elimination of one group of the previous ownership interests. Pooling-of-interests accounting has been tied closely to the continuity of ownership interests. As the pooling concept evolved, however, the insistence on continuity of ownership interests gradually diminished, as exemplified by use of convertible securities and by the part-purchase, part-pooling approach.

Opinion No. 16 did not provide, among its criteria, for a continuity of ownership interests. However, early experience under Opinion No. 16 indicated that incoming shareholders often were "bailed out," or received cash, shortly after the combination. As a result, the SEC, in Accounting Series Release No. 135, requires certain shareholders (affiliates) receiving shares in a combination to retain them at least until operating results of the combined entity for 30 days have been reported. The intent of this limiting provision appears to be to retain continuity of interests as a criterion of pooling-of-interests accounting, at least for a brief period of time, for shares issued to affiliates.

Post-Year-End Poolings. On occasion, pooling accounting prior to Opinion No. 16 resulted in a company incorporating the assets and earnings of a company into its financial statements for a period even though it had no financial interest in the company during that period. Assume that A Company has a fiscal year ending December 31, and assume further that it contemplates a combination with B Company. The combination may be consummated under a variety of conditions with varying effects on financial presentations.

Thus, A Company may purchase B Company for cash on October 1, in which case A Company will include the assets and liabilities of B Company in its balance sheet at December 31 and will include the operations and earnings of B Company from October 1 to December 31 in its income statement. If the combination took place on November 15, the result would be the same, except that the income statement would include the earnings of B Company only from November 15. If the combination took place in January or later in the following year, even though it was prior to the date the auditors of A Company completed their examination, the combination would not affect the A Company financial statements at December 31. Disclosure of the combination might be accomplished by footnote if it were material.

On the other hand, A Company may bring about its combination with B Company in such a manner that pooling-of-interests accounting is appropriate. Under the pooling concept the result was the same whether the combination was effected on October 1, November 15, in the following January, or at any other date prior to the date the auditors of A Company complete their examination of the December 31 financial statements. This result was to include the assets and liabilities of B Company in the balance sheet of the combined companies as of December 31 and to include the operations and earnings of B Company in the income statement of the combined companies for the entire year. Thus, under pooling accounting the earnings of B Company for a year could be reported in a combined income statement of A Company and B Company for that year even if the two companies did not effect the combination until after the end of the year being reported on. Opinion No. 16, however, concludes that the combination must be consummated prior to the end of the fiscal year for the operations of the two companies to be reported on a combined basis for that fiscal year. Post-year-end poolings no longer are permissible.

Restatement of Prior Years' Data. A somewhat related problem arises in the presentation of comparative financial data subsequent to a business combination. If the combination is accounted for as a purchase, no restatement is made for previously reported data. The operating results of the year of combination and the financial position after combination would be compared with the previously reported operating results and financial position for earlier years. Full disclosure would be made of the combination, and pro forma information would be presented as if the companies had been combined for the periods being reported upon.

If the combination is accounted for as a pooling of interests, however, the pooling concept indicates a need to restate the financial data reported for periods prior to the combination. Such restatement would be necessary to present the financial data for the prior years on the basis that the combined entities had always been one company. Comparisons made between data for the year of combination and those for earlier periods would then include information for all units currently a part of the combined entity. In practice, however, restatements of prior years' data have sometimes not been made, on the basis that the newly combined unit is immaterial to the total enterprise. Comparisons made between the current year's data and those for prior years will not be misleading in the absence of restatement because of the immaterial effect that restatement would have.

Standards of materiality, however, are not well defined. Gradually the AICPA, through Opinions No. 6 and 10 of the Accounting Principles Board, reinforced the policy of restatement of prior years' data if such data are presented in periods after a pooling-of-interests combination. The SEC has similarly supported such restatements. Under the pooling concept the usefulness of comparative data would appear to rest importantly on the restatement of the data for earlier years to encompass that of newly combined units.

SUMMARY

Growth through business combination has become an integral part of American economic development. Combinations have created a number of accounting problems related to: (1) accounting for the combination transaction, (2) accounting for operations subsequent to the combination, and (3) reporting the results of operations and financial position of the combined companies in a manner to permit comparisons with prior years. An overriding problem is related to the need to identify the characteristics of the combination so as to classify it appropriately for accounting purposes. Innovations in combination approaches and in types of securities used to effect the combination hindered clear identification in many cases. As a result, the APB issued Opinion No. 16 in an attempt to eliminate certain alleged abuses and to limit pooling accounting to combinations meeting all the specified criteria. Experience in applying Opinion No. 16 indicates, however, that some of the criteria are more arbitrary than sound. Numerous interpretations have been issued to guide practitioners, and the Financial Accounting Standards Board, the successor to the Accounting Principles Board, continues to assess the need for revised standards to account for business combinations.

BIBLIOGRAPHY

Accounting Principles Board (AICPA), *Status of Accounting Research Bulletins*, Opinion No. 6 (APB, 1965).

——, *Omnibus Opinion—1966*, Opinion No. 10 (APB, 1966).

——, *Business Combinations*, Opinion No. 16 (APB, 1970).

——, *Intangible Assets*, Opinion No. 17 (APB, 1970).

Alberts, W. W., and J. E. Segall (eds.), *The Corporate Merger* (University of Chicago Press, Chicago, 1966).

Briloff, A., "Dirty Poolings," *The Accounting Review*, July 1967.

Catlett, G. R., and N. O. Olson, *Accounting for Goodwill*, Accounting Research Study No. 10 (AICPA, 1968).

Committee on Accounting Procedure (AICPA), *Restatement and Revision of Accounting Research Bulletins*, Accounting Research Bulletin No. 43 (CAP, 1953).

———, *Business Combinations,* Accounting Research Bulletin No. 48 (CAP, 1957).

Gunther, S. P., "Poolings—Purchases—Goodwill: A Review of APB Opinions 16 and 17," *New York Certified Public Accountant,* January 1971.

———, "Lingering Pooling Problems," *CPA Journal,* June 1973.

Lev. B., "Microeconomic Consequences of Corporate Mergers," *Journal of Business* (University of Chicago), January 1972.

McCarthy, G. D., and R. E. Healy, *Valuing a Company: Practices and Procedures* (Ronald Press Company, New York, 1971).

Nurnberg, H., C. P. Stickney, and R. L. Weil, "Combining Stockholders' Equity Accounts under Pooling of Interests Method," *The Accounting Review,* vol. 50, no. 1 (January 1975), pp. 179–183.

Sapienza, S. R., "Business Combinations and Enterprise Valuation," *Journal of Accounting Research,* Spring 1964.

———, "Examination of AICPA Research Study No. 5—Standards for Pooling," *The Accounting Review,* July 1964.

Wyatt, A. R., *A Critical Study of Accounting for Business Combinations,* Accounting Research Study No. 5 (AICPA, 1963).

———, "Inequities in Accounting for Business Combinations," *Financial Executive,* December 1972.

Wyatt, A. R., and D. E. Kieso, *Business Combinations: Planning and Action* (International Textbook Co., Scranton, Pa., 1969).

CHAPTER 34

Consolidated

Statements

James A. Largay III
Arthur Andersen & Co. Alumni Professor of
Accounting, Lehigh University

MEANING AND PURPOSE OF CONSOLIDATED STATEMENTS

When a corporation owns more than 50 percent of the voting stock of another corporation and the two corporations remain as separate legal entities, a parent/subsidiary relationship exists between the two corporations. In effect, the parent's shareholders become the *controlling ownership interest* in a collection of economic resources and obligations spanning two or more legally separate corporations. Fair presentation of the financial affairs of such affiliated corporations to the controlling shareholders generally requires the preparation of consolidated statements. Indeed, the purpose of consolidated financial statements is to report the financial affairs of two or more affiliated corporations as if they were a *single unified economic entity.* The Accounting Principles Board pointed out in Statement No. 4 [1970, par. 194]:

> Consolidated financial statements present the financial position and results of operations of a parent company and its subsidiaries essentially as if the group were a single enterprise comprised of branches or divisions. The resulting accounting entity is an economic rather than a legal unit, and its financial statements are considered to reflect the substance of the combined economic relationships to an extent not possible by merely providing the separate financial statements of the corporate entities comprising the group.

Consolidation Policy. Although ownership of a majority of a company's outstanding voting shares (either directly or indirectly) is a *necessary* condition for consolidation, Accounting Research Bulletin No. 51 [1959, pars. 2, 3] notes that this is *not* a *sufficient* condition for consolidation for the following reasons:

1. Control may be *temporary* in that the stock acquisition may have been made to facilitate other business ventures and not as a long-term investment with a commitment of managerial resources.

2. Control may be *nominal* and not effective. For example, the affairs of a company in financial difficulty may be controlled by fiduciaries, not by the majority shareholders. A foreign subsidiary located where the political regime is unstable or hostile may find its assets controlled by local authorities, despite wishes of the majority shareholders.

3. Fair presentation of the financial affairs of a subsidiary in an unrelated line of business may be better achieved by presenting separate financial information or statements for that subsidiary and excluding it from consolidation. This happens quite frequently when a manufacturing company owns a finance company. The asset and liability structures and operations of the two are often so different that the finance subsidiary is not consolidated with the manufacturing parent.

These exceptions to the general rule that majority-owned companies are to be consolidated are not unusual. Of the 600 companies surveyed in *Accounting Trends and Techniques* in 1979 [AICPA, 1979, p. 49] 163 indicated that they did not consolidate all subsidiaries. Most of these nonconsolidated subsidiaries were finance-related.

As a significant accounting policy, a company's consolidation policy must be disclosed as required by APB Opinion No. 22 [1972]. To illustrate this, a recent annual report of American Brands stated, in part:

> The consolidated financial statements include the accounts of the Company and all subsidiaries other than The Franklin Life Insurance Company, which is accounted for by the equity method.

Elimination of Intercompany Relationships. Fundamental to the preparation of consolidated financial statements is the need to *eliminate* or *remove* the effects of financial transactions or relationships among the components of the consolidated entity. In this way, the financial statements for the consolidated entity are guided by the same accounting principles that guide any financial statements—namely, that information (revenues, expenses, assets, liabilities, etc.) is reported based on *transactions with outside parties*.

As a result, consolidation procedures employ *eliminating entries*—often made on a worksheet—to neutralize, reverse, or remove an existing intercompany financial relationship between two or more affiliated corporations. Although eliminating entries are made to prepare consolidated statements, it must be remembered that such entries have no *substantive effect* on the economic or legal relationships between the separate legal entities in an affiliated group. Consequently, eliminating entries do not affect the internal accounting records of any of the affiliated companies and are *not booked*. For example, a loan made by P Company to S Company will be eliminated in consolidation when the accounts of P and S are brought together. S Company's legal obligation to repay the amount borrowed is not forgiven. Rather, from the viewpoint of the controlling interest, an offsetting internal receivable and payable exist and must be eliminated because outside parties are not involved.

Eliminating entries made in consolidation achieve two basic objectives, which follow from the single-entity concept:

1. Elimination of transactions among affiliated companies avoids the double counting of assets, liabilities, revenues, and expenses that would otherwise exist.

2. Any gains or losses arising from transactions between affiliated corporations are eliminated if unconfirmed through subsequent external transactions on the grounds that internal transactions are, by their very nature, not arms'-length and realization has not been achieved.

Relationship to Accounting for Business Combinations. Accounting for business combinations was discussed in Chapter 33 of this handbook. In that chapter, application of the *purchase* and *pooling-of-interests* approaches to accounting for mergers and acquisitions was emphasized in that one or more of the combining companies ceased to exist as a separate legal entity and was absorbed into the surviving company. Consequently, a major concern was with valuation of the acquired company's assets and liabilities for the purpose of recording them on the books of the acquiring company. In a *purchase* combination, the assets and liabilities acquired were recorded at their *fair values* and the value of the consideration given substantiated the existence (or lack thereof) of purchased *goodwill*. The *pooling-of-interests* method views fair values as irrelevant and carries over the assets and liabilities "acquired" at their *book values* to the "acquired" company.

These rules governing accounting for business combinations are contained mostly in APB Opinion No. 16 [1970] and the many unofficial interpretations thereof. Moreover, they pertain with equal force to combinations that result in a parent/subsidiary relationship instead of the absorption of the acquired company. Because consolidated financial statements generally follow such combinations, the same principles that affected asset and liability valuations recorded at the time of merger affect the asset and liability valuations reported in consolidated statements. The difference is that departures from book value appear only in the consolidated statements and not on the books of any company. Allocation of investment cost among assets and liabilities is now done on the *consolidated financial statement working paper.*

CONSOLIDATED BALANCE SHEET AT DATE OF BUSINESS COMBINATION

We begin our overview of the preparation of consolidated statements by assuming that a consolidated balance sheet is prepared on the date that the parent company P obtains its controlling interest in the subsidiary company S. Although this need not happen in practice, by making this assumption we postpone the issues arising in the consolidation of income statements. Moreover, the date of business combination is important in its own right, because in a purchase combination it is the date at which the fair values of properties acquired and obligations assumed must be established. Even so, varying degrees of complexity can exist depending on the relationship between the investment cost and the book value of the net assets acquired and on whether the subsidiary is wholly or partially owned (i.e., a minority interest is present).

The simplest case is one in which investment cost equals the book value of the net assets acquired, the fair values of all assets and liabilities approximate their book values, and there is no minority interest.

Investment Cost = Fair Value = Book Value; No Outside Interests. On January 1, 19X1, the condensed balance sheets of P Company and S Company, immediately prior to the stock acquisition of S by P, are given in Exhibit 1. The assumption of equality among investment cost, book values, and fair values of the assets and liabilities acquired makes this case appropriate for purchase and pooling combinations. An actual pooling, of course, requires no such assumption; the accounting simply ignores any differences between book and fair value.

Acquisition of shares via purchase. On January 2, 19X1, P Company acquired all the outstanding stock of S Company in exchange for $100,000 cash and 20,000 shares of $1-par-value stock worth $400,000, recording the acquisition as follows.

Books of P Company

Investment in S	500,000	
Cash		100,000
Common Stock		20,000
Additional Paid-in Capital		380,000

EXHIBIT 1

P COMPANY AND S COMPANY
Condensed Balance Sheets at January 1, 19X1
(pre-combination)

	P Company	S Company
Assets		
Cash and receivables	$1,000,000	$ 200,000
Inventory	800,000	150,000
Plant assets (net)	2,500,000	900,000
Total assets	$4,300,000	$1,250,000
Liabilities and Shareholders' Equity		
Current liabilities	$ 500,000	$ 250,000
Noncurrent liabilities	1,000,000	500,000
Common stock, par value $1	200,000	50,000
Additional paid-in capital	700,000	150,000
Retained earnings	1,900,000	300,000
Total liabilities and shareholders' equity	$4,300,000	$1,250,000

Immediate preparation of a consolidated balance sheet requires that the following working paper elimination be made.

Consolidated Financial Statement Working Paper

Common Stock—S	50,000	
Additional Paid-in Capital—S	150,000	
Retained Earnings—S	300,000	
Investment in S		500,000

The above eliminating entry is fundamental to all consolidations. P's ownership of S's stock is a mere surrogate for ownership of the underlying assets and liabilities of S. This elimination has the effect of *substituting* the assets and liabilities of S for the Investment in S in the consolidated balance sheet. Without such an elimination, the net assets of S would be counted *twice*. Similarly, the shareholders' equity of S must be eliminated in consolidation. The shares of S are held internally and are effectively retired. Because the equity of the controlling interest is fully expressed in the shareholders' equity of P, failure to eliminate the shareholders' equity of S would result in counting it twice. Finally, under purchase accounting, S's retained earnings at date of business combination are not part of consolidated retained earnings and are eliminated.

Pooling of interests. Instead of the preceding assumptions, assume that on January 2, 19X1, P Company exchanged 25,000 shares of its $1-par-value stock for all of the outstanding shares of S Company in a combination qualifying as a pooling of interests. P's entry to record the pooling would be as follows.

Books of P Company

Investment in S	500,000	
Common Stock		25,000
Additional Paid-in Capital		175,000
Retained Earnings		300,000

Pooling-of-interest rules generally require that, after the pooling, P Company's contributed capital accounts equal the sum of the separate P and S contributed capital accounts. Because S Company's contributed capital of $200,000 (= $50,000 + $150,000) exceeds the par value of the newly issued P Company stock by $175,000 (= $200,000 − $25,000), this amount is recorded by P as additional paid-in capital (APIC). The entry also reflects P's pickup of S Company's retained earnings. Consolidated retained earnings under a pooling include P's share of all of S's retained earnings. In the illustrative entry the pickup is made when the pooling is recorded to facilitate the consolidation process. Alternatively, the same result could be achieved by a working paper extension.

Assuming a consolidated balance sheet is prepared at date of pooling, the working paper elimination is as follows.

Consolidated Financial Statement Working Paper

Common Stock—S	50,000	
Additional Paid-in Capital—S	150,000	
Retained Earnings—S	300,000	
Investment in S		500,000

The principles behind the elimination parallel those in the purchase case. S Company's retained earnings are eliminated here because they were recorded by P at the time of the pooling.

Formal consolidated balance sheets. Combining the accounts of P and S after making the appropriate working paper elimination leads to the consolidated balance sheets presented in Exhibit 2.

Because of the assumption that investment cost equaled the book value and fair value of S's net assets and liabilities, consolidated assets and liabilities under purchase and pooling are virtually identical. The difference of $100,000 follows from the use of $100,000 cash in the purchase transaction. The composition of consolidated shareholders' equity, however, is quite different in two respects. First, consolidated retained earnings is greater under pooling because of the inclusion of S Company's retained earnings prior to the combination. Second, the consolidated contributed capital accounts differ. Under purchase accounting, APIC reflects the excess of fair value of the stock issued over its par value; whereas in pooling, the increment to APIC is the excess of the book value of S's contributed capital accounts over the par value of the P stock issued.

Investment Cost = Fair Value = Book Value; Minority Interest Present. It is quite common for a parent company to own less than 100 percent of the subsidiary's outstanding voting stock. In such situations, the controlling interest controls all of the subsidiary's assets and liabilities but does not own all of the stock. The equity interest of outside shareholders in consolidated net assets (i.e., a pro rata share of S Company's net assets at book value) is disclosed in the consolidated balance sheet by an account entitled Minority Interest in Subsid-

EXHIBIT 2

P COMPANY AND SUBSIDIARY S COMPANY
Consolidated Balance Sheet at January 2, 19X1

	Purchase	Pooling
Assets		
Cash and receivables	$1,100,000	$1,200,000
Inventory	950,000	950,000
Plant assets (net)	3,400,000	3,400,000
Total assets	$5,450,000	$5,550,000
Liabilities and Shareholders' Equity		
Current liabilities	$ 750,000	$ 750,000
Noncurrent liabilities	1,500,000	1,500,000
Common stock, par value $1	220,000	225,000
Additional paid-in capital	1,080,000	875,000
Retained earnings	1,900,000	2,200,000
Total liabilities and shareholders' equity	$5,450,000	$5,550,000

iary. Precisely where this account appears in the consolidated balance sheet varies in practice. Some companies report it as a noncurrent liability, although it fails to satisfy some of the conventional liability tests. According to *Accounting Trends and Techniques* [AICPA, 1979, pp. 49, 191] of 590 firms issuing consolidated statements in 1979, 154 included minority interest among noncurrent liabilities; of 591 in 1978, 150 did so. Other companies report it as a component of consolidated shareholders' equity or in a special category between noncurrent liabilities and shareholders' equity. Because the issue is fundamentally one of disclosing the extent of outside ownership interests in consolidated net assets, clear disclosure in or near consolidated shareholders' equity seems appropriate.

The example from the last section can also illustrate entries made by P Company to record acquisition of a 90 percent interest in S Company by purchase and pooling. Assume that P gives $90,000 and 18,000 shares of $1-par-value common stock worth $360,000 in the purchase case and 22,500 shares of $1-par-value common stock in the pooling.

Books of P Company

	Purchase		Pooling	
	Dr.	Cr.	Dr.	Cr.
Investment in S	450,000		450,000	
Cash		90,000		
Common stock		18,000		22,500
Additional paid-in capital		342,000		157,500
Retained earnings (.9 × $300,000)				270,000

In consolidation, the same eliminating entry may be used in both the purchase and pooling cases. The entry eliminates the investment account against P's share of S Company's shareholders' equity and reclassifies the remaining amount, which pertains to the outside shareholders, as Minority Interest in S.

Consolidated Financial Statement Working Paper

Common Stock—S	50,000	
Additional Paid-in Capital—S	150,000	
Retained Earnings—S	300,000	
Investment in S		450,000
Minority Interest in S.............................		50,000

Investment Cost ≠ Book Value; No Outside Interests. The more realistic situation encountered in a purchase combination is that the investment cost—normally the fair value of the consideration exchanged for S's stock—differs from the book value of the stock or net assets acquired. Moreover, the fair values of S's individual assets and liabilities may differ from their book values. In a purchase combination, the accountant's objective is to see that, in consolidation, S's assets and liabilities are stated at their fair values. To do so involves allocating the purchase price (investment cost) among S's identifiable assets and liabilities in accordance with their fair values. Any amount unallocated in this way is reported on the consolidated balance sheet as *goodwill.* (It must be amortized by the straight-line method over a period not to exceed 40 years;[1] see Chapter 21.) In contrast, if the fair value of S's net assets exceeds the investment cost—the "negative goodwill" case—further allocation among noncurrent assets, excluding long-term investments in marketable securities, is required in order that the net assets acquired be reported at their acquisition cost. This denies the existence of a "bargain purchase" and the recognition of a "gain on acquisition."

One systematic approach to allocating the purchase price among S's assets and liabilities calls for allocating the *difference* between investment cost and book value to the existing book values of S's assets and liabilities. If investment cost exceeds book value, a *purchase premium* exists; a *purchase discount* arises if book value exceeds investment cost.

To illustrate the procedure, recall the balance sheet data for P Company and S Company in Exhibit 1. We now assume that P acquires all of S's stock by issuing 30,000 shares of $1-par-value stock worth $600,000 and also disburses $300,000 cash to the former shareholders of S. Because the book value of S's shareholders' equity is $500,000, the purchase price reflects a purchase premium of $400,000 (= $600,000 + $300,000 − $500,000). Estimated fair values of certain of S's assets and liabilities differ from their book values, as shown below.

Assets (Liabilities) of S Company		
	Book value	Fair value
Inventory	$ 150,000	$ 200,000
Plant assets (net)	900,000	1,100,000
Noncurrent liabilities	(500,000)	(430,000)

Computation and allocation of the purchase premium are presented in a schedule designed for that purpose in Exhibit 3.

The entry made by P to record the acquisition of S's stock and the working paper eliminations to be made if a consolidated balance sheet were prepared immediately would be as follows.

Books of P Company

Investment in S	900,000	
Cash		300,000
Common Stock		30,000
Additional Paid-in Capital		570,000

Consolidated Financial Statement Working Paper

Inventory	50,000
Plant Assets (net)	200,000

---

[1] See APB Opinion No. 17 [1970, pars. 27, 29, 30].

Noncurrent Liabilities	70,000	
Goodwill.	80,000	
Investment in S		400,000

To allocate the purchase premium among the assets and
liabilities of S Company in accordance with their fair values and record the unallocated portion as goodwill.

Common Stock—S.	50,000	
Additional Paid-in Capital—S	150,000	
Retained Earnings—S	300,000	
Investment in S		500,000

To eliminate the balance in the investment account, which
now equals the book value of the shareholders' equity
acquired, against the shareholders' equity accounts of S
Company.

The negative goodwill case can also be illustrated here. *Negative goodwill* is said to exist if the investment cost (IC) is *less than* the fair value of the net assets acquired (FV). Moreover, negative goodwill can arise regardless of the rela-

---

EXHIBIT 3

P COMPANY AND S COMPANY
Schedule for Computation and Allocation of the Purchase Premium Arising in the Stock Acquisition on January 2, 19X1

Cost of the acquisition:	
Fair value of stock given	$600,000
Cash given	300,000
Total cost of the acquisition	$900,000
Book value of the net assets or shareholders' equity acquired:	
Common stock	$ 50,000
Additional paid-in capital	150,000
Retained earnings	300,000
Total book value of S Company	$500,000
Purchase premium	$400,000

Assets and liabilities of S Company	Fair value	Book value	Fair value minus book value	Allocation based on P's interest (100%)
Cash and receivables	$ 200,000	$ 200,000		
Inventory	200,000	150,000	$ 50,000	$ 50,000
Plant assets (net)	1,100,000	900,000	200,000	200,000
Current liabilities	(250,000)	(250,000)		
Noncurrent liabilities.	(430,000)	(500,000)	70,000	70,000
	$ 820,000	$ 500,000	$320,000	$320,000
Goodwill				80,000
Total purchase premium				$400,000

---

tionship between IC and the book value of the net assets acquired (BV). For example, if IC > BV and FV > IC, then both negative goodwill and a purchase premium are present. After the initial allocation of the purchase premium or discount (as in Exhibit 3), negative goodwill must be accounted for as follows:

1. Allocate it among the noncurrent assets of S Company, except long-term investments in marketable securities, in accordance with their fair values. This is the second stage of what is now a two-stage process to allocate the purchase premium.

2. If any unallocated negative goodwill remains (i.e., the eligible noncurrent account balances are driven to zero), it is accounted for as a deferred credit and, following APB Opinion No. 17, is amortized over a period not to exceed 40 years.

Returning to our numerical example, suppose that P had acquired all of S's stock in a purchase combination by issuing 30,000 shares of its own $1-par-value common stock valued at $600,000. Because S's shareholders' equity has a book value of $500,000, a purchase premium of $100,000 exists. Allocating this purchase premium to the assets and liabilities of S Company, as shown in the lower part of Exhibit 3, results in a net upward revaluation of $320,000. This exceeds the purchase premium by $220,000 (= $320,000 − $100,000), and produces negative goodwill of that amount. Now, suppose that S's Plant Assets (net) account has the following components, in terms of book values and estimated fair values.

	Book value	Fair value	Percent of total fair value
Buildings (net)	$400,000	$ 550,000	50
Equipment (net)	300,000	330,000	30
Land	200,000	220,000	20
Total plant assets (net)	$900,000	$1,100,000	100

Final allocation of the purchase premium and negative goodwill is given below. The fair values were assigned to the plant assets in the first stage of the purchase premium allocation (see Exhibit 3; the detailed account balances given above were omitted there).

Account	Percent of fair value (1)	Negative goodwill allocation (2) = (1) × $220,000	Original purchase premium allocation (3)	Final allocation (4) = (3) − (2)
Buildings (net)	50	$110,000	$150,000	$ 40,000
Equipment (net)	30	66,000	30,000	(36,000)
Land	20	44,000	20,000	(24,000)
Totals.	100	$220,000	$200,000	$(20,000)

Consider now the entry made by P Company to record the acquisition of S for stock valued at $600,000 and the working paper entries needed to consolidate the balance sheets of P and S at date of acquisition.

Books of P Company

Investment in S	600,000	
Common Stock		30,000
Additional Paid-in Capital		570,000

Consolidated Financial Statement Working Paper

Inventory	50,000	
Buildings (net)	40,000	
Noncurrent Liabilities	70,000	
Equipment (net)		36,000
Land		24,000
Investment in S		100,000

To allocate the purchase premium among the assets and liabilities of S Company in accordance with their fair values as modified by the negative goodwill allocation.

Common Stock—S	50,000	
Additional Paid-in Capital—S	150,000	
Retained Earnings—S	300,000	
Investment in S		500,000

To eliminate the balance in the investment account against the shareholders' equity accounts of S Company.

Rationale for the treatment of negative goodwill. The negative goodwill case arises because of a discrepancy between the investment cost and the estimated fair value of the net assets acquired. If the fair value of the consideration given by P in the acquisition is reliable, it becomes the basis for recording the acquisition. Because the acquisition is presumed to be the outcome of an arms'-length bargaining process, there is little evidence to support the interpretation that P made a "bargain purchase" and that a "gain on acquisition" should be recorded. Noncurrent assets, other than long-term investments in marketable securities, become the dumping ground for negative goodwill, because estimates of their fair values are likely to be more subjective and less reliable than those for current assets, liabilities, and long-term investments in marketable securities.

Investment Cost ≠ Book Value; Minority Interest Present. Earlier the accounting where a minority interest existed and investment cost equaled book value was considered. In this section, alternative views of valuing the minority interest, where investment cost does not equal book value, are discussed along with the necessary working paper entries.

Alternative approaches to valuing the minority interest. An interesting theoretical issue arises when P acquires a less-than-100 percent interest in S for an amount different from the book value of the shares acquired. Specifically, what are the implications of the price paid by P for valuation of the minority interest in S? Three alternative consolidation theories lead to different minority interest valuations.[2]

1. The *parent (or proprietary) theory* of consolidated statement views consolidated statements as an extension of parent company statements. The parent records at cost only what it purchases. If 80 percent of S's stock is acquired, only 80 percent (the parent's share) of S's assets and liabilities are shown at their fair values. Because the minority's share continues to be carried at book value, the minority interest simply equals 20 percent of S Company's shareholders' equity, at book value. This treatment is one of those in accord with current generally accepted accounting principles.[3]

2. The *entity theory*[4] of consolidated statements regards the collection of assets and liabilities controlled by P as indivisible; equal treatment is afforded to both the controlling and minority shareholders. From the price paid by P for a fractional interest in S is inferred the total value of S as an entity. Thus, 100 percent of S's assets and liabilities are carried in consolidated statements at their fair values, and any goodwill pertains proportionately to all shareholders. Under this theory, the value assigned to the minority interest is based on the price paid by P for its controlling interest. This method is rarely used in practice.

3. The *entity theory modified* is a form of compromise position. It seeks to disclose the total fair value of all assets and liabilities acquired by P and requires that the minority's proportionate share of those assets and liabilities be stated at the same basis in consolidation as the parent's share—fair value. This view is consistent with the entity theory. The departure lies in the treatment of goodwill. Purchased goodwill, it is argued, represents an unidentifiable intangible asset acquired by the parent. Its value is derived solely from the price paid by the parent, and no evidence exists for assigning goodwill to the minority interest. In other words, the identifiable assets and liabilities have total estimated fair values that are recorded in part (parent theory) or in whole (entity theory), but goodwill, because it is not identifiable, exists only to the extent that it has been verified by P's acquisition cost. Therefore, this modification of the entity theory assigns to the minority interest its proportionate share of the fair value of S's identifiable net assets, but purchased goodwill is not included in the minority interest. This method is one of those in accord with current generally accepted accounting principles.[5]

Returning to our numerical example, suppose that P acquired 80 percent of S's stock for stock worth $600,000 and cash of $100,000. The book value of S's shareholders' equity is $500,000. From Exhibit 3, we see that the fair value of

---

[2]For a general discussion of these theories, see Beams [1982], chap. 12.

[3]See FASB Discussion Memorandum [1976], p. 107.

[4]A comprehensive development of this view of consolidated statements is given by Moonitz [1944].

[5]See FASB Discussion Memorandum [1976], p. 107.

S's identifiable net assets amounts to $820,000, of which P's share is $656,000 (= .8 × $820,000). Moreover, the total value of S implied by the $700,000 paid by P for an 80 percent interest is $875,000 (= $700,000/.8). Consider how S's identifiable net assets, goodwill, and the minority interest in S would appear under the three consolidation theories.

	S's identifiable net assets	Goodwill	Minority interest in S
Parent theory	$656,000	$44,000 (1)	$100,000 (2)
Entity theory	820,000	55,000 (3)	175,000 (4)
Entity theory modified	820,000	44,000 (1)	164,000 (5)

(1) $44,000 = $700,000 − (.8 × $820,000).
(2) $100,000 = .2 × $500,000.
(3) $55,000 = $875,000 − $820,000.
(4) $175,000 = .2 × $875,000; because .2 of $820,000 = $164,000, there is goodwill of $11,000 (= $175,000 − $164,000) included in the minority interest.
(5) $164,000 = .2 × $820,000.

Recording the minority interest in consolidation. As indicated, the Investment in S account includes (1) the book value of S's net assets acquired by P and (2) any increment (decrement) of the amount paid over (under) the book value in (1). Following the parent theory, after reclassification and allocation of any purchase premium or discount, elimination of the investment account against the shareholders' equity of S does not remove the entire shareholders' equity. The balance remaining is the book value of the Minority Interest in S and must be reclassified as such on the consolidated financial statement working paper. Here, this reclassification is combined with the investment elimination in a working paper entry. In the case just discussed, P acquired 80 percent of S's stock for $700,000, debiting Investment in S with that amount. The total book value of S's stock is $500,000, of which $400,000 pertains to P.

First, reclassify and allocate the purchase premium of $300,000 [= $700,000 − (.8 × $500,000)]. The amounts assigned to identifiable assets and liabilities equal *80 percent* of those in the right-hand column of Exhibit 3.

Consolidated Financial Statement Working Paper

Inventory	40,000	
Plant Assets (net)	160,000	
Noncurrent Liabilities	56,000	
Goodwill	44,000	
Investment in S		300,000
To allocate the purchase premium to the assets and liabilities of S Company.		

Next, eliminate the Investment in S against the shareholders' equity accounts and establish the minority interest.

Consolidated Financial Statement Working Paper

Common Stock—S	50,000	
Additional Paid-in Capital—S	150,000	
Retained Earnings—S	300,000	
Investment in S		400,000
Minority Interest in S		100,000

To eliminate the Investment in S against the shareholders'
equity of S Company and establish the minority interest.

Under the entity and modified entity theories, the full amount of the fair value of S's assets and liabilities acquired would be recognized. Under the entity approach the full amount of goodwill implicit in the transaction would be recognized.

Consolidated Financial Statement Working Paper

Inventory	50,000	
Plant Assets (net)	200,000	
Noncurrent Liabilities	70,000	
Goodwill	55,000	
Investment in S		375,000

The elimination entry would then be

Consolidated Financial Statement Working Paper

Common Stock—S	50,000	
Additional Paid-in Capital—S	150,000	
Retained Earnings—S	300,000	
Investment in S		325,000
Minority Interest in S		175,000

Under the modified entity approach, only the $44,000 of goodwill applicable to P's purchase would be recognized:

Consolidated Financial Statement Working Paper

Inventory	50,000	
Plant Assets (net)	200,000	
Noncurrent Liabilities	70,000	
Goodwill	44,000	
Investment in S		364,000

The elimination entry would then be

Consolidated Financial Statement Working Paper

Common Stock—S	50,000	
Additional Paid-in Capital—S	150,000	
Retained Earnings—S	300,000	
Investment in S		336,000
Minority Interest in S		164,000

CONSOLIDATED STATEMENTS AFTER DATE OF BUSINESS COMBINATION

The full set of financial statements—balance sheet, statement of income and retained earnings, and statement of changes in financial position—must be prepared for P and its subsidiaries at reporting dates after the controlling interest is acquired. The procedures needed to accomplish this are discussed next.

Consolidating the Statements of Income and Retained Earnings. Because P and S remain as legally separate corporations, the method used by P to account for its investment in S as an intercorporate investment affects the procedures at subsequent consolidation points. P would normally use the *equity method,* as described in APB Opinion No. 18 [1971], although the *cost method* may be used if only consolidated statements are to be issued. Because the two methods call for P to make different entries on its books, consolidation procedures differ. Nevertheless, the resulting consolidated statements are identical, regardless of the accounting method employed by P.

The equity method. Under the equity method, P increases (decreases) the Investment in S account for its share of S's reported periodic net income (loss). The investment account is decreased by P's share of S's dividends declared during the period. This periodic accrual of equity method income—the *equity method accrual*—is often complicated because APB Opinion No. 18 [1971, par. 19] views application of the equity method as a *one-line consolidation.*

Under this one-line consolidation concept, net income and retained earnings reported by P under the equity method are equal to consolidated net income and consolidated retained earnings, respectively. Consequently, any adjustments that enter into the determination of consolidated net income, such as amortization of a purchase premium or discount or the elimination of unconfirmed intercompany profits or losses, must also be reflected in the equity method accrual.

As an example, consider the following data (intercompany transactions are discussed in a later section). Suppose that P acquired an 80 percent interest in S on January 2, 19X1, for $500,000, an amount $100,000 more than the book value of the shares acquired. Further assume that $60,000 of the $100,000 purchase premium is allocated to plant assets with a remaining life of 10 years, and the remaining $40,000 is assigned to goodwill having an indeterminate life. S reports net income of $55,000 for 19X1 and declares and pays $20,000 in dividends. The plant assets are being depreciated by the straight-line method and the goodwill is to be amortized by the straight-line method as required by APB Opinion No. 17 over the maximum life permitted—40 years. P calculates its equity method accrual for 19X1 as follows.

P's share of S's reported net income (.8 × $55,000)	$44,000
Less amortization of purchase premium:	
Plant assets ($60,000/10)	$ 6,000
Goodwill ($40,000/40)...................................	1,000
Total purchase premium amortization	$ 7,000
P's equity method accrual	$37,000

P's share of S's dividends ($16,000 = .8 × $20,000) would be recorded during the year and the equity method accrual recorded at year-end as given below.

Books of P Company

Cash	16,000	
Investment in S		16,000
Investment in S	37,000	
Income from Subsidiary		37,000

After these entries are recorded, P's separate income statement includes the $37,000 equity method accrual, equal to P's share of S's reported net income less the periodic purchase premium amortization. Because the revenue and expense accounts of P and S are simply added together in consolidation, P's share of S's net income would be counted twice unless action is taken to prevent this. Hence a working paper elimination is needed to remove the double counting.

Consolidated Financial Statement Working Paper

Income from S	37,000	
Investment in S		37,000
To eliminate P's equity method accrual.		

Similarly, the receipt of intercompany dividends must be eliminated. After this is done, the Investment in S and the Retained Earnings—S (before closing entries are made) accounts will be restated to their balances at January 1, 19X1.

Consolidated Financial Statement Working Paper

Investment in S	16,000	
Dividends—S (or Retained Earnings—S)		16,000
To eliminate P's share of S Company's dividends.		

The cost method. If the parent company accounts for its investments in subsidiaries by the cost method, the investment account balance is not disturbed during the year and P's $16,000 share of S's dividends is recorded as dividend revenue, as follows.

Books of P Company

Cash	16,000	
Dividend Revenue		16,000

In consolidation, a working paper entry is also needed under the cost method to remove the intercompany dividends.

Consolidated Financial Statement Working Paper

Dividend Revenue	16,000	
Dividends—S (or Retained Earnings—S)		16,000
To eliminate P's share of S Company's dividends.		

This entry is made to avoid double counting of S's dividends in consolidation. The consolidated income statement includes S's revenues and expenses. Dividends represent the parent's realization of the subsidiary's income included in the consolidated income statement and must be removed so that income is recognized only once.

After the above eliminating entries needed under the equity or cost method are made, the purchase premium is allocated, the investment account is eliminated, and the current year purchase premium amortization is entered on the working paper. Because all entries other than the one needed to record the purchase premium amortization for 19X1 have been illustrated previously, only the one entry is given below. In the example, recall that allocation of the purchase premium increases depreciable plant assets by $60,000 and amortizable goodwill by $40,000. The respective 19X1 amortization amounts of $6,000 and $1,000 were computed when P's equity method accrual was determined. Note that elimination of the equity method accrual also removed the purchase premium amortization reflected therein.

Consolidated Financial Statement Working Paper

Depreciation Expense	6,000	
Amortization Expense.	1,000	
Plant Assets (net)		6,000
Goodwill		1,000
To record purchase premium amortization for 19X1.		

At consolidation points *after* the year of acquisition, an additional working paper entry is needed if P uses the *cost method* to account for the Investment in S. The balance in the investment account under the cost method is *not* adjusted by entries reflecting P's share of the change in S's retained earnings, as it is under the equity method. Therefore, a working paper entry is needed to restate the investment account and the retained earnings of P to the equity basis as of the beginning of the current year so that the investment account can be cleanly eliminated against S's beginning shareholders' equity.

Now the revenue and expense accounts of P and S are combined to obtain the consolidated totals. If intercompany revenues and expenses are also present, they are eliminated as shown in a subsequent section. *Consolidated net income* equals the net income of P from its own operations plus P's share of S's net income less any purchase amortization. If minority interest is present, its share of the subsidiary's net income must be deducted in determining consolidated net income as described in the next section.

The consolidated statement of retained earnings discloses beginning consolidated retained earnings plus consolidated net income for the year minus dividends declared to the *controlling interest* (P's shareholders). If P uses the equity method, the consolidated statement of retained earnings is identical to P's own statement of retained earnings.

Procedures when a minority interest is present. Working paper elimination of P's entries made under the equity method adjusts the investment account to its beginning-of-year balance. It is eliminated against S's beginning-of-year shareholders' equity accounts and the minority interest is established as of that date. Because the minority shares in both S's income and dividends, the following working paper entry is needed to reflect the *change in the minority interest during the current year*. The numbers reflect the minority's 20 percent shares of S's 19X1 net income and dividends, $55,000 and $20,000, respectively.

Consolidated Financial Statement Working Paper

Minority Interest in Net Income	11,000	
Dividends—S (or Retained Earnings—S)		4,000
Minority Interest in S............................		7,000
To record the change in the minority interest during 19X1.		

The Minority Interest in Net Income appears in the consolidated income statement as a deduction in computing consolidated net income. S's dividends are now fully eliminated, and the book value of the Minority Interest in S, which grew by $7,000 during 19X1, is shown in the consolidated balance sheet at its year-end balance of $107,000 [= .2($500,000 + $55,000 − $20,000)].

Assume that P Company reported net income from its own operations (i.e., excluding the equity method accrual) of $200,000 in 19X1. Given that S's reported net income was $55,000 and that purchase premium amortization of $7,000 was expensed, the lower part of the consolidated income statement appears as follows.

Income before minority interest in net income	$248,000
Minority interest in net income...................	11,000
Consolidated net income......................	$237,000

Observe that consolidated net income of $237,000 equals P's recorded net income of $237,000 (= $200,000 + $37,000), including the equity method accrual.

Business Combinations during an Accounting Period. Many business combinations occur during an accounting period, rather than at the beginning or end of one. No special problems are created in an intraperiod *pooling*, because the pooling rules call for consolidated net income to include P's share of S's net income for the entire year. In a *purchase*, however, the subsidiary's earnings begin accruing to the controlling interest only *after* the date of business combination. Therefore, consolidated net income must exclude any of the subsidiary's income earned prior to the acquisition by P. Two alternative treatments in the consolidated income statement are available to achieve this result.

1. Include only the subsidiary's revenue and expenses arising *after* date of acquisition in the consolidated income statement and base the minority interest in net income on S's postacquisition earnings. This calls for closing S's books at date of acquisition and eliminating S's retained earnings at that date.

2. Report the subsidiary's revenues and expenses for the *entire year* and show a deduction for *preacquisition earnings*—P's share of the subsidiary's net income prior to date of acquisition—in the consolidated income statement. S's

books are not closed at date of acquisition, and its retained earnings at the beginning of the year will be eliminated.

Although Accounting Research Bulletin No. 51 [CAP, 1959, par. 11] expresses a preference for the second treatment, both will be illustrated. Suppose that P acquires a 90 percent interest in S on September 30, 19X1. P and S report on a calendar-year basis. S's earnings and dividends occurred evenly over the year and amounted to $100,000 and $40,000, respectively. Total revenues and expenses for the two companies (from their own operations) are given next.

	P Company	S Company
Revenues	$1,000,000	$400,000
Expenses	800,000	300,000
Net income from own operations	$ 200,000	$100,000

Comparative consolidated income statements prepared under the two alternative treatments for the intrayear combination follow.

	P and S consolidated	
	Method 1	Method 2
Revenues	$1,100,000 (1)	$ 1,400,000
Expenses	(875,000) (2)	(1,100,000)
Minority interest in net income	(2,500) (3)	(10,000) (4)
Preacquisition earnings		(67,500) (5)
Consolidated net income	$ 222,500	$ 222,500

(1) $1,100,000 = $1,000,000 + .25 × $400,000.
(2) $875,000 = $800,000 + .25 × $300,000.
(3) $2,500 = .1 × .25 × $100,000 (for 3 months).
(4) $10,000 = .1 × $100,000 (for 12 months).
(5) $67,500 = .9 × .75 × $100,000.

The working paper entries made in method 1 cause no special problems. Minority Interest in Net Income is $2,500 for the period after acquisition and the change in the minority interest amounts to $1,500, reflecting the minority's share of S's dividends for 3 months, $1,000 (= .1 × .25 × $40,000). Under method 2, however, the investment elimination entry incorporates the preacquisition earnings of $67,500 (a debit) and P's share of S's preacquisition dividends (a credit) of $27,000 (= .9 × .75 × $40,000). Taken together, they reflect elimination of P's share of the change in S's retained earnings during the preacquisition period, $40,500 [= $67,500 − $27,000 = .9 × .75 ($100,000 − $40,000)].

Consolidated Statement of Changes in Financial Position. The technique for preparing a consolidated statement of changes in financial position (SCFP) parallels that in the single-entity case. Comparative consolidated balance sheets, the intervening consolidated statement of income and retained earnings, and supplementary information regarding asset dispositions, debt issues, and so on, are the essential ingredients. Some items frequently appearing in a consolidated SCFP, however, deserve special mention.

1. In determining funds provided by operations, amortization of goodwill arising in consolidation must, like depreciation expense, be added back to consolidated net income.

2. Minority Interest in Net Income, a nonfund expense deducted in computing consolidated net income, must be added back in computing funds provided by operations. Similarly, the minority interest in a subsidiary's net loss must be subtracted from consolidated net income.

3. Dividends paid to minority shareholders are shown as a nonoperating use of funds, separate from P's dividends.

4. Purchase of additional subsidiary shares in the open market constitutes a nonoperating use of funds. In contrast, if the shares are purchased directly from the subsidiary, there is no effect on consolidated funds.

INTERCOMPANY TRANSACTIONS

Affiliated corporations often engage in transactions with each other, referred to as *intercompany transactions*. Because these transactions do not involve outside parties and generally cannot be considered arms'-length, their effects must be eliminated when consolidated statements are prepared. Recall that the purpose of consolidated statements is to present the financial affairs of corporations under common control as those of a single unified economic entity, thereby reflecting the results of transactions with external parties. The two general types of intercompany transactions and intercompany bondholdings are discussed below.

Intercompany Revenues and Expenses. Sales of goods or services between affiliated corporations produce offsetting revenues and expenses on the books of the companies involved. Because the transacting companies have already recorded (or will record) purchase or sale transactions with outside parties, the intercompany revenue and expense are eliminated in their entirety in consolidation. Moreover, if any intercompany receivables or payables exist (e.g., unpaid invoices, advances, or loans), they too must be eliminated because no outside parties are involved. Elimination of such transactions avoids *double counting* of revenues, expenses, assets, and liabilities. Note that the percentage of P's ownership of S is irrelevant—the *total* recorded amount is eliminated.

For example, suppose that P Company performs computer analysis for S Company and bills S $20,000 per month for this service. Two months' charges remain unpaid at year-end. Further suppose that S sells component parts to P, which P incorporates in merchandise that it sells externally. During the year, S billed P $430,000 for these component parts, of which $70,000 had not been paid at year-end. The necessary working paper eliminations are given next.

Consolidated Financial Statement Working Paper

Computer Service Revenue	240,000	
Computer Service Expense		240,000

To eliminate intercompany computer service revenue and expense; $240,000 = 12 \times \$20,000$.

Merchandise Sales	430,000	
Merchandise Purchases (or Cost of Goods Sold)		430,000

To eliminate intercompany sale of component parts.

Accounts Payable	110,000	
Accounts Receivable		110,000

To eliminate intercompany payables and receivables; $110,000 = (2 \times \$20,000) + \$70,000$.

Without these eliminations, consolidated revenues and expenses would be overstated by $670,000 (= \$240,000 + \$430,000)$ and consolidated assets and liabilities by $110,000.

Unconfirmed Profits or Losses on Intercompany Asset Transfers. An additional problem arises when assets are sold within an affiliated group at prices different from cost on the books of the selling company. If those assets remain *within* the affiliated group at year-end, any profit or loss tentatively recorded by the selling affiliate is *unconfirmed* by external transactions and must be eliminated. Put another way, the internally transferred assets must be stated at acquisition cost to the consolidated entity. GAAP do not permit upward revaluation of assets unless the change in valuation is signaled by a completed market transaction. Even declines are generally not recorded unless the lower-of-cost-or-market rule is operative, as with inventories and marketable equity securities. In the discussion that follows, the focus is on intercompany *profit;* the same principles apply with equal force to intercompany losses.

It is generally agreed that the presence of a minority interest does not affect the amount of unconfirmed intercompany profit to be eliminated—it *all* must be removed. Although Accounting Research Bulletin No. 51 permits total elimination of the intercompany profit against the controlling interest, even if the selling company is a partially owned subsidiary, common practice eliminates the unconfirmed intercompany profit proportionally from both the controlling and minority interests if the seller is a partially owned subsidiary.[6]

In addressing these issues and the related consolidation procedures, it is helpful to distinguish between *downstream sales*—from parent to subsidiary—and *upstream sales*—from subsidiary to parent. Having made this distinction, unconfirmed intercompany profit on downstream sales is eliminated entirely against the controlling interest. Unconfirmed intercompany profit on upstream sales is eliminated proportionately against the controlling and minority interests; the Minority Interest in Net Income is reduced by the minority's proportionate share of eliminated unconfirmed profit on upstream sales.

---

[6]Accounting Research Bulletin No. 51 [CAP, 1959], par. 14. Refer, however, to Smolinski [1963].

Effect on the equity method accrual. Recall that APB Opinion No. 18 views application of the equity method as a *one-line consolidation*, reflecting all items that influence the determination of consolidated net income. The effect of purchase premium amortization on P's equity method accrual was discussed in a previous section. If unconfirmed intercompany profits are present, the equity method accrual is determined as follows, assuming that P owns 80 percent of S.

Computation of P's Equity Method Accrual

80% of S Company's reported net income	XXX
Less purchase premium amortization	(XX)
Less 100% of unconfirmed intercompany profit on downstream sales	(XX)
Less 80% of unconfirmed intercompany profit on upstream sales	(XX)
P's equity method accrual	XXX

Similarly, the Minority Interest in Net Income is determined as shown below.

Computation of Minority Interest in Net Income

20% of S Company's reported net income	XX
Less 20% of unconfirmed intercompany profit on upstream sales	(X)
Minority Interest in Net Income	XX

Therefore, the 20 percent portion of unconfirmed intercompany profit on upstream sales is charged against the minority interest by reducing the Minority Interest in Net Income, decreasing that deduction in the consolidated income statement. Moreover, consistent application of the equity method by P results in P's books reflecting net income and retained earnings equal to the respective consolidated amounts.

Income tax effects. If P Company and its subsidiaries file a consolidated income tax return, unconfirmed intercompany profits and losses are eliminated on the return and no special accounting problems result. In contrast, if the affiliates file separate income tax returns, unconfirmed intercompany profits and losses are *not* eliminated for tax purposes, and timing differences between consolidated net income for public reporting purposes and the affiliates' combined tax return incomes arise. The interperiod tax allocation provisions of APB Opinion No. 11 [1967] become operative. For example, if taxes are paid on intercompany profits eliminated in consolidation, these taxes must be classified as *prepaid* in consolidation. When the intercompany profit is confirmed in a subsequent period, the taxes previously paid must be recognized as a current period expense. In the next section, a numerical example illustrates the consolidation procedures necessary to deal with unconfirmed intercompany profits and the related tax effects.

Unconfirmed Intercompany Profits: An Example. Assume that P owns 80 percent of S's shares, purchased at book value several years ago, and accounts for them using the *equity method*. During the current year, 19X2, the following intercompany transactions occurred.

1. Intercompany merchandise transactions.

	P Company	S Company
Intercompany merchandise sales . .	$400,000	$150,000
Unconfirmed intercompany profit in beginning inventory	10,000	20,000
Unconfirmed intercompany profit in ending inventory	8,000	30,000

2. On January 2, 19X2, S sold a piece of equipment to P for $80,000. The equipment cost $60,000 two years ago and is being depreciated by the straight-line method over 10 years. Accumulated depreciation at date of sale was $12,000; S recorded a gain of $32,000. P owns the equipment at the end of 19X2 and has recorded depreciation of $10,000 (= $80,000/8).

3. On June 30, 19X2, P sold a parcel of land to S for $40,000. P had purchased the land for $30,000 during 19X1 and recorded a $10,000 gain. S owns the land at year-end.

4. P and S reported net incomes from their own operations in 19X2 of $300,000 and $200,000, respectively.

5. Both companies file separate income tax returns and face a marginal tax rate of 40 percent. (The possible capital gains treatment of the sales of land and equipment are ignored for simplicity.) Working paper eliminations are presented in sequence below.

Consolidated Financial Statement Working Paper

(1) Sales   550,000

  Cost of Goods Sold   550,000

  To eliminate intercompany merchandise sales.

(2) Retained Earnings—S   10,000

  Investment in S   20,000

  Cost of Goods Sold   30,000

  To eliminate intercompany profit in beginning inventory by reducing Cost of Goods Sold. The portion pertaining to S was recorded as profit in 19X1 and must be removed from S's retained earnings. The $20,000 relating to P was credited to the investment account via the 19X1 equity method accrual and now must be added back.

(3) Income Tax Expense   12,000

  Retained Earnings—S   4,000

  Investment in S   8,000

  To show the related income taxes as an expense of the current period. The credits to Retained Earnings—S and Investment in S are needed to adjust

the profits eliminated in (2) to an aftertax basis;
$4,000 = .4 \times $10,000; $8,000 = .4 \times $20,000.

(4) Cost of Goods Sold	38,000	
Inventory		38,000
To eliminate unconfirmed intercompany profits in ending inventory, thereby increasing the Cost of Goods Sold.		

(5) Prepaid Income Taxes	15,200	
Income Tax Expense		15,200
To classify as prepaid the income taxes accrued or paid on the intercompany profits eliminated from the ending inventory; $15,200 = .4 \times $38,000.		

(6) Gain on Sale of Land	10,000	
Land		10,000
To eliminate the unconfirmed gain on the intercompany sale of land and reduce the land to its original acquisition cost.		

(7) Prepaid Income Taxes	4,000	
Income Tax Expense		4,000
To classify as prepaid the income taxes accrued or paid on the eliminated intercompany gain from the sale of land; $4,000 = .4 \times $10,000.		

(8) Gain on Sale of Equipment	32,000	
Equipment		20,000
Accumulated Depreciation—Equipment		8,000
Depreciation Expense—Equipment		4,000
To eliminate the unconfirmed intercompany gain on the sale of equipment and adjust Equipment, Accumulated Depreciation, and Depreciation Expense to their original acquisition cost bases.		

Entry (8) deserves some additional explanation. Had the equipment *not* been sold, S's books would show depreciation expense of $6,000 (= $60,000/10) and accumulated depreciation of $18,000 (= 3 \times $6,000). P's books show accumulated depreciation and depreciation expense of $10,000 (= $80,000/8); entry (8) adjusts these amounts to $18,000 and $6,000, respectively. The gain is assumed confirmed as the equipment is depreciated. Thus the $4,000 reduction in recorded depreciation expense, one-eighth of the $32,000 gain assumed confirmed, is attributed to S Company, the seller.

(9) Prepaid Income Taxes	11,200	
Income Tax Expense		11,200
To classify as prepaid the income taxes accrued or paid on the unconfirmed portion of the gain on sale of equipment; $11,200 = .4 ($32,000 - $4,000).		

The equity method accrual and consolidated net income. P's equity method accrual is computed next.

Computation of the Equity Method Accrual

80% of S's reported net income of $200,000	$160,000
Less unconfirmed intercompany profits on downstream sales; $20,000 =	
−$20,000 + $30,000 + $10,000	(20,000)
Plus net tax reduction on the above; $8,000 = .4 ×$20,000	8,000
Less 80% of the unconfirmed intercompany profits on upstream sales; $20,800	
= .8(−$10,000 + $8,000 + $32,000− $4,000)	(20,800)
Plus the net tax reduction on the above; $8,320 = .4 × $20,800	8,320
Equity method accrual for 19X2	$135,520

Consolidated net income for 19X2 is $435,520 (= $300,000 + $135,520). After computing the minority interest in net income, another way of determining consolidated net income is illustrated.

Computation of Minority Interest in Net Income

Net income reported by S Company	$200,000
Less intercompany profits on upstream sales; $26,000 = −$10,000 +	
$8,000 + $32,000 − $4,000	(26,000)
Plus net tax reduction on the above; .4 × $26,000	10,400
Adjusted net income of S Company	$184,400
Multiplied by the minority ownership interest	× .2
Minority interest in net income	$ 36,880

Computation of Consolidated Net Income

Total net income reported by P and S...............................	$500,000
Less net unconfirmed intercompany profits; $46,000 = −$30,000 +	
$38,000 + $10,000 + $32,000 − $4,000	(46,000)
Plus net tax reduction on the above; .4 × $46,000	18,400
Less minority interest in net income computed above	(36,880)
Consolidated net income	$435,520

Intercompany Bondholdings. If one affiliate acquires newly issued bonds directly from the issuing affiliate, their cost equals the proceeds received by the issuer. In this case, the intercompany bond accounts, whether or not at par, will be equal and offsetting. Furthermore, the purchaser's periodic interest revenue equals the issuer's period interest expense, as long as both affiliates account for any unamortized discount or premium in the same way (which they should). Thus the intercompany bond accounts and the related intercompany interest revenue and expense can be easily eliminated at each consolidation point, as the bonds are *constructively retired* from the consolidated point of view.

In contrast, when the bonds of an affiliate are purchased in the open market, changes in interest rates since date of original issue will normally result in unequal intercompany bond accounts *and* unequal periodic intercompany interest revenue and expense. This set of circumstances produces the following considerations in consolidation.

1. In the year the bonds are acquired by the affiliate, a consolidated gain arises if the purchaser's cost is *less* than the issuer's liability. Conversely, a consolidated loss arises if the purchaser's cost is *greater* than the issuer's liability.

This gain or loss is recognized in consolidation when the intercompany bond accounts are eliminated.

2. Periodic intercompany interest revenue and expense as recorded by the affiliates differ because amortization of the purchaser's premium or discount on the bond investment will not equal amortization of the issuer's premium or discount on the bond liability.

3. In the years following acquisition of the bonds, care must be taken to ensure that the consolidated gain or loss recognized in consolidation in the year the bonds were acquired is not counted again as the affiliates amortize their respective premium or discount.

Several of these complexities are illustrated next.

On January 2, 19X2, P purchases $200,000 par value of S Company's 8 percent bonds for $185,000 cash in the open market, a discount of $15,000 below par. The bonds mature in 10 years and are carried on S's books at January 2, 19X2, at $210,000, reflecting an unamortized premium of $10,000. P owns 80 percent of S, and both companies use the straight-line method of amortization. At December 31, 19X2, the two companies' accounts include the following:

	P Company	S Company
Investment in bonds (par)	$200,000	
Discount on investment in bonds	(13,500)	
Bonds payable (par)		$(200,000)
Premium on bonds payable		(9,000)
Interest (revenue) expense	(17,500)	15,000

A consolidated gain of $25,000 was realized on January 2, 19X2, when the bond liability, carried at $210,000, was constructively retired at a cost of $185,000. Alternative views exist regarding the assignment of this gain: (1) assign it to the controlling interest because P presumably makes major investment and financing decisions for the group; (2) assign it to the issuer (S, in this case) on the grounds that P is acting as S's agent; (3) allocate it between P and S in accordance with their relative discount or premium. The third approach seems the most reasonable. Unless the bonds are actually retired, P and S will record a portion of the gain or loss each year until maturity as their respective discount or premium is amortized. The following working paper elimination is needed to remove the intercompany bond holding in consolidation at December 31, 19X2.

Consolidated Financial Statement Working Paper

Bonds Payable	200,000	
Premium on Bonds Payable	9,000	
Discount on Investment in Bonds	13,500	
Interest Revenue	17,500	
Investment in Bonds		200,000
Interest Expense		15,000
Gain on Retirement of Consolidated Debt		25,000

To eliminate the intercompany bondholding, the intercompany interest revenue and expense, and to recognize the gain on constructive retirement of the bonds.

Of the total $25,000 gain, $15,000 pertains to P and $10,000 to S. Moreover, $2,500 of the gain was recorded in 19X2 by the two companies as evidenced by the $2,500 difference between intercompany interest revenue and expense, due to amortization of the discount and premium. P's equity method accrual (and consolidated net income) is therefore increased by $20,700 (= $15,000 + .8 × $10,000 − $1,500 − .8 × $1,000). Similarly, the minority interest in net income is increased by $1,800 [= .2 ($10,000 − $1,000)]. In each subsequent year until maturity, the equity method accrual (and consolidated net income) and the minority interest in net income will be decreased by $2,300 and $200, respectively, in order that the total gain of $25,000 is not counted twice.

SUBSIDIARIES WITH PREFERRED STOCK

Valuation of the parent's interest in a subsidiary's common shareholders' equity is complicated if the subsidiary also has outstanding preferred stock. At acquisition, recognition must be given to the call price (or liquidation value if no call price exists) of the preferred stock and to any dividends in arrears on cumulative preferred stock, thereby affecting the amount of any purchase premium or discount on the investment in common. In consolidation, the corrected book value of the preferred stock must be established and disclosed as Minority Interest in Preferred. A working paper entry debiting Retained Earnings—S and crediting Preferred Stock may be necessary to reflect any prior year dividends in arrears and any excess of call price over par value. Furthermore, if the current year's dividends on cumulative preferred stock are in arrears, Minority Interest in Net Income must be charged and Preferred Stock credited for the arrearage on the working paper.

Parent's Investment in Subsidiary's Preferred Stock. Two issues arise when the parent acquires all or part of the subsidiary's outstanding preferred stock.

1. How should any difference between the cost and book value (properly computed) of the internally held preferred shares be treated in consolidation?
2. How should the investment in preferred stock be accounted for?

Suppose that the parent purchases the preferred stock for more than book value, implying a purchase premium. Because the market value of preferred stock is related to changes in interest rates, as opposed to changes in the value of the issuer's underlying assets and liabilities, the purchase premium (or discount) should not be allocated among the subsidiary's assets and liabilities, unlike the purchase premium on an investment in common. Rather, the purchase premium is viewed as a loss on the constructive retirement of preferred stock. Because this is analogous to the acquisition of treasury stock, when the Investment in Preferred is eliminated against the related portion of the subsidiary's Preferred Stock in consolidation, the purchase premium should be charged to Additional Paid-in Capital.

It is reasonable for the parent to carry the Investment in Preferred at *equity*, which follows from P's control over S's preferred dividend policy. Thus, if the preferred stock is *cumulative,* P's share of the annual preferred dividend (whether declared or not) is included in P's equity method accrual and the Investment in Preferred is increased accordingly. The investment account is reduced when the preferred dividends are declared. On the consolidated income statement, the Minority Interest in Net Income reflects the preferred dividends only on the shares held externally.

CHANGES IN DEGREE OF CONTROL

Changes in the parent's ownership interest in the subsidiary may occur because: (1) the parent purchases or sells additional subsidiary shares on the open market; (2) the subsidiary issues additional shares; or (3) the subsidiary engages in treasury stock transactions. These are discussed in turn.

Purchase or Sale by Parent. If the parent purchases additional blocks of the subsidiary's stock in the open market, the cost of each block must be compared with the book value of the subsidiary's shareholders' equity to determine the existence of a purchase premium or discount. Records should be kept for each block of stock purchased, indicating the portions of each purchase premium (or discount) allocated to reflect the fair value of the subsidiary's assets and liabilities, and goodwill. The same is true when the parent *achieves control* through a series of purchases. This procedure is consistent with an AICPA unofficial accounting interpretation of APB Opinion No. 17, *Goodwill in a Step Acquisition* [AICPA, 1973]. In effect, a parent achieving control in this way passes through the "equity method range," which, under APB Opinion No. 18, requires computation and amortization of fair values and goodwill. This supersedes the old "convenience" provision of Accounting Research Bulletin No. 51 [CAP, 1959, par. 10, in which the date of the latest purchase that leads to control may be used as the date of acquisition for the entire interest.

The principal problem arising when the parent sells some of its holdings relates to identifying the book value of the shares sold. When several blocks have been acquired at different dates, each block will normally have a different book value because the cost is different and the amount of unamortized purchase premium or discount differs. All blocks, however, should be carried at equity. When the shares are sold, the investment account is credited for their book value (based on specific identification, average cost, or a systematic policy such as first-in, first-out) and the unamortized purchase premium is adjusted. Gain or loss, equal to the difference between the proceeds and the book value of the shares sold, is recognized in the consolidated income statement. At subsequent consolidation points, amortization of the remaining purchase premium continues.

Issuance of Shares by the Subsidiary. If, as a result of new stock issues by the subsidiary, the parent's ownership interest changes, an accounting problem arises. Suppose that the subsidiary issues additional shares at more than book value, causing the parent's ownership interest to decline from 90 percent to 80 percent. Because the total book value of the subsidiary's shareholders' equity rises by more than a proportional increase in the existing book value, the book value of the parent's reduced interest also rises. In effect, the minority shareholders contribute capital that proportionately accrues to the controlling interest. The parent has clearly realized a gain. Yet such a "gain" is normally treated as additional paid-in capital (i.e., as a capital transaction) by the parent, following a position taken by the SEC—"No profits on the person's own equity securities, or profits of its affiliates on their own equity securities, shall be included under this caption" (i.e., *profits on securities*) [Rappaport, 1972, p. 18-28]. This matter is illustrated next.

Suppose that P owns 900,000 of S's 1,000,000 shares, each having a book value (to P and S) of $10. S issues 125,000 new shares for $15 each, a total of $1,875,000, none of which are purchased by P and P's ownership interest falls to 80 percent (= 900,000/1,125,000). The effect on the book value of P's interest is as follows.

	S Company	
	Before stock issue	After stock issue
Book value of shareholders' equity	$10,000,000	$11,875,000
P's ownership interest	(×) .9	(×) .8
Book value of P's interest	$ 9,000,000	$ 9,500,000
Gain realized by P = $9,500,000 − $9,000,000		$ 500,000

Note that a similar result would have occurred if P had sold 100,000 of its S Company shares for $1,500,000. Yet practice generally treats the two "gains" differently. If P sells the shares, the gain is recognized in the income statement; but if S sells the shares, the gain is entered directly in Additional Paid-in Capital. Both transactions produce identical economic gains to the parent, and both should be given the same accounting treatment, preferably by recording them in income.

Subsidiary Treasury Stock Transactions. Purchase of treasury stock by the subsidiary at more or less than book value produces results similar to the above, although the parent's percentage ownership interest rises rather than falls. If the treasury shares are acquired at *more* than book value, the subsidiary's shareholders' equity decreases by *more* than the increase in the parent's ownership interest, producing a *loss*. In contrast, if the shares are purchased for *less* than their book value, the subsidiary's shareholders' equity is reduced by *less* than the increase in the parent's ownership interest, producing a *gain*. Despite the similarity to the case where the subsidiary simply issues more shares, it is difficult to justify recognizing a gain or loss on a "purchase," so the increase or

EXHIBIT 4   Indirect Holdings. Alpha (α) Refers to the Ownership Percentage. For Example, α_{PS} Is the Percentage of S's Shares Owned by P.

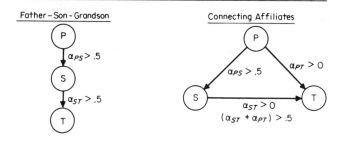

Father – Son – Grandson

Connecting Affiliates

decrease in the investment account should be credited or debited to Additional Paid-in Capital.

COMPLEX OWNERSHIP RELATIONSHIPS

To this point, the discussion of consolidated statements has been limited to situations in which the parent has a direct investment in one or more subsidiaries. Of course, the relationships among affiliates may be more complex: The subsidiary may itself be a holding company with one or more subsidiaries (*indirect holdings*, Exhibit 4); or some or all of the affiliates may own shares in each other (*mutual holdings*, Exhibit 5).

Indirect Holdings. Consolidation of indirect holdings involves an important conceptual accounting problem and an important procedural technique. The *conceptual problem* arises when the parent acquires a subsidiary that *already* is a holding company; that is, it has one or more subsidiaries of its own. In this case, the price paid by P for its interest in S is often influenced by the fact that S controls T. In other words, are the fair values of T's assets and liabilities relevant in determining the price paid for S? (Note that this issue does not arise if P controls S *before* S acquires controlling interest in T.) Two alternative

EXHIBIT 5   Mutual Holdings

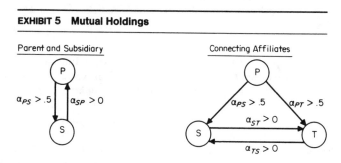

Parent and Subsidiary

Connecting Affiliates

approaches exist to the allocation of a purchase premium when P acquires S, a holding company. One approach attributes the entire purchase premium to S and disregards any changes in the fair values of T's assets and liabilities (i.e., S's Investment in T is fairly stated). The second approach views the acquisition of S as securing a controlling interest in the assets and liabilities of *both* S and T; hence, both must be considered in the purchase premium allocation process.

For example, suppose that P acquires an 80 percent interest in S for $6,000,000 cash. S has a 70 percent interest in T, carried at equity of $1,600,000. Condensed balance sheet data for S and T when P acquires the stock of S are given below.

| | Balance sheet data when P acquires 80% of S | | | |
| | S Company | | T Company | |
	Book value	Fair value	Book value	Fair value
Various assets (net).	$4,000,000	$5,000,000	$2,000,000	$2,800,000
Investment in T	1,600,000			
Total net assets (= shareholders' equity).	$5,600,000		$2,000,000	

Because 70 percent of T's shareholders' equity is $1,400,000, the Investment in T includes an unamortized purchase premium of $200,000, which is assumed to relate to T's net assets, not goodwill. If P's purchase premium of $1,520,000 (= $6,000,000 − .8 × $5,600,000) is allocated entirely to S, net asset revaluations will be $800,000 [= .8 × ($5,000,000 − $4,000,000)] and goodwill amounts to $720,000 (= $1,520,000 − $800,000).

Alternatively, if P's purchase premium in S is allocated to *both* S and T, the amount of goodwill is cut in half, as shown below.

(1) Amount attributed to S's undervalued net assets [.8($5,000,000 − $4,000,000)]	$ 800,000
(2) Amount attributed to T's undervalued net assets [.7($2,800,000 − $2,000,000)]	560,000
(3) Amount of (2) already included in the Investment in T . .	(200,000)
(4) Unallocated purchase premium attributed to goodwill	360,000
Total purchase premium	$1,520,000

Allocation of the purchase premium among the assets and liabilities of both S and T is preferable as long as reliable estimates of fair values can be obtained for T's assets and liabilities. On a consolidated financial statement working paper, the amount of P's purchase premium in S attributable to T, $360,000 (= $560,000 − $200,000), is reclassified from the Investment in S to the Investment in T at the beginning of the consolidation process.

The *procedural technique* in consolidating an indirect holding pertains to the order of consolidation: Consolidate S and T *before* consolidating P and S. This is helpful because P's equity method accrual, S's equity method accrual, and the minority interest in S's and T's net incomes are based in part on the elimination of unconfirmed intercompany profits relating to S and T. In a complex consolidation, of course, detailed schedules could be prepared to support summary eliminating entries, thereby removing the need for any specific order of consolidation.

Mutual Holdings. Also known as *bilateral* or *reciprocal* holdings, *mutual* holdings arise when one or more subsidiaries own stock in the parent or in each other.[7] The basic mutual holding relationships are diagrammed in Exhibit 5.

No minority interest. No special problems relate to mutual holdings when no minority interest is present. No allocation of income among the affiliates is necessary because it all pertains to the controlling interest. In the *parent/subsidiary* case, the shares of P owned by S are reclassified as *treasury stock* in consolidation; any purchase premium or discount implicit in the price paid by S for P's shares is considered part of the cost of the treasury stock and is not allocated or amortized. The treasury stock interpretation is not relevant in the *connecting affiliates* case because none of P's shares are held internally. Rather, any purchase premium or discount implicit in the subsidiaries' investments in each other must be allocated and amortized in consolidation, *just as if the parent company had acquired the shares directly.* As long as no minority interest is present, the subsidiaries' investments in the parent or in each other may be carried at cost with attendant elimination of any intercompany dividends.

Parent/subsidiary: minority interest present. The basic issue concerns how to allocate the total net income of the affiliates among the controlling and minority interests. In the *parent/subsidiary* case, there are two alternatives, which in general lead to different consolidated results.

Under the *treasury stock method*, supported by an early position taken by the American Accounting Association [Committee on Accounting Concepts and Standards, 1957, p. 44], the minority interest in the subsidiary's net income includes a pro rata share of any dividend revenue from the parent but does not include any of the parent's net income. The Investment in P is carried at *cost* and is reclassified in consolidation as Treasury Stock. For example, suppose that P owns 80 percent of S and S owns 10 percent of P. During the year, the following occurred.

	P Company	S Company
Net income from own operations	$200,000	$80,000
Dividends declared and paid	60,000	20,000

Pursuant to the treasury stock method, P's equity method accrual amounts to $62,800 [= .8 × $80,000 − .2 × $6,000 (the minority's share of P's dividends received by S)] and consolidated net income is $262,800 (= $200,000 + $62,800).

---

[7]Issues related to this general problem are discussed in detail by Weil [1973].

The minority interest in net income is $17,200 [= .2($80,000 + $6,000)]. Thus consolidated net income of $262,800 plus the minority interest in net income of $17,200 equals the combined income of the affiliates from their own operations, $280,000.

In contrast, the *traditional allocation method* calls for carrying the Investment in P at *equity* so that the minority interest shares in P's net income, not S's dividend revenue from P. Note that P's total earnings under the equity method depend in part on S's earnings. But because S owns some of P's shares, S's earnings under the equity method (and the minority interest in S's earnings) also depend on P's earnings. Thus there exists a circularity or interdependence between the earnings of P and S because each is influenced by the other. Proper allocation of the combined earnings of P and S between the controlling and minority interests is facilitated by the use of simultaneous equations that take into account the interdependence between P and S. The following general relationships are used.

$$P^* = \text{P Company's net income on an equity basis}$$
$$S^* = \text{S Company's net income on an equity basis}$$
$$Y_P = \text{net income of P from its own operations}$$
$$Y_S = \text{net income of S from its own operations}$$
$$\alpha_{PS} = \text{percentage of S's shares owned by P}$$
$$\alpha_{SP} = \text{percentage of P's shares owned by S}$$

P^* and S^* can be expressed as follows.

$$P^* = Y_P + \alpha_{PS}S^* \quad \text{and} \quad S^* = Y_S + \alpha_{SP}P^*$$

Note that $(P^* + S^*) > (Y_P + Y_S)$ as some income is double-counted. Therefore, P^* and S^* are *tentative* and will be reduced to reflect the controlling and minority interests in these equity basis net incomes. The technique is illustrated using the data presented previously in connection with the treasury stock method.

$$P^* = \$200,000 + .8S^* \qquad\qquad (1)$$

$$S^* = \$80,000 + .2P^* \qquad\qquad (2)$$

Substituting (2) into (1), we have

$$P^* = \$200,000 + .8(\$80,000 + .2P^*)$$
$$.84P^* = \$264,000$$
$$P^* = \$314,286$$

and

$$S^* = \$80,000 + .2(\$314,286)$$
$$= \$142,857$$

These amounts must be reduced as follows.

P Company's net income on an equity basis (P^*)	$314,286
Less amount attributable to S (.2 × $314,286)	(62,857)
Controlling interest's share of combined income	$251,429

S Company's net income on an equity basis (S^*).	$142,857
Less amount attributable to P (.8 × $142,857).	(114,286)
Minority interest in net income	$ 28,571
Combined net income of P and S from their own operations	$280,000

Comparing the results from application of the treasury stock and traditional allocation methods, we have

	(1) Treasury stock method	(2) Traditional allocation method	(3) (1)/(2) (%)
Controlling interest's share of combined income	$262,800	$251,429	104.5%
Minority interest's share of combined income	17,200	28,571	60.2

Column (3) shows that the results of the two methods, both generally accepted, can be materially different.

Under the traditional allocation method, both P and S carry their investments in each other's stock at equity. P's equity method accrual is $51,429, the amount needed to increase P's income from its own operations, $200,000, up to the controlling interest's share of combined income, $251,429. S Company will record $62,857, increasing its income from its own operations, $80,000, to the equity basis amount of $142,857.

Despite the conceptual appeal of the traditional allocation method in a parent/subsidiary mutual holding, the *treasury stock method* is more appropriate for two reasons.

1. From the standpoint of the controlling interest, any shares of P held by S have all the essential characteristics of treasury stock.

2. In most situations, use of the equity method to account for S's investment in P seems improper. This follows from the notion explained in APB Opinion No. 18 and elaborated on in FASB Interpretation No. 35 [1981], that the equity method is appropriate only if the investor can exercise significant influence over the investee. This is hardly true in the present case because P (the investee) controls S (the investor). Of course, if the minority shareholders of S also control large blocks of P's stock, the equity method—and the traditional allocation method—may well be appropriate.

Connecting affiliates: minority interest present. In this case, the subsidiaries hold no shares of the parent and the traditional allocation method must be used by S and T to determine their equity basis incomes. Although one could argue against use of the equity method by S and T on the grounds that they are *both* controlled by P, it must be remembered that P's control over S and T is related to its direct interest in S and T *and* to its indirect interest in the S and T mutual holding. Consequently, P's equity method accrual and the controlling interest's share of combined income are influenced by the circularity between S and T.

To solve the problem, simultaneous equations similar to those presented in the last section are solved for S^* and T^*. The controlling interest's share of combined income equals P's net income from its own operations plus P's respective percentage shares of S^* and T^*. The minority interest in net income consists of the minority ownership percentages in S and T multiplied by S^* and T^*, respectively.

CONSOLIDATION OF FOREIGN SUBSIDIARIES

Consolidated statements are generally appropriate for U.S. companies with foreign subsidiaries. The foreign entity's statements must first be measured in the foreign currency according to U.S. generally accepted accounting principles and then translated into dollars for consolidation with the U.S. parent. The translation principles are explained in Chapter 35 of this handbook.

The case for consolidation of foreign subsidiaries is not clear-cut. Chapter 12 of Accounting Research Bulletin No. 43 [CAP, 1953, chap. 12] expresses concern over the inclusion of translated foreign operations in U.S. company statements. Foreign operations are inherently risky—distant geographical locations subject to foreign sovereign states—and care should be taken in deciding whether to report foreign earnings in excess of amounts remitted or available for unrestricted transmission to the United States. The U.S. company *must* have effective control over the assets of its foreign operations to justify consolidation. If the foreign political regime is hostile and the realization of the foreign assets uncertain, or if controls over the conversion of foreign currency into dollars or other acceptable international reserves exist, consolidation may not be appropriate and the foreign operations should be reported according to one of the alternative formats described in Chapter 12 of Accounting Research Bulletin No. 43.

BIBLIOGRAPHY

Accountants International Study Group, *Consolidated Financial Statements: Current Recommended Practices in Canada, the United Kingdom, and the United States* (Curwen Press, Plainstow, England, 1973); also available from the AICPA.

Accounting Principles Board (AICPA), *Accounting for Income Taxes*, Opinion No. 11 (APB, 1967).

———, *Business Combinations*, Opinion No. 16 (APB, 1970).

———, *Intangible Assets*, Opinion No. 17 (APB, 1970).

———, *Basic Concepts and Accounting Principles underlying Financial Statements of Business Enterprises*, Statement No. 4 (APB, 1970).

———, *The Equity Method of Accounting for Investments in Common Stock*, Opinion No. 18 (APB, 1971).

———, *Disclosure of Accounting Policies*, Opinion No. 22 (APB, 1972).

American Institute of Certified Public Accountants, *Goodwill in a Step Acquisition*, an unofficial interpretation of APB Opinion No. 17 (AICPA, 1973).

———, *Accounting Trends and Techniques* (AICPA, 1979).

Beams, F. A., *Advanced Accounting*, 2d ed. (Prentice-Hall, Englewood Cliffs, N.J., 1982).

Committee on Accounting Concepts and Standards, *Accounting and Reporting Standards for Corporate Financial Statements* (American Accounting Association, Columbus, Ohio, 1957).

Committee on Accounting Procedure (AICPA), *Restatement and Revision of Accounting Research Bulletins*, Accounting Research Bulletin No. 43 (CAP, 1953).

————, *Consolidated Financial Statements*, Accounting Research Bulletin No. 51 (CAP, 1959).

Financial Accounting Standards Board, *Accounting for Business Combinations and Purchased Intangibles*, Discussion Memorandum (FASB, 1976).

————, *Criteria for Applying the Equity Method of Accounting for Investments in Common Stock*, Interpretation No. 35 (FASB, 1981).

Griffin, C. H., T. H. Williams, and K. D. Larson, *Advanced Accounting*, 4th ed. (Richard D. Irwin, Homewood, Ill., 1980).

Huefner, R.J., and J. A. Largay III, *Advanced Financial Accounting* (Dryden Press, Hinsdale, Ill., 1982).

Moonitz, M., *The Entity Theory of Consolidated Statements*, American Accounting Association Monograph No. 4 (AAA, 1944).

Rappaport, L.H., *SEC Accounting Practice and Procedure*, 3d ed. (Ronald Press Company, New York, 1972).

Smolinski, E. J., "The Adjunct Method in Consolidations," *Journal of Accounting Research*, vol. 1, no. 2 (1963), pp. 149–178.

Weil, R. L., "Reciprocal or Mutual Holdings: Allocating Earnings and Selecting the Accounting Method," *The Accounting Review*, vol. 48, no. 4 (October 1973), pp. 749–758.

CHAPTER **35**

Foreign Exchange

Transactions

and Translations

Hector R. Anton
Retired Partner, Deloitte Haskins & Sells
Director, V. C. Ross Institute of Accounting
Research, New York University

Prior to issuance of Financial Accounting Standards Board (FASB) Statement of Financial Accounting Standards (SFAS) No. 8, *Accounting for the Translation of Foreign Currency Transactions and Foreign Currency Financial Statements*, in 1975, foreign currency translation was guided by Chapter 12 of Accounting Research Bulletin (ARB) No. 43, *Foreign Operations and Foreign Exchange*, dated June 1953, as modified by paragraph 18 of Accounting Principles Board (APB) Opinion No. 6. Chapter 12 of ARB No. 43 called for the translation of current assets and liabilities at the current rate and noncurrent assets and liabilities at historical rates, the so-called *current–noncurrent method*. In certain circumstances various alternatives were permitted, however, including the inclusion of inventory at historical rates, and the restatement of long-term debt or capital stock issued in connection with long-term assets at new rates if permanent changes in the rate took place; exchange losses and realized gains were included in income, but unrealized gains were included in income only to the extent that they offset exchange losses previously included in net income. Moreover, APB Opinion No. 6 specified that "translation of long-term receivables and long-term liabilities at current rates is appropriate in many circumstances." This, in effect, permitted (but did not require) the *monetary–nonmonetary* method of translation.

Discontent with the number of alternative accounting practices that arose after the issuance of Chapter 12 of ARB No. 43 as modified led the Accounting Principles Board to restudy the issue. The APB issued an Exposure Draft in December 1971 that was intended to give guidance in dealing with this problem. An Accounting Research Study of the AICPA was in progress at the time, and it was concluded that the APB should await the publication of the Research Study before issuing a definitive Opinion. Later, it became apparent that the FASB would supersede the APB. SFAS No. 8, issued in October 1975, governed practice until fiscal years beginning after December 15, 1982, when SFAS No. 52, *Foreign Currency Translation,* issued in December 1981, became required.

Those who wish to review various concepts, principles, and methods should refer to the FASB Discussion Memorandum on this subject dated February 21, 1974. In March 1974, the FASB released a Financial Statement Model on Accounting for Foreign Currency Translation prepared by its research staff for illustrative purposes. Those wishing to study further the "cause and effect" of various methods in use prior to the issuance of SFAS No. 8 will find this material useful.

From the beginning, certain provisions of SFAS No. 8 were not well received. Partly this was due to poor timing; about the time that SFAS No. 8 was issued, the U.S. dollar and many other currencies were permitted to float freely in the market. The results were (1) fluctuating exchange rates, and (2) the weakening of the U.S. dollar relative to certain of its major trading partners. Also, reported inflation occurred in many countries, and the differential inflation rates affected the exchange rates. In any event, SFAS No. 8 was widely criticized on the following grounds:

> That it unduly emphasized fluctuations in exchange rates by reporting exchange gains and losses and translation adjustments in current income
>
> That it failed to recognize extensive economic hedges of foreign exchange risk exposure
>
> That it resulted in reported (accounting) foreign currency exposure that was inconsistent with the concurrent economic exposure

In January 1979, the FASB added to its agenda a project to reconsider SFAS No. 8. On August 28, 1980, the FASB, by a narrow 4–3 vote issued an Exposure Draft, *Foreign Currency Translation* (the 1980 Exposure Draft), which provided the basis for written comments and testimony at public hearings. The 1980 Exposure Draft called for significant and basic changes in accounting and reporting from those required by SFAS No. 8 and it, in turn, was widely criticized, hotly disputed, and became a divisive issue among corporate accounting executives. The FASB spent the next year in trying to meet criticisms directed at the 1980 Exposure Draft, and on June 30, 1981, it issued a revised Exposure Draft, *Foreign Currency Translation* (the Exposure Draft), again by a 4–3 vote. This revised Exposure Draft was similar to the 1980 Exposure Draft but provided ad hoc solutions to several vexing problems. The FASB continued its deliberations for another 6 months, and in December 1981, again by a 4–3 vote, issued SFAS No. 52. SFAS No. 52's basis is drastically different from that of SFAS No. 8, but in at least two major areas—translation of financial statements of foreign entities operating in hyperinflationary economies and translation of financial statements of foreign entities whose functional currency is a currency other than that of its books of record—SFAS No. 52 requires procedures that are prescribed, with minor modifications, by SFAS No. 8. Accordingly, substantial use of the temporal (monetary-nonmonetary) basis will continue.

OBJECTIVES OF FOREIGN CURRENCY TRANSLATION

According to SFAS No. 52, the translation of the financial statements of each component foreign entity of an enterprise should:

> Provide information that is generally compatible with the expected economic effects of a rate change on an enterprise's cash flows and equity, and
>
> Reflect in consolidated statements the financial results and relationships of the individual consolidated entities as measured in their functional currencies in conformity with U.S. generally accepted accounting principles (GAAP).

To accomplish these objectives, SFAS No. 52 uses the current rate method to translate foreign entities' financial statements from the functional currency to the reporting currency of the consolidated entity. These methods are discussed in detail below.

SFAS No. 52's objectives, which were rejected in SFAS No. 8 (paragraphs 79, 93, and 97), avoid *remeasurement* into the reporting currency (presumably the U.S. dollar) except in the two major cases of hyperinflation and differing functional currency noted above. In these situations, the objective of SFAS No. 8, "to measure and express (a) in dollars and in conformity with U.S. generally accepted accounting principles the assets, liabilities, revenue or expenses that are measured or denominated in foreign currency," governs. This objective leads to the single-entity perspective of consolidated financial statements and to the use of the temporal method. The remeasurement process is discussed on pages 35-10 and 35-43.

FOREIGN CURRENCY FINANCIAL STATEMENTS

Paragraph 4 of SFAS No. 52 states that:

> Financial statements are intended to present information in financial terms about the performance, financial position and cash flows of an enterprise. For this purpose, the financial statements of separate **entities** within an enterprise, which may exist and operate in different economic and currency environments, are consolidated and presented as though they were the financial statements of a single enterprise.

Basic translation procedures apply equally to consolidated and unconsolidated subsidiaries, to branches, to more limited types of foreign operations, to investees accounted for by the equity method, and to unsettled transactions receivable or payable in foreign currency. The problems of the propriety of including foreign subsidiaries in consolidated financial statements and the reporting of an investment in and earnings of unconsolidated subsidiaries are discussed in general in Chapter 34.

For the translation of foreign currency statements, the following steps are ordinarily required:

Conform foreign currency statements to U.S. GAAP.

Ascertain the functional currency.

Remeasure any foreign currency statements into the functional currency, if:
   The foreign currency statements are those of a foreign entity operating in a hyperinflationary economy;
   The foreign currency statements are those of a foreign entity whose books of record are not maintained in its functional currency.

Translate the foreign currency financial statements (in functional currency) into the reporting currency using the current rate method.

Definitions. Certain terms used extensively throughout the succeeding discussion are defined below. The section of this chapter relating to selection of exchange rates should be read in conjunction with the definitions of the principal exchange rates commonly applied in practice (closing free exchange rate, average free exchange rate for the month, historical exchange rate).

Appendix E of SFAS No. 52 is a glossary of terms. The terms "temporal method" and "monetary/nonmonetary" are not used in SFAS No. 52, but because of their common usage, those definitions are retained in the supplementary glossary that follows.

Average free exchange rate for the month—Arithmetic average of daily free exchange rates for a month. The rate for each day is usually the average of the high and low quotations for that day. In cases of extreme fluctuation, weighted averages may be desirable (temporarily).

Average monthly free exchange rate—Arithmetic average of the rates quoted for the last day in each month for the period.

Black market rates—Exchange rates for buying or selling currency established by unauthorized dealers in foreign exchange, often in violation of governmental regulations, and almost invariably higher for purchasing a hard currency than the official or free rate for the same currency.

Blocked accounts—Bank accounts of nonresidents restricted by the monetary authorities of the country in which the accounts are located. Generally, the funds may be used within the country but cannot be exported or exchanged for other currencies.

Blocked currency—Currency completely restricted as to its exchange for dollars or other currencies except through special permission from the government imposing the restriction.

Composite rate—Rate expressing the relationship of translated units of one currency to units of another currency for the same item. In the United States, such rates are calculated by dividing the dollar balance of an account by its corresponding foreign currency balance.

Convertible currency—Currency that may be used without restriction, by both residents and nonresidents, for all trade and capital transactions and payments with any other country.

Devaluation—Governmental action lowering the value of the country's currency, either by reduction of its gold or silver backing or of its equivalent value in terms of other currencies.

Dividend rate—Exchange rate at which a company pays dividends to nonresident shareholders.

Dual currency records—Accounting records maintained simultaneously both in the local currency and in the foreign currency in which a specific transaction occurred. Normally, dual currency records need be maintained only for unsettled foreign currency accounts receivable and payable (and, of course, the parent's investment).

Free rates—Exchange rates at which local, U.S., Swiss, or other banks will buy or sell a currency.

Monetary assets and liabilities—An asset or liability that (1) is cash, (2) is a claim collectible in a fixed amount of cash, (3) is an obligation payable in a fixed amount of cash, or (4) is a valuation account for such an asset or liability. The fact that a monetary asset or liability is recorded at an estimated amount does not make it nonmonetary.

Multiple exchange rates—Several official exchange rates applicable to the same foreign currency. These various rates apply to specific transactions and are designed to encourage or discourage imports or exports of certain commodities and to conserve the country's supply of foreign currencies. The term may be applied to official and free rates for the same foreign currency.

Nonmonetary assets and liabilities—All assets and liabilities that are not monetary (the equity accounts are considered separately).

Official rate—Exchange rate at which the central bank or other monetary authority of a country will buy or sell its local currency.

Penalty rate—Official exchange rate applicable to particular transactions and designed to discourage such transactions. Such a rate is higher for purchasing dollars than the official rate for unregulated transactions.

Preference rate—Official exchange rate applicable to particular transactions and designed to encourage such transactions. Such a rate is lower for purchasing dollars than the official rate for unregulated transactions.

Prevailing rate—Exchange rate in effect at the time a specific transaction occurred, or, at which local currency was converted into a foreign currency (same as historical rate).

Remittance rates—Exchange rates at which foreign funds are remitted or may be remitted to another country.

Repatriation—Requirement of a government for a foreign company that makes export sales and receives payment in dollars to use a stated percentage of the dollars received from these sales to purchase currency of that country. Sometimes the government sets a special penalty rate at which the currency must be purchased and/or sets the sales price for the sole purpose of computing the amount returnable regardless of the actual negotiated sales price.

Unrealized exchange gain or loss—Gain or loss arising in translation of financial statements because of the effects of exchange rate fluctuations between the local currency and the dollar on the local currency monetary items. When deferrals of translation adjustments are prohibited, as in SFAS No. 8, the term has no application.

Year-end rate—Quoted exchange rate at the end of a company's fiscal year.

Conversion versus Translation. The difference between conversion and translation is important. *Conversion* is the actual exchange of currency of one country for that of another. A remittance of U.S. dollars to the United Kingdom is converted into sterling at the rate prevailing at the time of the remittance; there is no question as to what exchange rate is applicable.

Translation is the restatement of amounts in a given currency in terms of another currency by applying an exchange rate. The accounts of a foreign subsidiary or branch are restated in terms of U.S. dollars by applying "appropriate exchange rates." Foreign currency accounts on the books of importers and exporters are restated in terms of the dollar by applying "appropriate exchange rates." The decision about which exchange rates are "appropriate" is governed by SFAS No. 8 and SFAS No. 52.

CONFORMING FOREIGN CURRENCY STATEMENTS TO U.S. GAAP

Prior to translation, financial statements of foreign entities that are prepared for purposes of combination, consolidation, or equity accounting should be prepared in conformity with U.S. GAAP. There is little, if any, specific guidance given in SFAS No. 52 for this conformity, but it poses few, if any, conceptual problems.

THE FUNCTIONAL CURRENCY

Functional currency is defined as the currency of the primary economic environment in which the foreign entity operates and generates net cash flows. Generally, if the operations of the entity are relatively self-contained and integrated within a country, the functional currency would be that of the currency of that country. However, if the entity operates as a branch, a sales agency, or otherwise as a direct or integral component or extension of the reporting parent or another entity within the consolidated group, the parent company's or other entity's currency would be the functional currency. Also, an entity may have more than one functional currency if it has more than one distinct and separable operation.

Deciding on the Functional Currency. Deciding which is the functional currency of currencies may be difficult in some instances. Appendix A of SFAS No. 52 provides general guidance on facts to be considered in identifying the functional currency; but management's judgment is required to assess the facts and circumstances of a particular foreign entity's operations and to choose the functional currency when the indicators are mixed. Once such a choice is made, it should be followed consistently unless the facts and circumstances change significantly. Changes in the functional currency are to be made prospectively and in accordance with APB Opinion No. 20. Appendix A offers the following guidelines:

> Arbitrary and unequivocal criteria may give superficial uniformity but may diminish the relevance and reliability of the resulting information. Accordingly, management's judgment is necessary; salient economic factors should be considered individually and collectively when determining the functional currency.
>
> Use the foreign currency as the functional currency if:
>> The foreign entity's cash flows are related to its individual assets and liabilities and primarily in the foreign currency and do not directly impact the parent's cash flows.
>> The sales prices for the foreign entity's products are determined primarily by local competition or local regulation and not primarily responsive on a current or short-term basis to changes in exchange rates.
>> There is an active local market for the foreign entity's products or services even though significant exports may exist.
>> Labor, materials, and other costs for the foreign entity's products or services are primarily local costs even though significant imports may exist.
>> Financing is determined primarily in foreign currency and funds generated by the entity's operations are sufficient to service debt.
>> There is a relatively low volume of intercompany transactions and there is not an extensive interrelationship between the operations of the foreign entity and its parent.
>
> Use the parent company's currency as the functional currency if cash flows related to the foreign entity's assets and liabilities directly impact the parent's cash flow and are generally available for remittance through intercompany account settlements.

The use of significant management control over the foreign entity and the use of the parent company's currency for decision-making purposes does not determine, per se, that the parent's currency is the functional currency.

Functional Currency and Hyperinflation. When the foreign entity operates in a hyperinflationary economy, defined by SFAS No. 52 as one that has a cumulative inflation of approximately 100 percent or more over a 3-year period, the functional currency is the reporting parent company's currency.

REMEASUREMENT OF FOREIGN CURRENCY STATEMENTS INTO THE FUNCTIONAL CURRENCY

Remeasurement of a foreign entity's assets, liabilities, revenues, expenses, and equity accounts into the functional currency is necessary when the entity's books of record are not maintained in its functional currency. The remeasurement is required before translation into the reporting currency. If the functional currency is the reporting currency, translation after remeasurement is, of course, unnecessary. The remeasurement process is intended to produce the same results on the foreign entity's books as if the record had been maintained in the functional currency. SFAS No. 8 had this same objective and, accordingly, SFAS No. 52 incorporated remeasurement rules that are identical to SFAS No. 8's translation rules.

Monetary and Nonmonetary Accounts.   The remeasurement process requires that historical exchange rates between the functional currency and another currency be used for remeasuring certain accounts and that the current rate be used for others. Appendix B of SFAS No. 52 specifies those accounts. Historical rates are to be used for nonmonetary balance sheet items and related revenue, expense, gain, and loss accounts. Items listed are marketable securities carried at cost, including debt not held for maturity; inventories carried at cost; prepaid expenses; property, plant, and equipment and accumulated depreciation thereon; patents, trademarks, licenses, and formulas; goodwill and other intangible assets; deferred charges and credits except deferred income taxes and life insurance policy acquisition costs; deferred revenue; common stock; preferred stocks carried at issuance price; cost of goods sold; depreciation of property, plant, and equipment; amortization of deferred charges other than deferred income taxes; and life insurance policy acquisition costs. The only change from SFAS No. 8 in this list is that previously all deferred charges and credits were considered nonmonetary items. All other accounts are to be remeasured using current rates at the balance sheet date for balance sheet accounts and at the average current rate during the period for income statement items.

Gains and Losses Resulting from Remeasurements.   Gains and losses resulting from the remeasurement process are to be included in current income in the functional currency statements. Application of the cost-or-market rule for inventories should be in conformity with Chapter 4 of ARB No. 43, *Inventory Pricing*. Inventories, in the remeasurement process, should first be remeasured to cost in the functional currency and that cost compared with market as stated in the functional currency. Application of this procedure may cause a write-down in the functional currency statements even though no write-down is made in the books of record. Similarly, assets other than inventory may require a write-down in the functional currency statements without a write-down in the books of record.

TRANSLATION OF FOREIGN CURRENCY FINANCIAL STATEMENTS

After the functional currency has been decided upon and any remeasurement necessary to convert to the functional currency has been accomplished, the foreign entity's financial statements are translated into the reporting company's currency. Under the net investment concept followed by SFAS No. 52, the reporting company is viewed as having an investment in a foreign business whose foreign currency earnings derived from its operations in its local economic, legal, and political climate, accrue to the benefit of the reporting enterprise in the amount of the dollar equivalent to those earnings.

The Current Rate Method. The translation implementing the net investment concept is accomplished by use of the current rate method whereby foreign currency financial statement elements are translated from the functional currency into the reporting currency by using the current exchange rate as of the date they are reported:

1. For assets and liabilities, the balance sheet date.

2. For revenues, expenses, gains, and losses, the dates on which those elements are recognized during the period. (For pragmatic reasons, these may be reasonably approximated by the use of an appropriate weighted-average exchange rate for the period.)

3. For changes in financial position, the balance sheet date except for changes resulting from revenues, expenses, gains, and losses, which are translated using exchange rates for the period.

Translation Adjustments and their Disposition. Increases or decreases in net assets resulting from changes in the exchange rate between balance sheet dates, and from changes between the weighted-average rate and the end-of-the-period rate, are termed "translation adjustments." These translation adjustments are not included in net income currently because they are not expected to result in cash flows to the reporting enterprise in the foreseeable future. Instead they are accumulated and reported separately in a separate component of shareholders' equity until sale or complete or substantially complete liquidation of the net investment in the foreign entity has taken place. Upon such an event, amounts accumulated in the separate component of equity may be realized; to the extent realized, these amounts are included as a gain or loss in income for the period in which the sale takes place. There are no special circumstances for which the sale and liquidation criteria do not apply. When recognized as income, translation adjustments are reported as part of the gain or loss from sale or liquidation of the net investment in the foreign entity.

The Statement of Changes in Financial Position. SFAS No. 52 does not prescribe either the form or content of the statement of changes in financial position and does not change the provisions of APB Opinion No. 19, *Reporting Changes in Financial Position*. A full discussion of this statement is given in Chapter 3.

FOREIGN CURRENCY TRANSACTIONS

Foreign currency transactions are transactions denominated in a currency other than the entity's functional currency. These transactions may produce foreign currency (cash) or receivables and payables that are denominated or fixed in terms of the foreign currency that will be received or paid. These transactions result from such activities as export or import of goods or services and from capital financings or other borrowings. An export sale by a British (foreign) entity to a German enterprise denominated in deutsch marks (DM) is such a foreign currency transaction because it results in a receivable denominated in DM where the functional currency is British pounds sterling. Likewise, if the British entity issues bonds denominated in dollars, for sale in the U.S. market, it results in a foreign currency transaction because the liability is denominated in other than the functional currency.

Forward Exchange Contracts. A forward exchange contract (forward contract) is an agreement to exchange different currencies at a specified future date and at a specified rate (the forward rate). "Currency swaps" are, in substance, forward contracts and are accounted for as such. Forward contracts are foreign currency transactions.

Foreign Exchange Gains and Losses. A change in the exchange rates between the functional currency and the currency in which the transaction is denominated will increase or decrease the amount of the functional currency expected to be received. Except as noted below (see "Foreign Currency Gains and Losses Excluded from Net Income"), any increase or decrease in the expected functional cash flow is considered as a foreign exchange gain or loss and is included in income for the period in which the transaction takes place, or if the transaction is unsettled, the period in which the exchange takes place.

Time of Transaction Basis. The "time of transaction" (or two-transaction) basis for translation is founded on the premise that once the transaction is recorded, the assets and liabilities, expenses and revenues arising in a foreign currency transaction are fixed in terms of dollars at the exchange rate prevailing on the date the transaction takes place. Exchange rate fluctuations subsequent to the original transaction date cause exchange gains and losses (with certain exceptions discussed below), as shown in Exhibit 1. Such exchange gains and losses are generally considered to be "realized" immediately if the change in the exchange rate is ascribed a quality of permanence. However, gains on unsettled transactions frequently resulted in a deferral of net exchange gains on such transactions until settled, prior to the issuance of SFAS No. 8. Paragraphs 16, 18, and 20 of SFAS No. 52 require the application of the time of transaction method and consequently the recognition of an exchange

EXHIBIT 1   Time of Transaction Illustrated

U.S. Importer—Dual Currency Record

	Local currency debit (credit)	U.S. dollars debit (credit)
June 19X1: Purchase of inventory, exchange rate 10:1		
Inventory		100
Payable, LC1,000	(1,000)	(100)
January 19X2: Settlement, exchange rate 11:1		
Payable, LC1,000	1,000	100
Cash		(91)
Gain on foreign exchange		(9)

Note: At year-end 19X1, assume the rate of exchange was LC11 to U.S. dollar. Importer should report the gain of $9 in 19X1 and not in the year of settlement, 19X2.

gain or loss at each balance sheet date to reflect the current exchange rate for any unsettled receivable or payable denominated in a foreign currency.

Time of Settlement Basis. The "time of settlement" (or one-transaction) basis is founded on the premise that a transaction is not complete so long as the monetary asset or liability arising therein is unsettled. An importer or exporter using the time of settlement basis for translating foreign currency accounts into dollars may, within limits, adjust nonmonetary assets and nonmonetary liabilities, expenses, and revenues for changes (as a result of exchange rate fluctuations) in the amounts of unsettled foreign monetary assets and liabilities arising in the same transaction. In the illustration above, the accounts would be adjusted under the time of settlement basis for the unsettled transaction as in Exhibit 2. This method is no longer acceptable, except for a gain or loss on a forward contract or other foreign currency transaction that is intended to hedge (on an aftertax basis) an identifiable foreign currency commitment—for example, an

EXHIBIT 2   Time of Settlement Illustration

U.S. Importer—Dual Currency Record

	Local currency	U.S. dollars debit (credit)
June 19X1:		
Inventory		100
Payable, rate 10:1	(1,000)	(100)
Close accounts for 19X1 with transaction not paid but rate weakened to 11:1		
Inventory		(9)
Payable		9

Note: If inventory had been sold by year-end, the credit would be taken to cost of goods sold.

agreement to purchase equipment. Such a gain or loss is deferred and included in the measurement of the related foreign currency transaction—for example, the cost of the equipment. The deferral is limited to the amount of the related commitment.

The requirement to apply the time of transaction method *to every situation* causes an unfortunate distortion of income, usually between adjacent periods, on the importation of unsold inventory where the payable in foreign currency is unsettled and the U.S. importer can raise the selling price to compensate for his additional cost of settlement following a strengthening of the foreign currency. The result is an unusual charge, say, to the fourth quarter of 19X1, followed by an unusually high gross profit in the first quarter of 19X2 when the item is sold at an increased U.S. dollar selling price, maintaining, from the merchant's point of view, a consistent U.S. dollar profit margin based on replacement cost and settlement of the foreign payable at a less favorable exchange rate. This method distorts even where the selling price is not raised. When the selling price is raised, the distortion is even more clear. Those charged with explaining variations in the results of operations among periods should keep this situation in mind. The distortion in this case could be avoided by not picking up the unrealized gain until the inventory is sold. In fact, competition may force a decrease in the selling price in the subsequent period, which should result in reporting a constant gross profit in dollars. Further, if the obligation is settled prior to the sale of the inventory, the gain could be deferred to the period of the sale of the inventory to avoid distortion between periods. Although this is acceptable, the Board has liberalized acceptable hedges, but hedging has a cost and it may have no effect on the changes in the subsequent dollar selling prices that contribute to variations in gross profit of an importer.

Foreign Assets and Liabilities of Foreign Corporations. The same problems are encountered by branches and subsidiaries of U.S. corporations as are encountered by U.S. corporations that are importers and exporters. Often, the "foreign" transaction is based on a contract to be settled in U.S. dollars, but settlement in any currency foreign to the foreign entity involves the same issue. SFAS No. 52 requires application of the time of the transaction method to such balances before the foreign entity financial statements are translated to U.S. dollars. This has the same disadvantage described in the previous section, but the applications should be identical.

Foreign Currency Gains and Losses Excluded from Net Income. SFAS No. 52 provides for the exclusion from net income of the following gains and losses on foreign currency transactions; these are reported separately and included with translation adjustments in the separate component of shareholders' equity:

Gains and losses attributable to a foreign currency transaction that is designated as, and is effective as, an economic hedge of a net investment in a foreign entity. (Expected future revenue streams in a foreign currency do not qualify as an accounting hedge of transaction gains and losses.)

Gains or losses attributable to intercompany foreign currency transactions and balances that are of a capital or long-term financing nature (which might include advances and demand notes payable) for which settlement is not planned or anticipated in the foreseeable future, when the entities to the transaction are consolidated, combined, or accounted for by the equity method in the reporting enterprise's financial statements.

HEDGES

A forward exchange contract or other foreign currency transaction may be designed as a hedge against identifiable foreign commitments—for example, in an agreement to purchase equipment, to take the output of a plant, or to use a ship to transport the enterprise's product. A gain or loss on a forward contract or other foreign currency transaction is deferred and included in the basis of the related foreign currency transaction (e.g., the purchase in the above example), except that losses are not deferred if such deferral could lead to recognition of losses in subsequent periods.

Intention to Hedge. A forward contract or other foreign currency transaction is considered to be intended to hedge an identifiable foreign currency commitment if it meets the following conditions:

The transaction is designated as, and effective as, a hedge of a foreign currency commitment.
The foreign currency commitment is firm.

Computing Gains and Losses on Forward Contracts. Gains and losses (whether deferred or not) are computed by multiplying the foreign currency amount of the forward contract by the difference between the spot rate at the balance sheet date and the spot rate at inception or the spot rate last used to determine gain or loss (the carrying amount from the last balance sheet date). Premium and discounts on forward contracts are accounted for separately and included in income only over the life of the contract, except when it is part of a deferral of the gain or loss on a hedged transaction. Accounting for hedged transactions begins as of the date the transaction is designated as a hedge.

Speculative Forward Contracts. A foreign currency contract that does not hedge an exposure is speculative. A gain or loss on a speculative forward contract is computed by multiplying the foreign currency amount of the contract by the difference between the forward rate available for the remaining life of the contract and the contracted rate or the carrying rate at the last balance sheet. Premium and discount on speculative forward contracts are not accounted for separately.

Hedges of Net Investments. A foreign currency transaction may be designated as, and be effective as, an economic hedge of a net investment in a foreign country. For example, a U.S. reporting enterprise with a British subsidiary enters into a loan agreement to borrow pounds sterling from a third party with the intent that the loan is a hedge of its investment in the British subsidiary.

The British loan is a liability, the net investment in the British subsidiary is an asset of the reporting enterprise, and the loan is a foreign currency transaction. The effect of changes in exchange rates will cause the translation adjustment for the loan and the net investment to move in opposite directions, so a hedge results. If the adjustments are equal, they are both deferred and reported in the accumulated equity adjustment component of shareholders' equity. If the adjustment from the loan exceeds the adjustment from the net investment, the excess is reported (as would be adjustments from the other uncovered foreign currency transactions) as an exchange gain or loss and included in current income for the period. Ordinarily, a transaction that hedges a net investment is denominated in the same currency as the functional currency of the net investment hedged (the pound sterling in the previous examples). Occasionally, the hedging transaction is denominated in a currency whose exchange rate generally moves in tandem with that of the functional currency.

INTERCOMPANY TRANSACTIONS

Intercompany Profits. An intercompany sale or transfer of goods or services, such as inventory or machinery, frequently produces intercompany profit for the selling unit, and the buying unit includes such profit in its cost of the asset. The intercompany profit is eliminated using the exchange rate in effect on the date of sale or purchase. Subsequent changes in the exchange rates are not attributable to intercompany profit.

Unsettled Intercompany Transactions. A difference between intercompany receivables and payables may result if unsettled intercompany transactions are subject to, and translated, using preference or penalty rates. That difference is treated as a receivable or payable in the enterprise's financial statements until eliminated by settlement.

Long-Term Financing or Capital Transactions. Exchange gains or losses arising from intercompany foreign currency transactions and balances that are of a long-term financing or capital nature, when the entities involved in the transaction are consolidated, combined, or accounted for by the equity method in the reporting entity's financial statements, are deferred and included with translation adjustments in the separate component of shareholders' equity. A "long-term investment" nature encompasses only investments (including advances and demand notes payable) for which settlement is not planned or anticipated in the foreseeable future. Gains and losses and other foreign exchange transactions, as previously explained, are included in the determination of current income.

LOCAL CURRENCY FINANCIAL STATEMENTS

Under SFAS No. 52, when the U.S. dollar is not the functional currency, all exchange gains and losses on U.S. dollar-denominated assets and liabilities other than intercompany balances that are of a long-term investment nature are included in current income. SFAS No. 52, however, does not govern statutory financial statements of a foreign branch or foreign subsidiary of a U.S. parent company. Although the time of transaction basis may be appropriate in hard-currency countries, its strict application in countries experiencing constant inflation is not practical. Where price-level financial statements are prepared in such countries, some relief is afforded. Where a foreign subsidiary purchases fixed assets or inventory from a country other than its functional currency country that remains unsold, the same distortion described above for a U.S. importer could arise under the time of transaction method. In some countries large projects cannot be financed locally, as the capital market simply will not support large borrowings.

The comments under the following three captions are not acceptable under U.S. generally accepted accounting principles, and any application in local currency financial statements is made only if the procedures are accepted in the country of the reporting company.

Purchase of Plant by Foreign Subsidiary. Assume that a foreign corporation that is a subsidiary of a U.S. company arranged for extended credit terms to obtain U.S. steel to build a plant in the foreign country. The price of the steel was $100,000 delivered at the plant site. The steel was delivered early in the year when the exchange rate was LC10 = $1, so construction in progress was charged LC1,000,000 and a liability account was credited in dual currency records in the amounts of LC1,000,000 and $100,000. At the end of the year the plant was still under construction and the exchange rate had deteriorated to LC12 = $1. Using the time of settlement basis, especially because the plant had not commenced operations, it would be proper to charge construction in progress and credit the liability account in the amount of an additional LC200,000, thereby avoiding recognition of an exchange loss of that amount. (If designated as a hedge, the same effect is obtained by debiting plant or a deferred charge account, which would then be amortized over the life of the plant.) Note that there is no need for a foreign branch or foreign subsidiary of a U.S. company to adjust the U.S. dollars first recorded, provided that the test outlined in the next section is met.

Limitations on Adjustments. The entry in local currency in the preceding example cannot be accepted even under the time of settlement basis or as designated if the result will be to increase the cost of the plant in local currency to an amount in excess of future economic value, that is, if the result will be to increase depreciation charges to a level that will preclude profitable operations in the foreign country in terms of local currency. It may be possible to apply the lower-of-cost-or-market rule in this case by restating plant costs incurred during the year using price-level restatement techniques, which are gaining acceptance in some foreign countries; the amount of exchange loss charged to construction in progress would be limited to the approximate amount by which the construction in progress account would have been increased by the price-level adjustment. Alternatively, it might be necessary to evaluate the reasonableness of the charge to construction in progress by studying budgets, forecasts, or other available data. Certainly the estimated local currency selling price of the product the new plant is expected to produce is the key to whether the additional LC200,000 may be charged to plant, or whether all or some portion should be charged off in local currency and then the $100,000 plant written down proportionately, or all the way to $83,333. Usually, however, local selling prices can be increased to absorb such additional charges. The U.S. dollar problem arises only in translation of branch and subsidiary financial statements.

If the liability were not discharged in subsequent years while the exchange rate continued to deteriorate, but the building was completed and operations were begun, continuing to charge the exchange losses to the asset account would result in steadily increasing annual depreciation charges in local currency, and the same test described in the previous paragraph would again be applied. Once a plant is complete and operating, however, subsequent exchange weakness is purely a financial charge against income resulting from unsettled foreign contracts and such treasury function risks are period charges in local currency. The longer the liability remains unsettled, the more there is a presumption that this is more appropriate.

Purchase of Inventory by Foreign Subsidiary. If the item obtained under a contract for settlement in U.S. dollars had been an inventory item, the reasonableness of charging the exchange loss to inventory would depend on the estimated net realizable amount in local currency of the inventory being more than the restated cost, which includes the additional local currency charge. If the liability were not discharged in subsequent years while the exchange rate continued to deteriorate, but the inventory items were being sold, it would be illogical to charge all the exchange losses to the inventory account and it would be impossible to adjust the local currency cost of goods sold in prior years. In this case, a period charge to exchange loss in local currency is required.

Dual Currency Records. Using the time of settlement basis, it is necessary to maintain dual currency records for each unsettled foreign currency transaction (both the debits and the credits); there is no shortcut. Using the time of transaction basis, dual currency records need be maintained only for foreign currency *monetary* assets and liabilities.

INCOME TAX CONSEQUENCES OF RATE CHANGES

Interperiod tax allocation is required in accordance with APB Opinion No. 11, *Accounting for Income Taxes*, which requires that income tax expense be allocated among income before extraordinary items, adjustments of prior periods (or of the opening balance in retained earnings), and direct entries to other accounts. See Chapter 36 for a full complete discussion of deferred income taxes.

Income Tax Allocation of Foreign Currency Translation Adjustments. The adjustments resulting from translation of foreign currency statements are considered timing differences if they otherwise meet the criteria of APB Opinion No. 11. The provisions of APB Opinion No. 23, *Accounting for Income Taxes—Special Areas*, and Opinion No. 24, *Accounting for Income Taxes—Investments in Common Stock Accounted for by the Equity Method (Other than Subsidiaries and Corporate Joint Ventures)*, are to be considered in determining the amount, if any, of deferred taxes. APB Opinion No. 23 provides that deferred taxes not be provided for unremitted earnings of a subsidiary in certain instances, deferred taxes in those instances are not provided on translation adjustments.

Income Tax Allocation of Foreign Exchange Transactions. Interperiod tax allocation is required if taxable exchange gains or tax-deductible exchange losses resulting from foreign exchange transactions are included in net income in a different period for financial purposes than for tax purposes. All gains or losses from foreign exchange transactions of this sort result in timing differences whether deferred, included in current income, or reported as a separate component in shareholders' equity.

TRANSLATION OF SPECIFIC EQUITY ACCOUNTS

SFAS No. 52 has little to say about translation of the equity accounts.

Minority Interests. Although normally classified as a liability (because it is not part of the parent company shareholders' equity), the portion of equity attributable to the minority interests is really a combined equity account. After all other items in the financial statements of a foreign company have been translated into dollars, minority interests should be computed as the minority percentage of ownership of the dollar equivalent of earnings and of the dollar equivalent of net assets based on the historical cost of the subsidiary (not the parent), adjusted if necessary to comply with accounting principles generally accepted in the United States and before consolidating entries ascribing excess costs and goodwill. (This assumes no outstanding preferred stock; see next section.) Accumulated translation adjustments attributable to minority interests are allocated to and reported as part of the total minority interests. It is not appropriate to translate minority interests at the current rate. There is no justification for a U.S. company to recognize a greater or lesser share of translated earnings than it is entitled to by its percentage of ownership of the company. If local currency minority interests were translated into dollars at the current rate, the U.S. company would recognize a greater equity than it is entitled to when exchange rates declined, and a smaller equity when the rates strengthened.

Preferred Stock. Preferred stock that is essentially a permanent shareholder investment is translated in the same manner as common stock, that is, at historical rates. If preferred stock not owned by the enterprise is carried at its liquidation value or if redemption is imminent, that preferred stock is translated at the current rate.

Common Stock and Additional Paid-in Capital. The historical cost of an investment must be used to evaluate adequately results of operations in relation to funds invested. Accordingly, capital stock and additional paid-in capital should be translated at the rate prevailing when contributed by the parent company and others. If stock was purchased for U.S. dollars, the original dollar cost should be maintained; if purchased with local currency assets, the stock should be translated at the rate in effect when the stock was acquired, that is, the historical rate. The foregoing assumes that the foreign subsidiary is a new operation. If a company acquires a foreign going concern, the same valuation problems arise as when a domestic going concern is acquired. After a business combination accounted for by the purchase method, the amount allocated at the date of acquisition to the assets acquired, and the liabilities assumed including goodwill and an excess of acquired net assets over cost are translated in conformance with SFAS No. 52. Most purchases of a foreign company should be treated as a tax-free purchase, making the evaluation of individual assets acquired complex (see paragraph 89 of APB Opinion No. 16, *Business Combinations*).

Retained Earnings. Retained earnings in dollars resulting from translation represent annual earnings as translated for each of the years of accumulation, reduced by dividends paid.

Dividends paid. Cash dividends to the parent company are normally translated at the remittance rate in effect when local currency is converted into dollars; payments to the minority interest, whether in local currency or some other currency, are translated at the same free exchange rate at the time of payment. The charge to retained earnings is grossed up for any taxes withheld, which should be translated at the free exchange rate at the time the dividends are paid.

Legal, general, and contingency reserves. Legal, general, and contingency reserves are usually mere appropriations of retained earnings arising from local law or custom. Frequently they are included in dollar equivalent consolidated retained earnings. However, such reserves usually constitute a restriction on the availability of retained earnings for dividend payments. The amount of such restriction can be calculated by use of the closing free exchange rate. Under generally accepted accounting principles, no exchange gain or loss arises from any translation adjustments to these reserves; there is merely a transfer between appropriated and unappropriated retained earnings. The appropriated retained earnings as translated is frequently used only to provide footnote information on dividend restrictions.

As a practical matter, the amount of local currency unappropriated retained earnings is the amount available for dividend declarations, and a memorandum translation of that amount at the closing free exchange rate provides the balance of unrestricted retained earnings (unrestricted by the reserve); any dollar equivalent retained earnings in excess of such unrestricted retained earnings could not be remitted and hence is in a measure restricted as far as dividends are concerned.

TRANSLATION OF SPECIFIC INCOME STATEMENT ACCOUNTS

Paragraph 12 of SFAS No. 52 governs the translation of revenue and expense accounts. The assumption is made that the financial statements are translated each month and that therefore (1) the beginning and ending dollar equivalent balance sheets are properly stated in accordance with the principles previously described, and (2) the average free exchange rate for the month is applicable to the translation of revenues and expenses arising in transactions occurring during the month. Accounting allocations such as depreciation, cost of sales, and amortization of deferred revenues and expenses also require translation at the current exchange rates applicable to the dates those applications are included in revenue and expenses. In a given situation, of course, the financial statements may be translated only quarterly, semiannually, or annually; an appropriate average free exchange rate for such period should then be applied to revenues and expenses arising in transactions occurring during that period, always remembering that ideally each such revenue or expense item would be translated at the free exchange rate on the day of the actual transaction. For example, it may be desirable to calculate a *weighted* average free exchange rate for the period, or to apply the free exchange rate at the time of the actual transactions to specific unusual, material items.

Sales. Sales should be translated at the average free exchange rate for the month. Transfers from nonmonetary liabilities (certain deferred income accounts) should be translated at the appropriate current exchange rates at dates of allocation.

Dividend Income. Cash dividends received on any local investments should be translated at the average free exchange rate for the month; income taxes on the dividends withheld at the source should be translated into dollars at the same exchange rate. The total amount of the dividend (including taxes withheld) should be shown as dividend income, and the amount of tax withheld should be classified as provision for income taxes.

Stock dividends may be reflected as revenue in local currency in accordance with requirements in some countries, but should not be translated into dollars under any circumstances. Any income taxes payable on stock dividends received should be translated at the average free exchange rate for the month and classified as provision for income taxes.

Interest Income. Translate interest income at the average free exchange rate for the month, including transfers from an unearned finance charges account that appears in the balance sheet as a valuation account against accounts receivable. If interest income were collected in advance, the transfer to interest income would be translated at the appropriate current exchange rates at dates of transfer.

Gain or Loss on Disposal of Properties. Any gain or loss resulting from disposals of properties should be based on the current dollar equivalent of cost of such assets and dollar equivalent of related accumulated depreciation at date of disposition, with local currency realization or net salvage value being translated into dollars at the average free exchange rate for the month in which the disposal occurs.

Gain or Loss on Disposal of Investments. If claim-type marketable securities and investments are disposed of for a local currency amount that differs from the amounts shown on the books (net of allowance for losses, if any), the difference is a gain or loss to be translated at the average free exchange rate for the month. However, if the claims were receivable in another foreign currency that was devalued prior to disposal of the investments, the book value would be adjusted to the new exchange rate as of the date of disposal before computing dollar equivalent gain or loss in order to avoid mixing exchange gains and losses with gain or loss on disposal of investments.

Any gain or loss resulting from disposal of equity-type marketable securities and investments should be based on dollar equivalent cost of such assets and any *dollar* provision for losses thereon, with local currency realization being translated into dollars at the average free exchange rate for the month in which the disposal occurs.

Costs and Expenses. Most current costs and expenses should be translated at the average free exchange rate for the month. Transfers from nonmonetary assets (such as beginning inventories, certain prepaid expenses and deferred charges, intangibles) should be translated at the appropriate current exchange rates at date of transfer.

Depreciation, Depletion, and Amortization. Depreciation was discussed previously with regard to translation of property, plant, and equipment. The same basic principles apply to depletion of natural resources and amortization of leasehold improvements.

Provisions for Losses on Receivables and Investments. Provisions for losses on receivables and claim-type investments should be translated at the average free exchange rate for the month. Calculating provisions for losses on equity-type investments was discussed earlier in connection with the translation of marketable securities and investments—equity securities.

Provision for Income Taxes. Translate at the average free exchange rate for the month. There is a tendency to disregard whether such taxes are paid in installments during the year or after the year-end.

Provision for deferred income taxes. Deferred taxes that relate to assets or liabilities are translated at the current rate. Deferred taxes related to other assets and liabilities and determined by the gross change method and deferred tax related to other assets and liabilities and determined by the net change method are both translated at the average rate of exchange for the period.

Exchange Gains and Losses. When the subsidiary has exchange gains or losses resulting from settled or unsettled transactions in foreign currencies (currencies other than the local currency and the dollar), such exchange gains or losses are translated at the average free exchange rate for the month.

To the consolidated entity, no exchange gain or loss on *dollar* monetary items results from fluctuations in the exchange rate between local currency and the dollar; therefore, if the subsidiary has recorded exchange gains or losses resulting from such fluctuations, the local currency amount thereof should not be translated. Foreign taxes payable (or the amount payable reduced by such fluctuations) are an element of consolidated tax expense.

Exchange gains and losses arising in translation because of the effects of exchange rate fluctuations between the local currency and the dollar on the local currency monetary items require immediate recognition in net income for the period in which the rate changes. The need for a provision for deferred taxes shall be determined in accordance with APB Opinion No. 23 relative to subsidiaries and APB Opinion No. 24 relative to investments in common stock accounted for by the equity method (other than subsidaries and corporate joint ventures).

Minority Interest in Earnings. Dividends paid to outsiders holding preferred stock are a charge against consolidated net income and should be translated at the free exchange rate at time of payment. The minority (common stock) interest in earnings is the applicable percentage of the subsidiary's total dollar equivalent net income (after dollar equivalent preferred dividends have been paid to both outsiders and the parent company).

Prior Period Adjustments. A prior period adjustment would be translated in the current year at the rate in effect when it is recorded (average free exchange rate for the month). If the adjustment is reflected retroactively in prior years in accordance with APB Opinion No. 9, *Prior Period Adjustments,* the effects are multiple. Assume a substantial assessment in 19X5 for income taxes applicable to 19X1 and 19X2. Income taxes payable and retained earnings at the end of each year since 19X1 will have to be adjusted; also minority interests (both the liability and the share of net income) in common stocks, if any. Income tax expense and net income for 19X1 and 19X2 will be altered.

On the theory that monetary liabilities should ideally be translated at the exchange rate to be in effect at the time they are discharged, the exchange rate in effect when the additional taxes are first assessed is objective evidence of the appropriate exchange rate, and the prior period adjustments should be reflected in the prior periods in terms of such later exchange rate. This eliminates alterations to previously calculated unrealized exchange gains and losses and thereby simplifies the adjustment procedure considerably.

SPECIAL SITUATIONS

Exchange Controls. Exchange rates fluctuate in accordance with the supply of and demand for a foreign currency in a given market. Many countries, especially the so-called developing ones, have instituted exchange controls to help keep supply and demand in balance. The controls range from virtually automatic licensing procedures to outright prohibition of remittances abroad and compulsory repatriation of assets owned abroad. In between are a number of controls (e.g., multiple exchange rates) that cause unusual translation problems. At the lower extreme of control (e.g., virtually automatic licensing procedures), no significant translation problem normally arises. At the upper extreme of control (e.g., outright prohibition of all remittances abroad), it may be questionable whether any value whatsoever should be assigned to assets in or related to the country involved.

Appropriate translation procedures when exchange controls exist must be evaluated individually, based on the facts involved in each situation. Sometimes translation, as such, is not really at issue. For example, if significant foreign cash accounts are restricted as to conversion and if using these funds for local payments is impracticable, they should be shown as noncurrent assets and reduced to estimated realizable amount; alternatively, these restricted funds may be excluded from the financial statements and disclosed in the notes only. Similarly, if remittances are restricted and if receivables are not likely to be collected within 1 year, they should be classified as long-term receivables and shown separately, if material, and estimated losses on receivables not protected by forward exchange contracts or other hedging devices should be provided for currently to reduce the receivables to estimated realizable amount. Similar problems arise in evaluating other foreign assets under tight exchange control conditions.

Black Markets. When meaningful exchange controls exist, it is probable that a black market also exists. Black market rates are established by unauthorized dealers in foreign exchange, often in violation of governmental regulations, and are almost invariably higher for purchasing a hard currency than the official or free rate for the same currency. Many of the transactions on the black market are speculative in nature. The volume of transactions at black market rates may be limited, and most businesses do not normally obtain funds at these rates. Therefore, translation of unsettled accounts or financial statements of foreign subsidiaries at black market rates would normally be inappropriate. Nonetheless, one in possession of relevant economic information and aware of the political factors involved in a particular situation may obtain from black market rates a useful indication of the future free exchange rate.

Multiple Exchange Rates. Regulation of the economy of some countries is undertaken through the medium of multiple exchange rates. A country having a free rate of 10 to 1 may offer a "preference" for the importation of certain goods by allowing remittance at a favorable or preference rate of 9 to 1. Government agencies often control (hold down) the selling prices locally of the company in consideration for the "preference" offered (entitlement) on request for foreign exchange to remit to the supplier (often the parent company). Upon the importation of such inventory, unrealized gains and losses between fiscal years will result unless the accountant takes special precautions. As long as the inventory and the account payable to the foreign supplier of the inventory item purchased at a preference rate are in balance, no unrealized exchange gains and losses can occur. Exhibit 3 shows one method of preventing unrealized gains and losses from occurring when inventory and accounts payable balances are not exactly equal. This illustrates one translation technique required to prevent the *overstatement* of profit by $.20 because of the treasury action of paying for importations in *advance* of sale.

The advantage of this technique is that it permits all sales and cost of sales figures to be translated at the free rate. This removes the requirement of specifically identifying the cost of those items that were purchased at a preferential rate. (Materials and supplies inventories may be handled similarly.)

Inventory purchased at a preference rate. If the supplier is paid by the foreign subsidiary at a preferred rate of exchange in advance of the inventory being sold, special accounting techniques are required to prevent the erroneous overstatement of profit by rigid line-by-line translation procedures in the period of remittance to the supplier, only to be followed by an equally erroneous "paper" loss in the period when the inventory is sold. Although the unrealized exchange gain at time of payment may be blocked from income by several mechanical methods, the one illustrated in Exhibit 3, in which an account receivable (in home country currency only) is used, is the easiest to operate, does not distort internal management reports in U.S. dollars, and an account receivable balance corresponds with the entitlements to "preference" that the treasurer has available and unused.

Inventory purchased at a penalty rate. Some countries tend to discourage importation of certain items by the application of a penalty rate. Thus, when the free rate is 10 to 1, the foreign exchange board may require the payment of 11 to 1 in connection with remittances abroad for classified luxury items. Again special techniques are required. Unrealized exchange gain would result in this situation from the sale locally (of the inventory item purchased at a penalty rate) in advance of payment for the item to the foreign supplier. Entries opposite to those illustrated in Exhibit 3 are appropriate. There should be no hesitancy to translate the inventory item at more dollars than the original dollar cost in the United States, because that is the purpose of the foreign government in discouraging such purchases. Of course, the inventory item should pass the cost-or-market test, using local selling price translated at the free rate to measure market as described previously.

Fixed assets purchased at a preference rate. Large numbers may be involved in the acquisition of fixed assets at a preference rate where clearly the

---

EXHIBIT 3 **Multiple Rates—Purchase of Inventory**

Opening balance sheet	P	$	Note
Cash	370	$5.0	A
. . . .	(60)	(.8)	C
	310	$4.2	
Inventory (three units of one item)	180	2.4	B
Account receivable		.6	B
. . . .		(.2)	C
Total assets	490	$7.0	
Intercompany payable:			
Three units purchased	(180)	$(3.0)	B
Payment for one unit	60	1.0	C
	(120)	$(2.0)	
Capital stock	(370)	(5.0)	A
Total liability and capital stock	(490)	$(7.0)	

Notes:
A Cash received for capital stock at 74/$—the free rate.
B Products imported at 60/$—the preferential rate. Liability is translated at the preferential rate, but the inventory is charged at the free rate, the dollar difference being carried as an account receivable. As a result, the inventory that cost $3.0 in the United States is carried at $2.4 in the foreign country.
C Payment of liability of $1 is made before inventory is sold. Credit is made to deferred charges at this time.

Statement of income	P	$
Sales—at the free rate	(60)	$ (.8)
Cost of sales—at the free rate	60	.8
Net income	0	$ 0

Closing balance sheet		
Cash—Opening balance plus sale proceeds	370	$ 5.0
Inventory—Opening balance less cost of sale	120	1.6
Account receivable—(.6 − .2)		.4
Total assets	490	$ 7.0
Intercompany payable	(120)	$(2)
Capital stock	(370)	(5)
Retained earnings	0	0
Total liability and capital stock	(490)	$(7.0)

---

foreign government was encouraging the acquisition of fixed assets by offering the "preference." Unless special techniques are employed, the amount of the "preference" in the acquisition of the fixed assets may be taken into income (an unrealized gain) and the fixed assets remain translated at an unrealistically high number which will develop "heavy" translated depreciation in subsequent periods (or may even cause a translated loss). Clearly no realizable gain resulted from acquiring the plant, and the government's "preference" should be reflected in a lower translation of the original cost. An example of a technique to prevent the reporting of the unrealized exchange gain at time of payment for the fixed asset is shown in Exhibit 4.

Profit is not made by purchasing equipment. Actually the foreign government is offering a subsidy (preference) to encourage the importation of the item. Therefore, the accountant should not be reluctant to translate the local currency used to acquire a tractor at $8,000 in the property accounts even when $10,000 was paid to the U.S. manufacturer. Conversely, if the foreign government wishes to restrict the importation of, say, automobiles, it may establish a penalty rate and the accountant should translate the excessive local currency used to acquire an automobile at $8,000 in the property accounts even when only $4,000 was paid to the U.S. dealer. These results are understandable because current assets (used) are translated at the free (or dividend remittance) rate.

A second important advantage under this technique is that all charges to fixed assets may be translated at the free rate. Mechanization leads to such considerations being given heavy weight.

Repatriation of Export Sales Proceeds. Certain export sales by foreign companies to U.S. dollar customers (including affiliated companies) are permitted by the foreign country on the basis that a given percentage of the dollar revenue

---

EXHIBIT 4   Multiple Rates—Purchase of Equipment

Opening balance sheet	P	$	Note
Cash........................	370	$ 5.0	A
....	(180)	(2.4)	C
	190	$ 2.6	
Equipment	180	2.4	B
Account receivable		.6	B
....		(.6)	C
	370	$ 5.0	
Payable to U.S. supplier	(180)	$(3.0)	B
....	180	3.0	C
	0	0	
Capital stock	(370)	(5.0)	A
	(370)	$(5.0)	

Notes:
A Cash received for capital stock at 74/$—the free rate.
B Equipment purchased at preferential rate—60/$. Liability is translated at the preferential rate but the equipment is charged with the free rate, the dollar difference being carried as an account receivable. As a result, equipment costing $3.0 in the United States is carried at $2.4 in the local country.
C Payment of entire liability at preferential rate.

will be returned (repatriated) to the foreign country for the purpose of purchasing its foreign currency. Certain foreign countries set the sales price for the sole purpose of computing the percentage to be returned, regardless of the actual negotiated sales price by the foreign company. Certain foreign countries also regulate the exchange rate at which the U.S. dollars will be converted into local currency. In effect such regulations are a form of taxation when the rate is unfavorable, yet it is not appropriate to classify any such dollar differences ("penalties") as taxes. This will result in fewer equivalent sales dollars being reported when the fewer local currency units received are translated at the free rate than are actually collected from U.S. customers.

MINIMIZING FOREIGN EXCHANGE LOSSES

Minimizing losses from unfavorable fluctuations in exchange rates or from periodic devaluations of foreign currencies is one of the chief treasury functions of any company holding assets in the form of foreign currency or realizable in foreign currency. Effective protection against such losses is a matter of constant surveillance of economic conditions in each country in which such assets are held, anticipating developments, and using the available means of protection as soon as it appears that the danger of loss outweighs the cost of such protection.

The Problem. The risk of foreign exchange loss is run not only by companies with bases of operations abroad, but also by any company with a receivable or payable to be collected or paid in a foreign currency. Foreign exchange problems vary from company to company, but all the companies presumably have the same objective: to maximize net income expressed in U.S. dollars. To meet this objective a decision must be made whether to hedge net assets held against a potential loss from foreign currency exchange fluctuations, and if so, what means should be used to hedge against such a potential loss.

The "exposure" of the trader is limited to the foreign currency receivable or payable; the exposure of the company operating abroad is far more complex.

Early Detection of Currency Weakness. Any company with "exposed" foreign assets to protect should establish an "early warning system" to detect the signs of currency weakness before unfavorable fluctuations in exchange rates transform local currency profits into dollar losses. Companies with the best record in protecting against foreign exchange losses are those that have head office-trained personnel assigned on a continuing basis to the task of monitoring economic developments abroad and attempting to forecast exchange rate trends for years in advance. Measures against foreign exchange losses are cheaper and easier to take when their need is anticipated. This function may well be a primary responsibility of local management, but periodic reports to the head office are recommended as a precautionary measure.

These are some of the signs of currency weakness that the surveillance system must detect and evaluate:

1. *Inflation.* Spiraling prices are the surest indicator of currency weakness. Although internal inflation is not always simultaneously reflected in a weakened exchange rate and even though governments can maintain an appearance of strength in their currencies, external devaluation tends strongly in the long run to parallel internal devaluation. Inflated real estate values may have particular significance because they may mean that real estate is being used as a haven for a currency in trouble.

2. *Money in circulation.* An increase in money in circulation disproportionate to the trend in gross national product is an early warning of inflation.

3. *National budget.* Recurring deficits generally precede local inflation.

4. *Rising interest rates.* Borrowing in the local currency is the chief defense against losses from foreign exchange. Rising interest rates may be the result of such defensive borrowings (for remittance abroad, or for investment in tangible assets) motivated by lack of confidence in the local currency. Eventually the interest cost may become higher than the expected loss from devaluation.

5. *Balance of trade.* Devaluation of the local currency is one remedy applied by governments to cure a decline in exports and to discourage imports.

6. *Balance of payments.* A favorable balance of trade can be more than offset by outward capital movements. If the net balance of payments continues to be unfavorable over a period of time, the government may try to stem the tide by devaluing the local currency.

7. *Foreign exchange quotations.* Rising costs of dollars for future delivery indicate that sellers of dollars have less confidence in the local currency and are commanding higher premiums for parting with their dollars. The existence of a black market for dollars points to the possibility of an official devaluation, as holders of dollars refuse to sell them at existing unrealistic official rates.

While the early warning system monitors events abroad, calculations of exposure to foreign exchange losses must be made at intervals dependent on the volatility of the currencies concerned. The more imminent the danger of loss, the more frequently should the exposure be calculated.

The seven matters discussed in the preceding paragraphs are relevant to an appraisal of the U.S. economy. When our domestic problems outrun those of a foreign country, we tend to say that the foreign currency will strengthen in relation to the U.S. dollar rather than saying that the U.S. dollar will weaken in relation to the foreign currency.

Measuring the "Exposure." Calculating the exposure at any given date is mainly a matter of segregating the assets and liabilities on the balance sheet in such a way as to bring to light the net amount of assets that are subject to a decrease in value in the event of currency deterioration. Cash and local currency receivables are the most exposed assets. Property and plant accounts are usually considered less exposed, on the generally accepted assumption that their value will usually rise in proportion to the devaluation of the local currency. The same theory applies to inventories to some degree, depending on whether the inventories are subject to price controls. Inventories not subject to price controls can generally be treated for this purpose in the same way as are property and plant, that is, excluded from the calculation. On the other hand, inventories subject to price controls might conservatively be handled in the same way as cash for an internal management report.

The preceding comments about inventories should be kept in mind when calculating exposure. A formula for that calculation follows:

Add:
A. Current assets (excluding prepaid expenses)
B. Investments to be recovered in fixed amounts of local currency
C. Long-term receivables, net of any allowances

Subtract:
D. Inventories not subject to price controls
E. U.S. dollar assets included in A, B, and C and not already eliminated through D
F. Local currency liabilities (including reserves such as pension reserves)

The algebraic sum of these items equals net assets exposed to risk of loss through exchange fluctuations. Effect should be given in these calculations to protection already obtained through forward exchange contracts.

The net assets exposed, as calculated in local currency, should then be translated into U.S. dollars at the exchange rate prevailing at both the balance sheet date and at the exchange rate forecast for any date ahead. The resulting difference between the asset values at the two dates is the loss on foreign exchange forecast for the period between the two dates unless preventive action is taken. The costs of protection against the loss should be investigated and weighed against the anticipated loss.

The calculation of exposure is illustrated in Exhibit 5. The frequency of the preparation of this report is dependent on the stability of the local currency in relation to the U.S. dollar.

Means of Protection. The means of minimizing foreign exchange losses when a foreign currency weakens and the guidelines to be followed when there is an exposure to such loss are enumerated below. Of course, not all of them are applicable or possible to follow in every case (when the foreign currency is expected to strengthen, an opposite course is usually indicated). The feasibility, cost, tax effects, and resulting benefits of each must be considered.

1. Convert local currency receivables into cash to the maximum extent through intensive collection efforts, reduction of credits terms, offering more generous discounts for prompt payment, and discounting the receivables through financial institutions.

2. Make maximum remittances abroad in the form of provisional dividends. Unremitted earnings increase net assets exposed.

3. Invoice export sales to harder currency countries in the currency of the buyer.

4. Pay U.S. dollar obligations to suppliers (including parent company or head office) promptly.

	Local currency
1. Total current assets (including prepaid expenses)......................	510,000
2. Add: Long-term receivables, less allowances	48,700
3.　Investments receivable in fixed local currency amounts..............	79,500
4.　Total (lines 1, 2, and 3)	638,200
5. Less: "Dollar" assets in above amounts (lines 1, 2, and 3)[a]	(65,800)
6.　Inventory amounts not under price control........................	(111,200)
7.　Prepaid expenses	(30,000)
8.　Total (lines 5 through 7)	(207,000)
9. Assets "exposed" (line 4 minus line 8)	431,200
10. Total current liabilities	(363,100)
11. Total long-term liabilities	(92,500)
12.　Total (lines 10 and 11)	(455,600)
13. Less: "Dollar" liabilities in above amounts (lines 10 and 11)[a]	174,900
14.　Liabilities covered (line 12 minus line 13).........................	(280,700)
15. Net assets exposed to exchange risk (line 9 minus line 14)	150,500

	U.S. dollars
16. Net assets exposed to exchange risk expressed in dollars in period-end exchange rate (.2000)...	$30,100
17. Forecast change in exchange rate by next report (present .2000 minus forecast .1500 = change)	.0500
18. Loss forecast if no action taken (line 15 times line 17)...................	$ 7,525
19. Loss since last report	$ 2,000

Notes:
[a]Derivation not shown here.

1. Local management should insert in the space at the foot of this exhibit their forecast and comments on the degree of confidence in the local currency and the treasury actions planned for the ensuing quarter (or year), if required, and amounts hedged, if any.

2. Intercompany receivables and payables should be excluded entirely from the foregoing calculation.

3. Effect should be given to protection already obtained through forward exchange contracts. Also, it may be advisable to adjust line 15 to reflect any anticipated change in the net monetary position before the exchange rate changes.

4. The estimated foreign tax benefit of additional local currency accruals in the future for settlement of dollar payables or the estimated taxes payable on gains from forward exchange contracts should be described.

Intercompany Accounts. It is important to note that intercompany receivables and payables should be excluded entirely for the exposure calculation. If a French subsidiary owes dollars to its U.S. parent, there is no exposure; there can be no exchange gain or loss on dollars in dollar financial statements. Carrying this situation one step forward: If a French subsidiary owes francs to its U.S. parent, there is also no exposure; a net gain or loss cannot arise when a company owes itself money, and consolidated statements presuppose the existence of a single reporting entity: furthermore, the U.S. parent is "long" the same number of francs that the French subsidiary is "short," which is a perfect hedge.

However, more should not be read into the preceding paragraph than is stated therein. The fact that a consolidated loss cannot result from intercompany accounts does not mean that protection from losses is not available from, for example, prompt payment by a foreign subsidiary of its dollar obligations. Although dollar payables do not reduce the exposure to losses on local currency assets, conversion of local currency assets into dollars does reduce exposure. In other words, payment of dollar obligations decreases local currency assets exposed and a reduction in net local currency exposed assets reduces risk.

The tax consequences in the different taxing authorities are another consideration in structuring the exposure to a change in the exchange rate. If a French subsidiary owes dollars rather than francs to its U.S. parent and the French franc weakens in relation to the U.S. dollar, the French subsidiary will have to charge income for the additional francs and a timing difference will arise until the account is settled. The tax consequence is in the French income tax in this case and will give rise to a tax benefit.

The foregoing comments about subsidiaries and intercompany accounts also apply to branches and intracompany accounts.

5. Maximize local payables through insistence on more generous credit terms from suppliers. Delay tax payments wherever possible.

6. Reduce the parent company or head office investment of hard currency and borrow locally for all purposes. The reasonableness of local interest rates (and their income tax effect) should be examined in the light of their relationship to the inflation or devaluation factor rather than to interest rates in other countries.

7. Purchase foreign exchange forward for hard currency obligations such as dividends, technical service fees, etc., that are known in advance.

8. Accumulate inventories (of types not subject to price controls). Arrange for payment in local currency, if possible; if not possible, purchase the hard currency forward.

9. Use currency or credit swaps in those instances where local financing cannot be arranged. (If hard currency financing cannot be avoided, it should be made in the form of loans rather than equity investment. Monetary authorities are more likely to provide hard currency for repaying a loan than for repatriating an equity investment.)

10. Convert local currency and remit in the form of hard currency as loans, advances on profits or royalties, deposits on purchases, etc., to the maximum extent possible. (Local tax effect might partially offset the protection from exchange loss.)

11. Invest unremittable funds in assets that are most likely to rise in value as the value of money deteriorates.

CRITICISMS OF SFAS NO. 52

Considerable criticism has resulted from the issuance of SFAS No. 52. This criticism erupted with the issuance of the 1980 Exposure Draft and continued with criticism of the 1981 Revised Exposure Draft. The FASB itself was badly split, 4–3. The minority, in general, reflects accurately this view of a significant portion of corporate accounting officials, professional accountants, and academics, including this author. The dissenting Board members do not support the statement for reasons discussed in the following sections.

Relationship to Preexisting Fundamental Concepts. The critics believe that SFAS No. 52 adopts objectives and methods that are at variance with fundamental concepts underlying present financial statements because the functional currency perspective challenges and rejects the U.S. dollar perspective that underlies existing theories of consolidation, historical cost and capital maintenance, and business combinations using the purchase method. Such a rejection of the U.S. dollar perspective has ramifications beyond a translation statement. Income from a consolidated U.S. entity exists only after recovery of historical costs measured in dollars. SFAS No. 52 changes that because it remeasures the U.S. dollar equivalent costs while an item is held (measured by changes in the exchange rate) and treats the remeasurement as a translation adjustment that will seldom, if ever, be reported in net income. This changes income measurement concepts in the basic financial statements, and modifies the measurement of changes in current cost in FASB Statement No. 33, *Financial Reporting and Changing Prices.*

The aggregation of results measured in various functional currencies and then translated in U.S. dollars by the use of current rate method, and disposition of translation adjustments to equity, abandons the principle that consolidated results should be measured from a single perspective, which is necessary for (1) valid additions and subtractions for measurement of both balance sheet items and net income, and (2) faithful representation of consolidated results in U.S. dollars and in conformity with the historical cost basis. Further, the Statement introduces a concept of realization different from any previously applied by indefinitely deferring from recognition of net income the effects of exchange rate changes from a U.S. dollar perspective on individual assets and liabilities even beyond the time that those assets and liabilities have ceased to exist. As a result, the effects of rate changes on current operating net revenues are recognized when they occur, but the results of rate changes from previous net revenues are not. This results in foreign currency sales being denominated as if in U.S. dollars without a consistent application on other items. Further, SFAS No. 52 accepts SFAS No. 8 methodology for some foreign operations, notably for companies operating in hyperinflationary economies and in other situations determined by management, particularly for vertically integrated companies, but criticizes that methodology.

Incompatibility of Underlying Premises. Critics believe that SFAS No. 52 is based on two premises that are inconsistent with each other and inconsistent with concepts underlying consolidated financial statements. The first premise is that it is the parent's net investment in foreign operations that is subject to risk rather than individual assets and liabilities, whereas the second premise retains the issuance of foreign statements as measured by the functional currency. The first premise is inconsistent with consolidated statements in that these present individual assets, liabilities, and so on, rather than net investments. The second premise, retaining the functional currency measurements, is inconsistent with the U.S. dollar perspective, which holds that translation gains and losses affect income in U.S. dollars. The critics further point out that the translation adjustments fail to meet any definition of an element of financial statements as set forth in Concepts Statement No. 3, *Elements of Financial Statements of Business Enterprises.*

Critics note that because exchange rates change, their use for translation purposes cannot result in maintaining period-to-period relationships reported in the functional currency. Further, the statement divides gains and losses from change in exchange rates into two components: one, transaction gains and losses, is considered to affect income, and the other is considered a translation adjustment. Transaction gains on a third currency are recognized even if the third currency weakens in relation to the dollar and will never increase U.S. dollar cash flow to U.S. investors and creditors.

Effects on Cash Flow Statements. U.S. investors and creditors should be provided information about performance on that basis. Changes between two foreign currencies are not relevant to U.S. investors' cash flows or may be incorrectly measured. Consolidated statements prepared under the functional currency basis also may exclude certain increments such as a gain on holding cash by a foreign operation when its functional currency has strengthened against the dollar.

Inflation Accounting. Remeasurement into the U.S. dollar is required when a foreign subsidiary is operating in a hyperinflationary economy. No such remeasurement is permitted for operations in economies that have a relatively lower rate of inflation. Accordingly, an inconsistency is introduced. The remeasurement for some but not all subsidiaries is contrary to both the single entity and the single unit of measure concepts.

Similar Accounting for Similar Circumstances. Critics also believe that SFAS No. 52 will not result in similar accounting in similar situations. It accepts the use of the dollar as the functional currency for many foreign operations, in addition to those in hyperinflationary environments. The statement permits wide interpretation of the criteria, which will result in wide discrepancies. Dissimilar accounting in similar situations will also result from the permissiveness in the application of hedging criteria—for example, an entity may or may not designate a transaction as a hedge at its discretion. Dissimilar accounting in similar circumstances may also arise in the initial adoption of the Statement because of the variety of methods permitted, including voluntary restatements.

APPENDIX A: ILLUSTRATION OF TRANSLATION OF FINANCIAL STATEMENTS OF A FOREIGN SUBSIDIARY[1]

Background. Abbot Corporation, a U.S. company, has a wholly owned subsidiary located in England that meets the criteria for treatment as a net investment under the provisions of SFAS No. 52. Specifically, the English subsidiary, Biltrite, Ltd., is engaged in the manufacture in England, and the sale throughout Europe, of industrial products. Biltrite is not dependent on the economic environment of the parent company's reporting currency. It is financed primarily by local currency borrowings or borrowings denominated in a currency other than that of the parent. The operations of Biltrite are expected to generate functional currency cash flows that are available to the parent for reinvestment or dividends. The parent is not directly affected by cash flows related to individual assets or liabilities of Biltrite. Further, the parent does not expect to withdraw its basic investment, although it might receive normal dividends.

Biltrite's balance sheets at July 31, 1980 and 1981 (Exhibit 6), statement of income and retained earnings (Exhibit 7), and funds statement (Exhibit 8) for the fiscal year ended July 31, 1981, conform with U.S. generally accepted accounting principles prior to translation into U.S. dollars.

---

[1]Adapted from Deloitte Haskins & Sells, *Foreign Currency Translation*, 1981.

EXHIBIT 6

BILTRITE, LTD.
Comparative Balance Sheets
July 31, 1980 and 1981
(000)

	1981	1980
Assets		
Current assets		
Cash	£ 1,000	£ 600
Accounts receivable (net of allowances)	2,000	2,500
Inventories (at lower of FIFO cost or market)	3,000	2,500
Total current assets	£ 6,000	£ 5,600

Property, plant, and equipment

	Cost	Accumulated depreciation	Net		
Land	£ 1,300		£1,300		£ 1,300
Building	10,000	£2,000	8,000		8,400
Machinery and equipment.	14,000	7,000	7,000		8,400
	£25,300	£9,000		£16,300	£18,100
Total assets.				£22,300	£23,700

	1981	1980
Liabilities and capital		
Current liabilities		
Notes payable	£ 1,000	£ 1,000
Accounts payable	4,000	3,700
Total current liabilities	£ 5,000	£ 4,700
Long-term liabilities		
Notes payable	£ 4,000	£ 7,000
Deferred income taxes	2,000	1,800
	£ 6,000	£ 8,800
Shareholders' equity		
Capital stock	£4,000	4,000
Retained earnings	7,300 → 11,300	6,200
Total liabilities and stockholders' equity	£22,300	£23,700

Additional Information

1. Biltrite was organized on July 31, 1976, as a wholly owned subsidiary of Abbot Corporation. All of the capital stock of Biltrite was issued on that date when the rate of exchange was $1.784.

2. Biltrite's capital stock has not changed since its organization.

EXHIBIT 7

BILTRITE, LTD.
Statement of Income and Retained Earnings
For the Fiscal Year Ended July 31, 1981
(000)

Sales		£20,000
Costs and expenses:		
Costs of sales	£12,000	
Depreciation[a]	1,800	
Selling, general, and administrative expenses	2,100	
Interest expense	840	16,740
Income before income taxes		£ 3,260
Income taxes		980
Net income		£ 2,280
Retained earnings, July 31, 1980		6,200
		£ 8,480
Dividends		1,180
Retained earnings, July 31, 1981		£ 7,300

[a] Annual depreciation:

Buildings	£ 400
M & E	1,400
	£1,800

EXHIBIT 8

BILTRITE, LTD.
Statement of Changes in Financial Position
For the Fiscal Year Ended July 31, 1981
(000)

Sources of funds:	
Funds provided by operations	
Net income	£2,280
Add: Depreciation	1,800
Deferred income taxes	200
Total	£4,280
Uses of funds:	
Dividends	£1,180
Retirement of long-term debt	3,000
Total	£4,180
Increase in working capital	£ 100

3. Sales are made and costs and expenses are incurred reasonably uniformly over the year.

4. Depreciation on the books is on a straight-line basis, useful lives being:

Buildings	25 years
Machinery and equipment	10 years

5. Foreign exchange rates for the British pound for the fiscal year July 31, 1981, are as follows:

July 31, 1980	$2.331
Average monthly rates:	
August 1980..............	$2.393
September 1980	$2.388
October 1980.............	$2.438
November 1980	$2.350
December 1980	$2.385
January 1981	$2.386
February 1981	$2.205
March 1981	$2.244
April 1981...............	$2.140
May 1981...............	$2.070
June 1981...............	$1.943
July 1981	$1.889
July 31, 1981	$1.835
Average of monthly average rates for the 12 months ended July 31, 1981.............	$2.237

6. Effective British corporate tax rate, 30 percent.

Translation. The translation of Biltrite's balance sheet calls for the use of the current year-end rate of 1.835, to translate all assets and liabilities, except shareholders' equity. Capital stock is translated at the rate in effect when the shares were issued. This procedure is necessary to keep the translation adjustment from affecting capital stock and to maintain a separate historical record of the adjustments. The translation of revenues, expenses, and dividends calls for the use of a weighted-average exchange rate assuming, of course, that the revenues and dividends are all generated in a relatively uniform pattern over the course of the year.

This treatment of the opening retained earnings conforms to the recommendation of Paragraph 144 of SFAS No. 52, that a separation need not be made as between the opening retained earnings balance and the accumulated adjustment account as of that date because that would require recomputation of all prior years' figures as if the Statement had been in effect. In the Board's judgment the benefits of recomputation do not justify the costs.

The translations of Biltrite's balance sheet, statements of income and retained earnings, and funds statement appear in Exhibits 9, 10, and 11. Exhibit 12 illustrates the computation needed to obtain the opening balance of the accumulated translation adjustment in the initial year of applying the current

EXHIBIT 9

BILTRITE, LTD.
Translation of Balance Sheet
July 31, 1981

	Balance sheet accounts stated in pounds (000)	Translation at current rate	Balance sheet accounts stated in dollars (000)	
Assets				
Cash	£ 1,000	$1.835[a]	$ 1,835	
Accounts receivable—net	2,000	1.835	3,670	
Inventories	3,000	1.835	5,505	
Land	1,300	1.835	2,386	
Buildings—net	8,000	1.835	14,680	
Machinery and equipment—net	7,000	1.835	12,845	
Liabilities and shareholders' equity				
Notes payable—current	£ 1,000	1.835		$ 1,835
Accounts payable	4,000	1.835		7,340
Notes payable—long-term	4,000	1.835		7,340
Deferred income taxes	2,000	1.835[b]		3,670
Capital stock	4,000	[c]		7,136
Retained earnings	7,300	[d]		15,600
Accumulated translation adjustment		[b]	2,000	
	£22,300	£22,300	$42,921	$42,921

[a]Rate of exchange July 31, 1981.
[b]In accordance with the Board's decision to account for adjustments as timing differences, deferred taxes should be determined according to the requirements of Opinions No. 11, 23, and 24. If the parent intended to repatriate the accumulated earnings of Biltrite, a provision for deferred tax at the effective rate of 48% would adjust the Accumulated Translation Adjustment account by $960 and decrease deferred taxes in the same amount. (See Exhibit 13.)
[c]Capital stock was issued on July 31, 1976, and has been reported in the amount of $7,136 since that date. No adjustment for currency translation is included in the capital stock account.
[d]See Exhibit 10.

rate method. The translation adjustment at 8/1/80, the beginning of the year of initial application of the current rate method, is obtained directly by translating the opening balance of net assets, applying the 7/31/80 exchange rate, and subtracting therefrom the sum of the capital stock translated at the historical rate, and retained earnings translated balance at 7/31/80. This approach does not separate out the amount of the accumulated adjustment in the opening retained earnings.

The adjustment for the fiscal year ended 7/31/81 is obtained by multiplying the opening balance of net assets by the change in exchange rates for the year. To this figure is added or subtracted the result of multiplying the change in net assets for the year by the difference between the year-end exchange rate and the weighted-average rate used to translate revenues and expenses.

Exhibit 13 is an analysis of the changes in the accumulated translation adjustment account as called for by paragraph 32 of SFAS No. 52. The analysis includes a provision for deferred taxes, which may be necessary under certain circumstances, to comply with paragraph 24 of the Statement. Notes to the financial statements appear as Exhibit 14.

EXHIBIT 10

BILTRITE, LTD.
Translation of Income Statement and Retained Earnings
July 31, 1981

	Income and retained earnings statement stated in pounds (000)	Translation rate—weighted average Y/E, 7/31/81	Income and retained earnings statement stated in dollars (000)
Sales	£20,000	$2.237	$44,740
Costs and expenses:			
Costs of sales	£12,000	2.237	$26,844
Depreciation	1,800	2.237	4,027
Selling, general, and administrative expenses	2,100	2.237	4,698
Interest expense	840	2.237	1,879
Income taxes	980	2.237	2,192
	17,720		39,640
Net income	£ 2,280		$ 5,100
Retained earnings—July 31, 1980	6,200	a	13,140
	£ 8,480		18,240
Dividends	1,180	2.237	2,640
Retained earnings—July 31, 1981	£ 7,300		$15,600

[a] As reported on July 31, 1980. The proposed Statement was adopted as of August 1, 1980. The use of this rate conforms with the approach called for by paragraph 10 of SFAS No. 52; therefore, no reclassification is made as between retained earnings and the separate component of shareholders' equity (the accumulated translation adjustment) prior to July 31, 1980.

EXHIBIT 11

BILTRITE, LTD.
Translation of Statement of Changes in Financial Position
July 31, 1981

	Statement of changes in financial position stated in pounds (£) (000)	Translation rate	Statement of changes in financial position stated in dollars ($) (000)
Sources of funds:			
Funds provided by operations			
Net income	£2,280	$2,237	$ 5,100
Add: Depreciation	1,800	2,237	4,027
Deferred income taxes	200	2,237	447
Total	£4,280		$ 9,574
Increase in deferred income taxes			
Decreases in noncurrent assets:		*a*	
Land		*a*	644
Building		*a*	4,005
Equipment		*a*	3,603
Total	£4,280		$17,826
Uses of funds:			
Dividends	£1,180	2,237	$ 2,640
Retirement of long-term debt	3,000	1,835	5,505
Other decreases in long-term debt		*a*	3,472
Decrease in deferred income taxes . . .		*a*	972
Decrease in accumulated translation adjustment		*a*	5,501
Total	£4,180		$18,090
Increase (decrease) in working capital .	£ 100		$ (264)

*a*Changes in translated amounts at end of period.

EXHIBIT 12   Calculation of Year-End Translation Adjustments with the Beginning Balance of Year of Adoption of Current Rate Method

Net assets at 7/31/80		£10,200	
Increase in rate of exchange in fiscal year ending 7/31/81			
Rate 7/31/81	$1.835		
Rate 7/31/80	2.331	×.496	$(5,059)
Addition to net assets for the fiscal year ended 7/31/81 from operations	$2,280		
Less dividends	1,180	£ 1,100	
Rate at 7/31/81	$1.835		
Average monthly rate	2.237	×.402	(442)
Addition to accumulated adjustment to year ended 7/31/81			$(5,501)
Accumulated transaction adjustments balance, 8/1/80			3,501
Accumulated adjustment balance, 7/31/81 (see Exhibit 9)			$(2,000)

The accumulated translation adjustment can also be calculated as follows:			
Net assets, 7/31/81	£11,300		
Rate of exchange, 7/31/81	×1.835		
		$20,736	
Less:			
Capital stock, 7/31/81 (Exhibit 9)	$ 7,136		
Retained earnings, 7/31/81 (Exhibit 10)[a]	15,600	22,736	
Accumulated translation adjustments, 7/31/80[b] . . .			$(2,000)

[a]Assume retained earnings from prior consolidation as of 7/31/80. If translated retained earnings are known at 7/31/80, based on approximation of the provisions of SFAS No. 52, that amount may be used.

[b]This balance is to be reduced by the tax effect amount needed to meet requirements of APB Opinions No. 11, 23, and 24, as needed, and that amount added to deferred taxes. If there is no intent to repatriate undistributed earnings of the foreign subsidiary, no taxes need be allocated on financial statement translation adjustments.

EXHIBIT 13

BILTRITE, LTD.
Analysis of Accumulated Translation Adjustments
July 31, 1981
(000)

Balance at 8/1/80	$ 3,501
Add: Aggregate adjustment for the fiscal year ended 7/31/81 resulting from the translation of foreign currency statements	(5,501)
Balance at 7/31/81	$(2,000)
If there is intent to repatriate undistributed earnings: Deduct: Provision for deferred income taxes at the effective rate of 48%	960
Balance at 7/31/81	$(1,040)

EXHIBIT 14 Notes to Financial Statements: Effects of Rate Changes on Reported Results

---

Paragraph 144 of SFAS No. 52 encourages management to supplement the disclosures required by the Statement with an analysis and discussion of changes on reported results of operations. The objective of this disclosure is to give users an understanding of the broad economic implications of rate changes. In the Biltrite illustration, the note to the financial statements describing the effects might be as follows:

> Biltrite's manufacturing operations are conducted entirely in England. Sales are made in England and throughout Europe. Raw materials are purchased largely in West Germany. During the past year the pound strengthened in relation to the dollar giving rise to an increase in the accumulated translation adjustment component of stockholders' equity. Operations were affected by the strengthening of the pound in relation to European currencies such as the West German mark and the Swiss franc. While raw materials imported from West Germany became cheaper, sales to European countries faced stiffer competition because our export products became relatively more expensive abroad. The results of these two factors, raw material costs decreases and sales decreases in this period, have to some extent offset one another in terms of effects on profit.

APPENDIX B: REMEASUREMENT INTO THE FUNCTIONAL CURRENCY

Assume that the Biltrite Co. (Appendix A) were only an agency for the U.S. parent or operated in a hyperinflationary economy. The following remeasurement into the functional currency (U.S. dollars) would be necessary.

Balance Sheet

Monetary assets, £3,000 at 1.835, the 7/31 current rate		$ 5,505
Monetary liabilities, £11,000 at 1.835, the 7/31 current rate		20,185
Net monetary credit		$(14,680)
Accounts at various historical costs:		
Land and buildings, £9,300 at 1.784	$16,591	
Machinery and equipment, £7,000 at 1.784	12,488	
Inventories, £3,000 at 1.967	5,901	34,980
Net assets		$ 20,300
Less: Capital stock	$ 7,136	
Retained earnings, 8/1/80 (Exhibit 10)	13,139	
Reported net income, net of dividends	2,232	22,507
Translation loss		$ (2,207)
Tax effect		1,059
Reportable translation loss in income		$ (1,148)

Income Statement

Sales, £20,000 at average current rate 2.237		$ 44,740
Cost of sales, £12,000 at historical rate, calculated as follows:		
Beg. inv. £2,500 at 2.330	$ 5,825	
Purchases £12,500 at average rate 2.237	27,963	
	$33,788	
Less ending inventory £3,000 at 1.967	5,901	$ 27,887
Depreciation, £1,800:		
Bldgs. £400 at 1.784	$ 714	
Mach., eq., and other £1,400 at 1.784	2,498	3,212
Other expenses, £3,920 at average rate 2.237		8,769
		$ 39,868
Net income		$ 4,872
Less dividend, £1,180 at 2.237		2,640
To retained earnings		$ 2,232

Note: The results of applying the proposed Statement under the current rate method and the temporal method (per SFAS No. 8, except that deferred taxes are classified as monetary) may be reconciled as follows:

Retained earnings, 7/31/81 per current rate	$15,600
Add: Accumulated adjustment	(2,000)
	$13,600
Less: Increase in nonmonetary assets from using historical rates ($34,980) to current rate ($35,416)	436
Retained earnings, 7/31/81 as remeasured in dollars, the functional currency (before tax effect)	$13,164
Retained earnings, 7/31/81 as remeasured in dollars, the functional currency (after tax effect)	$14,223

BIBLIOGRAPHY

Dukes, R. E., *An Empirical Investigation of the Effects of Statement of Financial Standards No. 8 on Security Return Behavior* (FASB, 1978).

Financial Accounting Standards Board, *Accounting for Foreign Currency Translation, Discussion Memorandum* (FASB, 1974).

———, *Financial Statement Model on Accounting for Foreign Currency Translation,* (FASB, 1974).

———, *Accounting for the Translation of Foreign Currency Transactions and Foreign Currency Financial Statements,* Statement of Financial Accounting Standards No. 8 (FASB, 1975).

———, *Foreign Currency Translation,* Statement of Financial Accounting Standards No. 52 (FASB, 1981).

Lorensen, L., *Reporting Foreign Operations of U.S. Companies in U.S. Dollars,* Accounting Research Study No. 12 (AICPA 1972).

National Association of Accountants, *Management Accounting Problems in Foreign Operations,* Research Report No. 36 (NAA, 1960).

Teck, A., "Control Your Exposure to Foreign Exchange," *Harvard Business Review,* January–February 1974, pp. 66–75.

———, "Using Computers for Foreign Exchange Tax Planning," *International Tax Journal,* Fall 1975.

Watt, G. C., "Unrealized Foreign Exchange Gains Arising from Funds Borrowed in Local Currency," *NAA Bulletin,* February 1965, pp. 3–11.

Wheeler, J. E., and W. H. Galliart, *An Appraisal of Interperiod Income Tax Allocation* (Financial Executives Research Foundation, New York, 1974).

CHAPTER 36

Accounting for

Corporate

Income Taxes

Hugo Nurnberg

*Professor of Accountancy, Baruch College of
the City University of New York*

INTRODUCTION

The net income figure of a corporation as reported in its published income statement is often used, together with other data, to evaluate its past performance and to form an opinion of its future prospects. The widespread impact of federal corporate income taxes with high tax rates makes them significant in the determination of net income. The exclusion of income taxes entirely would nearly double the net income figures of many corporations; their partial exclusion would have proportional results. This chapter examines the nature and financial reporting of federal corporate income taxes. Although not considered extensively in this chapter, the same financial reporting standards apply to state and foreign corporate income taxes.

NATURE OF INCOME TAX

The conceptualization of income taxes as an expense or a distribution of income depends on whether the proprietary or entity theory is assumed. Thus, from the shareholders' viewpoint, income taxes are an expense that should be included in computing net income available for distribution as dividends without impairing capital. But from the viewpoint of the corporate entity, income taxes are a distribution of income somewhat akin to dividends, and net income before income taxes is the more significant basis for evaluating past performance. Both theories have merit, but most theorists implicitly or explicitly assume the proprietary theory, whereby income taxes are viewed as an expense, and this conceptualization is explicitly assumed in the authoritative pronouncements of financial accounting standards in the United States [APB Opinion No. 11, 1967, par. 14(b)]. Accordingly, income taxes are viewed henceforth as an expense.

FLOW-THROUGH VERSUS TAX ALLOCATION

Historically, the income tax expense reported in the income statement was equal to the income tax assessable on taxable income for the same year, and the income tax liability reported in the balance sheet was equal to the unpaid balance. This procedure is known as the *flow-through method*. As tax rates have increased, income tax expense has assumed greater importance in the computation of net income. Differences in the treatment of revenue and expense items for book and tax purposes also became more common. More and more accountants became concerned with fluctuations in income tax expense for a series of years that resulted from such differences when the flow-through method was used. A new financial reporting procedure was developed to eliminate these fluctuations known as *income tax allocation*. (Alternative designations include *income tax normalization* and *tax effect accounting*.) Income tax allocation became controversial immediately upon its introduction.

DIFFERENCES BETWEEN PRETAX BOOK INCOME
AND TAXABLE INCOME

Despite the many revenues and expenses common to both, pretax book income and taxable income are essentially different—although reconcilable—quantities. Pretax book income is the sum of the revenues (and gains) less the sum of the expenses (and losses) other than income tax expense determined in accordance with generally accepted accounting principles. Taxable income, on the other hand, is defined statutorily by income tax laws and regulations.

Under the provisions of the income tax laws of most countries, there are some choices in methods of reporting certain transactions for tax purposes, the choices residing with the management of the corporation. Similarly, several alternatively acceptable accounting principles and procedures may be available for reporting certain transactions for book purposes, the choices again residing with the management. Thus, many of the differences between pretax book income and taxable income are discretionary.

Whether discretionary or not, differences between pretax book income and taxable income arise because of the different purposes to which the measurement of each is directed. Differences in the treatment of the same revenues (or gains) and expenses (or losses) promise to remain, although individual differences may be eliminated as new ones arise. Despite these differences, pretax book income may be reconciled with taxable income. Indeed, any comprehensive classification of these differences simultaneously entails a reconciliation of the two.

Differences between pretax book income and taxable income have been classified [see Nurnberg, 1971, pp. 14–21] as (1) permanent differences; (2) interpretive differences; and (3) timing differences.

Permanent Differences. Permanent differences encompass revenues (and gains) and nontax expenses (and losses) included in taxable income but forever excluded from either pretax book income or retained earnings, and revenues (and gains) and nontax expenses (or losses) included in either pretax book income or retained earnings but forever excluded from taxable income. Permanent differences are classifiable into four categories, depending on whether the items represent revenues (or gains) or expenses (or losses), and whether the items are recognized only for book purposes or only for tax purposes. Examples of permanent differences are enumerated in Exhibit 1.

For the most part, permanent differences present no special financial reporting problems, because all of the tax consequences are worked out in the year in which the differences occur. For example, the exclusion of interest on municipal bonds from taxable income is absolute—it will not be included in taxable income for some other year. As a result, the financial reporting of

---

EXHIBIT 1   Permanent Differences

---

1. Revenues (or gains) included in pretax book income but forever excluded from taxable income:
   Interest on tax-exempt bonds
   Certain proceeds from officer life insurance policies
   Certain gains from involuntary conversions
   Certain undistributed earnings of subsidiaries, joint ventures, and investees
   Gains in excess of amount taxed due to original tax basis in excess of original book basis
2. Expenses (or losses) reducing pretax book income but never a deduction from taxable income:
   Business expense for personal use
   Political campaign contributions
   Fines, bribes, penalties
   Officers' life insurance premium expense
   Losses in excess of amount tax deductible due to original book basis in excess of original tax basis
3. Revenues (or gains) included in taxable income but forever excluded from pretax book income:
   Gains in excess of amount recognized for book purposes due to original book basis in excess of original tax basis
4. Expenses (or losses) reducing taxable income but never an expense in computing pretax book income:
   Percentage depletion in excess of cost depletion
   Dividends received deduction[a]
   Losses in excess of amount recognized for book purposes due to original tax basis in excess of original book basis

---

[a]Assume that a corporation receives $100 of dividends qualifying for the 85 percent dividend exclusion. On the tax return the corporation will report $100 of revenue and a deduction of $85; technically, then, this is a type 4 permanent difference. One may think of the $85 as being a permanent difference of type 1, book revenue never taxed, even though it is not treated this way on the tax return.

income taxes in the presence of permanent differences does not differ depending on whether the flow-through method or income tax allocation is employed; under both procedures, income tax expense remains equal to the income tax assessable on taxable income for the same year.

Interpretive Differences. Interpretive differences encompass revenues (and gains) and nontax expenses (and losses) included in taxable income but excluded from pretax book income and included directly in retained earnings (or some other element of shareholders' equity) for the same year. Examples of interpretive differences involving direct adjustments of retained earnings include prior period adjustments for corrections of errors and realization of previously unrecorded tax benefits of preacquisition operating loss carry-forwards of purchased subsidiaries, and changes in accounting principles reported retroactively. Examples of interpretive differences involving direct adjustments of other shareholders' equity accounts include certain employee stock option plans and realization of previously unrecorded tax benefits of operating loss carry-forwards arising prior to a quasi-reorganization.

Timing Differences. Timing differences encompass revenues (and gains) and expenses (and losses) included in taxable income for one year but included in pretax book income for another year. Timing differences are classifiable into four categories:

1. Revenues (and gains) recognized *earlier* for tax purposes than for book purposes
2. Expenses (and losses) recognized *earlier* for tax purposes than for book purposes
3. Revenues (and gains) recognized *later* for tax purposes than for book purposes
4. Expenses (and losses) recognized *later* for tax purposes than for book purposes

Examples of timing differences classified into these four categories are enumerated in Exhibit 2.

By definition, timing differences originate or arise in one year and reverse or turn around in another year. Thus, timing differences that increase (decrease) pretax book income relative to taxable income in the year of origination inevitably decrease (increase) pretax book income relative to taxable income in the year of reversal. It is not always obvious, however, just when the reversal will occur. On the other hand, permanent differences never reverse.

A problem with respect to distinguishing between permanent differences and timing differences relates to certain initial differences between pretax book income and taxable income that may not reverse until indefinite future periods or may never reverse. Reversal of the initial differences is difficult to predict, because the events that create the initial differences are controlled by the taxpayer and frequently require that the taxpayer take specific action for reversal to occur. For example, earnings of subsidiaries may be taxable to the parent company at the time of remittance, which is subject to the control of the parent company, although the parent company may recognize these earnings for book

---

EXHIBIT 2 Timing Differences

---

1. Revenues (and gains) recognized earlier for tax purposes than for book purposes:
    Taxable when received but deferred on books until earned
        Prepaid interest, rental, commission, subscription, advertising, and royalty revenue
        Sales of coupon books entitling purchaser to services
        Theater ticket, transportation ticket, and token sales
        Certain membership fees
        Tuition fees
    Taxable when earned but deferred on books until received (rare)
        Long-term contracts taxed on percentage-of-completion basis, booked on completed contract basis
2. Expenses (and losses) recognized earlier for tax purposes than for book purposes:
    Tax deductible when paid but deferred on books until benefits expire
        Advertising expense
        Preoperating costs
        Salaries, wages, commissions, and fees paid in advance, including payroll taxes thereon
    Amortizable faster for tax purposes than for book purposes
        Organization cost
        Depreciation
        Intangible drilling cost
3. Revenues (and gains) recognized later for tax purposes than for book purposes:
    Accrued in accounts as earned but taxable later when received
        Installment sales booked at time of sale, taxed pro rata as collected
        Long-term contracts booked on percentage-of-completion basis, taxed on completed contract basis
        Undistributed earnings of subsidiaries, joint ventures, and investees accrued as earned but taxed as received
4. Expenses (and losses) recognized later for tax purposes than for book purposes:
    Accrued in accounts as incurred but tax deductible later when paid
        Sales discounts and returns
        Sales, freight, and customer advertising allowances
        Warranty and guarantee expense
        Deferred compensation and incentive bonuses
        Settlement cost of pending litigation
        Estimated cost of major repairs and maintenance
        Write-downs to net realizable value
    Amortizable faster for book purposes than for tax purposes (rare)
        Organization cost
        Depreciation
        Intangible drilling costs

---

purposes in accordance with the equity method as the earnings are realized by the subsidiary. Such differences may be classified as timing differences by contemplating the ultimate liquidation of the subsidiary, but this is contrary to the going-concern assumption in many cases. Alternatively, such differences may be classified as either permanent differences or timing differences, depending on the circumstances and experience of the subsidiary company with respect to remittances to the parent company.

BASIC APPROACHES TO REPORTING TAX
EFFECTS OF INTERPRETIVE DIFFERENCES

Two basic approaches have been suggested to report the tax effects of interpretive differences. Under *intraperiod* income tax allocation, the tax effects of revenues (and gains) and nontax expenses (and losses) included directly in retained earnings (or some other shareholders' equity account) are matched or netted against these items in the statement of changes in retained earnings (or statement of changes in some other shareholders' equity account), and the remaining tax is reported as expense in the income statement. Under the *flow-through method*, on the other hand, the entire income tax assessable on taxable income is reported as expense in the income statement for the same year, notwithstanding the presence of interpretive differences.

Intraperiod income tax allocation is contrasted with the flow-through method in Exhibit 3, where it is assumed that pretax book income is $1,000, the beginning balance of retained earnings is $5,000, and the corporate income tax rate is a flat 40 percent.[1] Taxable income is $1,200 in case 1 (including $200 of taxable revenues representing a correction of prior periods' income), whereas in case 2 it is $700 (including $300 of tax-deductible expenses representing a correction of prior periods' income). The data are tabulated in Exhibit 3, where the results under the flow-through method are indicated in the F columns, and the results under intraperiod income tax allocation are indicated in the A columns.

In case 1, the income tax currently payable is 40 percent of $1,200, or $480.

---

[1]The complexities of the graduated rate exemption are considered on pp. 36-23 to 36-26.

EXHIBIT 3   Intraperiod Allocation versus Flow-Through

	1		2	
	A	F	A	F
Income statement				
Pretax book income	$1,000	$1,000	$1,000	$1,000
Income tax expense	400	480	400	280
Posttax book income	$ 600	$ 520	$ 600	$ 720
Retained earnings statement				
Beginning balance	$5,000	$5,000	$5,000	$5,000
Add: Posttax book income	600	520	600	720
Prior period adjustment	200	200		
Tax effect	(80)			
	$5,720	$5,720	$5,600	$5,720
Less: Prior period adjustment			300	300
Tax effect			(120)	
Ending balance	$5,720	$5,720	$5,420	$5,420

EXHIBIT 4   Intraperiod Allocation versus Flow-Through

Partial income statement	A	F
Pretax book income from continuing operations	$3,000	$3,000
Income tax expense	1,200	800
Posttax book income from continuing operations	$1,800	$2,200
Extraordinary loss		1,000
Extraordinary loss net of $400 tax benefit	600	
Net income	$1,200	$1,200

Under flow-through, the entire $480 is reported as income tax expense in the income statement. Under intraperiod income tax allocation, 40 percent of $200, or $80, is reported as an offset to the $200 prior period adjustment in the retained earnings statement, and the remaining $400 is reported as income tax expense in the income statement. In case 2, the income tax currently payable is 40 percent of $700, or $280. Under flow-through, the $280 is reported as income tax expense in the income statement. Under intraperiod income tax allocation, 40 percent of $300, or $120, is reported as an offset to the $300 prior period adjustment in the retained earnings statement, and $400 is reported as income tax expense in the income statement—even though the income tax currently payable is only $280.

Intraperiod income tax allocation also refers to procedures for allocating income taxes between pretax book income from continuing operations and income from discontinued operations, extraordinary items, and cumulative adjustments for changes in accounting principles. This is contrasted with the flow-through method in Exhibit 4, where it is assumed that pretax book income is $3,000, an extraordinary loss is $1,000, and the income tax rate applicable to both is 40 percent. Accordingly, taxable income is $2,000, and the tax assessable thereon is $800. The data are tabulated in Exhibit 4, where the results under interperiod income tax allocation are indicated in the A column and the results under the flow-through method are indicated in the F column. Note that income tax expense bears a normal relationship to pretax book income from continuing operations under intraperiod income tax allocation but not under the flow-through method.

BASIC APPROACHES TO REPORTING TAX EFFECTS OF TIMING DIFFERENCES

Several approaches have been suggested to account for the tax effects of timing differences. Under the *deferred* and *liability methods* of interperiod allocation, tax payments and refunds are allocated among years in order to match the tax effects of revenues (or gains) and expenses (or losses) with the years in which they are recognized for book purposes. *Deferred tax credits* (or *deferred tax liabilities*) are recognized for the tax effects of the earlier recognition of revenues and later recognition of expenses for book purposes than for tax purposes, and *deferred tax debits* (or *deferred tax assets*) are recognized for the tax effects of the later recognition of revenues and earlier recognition of expenses for book purposes than for tax purposes. "Let the tax follow the income" is the guiding principle of interperiod income tax allocation.

Under the *net-of-tax method* of interperiod income tax allocation, timing differences are considered a problem in accounting for the revenues (or gains) and nontax expenses (or losses) themselves, together with the related assets and liabilities; accordingly, these items are adjusted for the tax effects of timing differences, and the annual reported income tax expense remains the income tax assessable on taxable income for the same year.

Finally, under the *flow-through method,* the tax effects of timing differences are ignored, and the annual reported income tax expense remains the income tax assessable on taxable income for the same year.

Interperiod income tax allocation is contrasted with the flow-through method in Exhibit 5, where it is assumed that pretax book income is $1,000 and encompasses $2,500 of revenues and $1,500 of expenses for both 19X1 and 19X2, and the corporate income tax rate is a flat 40 percent. In case 1, taxable income is $1,400 in 19X1 and $600 in 19X2 ($400 of revenues are collected and taxed in 19X1 but recognized on the books in 19X2). In case 2, taxable income is $900 in 19X1 and $1,100 in 19X2 ($100 of expenses are paid and tax deducted in 19X1 but expired and recognized on the books in 19X2). In case 3, taxable income is $800 in 19X1 and $1,200 in 19X2 ($200 of revenues are earned and recognized on the books in 19X1 but collected and taxed in 19X2). In case 4, taxable income is $1,300 in 19X1 and $700 in 19X2 ($300 of expenses are incurred and recognized on the books in 19X1 but paid and tax deducted in 19X2). The data are tabulated in Exhibit 5, where the results under the flow-through method are indicated in the F columns, the results under either the deferred or liability method of interperiod income tax allocation are indicated in the A columns, and the results under the net-of-tax method of interperiod income tax allocation are indicated in the N columns.

In case 1, $400 of revenues included in taxable income for 19X1 are included in pretax book income for 19X2. Under the flow-through method, no cognizance is taken of this timing difference; income tax expense each year remains equal to the income tax assessable on taxable income for the same year—40 percent of $1,400, or $560, for 19X1, and 40 percent of $600, or $240, for 19X2. Under either the deferred or liability method of interperiod income tax allocation, income taxes equal to 40 percent of $400, or $160, are deferred on the books at the end of 19X1 and expensed at the end of 19X2. Accordingly, income tax expense for 19X1 is $160 less than the $560 income tax then payable, and income tax expense for 19X2 is $160 more than the $240 income tax then payable. Either a deferred tax debit or a deferred tax asset of $160 is recognized on the books at the end of 19X1 and written off at the end of 19X2 depending, respectively, on whether the deferred or liability method is employed. Finally, under the net-of-tax method, income tax expense for each year remains equal to the income tax then payable, and reported revenues are increased by $160 for 19X1 and decreased by $160 for 19X2.

In case 2, $100 of nontax expenses included in taxable income for 19X1 are included in pretax book income for 19X2. Under the flow-through method, no

EXHIBIT 5 Interperiod Allocation versus Flow-Through

	1			2			3			4		
	F	A	N	F	A	N	F	A	N	F	A	N
19X1 income statement												
Revenues—unadjusted	$2,500	$2,500	$2,500	$2,500	$2,500	$2,500	$2,500	$2,500	$2,500	$2,500	$2,500	$2,500
Tax effect adjustment			160						−80			
Revenues—adjusted	$2,500	$2,500	$2,660	$2,500	$2,500	$2,500	$2,500	$2,500	$2,420	$2,500	$2,500	$2,500
Expenses—unadjusted	$1,500	$1,500	$1,500	$1,500	$1,500	$1,500	$1,500	$1,500	$1,500	$1,500	$1,500	$1,500
Tax effect adjustment						40						−120
Expenses—adjusted	$1,500	$1,500	$1,500	$1,500	$1,500	$1,540	$1,500	$1,500	$1,500	$1,500	$1,500	$1,380
Pretax book income	$1,000	$1,000	$1,160	$1,000	$1,000	$ 960	$1,000	$1,000	$ 920	$1,000	$1,000	$1,120
Income tax expense:												
Income tax currently payable	$ 560	$ 560	$ 560	$ 360	$ 360	$ 360	$ 320	$ 320	$ 320	$ 520	$ 520	$ 520
Add: Accrual of 19X2		−160			40			80			−120	
Deduct: Deferral to 19X2.												
Total income tax expense	$ 560	$ 400	$ 560	$ 360	$ 400	$ 360	$ 320	$ 400	$ 320	$ 520	$ 400	$ 520
Posttax book income	$ 440	$ 600	$ 600	$ 640	$ 600	$ 600	$ 680	$ 600	$ 600	$ 480	$ 600	$ 600
19X2 income statement												
Revenues—unadjusted	$2,500	$2,500	$2,500	$2,500	$2,500	$2,500	$2,500	$2,500	$2,500	$2,500	$2,500	$2,500
Tax effect adjustment			−160						80			
Revenues—adjusted	$2,500	$2,500	$2,340	$2,500	$2,500	$2,500	$2,500	$2,500	$2,580	$2,500	$2,500	$2,500
Expenses—unadjusted	$1,500	$1,500	$1,500	$1,500	$1,500	$1,500	$1,500	$1,500	$1,500	$1,500	$1,500	$1,500
Tax effect adjustment						−40						120
Expenses—adjusted	$1,500	$1,500	$1,500	$1,500	$1,500	$1,460	$1,500	$1,500	$1,500	$1,500	$1,500	$1,620
Pretax book income	$1,000	$1,000	$ 840	$1,000	$1,000	$1,040	$1,000	$1,000	$1,080	$1,000	$1,000	$ 880
Income tax expense:												
Income tax currently payable	$ 240	$ 240	$ 240	$ 440	$ 440	$ 440	$ 480	$ 480	$ 480	$ 280	$ 280	$ 280
Add: Deferral from 19X1		160			−40			−80			120	
Deduct: Accrual to 19X1.												
Total income tax expense	$ 240	$ 400	$ 240	$ 440	$ 400	$ 440	$ 480	$ 400	$ 480	$ 280	$ 400	$ 280
Posttax book income	$ 760	$ 600	$ 600	$ 560	$ 600	$ 600	$ 520	$ 600	$ 600	$ 720	$ 600	$ 600

cognizance is taken of this timing difference; income tax expense each year remains equal to the income tax assessable on taxable income for the same year—40 percent of $900, or $360, for 19X1, and 40 percent of $1,100, or $440, for 19X2. Under either the deferred or liability method of interperiod income tax allocation, income taxes equal to 40 percent of $100, or $40, are accrued and expensed on the books at the end of 19X1 although not paid until the end of 19X2. Accordingly, income tax expense for 19X1 is $40 more than the $360 income tax then payable, and income tax expense for 19X2 is $40 less than the $440 tax then payable. Either a deferred tax credit or a deferred liability of $40 is recognized on the books at the end of 19X1 and written off at the end of 19X2 depending, respectively, on whether the deferred or liability method is employed. Finally, under the net-of-tax method, income tax expense for each year remains equal to the income tax then payable, and reported nontax expenses are increased by $40 for 19X1 and decreased by $40 for 19X2.

In case 3, $200 of revenues included in taxable income for 19X2 are included in pretax book income for 19X1. Under the flow-through method, no cognizance is taken of this timing difference; income tax expense each year remains equal to the income tax assessable on taxable income for the same year—40 percent of $800, or $320, for 19X1, and 40 percent of $1,200, or $480, for 19X2. Under either the deferred or liability method of interperiod income tax allocation, income taxes equal to 40 percent of $200, or $80, are accrued and expensed in the accounts at the end of 19X1 although not paid until the end of 19X2. Accordingly, income tax expense for 19X1 is $80 more than the $320 income tax then payable, and income tax expense for 19X2 is $80 less than the $480 income tax then payable. Either a deferred tax credit or a deferred tax liability of $80 is recognized on the books at the end of 19X1 and written off at the end of 19X2 depending, respectively, on whether the deferred or liability method is employed. Finally, under the net-of-tax method, income tax expense for each year remains equal to the income tax then payable, and reported revenues are decreased by $80 for 19X1 and increased by $80 for 19X2.

In case 4, $300 of expenses included in taxable income for 19X2 are included in pretax book income for 19X1. Under the flow-through method, no cognizance is taken of this timing difference; income tax expense each year remains equal to the income tax assessable on taxable income for the same year—40 percent of $1,300, or $560, for 19X1, and 40 percent of $700, or $280, for 19X2. Under either the deferred or liability method of interperiod income tax allocation, income taxes equal to 40 percent of $300, or $120, are deferred on the books at the end of 19X1 and expensed at the end of 19X2. Accordingly, income tax expense for 19X1 is $120 less than the $520 income tax then payable, and income tax expense for 19X2 is $120 more than the $280 income tax then payable. Either a deferred tax debit or a deferred tax asset of $120 is recognized on the books at the end of 19X1 and written off at the end of 19X2, depending, respectively, on whether the deferred or liability method of interperiod income tax allocation is employed. Finally, under the net-of-tax method, income tax expense for each year remains equal to the income tax then payable, and reported expenses are decreased by $120 for 19X1 and increased by $120 for 19X2.

A comparison of the income statements under the flow-through method and the three methods of interperiod income tax allocation reveals the following:

1. Pretax book income is the same under the flow-through, deferred, and liability methods but different under the net-of-tax method.

2. Income tax expense equals the income tax payable on taxable income for the same year under the flow-through and net-of-tax methods, whereas it is based on pretax book income under the deferred and liability methods.

3. Net income and net assets are the same under all three methods of interperiod income tax allocation when, as is assumed in this illustration, the income tax rate is constant for all years and no portion of the income tax effects under the net-of-tax method is included in overhead burden rates and inventory cost.

4. Although not illustrated in Exhibit 5, disclosure in the financial statements of the tax effects of timing differences differs in location and detail under each of the three methods of interperiod income tax allocation.

CONTROVERSIES OVER INTRAPERIOD INCOME TAX ALLOCATION

As first proposed, intraperiod income tax allocation was subject to widespread controversy. Although sanctioned by the American Institute of (Certified Public) Accountants [CAP Accounting Research Bulletin No. 23, 1944], the Securities and Exchange Commission [Accounting Series Release No. 53, 1945] initially took exception to intraperiod income tax allocation. Specifically, the Commission maintained that intraperiod income tax allocation was contrary to accounting as traditionally conceived; that it was contrary to the historical cost convention and to the prescription against normalizing periodic net income; that it was not subject to objective measurement but rather involved the hypothecation of reality; that the actual facts of the situation were obscured; and that no other expense was allocated on the basis of applying to a given transaction so much of the expense as would not have occurred if the transaction to which the expense was attributed had not taken place. Critics raised far fewer objections to intraperiod income tax allocation between two positive incomes, whereby the total initial tax charge was allocated as two smaller tax charges, than to intraperiod allocation between a positive and a negative income, whereby the total initial tax charge was allocated as a negative tax charge (or tax savings) and a positive tax charge in excess of the initial tax charge by the absolute amount of the negative tax charge.

With the passage of time, however, intraperiod income tax allocation became a widely used accounting practice, and now constitutes a required generally accepted accounting principle [APB Opinion No. 11, 1967, par. 52]. A few critics remain, however, who still raise such objections to intraperiod income tax allocation [see, e.g., Chambers, 1968, pp. 106–110]. Additionally, complexities arise in applying intraperiod income tax allocation to two or more income items whenever the exclusion of one or more items changes taxable income to a level where the applicable income tax rate also changes.

CONTROVERSIES OVER INTERPERIOD INCOME TAX ALLOCATION

Most accounting theorists appear to favor either the flow-through method or the consistent use of one of the three methods of interperiod income tax allocation enumerated above, but opinion is divided among the latter as to whether the favored method of interperiod income tax allocation should be used for all or only some timing differences. Other theorists favor one method of interperiod income tax allocation for some timing differences and another method of interperiod income tax allocation for other timing differences. That is, both the nature and extent of interperiod income tax allocation are subject to controversy.

Purpose of Interperiod Allocation. Fluctuations in reported income tax expense and posttax book income for a series of years due solely to timing differences may result under the flow-through method but are eliminated under interperiod income tax allocation. Proponents of interperiod allocation desire to eliminate these fluctuations, not to smooth posttax book income per se, but rather to increase the comparability of posttax book income for a series of years. That is, financial statements prepared in accordance with interperiod income tax allocation are held to be more comparable and informative than financial statements prepared in accordance with the flow-through method.

Opponents of interperiod income tax allocation argue to the contrary. They contend that fluctuations in reported income tax expense and posttax book income due to timing differences should be recognized, and that to do otherwise is contrary to the generally accepted proscription against income smoothing. Opponents argue further that financial statements prepared in accordance with interperiod income tax allocation are more confusing than enlightening; that such statements obscure the efforts of management to minimize current taxes; that the procedure is a bookkeeping gimmick that is too complex to be practicable; and that disclosure of timing differences in footnotes alone is all that should be required.

In refutation, proponents of interperiod income tax allocation contend that, contrary to outward appearances, interperiod income tax allocation is intended to measure income in accordance with the principles of accrual accounting, not merely smooth income, and that smoothing charges may be leveled against many other accrual accounting procedures on the same basis. Moreover, the added complexities of interperiod income tax allocation in particular—and accrual accounting in general—are held to be irrelevant or at least an insufficient reason for rejecting either. Proponents argue further [see, e.g., Keller, 1961, pp. 112–113] that timing differences effect postponements or accelerations in the payment of the same total tax over the life of the corporation. Accordingly, timing differences are a *financial* management consideration presumably to be reported in the funds statement; only the interest inherent in such postponements or accelerations is an *operational* management consideration properly reported in the income statement. Because the flow-through method does not distinguish between the two, it is criticized as enabling management to manipulate the calculation of posttax book income by merely changing tax policies.

Unfortunately, most of the arguments cited thus far are merely opposing assertions concerning the comparative utility of different data on the same transactions accumulated in accordance with different accounting procedures. The *definitive* resolution of these arguments must await the development of more sophisticated measures of data utility than are currently available.

On the other hand, some of the implications of recent empirical research on the relationship of accounting numbers and security prices may provide some information for evaluating the desirability of alternative accounting methods in general and interperiod income tax allocation versus flow-through in particular. Suppose that the choice between alternative accounting methods is such that accounting numbers (such as posttax book income) produced by one method can be almost costlessly transformed by a user to accounting numbers consistent with the other method; if such transformations are less costly when one method is used for reporting purposes than the other method, then the first method should be used. Consistent with this reasoning, Gonedes and Dopuch suggest [1974, pp. 115–116] that it is relatively easy for users to convert interperiod allocation earnings to flow-through earnings but not vice versa, hence that interperiod income tax allocation is to be preferred to flow-through. Alternatively, if the additional cost to a firm of reporting accounting numbers consistent with one method is trivial once accounting numbers consistent with another method are already reported, Gonedes and Dopuch suggest [1974, p. 116] that both sets of numbers should be reported rather than wasting resources by deliberating over which method should be used. Social costs and benefits must be considered in addition to private costs and benefits, however, when the choice of accounting methods affects the information production costs of users external to the firm. Inherent in this reasoning are several other implications of recent empirical research: that evidence of stock market efficiency suggests that there is no information overload problem in the aggregate; and that the availability of several accounting numbers consistent with alternative accounting methods, such as both interperiod allocation earnings and flow-through earnings, will not confuse external users in the aggregate or affect capital market equilibrium.

Interperiod Allocation and Basic Accounting Concepts. Basic accounting concepts have been cited both to support and refute interperiod income tax allocation. Thus, Keller [1961, pp. 117–131] argues that the corporate income tax is a tax on income by definition; that the government intends to tax all income with minor exceptions; that the earning of income gives rise to the tax; that the tax should be accrued or deferred as income is accrued or deferred in the accounts, not as income is recognized for tax purposes; hence, that interperiod income tax allocation is consistent with the basic premises of accrual accounting, whereby expenses are recognized when incurred, not when paid. It is also suggested that to argue otherwise is comparable to favoring the recognition of revenue and other expense on the accrual basis but income tax expense on the cash basis—an inherently inconsistent and untenable position.

Once again, opponents of interperiod income tax allocation argue to the contrary. They reject as invalid the contention that the earning of income gives rise to the tax; rather, they [see, e.g., Chambers, 1968, pp. 104-106] maintain that the tax is an expense only to the extent assessed. This position has been supported by contending that the tax is not a tax on income but rather an excise tax using taxable income as defined by tax laws and regulations as the tax base, and that the intent of enacting timing differences is to increase or decrease taxes, not just accelerate or postpone their payment. Moreover, the manner of calculating the tax is held to be a consideration apart from the financial accounting to be accorded it; few would favor interperiod income tax allocation if the tax were assessed on another basis, hence the tax should not be allocated merely because it is assessed on taxable income. Furthermore, opponents of interperiod income tax allocation note that deferred tax assets and liabilities have no legal existence, and that their recognition is a significant departure from the historical cost convention; no transaction has occurred, hence the recognition of deferred tax assets or debits and deferred tax liabilities or credits is inherently subjective and dependent on tenuous forecasts of future taxable income and future tax rates.

In rejoinder, proponents of interperiod income tax allocation argue that balance sheet debits and credits resulting from interperiod income tax allocation are assets (or deferred debits or liability valuation adjustments) and liabilities (or deferred credits or asset valuation adjustments) within the necessarily economic concept of each that is adopted for financial accounting purposes; despite the absence of a legal status, these items may be associated with valuable services received by the government, and the lack of an ascertainable relationship between the value of these services and the amount of income taxes is irrelevant to the validity of their existence. Additionally, it has been suggested [Nurnberg, 1971, p. 39] that whether the income tax is in fact a tax on income or an excise tax is irrelevant to the determination of the financial accounting that should be accorded to it, as long as both types of taxes are expenses; and that whether timing differences entail permanent increases and decreases or accelerations and postponements of income taxes depends on the underlying cash flows, not the intent of governments in allowing such timing differences to exist.

Finally, some [see, e.g., Moonitz and Nelson, 1960, pp. 214-215] argue that interperiod income tax allocation may be justified even if it is inconsistent with more basic financial accounting concepts, for financial accounting is in a continuous state of transition, and existing concepts may require reformulation.

From the preceding review of the theoretical literature, it is apparent that different concepts of assets and liabilities underlie the contradictory analyses. Thus, many opponents of interperiod income tax allocation implicitly adopt somewhat legally oriented concepts of each, whereby income tax expense is affected only to the extent that income taxes are paid or legally payable and income tax refunds are received or legally secured. On the other hand, proponents of interperiod income tax allocation implicitly adopt broader concepts of assets and liabilities, and come to different conclusions. Resolution of these contradictory analyses requires the adoption of identical underlying concepts, else the disputants will continue to discuss different things.

Extent of Interperiod Allocation. Despite the many basic conceptual issues remaining unresolved, several commentators suggest that only the extent of interperiod income tax allocation continues to be questionable. Thus, interperiod income tax allocation is subject to far more controversy when applied to all timing differences than when applied only to certain timing differences. Indeed, much of the literature is devoted exclusively to an examination of the merits of a *comprehensive* versus *partial* approach to interperiod income tax allocation.

Indefinite deferral hypothesis. A partial approach is exemplified by the indefinite deferral hypothesis, formulated by Davidson [1958, pp. 175–180] and paraphrased as follows: If plant acquisitions each year equal or exceed plant acquisitions of the preceding year and the depreciation provisions of the income tax laws remain as generous as they are now—two assumptions that Davidson contends are quite reasonable—then accelerated tax depreciation will indefinitely equal or exceed straight-line book depreciation and any deferred tax liability (or credit) recognized under the deferred or liability method of interperiod income tax allocation will remain constant or increase, hence will never be paid. Accordingly, the recognition of a deferred tax liability (or credit) is held to be unwarranted, for none exists. Rather, interperiod income tax allocation is held to be appropriate only for those firms not maintaining regular plant acquisition policies, such as firms owning one or few assets, new firms, and declining or moribund firms, because tax depreciation will not indefinitely equal or exceed book depreciation, whereupon the deferred tax liability (or credit) will decrease, indicating that it exists and is paid. For declining or moribund firms, moreover, the recognition of deferred tax liabilities (or credits) is required only in the unlikely event that the dying years are profitable, for otherwise no taxes, let alone deferred taxes, will be paid. And where the recognition of deferred tax liabilities (or credits) is appropriate, Davidson argues that they should be measured by their present values, not their nominal maturity values. Indeed, because of their near-indefinite term, others suggest that the present values of most deferred tax liabilities (or credits) are too nominal to merit recognition in the accounts.

Several empirical studies substantiate Davidson's contention that for publicly owned corporations, the deferred tax liability (or credit) account rarely decreases due to income tax payments arising from reversals of depreciation timing differences.

Notwithstanding the empirical evidence in support of the indefinite deferral hypothesis, writers have rejected it on analytical grounds for several reasons. First, it has been rejected by those [see, e.g., Jaedicke and Nelson, 1960, p. 278] who reject its underlying assumptions—namely, the maintenance of a regular plant acquisition policy and the continuation of the favorable provisions of the income tax laws. Second, whereas interperiod income tax allocation is held to be tenuous due to its reliance on assumptions concerning future tax rates and future taxable income, others note that the indefinite deferral hypothesis presumes an even greater knowledge of the future.

Most telling, however, is the refutation of the indefinite deferral hypothesis by Jaedicke and Nelson. While accepting its underlying assumptions, Jaedicke and Nelson note [1960, pp. 278–279] that the hypothesis ignores the turnover of deferred tax liabilities (or credits). Thus, old portions of deferred tax liabilities (or credits) are continuously extinguished as new portions arise, this cycle occurring concurrently with the acquisition, use, and retirement of depreciable assets, although the aggregate balance may remain constant or even increase. Accordingly, not recognizing deferred tax liabilities (or credits) is analogous to not recognizing accounts payable, which similarly turn over concurrently with the acquisition and sale of merchandise, although the aggregate balance may remain constant or increase.

Davidson [1966, p. 118] denies the validity of this analogy:

> Accounts payable arise from actual, specific transactions in which identifiable goods or services are received. Each account is owed to a designated party and the amount of the obligation and the due date are usually set forth unambiguously on the written document that serves as the basis for the recognition of the payable. Actual cash payments to creditors are made regularly, even though other payables may at the same time be taking the place of those liquidated. The legal necessity to make the payments is not conditioned by any question about future operations being profitable. The "roll over" of transactions in accounts payable is real and undeniable.
>
> The most important distinction, of course, is that the deferred tax accrual results not from an actual event but from a hypothesis. Accounting deals with events, and those who would modify the recording of actual events (the payment of taxes) bear the burden of demonstrating that their modifications will increase the usefulness of the reports to management, investors, or other users. This is not accomplished by vague analogies to the roll over of items like accounts payable that do describe actual and discrete events.

In effect, Davidson denies the validity of imputing incremental tax effects to individual depreciable assets—an implicit assumption underlying Jaedicke's and Nelson's analysis as well as income tax allocation in general. He argues that taxes are levied on operations as a whole, not transaction by transaction.

A significant minority of accountants concur with Davidson and favor a partial approach to interperiod income tax allocation, particularly for recurring depreciation timing differences. They reject the notion that deferred tax liabilities turn over and argue instead that deferred tax liabilities should be recognized in the accounts only to the extent that reductions in their aggregate balances are anticipated in the foreseeable future.

Deferred tax assets. The less-than-general acceptance of comprehensive interperiod income tax allocation results, apart from the indefinite deferral hypothesis, largely from the continued adherence to the doctrine of conservatism, whereby expenses and losses are recognized in the accounts more readily than revenues and gains. Despite its well-known inconsistencies, the doctrine of conservatism continues to pervade accounting theory and, to an even greater extent, accounting practice. For example, until the end of 1967, interperiod allocation for depreciation timing differences was required in the United States only if deferred tax liabilities (or deferred tax credits or asset contra valuation increases)—but not deferred tax assets (or deferred tax debits or asset contra valuation decreases)—resulted therefrom [APB Opinion No. 1, 1962, par. 5]. This inconsistent procedure was defended as being fully consistent with the doctrine of conservatism, despite the resulting understatement of income and shareholders' equity; however, the recognition of deferred tax liabilities (or deferred tax credits or asset contra valuation increases) was not required to the extent that deferred tax assets (or deferred tax debits or asset contra valuation decreases) were also omitted. In effect, liabilities were netted against assets, but in a capricious manner that often impaired the comparability of the income figures for a series of years. Moreover, prior years' income and shareholders' equity remained understated to the extent that deferred tax assets exceeded deferred tax liabilities. Although this application of the doctrine of conservatism is no longer acceptable in either the United States or Canada, it still constitutes acceptable practice in other countries [see, e.g., IASC, International Accounting Standard No. 12, 1979].

Net operating loss carry-forwards. The most significant remaining application of the doctrine of conservatism to interperiod income tax allocation relates to net operating losses.

Under federal income tax laws, net operating losses may be carried back against taxable income for a period of years preceding the loss year and carried forward against taxable income for a longer period following the loss year. A logical corollary to comprehensive interperiod income tax allocation for timing differences is that the benefits of loss carry-backs and carry-forwards are attributable to the loss year. This is no longer in dispute for *carry-backs*, which are invariably identified with the loss year which, for *carry-backs*, is also the year of realization. But a rather conservative bias precludes recognizing almost all *carry-forwards* prior to realization, unless realization is assured beyond any reasonable doubt in the loss year.

Three methods have been suggested to account for the tax benefits of loss carry-forwards:

1. Recognition in the year of realization as extraordinary items
2. Recognition in the year of loss with the concomitant recognition of a carry-forward asset
3. Recognition in the year of realization as a prior period adjustment

Recognition in the year of realization as an extraordinary item is consistent with the aforementioned conservative bias, whereas recognition in the year of loss with the concomitant recognition of a carry-forward asset is not. Recognition in the year of realization as a prior period adjustment is also consistent with the conservative bias, but with the tax benefits of the carry-forward loss ultimately attributed to the loss year, so that the series of revised posttax book incomes are identical to the series that would result if the carry-forward benefits were recognized in the loss year. Otherwise, the issues involved in accounting for previously unrecognized carry-forward benefits upon realization are comparable to those concerning the all-inclusive versus current operating performance concepts of income.

Indefinite reversal timing differences. It has already been noted that certain initial differences between pretax book income and taxable income may not reverse until indefinite future periods or may never reverse. Examples of such differences in the United States include undistributed earnings of subsidiaries, general reserves of stock savings and loan associations, policyholders' surplus of stock life insurance companies, deposits in statutory reserve funds of U.S.

steamship companies, amortization of purchased goodwill, and stock option compensation expense. Because it is unclear whether these initial differences are permanent differences or timing differences, it is unclear whether interperiod income tax allocation is applicable to them. Indeed, under generally accepted accounting principles in the United States, management has almost unlimited discretion to recognize or not recognize deferred income taxes for some of these differences, notwithstanding the authoritative presumption [APB Opinion No. 23, 1972] in favor of comprehensive interperiod income tax allocation for some of these items. Accordingly, it has been contended that interperiod income tax allocation no longer is applied comprehensively in the United States or, more accurately, is applied comprehensively to some timing differences and partially to other timing differences.

But this is a matter of definition. Although the indefinite reversal of these differences introduces additional complexities into the financial accounting for income taxes, these complexities are not unique, but rather reflect estimation problems much akin to estimating service lives of depreciable assets or bad debts on credit sales. Consistent with comprehensive interperiod income tax allocation, not recognizing deferred income taxes for indefinite reversal timing differences is unacceptable for all periods shorter than infinity; some estimate is better than no estimate at all.

Investment tax credit. Under the Internal Revenue Code, income tax credits are available for investments in certain types of property, in addition to depreciation deductions otherwise available. The investment credit rates have changed from time to time, and there is an overall limitation as to the total amount of investment tax credits available, computed as a percentage of the income tax otherwise payable.

Once the amount of the investment tax credit is computed, financial accounting questions must be resolved concerning its conceptual nature and, if appropriate, the timing of its inclusion in posttax book income.

In APB Opinion No. 2 [1962], the Accounting Principles Board suggested that the investment tax credit may be viewed as either (1) a subsidy by way of contribution of capital from the government; (2) a reduction of asset cost; or (3) a reduction of income tax expense. The subsidy concept was summarily rejected on the assumption that the credit should be included in income; the asset cost reduction concept was favored; and the income tax expense reduction concept was accepted as a less preferable alternative to the asset cost reduction concept, provided that the effects of the credit were included in income over the life of the asset, consistent with the asset cost reduction concept. Spreading the benefits of the credit over the life of the related asset became known as the *deferral method*; including the benefits of the credit immediately in income in the year in which the related asset is acquired became known as *flow-through* method.

Initially, a small majority of publicly owned corporations elected to use the flow-through method rather than the deferral method, notwithstanding the stated preference of the Accounting Principles Board for the latter. (At that time, pronouncements of the APB were more in the nature of recommendations than requirements.) To some extent, the SEC undermined this stated preference of the APB for the deferral method by issuing Accounting Series Release No. 96 [1963], wherein the Commission sanctioned both deferral and flow-through as acceptable alternatives, whereupon the APB relented and also sanctioned both methods in APB Opinion No. 4 [1964]. Subsequent attempts by the APB to achieve uniformity culminated in the enactment of the Revenue Act of 1971, wherein the Board was prohibited from sanctioning deferral to the exclusion of flow-through. Currently, a large majority of publicly owned corporations use the flow-through method.

In addition to the basic investment tax credit, additional income tax credits are available to corporations that invest in qualified energy property or qualified rehabilitated property, as well as to corporations that have specified employee stock ownership plans; these additional credits merely affect the computation of the investment tax credit, which is still accounted for consistent with deferral or flow-through. On the other hand, still additional income tax credits in addition to the wage expense deduction are available for wages paid to certain employee groups in training or engaged in research or experimentation; these income tax credits are invariably included in posttax book income as reductions of income tax expense in the year in which taken for tax purposes, consistent with flow-through, because there is little or no basis for deferring them to later periods.

When enacted in 1962, the tax basis of the asset was reduced by the full amount of the investment tax credit, and depreciation for tax purposes was computed on this lower amount. The required tax basis reduction was eliminated in 1964. Starting in 1983, however, the tax basis of the asset is reduced by one-half of the investment credit in some cases. There is some question whether the reduction in the tax basis caused by the investment tax credit functions as a permanent difference or as a timing difference.

INTRAPERIOD INCOME TAX ALLOCATION AND GENERALLY ACCEPTED ACCOUNTING PRINCIPLES

Consistent with APB Opinions No. 20 [1971] and 30 [1973], intraperiod income tax allocation is required for the following income statement items:

1. Income or loss from continuing operations
2. Income or loss from operations of a discontinued segment of a business
3. Gain or loss from disposal of a segment of a business
4. Extraordinary gains and losses
5. Cumulative effect of changes in accounting principles

APB Opinion No. 30 [1973, par. 26] explicitly prohibits intraperiod income tax allocation for unusual or infrequently occurring items that do not qualify as extraordinary items under the criteria of that pronouncement.

Intraperiod income tax allocation is also required for prior period adjustments and cumulative effects of changes in accounting principles reported directly in the retained earnings statement, as well as for direct adjustments of other shareholders' equity accounts for stock option compensation expense, unrealized gains and losses on long-term investments in marketable securities, and unrealized gains and losses on foreign currency translations.

INTERPERIOD INCOME TAX ALLOCATION AND GENERALLY ACCEPTED ACCOUNTING PRINCIPLES

In the United States, APB Opinion No. 11 [1967] requires *comprehensive* application of the *deferred* method of interperiod income tax allocation for *all* timing differences other than certain indefinite reversal timing differences; the flow-through, liability, and net-of-tax methods and partial application of any method of interperiod income tax allocation are explicitly prohibited. In arriving at its position, the APB concluded [pars. 34-35] that comprehensive interperiod income tax allocation " . . . is an integral part of the determination of income tax expense," and " . . . the deferred method . . . provides the most useful and practical approach to interperiod tax allocation and the presentation of income taxes in financial statements." Note that this position is more of an assertion than a reasoned conclusion. Subsequently, the exceptions for certain indefinite reversal timing differences were eliminated in APB Opinions No. 23 and 24 [1972] and FASB Statement No. 19 [1977]. Discounting deferred tax balances is prohibited by APB Opinion No. 10 [1966].

Comprehensive application of the deferred method is also required in Canada [CICA, 1967], but only partial application of the liability method is recommended in the United Kingdom and Ireland [ASC, 1978], and only partial application of either the deferred or liability method is recommended by the International Accounting Standards Committee [1979].

Permanent versus Timing Differences. Detailed authoritative pronouncements have been issued for distinguishing circumstances in which specific indefinite reversal differences are to be treated as permanent differences from circumstances in which indefinite reversal differences are to be treated as timing differences.

In Opinion No. 17 [1970], the Accounting Principles Board concluded [par. 30] that the amortization of purchased goodwill or other purchased intangible assets for book purposes but not for tax purposes does not constitute a timing difference and, by implication, therefore constitutes a permanent difference. It follows, moreover, that upon the disposition of such assets, another permanent difference arises.

In Opinion No. 23 [1972], the Accounting Principles Board examined indefinite reversal differences relating to the undistributed earnings of subsidiaries (including Domestic International Sales Corporations), the undistributed earnings of corporate joint ventures, "bad debt reserves" of savings and loan associations, and "policyholders' surplus" of stock life insurance companies. Because of the special provisions of the Internal Revenue Code that are unique to these special items, a corporation might postpone indefinitely the payment of income taxes on certain differences between pretax book income and taxable income that would otherwise require interperiod income tax allocation for financial accounting purposes. Additionally, the corporation would have to take specific action for income tax purposes before income taxes on these indefinite reversal timing differences become payable, and the income taxes may never become payable unless the corporation takes these specific actions. For indefinite reversal differences relating to the undistributed earnings of subsidiaries and corporate joint ventures, the Board concluded [pars. 10–17] that it should be presumed that the undistributed earnings will be transferred to the parent or corporate joint venturer, hence constitute timing differences on which deferred income taxes should be accrued; but that this presumption may be overcome, and no deferred income taxes need be accrued, if sufficient evidence is available to show that the undistributed earnings will be reinvested indefinitely in the subsidiary or corporate joint venture, or will be remitted to the parent or corporate joint venturer in a tax-free liquidation. For indefinite reversal differences relating to "bad debt reserves" of savings and loan associations and "policyholders' surplus" of stock life insurance companies, the Board concluded [pars. 23, 28] that the accrual of deferred income taxes should not be made, hence that these differences should be treated as permanent differences; but if circumstances indicate that the corporation is likely to pay income taxes on these differences, either currently or in a later year, because of known or expected actions, deferred income taxes should be accrued, in which case these differences are treated as timing differences.

In Opinion No. 24 [1972], the Accounting Principles Board examined indefinite reversal differences relating to the undistributed earnings of investees (other than subsidiaries and corporate joint ventures) accounted for by the equity method. The Board noted [par. 6] that some commentators believe that income taxes should be provided only on the portion of the undistributed earnings of investees that represent timing differences but not on the portion that represent permanent differences. Nevertheless, the Board concluded [par. 7] that the undistributed earnings of investees are related either to probable future distributions of dividends or to anticipated realization on disposal of the investments and therefore have the essential characteristic of timing differences on which deferred income taxes should be accrued. In reaching this conclusion, the Board noted that the ability of an investor to exercise significant *influence* over an investee differs significantly from the ability of a parent corporation to *control* the investment policies of a subsidiary, and that only *control* justifies the conclusion that the undistributed earnings may be invested for indefinite periods. This seemingly inconsistent position no doubt also reflects a conservative bias, whereby the Board preferred to require the accrual of deferred income taxes that might never be paid, rather than permit the nonaccrual of deferred income taxes that might be paid.

In Statement No. 19 [1977], the Financial Accounting Standards Board concluded [pars. 61–62] that comprehensive interperiod income tax allocation by the deferred method should be followed by oil and gas producing companies for intangible drilling and development costs and other costs incurred that are included in taxable income and pretax book income for different periods. Additionally,

> ... the so-called interaction of book/tax timing differences with any anticipated future excess of statutory depletion allowed as a tax deduction over the amount of cost depletion otherwise allowable as a tax deduction shall not be recognized in determining the appropriate periodic provision for income taxes. Accordingly, the excess of statutory depletion over cost depletion for tax purposes shall be accounted for as a permanent differ-

ence in the period in which the excess is deducted for income tax purposes; it shall not be anticipated by recognizing interaction.

In Interpretation No. 22 [1978], the Financial Accounting Standards Board concluded [par. 11] that the amortizations of the costs of railroad gradings and tunnel bores that are reported differently for tax and book purposes constitute timing differences for which comprehensive interperiod income tax allocation is required, notwithstanding similarities of these differences with indefinite reversal differences, which are treated as timing differences in some circumstances but as permanent differences in other circumstances.

Neither the APB nor the FASB reached a conclusion as to whether deposits in capital construction funds or statutory reserve funds by U.S. steamship companies constitute permanent differences or timing differences for which interperiod income tax allocation is required.

In Statement No. 31 [1979], the Financial Accounting Standards Board concluded [par. 5] that the United Kingdom "stock relief" legislation, which permits corporations to deduct, for purposes of determining taxable income, increases in the carrying amount of inventory, should be treated as a timing difference unless it is probable that the tax benefit will not be recaptured prior to the end of the 6-year recapture period. With more recent changes in U.K. tax law, such recapture becomes unlikely; hence, no timing difference need be recognized.

Finally, in a proposed statement of financial accounting standards, the FASB concluded [1982b, par. 2] that the reduction of the tax basis due to the investment credit functions as a timing difference and that firms that account for investment tax credits under the flow-through method should recognize deferred income taxes equal to the tax effects of this basis reduction.

Differential Calculation of Deferred Tax. APB Opinion No. 11 [1967, par. 36] calls for measuring the tax effect of a timing difference by the differential between income taxes computed with and without inclusion of the transaction creating the difference between taxable income and pretax book income. In computing such differentials, taxable income is defined as the excess of revenues over deductions or the excess of deductions over revenues to be reported for income tax purposes for the period, except that deductions do not include net operating loss carry-backs or carry-forwards. Accordingly, in theory, a separate calculation is required for each originating timing difference in order to compute the income tax that would have resulted both with and without the timing difference. In practice, the same result will often be forthcoming if the marginal current income tax rate is simply applied to the amount of the timing difference, but the same result will not be forthcoming by use of this *short-cut method* in all circumstances. Specifically, differences may result under the short-cut method as a result of the effect of the graduated rate exemption, investment credits, foreign tax credits, the existence of an operating loss for the period, or the fact that an operating loss would have been incurred if the timing difference were excluded.

The different calculations under the *with and without method* required by APB Opinion No. 11 are illustrated in Exhibit 6, where it is assumed that the

EXHIBIT 6   With and Without Method

	19X1	19X2
Pretax book income	$120,000	$150,000
Excess tax depreciation	30,000	40,000
Taxable income	$ 90,000	$110,000
Income tax computed on pretax book income without timing difference ($120,000 for 19X1 and $150,000 for 19X2):		
$25,000 @ 15%	$ 3,750	$ 3,750
$25,000 @ 18%	4,500	4,500
$25,000 @ 30%	7,500	7,500
$25,000 @ 40%	10,000	10,000
$20,000 @ 46%	9,200	
$50,000 @ 46%		23,000
Total	$ 34,950	$ 48,750
Income tax computed on pretax book income with timing difference ($90,000 for 19X1 and $110,000 for 19X2):		
$25,000 @ 15%	$ 3,750	$ 3,750
$25,000 @ 18%	4,500	4,500
$25,000 @ 30%	7,500	7,500
$15,000 @ 40%	6,000	
$25,000 @ 40%		10,000
$10,000 @ 46%		4,600
Total	$ 21,750	$ 30,350
Deferred tax provision:		
$34,950 − $21,750	$ 13,200	
$48,750 − $30,350		$ 18,400

income tax rate is 15 percent on the first $25,000 of taxable income, 18 percent on the next $25,000 of taxable income, 30 percent on the next $25,000 of taxable income, 40 percent on the next $25,000 of taxable income, and 46 percent on taxable income above $100,000. Note that under the short-cut method, the deferred tax provision would have been computed as 46 percent of $30,000, or $13,800, for 19X1, and 46 percent of $40,000, or $18,400, for 19X2; the computation for 19X2 would be correct, but the computation for 19X1 would be incorrect. The amount deferred for 19X1 is not 46 percent of the $30,000 depreciation timing difference for that year, because of the interplay of the graduated rate exemption; rather, the amount deferred for 19X1 is 46 percent of $20,000, or $9,200, plus 40 percent of $10,000, or $4,000, or $13,200 in total.

When two or more types of timing differences are present, two approaches are available for making this differential calculation of the deferred tax provision. Under the *aggregate method,* one computation is made with and without all timing differences, with the resulting differential tax effect representing the deferred tax provision for the period; it may be necessary to apportion the deferred tax provision to the different types of timing differences in order to be able to amortize the deferred tax balances as the timing differences reverse. Under the *separate item method,* a with and without computation is required for each timing difference or each group of similar timing differences, with the sum of the resulting differential tax effects of the individual timing differences representing the deferred tax provision for the period. Different provisions for deferred taxes may result under the aggregate and separate item methods.

Specific guidance is provided in the authoritative pronouncements for making the differential calculation of deferred income taxes in special circumstances. For example, in computing the deferred income taxes on the undistributed earnings of a subsidiary, APB Opinion No. 23 [1972, par. 10] suggests that the assumption may be made that the undistributed earnings were distributed in the current period and the parent company received the benefit of all available tax planning alternatives and available tax credits and deductions, such as the dividends received deduction; and that the income tax expense of the parent company should also include the income taxes that would have been withheld if the undistributed earnings had been remitted as dividends. To illustrate, consider a parent company that acquires 70 percent of the voting common stock of a subsidiary company for $300,000 in cash, when the underlying book value of the acquired stock is $250,000, and the excess of cost over book value is attributable to intangible assets having a remaining useful life of 10 years from date of acquisition. The subsidiary company generates a pretax net income of $100,000 and a posttax net income of $60,000 for the year following acquisition, given a flat 40 percent income tax rate. Although the subsidiary pays no dividend currently, it intends to pay dividends in the future and, accordingly, deferred income taxes should be accrued on the parent company's share of subsidiary income, as follows:

Parent company's share of subsidiary income [$60,000(70%)]	$42,000
Less: Amortization of excess of cost over book value [$50,000(⅒)]	5,000
Pretax income on subsidiary investment	$37,000
Deferred income taxes:	
Parent company's share of subsidiary net income	$42,000
Dividends received deduction [$42,000(85%)]	35,700
Income subject to tax	$ 6,300
Deferred income tax [$6,300(40%)]	$ 2,520

The $2,520 deferred income tax should be included as part of the income tax expense of the parent company, whether the parent company issues consolidated or unconsolidated statements; allocation of this item to the pretax income on subsidiary investment is not permitted. Under generally accepted accounting principles, the $40,000 income tax expense of the subsidiary may be partially or entirely included in consolidated income tax expense, whether the subsidiary is consolidated or unconsolidated.

The differential calculations discussed in this section should take into consideration all taxes based on income—federal, foreign, state, and local. As a practical matter, however, where corporations are subject to a number of jurisdictions with income taxes, the tax rates to be used in this differential calculation are often determined by increasing the federal income tax rate by the percentage equivalent to the effect of the income taxes imposed by the other jurisdictions. Alternatively, if the overall effect on posttax book income is not material, the income taxes imposed by these other jurisdictions are accounted for consistent with the flow-through method, and only federal income taxes are subject to interperiod allocation.

Gross Change Basis or Net Change Basis with Tax Rate Changes. Whenever there is only one item that causes a timing difference between taxable income and pretax book income, it is relatively easy to compute the exact income tax effect, the buildup of the deferral, and the turnaround. Indeed, this method is called the *individual item method,* and involves the following steps:

1. For each timing difference, compute the initial tax effect and the subsequent reversal.
2. Reduce or "draw down" an equivalent amount of deferred taxes previously provided as the particular timing difference reverses.

If many items cause timing differences, a considerable amount of record keeping is required under the individual item method. Accordingly, this method is usually applied only where there are a few large timing differences.

More often, a corporation has a multitude of transactions treated differently for tax purposes than for book purposes, with some timing differences originating while other timing differences reverse. When it becomes impracticable to identify, follow, and account for each individual timing difference, one of two acceptable alternative methods may be applied, consistent with APB Opinion No. 11 [1967, par. 37], to simplify the computation of the deferred tax; these two methods are referred to as the *group of similar items gross change basis* and the *group of similar items net change basis* or, more simply, the *gross change method* and the *net change method.*

Under the *gross change method,* the net change in deferred income taxes for a period equals the sum of (1) originating timing differences at the *current* tax rate, less (2) reversing timing differences at historical tax rates, and involves the following steps:

1. Group similar timing differences, such as all depreciation timing differences and all warranty expense timing differences.
2. Compute the tax effects of originating timing differences using the current tax rate.
3. Compute the tax effects of reversing timing differences using appropriate historical tax rates.
4. The difference between steps 2 and 3 represents the net change in deferred income taxes for the period.

Under the *net change method,* income tax effects are *not* computed for specific timing differences as they originate and reverse. Rather, similar types of timing differences are grouped together, whether originating or reversing within the period, and the income tax effect is computed for the net change in the aggregate timing differences for the period. Deferred tax balances are not

EXHIBIT 7   Different Approaches to Tax Rate Changes

Deferred method—gross change basis

Pretax book income			$1,000,000
Income tax expense:			
Income taxes payable (assumed)		$425,000	
Add: Tax effect of originating timing difference [$350,000(50%)]	$175,000		
Less: Tax effect of reversing timing difference [$200,000(40%)]	80,000	95,000	
Total income tax expense . . .			520,000
Posttax book income			$ 480,000
Deferred tax credit:			
January 1, 19X6, balance			$ 480,000
Add: Tax effect of originating timing differences		$175,000	
Less: Tax effect of reversing timing differences		80,000	95,000
December 31, 19X6, balance . .			$ 575,000

Deferred method—net change basis

Pretax book income			$1,000,000
Income tax expense:			
Income taxes payable (assumed)		$425,000	
Add: Tax effect of net timing difference [$150,000(50%)] . .		75,000	
Total income tax expense . . .			500,000
Posttax book income			$ 500,000
Deferred tax credit:			
January 1, 19X6, balance			$ 480,000
Add: Tax effect of net timing difference			75,000
December 31, 19X6, balance . .			$ 555,000

Liability method

Deferred tax liability:			
December 31, 19X6, balance [$1,350,000(50%)]			$ 675,000
January 1, 19X6, balance [$1,200,000(40%)]			480,000
Increase for year			$ 195,000
Pretax book income			$1,000,000
Income tax expense:			
Income taxes payable (assumed)		$425,000	
Add: Increase in deferred tax liability for year		195,000	
Total income tax expense . . .			620,000
Posttax book income			$ 380,000

amortized under the net change method in periods in which the aggregate timing differences increase; they are amortized under this method only in periods in which the aggregate timing differences decrease, but never in excess of the cumulative amounts previously provided. Thus, if all of the timing differences of a particular group reverse in one period, the entire related deferred tax balance should be amortized regardless of the amount determined by using the current tax rate computation.

The different calculations that result under the gross change method and the net change method are illustrated in Exhibit 7, where it is assumed that the corporate income tax rate is 40 percent for the years 19X1 through 19X5 but changes to 50 percent in 19X6. For the years 19X1 through 19X5, cumulative depreciation expense for tax purposes exceeds cumulative depreciation expense for book purposes by $1,200,000; given the 40 percent income tax rate for these years, the deferred tax balance at December 31, 19X5, is 40 percent of $1,200,000, or $480,000. During 19X6, $200,000 of the $1,200,000 cumulative timing differences reverses, and $350,000 of new timing differences originate. Accordingly, the reconciliation of pretax book income and taxable income as well as the computation of income taxes payable for 19X6 are as follows:

Pretax book income		$1,000,000
Originating timing differences	$350,000	
Reversing timing differences	200,000	150,000
Taxable income		$ 850,000
Income taxes payable (50%)		$ 425,000

In order to comprehend more fully how the deferred method of interperiod income tax allocation handles changes in income tax rates under the gross and net change methods, the results under the liability method of interperiod income tax allocation are also presented in Exhibit 7, even though this method is no longer sanctioned under generally accepted accounting principles.

At the end of 19X6, the cumulative timing differences total $1,350,000. Consistent with the liability method, the deferred tax balance at the end of 19X6 must be 50 percent of $1,350,000, or $675,000; because the deferred tax balance at the beginning of 19X6 is $480,000, the deferred tax provision for 19X6 must be the difference, or $195,000, which includes a $120,000 catchup adjustment of 50 percent less 40 percent, or 10 percent on the $1,200,000 cumulative timing differences as of the beginning of the period. Accordingly, reported income tax expense is $620,000 for 19X6 under the liability method, resulting in a reported effective income tax rate of 62 percent.

Under the deferred method of interperiod income tax allocation, deferred tax balances do not represent assets and liabilities in the usual context, and no attempt is made to adjust the deferred tax balances for the cumulative effect of tax rate changes. Accordingly, the deferred tax balance at the end of 19X6 is $575,000 under the gross change method or $555,000 under the net change method, and no longer bears a normal relationship to the $1,350,000 cumulative timing differences at that time. On the other hand, reported income tax expense is $520,000 for 19X6 under the gross change method, resulting in a reported effective income tax rate of 52 percent. Reported income tax expense is $500,000 for 19X6 under the net change method, resulting in a reported effective income tax rate of 50 percent. The 52 percent or 50 percent reported effective income tax rates under the deferred method appear much more reasonable, given the statutory rate of 50 percent, than the 62 percent reported effective income tax rate under the liability method. It is largely for this reason that the Accounting Principles Board favored the deferred method over the liability method in Opinion No. 11, particularly when it is remembered that this pronouncement was issued at a time when income tax rates were increasing from 48 percent to 52.8 percent. In effect, the APB favored prospective rather than cumulative adjustment for changes in income tax rates in Opinion No. 11 [1967], much as it favored prospective rather than cumulative adjustment for actuarial gains and losses on pension plans [Opinion No. 8, 1966] and for changes in accounting estimates [Opinion No. 20, 1971].

The computation of the tax effects of reversing timing differences under the gross change method is in terms of the appropriate historical tax rates in effect when the timing differences originated. If the deferred tax balances consist of layers accumulated at different historical tax rates, either FIFO (first-in, first-out), LIFO (last-in, first-out), or average tax rate assumptions may be used as a basis for choosing the historical tax rates to be applied to the reversing timing differences. These assumptions are also made under the individual item method. Indeed, the gross change method is similar to the individual item method in that the tax effects of reversing timing differences are computed at the same tax rate in effect when they originated; the methods differ in that the gross change method groups similar timing differences, whereas the individual item method does not. The different calculations of the tax effects of reversing timing differences consistent with the FIFO, LIFO, and average tax rate assumptions under the gross change method are illustrated in Exhibit 8, where it is assumed that the corporate income tax rate changes from 40 to 50 percent at the beginning of 19X3. As seen more clearly in Exhibit 8, the tax effect of the reversing timing difference is measured entirely at the 40 percent tax rate under the FIFO assumption, partly at the 50 percent tax rate and partly at the 40 percent tax rate under the LIFO assumption, and at the 43 percent average rate under the average assumption.

Under the net change method, on the other hand, the tax effect of the reversing timing difference is merely 50 percent of $40,000, or $20,000, and this computation is made without the need for a tax rate flow assumption. For this reason, the net change method is easier to apply. But note what happens under the net change method if the amount of the reversing timing difference in 19X5 is $90,000 rather than $40,000. If the tax effect is computed as 50 percent of $90,000, or $45,000, the deferred tax balance would be reduced below zero; therefore, the tax effect of the $90,000 reversing timing difference is limited to $43,000, the cumulative deferred tax balance at the beginning of 19X5, and the tax effect of the remaining $10,000 timing difference will be zero.

Because of these problems, both short-run and long-run effects must be considered. If cumulative timing differences increase continuously over a number of years or level off, tax rate changes will have no significant effect on net income as a result of using the net change method. Because this is usually the

---

EXHIBIT 8 **Amortizing Deferred Taxes**

Underlying data

			Deferred tax	
Year	Rate	Timing difference	Annual change	Balance
19X1......	40%	$ 30,000	$12,000	$12,000
19X2......	40%	40,000	16,000	28,000
19X3......	50%	20,000	10,000	38,000
19X4......	50%	10,000	5,000	43,000
19X5......	50%	(40,000)		

Gross change method—FIFO assumption
$$\$(30,000) \times 40\% + \$(10,000) \times 40\% = \$(16,000)$$

Gross change method—average rate assumption[a]
$$\$(40,000) \times 43\% = \$(17,200)$$

Gross change method—LIFO assumption
$$\$(10,000) \times 50\% + \$(20,000) \times 50\% + \$(10,000) \times 40\% = \$(19,000)$$

Net change method
$$\$(40,000) \times 50\% = \$(20,000)$$

$$^{a}43\% = \frac{\$43,000}{\$30,000 + \$40,000 + \$20,000 + \$10,000}$$

case and the net change method is easier to apply, it is far more widely used. But if cumulative timing differences are expected to reverse frequently, tax rate changes during reversal periods may result in reported income tax expense that is considerably different than the amount expected for the statutory tax rate under the net change method, and the gross change or individual item method may be more appropriate. If there are never any reversals, the two methods yield the same results. Once again, whichever method is chosen must be used consistently from period to period.

Net Operating Losses. In Opinion No. 11 [1967, pars. 44–46], the Accounting Principles Board concluded that the tax benefits of loss carry-backs should be recognized in the loss year, but that the tax benefits of loss carry-forwards should not be recognized until they are realized, unless realization is assured beyond any reasonable doubt at the time the loss carry-forward arises. When the tax benefits of loss carry-forwards are not recognized until realized in full or in part in subsequent periods, the tax benefits should be reported in those periods as extraordinary items. In those rare cases in which realization of the tax benefits of loss carry-forwards is assured beyond any reasonable doubt, the potential benefits should be recognized as an asset and included in the determination of posttax book income of the loss period. The amount of the asset (and the tax benefits) should be computed at the tax rates expected to be in effect at the time of contemplated realization; the tax rates referred to here are those tax rates that, at the time the loss benefit is recognized for book purposes, have been enacted to apply to the periods in which realization of the carry-forward is anticipated.[2] If applicable tax rates change from those used to measure the tax benefits of the carry-forward at the time of recognition, the effect of the tax rate change should be accounted for in the period of the change as an adjustment of the asset and income tax expense.

According to APB Opinion No. 11, realization of the tax benefits of a loss carry-forward appears to be assured beyond any reasonable doubt when both of the following conditions exist:

1. The loss results from an identifiable, isolated, and nonrecurring cause, and the company either has been continuously profitable over a long period or has suffered occasional losses that were more than offset by taxable income in subsequent years.

2. Future taxable income is virtually certain to be large enough to offset the loss carry-forward and will occur soon enough to assure the realization within the carry-forward period.

Circumstances contemplated in which these criteria are met include net operating losses due to (1) the disposal of a segment of a business, where the other segments are profitable; (2) isolated and nonrecurring catastrophes; and (3) temporary government restrictions on imports, exports, or production. In Staff Accounting Bulletin No. 8 [1976], the Securities and Exchange Commission further clarified these criteria by stating that a carry-forward asset should not be recorded unless the reporting company has a very strong earnings history, the loss was not caused by a general economic or industry decline, the company has reasonable alternative tax strategies available, and a forecast based on reasonable assumptions indicates more than enough future income to offset the loss carry-forward.

Preexisting deferred tax credits. At the time that a net operating loss carry-forward arises, net deferred tax credits may exist as a result of timing differences of prior periods. In the *unusual* case when the tax benefits of the loss carry-forward are assured beyond any reasonable doubt, and a carry-forward asset is recognized in the loss year, the preexisting deferred tax credit balances should be amortized in future periods as the underlying timing differences reverse.

On the other hand, in the *usual* case when the tax benefits of the loss carry-forward are not assured beyond any reasonable doubt and a carry-forward asset is not recognized in the loss year, preexisting net deferred tax credits should be eliminated to the extent of the lower of (1) the potential tax benefits of the loss carry-forward, or (2) the amount of the net deferred tax credits that would otherwise be amortized during the carry-forward period; if the tax benefits of the loss carry-forward are realized subsequently, the amounts eliminated should be reinstated (at the then current tax rates) on a cumulative basis

---

[2] Note that under APB Opinion No. 11, deferred tax debits and credits are measured in terms of current tax rates, notwithstanding tax rate changes applicable to the periods in which the underlying timing differences reverse, whereas net operating loss carry-forward assets are measured in terms of such future tax rates.

EXHIBIT 9   Carry-forwards and Timing Differences

	19X1	19X2	19X3	19X4	19X5	Total
			Tax returns			
Revenues	$2,000	$2,000	$ 2,000	$2,000	$2,000	$10,000
Expenses:						
Depreciation—ACRS	$ 375	$ 570	$ 555	$ —	$ —	$ 1,500
Other	1,000	1,000	2,700	1,000	1,000	6,700
Total	$1,375	$1,570	$ 3,255	$1,000	$1,000	$ 8,200
Taxable income	$ 625	$ 430	$ (1,255)	$1,000	$1,000	$ 1,800
Loss carry-back	(625)	(430)	1,055			-0-
Loss carry-forward			200	(200)		
Balance	$ -0-	$ -0-	$ -0-	$ 800	$1,000	$ 1,800
Tax paid	$ 250	$ 172	$ (422)	$ 320	$ 400	$ 720
			Timing differences			
Tax depreciation—ACRS	$ 375	$ 570	$ 555	$ -0-	$ -0-	$ 1,500
Book depreciation—SL	300	300	300	300	300	1,500
Timing differences	$ 75	$ 270	$ 255	$ (300)	$ (300)	$ -0-
Tax effect (40%)	$ 30	$ 108	$ 102	$ (120)	$ (120)	$ -0-
			Books—realization assured			
Revenues	$2,000	$2,000	$ 2,000	$2,000	$2,000	$10,000
Expenses:						
Depreciation—SL	$ 300	$ 300	$ 300	$ 300	$ 300	$ 1,500
Other	1,000	1,000	2,700	1,000	1,000	6,700
Total	$1,300	$1,300	$ 3,000	$1,300	$1,300	$ 8,200
Pretax book income	$ 700	$ 700	$ (1,000)	$ 700	$ 700	$ 1,800
Income tax expense:						
Paid (refunded)	$ 250	$ 172	$ (422)	$ 320	$ 400	$ 720
Reduction anticipated due to carry-forward			(80)	80		-0-
Deferred	30	108	102	(120)	(120)	-0-
Total	$ 280	$ 280	$ (400)	$ 280	$ 280	$ 720
Posttax book income	$ 420	$ 420	$ (600)	$ 420	$ 420	$ 1,080
Deferred tax credit, December 31	$ 30	$ 138	$ 240	$ 120	$ -0-	
Carry-forward asset, December 31	$ —	$ —	$ 80	$ -0-	$ -0-	
			Books—realization not assured			
Revenues	$2,000	$2,000	$ 2,000	$2,000	$2,000	$10,000
Expenses:						
Depreciation—SL	$ 300	$ 300	$ 300	$ 300	$ 300	$ 1,500
Other	1,000	1,000	2,700	1,000	1,000	6,700
Total	$1,300	$1,300	$ 3,000	$1,300	$1,300	$ 8,200
Pretax book income	$ 700	$ 700	$ (1,000)	$ 700	$ 700	$ 1,800
Income tax expense:						
Paid (refunded)	$ 250	$ 172	$ (422)	$ 320	$ 400	$ 720
Reinstatement (elimination) due to carry-forward			(80)	80		-0-
Deferred	30	108	102	(120)	(120)	-0-
Total tax expense	$ 280	$ 280	$ (400)	$ 280	$ 280	$ 720
Posttax book income	$ 420	$ 420	$ (600)	$ 420	$ 420	$ 1,080
Deferred tax credit, December 31	$ 30	$ 138	$ 160	$ 120	$ -0-	

concurrently with, and to the extent that, the tax benefits of the loss carry-forward are realized.

The accounting for the tax benefits of net operating loss carry-forwards interacting with preexisting timing differences is illustrated in Exhibit 9, where 19X3 is the loss year, and the preexisting timing difference arises from the computation of depreciation. Specifically, the depreciable asset is acquired on the first day of 19X1 at a cost of $1,500, has a 5-year estimated useful life, and no salvage value. The asset falls in the 3-year class of assets under the ACRS rules in the tax law. For book purposes, depreciation is recognized on a straight-line basis over 5 years. For tax purposes, depreciation is recognized on an accelerated cost recovery basis, using the prescribed cost recovery allowances for 3-year class assets of 25, 38, and 37 percent for 19X1, 19X2, and 19X3, respectively. As indicated below, the revenues are a constant $2,000 per year, the other nontax expenses are a constant $1,000 per year except in 19X3, when they are $2,700, which causes the net operating loss to arise, and the income tax rate is a flat 40 percent for all years.

In the *unusual* case in which the realization of the tax benefits of the loss carry-forward is assured beyond any reasonable doubt, an $80 carry-forward asset is recognized at the end of 19X3, the loss year, and amortized at the end of 19X4, when the benefits are realized; and deferred taxes continue to be

---

EXHIBIT 10   Journal Entries for Carry-Forward and Timing Differences

	Realization assured		Realization not assured	
19X1 Income Tax Expense	280		280	
Deferred Tax Credit		30		30
Cash		250		250
19X2 Income Tax Expense	280		280	
Deferred Tax Credit		108		108
Cash		172		172
19X3 Receivable for Tax Refund	422		422	
Carry-Forward Asset	80		—	
Deferred Tax Credit	—		80	
Deferred Tax Credit		102		102
Income Tax Expense		400		400
19X4 Income Tax Expense	280		280	
Deferred Tax Credit	120		120	
Cash		320		320
Carry-Forward Asset		80		—
Deferred Tax Credit		—		80
19X5 Income Tax Expense	280		280	
Deferred Tax Credit	120		120	
Cash		400		400

accrued on the originating timing difference in 19X3 and are amortized in 19X4 and 19X5 as the timing differences reverse. On the other hand, in the *usual* case in which the realization of the tax benefits of the loss carry-forward is not assured beyond any reasonable doubt, no carry-forward asset is recognized, but $80 of deferred tax credits are eliminated at the end of 19X3, the loss year, and reinstated at the end of 19X4, when the benefits of the carry-forward are realized; and the $240 of deferred tax credits are amortized in the usual manner, $120 in 19X4 and $120 in 19X5. Note that the amount of the deferred tax credit that is eliminated at the end of 19X3 is limited to $80, the amount of the potential tax benefits of the carry-forward, rather than $138, the deferred tax credit balance. Journal entries are provided in Exhibit 10 to clarify these relationships further.

The justification for recognizing net operating loss carry-forwards indirectly by eliminating preexisting deferred tax credits is noted by Bevis and Perry [1969, p. 25], as follows:

> [I]t would be unrealistic to require recognition of deferred tax credits while at the same time denying recognition of deferred tax charges, in the form of a loss carry-forward. This follows because both the deferred credits and the deferred charges [for the carry-forward] will reverse during the same future accounting periods.

In effect, a consistent set of assumptions underlies the accounting for net operating loss carry-forwards and preexisting deferred tax credits.

As noted earlier, conservatism underlies the nonrecognition of carry-forward assets unless realization is assured beyond any reasonable doubt. But the elimination of preexisting deferred tax credits to the extent of unrecognized carry-forward assets may not be conservative at all, because debt–equity ratios are improved under this procedure relative to the full recognition of both deferred tax credits and carry-forward assets; the elimination procedure is a system of offsetting assets and liabilities, and results in the understatement of both.

Preexisting deferred tax debits. At the time that a net operating loss carry-forward arises, net deferred tax debits may exist as a result of timing differences of prior periods. To the extent that the deferred tax debits arose in the carry-back years, they would normally be eliminated through carry-back of the net operating loss, but deferred tax debit balances arising prior to the carry-back years may still remain. In the unusual case when the tax benefits of the loss carry-forward are assured of realization beyond any reasonable doubt, the preexisting deferred tax debit balances should continue to be carried forward in the accounts. But in the usual case when the tax benefits of the loss carry-forward are not assured of realization beyond any reasonable doubt, it may no longer be appropriate to carry forward the deferred tax debit balances in the accounts. In these situations, Bevis and Perry suggest [1969, p. 26] that the net deferred tax debit balances should be evaluated as to their realizability in the same manner as are other assets.

Concurrent timing differences. In other situations, timing differences may originate in the same period in which a net operating loss arises. If the net operating loss is *larger* for tax purposes than for book purposes, the underlying timing differences would normally result in the recognition of deferred tax credits in the financial records. If the realization of the tax benefits of the net operating loss is assured beyond any reasonable doubt, both the carry-forward asset and the deferred tax credits should be recognized in the accounts. If realization of the tax benefits of the net operating loss is not assured beyond any reasonable doubt, no carry-forward asset should be recognized, and the deferred tax credits that would otherwise be recognized (or preexisting deferred tax credits) should be eliminated, using the procedures discussed previously.

On the other hand, if the net operating loss is *smaller* for tax purposes than for book purposes, the underlying timing differences would normally result in the recognition of deferred tax debits in the financial records. If the realization of the tax benefits is assured beyond any reasonable doubt, both the carry-forward asset and the deferred tax debits should be recognized in the accounts. If the realization of the tax benefits of the net operating loss is not assured beyond any reasonable doubt, no recognition should be given in the accounts to either the carry-forward or the deferred tax debit, inasmuch as the tax effects of the timing differences would be zero under the with and without method.

When the realization of the tax benefits of a net operating loss is not assured beyond any reasonable doubt and, therefore, no carry-forward asset is recognized, the measurement of periodic posttax book income becomes somewhat ambiguous if deferred tax credits of an equal amount are not eliminated, the tax benefits of the loss carry-forward are only partially realized, or the write-off of preexisting deferred tax debits or carry-forward assets is required [see Laibstain, 1971; and Wolk and Tearney, 1973]. The ambiguities inherent in such situations require arbitrary financial accounting solutions too numerous for individual examination.

Other Unused Deductions and Credits. The basic accounting concepts underlying the accounting for net operating losses, as prescribed in APB Opinion No. 11 and detailed above, also apply to other unused deductions and credits for tax purposes that may be carried backward or forward in determining taxable income or income taxes payable, such as capital losses, contribution carryovers, foreign tax credits, and investment tax credits.

Capital loss carry-forwards. Under current federal income tax laws and regulations, corporations may deduct capital losses only to the extent of capital gains; capital losses not deductible under this provision may be carried back 3 years and carried forward 5 years. Because of the limitations inherent in the deductibility of capital losses, whether or not a tax benefit of a capital loss is assured of realization beyond any reasonable doubt depends on a number of subjective evaluations concerning the following:

1. The intent of management regarding the timing of the disposal of other capital assets

2. The probable proceeds from both gain and loss assets when they are disposed

3. The amount of existing capital gains against which capital loss carry-backs may be utilized

4. The amount of anticipated capital gains against which capital loss carry-forwards may be utilized

Additionally, the appropriate tax rate to use in calculating the tax benefits of capital losses depends on the nature of the net capital gains against which the capital losses are offset.

Consistent with FASB Statement No. 12 [1975, par. 22], unrealized gains and losses on marketable securities constitute timing differences subject to interperiod income tax allocation, whether the unrealized gains and losses are reported in the income statement or in the equity section of the balance sheet. Presumably, deferred tax credits should be accrued on net unrealized gains. FASB Statement No. 12 notes, however, that deferred tax debits should be accrued on net unrealized losses only when there exists assurance beyond any reasonable doubt that the tax benefits will be realized by offset of the loss against capital gains of prior or subsequent periods. As a practical matter, the tax benefits of almost all capital loss carry-forwards are not recognized in the accounts until realized. The authoritative literature does not require the presentation of the tax benefits of previously unrecognized realized capital loss carry-forwards as extraordinary items.

Unused investment credits. Prior to the Revenue Act of 1978, the maximum investment tax credit allowable was generally 100 percent of the first $25,000 of federal income taxes payable plus 50 percent of the remaining federal income taxes payable. The Revenue Act of 1978 changed the percentage limitations generally applicable to the remaining federal income taxes payable to 60 percent for 1979, 70 percent for 1980, 80 percent for 1981, and 90 percent for 1982; but the Tax Equity and Fiscal Responsibility Act of 1982 changed the percentage limitations again to 85 percent for 1983 and thereafter. If the investment tax credit is not used up because it exceeds the amount allowed for the year, it may be carried back to the 3 prior years and carried forward to the 15 subsequent years. In figuring the tax limitation, investment tax credits carried over are used first and then investment tax credits earned currently, consistent with first-in, first-out; after that, any carry-back credits may be applied. If there are any unused investment tax credits from 2 or more years, they are used up in the order in which they occur, again consistent with first-in, first-out. The investment tax credit allowable for the current year, plus any carryover investment tax credits, cannot exceed the general tax limitations.

Consistent with the deferred method of interperiod income tax allocation and the flow-through method of accounting for investment tax credits, the investment tax credit is recognized before it is realized as an offset against federal income taxes payable under the with and without method. In FASB Interpretation No. 25 [1978, par. 7], the FASB concluded that " . . . this practice should not be changed without a reconsideration of accounting for income taxes."

Accordingly, the FASB attempted to clarify the computational guidelines for recognizing investment credits for book purposes under the flow-through method, including the limitations on recognizing unused investment credits, as follows [FASB Interpretation No. 25, 1978, par. 10]:

> The tax benefit of investment tax credits becoming available in the current period (excluding investment tax credits carried back to previous years) or carried forward from a prior period shall be recognized in measuring income tax expense for the current period by the deferred method to the

extent that the benefit would have been realized if taxes payable had been based on pretax accounting income adjusted for permanent differences. In addition, any remaining unused investment tax credit shall be offset against existing net deferred tax credits to the extent that those net deferred tax credits would reverse during the investment tax credit carryforward period, disregarding any timing differences that may originate in that carryforward period. The statutory limitation on offsets of the investment tax credit against federal income taxes payable shall be applied to each determination of amounts of investment tax credit to be recognized. . . .

The FASB noted [Interpretation No. 25, 1978, fn. 2] that "[t]he tax benefit of investment tax credits carried back to previous tax years and realized as a refund of federal income taxes previously paid is added to the amount of investment tax credits recognized in measuring income tax expense for the current period."

Additional clarification was required as a result of the change in the percentage limitations under the Revenue Act of 1978, and resulted in FASB Interpretation No. 32 [1980], in which the FASB clarified the application of paragraph 10 of Interpretation No. 25 with respect to the statutory limitations to be used in recognizing unused investment credits, as follows [Interpretation No. 32, pars. 2–3]:

> The percentage limitation on the amount of federal income tax payable that can be offset by investment tax credits under the with-and-without computation is the statutory percentage limitations in effect for the year for which the computation is being made.
>
> The limitations to be used in recognizing investment tax credits in addition to that recognized in the "with-and-without" computation shall be the statutory percentage limitations applicable to the years in which previously recorded deferred tax credits are expected to reverse.

The FASB noted that only net deferred tax credits that have not been previously offset and that will reverse during the investment credit carry-forward period (disregarding any timing differences that may originate in that carry-forward period) should be offset by investment tax credits; additionally, net deferred tax credits that were offset in prior years should not be adjusted to reflect recently enacted changes in the statutory percentage limitations.

Some commentators questioned the rationale for limiting investment tax credits recognized under the with and without method to the limitation in effect for the year in which the computation is being made, but using future limitations in offsetting investment tax credits against existing net deferred tax credits. The FASB concluded, however, that the use of different percentage limitations is consistent with the deferred method of interperiod income tax allocation and the method of currently recognizing the tax benefits of net operating loss carry-forwards as offsets against existing net deferred tax credits [Interpretation No. 32, 1980, pars. 12–13]:

> The deferred method of interperiod tax allocation uses the tax rates currently in effect, does not consider future tax rates, and does not adjust for subsequent changes in rates. . . . Therefore, the amount of investment tax

credit recognized in the "with-and-without" computation is determined by applying the limitation in effect for the year for which the computation is being made. . . . Deferred tax credits offset in the "with-and-without" computation are considered fully offset.

In determining the amount of investment tax credit to be recognized as an offset against existing net deferred tax credits, prospective percentage limitations are applied to existing net deferred tax credits from prior years that have not been previously offset. Prospective limitations are applied only to existing net deferred tax credits not previously offset because application of prospective limitations to existing net deferred tax credits that have been previously offset would result in subsequently adjusting the limitation applied in the "with-and-without" computation. This concept . . . is similar to recognizing currently the tax benefit of an operating loss carryforward as an offset against existing net deferred tax credits.

When the tax benefit of an unused investment tax credit that was recognized for book purposes by offset against net deferred tax credits is subsequently realized for tax purposes as a reduction of federal income taxes payable, an equivalent amount of deferred tax credits should be reinstated in the accounts and amortized in the periods in which the related timing differences reverse.

A lengthy example of the application of the percentage limitations under FASB Interpretation No. 32 is contained in an appendix to that pronouncement.

FASB Interpretations No. 25 and 32 apply to firms that use the flow-through method to account for investment tax credits. These pronouncements in no way modify the alternative method of amortizing realized investment tax credits over the productive lives of the related assets, consistent with the deferral method. As noted more fully in APB Opinion No. 2 [1962, par. 16], the amount of any unused investment tax credit may be recognized as an asset and added to the realized investment tax credit under the deferral method to the extent that the unused credit is carried back, but the carry-forward of an unused investment tax credit should ordinarily be recognized for book purposes under the deferral method only as realized.[3]

Under APB Opinion No. 2 [1962], as amplified by FASB Interpretation No. 25 [1978, par. 14], unused investment tax credits may not otherwise be recognized as assets.

Consistent with FASB Interpretation No. 25 [1978, pars. 15–16], goodwill recognized in purchase-type business combinations should be reduced in the period of realization by the amount of income tax benefits realized from unused investment tax credits of acquired corporations. Goodwill should not be reduced retroactively to the date of the business combination, and posttax book incomes of previous periods should not be retroactively restated for the revised goodwill. Rather, the revised goodwill should be amortized over the remaining amortization period. If the amount of income tax benefits exceed the remaining unamortized goodwill from the business combination, they should be applied

---

[3]Consistent with the broader provisions of APB Opinion No. 11 [1967], however, it is permissible to recognize some investment tax credit carry-forwards prior to realization under the deferral method, by elimination of preexisting deferred tax credits, whereupon the percentage limitations enumerated in FASB Interpretation No. 32 [1980] presumably would apply.

to reduce any remaining unamortized noncurrent assets acquired, but these assets should not be reduced retroactively to the date of the business combination, and posttax book incomes of previous periods should not be retroactively restated for revised depreciation, depletion, or amortization expense. If the remaining unamortized noncurrent assets are reduced to zero, any remaining tax benefits from the unused investment tax credit should be recorded as a deferred credit and amortized systematically to income over the estimated period to be benefited, not to exceed 40 years.

Sale or Purchase of Tax Benefits. Under the Economic Recovery Tax Act of 1981, the tax benefits relating to certain property are separable from the property and can be transferred from the seller to the buyer through a tax lease transaction. These tax leases do not transfer substantially all of the benefits and risks of ownership and, accordingly, should not be accounted for as capital leases. Rather, the FASB concluded [1981, pars. 4-5; 1982a, pars. 5-6] that these tax leases should be accounted for as the sale or purchase of tax benefits.

Initially, the FASB proposed [1981, pars. 7-15] a dual-transaction approach, whereby the accounting for the purchase and sale of investment tax credits was distinguishable from the accounting for the purchase and sale of ACRS depreciation deductions. Subsequently, the FASB proposed a single-transaction approach for transfers of both investment tax credits and ACRS depreciation deductions; it is this single-transaction approach that is discussed below.

Sale of tax benefits. The FASB concluded [1982a, par. 7] that the seller of tax benefits should report the adjusted sales price in pretax book income in the period in which the tax lease transaction occurs, and recognize deferred income taxes on the adjusted sales price. Because the seller has not transferred the right to use the property to the buyer, the seller should continue to report the property among its long-term assets and depreciate it for book purposes. On the other hand, for tax purposes, the seller recognizes rental expense on the tax lease and interest revenue on the note receivable from the buyer. For the total transaction, the sum of the total depreciation charges less the adjusted sales price equals the sum of the total rental expense less the total interest revenue, hence functions as a timing difference.

Purchase of tax benefits. The FASB concluded [1982a, pars. 8-10] that the buyer of tax benefits should report in pretax book income interest revenue on the unrecovered adjusted purchase price in those periods in which the adjusted purchase price increased by any interest revenue recognized thereon exceeds the cumulative realized tax savings; the rate of interest should not exceed the lower of the buyer's aftertax incremental borrowing rate or the aftertax short-term investment rate. If the adjusted purchase price increased by any (imputed) interest revenue recognized thereon is *greater* than the anticipated tax savings from the transaction, the difference should be amortized using a compound interest method in periods in which the buyer's cumulative realized tax savings exceed the adjusted purchase price and imputed interest revenue—that is, in the periods in which the buyer has recovered its investment in tax benefits. On the other hand, if the adjusted purchase price increased by any (imputed) interest revenue recognized thereon is *less* than the anticipated tax saving from the transaction, the difference should be amortized using a compound interest method in periods in which the adjusted purchase price and imputed interest revenue thereon exceeds the cumulative realized tax savings—that is, in the periods in which the buyer has a positive investment in tax benefits. Deferred income taxes should be provided for any differences between pretax book income and taxable income that arise from the tax lease transaction.

Neither the seller nor the buyer should report in its balance sheets any receivables or payables with respect to tax lease transactions to the extent that the right of offset exists for payments to one another. Both should disclose the nature and financial effects of any sales or purchases of tax benefits.

The rationale for this accounting [FASB, 1982a, pars. 33–34] is the belief that the buyer of tax benefits makes an investment in a right to future tax benefits that either eliminates or defers cash payments to the government. The principal benefit is the right to the temporary use of cash that would otherwise be paid in taxes. In the early periods of the transaction, the investment tax credit and the tax effect of ACRS deductions and interest expense exceed the tax effect of rental revenue, resulting in tax savings; in the later periods, the tax effect of rental revenue exceeds the tax effect of interest expense, resulting in tax payments. Accordingly, the investment in tax benefits should be reduced as the investment is recovered in the form of tax savings. Because interest is implicit in the investment decision, imputed interest revenue should be recognized on the investment.

As a result of the enactment of the Tax Equity and Fiscal Responsibility Act of 1982, the purchase and sale of tax benefits under tax leases is virtually eliminated as a desirable tax strategy, and the FASB chose not to issue a final pronouncement in this area.

FINANCIAL STATEMENT PRESENTATION

Various pronouncements of the Accounting Principles Board, the Financial Accounting Standards Board, and the Securities and Exchange Commission specify minimum disclosure requirements in the financial statements and footnotes thereto.

Balance Sheet Presentation. Separate classification of the following income tax accounts is required in the balance sheet:

1. Income taxes estimated to be currently payable
2. Net amount of current deferred tax debits and current deferred tax credits relating to timing differences
3. Net amount of noncurrent deferred tax debits and noncurrent deferred tax credits relating to timing differences
4. Refundable income taxes arising from carry-backs of net operating losses, investment tax credits, and similar items
5. Future income tax benefits arising from carry-forwards of net operating losses and similar items, which have been recognized for book purposes because realization is assured beyond any reasonable doubt

6. Unamortized investment tax credits, if the deferral method of accounting for investment tax credits is employed

If a deferred tax debit or credit is related to a nontax asset or liability, it should be classified as current or noncurrent based on the classification of the related asset or liability; in this context, a deferred tax debit or credit is related to an asset or liability if reduction of the asset (by amortization, sale, or other realization) or reduction of the liability (by amortization, payment, or other satisfaction) causes the underlying timing difference to reverse. If a deferred tax debit or credit is not related to a nontax asset or liability because there is no associated nontax asset or liability or because reduction of an associated nontax asset or liability will not cause the underlying timing difference to reverse, the deferred tax debit or credit should be classified as current or noncurrent based on the expected reversal date of the specific underlying timing difference, applying the same criteria used for classifying other nontax assets and liabilities. Deferred income taxes arising from timing differences involving installment sales, depreciation, and unremitted foreign earnings of unconsolidated subsidiaries accounted for by the equity method relate to individual nontax assets—specifically, installment receivables, depreciable assets, and investments in subsidiaries, respectively; accordingly, these deferred income taxes should be classified consistently with the classification of these related nontax assets. On the other hand, deferred income taxes arising from timing differences involving certain accounting changes, long-term construction contracts, capital leases, and unremitted foreign earnings of consolidated subsidiaries do not relate to individual nontax assets or liabilities, hence should be classified consistent with the expected reversal of the underlying timing differences themselves.

Assets recognized for refundable income taxes due to net operating loss carry-backs and assets recognized for anticipated future income tax benefits due to net operating loss carry-forwards should be classified as current or noncurrent, depending on whether or not realization is anticipated within the next year or operating cycle.

No authoritative pronouncement has been issued on the appropriate balance sheet classification of unamortized investment tax credits accounted for under the deferral method.

Income Statement Presentation. Separate classification of the following components of the reported income tax expense for the period is required in the income statement:

1. Income taxes estimated to be payable
2. Income tax effects of timing differences
3. Income tax effects of net operating losses
4. Income tax effects of investment credits, whether the flow-through method or the deferral method is used

These amounts should be allocated to income from continuing operations, income from discontinued operations, extraordinary items, and cumulative adjustments for changes in accounting principles, and may be presented as separate amounts in the income statement or, alternatively, as combined amounts with disclosure of the components parenthetically or in a footnote.

When the income tax benefits of a net operating loss carry-forward are realized in full or in part and have not been previously recognized in the accounts, the benefits should be reported as an extraordinary item for the period in which realized.

Income tax effects of prior period adjustments of retained earnings, as well as direct adjustments of other shareholders' equity accounts, should be excluded from the income statement and reported as adjustments of such items in the financial statements in which such items are themselves reported.

Funds Statement Presentation. To the extent that the deferred tax provision in the income statement affects noncurrent deferred tax debits and credits, an adjustment is required in the funds statement in computing working capital from operations. Specifically, working capital from operations is more (less) than posttax book income by the increase (decrease) in net noncurrent deferred tax credits and the decrease (increase) in net noncurrent deferred tax debits. Similar adjustments should also be made for nonoperating sources and uses of funds that are appropriately reported on a net-of-tax basis in the funds statement in accordance with intraperiod income tax allocation, at least to the extent that the income tax consequences affect noncurrent deferred tax debits and credits.

The authoritative pronouncements do not indicate, however, just which nonoperating sources and uses of funds should be reported on a net-of-tax basis, and which should not. It seems clear that because extraordinary items are reported net of tax in the income statement, the counterpart nonoperating sources or uses of funds should be reported net of income taxes in the funds statement, consistent with intraperiod income tax allocation. On the other hand, unusual or infrequently occurring items that are not extraordinary items are reported gross of income taxes and included in net income from continuing operations in the income statement, but are often reported as nonoperating sources and uses of funds in the funds statement. APB Opinion No. 30 [1973, par. 26] clearly prohibits intraperiod income tax allocation for unusual or infrequently occurring items in the income statement. One commentator [Giles, 1975] has implicitly interpreted this pronouncement to call for the reporting of these nonoperating sources and uses of funds gross of income taxes in the funds statement, but APB Opinion No. 30 [1973] pertains only to the income statement. Accordingly, it appears equally reasonable to report these nonoperating sources and uses of funds net of income taxes in the funds statement; see Nurnberg [1983].

Other Disclosure Requirements. Certain other disclosures are required in addition to those made within the body of the financial statements, as follows:

1. Method of accounting for income taxes, including timing differences and investment tax credits
2. Amounts of unrecognized net operating loss carry-forwards, investment

tax credit carry-forwards, and any other unused deductions and credits, together with expiration dates and amounts which, upon recognition, would be credited to deferred tax accounts

3. Cumulative amount of undistributed earnings of subsidiaries and corporate joint ventures on which deferred income taxes are not accrued, and reasons for nonaccrual

---

EXHIBIT 11　Disclosures Required by Regulation S-X

Net income before income tax expense is $15,000 and is comprised of the following components:

Domestic	$12,600
Foreign	2,400
Total	$15,000

Income tax expense is $5,820 and is comprised of the following components:

	U.S. federal	Foreign	State and local	Total
Current expense	$2,312	$360	$400	$3,072
Deferred expense	2,328	420	-0-	2,748
Total	$4,640	$780	$400	$5,820

Deferred income tax expense results from timing differences in the recognition of revenue and expense for tax and financial statement purposes. The sources of these differences and the tax effect of each were as follows:

Excess of tax over book depreciation	$ 600
Preoperating costs expensed on tax return and deferred on books	1,440
Revenue recognized on completed contract basis on tax return and on percentage-of-completion basis on books	960
Tax-deductible inventory reserve provided in foreign tax jurisdiction	420
Warranty cost charged to expense on books but not deductible until paid	(672)
Total deferred expense	$2,748

Total income tax expense amounted to $5,820 (an effective rate of 38.8%), a total less than the amount of $6,900 computed by applying the U.S. federal income tax rate of 46% to income before taxes. The reasons for this difference are as follows:

	Tax effect	Percent of pretax income
Computed "expected" tax expense	$6,900	46.0%
Increases (reductions) in taxes resulting from:		
Foreign income subject to foreign income tax but not expected to be subject to U.S. tax in foreseeable future	(372)	(2.5)
Tax-exempt municipal bond interest	(720)	(4.8)
Investment tax credit	(700)	(4.7)
Goodwill amortization not deductible for tax purposes . . .	684	4.6
State and local income taxes, net of federal income tax benefit	208	1.4
Benefit from income tax at capital gains rate	(180)	(1.2)
Actual tax expense	$5,820	38.8%

4. Reasons for significant variations in the customary relationships between income tax expense and pretax book income, if not otherwise apparent

Additional disclosures are required in the financial statements included in the annual shareholders' reports of companies registered under the 1934 Securities Exchange Act, consistent with Regulation S-X, as follows:

1. Income tax effects of various types of timing differences and net operating losses
2. Amounts of foreign and domestic pretax income
3. Amounts of federal, foreign, and other income taxes
4. Reconciliation of reported effective income tax rate and federal statutory income tax rate

The separate disclosure of the income tax effects of each of the various types of timing differences and net operating losses is required unless the individual amounts are less than 15 percent of the deferred provision in the income statement for the year; if no individual type of timing difference is more than 5 percent of the amount computed by multiplying the income before tax by the applicable federal statutory income tax rate and the aggregate amount of timing differences is less than 5 percent of such computed amount, disclosure of the separate types of timing differences may be omitted. Similarly, the separate disclosure of amounts of U.S. federal income taxes, foreign income taxes, and other income taxes is required unless the amounts applicable to foreign and other income taxes do not exceed 5 percent of the total for the component. A simple example of these required disclosures is found in Exhibit 11. Note that the reconciliation of the statutory and effective income tax rates does not include the income tax effects of timing differences, which are already included in the computation of the deferred tax provision and the effective tax rate.

INTERIM FINANCIAL REPORTING

In Opinion No. 28 [1973, par. 9], the Accounting Principles Board concluded that " ... each interim period should be viewed primarily as an integral part of an annual period." That is, the APB subscribed to the integral view of interim financial reporting, whereby the fiscal year is the focal point of interim financial reports, and expenses are assigned to interim periods based on assumed or estimated relationships to total annual revenues and expenses.

In applying this integral view, APB Opinion No. 28 [par. 19] calls for the measurement of interim period income tax expense based on an estimate of the annual effective income tax rate for the fiscal year encompassing the interim period, as follows:

Estimated Annual Effective Tax Rate

$$= \frac{\text{Estimated Tax on Estimated Ordinary Income for Year}}{\text{Estimated Ordinary Income for Year}}$$

In this context, ordinary income or loss refers to income or loss from continuing operations before income taxes, excluding significant unusual or infrequently occurring items, extraordinary items, discontinued operations, and cumulative effects of changes in accounting principles; and the estimated tax on estimated ordinary income is inclusive of anticipated investment tax credits, foreign tax rates, percentage depletion, capital gains rates, and other available tax planning alternatives. By computing the annual effective income tax rate in this manner, the effect of special tax rates and tax credits pertaining to ordinary income is spread over all interim periods, consistent with the integral view of interim financial reporting, rather than recognized in the interim period in which the transaction occurs that is subject to the special tax rates or tax credits.

The income tax expense for an interim period is equal to the estimated annual effective income tax rate multiplied by the ordinary income for the year to date, less income tax expense recognized in previous interim periods, plus any income tax pertaining to unusual or infrequently occurring items, extraordinary items, discontinued operations, and cumulative effects of changes in accounting principles of that interim period. This year-to-date computation automatically adjusts for changes in estimates on a cumulative basis through succeeding interim periods of a fiscal year, consistent with the interim reporting of other changes in accounting estimates.

The tax benefits of losses that occur in the early interim periods of a fiscal year should be recognized only if realization is assured beyond any reasonable doubt, if carry-back of such losses (or the elimination of preexisting net deferred tax credits) is not possible. An established seasonal pattern of losses in early interim periods, offset by income in later interim periods, constitutes evidence that realization is assured beyond any reasonable doubt, unless other evidence indicates that the established seasonal pattern will not prevail. Consistent with the cumulative adjustment treatment of changes in accounting estimates, when the tax benefits of losses that arise in early interim periods of a fiscal year are not recognized in those interim periods, no provision for income tax expense should be made for income that arises in later interim periods of the same fiscal year, until the tax benefits of the previous interim period losses are utilized; the tax benefits of interim period losses accounted for in this manner should not be reported as extraordinary items in the later interim periods.

The complexities inherent in following these broad provisions of APB Opinion No. 28 [1973] led to the issuance by the Financial Accounting Standards Board of the much lengthier Interpretation No. 18 [1977], in which these broad provisions are clarified.

BIBLIOGRAPHY

Accounting Principles Board (AICPA), *New Depreciation Guidelines and Rules*, Opinion No. 1 (APB, 1962).
———, *Accounting for the "Investment Credit,"* Opinion No. 2 (APB, 1962).
———, *Accounting for the "Investment Credit,"* Opinion No. 4 (APB, 1964).
———, *Accounting for the Cost of Pension Plans*, Opinion No. 8 (APB, 1966).
———, *Omnibus Opinion—1966*, Opinion No. 10 (APB, 1966).

———, *Accounting for Income Taxes*, Opinion No. 11 (APB, 1967).

———, *Intangible Assets*, Opinion No. 17 (APB, 1970).

———, *Accounting Changes*, Opinion No. 20 (APB, 1971).

———, *Accounting for Income Taxes—Special Areas*, Opinion No. 23 (APB, 1972).

———, *Accounting for Income Taxes—Investments in Common Stock Accounted for by the Equity Method (Other than Subsidiaries and Corporate Joint Ventures)*, Opinion No. 24 (APB, 1972).

———, *Interim Financial Reporting*, APB Opinion No. 28 (APB, 1973).

———, *Reporting the Results of Operations—Reporting the Effects of Disposal of a Segment of Business, and Extraordinary, Unusual and Infrequently Occurring Events and Transactions*, Opinion No. 30 (APB, 1973).

Accounting Standards Committee, *Accounting for Deferred Taxation*, Statement of Standard Accounting Practice, No. 15 (Institute of Chartered Accountants in England and Wales, 1978).

Bevis, A., and R. Perry, *Accounting for Income Taxes*, Accounting Interpretations of APB Opinion No. 11 (AICPA, 1969).

Black, H. A., *Interperiod Allocation of Corporate Income Taxes*, Accounting Research Study No. 9 (AICPA, 1966).

Canadian Institute of Chartered Accountants, *Handbook*, Sec. 3470 (CICA, Toronto, 1967).

Chambers, Raymond J., "Tax Allocation and Financial Reporting," *Abacus*, December 1968, pp. 98–123.

Committee on Accounting Procedure (AICPA), *Accounting for Income Taxes*, Accounting Research Bulletin No. 23 (CAP, 1944).

Davidson, S., "Accelerated Depreciation and the Allocation of Income Taxes," *The Accounting Review*, April 1958, pp. 173–180.

———, "Comments," in H. A. Black, *Interperiod Allocation of Corporate Income Taxes*, Accounting Research Study No. 9 (AICPA, 1966), pp. 117–119.

Financial Accounting Standards Board, *Accounting for Certain Marketable Securities*, Statement of Financial Accounting Standards No. 12 (FASB, 1975).

———, *Prior Period Adjustments*, Statement of Financial Accounting Standards No. 16 (FASB, 1977).

———, *Accounting for Income Taxes in Interim Periods*, FASB Interpretation No. 18 (FASB, 1977).

———, *Financial Accounting and Reporting by Oil and Gas Producing Companies*, Statement of Financial Accounting Standards No. 19 (FASB, 1977).

———, *Applicability of Indefinite Reversal Criteria to Timing Differences*, FASB Interpretation No. 22 (FASB, 1978).

———, *Accounting for an Unused Investment Tax Credit*, FASB Interpretation No. 25 (FASB, 1978).

———, *Reporting Tax Benefits Realized on Disposition of Investments in Certain Subsidiaries and Other Investees*, FASB Interpretation No. 29 (FASB, 1979).

———, *Accounting for Tax Benefits Related to U.K. Tax Legislation Concerning Stock Relief*, Statement of Financial Accounting Standards No. 31 (FASB, 1979).

———, *Application of Percentage Limitations in Recognizing Investment Tax Credit*, FASB Interpretation No. 32 (FASB, 1980).

———, *Balance Sheet Classification of Deferred Income Taxes*, Statement of Financial Accounting Standards No. 37 (FASB, 1980).

———, *Accounting for the Sale or Purchase of Tax Benefits through Tax Leases*, Proposed Statement of Financial Accounting Standards (FASB, 1981).

———, *Accounting for the Sale or Purchase of Tax Benefits through Tax Leases*, Proposed Statement of Financial Accounting Standards (FASB, 1982a).

———, *Accounting for the Reduction in the Tax Basis of an Asset Caused by the Investment Tax Credit*, Proposed Statement of Financial Accounting Standards (FASB, 1982b).

Gilles, L. H., Jr., "Property Disposals on Statements of Changes in Financial Position," *The CPA Journal*, September 1975, pp. 57–58.

Gonedes, N. J., and N. Dopuch, "Capital Market Equilibrium, Information Production, and Selecting Accounting Techniques: Theoretical Framework and Review of Empirical Work," *Studies on Financial Accounting Objectives: 1974*, supplement to *Journal of Accounting Research*, vol. 12 (1974), pp. 48–129.

International Accounting Standards Committee, *Accounting for Taxes on Income*, International Accounting Standard No. 12 (IASC, 1979).

Jaedicke, R. K., and C. L. Nelson, "The Allocation of Income Taxes—A Defense," *The Accounting Review*, April 1960, pp. 278–281.

Keller, T. W., *Accounting for Corporate Income Taxes*, Michigan Business Studies, vol. XV, no. 2 (Bureau of Business Reasearch, University of Michigan, Ann Arbor, 1961).

Laibstain, S., "A New Look at Accounting for Operating Loss Carryforwards," *The Accounting Review*, April 1971, pp. 342–351.

Moonitz, M., and C. L. Nelson, "Recent Developments in Accounting Theory," *The Accounting Review*, April 1960, pp. 206–217.

Nair, R. D., and J. J. Weygandt, "Let's Fix Deferred Taxes," *The Journal of Accountancy*, November 1981, pp. 87–102.

Nurnberg, H., *Cash Movements Analysis of the Accounting for Corporate Income Taxes* (Division of Research, Graduate School of Business Administration, Michigan State University, East Lansing, 1971).

———, "Issues in Funds Statement Presentation," *The Accounting Review*, October 1983.

Securities and Exchange Commission, *In the Matter of "Charges in Lieu of Taxes"—Statement of the Commission's Opinion Regarding "Charges in Lieu of Taxes" and "Provisions for Income Taxes" in the Profit and Loss Statement*, Accounting Series Release No. 53 (SEC, 1945).

———, *Accounting for the "Investment Credit,"* Accounting Series Release No. 96 (SEC, 1963).

———, *Notice of Adoption of Amendment to Regulation S-X to Provide for Improved Disclosure of Income Tax Expense*, Accounting Series Release No. 149 (SEC, 1973).

———, *Corrections or Changes to Bulletin No. 1—New Interpretations*, Staff Accounting Release No. 8 (SEC, 1976).

———, *Regulation S-X* (SEC, 1981).

Stickney, C. P., "Current Issues in the Measurement and Disclosure of Corporate Income Taxes," *The Accounting Review*, April 1979, pp. 421–433.

Stickney, C. P., R. L. Weil, and M. A. Wolfson, "Income Taxes and Tax Transfer Leases: General Electric's Accounting for a Molotov Cocktail," *The Accounting Review*, April 1983, pp. 439–460.

Wolk, H. I., and M. G. Tearney, "Income Tax Allocation and Loss Carryforwards: Exploring Unchartered Ground," *The Accounting Review*, April 1973, pp. 292–299.

CHAPTER **37**

SEC Procedures

and Regulations

K. Fred Skousen
Director, School of Accountancy, Brigham Young University

EXHIBIT 1   Securities and Exchange Commission Organization Chart. *Source: The Work of the Securities and Exchange Commission, U.S. Government Printing Office, Washington, D.C., March 1978.*

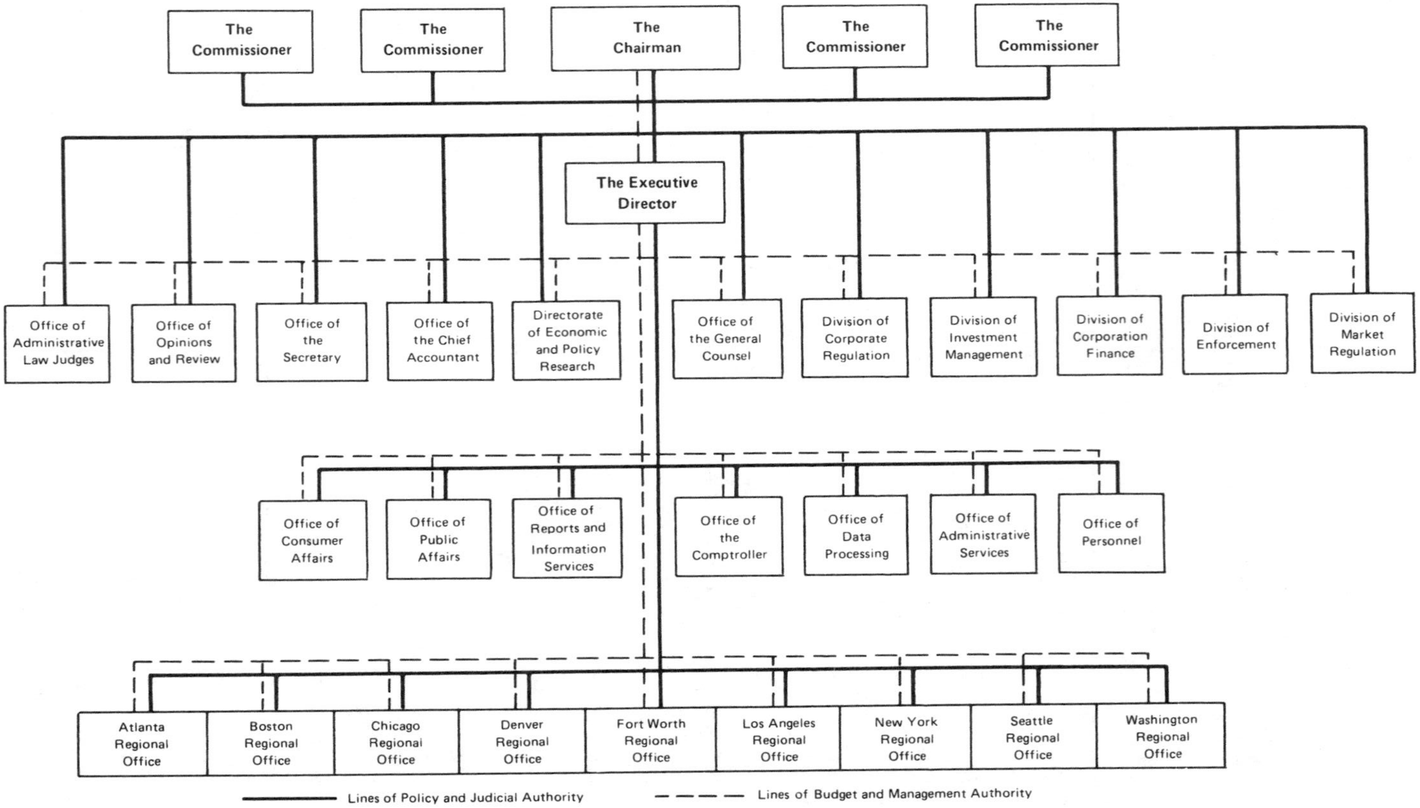

Lines of Policy and Judicial Authority

Lines of Budget and Management Authority

The Commissioner

The Commissioner

The Chairman

The Commissioner

The Commissioner

The Commissioner

The Executive Director

Office of Administrative Law Judges

Office of Opinions and Review

Office of the Secretary

Office of the Chief Accountant

Directorate of Economic and Policy Research

Office of the General Counsel

Division of Corporate Regulation

Division of Investment Management

Division of Corporation Finance

Division of Enforcement

Division of Market Regulation

Office of Consumer Affairs

Office of Public Affairs

Office of Reports and Information Services

Office of the Comptroller

Office of Data Processing

Office of Administrative Services

Office of Personnel

Atlanta Regional Office

Boston Regional Office

Chicago Regional Office

Denver Regional Office

Fort Worth Regional Office

Los Angeles Regional Office

New York Regional Office

Seattle Regional Office

Washington Regional Office

37-2

THE SEC AND THE LAWS IT ADMINISTERS

The Securities and Exchange Commission (SEC) was established by law in 1934 to regulate the distribution and trading of securities in the United States. It attempts to ensure that investors have "full and fair" disclosure of pertinent information in connection with security offerings. This chapter describes the nature of the SEC and some of its important procedures and regulations.

Organizational Structure. The SEC is an independent regulatory agency of the U.S. government. It is composed of five commissioners appointed by the President with the consent of the Senate. One commissioner is designated as the chairman by the President. No more than three commissioners may be members of the same political party.

The Commission is assisted by a professional staff organized into divisions and offices directly responsible to the Commission, as shown in Exhibit 1. Regional office functions are generally limited to broker-dealer matters, suspected trading violations, and handling the abbreviated Regulation A filings for offerings not exceeding $1,500,000. All other activity of the Commission takes place in Washington, D.C.

Accountants generally have more contact with the Division of Corporation Finance than with any other group. This Division handles the direct case work of reviewing companies' filings of registration statements, proxy statements, and periodic reports. The Division is organized along industry lines into a number of branches, each of which contains accountants, lawyers, security analysts, and examiners. Upon completion of its review of a filing, the Division customarily issues a "letter of comment" outlining deficiencies to be corrected or additional information to be furnished before reports are cleared or registrations become effective. Some comments tend to be trivial; others are significant and even precedent-setting. If the registrant or its accountants do not agree with the accounting positions expressed in the letter of comment, the SEC staff is open to discussion to try to resolve the differences. The chief accountant of the division (a position different from the chief accountant of the SEC; see below) has the authority to reverse the original determination.

In an attempt to reduce delays in the processing of registration statements, the SEC has adopted a system of "selective review." First-time issues will continue to receive a thorough review as described above. Repeat offerings of established companies, however, will be reviewed only on a selective basis. Also, as noted in ASR No. 303, Form S-8 filings automatically become effective without staff review. The result is that some registration statements will not be reviewed at all, whereas others will receive careful attention. This will allow the SEC to concentrate its efforts on the highest-priority areas. Under this approach, companies are notified promptly after filing whether or not their registration statements will be reviewed. This procedure in no way changes the responsibilities of the participants in the offering as to the accuracy of the disclosures.

The chief accountant of the Commission, as distinguished from the chief accountant of the Division of Corporation Finance, operates at a policy level as the principal staff advisor to the Commission on all matters of accounting and auditing. More than anyone else in the agency, the chief accountant of the Commission determines how much influence the SEC has on accounting principles and auditing practice.

Legislative Basis. The SEC functions with broad powers under the authority of several laws. Its legal framework includes the Securities Act of 1933; the Securities Exchange Act of 1934; the Public Utility Holding Company Act of 1935; the Trust Indenture Act of 1939; the Investment Company Act of 1940; the Investment Advisers Act of 1940; the Bankruptcy Reform Act of 1978; the Securities Investor Protection Act of 1970; and the Foreign Corrupt Practices Act of 1977. The accountant is usually most concerned with the 1933 and 1934 Securities Acts, and more recently with the Foreign Corrupt Practices Act of 1977.

The Securities Act of 1933. The Securities Act of 1933 is concerned primarily with the initial distribution of securities rather than with subsequent trading in securities. The law provides for the registration of securities with the Commission before they may be sold to the public.

The 1933 Act is a disclosure statute designed to give the prospective investor an adequate basis for making investment decisions and to prevent misrepresentation or fraud in the sale of securities. These objectives are generally accomplished by requiring disclosure of specified financial and other information regarding the issuer of securities.

Required disclosure is provided by means of a registration statement, which includes a prospectus. The prospectus (which is Part I of the registration statement) must be furnished to the buyer of the registered security. Preliminary "red herring" prospectuses are frequently used to permit formation of underwriting syndicates and to provide information to interested parties in advance of the actual offering.

The preparation of a registration statement is a complicated, technical process. To the management of a first-time offeror, it can well be a traumatic, albeit frequently satisfying, experience.

The Securities Exchange Act of 1934. The 1934 Act provides for registration of national securities exchanges, securities listed on exchanges, and broker-dealers. It is concerned primarily with the trading of securities that have been previously distributed. The law also regulates proxy solicitations, tender offer solicitations, and controls the use of margins in security trading.

Although the 1934 Act calls for registration of securities not covered by the 1933 Act, its principal significance to registrants is the continuing reporting requirements it places on them. Most companies having securities registered under the 1933 Act or the 1934 Act must file annual reports, quarterly reports, and certain other reports relating to the occurrence of specified events. The annual report now requires essentially as much financial data as a registration statement.

The Foreign Corrupt Practices Act of 1977. The Foreign Corrupt Practices Act (FCPA) was enacted to control questionable or illegal foreign payments by U.S. companies. By amendment to the 1934 Act, however, it also included a significant requirement that all public companies must maintain accurate accounting records and an adequate system of internal control. Although the FCPA did not alter existing disclosure requirements, it does make more explicit the responsibilities of management with respect to accounting records. It also subjects companies (including accountants) to civil liability and potential criminal prosecution under federal securities laws.

SEC REGISTRATION AND REPORTING

The SEC does not judge the merits of securities offered for sale. That investment decision remains with the investor. Furthermore, the registration process does not guarantee completeness or accuracy of disclosures. Those are the responsibilities of the registrant and the individuals involved (management, underwriters, accountants, attorneys, etc.). The SEC's role is to determine if there is satisfactory compliance with the applicable statutes and regulations, and to enforce penalties for presenting false or misleading information or other fraudulent acts.

The preparation of a registration statement for filing under the Securities Acts is almost invariably a combined operation. Representatives of the management of the registering company, the underwriters, the independent public accountants, counsel for the company, counsel for the underwriters, and, occasionally, engineers or appraisers all have important roles in preparing the registration document. When the registration statement has been completed, an executed copy, together with conformed copies and exhibits, is taken or mailed to the SEC in Washington, D.C., for "filing" with the Commission.

Processing a Registration Statement. A registration statement is processed in the Division of Corporation Finance, which reviews the document to see if it contains any untrue statements or omissions of material facts that make the information presented misleading—in short, if there has been full and fair disclosure. In the processing, the registration statement is reviewed by a group working individually and collectively under the supervision of an assistant director of the Division. The group usually includes a lawyer, an accountant, and a financial analyst; a copy of the registration statement is furnished to each of them. If necessary or desirable, they consult with other experts (such as mining engineers or petroleum engineers) or with other departments of the government. The reviewers prepare memoranda of their findings.

The SEC's letter of comment, customarily sent upon completion of the review, sets forth in detail those matters that the staff feels require revision or expansion. Sometimes the letter requests supplemental information, which upon receipt and review by the staff may produce additional comments. The SEC's comments are carefully considered by everyone concerned with the registration statement.

Matters having to do with financial statements, schedules, and exhibits are usually delegated to the issuer's financial and accounting personnel and the attesting accountants in order that an agreement may be reached on what to do about the SEC's comments. In the majority of cases, the registration statement is amended in accordance with the letter of comment. However, if the comments relate to revision of the financial statements and the registrant desires to discuss or possibly rebut the suggested changes, the SEC staff is available for telephone discussion or an appointment in Washington. In many cases, the comments may be modified or withdrawn, or supplemental information may satisfy them.

When there is agreement as to the changes to be made, an amendment is filed and the changes are examined by the staff. In some cases, a further letter of comment is necessary.

By the time a registration statement is filed, the issuer and the underwriter usually agree as to the nature of the security to be sold. In almost all cases, however, the issuer and the underwriter do not initially agree as to the price at which the securities are to be offered to the public, the underwriter's discount of commission, or the net proceeds to the issuer. If the registration statement relates to preferred stock or bonds, there is usually no agreement at the time of initial filing as to the precise terms, the interest rate, or the dividend rate, an assumed price being used for the purpose of filing. These matters usually are still undecided at the time of filing amendments that cure the deficiencies, if any.

While the registration statement and any amendments are in process of preparation, negotiations are conducted leading to the final underwriting agreement. At the appropriate time, the underwriting agreement is completed and signed by authorized representatives of the issuer and the underwriter. At this time, another amendment to the registration statement is prepared, which fills in the blank spaces in previous SEC filings relating to such items as the interest rate, the dividend rate, the public offering prices, the underwriter's discount or commission, and the net proceeds to the company. This is called the "price amendment," and at the time of its filing the issuer and the underwriter customarily request acceleration (waiver of 20-day waiting period) so that the proposed offering to the public may be made promptly and the company may receive the proceeds.

Filing under the 1933 Act. Generally a company that seeks to raise capital through an initial public offering of securities must file a registration statement under the 1933 Act. *Form S-1* has been the form most commonly used to register such securities, although there are more than 20 different forms for various types of companies and specific circumstances. Certain information is common to all forms, for example, the nature and history of the business; capital structure; description of significant contracts such as profit-sharing plans; description of securities being registered; salaries and security holdings of key officers and directors; major elements of the underwriting agreement; estimate of net proceeds and expected uses of the funds; and detailed financial information. A listing of the items of information required in Form S-1 provides a good indication of the types of and quantity of data to be submitted to the SEC through the registration process:

Part I. Information required in both Form S-1 and the prospectus
    Item 1.   Offering price information and distribution spread
    Item 2.   Plan of distribution, names of underwriters and their participations, and nature of the underwriters' obligation

Item 3.　Use of proceeds to registrant

Item 4.　Sales of securities other than for cash

Item 5.　Capital structure

Item 6.　Selected financial data; management's discussion and analysis of financial condition and results of operation

Item 7.　State and date of incorporation and type of organization of the registrant

Item 8.　Parents of the registrant and basis of control

Item 9.　Description of the business

Item 10.　Description and location of principal plants, mines, and other physical properties.

Item 11.　If organized within 5 years, names of and transactions with promoters

Item 12.　Pending legal proceedings other than routine litigation

Items 13, 14, 15.　Information as to capital stock, funded debt, or other securities being registered

Item 16.　Names of directors and executive officers and their principal occupations

Item 17.　Management remuneration and transactions

Item 18.　Security ownership of certain beneficial holders and management

Item 19.　Financial statements and supplementary data

Item 20.　Brokerage allocation

Part II.　Information required in Form S-1 but not required in the prospectus

Item 21.　Arrangements limiting, restricting, or stabilizing the market for securities being offered

Item 22.　Expenses of the issue

Item 23.　Relationship with registrant of experts named in the registration statement (including accountants)

Item 24.　Sale of securities to special parties

Item 25.　Recent sales of unregistered securities

Item 26.　List of subsidiaries of the registrant

Item 27.　Franchises or concessions held by the registrant and subsidiaries

Item 28.　Indemnification arrangements for officers and directors

Item 29.　Accounting for proceeds from sale of capital stock being registered

Item 30.　List of financial statements and exhibits

The financial statements called for in a registration statement are the traditional balance sheet (2 years), income statements (3 years), statements of additional paid-in capital (3 years), statements of retained earnings (3 years), and statements of changes in financial position (3 years). Financial statements of an interim period of the current fiscal year are also required if the prospectus is prepared other than at year-end. Financial statements for the 3 years are required to be certified, but interim statements may normally be presented on an unaudited basis. Consolidated statements are usually called for, with separate statements of the parent company required under certain circumstances.

Prescribed schedules must be furnished in support of balance sheets and income statements. The schedules provide additional information on such matters as plant additions and retirements; receivables from directors, officers, and employees; long-term debt; indebtedness to and from affiliates; and stock reserved for warrants or other rights.

The interim period since the end of the preceding fiscal year is commonly called the "stub" period. Information about the stub period normally represents the latest available information about the company's operations. Because data from this interim period are not required to be audited, and generally are not, a special burden is placed on company management, especially the chief financial officer, to make sure that the information presents fairly the net income and other data of the interim period. The same responsibilities exist whether the information is in the form of full financial statements or merely capsule (i.e., paragraph) data. If there are any adjustments other than normal recurring accruals, management is required to submit a supplemental letter to the SEC describing in detail the nature and amount of adjustments entering into the determination of the amounts shown.

Management's responsibility for fair presentation of the interim period is not lessened by the fact that their independent public accountants have performed review procedures with respect to the unaudited period and have issued a "comfort letter" to the underwriters. Such letters generally state that they are ". . . solely for the information of, and assistance to, the underwriters in conducting and documenting their investigation of the affairs of the Company. . . ."

The "comfort letter" runs to material not covered by the auditors' opinion and involves "negative assurance" from the auditors that, as a result of limited, specified procedures, nothing has come to their attention that caused them to believe that the unaudited financial statements were not prepared in conformity with generally accepted accounting principles applied on a consistent basis. The "specified procedures" to be followed by the auditors are generally determined by the underwriters. The types of information usually covered by negative assurance are as follows:

1. Unaudited financial statements included in the registration statement

2. Subsequent changes in the company's capitalization, long-term debt, and certain other financial statement items

3. Tables, statistics, and other designated financial information in the registration statement

Although *Form S-1* has been the usual vehicle for first-time registration by a commercial or industrial company, a number of other forms may or must be used under certain conditions. The following describes some of the major forms that have been used for registration under the 1933 Act.

Form S-2 has been used by commercial and industrial companies in the development stage. This form, now superseded, requires traditional financial statements to the extent that they are appropriate.

Form S-5 is used to register securities of open-ended management investment companies under the Investment Company Act of 1940. (*Form S-4* is used for closed-end funds.) Financial statements required include statements of assets and liabilities, operations, changes in net assets, realized gain or loss on investments, and unrealized appreciation or depreciation of investments.

Form S-7 was used by specified or defined mature, stable, profitable companies. Because of the nature of the registrants some of the disclosure requirements were relaxed under Form S-7. It has been replaced; see page 37-12.

Form S-8 may be used to register securities to be offered to employees pursuant to a stock purchase, savings, option, or similar plan. In addition to information about the company, the form requires considerable information about the plan, including its financial statements. The requirement for comparative financial statements can usually be met by incorporating by reference the company's published annual report.

Form S-9 is used for registration of nonconvertible, fixed-interest debt securities by large utility and other companies. With this form, the number of items of information required in the prospectus is reduced.

Form S-15 is an optional, and experimental, form that can be used to register securities issued in certain business combinations. It calls for an abbreviated prospectus to be accompanied by a copy of the latest annual report to shareholders.[1]

Form S-16, adopted in 1971 in the nature of an experiment, and now superseded, provided a simpler method of registration for companies entitled to use Form S-7. The basic technique is to incorporate by reference material filed under the 1934 Act for major portions of the normal disclosure requirement. The incorporated material consists of the latest annual report or the latest prospectus that contains attested financial statements for the latest fiscal year, all reports filed since the end of the fiscal year (Forms 8-K, 10-Q), and the proxy statement for the latest annual meeting of shareholders and any subsequent special meeting. Management is required to describe any materially adverse change in the registrant's affairs since the end of the latest fiscal year, and the company's auditors must consent to the use of their opinions contained in the material incorporated by reference.

To summarize, the principal objective of preparing a registration statement for a public offering under the 1933 Act is to present all pertinent facts and figures that are needed by a prospective investor to make a judgment about a company's securities. Although their interests and functions vary, company management, their attorneys, their independent public accountants, the underwriters and their attorneys all should strive for full disclosure.

Filing under the 1934 Act. Although the registration process of the 1934 Act is similar to that of the 1933 Act, there are several differences in the registration procedures and reporting requirements. The 1933 Act regulates the primary capital market, requiring registration for all initial offerings of securities for public sale. The registration is for a specific block of securities to be sold at a set price, and a prospectus is required to be given each potential shareholder prior to the sale.

The 1934 Act deals with the trading of securities in the secondary capital markets. Entire classes of securities, as well as brokers, dealers, and stock

---

[1] Form S-14 is available to issuers who qualify for use of Form S-15, but prefer to include the annual report information in the prospectus rather than send a copy of the annual report.

exchanges, are registered under the 1934 Act. In addition, the 1934 Act requires continuous disclosures of company activities through annual, quarterly, and special reports, as discussed in the next section. The broad provisions of the 1934 Act also extend to insider trading requirements, proxy solicitation rules, and the regulation of tender offers.

Generally, the types of companies that must register under the 1934 Act include:

1. Companies whose securities are listed on a national securities exchange under Section 12(b) of the Securities Exchange Act of 1934

2. Companies whose securities are traded over the counter and are registered under Section 12(g) (generally companies with more than 500 shareholders and total assets in excess of $3,000,000)

3. Companies that have registered a security under the 1933 Act (required to file periodic reports for the fiscal year in which the registration statement became effective and for each subsequent year in which there are 500 or more security holders at the beginning of the year)

There are 10 separate categories of report forms under the 1934 Act. *Form 10* is for registration of a class of securities for which no other form is specified. The principal annual report form is *Form 10-K*; the quarterly form is *Form 10-Q*; and the special event form is *Form 8-K*.

THE SEC'S INTEGRATED DISCLOSURE SYSTEM

Companies that register with the SEC traditionally have had to refer to several sources to ascertain the requirements, rules, and procedures for reporting. For example, *Regulation S-X* prescribes the form and content of the financial statements. *Regulation S-K* governs the nonfinancial statement disclosures. Each form specifies the particular items of information required. The SEC's *Accounting Series Releases* are statements of policy and interpretations of SEC procedures. The *Staff Accounting Bulletins* provide additional interpretations by the Commission staff, and the *Guides for Preparation and Filing Registration Statements* give specific rules to be followed.

The problem of knowing which information to present and in what manner is made more complex because the SEC requirements have not necessarily been consistent with generally accepted accounting principles required for external financial reporting. In order to simplify financial reporting and remove some of the inconsistencies, the SEC has now adopted an *integrated disclosure system.*

The objectives of the SEC's integrated disclosure system are to: (1) improve disclosures to investors and other users of financial information; (2) achieve a single disclosure system at reduced cost; and (3) reduce inconsistencies and current impediments to combining reports to shareholders with official SEC filings.

To accomplish these objectives, the SEC has taken several steps. It has adopted amendments to Form 10-K, Form 10-Q, and to the proxy rules, has expanded and modified Regulation S-K, has made a general revision of Regulation S-X, has deleted many of the Guides and incorporated others into Regulation S-X and Regulation S-K, is experimenting with a new Form S-15, and has adopted three new registration forms that replace several of the old forms, including Forms S-1, S-7, and S-16. The result is intended to be a more streamlined disclosure system that can be used for both registration of security issues and continuous reporting to the SEC as well as to shareholders.

The underlying premise of the integrated disclosure system is that investors and other users of financial information need a *basic information package.* Such a package should include audited financial statements, a summary of selected financial data, and a meaningful description of an enterprise's business and financial condition. This information must be presented in Form 10-K and in the annual report to shareholders. Because essentially the same information is required, this approach encourages incorporation by reference and the combination of the annual report to shareholders and Form 10-K into one document.

Annual Report to Shareholders. The main thrust of the new reporting system is to standardize disclosure items and make them consistent with similar requirements in SEC filings. Additional information now required in the annual report to shareholders includes an expanded discussion and analysis by management, a new summary of selected financial data, and one additional year (3 instead of 2) of statements of income and changes in financial position. These changes became effective for financial statements issued after December 15, 1980.

Form 10-K. The main changes to Form 10-K and related modifications to Regulation S-K and the proxy rules are (1) a revised management discussion and analysis of the entity's financial condition and results of operations (this discussion is to focus on the liquidity position and capital resources of the company, and on the impact of inflation and changing prices on the enterprise); (2) deletion of the summary of operations and addition of a summary of selected financial data; and (3) the requirement of signatures by the registrant's principal executive officer(s), principal financial officer, controller or principal accounting officer, and at least the majority of the board of directors.

To illustrate the type of disclosures required, the revised Form 10-K is structured as follows:

General Instructions
Cover Page
Part I
    Item 1. Business
    Item 2. Properties
    Item 3. Legal Proceedings
    Item 4. Submission of Matters to a Vote of Security Holders
Part II
    Item 5. Market for the Registrant's Common Equity and Related Shareholder Matters
    Item 6. Selected Financial Data

Item 7. Management's Discussion and Analysis of Financial Condition and Results of Operations

Item 8. Financial Statements and Supplementary Data

Item 9. Disagreements on Accounting and Financial Disclosure

Part III

Item 10. Directors and Executive Officers of the Registrant

Item 11. Management Remuneration and Transactions

Item 12. Security Ownership of Certain Beneficial Owners and Management

Part IV

Item 13. Exhibits, Financial Statement Schedules, and Reports on Form 8-K

Signatures

The information in Parts I and II, at the registrant's option, may be incorporated by reference from the annual report to shareholders.

New Forms S-1, S-2, and S-3. As part of the consolidation effort, the SEC has adopted a three-tier system of new securities forms, referred to as S-1, S-2, and S-3. Form S-3 is available for financially stable companies and essentially takes the place of old Forms S-7 and S-16. Form S-2 is available to companies that cannot qualify in all respects for Form S-3, but that can meet certain criteria for longevity of reporting and financial stability. Form S-1 would continue to be the basic long-form registration, similar to old Form S-1. It would allow only a minimum of incorporation by reference from other documents. These new forms rescind existing Forms S-1, S-2, S-7, and S-16. As an illustration of the changes, Exhibit 2 summarizes the general disclosure requirements under the new registration forms. In effect, the SEC is applying the efficient market theory. Companies that are well established, with high-quality corporate reports (including 1934 Act reports) that are widely disseminated in the market, are not required to provide as much data as are companies without such a track record and for which the applicable financial data are not generally available to help investors make decisions.

Form 10-Q. The principal form used for quarterly reporting to the SEC is Form 10-Q. It also has been revised as part of the SEC's integrated disclosure system. The changes made are intended to integrate quarterly reports to shareholders with Form 10-Q, and make the reporting for interim periods consistent with those for annual reporting. Thus, management's discussion of interim periods must cover material changes in financial condition and specifically address liquidity and capital resources.

Companies can incorporate by reference all or part of the financial information from their quarterly reports to shareholders into Form 10-Q. Essentially, the new interim requirements conform to the 10-K rules and the condensed balance sheet for the current quarter is to be accompanied by one for the prior fiscal year-end instead of last year's corresponding quarter.

Special Reporting. Two commonly used special reports are proxy statements and current reports (Form 8-K).

Proxy statements transmit information to shareholders in the course of soliciting their proxy to vote their shares at a meeting of shareholders.

Certified financial statements generally must be included in the proxy statement if action is to be taken at the shareholders' meeting with respect to any of the following matters:

Authorization or issuance of securities other than for exchange
Modification or exchange of securities
Mergers, consolidations, acquisitions, sale of assets, liquidations, and similar matters

Although considerable flexibility is permitted, the financial statements required are essentially the same as those required for a registration statement except for the omission of certain supporting schedules and other items.

The proxy rules require that the consolidated financial statements included in a proxy statement be in conformity with the requirements of Form 10, the form for original registration under the 1934 Act. Parent company financial statements of the registrant are not generally required in a proxy statement. Financial statements of the company to be acquired, however, should be included on both a consolidated basis and a parent company basis.

The reason for this distinction is that Item 15(a) of the proxy rules, which relates to the registrant, calls for financial statements of "the issuer and its subsidiaries." That phrase has been construed by the SEC staff to relate to consolidated financial statements only. The SEC is not, however, precluded from asking for parent company financial statements under the blanket authority given them by Item 15(c). Requirements relating to the company to be acquired are governed by Item 15(b), which calls for financial statements of "each person" as would currently be required on Form 10. Technically, therefore, this requires parent company financial statements of companies to be acquired, unless a proper reason for omission exists.

Although the registrant's consolidated financial statements are required to be audited, the proxy rules specify that the financial statements of the company to be acquired shall be "certified if practicable." This bit of leniency enables registrants to proceed with acquisitions of companies that have never been audited, whereas a more stringent rule by the SEC might preclude such acquisitions.

The SEC staff is also somewhat lenient in the area of interim financial statements and in permitting omission of financial statements of consolidated subsidiaries and 50 percent or less owned companies in proxy statements. This leniency is tempered by the degree of significance of the matter for which omission is requested in relation to the matter to be voted on at the meeting. Requests for such omissions may be presented informally to the staff.

Other than these types of differences, the SEC generally endeavors to apply Form S-1 financial statement disclosure concepts to proxy statements. This is an administrative practice and is not set forth in the rules.

EXHIBIT 2 Summary of Reporting Requirements for Forms S-1, S-2, and S-3ᵃ

Item	Source	Form S-1	Form S-2	Form S-3
		Part I. Prospectus content		
Distribution spread	Form S-7, modified	Item 1	Item 1	Item 1
Summary information (includes summary financial data)	New	Item 2	Item 2	Item 2
Plan of distribution	Forms S-7, S-16	Item 3	Item 3	Item 3
Use of proceeds to issuer	Form S-1, modified	Item 4	Item 4	Item 4
Selling security holders	Form S-16, modified	Item 5	Item 5	Item 5
Description of securities to be registered .	Forms S-1, S-7, S-16, modified	Item 6	Item 6	Item 6
Information with respect to the issuer		Item 7	Item 7	Not required. All periodic reports are incorporated by reference.
			Form S-2 users generally have the option to deliver the annual shareholders' report and subsequent quarterly reports to provide this information. Also, periodic reports are incorporated by reference. Only consolidated financial statements are required.	
(a) Description of business	Regulation S-K, Item 1			
(b) Financial statements	Regulation S-X			
(c) Industry segment information	Regulation S-K, Item 1			
(d) Beneficial ownership	Regulation S-K, Item 6			
(e) Market and dividend data	Regulation S-K, Item 9			
(f) Management's discussion and analysis	Regulation S-K, Item 11			
(g) Supplemental financial data	Regulation S-K, Item 12			

(a) Subsequent material changes
(b) Availability of 1934 Act reports
(c) National exchange listing
(d) Undertaking to offer periodic reports incorporated by reference

Part II. Information not required in prospectus

	New	Item 9 Part III of Form 10-K and Item 4 of Part I of Form 10-K, if necessary	Item 9 Same as Form S-3, plus certain portions of annual shareholders' report	Item 8 Requires all 1934 Act periodic reports—10-K, 10-Q, 8-K
Incorporation of certain information by reference				
Other expenses of issuance and distribution.	Forms S-7, S-16	Item 10	Item 10	Item 9
Interest of experts named	Forms S-7, S-16	Item 11	Item 11	Item 10
Indemnification of directors and officers	Form S-7	Item 12	Item 12	Item 11
Other documents filed; exhibits	Form S-7, and Item 7 of Regulation S-K	Item 13	Item 13	Item 12
Recent sales of unregistered securities	Form S-1	Item 14	Not required	Not required
Undertakings	Form S-7, modified	Item 15	Item 15[b]	Item 13
Signatures	Forms S-1, S-7, S-16 (same as recently revised Form 10-K)	Required	Required	Required

[a] SOURCE: Adapted from Ernst and Whinney, *Financial Reporting Developments: SEC Registrations—Proposed Forms A, B and C,* December 1980.
[b] There is no Item 14 for Form S-2.

37-15

Form 8-K (current report) must be filed only when certain significant events occur. Following is the type of information that must be filed:

1. Changes in control of the registrant
2. Acquisition or disposition of a significant amount of assets other than in the ordinary course of business
3. Material legal proceedings
4. Changes in registered securities
5. Changes in collateral for registered securities
6. Material defaults on senior securities
7. Material increases in amounts of outstanding securities
8. Material decreases in amounts of outstanding securities
9. Granting or extension of options to purchase securities of the registrant or its subsidiaries
10. Extraordinary item charges and credits, other material charges and credits to income of an unusual nature, material provisions for loss, and restatements of capital share account
11. Submission of matters to a vote of security holders
12. Changes in registrant's certifying accountant
13. Other materially important events
14. Financial statements of acquired businesses reported in Item 2

Of particular interest to independent accountants is Item 12, which apparently is designed to deter companies from changing auditors for the purpose of getting new ones who are more sympathetic to their views than the old ones. The complete instructions for Item 12 state:

Item 12. Changes in Registrant's Certifying Accountant

If an independent accountant who was previously engaged as the principal accountant to audit the registrant's financial statements resigns (or indicates he declines to stand for re-election after the completion of the current audit) or is dismissed as the registrant's principal accountant, or another independent accountant is engaged as principal accountant, or if an independent accountant on whom the principal accountant expressed reliance in his report regarding a significant subsidiary resigns (or formally indicates he declines to stand for re-election after the completion of the current audit) or is dismissed or another independent accountant is engaged to audit that subsidiary:

(a) State the date of such resignation (or declination to stand for re-election), dismissal, or engagement.

(b) State whether in connection with the audits of the two most recent fiscal years and any subsequent interim period preceding such resignation, dismissal, or engagement, there were any disagreements with the former accountant on any matter of accounting principles or practices, financial statement disclosure, or auditing scope or procedure, which disagreements if not resolved to the satisfaction of the former accountant would have caused him to make reference in connection with his report to the subject matter of the disagreement(s); also, describe each such disagreement. The disagreements required to be reported in response to the preceding sentence include both those resolved to the former accountant's satisfaction and those not resolved to the former accountant's satisfaction. Disagreements contemplated by this rule are those which occur at the decision-making level; i.e., between personnel of the registrant responsible for presentation of its financial statements and personnel of the accounting firm responsible for rendering its report.

(c) State whether the principal accountant's report on the financial statements for any of the past two years contained an adverse opinion or a disclaimer of opinion or was qualified as to uncertainty, audit scope, or accounting principles; also describe the nature of each such adverse opinion, disclaimer of opinion, or qualification.

(d) The registrant shall request the former accountant to furnish the registrant with a letter addressed to the Commission stating whether he agrees with the statements made by the registrant in response to this item and, if not, stating the respects in which he does not agree. The registrant shall file a copy of the former accountant's letter as an exhibit with all copies of the Form 8-K required to be filed pursuant to General Instruction F.

SEC INFLUENCE ON ACCOUNTING PRINCIPLES

Although the SEC has the authority to prescribe the accounting principles to be followed in financial statements filed with it, the Commission has not, with certain exceptions, invoked its authority to dictate accounting principles to be followed by registrants. In Regulation S-X it has set forth its requirements as to the form and content of financial statements filed under the several laws administered by it. In its decisions and in the Accounting Series Releases it has stated its rules concerning a limited number of accounting principles and practices. Under the Holding Company Act it has promulgated two uniform systems of accounts that are applicable to a small number of companies. Under the Investment Advisers Act it has specified the books, records, and other information that must be maintained by investment advisors subject to the Act. As to the large body of accounting principles underlying the preparation of financial statements, however, the SEC has for the most part been content to rely on generally accepted principles of accounting as they exist or evolve with the passage of time.

The job of developing and modernizing generally accepted accounting principles fell originally to the accounting profession, particularly the American Institute of Certified Public Accountants through its Committee on Accounting Procedure and later its Accounting Principles Board. Since 1973 the primary organization charged with the development of generally accepted accounting principles has been the Financial Accounting Standards Board.

In testifying before a congressional subcommittee in 1964 on efforts to eliminate or reduce accounting alternatives, former SEC Chairman William L. Cary said that the Commission had encouraged the accounting profession to exercise leadership in accounting and auditing matters but, at the same time, had not hesitated to criticize and prod, to take exception to accounting presentations, and to discipline members of the profession when circumstances warranted. The policy of reliance on the profession for the enunciation of accounting principles was formalized in Accounting Series Release No. 150, adopted in 1973. It states:

Release No. 150, December 20, 1973, 38 F.R. 1260
Statement of Policy on the Establishment and Improvement of
Accounting Principles and Standards

Various Acts of Congress administered by the Securities and Exchange Commission clearly state the authority of the Commission to prescribe the methods to be followed in the preparation of accounts and the form and content of financial statements to be filed under the Acts and the responsibility to assure that investors are furnished with information necessary for informed investment decisions. In meeting this statutory responsibility effectively, in recognition of the expertise, energy, and resources of the accounting profession, and without abdicating its responsibilities, the Commission has historically looked to the standard-setting bodies designated by the profession to provide leadership in establishing and improving accounting principles. The determinations by these bodies have been regarded by the Commission, with minor exceptions, as being responsive to the needs of investors.

The body presently designated by the Council of the American Institute of Certified Public Accountants (AICPA) to establish accounting principles is the Financial Accounting Standards Board (FASB). This designation by the AICPA followed the issuance of a report in March 1972 recommending the formation of the FASB, after a study of the matter by a broadly based study group. The recommendations contained in that report were widely endorsed by industry, financial analysts, accounting educators, and practicing accountants. The Commission endorsed the establishment of the FASB in the belief that the Board would provide an institutional framework which will permit prompt and responsible actions flowing from research and consideration of varying viewpoints. The collective experience and expertise of the members of the FASB and the individuals and professional organizations supporting it are substantial. Equally important, the commitment of resources to the FASB is impressive evidence of the willingness and intention of the private sector to support the FASB in accomplishing its task. In view of these considerations, the Commission intends to continue its policy of looking to the private sector for leadership in establishing and improving accounting principles and standards through the FASB with the exception that the body's conclusions will promote the interests of investors.

In Accounting Series Release No. 4 (1938) the Commission stated its policy that financial statements prepared in accordance with accounting practices for which there was no substantial authoritative support were presumed to be misleading and that footnote or other disclosure would not avoid this presumption. It also stated that, where there was a difference of opinion between the Commission and a registrant as to the proper accounting to be followed in a particular case, disclosure would be accepted in lieu of correction of the financial statements themselves only if substantial authoritative support existed for the accounting practices followed by the registrant and the position of the Commission had not been expressed in rules, regulations or other official releases. For purposes of this policy, principles, standards and practices promulgated by the FASB in its Statements and Interpretations[1] will be considered by the Commission as having substantial authoritative support, and those contrary to such FASB promulgations will be considered[2] to have no such support.

In the exercise of its statutory authority with respect to the form and content of filings under the Acts, the Commission has the responsibility to assure that investors are provided with adequate information. A significant portion of the necessary information is provided by a set of basic financial statements (including the notes thereto) which conform to generally accepted accounting principles. Information in addition to that included in financial statements conforming to generally accepted accounting principles is also necessary. Such additional disclosures are required to be made in various fashions, such as in financial statements and schedules reported on by independent public accountants or as textual statements required by items in the applicable forms and reports filed with the Commission. The Commission will continue to identify areas where investor information needs exist and will determine the appropriate methods of disclosure to meet these needs.

It must be recognized that in its administration of the Federal Securities Acts and in its review of filings under such Acts, the Commission staff will continue as it has in the past to take such action on a day-to-day basis as may be appropriate to resolve specific problems of accounting and reporting under the particular factual circumstances involved in filings and reports of individual registrants.

The Commission believes that the foregoing statement of policy provides a sound basis for the Commission and the FASB to make significant contributions to meeting the needs of the registrants and investors.

By the Commission.

George A. Fitzsimmons
Secretary

[1] Accounting Research Bulletins of the Committee on Accounting Procedure of the American Institute of Certified Public Accountants and effective opinions of the Accounting Principles Board of the Institute should be considered as continuing in force with the same degree of authority except to the extent altered, amended, supplemented, revoked or suspended by one or more Statements of Financial Accounting Standards issued by the FASB.

[2] It should be noted that Rule 203 of the Rules of Conduct of the Code of Ethics of the AICPA provides that it is necessary to depart from accounting principles promulgated by the body designated by the Council of the AICPA if, due to unusual circumstances, failure to do so would result in misleading financial statements. In such a case, the use of other principles may be accepted or required by the Commission.

The above statement of policy does not alter the Commission's or the staff's intention to require such accounting or disclosures as may be necessary in their opinion to avoid misleading inferences in particular cases.

Accounting Series Releases. Accounting Series Releases (ASRs) have been used by the Commission or its chief accountant to publish views on various accounting principles and disclosure matters. (ASRs also have been used to publicize disciplinary actions against accountants, a subject covered later.) Some of the more recent ASRs that dealt with accounting principles are the following:

ASR	Year	Subject
118......	1970	Accounting for investment securities by registered investment companies
130......	1972	Pooling-of-interests accounting
134......	1973	Accounting for catastrophe reserves
135......	1973	Pooling-of-interests accounting
146......	1973	Effect of treasury stock transactions on accounting for business combinations
162......	1974	Use of GAAP by limited partnerships
163......	1974	Capitalization of interest by nonutility companies
185......	1975	Use of GAAP by bank holding companies and banks
253......	1978	Reserve recognition accounting
268......	1979	Concerning redeemable preferred stock
289......	1981	SEC reverses position on reserve recognition accounting

Accounting Disclosures. In keeping with the general thesis that the SEC's major responsibility involves full and adequate disclosure to investors, the SEC has frequently taken the lead in requiring certain accounting disclosures. A notable example was the required (ASR No. 190) disclosure of replacement cost data by certain large registrants. Since the issuance of FASB Statement No. 33, ASR No. 190 has been rescinded.

Occasionally, the SEC pointedly states that its accounting disclosure requirement is being promulgated because the Accounting Principles Board or the Financial Accounting Standards Board has failed to give sufficient attention to the matter. ASRs No. 147, 148, and 149 (see below), issued in 1973, are examples of such a situation.

Among ASRs dealing with disclosure matters, in addition to ASR No. 190 just mentioned, are the following:

ASR	Year	Subject
113......	1969	Disclosure problems relating to restricted securities held by investment companies
117......	1970	Statements of source and application of funds
138......	1973	Unusual charges and credits to income
142......	1973	Reporting cash flow and other related data
147......	1973	Improved disclosure of leases
148......	1973	Disclosure of compensating balances and short-term borrowing arrangements
149......	1973	Improved disclosure of income tax expense
151......	1974	Disclosure of inventory profits reflected in income in periods of rising prices
164......	1974	Defense and other long-term contract activities
166......	1974	Disclosure of unusual risks and uncertainties in financial statements
169......	1975	Disclosure problems relating to the adoption of the LIFO inventory method
177......	1975	Quarterly reporting
194......	1976	Disagreements with former accountants
281......	1980	Conform interim requirements of 1933 and 1934 Acts
284......	1980	Technical amendments to certain rules, forms, and schedules
286......	1981	Revised Form 10-Q as part of integrated disclosure system

Regulation S-X. Regulation S-X is the principal accounting regulation of the SEC in its administration of the Securities Act of 1933, the Securities Exchange Act of 1934, the Public Utility Holding Company Act of 1935, and the Investment Company Act of 1940. Promulgated originally in 1940, the regulation has undergone several revisions. A public accountant who becomes involved in certifying financial statements intended for filing under any of these Acts should have an up-to-date copy of Regulation S-X at hand. Similarly, no corporate financial officer should undertake registration of SEC reporting responsibilities without having ready access to Regulation S-X.

In addition to certain requirements as to independence and accountants' reports, Regulation S-X deals principally with the form and content of financial statements and supporting schedules, as distinguished from the accounting principles that are applied to business transactions in arriving at the dollar amounts to be presented. For guidance as to which financial statements are to be included in the various types of filings, one must generally look to the instructions applicable to the particular form involved.

The rules contained in Regulation S-X are too voluminous to present in detail here. Its contents are listed in Exhibit 3.

Regulation S-K. The establishment of Regulation S-K was one of the first steps taken by the SEC in implementing its integrated disclosure system. Whereas Regulation S-X dictates the form and content of the financial statements, Regulation S-K governs the nonfinancial statement disclosures. Revisions in S-X and S-K now require identical disclosures in documents filed with the SEC (Form 10-K) and distributed to shareholders (annual report). Regulation S-K is continually being revised and expanded. The SEC's plan is (1) to categorize by subject matter the uniform disclosure items in Regulation S-K; (2) to add certain requirements with respect to the distribution of securities; and (3) to eliminate most of the guides for the preparation and filing of registration statements and reports by incorporating them into Regulation S-K or the general rules and regulations of the Acts themselves. Under this proposal, Regulation S-K would be divided into the following seven sections:

1. Application
2. Business
3. Financial information
4. Management
5. Securities of the registrant
6. Distribution of securities
7. Other

Staff Accounting Bulletins. Staff Accounting Bulletins are the chief accountant's informal statements of internal accounting policies currently being followed by the SEC staff. These statements are now being issued to the public in an effort to expose, for the first time, general policies of the SEC with respect to questions of accounting. They are not identified as holdings in particular cases, although such holdings are the genesis of virtually all SEC policy. The

EXHIBIT 3   Contents of Regulation S-X

Subject	Content
Article 1: Application of Regulation S-X	Applicability and definitions of terms used in Regulation S-X
Article 2: Qualifications and Reports of Accountants	Qualifications and independence of accountants and requirements for accountants' certificates
Article 3: General Instructions as to Financial Statements	General rules that should be considered in applying specific provisions of the regulation
Article 4: Consolidated and Combined Financial Statements . .	Rules governing the presentation of consolidated and combined financial statements
Article 5: Commercial and Industrial Companies.	
Article 5A: Commercial, Industrial, and Mining Companies in the Promotional, Exploratory, or Development Stage.	Specific provisions applicable to the financial statements and supporting schedules of the indicated types of companies
Article 6: Management Investment Companies.	
Article 6A: Unit Investment Trusts . .	
Article 6B: Face-Amount Certificate Investment Companies	
Article 6C: Employee Stock Purchase, Savings, and Similar Plans	
Article 7: Insurance Companies Other Than Life Insurance Companies	
Article 7A: Life Insurance Companies	
Article 8: Committees Issuing Certificates of Deposit	
Article 9: Bank Holding Companies and Banks	
Article 10: Interim Financial Statements	Exceptions to general form and content prescribed by other sections
Article 11: Statements of Other Stockholders' Equity	Content of statements of other stockholders' equity (paid-in additional capital and retained earnings)
Article 11A: Statement of Source and Application of Funds (changes in financial position)	Form and content of statements of changes in financial position
Article 12: Form and Content of Schedules	Rules governing the form and content of supporting schedules to financial statements

Bulletins do not have the "Commission's" official approval and thus do not have the force of law (Staff Accounting Bulletin No. 1, SEC, 1975).

SEC INFLUENCE ON AUDITING PRACTICE

The SEC has significantly influenced the way auditors practice their profession. Most of the larger clients of the big accounting firms are registered with the SEC; accounting firms are cautious not to run afoul of the SEC in a manner that might cause embarrassment or other adverse consequences to their clients.

Disciplining of Auditors. The Commission can set the qualifications for accountants and can decide if they are truly independent of the companies they are auditing. Under Rule 2(e) of its Rules of Practice (disciplinary rules for governing professionals), the Commission may deny, temporarily or permanently, the privilege of appearing or practicing before it to any person who is found by the Commission (1) not to possess the requisite qualifications to represent others; or (2) to be lacking in character or integrity or to have engaged in unethical or improper professional conduct; or (3) to have willfully violated, or willfully aided and abetted the violation of, any provision of the federal securities laws, or the rules and regulations thereunder. In addition to suspending accountants, other disciplinary actions taken by the Commission include censure requiring quality control reviews and programs and forbidding the taking of new clients who file or are contemplating filing with the Commission. There have been cases where the Commission has recommended criminal proceedings to the Department of Justice. Regardless of which type of action is taken by the Commission, the greatest harm to accountants is likely to be the damage to their reputations.

A sample of disciplinary actions by the SEC against accountants, as disclosed by publication in Accounting Series Releases, are the following:

ASR	Date	Subject
153......	2/25/74	Quality of auditing; censure, quality review program, peer review, nonacceptance of new SEC clients by one office of firm for 12 months, nonacceptance of any new real estate SEC clients by any office of firm for 12 months
157......	7/08/74	Withholding of information from Commission; censure
173......	7/02/75	Quality of auditing; peer review, adoption of specified audit procedures, study of specified method of accounting, nonacceptance of new SEC clients for 12 months, follow-up peer review for 2 succeeding years
191......	3/30/76	Quality of auditing; censure, peer review
288......	2/26/81	Quality of auditing; censure

Setting of Auditing Standards. As in the case of accounting principles, the Commission prefers to let the accounting profession set its own auditing standards. However, the SEC has not hesitated to influence auditing practice by encouraging and motivating the profession to modify and improve its auditing procedures. The McKesson & Robbins case illustrates of how an initial SEC review subsequently led to action by the accounting profession to prescribe confirmation of receivables and observation of inventories as standard auditing procedures. Other examples include the procedures to be followed by auditors upon subsequent discovery of events affecting their opinions on financial statements (Staff Accounting Bulletin No. 47) and the disclosures to be made concerning the independence of accountants (ASR No. 234, No. 250, and No. 291).

Liability of Accountants. Closely related to the SEC's role in establishing accounting principles and auditing standards is the professional legal liability that is associated with the securities acts. During recent years many accountants have been sued for a variety of reasons, and some have even been convicted of criminal offenses. In most cases the accountant's professional service to a publicly owned company was involved. Under the 1933 Act [Section 11(a)], accountants are liable for association with misleading registration statements. Further, the accountant may be held liable for ordinary negligence to any person acquiring the securities, and must prove through a "due diligence" defense that reasonable care was exercised in the performance of professional duties. Under the 1934 Act [Section 18 and Section 10(b)], the accountant may also be held liable for incorrect or misleading information in connection with SEC filings, including the periodic reports—10-K; 10-Q; 8-K. Readers who desire to gain additional information on this subject are directed to the following important cases:

Case	Citation
Yale Express	*Fisher et al. v. Kletz et al.*, 266 F. Supp. 180 (S.D., N.Y., 1967)
BarChris	*Escott et al. v. BarChris Construction Corp. et al.*, 283F. Supp. 643 (S.D., N.Y., 1968)
Continental Vending	*U.S. v. Simon et al.*, 425 F. 2d. 796 (2nd Cir. 1969)
Tenants' Corporation	*1136 Tenants' Corporation v. Max Rothenberg & Company*, 319 N.Y.S. 2d 1007 (1970)
National Student Marketing	*U.S. v. Natelli*, 526 F. 2d 1160 (2nd Cir. 1975)
Hochfelder	*Ernst & Ernst v. Hochfelder*, 425 U.S. 185 (U.S. Supreme Court, 1976)

BIBLIOGRAPHY

Poloway, M., and D. Charles, *Accountants' SEC Practice Manual* (Commerce Clearing House, Chicago, annual).

Previts, G. J. (ed.), *The Development of SEC Accounting* (Addison-Wesley Publishing Company, Reading, Mass., 1981).

Rappaport, L. H., *SEC Accounting: Practice and Procedure,* 3d ed. (Ronald Press Company, New York, 1972).

SEC Compliance (Prentice Hall, Englewood Cliffs, N.J., annual).

Skousen, K. Fred, *An Introduction to the SEC,* 3d ed. (South-Western Publishing Co. Cincinnati, Ohio, 1983).

CHAPTER 38

Cost Analysis

Gordon Shillinglaw
Professor of Accounting, Graduate School of Business, Columbia University

Cost is the amount of resources sacrificed to achieve a particular objective. These resources are usually measured in monetary terms. Cost analysis therefore can be defined as the estimation in monetary terms of the amounts of resources that have been or will be consumed to accomplish some objective. The objective may be the operation of a factory, the manufacture and sale of a particular product, or the provision of delivery service to one class of customers.

The primary purpose of cost analysis is to provide management with data for use in decision making. It may also be undertaken to provide data that will help explain management's actions or decisions to other parties. The principles and methods outlined in this chapter are designed to suit the decision-making purpose. Departures from these principles and methods for other purposes will depend on the purpose of the analysis and the specific requirements of the user.

THE INCREMENTAL PRINCIPLE

Decisions always require comparisons of alternatives. Any choice between two alternatives must be based on real or perceived differences between them. These differences are referred to as *differentials* or *increments*; the requirement that data for decisions should be estimates of increments is called the *incremental principle*. Absolute figures are useful in decision making only to the extent that they can be converted into differential data.

Emphasis on Cash Flows. The analytical problem in decision making is to estimate the costs and benefits of each alternative that has been identified and then find the alternative for which the benefit–cost relationship best satisfies the decision rule that management has decided to apply. In most cases, the analyst tries to measure both costs and benefits in monetary terms. More specifically, the question is how the choice between any two alternatives is likely to affect the flow of cash into or out of the organization.

The focus on cash is fundamental. Resources received in nonliquid form seldom can be used to pay creditors, employees, or owners. For example, shares of stock in other companies ordinarily cannot be used conveniently to pay the company's debts, pay dividends, or buy new equipment. Only cash can be used for these purposes. For this reason, the monetary increment or incremental gain must be measured by the effect of the decision on the future net cash flow—the margin between receipts and outlays of cash.

Net cash flow is not the same as accounting net income. For example, suppose that a company has 100,000 plastic rings in inventory, originally purchased for use in a product the company no longer manufactures. These rings originally cost 10 cents each. They have no current scrap value. A company engineer has just discovered that these rings can be used in another product that ordinarily incorporates rings of a cheaper quality, available at a price of 2 cents each. For income measurement, the use of the old, more expensive rings might be recorded by a transfer to expense of 100,000 × $.10 = $10,000. For the decision, however, management should know that use of these rings would require no cash outlay at all. In cost analysis, whenever cash flow and income figures differ, the cash flow figure should be used.

Steps in Cash Flow Analysis. Assuming that the increments can be estimated with reasonable certainty, the basic approach to analysis is as follows:

1. Identify and describe the alternatives.
2. Decide which determinants of cash flow will be affected by the decision.
3. Estimate values for each of these determinants under each alternative.
4. Select the alternative with the most favorable (least unfavorable) cash flow.
5. List intangible factors that might reinforce or lead away from this choice.

If uncertainty is substantial and either the apparent probabilities of high and low errors are unequal or management's attitude toward gains and losses is asymmetric, then step 3 should be repeated for other possible outcomes. If possible, probabilities should be attached to each of these outcomes.

If the alternatives differ in the timing of the inflows and outflows of cash, the problem is an investment problem and the cash flows occurring at different points of time must be translated into their time-adjusted equivalents. This is typically accomplished by discounting the cash flows to find their present value at some common date (see Chapter 9). Once this has been done, steps 4 and 5 above can be performed on the time-adjusted data.

Incremental Cost. The cost estimates that are relevant to incremental analysis are estimates of differential or incremental cost. Incremental cost is the difference in total cash outlays that will result from selecting one alternative instead of another.

For example, a café proprietor is studying the profitability of reopening a billiard room in the rear of the café. The billiard tables have been unused for several years but are in usable condition. The monthly cost estimates are as follows:

Costs	Operate the billiard room	Do not operate the billiard room
Food and beverages......	$11,000	$10,000
Salaries and wages	3,550	2,750
Supplies................	400	300
Utilities and heat	250	200
Rent....................	1,500	1,500
Insurance...............	100	100
Miscellaneous	200	150
Total	$17,000	$15,000

The incremental cost in this case is $17,000 — $15,000, or $2,000 a month.

The term "incremental cost" is often used in another sense, to refer to the elements of cost that will change as a result of the decision. For example, in this illustration the only costs affected by the decision are the costs of food and beverages, salaries and wages, supplies, utilities and heat, and miscellaneous resources consumed. The analysis can be simplified slightly in this case, significantly in others, by eliminating the unaffected items completely. The simplified comparison would be as follows:

Costs that will change	Operate the billiard room	Do not operate the billiard room
Food and beverages	$11,000	$10,000
Salaries and wages	3,550	2,750
Supplies	400	300
Utilities and heat	250	200
Miscellaneous	200	150
Total	$15,400	$13,400

Sunk cost. Any cost element that is unaffected by management's choice between alternatives is a sunk cost. In the first table above, two of the elements were sunk:

Rent	$1,500
Insurance	100

Reopening the billiard room would leave these costs unchanged. Even though the accounting system might allocate some of these costs to the billiard room, such allocations do not represent incremental cash outlays and should be ignored.

Negative increments. The cost differences in the preceding examples were additions to cost. Incremental cost may also be negative; that is, a management decision may reduce costs. This reduction may be referred to as a cost saving, but the analytical method is still incremental. For example, if the café proprietor is now operating the billiard room and wishes to know how much could be saved by closing it, the incremental cost should be measured by the amounts of cash outlays that will be made only if the billiard room remains open.

Future cost. Resources that are to be used under one or more alternatives should be measured at their anticipated prices, not at prices that have been paid in the past. For example, a company purchased 50,000 pounds of a certain material last year at $.50 a pound. The company uses this material as a raw material for several products. If 20,000 pounds are used to fill an order for a special product, the company will have to buy 20,000 pounds at the current price of $.60 a pound to rebuild its inventories of this material to the desired level. In this case, the cash outlay required by the special order would be 20,000 pounds × $.60 = $12,000. The historical cost figure of $.50 a pound has no relevance because it does not measure the future cash outlay that acceptance of the order would entail.

Opportunity Cost. Replacement cost per unit is not always the relevant multiplier to use in incremental analysis. An earlier paragraph cited a case in which the incremental cash outlay from the use of a stock of plastic rings was zero. In this case, replacement cost was irrelevant because acceptance of the proposal would not obligate the company to replace the items used.

The general concept that applies in situations like this is the concept of opportunity cost. For cash flow analysis, the cost of a nonmonetary asset already owned by the company should be measured by the amount of cash that must be sacrificed to make this asset available for its proposed use. This is its opportunity cost.

Measuring opportunity cost. One possible measure of opportunity cost is the asset's current liquidation value. This is applicable if the best alternative to the asset's proposed use is to sell it. A decision not to sell is equivalent from a cash flow viewpoint to a decision to buy.

A second possible measure of opportunity cost is replacement cost. This is applicable if use of the asset will require the company to buy a replacement unit for use elsewhere in the company.

A third possibility is the asset's present value in some alternative use. This present value figure is the relevant measure of opportunity cost if it is greater than the asset's current liquidation value and if the proposed diversion of the asset will not necessitate purchase of a replacement asset for the alternative use.

The opportunity cost concept applies to services as well as to tangible assets. For example, a proposal that will require a member of the sales staff to spend one day a week in the office should be charged with an amount equal to the value to the company of the sales that would be made if the day were spent calling on customers.

Separate Costs for Separate Purposes. It should be clear from these definitions that the amount of incremental cost depends on the decision to be made and the alternatives being compared. For example, the plant manager's salary is a sunk cost if the problem is to decide whether or not to install additional materials handling equipment, but it is presumably an incremental cost if abandonment of the plant is in question, and it may be partly incremental if the question is whether or not to double the plant's capacity.

COST–VOLUME RELATIONSHIPS

The immediate objectives of cost analysis are to identify the determinants of cost and to quantify their effects. One important cost determinant is operating volume, expressed as a rate per period of time (for example, hours per week, pounds per day).

Variable Costs. Costs that change in response to small changes in volume are known as *variable* costs. Exhibit 1 shows two of the many possible patterns of cost variation. The straight line in Exhibit 1 represents a cost that changes in direct proportion to changes in volume—for example, a royalty charge computed at a constant amount per unit sold. In contrast, the curved line shows costs rising sharply at first, then more gradually as volume achieves normal operating levels, and then sharply again as operations begin to approach capacity limits.

Marginal Costs. The average variable cost per unit computed from the straight line in Exhibit 1 will be the same at all operating volumes. For a cost described by the curved line, however, average unit cost will vary, as shown in column (3) of Exhibit 2.

Of even more significance are the figures shown in column (4) of Exhibit 2. These represent marginal cost, the added cost that results from the production of one additional unit of goods or services per period of time. In this case, marginal cost first decreases due to economies of larger production quantities, then levels off, and finally increases as diseconomies set in in the upper reaches of the output range.

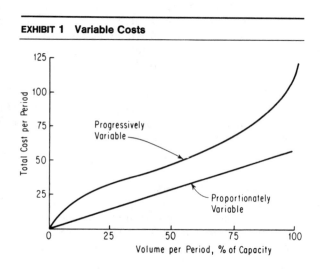

EXHIBIT 1   Variable Costs

EXHIBIT 2   Average Variable Cost and Marginal Cost

(1) Weekly volume (000 units)	(2) Weekly cost ($000)	(3) Average variable cost [(2) ÷ (1)]	(4) Marginal cost [(2) − line above in (2)]
1.	$ 3.50	$3.50	$3.50
2.	6.75	3.37	3.25
3.	9.75	3.25	3.00
4.	12.75	3.19	3.00
5.	16.00	3.20	3.25
6.	19.50	3.25	3.50
7.	23.50	3.36	4.00
8.	28.25	3.53	4.75

Measuring volume. Volume in this illustration has been measured in "units," with no indication of what kinds of units are referred to. The most obvious choice is the number of units of goods or services produced. This can be used for operations that produce only a single product or service, but something else must be found when output is diverse. The usual solution is to use some form of input measure, such as direct labor hours or pounds of material used. The best input unit to use is the one correlating most closely with cost variations, but a less accurate measure may be used if it can be made available more cheaply than the preferred measure. This question will be examined more fully in Chapter 40.

Fixed Costs. Costs that do not change as a necessary result of relatively small changes in volume are known as *fixed* costs. For analytical purposes it is useful to recognize two broad classes of fixed costs: capacity costs and programmed costs. •

Capacity costs. Many of the resources consumed in a period are consumed to provide or maintain the organization's capacity to produce or sell. These are known as *capacity* costs or *supportive* costs.

Capacity has three dimensions: physical capacity, provided by buildings, machinery, furniture, and so on; organizational capacity, provided by management, supervisory, and staff personnel; and financial capacity, provided by working capital and other financial resources. In all three senses, capacity can be changed only slowly. It takes time to conceive of the need for new facilities, arrange for financing, complete facilities construction or acquisition, provide the necessary staff and personnel, and put all of these resources to work. Capacity reductions also take time. This means that during any short period of time, the firm must operate with a relatively constant stock of productive resources, including organizational and financial resources.

As volume increases, average capacity cost per unit will decline. A cost that will amount to $2,000 a month, no matter what the operating volume, will average $1 a unit if volume is 2,000 units a month or $.50 a unit at a volume of 4,000 units. The effect on average total cost will depend on the relative importance of capacity costs and the shape of the variable cost function. If variable costs tend to be proportional to volume, average total costs will decline almost indefinitely as output expands. If average variable costs increase with increases in volume, however, this increase will offset the decline in average capacity costs at some stage, and average total cost will begin to rise.

Capacity costs can be classified further into *standby* costs and *enabling* costs. Standby costs are those that will continue to be incurred if operations or facilities are shut down temporarily. Examples are depreciation, property taxes, and some executive salaries. Enabling costs are those that can be avoided by a temporary shutdown but must be incurred if operations are to take place. Some of these are likely to be constant over the entire output range; others are likely to vary in steps. For example, one departmental supervisor may be adequate for single-shift operation, but operation of a second shift will require a second supervisor.

Step-variable capacity costs would be classified by an economist as variable costs; executives and accountants classify them as fixed within the capacity range they support. Some accountants call these *semifixed* costs. If the steps are sufficiently small, however, they may be averaged for most analytical purposes and treated as part of the variable costs.

Programmed costs. Fixed costs include a second category, fundamentally different from the first. These are costs established by autonomous management decisions to meet objectives other than the fulfillment of service demands. Costs in this group are known by a variety of names, including programmed costs, discretionary costs, and managed costs. Some programmed costs are incurred to obtain and retain sales orders; the cost leads to volume rather than the other way around. Some are incurred to achieve other kinds of results unrelated to current operating volume—ideas for new products, for example. Still others yield services to management and can be justified only by management's perception of the value of these services—for example, financial reporting systems.

Programmed costs tend to be budgeted at specified levels for individual time periods. Once the budget is set, programmed cost per unit will be low if volume is high and high if volume is low. The size of the programmed cost budget, however, should be determined by estimates of the effectiveness of these costs in achieving the objectives desired by management. If increases in budgeted spending seem likely to increase volume by a larger percentage than the increase in spending, average cost will fall. If additional spending produces a less than proportional increase in volume, however, average cost will rise. This is illustrated in the following table:

Total programmed cost	Volume achieved	Average programmed cost	Total programmed cost	Volume achieved	Average programmed cost
$10	50	$.20	$50	280	.18
20	125	.16	60	300	.20
30	200	.15	70	310	.23
40	250	.16			

The concept of marginal cost has no meaning in connection with programmed costs. Marginal costs measure the effects of increasing volume: programmed costs do not change as a result of changes in volume and therefore cannot be marginal with respect to those changes.

Semivariable Costs. Some cost elements have both fixed and variable components. For example, some consumption of electric power is independent of operating volume, whereas another component is likely to vary directly with volume.

Fixed Costs and Sunk Costs. Knowledge of cost behavior is important in incremental analysis whenever two alternatives differ in the rate of utilization of existing facilities and organization. It should not be assumed, however, that fixed costs are always sunk costs or that variable costs are always incremental.

For example, property taxes are usually fixed costs. They will not be increased if the company is able to obtain additional volume to utilize plant capacity more fully. For a plant utilization decision, therefore, property taxes are not only fixed; they are also sunk costs. In the decision to expand the plant's operating capacity, however, these fixed costs are no longer entirely sunk, because a larger plant will carry a greater assessed valuation and therefore greater property taxes.

Similarly, in making some decisions, variable costs are not always incremental costs. For example, if the company is considering whether to rent or own its manufacturing plant, total variable manufacturing costs are unlikely to be affected by the choice. They must be treated as sunk costs for the purpose of reaching this specific decision.

ANALYSIS OF JOINT COSTS

When the processing of a single input or set of inputs yields two or more products, these products are referred to as joint products. Gasoline and fuel oil are joint products.

The existence of joint products creates the phenomenon of joint costs—the costs of those input factors that are necessary for the manufacture and separation of all the joint products as a group. Costs incurred for the production of an individual joint product are known as separable costs or specific costs. Livestock, purchasing, and slaughtering costs are true joint costs of all the products that will eventually be marketed by a meatpacker, but tanning costs are specific costs of the tanned cowhides produced.

Joint Products as a Group. For the group of joint products as a whole, the question is whether the total revenue to be derived from the sale of all joint products, less any processing and distribution costs necessary to place these products in marketable form, is adequate to cover the incremental costs of the joint inputs. For example, the decision to work a mine that produces ore containing gold, zinc, and lead must be based on consideration of the volumes produced and the market prices of all three metals.

A related problem is to determine the maximum price the company can afford to pay for joint inputs of a given grade or specification. This will depend on the relative yield of each product to be derived from the joint inputs. For example, in buying raw materials that vary in quality, the price that can be paid will be higher on grades that yield a greater proportion of high-value products. The maximum purchase price is a function of the total value of all the joint products, less all the joint costs of processing or conversion.

Individual Joint Products. Once it has been determined that joint production is profitable, the next question is how far to process each of the joint products. For example, should cowhides be tanned or should they be sold untanned? For this kind of decision, the question is whether the sale value of the product can be increased by more than the additional costs of separate processing. The cost of the steer no longer has any meaning for this decision. What is relevant is opportunity cost, in this case the amount that could be realized from the sale of the untanned hides. If hides can be sold untanned for $.50 a pound, then $.50 a pound is the opportunity cost of any hides that are retained for further processing. The relevant comparison is as follows:

Market value of tanned hides		$.70
Less: Market value of untanned hides	$.50	
Incremental separate processing cost	.15	.65
Incremental processing profit		$.05

Accounting Allocations of Joint Costs. Most accounting systems allocate joint costs among the joint products in proportion to their relative values. The purpose of this allocation is to derive unit costs for use in costing inventories for external financial reporting. Unit costs derived in this way do not represent incremental cost, and should be totally ignored in managerial decision making.

APPLICATION OF COST DATA TO DECISIONS

Most of the cost data that are developed routinely by an accounting system are multipurpose data. They are used for such diverse purposes as financial reporting to shareholders, income tax calculations, departmental performance review, and managerial decision making. No one method of organizing the data can be perfect for all applications, and accounting data therefore often need to be modified to meet the needs of the decision maker. Examination of six different kinds of decision situations should indicate the problems encountered in adapting figures from the data bank:

1. Using idle capacity
2. Rationing scarce capacity
3. Pricing new products
4. Selecting customers
5. Replacing equipment
6. Selecting an order quantity

Using Idle Capacity. Most organizations always have some idle capacity in at least one major productive facility; most have idle capacity in all departments at least some of the time. Utilization of this idle capacity can be a source of increased profit.

Order acceptance. A relatively simple capacity utilization problem arises when a potential customer offers to place a single order for a specified amount of goods or services. In this case the programmed fixed costs are all sunk; management needs only estimate the incremental costs of filling the order and the possible effects on future prices and future orders.

The only cost that is relevant to a decision to accept an order for a single additional unit of product is its marginal cost. The incremental cost of larger orders is the sum of the marginal costs of the incremental units. For example, if one more unit will cost $2.50 and a second additional unit will cost $2.60, the total incremental cost is $5.10.

The shape of the marginal cost curve is seldom known with much precision. Fortunately, the analyst is often able to assume that marginal cost is constant and equal to average variable cost for much of the output range. When this assumption is valid, the incremental cost of a small change in volume can be approximated by multiplying average variable cost by the amount of the change. When the incremental volume is greater, however, increments in capacity costs must be considered and incremental variable cost may be either greater or less than the average. Particular attention should be paid to such cost elements as overtime premiums, warehousing labor, delivery labor, and factory supervision.

The total effect of a large number of small orders will be similar to that of a single large order, although the effect on order handling costs and machine setup costs may be greater. If management is likely to be faced with the problem of accepting or rejecting a number of such orders, the relevant cost information consists of variable cost per unit, if this can safely be assumed to be constant, and the amount of the increase in fixed costs that can be expected to accompany volume increases of various magnitudes.

Estimates of incremental cost are usually stated as average cost per unit, and management may insist on a single unit cost estimate. In such cases, the accountant should obtain the best available estimate of the sensitivity of sales to price. If volume is highly sensitive, then the average cost should include estimates of changes in fixed costs as well as in the variable costs. If volume is relatively insensitive, then average variable cost is likely to be more relevant.

Program expansion. The firm may be able to affect the flow of customer orders by changing the scope or direction of its marketing programs. Decisions to increase marketing program costs to produce capacity-absorbing orders require examination of two variables that do not enter into simple order acceptance decisions; incremental program costs and marketing response functions.

Incremental program costs are relatively easy to estimate because they are usually specified in the proposal—hire an extra salesperson, spend more on advertising, and so on. The difficult task is to estimate the response functions— that is, the effects of the incremental program costs on the volume of firm orders received. Historical data provide rough estimates of average responses but seldom reveal much about the incremental responses. Because of this uncertainty, estimators are often asked to provide optimistic and pessimistic forecasts as well as their primary predictions. These permit management to judge the sensitivity of results to errors of estimation and therefore the riskiness of the decisions. A further refinement is to require the submission of a rough probability estimate for each of several possible volumes, thereby permitting the construction of decision trees, payoff tables, and estimates of expected value.

For all of these cases, the estimated incremental profit is typically measured by deducting from incremental revenues the incremental costs of obtaining them (programmed costs) and the incremental costs of manufacturing and delivering the goods or services. The increments in manufacturing and delivery costs are estimated on the same bases as in the order acceptance decisions discussed above.

Rationing Scarce Capacity. When capacity is scarce, management must choose between alternative uses of this capacity. In such cases, the costs of the scarce input ordinarily should be ignored. For example, if management must decide whether to sell a product in limited supply to one customer at a price of $2.00 or to another at a price of $2.20, the decision can be made without any factory cost data at all. Total manufacturing cost will be the same under either alternative.

Single capacity constraint. A figure that is often used in capacity rationing decisions is the contribution margin (net price minus average variable cost) per unit of capacity. For example, if production is limited by the amount of product that can be processed in the forming department, the profitability of each product might be computed in the following way:

$$\text{Contribution Margin per Hour} = \frac{\text{Price} - \text{Average Variable Cost per Unit}}{\text{Forming Hours Required per Unit}}$$

Forming department capacity could then be allocated first to the product with the highest contribution margin ratio, and so on down the ladder until all capacity was utilized.

This solution can be attacked on both analytical and marketing grounds. From an analytical viewpoint, average variable cost may not be a good measure of the incremental cost of manufacturing and distributing individual products. Some products that use little forming department time may require large amounts of time in other departments. If product volume is big enough, some of the fixed costs of these other departments may be properly included in incremental cost.

The policy of granting complete priority to highest-margin products can also be criticized on marketing grounds. Sales of one product may be linked to sales of another; sales in the future may depend on the company's willingness and ability to fill orders now. In other words, the profit index may either over- or understate a product's true relative profitability.

Even so, the contribution margin figures may be useful for marginal adaptations of the production and sales plan. A high contribution margin means that the company can afford to spend more to make a sale. If contribution margin is $5 for product X and $2.50 for product Y, the sales staff presumably should be instructed to work on product X whenever the likelihood of making a sale of X is better than half the likelihood of making a sale of Y.

Multiple capacity constraints. The problem becomes even more complex if more than one capacity limitation is operative. For example, one product may have a relatively high profit per forming department hour but a low margin per finishing department hour. The gain from effective utilization of forming capacity may be more than offset by inefficiency or suboptimization in the use of finishing capacity.

To take a simple case, assume that the company has two products, each of which is processed in the same two production departments. The available data are as follows:

Product	Contribution margin per unit	Machine hours required per unit		Order backlog (units)
		Dept. X	Dept. Y	
A	$10	4	2	1,000
B	6	1	3	2,500

Capacity is 4,500 hours in department X and 7,500 hours in department Y.

Product A is the more profitable of the two, and one solution would be to produce the 1,000 units of product A, filling in with product B until one department's capacity was reached. Department X's capacity would be critical in this case, and the solution would be as follows:

Product	Output (units)	Capacity utilized (machine hours)		Contribution margin
		Dept. X	Dept. Y	
A	1,000	4,000	2,000	$10,000
B	500	500	1,500	3,000
Total		4,500	3,500	$13,000
Capacity available		4,500	7,500	
Idle capacity		0	4,000	

The existence of idle capacity in department Y suggests that it might be profitable to shift some production from A to B, which uses department Y more intensively. If 1 unit of A were to be dropped, this would permit production of 4 units of B because it would release 4 hours of department X capacity. Four units of B contribute $24 of profit instead of $10, for a net gain of $14 for every unit of A that is dropped.

A second possible solution, therefore, would be to produce as much product

B as department Y could handle. One unit of product B requires 3 hours in department Y and thus department Y's capacity would be completely absorbed by 2,500 units of product B and would contribute $15,000 in profit. This is better than the first solution, but this time some of department X's capacity would be idle:

Product	Output (units)	Capacity utilized (machine hours) Dept. X	Dpet. Y	Contribution margin
A	0	0	0	0
B	2,500	2,500	7,500	$15,000
Total		2,500	7,500	$15,000
Capacity available		4,500	7,500	
Idle capacity		2,000	0	

Once again the opportunity cost analysis is revealing. If a unit of product B were to be withdrawn, this would release capacity in department Y to make 1½ units of product A. The gain would be $15 (= 1½ × $10); the loss would be $6. Thus a net gain of $9 would result from this shift.

The optimum solution obviously lies somewhere between these extremes. When department X is underutilized, it pays to substitute product A for product B. When department Y is underutilized, it pays to substitute product B for product A. This suggests that the optimum solution will be reached when both departments are fully utilized.

One way to reach this solution is to use the substitution ratio in department Y. By cutting back 1 unit of product B, capacity is released for 1½ units of product A. This substitution will keep department Y fully occupied and will use 5 hours of department X's idle capacity:

Added production of A: 1½ × 4	6 hours
Less: Reduced production of B: 1 × 1	1 hour
Net increase in use of Department X	5 hours

Because department X has an idle capacity of 2,000 hours, this means that both departments will be fully utilized if 400 units of B are subtracted from the second solution. This will release enough capacity to produce 600 units of A. The total contribution margin under this solution is

$$600 × \$10 + 2,100 × \$6 = \$18,600$$

which is $3,600 greater than the better of the two previous solutions. This could have been predicted because the benefit from substituting 1½ units of A for 1 unit of B was found to be $9, and we made 400 of these substitutions.

The feasibility of the solution can be checked by deriving the input requirements:

Product	Units produced	Hours required Dept. X	Hours required Dept. Y
A	600	2,400	1,200
B	2,100	2,100	6,300
Total		4,500	7,500

The same solution can also be derived algebraically in this case. Full utilization of department X can be represented by the equation

$$4A + 1B = 4,500$$

The full utilization equation for department Y is

$$2A + 3B = 7,500$$

Two equations in two unknowns can be solved simultaneously to yield the values for A and B that we have already derived.

This is a special case of the kind of problem for which linear programming is ideally suited. Linear programming is a device that yields a solution to a resource allocation problem when an algebraic solution is unobtainable, that is, when the number of unknowns exceeds the number of equations.

Pricing New Products. Cost figures can enter into product pricing decisions in two ways: (1) in conjunction with price–volume estimates, to identify the most profitable sales volume; and (2) in conjunction with estimates of desired profit margins, to identify normal or target prices.

Profit–volume pricing. If satisfactory estimates of the price sensitivity of a product's sales can be obtained, a profit-maximizing price can be selected. In the following table, for example, where unit variable cost is $3.10 and fixed costs are $165,000, $6 is the profit-maximizing price:

(1) Price	(2) Units sold	(3) Sales [(1) × (2)]	(4) Cost	(5) Profit [(3) − (4)]
$5	100,000	$500,000	$475,000	$25,000
6	80,000	480,000	413,000	67,000
7	50,000	350,000	320,000	30,000

Costs for this kind of analysis should include any costs that will be affected by a change either in price or in volume. Factory materials cost, for example, will be affected by volume, whereas sales commissions will respond to changes in both prices and volume. Costs that are related to the product but unrelated to price or volume, such as some forms of advertising or market research, can be ignored. They enter into any evaluation of the desirability of introducing the product into the market, but are irrelevant to price-volume analysis.

Changes in marketing cost should be included in this kind of analysis only if they are related to product price. A marketing cost does not change because volume changes; instead, it may change in order to produce a volume change. Pricing analysis is not concerned, however, with choosing the optimum amount of marketing effort; only if price and marketing effort are interdependent should changes in marketing cost be introduced into the pricing analysis.

To put this another way, the costs and volume shown for each price should represent the estimated optimum amount of marketing effort at that price. If adding $50,000 to marketing effort would increase sales at a $5 price from 100,000 to 150,000 units, for example, this would be a better combination than the original estimate, as the following table shows:

	Revenues	Costs	Profit
Low effort (data from table above)	$500,000	$475,000	$25,000
High effort	750,000	680,000	70,000

In other words, a $5 price appears to be more profitable than a $6 price because, with effort, it will bring in a profit $70,000 higher than the amount available at any other price.

Cost formula pricing. Difficulties in estimating the price-volume relationship limit the direct application of profit-volume pricing. Another limiting factor in many cases is the dependence of sales in one period on price in previous periods. Price may be kept deliberately below the short-term optimum so as to achieve a greater penetration of the market and impede the entry and growth of competitors during the early stages of the product's life cycle.

In either of these circumstances, company price setters often rely heavily on cost-plus pricing formulas. The basic justification for the widespread use of such formulas is that they help the decision maker predict either the competitor's costs or a competitive price. For example, if the firm has been operating for some time in a market in which markups over cost average 50 percent, it may be able to assume that the same relationship will hold on new products.

This kind of thinking is particularly valid in oligopolistic industries. Recognizing that price competition is likely to be self-defeating, the pricer may set a price that is expected not to attract competitors unduly and then focus competitive efforts on other factors such as delivery, credit terms, and so forth.

Formula pricing does not necessarily mean that market forces are ignored in pricing new products. Anyone who is at all familiar with department store operations, for example, knows that percentage markups over cost vary from department to department and often for different lines of merchandise within a given department. Most differences in markup reflect well-established customs in the trade which guide the pricer toward a competitive price. Furthermore, the customary markups change from time to time, and most department store buyers who make the pricing decisions are free to alter the markup if they see a reason to do so.

Cost-based pricing formulas in manufacturing firms are likely to be "full cost" formulas, in which full cost is defined as estimated or standard manufacturing costs. Although formulas based on variable product cost can be constructed, they ignore differences in input requirements that may be very important. A product requiring a great amount of machine time but little labor time will pass through departments in which fixed overhead is relatively high. Products requiring only simple assembly operations ordinarily require far less fixed overhead. In the short run, the price of the first kind of product can be reduced substantially without creating an incremental loss; in the longer period, however, heavy overhead requirements may give it far more price protection than the simple assembled product. At least some of the fixed costs, in other words, are likely to be relevant to the pricing decision.

The development of factory unit cost estimates for use in formula pricing is described in detail in Chapter 40. Costs derived from such systems should be examined to make sure that they include only those costs reasonably attributable to the product. Exhibit 3, for example, shows a simple two-tier cost structure. Full product cost would include provisions for the categories of nonattributable costs described in the two blocks at the bottom of Exhibit 3. Because these are not attributable to individual products, they should be excluded from the pricing base. These costs must be covered by the margins on all products combined, but the contributions made by individual products need not be identical.

The amount of fixed cost included in product cost will depend on the operating volume over which the fixed costs are to be spread. High volume means low unit fixed cost, and vice versa. A good starting point is "designed capacity." For factory costs, this is the average operating level assumed by the designers when they were deciding how big a plant to build. It will typically be less than

EXHIBIT 3   Relationship between Service Department Cost and Product Cost

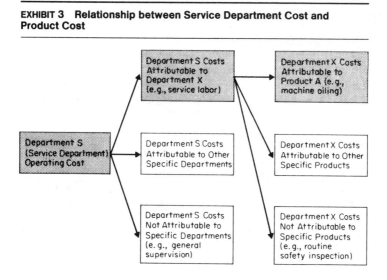

maximum physical capacity and will depend to some extent on industry practice as to the number of shifts worked in a normal week.

This is not to imply that price and volume are totally independent of each other. Pricing formulas are used partly because price-volume relationships are unknown and partly to establish long-term targets. If setting price at the target level would preclude the attainment of normal volume or something close to it, the product's long-term survival prospects are dim and management should know this.

A refinement of cost-based formula pricing is return-on-investment pricing. This differs only in that the cost base includes an estimate of the required implicit interest on the amount of capital attributable to each individual product. The general approach is the same.

Full cost formulas seldom incorporate sophisticated estimates of selling and administrative costs. These costs, if included at all, enter the formulas through simple averages, such as overall percentages of manufacturing cost. These averages will be inadequate if selling and administrative costs are strongly affected by product characteristics. The price that will produce a normal return on investment at normal volume will vary with the amount of marketing effort required to achieve that volume. Most marketing costs are programmed costs, of course, unresponsive to changes in the rate of production or sales. Such costs do not enter into profit-volume pricing, but they have to be a factor in decisions to market the product in the first place or retain it on a continuing basis. A product that cannot cover the costs attributable to it cannot survive indefinitely.

Selecting Customers. Customers and potential customers may be classified by location, by industry, by function (wholesaler vs. retailer), or by other characteristics. Knowledge of the cost of serving customers in a particular group may be the basis for deciding to charge them higher prices or perhaps not to sell to them at all.

Customer profitability analysis consists of four steps:

1. Classify the customers into groups.
2. Measure the product mix and volume for each group.
3. Estimate the manufacturing costs attributable to the products bought by each group.
4. Estimate the nonmanufacturing costs attributable to each group.

The third and fourth steps deserve special attention here.

Estimates of manufacturing costs. The basic question in this kind of analysis is how much cost would be eliminated if a particular customer group were to be dropped. This is the concept referred to earlier as attributable cost.

Factory costs can seldom be attributed directly to specific customer groups. They must first be attributed to products, and these in turn can be identified with different customer groups. Most companies use standard factory cost to represent attributable factory costs. The assumption that standard cost is a good approximation to attributable cost should be examined carefully if fixed costs constitute a large portion of factory costs. Indivisible fixed costs that cannot be traced to specific products should not be attributed to those products. Furthermore, a fixed cost that can be traced to a particular product but is highly indivisible ordinarily should not be attributed to a customer group. Such a cost can be eliminated only by dropping the product entirely, not by cutting out some of the consumers of that product.

Estimates of nonmanufacturing costs. Nonmanufacturing costs should be classified into two categories for customer profitability analysis. In the first category are the various kinds of programmed costs, such as marketing research and product research. Some of these can be traced directly to specific customer groups, such as the salaries and expenses of sales staff who call only on customers in a single group. Most of the others are not readily attributable to individual customer groups, however, and should be included in the analysis only insofar as meaningful measures of attributability can be developed. Average cost per sales call, for example, is likely to be a very poor measure of the cost of soliciting customer orders—only a special analysis of the effects of dropping a customer group can identify the attributable portion of these costs.

The second category of nonmanufacturing costs consists of the costs of organization support and order-filling activities. For broad support activities, such as the costs of corporate executive offices, cost attributability to customer groups is minimal. For others, the two-stage analysis diagrammed in Exhibit 4 is appropriate. The first stage is to identify the cost of performing the individual service functions such as invoice writing, payroll preparation, and customer delivery to calculate a cost per unit of functional service. The second stage is to estimate the number of units of functional service required by each customer group.

In the first stage, the company must identify the costs of performing individual functions and state these as unit costs—for example, cost per order or cost per payroll line. The unit cost divisor may be the number of service units produced (for example, number of paychecks) or a more abstract determinant of cost (for example, dollar value of items in storage). In either case, this divisor is referred to as the function's governing factor.

EXHIBIT 4   Assignment of Nonmanufacturing Costs to Revenue Segments

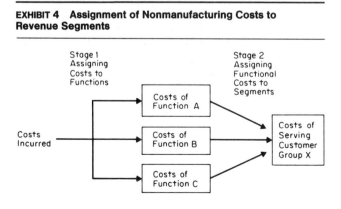

In the second stage, every functional cost that has a governing factor that depends on the number, size, or other dimension of customer orders should be identified. Other items should be excluded from the analysis. The cost of writing a customer invoice, for example, is clearly an order-related cost; the salary of the marketing vice-president just as clearly is not.

As an illustration, suppose that the problem is to investigate the cost of processing small orders. None of the nonmanufacturing costs can be traced directly to small orders; for example, all order clerks handle orders of all sizes, so all costs have to go through the two-stage analysis shown in Exhibit 4.

For example, suppose that functional cost analyses have revealed the following unit cost totals:

Governing factor	Unit cost
Number of orders	$2.00 per order
Value of orders	.005 per dollar
Number of product units ordered	.03 per unit
Number of order lines	.10 per line

This table, of course, represents the summation of all of the functional cost elements governed by each of the factors listed; a full example would have to list each function separately.

The next step is to find out how many units of each of these governing factors are associated with orders of various sizes. Suppose that a sample of orders yields the following statistics:

		Number of governing factor units		
Size class	Orders	Order value	Product units	Order lines
$ 1–$ 99	50,000	$ 1,000,000	200,000	100,000
100– 199	20,000	2,600,000	500,000	60,000
200– 499	20,000	5,600,000	1,100,000	80,000
500 and up	10,000	6,000,000	1,200,000	50,000
Total	100,000	$15,200,000	3,000,000	290,000

Because the question in this case is how much it costs to obtain and service an order, these statistics next should be restated as averages, as follows:

		Average number of governing factor units per order		
Size class	Orders	Order value	Product units	Order lines
$ 1–$ 99	1	$ 20	4	2.0
100– 199	1	130	25	3.0
200– 499	1	280	55	4.0
500 and up	1	600	120	5.0
Average	1	$152	30	2.9

The final step is to multiply these statistics by the unit cost figures cited earlier. The end result is the unit cost of an order, as summarized below:

Size class	Each order	Value of the order	Number of units in the order	Number of order lines	Total cost per order
		Servicing costs attributed to			
$ 1–$ 99	$2.00	$ .10	$ .12	$ .20	$2.42
100– 199	2.00	.65	.75	.30	3.70
200– 499	2.00	1.40	1.65	.40	5.45
500 and up	2.00	3.00	3.60	.50	9.10
Average	$2.00	$ .76	$ .90	$ .29	$3.95

Replacing Equipment. Equipment is ordinarily replaced to achieve one or more of three results:

1. Lower costs
2. Greater volume
3. Greater versatility

If the motive is greater volume or greater versatility, incremental revenues will be important to the decision. In all cases, however, cost differences are likely to be substantial and should not be overlooked.

Equipment replacement decisions differ from the decisions discussed above in that costs must be estimated separately for two or more different time periods. The reason is that a cost saving or other cash inflow that will take place 5 years ahead is worth less to the company than an immediate saving. For example, Exhibit 5 shows the present value of the cost savings expected at the end of each year from two different machines. This present value represents the amount that these savings are worth to a company that expects aftertax earnings of 12 percent on its investment. (See interest tables in the Appendix.) Each machine has an expected life of 5 years, but the savings on machine B are expected to build up gradually as production volume increases, whereas machine A gets its maximum benefit immediately. The lifetime savings from the two machines are identical, but machine A has a higher present value because near money is worth more than distant money. The company will receive $65 more at the end of year 1 with machine A than with machine B. If this amount can be invested for 4 years at a rate of return of 12 percent, it will be worth more to the company than a similar benefit 4 years later.

The cost saving from replacement is the difference in cash flow each year between the cost of operating the present machine and operating the replacement. Forecasts of these amounts must be made for each period prior to the date when the replacement machine, in its turn, will be replaced or retired.

Most equipment-related costs fall into the categories of setup labor, production labor, production materials, maintenance labor and materials, materials handling labor, employee fringe benefits, power, tooling and fixtures, insur-

---

EXHIBIT 5   Present Value of Cost Savings

Year	Machine A		Machine B	
	Cost saving	Present value at 12%	Cost saving	Present value at 12%
1.........	$100	$ 89	$ 35	$ 31
2.........	90	72	45	36
3.........	70	50	60	43
4.........	45	29	80	51
5.........	10	6	95	54
Total......	$315	$246	$315	$215

---

ance, and taxes. These elements must be estimated both for the existing machine and for the proposed replacement.

Three cautions need to be observed in replacement cost analysis. First, even though factory overhead or burden rates are often developed on a direct labor base, overhead cost savings cannot be determined by multiplying labor savings by the overhead rate. Profitable replacement often requires the partial substitution of overhead costs for direct labor costs; that is, total savings will be less than direct labor savings rather than greater.

Second, annual depreciation on existing equipment is not "saved" if the machine is replaced. Depreciation charges, as ordinarily calculated, are allocations of original cost (or replacement cost, in some instances). As such they represent sunk costs. The depreciation figure that is relevant to a replacement decision is the future decline that will take place in the disposal value of the equipment if it is not replaced now.

Similarly, the current book value of the existing equipment is a sunk cost that need not be covered by the anticipated cash savings from the operation of the new machine. Only the present salvage value of the old machine is relevant, because this measures the cash the company could receive if it were to replace the equipment now. The incremental cash flows associated with the purchase and salvage values of machines in a replacement decision are thus as shown in the accompanying table:

	Alternative A: Keep old machine	Alternative B: Replace with new machine	Difference
At time of replacement......	0	− cost of new machine + salvage of old machine now	− cost of new machine + salvage of old machine now
At end of estimated life of new machine	+ salvage of old machine at end of life	+ salvage of new machine at end of life	+ (salvage of new machine − salvage of old machine) at end of life

The third caution in this kind of analysis is that costs of floor space occupied should be computed on an incremental basis. In many cases, an increase in floor space requirements will lead to no increase in total occupancy costs; in such cases, the incremental cost is zero. Similarly, if the new machine occupies less space than the present machine, the actual cash saving may be zero. In each case, the question is whether total company space costs will increase or decrease. The present average cost per square foot of floor space is almost never a good basis on which to forecast this increment.

Selecting an Order Quantity. The decision as to how much merchandise or material to purchase in a single order requires cost estimates of a slightly different kind. The act of purchasing the goods leads to a one-time purchasing cost. In most cases, the purchasing agent's own salary should be treated as a sunk cost, irrelevant to the decision and therefore excluded from the analysis. Incremental purchasing costs consist of such items as telephone charges, clerical salaries, postage, and forms costs. Unless each purchase requires special activities such as the preparation and reproduction of diagrams, blueprints, and so on, incremental purchasing costs are likely to be very low.

Of greater significance are inventory carrying costs—mainly the costs of storage space, insurance, spoilage, and interest. The greater the inventory, the greater the carrying costs per period. Most of these costs can be expected to vary proportionately with the size of the inventory. Care must be exercised to see that space costs are estimated on an incremental basis (see final paragraph under "Replacing Equipment" above).

One simple order-size formula utilizing this kind of data is as follows:

$$EOQ = \sqrt{\frac{2DP}{CR}}$$

where EOQ = optimum number of units per purchase order
D = total number of units needed per year
P = ordering cost per purchase order
R = purchase price per unit
C = carrying cost per dollar of average inventory
CR = carrying cost per unit per year

As this formula indicates, the larger the annual requirements or the larger the order cost per order, the larger the order should be. Conversely, greater carrying costs call for smaller purchase lots because smaller and more frequent purchase lots reduce the average inventory quantity.

METHODS OF ANALYSIS

Cost data for decision analyses often can be found in the company's records of past cost experience. Sometimes the best analytical technique is to apply trend factors to the historical cost figures. Cost relationships are likely to be more complex than this would imply, however, and more sophisticated techniques are frequently necessary. Some of these techniques build on data already in the cost files; others require the generation of new data. Five groups of techniques deserve a brief introduction:

1. Statistical regression analysis
2. Observation
3. Synthesis of work elements
4. Personal judgment
5. Time pattern analysis

Statistical Regression Analysis. Statistical regression analysis is widely used to estimate the historical relationship between costs and volume. The result is typically stated in the form

$$C = a + bV$$

where C = total cost per period
a = fixed costs per period
b = average variable cost per unit of volume
V = volume per period

The line of relationship sometimes can be estimated adequately by plotting a set of historical observations on a sheet of graph paper and drawing a line that seems to fit the observations best (as in Exhibit 6). In other cases, mathematical analysis becomes necessary, usually by the method of least squares. This consists of finding a line such that the sum of the squares of the vertical deviations from the line will be at a minimum.

Regression analysis can also be applied to estimate the effects on cost of more than one variable. Analysis of this kind is known as multiple regression analysis, and leads to a formula of the form

$$C = a + bV + cX$$

in which X stands for the value of some variable other than volume (for example, external temperature) and c represents the rate of variation of cost with

EXHIBIT 6   Graphic Method for Analyzing Cost Variability

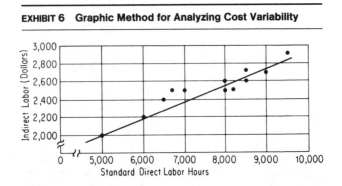

variations in this other variable. See Chapter 11 for a more extended discussion.

Observation. When historical data are out of date or unreliable, or when volume is not the main variable in the decision, the analyst may be able to estimate costs on the basis of observations made specifically for that purpose. These observations are ordinarily made by industrial engineers and are of two types:

1. Observation of existing operations
2. Experimentation

Observation of existing operations. The two most common kinds of observations are (1) time studies or time-and-motion studies and (2) work sampling. Time-and-motion studies are widely used in manufacturing operations as part of methods improvement programs or in the establishment or revision of incentive wage rates. Work sampling is most commonly applied to clerical operations as part of methods improvement programs.

In a time study, engineers use stopwatches to measure the amounts of time required for specific operations. They then apply leveling factors to adjust for differences between the observed performance and what they judge to be normal performance. They then add standard allowances for such factors as fatigue, rest time, and production interruptions.

In work sampling, in contrast, no attempt is made to time individual operations. Instead, the engineer accumulates a set of cross-section observations, each showing what the various employees were doing at a particular point in time. The total amount of time required for a given function is then estimated by multiplying the total time spent on all functions by the percentage indicated by the sample for this particular function.

Time studies are most useful when the individual task consumes a substantial amount of time and can be expected to be repeated many times. Work sampling is useful when a given task takes a relatively short time and the nature of the task is likely to change substantially from one period to the next.

Both methods assume that costs vary proportionately with volume. Techniques analogous to time studies can be used to measure the consumption of materials and some additional cost elements other than labor; work sampling is used only to identify labor requirements and utilization.

Experimentation. Experimental production runs are sometimes made to provide the basis for time studies or time and motion studies. Aside from this, experimentation is seldom used for cost estimation, mainly because experimental data often cannot be obtained without reducing existing operating efficiency.

Experimentation is most practical when operations are highly divisible. This permits the company to change a small part of its operations without disrupting the entire system. It also permits the use of the unaffected operations as a control against which to measure the experimental results.

Synthesis of Work Elements. A third main method of estimation is the synthesis of work elements. The prime example is the construction of cost estimates from commercially available tables of the amount of time required to perform basic physical motions, for example, methods-time measurement (MTM) systems.

The same approach underlies the construction of standard costs for a new product from the standard costs of an existing product. Labor and materials data for identical operations or parts can be transferred bodily for this purpose.

Personal Judgment. In the end, all cost estimates are personal judgments of the future effects of present decisions. Even if the highly precise statistical regression technique is used, the indicated cost-volume relationship is likely to be rejected if it does not seem reasonable.

Personal judgment is also used, however, as a direct method of deriving cost estimates. First, the analyst can examine a standard list of accounts and estimate the amount of cost likely to be charged to each account under specified conditions. This is sometimes called the "inspection of accounts" method. Although highly unsophisticated, this approach should not be totally scorned. Most judgmental estimates are based on personal experience. The estimates of shrewd analysts may have a stronger factual foundation than statistical regression analyses.

Personal judgment also enters into cost estimation in another guise, through the engineering estimate. Engineers will be asked to compute the cost of operating a machine that the company has never owned. By studying the machine and the performance characteristics specified by the manufacturer, the experienced engineer can draw on previous experience to derive a fairly accurate cost estimate.

The personal judgment method is undoubtedly the most widely used. It can also be called the method of historical analogy. The human mind stores data from the past and delivers them when they are needed. Even experimental methods generate data that are historical by the time they are accumulated. The advantage of the more sophisticated methods is that the process by which the data are converted into cost estimates is more visible, with assumptions, adjustments, and allowances specified as clearly as the analysis demands. Judgmental estimates are more difficult to document and to trace back to the underlying assumptions.

Time Pattern Analysis. All of these methods of analysis ignore the possibility that cost performance will change from period to period. One cause of such changes is that equipment often declines in efficiency as it gets older. This can be highly important for equipment replacement decisions. Data on cost-age patterns can be derived from equipment maintenance records, using a form of regression analysis.

Another cause of changes in cost performance is the so-called learning curve. Aircraft manufacturers discovered that unit cost declined as a function of the cumulative number of units produced, and that this decline could be predicted fairly accurately. These patterns were reflected in learning curves, showing the percentage decline in unit costs that could be expected from a given percentage increase in cumulative output. Thus an 80 percent learning curve was one in which doubling cumulative output would reduce cumulative unit cost by 20 percent. If the first 1,000 units cost a total of $10,000 to produce, or $10 a unit, the average cost of the first 2,000 units would be expected to be $8. To achieve this, of course, the cost of the second 1,000 units would have to be only $6,000, or $6 each.

Identification of the cost improvement pattern may be extremely useful in product pricing. In bidding on orders for custom products, for example, it can provide the basis for quantity discount schedules. In other situations, bidders who base bids on costs of the first units may find themselves priced out of the market.

COST–PROFIT DIAGRAMS

The results of a cost analysis are almost always shown in one or more summary tables of figures. The meaning of these data often can be made clearer, however, by presenting them in pictorial form. Two closely related devices used for this purpose are the profit–volume chart and the breakeven diagram.

Profit–Volume Charts. Decisions are often highly sensitive to the estimates of sales or production volume. The profit–volume chart is one device for visualizing the anticipated impact on profit of variations in operating volume.

Exhibit 7 shows one kind of profit–volume diagram. In this case, the volume of sales is measured along the horizontal axis, and total costs and total revenues for each sales volume are represented by the vertical distances above the base line. The vertical distance between the total revenue and total cost lines represents the expected profit or loss at that volume (indicated by the shaded areas on the chart).

In this traditional form, the total cost line is depicted as a straight line extend-

EXHIBIT 7   Profit–Volume Chart

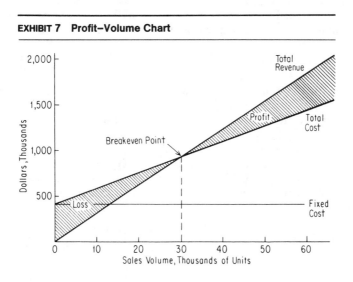

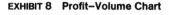

EXHIBIT 8   Profit–Volume Chart

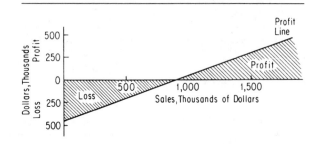

ing from zero volume to the highest volume shown on the chart. As we have already seen, this is an oversimplification. Variable cost rates are computed for a limited portion of the total output range, covering perhaps that 30 to 40 percent of the total range within which the company expects to operate. Although the straight-line cost function is reasonably representative within this range, the profit spreads to the left and right of this range have little meaning and are introduced only to facilitate the explanation of the nature of fixed costs.

These estimates are shown in a slightly different way in Exhibit 8. Separate lines for costs and revenues are eliminated by plotting the profits only. Volume is again measured along the horizontal axis, and profit or loss is represented by the vertical spread between the profit line and the zero-profit baseline.

The Breakeven Point. Some profit–volume charts are referred to as breakeven charts. In the diagram in Exhibit 7, for example, the breakeven point is the volume at which the total revenue and total cost lines cross. If the cost function can be assumed to be linear within much of the volume range, the breakeven volume can be calculated by solving the following equation:

$$\text{Breakeven Volume} = \frac{\text{Total Fixed Cost}}{\text{Contribution Margin per Volume Unit}}$$

In multiproduct operations, volume ordinarily is measured in sales dollars; contribution margin therefore will be stated as a percentage of sales. This percentage varies as the product mix changes, because the contribution margin varies from product to product. Any breakeven volume calculation therefore must be based on a specified product mix.

The profit–volume chart can be modified to include specified profit or return-on-investment targets among the fixed charges to be covered by total contribution margin. If aftertax profit targets are used, the tax rate must be introduced into the equation:

$$\text{Breakeven Volume} = \frac{(1 - \text{Tax Rate}) \times \text{Fixed Cost} + \text{Aftertax Profit Target}}{(1 - \text{Tax Rate}) \times \text{Contribution Margin per Unit}}$$

Using the Profit–Volume Diagram. The profit–volume diagram can help the manager in decision making by showing the sensitivity of profit to variations in volume. It can also be used to illustrate the comparison between two alternative decisions. For example, Exhibit 9 shows the estimated effect on profit of a change in product selling prices. The broken line in this exhibit represents the profit obtainable at various levels of sales at prices that are 10 percent higher than current prices, represented by the solid line. This shows that although increased prices are expected to reduce physical sales volume, dollar profit is expected to increase.

Many managers find the breakeven point useful as a partial measure of the risks involved in a particular course of action. A decision that will raise the breakeven point is often presumed to be riskier than other decisions. This notion is often implemented by the calculation of the margin of safety, or the spread between anticipated volume and the breakeven volume.

Crossover Diagrams. The breakeven concept can also be applied in crossover diagrams. For example, Exhibit 10 shows the relative advantage and disadvantage of using a special-purpose machine instead of a general-purpose machine at each likely length of production run. The special-purpose machine has a high setup cost and low running costs. The general-purpose machine has high running costs but a low setup cost. The length of run at which the costs of the two alternatives are equal is the crossover point. The diagram shows the planner which machine will be more economical for any given production run.

EXHIBIT 9   Effect of Price Change on Profit

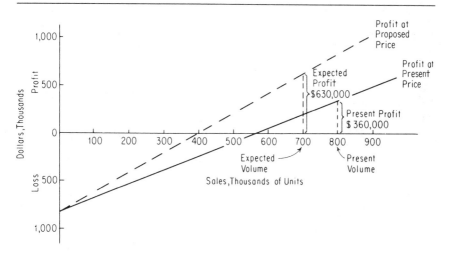

EXHIBIT 10 Guide to Production Scheduling

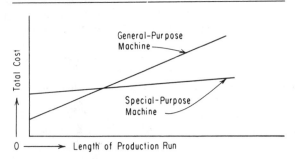

BIBLIOGRAPHY

Andress, F. J., "The Learning Curve as a Production Tool," *Harvard Business Review,* January-February 1954, pp. 87-97.

Conley, P., "Experience Curves as a Planning Tool," *IEEE Spectrum,* June 1970, pp. 63-68.

DeCoster, D. T., K. V. Ramanathan, and G. L. Sundem (eds.), *Accounting for Managerial Decision Making,* 2d ed. (Melville Publishing Co., Los Angeles, 1978).

Dopuch, N., J. G. Birnberg, and J. Demski, *Cost Accounting: Accounting Data for Management's Decisions,* 2d ed. (Harcourt Brace Jovanovich, New York, 1974).

Hartley, R. V., "Some Extensions of Sensitivity Analysis," *The Accounting Review,* April 1970, pp. 223-234.

————, "Decision Making with Joint Products," *The Accounting Review,* October 1971, pp. 746-755.

Horngren, C. T., *Cost Accounting: A Managerial Emphasis,* 5th ed. (Prentice-Hall, Englewood Cliffs, N.J., 1982).

Johnson, G. L., and S. S. Simik, II, "Multiproduct C.V.P. Analysis under Uncertainty," *Journal of Accounting Research,* Autumn 1971, pp. 278-286.

Rappaport, A. (ed.), *Information for Decision Making, Quantitative and Behavioral Dimensions,* 2d ed. (Prentice-Hall, Englewood Cliffs, N.J., 1975).

Shillinglaw, G., *Managerial Cost Accounting,* 5th ed. (Richard D. Irwin, Homewood, Ill., 1982).

Solomons, D. (ed.), *Studies in Cost Analysis,* 2d ed. (Richard D. Irwin, Homewood, Ill., 1968).

Weil, R. L., "Allocating Joint Costs," *American Economic Review,* December 1968, pp. 1342-1345.

Zimmerman, J. L., "The Costs and Benefits of Cost Allocations," *The Accounting Review,* July 1979, pp. 504-521.

CHAPTER 39

Budgets and

Controls

Michael W. Maher
Associate Professor of Accounting,
University of Michigan

This chapter discusses the use of budgets and methods of control in organizations. The first part of the chapter deals with budgeting for, and control of, ongoing operations. The uses of flexible budgets, standard costs, and variance analysis are also discussed.

The second part of the chapter deals with management control of decentralized operations. Topics include advantages and disadvantages of decentralization, performance measurement methods, and transfer pricing.

THE BUDGETING AND CONTROL PROCESS

The budgeting and control process is made up of the following phases (see Exhibit 1):

Setting organizational goals
Strategic planning
Capital budgeting
Operating budgeting
Comparison with actual results
Performance evaluation
Revision of goals, plans, and budgets

EXHIBIT 1 Overview of the Budgeting and Control Process

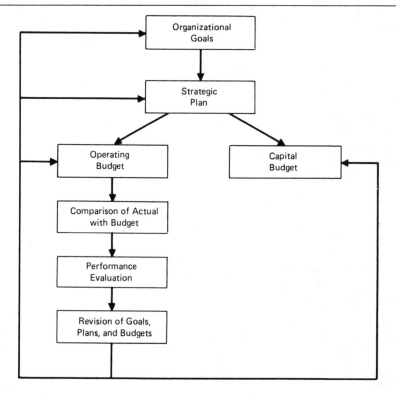

Organizational Goals. Organizational goals are the broad objectives established by management toward which employees work. Following is an example of such goals as recently stated by a manufacturing company's management:

> Our long-range objective is to increase earnings consistently while maintaining our current share of market sales, and maintain an ROI which is within the top one-third of our industry. We plan to achieve these goals while providing our customers with high-quality products, and meeting our social responsibilities to our employees and the communities in which they live.

Strategic Plan. The strategic plan states the method or strategy for achieving organizational goals. For example, the previously mentioned manufacturing company's strategies include the following:

1. *Cost control.* Optimize contribution from existing product lines by holding product cost increases to less than the rate of inflation. This will involve introducing new machinery proposed in the capital budget as well as replacing our five least efficient plants over the next 5 years.

2. *Market share.* Maintain our market share by providing a level of service and quality comparable to our top competitors. This requires improving our quality control such that customer complaints and returned merchandise is reduced from a current level of 4 percent to 1 percent within 2 years.

Strategic plans include long-range forecasts (typically 5 years or more) of sales, including new products, production and capacity requirements, aggregate levels of costs, and financing requirements. Strategic plans include consideration of the major capital investments required to maintain present facilities, increase capacity, or diversify to other products. In short, the strategic plan states long-run methods (strategy) for achieving organizational goals. Capital and operating budgets, as discussed later, are more specific, more detailed, and (particularly the operating budget) focus on near-term time periods.

To see the relation between strategic plans and budgets, consider the decisions by General Motors to produce the X-car and J-car product lines. The X-car and J-car product lines were part of a strategy for meeting new government regulations, rising foreign competition, and changing demands of consumers (partly because of increasing gasoline prices). Strategic planning required forecasts in the early 1970s of market demand, production capacity requirements, and financing needs for the late 1970s and 1980s. In short, strategic plans are long range, they are not too detailed, and they are usually organized around product lines.

The relation between strategic plans and budgets is shown in Exhibit 2. The output of strategic plans[1] (e.g., product line revenues, expenses, cash flows, and capital needs) are assigned to responsibility centers (e.g., divisions and plants). Thus the Chevrolet Division of General Motors has the Citation X-car, Oldsmobile has the Omega, and so forth. Needed capital investment is budgeted to each responsibility center using the capital budget. Operating budgets provide detailed annual profit plans and cash flow projections. In most companies, the

---

[1]These outputs of strategic planning are often called *programs.*

EXHIBIT 2   Relation of Strategic Plans to Budgets

Budgets organized by responsibility centers (e.g., divisions)	Strategic plans organized by product line				
	X-Car	J-Car	Etc.		
Chevrolet Division	XX	XX			
Pontiac Division	XX	XX			
Etc.					

---

operating budget for the next year is quite detailed, whereas the budgets for the following years are less detailed. Operating budgets for each of 5 years are common, with the understanding that the budget in (say) years 3 through 5 are "blue-sky" estimates. This gives managers an opportunity to plan several years ahead and to commit their plans to paper without being held strictly accountable for attaining or bettering those plans.

The relationships among organizational goals, the strategic plan, the capital budget, and the operating budget provide an "ideal" framework for budgeting, but one that is not always found in organizations. The operating budget is sometimes just an update of the previous year's budget, with an adjustment for inflation. This is a low-cost, but low-benefit way to budget that does not relate the budget to goals and strategies. The ideal budget is a "blueprint" for achieving some set of financial and other goals, within resource constraints, just as an architect's or engineer's blueprint provides a plan for achieving some physical goals, within resource constraints.

Capital Budget. Capital budgeting decisions are important because they tie organizations to long-term commitments that are not easily changed. For example, a capital budgeting decision by National Steel to install a continuous slab caster was a long-run decision that commits it to a particular production process. Capital budgeting decisions are also important because of the size of the amounts involved.

The capital budgeting process consists of the following five steps.

1. *Identify opportunities for capital expenditures.* Opportunities for capital expenditures can be classified as (a) those dealing with ongoing operations, including replacement, cost-saving methods, and quality improvement methods; and (b) those dealing with major changes in operations, including adding or dropping product lines, and opportunities for vertical or horizontal integration. Ideas about new opportunities for ongoing operations often come from operating personnel—those closest to day-to-day activities. Ideas about major changes in operations usually come from top management and high-level staff positions.

2. *Identify alternatives and estimate results.* Many opportunities will be

dropped early because they are totally infeasible or inappropriate. For the remaining opportunities under consideration, all possible alternatives are identified, and the results that would occur if the alternative was implemented are estimated. Because of the uncertainty inherent in this process, an "optimistic," "pessimistic," "most likely," and perhaps other estimates are frequently made. If computer simulation techniques are available, it is possible to assign probabilities to events and simulate a large number of possibilities (for example, see Hertz [1964]).

3. *Evaluate alternatives and make decisions.* This step requires selection of the most appropriate alternative. Choices are usually based on a combination of financial factors, including the amount and timing of estimated cash flows, and the riskiness of the project; and nonfinancial factors, including regulatory requirements, employee safety, corporate image, and community responsibility. Although these decisions require considerable judgment, techniques such as discounted cash flow analysis help quantify the financial analysis. (For a thorough discussion of these techniques, see Brealey and Myers [1981].)

4. *Prepare the capital budget.* After decisions about acceptable projects have been made, the acceptable projects are pulled together in the capital budget. After approvals have been obtained from management and the board of directors (or legislators in governmental units), the budget becomes the expenditure authorization. Internal control systems require another round of reviews and approvals before expenditures above the authorized level can be made.

5. *Follow-up and performance review.* An important but sometimes omitted step is the follow-up and performance review. This step has three purposes: (a) to ascertain whether the expenditure of funds was made in accordance with intentions and authorizations; (b) to evaluate the success of the capital project (e.g., were expected cost savings realized?); and (c) to evaluate the capital budgeting process (e.g., were cash flow estimates biased?).

This step completes the capital budgeting cycle, from opportunity identification through follow-up and performance review.

OPERATING BUDGETS

This section focuses on developing the 1-year operating budget. As previously indicated, this budget is simply a formal quantitative statement of management's objectives and plan of action for the future. In this chapter,we consider the principal uses of such budgets and demonstrate how they are developed for a typical business firm.

Uses of Operating Budgets. Budgets are useful tools for (1) planning, (2) control, and (3) employee motivation.

Tool for planning. After management selects the best alternatives with respect to products, prices, levels of output, production techniques, and so on, these choices are translated into a formal, integrated plan of action. This is one of the most important purposes of the budgeting process. It forces management to take each of the choices made and to make sure that it coordinates with other alternatives selected. It also presents management with a comprehensive picture of the expected effects of its decisions on the firm as a whole. Put another way, budgets are estimates of financial statements prepared before the actual transactions occur.

When used as a tool for planning, budgets are generally static. That is, the budgets are developed for a particular expected level of activity, usually sales or production in units. A single set of estimates is derived for sales, manufacturing costs, selling and administrative expenses, and profit. Such budgets are referred to as *static budgets*.

Tool for control. Budgets provide estimates of what performance is expected to be. As such, they serve as criteria or standards for evaluating performance. A comparison of budgeted and actual amounts provides a basis for evaluating past performance and guiding future action. To be effective as tools for control, the budgets must be initially developed for individual responsibility centers. Budgets will be developed for production, marketing, purchasing, administration, and so on. They will then be integrated into a master budget for the firm as a whole. In this way, the performance of each responsibility center can be evaluated with respect to those activities over which it had control during a particular period.

Flexible budgets. When used as tools for control, budgets are generally *flexible*. That is, the budget for each responsibility center is expressed in the form of a particular level of fixed cost that is expected to be incurred regardless of the level of activity and a variable cost per unit of activity that can change *in total* as the level of activity changes. The "flex" in a flexible budget is with respect to variable costs (i.e., those costs that vary with changes in activity levels). The budget for fixed costs is static.

Example. Studies of past cost behavior indicate that the Assembling Division of Standard Manufacturing Corporation should incur total fixed costs of $100,000 and variable costs of $10 per unit next period. For planning purposes, Standard estimates that 50,000 units will be produced by the Assembling Division. The static cost budget for the division used for planning purposes is therefore $600,000 [= $100,000 + ($10 × 50,000)]. Suppose, however, that due to unexpected demand during the period, the Assembling Division produced 70,000 units. It is not particularly useful *for control purposes* to compare the actual cost of producing 70,000 units with the expected cost of producing 50,000 units. The underlying levels of activity are different. To evaluate actual performance, the budget, or standard, must be expressed in terms of what costs should have been to produce 70,000 units. This is where the flexible budget comes in. It indicates that manufacturing costs should have been $800,000 [= $100,000 + ($10 × 70,000)] during the period. This is the most appropriate standard for control. Note that the estimates of fixed and variable costs form the inputs into both the static budget for planning and the flexible budget for control.

Tool for employee motivation. The importance of the human factor in the planning and control process is well known. Standards, or budgets, can serve as motivating devices for employees if the standards are set at levels that are tight but currently attainable with reasonably efficient performance. It is desirable that the budgets used for planning and control also serve as tools for employee motivation. In this way, a single budgeting and accounting system can be designed that will serve multiple purposes. In some instances, however, the budget of what costs are *expected to be* for planning purposes may be different from the level of costs that, when used as a standard for evaluating performance, will best motivate employees. In these cases, the budgeting and accounting system must be adaptable if it is to serve all purposes.

The Master Budget. The master budget, sometimes called the *comprehensive budget*, is a complete blueprint of the planned operations of the firm for a period. It emphasizes the relationship of the various inputs in all areas of the company to final output and sales. Its preparation requires a recognition of the interrelationships among the various units of a firm. For example, to prepare a master budget requires knowing how a projected increase in sales of product A affects each of the following: the several producing departments; the selling, general, and administrative effort; and the financial position of the company.

Preparation of a master budget is a difficult, complex process that requires much time and effort by management at all levels. The difficulties of fitting all pieces together may be great, especially the first few times a master budget is prepared. Despite these difficulties, or perhaps because of them, the master budget is an effective instrument for planning and control. Its value has been proved so often that almost all firms of any size recognize master budget preparation as a vital task of management.

No simple example can effectively convey the complexity of the process, but the illustration in the following pages is designed to indicate some of the problems and possible solutions.

A word of caution about uniformity may be in order before beginning the illustration. Managements are highly individualistic in their choices of budget titles, order of arrangement, number of supporting schedules, and similar stylistic matters. Many corporate budgets, as well as other texts and budget manuals, will differ in format from the illustration that follows, but all will have as their goal helping management to plan and control operations more effectively.

The budget preparation process will be illustrated for Victoria Corporation for a single period. The period could be a month, a quarter, or a full year. Victoria Corporation produces one product that sells for $6 per unit. An organization chart of Victoria Corporation is presented in Exhibit 3. Each box in the organization chart is viewed as a responsibility center. The production, marketing, and corporate staff departments should probably be broken down further into additional responsibility centers. In order to keep the illustrations simple, we shall not do this.

Knowing where to start in preparing a master budget may be a problem, but generally there is one crucial factor that determines the level of activity. For most firms the crucial factor is the volume of anticipated sales, but it could also be in the availability of certain raw materials, of the supply of labor, or of factory capacity. In the case of the Victoria Corporation, we assume that budgeted sales is the crucial factor. We start with the sales budget; the other budgets build on the sales budget and relate to one another.

Sales budget. The sales budget is presented in Exhibit 4. Responsibility for preparing this budget usually falls on the chief marketing officer of the firm. The marketing official will rely on input from the market research group as well

EXHIBIT 3   Organization Chart for Victoria Corporation

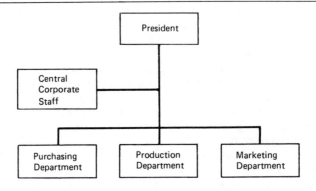

EXHIBIT 4

VICTORIA CORPORATION
Sales Budget
for Period 1

	Amount
70,000 units @ $6	$420,000

---

as from salespersons or district managers in the field. The discussions among sales groups in budget preparation frequently serve to bring out problems in the firm's selling and advertising programs and to broaden the participants' thinking about the firm's place in the market.

Previous sales experience is usually the starting point for sales budget estimates. These historical data are then modified to recognize market trends, anticipated changes in general economic conditions, altered advertising plans, and any other factors deemed relevant. In the end, it is the sales executive, relying on experience and knowledge, who must make the final decisions on the precise quantities and dollar amounts to be shown in the sales budget for each product.

Production budget. The sales budget plus estimates of desired ending inventories form the basis of the production budget for the Victoria Corporation shown in the top part of Exhibit 5. The number of units desired in the ending inventory usually reflects some early estimates of sales to be made in the next period beyond the one being budgeted. The number of units in ending inventory may differ from the quantity considered optimum by sales projections for next period as the indirect result of efforts to keep production balanced period by period and thereby keep the basic labor force employed on a regular basis.

The quantity of each product to be produced is budgeted by using a variant of the familiar inventory equation:

$$\text{Number of Units Sold} + \text{Units in Ending Inventory} - \text{Units in Beginning Inventory} = \text{Units to Be Produced}$$

The costs to be incurred in producing the desired number of units of product A and product B are shown in the lower part of Exhibit 5. The costs are divided into three categories: (1) direct materials, (2) direct labor, and (3) manufacturing overhead.

Direct materials. Direct materials are raw materials that are traceable to, or directly associated with, individual units produced. Direct materials are almost always a variable cost item. Each unit requires 1 pound of direct materials per finished unit. The quantities of raw material required per unit are based on engineering studies of material usage. The cost per pound or per ounce of the raw materials used is based on studies of past cost behavior and current price lists of suppliers.

EXHIBIT 5

VICTORIA CORPORATION
Production Budget
for Period 1

	Total
Units to be produced	
Budgeted sales, in units (see sales budget)	70,000
Desired ending inventory (assumed)	8,000
Total units needed	78,000
Beginning inventory (known at the time budget is prepared)	8,000
Units to be produced	70,000
Cost expected to be incurred	
Direct materials: Plastic (1 lb per unit @ $1.00/lb)	$ 70,000
Direct labor (⅙ hour per unit @ $20/hour).......................	175,000
Manufacturing overhead:	
Indirect labor ($.10 per unit).................................	7,000
Supplies ($.04 per unit)	2,800
Power ($1,000 per period plus $.03 per unit)....................	3,100
Maintenance ($13,840 per period)	13,840
Rent ($6,000 per period)	6,000
Insurance ($1,000 per period)	1,000
Depreciation ($10,360 per period)	10,360
Total	$289,100
Total cash outlays	
Direct materials (see raw materials purchases budget, Exhibit 6)	$ 70,000
Direct labor (from above).....................................	$175,000
Manufacturing overhead (total less depreciation)....................	$ 33,740

Direct labor. Direct labor represents work performed that is traceable directly to particular units of product. Relying on engineering time and motion studies and studies of past cost behavior, it is estimated that a unit requires 7.5 minutes of labor time. This estimate allows for periodic rest periods but is sufficiently tight so that employees are motivated to perform efficiently. The standard wage rate, including fringe benefits, for production workers in Victoria Corporation's plant is $20.00 per hour and is set by negotiation with the local labor union.

Manufacturing overhead. Unlike direct material and direct labor, manufacturing overhead costs are not traceable directly to particular units produced. Rather, these costs either give a firm the capacity to produce (fixed manufacturing overhead costs) or represent costs that vary with, but are not traceable directly to, the units produced (variable manufacturing overhead costs). As shown in Exhibit 5, indirect labor and supplies are variable manufacturing overhead costs. Power is a semivariable, or mixed, cost, having both variable and fixed components. Maintenance, rent, insurance, and depreciation are fixed manufacturing overhead costs.

Summary of production budget. The production budget shown in Exhibit 5 serves as a plan of action for the production department for the period. The production manager must schedule production so that 70,000 units are manufactured. The production budget also serves as a gauge for evaluating the performance of the production department at the end of the period. If production in units proceeds according to plan, then the production department should incur costs of $289,100 during the period. If the level of production differs from the projected amounts, then the flexible budget amounts must be applied to determine the amount of costs that should have been incurred. The flexible budget for the production department is

$$\begin{array}{l} \text{Total Cost} \\ \text{for Production} \\ \text{Department} \end{array} = \$32,200 + \left(\$3.67 \times \begin{array}{l}\text{Units} \\ \text{Produced}\end{array}\right)$$

The fixed cost amount is the sum of the estimates for power, maintenance, rent, insurance, and depreciation ($32,200 = $1,000 + $13,840 + $6,000 + $1,000 + $10,360). The variable cost amount is the sum of the estimates for direct materials, direct labor, indirect labor, supplies, and power ($3.67 = $1.00 + $2.50 + $.10 + $.04 + $.03).

Raw materials purchases budget. The purchasing of raw materials is the responsibility of the purchasing department in Victoria Corporation. Exhibit 6 presents the raw materials purchases budget. The production budget along with the estimates of beginning and ending inventories of raw materials serve as the basis for the raw materials purchases budget. The quantity of each class of materials to be purchased is budgeted by multiplying the quantity of that class of raw material in each unit of product to be produced by the same variant of the familiar inventory formula that was used in deriving the production budget. The number of units of each class of raw materials to be purchased each period is shown in the top part of Exhibit 6. The budget indicating the estimated cost of those purchases is shown in the lower part of Exhibit 6. For simplicity in presentation, it is assumed in Exhibit 6 that payments to suppliers equal pur-

EXHIBIT 6

VICTORIA CORPORATION
Raw Materials Purchases Budget
for Period 1

Quantities to be purchased (lb)	
Units to be used (see production budget)	70,000
Planned ending inventory (assumed)	10,000
Units needed	80,000
Beginning inventory (known at the time the budget is prepared)	10,000
Units to be purchased	70,000
Cost to be incurred	$70,000

chases each period. That assumption is probably unrealistic. A procedure for dealing with time lags in payments is illustrated later in the receivables and collections budget (see Exhibit 11). The same procedure could have been used for accounts payable to suppliers.

Selling expense budget. The budget for selling expenses for the Victoria Corporation's marketing department is shown in Exhibit 7. All of the items except commissions and shipping costs are estimated to be fixed. Commissions are 2 percent of sales dollars and shipping costs are $.02 per unit shipped. Note that variable selling costs vary with sales dollars and shipments made, whereas variable manufacturing costs vary with units produced.

Central corporate administrative expense budget. All of the central corporate administrative expenses shown in Exhibit 8 are fixed. Not all of them require current cash outlays. Depreciation of office equipment is an expense that does not require a current expenditure but is the allocation of part of the cost of a long-term asset to the current period.

Capital budget. The capital budget, Exhibit 9, shows the Victoria Corporation's plan for acquisition of depreciable, long-term assets during the next

EXHIBIT 7

VICTORIA CORPORATION
Selling Expense Budget

	Period 1
Salaries ($25,000 per period)	$25,000
Commissions (2% of sales; see Exhibit 4)	8,400
Advertising ($30,000 per period)	30,000
Sales office costs ($8,400 per period)	8,400
Shipping costs ($.02 per unit shipped; see Exhibit 4)	1,400
Travel ($2,000 per period)	2,000
Total selling expense budget (= cash outlay)	$75,200

EXHIBIT 8

VICTORIA CORPORATION
Central Corporate Administrative Expense Budget

	Period 1
President's salary	$10,000
Salaries of other staff personnel	17,000
Supplies	2,000
Heat and light	1,400
Rent	4,000
Donations and contributions	1,000
General corporate taxes	8,000
Depreciation—staff office equipment	1,400
Total central corporate administrative budget	$44,800
Less: Depreciation[a]	1,400
Budgeted cash outlays	$43,400

[a]Note that all items except depreciation are fixed costs requiring current cash outlays.

EXHIBIT 9

VICTORIA CORPORATION
Capital Budget

	Period 1
Acquisition of new factory machinery	$12,000
Miscellaneous capital additions	2,000
Total capital budget	$14,000
Borrowings for new machinery (notes payable)[a]	10,000
Current cash outlay	$ 4,000

[a]Notes payable to be repaid at the rate of $4,000 per period.

period. The company plans to purchase major items of equipment. Part of the cost will be financed by the issuance of notes payable in a later period to equipment suppliers. The note issuance is deducted from the cost of the acquisitions to determine current cash outlays for equipment. An alternative, accepted treatment would have viewed the note issuance as a cash inflow with the entire cost of the equipment included in cash outflows.

Cash outlays budget. A schedule of the planned cash outlays for period 1 is presented in Exhibit 10. The first six items are taken from the cash outlay lines of earlier exhibits. The agreement with the equipment suppliers calls for payment of $4,000 per period plus interest. The amount shown for interest also includes interest on the short-term notes. Each period the Victoria Corporation pays the income taxes accrued in the previous period. Income taxes payable at the start of period 1 are shown on the actual balance sheet (column 1 of Exhibit 14). Dividends at the rate of $.50 per share are declared and paid each period.

Receivables and collections budget. Most of the sales of each period are collected in the period of sale, but there is some lag in collections. The budget for cash collections from customers is shown in Exhibit 11. Collections for sales

---

EXHIBIT 10

VICTORIA CORPORATION
Cash Outlays Budget

	Period 1
Materials (Exhibit 6)	$ 70,000
Labor (Exhibit 5)	175,000
Manufacturing overhead (Exhibit 5)	33,740
Selling expenses (Exhibit 7)	75,200
Central corporate administrative expenses (Exhibit 8)	43,400
Capital expenditures (Exhibit 9)	4,000
Payments on equipment notes[a]	4,000
Repayment of short-term notes[b]	13,000
Interest[b]	3,000
Income taxes[c]	6,200
Dividends[d]	5,000
Total cash outlays	$432,540

[a]Equipment notes are repayable at the rate of $4,000 per period.
[b]Assumed for purposes of illustration.
[c]Income taxes on earnings of previous period are paid in current period. The amount is assumed in this case.
[d]Dividends at the rate of $.50 per share are declared and paid each period.

EXHIBIT 11

VICTORIA CORPORATION
Receivables and Collections Budget

	Period 1
Accounts receivable, start of period:	
From immediately preceding period (15% of $400,000)	$ 60,000
From second previous period (3% of $380,000)	11,400
Total	$ 71,400
Sales of this period	420,000
Total receivables	$491,400
Collections:	
Current period (85% of $420,000)	$357,000
Previous period (12% of $400,000)	48,000
Second previous period (3% of $380,000)	11,400
Total collections	$416,400
Accounts receivable, end of period	$ 75,000

of a given period normally occur as follows: 85 percent in the period of sale, 12 percent in the next period, and 3 percent in the second period after the period of sale. It would be possible to introduce sales discounts and estimates of uncollectible accounts into the illustration, but they are omitted for simplicity. The accounts receivable at the start of period 1 of $71,400 are shown on the actual balance sheet (column 1 of Exhibit 14). The amount represents 15 percent of the sales of $400,000 of the previous period ($60,000 = .15 × $400,000) and 3 percent of the sales of $380,000 of the second previous period ($11,400 = .03 × $380,000). Collections in period 1 are budgeted at 85 percent of that period's sales ($357,000 = .85 × $420,000, see Exhibit 4), plus 12 percent of the previous period's sales ($48,000 = .12 × $400,000, leaving 3 percent to be collected in period 2), plus 3 percent of the sales of the second previous period ($11,400 = .03 × $380,000).

Cash budget. Cash flow is the lifeblood of any business. No budget is more important for planning purposes than the cash budget, illustrated in Exhibit 12. This budget is significant because it helps management in planning to avoid unnecessary idle cash balances on the one hand, or unneeded, expensive borrowing on the other. Most companies prepare a cash budget rather than a budgeted statement of changes in financial position.

The budgeted amounts for cash outflows and collections from customers are taken from Exhibits 10 and 11, respectively. The other income is made up of interest and miscellaneous revenues. It is estimated to be $2,000 for the period.

Budgeted (pro forma) income and retained earnings statement. All of the previous budget information is pulled together in the budgeted income and retained earnings statement and the budgeted balance sheet. The former is illustrated in Exhibit 13. It is at this stage in the budgeting process that management's attention switches from decision making, planning, and control to external reporting to shareholders. That is, management becomes particularly interested in how the results of its decisions will be reflected in the income statement and balance sheet. Accordingly, the budgeted income statement and

---

EXHIBIT 12

VICTORIA CORPORATION
Cash Budget

Period 1

Cash receipts:	
Collections from customers (Exhibit 11)	$ 416,400
Other income	2,000
Total receipts	$ 418,400
Cash outflows (Exhibit 10)	432,540
Increase (decrease) in cash during period	$ (14,140)
Cash balance at start of period	69,800
Cash balance at end of period	$ 55,660

EXHIBIT 13

VICTORIA CORPORATION
Budgeted (Pro Forma) Income and Retained Earnings
Statement

Sales (70,000 units @ $6).	$420,000
Cost of goods sold (70,000 units @ $4.13)	289,100
Gross margin	$130,900
Selling expense	$ 75,200
Central corporate administrative expense	44,800
Total other operating expenses.	$120,000
Operating income.	$ 10,900
Other income	2,000
	$ 12,900
Interest expense.	3,000
Pretax income	$ 9,900
Income taxes[a]	3,861
Net income	$ 6,039
Dividends	5,000
Increase in retained earnings.	$ 1,039
Retained earnings at start of period	56,500
Retained earnings at end of period.	$ 57,539

[a] Amount assumed for this case.

balance sheet are often prepared in accordance with generally accepted accounting principles.

There is one major item that is likely to be treated differently for decision making, planning, and control purposes as compared to the treatment required under generally accepted accounting principles: the accounting for fixed manufacturing overhead costs. Generally accepted accounting principles require that fixed manufacturing overhead costs be allocated to the units produced. These costs do not become expenses until the period in which the units are sold. Fixed manufacturing overhead costs have been treated as expenses of the period in which the costs were incurred this far.

To prepare a budgeted income statement, retained earnings statement, and balance sheet for Victoria Corporation, we assume that each unit is allocated $.46 (= $32,200/70,000 units) of fixed manufacturing overhead cost. The cost of goods sold is therefore $4.13 per unit (= $3.67 variable cost + $.46 fixed cost).

Compilation of all of the data for the period indicates a budgeted income of $6,039. If top management finds this budgeted result satisfactory, and adequate cash can be made available to carry out the operations as indicated by Exhibit 12, the master budget will be approved. If the budgeted results are not considered satisfactory, much additional thought and many additional meetings will be devoted to considering ways in which the budgeted results might be improved through cost reductions or altered sales plans.

Budgeted Balance Sheet. The final exhibit of this series, Exhibit 14, shows the actual balance sheet at the start of the period and the budgeted balance sheet at the end of the period. Here, as in the budgeted income statement, management will have to decide whether the budgeted overall results will be acceptable. Will cash balances be satisfactory? Is the receivables turnover up to plan? Will the final capital structure and debt-to-equity ratio conform to management's desires? If the budgeted balance sheet and income statement are satisfactory, they will become the initial benchmarks against which actual performance in the ensuing period is checked.

Summary of the master budget. The master budget is a summary of management's plans for the period covered. Preparing the master budget is usually

---

EXHIBIT 14

VICTORIA CORPORATION
Budgeted Balance Sheet

	Start of period 1 (actual)	End of period 1 (projected)
Assets		
Current assets:		
Cash (Exhibit 12)	$ 69,800	$ 55,660
Accounts receivable (Exhibit 11)	71,400	75,000
Finished goods (Exhibit 5)	33,040[a]	33,040[a]
Raw materials (Exhibit 6)	10,000[b]	10,000[b]
Total current assets	$ 184,240	$173,700
Long-term assets:		
Equipment and other long-term assets	460,000	474,000
Accumulated depreciation	(162,000)	(173,760)
Total assets	$ 482,240	$473,940
Equities		
Current liabilities:		
Accounts payable	$ 96,540	$ 96,540
Short-term notes and other payables[c]	41,000	28,000
Income taxes payable (Exhibit 10)	6,200	3,861
Total current liabilities	$ 143,740	$128,401
Long-term liabilities:		
Long-term equipment notes	82,000	88,000
Total liabilities	$ 225,740	$216,401
Shareholders' equity:		
Capital stock ($20 par value)	$ 200,000	$200,000
Retained earnings	56,500	57,539
Total shareholders' equity	$ 256,500	$257,539
Total equities	$ 482,240	$473,940

[a] 8,000 units @ $4.13 per unit ($4.13 = $3.67 variable cost plus $.46 allocated fixed cost).
[b] 10,000 units @ $1.00.
[c] Assumed for purposes of illustration.

a complex, dynamic process requiring the participation of all managerial groups from local plant and sales managers to the top executives of the company. Once the budget is prepared and adopted, it becomes a major planning and control instrument. Master budgets are almost always static budgets; that is, they consider the likely results of operations at the one level of operations specified in the budget. This may facilitate the planning process, but it weakens the effectiveness of the budget as a control device if the scale of operations deviates from the planned level. Under those circumstances, flexible budgets are necessary. Flexible budgets consider the varying amounts of revenues and costs that are appropriate at various levels of operations. The use of flexible budgets is described in more detail below.

USING THE BUDGET FOR PERFORMANCE EVALUATION AND CONTROL

This section shows how actual results are compared with budgets and are derived for performance evaluation. The emphasis is on the use of the budget to control operations, hence only the master budget income statement is discussed.

Comparison of Actual Results with the Flexible and Master Budgets. An overview comparison of the master budget with the flexible budget and with actual results is presented in the following example. This overview ties the results of the planning process that results in the master budget with flexible budgeting, and it forms the basis for analyzing differences between plans and actual results.

Exhibit 15 compares the flexible budget with the master budget income statement for Victoria Corporation. The master budget is based on the income statement in Exhibit 13, from sales through operating income. To review, some of the important amounts are as follows:

Sales price per unit	$6.00
Sales volume per period	70,000 units
Variable manufacturing costs per unit	$3.67
Variable selling costs per unit (2% sales commission plus $.02 per unit shipping costs)	$.14
Fixed manufacturing costs per period	$32,200
Fixed selling and administrative costs per period	$110,200

The flexible budget is based on the actual activity.[2] During period 1, 80,000 units were produced and sold. The difference of $21,900 between operating income in the master budget and the flexible budget is due to this 10,000 unit difference

---

[2]The relevant activity variable is sales volume, because this is an income statement. The relevant activity variable would be production volume if the objective were to compare the flexible *production* budget with the master production budget. Sales and production volumes are assumed to be equal throughout this example.

EXHIBIT 15

VICTORIA CORPORATION
Flexible Budget and Activity Variance

	Flexible budget (based on actual activity of 80,000 units sold)	Activity variance (based on variance in sales volume)	Master budget (based on a prediction of 70,000 units sold)
Sales	$480,000[a]	$60,000 F	$420,000[b]
Less: Variable manufacturing costs....	293,600[c]	36,700 U	256,900[d]
Variable selling and administrative expense	11,200[e]	1,400 U	9,800[f]
Contribution margin................	$175,200	$21,900 F	$153,300
Less: Fixed manufacturing costs......	32,200		32,2C0
Fixed selling and administrative expense	110,200		110,200
Operating income.................	$ 32,800	$21,900 F	$ 10,900

[a]80,000 units sold @ $6.00.
[b]70,000 units sold @ $6.00.
[c]80,000 units sold @ $3.67.
[d]70,000 units sold @ $3.67.
[e]80,000 units sold @ $.14.
[f]70,000 units sold @ $.14.
U denotes "unfavorable" variance.
F denotes "favorable" variance.

in activity from the sales plan of 70,000 units. This amount, which results from the 10,000 unit increase times the budgeted contribution margin per unit of $2.19 (= $6.00 − $3.67 − $.14), is called an *activity* variance or sales volume variance.

What is the meaning of "favorable" and "unfavorable?" Note the use of *F* (favorable) and *U* (unfavorable) beside each of the variances in Exhibit 15. These terms describe the impact of the variance on the budgeted operating income. A *favorable* variance means the variance would *increase* operating income, holding all other things constant. An *unfavorable* variance would *decrease* operating income, holding all other things constant. These terms are not used in a normative sense; thus a "favorable" variance is not *necessarily* good and "unfavorable" variance is not *necessarily* bad. Further note the variable cost variances—both are labeled "unfavorable." Does this reflect unfavorable conditions in the company? Highly unlikely! These are costs that are expected to increase with the increase in sales volume from the planned volume. These differences are labeled "favorable" or "unfavorable." However, attaching any normative meaning to those terms requires investigation of the circumstances causing the variances.

The information presented in Exhibit 15 has a number of uses. First, it isolates the increase in operating income from the master budget caused by the increase in activity over the level planned. Sales variances are usually the responsibility of the marketing department, so this information may be useful feedback to personnel in that department, and it may be informative for evaluating their performance. Second, the resulting flexible budget shows budgeted sales, costs, and operating income *after* taking into account the activity increase, but *before* considering differences in *unit* selling prices, differences in *unit* variable costs, and differences in fixed costs from the master budgets. Assume that the actual results for period 1 are as follows:

Sales price per unit	$6.10
Sales volume for the period	80,000 units
Variable manufacturing costs per unit	$3.82
Variable selling and administrative expense per unit	$.16
Fixed manufacturing costs for the period	$34,000
Fixed selling and administrative expenses for the period	$109,000

Now the actual results can be compared with both the flexible budget and the master budget as shown in Exhibit 16. Columns (5), (6), and (7) are carried forward from Exhibit 15.

Column (1) in Exhibit 16 is calculated from the facts presented above. Column (2) summarizes production and manufacturing variances, which are discussed in more detail later. Column (3) shows selling and administrative variances. Both have been divided into fixed and variable portions, and would be presented in more detail to the managers of centers having responsibility for them. These variances are also called "input variances" because they are deviations in costs and efficiencies.

Variance Analysis. As shown in Exhibit 16, the total variance in operating income from the original plan was $15,700 favorable. The next step is to investigate and analyze those variances to find their cause, to ascertain whether corrective steps need be taken, and to use them for rewarding or penalizing employees, where approriate.

The use of variances fits the *management by exception* philosophy, which is to focus managerial attention on exceptions, or variances, from the norm. The question is how large a variance must be before it should be investigated. The conceptual answer is straightforward: Investigate variances when the benefits from investigation exceed the costs. It is quite difficult to measure such benefits and costs, however, so decisions about the value of investigating variances rely considerably on managerial judgments. (For discussions of statistical methods for variance investigations, see Kaplan [1975] and Baiman and Demski [1980].)

Responsibility for Variances

Marketing. Marketing is usually assigned responsibility for the sales volume (activity), sales price, and selling expense variances. Thus, the marketing department at Victoria Corporation would be assigned the following variances. (For illustrative purposes, assume that one-half of the $1,200 favorable fixed

EXHIBIT 16

VICTORIA CORPORATION
Comparison of Actual to Budget

	Actual (based on actual activity of 80,000 units sold) (1)	Purchasing and manufacturing variances (2)	Selling and administrative expense variances (3)	Sales price variances (4)	Flexible budget (based on actual activity of 80,000 units sold) (5)	Activity (sales volume) variance (6)	Static budget plan (based on a plan of 70,000 units sold) (7)
Sales	$488,000^a			$8,000 F	$480,000^b	$60,000 F	$420,000^c
Less: Variable manufacturing costs	305,600^d	$12,000 U			293,600^e	36,700 U	256,900^f
Variable selling expense	12,800^g		$1,440 U	160^h U	11,200^i	1,400 U	9,800^j
Contribution margin	$169,600	$12,000 U	$1,440 U	$7,840 F	$175,200	$21,900 F	$153,300
Less: Fixed manufacturing costs	34,000	1,800 U			32,200		32,200
Fixed selling and administrative expense	109,000		1,200 F		110,200		110,200
Operating income	$ 26,600	$13,800 U	$ 240 U	$7,840 F	$ 32,800	$21,900 F	$ 10,900

Total variance from flexible budget = $6,200 U

Total variance from budget plan = $15,700 F

^{a}80,000 units sold @ $6.10 per unit.
^{b}80,000 units sold @ $6.00.
^{c}70,000 units sold @ $6.00.
^{d}80,000 units sold @ $3.82 per unit.
^{e}80,000 units sold @ $3.67.
^{f}70,000 units sold @ $3.67.
^{g}80,000 units sold @ $.16 per unit.
^{h}$8,000 favorable price variance × 2% (sales commission).
^{i}80,000 units sold @ $.14.
^{j}70,000 units sold @ $.14.
U denotes "unfavorable" variance.
F denotes "favorable" variance.

selling and administrative expense variance is assigned to marketing and one-half to administration.)

Sales volume.................	$21,900 *F*
Sales price	$ 8,000 *F*
Variable selling expense........	$ 1,600 *U*
Fixed selling expense	$ 600 *F*

Marketing may be credited with the $21,900 *F* sales volume variance. (Sales volume also may be a function of other factors, such as unexpected changes in the market or unexpected changes in competitors' behavior.) This is a contribution margin variance, because it is the difference between unit sales price and the variable cost of each unit sold. While each unit sold generates $6.00 of revenue, each unit has a budgeted, or standard variable production cost of $3.67, a budgeted shipping cost of $.02 per unit, and a budgeted sales commission of $.12 (= 2 percent times $6.00). Thus, the contribution margin expected from each unit is $2.19 (= $6.00 − $3.67 − $.02 − $.12). The *standard* variable cost is used instead of *actual* to avoid mixing the effect of sales volume with variances from standard costs and expenses.

Marketing also may be credited with the sales price variance. Note that the favorable sales price variance of $8,000 is partially offset by the increase in sales commission (2 percent of $8,000 = $160) because of the higher-than-budgeted sales price. The total variable selling expense variance is $3,000 unfavorable, but $1,400 is due to the sales volume variance and $160 is due to the sales price variance. So only $1,440 unfavorable variable selling expense and $600 favorable fixed selling expense remain to be explained.

Administration. Administration is assigned a $600 favorable variance. Administrative variances are often the hardest to manage because, unlike manufacturing costs, administrative expenses are not *engineered*; that is, a well-defined causal relation between administrative input and administrative output rarely exists.

Purchasing. A common method of evaluating the performance of the purchasing department is by the materials price variance [Mautz et. al., 1980, p. 172].

For illustrative purposes, assume that Victoria Corporation actually purchased 81,000 pounds of direct raw materials at $1.05 per pound. Recall that the standard cost was $1.00 per pound. Purchasing would be charged with an unfavorable price variance of $4,050 [= ($1.05 − $1.00) × 81,000 pounds].

Manufacturing. Manufacturing would be charged with the variable manufacturing cost variance that was not assigned to purchasing, or $7,950 unfavorable (= $12,000 *U* − $4,050 *U* assigned to purchasing), and with the $1,800 unfavorable fixed manufacturing cost variance. Variable manufacturing cost variances are often partitioned into a *price* and *efficiency* component. The price component is the difference between the budget, or standard, prices and the actual price paid for each unit of input, whereas the efficiency variance is a measure of the efficiency with which inputs are used to produce output. To demonstrate this point, suppose that Victoria Corporation's $12,000 unfavorable variable manufacturing variance consists of the following (for illustrative purposes, assume that 80,000 units were produced):

	Actual	Standard budget allowed
Direct materials	81,000 lb @ $1.05 = $85,050	80,000 lb @ $1.00 = $80,000
Direct labor	10,100 hr @ $20.50 = $207,050	10,000 hr (= 80,000 units × ⅛ hr) @ $20.00 = $200,000
Variable manufacturing overhead	$13,500	80,000 units @ $.17 = $13,600

The price and efficiency variances for direct materials and direct labor are as follows:

	Price	Efficiency
Direct materials	($1.05 − $1.00) × 81,000 lb = $4,050 U (This variance is assigned to purchasing.)	$1.00 × (81,000 lb − 80,000 lb) = $1,000 U
Direct labor...........	($20.50 − $20.00) × 10,100 hr = $5,050 U	$20.00 × (10,100 hr − 10,000 hr) = $2,000 U

Efficiency variances are based on the differences between the actual quantity of an input used and the standard amount allowed for each unit produced (e.g., one-eighth direct labor hour) times the number of units produced (e.g., 80,000 units). The direct labor efficiency variance in quantities is 100 hours; in dollars it is 100 hours times the $20.00 budgeted per hour labor rate, or $2,000.

In short, a variance report for manufacturing might look like the following:

Variable Manufacturing Costs Variances	
Raw materials: Efficiency	$1,000 U
Direct labor: Price	5,050 U
Efficiency	2,000 U
Variable manufacturing overhead	100 F
Total	$7,950 U
Fixed manufacturing overhead	1,800 U
	$9,750 U

Adding the $9,750 unfavorable manufacturing variance to the $4,050 unfavorable purchasing variance noted earlier gives the $13,800 unfavorable total purchasing and manufacturing variance in column (2) of Exhibit 16.

This overview of manufacturing variances provides the essential calculations for management use of variances. Most companies calculate and analyze variances in much more detail than presented here.

Summary and overview. Exhibit 17 is a diagram of the variances discussed. It breaks down the $15,700 total favorable variance into components and shows their assignment to responsibility centers.

EXHIBIT 17   Victoria Corporation Variance Diagram

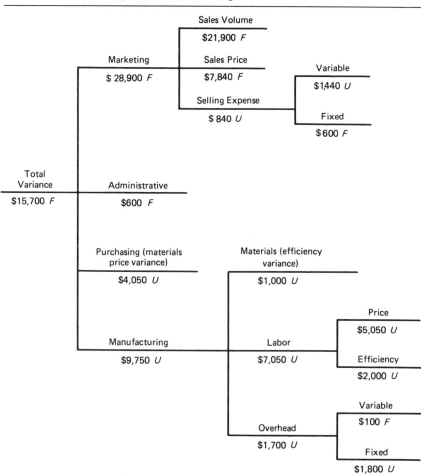

Behavioral Issues in Setting Standards for Budgets. There are two principal factors of concern in setting standards for budgets: (1) the extent of employee participation in setting standards, and (2) the tightness of the standards.

Employee participation. There is an extensive literature, both theoretical and empirical, on the question of if, and to what extent, employees should participate in the setting of standards against which their performance will be evaluated. No clear-cut conclusions can be drawn from the literature to date. An appreciation of the issues involved might be obtained by considering some of the questions that have been addressed in this research:

1. Does participation lead employees to feel that they are a more integral part of an organization and, because of this ego involvement, result in improved performance?

2. Does participation lead merely to greater group cohesiveness among employees, which can then work either to the advantage or disadvantage of the firm depending on the group's feeling about the benefits of the participation?

3. Are the results of participation different in the following two situations?

(a) Employees merely provide inputs to the standard-setting process but have no voice in the actual standards setting.

(b) Employees both supply inputs and participate in setting specific standards.

4. Are the results of participation different depending on the managerial style of supervisors (authoritarian, democratic) and the personality characteristics of employees?

5. Are the results of participation different depending on the educational backgrounds and technical skills of employees and the nature of the tasks (production versus research and development or legal services)?

6. How is participation related to the creation of slack in organizations (a term referring to the difference between the resources available to a firm and the amount necessary to maintain the organization coalition of individuals and groups)?

Interested readers may consult Stedry [1960] or Milani [1975].

Tightness of standards. Standards for performance may be set very loose and be met a large percentage of the time or set very tight and be met only a small percentage of the time. Empirical research tends to suggest that employees underperform when standards are set too loose. Introducing a moderate level of tension by way of tighter standards leads to higher employee motivation and thereby better performance. The principal question, then, is just how tight the standards should be. Two types of standards have been described in the literature: (1) ideal standards, and (2) normal or currently attainable standards.

Ideal standards are those that can be met under the most efficient operating conditions for existing resources (plant, equipment, employees). Ideal standards are used when management feels that such standards provide the best incentive to good performance. Generally, however, empirical research tends to show that standards do not provide an incentive to perform well unless the employee whose performance is measured against the standard perceives the standard to be reasonable and attainable [Stedry, 1960; Holstrum, 1971]. Ideal standards can be criticized, then, because employees may lose initiative for seeking more efficient performance and become discouraged because the standards are seldom achievable.

Normal or *currently attainable standards* are those that can be met under reasonably efficient operating conditions with provision for normal spoilage, rest periods, and other time that is lost because of, for example, normal machine breakdowns. Normal standards are, by definition, those that management can reasonably expect, but stringent enough so that workers who achieve them have reason to be satisfied with their performance.

It is difficult to generalize as to how tight standards should be. All that can be said is that there are dangers in setting the standards too loose or too tight. Standards that are currently attainable but sufficiently tight to motivate employees are probably best. Such standards are easy to define in principle. It takes a wise and capable management to translate them into effective performance norms in practice.

PERFORMANCE MEASUREMENT AND CONTROL IN DECENTRALIZED ORGANIZATIONS

The remainder of this chapter deals with performance measurement and controls in decentralized units. Delegation of managerial duties is common in all but very small organizations. The major advantages of delegation are as follows:

1. Delegation allows local personnel to respond quickly to a changing environment.
2. Delegation frees top management from detailed operating decisions.
3. Delegation divides large, complex problems into manageable pieces.
4. Delegation helps train local managers and provides a basis for evaluating their decision-making performance.
5. Delegation motivates. Ambitious managers are likely to be frustrated if they only implement the decisions of others.

Delegation has disadvantages, however. Local managers may make decisions that are not "congruent" with the preferences of top management. Thus, organizations incur costs of monitoring and controlling the actions of local managers and other employees. In this section we discuss some of the methods available for monitoring and controlling employees in decentralized organizations.

Criteria for Divisional Performance Measurement.[3] Control systems are likely to be more effective if a quantitative measure can be designed that captures the relevant aspects of performance. This statement is equally applicable in the case of divisional performance control. What are the desirable dimensions of a divisional performance measure?

One desirable attribute is that the measure provides a common basis for comparing and evaluating the performance of divisions operating in widely different geographical and product markets. This is critical from the standpoint of top management. Because a principal goal of all divisions is generating profits, the measure commonly used is based on divisional income or profits.

A second desirable attribute is that the divisional performance measure be as independent as possible from performance achieved in other parts of the company. This attribute is desirable so that responsibility can be pinpointed and divisional managers can be held accountable only for activities over which

---

[3]The term "division" is used by different companies to mean different things. Some companies use the term to refer to segments organized according to product groupings, whereas other companies use it in reference to geographical areas served. We use the term "division" to refer to a segment that conducts both manufacturing and marketing activities. It therefore constitutes a *profit center* because it has responsibility for both revenues and expenses.

they have some degree of control. A divisional performance measure will not be independent if a portion of one division's costs or part of the central corporate headquarters costs are allocated to another division. If the division had no control over these costs, then they should not affect top management's evaluation of the division's performance.

A third desirable attribute is that the divisional performance measure indicate as closely as possible the contribution the division makes to company-wide results. This contribution may be somewhat different from the amount over which the division has control. One obvious example is the salary of the divisional manager. The amount of the salary is likely to be determined by top management and therefore not be controllable by the division manager. It is a necessary cost, however, that must be covered before the division can contribute to the profits of the company and should, therefore, be included in any performance measure. Another example relates to interdivisional conflict. Suppose that a division purchased materials externally rather than buying from a division having idle capacity, and by purchasing externally, the profits of the two divisions together are less than if the materials had been purchased internally. Should the performance measure for each division reflect the results of its actual transactions? Or should the cost of idle capacity in the one division be charged against the profits of the other division? There are no easy answers to these questions. Top management needs to be informed of situations where actions of individual divisions are detrimental to overall company performance.

Return on Investment as the Performance Measure. Given that one of the principal goals of the divisions is to contribute to the profits of the company, it is not surprising that divisional income is commonly used as a measure of performance. Divisional income by itself, however, does not provide a basis for comparing the performance of various divisions. For example, the fact that division A had income of $50,000 does not necessarily mean that it was more successful than division B, which had income of $40,000. The difference between these profit levels could be attributable entirely to a difference in the size of the divisions. Some means must therefore be used to scale the divisional profit amounts. The most common approach is to divide divisional income by some measure of the amount of capital invested in the division. The result is referred to as divisional return on investment, or ROI, and is calculated as follows:

$$\text{Divisional Return on Investment (ROI)} = \frac{\text{Divisional Income}}{\text{Divisional Investment}}$$

If the investments of division A and division B in the preceding example were $500,000 and $250,000, respectively, then the ROIs would be 10 percent (= $50,000/$500,000) and 16 percent (= $40,000/$250,000). Thus, division B was more successful given its investment base than was division A, even though division A generated a larger absolute amount of profit.

There are several important questions that must be answered before ROI can be applied as a control measure:

1. How are revenues measured, particularly when part of a division's output is transferred to another division rather than being sold externally?

2. Which expenses are deducted in determining divisional income—only those that are controllable by the division or also a portion of central corporate expenses?

3. How is investment to be measured—total assets or net assets, at historical cost or current replacement cost?

These questions are considered in the sections that follow.

Transfer Pricing. In cases where, because of the nature of the product, none of a division's output can be sold to another division and all of the output is therefore sold externally, there are few unique revenue measurement problems beyond those encountered in financial accounting. That is, accounting policy questions must be made regarding whether revenue will be recognized as production takes place, at the point of sale, or as cash is collected. The only concern with the measurement of divisional revenues in this case is that all divisions follow the same accounting methods, thereby enhancing the comparability of the measures of ROI.

In cases where one division's output can be or is sold to another division, we are confronted with what is called the *transfer pricing problem*. The "price" assigned to the interdivisional transfer of goods or services represents a revenue of the selling division and a cost of the buying division.[4] Should the transfer price be set equal to the manufacturing cost of the selling division? Or should the transfer price be the amount at which the selling (buying) division could sell (purchase) the good or service externally? Or should the transfer price be a negotiated amount somewhere between the selling division's cost of manufacturing and the external market price?

A superficial consideration of the transfer pricing problem might suggest that the selection of a transfer price is of little consequence. After all, what comes out of one corporate pocket goes into another. This simplistic viewpoint ignores the fact that the amount of the transfer price may affect certain divisional decisions, which in turn affect the overall profitability of the company. For example, suppose that a transfer price is set at $10 per unit and there is no external market for the product. If the buying division feels that this price is too high, it may take less than it would at a lower price. In this case the buying division may be doing what is best from the standpoint of its own profitability, but the actions of the two divisions together may not be best for the company as a whole. The

---

[4]Only rarely will cash equal to the transfer price actually change hands. Transfer prices are set primarily so that performance of the selling division can be assessed as of the time of the transfer rather than waiting several periods until all manufacturing is completed and the good is sold to someone outside of the company. Even then it would be necessary to divide the income among the several divisions that participated in producing and selling the good.

simplistic view of the transfer pricing problem also ignores the real possibility that a transfer price arbitrarily set by central corporate headquarters may undermine the entire divisional organizational structure. Division managers are supposed to be free, within limits, to make manufacturing and marketing decisions as if they were separate companies. If the return, or profit, from a significant portion of its operations is dictated by the transfer price imposed by top management, the division manager may become frustrated and the benefits of divisionalization will be lost. The selection of an appropriate transfer price can therefore have a significant impact.

On what basis should a transfer price be selected? The goal should be the selection of a transfer price that maximizes the profits of the firm as a whole. An effective transfer pricing scheme will also lead to maximizing divisional profits. Where company-wide and divisional profitability are in conflict, the best interests of the company's owners require attending to overall company profits.

In the sections that follow, we consider several types of transfer prices and discuss the conditions when each type might be appropriate. It is sufficient to point out here that there is no single type of transfer price that satisfies the goal, or ideal, in all cases.

Cost-based transfer prices. One possibility is to base the transfer price on the actual average unit cost of the selling division. This measure is subject to numerous criticisms, however. First, average unit costs will fluctuate from month to month in response to changes in costs. This will require the buying division continually to reassess how much it is willing to purchase from the selling divisions, making production planning decisions more difficult. Second, for a highly automated division, average cost can fluctuate widely in response to changes in volume. This is because the fixed costs are spread over a varying number of units. Thus, production-level decisions by the selling division will affect the profitability of the buying division. Third, transfer prices will be affected by changes in efficiency in the selling division, so that gains and losses in efficiency will be passed on to other divisions. For example, suppose that the selling division is able to reduce average unit cost by more efficient routing of work through the manufacturing process. The benefits of this reduction are passed on to the buying division by way of a lower acquisition cost (i.e., transfer price), with a related improvement in the buying division's ROI. The improved efficiency would not be reflected in the selling division's ROI. There is an even more important criticism of average unit cost in the case of losses in efficiency. If management of the selling division knows that all costs can be passed on in the transfer price, there may be little incentive to control costs or improve efficiency. A fourth criticism of using average unit cost as a transfer price is that it does not permit the selling division to show a return, or profit, on goods or services sold to other divisions (i.e., revenue = costs). This creates an incentive for the selling division to market its products externally rather than supplying them to another division. It also creates incomparability in the ROIs across divisions, depending on the extent that interdivisional transfers of goods or services take place.

The use of standard, rather than actual, costs will minimize the effects of the first three criticisms above. Standard costs will be less volatile so that transfer prices can remain constant for longer periods. Also, gains and losses in efficiency are not passed on to the buying division. However, the selling division will report a profit only if it is able to produce at less than standard cost. Thus, the use of standard cost as a transfer price is subject to the fourth criticism above.

There are some benefits of using a cost-based transfer price. In situations where there is no external market, it may be the only objective basis for setting a transfer price. This might occur, for example, where the output of one division is a semiprocessed product requiring additional work by a buying division. Information on the cost of manufacturing a product also provides a basis on which the buying and selling divisions can negotiate a transfer price, an approach to be discussed after the use of market prices is considered.

Market prices as transfer prices. The use of an external competitive market price meets most of the requirements of an ideal system. First, use of a market price implies the existence of an external market. Divisions are free to transact either among themselves or in the external market, thereby increasing the freedom of the divisions. Use of a market price also helps assure profit independence of the divisions. Any gains or losses in efficiency of the selling division do not get passed on to the buying division. Use of competitive market prices is also relatively free from argument, thereby saving administrative costs.

Market prices, however, are not always the ideal transfer prices. In some instances, market prices do not exist. Some of the benefits mentioned above, such as profit independence and attribution of gains and losses in efficiency to the selling division, will therefore be reduced. This is likely to be the case for unique products passing between divisions in semiprocessed form.

Probably the most important criticism of a policy of using market prices is that it may lead to decisions by divisions that are not in the best interests of the company as a whole. Permitting divisions to sell and purchase externally rather than internally results in additional transaction costs from entering the market twice. These costs would be saved if the divisions dealt with each other. To reflect these additional transaction costs, some firms set the transfer price equal to the external market price but reduce it by an estimate of the normal transaction costs. Another case where use of market prices can lead to less than optimal decisions occurs when short-run market demand exceeds the supply available at prevailing prices. For example, assume that a selling division has the capacity to produce 100,000 units per year and can sell these units either to another division within the firm or on the external market. Market demand is such that if the buying division does not purchase at least 75,000 units from the selling division, it will have to curtail its operations significantly. In this situation it is in the best interests of the firm for the selling division to supply the needed units to the buying division rather than to have the selling division indifferent as to its customer. The external market price must be adjusted somehow to induce the intracompany transfer.

A major problem in using market prices arises when market price exceeds variable cost of the selling division and the selling division has unused capacity. Under these circumstances, firm-wide profits can be maximized only if the buying division buys all of its needs from the selling division. If there is no cost-saving advantage in buying from the selling division, the motivation of the buying division to do so is reduced. Under these circumstances, negotiated transfer prices may be required.

Negotiated transfer prices. Transfer prices based on cost represent a lower limit on the price that selling divisions are willing to accept. Transfer prices based on market prices represent an upper limit on the price that buying divisions are willing to absorb. The difference between these two prices is the total margin on the transfer. Many firms permit divisional managers to negotiate among themselves as to how the margin is to be split. If both divisions are free to deal either with each other or in the external market, then the negotiated price will likely be close to the external market price. If all of a selling division's output cannot be sold on the external market (i.e., a portion must be sold to the buying division), then the negotiated price will likely be less than the market price and the total margin will be shared by the divisions. The use of negotiated transfer prices is consistent with the concept of decentralized decision making in divisionalized firms.

One of the principal disadvantages of negotiated transfer prices is that significant time may be required by the divisions to carry out the negotiating process. Also, interdivision hostility may result, which could hurt overall company performance.

As we mentioned previously, no particular transfer pricing scheme is best in all circumstances. The choice revolves around such factors as the degree of market competition, the relationship between short-run supply and demand, the extent top management chooses to interfere in divisional decisions, and other factors.

Measuring Divisional Expenses. The computation of divisional ROI requires that certain expenses be deducted from divisional revenues to obtain divisional net income. Four types of expenses are considered: (1) controllable direct expenses, (2) noncontrollable direct expenses, (3) controllable indirect expenses, and (4) noncontrollable indirect expenses.

Controllable direct expenses. Expenses in the first category include those that are traceable directly to, and are controllable by, the division. Raw materials used in manufacturing the division products, salaries and wages of manufacturing and marketing personnel within the division, and depreciation on the division's equipment are examples of expenses that are likely to be controllable and direct. There is little question that these expenses should be deducted from revenues in determining divisional income. It may be desirable, however, to report variable and fixed expenses separately on the divisional income statement. This possibility is discussed later in the chapter.

Noncontrollable direct expenses. The salary of the divisional manager is an example of a noncontrollable direct expense. Top management generally controls the amount of this expense item. From the standpoint of top management, this expense is a necessary incremental cost of operating a division and one that must be covered if a division is to contribute to the profits of the whole company. These expenses should therefore be deducted in determining divisional income.

Controllable indirect expenses. Costs incurred at central corporate headquarters, called common costs, indirectly benefit all divisions within the firm.

These common costs can be classified into two groups: (1) costs of central corporate administration, such as the president's salary; and (2) costs of providing centralized services, such as data processing, product development, and training. Costs in the first group are largely beyond the control of the divisions. Costs in the second group are at least partially controllable by the divisions to the extent that they have discretionary use of the services of these centralized service departments.

A response to the question about whether or not the costs of centralized service departments should be allocated to the divisions will likely revolve around the extent to which the divisions have the choice of either using the centralized services or acquiring similar services from an external source. If decision making is fully decentralized, the divisions will have this choice. In this case, the divisions should be "charged" for the use of centralized services just as if the services were purchased externally. The divisional net income of one division should not be higher than another simply because the first division uses centralized services and the second division acquires the services externally.

In situations where divisional managers are required to use centralized services, the question of whether the costs of providing these services should be allocated to the divisions becomes more complex. The division manager may resent such an allocation because there is no opportunity for going outside if the "charges" become too high. Also, the total amount of centralized costs to be allocated to the divisions depends on the amount of services required by other divisions, as well as certain top-management decisions as to minimum levels of service capacity that will be maintained regardless of demand. Thus, the costs are largely noncontrollable by the division manager. From the viewpoint of top management, the centralized service departments are maintained for the benefit of the divisions. The decision to operate such departments was probably made after considering the costs of decentralizing these services into the divisions as well as the costs of acquiring the services externally. Centralization was selected because it was the least costly or most efficient alternative for the company as a whole. Because these are incremental, although somewhat indirect, costs of operating divisions, top management will argue that these costs should be allocated to the divisions.

Whether or not these costs are allocated will likely revolve around the behavioral reactions of division managers. Top management must communicate the reasons for such allocations to the division managers and indicate just how assessments of divisional performance will be affected by the allocations. Some companies calculate divisional net income both before and after allocations of centralized service department costs. The preallocation figure plays a heavier role in evaluating the month-to-month performance of the divisions. The divisions, however, are expected over longer periods to have a positive margin after allocation to ensure that the central service costs are being adequately covered.

Once a decision has been made to "charge" the divisions for centralized services, the next question concerns the amount to be charged. Most companies do not treat their centralized service departments as profit centers. That is, the amount charged to the division is based on the costs incurred by the service departments. Treating the service departments as cost centers, rather than as profit centers, is based on the rationale that the service departments are operated to provide support to the divisions and not to generate profit. The amount charged, or the transfer price, is therefore based on cost. The costs are allocated to the divisions using an allocation base that varies most closely with the cost item. For example, data processing costs may be allocated based on computer time used. Training costs may be allocated based on the number of employees hired per year. Use of a cost-based transfer price here is subject to many of the same criticisms as the transfer pricing scheme discussed earlier. As a means of inducing service departments to control the amount of costs incurred, some companies charge the divisions for the standard, rather than actual, costs of the services.

Noncontrollable indirect expenses. The considerations that bear on the question of allocating centralized service department costs have little relevance in the case of noncontrollable indirect expenses. Divisions cannot control the amount of top management's attention that is given to individual divisions, general corporate policy, and external relations. There are no equivalent "acquire internally–acquire externally" decisions that divisions must make. Different arguments must be offered for and against allocation of central corporate expenses.

The most frequently cited arguments against allocation relate to the divisions' inability to control the amount of costs incurred and to the arbitrary allocation bases that must be used. For example, on what basis should the president's salary be allocated to the divisions—sales, number of employees, square footage of space used? Any allocation base is likely to be meaningless. It will be difficult for top management to evaluate division managers effectively if the divisional net income figure includes elements that are both controllable and noncontrollable by the managers being evaluated.

The most frequently cited argument for allocation is that, unless these costs are allocated to the divisions, the divisions will underprice their products and cause the firm as a whole to operate at a loss. That is, the revenues generated by the divisions will be insufficient to cover both the direct expenses of the divisions and the indirect expenses incurred at central headquarters. This argument is not particularly convincing in the short run. Prices are likely to be constrained by competitive market conditions. These prices will be the same whether central corporate expenses are allocated or not. Over the long run, these central corporate expenses must be covered by the divisions and a stronger case can therefore be made for allocation. As a basis for evaluating the month-to-month performance of divisional managers, however, attention should be directed to the divisional contribution to coverage of central corporate expenses and profit (i.e., divisional income before allocation of central corporate expenses). If divisions seek to optimize this divisional contribution amount, they will also optimize divisional income after allocation of central corporate expenses, however they may be allocated.

Measuring Divisional Investment. As we pointed out earlier, it is inappropriate for top management to evaluate divisional performance by simply comparing net income across divisions. If this is done, the larger divisions are likely to look better. It is desirable to scale the divisional income amounts to recognize differences in the size of the divisions. Most companies use some measure of capital employed, or invested, in each division. Our concerns in this section are (1) what assets are to be included in the investment base, and (2) what basis of valuation is to be used.

Assets included in the investment base. Two guidelines can be suggested in selecting assets to be included in the investment base. First, consistent with the use of divisional net income as the numerator of ROI, the assets included should be those for which divisions have significant control. For assets physically located in a division and used only in the division's operations, there is little question that they should be included. More difficult problems arise with respect to assets shared with other divisions (e.g., a manufacturing plant) and assets acquired by centralized services departments (e.g., equipment used in personnel training). Where reasonable bases can be obtained for allocating shared assets, they should be included in the investment base. For example, the cost of a shared manufacturing plant might be allocated between divisions based on square footage used. Where only highly arbitrary allocation bases are possible, it is best not to attribute common investment facilities to the divisions. For example, equipment used in personnel training is probably best left unallocated.

The second general guideline for selecting assets to be included in the investment base is consistency. Whatever base a firm selects, it should follow it consistently across time and across divisions. This will at least stabilize the effects of any biases in the investment base.

Valuation of assets in the investment base. Once a decision has been made regarding which assets are to be included in the investment base, a monetary amount must be assigned. Most firms use acquisition cost as the valuation basis. The necessary amounts can be obtained directly from the company's records and accounts. Also, this valuation basis is consistent with the measurement of cost of goods sold and depreciation expense in the numerator of ROI.

The use of book values of assets, particularly fixed assets, in the denominator of ROI can have undesirable results. A division with old, low-cost, and almost fully depreciated assets may be reluctant to replace the assets with newer, more efficient, but more costly assets. (Replacing old assets with new ones decreases the numerator—income—of the ROI calculation because of increased depreciation charges. It also increases the denominator—cost of total assets—of the ROI calculation. These two effects combine to reduce calculated ROI.) If use of book values in the investment base does have this effect on divisional investment behavior, there are at least two possible ways to deal with the problem. One is to state all assets gross, rather than net, of accumulated depreciation. Assets will therefore be stated at their full acquisition cost regardless of age. Another approach is to state assets at their current replacement cost in new condition. In this case, the investment base will be stated at the same amount whether or not the division replaces the old assets. Use of either acquisition cost or current replacement cost of assets in new condition, however, does not provide an accurate measure of the capital invested in the division. The best approach here, as in previous cases, is to select the measurement methods that most accurately reflect performance, effectively communicate the reasons for using these measurement methods to divisional personnel, and then apply them consistently over time. If there is a ready market for used assets of the type in use, the current disposal (exit) value of the assets is probably the single best measure for these purposes.

Interpreting Divisional ROI. In previous sections we have discussed some of the factors to be considered in calculating ROI. In this section we discuss several additional considerations in using and interpreting ROI as a basis for evaluating divisional performance.

Single versus multiple ROIs. We suggested that a firm should settle on the way it is going to calculate ROI and then use it consistently. There is a tendency, however, to place too much emphasis on this single statistic. This is particularly a problem when the divisional performance report is being used for several different purposes. In this section, we suggest a format for a divisional performance report based on the ROI measure that can be used for several different purposes. Exhibit 18 presents a divisional performance report in the suggested format.

Sales and divisional expenses. The statement distinguishes between sales to outsiders and those to other divisions. The purpose of this distinction is to show the extent to which the division is dependent on orders from other divi-

---

EXHIBIT 18   Suggested Format for a Divisional Performance Report[a]

		Dollars	ROI
Revenues:			
Sales to outside customers.............................		$XXX	
Sales to other divisions		XXX	
Total revenues...................................		$XXX	
Less controllable expenses:			
Variable direct	$XXX		
Variable indirect.................................	XXX	XXX	
Contribution margin		$XXX	
Fixed direct	$XXX		
Fixed indirect	XXX	XXX	
Equals controllable profit margin....................		$XXX	XX.X%
Less noncontrollable direct expenses		XXX	
Equals divisional contribution to central corporate expenses......................................		$XXX	XX.X%
Less allocated share of central corporate expenses.....		XXX	
Income before income taxes		$XXX	[b]
Less income taxes		XXX	
Net income after income taxes.....................		$XXX	[b]

[a]The actual performance report should include columns for both budgeted and actual amounts.
[b]An ROI measure is inappropriate here, because it is difficult to allocate the cost of shared central corporate facilities to each of the divisions in a meaningful way.

sions for its business. The statement also indicates the variable and fixed cost structure under the control of the division. This information might be used for breakeven and other cost-volume-profit analysis.

Profit margins. The controllable profit margin and the corresponding ROI are measures of the return generated from decisions made within the division. The controllable profit margin and its corresponding ROI are the best measure for evaluating the performance of the division manager. When noncontrollable direct expenses, such as the division manager's salary, are deducted from the controllable profit margin, we obtain the division's contribution to central corporate expenses and its corresponding ROI. These are the best measures for top management to use in evaluating a division (as contrasted to the division manager) in relation to other divisions and to the company as a whole.

Allocation of central corporate expenses. We suggested earlier that it is undesirable to allocate central corporate expenses to divisions if the purpose is to obtain a measure for evaluating divisional performance. Divisions do not have control over these costs and, therefore, should not be held accountable for them. However, divisional personnel must be conscious of the need to provide a positive contribution margin to the coverage of central corporate expenses and to profits. One means of communicating this to divisional personnel is to show on the performance report the relationship between the division's contribution and the amount which top management feels is an equitable share of central corporate expenses.

In addition to subtracting a share of central corporate expenses, some firms also deduct an amount for interest on the capital used by the division. This is typically a charge for implicit, rather than explicit, interest, because no cash payments are made by the division. Instead, the charge represents a minimum desired rate of return that the division should generate. Inclusion of this implicit interest indicates to the division the relationship between the divisional return, or contribution, and the amount expected by top management.[5]

To illustrate, assume that the divisional contributions to profit earned by division A and division B are $100,000 and $120,000, respectively, and that the investment of both divisions is $500,000. If top management expected a return of 14 percent on the capital employed, the divisions' income after interest on capital would be computed as in Exhibit 19. After interest imputation, the relative performance of divisions can appear somewhat different from before the imputation.

Allocation of income taxes. One question that has not been considered is the treatment of income taxes. In the vast majority of cases, income taxes are assessed on the taxable income of the company as a whole rather than on each division. Should these income taxes be allocated to individual divisions?

There are two principal arguments for interdivisional allocation of income taxes. First, managers should be encouraged to make decisions keeping in mind the income tax consequences. For example, consideration should be given to

---

[5]Solomons [1965, pp. 63ff.] refers to divisional income after subtracting a charge for the use of capital as "residual income."

EXHIBIT 19   Inclusion of Implicit Interest Charge in Divisional ROI Calculation

	Division A	Division B
Divisional contribution to profits	$100,000	$120,000
Interest on capital employed, .14 × $500,000	(70,000)	(70,000)
Divisional income (= residual income)	$ 30,000	$ 50,000
Return on investment after interest imputation:		
$30,000/$500,000	6%	
$50,000/$500,000		10%
Return on investment without interest imputation:		
$100,000/$500,000	20%	
$120,000/$500,000		24%

---

the investment tax credit, the tax savings from depreciation deductions through accelerated cost recovery, and the tax consequences of selling versus trading in old equipment in capital budgeting decisions. To the extent that division managers have authority to make these types of decisions, they should be held accountable for the income tax consequences. Second, Congress has granted income tax incentives for firms to invest in certain risky industries (e.g., oil exploration). The decision by a firm to organize a division to operate in such an industry must have taken these income tax incentives into consideration. Because these income tax benefits were considered by top management when it developed its expectations about the profitability of the division, they should be considered when management evaluates the division's performance.

The arguments against allocation are similar to those against allocating central corporate expenses. The amount of income taxes assessed is often beyond the control of divisional managers. In addition, the amount of income taxes that would be paid on divisional income if it were a separate taxable entity may be different from the amount actually assessed when it is aggregated with income of other divisions. For example, a limit is placed on the amount that can be deducted for charitable contributions. If one division contributes more than the maximum in a given year, and income taxes are assessed on the division, it will be unable to deduct the excess contributions in determining taxable income. However, as long as other divisions contribute less than the maximum, the full amount of the division's contributions will be deductible when aggregated at the company-wide level. Thus, the income taxes of one division are not independent of income generated by other divisions.

If, for a particular firm, the arguments against allocation are stronger, our suggested divisional performance report would end with "Income before Income Taxes." If, on the other hand, the arguments for allocation are stronger, the income taxes would probably be placed under controllable expenses. Our placement of income taxes at the bottom of the report is a compromise between the two positions. Recognition is given to the fact that allocation of income taxes is as difficult as that for central corporate expenses. However, it emphasizes to division managers the importance of income taxes in decisions and the need that they be covered before profits are generated for the owners.

Separating return on investments. The rate of return on investment can be separated into profit margin and asset turnover components.

$$\text{Return on Investment} = \text{Profit Margin Percentage} \times \frac{\text{Investment Turnover}}{\text{Ratio}}$$

$$\frac{\begin{array}{c}\text{Controllable Profit}\\\text{Margin (or other}\\\text{divisional income}\\\text{measure)}\end{array}}{\text{Divisional Investment}} = \frac{\begin{array}{c}\text{Controllable Profit}\\\text{Margin (or other}\\\text{divisional income}\\\text{measure)}\end{array}}{\text{Divisional Revenues}} \times \frac{\begin{array}{c}\text{Divisional}\\\text{Revenues}\end{array}}{\begin{array}{c}\text{Divisional}\\\text{Investment}\end{array}}$$

To illustrate the usefulness of separating the ROI, assume the following information about division A:

Year	Sales	Net income	Investment
19X0......	$1,000,000	$100,000	$ 500,000
19X1......	2,000,000	160,000	1,000,000
19X2......	4,000,000	400,000	2,500,000

The ROI for each of the 3 years and the associated profit margin percentages and investment turnover ratios are shown below.

Year	ROI	=	Profit margin percentage	×	Investment turnover ratio
19X0......	20%	=	10%	×	2.0
19X1......	16%	=	8%	×	2.0
19X2......	16%	=	10%	×	1.6

The profit margin percentage provides information for assessing divisional management's ability to combine inputs to generate outputs. That is, various cost inputs (materials, labor, depreciation) are combined to generate revenue outputs (sales of goods and services). The profit margin percentage indicates the portion of each dollar of revenue that is in excess of the costs incurred. It is often used as a measure for assessing efficiency in producing and selling goods and services. The profit margin percentage for division A in the example above decreased from 10 percent to 8 percent between 19X0 and 19X1. Because the investment turnover ratio remained the same between the two years, it appears that the decrease in ROI is caused by an inability to control costs or an inability to raise selling prices as costs have increased, or both.

We indicated earlier that divisional income is divided by investment as a means of scaling divisions of different size so that their performance measures are more comparable. When ROI is disaggregated, however, useful information can be obtained on how effectively the capital invested in the division has been used. The investment turnover ratio indicates the dollars of revenue that the division was able to generate for each dollar of invested capital. Returning to the example above, division A was unable to increase its ROI between 19X1 and 19X2, despite an increase in its profit margin percentage, because its investment turnover ratio decreased. The division was unable to generate $2 of revenue for each dollar invested in 19X2 as it had done in previous years.

More useful information is likely to be provided by studying profit margin percentages and investment turnover ratios for a given division over several periods than by looking at these ratios for all divisions in a particular period. This is caused by the fact that some divisions, because of the nature of their activities, require more capital than others. For example, a division involved in manufacturing and selling heavy equipment is likely to require more capital than one selling management consulting or advertising and promotion services. The investment turnover ratios of these two divisions are inherently likely to be quite different and not a cause of concern for top management. A significant change in the ratio of either division between two periods, however, may signal the need for corrective action. For example, a significant decrease in investment turnover for the manufacturing division may indicate excess capacity and suggest disposal of some facilities.

Setting minimum desired ROIs. If the ROI is to serve as an effective measure for controlling divisional performance, a standard, or desired, rate must be set each period. Some firms merely use the actual ROI of the preceding period as the standard. This is common practice where top management emphasizes trends or changes in ROI over time. Use of the actual ROI of a preceding period as a standard is subject to several important criticisms. Past performance might have been poorer than it should have been. Improvement on poor performance may still not be satisfactory. Moreover, even if past performance was considered satisfactory, conditions might have changed in such a way that what was satisfactory for the last period may not be satisfactory for this period.

Another approach is to specify a minimum desired ROI for each division, given their particular operating characteristics. One company [Hughes, 1970, p. 56], for example, computes a minimum rate of return for various classes of divisional assets and then aggregates to obtain a required ROI. Fixed assets are required to generate a return of 22 percent, inventories 14 percent, and accounts receivable 7 percent. If a division had $500,000, $400,000, and $100,000 invested on average in these three types of assets, respectively, its minimum required ROI would be 17.3 percent {= [(.22 × $500,000) + (.14 × $400,000) + (.07 × $100,000)]/($500,000 + $400,000 + $100,000)}. Specifying a different rate of return is an attempt to adjust for different degrees of risk from investing in each type of asset.

Summary of Control Systems in Decentralized Organizations. We have discussed the most important factors to be considered in designing a divisional control system. The variety of ways of treating transfer prices, central corporate expenses, income taxes, the investment base, investment valuation, and other variables may be unsettling. It must be emphasized, however, that there is no single "correct" way to calculate ROI or any other divisional performance measure. Each firm must design the performance measure to suit its particular needs. The most critical factor to keep in mind is that a balance must be maintained between divisional decision-making autonomy and top management concern for the welfare of the company as a whole.

BIBLIOGRAPHY

Baiman, S., and J. Demski, "Variance Analysis Procedures as Motivational Devices," *Management Science*, vol. 26, no. 8 (August 1980), pp. 840–848.

Brealey, R., and S. Myers, *Principles of Corporate Finance* (McGraw-Hill Book Company, New York, 1981).

Hertz, D. B., "Risk Analysis in Capital Investment," *Harvard Business Review*, vol. 42 (January–February 1964), pp. 95–106.

Holstrum, G., "The Effect of Budget Adaptiveness and Tightness on Managerial Decision Behavior," *Journal of Accounting Research*, vol. 9, no. 2 (Autumn 1971), pp. 268–277.

Hughes, D., "The Behavioral Aspects of Accounting Data for Performance Evaluation at Burlington Industries, Inc.," in T. Burns (ed.), *The Behavioral Aspects of Accounting Data for Performance Evaluation* (Ohio State University College of Administrative Science, Columbus, 1970).

Kaplan, R., "The Significance and Investigation of Cost Variances: Survey and Extensions," *Journal of Accounting Research*, vol. 13, no. 2 (Autumn 1975), pp. 311–337.

Mautz, R., W. Kell, M. Maher, A. Merten, R. Reilly, D. Severance, and B. White, *Internal Control in U.S. Corporations* (Financial Executives Research Foundation, New York, 1980).

Milani, K., "The Relationship of Participation in Budget-Setting to Industrial Supervisor Performance and Attitudes: A Field Study," *The Accounting Review*, vol. 50, no. 2 (April 1975), pp. 274–284.

Solomons, D., *Divisional Performance Measurement and Control* (Financial Executives Research Foundation, New York, 1965).

Stedry, A., *Budget Control and Cost Behavior* (Prentice-Hall, Englewood Cliffs, N.J., 1960).

CHAPTER 40

Accounting for

the Rate-Regulated

Enterprise

Richard N. Hildahl
Partner, Ernst & Whinney

GENERAL CONSIDERATIONS

Accounting practices for rate-regulated industries are founded on the same principles as those that govern financial reporting in general. Nevertheless, because rate regulation requires specific practices different from those used by nonregulated companies, regulatory accounting may be considered a specialized field in itself.

To understand the practices used in regulatory accounting, however, it is necessary first to understand three basic conditions that give rise to these practices. First, rate regulation exists because the regulated companies have economic and operating characteristics that set them apart from other business enterprises. Second, rate regulation in many instances prescribes the accounting practices to be followed by the regulated industry. Third, because regulators rely on accounting data in the process of evaluating and setting rates charged for services by the regulated enterprises, regulatory accounting not only *reports* the results of the company's operations, but can actually *influence* those results.

Characteristics of the Rate-Regulated Enterprise. In general, rate regulation is applied by government to those industries whose services involve the public interest, but exhibit extreme economies of scale. Because efficient production requires a single "natural monopolistic" supplier, the normal forces of the competitive marketplace cannot operate freely to regulate supply, demand, and pricing. These industries, usually electric, gas, telephone, and water companies, are termed public utilities and are traditionally subject to rate regulation by federal, state, or local agencies. Though the industries differ from each other in many ways, and individual companies within each industry may also differ, all share a particular set of economic characteristics:

1. They are natural monopolies; that is, a single large firm serving a given market can provide more service more efficiently at a lower average cost than could several smaller firms competing in the same market. The natural monopoly is also capital intensive and characterized by relatively high fixed costs (depreciation, interest, insurance, and property taxes).

2. Their customers have few, if any, alternatives to the essential service provided by the utility.

3. They often deal in a single service.

4. Their services are generally nonstorable or storable only to a highly limited degree.

5. They are often site restricted by the physical and economic characteristics of their assets.

Clearly, any number of non-rate-regulated entities may exhibit one or more of these characteristics; a public utility is generally so classified only when it exhibits the full set. Frequently, however, when a nonutility industry displays several of these characteristics, government may become concerned about the ability of competition to regulate those activities and may apply some form of rate regulation, though the form and intensity of the regulation may vary widely according to the industry and to economic and historical considerations. Even among traditional utilities, the form and degree of rate regulation may change over time as a result of economic or technological developments. Later, this chapter discusses special considerations for rate-regulated, but nonutility, enterprises.

Traditional public utility rate regulation, however, is centered on the costs of providing the utility service. That is, utility rate making seeks, as its primary objective, to compute the total amount of revenue a company must realize from its operations to meet its short- and long-term needs. At the same time, it is also seeking to provide efficient service to all customers at rates that regulators will deem "just and reasonable."

To achieve this objective, most utility commissions consider the company's total revenue requirements as the total of the operating expenses, depreciation, and taxes, plus a percentage return on the company's investment in its facilities. This procedure may be stated as an equation called the standard rate-making formula:

Revenue Requirement = Rate Base × Rate of Return
+ Income Tax Allowance + Operating Expense + Depreciation

Influences of Rate Regulation on Accounting Practices. Rate regulation, which results in the regulation of a utility's revenues, directly affects accounting practices, because the regulators rely heavily on the company's accounting information. Therefore, the manner and completeness with which that information is presented for rate-making purposes will often determine the amount of the allowed revenue requirement.

Further, however, many regulatory commissions also have direct authority over the regulatory accounting practices of the companies within their jurisdictions. Thus the regulatory accountant must comply with agency requirements, often at both state and federal levels, and, insofar as the regulated entity engages in financing, with requirements of the Securities and Exchange Commission or, where appropriate, state agencies.

The regulators use accounting data to evaluate the fairness of rates charged by a particular enterprise and, in some cases, to determine appropriate rates of return on investment for the regulated industry as a whole. Therefore, a primary concern is that accounting practices be substantially uniform throughout each regulated industry. Also, in order to evaluate rates proposed by a particular enterprise, regulators compare that enterprise's operations with those of other enterprises offering similar services. Hence, comparability of accounting data is a second major concern.

Of course, uniformity and comparability are major concerns for financial reporting in nonregulated industries as well. But because regulatory accounting information is used for rate making as well as for financial reporting, the accounting uniformity and comparability required by regulators may differ significantly from that required by generally accepted accounting principles (GAAP). Accounting information required by one regulatory agency may even differ from that required by another agency. To ensure both uniformity and comparability in the accounting systems of regulated companies, most regulatory agencies require the use of *uniform systems of accounts* (USOAs) and compliance with interpretive orders pertaining to those systems. For electric and gas utilities, uniform systems have been issued by both the National Association of Regulatory Utility Commissioners (NARUC), and for those companies regulated at the national level, by the Federal Energy Regulatory Commission. These systems are virtually identical, and most state regulatory commissions adopt one or the other.

State and municipal agencies regulating water utilities frequently prescribe the NARUC system developed for that industry, and most telephone companies follow the USOAs issued by the Federal Communications Commission (FCC). The FCC requires USOAs for all telephone utilities with interstate operations, and these have been generally adopted for intrastate operations as well. Although USOAs differ according to the nature of the industries for which they were developed, they share many common characteristics. Most group companies by size into classes A through D, usually based on gross revenues; requirements for smaller companies are less complicated. All uniform systems are quite detailed, with specific instructions for using each account.

When necessary, interpretations are issued by NARUC (Interpretations of Uniform Systems of Accounts for Electric, Gas and Water Utilities) and by the chief accountants of the federal commissions (Accounting Releases). These interpretations at the federal level are frequently adopted on the state and local levels as well.

The accounts included in any USOA are similar to those that might be used by a nonregulated company, except that, in general, there are more of them and their use is more closely restricted. An excerpt from the FCC USOA for class A telephone companies illustrates the level of detail required in recording maintenance expenses:

§31.604 Repairs of central office equipment.
   (a) This account shall include the cost of repairing central office equipment.
   (b) This account shall include also the pay and expenses of plant department forces engaged in maintaining and operating equipment for producing electricity for transmitting traffic and operating signals.

ITEMS
(Note §31.01-8)

Adding acid and water to batteries and reading specific gravity, current drain, and voltage of batteries.
Cleaning equipment.
Disconnecting and reconnecting customers' lines in central offices for temporary periods of nonuse or for nonpayment of bills.
Disconnecting customers' lines in central offices due to termination of service.
House service. (Note also account 707.)
Lubrication, adjustment, and cleaning of power equipment, including the lubrication and cleaning of drive motors and driving mechanism in panel offices.
Operating prime movers, generators, and motors.
Reading and recording information from message registers and traffic load counters located in central offices.

Rearranging and replacing frame cross-connection wires. (See also Note A to this account.)

Removing sediment from storage batteries and the cost of repairing storage batteries, including replacement of minor items.

Repairing used central office equipment for reuse.

Replacement of central office dry cell batteries.

Replacing minor items of central office equipment, including labor and material used and the removal and recovery of the items retired less salvage recovered, except when such items are replaced through the replacement of retirement units. (Note also §31.2-25.)

Starting, stopping, and watching operation of power equipment.

Supplies, such as acid, caustic soda, cheesecloth, commutator paste, dry cells, electrolyte, kerosene, oil, and waste.

Tools and other individual central office equipment—items of small value or short life, cost and repairs of. (Note also §31.2-20(d).)

Training employees for central office repair work.

Underlining switchboard jacks, renewing switchboard markings, and placing and changing number plates and designation strips, not incident to construction. (See also Note C to this account.)

NOTE A: The cost of work on central office frames incident to routine station and line turnover and growth, including the placing, removing, or rearrangement of cross-connections (including the cost, less salvage, of the cross-connection wire, heat coils, protector blocks, etc.), and the opening and closing of lines on the frame, may be currently charged direct to this account and, before the close of the calendar year, adjustment made between this account and account 221 for the net increase in central office investment or between account 221 and account 171 for the net decrease in such investment, due to increase or decrease in lines.

NOTE B: The pay and expenses of test-board men and other employees in central offices engaged in testing circuits in connection with the maintenance of plant, such as testing with station repairmen, cablemen, etc., shall be charged to account 603. Similar costs in connection with construction projects shall be included in the telephone plant account appropriate for the class of plant tested.

NOTE C: The pay of clerks of the traffic department when engaged in such work shall be charged to account 624. The cost of placing number plates, designation strips, making switchboard markings, and similar work in connection with central office construction shall be included in account 227. (Note also §31.6-63.)

NOTE D: The cost of power produced for house service purposes shall be charged to account 707 or other account, as may be appropriate.

NOTE E: The cost of electricity purchased and the cost of coal, gas, gasoline, oil, and other fuel used in the generation, conversion, and storage of current for transmitting traffic and operating signals shall be included in account 610. [FCC, Maintenance Exp. Account 602:1.]

In addition, the nature of rate regulation requires that the regulatory accountant follow cost allocation procedures far more detailed and complicated than any normally used by nonregulated business. In all areas, successful operation under regulation demands the most thorough record keeping available to a company on a cost-effective basis.

Effects of Accounting Practices on Results of Operations. Because regulators rely on accounting data in evaluating rates and in determining a utility's revenue requirement, accounting for rate-making purposes must reflect:

All costs associated with the provision of a particular service,

All appropriate costs incurred in relation to every construction project, and

All significant time delays involved in the receipt of revenues and payment of expenses.

If these elements are not completely reflected and supported, the regulatory commission may see the company's operations as more profitable than they actually are and may set rates too low to permit the company's continued financial well-being.

Although a realistic picture of any company's economic status is also a goal of GAAP, such accuracy is particularly important in the regulated setting, where regulators have direct control over an entity's rate levels and ultimate profitability. To understand clearly how accounting practices can influence a utility's results of operations, it is necessary to outline briefly the general utility rate-making methodology.

HOW UTILITY RATE MAKING WORKS

Traditionally, public utilities have been regulated according to a basic rate base rate-of-return methodology. This methodology, as noted earlier, equates a company's total revenue requirement with the total of operating expenses, depreciation, and taxes, plus a percentage return on the company's total investment in its facilities,[1] using the basic formula:

Revenue Requirement = Rate Base × Rate of Return
+ Income Tax Allowance + Operating Expense + Depreciation

The total investment is commonly termed the "rate base." Because the amount of the company's investment in its property in service (less depreciation) often forms more than 90 percent of the rate base on which the company is allowed to earn a return, it is imperative that *all* property be fully reflected in the plant accounts and that its valuation be reported as realistically as possible. This unusual emphasis on property investment helps create the major differences between regulatory accounting procedures and financial accounting procedures.

The determination of the rate base is made on the basis of a specific "test period," historically the most recent 12-month period for which complete records are available. This test period is then adjusted or "normalized" to reflect known and measurable changes that will occur during the period for which the proposed rates will be in effect.

---

[1] This rate-making concept was first expressed in *Smith v. Ames* (1898), 169 U.S. 466 (U.S. Supreme Court), and, although challenged on various occasions, has governed the actions of most regulatory agencies to the present day.

All components of the rate base are scrutinized in terms of the test period. When the company's total investment in property has been computed, rates are established that are intended to allow the utility an opportunity to recover all its costs plus a reasonable percentage return on its investment. This percentage is termed the "allowed rate of return." It may vary considerably, but it is established for each company by the regulatory commissions according to general industry guidelines, comparisons with earnings in nonregulated industries, and, sometimes, considerations of circumstances unique to the particular company.

Exhibit 1 illustrates the working of the major elements of the rate-making process.

Rate Base. One of the most difficult tasks facing a regulatory commission is determining the proper rate base, that is, the appropriate value of the company's investment in its property and plant. Property and plant include both tangible and intangible items. Tangible items include land and land rights, rights of way, and buildings and equipment used for production, transmission, administration, and distribution. Intangible items may include such items as fees, franchises and licenses, patents, organizational expenses, and legal fees.

EXHIBIT 1

PACIFIC GAS AND ELECTRIC COMPANY
Gas Department
PACIFIC GAS TRANSMISSION COMPANY
Cost of Service
Test Year

Line no.	Item	Staff (A)	Utility (B)	Utility exceeds staff (C)	Percent (D)
			(in thousands of dollars)		
1.	Operating expenses	$ 8,220	$ 8,485	$265	3.2%
2.	Maintenance	2,505	2,601	96	3.8
3.	Depreciation	10,534	10,534		
4.	Ad valorem taxes	1,381	1,381		
5.	Income taxes	6,124	6,124		
6.	Payroll and other taxes	312	312	___	___
7.	Total expenses	$29,076	$29,437	$361	1.2%
8.	Return	10,792	10,792	___	___
9.	Total cost of service	$39,868	$40,229	$361	.9%
10.	Less allocation to Northwest Pipeline	(1,167)	(1,178)	(11)	.9
11.	Cost to PG&E	$38,701	$39,051	$350	.9%

EXHIBIT 2

40-8

PACIFIC GAS & ELECTRIC COMPANY
Gas Department
Weighted-Average Depreciated Rate Base
Test Year

Line no.	Account no.	Item	Staff (A)	Utility (B) (in thousands of dollars)	Utility exceeds staff Amount (C)	Utility exceeds staff Percent (D)
1.		Total weighted-average gas plant	Weighted-average gas plant $2,268,147	$2,374,933	$106,786	4.7
		Working capital				
		Materials and supplies:				
2.		Production fuel	$ 17	$ 17	$ 0	0.0
3.		Other	14,196	14,196	0	0.0
4.		Current gas underground	206,224	206,224	0	0.0
5.		Gas line pack	4,849	4,849	0	0.0
6.		Prepaid gas	0	39,393	39,393	0.0
7.		Working cash allowance	42,769	51,077	8,308	19.4
8.		Gas exploration	0	0	0	0.0
9.		Conservation capital	0	64,170	64,170	0.0
10.		Total working capital	$ 268,055	$ 379,926	$111,871	41.7
		Adjustments				
11.		Customer advances for construction	$ -40,121	$ -40,121	0	0.0
12.		Accumulated deferred taxes on income	-228	-228	0	0.0
13.		Deferred investment tax credit	-6,642	-362	$6,280	-94.5
14.		Total adjustments	$ -46,991	$ -40,711	$6,280	-13.4
15.		Total working capital and adjustments	$2,489,211	$2,714,148	$224,937	9.0
		Deductions				
16.		Weigted-average depreciation reserve	$ 842,129	$ 840,614	$ -1,515	-0.2
17.		Total deductions	$ 842,129	$ 840,614	$ -1,515	-0.2
18.		Total weighted-average depreciated rate base	$1,647,082	$1,873,534	$226,452	13.7

All of these items are appropriately capitalized as part of the company's investment in property, according to the general rule that the expenditure must have a service life of more than 1 year. Because of the influence of the rate base in determining the allowed return, most prescribed USOAs stipulate precisely all cost components to be properly reflected in the Property and Plant accounts.

Other components frequently included in the rate base are as follows:

Plant held for future use. This component includes such items as land acquired in advance of planned expansion projects. If the use is to occur after some time period arbitrarily set by the regulators, this component is sometimes disallowed from the rate base.

Working capital components. Although this investment generally represents a small part of the rate base, controversies sometimes arise over precise items to be included. In general, working capital for *regulatory* purposes includes the average amount of capital, apart from other rate base items, to bridge the time lag between the expenditure of funds needed to provide service and the receipt of revenues from that service. This definition of working capital clearly differs from the usual accounting definition, that is, the difference between current assets and current liabilities. Other working capital components can include:

Inventories. Three categories, fuel, materials and supplies, and construction materials in inventory, are generally included in rate base because they represent a permanent investment, even though actual dollar amounts vary over time.

Prepayments not recognized elsewhere.

Bank balances.

Miscellaneous rate base items: leasehold improvements, acquisition adjustments (debit or credit differences between the actual purchase price of a property and its value as determined by regulators), and extraordinary retirements (property retired from service long before it is fully depreciated).

Exhibit 2 presents the components of a gas utility's rate base as it was presented to the California Public Utilities Commission.

Valuation of Property in the Rate Base. Because the regulated company's investment in property represents by far the largest portion of its rate base and because the value of the rate base ultimately determines how much the regulated company will be permitted to earn (provided that there are no major competitive constraints as well), historically there has been much controversy among regulators, courts, and regulated companies about the most appropriate methods for determining the current value of property. The two measures most widely used historically have been the *original cost* method and the *fair value* method. Individual regulatory commissions generally choose one of these methods, based on the precedential "end-result" doctrine formulated in the Hope Case [*Federal Power Commission v. Hope Natural Gas Co.*, 320 U.S. 591 (1944)]. This doctrine holds that a regulatory body may choose either method in any given case provided that the method used produces results that are fair to the consumer and reasonable for the investor.

The original cost method is now most widely used. In the case of purchased property, the value is listed as the cost of the property at the time it was first dedicated to public service. Thus, if a regulated utility purchases property from another utility, the accountant must record the property's cost to the company that *first* used it for public service, no matter what the present owner paid for it. Any difference between the purchase price of the property and its original cost is recorded separately as an "acquisition adjustment." This adjustment may be partially or fully included in the rate base according to the practice of the particular agency having jurisdiction and the facts and circumstances surrounding the specific acquisition. Acquisition adjustments were adopted in the 1930s to eliminate the practice by some companies of transferring assets at inflated prices to boost rate base and increase allowed returns.[2]

Whenever a company has been engaged in a construction project rather than a purchase, a major component of the revenues will be an allowance for funds used during construction (AFUDC), which, for a utility, includes an allowance for the cost of both debt funds *and* equity funds devoted to the project during construction. Construction Work in Progress (CWIP) has generally been excluded from the rate base on the basis that it does not affect the provision of service to current customers. However, current conditions for many utilities, such as major new power projects, require such an enormous investment in construction at current high costs of capital that capitalized AFUDC can range to 70 percent and more of reported net income. Some regulators now believe that consumers are better off paying for these financing costs now rather than paying additional financing costs over the life of the assets. As a result, some commissions now allow CWIP in the rate base while discontinuing capitalization of AFUDC.[3]

The following schedule presents the current FERC formulas for the computation of AFUDC:

$$A_i = s\left(\frac{S}{W}\right) + d\left(\frac{D}{D + P + C}\right)\left(1 - \frac{S}{W}\right)$$

$$A_e = \left(1 - \frac{S}{W}\right)\left[p\left(\frac{P}{D + P + C}\right) + c\left(\frac{C}{D + P + C}\right)\right]$$

---

[2]For further information on acquisition adjustments, refer to Bonbright [1961, pp. 175–178 and 216–218].

[3]U.S. Federal Power Commission Amendments to Uniform System of Accounts for Public Utilities and Licenses and for Natural Gas Companies (Classes A, B, C, and D) to Provide for the Determination of Rate for Computing the Allowance for Funds Used during Construction and Revisions of Certain Schedule Pages of FPC Reports, U.S. FPC Order No. 561, U.S. FPC Order No. 561A.

The components of the formula are as follows:

A_i = allowance for borrowed funds used during construction rate
A_e = allowance for other funds used during construction rate
S = average short-term debt
s = short-term debt interest rate
D = average long-term debt
d = long-term debt interest rate
P = average preferred stock
p = preferred stock cost rate
C = average common equity
c = common equity cost rate
W = average construction work in progress balance

The original cost approach to determining rate base is used by most federal jurisdictions, and by latest estimate, 45 states.[4] Its popularity is due largely to the fact that original cost amounts are readily accessible and easily documented.

An original cost rate base, however, contains no provision for the effects of operating in an inflationary economy. Any adjustments for the effects of inflation must therefore be reflected in the rate of return allowed on the rate base. Opponents of original cost methodology argue that the high percentage rates of return necessary to reflect inflation properly also produce an inflated and distorted picture of the company's earnings. For example, a 23 percent rate of return (including a 10 percent inflation adjustment) on an original cost rate base makes a regulated company appear more profitable than would a 13 percent rate of return on a rate base that already contains an inflation adjustment in its property valuation.

Critics of the original cost methodology frequently advocate some form of "fair value" rate base, by which the regulated company's property is valued either at "replacement cost" (the cost of constructing facilities of identical capacity using current technology and equipment) or at "reproduction cost new" (the cost of reproducing identical facilities at current market prices). Proponents of these approaches contend that the resulting rate base would more accurately reflect the costs of doing business in the contemporary economic environment and that the resulting lower rates of return granted on this rate base would reflect the company's financial health more realistically.

This controversy resembles current discussions in the financial accounting community over application of current cost accounting methods for financial reporting. In both cases, a major problem is the difficulty involved in arriving at the current value of property, especially in areas where technology has changed rapidly. Questions arise as to the most appropriate indices and to the

---

[4]The ICC still uses what is basically a "fair market value" approach to some of the industries it regulates as do a few state jurisdictions. NARUC annually publishes a report on utility and carrier regulation where current trends can be observed.

best means for achieving consistency, uniformity, and comparability within individual industries and in comparing different industries.

Test Period Cost of Service. In addition to receiving a fair return on its investment or rate base, the regulated entity is entitled to recover in rates to customers all reasonable and necessary costs involved in providing service. In order to ensure that proposed rates will enable the company to recover its costs, a means must be found to measure those costs. For this purpose regulators generally prescribe the use of a test period to be used in measuring the results of operations. The two key questions involved in this process are these:

1. What time period will be used as a measure?
2. What revenues and expenses will be allowed in determining operating income for the test period selected?

Three basic types of test periods may be used, either separately or in various combinations: (1) the historical average test year, usually the most recent 12-month period for which complete records are available; (2) the year-end approach; and (3) the projected future test year.

Generally the same test period used for determining the cost of service will also be used for determining the rate base. One instance in which this approach would not work would be when using a year-end investment rate base along with the operating results from the preceding 12 months, unadjusted to match the year-end investment. Such a combination could produce a significant mismatching, because the rate base at the end of the period could contain major additions intended only for future use.

Such a mismatch is sometimes retained to offset regulatory lag in cases when the company's earnings are declining. Such declines, called attrition, result when a company experiences rapid plant growth and increased costs due to that growth and to inflation, while still operating under rates fixed during a previous time period when costs were lower.

Historical test year. The historical average test year traditionally was the most common approach to measuring cost of service. This approach is based on a presumption that the conditions under which the company operated during the test year will remain constant during the period for which proposed rates will be in effect. As noted above, it generally uses the most recent 12-month period for which complete financial data are available. Rate base is computed for each month using a basic 13-month averaging approach (the beginning and end of each number for a year) and is thus compared to earnings. Cost of service, including expense, depreciation, taxes, and return, is prepared in conjunction with this average rate base, based primarily on recorded results for that period.[5]

Because, however, the rates proposed on this basis are to be in effect for a future time period, the historical period must be adjusted, or "normalized," to

---

[5]The NARUC publication, *Annual Report on Utility and Carrier Regulation,* is an excellent reference for ascertaining those items that various state agencies will allow in rate base.

reflect as well all measurable expenses known and expected to occur during the time the rates will be effective. For example, if a labor contract is scheduled to expire during the succeeding period and will be renegotiated on a higher basis, that increased cost will be included in the normalized test year. Thus, by including such measurable future costs, the historical test year can be made more representative of the near future and ensure that future costs will be recovered in rates.

The advantages of this system are that it depends on recent actual data easily obtained and that it can consistently relate investment to operating results. Its major disadvantage is that it depends on past conditions for measuring future revenue needs. Although adjustments are permitted for known and measurable changes in costs, regulators tend to object to estimates and to disallow extensive adjustments to the test year. In a rapidly changing economic environment, increased costs tend to outrun the provisions made for them, so that it is not uncommon that new rates become insufficient to cover costs even a few months after they become effective. Thus a regulated entity may consistently find itself in a "catch-up" position, in which it never fully makes up for earnings lost due to attrition and regulatory lag.

Year-end test period. The "year-end" approach has an advantage over the historical test year in that it minimizes the time lag between the test period and the application of new rates. Although it uses historical data as far as possible, it also allows more extensive adjustments.

A major difference between this approach and the historical test year is that new property added during the test year is included in rate base, and, if that property will also produce additional revenues, some jurisdictions include the projected revenues and expense in estimating financial results. Thus the final picture of the results of operation is somewhat more future-oriented than that produced by the historical test year.

Projected future test period. The use of a projected or future test period varies in use according to jurisdictions. Regulators in general oppose using a totally projected test year because it relies too heavily on budget estimates and projections and is difficult to verify. However, as projection techniques become more sophisticated and regulators become more familiar with their reliability, this resistance is beginning to erode.

Many agencies now accept partially projected test periods—that is, test periods that begin a few months before proposed new rates are filed and end several months after the filing. Thus the regulators have the advantage of seeing actual financial results for the first part of the test period and projections for the remainder, both for revenues, expenses, and the rate base. This approach retains some of the advantages of verifiability while still recognizing the volatility of the current business environment and minimizing attrition due to regulatory lag. A number of regulatory commissions are currently experimenting with alternative techniques to recognize timely changes in cost patterns.[6]

---

[6]Examples include the FERC's proposal in the TAPS case for a variable tariff methodology and the National Energy Board of Canada classes of rate cases, which allow for expedited proceedings if controversial items are not involved. The California Public Utilities Commission is experimenting with similar plans.

Cost-of-Service Components. In determining a regulated entity's cost of services and revenues, regardless of the type of test period used, regulators must consider the following components and determine what sorts of normalization adjustments to each component shall be required: revenues, operating expenses, depreciation and amortization, income and other taxes, unusual or nonrecurring expenses, capitalized general and administrative expenses, and management and intercompany fees.

For example, revenues may be representative of the test period used and of normal conditions. However, depending on the business cycles applicable to a particular company or a particular industry, adjustment may be required to match revenues of the test period with usage levels as measured for rate base determination. Other adjustments may be necessary to reflect rate changes during the test period, major changes in customer number and composition during and after the test period, variations in consumption that occur in cycles larger than the period covered by the test year, abnormal weather conditions, revenues unbilled at the end of the period or recorded at the beginning of the period but representing previous sales, or any extraordinary or nonrecurring items. An increasingly important phenomenon is the recognition by regulatory commissions of "demand curtailment" by consumers as a result of escalating prices.

Operating expenses. Operating expenses normally allowed by regulators are those provided for in the USOAs pertaining to the particular industry. Items not included in the USOA are generally considered on a case-by-case basis and are deemed includible by regulators only as the regulated company is able to provide supporting documentation. Current examples of such costs could include accruals for decommissioning of facilities and for environmental restoration requirements.

Depreciation. Depreciation is a major element in cost of service because of the capital-intensive nature of utilities. Utilities generally have developed highly sophisticated methods for computing this element.[7] Although many companies use accelerated depreciation for tax purposes, regulators almost universally apply straight-line depreciation for rate-making purposes because it is considered the most reasonable means of allocating investment costs over generations of ratepayers.

Because public utilities' assets generally consist of mass property (numerous like assets with homogeneous life characteristics), regulatory authorities have historically prescribed that regulated companies use straight-line group depreciation practices. Under these practices, the straight-line depreciation rate for a category of investment may be defined as

$$\text{Depreciation Rate} = \frac{100\% - \text{NS/OC}}{\text{ASL}}$$

where NS represents net salvage (gross salvage less cost of removal), OC represents original cost, and ASL is the estimated average service life of the property.

---

[7]For further information, refer to the National Association of Regulatory Utility Commissioners, *Depreciation Practices for Small Telephone Utilities* (NARUC, Washington, D.C., 1975).

With the unit plan of depreciation, a gain or loss on the disposal of an asset is recognized in the year of retirement. Group depreciation practices, however, explicitly take net salvage into consideration in the depreciation rate. When the asset is retired from the group, the cost of removal is debited and the gross salvage proceeds are credited to the accumulated depreciation account.

Under average service life conventions, a weighted-average life for the group is developed. This group may be defined as all assets or all assets placed in a given year (vintage group). Or the vintage group may be further subdivided into groups of assets having expected equal lives (equal life groups). The average service life is then developed by weighting all of the groups by their respective lives and summing.

Amounts allowed are sometimes restricted to those actually recorded for the test period. In other cases, a company may be allowed to adjust for a full year's depreciation on year-end property. Additional adjustments may be made to reflect changes in the depreciation rate when these occur during or shortly after the test period.

Income taxes. Appropriate regulatory treatment of income taxes has been especially controversial in recent years, particularly regarding the proper rate-making treatment of permanent tax savings produced by the investment tax credit (ITC) and the tax timing differences that result from using accelerated depreciation for tax purposes (ADIT).[8] It is sufficient to note for this discussion that the objective is to provide an allowance for income taxes that will permit a reasonable opportunity for the utility to earn the allowed rate of return *after* income taxes.

Other. Miscellaneous items that are sometimes, but not normally, included in cost of service for a regulated enterprise are charitable contributions, merchandising costs, and unusual nonrecurring items.

Rate-of-Return Considerations. The beginning of this section discusses the fact that, if regulatory agencies use typical, utility-type rate-making methodologies, the total revenue requirement will include a profit component. This profit component is called a *return,* and it is usually computed by multiplying some measure of the investment in assets by the allowed rate of return. In general, regulated companies are allowed to recover costs of operation and to earn an additional return component that covers the cost of capital used to support the investment in the regulated enterprise.

Regulated companies often require large amounts of capital from investors before operations can begin. Investors would be unwilling to supply funds unless they could expect to receive compensation for the use of their funds, as they have alternative invesment opportunities. If funds are to be attracted from investors, then regulated companies must compete successfully with the alternatives available to investors. That is, regulated companies must be able to provide returns that are commensurate with the risks that investors must bear.

---

[8]For further discussion of these issues, refer to the FERC's Order No. 144, a major rulemaking proceeding: U.S. Federal Energy Regulatory Commission, Tax Normalization for Certain Items Reflecting Timing Differences in Recognition of Expenses or Revenues for Rate-Making and Income Tax Purposes: Final Rule, U.S. FERC Order No. 144.

Methods of ascertaining a fair rate of return vary widely among regulatory agencies and industries. The rate of return allowed results in a ceiling on prices of services. Regulated companies must still bear business risk, and it is possible that, because of various economic circumstances, the companies are unable to earn the returns that are permitted by agencies.

Whatever specific method a particular regulatory body may use for determining an appropriate rate of return for either a company or an industry, there are, nevertheless, certain general criteria. Legal requirements prohibit any regulatory agency from establishing rates that are confiscatory in nature. Decisions of the U.S. Supreme Court establish legal guidelines, and, the most commonly cited cases are the *Bluefield*[9] and *Hope*[10] cases. The criteria established for determining the reasonableness of returns allowed for equity investors are described below.

The return should be high enough to maintain credit availability and confidence in the financial integrity of the company.

The return should allow the company to attract additional capital at reasonable terms.

The return should provide the enterprise and its investors with an opportunity to earn a return on the value of used and useful property commensurate with the returns available on alternative investments with similar risks.

In measuring the allowed rates of return, regulators generally consider the capital structure of a regulated company. Debt capital provides specific contractual rates of interest; hence, it is not difficult to measure the return on existing debt. If additional borrowings are anticipated, however, then the allowed returns would need to be sufficient to cover interest obligations that might be unknown at the time rates are set. Therefore, the allowed returns often depend on the proportion and terms of both existing and anticipated debt in the capital structure.

Besides debt, a regulated company will have other classes of long-term capital in its structure. Preferred stock usually carries specific contractual dividend rates. The rate of return to be allowed for common stock is one of the most controversial issues in rate determination. There are various techniques used to measure appropriate rates of return, but many involve comparisons to other firms considered to be of comparable risk. Once the comparison firms are established, there are some specific methods used to estimate fair rates of return. Some of the most commonly used techniques are described below.

Comparable earnings. Under the comparable earnings method, the earnings achieved by the comparison firms are used as a guideline for measuring allowed returns.

Discounted cash flow analysis. Using market prices, dividend yields, and various assumptions, a discount rate is computed that would make the present value of dividends equal the current market price of the stock.

---

[9] *Bluefield Water Works & Improvement Co. v. West Virginia Public Service Commission,* 262 US 679, 692-3 (1923).

[10] *Federal Power Commission v. Hope Natural Gas Co.,* 320 US 591, 88L ed. 333; 51, PUR (NS) 192, 200, 201 (1944).

Risk premium analysis. Under the risk premium analysis method, a risk measure is estimated for a company by a variety of techniques. The allowed rate of return is then set by adding a premium to the returns offered by low-risk alternative investments such as government bonds.

Each method has advantages and disadvantages, and much of the eventual allowed return depends on the judgment of regulators.

Rate Design Considerations: Cost Allocation Problems.

After overall revenue requirements have been set, a utility must establish the proportions of the requirement to be recovered in rates from each service jurisdiction and each class of customer.

Most rate-regulated industries must provide services to a wide range of customer classes: large and small industries, commercial organizations of various sizes, public service organizations, small businesses, and residential customers. Regulation requires that service rates be set as "equitably" as possible for each class of customer while at the same time producing overall returns that meet the revenue requirements of the company. Clearly, it would be inequitable for a company to charge identical rates to all customers receiving uneven levels of service, yet it would be impossible to design individual tariffs for each.

One basic principle applied in developing a rate structure is known as the *cost causer/cost payer* concept; that is, regulators hold that proper rate design will produce rates to each individual class of customers that are proportionate to the costs of serving that class. This principle was articulated by the FCC in Docket No. 18128, relating to the American Telephone and Telegraph Company, Long Lines Department.

Implementation of this principle involves two basic phases: dividing customers into appropriate classes and groups, and allocating costs related to each group. For example, a regulated company may first divide its customers into broad classes, usually "industrial," "commercial," and "residential." Then, depending on the nature of services provided, the company may further divide these classes into groups, usually based on volume and type of usage. For example, an electric utility may subdivide its residential customers into groups using electric water heaters, electric heating, and so on, on the basis that these services have certain costs associated directly with them or are of particular value to its customers.

The second phase, of particular relevance for accounting purposes, is the proper allocation of costs among customers. In addition to allocating costs to their appropriate time periods, it is also necessary to allocate all investment and operating costs to the particular services and users with which they are associated. Because most facilities are shared by various groups and classes of customers and costs cannot be assigned directly, they are generally allocated based on percentage of use measurements. This is a complex procedure whose success depends heavily on the quantity and quality of property records maintained by the regulated company. A typical utility will be more or less complex according to the size of the utility, the range of services provided, and the variety of customers within the service area.

Operating expenses, depreciation, and taxes are frequently not allocable directly to any particular group of customers. Therefore, depreciation and accumulated depreciation, for example, are usually assigned first by the category of plant to which they apply and then included in the allocation of plant cost by customer group.

Factors commonly applied in the allocation process include demand (capacity) costs, commodity (variable) costs, and customer costs. Demand costs are associated with plant investment and represent the level of operation necessary to meet maximum service requirements. Maximum service levels must be used even if they are not required at the time of allocation, because the cost of maximum service continues in order to have plant capacity available when needed. Declining customer usage does not decrease these costs. For example, an electric plant must be able to generate enough power to meet peak demand levels even during times of the day and seasons of the year when usage is relatively low. These fixed costs are usually allocated by customer class on the basis of each class's level of use during the peak demand periods, and can be measured in various ways.

Commodity or variable costs are related to functions that change according to usage of the system. Fuel and power expenses, for example, are incurred only when a system is in use. They can easily be allocated according to which customers are using the system at a particular time and to what degree they are using it.

Customer costs pertain to such items as administrative and billing costs and are thus closely related to fixed costs. They are usually assigned to customer classes according to the ratio of customers in each class to the total number of customers served.

Many regulated enterprises operate in dual jurisdictions—at both the federal and state levels. The telephone industry is a good example. Interstate long-distance rates are regulated by the FCC, whereas state long-distance rates and local exchange rates are regulated at the state level. Thus major telephone utilities are required to "separate" their plant and costs between the dual jurisdictions and in many instances between the services they provide. These requirements significantly influence the level of detail in utility accounting practices. Many other considerations affect individually regulated companies: the nature of a particular industry, the geographic area it serves, the economics of that area, and its demographics.

Summary. This brief description of the rate-making process indicates that regulatory accounting should reflect the results of actions of the regulators in order to present fairly the results of operations. For example, if a nonregulated enterprise abandoned a plant, it would be written off immediately for financial reporting purposes. For a utility under similar circumstances, where a regulatory commission approved the construction initially and then approved the abandonment because of changes in demand and permitted future recovery of the costs, the utility may set up a deferred charge and amortize such costs over future periods. The regulatory body's action has produced future rights for the utility that should be reflected on the financial statements. This example illustrates the essence of regulatory accounting.

SPECIAL CONSIDERATIONS FOR REGULATORY ACCOUNTING

New technologies, the effects of an inflationary economy, and changing degrees and kinds of economic regulation make regulatory accounting a dynamic field. The accountant in a regulated enterprise must continually keep abreast of many conditions that can affect the health of the company and alter the financial effects of its accounting methods.

This section explains the conceptual basis under GAAP that allows for the special considerations of regulatory accounting. Our discussion begins with an analysis of the Financial Accounting Standards Board's Statement of Financial Accounting Standards (SFAS) No. 71, *Accounting for the Effects of Certain Types of Regulation* [FASB, 1982].

As an example, we shall discuss AFUDC. A presentation of financial statements follows.

FASB Statement No. 71. The major document available to the regulatory accountant for preparing general-purpose financial statements is the FASB's SFAS No. 71, which gives guidance for public utilities and certain other rate-regulated companies.

The Statement applies primarily to public utilities that provide services or products subject to rate setting by independent, third-party regulators. The rates must be set to recover the utility's specific costs, and be chargeable to and collectible from customers, not the regulator itself.

SFAS No. 71 generally endorses the principal accounting practices that those entities currently follow. Several of its key points are as follows:

It requires, if the rate-setting process for a regulated enterprise gives assurance that incurred costs will be recovered eventually, that those incurred costs be deferred until the corresponding revenues are recognized.

Regulated enterprises must charge refunds to current income when these amounts can be estimated, instead of retroactively adjusting income in the year they were collected.

If rates are set to cover future costs, current receipts must be recorded as liabilities until their associated costs have been incurred.

If rates are based on allowable costs that include an allowance for the cost of funds used during construction (consisting of an equity component and a debt component), the company should capitalize and increase net income by the amount used for rate-making purposes—instead of capitalizing interest in accordance with SFAS No. 34, *Capitalization of Interest Cost.*

If rates are based on allowable costs that include reasonable inter-company profits, the company should not eliminate those inter-company profits in its financial statements.

It continues the practice of not eliminating from net income certain profits on sales to regulated affiliates.

It requires regulated enterprises to capitalize leases if SFAS No. 13 tests are met. It provides, however, a 4-year transition period before retroactive application is required.

It prohibits prior period adjustments for refunds to customers. This Statement may require that a cost be accounted for differently than that required in another authoritative pronouncement. In that event, SFAS No. 71 supersedes any other, because it reflects solely the economic effects of the rate-making process.

It is effective for fiscal years beginning after December 15, 1983, except for the standards applying to the capitalization of leases.

To understand more clearly the problems that arise when financial and regulatory accounting practices conflict, it is helpful to focus on a single accounting category and to examine the implications of the various approaches: the treatment of interest during construction (IDC) or, as it is termed for public utilities, "allowance for funds used during construction" (AFUDC).

Treatment of interest during construction. In October 1979 the Financial Accounting Standards Board issued its Statement of Financial Accounting Standards No. 34, *Capitalization of Interest Cost*, which is summarized as follows: This Statement establishes standards for capitalizing interest cost and the amounts to be capitalized. See the discussion in Chapters 19 and 20 of this handbook.

For most public utilities, the applicable USOAs specify that capitalized costs of construction shall include an allowance for funds used during construction (AFUDC) based on the cost of all equities—the so-called cost of capital. Thus most industries classified as public utilities capitalize not only interest costs on debt funds used for construction, but also an interest rate on equity funds. This rate is normally called the *opportunity cost*, that is, an average rate of interest that the company *could* have earned if it had invested those equity funds elsewhere and that it has lost or foregone by committing those funds to the construction project.

This practice, which is clearly contrary to practices followed under GAAP by nonregulated companies, ensures that: (1) the full cost of the construction, including the cost of capital tied up during construction is recognized for rate setting and financial reporting; (2) the utility is at least partially protected against costs associated with construction projects; (3) present consumers do not bear the costs of projects properly associated with future consumers; and (4) the capitalization practice allows the utility an opportunity to recover, through depreciation and returns on undepreciated amounts, its costs whenever the new facilities are placed in service.

The practice of recognizing AFUDC has long been accepted by the utility industry in theory. But in recent years, largely because of increases in construction activity, AFUDC amounts have grown to have substantial impact on utility financial reporting. They have raised considerable concern for regulators and for the industries themselves, particularly with regard to the equity interest amounts. Whereas the computation of interest on debt is based on the actual recorded costs of the borrowed funds, the measurement of the opportunity costs of equity funds has become increasingly controversial. Though there is general agreement that these costs are real, the amounts reported are necessarily hypothetical.

In an effort to eliminate this problem for the utilities it regulates, the FPC in February 1977 issued its Order No. 561 to improve disclosure regarding these practices. It requires segregation of borrowed funds from other funds, stipulating that borrowed funds be reflected in the interest charges section of the income statements and other funds remain under "Other Income and Deductions." The Order also prescribed a maximum allowable AFUDC rate and a uniform method of computing it.

This Order, together with SFAS No. 71, has permitted those utilities regulated by the FERC to achieve a considerable congruence in regulatory and financial reporting methods. However, in the treatment of AFUDC, an additional problem has arisen as to the appropriate reflection of the tax effects of interest associated with construction.

To shield a regulated entity's operations from the impact of construction costs, all items associated with construction are separated from operating costs. Many companies do not, however, separate these costs completely, because they do not properly allocate the income tax effects associated with the construction funds. When a company has large construction projects, these tax effects can be significant.

Different regulatory agencies apply differing approaches to AFUDC. For example, for telephone companies, the Federal Communications Commission allows capitalization of CWIP on construction projects lasting less than 1 year. Agencies also vary considerably in the dollar amounts they permit to be capitalized, and individual agencies may raise or lower these limits over time.[11] Practices may range from permitting capitalization on amounts of CWIP from a minimum of $50 to balances exceeding hundreds of thousands of dollars and may vary considerably with regard to the particular categories of costs included.

Financial Statements. The format of the financial statements of regulated and nonregulated industries reflects the different economic and accounting characteristics of these two groups. A comparison of the income statement and balance sheet for a regulated company (in this case a company in telecommunications) with those for a nonregulated company demonstrates, through the differences in emphasis, these issues. The statement of changes in financial position, though somewhat different for a regulated firm, is not illustrated here.

Income statement. As the income statement is a measure of the financial activities of a company over a period of time, it reflects the company's ability to operate profitably. Its format is chosen to present the results of operations as clearly as possible. The income statement for the regulated company (Exhibit 3) is broken into two basic categories: above-the-line and below-the-line revenues and expenses. Above-the-line expenses are those expenses that are necessary for the provision of current service. These are the costs for which regulators allow recovery through established rates. All expenses for which regulators do not allow recovery are classified as below-the-line expenses.

---

[11]In 1981 the FCC reconsidered its capitalization limits.

EXHIBIT 3

Income Statement
TELECOMMUNICATIONS COMPANY
Year 19X1
(in thousands of dollars)

Operating revenues:	
Local service	
Service and equipment	$1,826,781
Message charges	396,372
Public telephones	94,866
Private lines	34,415
Toll service	
Private lines	351,385
Message charges	2,940,110
Special service	396,860
Directory advertising and other	299,985
Less: Provision for uncollectibles	(84,307)
Total operating revenues	$6,256,467
Operating expenses:	
Maintenance	$1,572,660
Depreciation	891,742
Network and operator services	522,447
Marketing and customer services	540,168
Financial operations	165,721
Directory	130,705
Provision for pensions and other employee benefits	661,004
Services received from parent	131,264
Other operating expense	49,815
Total operating expenses	$4,665,526
Net operating revenues	$1,590,941
Operating taxes:	
Federal income taxes	$ 233,121
State income taxes	96,095
Property taxes	133,459
Payroll-related and other taxes	145,091
Total operating taxes	$ 607,766
Operating income	$ 983,175
Other income:	
Interest charged construction	$ 44,547
Miscellaneous income and deductions	(293)
Total other income	$ 44,254
Income before interest	$1,027,429
Interest deductions	583,418
Net income	$ 444,011
Preferred dividend requirement	55,389
Income applicable to common stock	$ 388,622

Examples are expenses incurred for future service or for operations that are not regulated. In contrast, the income statement for the nonregulated company (Exhibit 4) shows no such distinction. In this statement all expenses are deducted from revenues, the question of allowability not being applicable.

A closer look at several specific revenues and expenses demonstrates why one format would be chosen over the other as representative of operations. One obvious dissimilarity is in the placement of income tax expense. On the nonregulated company's income statement, tax expense is placed at the end of the statement after a pretax income subtotal has been made for all other revenues and expenses. This is because the tax is calculated after all other expenses (allowable for tax purposes) have been deducted from all revenues. As Exhibit 3 shows, however, a regulated company's income statement places income tax after operating expenses and before a total is made for operating income and before any below-the-line expenses or revenues. The difference in placement reflects the fact that regulators allow recovery of taxes in the rates they set. Therefore tax expense is an above-the-line expense and should be placed before below-the-line items.

The reporting of interest expense also reflects the difference between above-the-line and below-the-line items. Interest is not treated as a recoverable cost in utility operations. Rather it is included in revenue requirements through the allowed rate of return. Thus in Exhibit 3 it appears below the "Operating income" line. For a nonregulated company, interest expense is included with all other expenses.

EXHIBIT 4

Income Statement
NONREGULATED COMPANY
Year 19X1
(in thousands of dollars)

Revenues:	
Net sales	$2,529,856
Equity earnings	6,666
Royalty income	6,404
Interest income	13,589
Gain on conversion	11,298
Total	$2,567,813
Costs and expenses:	
Cost of sales	$1,807,048
Selling, administrative, and general	
expenses	487,674
Interest expense	62,601
Other expenses	3,679
Total	$2,361,002
Pretax earnings	$ 206,811
Income taxes	74,451
Net earnings	$ 132,360

EXHIBIT 5

TELECOMMUNICATIONS COMPANY
Balance Sheet
(in thousands of dollars)

	December 31, 19X1	December 31, 19X0
Assets		
Telephone plant:		
In service[a]	$17,127,575	$15,176,646
Under construction[a]	796,857	616,166
Other (held principally for future use)	1,544	4,679
	$17,925,976	$15,797,491
Less: Accumulated depreciation	3,370,123	3,088,837
Total	$14,555,853	$12,708,654
Current assets:		
Cash and temporary cash investments	$ 79,509	$ 59,920
Receivables—Less allowance for uncollectibles, $20,890 in 19X1, $15,072 in 19X0	910,525	839,969
Materials and supplies	144,447	107,382
Prepayments	17,026	16,846
Federal income tax benefits	221,100	169,552
Total	$ 1,372,607	$ 1,193,669
Deferred charges	$ 240,225	$ 177,175
Total assets	$16,168,685	$14,079,498

A third area of interest is the distinction between revenues placed at the top of the statement and those categorized as "Other income." The distinction between these two items for both regulated and nonregulated industries is that "Other income" encompasses income that is not directly attributable to operations. However, the definition of operations is not the same for regulated and nonregulated industries. "Operating revenues" in Exhibit 3 is broken down into categories of service; therefore it is easy to see from the captions that these revenues all stem from current telephone services only. All other revenues are included in the below-the-line item, "Other income." Specifically, "Interest charged construction" is a credit for interest that is accumulated on funds used for construction of property to be used for future service. It is capitalized into the property account as a cost of construction. As it is for service to be rendered, it is not considered above-the-line income despite the fact that it is income deriving from the regulated service.

Nonregulated industries have a more flexible definition of operating revenues. Exhibit 4 displays the various types of revenue aside from product sales revenue that are included. Equity earnings, royalty income, and interest income are all revenues that might be collected by regulated industries but would be considered as "Other income."

Balance sheet. The balance sheet of a regulated company reflects the unique economic and accounting issues faced by regulated industries. Hence,

EXHIBIT 5   (cont.)

TELECOMMUNICATIONS COMPANY
Balance Sheet
(in thousands of dollars)

	December 31, 19X1	December 31, 19X0
Liabilities and equities		
Common shareholders' equity:		
Common shares	$ 3,010,499	$ 3,010,499
Capital-in-excess	421,397	421,397
Reinvested earnings	1,138,601	1,045,234
Total	$ 4,570,497	$ 4,477,130
Nonredeemable preferred shares	$ 102,500	$ 102,500
Preferred shares subject to mandatory redemption	625,001	520,813
Long- and intermediate-term debt	6,152,500	5,265,000
	$ 6,880,001	$ 5,888,313
Current liabilities:		
Accounts payable		
Affiliate	$ 194,120	$ 140,644
Revenue refund	467,394	353,235
Other	410,753	367,779
Interest accrued payable	163,070	124,351
Dividends payable	80,220	80,220
Advanced billings and customer deposits	131,166	112,901
Taxes payable	78,638	48,095
Debt maturing within 1 year	585,341	402,877
Taxes and interest payable	1,630,068	1,256,956
Total	$ 3,740,770	$ 2,887,058
Deferred credits:		
Accumulated deferred income taxes	$ 677,772	$ 581,764
Unamortized investment tax credit	247,813	211,817
Other	51,832	33,416
Total	$ 977,417	$ 826,997
Commitments	—	—
Total liabilities and equitities	$16,168,685	$14,079,498

[a] *Interest charged on construction*—Regulatory authorities allow the Company and its subsidiaries to provide for a return on capital invested in telephone construction projects expected to be completed in excess of 1 year from the time construction starts by accruing interest charged construction as an item of income during the construction period and as an addition to the cost of the plant constructed. Such income is not realized in cash currently but will be realized over the service life of the plant as the resulting higher depreciation expense is recovered in the form of increased revenues.

it differs in many ways from that of a nonregulated company. Exhibit 5 displays the balance sheet for the telecommunications company whose income statement was discussed earlier. Exhibit 6 shows the balance sheet of a nonregulated company. A glance at the exhibits reveals the obvious dissimilarities in format; a closer look, however, reveals that there are other, less obvious, but significant differences as well.

EXHIBIT 6

NONREGULATED COMPANY
Balance Sheet
(in thousands of dollars)

	December 31, 19X1	December 31, 19X0
Assets		
Current assets:		
Cash	$ 22,631	$ 40,550
Marketable securities	1,133	2,385
Accounts receivable—Less: Allowance for uncollectibles, $7,685 in 19X0	405,741	355,444
Inventories	536,504	486,013
Other current assets	91,947	63,587
Total	$1,057,956	$ 947,979
Investments and other assets:		
Unconsolidated financial subsidiary	$ 30,903	$ 24,449
Unconsolidated real estate subsidiary	22,870	7,074
Unconsolidated joint venture	46,873	
Affiliated companies and other investments	61,143	56,659
Other assets	57,490	73,244
Total	$ 219,279	$ 161,426
Property, plant, and equipment:		
Land	$ 33,337	$ 29,019
Buildings	283,182	261,266
Machinery and equipment	560,171	486,879
Construction in progress	86,165	82,781
Total	$ 962,855	$ 859,945
Less: Allowance for depreciation and amortization	319,626	289,605
Total	$ 643,229	$ 570,340
Goodwill	$ 95,866	$ 96,460
Total assets	$2,016,330	$1,776,205
Equities		
Current liabilities:		
Notes payable	$ 42,320	$ 69,380
Accounts payable and accrued expense	358,144	340,883
Income taxes	11,440	31,414
Current maturities of long-term debt	15,760	17,000
Total	$ 427,664	$ 458,677
Long-term debt	$ 569,646	$ 376,035
Deferred income taxes	57,122	59,529
Other deferred credits	26,123	25,126
Total	$ 652,891	$ 460,690
Shareholders' equity:		
Preferred stock	$ 674	$ 905
Common stock	139,812	137,225
Additional paid-in capital	240,228	237,199
Retained earnings	555,262	481,710
Less: Treasury stock	(201)	(201)
Total	$ 935,775	$ 856,838
Total equities	$2,016,330	$1,776,205

The general classification of assets within the balance sheet is similar in both exhibits, however, the order is different. In Exhibit 5 the first category is "Telephone plant," which is followed by "Current assets." Exhibit 6 shows the standard format used by nonregulated industries. There, "Current assets" is first whereas "Investments" and "Property, plant, and equipment" follow. The difference stems from the relative importance of current and noncurrent assets. The plant account is crucial to a regulated company because it is a major component of the rate base from which the allowed return is calculated. The amount of current assets is minor in comparison, because rate-regulated industries do not tend to produce storable goods; therefore, their current assets inventory is small. This is in contrast to nonregulated industries. The emphasis there is on current assets because they are related directly to revenues. Nonregulated industries often have large current asset inventory accounts of the goods they produce or sell. Property, plant, and equipment is necessary, also, for a nonregulated company. However, it is not related directly to revenues as it is for regulated companies and so has a less prominent position in the balance sheet. A comparison of the numerical portion of total assets made up of current assets (particularly inventories) and that portion made up of property, plant, and equipment for the telecommunications company in Exhibit 5 and the nonregulated company in Exhibit 6 emphasizes the different roles that current and noncurrent assets have.

A further point with regard to the plant account is the type of segregation made within that category. The nonregulated company divides property into "Land," "Buildings," "Machinery and equipment," and "Construction in progress." The detail is by type of property, plant, and equipment. The telecommunications company reflects the practice of regulated industries by dividing "Telephone plant" into "In service," "Under construction," and "Other (held principally for future use)." This segregation emphasizes that the importance of property is whether or not it is used for current service and therefore included in the rate base.

On the liabilities and owners' equities side of the balance sheet, further dissimilarities appear. The owners' equity section comes first in Exhibit 5 and is last in Exhibit 6. This inversion emphasizes the importance to the rate of return earned by a regulated company of shareholders' equity and long-term debt relative to that of current liabilities. This format is common among the balance sheets of regulated companies, although a few companies use other formats that more closely follow those used by nonregulated companies. As with current assets, current liabilities for a nonregulated company are connected directly to its primary operations and are therefore placed first.

An interesting detail is found in the "Accounts payable" section of Exhibit 5. A specific effort is made to distinguish the accounts payable of affiliates from other payables. This separation is more commonly found in regulated industries' statements than in those of nonregulated industries because of the close scrutiny given to the interaction of affiliates by rate regulators.

Another important item is the "Unamortized investment tax credit" account under "Deferred credits" in Exhibit 5. Although the treatment of the investment tax credit (ITC) is a controversial issue in the regulated sphere, most regulated companies amortize the credit over the life of the related asset. The alternative is to flow it through income immediately, thus benefiting current rate payers only. Most nonregulated companies use the flow-through method, so a deferred investment credit account is more apt to be seen on balance sheets of rate-regulated companies.

Prior to December 1982 and the FASB's issuing Statement No. 71, the Addendum to APB Opinion No. 2 was a rate-regulated enterprise's only guidance. The Addendum to APB Opinion No. 2 recognized the financial implications of rate regulation for regulated industries, and most persons responsible for the accounting and financial reporting of these industries generally agreed with its rationale: that rate-making treatment must be reflected in financial statements if those statements were to present an economically realistic picture of these industries.

However, confusion and controversy persisted regarding the concepts contained in the Addendum as well as regarding its proper application. Critics of the Addendum contended that: (1) its rationale was insufficiently explained; (2) it was unclear as to which industries it applied (some industries it cited had rarely used it; others not cited had characteristics that might have warranted its application); (3) its "matching" and "cost recoverability" concepts needed more specific criteria for application; and (4) it was income statement-oriented and left balance sheet treatment of some items unsettled.

Accordingly, in 1977, both the Securities and Exchange Commission and the AICPA Accounting Standards Division requested that the Financial Accounting Standards Board (FASB) reexamine the Addendum and either amend it if necessary or provide more specific interpretation. The FASB began to comply with these requests. In December 1979 the Board issued a Discussion Memorandum on the Effect of Rate Regulation on Accounting for Regulated Enterprises and circulated the document for public comment. The issues raised were numerous and complex, but, because of their importance, the main ones are listed here:

> Issue 1: Should accounting prescribed by regulatory authorities be considered in and of itself generally accepted for purposes of financial reporting by rate-regulated enterprises?
>
> Issue 2: Does rate regulation introduce an economic dimension in some circumstances that should affect the application of generally accepted accounting principles to rate-regulated enterprises?
>
> Issue 3: Should any pronouncement issued by the Board identify specific industries affected?
>
> Issue 4: Should the effects of rate-making transactions applicable to prior periods be accounted for as prior period adjustments? If so, should the matter be included in a pronouncement coming out of this project, or should it be covered in an amendment to or interpretation of FASB Statement No. 16, *Prior Period Adjustments?*
>
> Issue 5: How should regulated enterprises give effect to changes in accounting principles when:
>
> 1. An FASB Statement requires retroactive application or a cumulative adjustment, but the change will be applied prospectively for rate-making purposes?
>
> 2. Following a change prescribed by the FASB, rates that had been established on a basis that reflected the prior principle continue in effect?

Issue 6: Should any pronouncement dealing with the impact of rate regulation specify mandatory application?

Issue 7: Does the rate-making process support reporting the contra credit to any capitalized cost of equity funds used in construction as current income?

Issue 8: Should the financial statements of a regulated enterprise disclose the effect of differences between those statements and what they would be if the enterprise were nonregulated? Should the same standards apply to both the balance sheet and the income statement?

Issue 9: What disclosures of rate-making treatment should be made if it is concluded that such treatment should not affect the application of generally accepted accounting principles? Specifically:

1. Should the effect of material differences in the way revenues and expenses are treated for rate-making purposes and for financial reporting purposes be disclosed?

2. Should the estimated impact of these differences on future revenues be disclosed? If so, how—by year, by bands of years, or in total? Should a similar impact on net income be disclosed?

3. Should material differences for property, plant, and equipment (or other assets and liabilities) between the amounts included in the balance sheet and amounts included in the rate base be disclosed?

Issue 10: What other information, if any, should be disclosed about rate making? Where in financial reporting should that additional information be disclosed?

Issue 11: Should any new standards on accounting for the impact of rate regulation be applied:

1. Retroactively by restating all prior periods presented?

2. Retroactively by including a cumulative adjustment in the current period?

3. Prospectively?

What these issues illustrate most clearly was the magnitude of the accounting community's attempt to find a consistent and economically realistic method of reporting for a group of industries whose influence on the public interest is pervasive.

ACCOUNTING CONSIDERATIONS FOR NONUTILITY INDUSTRIES SUBJECT TO RATE REGULATION

As noted at the beginning of this chapter, a number of industries not classified as public utilities display a sufficient number of the characteristics common to public utilities that government has chosen at different times and to different degrees to impose rate regulation. Among these industries are trucking, railroads, certain shipping industries, cable television, and certain health care and insurance industries.

For these industries, the degree of regulation is generally less focused on the precise level of rates and more on ensuring that there are no discriminatory rules or practices or predatory pricing and that there is equal access to facilities. Rules are designed to ensure that suppliers do not discriminate and that users are charged equitably for similar services. Equal access ensures that shippers, if they have met the common carriers' requirements, cannot be denied the right to use the facility equally. Predatory pricing is a strategy employed by a dominant company (monopoly) to preserve its control as it operates in a specific market or territory. This strategy is used to drive out potential competitors by undercutting the existing price level and forcing them into a situation where they cannot financially survive.

The range of rate-regulatory methodologies applied to these industries is too great for detailed discussion here. However, the accounting problems posed by the "in between" status of these industries are perhaps the most complicated any accountant can face.

The characteristics or nature of these industries frequently are such that, though they are regulated, the presence or potential of either direct or intermodal competition exists. The Interstate Commerce Act calls on the Interstate Commerce Commission (ICC) to consider the following items in its regulation to ensure the development, coordination, and preservation of an adequate transportation system necessary:

(1) To recognize and preserve the inherent advantage of each mode of transportation;

(2) To promote safe, adequate, economical, and efficient transportation;

(3) To encourage sound economic conditions in transportation, including sound economic conditions among carriers;

(4) To encourage the establishment and maintenance of reasonable rates for transportation without unreasonable discrimination or unfair or destructive competitive practices;

(5) To cooperate with each State and the officials of each State on transportation matters; and

(6) To encourage fair wages and working conditions in the transportation industry.

These regulatory accounting problems that face accountants can be illustrated, at least partially, by examining the situation of one of the least complex of these rate-regulated industries, petroleum pipelines. Oil pipeline technology is relatively simple and has remained stable. Like utilities, this industry is capital-intensive and subject to economies of scale. It deals in a single service, the transportation of petroleum and petroleum products. Also like utilities, oil pipelines have generally immobile assets: Lines must run from fixed sources of supply to fixed areas of demand, and it is generally uneconomical to try to move a line from one place to another as one oilfield is depleted and another opens up.

Unlike utilities, however, oil pipelines serve fewer classes of customers directly. Further, they do not operate under franchise agreements and do not have an exclusive franchise area. And as such, from an accounting point of view, there is less assurance of future recovery of costs. Accordingly, most of these enterprises historically have adopted a practice by which there was a distinction between those accounting practices that would be appropriate for rate-making purposes and that would be appropriate for financial reporting purposes.

Two brief examples provide a general idea of the current accounting issues related to regulated but nonutility industries.

Railroad Accounting—Betterment Versus Depreciation Accounting. At the present time the ICC requires railroads to use betterment accounting for their track structure. Betterment accounting (retirement-replacement-betterment accounting) provides that all costs of maintaining the track structure (including replacing track in kind) will be charged to "Expense" unless there is a "betterment." The initial cost of the track is left undisturbed on the balance sheet until the track is retired from service or abandoned. Costs incurred to improve the productive capacity of track (e.g., replacing 100-pound rail with 120-pound rail) are capitalized. No depreciation is recorded for the track structure.

The ICC has issued a notice of proposed rule making (Docket No. 36988, Alternative Methods of Accounting for Railroad Track Structures) to change to depreciation accounting. It is summarized as follows:

> The ICC proposes to change its method of accounting for track structure from Retirement Replacement Betterment (RRB) to ratable depreciation accounting. The objectives in changing methods of accounting for track are to improve reporting of the loss in service potential resulting from the use of track assets, to improve the quality of reported earnings through better matching of revenues and expenses, and to make financial reports comparable with other industries.

Oil Pipelines—Utility Accounting or Not? In 1977, jurisdiction of oil pipelines was transferred from the ICC to the Federal Energy Regulatory Commission (FERC). Under ICC-prescribed accounting, there was always a distinction between accounting for rate making and for financial reporting. For example, for rate making, oil pipelines recognize a full allowance for funds used during construction through the valuation process. However, the USOA permits only interest on debt to be capitalized for financial reporting purposes.

The FERC is currently studying whether to have oil pipelines adopt accounting procedures similar to gas pipelines. For gas pipelines, rate-making conventions such as AFUDC are reflected for financial reporting purposes as well. The basic question is whether, in the absence of a protected franchise area and given the risks associated with the industry, one would have adequate assurance of future recovery to use utility capitalization practices for financial reporting purposes.

Given the problems involved in accounting for such a relatively uncomplicated industry as oil pipelines, it becomes obvious that for other rate-regulated nonutility industries, setting and maintaining appropriate and complete accounting practices can be a major challenge, particularly when the shape and intensity of rate regulation itself is in a state of flux.

Accounting for Changing Degrees of Regulation. A contemporary issue is how to account for changing degrees of regulation. There is a trend in more and more industries to replace regulation with competition. When this happens, the enterprise must reflect this fact in its accounting practice. For example, when the ICC allowed expanded competition in the trucking industry and did away with the franchise areas, the companies that had capitalized costs associated with their franchise were required (SFAS No. 44) to write those off immediately.

Another example of where changing degrees of regulation have accounting implications is in the telecommunications industry. The FCC has opened several services to competition. One such service is the provision of station equipment. Opening this to competition had implications for the service life of such equipment, and also suggests that the accounting practices for such property should reflect those for nonutility enterprises.

Deregulation does not necessarily mean an easing of accounting requirements. Specifically in the case of telecommunications, because of the FCC's concern that there not be cross-subsidization of competitive services by monopoly services and further that there not be predatory pricing on individual services, it has proposed an extensive system of accounts to track both competitive and monopoly services.

BIBLIOGRAPHY

Bonbright, J. C., *Principles of Public Utility Rates* (Columbia University Press, New York, 1961).

Culpepper, R. C., "A Study of the Effect of Certain Alternative Accounting Methods on Regulatory Decisions in the Gas Utility Industry," Ph.D. dissertation, University of Arkansas, 1969.

Farris, M. T., and R. J. Sampson, *Public Utilities Regulation, Management, and Ownership* (Houghton Mifflin Co., Boston, 1973).

Financial Accounting Standards Board, *Accounting for the Effects of Certain Types of Regulation*, Statement of Financial Accounting Standards No. 71 (FASB, 1982).

Foster, J. R., and B. S. Rodez, *Public Utility Accounting* (Prentice-Hall, Englewood Cliffs, N.J., 1951).

Livingston, J. L., "The Effects of Alternative Accounting Rate of Return Decisions in the Electric Utility Industry," Ph.D. dissertation, Stanford University, 1966.

Modisette, J. P., "An Evaluation of Current Accounting Practices in the Privately Owned Electric Power and Light Industry," Ph.D. dissertation, Louisiana State University, 1962–1963.

National Association of Regulatory Utility Commissioners, *Uniform System of Accounts for Class A and B Gas Utilities.*

———, *Uniform System of Accounts for Class A and B Water Utilities.*

———, *Uniform System of Accounts for Class C Water Utilities.*

———, *Uniform System of Accounts for Radio Common Carriers.*

Phillips, C., Jr., *The Economics of Regulation* (Richard D. Irwin, Homewood, Ill., 1969).

Quick, G. D., "A Computer Simulation Analysis of Alternative Methods of Accounting for Utility Construction Work in Progress," Ph.D. dissertation, University of Florida, 1974.

Reeser, M. P., *Introduction to Public Utility Accounting* (American Gas Association, Arlington, Va., 1976).

Salmonson, R. F. (ed.), *Public Utility Accounting: Models, Mergers, and Information Systems* (MSU Public Utilities Studies, East Lansing, Mich., 1971).

Sampson, R. J., *Public Utilities: Regulation, Management, Ownership* (Houghton Mifflin Co., Boston, 1973).

Suelflow, J. E., *Public Utility Accounting: Theory and Application* (MSU Public Utilities Studies, East Lansing, Mich., 1973).

Troxel, E., *Economics of Public Utilities* (Holt, Rinehart and Winston, New York, 1947).

U.S. Federal Communications Commission, *Uniform System of Accounts for Class A and B Telephone Companies.*

U.S. Federal Power Commission [Federal Energy Regulatory Commission], *Uniform System of Accounts Prescribed for Natural Gas Companies (Classes A, B, C, and D).*

————, *Uniform Systems of Accounts Prescribed for Public Utilities and Licensees, Classes A, B, C, and D.*

U.S. Interstate Commerce Commission, *Uniform System of Accounts for Pipeline Companies.*

CHAPTER 41

Governmental

Accounting

and Financial

Reporting

Allan R. Drebin
Professor of Accounting and Information Systems, Northwestern University

CONCEPT OF FUND ACCOUNTING

Nature of Governmental Units. Governmental units are established and exist to provide a wide variety of services to the public. Although some services provided by governments may be similar to those offered by business, most are essentially "public goods" that a firm organized for profit could not be expected to provide.

Although governmental units may possess some of the characteristics of business or not-for-profit organizations, they also have their own unique qualities: Public officials are elected by and responsible to the citizens, whose votes are based on the number of persons voting rather than on relative financial contribution. In turn, these public officials are granted limited authority over the public within their respective jurisdictions, including the following three major powers:

1. The authority to enact legislation by which the constituency must abide
2. The authority to levy taxes to support the activities of government
3. The authority to conduct monopoly enterprises in certain operations where charges are made to the users of certain services or products based on the amount of service or product received (e.g., public utilities) [AAA, 1971]

Because most governmental activities are not controlled by market forces, and there are no equity owners to guide operations, other controls are necessary to assure that actions taken are consistent with the interests of society. Thus, governmental units are subject to legal constraints imposed by the electorate or their representatives. Although states are regarded as "sovereign," their powers are limited by their own constitutions and statutes. Local governments—counties, cities, special districts, etc.—are instrumentalities of the states and may perform only those functions their state governments have specifically authorized them to do.

This structure of government creates a need for special types of accounting and financial information. Because of the lack of a market mechanism, resources are allocated through a budgetary procedure. Although it may be regarded as a managerial planning device, the budget of a governmental unit is also a law, referred to as an appropriations ordinance or act. Thus, deviations from the budget are not viewed merely as indicators of ineffective management, but as illegal acts. Accounting information is necessary to permit oversight bodies and other interested parties to monitor compliance with budgetary authorizations.

To control the resource allocation process further, constraints may be placed on the purposes for which particular resources may be used. Thus governmental resources are not fungible, and excess money from one function may not be available for use in a different function. Accounting and financial reporting must therefore reflect the restrictions imposed on the use of certain resources. This is generally accomplished through the use of "fund" accounting.

Fund accounting is a system in which the financial activities of a governmental unit are partitioned into several separate entities, called funds, for purposes of recording information and reporting financial position and results of operations. The objective of the system is to assure and report on compliance with finance-related legal and contractual restrictions. The accounting and reporting implications of this process are discussed later in this chapter.

Sources of Governmental Accounting Principles. Because of their sovereignty under the federal Constitution, individual states have the power to determine the principles to be used in their own accounting and financial reporting. They are not subject to the jurisdiction of the Securities and Exchange Commission (SEC) or any other federal agency. Furthermore, as local government units are all instrumentalities of some state government, their accounting procedures may be prescribed by their state governments.

Nevertheless, state and local governments have found it to their advantage to use generally accepted accounting principles (GAAP) in their financial reporting. These principles are favored by the securities markets, may be required by granting agencies, and provide better comparability of financial reports among jurisdictions.

At the present time, generally accepted accounting principles for state and local governments are those established by the National Council on Governmental Accounting (NCGA). Its Statement 1, *Governmental Accounting and Financial Reporting Principles,* and subsequent Statements and Interpretations (see Bibliography) are regarded as the authoritative pronouncements setting basic principles for state and local government accounting and financial reporting.

The NCGA has no enforcement powers, and its pronouncements have not been universally adopted, although virtually all governmental units use some variation of these principles. Recognizing the need for a more effective standard-setting structure, an ad hoc committee of interested groups has proposed the establishment of a Governmental Accounting Standards Board (GASB). The GASB would parallel the FASB, and would be a part of the same organizational structure, the Financial Accounting Foundation. It would establish financial accounting standards for all state and local governmental bodies that do not have counterparts in the private sector. Standards for units similar to privately owned enterprises (such as utilities, hospitals, and universities) would be set jointly by the FASB and GASB.

Although the proposed structure has received widespread support from most of the organizations that would be expected to participate in its operation and funding, the GASB has not yet become operational. Until superseded by possible pronouncements of the GASB, statements promulgated by the NCGA may be regarded as GAAP.

Similarities of Governmental Accounting and Accounting for Commercial Enterprises. The basic concepts of governmental accounting in terms of a debit-and-credit double-entry system of accounts and periodic determination of financial position and results of operation may appear similar to those followed in commercial accounting. The basic objective of commercial accounting, however, is to permit the periodic determination of income, which is not relevant to the evaluation of most governmental activities. Governmental units do not issue equity securities, and profit maximization is not their objective.

To the extent that governmental units engage in activities similar to those of commercial enterprises, the accounting and financial reporting for such activities are dealt with through "proprietary" funds, which use accounting principles similar to those used in business. The periodic matching of costs and revenues in such funds reflects the degree to which capital has been maintained, which is an objective of these activities. On the other hand, accounting and financial reporting for governmental activities are dealt with through "governmental" funds whose measurement focus is on flows and balances of short-term financial resources. These are the resources available for spending and appropriation, and much of governmental accounting is oriented toward providing this information.

This does not suggest that governmental accounting is done on a cash basis, however. Although some jurisdictions may use a cash basis of accounting, generally accepted accounting principles require the use of the accrual concept for financial reporting. Thus short-term financial resources such as taxes receivable are accrued when they become "measurable and available," even though collections might not occur until subsequent periods.

Other concepts generally applied in commercial accounting are also pertinent to governmental accounting. The monetary expression of accounts is based on historical cost, data reliability is checked through internal control, and the concepts of materiality and objectivity also apply.

Differences between Governmental Accounting and Accounting for Commercial Enterprises. Although there are many similarities between accounting and financial reporting for governmental units and for commercial enterprises, there are also some significant differences stemming from their differing objectives. Commercial enterprises incur costs in order to produce revenue. This creates a cause-and-effect relationship, leading to the significance of income determination.

Governmental units exist to provide services to the citizens they serve. They exercise their taxing powers and other means of raising revenues and spend these resources to provide desired services. Usually, these services are limited to those that can be provided most effectively through governmental action or for which the citizens have felt a need that has not been met through private enterprise. The objective is to render maximum service at a reasonable cost, because available resources are generally insufficient to provide all services desired.

Such limitations of resources have resulted in the development of budgetary planning and control in governmental units. Budgets were developed and used in government long before they were generally used by commercial enterprises. For those governmental activities controlled by a budget, the presentation of operating results without budgetary comparisons is considered to be incomplete disclosure.

Operating statements, then, usually present the actual amounts of revenues and expenditures compared with the budget. Because the basis of budgeting legally required in many jurisdictions may differ from that generally accepted for financial reporting, the budgetary comparisons must be reported in a manner that reveals the degree to which budgetary mandates have been complied with.

The focus of governmental operating statements is on *expenditures* rather than expenses. The expenditure measurement focus reports the using up of appropriable resources as opposed to the using up of assets during a period. For example, inventories, which are frequently a major factor in measuring income of a commercial enterprise, are relatively unimportant in governmental activities. Thus the acquisition of inventory items may be treated as an expenditure during a period, even though the items are still on hand at the end of the period. Similarly, assigning the cost of assets with lives extending over several years to accounting periods through depreciation is not followed, except in proprietary-type operations. Because governmental economic viability does not generally rest on financial condition (in a balance sheet sense) but on the power to tax, valuation of assets is not significant. Instead the emphasis is placed on reporting the resources that will be available for appropriation, that is, cash and items that are expected to become cash within the budgetary cycle. Consequently, balance sheets of governmental funds usually display only current assets and current liabilities.

The definition of the reporting entity is a particular problem in governmental accounting. Because there are no ownership interests, the commercial accounting rules for inclusion of subsidiary companies in consolidated statements, or for using the equity method, do not apply. Frequently, several jurisdictions with separate governing boards may provide different services to the same constituency. In addition, the need to convey the restrictions implicit in fund segregation militates against consolidated reports, which are widely used in commercial accounting.

Overriding all these causes for differences between commercial and governmental accounting is the need to demonstrate that legal requirements and restrictions have been complied with. Indeed, these laws often specify that certain accounting procedures must be followed. In any case, they must constantly be kept in mind in developing the accounting and reporting systems. For example, a government generally may not spend except in accordance with appropriations passed by its governing body. Budgetary comparisons indicate compliance by exhibiting the fact that expenditures, category by category, are not greater than the amount appropriated. Similarly, segregation of resources for specified purposes into separate funds aids in demonstrating that they have been expended only for those specified purposes.

Some critics of governmental reporting suggest that the complexity introduced by segmenting information into fund-type categories may limit the usefulness of the statements. They propose the addition of consolidated financial statements, focusing on results achieved by the organization as a whole, to help the reader understand the operations of the governmental unit. Such statements are not permitted under current GAAP, but may be prepared as supplementary reports.

There may be conflicts between generally accepted accounting principles and legal reporting requirements. NCGA Statement 1 recommends:

> The basic financial statements of governmental units should be prepared in accordance with GAAP.... Where financial statements prepared in conformity with GAAP do not demonstrate finance-related legal and contractual compliance, the governmental unit should present such additional schedules and narrative explanations in the comprehensive annual financial report as may be necessary to report its compliance responsibilities and accountabilities [NCGA, 1979, p. 5].

BASIC PRINCIPLES

The NCGA in Statement 1 has recommended the following 12 principles. These principles do not represent either a complete or separate body of accounting principles, but are a part of the entire body of generally accepted accounting principles and deal specifically with governmental units. Each is accompanied by a short explanation.

1. Accounting and Reporting Capabilities

> A governmental accounting system must make it possible both: (a) to present fairly and with full disclosure the financial position and results of financial operations of the funds and account groups of the governmental unit in conformity with generally accepted accounting principles; and (b) to determine and demonstrate compliance with finance related legal and contractual provisions.

One requirement of accounting for a governmental unit is to demonstrate that it has conducted its financial affairs in compliance with all the legal provisions imposed on it. The sources of these provisions are, among others, state constitutions, statutes enacted by state legislatures, charters, ordinances, and resolutions of the unit's own governing body. Such provisions include restrictions on purposes for which the derived revenues may be expended and rate limits on taxes. The most specific, and one of the most important enactments affecting financial operations, is the annual budget.

Demonstrating compliance is not sufficient, however. The accounting system must also have the capability of providing information on financial position and results of operations of the funds and account groups. To permit such determinations, the fund structure, the budget document, the chart of accounts, and related procedures must all be coordinated. Accounting for actual revenues and expenditures must accord with the budget in terms of fund structure and chart of accounts to permit comparison of actual fiscal operations with the authorizations of the governing body. In addition, the accounts must make it possible to report revenues and expenditures on a basis that fairly presents the results of financial operations.

It is essential that readily understood information be made available in sufficient detail to provide a comprehensive portrayal of the financial position of a governmental unit and of its operating results. The system should encompass the preparation of balance sheets, and of periodic statements of revenues and expenditures. The degree of detail included in such statements may vary according to the class of the reader for whom the statements are intended, ranging from condensed summaries for members of the public (but without limitation on their right of access to additional detail if they desire it) to highly detailed statements of departmental revenues and expenditures for operating heads of departments.

2. Fund Accounting Systems

Governmental accounting systems should be organized and operated on a fund basis. A fund is defined as a fiscal and accounting entity with a self-balancing set of accounts recording cash and other financial resources together with all related liabilities and residual equities or balances, and changes therein, which are segregated for the purpose of carrying on specific activities or attaining certain objectives in accordance with special regulations, restrictions, or limitations.

For reasons set forth earlier, it is necessary to segregate the accounting for various activities of governmental units into separate funds. Each fund must have its own self-balancing set of accounts within the accounting records, although there need not be a physical segregation of assets (such as bank accounts) unless required by law or by contractual terms. Each of these funds may have transactions within itself, with external parties, or with other funds of the same governmental unit. In the latter case, it is essential that the integrity of each of the funds be maintained, requiring that interfund receivable and payable accounts be provided, and that each interfund transaction be recorded as a complete debit-and-credit entry within each of the affected funds so that each individual fund remains in balance. Funds may be established by constitutional or statutory provisions, charter, ordinances, or provisions of contracts such as grants or bond indentures. They may exist to account either for specific sources of revenues or for specific activities.

3. Types of Funds

The following types of funds should be used by state and local governments:

Governmental Funds

(1) *The General Fund*—to account for all financial resources except those required to be accounted for in another fund.

(2) *Special Revenue Funds*—to account for the proceeds of specific revenue sources (other than special assessments, expendable trusts, or for major capital projects) that are legally restricted to expenditure for specified purposes.

(3) *Capital Projects Funds*—to account for financial resources to be used for the acquisition or construction of major capital facilities (other than those financed by proprietary funds, Special Assessment Funds, and Trust Funds).

(4) *Debt Service Funds*—to account for the accumulation of resources for, and the payment of, general long-term debt principal and interest.

(5) *Special Assessment Funds*—to account for the financing of public improvements or services deemed to benefit the properties against which special assessments are levied.

Proprietary Funds

(6) *Enterprise Funds*—to account for operations (a) that are financed and operated in a manner similar to private business enterprises—where the intent of the governing body is that the costs (expenses, including depreciation) of providing goods or services to the general public on a continuing basis be financed or recovered primarily through user charges; or (b) where the governing body has decided that periodic determination of revenues earned, expenses incurred, and/or net income is appropriate for capital maintenance, public policy, management control, accountability, or other purposes.

(7) *Internal Service Funds*—to account for the financing of goods or services provided by one department or agency to other departments or agencies of the governmental unit, or to other governmental units, on a cost-reimbursement basis.

Fiduciary Funds

(8) *Trust and Agency Funds*—to account for assets held by a governmental unit in a trustee capacity or as an agent for individuals, private organizations, or other governmental units, and/or other funds. These include (a) Expendable Trust Funds, (b) Nonexpendable Trust Funds, (c) Pension Trust Funds, and (d) Agency Funds.

Most of these types of funds represent sources of revenues or activities that are more or less continuous and repetitive. They are generally controlled by annual or biennial budgets and should be accounted for on the basis of the fiscal year as the basic accounting period. However, Capital Projects Funds and Special Assessment Funds are used to finance and account for projects that may extend over several years. Accounting records and reports must exhibit the cumulative total cost of each such project together with sources and amounts of the capital to finance them. Because it is necessary to report progress periodically, such funds also require at least annual closings and reporting. The governmental funds generally have an expenditure measurement focus, whereas proprietary funds measure expenses in accordance with their focus on capital maintenance.

4. Number of Funds

Governmental units should establish and maintain those funds required by law and sound financial administration. Only the minimum number of funds consistent with legal and operating requirements should be established, however, since unnecessary funds result in inflexibility, undue complexity, and inefficient financial administration.

It is important that the number of funds used be kept at a minimum consistent with legal requirements and the need to demonstrate compliance with finance-related restrictions. A proliferation of funds would unduly complicate financial reporting, and possibly result in a misleading portrayal of financial constraints. Not all governmental units will find it necessary to establish funds within all eight of the categories enumerated under principle 3.

5. Accounting for Fixed Assets and Long-Term Liabilities

A clear distinction should be made between (a) fund fixed assets and general fixed assets and (b) fund long-term liabilities and general long-term debt.

a. Fixed assets related to specific proprietary funds or Trust Funds should be accounted for through those funds. All other fixed assets of a governmental unit should be accounted for through the General Fixed Assets Account Group.

b. Long-term liabilities of proprietary funds, Special Assessment Funds, and Trust Funds should be accounted for through those funds. All other unmatured general long-term liabilities of the governmental unit should be accounted for through the General Long-Term Debt Account Group.

The accounts of a governmental fund usually include only current assets and current liabilities related to the operation of that particular fund because of the focus on the amount available for future appropriation. Resources of an operating fund that have already been expended, including those expended for fixed assets, are not available for future appropriation, so fixed assets are not carried in governmental funds, but are accounted for in a separate group of accounts.

The General Fixed Assets Account Group consists of a self-balancing group of accounts but is not considered to be a fund. It is, rather, a vehicle for recording and reporting the cost of all the fixed assets of the governmental unit that are not employed in the operation of commercial-type activities or held in trust. The credit balance accounts in this group show the sources of financing for the fixed assets.

Exceptions to the principle of segregating fixed asset accounts are necessary with respect to Internal Service Funds, Enterprise Funds, and certain Trust

Funds. These exceptions are required because of the purposes generally served by each of these funds. For example, in an Enterprise Fund the revenues of the fund are generally intended to cover all costs of providing the service for which the enterprise was established. It is necessary that depreciation be included among the costs to demonstrate that all costs have been covered and to avoid impairment of the fund's capital. In addition, the fixed assets of the Enterprise Fund may be pledged under bond ordinances related to their financing.

Similarly, the general long-term debt of the governmental unit should be accounted for in a separate, self-balancing group of accounts. Obligations issued on the basis of the general credit and taxing powers of the governmental unit should be accounted for in the General Long-Term Debt Account Group. The related debit balance accounts are the Amount Available in Debt Service Funds and the Amount to Be Provided for Payment of Bonds. Revenue bonds, on the other hand, are normally accounted for in the respective Enterprise Funds established for the operation of the facilities that they financed.

6. Valuation of Fixed Assets

Fixed assets should be accounted for at cost or, if the cost is not practicably determinable, at estimated cost. Donated fixed assets should be recorded at their estimated fair value at the time received.

"Cost" is used in this context to mean the purchase price or construction cost of each asset, including the charges necessary to place it on location and ready for operation. It includes, therefore, costs of site preparation, transportation, professional fees, and any other charge attributable directly to the acquisition of the asset. In some cases it may include interest costs incurred during a period of construction. Governmental units frequently receive properties by gift or by dedication from land developers and others. The fair market value of such assets at the date they are received should be recorded as their cost.

It is important that proper accounting control be established over all the assets of the governmental unit. If fixed asset records are inadequate, an inventory should be taken of all fixed assets owned and an estimate made of the original costs of such assets. These assets should then be recorded at estimated cost to establish accounting control.

7. Depreciation of Fixed Assets

a. Depreciation of general fixed assets should not be recorded in the accounts of governmental funds. Depreciation of general fixed assets may be recorded in cost accounting systems or calculated for cost finding analyses; and accumulated depreciation may be recorded in the General Fixed Assets Account Group.

b. Depreciation of fixed assets accounted for in a proprietary fund should be recorded in the accounts of that fund. Depreciation is also recognized in those Trust Funds where expenses, net income, and/or capital maintenance are measured.

Because of the nature of the operations of proprietary funds and the desire to measure cost of operations and the maintenance of capital in such funds, depreciation generally is recorded as an expense in those funds. A number of other activities are carried on by governmental units in funds other than proprietary funds where it is desirable to know the costs of providing certain services or of accomplishing certain tasks. In a study to determine such costs, it may be necessary to include a charge for depreciation of the assets used for such purposes over their estimated useful lives. It may thus be desirable to maintain this information in the accounting records, but it would not be appropriate to include it in operating statements of funds that have a spending measurement focus.

8. Accrual Basis in Governmental Accounting

The modified accrual or accrual basis of accounting, as appropriate, should be utilized in measuring financial position and operating results.

a. Governmental fund revenues and expenditures should be recognized on the modified accrual basis. Revenues should be recognized in the accounting period in which they become available and measurable. Expenditures should be recognized in the accounting period in which the fund liability is incurred, if measurable, except for unmatured interest on general long-term debt and on special assessment indebtedness secured by interest-bearing special assessment levies, which should be recognized when due.

b. Proprietary fund revenues and expenses should be recognized on the accrual basis. Revenues should be recognized in the accounting period in which they are earned and become measurable; expenses should be recognized in the period incurred, if measurable.

c. Fiduciary Fund revenues and expenses or expenditures (as appropriate) should be recognized on the basis consistent with the fund's accounting measurement objective. Nonexpendable Trust and Pension Trust Funds should be accounted for on the accrual basis; Expendable Trust Funds should be accounted for on the modified accrual basis. Agency Fund assets and liabilities should be accounted for on the modified accrual basis.

d. Transfers should be recognized in the accounting period in which the interfund receivable and payable arise.

Accounting should provide information that permits periodic reporting of significant data. The time at which a transaction is recorded therefore becomes important. The accrual basis is generally used in accounting for transactions because it relates revenues and expenditures to the time periods in which the revenues arise or the benefits of the expenditures are received.

The principle quoted above recommends full accrual basis accounting for proprietary fund types and the modified accrual basis for governmental fund types. The modified accrual basis is recommended for governmental funds because of their expenditure measurement focus. In addition, some of their revenue sources are difficult to estimate prior to their receipt. Examples of these sources include current income taxes, sales taxes, gross receipts taxes, and many service fees. Revenue sources that give rise to legally enforceable claims and are readily subject to accurate estimate (such as property taxes and grants or transfers from other governmental units) should be recorded on an accrual basis. Property taxes should be included as revenues not later than the time at which they are billed to the taxpayers. In some cases, they should be accrued at an earlier time (e.g., when the local governmental unit acts upon a levy ordinance and a higher level of government takes over the process of billing and collecting the tax). The "available" criterion has been interpreted by NCGA to require that property taxes be collectible within 60 days following the close of a fiscal year to permit recognition as revenue that year. Where property taxes are recorded on the accrual method, an allowance for the estimated amount of uncollectible taxes should be provided.

An exception is made to the full accrual basis in the case of general debt interest costs that are recorded in Debt Service Funds. Principal and interest payments on bonds are known in advance. Tax levies are provided in the amounts required to meet these fixed obligations. Under these circumstances, it is felt that the accrual of interest would not serve a useful purpose.

9. Budgeting, Budgetary Control, and Budgetary Reporting

a. An annual budget(s) should be adopted by every governmental unit.

b. The accounting system should provide the basis for appropriate budgetary control.

c. Budgetary comparisons should be included in the appropriate financial statements and schedules for governmental funds for which an annual budget has been adopted.

Because a governmental unit may have a limited ability to tax or to provide revenue by other means, and because it must use its ability to tax judiciously to maintain the economic well-being of its constituents, it is essential that it plan carefully what services it expects to provide, what the cost of those services will be, and the sources of revenues from which they will be financed. After adoption by the appropriate legislative body, such a plan constitutes a budget for the year's operation.

After the budget has been prepared and adopted, the accounting system should provide budgetary control over revenues and expenditures. To do this effectively, the budget and the accounts must be prepared and maintained on a coordinated basis. The funds and programs maintained in the accounting records and the chart of accounts for each fund must relate to the fund structure contemplated by the budget and with the line items of estimated revenues and appropriations. Similarly, the timing basis should correspond as between the budget and the accounts. It is recommended that both budgeting and accounting be done on an accrual basis for major items of revenues and expenditures. Revenues "susceptible to accrual" should be included in the period in which they are earned or for which they are levied. Expenditures (with the exception of accrued interest on general-obligation bonds) should be included in the period in which liabilities for goods or services are incurred.

Revenue estimates and budget appropriations should be recorded in the accounts at the beginning of the fiscal year. Commitments in the form of purchase orders or contracts for services are recorded as encumbrances at the time they are approved. Thus recording the estimated amount of the commitment provides a means to prevent overexpenditure of appropriations by establishing control over committed amounts.

10. Transfer, Revenue, Expenditure, and Expense Account Classification

  a. Interfund transfers and proceeds of general long-term debt issues should be classified separately from fund revenues and expenditures or expenses.
  b. Governmental fund revenues should be classified by fund and source. Expenditures should be classified by fund, function (or program), organization unit, activity, character, and principal classes of objects.
  c. Proprietary fund revenues and expenses should be classified in essentially the same manner as those of similar business organizations, functions, or activities.

When each fund is viewed as a separate fiscal entity, the transfer of resources from one fund to another might be regarded as revenue of the receiving fund and an expenditure of the paying fund. From the individual fund perspective, the receipt of resources from another fund is the same as from any other source. From the standpoint of the governmental unit as a whole, however, such exchanges would be viewed merely as internal transfers, having no effect on the total resources available to the unit. Although individual funds are regarded as separate entities, readers of financial reports who are interested in the governmental unit as a whole might be confused if interfund transactions were classified as revenues and expenditures. Thus the term "transfers" is applied to such transactions, and their effects are shown separately in reports of financial operations.

As used in this principle, the term "fund" means an accounting subdivision of the governmental unit, and the term "source" means the nature of the revenue item. Revenues may also be classified by subunits through which their collection was effected.

In accounting for expenditures, "fund" has the same meaning as that described above; "function" means the purpose for which a group of activities or programs is carried out, such as public safety, sanitation, or education. The "organization unit" might be a department, bureau, or division of the governmental structure. Each organization unit will be charged with the responsibility for carrying out one or more activities or programs. "Character" of expenditures refers to the differentiation of outlays for current services from capital outlays or debt redemptions. "Objects" refer to the articles purchased or the services obtained, such as personal services, contractual services, and commodities.

11. Common Terminology and Classification

  A common terminology and classification should be used consistently throughout the budget, the accounts, and the financial reports of each fund.

Unless accounts are kept and reported on the same basis as was contemplated at the time of adoption of the budget, the control aspects of the budgetary process will be ineffective. In addition, the development of data to guide the preparation of the budget for the succeeding year may be facilitated by using compatible accounts for budgeting and financial reporting.

12. Interim and Annual Financial Reports

a. Appropriate interim financial statements and reports of financial position, operating results, and other pertinent information should be prepared to facilitate management control of financial operations, legislative oversight, and, where necessary or desired, for external reporting purposes.

b. A comprehensive annual financial report covering all funds and account groups of the governmental unit—including appropriate combined, combining, and individual fund statements; notes to the financial statements; schedules; narrative explanations; and statistical tables—should be prepared and published.

c. General-purpose financial statements may be issued separately from the comprehensive annual financial report. Such statements should include the basic financial statements and notes to the financial statements that are essential to fair presentation of financial position and operating results (and changes in financial position of proprietary funds and similar Trust Funds).

Fiscal control can be achieved only if actual financial results are compared to budgetary expectations and reported in a timely fashion, accurately, and with full disclosure. Many users of governmental financial reports are also interested in knowing the financial position and results of operations of the governmental unit. An expanded discussion of these reporting requirements is in the "Financial Reporting" section of this chapter.

THE PROCESS OF FUND ACCOUNTING

The principles of double-entry bookkeeping are applied in fund accounting for governmental units. The accounting equation is stated as "assets = liabilities + fund equity." "Fund equity" is equivalent algebraically to the "owners' equity" used in commercial accounting, although it does not represent an ownership interest. It is usually referred to as "Fund Balance" in governmental funds, and "Contributed Capital" and "Retained Earnings" in proprietary funds. Confusion sometimes results where a transaction affects two or more funds. It must be remembered, in such cases, that the accounting equation applies to each individual fund and the entry must include equal debits and credits for *each* of the funds affected.

The use of budgetary accounts for financial control in fund accounting also introduces some added entries. Such entries and others, more or less unique to governmental accounting, are explained and illustrated in the following paragraphs for each class of fund.

The General Fund. The General Fund accounts for all revenues and expenditures that are not required to be accounted for in another fund. Because of the nature of their operations, most governmental units receive a wide variety of revenues and expend their assets to provide the basic services that the governmental unit was organized to provide. The largest part of their revenues and expenditures generally flow through the General Fund. Other names are sometimes used, such as "Corporate Fund," "Education Fund" in the case of a school district, or some other name related to the general activities of the governmental unit.

Budget adoption. Accounting for the General Fund usually gives formal recognition to the budgetary process. A governmental unit has no authority to expend any of its General Fund resources unless a budget or an appropriation bill or ordinance has been passed. Sound financial management, as well as legal constraints, makes it imperative that the budgetary information be recorded in the accounts to facilitate periodic reports comparing actual with budget. For managerial purposes it is also important to keep track of available budgetary authorizations. Although purchase orders and other commitments might not be regarded as transactions in the usual accounting sense, they do use up the governmental unit's authority to spend, and management must continually monitor the status of this item.

At the beginning of the fiscal year the adoption of the budget should be recorded in the accounts as follows:

Estimated Revenues	500,000	
Appropriations		480,000
Fund Balance		20,000

The credit to the Fund Balance account arises in this example from the excess of estimated revenues over planned expenditures; an excess of appropriations over estimated revenues, which could occur if there were a balance remaining from the prior year, would result in a debit. The details of this entry by specific revenue sources and accounts would be recorded in subsidiary ledgers, or substituted for the above entry where the detailed accounts are carried as part of the general ledger.

Recording taxes and other revenues. After adopting the budget, the governing body usually enacts a tax levy. In the case of property taxes, the tax levy is divided by the total assessed valuation of all property subject to the tax to produce a tax rate. (The rate may be limited by law.) The tax rate is extended against the assessed valuation of the property of all individual property owners in a tax roll and a bill is sent to each owner. The tax levy is recorded as revenue and a receivable, partially offset by an allowance for uncollectible taxes at the time the amount becomes measurable and available. This is accomplished by the following entry:

Taxes Receivable—19X1 Levy	300,000	
Estimated Uncollectible Taxes, 19X1 Levy		12,000
Current Tax Revenue		288,000
To record current property tax levy for the year.		

Tax collections are recorded as follows:

Cash	170,000	
Taxes Receivable—19X1 Levy		170,000
To record current property tax collections.		

Some taxes are not collected by their due date, become delinquent, and may result in the imposition of penalties and interest. In due course, the delinquent taxes may be converted into tax liens by court order, further subjecting the property owner to payment of court costs. Entries may be required to record the change in status and the additional amounts collectible (subject to appropriate allowances for losses in collection) if the unit itself is involved directly in the tax collection process and entitled to such additional amounts. In some cases the unit (such as a school district) may not bill and collect its own tax levy, this function being performed by some other unit (such as the county government). Eventually (usually after 3 to 5 years) the losses through failure to collect are recognized by the following entry:

Estimated Uncollectible Taxes, 19X1 Levy	12,000	
Fund Balance	3,000	
Taxes Receivable—19X1 Levy		15,000
To write off uncollectible taxes on 19X1 levy.		

The amount by which the actual losses differ from the allowance is debited or credited to the Fund Balance account.

Other revenue items would be accounted for in a similar manner except that no accruals are made for some items of revenue, because they cannot be anticipated or because they are minor sources of revenue. The following entry records receipt of such an item that was not previously accrued:

Cash	10,000	
Revenues		10,000
To record revenue received not previously accrued.		

Recording encumbrances and expenditures. As purchase orders are issued, amounts appropriated become obligated to pay for the items ordered. These obligations are termed "encumbrances." It is customary in governmental accounting to record encumbrances at the time of issuance of purchase orders in the amount of the estimated cost of the item. Encumbrances may be recorded in the accounts as follows:

Encumbrances.	25,000	
Fund Balance Reserved for Encumbrances		25,000
To record order placed for materials.		

Detailed entries should be made to the individual appropriation accounts affected, thereby reducing the amount available for future encumbrances or expenditures for that item.

Salary appropriations (and some others with similar characteristics) for full-time employees are not usually encumbered prior to the recording of actual liabilities. Unlike appropriations for such items as supplies and equipment, salaries are usually established in advance and controlled through administrative and personnel practices (such as authorized staffing tables) that prevent overexpenditure.

When materials and services are received in fulfillment of purchase orders, the encumbrance matures into a liability for the actual amount. Two entries are then required. The first reverses the encumbrance previously recorded:

Fund Balance Reserved for Encumbrances	25,000	
Encumbrances		25,000
To reverse encumbrances for materials received.		

The second entry records the actual liability:

Expenditures	24,000	
Vouchers Payable		24,000
To record vouchers issued for materials received.		

Materials may also be ordered for inventory and accounted for in the same manner as in commercial accounting. Their purchase would be recorded as a debit to Inventory of Supplies and a credit to Vouchers Payable at the time the material is received. At the time of issuance from inventory for usage, an entry charging Expenditures and crediting Inventory of Supplies would be recorded. Normally, however, such purchases are treated as expenditures at the time the materials are received. Many other transactions of types similar to those encountered in commercial accounting may arise, such as billings for services rendered, investment of excess cash, and loans between funds. In recording interfund loans, it must be remembered that a complete debit-and-credit entry must be made in each of the two funds affected.

Closing the accounts. At the end of the accounting period, appropriation accounts are closed by the following entry:

Appropriations	480,000	
Expenditures		402,000
Encumbrances		42,000
Fund Balance		36,000
To close out 19X1 appropriations, expenditures, and encumbrances to fund balance.		

Note that the above entry closed a $42,000 debit balance of encumbrances. This implies that a remaining balance of $42,000, representing unfilled purchase commitments, is still carried in the Fund Balance Reserved for Encumbrances, which is not closed out but continues to be carried in the records. In a subsequent year when the related materials are received, the expenditures would be recorded as follows:

Expenditures—19X1	40,000	
Vouchers Payable		40,000
To record liability for material received in 19X2 that had been ordered in 19X1 at an estimated cost of $42,000.		

The following entry would be recorded in 19X2 to close out the reserve for encumbrances for the year 19X1:

Fund Balance Reserved for Encumbrances—19X1	42,000	
Expenditures—19X1		40,000
Fund Balance		2,000
To close expenditures chargeable to prior year's reserve		
for encumbrances.		

Actual and estimated revenues would also be closed at the end of the fiscal year of 19X1 by the following entry:

Revenues	512,000	
Estimated Revenues		500,000
Fund Balance		12,000
To close out 19X1 actual and estimated revenues.		

Fixed assets. With the exception of proprietary funds, a clear distinction should be made between the accounts relating to current assets and liabilities and those relating to fixed assets and liabilities. Therefore, although the General Fund may purchase fixed assets from its revenues, these assets, once acquired, are not carried in the accounts of the General Fund. At the time of their acquisition, the General Fund records their purchase as an expenditure. At the same time, or at the end of the fiscal period, these assets are recorded in a separate self-balancing group of accounts called the General Fixed Assets Account Group (discussed subsequently). The basic principles illustrated above in accounting for the General Fund apply also to the other governmental funds, with the additional comments and exceptions noted in the following paragraphs.

Special Revenue Funds. Special Revenue Funds are established by legal requirements to account for revenues derived from a specific revenue source limited to specific uses. The distinguishing characteristic of these funds is that their revenues are earmarked to finance particular activities or functions. Examples of such funds are those established to account for motor fuel taxes, which may be used only for the maintenance of streets and highways, and those used to account for the proceeds of intergovernmental grants whose terms impose special restrictions and accountability requirements. Special revenue funds may be administered by the same administrative and legislative officials as the other activities of the unit, or they may be administered by an independent or semi-independent board or commission. Special Revenue Funds may be distinguished from Enterprise Funds in that their function is usually financed mostly by tax revenues. If the activity is financed entirely or predominately by user charges that are intended to recover the full cost of the operation, or if the governing body has decided that the measurement of income is appropriate for capital maintenance or public policy, it should be classified as an Enterprise Fund.

The accounting principles illustrated above for the General Fund apply also to Special Revenue Funds. The details of their budgets and charts of accounts should follow that for the General Fund.

Capital Projects Funds. Capital Projects Funds account for financial resources to be used for the acquisition or construction of major capital facilities by a governmental unit, except those financed by Special Assessment, Enterprise, or Trust Funds. The sources of these funds may be the proceeds of general-obligation debt, grants from agencies or other governmental units, accumulated tax revenues levied for such purposes, or transfers from other funds. Most often capital projects are budgeted and authorized on an individual basis and separate funds are set up for each project, although a series of related projects may be accounted for in one combined fund. If one bond issue is used to finance a series of related projects, then only one Capital Projects Fund would ordinarily need to be used. However, if each project is separately authorized and financed, it becomes necessary to show that the proceeds of each bond issue were spent only for the specific purposes authorized and therefore separate funds must be established. Capital Projects Funds ordinarily are established only to account for the acquisition or construction of major permanent facilities having relatively long lives. They are not used for the acquisition of equipment, which is usually financed from current revenues or by short-term obligations.

Budgeting for capital projects differs somewhat from that of the General Fund in that a capital budget is adopted that consists of a plan of proposed capital outlays and the means of financing them. It may cover a single fiscal year. More frequently, it covers a period of 4 to 6 years in the future, although it is normally revised annually and extended for an additional year into the future. Each year that part of the capital budget pertaining to the current fiscal year is incorporated into the annual budget for the forthcoming year. When the annual budget is adopted, the capital projects contemplated become appropriations and constitute authority to make expenditures on the projects so authorized.

When the financing for a project is to be derived from the sale of a bond issue, the initial journal entry in the Capital Projects Fund would be a debit to Cash for the proceeds of the issue and a credit to Other Financing Sources for the par value of the bonds. The proceeds are not called revenue because they do not increase the net worth of the governmental unit as a whole, but they do result in an increase in the Fund Balance of the Capital Projects Fund because they increase the fund's assets without a corresponding increase in liabilities. The liability for the bonds issued is not recognized by the Capital Projects Fund, but is recorded in the General Long-Term Debt Account Group.

The proceeds from the sale of a bond issue frequently include a premium. The premium represents an adjustment of the interest rate and must normally be transferred to the Debt Service Fund. In some jurisdictions, however, these additional proceeds may, by statute, be expended to finance the project. Proceeds of bond issues and other cash accumulated to finance a project may not be needed for considerable periods of time. Under these circumstances, investments are frequently made and interest is earned until the cash is needed to pay for the construction costs. Generally, if permitted by statute, the interest earned is retained in the Capital Projects Fund and used along with other cash available to meet authorized project expenditures. Sometimes the interest earned is transferred to the appropriate Debt Service Fund or to the General Fund to offset the interest costs of the bonds issued to finance the project.

The cost of completed projects should be recorded in the General Fixed Assets Account Group. In other respects, the accounting entries to record construction and other acquisitions of capital assets follow those described for the General Fund.

Debt Service Funds. Debt Service Funds account for the accumulation of resources necessary for the payment of principal and interest on general-obligation bonds. General-obligation bonds are those for whose payment the full faith and credit of the issuing unit are pledged and are generally payable from taxes and other general revenues. Debt Service Funds are used only when a contractual obligation such as a bond indenture requires the provision of a sinking fund to retire long-term debt. Thus they would not be required for serial bonds or other debt to be serviced from current revenues. Debt Service Funds are not used for debt payable from special assessments or debt issued for the benefit of a governmental enterprise from whose revenues it will be serviced.

Although debt service on general-obligation bonds may be financed from other sources, most bonds are serviced from the proceeds of general property taxes. The authorization to issue such bonds may include simultaneously the levy required to service them for all the years that they will be outstanding. All debt service requirements should be budgeted regularly as part of the annual budget. Each bond issue constitutes a separate obligation and generally has its own property tax levy to support it and its own legal restrictions and service requirements. Appropriate provisions must be made to develop information with respect to the status of each issue and its related revenues. If legally required, it may be necessary to have a separate fund for each individual bond issue. Having numerous funds, however, unduly complicates the accounting process; therefore, the minimum number of Debt Service Funds consistent with legal and contractual requirements should be established.

During the accumulation phase, the Debt Service Fund records the receipt of revenues from taxes or other sources, the investment of available cash, and the earnings on investments. During this phase, Fund Balance will continually increase. In the year in which the bonds mature, a liability is recognized in the amount of the obligation, with the offsetting debit to Expenditures, which will reduce Fund Balance. After the obligations have been paid, the particular debt service fund is closed, and any remaining balance is transferred to the General Fund or otherwise disposed of in accordance with legal provisions.

The following entries illustrate the accounting for the accumulation to retire a term bond issue in a Debt Service Fund:

Required Contributions	220,000	
Required Earnings	27,500	
Fund Balance		247,500

To record budget based on actuarial calculations and indenture provisions.

Taxes Receivable—19X1 Levy	173,000	
Estimated Uncollectible Taxes		3,000
Revenues		170,000
To record property tax levy for year.		

Due from General Fund	50,000	
Other Financing Sources		50,000
To record contribution from General Fund.		

Cash	200,000	
Taxes Receivable—19X1 Levy		150,000
Due from General Fund		50,000
To record collection of taxes and General Fund contribution.		

Investments	200,000	
Cash		200,000
To record investment of cash balances.		

Cash	26,000	
Earnings on Investments		26,000
To record receipt of earnings on investments.		

Revenues	170,000	
Other Financing Sources	50,000	
Required Contributions		220,000
To close revenue and contributions accounts.		

Earnings on Investments	26,000	
Fund Balance	1,500	
Required Earnings		27,500
To close investment earnings account.		

The following additional entries would be made in the year in which the bonds mature:

Expenditures	1,000,000	
Matured Bonds Payable		1,000,000
To recognize bond liability.		

Cash	980,000	
Investments		980,000
To record liquidation of investments.		

Matured Bonds Payable	1,000,000	
Cash		1,000,000
To record redemption of bonds at maturity.		

Special Assessment Funds. Special Assessment Funds are employed to account for the financing and construction of public improvements for the principal benefit of certain property owners. These improvements (such as paving of residential streets, curbs and gutters, and sidewalks) are paid for, either completely or in large part, by the owners of adjacent property. The limited area of benefit is the essential characteristic that distinguishes such improvements from those that benefit the entire community and are paid for out of general revenues or through general-obligation bonds.

Each separate local improvement project must be accounted for through a separate fund, because the related special assessment bonds or warrants are payable only from the collections assessed against benefited property owners. The fact that some part of the total cost of the project may be deemed to represent a public benefit payable from the General Fund (or that the bonds carry an additional pledge of the full faith and credit of the municipality) does not alter the need to create a separate fund for each project.

Each Special Assessment Fund accounts for the expenditure of the proceeds of the sale of bonds in defraying construction costs of the designated improvement, and also accounts for the collection of the assessments levied against individual property owners.

Generally, the property owners have an option of paying the full assessment immediately or of paying in installments, together with interest, over a period of several years. If the assessment includes such an installment feature, the related bonds issued to finance the project may also be payable in installments over the same period of time as the assessments are to be collected. Each bond may be payable in installments, or the entire issue may be callable serially by number. Accounting for the latter form is simpler because it eliminates the need for maintaining a record of bonds payable by installment maturities.

Because the bonds issued to finance the project are a liability of the fund that accounts for the expenditure of their proceeds, each Special Assessment Fund must continue in existence until the bonds are fully retired. After completion of the construction financed by the fund, the accounting consists of recording collections on assessments receivable and the servicing of the outstanding bonds. Upon final retirement of the bonds, any balance that remains should be disposed of in accordance with applicable legal provisions.

Journal entries illustrating the operation of a Special Assessment Fund are as follows:

Special Assessments Receivable—Current	10,000	
Special Assessments Receivable—Deferred	90,000	
Due from General Fund	10,000	
Revenues		10,000
Deferred Revenues		90,000
Other Financing Sources		10,000
To record approved special assessments against property owners (payable in 10 installments) and amount due from General Fund for city's contribution.		
Cash	90,000	
Bonds Payable		90,000
To record proceeds from sale of special assessment bonds at par.		
Cash	19,500	
Special Assessments Receivable—Current		9,500
Due from General Fund		10,000
To record collections on special assessments and city's contribution from General Fund.		

Special Assessments Receivable—Delinquent	500	
Special Assessments Receivable—Current		500
To record delinquencies in payment of assessments.		

Expenditures	105,000	
Contracts Payable		105,000
To record construction cost under contract with Hard Rock Construction Company.		

Expenditures	5,000	
Due to General Fund		5,000
To record construction cost of work done by Street Department.		

Contracts Payable	105,000	
Due to General Fund	5,000	
Cash		110,000
To record payment of construction costs.		

Interest Receivable	4,612	
Interest Revenue		4,612
To record interest receivable on deferred assessments.		

Interest Expense	4,500	
Interest Payable		4,500
To record interest payable on special assessment bonds.		

Interest Revenue	4,612	
Interest Expense		4,500
Fund Balance		112
To close interest revenue and expense accounts to fund balance.		

Revenues	10,000	
Other Financing Sources	10,000	
Fund Balance	90,000	
Expenditures		110,000
To close revenues, expenditures, and other financing sources to fund balance.		

Note that the above entries result in a negative Fund Balance of $90,000 (excluding the $112 due to the interest differential), despite the fact that construction costs were exactly equal to the amounts assessed against property owners plus the General Fund contribution. This is caused by the application of governmental fund-type concepts to the particular circumstances of the Special Assessment Fund.

Note that the deferred portion of special assessments is not recognized as current revenue but is set up as a liability, "Deferred Revenue." It is balanced by the asset account, Special Assessments Receivable—Deferred. The obligation that these deferred collections will be used to retire is also recognized as a liability—Bonds Payable—in the Special Assessment Fund. This anomaly does not occur in the other governmental fund types because long-term obligations are not recognized in those funds but in the separate General Long-Term Debt Account Group.

This may cause confusion, as readers of Special Assessment Fund statements may become alarmed over the appearance of a deficit. This problem disappears over the life of the fund as the Deferred Receivables become current and are recognized as revenue. However, many accountants have expressed concern over this issue, and it is likely that action will be taken to revise generally accepted accounting principles to eliminate the problem. One way of overcoming this would be to recognize the deferred portion of taxes receivable as revenue at the time the taxes are levied. Although they will not provide current resources, they will provide the resources that are to be used to retire liabilities of the fund.

Upon completion of the construction phase of the project, an entry would be made in the General Fixed Assets Account Group to record the cost of the improvement as an asset, with an offsetting credit to the account, Investment in General Fixed Assets—Special Assessments.

Enterprise Funds. Enterprise Funds are established to account for self-supporting services carried on by governmental units, or activities for which the governing body has decided that the determination of income is important for purposes such as capital maintenance or public policy. The most frequent examples of such enterprises are municipally owned public utilities providing water, gas, or electricity. Other examples include transit systems, port facilities, airports, hospitals, and parking facilities. Some of these activities may be partially supported by general tax revenues. In such instances, the principal source of revenues and the intent of the governing body should determine whether the activity is to be accounted for as a Special Revenue Fund or as an Enterprise Fund. Note that the prerogative of the governing body to decide whether a particular activity should be accounted for through an Enterprise Fund may result in similar activities being treated differently among various jurisdictions. Once such a decision has been made with respect to a particular activity, however, it should be followed consistently because the accounting practices for the two categories of funds are different and will reflect different operating results.

The accounting for Enterprise Funds generally follows the accounting principles and procedures appropriate for a commercial enterprise engaged in the same activity. Frequently their operations are subject to the same budgetary procedures as the General Fund, except that expenditures should not be controlled by rigid appropriations. Expenditures will vary with the levels of demand for service, which in turn will produce corresponding levels of revenue.

Because the facilities of Enterprise Funds are frequently financed by revenue bonds (which require measurement of the operating results of the related self-supporting enterprise), it is necessary to establish a separate fund for each such enterprise to ensure that the resources of one are not illegally or improperly utilized by another.

These enterprises frequently have segregations of assets within their respective funds that constitute restricted assets and are sometimes referred to in the language of revenue bond ordinances as "funds" or "accounts." For example, proceeds of bond issues are often required to be segregated in Construction

Funds; money accumulating to retire bonds may be required to be segregated as a Sinking Fund; protective covenants included for the benefit of bondholders may require segregation into several other "funds" such as Debt Service, Depreciation, Reserve, and Contingency. These "funds" should be called "accounts" to avoid confusion with the general use of the term "fund" in governmental accounting.

Enterprise Funds may provide services for other governmental departments (such as providing water for their use) and in turn receive services (such as administrative or clerical assistance) from them. All these interfund relationships make it important to adhere strictly to the concept of individual fund entities; services rendered by an Enterprise Fund to other funds, or vice versa, should not be disregarded or canceled out. A billing should be made for the services on the same basis as they would be handled with other users. This is often required to comply with the provisions of revenue bond ordinances and, in any case, it is desirable in order to permit valid comparisons of operating results among comparable enterprises.

In accounting for Enterprise Funds, it is important that the accrual method of accounting be followed because it is necessary to measure operating results on a full cost of services basis. Fixed assets frequently constitute a large percentage of the total assets and represent the primary source of the enterprise's earning power. They are recorded as part of the assets of the Enterprise Fund and periodic charges are made against the operating revenues for their depreciation. A clear distinction must be made between operating revenues and items that are nonoperating income or contributions to the capital of the Enterprise Fund.

Internal Service Funds. Internal Service Funds provide specified services or commodities for other departments of the governmental unit that establishes them or for other governmental units. Such funds have sometimes been referred to in the past as "working capital funds" or "intragovernmental service funds." Internal Service Funds render services only to other departments of the governmental unit, which distinguishes them from Enterprise Funds and other funds established to render services directly to the general public. Common examples of such funds are purchasing and supply departments, central garage and motor pool, and so on.

The capital to establish an Internal Service Fund can come in the form of long-term advances or permanent contributions from other funds or from the proceeds of sale of general-obligation bonds. As the Internal Service Fund provides services to various departments, it is reimbursed by transfers from the budget appropriations of the departments served. The concept of the Internal Service Fund requires that it recover its complete costs of operation, including all administrative costs, without producing any significant profit. The expenditures to be incurred through an Internal Service Fund are ultimately reimbursed by other funds and become expenditures to them. Such expenditures must be covered by appropriations in the respective funds utilizing the services of the Internal Service Fund. Budgetary control over the operations of the Internal Service Fund is therefore exercised through the accounts of the fund being served, and no separate appropriations are made for the Internal Service

Fund itself. In the interest of sound financial management, however, a plan of operation should be prepared for each Internal Service Fund each fiscal year.

The accounting entries for an Internal Service Fund are similar to those of a comparable commercial enterprise. Its billing to the other departments would be recorded as a debit to an account entitled Due from General Fund, for example, and a credit to a revenue account.

Fiduciary Funds. Trust and Agency Funds are established to account for cash and other assets received by a governmental unit in the capacity of trustee, custodian, or agent except in those cases in which the source is related to operation of an Enterprise Fund. Although a distinction can be made between a Trust Fund and an Agency Fund, in both cases the governmental unit operates in a fiduciary capacity and, for this reason, both types are considered together. Trust Funds may be further classified as being expendable or nonexpendable. Expendable Trust Funds are those in which both principal and income therefrom may be expended for the purposes designated in the trust documents. A common example of an Expendable Trust Fund is that established for pension and retirement systems for employees of the governmental unit. Nonexpendable Trust Funds are those in which the principal or corpus must be preserved intact and only the income may be used for the designated purposes. For this reason, it is important to maintain the accounts of a Nonexpendable Trust Fund in such a way as to identify the amount of its corpus or principal and the accumulated but unspent income. A separate self-balancing set of accounts should be maintained for each Fiduciary Fund. To demonstrate that the terms of the trust documents or the agency agreement (expressed or implied) have been complied with, separate financial statements of each such fund should also be prepared.

Generally, budgets are not prepared with respect to Fiduciary Funds and budgetary accounts are not maintained. There are certain exceptions, such as a Retirement Fund that accounts for its own operating outlays in addition to the payment of retirement benefits, or a fund for other purposes supported partly by general tax revenues, in which budgets and budgetary accounts should be adopted.

The accounting for most Trust Funds and Agency Funds is relatively simple, consisting primarily of recording cash receipts and disbursements. Upon receipt, the Cash account is debited and the Fund Balance credited. An expenditure is recorded in the opposite manner. Appropriate subaccounts should be maintained in such Agency Funds as Performance Deposit Funds to permit identification of the various individuals for whom the deposits are being held. Many Agency Funds act only as conduits (such as those for employee benefit plan deductions and payroll deductions), and therefore have no balances at the end of the year.

Nonexpendable Trust Funds. Accounting for Nonexpendable Trust Funds and for Employee Retirement Funds is more complex. As mentioned above, the accounts for a Nonexpendable Trust Fund must be established in such a manner as to demonstrate compliance with the terms of the trust instrument, including measurement of net income in accordance with the terms specified by the donor. In distinguishing between corpus and income, the same principles apply in the case of governmental Trust Funds as those concerning fiduciary accounting in general.

Employee Retirement Funds. Accounting for an Employee Retirement Fund should be designed to show the amount and source of its assets that have been set aside for retirement benefits, and its liabilities as determined by an actuarial evaluation. In other words, the accrual basis of accounting should be employed to provide full disclosure of financial position on both a current and long-term basis. Revenues earned but not received and payments due but not disbursed should be shown as current assets and current liabilities, respectively, on the balance sheet.

The most important aspect of accounting for a retirement system is the measurement and recording of its actuarial characteristics. Actuarial studies should be conducted by professional actuaries for all public retirement systems to measure the estimated liability for the authorized allowances and benefits to be provided under the plan. Reserve accounts should be recorded on the books to demonstrate compliance with legal requirements. The actual assets held by the fund to provide for payment of employee benefits should be reported; in addition, the accounting records and statements should show the amount of assets (based on an actuarial study) that should be in the fund to pay benefits to current employees as they become eligible for such payments. If such accounts are maintained, a credit balance in the Fund Balance account will indicate that the fund is fully funded. A debit balance will indicate that a deficit exists and financing must be provided in the future to permit the fund to meet its commitments.

In addition to the basic financial statements, an Employee Retirement Fund also requires a statement setting forth an analysis of changes in its actuarial and other reserves. Because of deficiencies in statutes or ordinances in some jurisdictions, the actuarial reserve basis of accounting for retirement systems may not be followed. In these cases, it is important that adequate disclosure be made in a note to the financial statements regarding the difference between the reserve requirements on a statutory basis and those on an actuarial basis.

General Fixed Assets Account Group. The General Fixed Assets Account Group is maintained to account for all the fixed assets of the governmental unit that are not accounted for in an Enterprise, Internal Service, or Trust Fund. A fixed asset for this purpose should be defined as a tangible item of property having a life longer than 1 fiscal year. In addition, it is customary to account for only those assets having a value in excess of some minimum amount, to avoid the necessity of maintaining detailed accounting and inventory records on units of property so small that the time and expense involved in the record keeping is not justified.

Most governmental units have a substantial investment in fixed assets, which may be in scattered locations. Sound administration and protection of such assets can be achieved only through the establishment of appropriate accounting records as well as periodic physical inventorying, particularly of movable equipment. Such procedures are essential to the fixing of responsibilities for custody on the part of individual public officials. A financial report of a governmental unit without complete and accurate fixed asset information is deficient.

The asset account classifications maintained for the General Fixed Asset Account Group are similar to those maintained for a commercial enterprise. The NCGA recommends the following major classes for statement presentation: Land, Buildings, Improvements Other Than Buildings, Machinery and Equipment, and Construction in Progress. Subdivisions of these accounts may be provided as appropriate to the needs of the specific governmental unit.

So that the General Fixed Assets Account Group may be self-balancing, credit balance accounts in the form of several "investment accounts" should be established to indicate the resources from which the assets were acquired. The following account titles have been recommended:

Investment in General Fixed Assets from:
   Capital Projects Funds
      General-Obligation Bonds
      Federal Grants
      State Grants
      ·Local Grants
   General Fund Revenues
   Special Revenue Fund Revenues
   Special Assessments
   Private Gifts

All entries in the General Fixed Assets Account Group (except for property received by gift) are counterparts to entries recording expenditures in the various funds. For property acquired through Capital Projects or Special Assessment Funds, an entry is recorded here as "Construction Work in Progress" at the end of the fiscal year if the project has not been completed. When the project is completed in a subsequent fiscal period, the costs incurred are transferred from Construction Work in Progress to the pertinent asset account. For assets acquired by General or Special Revenue Funds, the entry may be made in the General Fixed Assets Account Group either at the time of the expenditure or on an accumulated basis at the end of the accounting period.

No entries are made in the General Fixed Assets Account Group during the life of an asset. The fixed assets are recorded at their acquisition cost until they are disposed of. Procedures must be provided for reports to be made to the accounting office upon disposition of an asset (through scrapping, abandonment, trade-in, or sale) so that proper adjustments may be made to remove the cost of the assets disposed of from the General Fixed Assets Account Group.

General Long-Term Debt Account Group. The General Long-Term Debt Account Group is a separate self-balancing group of accounts in which all the unmatured, long-term indebtedness backed by the full faith and credit of the governmental unit is recorded. A revenue bond issued by an Enterprise Fund and payable only from its revenues is recorded in the Enterprise Fund. A general-obligation bond issued for the benefit of a governmental enterprise, and serviced by earnings of the enterprise, should also be included in the affected Enterprise Fund.

Another special case is that of a special assessment bond that carries a secondary pledge of the governmental unit's full faith and credit. In this case the direct liability should be included only in the Special Assessment Funds, but the contingent liability should be indicated by a footnote in the Statement of General Long-Term Debt.

At the time debt is issued, an entry should be made in the General Long-Term Debt Account Group to record the liability by a credit to Bonds Payable for the principal amount of the debt. The offsetting debit is to an account entitled Amount to Be Provided for Payment of Bonds. After the entry to record the issuance of the bonds has been made, transactions are recorded in the General Long-Term Debt Account Group to complement those in the various Debt Service Funds. Increases in the Debt Service Fund balances available for payments on long-term debt are recognized in the General Long-Term Debt Account Group by a debit to the account Amount Available in Debt Service Funds and a credit to the account Amount to Be Provided for Payment of Bonds. As bonds are retired through a Debt Service Fund, a simultaneous entry is made in the General Long-Term Debt Account Group debiting Bonds Payable and crediting either Amount to Be Provided for Payment of Bonds or Amount Available in Debt Service Funds.

FINANCIAL REPORTING

Objectives of Financial Reporting. Financial reports for governmental units must be prepared with the objective in mind of providing full disclosure on a timely basis of all material facts relating to their financial position and results of operation. As with any organization, financial statements of a governmental unit are used by different groups, each of which has its own particular needs. The financial statements of governmental units are of primary interest to administrative personnel, governing and oversight bodies, investors, and the general public. Generally, no set of financial statements is developed solely for the use of one of these groups to the exclusion of the others. Consequently, the needs of each group must be kept in mind in designing and preparing financial statements and schedules. Different levels of summarization of the financial information may be used to accommodate the relative degree of detail needed by each group. Financial information may be presented first in the form of balance sheets, statements of revenues, expenditures, and changes in fund balance, and so on. These in turn would be supplemented by footnotes and schedules setting forth the details of the various items appearing in the summary financial statements.

Annual Financial Reports. NCGA Statement 1 recommends:

> Every governmental unit should prepare and publish, as a matter of public record, a comprehensive annual financial report (CAFR) that encompasses all funds and account groups. The CAFR should contain both (1) the general-purpose financial statements (GPFS) by fund type and account group, and (2) combining statements by fund type and individual fund statements.

The CAFR is the governmental unit's official annual report and should also contain introductory information, schedules necessary to demonstrate compliance with finance-related legal and contractual provisions, and statistical data.

The different levels of detail and summarization have been illustrated by the NCGA in the financial reporting "pyramid" shown in Exhibit 1. Although condensed summary data may be sufficient to meet the needs of some users, the CAFR must include details of individual funds and account groups, as well as supplementary disclosures and schedules. The general-purpose financial statements are a component of the CAFR, and are regarded as "liftable" so that they may be used separately as the primary reporting vehicle for users who do not need the supporting detail. The accounting system must provide basic transactions data so that summarized schedules in the CAFR can be verified by audit, and to enable the preparation of special-purpose reports.

The financial statements and schedules required in the CAFR include the following:

a. A combined balance sheet—all fund types and account groups. This is usually displayed in a columnar format with a total column, as illustrated in

EXHIBIT 1   The Financial Reporting "Pyramid"

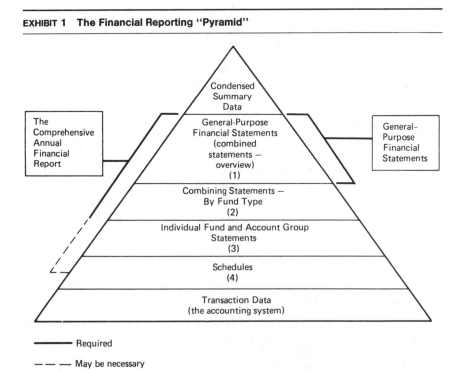

The Comprehensive Annual Financial Report

Condensed Summary Data

General-Purpose Financial Statements (combined statements — overview) (1)

General-Purpose Financial Statements

Combining Statements — By Fund Type (2)

Individual Fund and Account Group Statements (3)

Schedules (4)

Transaction Data (the accounting system)

———— Required

— — — May be necessary

Exhibit 2. The total column is captioned "memorandum only" because aggregating amounts from funds with differing measurement principles does not provide meaningful totals. In addition, the figures in the total column should not be regarded as comparable to "consolidated" statements because no adjustments or eliminations are made for interfund balances.

b. *Combining balance sheets for all funds of each type.* Because the combined balance sheet includes data aggregated by fund type, these statements provide the details of financial position of individual funds. A combining balance sheet for all Special Revenue Funds is illustrated in Exhibit 3. Note that the total column of this statement agrees with the column for Special Revenue Fund types in the combined balance sheet. In addition, separate balance sheets and schedules may be necessary for individual funds and account groups if the combining balance sheets do not sufficiently indicate financial position and compliance with finance-related legal and contractual requirements.

c. *A combined statement of revenues, expenditures and changes in fund balances—all governmental fund types.* This is an aggregate operating statement in which all governmental fund types are combined. Note that proprietary and fiduciary fund types are excluded from this statement because their measurement focus (expense rather than expenditure) makes their operating results incompatible. This statement is illustrated in Exhibit 4.

d. *Combined statement of revenues, expenditures and changes in fund balances—budget and actual—general and special revenue fund types.* This statement provides a comparison of actual operations with the budget for fund types that normally have a legally adopted annual budget. Other governmental fund types—capital projects, special assessment, and debt service—are oriented toward projects of several years' duration, so annual operating results are not comparable. This statement is illustrated in Exhibit 5.

e. *Combining statements of revenues, expenditures and changes in fund balances for each governmental fund type.* This statement for Special Revenue Funds is illustrated in Exhibit 6. The total column on this statement agrees with the Special Revenue Funds column in the combined statement in Exhibit 4. In addition, individual fund operating statements may be necessary to demonstrate compliance with finance-related legal and contractual provisions.

f. *Combined and combining statements of revenues, expenses and changes in retained earnings for all proprietary fund types.* Operating results for proprietary funds can be combined because they have a similar measurement focus. In addition, fiduciary funds that have an expense measurement focus may also be reported in this combined statement as illustrated in Exhibit 7. However, the results of operations of each fund must also be displayed separately so that individual fund operations can be analyzed.

g. *Operating statements for fiduciary fund types.* Expendable Trust Funds are regarded as comparable to governmental funds and should be reported in the same manner. Nonexpendable Trust and Pension Trust Funds are regarded as comparable to proprietary funds and should be reported similarly. At the general-purpose financial statement level, fiduciary fund operating statements may either be presented separately or within the combined statements of the governmental and proprietary funds, as appropriate.

EXHIBIT 2

CITY OF A
Combined Balance Sheet—All Fund Types and Account Groups
June 30, 19X1
(in thousands)

	Governmental fund types				Proprietary fund types		Fiduciary fund type	Account groups		Total (memorandum only)	
	General	Special revenue	Debt service	Capital projects	Enterprise	Internal service	Trust and agency	General fixed assets	General long-term debt	19X1	19X0
Assets											
Cash and investments	$ 9,303	$3,080	$545	$4,992	$ 16,073	$ 22	$7,553			$ 41,568	$ 40,786
Accounts receivable, net	1,313	2,231	24	2,017	8,262	67				13,914	9,793
Accrued interest receivable	200	99	10	95	1,247					1,651	1,510
Due from other funds	628				242					870	933
Inventories					1,557	125				1,682	1,327
Prepaid expenses and other assets	84				290					374	2,914
Deposits	676	29				4				709	1,244
Restricted cash and investments	2,065	355			29,451					31,871	48,101
Deferred charges					3,958					3,958	3,302
Property, plant, and equipment, net					170,165	4,598		$35,799		210,562	172,460
Amount available for retirement of general long-term debt									$ 643	643	563
Amount to be provided for retirement of general long-term debt									4,002	4,002	4,678

Liabilities:

										Total	Total
Accounts payable	$ 1,551	$ 427		$ 912	$ 14,952	$ 256				$ 18,098	$ 17,042
Accrued liabilities	5,159	208		2,554	2,308	717				10,946	7,252
Deposits	1,419				1,104					2,523	2,841
Due to other governments	31						$7,510			7,541	8,526
Due to other funds	91				326	453				870	933
Deferred compensation payable	2,065									2,065	1,419
Deferred revenue		624		291						915	1,965
Advances for construction					1,443					1,443	90
Long-term debt					100,346			$4,645		104,991	98,338
Total liabilities	$10,316	$1,259		$3,757	$120,479	$1,426	$7,510	$4,645		$149,392	$138,406
Fund equity:											
Contributed capital					$ 51,586	$3,829				$ 55,415	$ 51,959
Investment in general fixed assets									$35,799	35,799	33,329
Fund balances transferred					33,909					33,909	33,909
Retained earnings:											
Reserved					3,666					3,666	2,990
Unreserved					21,605	(439)				21,166	13,925
Fund balances:											
Reserved	$ 3,953	$ 610					$ 22			4,585	4,994
Unreserved		3,925	$579	$3,347			21			7,872	8,099
Total fund equity	$ 3,953	$4,535	$579	$3,347	$110,766	$3,390	$ 43		$35,799	$162,412	$149,205
	$14,269	$5,794	$579	$7,104	$231,245	$4,816	$7,553	$4,645	$35,799	$311,804	$287,611

EXHIBIT 3

CITY OF A
Combining Balance Sheet
All Special Revenue Funds
June 30, 19X1
(in thousands)

	Gas tax	Comprehensive employment and training act	Community development block grant	Federal revenue sharing	Parksites and playground	Sewer construction and maintenance	Miscellaneous grants	Total 19X1	Total 19X0
Assets									
Cash and investments	$ 701	$ 32		$ 551	$ 11	$1,462	$323	$3,080	$3,148
Accounts receivable	859	757		545	23		47	2,231	1,556
Accrued interest receivable	29			30		33	7	99	43
Deposits		29						29	217
Restricted cash and investments			$291		64			355	329
	$1,589	$818	$291	$1,126	$ 98	$1,495	$377	$5,794	$5,293
Liabilities and fund balances									
Accounts payable	$ 93	$173	$105		$ 54		$ 2	$ 427	$ 920
Accrued liabilities	23	70	100		4	$ 9	2	208	145
Deferred revenue		575			49			624	568
Total liabilities	$ 116	$818	$205		$ 107	$ 9	$ 4	$1,259	$1,633
Fund balances (deficit):									
Reserved	$ 306		$ 76	$1,126	$ 173	$ 55	$373	$ 610	$1,696
Unreserved	1,167		10		(182)	1,431		3,925	1,964
Total fund balances (deficit)	$1,473		$ 86	$1,126	$ (9)	$1,486	$373	$4,535	$3,660
	$1,589	$818	$291	$1,126	$ 98	$1,495	$377	$5,794	$5,293

EXHIBIT 4

CITY OF A
Combined Statement of Revenue, Expenditures, and Changes in Fund Balances
All Governmental Fund Types
Year Ended June 30, 19X1
(in thousands)

	General	Special revenue	Debt service	Capital projects	Total (memorandum only) 19X1	19X0
Revenue:						
Property taxes	$ 4,288		$1,256		$ 5,544	$ 5,187
Sales and use taxes	17,482				17,482	15,001
Licenses, fees, and permits	3,415	$ 419			3,834	3,178
Intergovernmental revenue	5,965	13,002		$ 9,123	28,090	23,943
Charges for services	7,850	7			7,857	6,836
Fines, forfeits, and penalties	1,663				1,663	1,018
Interest and rentals	824	561	52	555	1,992	1,532
Other	1,478	590		221	2,289	1,892
	$ 42,965	$ 14,579	$1,308	$ 9,899	$ 68,751	$ 58,587
Expenditures:						
General government	$ 3,821	$ 3,434		$ 7	$ 7,262	$ 6,892
Nondepartmental	164	2,493		165	2,822	5,171
Public safety	23,661	187		101	23,949	21,476
Public works	17,371	3,651		14,173	35,195	30,126
Culture and recreation	5,753	1,338		179	7,270	6,860
Debt service:						
Principal retirement			$1,050		1,050	1,045
Interest and fiscal charges			125		125	161
	$ 50,770	$ 11,103	$1,175	$ 14,625	$ 77,673	$ 71,731
Excess of revenue over (under) expenditures	$ (7,805)	$ 3,476	$ 133	$ (4,726)	$ (8,922)	$(13,144)
Other financing sources (uses):						
Operating transfers in	$ 674	$ 480		$ 2,407	$ 3,561	$ 3,471
Operating transfers out	(730)	(3,081)			(3,811)	(3,726)
	$ (56)	$ (2,601)		$ 2,407	$ (250)	$ (255)
Excess of revenue and other sources over (under) expenditures and other uses	$ (7,861)	$ 875	$ 133	$ (2,319)	$ (9,172)	$(13,399)
Fund balances at beginning of year	3,276	3,660	446	5,666	13,048	19,852
Transfers from other funds	8,538				8,538	6,595
Fund balances at end of year	$ 3,953	$ 4,535	$ 579	$ 3,347	$ 12,414	$ 13,048

EXHIBIT 5

CITY OF A
Statement of Revenue, Expenditures, and Changes in Fund Balances (Deficit)
Budget and Actual
General and Special Revenue Fund Types
Year Ended June 30, 19X1
(in thousands)

	General fund			Special revenue funds			Total (memorandum only)		
	Budget	Actual	Variance—favorable (unfavorable)	Budget	Actual	Variance—favorable (unfavorable)	Budget	Actual	Variance—favorable (unfavorable)
Revenue:									
Property taxes	$ 4,483	$ 4,288	$ (195)				$ 4,483	$ 4,288	$ (195)
Sales and use taxes	17,500	17,482	(18)				17,500	17,482	(18)
Licenses, fees, and permits	3,334	3,415	81	$ 906	$ 419	$ (487)	4,240	3,834	(406)
Intergovernmental revenue	5,948	5,965	17	15,788	13,002	(2,786)	21,736	18,967	(2,769)
Charges for services	8,109	7,850	(259)		7	7	8,109	7,857	(252)
Fines, forfeits, and penalties	1,515	1,663	148				1,515	1,663	148
Interest and rentals	928	824	(104)	235	561	326	1,163	1,385	222
Other	1,802	1,478	(324)	491	590	99	2,293	2,068	(225)

Nondepartmental	1,314	164	1,150	2,688	2,493	195	4,002	2,657	1,345
Public safety	24,061	23,661	400	215	187	28	24,276	23,848	428
Public works	17,375	17,371	4	8,801	3,651	5,150	26,176	21,022	5,154
Culture and recreation	6,246	5,753	493	2,424	1,338	1,086	8,670	7,091	1,579
	$ 53,484	$ 50,770	$ 2,714	$ 17,692	$ 11,103	$ 6,589	$ 71,176	$ 61,873	$ 9,303
Excess of revenue over (under) expenditures	$ (9,865)	$ (7,805)	$ 2,060	$ (272)	$ 3,476	$ 3,748	$(10,137)	$ (4,329)	$ 5,808
Other financing sources (uses):									
Operating transfers in	$ 1,137	$ 674	$ (463)		$ 480	$ 480	$ 1,137	$ 1,154	$ 17
Operating transfers out	(232)	(730)	(498)	$ (3,537)	(3,081)	456	(3,769)	(3,811)	(42)
	$ 905	$ (56)	$ (961)	$ (3,537)	$ (2,601)	$ 936	$ (2,632)	$ (2,657)	$ (25)
Excess of revenue and other sources over (under) expenditures and other uses	$ (8,960)	$ (7,861)	$ 1,099	$ (3,809)	$ 875	$ 4,684	$(12,769)	$ (6,986)	$ 5,783
Fund balances at beginning of year	3,276	3,276		3,660	3,660		6,936	6,936	
Transfers from other funds	8,035	8,538	503				8,035	8,538	503
Fund balances (deficit) at end of year	$ 2,351	$ 3,953	$ 1,602	$ (149)	$ 4,535	$ 4,684	$ 2,202	$ 8,488	$ 6,286

EXHIBIT 6

41-38

CITY OF A
Combining Statement of Revenue, Expenditures, and Changes in Fund Balances (Deficit)
All Special Revenue Funds
Year Ended June 30, 19X1
(in thousands)

	Gas tax	Comprehensive employment and training act	Community development block grant	Federal revenue sharing	Parksites and playgrounds	Sewer construction and maintenance	Miscellaneous grants	Total 19X1	Total 19X0
Revenue:									
Intergovernmental revenue	$3,004	$4,229	$3,045	$2,226	$341		$157	$13,002	$12,054
Developers' fees					247	$171	1	419	544
Charges for services	7							7	34
Interest and rentals	135		23	177		184	42	561	410
Other	166		10	6	363	45		590	345
	$3,312	$4,229	$3,078	$2,409	$951	$400	$200	$14,579	$13,387
Expenditures:									
General government		$3,431	$3	$9			$25	$3,434	$3,050
Nondepartmental		196	2,263				25	2,493	1,595
Public safety		113	36				38	187	448
Public works	$2,341	225	650	170	$15	$201	49	3,651	5,192
Culture and recreation	264	264	81		953		40	1,338	1,682
	$2,341	$4,229	$3,033	$179	$968	$201	$152	$11,103	$11,967
Excess of revenue over (under) expenditures	$971		$45	$2,230	$(17)	$199	$48	$3,476	$1,420
Other financing sources (uses):									
Operating transfers in (out), net	(374)			(2,407)	180			(2,601)	(3,372)
Excess of revenue and other sources over (under) expenditures and other uses	$597		$45	$(177)	$163	$199	$48	$875	$(1,952)
Fund balances (deficit) at beginning of year	876		41	1,303	(172)	1,287	325	3,660	5,612
Fund balances (deficit) at end of year	$1,473		$86	$1,126	$(9)	$1,486	$373	$4,535	$3,660

EXHIBIT 7

CITY OF A
Combined Statement of Revenue, Expenses, and Changes in Retained Earnings (Deficit) /Fund Balance
All Proprietary Fund Types and Similar Trust Funds
Year Ended June 30, 19X1
(in thousands)

	Proprietary fund types		Fiduciary fund type	Total (memorandum only)	
	Enterprise	Internal service	Museum and library	19X1	19X0
Operating revenue:					
Charges for services	$105,757	$5,690		$111,447	$89,303
Other	1,716	152	$ 5	1,873	1,710
	$107,473	$5,842	$ 5	$113,320	$91,013
Operating expenses:					
Cost of water/purchased power	$ 76,024			$ 76,024	$62,492
Maintenance, operations, and administration	16,751	$5,466	$ 14	22,231	18,222
Depreciation and amortization	3,394	1,213		4,607	3,824
Other	48			48	94
	$ 96,217	$6,679	$ 14	$102,910	$84,632
Income (loss) from operations	$ 11,256	$ (837)	$ (9)	$ 10,410	$ 6,381
Nonoperating revenue (expenses):					
Interest revenue	$ 6,266		$ 6	$ 6,272	$ 2,664
Transient occupancy tax	4,922			4,922	4,193
Interest expense	(4,437)	$ (109)		(4,546)	(2,509)
Visitor and Convention Bureau expense	(696)			(696)	(571)
Other income	100			100	
	$ 6,155	$ (109)	$ 6	$ 6,052	$ 3,777
Income (loss) before operating transfers and extraordinary item	$ 17,411	$ (946)	$ (3)	$ 16,462	$10,158
Operating transfers in		250		250	254
Net income (loss) before extraordinary item	$ 17,411	$ (696)	$ (3)	$ 16,712	$10,412
Extraordinary gain on refunding of long-term debt					4,337
Net income (loss)	$ 17,411	$ (696)	$ (3)	$ 16,712	$14,749
Retained earnings/fund balance at beginning of year	16,752	163	46	16,961	8,969
Transfers (to) from other funds	(8,892)	94		(8,798)	(6,758)
Retained earnings (deficit)/fund balance at end of year	$ 25,271	$ (439)	$ 43	$ 24,875	$16,960

BIBLIOGRAPHY

American Accounting Association, Report of the Committee on Concepts of Accounting Applicable to the Public Sector, 1970–71 (AAA, 1971).

American Institute of Certified Public Accountants, Accounting Standards Division, *Accounting and Financial Reporting by Governmental Units*, Statement of Position 80-2 (AICPA, 1980).

American Institute of Certified Public Accountants, Committee on Governmental Accounting and Auditing, *Audits of State and Local Governmental Units* (AICPA, 1974).

Anthony, R. N., *Financial Accounting in Nonbusiness Organizations* (FASB, 1978).

Comptroller General of the United States, *Standards for Audit of Governmental Organizations, Programs, Activities & Functions* (U.S. General Accounting Office, Washington, D.C., 1981).

Davidson, S., D. O. Green, W. Hellerstein, A. Madansky, and R. L. Weil, *Financial Reporting by State and Local Government Units* (University of Chicago, Chicago, 1977).

Drebin, A. R., "Governmental vs. Commercial Accounting: The Issues," *Governmental Finance*, November 1979, pp. 3–8.

———, "Is Accounting That's Good for General Motors Good for Detroit?," *The Government Accountants Journal*, Spring 1981, pp. 28–33.

Drebin, A. R., J. L. Chan, and L. C. Ferguson, *Objectives of Accounting and Financial Reporting for Governmental Units: A Research Study* (National Council on Governmental Accounting, Chicago, 1981).

Ernst & Whinney, *How Cities Can Improve Their Financial Reporting* (E&W, Cleveland, 1979).

Hay, L. E., *Accounting for Governmental and Nonprofit Entities*, 6th ed. (Richard D. Irwin, Homewood, Ill., 1980).

Henke, E., *Introduction to Nonprofit Organization Accounting* (Kent, Boston, 1980).

Lynn, E. S., and R. J. Freeman, *Fund Accounting: Theory and Practice*, 2d ed. (Prentice-Hall, Englewood Cliffs, N.J., 1983).

Municipal Finance Officers Association, *Governmental Accounting, Auditing and Financial Reporting* (MFOA, Chicago, 1980).

National Council on Governmental Accounting, *Governmental Accounting and Financial Reporting Principles*, Statement 1 (Municipal Finance Officers Association of the United States and Canada, Chicago, 1979).

———, *Grant, Entitlement, and Shared Revenue Accounting and Reporting*, Statement 2 (MFOA, 1979).

———, *Defining the Governmental Reporting Entity*, Statement 3 (MFOA, 1981).

———, *Accounting and Financial Reporting for Claims and Judgments and Compensated Absences*, Statement No. 4 (MFOA, 1982).

Solomons, David (ed.), *Improving the Financial Discipline of States and Cities* (Council of Arthur Young Professors, Reston, Va., 1980).

State Government Accounting Project, *Preferred Accounting Practices for State Governments* (Council of State Governments, Lexington, Ky., 1983).

Steinberg, H. I., "A New Look at Governmental Accounting," *Journal of Accountancy*, March 1979, pp. 46–55.

CHAPTER 42

Accounting for

Nonprofit

Organizations

Timothy J. Racek
Partner, Arthur Andersen & Co.

STATE OF THE ART

Accounting for nonprofit organizations (excluding governmental entities and those organized for the economic benefit of their members) has evolved slowly, and at times with painfully conflicting concepts. Accounting principles have often been adopted to meet management objectives, which differ from time to time and from entity to entity. The result is a relative lack of consistency in accounting for similar transactions and in forms of reporting similar results of operations and financial position. For example, the American Institute of Certified Public Accountants has issued four different sets of guidelines for accounting in this sector [AICPA, 1972, 1973, 1974b, 1978d].

Scope of the Industry. Although nonprofit organizations are alike in that the accumulation of wealth for owners is not an objective, they differ considerably in their purposes. These differences give rise to differing elements of resources needed to achieve their underlying purposes, differing organizational structures, and differing operating philosophies. As a result, the nonprofit sector comprises organizations that differ in almost every way, other than the lack of a long-term profit motive. Thus, need exists for a logical and consistent basis of accounting that will be useful both for a local church group and a complex teaching hospital. The Financial Accounting Standards Board (FASB) is currently attempting to meet this need.

Statement of Financial Accounting Concepts No. 4. The FASB has recognized the need to deal with the relative lack of consistency and authoritative guidance in nonprofit organization financial reporting and has initiated a long-term effort to deal with the problem. The first result of this effort was the issuance in 1980 of Statement of Financial Accounting Concepts (SFAC) No. 4, *Objectives of Financial Reporting by Nonbusiness Organizations.* This identifies the objectives of nonbusiness financial reporting and the related underlying concepts of financial accounting. These concepts will be used by the Board in the future development of financial accounting and reporting standards that will constitute authoritative guidance.

Certain of the key findings of SFAC No. 4 are as follows:

1. Only one conceptual framework will be developed, covering both business and nonbusiness organizations. However, appropriate provisions will be made for differences between the two groups in reporting objectives and concepts.

2. The decision as to applicability of the concepts to government has been deferred pending further developments in the structure for standards development in that sector.

3. Objectives of nonbusiness financial reporting are stated in terms of meeting the needs of users to make decisions regarding resource allocation; assessment of services; assessment of management stewardship and performance, and the related need for information about economic resources, obligations, net resources, and changes; including resource flow and service efforts and accomplishments.

4. Although purposely nonspecific in almost every area, the FASB did indicate that accrual accounting provides better information than does cash basis accounting.

Pervasive Issues. The FASB has initiated the next step in development of nonbusiness accounting principles by establishing a staff project to develop a second concepts statement to be used as a basis for resolving underlying pervasive issues. This is a particularly critical project, because the issues to be decided will ultimately determine the degree to which changes must be made in present reporting practices.

Among the key pervasive issues that may be addressed are the following.

Depreciation. Should nonbusiness organizations depreciate the cost of their fixed assets? Under present AICPA guidance, colleges and universities do not depreciate their educational plant, whereas AICPA guidance for all other nonbusiness organizations requires recognition of depreciation as a cost of conducting their nonprofit and supporting service activities. A key aspect of the issue is the degree to which it is desirable to report the full cost of providing services, including the cost associated with the use of facilities.

Income recognition. Should restricted contributions be recognized as support in the operating statement when received, or should they be deferred and reflected in operations only when spent for the restricted purposes? If deferred, should they be shown as a liability in the balance sheet or credited directly to equity? Existing AICPA guidance differs significantly on these issues. For example, voluntary health and welfare organizations report restricted contributions as support in the statement of operations when received. Most hospitals reflect such gifts as direct credits to restricted fund balances and later report contributions and related expenses in the operating statement when the resources have been used.

Investments. Should investments be carried at cost (or the lower of cost or market) or at market? At present, most nonprofits have an option as to which method to use, resulting in considerably different results depending on which is elected.

Form of financial statements. Should financial statements reflect each fund separately, or may they be combined? If shown separately, is a columnar presentation with a total column acceptable? Should the operating statement reflect a "bottom line"? Should the results of fund-raising efforts be reported separately from other revenue and service activities? Again, existing practice differs on all of these issues.

Reporting entity. The FASB may also develop the conceptual base needed to resolve problems of defining the reporting entity. Related issues range from the degree to which an individual fund might possibly be viewed as a separate entity, to issues involving reporting by related organizations that do not involve the classic control elements of stock ownership common to business organizations.

Standards Development. Upon completion of its conceptual projects, the FASB will proceed with the issuance of standards that will constitute generally accepted accounting principles and, presumably, result in modification and extraction by the FASB of the current AICPA nonbusiness audit guides and statements of position. In the meantime, the AICPA pronouncements constitute generally accepted accounting principles for the respective organizations.

Hospital Audit Guide. The *Hospital Audit Guide* and related Statements of Position provide guidance in hospital financial reporting. It is based on the concept that generally accepted accounting principles for business should be applicable, other than for transactions such as contributions, which are unique to the nonprofit area.

Audits of Colleges and Universities. *Audits of Colleges and Universities* and related Statements of Position build on many of the concepts developed over the years by the National Association of College and University Business Officers. Its basic focus is that colleges and universities differ in such significant ways from business enterprises that different concepts are required in financial reporting. As a result, there is a requirement for extensive fund reporting, data regarding totals of all funds is discouraged, and the operating statements mix plant financing activities with income and expenses.

Audits of Voluntary Health and Welfare Organizations. The preface to *Audits of Voluntary Health and Welfare Organizations* indicates that the organizations to which it is intended to apply include "those nonprofit organizations that derive their revenue primarily from voluntary contributions from the general public to be used for general or specific purposes connected with health, welfare or community services." Although decisions on applicability are sometimes difficult in practice, presumably only those organizations that receive more than half of their income from public contributions and are involved in health, welfare, or community services are covered.

This guide supports the work done by the National Health Council, Inc., the National Assembly of National Voluntary Health and Social Welfare Organizations, Inc., and United Way of America. It approaches financial reporting from the standpoint of accountability, thereby presenting an all-inclusive statement of operations with columns to reflect donor restrictions on resources and a total column.

Accounting Principles and Reporting Practices for Certain Nonprofit Organizations—SOP 78-10. Statement of Position 78-10 of the AICPA provides guidance for those nonprofit organizations not covered by the other guides. Because the FASB had initiated its nonbusiness conceptual framework project at the time the SOP was issued, no effective date was set. This was done to avoid the possibility that covered organizations would be required to adopt the recommendations of the SOP and then amend them again when FASB issues nonbusiness standards.

Statement of Financial Accounting Standards No. 32, *Specialized Accounting and Reporting Principles and Practices in AICPA Statements of Position and Guides on Accounting and Auditing Matters.* However, the FASB did acknowledge the issuance of the SOP and indicated in Statement of Financial Accounting Standards No. 32 that the specialized accounting and reporting principles and practices contained in SOP 78-10 are preferable for purposes of justifying a change in accounting principles for those organizations that voluntarily elect to follow its guidance. SFAS No. 32 also includes the other three guides (hospitals, colleges, and health and welfare) in its listing of AICPA guidance that constitutes preferable principles for purposes of justifying a change in principle by the organizations to which those guides apply.

FUNDAMENTALS OF NONPROFIT ACCOUNTING

Accounting for nonprofit organizations may be approached by focusing on those aspects that differ from commercial accounting. From this view, such areas as sales, cost of sales, related inventory, and receivables should employ normal commercial principles. Special guidance is needed solely in those areas affected by the basic nonprofit nature of the entity and transactions that do not normally take place in the business world. Because the FASB is currently attempting to resolve the proper accounting for these pervasive differences, detailed discussion of these matters will not be given here. The following review of fund accounting provides a basic guide to the nonprofit accounting process.

Fund Accounting. Most nonprofit organizations employ some type of fund accounting to assure that third-party restrictions on uses of contributed resources are honored. This is a bookkeeping practice whereby separate self-balancing sets of asset, liability, equity, income, and expense accounts are set up to account separately for restricted gifts (or groups of gifts with similar restrictions). Funds commonly include the following:

Unrestricted or General Fund
Endowment Fund
Plant Fund
Current Restricted Fund
Other funds: Annuity Fund, Life Income Fund, Custodial Fund, etc.

Unrestricted or general fund. With rare exceptions, all nonprofits maintain an unrestricted fund to account for resources that may be used fully at the discretion of the governing board. Although the board may designate portions of the fund balance to be used for specific purposes (or to be invested), such designations normally may be rescinded by the board. As a result, even though subfunds may be established, the identification of unrestricted resources must be maintained to permit proper reporting in the financial statements.

All entries to record transactions by the nonprofit entity must identify first the fund affected by the transaction and then the normal information regarding the specific accounts that are affected. Receipt of an unrestricted $100 cash contribution is recorded by the following entry:

Unrestricted Fund

Cash	100	
Contributions		100
To record receipt of unrestricted contribution.		

Because nonprofit organizations do not have shareholders, contributed capital and retained earnings accounts are not used. Rather, equity is most often reflected in an account designated Fund Balance. (However, the FASB is presently considering use of alternative terms, such as Net Assets.) The net results of operations are transferred to equity at the end of the period. In the absence of other transactions, the $100 Contributions account balance would be closed as follows:

Unrestricted Fund

Contributions	100	
Fund Balance		100
To close income accounts for the year to fund balance.		

Endowment fund. Gifts that require the entity to invest and maintain the principal in perpetuity are recorded in endowment funds. Those that require investment for a specified period of time are referred to as term endowments. Receipt of a $10,000 endowment gift would be recorded as follows:

Endowment Fund

Cash	10,000	
Contributions		10,000
To record receipt of endowment gift.		

Interest and dividends earned from endowment investments may be available for unrestricted use or, if specified by the contributor, restricted for specific purposes. Normally, such investment income is recorded upon receipt directly in the fund in which it will be spent and is *not* reflected in the endowment fund. For example, receipt of $500 of interest from an endowment that does not specify how the income is to be used would be recorded as follows:

Unrestricted Fund

Cash	500	
Investment Income		500
To record receipt of unrestricted endowment investment income.		

However, capital gains and losses normally are accounted for in the endowment fund following concepts originally applicable to trust accounting, which segregate income and principal transactions. Under those concepts, purchases and sales of securities are deemed to be capital transactions and related gains and losses affect the Endowment Fund balance. Certain state laws now permit the governing board to decide whether net aggregate capital gains may be used for operating purposes. If such decisions are made, the amounts made available should be reflected as interfund transfers. For example, if $1,000 of accumulated capital gains were transferred from the Endowment Fund Cash account to the Unrestricted Cash account, the entries would be as follows:

Endowment Fund

Transfer to Unrestricted Fund	1,000	
Cash		1,000

Unrestricted Fund

Cash	1,000	
Transfer from Endowment Fund		1,000
To record transfer of accumulated capital gains from endowment to unrestricted fund, as approved by governing board.		

At year-end, the interfund transfer accounts are closed to the respective fund balance accounts in the same way that income and expense accounts are closed.

Many nonprofit organizations pool liquid assets of the respective funds for investment purposes. In these cases, records must be maintained of the equity of the respective funds (and of the individual restrictions on the use of income of specific endowments) in the pool to permit proper allocation of income as well as gains and losses. The AICPA audit guide for voluntary health and welfare organizations discusses this process and illustrates proper accounting. Use of a separate endowment fund in the financial statements helps report on stewardship in accordance with contributors' wishes and also makes clear that these resources are not available to fund current operations.

Plant fund. Many nonprofit organizations use a Plant Fund to reflect unspent gifts restricted by contributors for fixed asset acquisition as well as amounts already expended for this purpose. Often the amounts expended are funded by a combination of donor-restricted and -unrestricted gifts. Amounts financed by unrestricted gifts are reflected as interfund transfers from the Unrestricted Fund to the Plant Fund.

Plant debt is normally reported in the Plant Fund. Depreciation may be shown directly in the Plant Fund or in the Unrestricted Fund. In the latter case, an amount equal to the depreciation charge is transferred from the Unrestricted Fund to the Plant Fund. The following illustrates this process:

Unrestricted Fund

Provision for Depreciation	12,000	
Transfer to Plant Fund		12,000

Plant Fund

Transfer from Unrestricted Fund	12,000	
Accumulated Depreciation		12,000
To reflect depreciation provision in the Unrestricted Fund and accumulated depreciation in the Plant Fund.		

The interfund transfer account balances are closed out to the respective fund balance accounts at the end of the period.

Use of a separate Plant Fund helps to communicate to the user of the financial statements both the amount of fixed assets for which the entity has stewardship responsibility and the relative lack of liquidity that is inherent in such assets.

Current restricted fund. The Current Restricted Fund is used to account for gifts restricted by contributors for specific operating purposes.

Often, organizations maintain one principal checking account for deposit of contributions and payment of bills. In these cases, interfund asset and liability accounts must be used to maintain accountability for donor-restricted contributions. For example, receipt by a voluntary health organization of a $500 gift restricted to research, which is deposited in the general operating bank account, would be recorded as follows:

Unrestricted Fund

Cash—Operating Account	500	
Due to Restricted Fund		500

Restricted Fund

Due from Unrestricted Fund	500	
Contributions—Restricted for Research		500
To record receipt of gift restricted for research which was deposited in general bank account.		

Expenses paid by the Unrestricted Fund on behalf of the Restricted Fund would be recorded by similar entries. At year-end, the interfund receivable and payable account balances may be reflected in the balance sheets of the respective funds. However, in those instances in which cash is available to settle the interfund debt resulting from use of a single operating cash account, the interfund balances may be eliminated by reclassifying cash to reflect the respective equities in this fungible asset.

Other funds. Similarly, other funds may be established to maintain control over resources with special accountabilities, such as the following:

1. *Annuity Fund*—Resources held to generate income at a specified rate for a third party with the remainder ultimately available for the nonprofit organization

2. *Life Income Fund*—Resources held to generate income, all of which is paid to a third party, with the principal ultimately available for the nonprofit organization

3. *Custodial Fund*—Resources managed at the direction of and for the benefit of others. The net asset balance is matched by a liability, rather than an equity, for the organization holding the resources.

BIBLIOGRAPHY

American Institute of Certified Public Accountants, *Hospital Audit Guide*, Industry Audit Guide (AICPA, 1972).

———, *Audits of Colleges and Universities*, Industry Audit Guide (AICPA, 1973).

———, *Financial Accounting and Reporting by Colleges and Universities*, Statement of Position 74-8 (AICPA, 1974a).

———, *Audits of Voluntary Health and Welfare Organizations*, Industry Audit Guide (AICPA, 1974b).

———, *Clarification of Accounting, Auditing, and Reporting Practices Relating to Hospital Malpractice Loss Contingencies*, Statement of Position (AICPA, 1978a).

———, *Accounting by Hospitals for Certain Marketable Equity Securities*, Statement of Position 78-1 (AICPA, 1978b).

————, *Financial Accounting and Reporting by Hospitals Operated by a Governmental Unit,* Statement of Position 78-7 (AICPA, 1978c).

————, *Accounting Principles and Reporting Practices for Certain Nonprofit Organizations,* Statement of Position 78-10 (AICPA, 1978d).

————, *Reporting Practices Concerning Hospital-Related Organizations,* Statement of Position 81-2 (AICPA, 1981a).

————, *Audits of Certain Nonprofit Organizations,* Industry Audit Guide (AICPA, 1981b).

Association of Science-Technology Centers, *Museum Accounting Guidelines* (Washington, D.C., 1976).

Financial Accounting Standards Board, *Objectives of Financial Reporting by Nonbusiness Organizations,* Statement of Financial Accounting Concepts No. 4 (FASB, 1980).

National Association of College and University Business Officers, *College and University Business Administration,* 4th ed. (Washington, D.C., 1982).

National Association of Independent Schools, *Accounting for Independent Schools,* 2d ed. (Boston, 1977).

National Health Council, Inc., National Assembly of National Voluntary Health and Social Welfare Organizations, Inc., and United Way of America, *Standards of Accounting and Financial Reporting for Voluntary Health and Welfare Organizations,* rev. ed. (New York, 1974).

Sumariwalla, R. D., *Accounting and Financial Reporting—A Guide for United Ways and Not-for-Profit Human Service Organizations* (United Way of America, Alexandria, Va., 1974).

U.S. Catholic Conference, *Accounting Principles and Reporting Practices for Churches and Church-Related Organizations* (Washington, D.C., 1983).

Compound Interest,

Annuity,

and Bond Tables

TABLE 1 Future Value of $1

$$F_n = P(1 + r)^n$$

r = interest rate; n = number of periods until valuation; $P = \$1$

Periods = n	¼%	½%	¾%	1%	1½%	2%	3%	4%	5%	6%	7%	8%	10%	12%	15%	20%
1	1.00250	1.00500	1.00750	1.01000	1.01500	1.02000	1.03000	1.04000	1.05000	1.06000	1.07000	1.08000	1.10000	1.12000	1.15000	1.20000
2	1.00501	1.01003	1.01506	1.02010	1.03023	1.04040	1.06090	1.08160	1.10250	1.12360	1.14490	1.16640	1.21000	1.25440	1.32250	1.44000
3	1.00752	1.01508	1.02267	1.03030	1.04568	1.06121	1.09273	1.12486	1.15763	1.19102	1.22504	1.25971	1.33100	1.40493	1.52088	1.72800
4	1.01004	1.02015	1.03034	1.04060	1.06136	1.08243	1.12551	1.16986	1.21551	1.26248	1.31080	1.36049	1.46410	1.57352	1.74901	2.07360
5	1.01256	1.02525	1.03807	1.05101	1.07728	1.10408	1.15927	1.21665	1.27628	1.33823	1.40255	1.46933	1.61051	1.76234	2.01136	2.48832
6	1.01509	1.03038	1.04585	1.06152	1.09344	1.12616	1.19405	1.26532	1.34010	1.41852	1.50073	1.58687	1.77156	1.97382	2.31306	2.98598
7	1.01763	1.03553	1.05370	1.07214	1.10984	1.14869	1.22987	1.31593	1.40710	1.50363	1.60578	1.71382	1.94872	2.21068	2.66002	3.58318
8	1.02018	1.04071	1.06160	1.08286	1.12649	1.17166	1.26677	1.36857	1.47746	1.59385	1.71819	1.85093	2.14359	2.47596	3.05902	4.29982
9	1.02273	1.04591	1.06956	1.09369	1.14339	1.19509	1.30477	1.42331	1.55133	1.68948	1.83846	1.99900	2.35795	2.77308	3.51788	5.15978
10	1.02528	1.05114	1.07758	1.10462	1.16054	1.21899	1.34392	1.48024	1.62889	1.79085	1.96715	2.15892	2.59374	3.10585	4.04556	6.19174
11	1.02785	1.05640	1.08566	1.11567	1.17795	1.24337	1.38423	1.53945	1.71034	1.89830	2.10485	2.33164	2.85312	3.47855	4.65239	7.43008
12	1.03042	1.06168	1.09381	1.12683	1.19562	1.26824	1.42576	1.60103	1.79586	2.01220	2.25219	2.51817	3.13843	3.89598	5.35025	8.91610
13	1.03299	1.06699	1.10201	1.13809	1.21355	1.29361	1.46853	1.66507	1.88565	2.13293	2.40985	2.71962	3.45227	4.36349	6.15279	10.69932
14	1.03557	1.07232	1.11028	1.14947	1.23176	1.31948	1.51259	1.73168	1.97993	2.26090	2.57853	2.93719	3.79750	4.88711	7.07571	12.83918
15	1.03816	1.07768	1.11860	1.16097	1.25023	1.34587	1.55797	1.80094	2.07893	2.39656	2.75903	3.17217	4.17725	5.47357	8.13706	15.40702
16	1.04076	1.08307	1.12699	1.17258	1.26899	1.37279	1.60471	1.87298	2.18287	2.54035	2.95216	3.42594	4.59497	6.13039	9.35762	18.48843
17	1.04336	1.08849	1.13544	1.18430	1.28802	1.40024	1.65285	1.94790	2.29202	2.69277	3.15882	3.70002	5.05447	6.86604	10.76126	22.18611
18	1.04597	1.09393	1.14396	1.19615	1.30734	1.42825	1.70243	2.02582	2.40662	2.85434	3.37993	3.99602	5.55992	7.68997	12.37545	26.62333
19	1.04858	1.09940	1.15254	1.20811	1.32695	1.45681	1.75351	2.10685	2.52695	3.02560	3.61653	4.31570	6.11591	8.61276	14.23177	31.94800
20	1.05121	1.10490	1.16118	1.22019	1.34686	1.48595	1.80611	2.19112	2.65330	3.20714	3.86968	4.66096	6.72750	9.64629	16.36654	38.33760
22	1.05647	1.11597	1.17867	1.24472	1.38756	1.54598	1.91610	2.36992	2.92526	3.60354	4.43040	5.43654	8.14027	12.10031	21.64475	55.20614
24	1.06176	1.12716	1.19641	1.26973	1.42950	1.60844	2.03279	2.56330	3.22510	4.04893	5.07237	6.34118	9.84973	15.17863	28.62518	79.49685
26	1.06707	1.13846	1.21443	1.29526	1.47271	1.67342	2.15659	2.77247	3.55567	4.54938	5.80735	7.39635	11.91818	19.04007	37.85680	114.4755
28	1.07241	1.14987	1.23271	1.32129	1.51722	1.74102	2.28793	2.99870	3.92013	5.11169	6.64884	8.62711	14.42099	23.88387	50.06561	164.8447
30	1.07778	1.16140	1.25127	1.34785	1.56308	1.81136	2.42726	3.24340	4.32194	5.74349	7.61226	10.06266	17.44940	29.95992	66.21177	237.3763
32	1.08318	1.17304	1.27011	1.37494	1.61032	1.88454	2.57508	3.50806	4.76494	6.45339	8.71527	11.73708	21.11378	37.58173	87.56507	341.8219
34	1.08860	1.18480	1.28923	1.40258	1.65900	1.96068	2.73191	3.79432	5.25335	7.25103	9.97811	13.69013	25.54767	47.14252	115.80480	492.2235
36	1.09405	1.19668	1.30865	1.43077	1.70914	2.03989	2.89828	4.10393	5.79182	8.14725	11.42394	15.96817	30.91268	59.13557	153.15185	708.8019
38	1.09953	1.20868	1.32835	1.45953	1.76080	2.12230	3.07478	4.43881	6.38548	9.15425	13.07927	18.62528	37.40434	74.17966	202.54332	1020.675
40	1.10503	1.22079	1.34835	1.48886	1.81402	2.20804	3.26204	4.80102	7.03999	10.28572	14.97446	21.72452	45.25926	93.05097	267.86355	1469.772
45	1.11892	1.25162	1.39968	1.56481	1.95421	2.43785	3.78160	5.84118	8.98501	13.76461	21.00245	31.92045	72.89048	163.9876	538.76927	3657.262
50	1.13297	1.28323	1.45296	1.64463	2.10524	2.69159	4.38391	7.10668	11.46740	18.42015	29.45703	46.90161	117.3909	289.0022	1083.65744	9100.438
100	1.28362	1.64667	2.11108	2.70481	4.43205	7.24465	19.21863	50.50495	131.5013	339.3021	867.7163	2199.761	13780.61	83522.27	117×10^4	828×10^5

TABLE 2 Present Value of $1

$$P = F_n(1 + r)^{-n}$$

r = discount rate; n = number of periods until payment; F_n = $1

Periods = n	¼%	½%	¾%	1%	1½%	2%	3%	4%	5%	6%	7%	8%	10%	12%	15%	20%
1	.99751	.99502	.99256	.99010	.98522	.98039	.97087	.96154	.95238	.94340	.93458	.92593	.90909	.89286	.86957	.83333
2	.99502	.99007	.98517	.98030	.97066	.96117	.94260	.92456	.90703	.89000	.87344	.85734	.86245	.79719	.75614	.69444
3	.99254	.98515	.97783	.97059	.95632	.94232	.91514	.88900	.86384	.83962	.81630	.79383	.75131	.71178	.65752	.57870
4	.99006	.98025	.97055	.96098	.94218	.92385	.88849	.85480	.82270	.79209	.76290	.73503	.68301	.63552	.57175	.48225
5	.98759	.97537	.96333	.95147	.92826	.90573	.86261	.82193	.78353	.74726	.71299	.68058	.62092	.56743	.49718	.40188
6	.98513	.97052	.95616	.94205	.91454	.88797	.83748	.79031	.74622	.70496	.66634	.63017	.56447	.50663	.43233	.33490
7	.98267	.96569	.94904	.93272	.90103	.87056	.81309	.75992	.71068	.66506	.62275	.58349	.51316	.45235	.37594	.27908
8	.98022	.96089	.94198	.92348	.88771	.85349	.78941	.73069	.67684	.62741	.58201	.54027	.46651	.40388	.32690	.23257
9	.97778	.95610	.93496	.91434	.87459	.83676	.76642	.70259	.64461	.59190	.54393	.50025	.42410	.36061	.28426	.19381
10	.97534	.95135	.92800	.90529	.86167	.82035	.74409	.67556	.61391	.55839	.50835	.46319	.38554	.32197	.24718	.16151
11	.97291	.94661	.92109	.89632	.84893	.80426	.72242	.64958	.58468	.52679	.47509	.42888	.35049	.28748	.21494	.13459
12	.97048	.94191	.91424	.88745	.83639	.78849	.70138	.62460	.55684	.49697	.44401	.39711	.31863	.25668	.18691	.11216
13	.96806	.93722	.90743	.87866	.82403	.77303	.68095	.60057	.53032	.46884	.41496	.36770	.28966	.22917	.16253	.09346
14	.96565	.93256	.90068	.86996	.81185	.75788	.66112	.57748	.50507	.44230	.38782	.34046	.26333	.20462	.14133	.07789
15	.96324	.92792	.89397	.86135	.79985	.74301	.64186	.55526	.48102	.41727	.36245	.31524	.23939	.18270	.12289	.06491
16	.96084	.92330	.88732	.85282	.78803	.72845	.62317	.53391	.45811	.39365	.33873	.29189	.21763	.16312	.10686	.05409
17	.95844	.91871	.88071	.84438	.77639	.71416	.60502	.51337	.43630	.37136	.31657	.27027	.19784	.14564	.09293	.04507
18	.95605	.91414	.87416	.83602	.76491	.70016	.58739	.49363	.41552	.35034	.29586	.25025	.17986	.13004	.08081	.03756
19	.95367	.90959	.86765	.82774	.75361	.68643	.57029	.47464	.39573	.33051	.27651	.23171	.16351	.11611	.07027	.03130
20	.95129	.90506	.86119	.81954	.74247	.67297	.55368	.45639	.37689	.31180	.25842	.21455	.14864	.10367	.06110	.02608
22	.94655	.89608	.84842	.80340	.72069	.64684	.52189	.42196	.34185	.27751	.22571	.18394	.12285	.08264	.04620	.01811
24	.94184	.88719	.83583	.78757	.69954	.62172	.49193	.39012	.31007	.24698	.19715	.15770	.10153	.06588	.03493	.01258
26	.93714	.87838	.82343	.77205	.67902	.59758	.46369	.36069	.28124	.21981	.17220	.13520	.08391	.05252	.02642	.00874
28	.93248	.86966	.81122	.75684	.65910	.57437	.43708	.33348	.25509	.19563	.15040	.11591	.06934	.04187	.01997	.00607
30	.92783	.86103	.79919	.74192	.63976	.55207	.41199	.30832	.23138	.17411	.13137	.09938	.05731	.03338	.01510	.00421
32	.92321	.85248	.78733	.72730	.62099	.53063	.38834	.28506	.20987	.15496	.11474	.08520	.04736	.02661	.01142	.00293
34	.91861	.84402	.77565	.71297	.60277	.51003	.36604	.26355	.19035	.13791	.10022	.07305	.03914	.02121	.00864	.00203
36	.91403	.83564	.76415	.69892	.58509	.49022	.34503	.24367	.17266	.12274	.08754	.06262	.03235	.01691	.00653	.00141
38	.90948	.82735	.75281	.68515	.56792	.47119	.32523	.22529	.15661	.10924	.07646	.05369	.02673	.01348	.00494	.00098
40	.90495	.81914	.74165	.67165	.55126	.45289	.30656	.20829	.14205	.09722	.06678	.04603	.02209	.01075	.00373	.00068
45	.89372	.79896	.71445	.63905	.51171	.41020	.26444	.17120	.11130	.07265	.04761	.03133	.01372	.00610	.00186	.00027
50	.88263	.77929	.68825	.60804	.47500	.37153	.22811	.14071	.08720	.05429	.03395	.02132	.00852	.00346	.00092	.00011
100	.77904	.60729	.47369	.36971	.22563	.13803	.05203	.01980	.00760	.00295	.00115	.00045	.00007	.00001	.00000	.00000

TABLE 3 Future Value of Annuity of $1 in Arrears

$$F = \frac{(1 + r)^n - 1}{r}$$

r = interest rate; n = number of payments

No. of Payments = n	¼%	½%	¾%	1%	1½%	2%	3%	4%	5%	6%	7%	8%	10%	12%	15%	20%
1	1.00000	1.00000	1.00000	1.00000	1.00000	1.00000	1.00000	1.00000	1.00000	1.00000	1.00000	1.00000	1.00000	1.00000	1.00000	1.00000
2	2.00250	2.00500	2.00750	2.01000	2.01500	2.02000	2.03000	2.04000	2.05000	2.06000	2.07000	2.08000	2.10000	2.12000	2.15000	2.20000
3	3.00751	3.01503	3.02256	3.03010	3.04523	3.06040	3.09090	3.12160	3.15250	3.18360	3.21490	3.24640	3.31000	3.37440	3.47250	3.64000
4	4.01503	4.03010	4.04523	4.06040	4.09090	4.12161	4.18363	4.24646	4.31013	4.37462	4.43994	4.50611	4.64100	4.77933	4.99338	5.36800
5	5.02506	5.05025	5.07556	5.10101	5.15227	5.20404	5.30914	5.41632	5.52563	5.63709	5.75074	5.86660	6.10510	6.35285	6.74238	7.44160
6	6.03763	6.07550	6.11363	6.15202	6.22955	6.30812	6.46841	6.63298	6.80191	6.97532	7.15329	7.33593	7.71561	8.11519	8.75374	9.92992
7	7.05272	7.10588	7.15948	7.21354	7.32299	7.43428	7.66246	7.89829	8.14201	8.39384	8.65402	8.92280	9.48717	10.08901	11.06680	12.91590
8	8.07035	8.14141	8.21318	8.28567	8.43284	8.58297	8.89234	9.21423	9.54911	9.89747	10.25980	10.63663	11.43589	12.29969	13.72682	16.49908
9	9.09053	9.18212	9.27478	9.36853	9.55933	9.75463	10.15911	10.58280	11.02656	11.49132	11.97799	12.48756	13.57948	14.77566	16.78584	20.79890
10	10.11325	10.22803	10.34434	10.46221	10.70272	10.94972	11.46388	12.00611	12.57789	13.18079	13.81645	14.48656	15.93742	17.54874	20.30372	25.95868
11	11.13854	11.27917	11.42192	11.56683	11.86326	12.16872	12.80780	13.48635	14.20679	14.97164	15.78360	16.64549	18.53117	20.65458	24.34928	32.15042
12	12.16638	12.33556	12.50759	12.68250	13.04121	13.41209	14.19203	15.02581	15.91713	16.86994	17.88845	18.97713	21.38428	24.13313	29.00167	39.58050
13	13.19680	13.39724	13.60139	13.80933	14.23683	14.68033	15.61779	16.62684	17.71298	18.88214	20.14064	21.49530	24.52271	28.02911	34.35192	48.49660
14	14.22979	14.46423	14.70340	14.94742	15.40538	15.97394	17.08632	18.29191	19.59863	21.01507	22.55049	24.21492	27.97498	32.39260	40.50471	59.19592
15	15.26537	15.53655	15.81368	16.09690	16.68214	17.29342	18.59891	20.02359	21.57856	23.27597	25.12902	27.15211	31.77248	37.27971	47.58041	72.03511
16	16.30353	16.61423	16.93228	17.25786	17.93237	18.63929	20.15688	21.82453	23.65749	25.67253	27.88805	30.32428	35.94973	42.75328	55.71747	87.44213
17	17.34429	17.69730	18.05927	18.43044	19.20136	20.01207	21.76159	23.69751	25.84037	28.21288	30.84022	33.75023	40.54470	48.88367	65.07509	105.9306
18	18.38765	18.78579	19.19472	19.61475	20.48938	21.41231	23.41444	25.64541	28.13238	30.90565	33.99903	37.45024	45.59917	55.74971	75.83636	128.1167
19	19.43362	19.87972	20.33868	20.81090	21.79672	22.84056	25.11687	27.67123	30.53900	33.75999	37.37896	41.44626	51.15909	63.43968	88.21181	154.7400
20	20.48220	20.97912	21.49122	22.01900	23.12367	24.29737	26.87037	29.77808	33.06595	36.78559	40.99549	45.76196	57.27500	72.05244	102.4436	186.6880
22	22.58724	23.19443	23.82230	24.47159	25.83758	27.29898	30.53678	34.24797	38.50521	43.39229	49.00574	55.45676	71.40275	92.50258	137.63164	271.0307
24	24.70282	25.43196	26.18847	26.97346	28.63352	30.42186	34.42647	39.08260	44.50200	50.81558	58.17667	66.76476	88.49733	118.1552	184.16784	392.4842
26	26.82899	27.69191	28.59027	29.52563	31.51397	33.67091	38.55304	44.31174	51.11345	59.15638	68.67647	79.95442	109.1818	150.3339	245.71197	567.3773
28	28.96580	29.97452	31.02823	32.12910	34.48148	37.05121	42.93092	49.96758	58.40258	68.52811	80.69769	95.33883	134.2099	190.6989	327.10408	819.2233
30	31.11331	32.28002	33.50290	34.78489	37.53868	40.56808	47.57542	56.08494	66.43885	79.05819	94.46079	113.2832	164.4940	241.3327	434.74515	1181.881
32	33.27157	34.60862	36.01483	37.49407	40.68829	44.22703	52.50276	62.70147	75.29883	90.88978	110.2181	134.2135	201.1378	304.8477	577.10046	1704.109
34	35.44064	36.96058	38.56458	40.25770	43.93309	48.03380	57.73018	69.85791	85.06696	104.1838	128.2588	158.6267	245.4767	384.5210	765.36535	2456.118
36	37.62056	39.33610	41.15272	43.07688	47.27597	51.99437	63.27594	77.59831	95.83632	119.1209	148.9135	187.1022	299.1268	484.4631	1014.34568	3539.009
38	39.81140	41.73545	43.77982	45.95272	50.71989	56.11494	69.15945	85.97034	107.7095	135.9042	172.5610	220.3159	364.0434	609.8305	1343.62216	5098.373
40	42.01320	44.15885	46.44648	48.88637	54.26789	60.40198	75.40126	95.02552	120.7998	154.7620	199.6351	259.0565	442.5926	767.0914	1779.09031	7343.858
45	47.56606	50.32416	53.29011	56.48107	63.61420	71.89271	92.71986	121.0294	159.7002	212.7435	285.7493	386.5056	718.9048	1358.230	3585.12846	18281.31
50	53.18868	56.64516	60.39426	64.46318	73.68283	84.57940	112.7969	152.6671	209.3480	290.3359	406.5289	573.7702	1163.909	2400.018	7217.71628	45497.19
100	113.44996	129.33370	148.14451	170.4814	228.8030	312.2323	607.2877	1237.624	2610.025	5638.368	12381.66	27484.52	137796.1	696010.5	783×10^4	414×10^6

$$P_A = \frac{1 - (1+r)^{-n}}{r}$$

r = discount rate; n = number of payments

No. of Payments = n	¼%	½%	¾%	1%	1½%	2%	3%	4%	5%	6%	7%	8%	10%	12%	15%	20%
1	0.99751	0.99502	0.99256	.99010	.98522	.98039	.97087	.96154	.95238	.94340	.93458	.92593	.90909	.89286	0.86957	.83333
2	1.99252	1.98510	1.97772	1.97040	1.95588	1.94156	1.91347	1.88609	1.85941	1.83339	1.80802	1.78326	1.73554	1.69005	1.62571	1.52778
3	2.98506	2.97025	2.95556	2.94099	2.91220	2.88388	2.82861	2.77509	2.72325	2.67301	2.62432	2.57710	2.48685	2.40183	2.28323	2.10648
4	3.97512	3.95050	3.92611	3.90197	3.85438	3.80773	3.71710	3.62990	3.54595	3.46511	3.38721	3.31213	3.16987	3.03735	2.85498	2.58873
5	4.96272	4.92587	4.88944	4.85343	4.78264	4.71346	4.57971	4.45182	4.32948	4.21236	4.10020	3.99271	3.79079	3.60478	3.35216	2.99061
6	5.94785	5.89638	5.84560	5.79548	5.69719	5.60143	5.41719	5.24214	5.07569	4.91732	4.76654	4.62288	4.35526	4.11141	3.78448	3.32551
7	6.93052	6.86207	6.79464	6.72819	6.59821	6.47199	6.23028	6.00205	5.78637	5.58238	5.38929	5.20637	4.86842	4.56376	4.16042	3.60459
8	7.91074	7.82296	7.73661	7.65168	7.48593	7.32548	7.01969	6.73274	6.46321	6.20979	5.97130	5.74664	5.33493	4.96764	4.48732	3.83716
9	8.88852	8.77906	8.67158	8.56602	8.36052	8.16224	7.78611	7.43533	7.10782	6.80169	6.51523	6.24689	5.75902	5.32825	4.77158	4.03097
10	9.86386	9.73041	9.59958	9.47130	9.22218	8.98259	8.53020	8.11090	7.72173	7.36009	7.02358	6.71008	6.14457	5.65022	5.01877	4.19247
11	10.83677	10.67703	10.52067	10.36763	10.07112	9.78685	9.25262	8.76048	8.30641	7.88687	7.49867	7.13896	6.49506	5.93770	5.23371	4.32706
12	11.80725	11.61893	11.43491	11.25508	10.90751	10.57534	9.95400	9.38507	8.86325	8.38384	7.94269	7.53608	6.81369	6.19437	5.42062	4.43922
13	12.77532	12.55615	12.34235	12.13374	11.73153	11.34837	10.63496	9.98565	9.39357	8.85268	8.35765	7.90378	7.10336	6.43255	5.58315	4.53268
14	13.74096	13.48871	13.24302	13.00370	12.54338	12.10625	11.29607	10.56312	9.89864	9.29498	8.74547	8.24424	7.36669	6.62817	5.72448	4.61057
15	14.70420	14.41662	14.13699	13.86505	13.34323	12.84926	11.93794	11.11839	10.37966	9.71225	9.10791	8.55948	7.60608	6.81086	5.84737	4.67547
16	15.66504	15.33993	15.02431	14.71787	14.13126	13.57771	12.56110	11.65230	10.83777	10.10590	9.44665	8.85137	7.82371	6.97399	5.95423	4.72956
17	16.62348	16.25863	15.90502	15.56225	14.90765	14.29187	13.16612	12.16567	11.27407	10.47726	9.76322	9.12164	8.02155	7.11963	6.04716	4.77463
18	17.57953	17.17277	16.77918	16.39827	15.67256	14.99203	13.75351	12.65930	11.68959	10.82760	10.05909	9.37189	8.20141	7.24967	6.12797	4.81219
19	18.53320	18.08236	17.64683	17.22601	16.42617	15.67846	14.32380	13.13394	12.08532	11.15812	10.33560	9.60360	8.36492	7.36578	6.19823	4.84350
20	19.48449	18.98742	18.50802	18.04555	17.16864	16.35143	14.87747	13.59033	12.46221	11.46992	10.59401	9.81815	8.51356	7.46944	6.25933	4.86958
22	21.37995	20.78406	20.21121	19.66038	18.62082	17.65805	15.93692	14.45112	13.16300	12.04158	11.06124	10.20074	8.77154	7.64465	6.35866	4.90943
24	23.26598	22.56287	21.88915	21.24339	20.03041	18.91393	16.93554	15.24696	13.79864	12.55036	11.46933	10.52876	8.98474	7.78432	6.43377	4.93710
26	25.14261	24.32402	23.54219	22.79520	21.39863	20.12104	17.87684	15.98277	14.37519	13.00317	11.82578	10.80998	9.16095	7.89566	6.49056	4.95632
28	27.00989	26.06769	25.17071	24.31644	22.72672	21.28127	18.76411	16.66306	14.89813	13.40616	12.13711	11.05108	9.30657	7.98442	6.53351	4.96967
30	28.86787	27.79405	26.77508	25.80771	24.01584	22.39646	19.60044	17.29203	15.37245	13.76483	12.40904	11.25778	9.42691	8.05518	6.56598	4.97894
32	30.71660	29.50328	28.35565	27.26959	25.26714	23.46833	20.38877	17.87355	15.80268	14.08404	12.64656	11.43500	9.52638	8.11159	6.59053	4.98537
34	32.55611	31.19555	29.91278	28.70267	26.48173	24.49859	21.13184	18.41120	16.19290	14.36814	12.85401	11.58693	9.60857	8.15656	6.60910	4.98984
36	34.38647	32.87102	31.44681	30.10751	27.66068	25.48884	21.83225	18.90828	16.54685	14.62099	13.03521	11.71719	9.67651	8.19241	6.62314	4.99295
38	36.20770	34.52985	32.95808	31.48466	28.80505	26.44064	22.49246	19.36786	16.86789	14.84602	13.19347	11.82887	9.73265	8.22099	6.63375	4.99510
40	38.01986	36.17223	34.44694	32.83469	29.91585	27.35548	23.11477	19.79277	17.15909	15.04630	13.33171	11.92461	9.77905	8.24378	6.64178	4.99660
45	42.51088	40.20720	38.07320	36.09451	32.55234	29.49016	24.51871	20.72004	17.77407	15.45583	13.60552	12.10840	9.86281	8.28252	6.65429	4.99863
50	46.94617	44.14279	41.56645	39.19612	34.99969	31.42361	25.72976	21.48218	18.25593	15.76186	13.80075	12.23348	9.91481	8.30450	6.66051	4.99945
100	88.38248	78.54264	70.17462	63.02888	51.62470	43.09835	31.59891	24.50500	19.84791	16.61755	14.26925	12.49432	9.99927	8.33323	6.66666	5.00000

NOTE: To convert from this table to values of an annuity in advance, determine the annuity in arrears above for one less period and add 1.00000.

TABLE 5 Bond Values in Percent of Par: 10 Percent Semiannual Coupons

$$\text{Bond Value} = 10/r + (100 - 10/r)(1 + r/2)^{-2n} \quad r = \text{Yield to Maturity}; \quad n = \text{Years to Maturity}$$

Years to maturity	Market yield percent per year compounded semiannually											
	8.0	9.0	9.5	10.0	10.5	11.0	12.0	13.0	14.0	15.0	20.0
0.5	100.9615	100.4785	100.2387	100.0	99.7625	99.5261	99.0566	98.5915	98.1308	97.6744	95.4545
1.0	101.8861	100.9363	100.4665	100.0	99.5368	99.0768	98.1666	97.2691	96.3840	95.5111	91.3223
1.5	102.7751	101.3745	100.6840	100.0	99.3224	98.6510	97.3270	96.0273	94.7514	93.4987	87.5657
2.0	103.6299	101.7938	100.8917	100.0	99.1186	98.2474	96.5349	94.8613	93.2256	91.6267	84.1507
2.5	104.4518	102.1950	101.0899	100.0	98.9251	97.8649	95.7876	93.7665	91.7996	89.8853	81.0461
5.0	108.1109	103.9564	101.9541	100.0	98.0928	96.2312	92.6399	89.2168	85.9528	82.8398	69.2772
9.0	112.6593	106.0800	102.9803	100.0	97.1339	94.3770	89.1724	84.3513	79.8818	75.7350	58.9929
9.5	113.1339	106.2966	103.0838	100.0	97.0393	94.1962	88.8419	83.8979	79.3288	75.1023	58.1754
10.0	113.5903	106.5040	103.1827	100.0	96.9494	94.0248	88.5301	83.4722	78.8120	74.5138	57.4322
15.0	117.2920	108.1444	103.9551	100.0	96.2640	92.7331	86.2352	80.4120	75.1819	70.4740	52.8654
19.0	119.3679	109.0250	104.3608	100.0	95.9194	92.0976	85.1540	79.0312	73.6131	68.8015	51.3367
19.5	119.5845	109.1148	104.4017	100.0	95.8854	92.0357	85.0509	78.9025	73.4701	68.6525	51.2152
20.0	119.7928	109.2008	104.4408	100.0	95.8531	91.9769	84.9537	78.7817	73.3366	68.5140	51.1047
25.0	121.4822	109.8810	104.7461	100.0	95.6068	91.5342	84.2381	77.9132	72.3985	67.5630	50.4259
30.0	122.6235	110.3190	104.9381	100.0	95.4591	91.2751	83.8386	77.4506	71.9216	67.1015	50.1642
40.0	123.9154	110.7827	105.1347	100.0	95.3175	91.0345	83.4909	77.0728	71.5560	66.7690	50.0244
50.0	124.5050	110.9749	105.2124	100.0	95.2666	90.9521	83.3825	76.9656	71.4615	66.6908	50.0036

TABLE 6 Bond Values in Percent of Par: 12 Percent Semiannual Coupons

$$\text{Bond Value} = 12/r + (100 - 12/r)(1 + r/2)^{-2n}$$

r = Yield to Maturity; n = Years to Maturity

Years to maturity	Market yield percent per year compounded semiannually										
	8.0	9.0	10.0	11.0	11.5	12.0	12.5	13.0	14.0	15.0	20.0
0.5	101.9231	101.4354	100.9524	100.4739	100.2364	100.0	99.7647	99.5305	99.0654	98.6047	96.3636
1.0	103.7722	102.8090	101.8594	100.9232	100.4600	100.0	99.5433	99.0897	98.1920	97.3067	93.0579
1.5	105.5502	104.1234	102.7232	101.3490	100.6714	100.0	99.3348	98.6758	97.3757	96.0992	90.0526
2.0	107.2598	105.3813	103.5459	101.7526	100.8713	100.0	99.1387	98.2871	96.6128	94.9760	87.3205
2.5	108.9036	106.5850	104.3295	102.1351	101.0603	100.0	98.9540	97.9222	95.8998	93.9312	84.8369
5.0	116.2218	111.8691	107.7217	103.7688	101.8620	100.0	98.1816	96.4056	92.9764	89.7039	75.4217
9.0	125.3186	118.2400	111.6896	105.6230	102.7585	100.0	97.3432	94.7838	89.9409	85.4410	67.1944
9.5	126.2679	118.8899	112.0853	105.8038	102.8449	100.0	97.2642	94.6326	89.6644	85.0614	66.5403
10.0	127.1807	119.5119	112.4622	105.9752	102.9266	100.0	97.1898	94.4907	89.4060	84.7083	65.9457
15.0	134.5841	124.4333	115.3724	107.2669	103.5353	100.0	96.6489	93.4707	87.5910	82.2844	62.2923
19.0	138.7357	127.0750	116.8679	107.9024	103.8283	100.0	96.3995	93.0104	86.8065	81.2809	61.0694
19.5	139.1690	127.3445	117.0170	107.9643	103.8565	100.0	96.3760	92.9675	86.7351	81.1915	60.9722
20.0	139.5855	127.6024	117.1591	108.0231	103.8832	100.0	96.3539	92.9272	86.6683	81.1084	60.8838
25.0	142.9644	129.6430	118.2559	108.4658	104.0822	100.0	96.1930	92.6377	86.1993	80.5378	60.3407
30.0	145.2470	130.9570	118.9293	108.7249	104.1960	100.0	96.1053	92.4835	85.9608	80.2609	60.1314
40.0	147.8308	132.3480	119.5965	108.9655	104.2982	100.0	96.0313	92.3576	85.7780	80.0614	60.0195
50.0	149.0100	132.9248	119.8479	109.0479	104.3316	100.0	96.0093	92.3219	85.7307	80.0145	60.0029

Index

Sidney Davidson has been Arthur Young Professor of Accounting, Graduate School of Business, University of Chicago, for over 20 years. He was a member of the Accounting Principles Board for 5 years, and is past president of the American Accounting Association, which named him Outstanding Educator. He has served as consultant to a number of business firms and government agencies, including the U.S. Treasury Department.

Roman L. Weil is Professor of Accounting and Director of the Institute of Professional Accounting, Graduate School of Business, University of Chicago. He has served as a consultant to businesses and government agencies, including the U.S. Treasury Department and the SEC.